2025

ACCOUNTING DESK BOOK

The Accountant's Everyday Instant Answer Book

Marty D. Van Wagoner, CPA

EDITION

Editorial Staff

Editorial	Barbara L. Post, J.D.
Production	Ranjith Rajaram, Prabhu Meenakshisundaram

This publication is designed to provide accurate and authoritative information in regard to the subject matter covered. It is sold with the understanding that the publisher is not engaged in rendering legal, accounting or other professional service. If legal advice or other expert assistance is required, the services of a competent professional person should be sought. All views expressed in this publication are those of the author and not necessarily those of the publisher or any other person.

ISBN: 978-0-8080-6036-9

No claim is made to original government works; however, within this publication, the following are subject to CCH Incorporated's copyright: (1) the gathering, compilation, and arrangement of such government materials; (2) the magnetic translation and digital conversion of data, if applicable; (3) the historical, statutory and other notes and references; and (4) the commentary and other materials.

Printed in the United States of America

2025 Accounting Desk Book

by Marty D. Van Wagoner

2025 Edition Highlights

2024 and 2023 were actually relatively quiet years, compared to the previous few years. There were a number of changes in accounting standards and a few tax changes, but not anything with any huge impact, as we have seen in periods before this one. 2020 and 2021 are years everyone who lived through will remember as long as they live. The coronavirus (a.k.a. COVID-19) pandemic affected everyone one way or another, not just in the U.S. but all over the world.

The FASB issued updates since the last publication covering various topics.

The GASB has issued Statements 102 and 103 since the last publication.

In late 2020 and early 2021, two laws were enacted to further address the pandemic caused by COVID-19. The first one was the Consolidated Appropriations Act, 2021. Additional laws with the same name were issued in 2022, 2023, and 2024. The second bill was the American Rescue Plan Act of 2021.

The IRS is still in constant attack with regard to security of taxpayers' data. There were also significant complaints from taxpayers about receiving calls and emails from persons impersonating the IRS agents. While the IRS has been very vigilant, its improvements in its security should be full of fervor to be effective. On the other hand, CPAs are encouraged to take courses that would prepare them against various types of identity theft, online fraud and data breaches. CPAs' databases have been also the target of these attacks.

CCH® CPELink

Wolters Kluwer's goal is to provide you with the clearest, most concise, and up-to-date accounting and auditing information to help further your professional development, as well as a convenient method to help you satisfy your continuing professional education requirements. CCH® CPELink* offers a complete line of webinars and self-study courses covering complex and constantly evolving accounting and auditing issues. We are continually adding new programs to help you stay current on all the latest developments. The CCH® CPELink self-study courses are available 24 hours a day, seven days a week. You'll get immediate exam results and certification. To view our complete accounting and auditing course catalog, go to: ***cchcpelink.com***.

Accounting and Auditing on CCH AnswerConnect

Welcome to Accounting and Audit Research on CCH AnswerConnect. Users can access all of their content — federal, state and international tax as well as accounting, audit and SEC material on the best most comprehensive research platform in the industry. Interpretive guidance written in plain English delivers information needed to financial reporting. Updated 5 times daily, Accounting and Audit on CCH AnswerConnect provides the most current information from the FASB, GASB, the AICPA, SEC and other standard setting bodies.

With CCH AnswerConnect, you maximize the efficiency of your research time while enhancing your results. Learn more about the content, our experts, and how you can request a FREE trial by visiting us at answerconnect.cch.com

10/24

*Wolters Kluwer is registered with the National Association of State Boards of Accountancy (NASBA) as a sponsor of continuing professional education on the National Registry of CPE Sponsors. State Boards of Accountancy have the final authority on the acceptance of individual course for CPE credit. Complaints regarding registered sponsors may be submitted to the National Registry of CPE Sponsors through its website: *www.nasbaregistry.org*.

Preface

Accounting information is complex, mirroring the complexity of the business, government, and non-profit activities it measures. It is difficult for those practicing the profession to be specialists in more than a few limited areas, let alone understand it all. Overlaying this problem is the growing influence of the international accounting community and its pursuit of convergence of accounting standards, with the intent of leading to uniform reporting around the world. In this complex and changing environment, it is essential that the accounting practitioner have at least a glancing knowledge of many areas.

In auditing in particular, but also in tax and other areas of accounting, the practitioner must understand the industry in which the client operates including the industry's specific regulatory environment. One of the goals of the *Accounting Desk Book* is to bring together in one source, changes and updates to areas of accounting and tax compliance from across the business spectrum. While it is difficult for anyone to be an expert in all areas of accounting, it is certainly possible to be aware of recent changes across a wide range of accounting and tax issues. It is not a textbook or a detailed reference on a niche within accounting. Rather, it spans traditional boundaries in accounting by providing current information on financial accounting, cost accounting, tax, non-profit, governmental, and international accounting as well as related information on investments, e-commerce, ethics, the Securities and Exchange Commission, insurance accounting and much more.

Because of its breadth of coverage, this work serves to introduce and update many topics. Nevertheless, in the case of other topics, on which comprehensive information is not always available, such as the treatment of independent contractors and tip income, its coverage is substantial. For many practitioners, the book proves most useful by offering a quick background update on an unfamiliar topic or area in which they have not practiced for a number of years. Chapters and sections most often begin with a simple explanation of particular accounting matters that even non-accountants should find very helpful, and then progresses to more complex matters and explanations. Consistent with this approach, the first two chapters provide a plain English overview of many basic accounting matters. The information in those two chapters is likely to be more beneficial to those with little or no accounting experience in any of the specific areas.

It is imperative that all accountants and auditors keep pace with new laws, regulations, official pronouncements and industry guidance affecting their practice. The *Accounting Desk Book* assists the accountant in efforts to understand and comply with both new and existing accounting rules and regulations. The importance of current information cannot be overemphasized. Coverage of topics, applications, examples, and definitions of terms is the goal of this volume. It avoids abstract theory, technical jargon, complex "legalese" and textbook-type prose, which can needlessly complicate discussion of the rules and procedures. All topics are covered in straightforward, plain English. Discussions throughout the *Accounting Desk Book* are mostly self-contained. A review of the topics does not require reference to other sources. The table of contents clearly sets forth the subjects discussed and the index helps locate needed information rapidly. The Word files for Chapter 23 can be found at *download.cchcpelink.com/ADB.docx*.

About the Author

Marty D. Van Wagoner has 36 years of experience in public accounting. He is currently managing partner of Mountainside Accounting & Consulting, with a focus on audits of private commercial companies, not-for-profit entities, and HOAs. He is also Professional-in-Residence Faculty at Utah Valley University and he teaches professional education courses across the country. He spent the first ten years of his career at KPMG, a "Big Four" global accounting firm, and most of the rest of his career as a partner in local firms, with an emphasis in audits of public international companies, as well as small private companies. After KPMG, he briefly worked at placement agencies and then was sole proprietor of an accounting and auditing firm. During that time, he spent four years as a professor at the University of Utah. He serves and has served on a variety of not-for-profit Boards. In addition to the *Accounting Desk Book*, he is the author of other books published by Wolters Kluwer. He has also served as President and in other officer and committee positions of the Utah Association of Certified Public Accountants (UACPA) and as a Council Member of the American Institute of Certified Public Accountants (AICPA). He received his BA in Accounting with a Spanish minor and his MBA from the University of Utah.

Acknowledgments

We express our appreciation to Geralyn Jover-Ledesma, Lois Ruffner Plank, Bryan R. Plank, and Christie Plank Ciraulo for their past authorship of the *Accounting Desk Book*. Because of their dedication, this book is *The Accountant's Everyday Instant Answer Book*.

Contents

Financial Reporting

Standards

Accounting Procedures

Niche Accounting

SEC Accounting and Oversight

Investments

Tax Matters

Appendices

PART I

Financial Reporting

The general objective of financial reporting is to provide relevant, reliable information on the resources, obligations, ownership, and activities of an organization. In order to be useful for decision makers, the information should be accurate, complete, comparable and understandable. Some basic features involved in financial accounting and reporting are the individual accounting entity, accrual basis accounting, the use of estimates, when needed, and the preparation of a full set of financial statements.

A full set of financial statements generally consists of a balance sheet, income statement, statement of changes in stockholders' equity, and statement of cash flows. A balance sheet is sometimes called a statement of financial position. An income statement is sometimes called a statement of operations (when both income and net losses are reported) or even a statement of net losses (when there is no net income). For certain types of entities, such as not-for-profit or governmental entities, it may be called a statement of activities or a statement of changes in net assets. These financial statements summarize a firm's operations and ending financial position. Analysts, investors, creditors and potential investors and creditors analyze these documents in their decision-making processes.

In this section, we provide guidance for financial reporting with a chapter for each of the basic financial statements, a chapter for presentation and disclosure related to these items, and a chapter for broad reporting issues that have a reporting impact across more than one of the financial statements.

CHAPTER 1

Balance Sheet

¶1000 Overview

The balance sheet, or statement of financial position, is often described as a "snapshot of the organization's financial position at a point in time." It is divided into sections for assets, liabilities, and equity. Assets and liabilities are further divided, in what is referred to as a classified balance sheet, into current- and long-term classifications, generally based on whether the item is realized or settled in less than a year or longer than a year. In rare cases, for certain industries where the operating cycle is longer than a year, the operating cycle is used as the dividing point rather than one year. This division into three sections is consistent with what is referred to as the accounting equation: Assets = Liabilities + Equity. This equation must always hold true for the balance sheet to properly be in balance. Assets and liabilities are usually presented in order of liquidity; that is, how quickly they are converted into cash.

This chapter will address the most common asset, liability, and equity accounts generally reported in a balance sheet. Leases impact the assets and liabilities on the balance sheet but they are not addressed in this chapter. Detailed guidance on accounting for leases may be found in Chapters 6 and 7.

¶1001   Cash and Cash Equivalents

Cash is nearly always the first item listed on the balance sheet, as it is the most liquid. Cash consists of cash on hand as well as amounts held in demand deposit accounts such as checking and savings. To better ensure accuracy of cash reported, organizations should have a monthly bank reconciliation performed for all accounts. In addition, any checks received, but not yet deposited, should be reported as part of the cash balance. Checks written, but not yet sent, should also be reported as part of the cash balance because they are still in the organization's control. Most accounting systems reduce the cash balance when a check is prepared by the system so "held checks" often require a manual adjustment at the end of a reporting period, with a reversing manual adjustment at the beginning of the subsequent period.

.01   Restricted Cash

Restricted cash is presented separate from other cash balances. It may be current or long-term, depending on the type and length of the restriction. A common type of restricted cash is a compensating balance required by a financial institution. A compensating balance exists, most commonly, when a loan is received from a financial institution that requires a certain amount or percentage of the loan to be held in an account in case a payment is missed. Management may set cash aside to be used for some purpose determined internally, but that is not the same as restricted cash. Cash identified by management or the Board of Directors for a specific purpose is most commonly called management or Board designated cash, as opposed to restricted cash, which is restricted by an outside party.

.02   Cash Equivalents

Cash equivalents, when present, are combined with cash on the balance sheet and in the statement of cash flows and are titled Cash and Cash Equivalents. They consist of highly liquid investments, readily convertible into known amounts of cash and so near their maturity (generally 90 days or less) that they present minimal risk of changes in value from changes in rates. They typically include instruments such as U.S. Treasury bills, commercial paper, certificates of deposit and short-term government bonds with a maturity of three months or less. Some instruments have characteristics of cash equivalents and investments. It can sometimes be difficult to make the classification. One consideration is the organization's use of the instrument. If the organization uses such an instrument like an investment, with the intent to record earnings from it, it should likely be classified as an investment. If the instrument is used as part of the organization's cash management, it should likely be classified as a cash equivalent, as long as it has the other characteristics of a cash equivalent.

¶1002   Accounts Receivable

Accounts receivable, also referred to as trade accounts receivable, result from normal operations of an entity when products or services are provided to a customer on credit instead of on a cash basis. Because most entities' operating cycle is less than one year, accounts receivable are generally expected to be collected in less than a year and, therefore, are almost always current assets. Terms of accounts receivable vary a great deal. They are sometimes due in 30 days. Sometimes in 60 or 90 days. A common report used to analyze accounts receivable (A/R) and their collectability is the A/R aging report. It breaks accounts receivable from each customer into categories such as current, over 30 days, over 90 days, etc. If the older receivable categories are growing over time, it should be a cause for concern among management.

.01   Allowance for Doubtful Accounts and Bad Debt Expense

Unfortunately, not all accounts receivable are always collected. A customer may go bankrupt or have other financial difficulties. Whatever the reason, organizations estimate the amount of A/R they believe will not be collected and create an allowance for doubtful accounts. This allowance is a contra asset. A balance sheet will either show an A/R amount that is net of the allowance, with the details in the footnotes, or it will show gross A/R, less an allowance, totaling net A/R. Bad debt expense is recorded to create an allowance, matching the expense with the revenue to which it relates. Later, when the account is actually written off, A/R and the allowance are reduced. This is different from income tax accounting, which only allows a deduction when the account is actually written off. An allowance is estimated using the specific identification method, a balance sheet method, or an income statement method. Specific identification is most often used by entities with fewer receivables. It consists of reviewing the A/R detail and specifically identifying those amounts expected to be uncollected and then recording an allowance for the total of those amounts. The balance sheet method uses a percentage of A/R to estimate the ending balance of the allowance and records bad debt expense to arrive at that ending balance. The income statement method uses a percentage of credit sales to estimate and record bad debt expense, without regard to where the allowance balance ends up. In the latter two methods, the percentage used is based on historical experience of the entity. The balance sheet method often breaks A/R into aging categories, as described above, with different percentages for each category. This results in an estimate with more precision.

.02   Financing with Accounts Receivable

Accounts receivable are sometimes used as a vehicle for financing. There are two primary ways this is done. A/R may be used as collateral on a loan. In that case, it simply requires footnote disclosure. Alternatively, A/R may be sold. This is often referred to as factoring of A/R. Financial entities that acquire such A/R are factors. The factor always charges a fee. The entity selling the A/R records that fee as a loss on the sale of A/R. In addition, A/R may be sold with recourse or without recourse. If it is sold without recourse, the buyer does not have the ability to take recourse against the seller; that is, the buyer cannot come back against the seller to demand payment for uncollected amounts. If the A/R is sold with recourse, the seller is then liable to the buyer for any amounts not collected. Therefore, the loss to the seller when A/R is sold with recourse should also include an estimate of the amount the seller expects to have to pay for uncollected balances.

¶1003   Inventory

Inventory is an asset held by an entity with the intent to sell it to a customer. Inventory is generally recorded at cost. However, cost may comprise more than just the cost of the product itself. The "cost" at which an asset is recorded and carried on an entity's books includes all costs incurred to get the asset to the location and condition needed for its intended purpose. That means shipping costs may be added to the cost of inventory but only freight in, not freight out, which would be a selling cost. Other costs, such as testing, may also be added to the cost of inventory. Inventory may be written down to below cost, as described below, but only in rare situations can inventory be stated above cost, such as for precious metals with a fixed monetary value and little or no cost of marketing. In such cases, disclosure is required. Cost or carrying value of inventory should also include any appropriately allocated labor and overhead costs. Labor costs include all or a portion of the salaries of those who work on the inventory. Overhead includes costs such as rent or depreciation of the building in which the inventory is manufactured, utilities, supervision, and any other costs related to the manufacture and storage of inventory.

.01   Categories

Inventory is classified into three general areas for reporting: raw materials, work in process (WIP), or finished goods. A distributor will generally only have finished goods because such an entity buys inventory only to resell it, with nothing added to it. A manufacturer, however, buys raw materials and then has employees and/or machinery manufacture those materials into something different that can be sold to customers. The titles of the categories are somewhat self-evident. Raw materials include items acquired to be used in manufacturing. WIP includes the inventory that is in some phase of the manufacturing process. Finished goods are completed items ready to be sold. Raw materials cost is mostly the cost of materials and includes little labor or overhead. Measuring the cost of WIP is perhaps the most complex because an assessment should be made of the level of completion in order to allocate the proper amount of labor and overhead put into the product to its level of completion at the measurement date. Finished goods will have all allocable labor and overhead included in its cost.

When inventory is sold, the inventory balance is reduced and costs of goods sold is reported on the income statement. Cost of goods sold also includes other related costs such as shrinkage (loss or theft of inventory), write-downs, etc.

.02   Valuation

A particular challenge is presented because inventory is purchased at differing amounts over time and from different places. As an example, assume three identical products are purchased—one for $6.50, another for $7.25, and a third for $8.10. A customer comes into the store, randomly grabs one of the products, and buys it. A sale would be recorded but which of the three amounts should be recorded for cost of goods sold if it is impossible to distinguish between the three items? Because of this challenge, we use inventory costing methods. Each of the costing methods used has advantages and disadvantages compared to the others. The common methods are the specific identification method, the weighted-average method, first-in first-out (FIFO), and last-in first-out (LIFO). Less commonly used methods are the retail method and others outside the scope of this work. The specific identification method is best used for large, discrete items of inventory where it is easy to track a specific item and identify when it is sold. The weighted-average method weights the cost of inventory items by the relative number of items at that cost. This approach tends to smooth the impact on the income statement and keep things more consistent over time. The FIFO method assumes the oldest items are sold first, while the LIFO method assumes the newest items are sold first. As might be imagined, these two methods have opposite impacts on the income statement. In a period of rising costs, which is most generally the case, FIFO results in a comparatively lower cost of goods sold and higher net income. LIFO would result in the opposite. Entities using LIFO are often tax-driven so they want lower net income in order to pay less in taxes. U.S. GAAP requires the use of LIFO for book purposes if it is used for tax purposes. So a company cannot get the "best of both worlds" by having the lowest net income for taxes and the highest net income for books, which is usually more desirable. It is important to note that the selection of cost flow need not represent any physical flow of inventory being sold, except in specific identification.

U.S. GAAP tends to be conservative. Generally, gains are not recognized until they actually happen but losses are recorded as soon as it is probable they will occur, even if in the future. This is the case with inventory. Although it was modified somewhat with an additional standard issued, it has long been the case that inventory is written down and a loss taken if its value reduces below the amount at which it is recorded. This concept has long been called the lower of cost or market (LCM). It was modified to the lower of cost or net realizable value (LCNRV). Because LIFO and the retail inventory method still require the more complex LCM, those rules will be reviewed, after which LCNRV rules will be described. The general concept behind LCM is that inventory must be written down and a loss taken when market value is lower than cost, or carrying value. The complexity arises from measuring market value. For LCM, three different amounts must be considered—net realizable value (NRV), replacement cost, and net realizable value less a normal profit margin. NRV is considered a ceiling above which market may not be measured. NRV less a normal profit margin is a floor. Replacement cost is considered market value as long as it does not go above the ceiling, in which case NRV would be used as market value, or below the floor, in which case NRV less a normal profit margin would be considered market value. Another way to look at it is to identify the three amounts just discussed and use the amount in the middle as market value. (If replacement cost goes above the ceiling, or NRV, then NRV would be the amount in the middle and would be used as market, etc.) Under the relatively new standard issued, for all inventory except when LIFO or the retail method is used, the calculation is simplified. Of the three measurements described above, only NRV is used—lower of cost or net realizable value (LCNRV). Replacement cost and NRV less a normal profit margin are not considered.

¶1004   Investments

Organizations sometimes use excess cash by investing it in order to earn a higher return than they would by leaving it in a bank account, or even by reinvesting it in its own operations. There are a variety of types of investments, but this discussion will focus on equity investments, such as the stock of another corporation, and debt investments, such as bonds.

FASB Accounting Standards Codification™ (ASC) Topic 320 provides guidance for investments in debt securities and ASC 321 for investments in equity securities. The guidance applies to marketable securities. Securities without readily available market values are generally recorded at cost. Debt securities can be classified as trading securities, available for sale, or held to maturity. Trading securities are those held with the intent to resell in a very short term. Held to maturity securities are those for which the organization has the intent and ability to hold until they mature. Available for sale securities are all others. Held to maturity securities are recorded at cost. The other two are adjusted to fair value at every reporting period. Unrealized gains and losses from trading securities are recognized in the income statement. Unrealized gains and losses from available for sale securities are recorded as other comprehensive income until realized (by sale of the security), after which the gain or loss is removed from other comprehensive income and recognized in the income statement. Equity securities are recorded at fair value at each reporting period, with unrealized gains and losses recognized in the income statement.

The investments described above are those for which the entity has no control nor significant influence, generally when the entity holds less than 20 percent voting ownership. Significant influence, usually considered to be 20 percent to 50 percent ownership, uses the equity method of accounting. Control, usually considered to be greater than 50 percent ownership, uses consolidation. Both of those types of investments are addressed elsewhere in these materials.

¶1005   Other Assets

There are a variety of other assets but the most commonly occurring are prepaid expenses. These arise when an entity pays an amount in advance. Two common examples are insurance and rent. For example, if a one-year insurance policy premium is paid on July 1, half the policy would cover part of the current year while the other half covers part of the subsequent year. So, it would be inappropriate, under U.S. GAAP accrual accounting to recognize all the expense in the current year. Therefore, a prepaid expense would be recorded as an asset and then adjusted to expense as the policy is "used up" over the period of the policy term. An analogy is to consider a glacier. As it melts into the sea, the glacier turns to water. Similarly, as assets are used up, they become expenses depicting such use. For prepaids (and accruals, discussed later) an adjustment is made at each reporting period to adjust it to the proper balance. If $1,000 is paid on July 1 for this annual insurance policy, it would initially be reported as a prepaid asset of $1,000. At year-end, because half the policy has passed, a year-end adjusting entry would be recorded to adjust the prepaid balance to $500 and recognize $500 as insurance expense.

¶1006   Property, Plant and Equipment

Whereas inventory consists of assets purchased with the intent to sell them to customers for profit, property, plant, and equipment (PPE), also referred to as fixed assets, is purchased to be used in the operations of an entity. Such assets generally consist of land, buildings, equipment, furniture, vehicles and other items generally expected to be in place for a longer term. As with other assets, PPE is recorded at cost, including all costs necessary to get the item into the location and condition necessary for its intended use and function. The process of recording an asset rather than an expense is called capitalization. All the expenditures that go into the cost of an asset are capitalized rather than expensed.

.01   Self-constructed Assets and Interest Capitalization

There are situations in which an entity will construct its own fixed assets. In such cases, as with inventory, labor and overhead should be allocated to the cost of the fixed asset. This includes the capitalization of interest costs, as applicable. These calculations can be somewhat complex. The idea is that if an entity must borrow money to build an asset, then the interest paid on that borrowed money should be capitalized as part of the cost of the asset. This is pretty obvious for a loan entered into specifically for the construction of that asset. However, somewhat less obvious is the requirement to capitalize interest related to other loans the entity has, even if not related to the asset under construction. The concept in this case is that the interest paid on other loans is an opportunity cost. If the asset were not being constructed, the cash being used toward construction of the asset could be used to pay down the loan more quickly and incur less interest. Therefore, even indirect interest is capitalized as part of the asset. Detailed guidance on the interest calculations may be found in the accounting standards.

.02   Depreciation

Fixed assets are capitalized as assets rather than expensed because they provide service over an extended period of time. Therefore, the costs of those assets are expensed in the income statement over the expected useful life of the asset. This process is called depreciation. Outside of accounting, depreciation is a word used to describe a decrease in value over time. Because of that, many misinterpret depreciation in accounting as a way to report a fixed asset closer to its market value. However, that is not the case. Depreciation in accounting has nothing to do with fair market value. It is solely a mechanism through which the cost of an asset can be allocated to and recognized over its estimated useful life. In order to do so, a depreciable base is calculated as asset cost minus salvage value, or the amount one is expected to get for any remaining asset at the end of its life. That depreciable base is expensed in accordance with a selected depreciation method. The most common depreciation method for U.S. GAAP, or book, purposes is the straight-line method, where an equal amount of expense is recorded each period. The expense is calculated by dividing the depreciable base into the number of periods in the estimated useful life. Other methods sometimes used are declining balance, units-of-production, or sum-of-the-years-digits. When depreciation expense is recorded to the income statement, a contra-asset account of accumulated depreciation is recorded to the balance sheet. PPE is then reported on the balance sheet net of accumulated depreciation.

.03   Impairment

Just as inventory is written down to market when it is lower than cost (see above), there are situations in which the value of PPE declines to below its book value and needs to be written down. For long-term assets, this is called impairment. There are two steps to determining impairment on PPE. First is a recoverability test. If the undiscounted sum of estimated future cash flows from that asset is less than its book value, it is impaired. If it is impaired, the amount of loss to be recorded is the amount by which fair value is less than book value.

If a fixed asset is held for sale, rather than being used in operations, no further depreciation should be recorded and it must be reported separately from operating assets in the financial statements.

¶1007   Intangible Assets and Natural Resources

Intangible assets include patents, copyrights, trademarks, franchises, etc. Recording these assets follows a similar process to that for fixed assets. It is important to note, however, that research and development costs are expensed as incurred and not capitalized as part of a patent or other intangible asset. Capitalized costs of intangible assets include purchase price (when acquired from an external party), legal fees, filing fees, etc. Another intangible asset is goodwill, which can only be recognized in conjunction with a business acquisition. This will be addressed along with business combinations in a later chapter.

Natural resources are items such as mines, wells, tracts of forest, etc. and follow guidance similar to that for other long-term assets. One additional feature that can add to the recorded cost of a natural resource is an asset retirement obligation, explained below.

.01   Finite and Indefinite Lives

Intangible assets are divided into those with finite useful lives and those with indefinite useful lives. Costs of intangible assets with finite useful lives are recognized over the assets' estimated useful lives, just as is done with depreciation. But for intangible assets, we call it amortization. It is the same with natural resources but we call it depletion and, most commonly, the units-of-production method is used. Intangible assets with indefinite useful lives are not amortized. They are regularly assessed for impairment but otherwise just stay on the books perpetually.

.02   Impairment

Impairment of intangible assets other than goodwill is simply a one-step process. If fair value is less than book value, an impairment loss is recognized for the difference. Assessment of impairment for goodwill is more complex. Goodwill only arises from a business acquisition. The acquired business that resulted in recognition of goodwill is the reporting unit to which that goodwill relates. To test goodwill for impairment, the fair value of the reporting unit is compared to its book value. If fair value is less than book value, an impairment loss is recorded for the difference, except that any recognized loss cannot be greater than the book value of the goodwill. Subsequent reversal of impairment losses is not allowed.

.03   Asset Retirement Obligations

An asset retirement obligation exists when there is a cost associated with retiring an asset, ending its useful life. An example is when a mine is dug, the mining company is required by local law or contract to restore the land to the same condition as before the mining began, or to build a park where the mine is. An estimate of that future cost is made by calculating an average of different possible costs weighted by their respective probabilities. A present value of that estimated, weighted-average future cost is calculated and added to the recorded cost of the asset. Interest is then accreted (added to) that present value over time so, at the end of the mining operation, the cost matches the estimate previously made. Any difference between the estimate and the amount actually incurred is treated as a change in estimate, described elsewhere in this text.

¶1008   Accounts Payable and Other Current Liabilities

Accounts payable, also referred to as trade accounts payable, result from normal operations of an entity when products or services are acquired from a supplier on credit instead of on a cash basis. Accounts payable are most commonly used for the purchase of inventory but are also used for other amounts owed to third parties. Because most entities' operating cycle is less than one year, accounts payable are generally expected to be paid in less than a year and, therefore, are almost always current liabilities. Terms of accounts payable vary a great deal. They are sometimes payable in 30 days. Sometimes 60 or 90 days. A common report used to analyze accounts payable (A/P) and their collectability is the A/P aging report. It breaks accounts payable to each supplier into categories such as current, over 30 days, over 90 days, etc. This is often a cash management tool, allowing management to prioritize which bills need to be paid and when.

Accrued expenses are similar to accounts payable. These are usually current liabilities and are recorded for amounts to be paid subsequent to the reporting period. They share characteristics of prepaid expenses. While prepaid expenses are paid up front and the benefit of what is paid for is received later, accrued expenses are the opposite—the benefit is received first and payment is made later. Similar to prepaid expenses, accrued expenses are often adjusted at year-end in order to have the correct amount of expense in the correct period and to have the correct amount on the balance sheet at the end of the reporting period.

.01   Purchase Commitments

Entities sometimes enter into agreements to purchase a certain amount of inventory at a specified price or over a specified time period. This is called a purchase commitment. The buyer's incentive for such an agreement is to lock in prices when the expectation is that prices will go up in the future, thereby saving money at the date of purchase. The seller's incentive is to lock in assured sales for the future, at the risk of losing a little money on those sales if prices do go up. Nothing is recorded when the agreement is signed because no product changes hands, neither does any consideration/money change hands. It just locks the entities into future amounts to be recorded. However, there is one aspect that does require a loss to be recognized before the transaction actually occurs. If, at the reporting period, the selling price of the product to be purchased drops below the commitment amount, a loss needs to be recognized at the date. This is consistent with conservative guidance to only recognize gains when they actually happen but to recognize losses when it becomes probable they will happen.

¶1009   Deferred Revenue

Whereas an accrual is recorded when an entity receives a benefit before it must actually pay for the benefit, a deferred revenue is when the company receives payment before it actually performs what is needed to earn that payment. Deferred revenue is sometimes referred to as unearned revenue. It is recorded as a liability because, when the payment is received, the entity is obligated to do something to earn that payment in the future. Hence, it is a future obligation, which is in the definition of a liability.

Deferred revenues have become somewhat more complex with the issuance of the new revenue recognition standard. More detail on this is provided in Chapter 2 on the income statement. The point pertinent to this discussion is that a company has an obligation to perform in any sales arrangement. That performance obligation must be satisfied in order to recognize revenue. If payment is received before the performance obligation is satisfied, the entity has a contract liability that is most often recorded as a deferred revenue. Under the new standard, some entities are ending up initially recording more deferred revenue on the balance sheet as a liability and less revenue on the income statement. It is critical to become familiar with the new standard in order to correctly account for transactions in accordance with the standard.

¶1010   Debt

When an entity borrows funds, a liability is recorded as debt on the balance sheet. The classification of debt as current or long-term is dependent on the amount of time until it will be paid back. Commonly, debt is reported as long-term with a current portion for the amount of principal expected to be repaid within one year after the reporting date.

Although debt for most entities arises from borrowing from a bank or other third party, entities will sometimes issue bonds. Bonds are a financing mechanism which essentially allows an entity to borrow money from individuals or whatever other entities that invest in those bonds. Bonds are almost always long-term and usually allow for interest-only payments over the life of the bond, with the entire principal paid back at maturity. The issuance of bonds is often a straightforward recording of a liability in the amount of the bonds' face value. However, there are times when bonds are issued with a stated interest rate that differs from the market interest rate at the time of issuance. This results in a premium or discount recorded with the bond liability. For example, if a bond has a certain stated rate but, by the time the bonds go through the approval process, the market rate has dropped, the issuer can charge extra for the bonds because they are paying higher interest than other instruments currently on the market. The amount charged is calculated using a present value formula for principal and interest payments that creates an effective interest rate equal to the market interest rate. This would be a premium on the sale of the bond. The opposite would result in a discount. A premium or discount is generally amortized to interest expense over the life of the bond. However, if a bond is callable; that is, if the bond issuer can require the holder to relinquish the bond for payment before its maturity date, any premium should be amortized only up to the earliest possible call date.

Sometimes debt, including bonds, is convertible into common stock at a stated amount per share. For example, a $1,000 bond may be convertible into shares of stock at the conversion price of $2 per share, which would result in the bondholder receiving 500 shares of stock at conversion. The conversion price is usually the market value of the stock at the date of bond issuance. In most cases, it is still just recorded as a bond liability at face value. The conversion information is disclosed in the footnotes. There is one level of complexity, however, when the conversion price differs from the market value of the stock, there could be a beneficial conversion feature that gives the bondholder a benefit over others who would purchase the stock. The accounting for a beneficial conversion feature is complex. If it may exist, the accounting standards should be consulted. This is especially the case if there is any variability in the conversion price as that could be an indicator that a beneficial conversion feature contains an embedded derivative.

¶1011   Equity

Equity is sometimes considered the net assets of an entity (assets minus liabilities). More commonly for commercial entities, it is referred to as the owners' claims on the entity's assets, whereas liabilities are creditors' claims on the entity's assets. Equity can be split into two categories: earned equity and owned equity. Earned equity is reflected in retained earnings—the accumulated net income of the entity less any dividends declared. Owned equity is reflected in the stock and additional paid-in capital accounts, which are recorded when funds are received from investors in exchange for a portion of ownership. Stock most often has an associated par value, which was assigned in the original articles of incorporation, though it may be changed by amendment. Historically, par value was important because of legal obligations related to par value. In today's world however, investors are more strongly protected from such liabilities so par value has little meaning. It is little more than a throwback to earlier days. Having said that, it is still widely used. When stock is sold, the par value is recorded in the stock account and any amount received in excess of par value goes into an additional paid-in capital account. If the stock has no par value, the entire amount is recorded as stock. At times, an entity buys back some of its own stock, resulting in a contra-equity account called treasury stock. Treasury stock is generally recorded at cost and subsequently relieved when the stock is retired or resold into the market. On the balance sheet, the equity section line items are usually common stock, preferred stock, additional paid-in capital, treasury stock, and retained earnings. There may also be accumulated other comprehensive income, which will be discussed in Chapter 2 on the income statement.

An entity may have more than one class of stock. The basic stock, which usually has voting rights, is common stock. Stock with different rights and characteristics is usually recorded as preferred stock. As with common stock, preferred stock may have a par value and it may not. It may have no voting rights or different voting rights. It may have preferential treatment for dividends or in liquidation. These aspects must all be disclosed in the footnotes.

Entities sometimes have instruments with characteristics of equity and characteristics of debt. For example, redeemable preferred stock is more like a liability than equity because the holder of the stock may require the entity to buy the stock back at a stated price so it is very much like debt and is, therefore, classified in liabilities rather than equity.

More detail related to equity is provided in Chapter 3 on the statement of stockholder's equity.

CHAPTER 2

Income Statement

¶2000   Overview

Whereas the balance sheet is a snapshot of an organization's assets, liabilities, and equity at a point in time, the income statement presents revenues, expenses, gains, and losses over a specified period of time. Most commonly, the period of time is a year. However, it might be a quarter, a month, or for the period from February 23 to April 14, for example. Any period may be used, as long as that period is clearly identified.

In recent years, new guidance has been released and implemented related to revenue recognition. Because this guidance is very pervasive in its impact on financial reporting, we will first discuss the new standard and then delve into other areas on the income statement.

It was the Financial Accounting Standards Board's (FASB's) intention for some time to develop a comprehensive statement on revenue recognition that is conceptually based and framed in terms of principles. This was done in partnership with the International Accounting Standards Board (IASB). In 2014, the completion of this project resulted in Accounting Standards Update (ASU) No. 2014-09, Revenue from Contracts with Customers. Both U.S. GAAP and international GAAP, as promulgated by the IASB, were modified in the process. The resulting guidance is general in scope in contrast to the FASB's prior rule-based approach which attempted to accommodate unique conditions in specific industries.

It was assumed that the new revenue recognition guidance would:

- Eliminate the inconsistencies in the existing authoritative literature and accepted practices.
- Fill the voids that have emerged in revenue recognition guidance in recent years.
- Provide guidance for addressing issues that arise in the future.

The overriding goal, as stated by the IASB, was to offer one measure of revenue recognition that is applicable across all industries, rather than attempting, as U.S. GAAP had done, to tailor the guidance to specific industries. Thus, while U.S. GAAP has employed different rules for certain industries, for example, the construction industry, the convergence with international GAAP will mean more general principles and principles that apply universally.

According to FASB, the core principle of the new guidance is to "recognize revenue to depict the transfer of promised goods or services to customers in an amount that reflects the consideration to which the entity expects to be entitled in exchange for those goods or services." The new standard calls for enhanced disclosures about revenue, providing guidance for transactions that were not previously addressed comprehensively (for example, service revenue and contract modifications). The codified FASB guidance on Revenue from Contracts with Customers is found in FASB's Accounting Standards Codification™ (ASC) Topic 606. The new guidance has specific impact on revenue generated in connection with performance obligations occurring over time, sales with a right of return, consignment sales, sales with options, the effects of warranty contracts, non-refundable upfront fees, bill-and-hold agreements, repurchase agreements, principal-agent issues, and customer acceptance.

While the new guidance is stated in a dramatically different format from older U.S. GAAP guidance—based on measuring changes in assets and liabilities—for most business transactions, the results will be the same, similar, or only marginally different. This is because in most business transactions there is a clear point at which an exchange of assets or services has taken place and little controversy about the timing of the revenue to be recognized. But in some industries the goods or services are provided over an extended period of time and the contract for providing those services may have intermediate steps. Consider the example of a real estate developer for a residential subdivision. Assume that the contractor has promised, in addition to streets, sewers and streetlights, to furnish the subdivision with a golf course, swimming pool community house, dog park, and tennis courts. Assume further that upon completion of the first homes in the development none of these special amenities has yet been completed or even started. The projected revenue from the sale of all the homes is expected to cover the costs of the homes as well as the costs to be incurred in connection with developing the golf course, swimming pool, etc. But the profit to be recorded from each home sale will be calculated when the home is transferred to the customer. Under prior guidance, the contractor would use the percentage of completion method, using an estimate of expenses incurred to date to total expenses, including the land and its development as well as the costs of the contracted-for amenities even though these costs have not yet been incurred. Under the new rules, it may be necessary to allocate the total price to be obtained from the sale of all the homes in part to a hypothetical sale of the other identifiable items in the project, such as the golf course.

In calculating the revenue to be recognized on any contract with a customer, the new guidance requires a five-step process:

1. Identify the contracts. This requires that the entity be able to identify each party's rights and the payment terms, and in some cases may require combining separate contracts into a single contract if two or more contracts were entered into with the same customer at the same time with the same economic objective. If a contract is modified after the rights and obligations associated with it have been determined, the effect of the modification(s) of those rights and obligations must be reassessed. In some circumstances, the modification of a contract must be treated as a separate contract. In the example of the home builder above, each home purchaser will have a separate contract with the builder.

2. Identify any separate performance objectives within the contracts. This requires a specific assessment of the goods or services promised in a contract and whether the contract calls for a distinct good or service or a series of distinct goods or services that have the same pattern of transfer. In the example of the home builder described above, this means that it may be necessary to identify then the home sale as one performance obligation and the other specifically contracted-for amenities, like the golf course, as a separate performance obligation on which to recognize revenue.

3. Determine the transaction price. This requires considering all the terms of the contract as well as customary business practices. The transaction price includes the total consideration the entity expects to receive and must be adjusted for the nature and timing of the receipt of the consideration. If the revenue contains a significant financing component, this must be separated out. If the amount to be received is variable, estimates will have to be made about the amount to be received. This variance can be caused by a number of factors including discounts, credits, rebates, incentives, performance bonuses, as well as penalties. The amount that is variable in a contract may be estimated using probability-weighted amounts or the most likely amount from a range of possibilities. In the above example of the contractor, the total transaction price is the sum of the individual prices on the individual homes. As in accounting generally, consistency in the use of a particular method is important.

4. Allocate the transaction price to the separate performance obligations. Once the full transaction price is determined it must be allocated to each of the performance obligations already identified. This must be done on a "relative stand-alone selling price basis." The stand-alone selling price is that at which the entity would sell the good or service separately; this amount may not be readily available but may have to be inferred from the total contract and the specific conditions of the sale. More than one method is available for determining the stand-alone selling price, including the adjusted market assessment approach, expected cost plus a margin approach, or a residual approach. If the contract has a variable component, the revenue from this component may be attributed to the whole contract or to a specific part, depending on the terms of the contract. In the above example of the home contractor, this may mean that each individual home will be treated as a separate contract obligation and that one or more of the individual amenities to be built, especially the golf course, will also be treated as a separate performance obligation. Although the golf course is not going to be sold to an outside buyer, the fact that each home purchaser's contract includes access to the golf course may mean that a separate hypothetical price may have to be allocated to the golf course.

5. Recognize revenue when each performance obligation is satisfied. An entity recognizes revenue when the control of the asset(s) being transferred is obtained by the customer. Control refers to the ability to direct the use of and receive the benefits from that asset. In some cases, the transfer will take place at a clearly designated time while in others, it will take place over time. In the latter case, the revenue is also recognized over time rather than, for example, at the completion of all the related transfers. Measurement of the progress toward transfer of control may be made by either the input method or the output method (explained below). In the above home builder example, this will mean recognizing revenue with the completion and sale of each home and may also require recognizing revenue, once the golf course is completed, on its transfer to the homeowners. This would require allocating part of the purchase price of each home to the purchase of a portion or right in the golf course (depending on the terms of the contract).

The input and output methods are alternatives for recognizing revenue. The output method recognizes revenue based on items produced and transferred to date to the customer. The input method recognizes revenue based on items used by the company to date in completing the work for the customer. Thus, the output method may use items such as tons of coal or barrels of oil produced while the input method may use costs or labor hours or other measures of work done to date.

Additional information on the new revenue recognition principles can be found in Chapters 7 and 11, respectively: "Actions of the Financial Accounting Standards Board" and "International Standards: Accounting."

A number of goals were enunciated for ensuring the comprehensive revenue recognition guidance meets the needs of financial statement users. Among these goals were removing inconsistencies and weaknesses in existing revenue recognition standards and practices; improving comparability of revenue recognition practices across entities, industries, jurisdictions, and capital markets; and simplifying the preparation of financial statements by reducing the number of requirements to which entities must refer.

¶2001   Historical Background of Revenue Recognition

The pace may have appeared to be relatively slow, but because of the amount of damage that can be and has been caused by firms manipulating revenue recognition in financial statements, any standard covering the topic should certainly be given careful thought and due process.

The Board also affirmed that its goal was to develop a comprehensive standard on revenue recognition that would apply broadly to *all* revenue arrangements. In connection with that decision, the Board agreed to pursue an approach under which performance obligations would be measured by allocating the customer consideration rather than at the fair value of the obligation (that is, the amount the reporting entity would be required to pay to transfer the performance obligation to a willing third party of comparable credit standing).

The Board continued discussing principles for revenue recognition as well as the implications of measuring performance obligations based on the customer consideration amount.

Accounting Standards Update (ASU) No. 2014-09 was issued to implement the new revenue recognition model in ASC 606. This model is covered in-depth in future chapters of this volume and must be followed, where applicable.

¶2002   SEC Revenue Recognition Measures Aid FASB Project

SEC sought to fill the gap in the accounting literature with SAB No. 101, *Revenue Recognition in Financial Statements*, which was issued in December 1999, and the companion document, *Revenue Recognition in Financial Statements Frequently Asked Questions and Answers*, which was issued in October 2000. SAB 101 was superseded by SAB 104, *Revenue Recognition*, in December 2003. SAB 104 states that if a transaction falls within the scope of specific authoritative literature on revenue recognition, that guidance should be followed. In the absence of such guidance, the revenue recognition criteria in Concepts Statement 5 (namely, that revenue should not be recognized until it is (a) *realized or realizable* and (b) *earned*) should be followed. However,

SAB 104 is more specific, stating additional requirements for meeting those criteria, and reflects the SEC staff's view that the four basic criteria for revenue recognition in AICPA SOP 97-2, *Software Revenue Recognition*, should be a foundation for all basic revenue recognition principles. Those criteria are:

- Persuasive evidence of an arrangement exists.
- Delivery has occurred.
- Collectability is probable.
- Fixed or determinable fee.

Some criticized SAB 101 on the basis that the criteria in SOP 97-2 were developed for a particular industry and that broader application of those criteria was neither contemplated nor intended. They asserted that that guidance might not be appropriate for certain recognition issues, including some that the EITF has considered. Others noted that a SAB is designed to provide the SEC staff's interpretive responses and not to change U.S. Generally Accepted Accounting Principles (U.S. GAAP). For that reason, SABs are issued without an invitation for comment. Many used SAB 104 and SOP 97-2 as general guidance for revenue recognition, even though it had been issued only for specific industries. Because of this, critics argued that SAB 101 (then SAB 104) had in fact changed U.S. GAAP by promulgating changes in industry practice without the full due process and deliberation that characterize the FASB's decision-making process. Even though the SEC guidance for revenue recognition applies only to SEC registrants, the FASB considers that the work done in developing and implementing SAB 101 has focused attention on revenue recognition issues and is useful in their project toward adopting a standard.

.01   Staff Accounting Bulletin No. 104

Staff Accounting Bulletin No. 104, *Revenue Recognition*, superseded SAB 101. It was adopted primarily to rescind accounting guidance contained in SAB 101 related to *multiple element revenue arrangements*, superseded as a result of the issuance of EITF 00-21. Additionally, SAB 104 rescinds the SEC's Revenue Recognition in Financial Statements Frequently Asked Questions issued with SAB 101 that had been codified in SEC Topic 13, *Revenue Recognition*. Selected portions of the FAQ have been incorporated into SAB 104. Although the wording of SAB 104 has changed to reflect the issuance of EITF 00-21, the revenue recognition principles of SAB 101 remain largely unchanged by the issuance of SAB 104.

.02   Revenue Recognition in SEC Topic 13

Because the accounting literature on revenue recognition includes both broad conceptual discussions and certain industry-specific guidance, the SEC has stated that if a transaction is within the scope of specific authoritative literature that provides revenue recognition guidance, that literature should be applied. However, in the absence of authoritative literature addressing a specific arrangement or a specific industry, the staff will consider the existing authoritative accounting standards as well as the broad revenue recognition criteria specified in the FASB's conceptual framework that contain basic guidelines for revenue recognition.

Based on these guidelines, revenue should not be recognized until it is realized or realizable and earned. Concepts Statement 5, paragraph 83(b), as originally issued, stated that "an entity's revenue-earning activities involve delivering or producing goods, rendering services, or other activities that constitute its ongoing major or central operations, and revenues are considered to have been earned when the entity has substantially accomplished what it must do to be entitled to the benefits represented by the revenues." Paragraph 84(a) continued, "the two conditions (being realized or realizable and being earned) are usually met by the time product or merchandise is delivered or services are rendered to customers, and revenues from manufacturing and selling activities and gains and losses from sales of other assets are commonly recognized at time of sale (usually meaning delivery)." In addition, paragraph 84(d) stated that "If services are rendered or rights to use assets extend continuously over time (for example, interest or rent), reliable measures based on contractual prices established in advance are commonly available, and revenues may be recognized as earned as time passes." Although Concepts Statement 5 has been amended, these ideas are still generally incorporated into newer statements and standards.

The staff believes that revenue generally is realized or realizable and earned when all of the following criteria are met:

- Persuasive evidence of an arrangement exists.
- Delivery has occurred or services have been rendered.
- The seller's price to the buyer is fixed or determinable.
- Collectability is reasonably assured.

Some revenue arrangements contain multiple revenue-generating activities. The staff believes that the determination of the units of accounting within an arrangement should be made prior to the application of the guidance in this SAB Topic by reference to the applicable accounting literature.

¶2003   Cautions for Accountants, Auditors, Investors

Nothing lends itself more readily to imaginative or downright fraudulent accounting than revenue recognition. As has been quite evident over the last couple of decades, accounting has faced more criticism than ever before. As a result, what was formerly a self-regulated profession has been deluged with rules and regulations. However, not all of these rules have managed to prevent willing companies from painting a rosier picture of revenues than is warranted. So, forewarned is forearmed. It is important for all those with a stake in financial reporting to understand where and how problems may exist in financial reporting. Fraud is often broken into two areas: asset misappropriation (stealing cash or other assets) and financial statement misrepresentation ("fudging" the numbers). Although the former happens much more often, the latter makes up a very high percentage of the dollar amounts of fraud. Revenue recognition frauds are the highest percentage of financial statement misrepresentations. The following may help users of financial statements avoid being fooled.

.01   Different Materiality Focus

The task of accountants, auditors, and investors is difficult enough without becoming overly concerned about immaterial items. This may be a reasonable position to take, but, as a large investment company cautions, the CPA/PFS and investors focusing on revenue growth should constantly be aware that they must adopt a view of what is or is not "material" that differs from that often adopted by auditors and general practice accountants.

In the interest of their clients, financial advisors need to measure materiality against the change in revenues because their revenue-multiple valuation metric is driven by *revenue growth rates*. In contrast, auditors and accountants tend to focus on the *total revenue figure* when thinking of materiality. These different perspectives can lead to different materiality assessments. What is immaterial to accountants and auditors may be quite material to investors and their advisors. The reverse is seldom, if ever, true. To think as an investor, the PFS must measure revenue materiality against the *change or trend in revenues*.

The most accurate identification of what is material is whether or not it will change the mind of a decision maker, a qualitative assessment. However, as a practical matter, the measure of materiality is usually calculated quantitatively using revenue or total assets.

.02   Avoiding Revenue Growth Traps

Because revenue growth is the primary driver of sustained profit growth, unusual revenue growth can be an indication of a costly trap for investors if it is the result of accounting fraud, manipulation, or excessively aggressive accounting practices. The 50 percent of the Securities and Exchange Commission accounting enforcement actions that involve revenue recognition are ample testimony to this fact. In a majority of these cases, investors suffered significant losses because they were overly impressed by a company's glowing revenue-growth story, which in the end turned out to be inflated.

In order to avoid revenue growth traps, investors need to know:

- How to measure materiality correctly.
- The common forms of revenue recognition manipulation.
- How to detect the common forms of revenue manipulation.
- The extent to which they can rely on auditor opinions and other forms of assurance, such as management certifications.

.03   Revenue Manipulations

Revenue misstatements come in a remarkable variety of frequently occurring practices. Auditors, accountants, financial advisors, and their clients should be aware of any number of questionable practices that may be used to paint a rosier picture than the facts warrant. The user of financial statements has a better chance of avoiding problems if he or she is aware of some of the more imaginative practices.

Common forms of revenue manipulations encompass:

1. Including in the current period revenue on products delivered and services rendered after the end of the period's cut-off date.
2. Convincing a company being acquired to slow down their selling activity in the period prior to their acquisition so that the deferred sales can be recognized after the company has been acquired.
3. Including inappropriate items in revenue, such as gains, financial income, and other items that are peripheral, incidental, or unrelated to the company's *major or central operations*.
4. Undisclosed side-letters between the seller and buyer, such as generous no-penalty return privileges that actually modify the sales arrangements.
5. Improper allocation of revenue to the various components of sales arrangements involving multiple deliverables over time, with the result that excessive revenue is recognized upfront.
6. Shipments to fictitious customers.
7. Recognizing revenues from contracts that are in essence consignment-type arrangements, such as:
   a. Bill-and-hold arrangements.
   b. Unusual deferred-payment schedules.
   c. Delivery to customer storage facilities paid for by the seller.
8. The buyer and seller enter into an underhanded reciprocal arrangement to boost revenue in which both parties record revenue or one party records revenue and the other an investment.
9. The seller is actually an agent but recognizes the full transaction value rather than just the agent's fees.
10. Net revenues are overstated because of inadequate provisions for deductions from gross revenues, such as provisions for returns and allowances.

Although revenue manipulation can be difficult to spot, it is often used in conjunction with other accounting schemes by a company bent on showing greater profit from year to year. It is sometimes easier to locate signs of other income manipulation schemes that may be part of a concerted effort to project better than actual operating results.

Two procedures that might have tipped the investor off in many of the famous revenue-inflating schemes of the past (as well as other income manipulation schemes) are formal analytical procedures simple to perform using an electronic spreadsheet—vertical analysis and horizontal analysis. Such analysis involves placing the items of income and expense from the company's most recent income statements (preferably at least five years) in a spreadsheet. The horizontal analysis is accomplished by determining the incremental difference from each year to the next for each item on the income statement and expressing this amount as a percentage. Thus, if commission expense increased from $10,000 last year to $12,000 this year, the $2,000 increase is shown as 20 percent. This amount of change can then be compared with the percentage change for this account in prior years or with changes in sales or payroll or other relevant accounts to see if the change is in proportion. Horizontal analysis will highlight increases or decreases in percentage for each line item on the income statement from year to year making it easy to spot trends that are out of line with expectations and require further investigation.

Vertical analysis begins with computing, for each year, what percentage each item on the income statement is of gross revenue—for example: gross profit, selling expense, and depreciation. Each item is then compared across time noting any changes in the percentage that a given statement item is to the gross revenue. As a general rule, the percentages should change little from year to year unless there is a compelling reason. If revenues are increasing from year to year, there is normally no *prima facie* reason that the gross profit or other expense items should decrease or fluctuate erratically. Vertical and horizontal analyses are typically used in tandem to spot items requiring further explanation. Horizontal analysis shows the percentage of change within an account and vertical analysis shows the relative percent each account is to gross revenue.

If a particular expense item is decreasing across the spreadsheet, it could be an indication of greater efficiency, *or* it could indicate that certain expenses are being capitalized that were previously written off. This occurs frequently in attempts to show a greater profit. Manipulation of cost of goods sold, deferral of operating expenses, and other schemes may be highlighted using this spreadsheet technique. Although spotting other income manipulation schemes does not directly imply that revenue is being inflated, the existence of these schemes are warning flags prompting further investigation of revenue recognition procedures in use.

¶2004   Expenses

Expenses are one of the six basic elements of financial accounting, along with assets, liabilities, owners' equity, revenue and net income. Expenses are determined by applying the expense recognition principles on the basis of relationships between acquisition costs [the term "cost" is commonly used to refer to the amount at which assets are initially recorded, regardless of how determined] and either the independently determined revenue or accounting periods. Since the point in time at which revenue and expenses are recognized is also the time at which changes in amounts of net assets are recorded, income determination is interrelated with asset valuation and expense recognition.

All costs are not expenses. Some costs are related to later periods, will provide benefits for later periods, and are carried forward as assets on the balance sheet. Other costs are incurred and provide no future benefit, having expired in terms of usefulness or applicability—these expired costs are called "expenses." All expenses, therefore, are part of the broader term "cost." These expired costs are not assets and are shown as deductions from revenue to determine net income.

Expenses are gross decreases in assets or gross increases in liabilities recognized and measured in conformity with U.S. GAAP that result from those types of profit-directed activities that can change an owner's equity.

.01 Recognizing Expenses

Three pervasive principles form the basis for recognizing expenses to be deducted from revenue to arrive at net income or loss:

1. Associating cause and effect ("matching")—For example, manufacturing cost of goods sold is measured and matched to the *sale* of the product. Assumptions must be made as to how these costs attach to the product—whether on machine hours, space used, or labor expended. Assumptions must also be made as to how the costs flow out (LIFO, FIFO, average costs).
2. Systematic and rational allocation—When there is no direct way to associate cause and effect and certain costs are known (or presumed) to have provided benefits during the accounting period, these costs are allocated to that period in a systematic and rational manner and to appear so to an unbiased observer. The methods of allocation should be consistent and systematic, though methods may vary for different types of costs. Examples are depreciation of fixed assets, amortization of intangibles depletion of natural resources and interperiod allocation of rent or interest. The allocation referred to here is not the allocation of expired manufacturing costs with the "cost" area to determine unit or job costs; it is rather the broader area of allocation to the manufacturing area from the unexpired asset ac-

count: Depreciation on factory building, rather than overhead-depreciation on Product A, B, or C.

3. Immediate recognition (period expenses)—Costs are expensed during an accounting period because:

   a. They cannot be associated on a cause-and-effect basis with revenue, yet no useful purpose would be achieved by delaying recognition to a future period,

   b. They provide no discernible future benefits, or

   c. They were recorded as assets in a prior period and now no longer provide discernible future benefits.

Examples are officers' salaries, advertising expenses, most selling expenses, legal fees (unless associated with acquisition or defense of certain intangible assets such as patents), and most general and administrative expenses.

¶2005   Other Revenues (and Expenses)

Expenses and revenue from *other* than sales of products, merchandise, or services should be separated from (operating) revenue and disclosed separately under Other Revenue (and Expenses). These are commonly referred to as ancillary or incidental expenses, rather than those related to the core operations of the entity.

¶2006   Imputed Interest on Notes Receivable or Payable

.01   Accounting Considerations

The American Institute of Certified Public Accountants (AICPA) sets forth the appropriate accounting when the face amount of certain receivables or payables ("notes") does not reasonably represent the present value of the consideration given or received in certain exchanges. The objective of these rules is to prevent the form of the transaction from prevailing over its economic substance. (*Present value* is the sum of future payments, discounted to the present date at an appropriate rate of interest.)

The FASB provides guidance for interest and imputed interest. ASC 835-30-25 states:

835-30-25-2   If determinable, the established exchange price (which, presumably, is the same as the price for a cash sale) of property, goods, or service acquired or sold in consideration for a note may be used to establish the present value of the note. When notes are traded in an open market, the market rate of interest and quoted prices of the notes provide the evidence of the present value. These methods are preferable means of establishing the present value of the note.

835-30-25-3 If an established exchange price is not determinable and if the note has no ready market, the problem of determining present value is more difficult. To estimate the present value of a note under such circumstances, an applicable interest rate is approximated that may differ from the stated or coupon rate. This process of approximation is called imputation, and the resulting rate is called an imputed interest rate. Nonrecognition of an apparently small difference between the stated rate of interest and the applicable current rate may have a material effect on the financial statements if the face amount of the note is large and its term is relatively long.

> Notes Exchanged for Cash or for Cash and Rights or Privileges

835-30-25-4 When a note is received or issued solely for cash and no other right or privilege is exchanged, it is presumed to have a present value at issuance measured by the cash proceeds exchanged. If cash and some other rights or privileges are exchanged for a note, the value of the rights or privileges shall be given accounting recognition as described in paragraph 835-30-25-6.

835-30-25-5 The total amount of interest during the entire period of a cash loan is generally measured by the difference between the actual amount of cash received by the borrower and the total amount agreed to be repaid to the lender. The difference between the face amount and the proceeds upon issuance is shown as either discount or premium. For example, if a bond is issued at a discount or premium, such discount or premium is recognized in accounting for the original issue. The coupon or stated interest rate is not regarded as the effective yield or market rate. Moreover, if a long-term non-interest-bearing note or bond is issued, its net proceeds are less than face amount and an effective interest rate is based on its fair value upon issuance.

835-30-25-6 A note issued solely for cash equal to its face amount is presumed to earn the stated rate of interest. However, in some cases the parties may also exchange unstated (or stated) rights or privileges, which are given accounting recognition by establishing a note discount or premium account. In such instances, the effective interest rate differs from the stated rate. For example, an entity may lend a supplier cash that is to be repaid five years hence with no stated interest. Such a non-interest-bearing loan may be partial consideration under a purchase contract for supplier products at lower than the prevailing market prices. In this circumstance, the difference between the present value of the receivable and the cash loaned to the supplier is appropriately regarded as an addition to the cost of products purchased during the contract term. The note discount shall be amortized as interest income over the five-year life of the note, as required by Section 835-30-35.

> Note Exchanged for Property, Goods, or Services

835-30-25-7   A note exchanged for property, goods, or service represents the following two elements, which may or may not be stipulated in the note:

    a.   The principal amount, equivalent to the bargained exchange price of the property, goods, or service as established between the supplier and the purchaser.

    b.   An interest factor to compensate the supplier over the life of the note for the use of funds that would have been received in a cash transaction at the time of the exchange.

835-30-25-8   Notes exchanged for property, goods, or services are valued and accounted for at the present value of the consideration exchanged between the contracting parties at the date of the transaction in a manner similar to that followed for a cash transaction.

835-30-25-9   The difference between the face amount and the present value upon issuance is shown as either discount or premium.

835-30-25-10   In circumstances where interest is not stated, the stated amount is unreasonable, or the stated face amount of the note is materially different from the current cash sales price for the same or similar items or from the fair value of the note at the date of the transaction, the note, the sales price, and the cost of the property, goods, or service exchanged for the note shall be recorded at the fair value of the property, goods, or service or at an amount that reasonably approximates the fair value of the note, whichever is the more clearly determinable. That amount may or may not be the same as its face amount, and any resulting discount or premium shall be accounted for as an element of interest over the life of the note.

835-30-25-11 In the absence of established exchange prices for the related property, goods, or service or evidence of the fair value of the note (as described in paragraph 835-30-25-2), the present value of a note that stipulates either no interest or a rate of interest that is clearly unreasonable shall be determined by discounting all future payments on the notes using an imputed rate of interest. This determination shall be made at the time the note is issued, assumed, or acquired; any subsequent changes in prevailing interest rates shall be ignored.

ASC 835-30-25-12, 25-13 also provide some general guides for determining an "appropriate" interest rate and the manner of amortization for financial reporting purposes.

IMPUTED INTEREST: When a sale is made for an amount that is collectible at a future time giving rise to an account receivable, the amount is regarded as consisting of a sales price *and* a charge for interest for the period of the payment deferral. ASC 835 requires that in the absence of a stated rate of interest, the present value of the receivable should be determined by reducing the face amount of the receivable by an interest rate that is approximated under the circumstances for the period that payment is deferred.

This rate is the *imputed rate.* It is determined by approximating the rate the supplier pays for financing receivables, or by determining the buyer's credit standing and applying the rate the borrower would have to pay if borrowing the sum from, say, a bank.

The process of arriving at the present value of the receivable is referred to as *discounting* the sum. If the total present value of the receivable (face amount plus the imputed interest) is less than the face amount, the difference between the face value of the receivable and its present value is recognized as a discount. If the present value exceeds the face amount of the receivable, the difference is recognized as a premium.

The sale is recorded as a debit to a receivable account, a credit to a discount on the receivable, and a credit to sales at the present value as reported for the receivable. The discount is amortized as a credit to interest income over the life of the receivable. On the balance sheet any unamortized discount at the end of the accounting period is reported as a direct subtraction from the *face amount* of the receivable.

Example: A seller ships merchandise totaling $10,000 to a customer with payment deferred for five years. Seller and customer agree to impute an interest charge of 10 percent for the $10,000. The journal entries follow.

Accounts Receivable	10,000	
Sales (Present value at 10%)		6,209
Unamortized Discount		3,791
(To record the sale of merchandise at the present value of the receivable)		

The *interest method* is applied to amortize the discount.

End of Year 1		
Unamortized Discount	620.90	
Interest Income (10% of $6,209.00)		620.90
End of Year 2		
Unamortized Discount	682.99	
Interest Income (10% of $6,829.90)		682.99
End of Year 3		
Unamortized Discount	751.29	
Interest Income (10% of $7,512.89)		751.29
End of Year 4		
Unamortized Discount	826.42	
Interest Income (10% of $8,264.18)		826.42
Unamortized Discount	909.06	
End of Year 5		
Unamortized Discount	909.06	
Interest Income (10% of $9,090.60)		909.06

At the end of five years full amortization of the discount has been recorded and the face amount of the receivable results. (*Note:* ASC 835 does not require the imputed interest method when "…receivables and payables arising from transactions with customers or suppliers in the normal course of business which are due in customary trade terms not exceeding approximately one year.")

¶2007   Earnings Per Share

According to ASC 260, a U.S. GAAP presentation of income requires that earnings per share (EPS) be calculated along with net income for public business entities. There are two separate calculations of EPS, one is the basic calculation using the weighted number of common shares outstanding for the year. The other is a "fully diluted" earnings per share, where the number of common shares used in the denominator of the calculation reflects potential dilution caused by the possible exercise of stock options, conversions of convertible bonds, conversions of convertible preferred stock or other stock transactions which could produce either more shares of common stock or less income into which the shares are divided.

Simple or Basic EPS. The calculation of basic EPS involves first modifying income if there are preferred shares of stock outstanding for the dividends to be paid on these shares. This reflects the fact that preferred shareholders are to be paid dividends prior to common shareholders and that once the preferred dividends have been paid, there will be fewer resources available to pay the common shareholders. Thus, although income itself is not actually reduced by the payment of preferred dividends, the net income figure used to compute EPS is reduced by subtracting the dividends on preferred shares. If the preferred stock is cumulative, the dividends are subtracted whether they have been declared for the year or not. When there are additional shares of common stock issued or repurchased during the year, the weighted average number of shares used in the denominator is computed by determining the effective number of shares outstanding for the periods before and after the issuance or repurchase of shares. Finally, if there is a stock split or stock dividend issued during the year, the number of common shares outstanding is retroactively increased back to the start of the year (or if prior years are being included in the financial statements, back to the beginning of those periods).

Fully Diluted EPS. The computation of fully diluted earnings per share can become complex depending on the contingent shares a corporation may be committed to issuing. If a corporation has incentive stock options, for example, the total number of shares that could arise through the exercise of the options and the subsequent issuance of additional shares must be computed. These shares are only added to the denominator if their overall effect is dilutive. Here a procedure referred to as the "treasury stock method" is used to determine potential dilution. This requires a calculation of the hypothetical proceeds resulting from the exercise of the stock options and the application of the proceeds received by the company from these options to the purchase of the company's own stock at its current market price on the date the options are exercised. This calculation will result in both an increase in the potential number of common shares outstanding from the exercise of the stock options and a decrease due to the hypothetical repurchase of treasury shares using the proceeds from the exercise of the options. Similar considerations are required for convertible debt, convertible preferred stock, and similar items with the potential to become common stock. For example, convertible debt uses the as if converted method, which adds the number of shares to be issued on conversion to the denominator and adds back to net income any interest expense incurred on that debt.

¶2008   Discontinued Operations

When an organization disposes of a component of its operations, whether by sale, closure, or discarding that component, and when certain criteria are met, related gains and losses are pulled out of other line items on the income statement and shown after net income from continuing operations, otherwise referred to as "below the line," net of taxes, combined into one line item. In order to qualify for classification as discontinued operations, the disposal of the component must represent a "strategic shift." That is, it can be dropping an entire product line; pulling out of an entire geographic region, etc. Also, in order to qualify as discontinued operations, the decision to dispose of the operations must result from a legal or regulatory body, such as a bankruptcy court, or by a resolution of the Board of Directors putting a plan of disposal in place from which there is a remote chance of any reversal of that plan. When discontinued operations are identified, there are two parts of the gain or loss. First is the income or loss from any ongoing operations during the reporting period from the date a plan was put into place to the disposal of the component or until year-end. Second is any gain or loss on sale or disposal. The total/net gain/loss is shown net of any applicable taxes.

¶2009   Comprehensive Income

Comprehensive income is all net income reported by an entity, including the net income from the income statement as well as other comprehensive income, consisting of certain unrealized gains and losses that go directly to equity without being shown in the income statement.

For a full discussion of comprehensive income, see Chapter 5, ¶5008.

CHAPTER 3
Stockholders' Equity

¶3000   Overview

"Stockholders' equity" is the most commonly used term to describe the section of the balance sheet encompassing the corporation's capital and retained earnings. Other terms used are "net worth," "net assets," or "capital and surplus" though the latter term is strongly discouraged by U.S. GAAP and its use is diminishing. Stockholders' equity consists of three broad source classifications:

1. Investments made by owners: Capital Stock (Common and/or Preferred)—at par value (legal value) or stated amount. Additional Paid-In Capital—"In Excess of Par," etc.
2. Income (loss) generated by operations: Retained Earnings—the accumulated undistributed annual profits (losses), after taxes and dividends.
3. Appraisal Capital—resulting from the revaluation of assets over historical cost (not in conformity with U.S. GAAP).

Changes in shareholders' equity, primarily in retained earnings, are caused by:

1. Periodic net income (loss) after taxes
2. Dividends declared
3. Prior period adjustments of retained earnings

4. Contingency reserves (appropriations of retained earnings)
5. Recapitalizations:
   a. Stock dividends and stock splits
   b. Changing par or stated value
   c. Reducing capital
   d. Quasi-reorganizations
   e. Stock reclassifications
   f. Substituting debt for stock
6. Treasury stock
7. Business combinations
8. Certain unrealized gains and losses (other comprehensive income)

¶3001   Capital Stock

Capital represents amounts contributed by the owners to the corporation. Although such contributions are sometimes made without increasing ownership, they are most commonly made in exchange for ownership in the corporation. Stock certificates are often prepared to be given in exchange for such contributions to represent ownership of a percentage of the corporation. Capital stock is the portion of equity in which this ownership is reported.

.01   Common Stock

The common stockholders are the residual owners of the corporation; that is, they own whatever is left after all preceding claims are paid off in a liquidation. By definition, common stock is "a stock which is subordinate to all other stocks of the issuer."

When a corporation has a single class of stock, it is sometimes called "capital stock" instead of "common stock." Three aspects of stock ownership are (1) dividends, (2) claims against assets on liquidation, and (3) shares in management (i.e. voting rights). As to these aspects of ownership, common stockholders usually have the following rights: (1) The amount of any/all dividend payments depends upon the profitability of the company. (2) Common stockholders have no fixed rights but, on the other hand, are limited to no maximum payment. (3) Their claim against the assets of the corporation on liquidation is last in the order of priority, following all creditors and all other equity interests. (4) The common stockholders, by statute, must have a (voting) voice in management. Their voice is often to the exclusion of all other equity interests, but they may also share their management rights with other classes of stock.

Common stock may be classified as par or no-par stock or class stock according to state law.

Par and No-Par Stock. Par stock is stock with a stated, legal dollar value, whereas no-par stock lacks such a given value. The distinction today is largely an academic one. However, state laws regarding stock dividends and stock splits and the adjustments of par value may affect the accounting treatment of such items.

Classes of Common Stock. Common stock may be divided into separate classes, such as class A or class B. Usually, the class distinction deals with the right to vote for separate directors, or one class may have the right to vote and one class may not. Class stock is a typical technique used where a minority group wishes to maintain control, while still giving ownership to others.

The equity section of a corporation's balance sheet must contain information on the number of shares of stock **authorized** under state law (stipulated in the articles of incorporation). In addition, the number of shares **issued** must be stated as well as the number of shares **outstanding**. The number of shares issued includes all shares sold to third parties, including those that have been purchased back by the company as treasury stock, as long as the shares have not been retired/cancelled. Thus, the number of shares outstanding refers only to those shares that are in the hands of stockholders, not including the shares owned by the company in its treasury.

.02 Preferred Stock

The second major type of capital stock is preferred stock, that which has some preference with regard to dividend payments or distribution of assets on liquidation. In the usual situation, preferred stock will have a preference on liquidation, to the extent of the par value of the stock. In addition, its right to dividends depends on whether it is classified as participating or nonparticipating, convertible, or cumulative or noncumulative.

Participating and Nonparticipating. If the preferred stock has limits on the dividends that can be issued each year (assuming a dividend is declared) and cannot share in any additional dividends over and above the stated amount or percentage of par value, it is nonparticipating preferred. If it is entitled to a share of any dividends over and above those to which it has priority, it is called participating. For example, a preferred may have the right to a 5 percent (of par) annual dividend and then share equally with the common stock in dividends after a dividend (equal to the preferred per-share dividend) has been paid to the common stockholders.

Cumulative and Noncumulative. A corporation that lacks earnings and profits, either current or accumulated, cannot pay dividends on its preferred on common stock. In that case, the question arises whether the past dividend must be paid in future years. If past dividends do accumulate and must be paid off, the stock is cumulative; otherwise, noncumulative.

The preferred may share voting rights equally with the common stock; it may lack voting rights under any circumstances; or it may have the right to vote only if either one or more dividend is passed. In the latter case, the preferred may have the exclusive right to vote for a certain number of directors to be sure that its interests as a class are protected.

Dividends are only accrued when declared by the board of directors. Care should be taken when computing earnings per share to reduce the earnings available for common dividends by the amount of dividends allocated to preferred stock including the current year's undeclared dividends on cumulative preferred stock.

Convertible Preferred Stock. Convertible preferred stock may, at the holder's option, be exchanged for common. The terms of the exchange and the conversion period are set forth on the preferred stock certificate. Thus, as an example, one share of $100 par preferred stock may be convertible beginning one year after issue into two shares of common if the conversion price is stated as $50. The preferred stockholder who converts will own two shares of common stock. A company will issue a convertible security at a time when it needs funds but for one reason or another cannot or does not wish to issue common stock. For example, in a weak stock market, common stock may be poorly received while a convertible preferred stock can be privately placed with a large institutional investor. The conversion privilege, from the point of view of the purchaser, is a "sweetener" since it affords the opportunity to take a full equity position in the future if the company prospers. The issuer may be quite satisfied to give the conversion privilege because it means that (assuming earnings rise) the preferred stock, with a prior and fixed dividend claim, will gradually be eliminated in exchange for common shares.

Accounting for a convertible preferred stock issuance follows the usual rules. That is, when the preferred stock is first issued, a separate capital account will be set up, to which will be credited the par value of the outstanding stock. When conversion takes place, an amount equal to the par value of the converted stock is debited to the preferred account. The common stock account will be credited with an amount equal to the par or stated value of the shares issued in exchange for the preferred. Any excess will go to capital surplus.

Both participating and convertible preferred stocks above must be taken into consideration when computing earnings per share.

.03   Par Value, Stated Capital, and Capital Stock Accounts

The money a corporation receives for its stock is in a unique category. It is variously referred to as "a cushion for creditors," "a trust fund," and similar expressions. The point is that in a corporation which gives its stockholders limited liability, the only funds to which the creditors of the corporation can look for repayment of their debts in the event the corporation suffers losses is the money received for stock, which constitutes the stated capital account. Consequently, most state corporation statutes require a number of steps to be taken before a corporation can reduce its stated capital. These steps include approval by the stockholders and the filing of a certificate with the proper state officer, so that creditors may be put on notice of the reduction in capital.

Stated capital is actually divided into separate accounts, each account for a particular class of stock. Thus, a corporation may have outstanding a class A common, a class B common, a first preferred, and a second preferred. Each class would have its own account, which would show the number of shares of the class authorized by the certificate of incorporation, the number actually issued and the consideration received by the corporation.

It is at this point that the distinction between par and no-par stock becomes important. Par stock is rarely sold for less than its par value, although it may be sold for more. In many states, it is illegal to sell stock at a discount from par, and even when not illegal, there may be a residual stockholder liability for that original discount to the creditors. In any case, an amount equal to the par value of the stock must be credited to its capital account, with any excess going into a surplus account.

In the case of no-par stock, the entire amount received for sale of the stock is recorded to the stock account. At times, no-par stock is given a stated value, either through its board of directors or at a stockholders' meeting, in which case the entity assigns part of the consideration received as stated capital for the stock and treats the rest as additional paid in capital. Treating part of the consideration received as stated capital is the equivalent of giving the stock a par value, even though there was no par value assigned in the articles of incorporation.

.04   Capital Stock Issued for Property

Where capital stock is issued for property in a non-cash transfer, measurement of owners' investment is usually determined by using the fair market value of the assets received (and/or the discounted present value of any liabilities transferred).

When the fair value of the assets transferred cannot be measured, the market value of the stock issued may be used instead for establishing the value of the property received. In more common terms, the value of whichever item has the more reliable fair value is used to value the transaction.

When the acquisition is an entire business, the principle of "fair value" is extended to cover all assets acquired (other than goodwill). If the fair *value* of the whole business is considered to be *more* than the individual values, that excess is considered to be goodwill. In other words, if the value of consideration given is higher than the fair value of the net assets received, goodwill is recorded. If the fair value of consideration given is less than the fair value of the net assets acquired, a gain on acquisition is recorded. See more guidance in the Business Combinations section of Chapter 6.

.05 Capital in Excess of Par or Stated Value

The term "capital surplus" is rarely used and its use is discouraged by U.S. GAAP as misleading to shareholders; the preferred terminology is "capital in excess of par" or, more commonly, "additional paid-in capital."

The capital in excess of par account is credited with capital received by the corporation which is not part of par value or stated capital. It is primarily the excess of consideration received over par value or the amount of consideration received for no-par stock which is not assigned as stated capital.

In addition, donations of capital to the corporation are credited to this account. If stated capital is ever reduced as permitted by law, the transfer is from the capital stock account to this capital in excess of par account.

This account is also credited for the excess of market value over par value for stock dividends (which are not stock splits) and for the granting of certain stock options and rights.

To further the description provided above, the concept of par value was originally put into place to protect creditors. Stockholders could be held personally liable to creditors for amounts up to par value. Security laws have changed over the years to better protect shareholders. Par value is largely meaningless now from a legal standpoint. However, it is still often used in keeping with tradition. Therefore, we must still be aware of the accounting that has been previously described.

¶3002 Retained Earnings

Terminology bulletins do not have authoritative status; however, they are issued as useful guides. Accounting Terminology Bulletin No. 1 recommended that:

1. The term "surplus" be abandoned.
2. The term "earned surplus" be replaced with such terms that indicate the source, such as:
   a. Retained Earnings,
   b. Retained Income,
   c. Accumulated Earnings, or
   d. Earnings Retained for Use in the Business.

Retained earnings are the accumulated undistributed past and current years' earnings, net of taxes paid and dividends declared.

Portions of retained earnings may be set aside for certain contingencies, appropriated for such purposes as possible future inventory losses, sinking funds, etc. A Statement of Changes in Retained Earnings is one of the basic financial statements *required* for fair presentation of results of operation and financial condition to conform with U.S. GAAP. It shows net income, dividends, and prior period adjustments. A Statement of Changes in Stockholders' Equity includes that required information and shows additional investments by owners, retirements of owners' interests and similar events (if these are few and simple, they may be put in the notes).

Regardless of how a company displays its undistributed earnings, or the disclosures thereof, for tax purposes, the actual earnings and profits which could have been or are still subject to distribution as "dividends" *under IRS regulations* may, under some circumstances, retain that characteristic for the purpose of ordinary income taxation to the ultimate recipient. U.S. GAAP reporting does not require disclosure of IRS earnings and profits calculations which determine the tax status of dividends.

¶3003   Prior Period Adjustments

Only the following rare types of items should be treated as prior period adjustments and *not* be included in the determination of current period net income:

1.   Correction of an error (material) in prior financial statements; and
2.   Realization of income tax pre-acquisition operating loss benefits of *purchased* subsidiaries.

Corrections of errors are *not* changes in accounting estimates. Error corrections are those resulting from:

1.   Mathematical errors;
2.   Erroneous application of accounting principles; and
3.   Misuse of, or oversight of, facts existing at a prior statement period.

Changes in accounting *estimates* result from *new* information or developments, which sharpen and improve judgment.

Litigation settlements and income tax adjustments *no longer* meet the definition of prior period adjustments. However, for *interim periods only* (of the current fiscal year), material items of this nature should be treated as prior interim adjustments to the identifiable period of related business activity.

Goodwill cannot be written off as a prior period adjustment.

Retroactive adjustment should be made of all comparative periods presented, reflecting changes to particular items, net income and retained earnings balances. The tax effects should also be reflected and shown. Disclosure of the effects of the restatement should be made.

Prior period adjustments must be charged or credited to the opening balance of retained earnings. They cannot be included in the determination of net income for the current period. For income tax purposes such changes must be disclosed in Schedule M-2 of form 1120.

Beginning Retained Earnings			1,000
Correction of Depreciation Error			
$300 × .50 (net of tax)			150
Adjusted Beginning Retained Earnings			1,150
Net Income			400
Ending—Retained Earnings			$1,550
Journal entry:			
Accumulated Depreciation	$300		
Taxes Payable		150	
Retained Earnings		150	

¶3004   Contingency

A "contingency" is defined as "an existing condition, situation, or set of circumstances involving uncertainty as to possible gain or loss to an enterprise that will ultimately be resolved when one or more events occur or fail to occur." Loss contingencies fall into three categories:

1. Probable
2. Reasonably possible
3. Remote

In deciding whether to accrue the estimated loss by charging income or setting aside an appropriation of retained earnings, or merely to make a disclosure of the contingency in the notes to the financial statement, the following standards have been set:

A charge is accrued as an expense and liability if *both* of the following conditions are met at the date of the financial statements:

1. Information available *before* the issuance of the financial statements indicates that it is probable the asset will be impaired or a liability incurred; and
2. A *reasonable* estimate of the loss *can* be made.

(When a contingent loss is probable but the reasonable estimate of the loss can only be made in terms of a range, the amount shall be accrued for the loss. When some amount within the range appears at the time to be a better estimate than any other amount within the range, that amount shall be accrued. When no amount within the range is a better estimate than any other amount, the minimum amount in the range shall be accrued.)

When a contingent loss is only *reasonably possible* or the probable loss cannot be estimated, an estimate of the *range* of loss should be made or a narrative description given to indicate that *no* estimate was possible. Disclosure should be made; but no accrual is recorded.

When the contingency is *remote*, disclosure is optional but should be made when it is in the nature of a guarantee. Additionally, even if the contingency is remote, it must be disclosed if it is expected to be resolved within one year or less and the impact on the entity could be catastrophic. Other remote contingencies are not required to be disclosed, but they may be, if desired, for more significant reporting.

General reserves for unspecified business risks are not to be accrued and no disclosure is required.

Appropriations for loss contingencies from retained earnings must be shown with the stockholders' equity section of the balance sheet, and clearly identified as such.

Examples of loss contingencies are:

1. Collectability of receivables.
2. Obligations related to product warranties and product defects.
3. Risk of loss or damage of enterprise property by fire, explosion, or other hazards.
4. Threat of expropriation of assets.
5. Pending or threatened litigation.
6. Actual or possible claims and assessments.
7. Risk of loss from catastrophes assumed by property and casualty insurance companies including reinsurance companies.
8. Guarantees of indebtedness of others.
9. Obligations of commercial banks under "standby letters of credit."
10. Agreements to repurchase receivables (or to repurchase the related property) that have been sold.

Handling of these loss contingencies depends upon the nature of the loss probability and the reasonableness of estimating the loss. (Gain contingencies are not booked, only footnoted.)

¶3005   Recapitalizations

Essentially, a recapitalization means changing the structure of the capital accounts. It can also mean a reshuffling between equity and debt. A recapitalization may be done voluntarily by the corporation; or it may be part of a reorganization proceeding in a court, pursuant to a bankruptcy or a reorganization petition filed by the corporation or its creditors.

In almost all cases of recapitalizations, stockholder approval is required at some point during the process. This is because a recapitalization may affect the amount of stated capital of the corporation or change the relationships between the stockholders and the corporation or between classes of stockholders. The different categories of recapitalizations are discussed in the following paragraphs.

.01   Stock Splits

A stock split involves dividing the outstanding shares into a larger number, as, for example, two for one in which each stockholder receives a certificate for additional shares equal to the amount of shares already held. The stock split is reflected in the corporate books by reducing the par value or the stated value of the outstanding shares. Thus, if shares with a par value of $10 are split two for one, the new par becomes $5. No entry is necessary, other than a memo entry. The stockholder adjusts his or her basis for the unit number of shares.

Reverse Split. The opposite of a stock split is a reverse split, which results in a lesser number of outstanding shares. Stockholders turn in their old certificates and receive a new certificate for one-half, for example, of former holdings. The par value or stated value is adjusted to show the higher price per share. A reverse split is sometimes used in order to increase the price of the stock immediately on the open market.

.02   Stock Dividends

As far as the stockholder is concerned, a stock dividend is the same as the stock split; the stockholder receives additional shares, merely changing the unit-basis of holding. But the effect is quite different from the point of view of the corporation. A stock dividend requires a transfer from retained earnings of the *market value* of the shares. Capital stock is credited for the par value and capital in excess of par value is credited for the excess of market price over par. (The stockholder who has the option of receiving cash must report the dividend as ordinary income.)

.03   Stock Split Effected in the Form of a Dividend

Usually, a stock distribution is either a dividend or a stock split. However, when the stock dividend is 25 percent or more, a third or hybrid classification is employed and the dividend is referred to as a large stock dividend.

In those instances where the stock dividend materially reduces the market value, U.S. GAAP and in particular an SEC rule requires the transfer or capitalization of a portion of the company's retained earnings. In addition, because certain states require that retained earnings must be capitalized in order to maintain par value, those types of transactions should be described by the corporation as a "stock split effected in the form of a dividend." The entry would then be a reduction of retained earnings and an increase in capital stock for the *par value* (not the market value) of the distribution. For income tax purposes, the corporation may be required to show this reduction of retained earnings as a Schedule M adjustment and may technically still have to consider it as available for ordinary rate ultimate distribution.

¶3006   Changing Par or Stated Value of Stock

This type of recapitalization involves changing from par to no-par or vice versa. This is usually done in conjunction with a reduction of stated capital and is effected by an amendment to the articles of incorporation. A corporation, for example, may decide to change its stock from par stock to no-par stock in order to take advantage of lower franchise fees and transfer taxes. Or no-par shares may be changed to shares having par value to solve legal problems existing under particular state statutes. A par value stock which is selling in the market at a price lower than its par must be changed if the corporation intends to issue new stock. This is necessary because of some state laws which prohibit a corporation from selling its par value stock for less than par value. In such a case, the corporation may reduce par value or may change the par to no-par; thereby, the new stock can be given a stated value equivalent to the price it can bring in the open market.

¶3007   Quasi-Reorganizations

Current or future years' charges should be made to the income accounts instead of to capital surplus. An exception to this rule (called "readjustment") occurs when a corporation elects to restate its assets, capital stock and retained earnings and thus avail itself of permission to relieve its future income account or retained earnings account of charges which would otherwise be made. In such an event, the corporation should make a clear report to its shareholders of the restatements proposed to be made, and obtain their formal consent. It should present a fair balance sheet as at the date of the readjustment, in which the readjustments of the carrying amounts are reasonably complete, in order that there may be no continuation of the circumstances which justify charges to capital surplus.

As an example of how this readjustment might occur, suppose that a company has a deficit in its retained earnings (earned surplus) of $100,000. By revaluing its assets upward, it is possible for this company to create a capital surplus account for the write-up to fair value, then write off the deficit in retained earnings to that account. From then on, a new retained earnings account should be established and the fact be disclosed for ten years.

¶3008 Stock Reclassifications

Another category of stock recapitalization involves reclassifying the existing stock. This means that outstanding stock of a particular class is exchanged for stock of another class. For example, several outstanding issues of preferred stock may be consolidated into a single issue. Or, common stock may be exchanged for preferred stock, or vice versa. The objective in this type of reclassification is to simplify the capital structure, which in many cases is necessary in order to make a public offering or sometimes to eliminate dividend arrearages on preferred stock by offering a new issue of stock in exchange for canceling such arrearages.

¶3009 Substituting Debt for Stock

One form of recapitalization that has become popular in some areas involves substituting bonds for stock. The advantage to the corporation is the substitution of tax-deductible interest on bonds for nondeductible dividends on preferred stock. Of course, where dealing with a closely held corporation, substituting debt for stock in a manner to give the common stockholders a pro rata portion of the debt may be interpreted for tax purposes as "thin" capitalization, and the bonds may be treated as stock, regardless.

Also, to attract new money into the corporation, it is advantageous to consider the issuance of convertible debt securities bonds—to which are attached the rights (warrants) to buy common stock of the company at a specified price. The advantages of this type of security are:

1. An interest rate that is lower than the issuer could establish for nonconvertible debt;
2. An initial conversion price greater than the market value of the common stock; and
3. A conversion price that does not decrease.

The portion of proceeds from these securities that can be applied to the warrants should be credited to paid-in capital (based on fair value of both securities) and discounts or premiums should be treated as they would be under conventional bond issuance.

¶3010 Treasury Stock

Treasury stock is stock that has previously been issued by a corporation but is no longer outstanding. It has been reacquired by the corporation and, as its name implies, held in its treasury. Treasury stock is not canceled because cancellation reduces the authorized issue of corporation stock.

.01   Treasury Stock Shown at Cost

When a corporation acquires its own stock to be held for future sale or possible use in connection with stock options, or with no plans or uncertainty as to future retirement of that stock, the cost of the acquired stock can be shown separately as a contra-equity, or deduction from the total of capital stock, capital surplus and retained earnings. Gains on subsequent sales (over the acquired-cost price) should be credited to additional paid-in capital or additional capital in excess of par and losses (to the extent of prior gains) should be charged to that same account, with excess losses going to retained earnings. State law should be followed if in contravention.

Although extremely rare, if adequately disclosed, it is permissible in some circumstances to show stock of a corporation held in its own treasury as an asset. For example, pursuant to a corporation's bonus arrangement with certain employees, treasury stock may be used to pay the bonus, and, in accordance with the concept of a current asset satisfying a current liability, that applicable treasury stock might be shown as current asset. However, dividends on such stock should not be treated as income while the corporation holds the stock. Furthermore, it should also be noted that even though it is permissible, it is not according to U.S. GAAP to report treasury stock as an asset.

Treasury stock has neither voting rights nor the right to receive dividends. (Note: treasury stock remains *issued* stock, but not *outstanding* stock). Treasury stock can either be retired or resold. Treasury stock is a contra-owners' equity account and is deducted from the stockholders' equity on the balance sheet.

When a company buys its own stock:		
Treasury Stock	XXX	
Cash		XXX
If the stock is resold:		
Cash	XXX	
Treasury Stock		XXX
(The credit is the amount paid for the stock when purchased by the corporation)		

If there is a difference between the corporation's acquisition of the stock and the resale price, the difference is debited or credited to an account Paid-In Capital from Treasury Stock Transactions for the amount of the difference between the proceeds of the resale and the amount paid by the corporation.

Under the cost method, treasury stock is shown as the last item before arriving at stockholders' equity, while under the par value method treasury stock reduces the common stock account directly under the capital stock section of stockholders' equity.

Statement of Changes in Stockholders' Equity. As noted above, a Statement of Retained Earnings shows the factors that caused retained earnings to increase or decrease during the period. An alternative, and more comprehensive presentation, is provided by a Statement of Changes in Stockholders' Equity. While it is not required that U.S. GAAP financial statements contain a Statement of Changes in Stockholders' Equity, many corporations prepare this statement as a means of disclosing in one place information about changes in all aspects of shareholders' equity, not merely retained earnings. Formal disclosure is required for changes in different classes of common stock, additional paid-in capital, dividends paid, retained earnings, prior period adjustments, treasury stock, and other comprehensive income. If the Statement of Changes in Stockholders' Equity is prepared, it replaces the Statement of Retained Earnings and eliminates the need to separately disclose in notes or parenthetically the other changes that occurred within stockholders' equity. If a corporation chooses to include a Statement of Changes in Stockholders' Equity, containing comprehensive income as well as changes in stock issuance, it must display this statement as a major financial statement.

In preparing a Statement of Changes in Stockholders' Equity the corporation will list separately columns for the number of common shares and their par or stated value (or if more than one class of common exists, a column for each), a column for the number and par value of preferred stock if any, columns showing additional paid-in capital for common, treasury, and preferred stock, a column for treasury stock, as well as columns for retained earnings and other comprehensive income. The notations to the left indicate the causes or sources of changes in each of these categories.

The topic of other comprehensive income is discussed in Chapter 5, "Presentation and Disclosure." It represents elements of income or expense not reported in the Income Statement but representing changes in the corporation's equity. Other comprehensive income includes items requiring revaluation of assets or liabilities resulting in balance sheet changes not currently reflected in the income statement. These include, for example, changes in the valuation account for available-for-sale securities or translation adjustments from converting the financial statements of a company's foreign operations to U.S. dollars. See Chapter 2, "Income Statement," for a full discussion of this topic.

Sample Format for Statement of Changes in Stockholders' Equity

Statement of Changes in Stockholders' Equity For the Year Ended 12/31/XX	Common Shares Issued	Stock Shares Amount	Additional Capital Common Stock	Paid-in Treasury Stock	Retained Earnings	Accumulated Other Comprehensive Income	Treasury Stock
Balances 1/1/XX	1,000	$2,000	$15,000	$50	$125,000	$4,000	($200)
Issued for cash	500	1,000	10,000				
Unrealized increase in value of available-for-sale securities						700	
Treasury stock acquired							(300)
Net income					35,000		
Cash dividends					(6000)		
Conversion debt to stock		25	50	250			
Stock options exercised		10	20	100			
Balances 12/31/XX	1,535	$3,070	$25,350	$50	$154,000	$4,700	($500)

.02   Treasury Stock Shown at Par or Stated Value

When treasury stock is acquired for the purpose of *retirement* (or constructive retirement), the stock should be shown at par value or stated value as a reduction in the equity section; the excess of purchase cost over par (stated) value should be charged to additional paid-in capital to the extent of prior gains booked for the same issue, together with pro rata portions applicable to that stock arising from prior stock dividends, splits, etc. Any remaining excess may be applied pro rata to either common stock or to retained earnings.

CHAPTER 4
Statement of Cash Flows

¶4000   Overview

The term "cash flow" refers to a variety of concepts, but its most common meaning is the net amount of cash and cash equivalents being transferred into and out of a business. The *concept* of cash flow can be used effectively as one of the major factors in funding operations, judging the ability to meet debt retirement requirements, to maintain regular dividends, and to finance replacement and expansion costs.

Assessing a company's cash flow is a valuable tool in evaluating the quality of earnings reported on the income statement. A statement of cash flow, one of the four statements required by U.S. GAAP, provides an analysis of the amount and source of cash flow, whether from operating, investing, or financing activities.

The statement of cash flows can be the most difficult to understand of the financial statements. The author believes it is significantly underutilized and is often difficult to understand because of the highly predominant use of the indirect method. The indirect method and the reason it contributes to this difficulty are described below.

¶4001   Importance of Cash Flow

The concept of cash flow was originated by security analysts. It has been stated that in evaluating the investment value of a company, cash flow is frequently regarded as more meaningful to them than net income.

Cash flow from operations data in financial summaries shows the liquid or near-liquid resources generated from operations that may be available for the discretionary use of management. Analysts have suggested that this is a useful measure of the ability of the entity to accept new investment opportunities, to maintain its current productive capacity by replacement of fixed assets, and to make distributions to shareholders without drawing on new external sources of capital.

While information about cash flow from operating activities is useful, it should be considered carefully within the framework of the complete statement of cash flows. This statement reflects management's decisions as to the use of these cash flows and the external sources of capital used in relation to investing and financing activities. The implication of considering or analyzing only the cash flows generated from the operations portion of a cash flows statement is that its use is entirely at the discretion of management. In fact, certain obligations (e.g., mortgage payments) may exist even if replacement of nondepreciating assets is considered unnecessary.

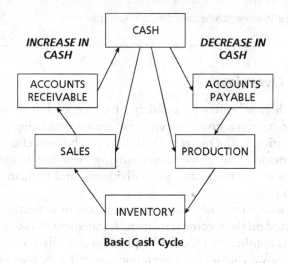

Basic Cash Cycle

In using cash flow as an analytic tool, care is required. For example, Corporation X has been capitalized with straight common stock. Corporation Y, the same size as Corporation X and comparable in other respects, has been capitalized 25 percent with common stock and 75 percent with debt. A cash flow equivalent to, say, 20 percent of each corporation's gross sales will seem to be four times as large in relation to Corporation Y's stock when compared with the common stock of Corporation X. Cash flow as a meaningful tool, therefore, will have more significance when related to industries and companies in which long-term debt is limited or at least taken into consideration in the analysis.

For industries where depreciation represents a material expense on the income statement, the cash flow statement accentuates the potential difference between a company's earnings and its cash flow from operations. Since depreciation is an expense that reduces income but does not use cash, the greater the amount of depreciation the greater will be the discrepancy between net income and cash flow from operations. Other noncash items with a similar impact are bad debt expense, stock-based compensation, and other gains and losses.

High cash flow is also the reason that some companies with meager earnings per share are able to pay cash dividends, sometimes in excess of earnings. The SEC has noted situations where investors were misled by these cash distributions in excess of net income when not accompanied by disclosure indicating clearly that part of the distribution represented a return *of* capital rather than a return *on* capital.

In the extractive industries such as oil, coal and other natural resources, the depletion allowance and amortization of development costs, in addition to depreciation, are responsible for increasing the extent of cash flow relative to net income.

Cash flow also helps analysts judge whether debt commitments can be met without refinancing, whether the regular cash dividend can be maintained despite ailing earnings, whether the extractive industries (i.e., oils and mining) will be able to continue exploration without raising additional capital, or whether additional facilities can be acquired without increasing debt or present capital.

Relative cash flow is an important factor in deciding whether to buy or lease. But it is not necessarily true that owning property creates funds for use in expansion. The cash made available to a corporation through operations will be similar whether the business property is owned or leased. Owned property acquired by borrowed capital will require periodic payments on the debt which will have to be met before funds are available for expansion.

¶4002   ASC 230, *Statement of Cash Flows*

ASC 230 originated from the issuance of Statement of Financial Accounting Standards No. 95 (FAS 95), issued in November 1987. FAS 95 established the standards for reporting cash flows in the financial statements. It superseded APB Opinion 19, *Reporting Changes in Financial Position*, and superseded or amended prior pronouncements. Specifically, ASC 230 requires disclosure of cash flows to be included in the full set of financial statements. The international accounting requirements (iGAAP) for a statement of cash flows are presented in IAS 7, Cash Flow Statements. The U.S. and IASB standards are substantially the same.

The Statement of Cash Flows breaks cash inflows and outflows into three categories. Those categories are operating activities, investing activities, and financing activities.

Business enterprises are encouraged to report cash flows from operating activities *directly* by disclosing the major sources of operating cash receipts and disbursements (the *direct* method). Enterprises can elect not to show operating cash receipts and disbursements, but will be required to disclose the same amount of net cash flow from operating activities *indirectly* by adjusting net income to reconcile the net cash flow from operating activities (the *indirect reconciliation method*) by eliminating the effects of:

- All deferrals of past operating cash receipts and payments.
- All accruals of expected future operating cash receipts and payments.
- All items that are included in net income that do *not* affect operating cash receipts and payments.

It should be noted that if the direct method is applied, a reconciliation of net income and net cash flow from operating activities is required to be provided in a separate schedule, except not-for-profit entities, for which this requirement was eliminated.

Although the FASB encourages use of the direct method, a vast majority of entities uses the indirect method. Because the reconciliation described in the preceding paragraph must be prepared by most entities, the direct method requires more information and effort than the indirect method. So organizations seldom use it. For investing and financing activities, both methods are exactly the same, showing cash coming in and going out. The only difference is in operating activities. The operating activities of a direct method statement are similar to investing and financing. That is, it shows cash coming in and going out. The operating section of an indirect method, however, is made up of noncash items. It begins with net income and adjusts out all the noncash items to end up with cash from operations. It is the author's opinion that someone with little or no expertise in a statement of cash flows may look at the statement and see that the entire first section, of what is supposed to be a statement of cash flows, is all made of items that are NOT cash flows. It is no wonder one can be confused! More detailed guidance on the two methods is provided below.

If a reporting company has foreign business operations, the cash flows statement must disclose the currency equivalent of foreign currency cash flows, applying the current exchange rate at the time of the cash flow. The effect of changes in the exchange rates is disclosed as a separate item in the reconciliation of beginning and ending balances of cash and cash equivalents.

Information about investing and financing activities not resulting in cash receipts or payments is to be disclosed separately.

.01   Terminology

Precise definitions to clarify the meaning of the terms related specifically to ASC 230 can be helpful to an understanding of the requirements.

Cash. Includes currency on hand, demand deposits with banks, and accounts with financial institutions that have the general characteristics of demand deposits; e.g., a depository that accepts deposits and permits withdrawals without prior notice or penalty.

Cash Equivalent. Short-term, highly liquid investments that are 1) readily convertible into known amounts of cash, and 2) near enough to maturity (see *Original Maturity*) that a change in the interest rate structure presents an insignificant risk of changes in the value of the investment.

Cash Flow. Cash receipts and cash payments resulting from investing, financing, or operating activities.

Direct Method. Shows the principal components to be operating cash receipts and payments; e.g., cash received from accounts receivable; cash paid to suppliers.

Financing Activities. Issuing stock; repurchasing stock; paying dividends; borrowing money; paying borrowings; long-term credit. In general, transactions to acquire and repay capital.

Indirect Method. Computation starts with net income that is adjusted for revenue and expense items *not* resulting from operating cash transactions (e.g., noncash transactions) to reconcile to net cash flow from operating activities. This method does not disclose operating cash receipts and payments.

Investing Activities. Making loans; collecting loans; acquiring and disposing of debt; acquiring and disposing of equity; acquiring and disposing of productive assets (e.g., plant and equipment).

Net Cash Flow. The arithmetic sum of gross cash receipts and gross cash payments which results in the net cash flow from operating activities.

Noncash and Investing Activities. Investing and financing activities that affect assets or liabilities, but do not result in cash receipts or cash payments.

Operating Activities. All transactions and other events that are not defined as investing or financing activities. Cash flows from activities which generally result from transactions and other events that enter into the determination of net income.

Original Maturity. An investment *purchased* three months from the maturity date.

NOTE: An investment *purchased more than three months from maturity is not* a cash equivalent, even though its remaining maturity on financial statement date is within the three months' rule.

.02   Summary

The summary that follows brings together in columnar format the significant requirements of ASC 230.

1.   The objective of ASC 230 is to provide detailed information about the cash receipts and cash payments of an enterprise during a specified accounting period.
2.   The statement of cash flows reports the cash effects of any enterprise's operations, investing transactions and financing transactions.

3. Related disclosures detail the effects of investing and financing transactions that affect an enterprise's financial position, but do not directly affect cash flows.
4. Net income and net cash flow from operating activities are reconciled to provide information about the *net* effects of operating transactions, other events, and financial activities.
5. The cash flows statement should explain the change during specified accounting period in cash and cash equivalents.
6. ASC 230 requires enterprises with foreign currency transactions (e.g., cash receipts and payments) to report the currency equivalent of foreign currency cash flows applying the exchange rates in effect at the time of the cash flows. (A weighted average exchange rate for the period for translation is permissible.)
7. Noncash transactions have a significant effect on the cash flows of a company and should be disclosed.

¶4003   Classification of Cash Receipts and Cash Payments

.01   Resulting from Operating Activities

Cash Inflows	Cash Outflows
Receipts from sale of goods and services.	Payments to suppliers.
Collections on accounts.	Payments on accounts.
Collections on short- and long-term notes and other credit arrangements.	Principal payments on short- and long-term payables.
Interest and dividend receipts.	Interest payments.
Other cash receipts that do not originate from investment or financing activities.	Other cash payments that do not originate from investment or financing activities.
Generally, the cash effects of transactions that enter into the determination of net income.	Payments to employees, tax payments, etc.

.02   Resulting from Investing Activities

Cash Inflows	Cash Outflows
Principal collections on loans (notes receivable).	Loans made (notes receivable). Payment for debt instruments of subsidiaries.
Sale of equity securities of other enterprises.	Purchases of equity securities of other enterprises.
Sale of plant, equipment, property, and other productive assets.	Purchases of plant, equipment, property, and other productive assets.

.03 Resulting from Financing Activities

Cash Inflows	Cash Outflows
Proceeds from new securities issued.	Repurchase of enterprise's equity securities.
Bonds, mortgages, notes, and other indebtedness.	Debt repayments; dividend payments.

¶4004 Direct Method—Discussion and Illustration

Two methods for preparing the statement of cash flows are provided by ASC 230, the direct method and the indirect method. While the direct method is preferred by the FASB, the indirect method is more widely used in practice. The direct method requires reporting the three major classes of gross cash receipts and gross cash payments, as well as their arithmetic sum to disclose the *net cash flow* from operating activities.

The rule allows reporting entities to detail cash receipts and payments to any extent considered to be meaningful. For example, payments to suppliers might be divided between raw material purchases and other major supplies used in the business. Wage and salary payments might be divided between manufacturing, selling, and administrative expenses. Sales receipts could be divided among different sources, with an "other" operating cash receipts, if any.

The reconciliation of net income to net cash flow from operating activities must be provided in a separate schedule.

Statement of Cash Flows Increase (Decrease) in Cash and Cash Equivalents

(Direct Method) Year Ended December 31, 20XX		
Cash flows from operating activities:		
Cash received from customers	$ 435,000	
Interest received	5,000	
Cash paid to employees and suppliers	(382,000)	
Interest paid	(13,000)	
Taxes paid	(20,000)	
Net cash flow from operations		$ 25,000

Cash flows from *investing* activities:		
Marketable securities purchases	$(32,500)	
Proceeds—marketable securities sales	20,000	
Loans made	(8,500)	
Loan collections	6,000	
Plant purchase	(80,000)	
Proceeds—sale of plant assets	37,500	
Net cash used in investing activities		$(57,500)
Cash flows from *financing* activities:		
Loan proceeds	$ 22,500	
Debt repayment	(27,500)	
Proceeds—Bond issue	50,000	
Proceeds—Common Stock issue	25,000	
Dividends paid	(20,000)	
Net cash provided by financing activities		$ 50,000
Net increase (decrease) in cash		$ 17,500

The following is a more comprehensive Statement of Cash Flow from operations applying the *direct* method. This approach includes the disclosure of noncash transactions in a separate schedule formatted beneath the statement.

Statement of Cash Flows Increase (Decrease) in Cash and Cash Equivalents

(Direct Method) Year Ended December 31, 20XX		
Cash flow from operations:		
Cash from receivables	$10,000,000	
Dividend receipts	700,000	
Cash paid to suppliers	2,000,000	
Wage and salary payments	4,000,000	
Interest payments	750,000	
Taxes	1,000,000	
Net cash flow from operations		$ 2,950,000

Cash flow from investing activities:		
Property and plant purchases	(4,000,000)	
Proceeds from sale of equipment	2,500,000	
Acquisition of Corporation X	(900,000)	
Securities purchases	(4,700,000)	
Securities sales	5,000,000	
Borrowings	(7,500,000)	
Collections on notes receivable	5,800,000	
Net cash outflow from investments		$(3,800,000)
Cash flow from financing activities:		
Increase in customer deposits	1,100,000	
Short-term borrowings (increase)	75,000	
Short-term debt payments	(300,000)	
Long-term debt proceeds	1,250,000	
Lease payments	(125,000)	
Common stock issue	500,000	
Dividends to shareholders	(450,000)	
Net cash provided by financing		$ 2,050,000
Foreign exchange rate change		100,000
Net increase (decrease) in cash		$ 1,300,000
Schedule—Noncash Investing and Financing Activities:		
Incurred lease obligation	$ 750,000	
Acquisition of Corporation X:		
Working capital acquired (except cash)	(100,000)	
Property and plant acquired	3,000,000	
Assumed long-term debt	(2,000,000)	
Cash paid for acquisition	$ 900,000	
Common stock issued in payment of long-term debt	$ 250,000	

¶4005   Indirect Method—Discussion and Illustration

The indirect method requires *net cash flow* to be reported indirectly with an adjustment of net income to reconcile it to net cash flow from operating activities. The adjustment requires:

1. The removal from net income of the effects of all deferrals of past operating cash receipts and payments.
2. The removal from net income of the effects of all accruals of expected future operating cash receipts and payments.
3. The removal from net income of the effects of items of all investing and financing cash flows.

The reconciliation can be reported *either* within the statement of cash flows *or* in a separate schedule, with the statement of cash flows reporting only the net cash flow from operating activities. However, if the reconciliation is disclosed in the cash flow statement, the adjustments to net income must be identified as reconciling items.

Statement of Cash Flows Increase (Decrease) in Cash and Cash Equivalents

(Indirect Method) Year Ended December 31, 20XX		
Cash flows from *operating* activities:		
Net cash flow from operating activities		$ 25,000
Cash flows from *investing* activities:		
Marketable securities purchases	$(32,500)	
Proceeds—marketable securities sales	20,000	
Loans made	(8,500)	
Loan collections	6,000	
Plant purchase	(80,000)	
Proceeds—sale of plant assets	37,500	
Net cash used in investing activities		$(57,500)
Cash flows from *financing* activities:		
Loan proceeds	$ 22,500	
Debt repayment	(27,500)	
Proceeds—Bond issue	50,000	
Proceeds—Common Stock issue	25,000	
Dividends paid	(20,000)	
Net cash provided by financing activities		$ 50,000
Net increase (decrease) in cash		$ 17,500

The following is a more comprehensive Statement of Cash Flow from operations applying the *indirect* method. This approach includes the disclosure of noncash transactions in a separate schedule formatted beneath the statement.

Statements of Cash Flows

(Indirect Method) Year Ended December 31, 20XX		
Net cash flow from operations		$ 2,950,000
Cash flow from investing activities:		
Property and plant purchases	(4,000,000)	
Proceeds from sale of equipment	2,500,000	
Acquisition of Corporation X	(900,000)	
Securities purchases	(4,700,000)	
Securities sales	5,000,000	
Borrowings	(7,500,000)	
Collections on notes receivable	5,800,000	
Net cash outflow from investments		$(3,800,000)
Cash flow from financing activities:		
Increase in customer deposits	1,100,000	
Short-term borrowings (increase)	75,000	
Short-term debt payments	(300,000)	
Long-term debt proceeds	1,250,000	
Lease payments	(125,000)	
Common stock issue	(500,000)	
Dividends to shareholders	(450,000)	
Net cash provided by financing		$ 2,050,000
Foreign exchange rate change		100,000
Net increase (decrease) in cash		$ 1,300,000
Schedule—Earnings to net cash flow reconciliation from operations:		
Net income	$ 3,000,000	
Noncash expenses, revenues, losses, and gains included in income:		
Depreciation and amortization	1,500,000	
Deferred taxes	150,000	
Net increase in receivables	(350,000)	
Net increase in payables	(200,000)	
Net increase in inventory	(300,000)	
Accrued interest earned	(350,000)	
Accrued interest payable	100,000	
Gain on sale of equipment	(600,000)	
Net cash flow from operations		$ 2,950,000

Schedule of noncash investing and financing activities:	
Incurred lease obligation	$ 750,000
Acquisition of Corporation X:	
Working capital acquired (except cash)	$ (100,000)
Property and plant acquired	3,000,000
Assumed long-term debt	(2,000,000)
Cash paid for acquisition	$ 900,000
Common stock issued in payment of long-term debt	$ 250,000

The preparation of the statement of cash flows using the indirect method requires computing the change in each account from the beginning of the year to the end. These differences form the basis for an analysis of the resulting effect on cash flows. The differences among current assets including inventory and accounts receivable as well as between current liabilities including accounts payable and accrued expenses represent either increases or decreases in cash flow relative to operating income. If accounts receivable have increased during the year, for example, this means that more revenue has been recorded during the year than can be accounted for by the receipt of cash. On the statement of cash flows this change is represented as a reduction in cash relative to income; the difference is thus subtracted from net income in arriving at cash flow from operating activities.

Particular care must be exercised in analyzing changes in fixed asset and investment accounts. Here the change from the beginning of the year to the end may represent a netting of increases and decreases. For example, an overall increase in a fixed asset account, upon analysis, may include the disposal of some assets and the acquisition of others. These changes must be segregated as the disposals will be shown as cash inflows from investing activities, while acquisitions will be shown as cash outflows from investing activities. In addition, any gains or losses resulting from the disposal of fixed assets or other investments must be shown in the changes in operating section of the cash flow statement since they represent increases or decreases to income that produced no corresponding increase or decrease in cash—the cash resulting from or used in the transaction has already been shown in the changes in investing activities. While changes in operating balance sheet items may be shown net, investing and financing items must be "grossed-up," showing increases separate from decreases.

In preparing the statement of cash flows, the accountant must be vigilant in relating new accounting standards or changes in accounting treatments to their respective effects on the statement of cash flows. For example, the treatment of share-based compensation such as stock options requires companies to deduct currently the expected value of employee compensation to be paid at a later time in stock. As a result, the expensing of share-based compensation on the U.S. GAAP income statement occurs without a corresponding cash outflow. This produces a non-cash item for the operating section of the statement of cash flows similar to the recognition of a loss on the sale of equipment.

¶4006   Bankers' Use of Financial Statements

The accountant needs to know how financial information is used and interpreted by different kinds of statement users who have different needs for credit information. The following review concerns accountants' relationships with banker clients and specific items in financial statements that bankers emphasize in their analysis of financial statements that accompany loan applications.

Of specific concern to a banker are the *trends*, both short-term and long-term, in the prospective borrower's operating results. Sales, liquidity, earnings, and the equity accounts give significant evidence of a company's operating performance since it has been in business and in the near-term trends in those indicators. Banks lend money; a business has inherent risks. The more complete, accurate, and timely the financial statements of the borrower are, the more acceptable are the borrower's statements in a risk-evaluation examination by a banker.

In the case of audited financial statements, the acceptability of financial statements and the verifiability of the information in the financial reports that accountants attest give the banker confidence in a borrower's accountant and in the integrity of the financial information furnished by the borrower. The audit report should be an unqualified opinion. There should be no violations of accounting principles (U.S. GAAP), no AICPA or SEC disclosure deficiencies, and no lack of accuracy and consistency with previous years' reports.

.01   Evaluation of Financial Ratios

While most ratios are valuable in measuring the financial excellence of a business, certain ratios, such as the current ratio, are emphasized for particular purposes. The following discussion covers the more common purposes for which ratios are used by bankers.

With respect to those commonly used by bankers, no one ratio can be said to be the most important, as they are all related to one another. For bank loan officers *the current ratio* is important because the nature of the banking business—deposits available upon demand—requires bank lending activity to be concerned predominantly with furnishing short-term loans, i.e., working capital loans. Banks as creditors attach importance to the *debt-to-net-worth ratio* and the borrower's ability to generate sufficient cash flow to service any current debt load.

.02   Management Evaluation

Management's primary interest is efficient use of the company's assets. Management is particularly interested in the turnover ratios, such as the inventory turnover and the relationship of working capital to total sales. To the extent that assets are not being used efficiently, the company is overinvesting and realizing a smaller return than possible on its equity. On the other hand, excessive turnover is dangerous because it puts the company in a vulnerable position. Bankers are also particularly interested in trend relationships shown in the income statements for the past years. Excessive selling expenses may indicate that commissions or other payments are out of line with the market. Bank creditors will also make a comparison between a loan applicant and its competitors in all areas to indicate where improvements in operations should be expected.

.03   Short-Term Creditors

As was stated earlier, a loan officer making short-term loans is particularly interested in the current ratio, since this is a measure of the borrower's working capital and ability to meet current debt obligations. Also discussed was the importance of the net-worth-to-debt ratio, which shows the relationship of the stockholders' investments to funds furnished by trade creditors and others, and shows a borrower's ability to stand up under pressure of debt. The sales-to-receivables ratio (net annual sales divided by outstanding trade receivables) shows the relationship of sales volume to uncollected receivables and indicates the liquidity of the receivables on the balance sheet. Another ratio important to a short-term lender is cost of sales to inventory, which shows how many times a company turns over its inventory, which shows whether inventories are fresh and salable and helps evaluate its liquidating value.

.04   Long-Term Creditors

Since the long-term lender is looking far into the future, a banker wants to be convinced that the company's earnings will continue at least at the current level. In addition, a lending officer will study the various working capital ratios to determine if the company will have sufficient cash when needed to amortize the debt. The ratio of total liabilities to the stockholders' equity is important because the long-term lender wants to be sure that the shareholders have a sufficient stake in the business. One ratio which is used by long-term lenders is the number of times fixed charges are earned. Fixed charges represent the interest payments on the lender's debt as well as any debt which has priority over it. When total earnings of the company are divided by total fixed charges (including preferred stock dividends, if any) the resulting figure represents the number of times fixed charges are earned.

¶4007   FASB Statements Amending the Cash Flow Statement

.01   No New Updates

The FASB has issued no new Updates related to the Statement of Cash Flows since 2016, when two Updates were issued. Implementation of those two Updates was required by 2020 for all entities.

CHAPTER 5
Presentation and Disclosure

¶5000   Fair Presentation in Conformity with U.S. GAAP

When a business is audited, the CPA's audit report attests to the fact that the financial statements are presented in conformity with U.S. GAAP. This means a number of things, but high in importance is the use of accrual basis accounting as opposed to cash basis, tax basis or some other comprehensive basis of accounting.

Fair presentation in conformity with U.S. GAAP requires that the following four criteria be met:

1. U.S. GAAP applicable in the circumstances have been applied in accumulating and processing the accounting information.
2. Changes from period to period in U.S. GAAP have been properly disclosed.
3. The information in the *underlying* records is properly *reflected* and *described* in the financial statements in conformity with U.S. GAAP.

4. A proper balance has been achieved between the conflicting needs to:
    a. Disclose the important aspects of financial position and results of operation in conformity with conventional concepts, and
    b. Summarize the voluminous underlying data with a limited number of financial statement captions and supporting notes.

¶5001   Twelve Principles of Financial Statement Presentation

1. *Basic Financial Statements.* At minimum, these statements must include:
    a. Balance Sheet, also referred to as Statement of Financial Position or, for certain entities, Statement of Net Assets
    b. Statement of Income, Statement of Operations, Statement of Activities, or Statement of Changes in Net Assets
        (1) When applicable, a Statement of Comprehensive Income should be included, either as a single, continuous statement or as a Statement of Income and a separate Statement of Other Comprehensive Income. This is only necessary when certain types of unrealized gains or losses are reported.
    c. Statement of Changes in Stockholders' Equity
    d. Statement of Cash Flows
    e. Disclosure of Accounting Policies
    f. Full Disclosure in Related Notes
        Information is usually presented for two or more periods. Other information also may be presented, and in some cases required (e.g., price-level statements, information about operations in different industries, foreign operations and export sales, major customers, and segment reporting). See FASB Accounting Standards Codification™ (ASC) Topic 205.
2. *The Balance Sheet.* A complete balance sheet must include:
    a. All assets
    b. All liabilities
    c. All classes of stockholders' equity
    d. See ASC 210
3. *The Income Statement.* A complete income statement must include:
    a. All revenues and expenses
    b. All gains and losses
    c. See ASC 220
4. *The Statement of Cash Flow.* A complete statement of cash flow includes and describes all important cash flow aspects of the company's operating, financing and investing activities. See ASC 230.
5. *Accounting Period.* The basic time period is one year, with very few exceptions. An interim statement is for less than one year.

6. *Consolidated Financial Statements.* In the context of a parent company and its subsidiaries, statements are presumed to be more meaningful than separate statements of the component legal entities. They are usually necessary when one of the group controls other(s), usually indicated by ownership (directly or indirectly) of over 50 percent of the outstanding voting stock. The information is presented as if it were a single enterprise.

7. *The Equity Method.* For unconsolidated subsidiaries (consolidation is used where the parent company has control, usually indicated by over 50 percent of ownership) where the investor has significant influence over investees (usually indicated by ownership between 20 percent and 50 percent of the voting stock), the equity method is used to report the amount of the investment on the investor's balance sheet. The investor's share of the net income or loss reported by the investee is picked up and shown as investment income and an adjustment of the investment account is made for all earnings subsequent to the acquisition. Dividends are treated as an adjustment (credit) to the investment account. This approach, ASC 323-10-15, employs the same ownership test, 20 percent or more, up to 50 percent, to indicate the use of the equity method is appropriate, in IAS 28, the IASB rule.

8. *Translation of Foreign Branches.* Data are translated into U.S. dollars by conventional translation procedures involving foreign exchange rates.

9. *Classification and Segregation.* These important components should generally be disclosed separately:

   a. Income Statement—Sales (or other source of revenue); Cost of Sales; Depreciation; General, Selling and Administration Expenses; Interest Expense; Income Taxes.

   b. Balance Sheet—Cash; Receivables; Inventories; Plant and Equipment; Payables; Debt; and Categories of Stockholder's Equity:

      (1) Par or stated amount of capital stock; Additional paid-in capital.

      (2) Retained earnings affected by:

         (a) Net income or loss,

         (b) Prior period adjustments,

         (c) Dividends, or

         (d) Transfers to other categories of equity.

      (3) Working capital—current assets and current liabilities should be classified as such to be able to determine working capital—useful for enterprises in manufacturing, trading and some service enterprises.

      (4) Current assets—cash and other assets that can reasonably be expected to be realized in one year or a longer business cycle.

      (5) Current liabilities—liabilities expected to be satisfied by the use of those assets shown as current; by the creation of other current liabilities; or in one year.

(6) Assets and liabilities—should *not* be offset against each other unless a legal right to do so exists, which is a rare exception.

(7) Gains and losses—arise from disposals of other than products or services and may be combined and shown as one item. Examples are the sale of equipment used in operations, gains and losses on temporary investments, non-monetary transactions and currency devaluations. Such items should be shown separately under their own titles.

(8) Net income—should be separately disclosed and clearly identified on the income statement.

(9) Earnings per share information is shown for net income and for individual components of net income. Earnings per share is only required reporting for public (SEC) companies.

(10) Earnings and losses from discontinued operations, shown net of tax after net income from operations, also referred to as "below the line."

10. *Other Disclosures (Accounting Policies and Notes).* These include:

    a. Customary or routine disclosures:

        (1) Measurement bases of important assets

        (2) Restrictions on assets

        (3) Restriction on owners' equity

        (4) Contingent liabilities

        (5) Contingent assets

        (6) Important long-term commitments not in the body of the statements

        (7) Information on terms of equity of owners

        (8) Information on terms of long-term debt

        (9) Other disclosures required by FASB or the AICPA

    b. Disclosure of changes in accounting policies

    c. Disclosure of important subsequent events—between balance sheet date and date of the opinion

    d. Disclosure of accounting policies ("Summary of Significant Accounting Policies")

    e. Disclosure of related parties, as well as related-party transactions and balances.

11. *Form of Financial Statement Presentation.* No particular form is presumed better than all others for all purposes. Several are used. Presentation commonly used in the industry, as well as needs of users, should be considered.

12. *Earnings Per Share.* For public business entities, this information must be disclosed on *the face of the Income Statement.*

Disclosure should consider:
  a. Changes in number of shares outstanding
  b. Contingent changes
  c. Possible dilution from potential conversion of:
      (1) Preferred stock
      (2) Options
      (3) Convertible bonds
      (4) Warrants

This information is disclosed both for basic earnings per share and for fully diluted earnings per share which adjusts the denominator for potentially dilutive shares arising from possible exercise of stock options, conversion of convertible debt to stock and the like. If the conversion of potentially dilutive securities is anti-dilutive—that is, the fully diluted earnings per share is actually greater than the basic earnings per share— the shares are reported as not being dilutive. The anti-dilutive EPS is not shown on the face of the income statement. See ASC 260.

¶5002   Disclosures Required in Financial Statements

The information on the balance sheet, income statement, and other financial statements is often referred to as being shown on the "face" of the financial statements. In order to understand what is behind those numbers, however, footnotes are also a required part of the financial statements. The face of the financial statements has to do with presentation and the financial statement footnotes are what is commonly referred to as disclosure.

For decades, the profession has been inundated with disclosure literature, rules, regulations, statements, government agencies' accounting regulations, court decisions, tax decisions, intellectualizing by academics, books and seminars, all concerning what disclosure is all about.

Auditors, when auditing financial statements, and preparers, when preparing financial statements, often use an accounting disclosure checklist. These are created to summarize, as much as possible, all that is required to be disclosed in financial statements. Having stated that, a great deal of professional judgment is still required. The criteria for what information must or need not be disclosed forces upon the independent accountant the responsibility to decide what constitutes a matter requiring disclosure, requiring an exercise of judgment in light of the circumstances and facts available at the time. The *auditor's* responsibility is confined to the expression of an opinion based upon an examination. The representations made through the statements are *management's* responsibility.

What is a material fact, and for whom does a disclosed fact have material significance? What substantive standards of disclosure must the accountant maintain? Who is to promulgate these standards? The profession? One or all of the governmental regulatory agencies? A federal board of accounting? The courts? The Congress?

One conclusion is clear, however. There is an unmistakable trend toward increasing demands upon the accounting profession for more financial information. What better evidence can be cited than the conclusion reached, over 50 years ago, of the AICPA Study Group on the Objectives of Financial Statements? The group's report said that "...financial statements should meet the needs of those with LEAST ability to obtain information."

FASB is making efforts to offset the increasing disclosure demands with its simplification project underway. Several standards have been issued to reduce or change the amount of disclosure required, though some additions are also still made.

The confusion between what is and is not *material* is caused by a widely held concept—different facts have different meanings for the individual user of financial information. Information that is important to one user may be insignificant to another.

> "All information must adapt *itself* to the perception of those towards whom the information is intended."

> -Anonymous

It is neither possible nor economically feasible, however, for an accountant to cover in the statements every single small detail concerning a client's business. Where should the accountant draw the line? (Not many years ago, a large accounting firm had to defend a lawsuit up to the U.S. Supreme Court at a cost of several million dollars because the accountant did not question the company's chief executive officer's policy that he, alone, open the company's mail.)

Recent trends in financial reporting reflect an increase in the amount of disclosure found in financial statements. The information is communicated in the footnotes, which are an integral part of the financial statements. Although the footnotes are usually drafted in somewhat technical language, they are the accountant's means of amplifying or explaining the items present in the main body of the statements.

Following is an overview of the most important disclosures required in financial statements with a brief comment on the substance of each requirement. See ASC 235.

.01   Accounting Policies

Footnote disclosure should set forth the accounting principles underlying the statements that materially affect the determination of financial position, changes in financial position, and results of operations. Also included are the accounting principles relating to recognition of revenue, allocation of asset costs to current and future periods, the selection from existing acceptable alternatives, such as the inventory method chosen, and any accounting principles and methods unique to the industry of the reporting entity.

As a general rule, the preferred position of the review of accounting policies is footnote No. 1 or 2, but a section summarizing the policies preceding the footnotes, or a description of the entity's primary operations, is acceptable.

.02   Who Decides What Information Is Material?

This decision is the responsibility of management working with the company's accountant. As a generalization, the *causes* for material changes in financial statement items *must* be noted to the extent necessary for users to understand the business as a whole. This requirement applies to all financial statements, not just to the income statement. The following items are considered material and must be recognized, either on the face of the financial statements or in the footnotes:

1. Sales and revenues. Increases or decreases in sales and revenues that are temporary or nonrecurring and their causes.
2. Unusually increased costs.
3. Informative generalizations with respect to each important expense category.
4. Financial expenses. Changes in interest expenses (and interest income); changes in the company's cost of borrowing; changes in the borrowing mix (e.g., long-term vs. short-term).
5. Other income and expense items. These may include dividend income from investees; the equity in the income or losses of investees or of unconsolidated subsidiaries.
6. Income taxes. The effective tax rate paid by corporations should be reconciled to the statutory rates. The reconciliation provides the basis for a description of the reasons for year-to-year variations in the effective tax rate to which a business is subject. Changes caused by the adoption of new or altered policies of tax-deferred accounting are considered material.
7. Material changes in the relative profitability of lines of business.
8. Material changes in advertising, research and development, new services, or other discretionary costs.

9. The acquisition or disposition of a material asset.
10. Material and unusual charges or gains, including credits or charges associated with discontinuance of operations.
11. Material changes in assumptions underlying deferred costs and the plan for the amortization of such costs.
12. The cost of goods sold, where applicable. The gross margin of an enterprise can be affected by important changes in sales volume, price, unit costs, mix of products or services sold, and inventory profits and losses. The composition of cost among fixed, semi-variable and variable elements influences profitability. Changes in gross margins by an analysis of the interplay between selling prices, costs, and volume should be explained.
13. Cash flow information.
14. Dilution of earnings per share.
15. Segmental reporting.
16. Rental expense under leases.
17. Receivables from officers and stockholders.

In some cases, a company is faced with a sensitive issue that requires disclosure in a footnote. Some examples are:
1. Related party transactions
2. Errors
3. Irregularities
4. Illegal acts

¶5003   Full Disclosure

The objectives of financial reporting are set forth in *FASB Concepts Statements*. The financial statements, notes to the financial statements, and necessary supplementary information are governed by FASB standards. Though not part of audited financial statements, financial reporting includes other types of information, such as *Management's Discussion and Analysis*, letters to stockholders, order backlogs, statistical data, and the like, commonly included in reports to shareholders.

Financial facts significant enough to influence the judgment of an informed person should be disclosed. The financial statements, notes to the financial statements, summary of accounting policies, should disclose the information necessary to prevent the statements from being misleading. The information in the statements should be disclosed in a manner that the intended meaning of the information is apparent to a reasonably informed user of the statements.

¶5004   Disclosure of Accounting Policies

A description of all significant accounting policies of the reporting entity should be included as an integral part of all financial statements. Whether these statements are issued in presenting the entity's financial position, changes in the financial position, or in showing results of operations in accordance with U.S. GAAP, a description of all significant accounting policies, methods and practices of the reporting entity should be included as an integral part of all financial statements. When it is appropriate to issue one or more basic financial statements without the others, these statements should also comprise the pertinent accounting policies. Not-for-profit entities should also present details of their accounting policies as an integral part of their financial statements.

.01   Content and Format of Disclosures

1. Disclosure of accounting policies should identify and describe the accounting principles employed by the reporting business and the methods of applying those principles which are important in the determination of financial position, changes in financial position, or results of operations. The disclosure should include decisions concerning applicability of principles relating to recognition of revenue and allocation of asset costs to current and future periods. The disclosure statement should comprise all the reasoning behind the choice of, or an explanation of, the accounting principles and methods employed that involve any of the following:
   a.   Selection of one practice over another from existing acceptable alternatives.
   b.   Principles and methods peculiar to the industry of the reporting firm, even when such principles and methods are characteristically followed in that industry.
   c.   Unusual or innovative applications of generally accepted accounting principles or of practices and methods peculiar to that industry.
2. Examples of disclosures commonly required in regard to accounting policies include those relating to basis of consolidation, depreciation methods, amortization of intangibles, inventory pricing, accounting for research and development costs and the basis for amortization thereof, translation of foreign currencies, recognition of profit on long-term construction-type contracts, recognition of revenue from franchising and leasing operations, and any other items deemed pertinent to give a complete picture of a firm's financial status.
3. The format follows a plan of having a separate *Summary of Significant Accounting Policies* preceding the notes to the financial statements or, in some cases, as the initial or second note of the statement.

¶5005   Disclosures Itemized

Following is an alphabetical listing of items requiring disclosure including short comments if applicable:

Accelerated Depreciation Methods—when methods are adopted.

Accounting Policies—(see the discussion of APB 22 at the end of this chapter.)

Allowances (depreciation, depletion, bad debts)—deduct from asset with disclosure.

Amortization of Intangibles—disclose method and period.

Amounts Available for Distribution—note the needs for any holdback retention of earnings.

Arrangements with Reorganized Debtor—disclose if a subsequent event.

Arrears on Cumulative Preferred Stock—the rights of senior securities must be disclosed on the face of balance sheet or in the notes.

Assets (interim changes in)—only significant changes required for interims.

Business Segments.

Cash-Basis Statements—fact must be disclosed in the opinion with delineation of what would have been had accrual basis been used, its significant variance.

Change in Stockholders' Equity Accounts—in a separate schedule. This does not include the changes in retained earnings statement, which is also a basic requirement.

Change to Declining Balance Method—disclose change in method and effect of it.

Changes, Accounting.

Commitments, Long-Term—disclose unused letters of credit, assets pledged as security for loans, pension plans, plant expansion or acquisition; obligations to reduce debt, maintain working capital or restrict dividend.

Commitments to Complete Contracts—only the extraordinary ones.

Consolidation Policy—method used.

Construction Type Contracts—method used.

Contingencies—disclose when reasonable possibility of a loss, the nature of, and estimated loss. Threats of expropriation, debtor bankruptcy if actual. Those contingencies which might result in gains, but not misleading as to realization. Disclosure of uninsured risks is advised, but not required. Gain contingencies should be disclosed, but not reflected in the accounts.

Contingencies in Business Combinations—disclose escrow items for contingencies in the notes.

Control of Board of Directors—disclose any stock options existing.

Corporate Officer Importance—disclose if a major sales or income factor to the company.

Current Liabilities—disclose why, if any, omitted (in notes).

Dating (Readjusted) Earned Surplus—no more than ten years is the term now required.

Deferred Taxes—disclose and also see Marty Van Wagoner, *Accounting for Income Taxes* (CCH 2025)

Depreciation and Depreciable Assets—disclose the following:

1. Depreciation expense for the period.
2. Balances of major classes of depreciable assets by nature or function.
3. Accumulated depreciation by classes, or in total.
4. A general description of the methods used in computing depreciation.

Development Stage Enterprises—are required to use the same basic financial statements as other enterprises, with certain additional disclosures required. Special type statements are not permissible.

Discontinued Operations—disclose separately below continuing-operating income, net of tax. Show separate EPS.

Diversified Company's Foreign Operations.

Earnings per share—see discussion in this text, but the following is also required in addition to the data stated there (does not apply to non-public enterprises):

1. Restatement for a prior period adjustment.
2. Dividend preference.
3. Liquidation preference.
4. Participation rights.
5. Call prices and dates.
6. Conversion rates and dates.
7. Exercise prices and dates.
8. Sinking fund requirements.
9. Unusual voting rights.
10. Bases upon which primary and fully diluted earnings per share were calculated.
11. Issues that are common stock equivalents.
12. Issues that are potentially dilutive securities.
13. Assumptions and adjustments made for earnings per share data.
14. Shares issued upon conversion, exercise, and conditions met for contingent issuances.

15. Recapitalization occurring during the period or before the statements are issued.
16. Stock dividends, stock splits or reverse splits occurring after the close of the period before the statements are issued.
17. Claims of senior securities entering earnings per share computations.
18. Dividends declared by the constituents in a pooling.
19. Basis of presentation of dividends in a pooling on other than a historical basis.
20. Per share and aggregate amount of cumulative preferred dividends in arrears.

Equity Method—as follows:
1. Financial statements of the investor should disclose in the notes, separate statements or schedules, or parenthetically:
    a. The name of each investee and percentage of ownership,
    b. The accounting policies of the investor, disclosing if, and why, any over 20 percent holdings are not under the equity method,
    c. Any difference between the carrying value and the underlying equity of the investment, and the accounting treatment thereof;
2. Disclose any investments which have quoted market prices (common stocks) showing same—do not write down;
3. Present summary balance sheet and operating information when equity investments are material;
4. Same as above for any unconsolidated subsidiaries where ownership is majority;
5. Disclose material effects of contingent issuances.

Extinguishment (Early) of Debt—gains or losses should be described, telling source of funds for payoff, income tax effect, per share amount.

Fiscal Period Differences (in Consolidating)—disclose intervening material.

Fiscal Year Change—disclose effect only.

Foreign Items—Assets, must disclose any significant ones included in U.S. statements; gains or losses shown in body of U.S. statement; disclose significant "subsequent event" rate changes; operations, adequate disclosure to be made of all pertinent dollar information, regardless of whether consolidating or not (for foreign subsidiaries).

Headings and Captions—may be necessary to explain.

Income Taxes (and Deferred Taxes)—(see Marty Van Wagoner, *Accounting for Income Taxes* (CCH 2025)).

Income Taxes of Sole Proprietor or Partnership—may be necessary to disclose personal taxes to be paid if the money will come from and put a drain on the firm's cash position.

Infrequent Events—show as separate component of income and disclose nature of them.

Interim Statements—(see discussion in Appendix E).

Inventories—disclose pricing policies and flow of cost assumption in "Summary of Significant Accounting Policies"; disclose changes in method and effect on income. Dollar effect based upon a change should be shown separately from ordinary cost of sales items.

Investment Tax Credits—disclose method used, with amounts if material. Also, disclose substantial carryback or carryforward credits.

Leases.

Legal Restrictions on Dividend Payments—put in notes.

Liability for Tax Penalties—if significant, disclose in notes. May have to take exception in opinion.

Market Value of Investments in Marketable Securities—should be written down to market value and up again, but not to exceed cost for entire portfolio per classification.

Noncumulative Preferred Stock—should disclose that no provision has been made because it is noncumulative.

Obligations (Short-Term)—disclose in notes reason any short-term obligations not displayed as current liabilities.

Partnerships, Limited—disclose fact that it is a limited partnership.

Patent Income—disclose if income is ending.

Pension Plans—must disclose the following:

1. Describe and identify employee groups covered by plan.
2. The accounting and funding policy.
3. The provision for pension cost for the period.
4. Excess, if any, of vested benefits over fund total; any balance sheet deferrals, accruals, prepays.
5. Any significant matters affecting comparability of periods presented.

Political Contributions—must disclose if material or not deductible for taxes, or if they are beneficial to an officer.

Price-Level Restatements.

Prior Period Adjustments—must disclose with tax effects. Must disclose in interim reports.

Purchase Commitment Losses—should be separately disclosed in dollars in income statement.

Purchase Option Cancellation Costs—yes, disclose.

Real and Personal Property Taxes—disclose if using estimates, and if substantial. All adjustments for prior year estimates should be made through the current income statement.

Real Estate Appraisal Value—for development companies, footnote disclosure might be useful.

Receivables, Affiliated Companies, Officers and Employees—should be segregated and shown separately from trade receivables.

Redemption Call of Preferred Stock—disclose in the equity section.

Renegotiation Possibilities—use dollars if estimable or disclose inability to estimate.

Research and Development Costs—disclosure must be made in the financial statements of the total research and development costs charged to expenses in each period for which an income statement is presented. Government-regulated enterprises should disclose the accounting policy for amortization and the totals expensed and deferred, but not the confidential details of specific projects, patents, new products, processes or company research philosophy. Applies the above provision for disclosure to business combinations.

Restricted Stock Issued to Employee—disclose circumstance and the restrictions.

Retained Earnings Transferred to Capital Stock—arises usually with "split-ups effected as dividends" and with stock dividends; must disclose and include schedule showing transfers from retained earnings to capital stock. Also, must disclose number of shares for EPS; must show subsequent event effects.

Sale and Leaseback.

Seasonal Business (Interim Statements)—must disclose, and advisable to include 12-month period, present and past.

Stock Dividends, Split-up—disclose and present as if it had occurred at the beginning of the earliest period presented.

Stock Options—disclose status. Has effect on EPS.

Stockholders' Buy/Sell Stock Agreements—disclose.

Subleases.

Termination Claims (War and Defense Contracts)—shown as current receivable, unless extended delay indicated; usually shown separately and disclosed if material, in income statement.

Treasury Stock—Shown in body of balance sheet (equity section ordinarily); should, in notes, indicate any legal restrictions.

Unconsolidated Subsidiaries—if using cost method, should also give independent summary information about position and operations.

Undistributed Earnings of Subsidiaries.

Unearned Compensation.

Unremitted Taxes—disclose only if going concern concept is no longer valid.

¶5006 Materiality

Financial statements are subject to the constraint of materiality. There have been attempts by authoritative rule-making bodies, scholars of accounting, users of financial statements, and others to develop quantitative criteria for determining the materiality of items in the financial statements. They postulate that if Item A is X percent of a total, Item A is material. If Item B is Y percent of a total, then Item B is material, but all efforts have proved fruitless, and there are no accepted quantitative standards that can be wholly relied upon for an unquestioned determination of whether an item is material or immaterial (and thus can be omitted from the financial statements or notes thereto).

The courts to some extent have helped. However, it should be cautioned that different jurisdictions in different geographic areas of the country have established many opinions and definitions of materiality. For example, the Tenth Circuit Court of Appeals ruled that information is material if "...the trading judgment of reasonable investors would not have been left untouched upon receipt of such information." (*Mitchell v. Texas Gulf Sulphur Co.*). In the "landmark" *BarChris* case, the judge said that a material fact is one "... which if it had been correctly stated or disclosed would have deterred or tended to deter the average prudent investor from purchasing the securities in question" (*Escott et al. v. BarChris Construction Corporation et al.*).

Principally, because the U.S. Supreme Court defined materiality in the *TSC Industries Inc. v. Northway Inc.* case, the following statement of the Court is considered to be an authoritative basis upon which to render a judgment of materiality:

> "An omitted fact is material if there is a substantial likelihood that a reasonable shareholder would consider it important in deciding how to vote. This standard is fully consistent with the general description of materiality as a requirement that the defect have a significant *propensity* to affect the voting process."

[Note: This decision dealt with omissions of material information.]

The Securities and Exchange Commission defines *material information:* "*The term material when used to qualify a requirement for the furnishing of information as to any subject, limits the information required to those matters as to which an average prudent investor ought reasonably to be informed.*"

Recent audit standards also address the meaning of materiality and strive to align it with the definitions adhered to by the Department of Justice and the Public Company Accounting Oversight Board (PCAOB).

.01   What Is Material?

The accountant must decide precisely what information requires disclosure. To do this, the accountant must exercise judgment according to the circumstances and facts concerning material matters and their conformity with U.S. Generally Accepted Accounting Principles (U.S. GAAP). A few examples of material matters are:
1. The form and content of financial statements.
2. Notes to the statements.
3. The terminology used in the statements.
4. The classification of items in the statements.
5. Amount of detail furnished.
6. The bases of the amounts presented (e.g., for inventories, plants, liabilities).
7. The existence of affiliated or controlling interests.

A clear distinction between materiality and disclosure should be noted. Material information involves both quantitative (data) and qualitative information. Additionally, the information must be disclosed in a manner that enables a person of "average" comprehension and experience to understand and apply it to an investment decision. Contra speaking, information disclosed in a manner that only an "expert" can evaluate is not considered within the meaning and intent of disclosure requirements.

Materiality should be thought of as an abstract concept. Many efforts to define the term can be found in the literature (e.g., accounting and auditing books, law books, and Regulation S-X). Nevertheless, in the final analysis, judgments with respect to what is material resulting from court decisions, SEC actions, accountants' interpretations, and corporate and financial officers' judgments have ultimately evolved into the subjective judgment of individuals (accountants and management) responsible for deciding what is and is not material.

¶5007   Special Purpose Frameworks

Most of the discussion has been related to financial statements presented in accordance with U.S. GAAP. However, other financial reporting frameworks may also be used.

Historically, these other frameworks were referred to as OCBOA (Other Comprehensive Basis of Accounting). Under newer standards, they are referred to as SPF (Special Purpose Frameworks). The most common SPFs are Cash Basis, Modified Cash Basis, and Tax Basis. There are also financial statements issued under a contractual basis or regulatory basis.

In addition to the frameworks just listed, in 2013, the AICPA issued its "Financial Reporting Framework for Small- and Medium-Sized Entities" (FRF for SMEs). This is one of two reporting frameworks presented during the year to accommodate the needs of non-public corporations. The FASB released its proposal for private company reporting, explained in more detail below. In contrast to the FASB activities, the FRF for SMEs is not U.S. GAAP, and is intended for small- and medium-sized corporations that are not required to report on a U.S. GAAP basis. Often the difference between the two proposals is whether the corporation is required to have its financial statements audited, and whether the audit must affirm conformity with U.S. GAAP.

The AICPA's proposal is based on U.S. GAAP, but modified to conform more closely to the reporting needs of small- and medium-sized businesses. Since it is optional and not required, there is no effective date. As an SPF, the names of the financial statements must not imply U.S. GAAP reporting. Thus, instead of a balance sheet, the corporation will present a Statement of Financial Position. Instead of an income statement, the guidance provides a Statement of Operations.

The AICPA's release of the FRF for SMEs sparked a controversy with the National Association of State Boards of Accountancy (NASBA) requesting that CPAs not implement the "guidance" because it had no official status as U.S. GAAP. The controversy led to discussions and an agreement. The NASBA and the AICPA issued the following joint statement: "The AICPA and NASBA have a shared belief that current U.S. Generally Accepted Accounting Principles (U.S. GAAP) may not always meet the needs of small private businesses and the users of their financial statements."

The FASB activities resulted in the Private Company Council (PCC), which was established as a result of the "Blue-Ribbon" Panel on Standard Setting for Private Companies created by NASBA, the AICPA and the Financial Accounting Foundation. This Council has developed and continues to develop an authoritative U.S. GAAP solution for private companies that is strongly supported. The PCC has made progress to date and both NASBA and the AICPA are committed to the PCC's success in developing a U.S. GAAP-based financial reporting model for all private companies. The PCC recommends standards or amendments to standards to the FASB, which then determines if they should be issued as a new Accounting Standards Update.

CPAs who report on financial statements prepared in accordance with U.S. GAAP, or a special purpose framework, such as the FRF for SMEs, will be held to the highest standards of professional practice by U.S. Boards of Accountancy.

¶5008   Reporting Comprehensive Income

According to ASC 220, the items that are required to be recognized under accounting standards as components of comprehensive income must now be reported in a financial statement that is displayed with the same degree of prominence as other financial statements.

.01   Comprehensive Income Defined

Comprehensive income is defined in FASB Concepts Statements as "... the change in equity (net assets) of a business enterprise during a period from transactions and other events and circumstances from non-owner sources. It includes all changes in equity during a period except those resulting from investments by owners and distributions to owners."

ASC 220 considers that comprehensive income consists of two major components—net income and "other comprehensive income." The latter refers to unrealized revenues, expenses, gains and losses that, according to U.S. GAAP, are included in comprehensive income but excluded from net income. They are direct debits or credits to owners' equity that do not involve transactions with owners, such as foreign currency translation gains and losses, unrealized gains or losses on marketable securities classified as available-for-sale, and minimum pension liability adjustments. Thus, comprehensive income is the total of net income plus the revenue, expense, gain and loss changes in equity during a period which now is not included in net income. When such items are realized, they are moved from other comprehensive income to the income statement.

.02   Equity Valuation Not Affected

This display and related disclosures do not influence equity valuations, nor is any new or additional information disclosed. The FASB does appear to believe that, used in conjunction with related disclosures and other information in the financial statements, the comprehensive income information could help the knowledgeable user in assessing an entity's activities, and the timing and extent of future cash flows. Further, the Board emphasizes that while a total comprehensive income figure is useful, information about its components may give more insight into an enterprise's activities.

.03   Format for Presentation of Comprehensive Income

One aspect for the accountant to consider is the best way to display this information to inform, but not confuse, the less sophisticated user of financial statements. There are two acceptable methods of displaying other comprehensive income:

1. An entity may present a single statement of comprehensive income. That statement would begin with a normal income statement and then add the other comprehensive income items to arrive at net comprehensive income.
2. An entity may present two separate statements. The first is an income statement. The second is a statement of comprehensive income that begins with

net income from the income statement and then lists the other comprehensive income items to arrive at net comprehensive income.

.04 Application of Requirements

ASC 220 applies to all companies that present a full set of general-purpose financial statements. Investment companies, defined benefit pension plans, and other employee benefit plans that are exempt from the requirement to provide a statement of cash flows by ASC 230, *Statement of Cash Flows*, are not exempt from requirements of ASC 220 if it applies in all other respects. However, it does not apply to organizations that have no items of comprehensive income in any period presented, or to not-for-profit organizations that are covered by ASC 958, *Not-for-Profit Entities*.

As mentioned above, the Statement suggests how to report and display comprehensive income and its components but does not provide guidance on items that are to be included. For this guidance, the existing and future accounting standards mentioned earlier will need to be consulted.

.05 Components of Comprehensive Income

At this time, eight items qualify, according to U.S. GAAP, as components of other comprehensive income that, under prior standards, bypassed the income statement and had to be reported as a balance within a separate component of equity in a statement of financial position.

1. Foreign currency translation adjustments.
2. Gains and losses on foreign currency transactions that are designated as, and are effective as, economic hedges of a net investment in a foreign entity, commencing as of the designation date.
3. Gains and losses on intercompany foreign currency transactions that are of a long-term-investment nature (i.e., settlement is not planned or anticipated in the foreseeable future), when the entities to the transaction are consolidated, combined, or accounted for by the equity method in the reporting enterprise's financial statements.
4. A change in the market value of a futures contract that qualifies as a hedge of an asset reported at fair value according to ASC 320, *Investments—Debt Securities*.
5. A net loss recognized under ASC 715, *Compensation—Retirement Benefits*, as an additional pension liability not yet recognized as net periodic pension cost.
6. Unrealized holding gains and losses on available-for-sale securities.
7. Unrealized holding gains and losses that result from a debt security being transferred into the available-for-sale category from the held-to-maturity category.

8. Subsequent decreases (if not an other-than-temporary impairment) or increases in the fair value of available for-sale securities previously written down as impaired.

.06 Terminology

The Statement does not require that the descriptive terms "comprehensive income," "total comprehensive income," or "other comprehensive income" be used in financial statements. It permits companies to use equivalent terms, such as "total non-owner changes in equity," "comprehensive loss" or other appropriate descriptive labels. It may be that most entities will choose to use alternative terms since "comprehensive income" still has a rather hollow ring to it.

.07 Cash Flow and Equity Valuation Not Affected

Inasmuch as all of the items included in other comprehensive income are non-cash items, the FASB decided that indirect-method cash flow statement presentation would continue to begin with net income as required by ASC 230, *Statement of Cash Flows*.

ASC 220 should clarify the extent to which revenue, expense, gain and loss items are being taken directly to owners' equity, but, as mentioned above, the display of comprehensive income and its components will not affect equity valuation. Unlike the requirements in ASC 280, *Segment Reporting*, which calls for greatly expanded reporting on segments, the requirements of ASC 220 call for no new data. Since informed investors have always examined owners' equity to evaluate the material now collected under the other comprehensive income items, the new display should have little impact on the public's conception of a company's financial condition.

¶5009 Restatements

The following alphabetical listing indicates those areas that require a restatement (with disclosure) for all prior periods presented in the comparative financial statements:

Appropriations of Retained Earnings—any change made for the reporting of contingencies requires retroactive adjustment.
Changes in Accounting Principle Requiring Restatement:
1. Change from LIFO to another method.
2. Change in long-term construction method.
3. Change to or from "full cost" method in the extractive industries.
4. Must show effect on both net income and EPS for all periods presented.
Change in Reporting Entity—must restate.
Contingencies—restate for the cumulative effect applying the rules for contingencies.

Earnings Per Share—the effect of all restatements must be shown on EPS, separating as to EPS from continuing operations, EPS from disposals, EPS from extraordinary items and EPS from net income.

Equity Method—restatement required when first applying the method, even though it was not required before.

Foreign Currency Translations—restate to conform with adoption of standards; if indeterminable, use the cumulative method. Disclose nature of restatement and effect (or cumulative effect) on income before extraordinary items, on net income, and on related per share amounts.

Income Taxes (Equity Method)—restate to comply.

Interim Financial Statements—restate for changes in accounting principle and for prior period adjustments. If it is a cumulative type change, the first interim period should show the entire effect; if in later period, full effect should be applied to the first period and restated for other periods. Leases.

Prior Period Adjustments—must restate the details affected for all periods presented, disclose and adjust opening retained earnings. Must also do it for interim reports.

Refinancing Short-Term Obligations—restatement is permitted, but not required.

Research and Development Costs—In conforming with standards, apply retroactively as a prior period adjustment. (*No* retroactive recapitalization of costs is permissible. Applies to *purchase* combinations also. Basic rule: expense as incurred.)

Revision based on FASB Opinions—retroactive restatement is not required *unless* the new standard *specifically* states that it is required. (Note that restatements are *not* required for a change from FIFO to LIFO, nor for a change in the method of handling investment tax credits.)

Statistical Summaries (e.g., five years, ten years)—restate all prior years involved in prior period adjustments.

Stock Dividends and Splits—must restate earnings per share figures and number of shares to give effect to stock dividends and splits *including* those occurring after close of period being reported on (for all periods presented).

¶5010   Disclosures About Segments of an Enterprise and Related Information

At the same time as the U.S. and Canadian groups were working together, the International Accounting Standards Committee (IASC), subsequently replaced by the International Accounting Standards Board (IASB), was also working closely with them to revise International Accounting Standard (IAS) 14, *Reporting Financial Information by Segment.* That statement was later replaced by

IFRS 8, *Operating Segments*, which closely resembles the FASB standard. Both the FASB and IASB now use the management approach to identify reportable segments, and segment disclosure is required.

.01   Reporting Requirements

Public corporations preparing consolidated financial statements are given guidance on the proper extent of reporting on the business segments aggregated to form the consolidated business.

ASC 280 sets forth stricter requirements than previously for the way a business reports financial and related information about reportable operating segments in annual and interim reports. The Statement does not apply to non-public business enterprises nor to not-for-profit organizations.

Reporting financial information under ASC 280 is based on the *management approach* in contrast to the *industry approach* that was previously used. While the previous guidance required reporting of information about major customers, and some data was provided on related product and service groups, it was felt that the industry approach was too subjective. So much discretion was left to the reporting company in the application of the previous Standard that unfavorable earnings figures could be hidden (by switching industry groupings around, for example).

Generally, this Standard requires that the information be reported on the same basis as the enterprise uses *internally* for evaluating segment performance and deciding how to allocate resources to segments. This leads to new data being disclosed by companies and should be useful to investment analysts and informed investors. They become privy to much of the operations information that goes to upper management to assist them in their decision making.

.02   Objectives of the Standard

It would appear that the FASB considers this a refinement of the general principles of good general-purpose financial reporting. The Board apparently feels that providing the required segment information will better the financial statement user's ability to:

- Understand the enterprise's performance.
- Estimate the enterprise's prospects relating to future cash flows.
- Arrive at better informed judgments about the enterprise as a whole.

.03   Operating Segment Disclosure Requirements

ASC 280 establishes standards for related financial and other disclosures in relation to:

- Products and services.
- Geographical areas.
- Major customers.

This information must be reported whether the business actually uses it in making operating decisions or not—unless preparing information that is not used internally would be impracticable. The enterprise must also:

1. Provide background information about the manner in which the operating segments were established.
2. Describe the particular products and/or services provided by each segment.
3. Explain any differences between the measurements used in reporting segment information and those used in their general-purpose financial statements.
4. Explain any changes in the measurement of segments from one reporting period to another.
5. Indicate shifts in a company's sources of profits, geographical risk, and investment requirements.

ASC 280 requires that a company provide for each reportable segment quantitative disclosure of two basic items—total assets and a measure of profit or loss. The newer standard defines neither segment profit (loss) not assets. Instead, as stated above, management is required to determine what is reportable based on how they operate their business. In addition, the company-wide disclosure must include the following for each segment, but only if management includes them in measuring segment profit or loss:

1. A measure of profit or loss and total assets for each segment reported.
2. Revenues from external customers allocated between those arising from the enterprise's country of domicile and those from foreign sources.
3. Interest revenue and interest expense.
4. Depreciation, depletion, and amortization and other significant non-cash items.
5. Income tax benefit or expense.
6. Extraordinary items and information on disposal of a segment.
7. Information about the extent of the enterprise's dependence on major customers—defined as customers providing 10 percent or more of the enterprise's revenues. It is not necessary to report the name of a major customer but it is required that such customer be associated with a particular segment.
8. Equity in net income of equity method investees.

.04 Management Approach

The *management approach* is based on the way management organizes the segments within a company for making operating decisions and assessing performance. Because of this, the segments should be evident from the structure of the company's organization. Therefore, financial statement preparers should be able to provide the additional required information without a great amount of additional time and effort.

The management approach should result in consistent descriptions of a company in its annual report since it focuses on financial information that an enterprise's decision makers have been using to make their decisions regarding company operations. The components that management establishes for that purpose are referred to in ASC 280 as operating segments.

According to the FASB, if management were to change the internal structure of their organization to the extent that the operating segment lines were altered, the changed reporting may be handled in one of two ways:

1. By restating segment information for earlier periods, including interim periods.
2. By disclosing segment information for the current period under both the old and the new bases of segmentation unless it is impracticable to do so.

.05 IASC's Revised Segment Reporting Standard

As mentioned, the release of the IASC's revised Standard on segment reporting was delayed while efforts were made to synchronize it with the new segment disclosure Standards developed by the FASB and Canadian standard setters. The original IAS 14 was revised and superseded by IFRS 8 to bring it into line with the common disaggregated disclosure requirements agreed upon by the IASC and the FASB, and embodied in ASC 280.

The IASC went along with the FASB/Canadian measures as far as to adopt the management approach in which a company's internal structure and its system of internal financial reporting to senior management is normally the basis for identifying reportable segments and, thus, for its segment disclosures. Unlike the two North American standards, IFRS 8 does allow management under some circumstances to depart from the management approach.

It also differs from them in another respect. The IASC Standard requires that segment data disclosures be prepared using the accounting policies adopted for the company's consolidated financial statements. In contrast, ASC 280 requires the same accounting as management uses internally to be used in its segment data disclosures.

.06　Operating Segments Defined

ASC 280 defines an operating segment as a component of an enterprise:

- That engages in business activities from which it may earn revenues and incur expenses.
- Whose operating results are regularly reviewed by the enterprise's chief operating decision maker regarding decisions about resources to be allocated to the segment and to assess its performance.
- For which discrete financial information is available.

(The term "chief operating decision maker" identifies a function, not a person with that title. The person's or persons' function is to allocate resources to and assess the performance of the company's segments. A chief operating decision maker is frequently a company's chief executive officer or chief operating officer, but it also could be a group of decision makers, for example, the company's president, executive vice presidents and others.)

.07　No More Secrets

As with other recent exposure drafts and standards, there was a storm of protest raised about the requirements. Most of the complaints were leveled at the increased disclosure requirements that respondents felt would result in competitive harm. They felt that the specificity of the required reporting would place them at a disadvantage by giving competitors and suppliers sufficient information to figure out their profit margins on particular products.

Strangely enough, when the SEC requested comment on whether the proposed revisions, if adopted, would have an adverse effect on competition, or would impose a burden on competition that was neither necessary nor appropriate in furthering the purposes of the Securities Act and the Exchange Act, no commenter addressed the issue. Therefore, based upon this apparent lack of concern and further study, the Commission determined that there would be no adverse effect on competition, and that the rule changes would not impose any unnecessary burden on competition that is not appropriate in furthering the purposes of the federal securities laws.

.08　Segment Quantitative Thresholds

In accordance with ASC 280, except as indicated below, a company must report separately information about an operating segment that meets any of the following quantitative thresholds:

1. Its reported revenue, including both sales to external customers and inter-segment sales or transfers, is 10 percent or more of the combined revenue, internal and external, of all reported operating segments. (The *revenue* test.)
2. The absolute amount of its reported profit or loss is 10 percent or more of the greater, in absolute amount, of one of the following:
    a. The combined reported profit of all operating segments that did not report a loss.
    b. The combined reported loss of all operating segments that did report a loss. (The *profitability* test.)
3. Its assets are 10 percent or more of the combined assets of all operating segments. (The *asset* test.)

Information about operating segments that do not meet any of the quantitative thresholds may be disclosed separately.

ASC 280 permits combining information about operating segments that do not meet the quantitative thresholds with information about other operating segments that do not meet the quantitative thresholds to produce a reportable segment only if the operating segments have similar economic characteristics and share a majority of the following aggregation criteria:

- The nature of the products and services.
- The nature of the production process.
- The type or class of customers for their products and services.
- The methods used to distribute their products or provide their services.
- If applicable, the nature of the regulatory environment (banking, insurance, or public utilities, for example).

If the total of external revenue reported by operating segments is less than 75 percent of the enterprise's total consolidated revenue, additional operating segments must be identified as reportable segments. This must be done even if the segments do meet the quantitative threshold criteria until at least 75 percent of total consolidated revenue is included in reportable segments. That is, once the 10 percent tests have been completed as above, if the external revenues of the segments thus identified do not constitute a substantial portion of the company's total operations (substantial portion being defined as 75 percent of its consolidated revenues), the difference must be made up with segments representing less than 10 percent of revenue, profitability, or assets, until the total of the original segments identified plus these smaller segments reaches 75 percent of the company's consolidated revenue.

Finally, an "all other" category is to be set up for disclosure about other business activities and operating segments that are not reportable under the previously mentioned quantitative threshold criteria. Sources of the revenue included in this category must be revealed.

.09   Rules for Single Segment Entities

ASC 280 includes disaggregated disclosure requirements for companies that have a single reportable segment and whose business activities are not organized on the basis of differences in related products and services or differences in geographical areas of operations. Disclosures about products and services, geographical areas, and major customers are required of these companies. As a result:

1. The expanded disclosure of operating segment income statements and asset data should enhance investors' understanding of an operating segment's performance, cash flows, and investment requirements.
2. The operating segment data presentation should be more consistent with other parts of a company's annual report.

.10   Other Aspects

Under ASC 280, the following take effect.

1. Disclosures about different parts of a business are required, but the basic income statement and balance sheet are not changed.
2. Entities may no longer claim that their business consists of only one segment if, in fact, it does not.
3. Operating segment data will be reported quarterly.
4. Reporting geographic operating data by countries should aid in the evaluation of performance and risk resulting from the global nature of present day business and commerce. The cultural, economic, political, and social data resulting from this disclosure and reporting should better serve top management as well as creditors and investors in evaluating a company as a whole—not just particular segments.
5. The FASB has taken the first big step in its consolidations projects. Consolidations policy and procedure, and unconsolidated entities are still to come.

In the final analysis, ASC 280 attempts to provide information for the user of financial statements about the different types of business activity in which a company engages, the different environments in which it operates, and the nature of its client base.

¶5011   Security and Exchange Commission Response to ASC 280

As a result of the promulgation of ASC 280, the Security and Exchange Commission adopted technical amendments to Regulations S-X, S-K, and Schedule 14A in order to bring SEC reporting requirements in line with new disclosures relating to a business enterprise's operating segments. These steps also required consistent changes to Form 20-F and a section of the Codification of Financial Reporting Policies (CFRP).

Since previous guidance had required corporations to disclose certain financial information by "industry segment" as defined in that statement and by geographic area, the SEC had adopted amendments to their rules to integrate information to be furnished with the narrative and financial disclosures required in various SEC disclosure forms.

The SEC agreed to adopt the rules in ASC 280 essentially as proposed. They believe that this is in keeping with their long-standing policy to rely upon the private sector for the promulgation of U.S. Generally Accepted Accounting Principles (U.S. GAAP). The Commission felt this step was also in line with their goal of integrating existing accounting information into the narrative disclosure in documents mandated by the federal securities laws. However, as frequently happens, the SEC retains some of their more stringent requirements while adopting the FASB rules.

.01   Description of Business—Item 101

In the past, SEC Regulation S-K had required issuers to disclose in the "business description" sections of documents that they filed with the Commission, pertinent financial information based on U.S. GAAP's old "industry segment" standard. Now, registrants report segment information in accordance with U.S. GAAP's operating segment standard.

Principal Products or Services. Historically, the SEC has required a discussion, by segment, of the principal markets for and methods of distribution of each segment's products and services. On the other hand, U.S. GAAP required, and continues to require, only disclosure of the types of products and services from which each segment derives its revenues, without reference to principle markets and distribution methods. The SEC continues to believe such information is also useful to investors; consequently, the provision is retained in their rules.

The SEC also requires registrants to disclose the amounts of revenues from each class of similar products and services based on quantitative thresholds. Specifically, the issuer must state the amount or percentage of total revenue contributed by any class of similar products or services that accounted for 10 percent or more of consolidated revenue in any of the last three fiscal years, or if total revenue did not exceed $50 million during any of those three fiscal years, 15 percent or more of consolidated revenue. The Commission amended their rules to conform with ASC 280 requirements, but retained some of their own previous provisions.

ASC 280 requires disclosure of revenues from external customers for each product and service or each group of similar products and services, regardless of amount, unless it is impracticable to do so. It appears, then, to require more disclosure than SEC rules. ASC 280 provisions result in *disclosure of a range of amounts of products and services, depending upon how a company defines a class of related products or services*. In fact, the SEC decided that ASC 280 could well require disclosure of amounts below the existing 10 percent threshold of SEC requirements.

However, the Commission believes that a clearly stated minimum threshold for disclosure is desirable. Such a measure should eliminate any possible ambiguity resulting from attempts to apply an unwritten materiality threshold to small amounts of reportable revenues. The SEC, therefore, decided to retain the thresholds.

Retroactive Restatement of Information. The SEC has required issuers to restate retroactively previously reported financial information when there has been a material change in the way they group products or services into industry segments and that change affects the reported segment information. ASC 280 provides that if an issuer changes the structure of its internal organization in a manner that causes the composition of its reportable segments to change, the issuer must restate the corresponding information for earlier periods unless it is impracticable to do so. In their final rule, the SEC conforms the language of Item 101 with the language of ASC 280 regarding when a company must restate information.

.02   Property—Item 102

Regulation S-K Item 102 requires descriptions of an issuer's principal plants, mines, and other "materially important" physical properties. Companies must identify the industry segment(s) that use the described properties. An updating of the item reflects ASC 280 financial statement reporting requirements.

.03   Management's Discussion and Analysis

Regulation S-K Item 303, which requires management to include a discussion and analysis of an issuer's financial condition and results of operations, provides:

"Where in the registrant's judgment a discussion of segment information or other subdivisions of the registrant's business would be appropriate to an understanding of such business, the discussion shall focus on each relevant, reportable segment or other subdivision of the business and on the registrant as a whole."

The Commission has in the past relied on the FASB's definition for segment disclosure in Management's Discussion and Analysis (MD&A), and intends to continue to rely on the FASB's standards, thereby allowing issuers to use the management approach under ASC 280. No rule change is necessary.

Under the language in Item 303, a multi-segment registrant preparing a full fiscal year MD&A should analyze revenues, profitability (or losses) and total assets of each significant segment in formulating a judgment as to whether a discussion of segment information is necessary to an understanding of the business.

Although the SEC did not adopt changes to the language of Item 303, they did amend the CFRP which provides informal guidance about MD&A. (See later in this chapter.) The revisions in Item 303 conform the Codification's language with that of ASC 280, and add a new footnote, that reads:

> Where consistent with the registrant's internal management reports, ASC 280 permits measures of segment profitability that differ from consolidated operating profit as defined by GAAP, or that exclude items included in the determination of the registrant's net income. Under ASC 280, a registrant also must reconcile key segment amounts to the corresponding items reported in the consolidated financial statements in a note to the financial statements. Similarly, the Commission expects that the discussion of a segment whose profitability is determined on a basis that differs from consolidated operating profit as defined by GAAP or that excludes the effects of items attributable to the segment also will address the applicable reconciling items in Management's Discussion and Analysis.

> For example, if a material charge for restructuring or impairment included in management's measure of the segment's operating profit or loss, registrants would be expected to discuss in Management's Discussion and Analysis the applicable portion of the charge, the segment to which it relates and the circumstances of its incurrence. Likewise, the Commission expects that the effects of management's use of non-GAAP measures, either on a consolidated or segment basis, will be explained in a balanced and informative manner, and the disclosure will include a discussion of how that segment's performance has affected the registrant's GAAP financial statements.

In short, SEC wants to make it clear that they expect a narrative discussion in MD&A of items that affect the operating results of a segment but that are not included in segment operating profit defined by management.

Where consistent with the registrant's internal management reports, ASC 280 permits measures of segment profitability that differ from consolidated operating profit as defined by U.S. GAAP, or that exclude items included in the determination of the registrant's net income. Under ASC 280, a registrant also must reconcile key segment amounts to the corresponding items reported in the consolidated financial statements in a note to the financial statements.

Similarly, the Commission expects that the discussion of a segment whose profitability is determined on a basis that differs from consolidated operating profit as defined by U.S. GAAP, or that excludes the effects of items attributable to the segment, will also explain the applicable reconciling items in MD&A.

For example, if a material charge for restructuring or impairment relates to a specific segment, but is not included in management's measure of the segment's operating profit or loss, registrants would be expected to discuss in MD&A:

- The applicable portion of the charge.
- The segment to which it relates.
- The circumstances relating to how and why the charge was incurred.

The Commission expects that the effects of management's use of non-U.S. GAAP measures, either on a consolidated or segment basis, will be explained in a balanced and informative manner, and the disclosure will include a discussion of how that segment's performance has affected the registrant's U.S. GAAP financial statements.

.04   Form 20-F

Form 20-F is the registration statement and annual report for foreign private issuers promulgated under the Securities Exchange Act of 1934. Form 20-F has permitted a foreign registrant that presents financial statements according to U.S. GAAP to omit previously required disclosures if it provides the information required by Item 1 of the form. A reference to ASC 280 replaces those previously required disclosures.

Much of the material required by the FASB Standards is supplied in Item 1, which requires registrants to disclose sales and revenues by categories of activity and geographical areas, as well as to discuss each category of activities that provides a disproportionate contribution to total "operating profit" of the registrant.

.05   Other Reporting Requirements

Geographic Areas. Now companies must disclose revenues from external customers deriving from:

- Their country of domicile.
- All foreign countries in total from which the company derives revenues.
- An individual foreign country, if material.

A company must also disclose the basis for attributing revenues from external customers to individual countries.

The Standard requires an issuer to disclose long-lived assets other than financial instruments, long-term customer relationships of a financial institution, mortgage and other servicing rights, and deferred policy acquisition costs. It is also necessary to include deferred tax assets located in its country of domicile and in all foreign countries, in total, in which the enterprise holds assets. If assets in an individual foreign country are material, an issuer must disclose those assets separately.

Even those companies whose segments were defined by geography, continue to report designated information based on geographic areas, unless the information is already provided as part of the reportable operating segment information required by the accounting standards. Consistent with ASC 280, rules no longer will require companies to disclose geographic information relating to profitability, unless their segments are defined by geographic areas, or export sales.

Major Customers. Even under previous guidance, U.S. GAAP has required disclosure of revenues from major customers. ASC 280 now requires issuers to disclose the amount of revenues from each external customer that amounts to 10 percent or more of an enterprise's revenue as well as the identity of the segment(s) reporting the revenues.

The accounting standards had never before required issuers to identify major customers. On the other hand, the SEC has historically required naming a major customer if sales to that customer equal 10 percent or more of the issuer's consolidated revenues and if the loss of the customer would have a material adverse effect on the issuer and its subsidiaries. The Commission believes that the identity of major customers is material information to investors.

This disclosure improves a reader's ability to assess risks associated with a particular customer. Additionally, material concentrations of revenues related to a particular customer may be judged more accurately. Consequently, the SEC continues to require this information.

¶5012 Segment Information Added to Interim Reports

U.S. GAAP historically has not required segment reporting in interim financial statements. In ASC 280, the FASB changed its position. Under the new accounting standards, issuers must include in condensed financial statements for interim periods the following information about each reportable segment:

1. Revenues from external customers.
2. Intersegment revenues.
3. A measure of segment profit or loss.
4. Total assets for which there has been a material change from the amount disclosed in the last annual report.
5. A description of differences from the last annual report in the basis of segmentation or in the basis of measurement of segment profit or loss.
6. A reconciliation of the total of the reportable segments measures of profit or loss to the enterprise's consolidated income before income taxes, extraordinary items, discontinued operations, and the cumulative effect of changes in accounting principles.

Thus, issuers must now disclose in interim financial statements, including those filed with the Commission, condensed financial information about the segments identified as reportable segments for purposes of their annual reports.

¶5013 Codification Update, Revised Section 501.06

The Codification of Financial Reporting Policies (CFRP) contains current Commission interpretive guidance relating to financial reporting and is updated whenever it is deemed necessary. In this case the new guidance information results from the technical amendments to Regulations S-X and S-K.

.01 Segment Analysis

In formulating a judgment as to whether a discussion of segment information is necessary to an understanding of the business, a multi-segment SEC registrant preparing a full fiscal year MD&A should analyze revenues, profitability, and the cash needs of its significant segments.

To the extent any segment contributes in a *materially disproportionate* way to those items, or where discussion on a consolidated basis would present an incomplete and misleading picture of the enterprise, *segment discussion* should be included.

Examples could include:

1. When there are legal or other restrictions upon the free flow of funds from one segment, subsidiary, or division of the registrant to others.
2. When known trends, demands, commitments, events, or uncertainties within a segment are reasonably likely to have a material effect on the business as a whole.
3. When the ability to dispose of identified assets of a segment may be relevant to the financial flexibility of the registrant.
4. Other circumstances in which the registrant concludes that segment analysis is appropriate to an understanding of its business.

.02   Financial Information About Segments

Each segment must report, as defined by U.S. GAAP, revenues from external customers, a measure of profit or loss and total assets. A registrant must report *this* information for each of the last three fiscal years or for as long as it has been in business, whichever period is shorter. If the information provided in response to this paragraph conforms with U.S. GAAP, a registrant may include in its financial statements a cross reference to this data instead of presenting duplicate information in the financial statements; conversely, a registrant may cross reference to the financial statements.

If a registrant changes the structure of its internal organization in a manner that causes the composition of its reportable segments to change, the registrant must restate the corresponding information for earlier periods, including interim periods, unless it is impracticable to do so.

Following a change in the composition of its reportable segments, a registrant must disclose whether it has restated the corresponding items of segment information for earlier periods. If it has not restated the items from earlier periods, the registrant is to disclose, in the year in which the change occurs, the segment information for the current period under both the old basis and the new basis of segmentation, unless it is impracticable to do so.

.03   Financial Information About Geographic Areas

1. The SEC registrant must state the following for the last three fiscal years, or for each fiscal year the registrant has been engaged in business, whichever period is shorter:
   a. Revenues from external customers attributed to:
      • The registrant's country of domicile.
      • All foreign countries, in total, from which the registrant derives revenues.

- Any individual foreign country, if material. The registrant must disclose the basis for attributing revenues from external customers to individual countries.
b. Long-lived assets, other than financial instruments, long-term customer relationships of a financial institution, mortgage and other servicing-rights, deferred policy acquisition costs, and deferred tax assets, located in:
   • The registrant's country of domicile.
   • All foreign countries, in total, in which the registrant holds assets.
   • Any individual foreign country, if material.
2. A registrant must report the amounts based on the financial information that it uses to produce the general-purpose financial statements. If providing the geographic information is impracticable, the registrant must disclose that fact. A registrant may wish to provide, in addition to the information required by this Section, subtotals of geographic information about groups of countries. If the disclosed information conforms with U.S. GAAP, the registrant may include a cross reference to this data instead of presenting duplicate data that is in its financial statements; conversely, a registrant may cross-reference to the financial statements.
3. A registrant is required to describe any risks attendant to the foreign operations and any dependence on one or more of the registrant's segments upon its foreign operations. Or the registrant might consider it more appropriate to discuss this information in connection with one or more of the segments in an individual foreign country.

¶5014   The SEC Questions Registrants' Application of Aggregation Policies

Segment disclosures, or disclosure of disaggregated information, have long been a source of pain for registrants, auditors, Commission staff, and standard setters. The Securities and Exchange Commission points out that the disclosures have also been a source of pain for users who should be benefiting from them. The SEC realizes that users are rarely united in terms of what information they would like to see in filings of public companies, but they do know that they want segment data. The FASB's progress with ASC 280, *Segment Reporting*, has increased the volume of segment data, but, as with standards in other areas, perhaps the follow-through from the preparers has not gone as far as the FASB had intended.

.01   Specific Provisions for Segment Aggregation

Members of the SEC's Chief Accountant's office consider that one of the reasons for this is that there are many companies that take advantage of ASC 280's provisions that allow for aggregation of operating segments. Although aggregation of immaterial segments is easy to understand and accept, it is more difficult for users to accept aggregation that occurs primarily because a company contends that material operating segments are so similar that they should be combined.

If the SEC registrant is following the *intent* of ASC 280, aggregation can occur only if each of the operating segments unquestionably meets certain requirements. Two or more operating segments may be aggregated into a single operating segment if:

1. Aggregation is consistent with the objective and basic principles of the Statement.
2. The segments have similar economic characteristics.
3. The segments are similar in each of the following areas:
   - The nature of the products and services.
   - The nature of the production processes.
   - The type or class of customer for their products and services.
   - The methods used to distribute their products or provide their services.
4. The segments sell their products or services in similar regulatory environments, for example, banking, insurance, or public utilities.

With all of these caveats, it would appear that this should be a high hurdle to aggregation. The FASB makes clear in the basis for conclusions to ASC 280 that aggregation is acceptable in certain situations because "separate reporting of segment information *will not add significantly* to an investor's understanding of an enterprise if its operating segments have characteristics so similar that they can be expected to have essentially the same future prospects." To put it bluntly, aggregation is permissible if presenting the information separately *would not provide the users with any additional useful information.*

.02   SEC Concerned About Unwarranted Aggregation

When the SEC has queried registrants about *why* the company aggregated segment data, the answer *has not* focused on whether the additional information would be useful to users or whether aggregation in the particular instance is consistent with the objectives and principles of ASC 280. Instead, the discussions have all revolved around whether each of the six objective criteria has been met and how the evaluation of similar economic characteristics should be performed. In addition, registrants often cite a complaint that they had made when segment disclosure was being debated before the adoption of ASC 280—the competitive harm that would befall the company if it disclosed additional information. It would appear that the registrant is more concerned about maintaining secrecy from its competitors than in gaining the respect of users or their financial statement for the *full and complete disclosure* of the financial condition of the entity.

¶5015   FASB Provides Additional Segment Guidance

In November 2023, the FASB issued Accounting Standards Update (ASU) No. 2023-07, *Segment Reporting* (Topic 280). The Update is applicable to public companies that are required to report segment information in accordance with ASC 280. The amendments:

1. Require that a public entity disclose, on an annual and interim basis, significant segment expenses that are regularly provided to the chief operating decision maker (CODM) and included within each reported measure of segment profit or loss (collectively referred to as the "significant expense principle").
2. Require that a public entity disclose, on an annual and interim basis, an amount for other segment items by reportable segment and a description of its composition. The other segment items category is the difference between segment revenue less the segment expenses disclosed under the significant expense principle and each reported measure of segment profit or loss.
3. Require that a public entity provide all annual disclosures about a reportable segment's profit or loss and assets currently required by ASC 280 in interim periods.
4. Clarify that if the CODM uses more than one measure of a segment's profit or loss in assessing segment performance and deciding how to allocate resources, a public entity may report one or more of those additional measures of segment profit. However, at least one of the reported segment profit or loss measures (or the single reported measure, if only one is disclosed) should be the measure that is most consistent with the measurement principles used in measuring the corresponding amounts in the public entity's consolidated financial statements. In other words, in addition to the measure that is most consistent with the measurement principles under U.S. generally accepted accounting principles (U.S. GAAP), the public entity is not precluded from reporting additional measures of the segment's profit or loss that are used by the CODM in assessing segment performance and deciding how to allocate resources.
5. Require that a public entity disclose the title and position of the CODM and an explanation of how the CODM uses the reported measure(s) of segment profit or loss in assessing segment performance and deciding how to allocate resources.
6. Require that a public entity that has a single reportable segment provide all the disclosures required by the amendments in this Update and all existing segment disclosures in ASC 280.

.01   To Aggregate the Segments or Not

In an attempt to solve some of the problems related to aggregation, the Emerging Issues Task Force published Issue No. 04-10, *Determining Whether to Aggregate Operating Segments That Do Not Meet the Quantitative Thresholds*. ASC 280 requires that a public business enterprise report financial and descriptive information about its reportable operating segments. Operating segments are components of an enterprise about which separate financial information is available that is evaluated regularly by the chief operating decision maker in deciding how to allocate resources and in assessing performance. Generally, financial information is required to be reported on the basis that it is used internally for evaluating segment performance and deciding how to allocate resources to segments. This particular issue focuses on how an enterprise should evaluate the aggregation criteria according to paragraph 17 of ASC 280 when determining whether operating segments that do not meet the quantitative thresholds may be aggregated in accordance with ASC 280.

.02   "Similar Economic Characteristics"

Issue No. 04-E, *The Meaning of Similar Economic Characteristics*, refers to ASC 280, which allows two or more operating segments to be aggregated if, among other things, "they have similar economic characteristics." Significant diversity exists as to what is meant by "similar economic characteristics." The particular issue in this instance is whether it is possible for two operating segments to have different long-term and future expected financial results and still have similar economic characteristics. The Task Force agreed to remove this Issue from the agenda, but asked the FASB staff to provide guidance on it in the anticipated FSP.

The consensus states that operating segments that do not meet the quantitative thresholds can be aggregated only if aggregation is consistent with the *objective* and *basic principles* of ASC 280, the segments have similar economic characteristics, and the segments share a majority of the aggregation criteria listed in ASC 280.

.03   Both Qualitative and Quantitative Factors Should Be Considered

In March 2005, the FASB staff did issue the proposed Statement of Position (FSP) 131-a, *Determining Whether Operating Segments Have "Similar Economic Characteristics,"* under ASC 280, *Segment Reporting*, to address the questions discussed earlier. The Board decided not to issue the proposed FSP because it did not appear to address different interpretations of existing U.S. GAAP that have resulted in diversity of financial reporting.

.04   Frequently Asked Questions

Evidently the FASB anticipates some questions are still going to ask regardless of how basically the requirements are spelled out.

Q1: Should both quantitative and qualitative factors be considered for purposes of determining whether the economic characteristics of two or more operating segments are similar?

A1: The FASB staff believes both quantitative and qualitative factors should be considered for purposes of determining whether the economic characteristics of two or more operating segments are similar. Even if the qualitative factors (including those listed in ASC 280) are virtually identical, the FASB staff believes it is still, necessary to evaluate the quantitative factors to determine whether the segments have similar economic characteristics. Quantitative factors could include performance measures such as gross margins, trends in sales growth, returns on assets employed, and operating cash flows. Qualitative factors could include nonperformance measures such as competitive and operating risks, currency risks, and economic and political conditions associated with each segment.

Q2: How should an enterprise identify the factors to consider for purposes of determining whether two or more operating segments have similar economic characteristics?

A2: The FASB staff believes that the factors that should be considered for purposes of determining whether operating segments have similar economic characteristics should be based on the primary factors that the chief operating decision maker (CODM) uses in allocating resources to individual segments. For example, if the CODM primarily uses gross margin, sales volume, and expected future sales growth to allocate resources to individual operating segments, those are the quantitative factors that should be considered for purposes of determining whether the operating segments have similar economic characteristics. The FASB staff would expect the quantitative and qualitative factors to be similar in order to conclude that the operating segments have similar economic characteristics; however, evaluating whether economic characteristics are similar is a matter of judgment that depends on specific facts and circumstances.

PART II
Standards

A variety of organizations set standards which accountants must follow. The Financial Accounting Standards Board (FASB) is the authoritative standard setter in the United States for private companies. The FASB establishes U.S. Generally Accepted Accounting Principles (U.S. GAAP). The U.S. Securities and Exchange Commission (SEC) has statutory (legal) authority over public companies in the U.S. The SEC requires public companies to follow FASB's standards, as well as additional standards set by the SEC. Also created by statute is the Public Company Accounting and Oversight Board (PCAOB) which sets standards and provides oversight for auditors of public companies.

The Governmental Accounting Standards Board (GASB) sets standards for governmental entities, much as the FASB does for private entities.

The International Accounting Standards Board (IASB) sets international accounting standards.

Although outside the scope of this book, it is worth mentioning organizations within the American Institute of Certified Public Accountants (AICPA). The Auditing Standards Board (ASB) of the AICPA sets standards for auditors of private entities. The Accounting and Review Services Committee (ARSC) of the AICPA sets standards for reviews, compilations, and preparations of financial statements. The ASB also issues standards for attestation engagements.

CHAPTER 6
Broad Accounting and Reporting Issues

¶6000   Business Combinations

Business combinations are accounted for under the acquisition method. Although the phrase commonly used in the market is "mergers and acquisitions" or "M&A," accounting is always done as one entity acquiring another when the entities are businesses. When the entities are not-for-profit entities that combine, it be treated as a "true merger," defined by ASC 958-805-20 as a "transaction or other event in which the governing bodies of two or more not-for-profit entities cede control of those entities to create a new not-for-profit entity." Such a transaction requires the carryover method of accounting, rather than the acquisition method, in which previous recorded amounts are carried forward into the new entity. It is important to point out, in order for a transaction to be accounted for as a business combination, the assets acquired and liabilities assumed must constitute a business. If the assets acquired are not a business, the transaction is accounted for as an asset purchase. A business is an integrated set of activities and assets capable of being managed to provide a return, such as dividends, lower costs, or other economic benefits. A business consists of inputs and processes that have the ability to contribute to the creation of outputs.

The acquisition method requires the following four steps:

a.   Identify the accounting acquirer

b.   Determine the acquisition date

c.   Recognize the identifiable assets acquired, liabilities assumed, and any noncontrolling interest in the acquiree at fair value

d.   If the acquisition price exceeds the net fair value of items in c., goodwill is recorded for the difference. If the acquisition price is lower than the net fair value, a gain from a bargain purchase is recorded.

.01   Identify the Accounting Acquirer

In a business combination, the entity that obtains control of the other entity is the accounting acquirer. A practical application of this concept is to identify which group controls the combined entity. The entity that was controlled by that group before the combination is the accounting acquirer. This may or may not be the same entity identified as the legal acquirer in the business combination documents. If the accounting acquirer is different than the legal acquirer, the transaction is deemed a reverse merger, described in more detail below.

.02   Determine the Acquisition Date

The acquisition date is the date on which the acquirer obtains control of the acquiree. It is usually the date assets and liabilities are legally transferred, also referred to as the closing date. However, certain contingencies or other events may indicate an acquisition date that differs from the closing date.

Sometimes, acquisitions are done in stages, or as a step acquisition. When this occurs, on the date the acquirer obtains control, it will remeasure its previous equity interest at the fair value on that date. Any resulting gain or loss from the remeasurement is recognized in earnings.

If information is incomplete by the end of the reporting period including a business combination, estimates will be included in the financial statements of that period. There is up to a one-year measurement period during which such estimates may be adjusted with a corresponding adjustment to goodwill, if applicable.

.03   Recognize Assets, Liabilities and Noncontrolling Interest at Fair Value

All assets and liabilities of the acquiree, as well as any noncontrolling interest that may exist (amounts controlled by other parties that are not the acquirer), are to be adjusted to fair value in acquisition. This may be done with appraisals, business valuations, or other similar methods. This adjustment is to allow the combination to be recorded on the acquirer's books.

There are times an acquiree would need to issue stand-alone financial statements and has the option to use push-down accounting. If an acquiree uses push-down accounting, it will report its assets and liabilities at their fair values on the acquisition date, as recorded by the acquirer.

.04   Record Goodwill or Gain on Acquisition

Most often referred to as the price paid by the acquirer for the acquiree, the consideration given must be determined. It may be as simple as a stated amount in the contract but it may have added complexity. Acquisition-related costs are separate from consideration given to obtain control of an acquiree. Such costs include finder's fees; advisory, legal, accounting, valuation, and other professional fees; and other administrative costs. Those costs are expensed in the period incurred. Costs of registering and issuing securities are recognized in accordance with other applicable U.S. GAAP.

When the acquisition price is determined, goodwill is recorded if that price is higher than the fair value of net assets and liabilities acquired, taking into account any noncontrolling interest. When the acquisition price is lower than that fair value, a gain on acquisition is recognized. Caution should be exercised in recording such a gain. The price just paid for something may be deemed as an indicator of the fair value of what was obtained. A gain on acquisition may be an indicator that the fair value of assets and liabilities may not have been accurately measured.

.05   Reverse Mergers

As previously noted, a reverse merger is a situation in which the accounting acquirer is the legal acquiree and the legal acquirer is the accounting acquiree. There are several situations in which this might occur but the most common is when a private operating company wishes to go public without going through an initial public offering (IPO). Such a private company may find a public shell—an entity that has registered with the SEC but has no operations. Public shells are sometimes created as such from inception or sometimes arise from a public operating company that went out of business but the owners kept the registration with the SEC active. This is most often done with the intent to sell the shell to a private company in a reverse merger. The agreement must be written in such a way that the public shell legally acquires the operating company, in order for the combined entity to remain a public entity. However, the operating company ends up having control and is, therefore, the accounting acquirer. This makes sense from a reporting standpoint. As described below, the income statement of an acquiree is only included in the consolidated financial statements from the acquisition date forward, while all the acquirer's historical information is included. In the situation described above, potential investors would be interested in the historical financial statements of the operating company, rather than the public shell. So it stands to reason that the operating company's historical financial statements are those presented.

A reverse merger allows an entity to go public without going through some of the cost, time, and scrutiny incurred in an IPO. Also, public shells have sometimes been used in a reverse merger and it was later found that old liabilities or other risks were attached to the shell. Consequently, the SEC and others are leery of such transactions and they are often considered very risky.

.06   Consolidation

When an entity acquires ownership of a portion of another entity, but does not gain significant influence or control, it is accounted for as an investment in that entity. This is usually indicated by less than 20 percent ownership. When significant influence is obtained, usually indicated by 20 percent to 50 percent ownership, the equity method of accounting is used. See descriptions of both those situations in the Investments section of Chapter 1. When control is obtained, usually indicated by over 50 percent ownership, the entities are consolidated. In consolidation, the assets and liabilities of the two entities are combined, as are revenues, expenses and other income statement items, with inter-entity transactions and balances eliminated. The investment in subsidiary on the parent's (acquirer's) books is eliminated against the equity of the subsidiary (acquiree). In the year of acquisition, the income statement of the parent is included for all periods presented but the income statement of the subsidiary is included from the acquisition date to the end of the period.

.07 Recent Updates

In August 2023, the FASB issued ASU 2023-05, Business Combinations— Joint Venture Formations (Subtopic 805-60): Recognition and Initial Measurement, requiring a joint venture to recognize and initially measure its assets and liabilities using a new basis of accounting upon formation to reduce diversity in practice and provide decision-useful information.

In October 2021, the FASB issued ASU 2021-08, Business Combinations (Topic 805): Accounting for Contract Assets and Contract Liabilities from Contracts with Customers, to improve accounting for required revenue contracts with customers in a business combination.

Another situation in which consolidation may be applicable is with variable interest entities. This is a complex concept so it has its own section, below.

¶6001   Variable Interest Entities

Just as derivatives received much of the blame for questionable accounting practices during the 1990s, special-purpose entities (SPEs) received much of the blame for the accounting profession's fall from grace during the early years of the 21st century. Yet both of these vehicles can serve, and have served, a useful and legitimate purpose. However, as is often suggested, as long as there is someone who is determined to show a profit regardless of what is right or wrong, a way will be found. The more legitimate appearing, the better to subvert! Measures have been taken in the past to see that derivatives are properly regulated, and the process continues.

Dealing with one vexing regulatory problem often results in having to deal with another. The guidance from the Financial Accounting Standards Board for consolidation and transfers will affect more than what goes on or comes off the financial statements. Entities consolidated under the new guidance must remember that they are subject to Section 404 of the Sarbanes-Oxley Act, so companies will have to evaluate the necessary changes to internal control, and their internal control assessment processes, to address those entities. Companies may also have to spend time informing their investors about the changes to the financial statements as a result of the new guidance, in addition to evaluating the effects on debt covenants and regulatory capital requirements, among others.

Variable Interest Entity guidance was originally issued as FASB Interpretation No. (FIN) 46, *Consolidation of Variable Interest Entities*, which was later included in ASC 810. It has been impacted by Accounting Standards Updates (ASUs). The following information continues to refer to FIN 46 and other original guidance to maintain a history of the development of the topic.

.01 ASU 2010-10 Defers FASB 167 Effective Date for Certain Investment Funds

In February 2010, the FASB issued ASU 2010-10, Consolidation (Topic 810): Amendments for Certain Investment Funds, primarily to address concerns with the application of Statement 167's consolidation guidance by reporting enterprises in the asset management industry. The concern is that the joint consolidation model under development by the FASB and the IASB may result in a different consolidation conclusion for asset managers with the result that an asset manager consolidating certain funds would not provide useful information to investors. Therefore, ASU 2010-10 deferred the effective date of the consolidation guidance of Statement 167 for certain investment funds indefinitely. However, Statement 167's *disclosure requirements* will continue to apply to all entities.

The amendments to the consolidation requirements resulting from the issuance of Statement 167 are deferred for a reporting entity's interest in an entity (1) that has all the attributes of an investment company or (2) for which it is industry practice to apply measurement principles for financial reporting purposes that are *consistent with* those followed by investment companies.

The deferral does not apply in situations in which a reporting entity has the explicit or implicit obligation to fund losses of an entity that could potentially be significant to the entity. The deferral also does not apply to interests in securitization entities, asset-backed financing entities, or entities formerly considered special purpose entities (QSPEs).

The deferral applies to a reporting entity's interest in an entity that is required to comply or operate in accordance with requirements similar to those in Rule 2a-7 of the Investment Company Act of 1940 for registered money market funds (MMFs).

An entity that qualifies for the deferral will continue to be assessed under the overall guidance on the consolidation of variable interest entities (VIEs) in Subtopic 810-10 (before the Statement 167 amendments) or other applicable consolidation guidance, such as the guidance for the consolidation of partnerships.

.02   Disclosures

The amendments in this Update do not defer the disclosure requirements in FASB 167. Accordingly, both public and nonpublic companies are required to provide the disclosures included in ASC 810, as amended by Statement 167, for all variable interest entities in which they hold a variable interest. This includes variable interests in entities that qualify for the deferral but are considered VIEs under the provisions in ASC 810 (before the Statement 167 amendments).

.03   Reminders on ASU 2010-10 Implementation

It is important to remember that FASB 167 does not change the definition of a VIE. However, it significantly modifies the key provisions of FIN 46(R). It targets when to assess an entity's relationship with a VIE (and thus the decision to consolidate), how to make that assessment, and it eliminates a number of exceptions, and expands related disclosures.

One modification of FASB 167 requires ongoing assessments of an entity's relationship with a VIE. FIN 46(R) required reconsideration of the initial consolidation determination only when certain "triggering events" occurred. In practice, this reconsideration happened rarely. According to FASB 167, a VIE's status under FIN 46(R) is to be reconsidered on an ongoing basis, such as when there is a change in voting or other rights "to direct the activities of the entity that most significantly impact the entity's economic performance."

Another new consideration is the qualitative nature of this ongoing assessment. FASB 167 re-defines a primary beneficiary of a VIE as an enterprise that has both of the following:

- The power to direct the activities of a VIE that most significantly impact the VIE's economic performance, and
- The obligation to absorb losses of the VIE that could potentially be significant to the VIE, or the right to receive benefits from the VIE that could potentially be significant to the VIE.

.04   Improving Financial Reporting for Various Entities

In an effort to end the abusive accounting for, to restore the legitimacy of, and to expand upon and strengthen existing accounting guidance on special-purpose entities, the Financial Accounting Standards Board (FASB) issued Interpretation 46 (FIN 46), *Consolidation of Variable Interest Entities*. The Interpretation addresses when a company should include the assets, liabilities, and activities of these entities in its financial statements.

Although many variable interest entities have commonly been referred to as special-purpose entities or off-balance-sheet structures, the guidance applies to a *larger group* of entities. The FASB explains that, in general, a variable interest entity is a corporation, partnership, trust, or any other *legal* structure used for business purposes that either:

- Does not have equity investors with voting rights; or
- Has equity investors that do not provide sufficient financial resources for the entity to support its activities.

A variable interest entity often holds financial assets, including loans or receivables, real estate, or other property. A VIE may be essentially passive or it may engage in research and development or other activities on behalf of another company. As pointed out, these types of entities can be put to perfectly legitimate use. Therefore, the Board's objective in FIN 46 is not to restrict the use of variable interest entities, but to improve financial reporting by companies involved with them.

Until now, one company generally has included another entity in its consolidated financial statements *only* if it controlled the entity through voting interests. However, the Board believes that if a business enterprise actually has a controlling *financial* interest (regardless of method of determination) in a variable interest entity, the assets, liabilities, and results of the activities of that variable interest entity should be included in consolidated financial statements with those of the business enterprise. Thus, FIN 46 changes present use by requiring a variable interest entity to be consolidated by a company if that company is subject to a majority of the risk of loss from the variable interest entity's activities or entitled to receive a majority of the entity's residual returns, or both.

.05   FASB Coins a Term

Leading up to FIN 46's final form, the FASB made several significant changes to the draft rule relating to the Interpretation. During a meeting in mid-October 2002, the Board agreed to discontinue the use of the term "special-purpose entities" in favor of the term "variable interest entities." The term coined by the FASB includes many, but not all, of the entities that were referred to in the past as special-purpose entities or off-balance-sheet structures, as well as additional entities.

FIN 46 began as an interpretation of FASB Accounting Research Bulletin (ARB) 51, *Consolidated Financial Statements*, which addresses consolidation by business enterprises of variable interest entities. The Exposure Draft that preceded this Interpretation referred to the entities being covered by its requirements as special-purpose entities. Because some entities that have been commonly referred to as SPEs may not be subject to this Interpretation, and other entities that have not commonly been referred to as SPEs may be subject to the Interpretation, the FASB decided to use the term "variable interest entity."

.06   VIEs and Exceptions Defined

The term is used for those entities having at least one of the following characteristics:

- The equity investment at risk is not sufficient to permit the entity to finance its activities without additional subordinated financial support from other parties. This is provided through other interests that are to absorb some or all of the expected losses of the entity.
- The equity investors lack one or more of the following essential characteristics of a controlling financial interest:
  - The direct or indirect ability to make decisions about the entity's activities through voting rights or similar rights.
  - The obligation to absorb the expected losses of the entity if they occur, which makes it possible for the entity to finance its activities.
  - The right to receive the expected residual returns of the entity if they occur, which is the compensation for the risk of absorbing the expected losses.

Exceptions. With only a few exceptions, the Interpretation applies to any business enterprise that has an ownership interest in, contractual relationship with, or other relationship with a VIE. The guidance in this Topic does not apply in any of the following circumstances:

a. An employer shall not consolidate an employee benefit plan subject to the provisions of Topic 712 or 715.

b. Except as discussed in paragraph 946-810-45-3, an investment company within the scope of Topic 946 shall not consolidate an investee that is not an investment company.

c. A reporting entity shall not consolidate a governmental organization and shall not consolidate a financing entity established by a governmental organization unless the financing entity meets both of the following conditions:

   1. Is not a governmental organization
   2. Is used by the business entity in a manner similar to a VIE in an effort to circumvent the provisions of the Variable Interest Entities Subsections.

d. A reporting entity shall not consolidate a legal entity that is required to comply with or operate in accordance with requirements that are similar to those included in Rule 2a-7 of the Investment Company Act of 1940 for registered money market funds.

   1. A legal entity that is not required to comply with Rule 2a-7 of the Investment Company Act of 1940 qualifies for this exception if it is similar in its purpose and design, including the risks that the legal entity was designed to create and pass through to its investors, as compared with a legal entity required to comply with Rule 2a-7.

   2. A reporting entity subject to this scope exception shall disclose any explicit arrangements to provide financial support to legal entities that are required to comply with or operate in accordance with requirements that are similar to those included in Rule 2a-7, as well as any instances of such support provided for the periods presented in the performance statement. For purposes of applying this disclosure requirement, the types of support that should be considered include, but are not limited to, any of the following:

      i. Capital contributions (except pari passu investments)

      ii. Standby letters of credit

      iii. Guarantees of principal and interest on debt investments held by the legal entity

      iv. Agreements to purchase financial assets for amounts greater than fair value (for instance, at amortized cost or par value when the financial assets experience significant credit deterioration)

      v. Waivers of fees, including management fees.

The following exceptions to the Variable Interest Entities Subsections apply to all legal entities in addition to the exceptions listed above:

a. Not-for-profit entities (NFPs) are not subject to the Variable Interest Entities Subsections, except that they may be related parties for purposes of applying paragraphs 810-10-25-42 through 25-44. In addition, if an NFP is used by business reporting entities in a manner similar to a VIE in an effort to circumvent the provisions of the Variable Interest Entities Subsections, that NFP shall be subject to the guidance in the Variable Interest Entities Subsections.

b. Separate accounts of life insurance entities as described in Topic 944 are not subject to consolidation according to the requirements of the Variable Interest Entities Subsections.

c. A reporting entity with an interest in a VIE or potential VIE created before December 31, 2003, is not required to apply the guidance in the Variable Interest Entities Subsections to that VIE or legal entity if the reporting entity, after making an exhaustive effort, is unable to obtain the information necessary to do any one of the following:

1. Determine whether the legal entity is a VIE
2. Determine whether the reporting entity is the VIE's primary beneficiary
3. Perform the accounting required to consolidate the VIE for which it is determined to be the primary beneficiary.

This inability to obtain the necessary information is expected to be infrequent, especially if the reporting entity participated significantly in the design or redesign of the legal entity. The scope exception in this provision applies only as long as the reporting entity continues to be unable to obtain the necessary information. Paragraph 810-10-50-6 requires certain disclosures to be made about interests in VIEs subject to this provision. Paragraphs 810-10-30-7 through 30-9 provide transition guidance for a reporting entity that subsequently obtains the information necessary to apply the Variable Interest Entities Subsections to a VIE subject to this exception.

d. A legal entity that is deemed to be a business need not be evaluated by a reporting entity to determine if the legal entity is a VIE under the requirements of the Variable Interest Entities Subsections unless any of the following conditions exist (however, for legal entities that are excluded by this provision, other generally accepted accounting principles [GAAP] should be applied):

1. The reporting entity, its related parties (all parties identified in paragraph 810-10-25-43, except for de facto agents under paragraph 810-10-25-43(d)), or both participated significantly in the design or redesign of the legal entity. However, this condition does not apply if the legal entity is an operating joint venture under joint control of the reporting entity and one or more independent parties or a franchisee.
2. The legal entity is designed so that substantially all of its activities either involve or are conducted on behalf of the reporting entity and its related parties.
3. The reporting entity and its related parties provide more than half of the total of the equity, subordinated debt, and other forms of subordinated financial support to the legal entity based on an analysis of the fair values of the interests in the legal entity.
4. The activities of the legal entity are primarily related to securitizations or other forms of asset-backed financings or single-lessee leasing arrangements.

A legal entity that previously was not evaluated to determine if it was a VIE because of this provision need not be evaluated in future periods as long as the legal entity continues to meet the conditions in (d).

There are also accounting alternatives for Entities under Common Control, detailed in ASC 810-10-15-17AC through AF.

.07   Specific Provisions of FIN 46

The FASB divided entities into two classes in the determination of which entities should be consolidated in the financial statements of another entity:

1. Those for which the consolidation decision is based on the controlling equity interests in the entity.
2. Those where the consolidation decision is based on interests *other than* controlling equity interests. (These are the interests now referred to as variable interests. Thus, these are the entities in which consolidation is subject to the nature of these variable interests. It is these, in particular, that are the subject of the Interpretation.)

FIN 46 addresses consolidation by business enterprises where equity investors do *not* bear the residual economic risks and rewards. These entities have been commonly referred to as special-purpose entities.

The underlying principle behind the new Interpretation is that, if a business enterprise has the majority financial interest in an entity (defined in the guidance as a variable interest entity), the assets, liabilities, and results of the activities of the variable interest entity should be included in consolidated financial statements with those of the business enterprise.

Majority-owned subsidiaries are entities separate from their parents that are subject to this Interpretation and may be VIEs.

The Interpretation explains how to identify variable interest entities. It also explains how an enterprise should assess its interest in an entity when deciding whether or not to consolidate that entity and include the assets, liabilities, noncontrolling interests, cash flows, and results of operations of a particular VIE in its consolidated financial statements.

.08   Determination of Status

The initial determination of whether an entity is a VIE and thus subject to the Interpretation is made at the time when an enterprise becomes involved with the entity through ownership, a contractual interest, or other pecuniary interest (i.e., the determination date). These interests can change with the entity's net asset value and may take a variety of forms, including but not limited to guarantees, options to acquire assets, purchase contracts, management or other service contracts, credit enhancements, leases, or subordinated loans. Equity interests with or without voting rights are considered variable interests if the entity is a VIE.

Also at the determination date, the enterprise should determine whether its investments or other interests will absorb any portions of the VIE's expected losses or receive any portions of the entity's expected residual returns. If so, they are indeed variable interests and subject to the Interpretation. VIEs whose variable interests effectively disperse risk among the parties involved need not be consolidated by any of the parties.

A company that consolidates a VIE is called the *primary beneficiary* of that entity. The FASB believes consolidation by a primary beneficiary of the assets, liabilities, and results of activities of VIEs will provide more complete information about the resources, obligations, risks, and opportunities of the consolidated company. To further assist financial statement users in assessing a company's risks, FIN 46 also requires disclosures about VIEs that a company is *not* required to consolidate but in which it has a significant variable interest.

.09   Difference between FIN 46 and Previous Practice

In the past, two enterprises generally have been included in consolidated financial statements because one enterprise controlled the other through voting interests. FIN 46 explains other methods of identifying variable interest entities and then indicates how an enterprise assesses its particular interests in a VIE to decide whether or not to consolidate that entity. FIN 46 requires existing unconsolidated variable interest entities to be consolidated by their *primary beneficiaries* if the entities do not effectively disperse risks among parties involved. The variable interest entities that do effectively disperse risks will not be consolidated, unless a single party holds an interest or combination of interests that effectively recombines risks that had previously been dispersed.

The ability to make decisions is not a variable interest, but it is an indication that the decision maker should carefully consider whether it holds sufficient variable interests to be the primary beneficiary. An enterprise with a variable interest in a VIE must consider variable interests of related parties and de facto agents as its own in determining whether it is the primary beneficiary of the entity.

.10   Measurement

Assets, liabilities, and noncontrolling interests of newly consolidated VIEs generally will be initially measured at their fair values except for assets and liabilities transferred to a variable interest entity by its primary beneficiary, which will continue to be measured as if they had not been transferred. If recognizing those assets, liabilities, and noncontrolling interests at their fair values results in a *loss* to the consolidated enterprise, that loss will be reported immediately as an extraordinary item. On the other hand, if recognizing those assets, liabilities, and noncontrolling interests at their fair values results in a *gain* to the consolidated enterprise, that amount will be allocated to reduce the amounts assigned to assets in the same manner as if consolidation resulted from a business combination.

However, assets, liabilities, and noncontrolling interests of newly consolidated variable interest entities that are under common control with the primary beneficiary are measured at the amounts at which they are carried in the consolidated financial statements of the enterprise that controls them (or would be carried if the controlling entity prepared financial statements) at the date the enterprise becomes the primary beneficiary. After initial measurement, the assets, liabilities, and noncontrolling interests of a consolidated variable interest entity will be accounted for as if the entity were consolidated based on voting interests. In some circumstances, earnings of the variable interest entity attributed to the primary beneficiary arise from sources other than investments in equity of the entity.

.11   Disclosure Requirements

An enterprise that holds significant variable interests in a variable interest entity but *is not the primary beneficiary* is required to disclose:

- The nature, purpose, size, and activities of the variable interest entity.
- The nature of its involvement with the entity and date when the involvement began.
- Its maximum exposure to loss as a result of involvement with the VIE.

The *primary beneficiary* of a variable interest entity is required to disclose the following, unless it also holds a majority voting interest in the VIE:

- The nature, purpose, size, and activities of the variable interest entity.
- The carrying amount and classification of consolidated assets that are collateral for the variable interest entity's obligations.
- Any lack of recourse by creditors (or beneficial interest holders) of a consolidated variable interest entity to the general credit of the primary beneficiary.

The primary beneficiary must, in addition, disclose all information that may be required by other standards. It is also important for a primary beneficiary to reconsider its status from time to time, particularly if:

- The VIE's governing documents or contractual arrangements among the involved parties change.
- The primary beneficiary sells or otherwise disposes of all or part of its interest to other parties.

A holder of beneficial interests that is *not a primary beneficiary* should also reconsider its status if the enterprise acquires newly issued interests in the entity or part of the primary beneficiary's interest in the VIE.

A cautionary note about disclosure: disclosures required by FASB 140 about a variable interest entity must be included in the same note to the financial statements as the information required by FIN 46. Information about VIEs may be reported in the aggregate for similar entities if separate reporting would not add material information.

.12   What Constitutes a Variable Interest?

An entity is a VIE and, therefore, subject to consolidation according to the provisions of FIN 46 if, by the way it is structured, either of two conditions exists:

1. The total equity investment as reported as equity in the entity's statements at risk is not sufficient to permit the entity to finance its activities without additional subordinated financial support from other parties. That is, the equity investment at risk is not greater than the expected losses of the entity. For this purpose, the total equity investment at risk:
    a.   Includes only equity investments in the entity that participate significantly in profits and losses, even if those investments do not carry voting rights.
    b.   Does not include equity interests that the entity issued in exchange for subordinated interests in other VIEs.
    c.   Does not include amounts provided to the equity investor by the entity or other parties involved with the entity (such as fees, charitable contributions, or other payments), unless the provider is a parent, subsidiary, or affiliate of the investor required to be included in the same set of consolidated financial statements as the investor.
    d.   Does not include amounts financed for the equity investor (for example, by loans or guarantees of loans) directly by the entity or by other parties involved with the entity, unless that party is a parent, subsidiary, or affiliate of the investor that is required to be included in the same set of financial statements of the investor.
2. As a group, the holders of the equity investment at risk lack any one of the following three characteristics of a controlling financial interest:
    a.   The direct or indirect ability to make decisions about an entity's activities through voting rights or similar rights. The investors do not have that ability through voting rights or similar rights if no owners hold voting rights or similar rights (such as those of a common shareholder in a corporation or a general partner in a partnership). In addition, the equity investors as a group also are considered to lack the characteristic of this condition if:

(1) The voting rights of some investors are not proportional to their obligations to absorb the expected losses of the entity, to receive the expected residual returns of the entity, or both.

(2) Substantially all of the entity's activities (for example, providing financing or buying assets) either involve or are conducted on behalf of an investor and any related parties of the investor that have disproportionately few voting rights. According to FIN 46, this provision is necessary to prevent a primary beneficiary from avoiding consolidation of a VIE by organizing the entity with non-substantive voting interests.

b. The obligation to absorb the expected losses of the entity if they occur. Investor or investors do not have that obligation if they are directly or indirectly protected from the expected losses or are guaranteed a return by the entity itself or by other parties involved with the entity.

c. The right to receive the expected residual returns of the entity if they occur. The investors do not have that right if their return is capped by the entity's governing documents or arrangements with other variable interest holders or with the entity.

Several of these provisions have been included in an attempt to forestall methods of circumventing the intent of the various rulings to provide a true financial picture for the benefit of the financial statement user in general and the investor in particular.

.13   Equity Investment at Risk

The determination of the total amount of equity investment at risk that is necessary to permit an entity to finance its activities is a matter of judgment. FIN 46 offers guidance, but each case must be determined based on its facts and circumstances. A VIE's expected losses and expected residual returns include:

- The expected variability in the entity's net income or loss.
- The expected variability in the fair value of the entity's assets (except as explained below in "Specified Assets"), if it is not included in net income or loss.
- Fees to the decision maker (if there is one).
- Fees to providers of guarantees of the values of all or substantially all of the entity's assets (including writers of put options and other instruments with similar results) and providers of guarantees that all or substantially all of the entity's liabilities will be paid.

.14   Ten Percent Guideline

An equity investment of *less than 10 percent* of the entity's total assets is *not* to be considered sufficient to permit the entity to finance its activities without subordinated financial support in addition to the equity investment *unless* the equity investment can be demonstrated to be sufficient in at least one of three ways:

1. The entity has demonstrated that it can actually finance its activities without additional subordinated financial support.
2. The entity has at least as much equity invested as other entities that hold only similar assets of similar quality in similar amounts and operate with no additional subordinated financial support. (This comparison should be very carefully researched and considered, not merely an attempt to validate a questionable decision.)
3. The amount of equity invested in the entity exceeds the estimate of the entity's expected losses based on reasonable quantitative evidence.

FIN 46 points out that some entities may require an equity investment greater than 10 percent of their assets to finance their activities. This is particularly true if they engage in high-risk activities, hold high-risk assets, or have exposure to risks that has not been adequately shown in the reported amounts of their assets or liabilities. It is unquestionably the responsibility of the enterprise to determine whether a particular entity with which it is involved needs an equity investment *greater than 10 percent* of its assets in order to finance its activities without subordinated financial support in addition to the equity investment. At the time of the Enron fiasco, the guideline was only 3 percent, and even this was not observed. Auditors and management must move very cautiously when deciding whether or not an entity must be consolidated.

.15 Specified Assets

A variable interest can be in the VIE or specified assets of the VIE, such as a guarantee or subordinated residual value.

A variable interest in specific assets of a VIE are considered to be a variable interest in the VIE only if:

- The fair value of the specific asset is more than 50 percent of the fair value of the VIE's total assets.
- The holder has another variable interest in the VIE as a whole, except where those other interests are insignificant or have little or no variability.

If an enterprise has a variable interest in specified assets that are essentially the only source of payment for specified liabilities or other specified interests of the VIE, the enterprise should treat that portion of the entity as a separate VIE. If this is the case and the holder is required to consolidate only this discrete piece of the VIE, the holders of other variable interests need not consider that portion to be part of the larger VIE.

.16   Who Should Consolidate Whom and When?

The consolidation policy rule appears on the surface, and from all the provisos, to be very complicated. However, once everything has been considered, it is relatively simple. An enterprise must consolidate a VIE if that enterprise has a variable interest (or a combination of variable interests) that will:

- Absorb a majority of the VIE's expected losses, if they occur.
- Receive a majority of the VIE's expected residual returns if they occur.
- Both.

   In the situation where one enterprise will absorb the majority of the expected losses and another enterprise will absorb the majority of the expected residual returns, the enterprise absorbing the losses must consolidate the VIE.

   The consolidating entity is called the primary beneficiary in the Interpretation. The determination of primary beneficiary status is made at the time the enterprise becomes involved in the VIE.

.17   Decisions Relating to Variable Interests

The initial determination of whether an entity is a variable interest entity needs to be *reconsidered* only if one or more of the following occur:

- The entity's governing documents or the contractual arrangements among the parties involved change.
- The equity investment or some part thereof is returned to the investors, and other parties become exposed to expected losses.
- The entity undertakes additional activities or acquires additional assets that increase the entity's expected losses.

.18   Determination Date

The initial determination of whether an entity is a variable interest entity is to be made on the date at which an enterprise becomes involved with the entity through ownership, a contractual interest, or other pecuniary interest. Such determination should be based on the circumstances occurring on that date, including future changes that are required in existing governing documents and existing contractual arrangements. An enterprise is not required to determine whether an entity with which it is involved is a variable interest entity if it is apparent that the enterprise's interest would not be a significant variable interest and if the enterprise, its related parties, and its de facto agents were not involved in forming the entity.

Any entity that previously did not require consolidation does not become subject to the Interpretation because it loses more than its "expected losses," resulting in a reduction of the equity investment.

.19   Related Parties

An enterprise's variable interest in a VIE includes the variable interests of any related parties in the same VIE. For the purposes of the Interpretation, related parties as identified in FASB 57, *Related Parties*, and certain other de facto agents of the variable interest holder are considered to be related parties. FASB 57 identifies related parties as:

- A parent company and its subsidiaries.
- Subsidiaries of a common parent.
- An enterprise or trust for the benefit of employees that is managed by or under the trusteeship of the enterprise's management.
- An enterprise and its principal owners, management, or members of their immediate families.
- Affiliates.

FIN 46 considers the following to be de facto agents of an enterprise:

- A party that cannot finance its operations without subordinated financial support from the enterprise (e.g., another VIE of which the enterprise is the primary beneficiary).
- A party that received its interests as a contribution or loan from the enterprise.
- An officer, employee, or member of the governing board of the enterprise.
- A party that has:
  — An agreement that it cannot sell, transfer, or encumber its interests in the entity without the prior approval of the enterprise.
  — A close business relationship like that between a professional service provider and one of its significant clients.

If two or more related parties hold variable interests in the same VIE, the following guidelines should be used to determine which is the primary beneficiary:

- If two or more parties with variable interests have an agency relationship, the principal is the primary beneficiary.
- If the relationship is not that of a principal and an agent, the party with activities that are most closely associated with the entity is the primary beneficiary.

.20 Fair Value Measurement

A primary beneficiary initially measures the assets, liabilities, and non-consolidated interests in a VIE at their *fair value* upon consolidation. There are two exceptions to this rule. Assets and liabilities transferred by a primary beneficiary to a newly consolidated VIE are measured at the same amount they would have been measured at if no transfer had occurred. If the primary beneficiary and the VIE are under common control, assets and liabilities transferred to the VIE are measured at their carrying amounts on the financial statements of the enterprise that controls the VIE. After the initial measurement, the assets, liabilities, and noncontrolling interests of a consolidated VIE are accounted for based on voting interests.

.21 Guidance Provided on Questions Raised by Users

Guidance in several areas was provided in July 2003 through five FASB Staff Positions (FSPs). The guidance in each of the FSPs was effective immediately for VIEs to which the requirements of the Interpretation had already been applied. The guidance was applied to other variable interest entities as a part of the adoption of FIN 46. If the guidance resulted in changes to previously reported information, the cumulative effect of the accounting change was to be reported in the first period ending after July 24, 2003.

These FSPs may be applied by restating previously issued financial statements for one or more years with a cumulative-effect adjustment as of the beginning of the first year restated.

Regardless of specific language used in FIN 46 that caused some readers to question whether a distinction was being drawn regarding certain types of health care organizations, this was not the intention. All not-for-profit organizations as defined in FASB 117, *Financial Statements of Not-for-Profit Organizations*, including health care organizations subject to the AICPA Audit Guide, are included within the scope of the exemption for not-for-profits. However, FIN 46 does point out that not-for-profit organizations may be related parties for purposes of applying certain portions of the Interpretation. In addition, as emphasized earlier in this chapter, a not-for-profit entity used by a business enterprise in a manner similar to a VIE in an effort to circumvent the provisions of Interpretation 46 is subject to the Interpretation.

A specified asset (or group of assets) of a variable interest entity and a related liability secured only by the specified asset or group are not treated as a separate VIE if other parties have rights or obligations related to the specified asset or to residual cash flows from the specified asset. The FSP explains that this is considered so because a separate VIE is deemed to exist for accounting purposes only if essentially all of the assets, liabilities, and equity of the deemed entity are separate from the overall entity and specifically identifiable. It is further explained that, essentially none of the returns of the assets of the deemed entity can be used by the remaining variable interest entity, and essentially none of the liabilities of the deemed entity are payable from the assets of the remaining VIE.

Transition requirements for initial application of FIN 46 provide that both of the following determinations should be made as of the date the enterprise became involved with the entity unless events requiring reconsideration of the entity's status or the status of its variable interest holders have occurred:

1. Whether an entity is a VIE.
2. Which enterprise, if any, is a VIE's primary beneficiary.

If a reconsideration event has occurred, each determination should be made as of the most recent date at which the Interpretation would have required consideration. However, if, at transition, it is impracticable for an enterprise to obtain the information necessary to make such a determination (as of the date the enterprise became involved with an entity or at the most recent reconsideration date), the enterprise should make the determination as of the date on which FIN 46 is first applied. If the VIE and primary beneficiary determinations are made in accordance with these conditions, then the primary beneficiary must measure the assets, liabilities, and noncontrolling interests of the VIE at fair value as of the date on which the Interpretation is first applied.

The two remaining June 2003 FSPs deal with the term "expected losses". The phrase "expected losses of the entity" as used in the Interpretation, is based on the variability in the entity's net income or loss and not on the amount of the net income or loss. Procedures in FIN 46 and Appendix A require that the outcomes used to calculate expected losses include (1) the expected unfavorable variability in the entity's net income or loss and (2) expected unfavorable variability in the fair value of the entity's assets, if it is not included in the net income or loss. (Even an entity that expects to be profitable will have expected losses when this criterion for determining expected losses is considered.) Detailed instructions for calculating expected losses are also provided.

.22   FIN 46(R)

As pointed out above, the "derivatives problem" has not been easily solved, nor has the SPE/VIE fiasco. Will it take a headline grabber like Orange County or Enron to furnish the FASB sufficient clout to require effective accounting for the costs of stock options? The FASB was not unaware of possible problems arising from the growing use of off-balance sheet vehicles before Enron succeeded in utilizing them in their creative accounting. Numerous Standards and other rulings had obviously failed to control the situation or were too easily subverted.

Interpretation 46 was a big step toward preventing misuse of SPEs. As noted above, the Board realized immediately that implementation guidance and additional interpretation would be necessary. Thus, in the summer of 2003, the several staff positions were published to help clarify the requirements. But after almost a year of working with it, financial statement preparers were still not interpreting FIN 46 as the Board had intended. If this were not such a high profile "case," this might be an ideal time to try out the principles-based approach to standard setting.

FIN 46(R) adopted in December 2003 is the next step in trying to make everything perfectly clear. Provisions re-emphasize those entities that are subject to consolidation as well as those that are not. It appears that, to make sure that they did not run into trouble, too many organizations were consolidating off-balance sheet entities erroneously. Therefore, the revision reiterates and emphasizes the types of organizations that are not required to consolidate, and spells out other exceptions to the scope of the Interpretation in the following manner:

- An enterprise with an interest in a variable interest entity or potential variable interest entity created before December 31, 2003, is not required to apply this Interpretation to that entity if the enterprise, after making an exhaustive effort, is unable to obtain the necessary information.
- An entity that is deemed to be a business (as defined in this Interpretation) need not be evaluated to determine if it is a variable interest entity unless one of the following conditions exists:
  — The reporting enterprise, its related parties, or both participated significantly in the design or redesign of the entity, and the entity is neither a joint venture nor a franchisee.
  — The entity is designed so that substantially all of its activities either involve or are conducted on behalf of the reporting enterprise and its related parties.
  — The reporting enterprise and its related parties provide more than half of the total of the equity, subordinated debt, and other forms of subordinated financial support to the entity based on an analysis of the fair values of the interests in the entity.
  — The activities of the entity are primarily related to securitizations, other forms of asset-backed financings, or single-lessee leasing arrangements.
- An enterprise is not required to consolidate a governmental organization and is not required to consolidate a financing entity established by a governmental organization unless the financing entity:
  — Is not a governmental organization.
  — Is used by the business enterprise in a manner similar to a variable interest entity in an effort to circumvent the provisions of this Interpretation.

.23   FASB's Explanation for the Revision

It would appear that FIN 46(R) is not so much a "revision" as a reemphasis of FIN 46. As mentioned above, many VIEs may have been consolidated that should not necessarily have been. On the other hand, users of financial reports would probably prefer this condition to one in which they are not, and, thus, information relating to them is more difficult to ascertain. It is because transactions involving variable interest entities have become increasingly common, and the relevant accounting literature is so fragmented and incomplete that the FASB has found it necessary to issue the Interpretation. The Board has pointed out that ARB 51 requires that an enterprise's consolidated financial statements include subsidiaries in which the enterprise has a controlling financial or voting interest. As has become evident, the voting interest approach is not effective in identifying controlling financial interests in entities that are not controllable through voting interests or in which the equity investors do not bear the residual economic risks.

Thus, the objective of the Interpretation is not to restrict the use of variable interest entities but to improve financial reporting by enterprises involved with variable interest entities. The Board believes that if a business enterprise has a controlling financial interest in a variable interest entity, the assets, liabilities, and results of the activities of the variable interest entity should be included in consolidated financial statements with those of the business enterprise.

.24   Relationship of FIN 46(R) to the Conceptual Framework

The Board evidently felt that after pulling together much of the diverse scattered rulings related to various forms of off-balance-sheet entities and attempting to control their financial reporting with Interpretations, it was important to tie the requirements to their roots. Thus, references to the appropriate Concepts Statements:

FASB Concepts Statements state that financial reporting should provide information that is useful in making business and economic decisions. Including variable interest entities in consolidated financial statements with the primary beneficiary will help achieve that objective by providing information that helps in assessing the amounts, timing, and uncertainty of prospective net cash flows of the consolidated entity.

Completeness is identified in FASB Concepts Statements as an essential element of representational faithfulness and relevance. Thus, to represent faithfully the total assets that an enterprise controls and liabilities for which an enterprise is responsible, assets and liabilities of variable interest entities for which the enterprise is the primary beneficiary must be included in the enterprise's consolidated financial statements.

FASB Concepts Statements define assets, in part, as probable future economic benefits obtained or controlled by a particular entity and defines liabilities, in part, as obligations of a particular entity to make probable future sacrifices of economic benefits. The relationship between a variable interest entity and its primary beneficiary results in control by the primary beneficiary of future benefits from the assets of the variable interest entity even though the primary beneficiary may not have the direct ability to make decisions about the uses of the assets. Because the liabilities of the variable interest entity will require sacrificing consolidated assets, those liabilities are obligations of the primary beneficiary even though the creditors of the variable interest entity may have no recourse to the general credit of the primary beneficiary.

¶6002　Derivatives

A derivative is something that derives (hence, the word "derivative") its value from something else. For example, a put or call option on stock only has value because the stock itself has value.

A derivative has certain characteristics. First is an underlying. An underlying is a price, rate or similar amount. It can be a stock price, commodity price, interest rate, credit rating, exchange rate, or a price or rate index of any of those items. Second is a notional amount. While the underlying is a price or rate, a notional amount is a quantity, like a number of shares, bushels, pounds, units, etc. A derivative may also have a payment provision, which is a fixed or determinable settlement to be made if a specific event happens.

A derivative has one or more underlyings and one or more notional amounts or payment provisions or both. It also requires little or no initial net investment. Finally, it requires net settlement set by the terms of the instrument, can be settled by a means outside the contract, or provides for delivery of an asset substantially equivalent to net settlement.

Derivatives are recorded as an asset or liability at fair value. Instruments may, themselves, be the derivatives, or instruments may contain embedded derivatives.

The concept of derivatives is incredibly complex and is outside the scope of this book. When dealing with such instruments, additional research should be done in ASC 815 and/or other guidance.

¶6003　Leases

Leases are one of the "Big Three" accounting standards issued in recent years. The other two were revenue recognition and financial instruments. Each of these three standards created an entirely new topic in the ASC. The changes are so extensive that amending previous topics was not adequate to address them. The previous topic for leases was ASC 840, while the new topic is ASC 842. The new lease standard came with the issuance of Accounting Standards Update (ASU) No. 2016-02, Leases (Topic 842). The effective date of the new standard for public business entities was fiscal years beginning after December

15, 2018. The date for other entities was extended with ASU 2019-10 to fiscal years beginning after December 15, 2020, as long as the entity had not issued financial statements with the standard already adopted. ASC 840 is completely superseded as of this writing, so we will refer to ASC 840 as the former standard and ASC 842 as the new standard.

Several ASUs have been issued subsequent to ASU 2016-02 to fine-tune and clarify issues that arose after the issuance and during implementation of ASU 2016-02. For more in-depth information on these clarifying items, the reader is referred to:

- ASU 2018-01, Leases (Topic 842): Land Easement Practical Expedient for Transition to Topic 842
- ASU 2018-11, Leases (Topic 842): Targeted Improvements
- ASU 2018-20, Leases (Topic 842): Narrow-Scope Improvements for Lessors
- ASU 2019-01, Leases (Topic 842): Codification Improvements
- ASU 2021-05, Leases (Topic 842): Lessors—Certain Leases with Variable Lease Payments
- ASU 2021-09, Leases (Topic 842): Discount Rate for Lessees That Are Not Public Business Entities
- ASU 2023-01, Leases (Topic 842): Common Control Arrangements

.01   Background

Accounting for leases has historically been a controversial issue. Some leases were recorded on the balance sheet as an obligation and an asset, while others were left off the balance sheet. Although few argued the point that a lease agreement met the requirements to be recorded as a liability, the argument went something like, "Yes, it probably should be a liability. But, if you make us record the liability, we'll also have to record an asset we don't own. It would be misleading to report such an asset as ours on the balance sheet." So certain leases continued to be left off the balance sheet.

Accounting for leases depends on whether it is the lessee reporting or the lessor. Lessor accounting did not change a great deal with the release of the new standard. But lessee accounting did. At least for those leases that were formerly left off the balance sheet.

Under the former lease standard, leases were classified as capital leases or operating leases. If any of the following criteria were met, the lease was capitalized, or shown on the balance sheet. If none of them were met, it was classified as operating:

1.   Ownership of the leased asset reverted to the lessee by the end of the lease
2.   The lessee could acquire the leased asset at a bargain purchase price

3. The present value of minimum future lease payments was equal to or greater than 90 percent of the fair value of the leased asset
4. The lease term is equal to or greater than 75 percent of the expected useful life of the leased asset

One can see there is a common theme in these criteria—a focus on the asset. If the lessee got the asset in the end, paid most of the value of the asset, or used the asset for most of its life, then it seemed acceptable to report the asset on the balance sheet, so the liability was also reported. If none of those were true, the argument was that it would be misleading to have an asset on the balance sheet, so no liability was reported, either. After a series of what were deemed accounting failures in the early 2000s, not only were new laws implemented, such as Sarbanes-Oxley and Dodd-Frank, there was also a greater push for transparency; a very strong push to get rid of items referred to as off-balance sheet financing. This was a large part of the impetus for the new lease standard.

Under the former lease standard, capital leases reported an asset and liability while operating leases did not. On the income statement, capital leases reported interest expense related to the lease obligation and amortization expense related to the leased asset. Operating leases reported a straight-line rent expense over the term of the lease.

For lessors, leases were classified as sales-type leases, direct financing leases, or operating leases. If any of the four criteria described for the lessee were true and two additional criteria were true, the lease would be either sales-type or direct financing. Those two additional criteria were that the lessor had no significant remaining obligation to perform under the lease and collectability was reasonably assured. Additionally, if there was seller's profit, the lease was a sales-type lease. If not, it was direct financing. Under the new standard, the classifications and accounting are substantially the same for lessors. Arriving at the classification differs slightly, but all else is similar.

.02 Lessee Classification

Under the new lease standard, even though all leases, except short-term leases, are reported on the balance sheet, there are still two classifications. Leases are now classified as finance leases or operating leases. If any of the following criteria are met, the lease is a financing lease. If none of them are met, it is classified as operating:

1. Lease transfers ownership of the underlying asset to the lessee by the end of the lease term
2. The lease grants the lessee an option to purchase the underlying asset that the lessee is reasonably certain to exercise
3. The lease term is for the major part of the remaining economic life of the asset, unless near the end of the economic life of the lease

4. The present value of the sum of the lease payments and any residual value guaranteed by the lessee equals or exceeds substantially all of the fair value of the underlying asset
5. The underlying asset is of such a specialized nature that it is expected to have no alternative use to the lessor at the end of the lease term

It is immediately evident, except the addition of the last item, the criteria are pretty much the same as they were previously. One of FASB's stated goals was to remove the "bright lines" from the old criteria. So "major part" is used instead of 75 percent and "substantially all" is used instead of 90 percent. However, the standard does state that a reasonable approach would be to conclude 75 percent is a major part and 90 percent amounts to substantially all. So, although bright lines are removed, the concepts really have not changed.

The obvious question is, "If all leases except short term leases (12 months or less) are recorded on the balance sheet, why have different classifications?" The answer is the impact on the income statement, as described in the following section.

.03   Lessee Accounting

Finance leases and operating leases have the same accounting for the balance sheet. A liability is recorded for the present value of lease payments. An asset is recorded in the same amount plus any initial direct costs and any up-front payments. The asset is called a right-of-use asset. This was primarily done to overcome the argument that the entity does not own an asset so none should be recorded. Accounting concept statements define an asset as something that provides future economic benefit. The right to use an asset does provide future economic benefit, even when the asset is not owned.

Income statement accounting for finance leases is substantially the same as accounting for former capital leases. The asset is amortized over the lease term or the asset's expected useful life, whichever is shorter. The lease obligation is amortized using the effective interest method, with payments reducing principal and recorded as interest expense.

Income statement accounting for operating leases arises from the desire for a consistent expense amount each period, just as in the former operating lease. The challenge is that an operating lease now has an asset and a liability that reduce over time. The reduction of the liability still follows the effective interest method. So, in order to get a straight-line lease expense, the reduction of the asset follows what is essentially the inverse of an accelerated depreciation method. Monthly lease expense is calculated by adding all amounts paid for the lease and dividing that total by the number of months in the lease. A debit to lease expense is recorded in that amount. A credit to cash is recorded for the amount of the payment. A debit to the lease obligation is recorded in accordance with an amortization table prepared according to the effective interest method. The remaining credit is a balancing amount credited to reduce the asset.

¶6004   Accounting for Income Taxes

This section provides an abbreviated "plain English" overview of the principles of Accounting for Income Taxes addressed in ASC 740.

Several ASUs have been issued clarifying issues impacting accounting for income taxes. For more in-depth information on these clarifying items, the reader is referred to:

- ASU 2013-11, Income Taxes (Topic 740): Presentation of an Unrecognized Tax Benefit When a Net Operating Loss Carryforward, a Similar Tax Loss, or a Tax Credit Carryforward Exists (a consensus of the FASB Emerging Issues Task Force)
- ASU 2015-17, Income Taxes (Topic 740): Balance Sheet Classification of Deferred Taxes
- ASU 2016-16, Income Taxes (Topic 740): Intra-Entity Transfers of Assets Other than Inventory
- ASU 2018-05, Income Taxes (Topic 740): Amendments to SEC Paragraphs Pursuant to SEC Staff Accounting Bulletin No. 118 (SEC Update)
- ASU 2019-12, Income Taxes (Topic 740): Simplifying the Accounting for Income Taxes
- ASU 2023-09, Income Taxes (Topic 740): Improvements to Income Tax Disclosures

The acronyms above will be used throughout the product and have the following meanings:

FASB	Financial Accounting Standards Board
ASC	Accounting Standards Codification
ASU	Accounting Standards Update
GAAS	Generally Accepted Auditing Standards
U.S. GAAP	Accounting Standards Generally Accepted in the United States of America
Topic 740	References to FASB ASC Topic 740 may be shortened to just Topic 740

Keep in mind that these materials primarily address the U.S. GAAP rules, not the Internal Revenue Code. In commonly used jargon, this addresses "book" accounting, not "tax" accounting. However, the very reason this topic is even an accounting issue is because there are differences in the way we account for things in accordance with U.S. GAAP and the way we account for things under tax laws. It is precisely those differences that give rise to the need for deferred tax assets and liabilities and the other issues that comprise this topic. Therefore, some understanding of tax law is needed to properly understand and apply the material. It is usually best to have those with tax expertise to work closely with those who have U.S. GAAP expertise in order to properly account for these items.

The basic steps we follow in accounting for income taxes are:

1. Calculate current taxes payable or receivable.
2. Identify differences between the book basis and tax basis of assets and liabilities.
3. Determine, for each difference, whether it will result in taxes paid in the future; that is, a future tax obligation; or a future tax benefit.
4. Apply an appropriate tax rate to the difference to calculate a deferred tax.
5. Classify differences that result in a future tax obligation as deferred tax liabilities and those that result in a future tax benefit as deferred tax assets.
6. Determine if a valuation allowance is needed for any or all deferred tax assets.

After addressing a few more basic concepts, we will address each of the steps above in more detail. We also will address items related to these steps, such as a net operating loss, which has a tax rate applied to it in order to calculate a deferred tax asset; and tax credits, carryforwards and carrybacks.

More detailed topics to be addressed include uncertainty in income taxes, intraperiod tax allocations, and disclosure requirements.

.01   Asset and Liability Method

We use the asset and liability approach to account for income taxes. This concept can actually be perceived in three different ways. First, we focus on the balance sheet and let changes run through the income statement. That is, we calculate the proper current and deferred assets and/or liabilities and adjust them by recording income tax expense or benefit on the income statement.

Second, we use the difference between the book basis and the tax basis of assets and liabilities for our calculations, not the difference between book revenue/expenses and taxable income/deductions.

Third, we use the definition of an asset and a liability to guide us in proper recognition. Perhaps this can best be shown with an example. The most commonly identified difference between books and taxes is depreciation. Generally, books use a straight-line approach and taxes use MACRS (Modified Accelerated Cost Recovery System), which is, as the name implies, an accelerated method. The following diagram shows how depreciation expense is recorded over time:

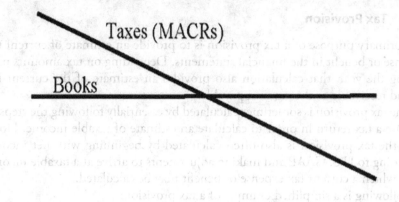

Think about it this way—because MACRS is used for taxes, the earlier years will provide a company a greater deduction, or benefit, for tax purposes than the book expense would give it. In later years, less depreciation will be taken for taxes than for books. We refer to that as the book-tax difference reversing. When it reverses, the company will have to pay more taxes than its books would indicate. Because it has to pay more in the future than would be expected from its net income, that is a future obligation. It meets the definition of a liability. This is a deferred tax liability. A difference that goes the other way would provide a future economic benefit to the company, which is the definition of an asset. This would be a deferred tax asset.

As noted above, we do not calculate deferred assets and liabilities on the differences in depreciation expense. Rather, the calculations are based on the differences in net fixed assets. This allows the differences to be identified based on accumulated information rather than just for one year, resulting in more proper measurement of the differences and their eventual reversals.

.02   Current Tax Assets and Liabilities

The first step to be taken in the process of accounting for income taxes is the calculation of a current tax asset or liability. This is simply the amount of tax refund or tax payable calculated on the tax return.

This concept is simple but there is a bit of a challenge in its implementation. The challenge is that a tax return is generally completed *after* the financial statements are prepared and, if those financial statements are audited, the tax return usually uses the completed, audited financial statements as a starting point for the income tax return. Therefore, an estimate is generally used in the preparation of the financial statements and the accuracy of that estimate is assessed by the auditors. A very common way of calculating that estimate is by preparing what is called a tax provision.

.03   Tax Provision

The primary purpose of a tax provision is to provide an estimate of current tax expense or benefit in the financial statements. Depending on tax amounts paid during the year, that calculation also provides an estimate of the current tax refund receivable or the amount payable.

The tax provision is sometimes calculated by essentially following the steps to prepare a tax return in order to calculate an estimate of taxable income. However, the tax provision is also often calculated by beginning with net income according to U.S. GAAP and making adjustments to arrive at a taxable income from which a current tax expense or benefit may be calculated.

Following is a simplified example of a tax provision:

Net income (U.S. GAAP)	$726,453
Adjustments to net income	
50 percent of meals and entertainment	16,274
Key man life insurance premiums	12,000
Interest income from non-taxable municipal bonds	(23,478)
Tax depreciation in excess of books	(63,552)
Bad debt expense in excess of write-offs	24,663
Non-deductible expenses recorded for reserves	48,559
Taxable income	$740,919
Multiplied by tax rate	21%
Estimated tax expense	$155,593
Less amounts paid during the year	144,000
Taxes payable (refund receivable)	$11,593

Note that this provision is simplified. There may be more adjustments to bring net income for U.S. GAAP to a taxable income. Also, the tax rate shown does not take into consideration any graduated tax rates, in accordance with current corporate tax law. In a period when graduated rates are applicable, they should be considered. Any applicable state or local tax rate should be considered, as well.

Although a tax provision is primarily used to estimate current amounts, it is also helpful in identifying deferred amounts, which will be discussed in detail later. The reason this is the case is that most differences have an impact on current and deferred taxes. To again use depreciation as an example, the difference between book depreciation expense for a year and tax depreciation expense for a year should be one of the adjustment items in the tax provision in order to calculate an estimate of taxable income. The difference between the tax basis and book basis of net fixed assets is used in calculating deferred tax amounts. The difference in the expense for the current year is a portion of the difference in the net asset due to the impact of accumulated depreciation. So the provision helps in the identification of temporary differences for deferred taxes, as well as in the calculation of current taxes.

.04 Identifying Tax Differences

The best way to identify tax differences is to have plenty of experience in this area and to know where to look. Of course, that is not very helpful for those who do not yet have that kind of experience.

A company may prepare a tax basis balance sheet and roll it forward from year to year. This can be a very helpful tool in identifying differences between books and tax. It is also helpful in ensuring accuracy in a company's tax return preparation. However, this seems to be seldom done—particularly in small companies.

In the absence of a tax balance sheet, one may look at the tax returns in previous years and compare them to the financial statements for those years. In particular, it is helpful to examine the Schedule M-1, which shows a reconciliation of income or loss per books with income per the return. If done appropriately, this will identify items with differences. In case such things are not available or if their accuracy may be uncertain, we will provide examples of the primary types of differences in ¶6004.06.

.05 Differences without Future Tax Consequences

Earlier we referred to the "reversing" of book-tax differences. We used an example involving depreciation, where more is usually deducted for taxes than books in an asset's early years, but the book expense is higher than the tax deduction in later years. However, some differences do not reverse. Traditionally, those differences were called "permanent differences." While Topic 740 still uses the term "temporary differences," it no longer uses the term permanent differences. It simply refers to such items as "differences without future tax consequences," or basis differences that are not temporary differences. To be honest, many practitioners still use the term permanent differences for such items.

Differences without future tax consequences do not result in deferred tax assets or liabilities because there is no future obligation or benefit arising from such differences. They will never reverse.

Examples of differences without future tax consequences are:

- Tax penalties and fines,
- The 50 percent limitation on deductibility of meals and entertainment,
- Key man life insurance premiums,
- Proceeds from key man life insurance policies,

- Interest income from investments in non-taxable municipal bonds,
- Nondeductible goodwill amortization under the purchase method for acquisitions,
- Certain start-up costs, such as the cost of raising capital for a new business,
- Special dividends received deduction,
- Book depreciation expense in excess of the amount allowed by tax law,
- Percentage depletion of natural resources in excess of their cost, and
- Certain compensation related to some forms of stock option plans.

In addition, Topic ASC 740 specifies certain items that may reverse in the foreseeable future, in which case they would result in deferred taxes, but generally do not. These items are rare, and some apply to old transactions. Examples provided for these items are:

- Basis of an investment in a foreign subsidiary or a foreign corporate joint venture that is essentially permanent in duration;
- Undistributed earnings of a domestic subsidiary or a domestic corporate joint venture that is essentially permanent in duration that arose in fiscal years beginning on or before December 15, 1992 using a last-in, first-out (LIFO) pattern;
- Bad debt reserves for tax purposes of U.S. savings and loan associations (and other qualified thrift lenders) that arose in tax years beginning before December 31, 1987; and
- Policyholders' surplus of stock life insurance entities that arose in fiscal years beginning on or before December 15, 1992.

Finally, there are certain other items identified as exceptions from the basic requirements of calculating deferred tax assets or liabilities from temporary differences:

- Deposits in statutory reserve funds by U.S. steamship entities;
- After-tax income for leveraged leases or allocation of purchase price in a purchase business combination to acquired leveraged leases;
- Intra-entity transfers of inventory from one tax-paying component to another of the same consolidated group; and
- Items remeasured from the local currency into the functional currency under certain conditions.

.06   Temporary Differences

In opposition to the section above, temporary differences are those which do reverse over time and will result in deferred tax assets or liabilities. These can be categorized into four basic areas, with a few additional items outside of those areas.

The four basic areas are:

1. Revenues or gains that are taxable *after* they are recognized in financial income;
2. Revenues or gains that are taxable *before* they are recognized in financial income;
3. Expenses or losses that are deductible *after* they are expensed in financial income; and
4. Expenses or losses that are deductible *before* they are expensed in financial income.

The additional items are:

1. Reduction in the tax basis of depreciable assets because of tax credits;
2. Investment tax credits accounted for by the deferral method;
3. Increase in tax basis of assets because of indexing whenever the local currency is the functional currency; and
4. Business combinations and combinations of not-for-profit entities.

Common examples of temporary differences in the four basic areas identified above are:

1. Revenues or gains that are taxable *after* they are recognized in financial income
    a. installment sales
    b. construction revenue when completed contract method is used for taxes and percentage-of-completion is used for books
    c. unremitted earnings of foreign subsidiaries
    d. unrealized gains on marketable securities
2. Revenues or gains that are taxable *before* they are recognized in financial income
    a. subscriptions received in advance
    b. rent received in advance, or any other similar revenue item when payment is received before the revenue is earned in accordance with financial accounting rules—generally titled deferred revenues or unearned revenues
3. Expenses or losses that are deductible *after* they are expensed in financial income
    a. product warranty liability
    b. allowance for doubtful accounts
    c. inventory obsolescence reserves and other similar liabilities
    d. many accruals
    e. liabilities for contingencies

    f.   amortization of goodwill and other intangible assets when the private
         company council option is used and the asset is amortized more quick-
         ly for books than for taxes
    g.   unrealized losses from marketable securities
    h.   impairment losses
4. Expenses or losses that are deductible *before* they are expensed in financial
    income
    a.   accelerated depreciation
    b.   amortization of goodwill and other intangible assets unless the private
         company council option is used
    c.   capitalized interest
    d.   certain software development costs

Keep in mind, although the categories above are related to differences in
revenues and expenses, temporary differences result from differences in assets
and liabilities. For example, the first example listed is installment sales. The
difference used to calculate deferred tax assets or liabilities would actually be
the difference in accounts receivable. Book basis accounts receivable would
include the entire amount of revenue for the items that have been sold, less
any payments already received, while tax basis accounts receivable would be
zero because revenue is only recognized when the installment payment is received. The difference in revenue during the year would be used in the calculation of the tax provision but the difference in accounts receivable would be
used to arrive at a deferred tax liability after following the additional steps in
the process.

.07   Are Differences Taxable or Deductible?

Once we are able to identify book-tax differences and the amount of those differences, we then need to determine if those differences result in payment of
higher taxes in the future or a reduction in the payment of future taxes.

Determining whether a difference is taxable or deductible refers to what will
happen in the future as a result of that difference. If more taxes will be paid in
the future, it is a taxable difference. If less taxes will be paid in the future, it is
a deductible difference. Returning to our depreciation example, an accelerated
depreciation method for tax purposes means a higher deduction is taken in early
years for tax purposes than the expense recorded for books. Net fixed assets are
reported at a higher amount for books than for taxes in those early years. In the
future, the difference will reverse between the book basis of those fixed assets and
their tax basis. When that happens, more expense will be taken for books than
the deduction taken for tax. So taxes will be paid on a higher taxable net income
than book net income in those future years. In other words, more tax will be paid

in the future than would have been paid using book net income. Therefore, it is a taxable difference because of that higher tax that will be paid in the future.

In contrast to the above example, consider accounts receivable, net of an allowance for doubtful accounts. Bad debt expense is recorded to establish or increase the allowance for doubtful accounts. That results in a decrease of net income. However, a deduction for tax purposes cannot be taken until the account receivable is actually written off. So a current book expense is recorded but the tax deduction will be taken in the future. So the difference between book and tax net accounts receivable would be a deductible difference.

.08   Applicable Tax Rate

After identifying whether temporary differences are taxable or deductible, an applicable tax rate needs to be applied to each difference in order to calculate a deferred tax asset or liability.

The applicable tax rate to be used in the U.S. federal tax jurisdiction is the regular tax rate. No alternative minimum tax rate should be used. The only consideration of alternative minimum tax is any credit carryforward that results. Such a credit carryforward will be reflected as a deferred tax asset like other credit carryforwards, which are addressed in ¶6004.10.

Ideally, the tax rate to be used would be the rate that will be applicable when the difference reverses. That would result in an accurate asset or liability. Since we may not be certain of the rate that will then be in place because of possible changes in tax law that could occur, we use existing law to determine the rate to be used. We must use rates identified by currently enacted tax law. If a law has been passed that identifies 25 percent as the tax rate for the current year and 27 percent in the next year, and the difference is expected to reverse in the next year, 27 percent would be the properly applicable tax rate to use. Estimates or expectations may not be used; only tax rates that have been enacted into law. A discounted basis may not be used so there are no time-value of money calculations used to calculate deferred assets or liabilities.

Additionally, graduated tax rates should be considered when applicable. If, during a period in which a difference is expected to reverse, an entity's taxable income falls in a range that would require the use of graduated tax rates, the rate to be used will be an average graduated tax rate expected to be applicable in the year of reversal.

.09   Deferred Tax Assets and Liabilities

After following each of the preceding steps, it is easy to arrive at deferred tax assets and liabilities. Applying the applicable tax rate to a taxable difference results in a deferred tax liability. Doing the same to a deductible difference results in a deferred tax asset.

.10   Net Operating Losses, Tax Credits, Carryforwards and Carrybacks

Temporary differences are not the only things that result in a deferred tax asset. Net operating losses (NOLs) and credits also result in deferred tax assets.

Net operating losses can generally be carried back or carried forward to offset net taxable income in a different year. A taxable loss may be carried back to the two preceding years and/or carried forward for the next 20 years.

When a company incurs a taxable loss and the previous two years have enough taxable income to fully offset the current year's loss, that loss is carried back to those previous years by the filing of an amended return. After applying a tax rate, a refund receivable is recorded but no deferred taxes result. When there is not adequate taxable income in previous years, so some or all of the net operating loss is carried forward, it results in a deferred tax asset because there would be a future benefit from the use of that NOL. In that case, the NOL would be multiplied by an applicable tax rate to calculate the resulting deferred tax asset.

Certain tax credits may also be carried back and/or forward. The same process is used for a credit as for an NOL except that no tax rate is applied. A loss reduces taxable income, which then has a tax rate applied to calculate the amount of tax. A credit reduces taxes directly, with no rate applied. Therefore, a credit carryback will result in a tax refund receivable in the amount of the credit. A credit carryforward results in a deferred tax asset of the same amount as the credit carryforward.

.11   Valuation Allowance

Any asset recorded assumes the asset will provide future benefit. If the future benefit of a deferred tax asset is questionable, a valuation allowance should be recorded to reduce the amount of the asset.

A valuation allowance is similar to an allowance for doubtful accounts related to accounts receivable or an inventory obsolescence reserve. It is a contra-asset used so the net book value of the asset reflects the amount at which the asset will be realized.

A valuation allowance is recorded for all or a portion of any deferred tax asset which is more likely than not to not be realized.

In assessing the need for a valuation allowance, an entity must consider positive and negative evidence that the asset will be realized. Information about an entity's financial position and results of operations are considered. When a deferred tax asset arises from an NOL or tax credit carryforward, additional items that may be considered are future settlement of deferred tax liabilities against which the deferred tax asset may be offset, future taxable income exclusive of reversing temporary differences and carryforwards, taxable income in prior carryback periods when carryback is permitted by law, and tax-planning strategies. Examples of tax planning strategies include the acceleration of taxable amounts, a change in the character of certain items from ordinary income to capital gain, or a change of certain items such as investments from tax-exempt to taxable. Tax-planning strategies must be prudent and feasible, an action the entity normally might not take but would do so in order to not lose the NOL or tax credit carryforward, and would result in realization of deferred tax assets.

Examples of negative evidence are a history of NOL or tax credit carryforwards expiring unused, losses expected in early future years, unsettled circumstances that could adversely affect future operations, and a carryback or carryforward period so brief that its use is doubtful.

Examples of positive evidence are existing contracts or firm sales backlog, excess of appreciated asset value over the tax basis of net assets, or a strong earnings history exclusive of the specific loss that caused the NOL, along with evidence such earnings are likely to return in the near future.

After consideration of positive and negative evidence, the practitioner must use professional judgment to make an assessment of the need for a valuation allowance and, if needed, the amount that should be recorded.

.12 Classification as Long-term or Short-term

In accordance with FASB ASC 740-10-45-4, in a classified statement of financial positions, an entity shall classify deferred tax liabilities and assets as noncurrent amounts.

.13 Putting It All Together

To review the basic steps we follow in accounting for income taxes:

1. Calculate current taxes payable or receivable.
2. Identify differences between the book basis and tax basis of assets and liabilities.
3. Determine, for each difference, whether it will result in taxes paid in the future; that is, a future tax obligation; or a future tax benefit.
4. Apply an appropriate tax rate to the difference to calculate a deferred tax.
5. Classify differences that result in a future tax obligation as deferred tax liabilities and those that result in a future tax benefit as deferred tax assets.
6. Determine if a valuation allowance is needed for any or all deferred tax assets.

Each of these steps is addressed in more detail in the preceding paragraphs. Now let us put them all together in a spreadsheet.

There are a variety of different models to follow in a variety of spreadsheets that have been developed. Following is just one example of such a spreadsheet. It lists the book basis and tax basis of each of the assets and liabilities that are different for books and taxes. The difference between those bases is calculated and classified as deductible or taxable. A tax rate is then applied to calculate deferred tax assets for those that are deductible and deferred tax liabilities for those that are taxable. If there is an NOL, it is then multiplied by the applicable tax rate to arrive at a deferred tax asset. Any tax credit carryforwards do not have a tax rate applied; they are simply recorded as deferred tax assets. After all amounts are totaled, it is determined whether or not a valuation allowance is needed. If so, it is calculated and deducted from the deferred tax asset, arriving at a net total of deferred tax assets and deferred tax liabilities.

Assets & liabilities	Book Basis	Tax Basis	Differences Deductible	Taxable	Tax Rate	Def Tax Assets	Def Tax Liabilities
Accounts Receivable	XXX	XXX	XXX		XX%	XXX	
Inventory	XXX	XXX	XXX		XX%	XXX	
Fixed assets	XXX	XXX		XXX	XX%		XXX
Accruals and reserves	XXX	XXX	XXX		XX%	XXX	
etc.							
Net Operating Loss			XXX		XX%	XXX	
Tax credit carryforwards						XXX	=
Totals						XXXX	XXXX
Valuation Allowance						(XXX)	
Net						XXXX	XXXX

Presentation of this information on the face of the financial statements and in the footnotes is further discussed in ¶6004.17.

.14   Uncertainty in Income Taxes

Whenever an income tax return is prepared, certain tax positions are taken. Sometimes, a taxing authority, including the IRS or a state or local taxing authority, may question those positions. A tax position is taken when a preparer decides how to identify, recognize, and measure taxable revenues and deductible expenses or other tax-related matters. Some tax positions are easily taken, with clear, strong support in tax law or cases. Other positions may be in more of a gray area and are more easily questioned.

ASC 740 requires the application of a more-likely-than-not criterion to recognize tax positions. That is, the likelihood of the tax position to be sustained upon examination is greater than 50 percent. In making such an assessment, the following presumptions are required:

- The tax position will be examined by the relevant taxing authority and that taxing authority has full knowledge of all relevant information. (Whether or not the position is actually examined is irrelevant. Application of the more-likely-than-not criterion requires us to *presume* it will be examined.)
- The technical merits of the tax position are derived from tax law, including legislation and statutes, legislative intent, regulations, rulings and case law, and their applicability to the tax position.
- Tax positions are evaluated individually, with no offset or aggregation with other positions.

When the more-likely-than-not criterion is not met in a particular period, the tax position should be monitored to see if the criterion is met in a later period. The change could result from a change in law, a change in facts and circumstances, passing of a statute of limitations, or effective settlement of the tax position through examination, negotiation or litigation.

With certain positions, there may be an incremental probability of the position being sustained. In such cases, we should look at the position in increments, not in total. For example, say a company claims a $100 deduction on its tax return. Instead of the possible amounts to be recognized being either the full $100 or zero, it might be more appropriate to recognize a portion of the total amount. Management may determine that only a portion will be disallowed, not the entire $100. Management may decide that there is only a 25 percent likelihood of the entire $100 being sustained. In contrast, management may also determine there is a 20 percent likelihood of $80 being sustained and a 20 percent likelihood that $60 will be sustained. It is important to consider the cumulative likelihood in order to determine when the more-likely-than-not threshold is satisfied. The threshold is certainly not satisfied for the full $100, which is only 25 percent. There is a cumulative probability of 45 percent that at least $80 will be sustained. There is a cumulative probability of 65 percent that at least $60 will be sustained, which has now passed the 50 percent mark. So $60 would be the amount that should be recognized as a deduction for this item.

Now let us look at the proper accounting for the situation described in the previous paragraph. Assume management is aggressive and claims the entire $100 deduction on the company's tax return. Are they being dishonest or unethical? Perhaps, but not necessarily. Being more aggressive does not always equate to being dishonest. Some people would rather not deal with an IRS investigation or have their positions questioned, so they may be more conservative. Others may believe they have a supportable position, even though it may be questioned, and are willing to negotiate, and maybe even litigate, with the IRS in support of their position. Given the example we have been using, some might claim $100 on a tax return, some $80, some $60 and some even less than that. The point is that there is a wide range of positions taken. We must know how to account for whatever position is taken.

For purposes of this discussion, we can identify positions that meet the more-likely-than-not criterion to be relatively certain positions. If an entity takes a position that does not meet that criterion, it would be deemed an uncertain tax position. As explained above, the entire position might not be an uncertain tax position— only the portion that does not meet the criterion. In the example above, if an entity claimed the entire $100 as a deduction on its tax return, $40 would be an uncertain tax position. Because it is more-likely-than-not an examination would overturn or disallow that portion of the position, we must assume that the taxes related to that portion of the deduction will later have to be paid, probably with interest and penalties, so we record a liability for the tax effect of that amount.

Traditionally, the diagram used to reflect deferred tax assets and liabilities has been as follows:

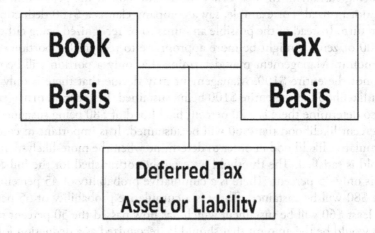

When considering uncertainty in income taxes, we add another box to the diagram:

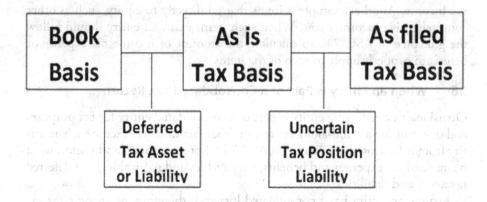

As described above, a liability arises from the difference between what is actually filed on the tax return and what meets the more-likely-than-not criterion and, therefore, what should be recorded. This amount is interchangeably called an Uncertain Tax Position Liability (UTP) or an Unrecognized Tax Benefit (UTB) because it is a benefit claimed on the return that should not be recognized. We will generally refer to it as a UTP.

The UTP cannot be netted against or appended to the deferred tax asset or liability except in one situation. When the deferred tax asset arises from an NOL, the UTP is netted against that deferred tax asset. Presumably, the deduction claimed on the tax return increases any tax loss taken so has increased the NOL. A reduction in that deduction would cause a reduction in the NOL so it can be used to offset, or reduce, the amount of the deferred tax asset arising from the NOL.

It may also be important to note that any uncertain tax position recorded in the financial statements requires a Schedule UTP to be filed with an entity's tax return.

.15   Intraperiod Tax Allocations

This topic is a bit more complex than can reasonably be addressed in a brief overview. Detailed information is provided later in the product. Suffice it to say for now that this is an area that does not impact many entities. Unfortunately, however, there are some it does impact, or *should* impact, but they do not properly implement it.

Intraperiod tax allocations become an issue when an entity has other taxable categories besides operating income. For example, an entity may have discontinued operations, which require gains and losses to be shown net of tax, after net income. Another example is items that go directly to equity, such as other comprehensive income items. When such items exist, an entity should follow the guidance in ASC 740 to calculate the amount of income tax expense or benefit to properly apply to each of the items.

.16   When an Entity Is Part of a Consolidated Tax Return

Occasionally, a reporting entity is part of a consolidated entity for tax purposes and does not file a stand-alone tax return. That fact does not excuse such an entity from following the guidance in ASC 740. Some reasonable allocation must be made of tax expenses and benefits, tax payables and receivables, and deferred tax assets and liabilities.

Assume an entity has a consolidated loss and, therefore, no income tax expense. It is not reasonable toa assume that all subsidiaries are able to individually report no tax expense. It may be the case that some entities in the group have losses and others have gains. Those with losses would likely report income tax benefits while those with gains would report income tax expense. The preferred method for making a proper allocation is to follow the guidance in ASC 740 for each entity and allocate the consolidated information pro rata, based on the separate calculations.

.17   Presentation and Disclosure

A key point about presentation is that deferred items are combined and presented differently on the balance sheet from the way they are presented in the footnotes. But we will first address current items.

On the income statement, there is generally a one-line item for income taxes or benefits related to ongoing operations. It includes current tax expenses and benefits, as well as deferred tax expenses and benefits. Those items are then broken out in more detail in the footnotes.

Current taxes payable or refunds receivable are reflected as such on the balance sheet. If an entity pays taxes in more than one tax jurisdiction, it may show both a refund receivable and a tax payable. Amounts due to or from separate tax jurisdictions are broken out separately. This is true of deferred taxes, as well.

Deferred taxes are combined and shown net on the balance sheet. If deferred tax assets exceed deferred tax liabilities, the net amount will be shown as a deferred tax asset, and vice versa. The only way there would ever be both a deferred tax asset and a deferred tax liability reported is if there is more than one tax jurisdiction. As with current taxes, deferred taxes are not netted together across separate tax jurisdictions.

Under the now-superseded guidance, when there were current and noncurrent deferred tax assets and liabilities, all current items were netted together and reflected as either a current deferred tax asset or a current deferred tax liability, depending on which amount was greater. Noncurrent items were also netted together and reflected as a noncurrent deferred tax asset or liability.

In contrast to balance sheet presentation, the footnote disclosure requires deferred tax assets to be combined and reported net of the valuation allowance. Deferred tax liabilities must also be combined.

Generally, it is expected that three tables are included in the income tax footnote. One is generally referred to as an expected-to-actual reconciliation. It begins with an expected tax, which is calculated by multiplying net income on the income statement by an expected tax rate. The subsequent lines adjust for all items that bring it to the actual amount of income tax expense or benefit shown on the income statement. Adjusting items may include things like state taxes, deferred tax expense or benefit, the effect of differences with no future tax consequence, etc.

The second table is a breakout of income tax expense or benefit between state and federal, as well as current and deferred.

The third table discloses deferred tax assets and the valuation allowance, as well as deferred tax liabilities.

Additional detailed disclosure requirements are presented later in the product.

CHAPTER 7
Actions of the Financial Accounting Standards Board

¶7000   Overview of FASB and Accounting Standards Codification™

The Financial Accounting Standards Board (FASB) was established in 1973 as an independent, private-sector, not-for-profit organization that establishes financial accounting and reporting standards for public and private companies and not-for-profit organizations that follow the U.S. Generally Accepted Accounting Principles (U.S. GAAP). The FASB is recognized as the authority in setting the standards for both public and nonpublic entities, though the Securities and Exchange Commission (SEC) has statutory authority to issue standards for public companies. The SEC relies upon the FASB standards and then adds to those standards as it deems necessary for public companies. The FASB develops financial accounting standards to promote a more uniform financial reporting that provides useful information to investors and the users of financial reports in general.

.01   Accounting Standards Codification™—The Single Source of Authoritative Nongovernmental U.S. GAAP

The FASB launched the FASB Accounting Standards Codification™ (ASC) as the single source of authoritative nongovernmental U.S. GAAP on July 1, 2009. The Codification is effective for interim and annual periods ending after September 15, 2009. All existing accounting standards documents are superseded as described in FASB Statement No. 168, The FASB Accounting Standards Codification™ and the Hierarchy of Generally Accepted Accounting Principles. All other accounting literature not included in the Codification is nonauthoritative.

The Codification reorganized the thousands of U.S. GAAP pronouncements into roughly 90 accounting topics and displays all topics using a consistent structure. It also includes relevant SEC guidance that follows the same topical structure in separate sections in the Codification. Though it should be mentioned that the SEC guidance in the Codification is included for convenience in doing research but cannot be considered authoritative for the SEC. That is to say, if the SEC issues or revises a standard and it takes a little while for that standard or modification to be added to the Codification, it should be obvious that the SEC standard overrides what would be in the Codification. Researchers working with public companies should compare Codification information to SEC Regulations to be certain they are using the most up-to-date guidance.

While the Codification did not change U.S. GAAP, it introduced a new structure—one that is organized in an easily accessible, user-friendly online research system. The FASB believed this system would:

- Reduce the amount of time and effort required to research an accounting issue,
- Mitigate the risk of noncompliance with standards through improved usability of the literature,
- Provide accurate information with real-time updates as new standards are released, and
- Assist the FASB with the research efforts required during the standard-setting process.

The Codification excludes governmental accounting standards. It codified all standards issued by a standard setter within levels A through D of the pre-Codification U.S. GAAP hierarchy, with non-SEC content listed below:

Financial Accounting Standards Board (FASB)
- Statements (FAS)
- Interpretations (FIN)
- Technical Bulletins (FTB)
- Staff Positions (FSP)
- Staff Implementation Guides (Q&A)

Emerging Issues Task Force (EITF)
- Abstracts
- Appendix D Topics
- Derivative Implementation Group (DIG) Issues
- Accounting Principles Board (APB) Opinions
- Accounting Research Bulletins (ARB)
- Accounting Interpretations (AIN)

American Institute of Certified Public Accountants (AICPA)
- Statements of Position (SOP)
- Audit and Accounting Guides (AAG)—only incremental accounting guidance
- Practice Bulletins (PB)
- Technical Inquiry Service (TIS)—only for Software Revenue Recognition

.02   History—"Disclosure Framework" Project Aimed at More Useful, Organized, and Consistent Disclosures

In July 2009, the FASB announced the addition of a new FASB agenda project aimed at establishing an overarching framework intended to make financial statement disclosures more effective, coordinated, and less redundant.

The project was added in response to requests and recommendations received from several constituents, including the Investors Technical Advisory Committee (ITAC) and the SEC Advisory Committee on Improvements to Financial Reporting (CIFR).

Many constituents expressed concerns about so-called "disclosure over-load." While clear and robust disclosures are essential to informative and transparent financial reporting—a critical component in maintaining investor confidence in the markets—improving the way such disclosures are integrated can help decrease complexity, the Board believes.

The aim of this project was to create a principles-based disclosure framework that would enable companies to communicate more effectively with investors, and to help eliminate redundant or otherwise outdated U.S. GAAP disclosure requirements. The objective of the project was not intended to be "additive," but to focus on developing a framework for improved U.S. GAAP disclosures. It was envisioned that a carefully developed framework would enable all entities to:

- Focus on making more coherent disclosures in their annual reporting package, and
- Move away from what some assert has become a compliance exercise.

Some specific financial reporting areas the project evaluated and addressed included whether the disclosure framework should:

- Apply to all entities or perhaps exclude private or nonprofit entities.
- Apply to interim reporting.
- Focus only on high-level principles.
- Focus only on notes to financial statements or extend to ways to better integrate information provided in financial statements, MD&A, and other parts of a company's public reporting package.

¶7001   The "Big Three" Recent Accounting Standards Updates

Over the last several years, financial statement preparers and users have been implementing what many of us call the Big Three Accounting Standards Updates. They are updates that provide such large, pervasive changes that an entirely new Codification Topic was added for each of them. Those Topics are Revenue Recognition, Leases, and Investments in Marketable Securities.

.01   Revenue Recognition

The superseded Revenue Recognition Topic was ASC 605. The new Topic introduced by Accounting Standards Update (ASU) No. 2014-09 was ASC 606, *Revenue from Contracts with Customers*, which completely superseded ASC 605. Revenue recognition is the most frequent cause of financial statement restatements. Having clear yet flexible guidance is thus critical. While both IFRS and U.S. GAAP provided their own guidance, each system had recognized limits. IFRS provided limited guidance for some complex transactions, while U.S. GAAP's industry-specific guidance could result in diverse treatment for economically similar transactions. One of the stated goals of the new guidance was to improve comparability "across entities, industries, jurisdictions and capital markets." According to the FASB, "The previous requirements of both IFRS and U.S. GAAP were different and often resulted in different accounting for transactions that were economically similar. Furthermore, while revenue recognition requirements of IFRS lacked sufficient detail, the accounting requirements of U.S. GAAP were considered to be overly prescriptive and conflicting in certain areas."

In the FASB Accounting Standards Codification™, the guidance on Revenue from Contracts with Customers is found under ASC 606. The core principle of the new standard, according to the FASB, is for companies to "recognize revenue to depict the transfer of goods or services to customers in amounts that reflect the consideration (that is, payment) to which the company expects to be entitled in exchange for those goods or services." The new standard calls for enhanced disclosures about revenue recognition, providing guidance for transactions that were not previously addressed comprehensively (for example, service revenue and contract modifications).

Generally, the new rules are applicable to all companies in all industries and will replace the industry-specific revenue guidance previously provided for software companies, construction contractors, real estate, asset management, telecommunications, and aerospace companies. The new requirements include more extensive disclosure of the specifics of contracts with customers so the readers of the financial statements can better understand how the company is recognizing revenue. Depending on the kind of customer contracts used, companies will need to supply information on the factors related to determining the transaction price as well as information about changes in contracts and obligations for future performance on contracts that remain open at the year-end. The complexities for companies dealing in long-term contracts and contracts involving multiple steps in measuring performance may be significant, depending on what procedures were previously followed.

The new guidance has specific impact on revenue generated in connection with performance obligations occurring over time, sales with a right of return, consignment sales, sales with options, the effects of warranty contracts, nonrefundable upfront fees, bill-and-hold agreements, repurchase agreements, and customer acceptance.

In calculating the revenue to be recognized on any contract with a customer, the new guidance requires a five-step process:

1. Identify the contract(s) with a customer. This requires that the entity be able to identify each party's rights and the payment terms, and in some cases may require combining separate contracts into a single contract if two or more contracts were entered into with the same customer at the same time. If a contract is modified after the rights and obligations associated with it have been determined, the effect of the modification(s) of those rights and obligations must be reassessed. In some circumstances, the modification of a contract must be treated as a separate contract.

2. Identify the separate performance obligations in each contract. This requires a specific assessment of the goods or services promised in a contract and whether the contract calls for a distinct good or service or a series of distinct goods or services that have the same pattern of transfer. An entity recognizes revenue when the control of the asset being transferred is obtained by the customer. Control refers to the ability to direct the use of and receive the benefits from that asset. In some cases, the transfer will take place at a clearly designated time, while in others it will take place in stages. In the latter case, the revenue is also recognized in stages rather than, for example, at the completion of all the related transfers. Measurement of the progress toward transfer of control may be made by either the input method or the output method (explained below).

3. Determine the transaction price. This requires considering all the terms of the contract as well as customary business practices. The transaction price includes the total consideration the entity expects to receive and must be adjusted for the nature and timing of the receipt of the consideration. If the revenue contains a significant financing component, this must be separated out. If the amount to be received is variable, estimates will have to be made

about the amount to be received. This variance can be caused by a number of factors including discounts, credits, rebates, incentives, performance bonuses, as well as penalties. The amount that is variable in a contract may be estimated using probability-weighted amounts or the most likely amount from a range of possibilities. As in accounting generally, consistency in the use of a particular method is important.

4. Allocate the transaction price to the separate performance obligations. Once the full transaction price is determined it must be allocated to each of the performance obligation stages already identified. This must be done on a relative stand-alone selling price basis. The stand-alone selling price is that at which the entity would sell the good or service separately; this amount may not be readily available but may have to be inferred from the total contract and the specific conditions of the sale. More than one method is available for determining the stand-alone selling price, including the adjusted market assessment approach, expected cost plus a margin approach, or a residual approach. If the contract has a variable component, the revenue from this component may be attributed to the whole contract or to a specific part, depending on the terms of the contract.

5. Recognize revenue when (or as) each performance obligation is satisfied.

The input and output methods are alternatives for recognizing revenue. The output method recognizes revenue based on the value to the customer of the company's work to date. The input method recognizes revenue based on the costs incurred by the company to date in providing the work to the customer. Thus, the output method is related to the ultimate contract price, while the input method is related to the total costs to the company.

In addition to employing the new revenue recognition method, companies will also have to determine, as of the financial statement date, how much revenue they will be reporting that they would not have been reporting under their previous method; or, the amount of additional revenue they would have been reporting under their former method of revenue recognition that they are not currently reporting under the new method. The reporting of this information is referred to as the "cumulative-effect transaction approach." An alternative to this approach is to retroactively adjust all reported financial information as if the new method had been employed all along. This alternative is called the "retrospective transaction approach." Companies may choose either method for their financial statements presented under the new guidance. For public companies, the retroactive approach may be more onerous because the SEC requires five years of restated financial statements. In the SEC's *Financial Reporting Manual*, section 1610.1, it is stipulated: "all periods presented in selected financial data to be presented on a basis consistent with the annual financial statements."

This consistency requirement means, for example, that "if a company adopts a new accounting standard that requires retrospective application ... the staff will expect the years prior to the annual financial statements – generally years 4 and 5 – to be presented on the same basis as the annual financial statements." This requirement may make the cumulative-effect transaction approach more palatable for public companies.

Public companies were scheduled to implement the new rules for fiscal years beginning after December 15, 2016, and nonpublic companies for fiscal years beginning after December 15, 2017. In 2015, however, the FASB postponed the effective dates for one year. All other entities are required to adopt ASC 606 for annual reporting periods beginning after December 15, 2018, and interim reporting periods within annual reporting periods beginning after December 15, 2019.

The amendments in ASU 2016-20 affect some aspects of the guidance issued in ASU 2014-09 as follows:

Issue 1: Loan Guarantee Fees: The amendments clarify that guarantee fees within the scope of Topic 460, *Guarantees*, (other than product or service warranties) are not within the scope of Topic 606.

Issue 2: Contract Costs—Impairment Testing: The amendments clarify that when performing impairment testing in Subtopic 340-40, *Other Assets and Deferred Charges—Contracts with Customers*, an entity should: (a) consider expected contract renewals and extensions; and (b) include both the amount of consideration it already has received but has not recognized as revenue and the amount it expects to receive in the future.

Issue 3: Contract Costs—Interaction of Impairment Testing with Guidance in Other Topics: The amendments clarify that impairment testing first should be performed on assets not within the scope of Topic 340, Topic 350, *Intangibles—Goodwill and Other*, or Topic 360, *Property, Plant, and Equipment* (e.g., Topic 330, *Inventory*), then assets within the scope of Topic 340, then asset groups and reporting units within the scope of Topic 360 and Topic 350.

Issue 4: Provisions for Losses on Construction-Type and Production-Type Contracts: The amendments require that the provision for losses be determined at least at the contract level. However, the amendments allow an entity to determine the provision for losses at the performance obligation level as an accounting policy election.

Issue 5: Scope of Topic 606: The amendments remove the term insurance from the scope exception to clarify that all contracts within the scope of Topic 944, *Financial Services—Insurance*, are excluded from the scope of Topic 606.

Issue 6: Disclosure of Remaining Performance Obligations: The amendments provide optional exemptions from the disclosure requirement for remaining performance obligations for specific situations in which an entity need not estimate variable consideration to recognize revenue. The amendments also expand the information that is required to be disclosed when an entity applies one of the optional exemptions.

Issue 7: Disclosure of Prior-Period Performance Obligations: The amendments clarify that the disclosure of revenue recognized from performance obligations satisfied (or partially satisfied) in previous periods applies to all performance obligations and is not limited to performance obligations with corresponding contract balances.

Issue 8: Contract Modifications Example: The amendments better align Example 7 with the principles in Topic 606.

Issue 9: Contract Asset versus Receivable: The amendments provide a better link between the analysis in Example 38, Case B and the receivables presentation guidance in Topic 606.

Issue 10: Refund Liability: The amendments remove the reference to the term contract liability from the journal entry in ASC 606, Example 40.

Issue 11: Advertising Costs: The amendments reinstate the guidance on the accrual of advertising costs and move the guidance to Topic 720, *Other Expenses*.

Issue 12: Fixed-Odds Wagering Contracts in the Casino Industry: The amendments: (a) create a new Subtopic 924-815, *Entertainment—Casinos—Derivatives and Hedging*, which includes a scope exception from the derivatives guidance for fixed-odds wagering contracts; and (b) includes a scope exception within Topic 815 for fixed-odds wagering contracts issued by casino entities. Fixed-odds wagering contracts are revenue transactions which should be recognized in accordance with Topic 606.

Issue 13: Cost Capitalization for Advisors to Private Funds and Public Funds: The amendments align the cost-capitalization guidance for advisors to both public funds and private funds in Topic 946, *Financial Services—Investment Companies*.

Narrow-Scope Improvements and Practical Expedients. The FASB issued ASU 2016-12 to clarify certain narrow areas and add some practical expedients relating to revenue from contracts with customers. The amendments do not change the core revenue recognition principle in ASC 606. The following are the amendments:

1. Collectability criterion assessment to determine whether the contract is valid and represents a substantive transaction on the basis of whether a customer has the ability and intention to pay the promised consideration in

exchange for the goods or services that will be transferred to the customer was clarified.

2. A new criterion to ASC 606-10-25-7 was added to clarify when revenue would be recognized for a contract that fails to meet the criteria in Step 1 of ASC 606-10-25-7. That criterion allows an entity to recognize revenue in the amount of consideration received when the entity has transferred control of the goods or services, the entity has stopped transferring goods or services and has no obligation under the contract to transfer additional goods or services, and the consideration received from the customer is nonrefundable.

3. An entity may exclude amounts collected from customers for all sales (and other similar) taxes from the transaction price, as an accounting policy election.

4. The measurement date for noncash consideration is contract inception.

5. A practical expedient that permits an entity to reflect the aggregate effect of all modifications that occur before the beginning of the earliest period presented in accordance with ASC 606 when identifying the satisfied and unsatisfied performance obligations, determining the transaction price, and allocating the transaction price to the satisfied and unsatisfied performance obligation was provided.

6. A completed contract for purposes of transition is considered a contract for which all (or substantially all) of the revenue was recognized under legacy U.S. GAAP before the date of initial application; an entity may apply the modified retrospective transition method either to all contracts or only to contracts that are not completed contracts.

7. An entity that retrospectively applies the guidance in ASC 606 to each prior reporting period is not required to disclose the effect of the accounting change for the period of adoption; however, an entity is still required to disclose the effect of the changes on any prior periods retrospectively adjusted.

Principal Versus Agent Considerations. ASC 606 was amended by ASU 2016-08 by improving the operability and understandability of the implementation guidance as to when an entity is considered a principal or an agent. Thus, an entity may determine whether it is a principal or an agent for each specified good or service promised to a customer. An entity may determine whether the nature of its promise is a good, service, or a right to a good or service. When another party is involved in providing goods or services to a customer, an entity that is a principal controls any of the following:

1. a good or another asset from the other party that it then transfers to the customer;

2. a right to a service that will be performed by another party, which gives the entity the ability to direct that party to provide the service to the customer on the entity's behalf; or

3. a good or service from the other party that it combines with other goods or services to provide the specified good or service to the customer.

Performance Obligations and Licensing. Further, the FASB issued ASU 2016-10 to clarify the following two aspects of ASC 606: (a) identifying performance obligations; and (b) the licensing implementation guidance.

The amendments add the following guidance:

1. Obligations if they are immaterial in the context of the contract with the customer.
2. An entity may account for shipping and handling activities that occur after the customer has obtained control of a good as an activity to fulfill the promise to transfer the good rather than as an additional promised service, as an accounting policy election.
3. Better articulation of the principle for determining whether promises to transfer goods or services to a customer are separately identifiable by emphasizing that an entity determines whether the nature of its promise in the contract is to transfer each of the goods or services or whether the promise is to transfer a combined item to which the promised goods and/or services are inputs.
4. Revised the related factors and examples to align with the improved articulation of the separately identifiable principle.
5. An entity's promise to grant a customer a license to intellectual property that has significant stand-alone functionality does not include supporting or maintaining that intellectual property during the license period.
6. An entity's promise to grant a customer a license to symbolic intellectual property (that is, intellectual property that does not have significant stand-alone functionality) includes supporting or maintaining that intellectual property during the license period.
7. An entity considers the nature of its promise in granting a license, regardless of whether the license is distinct, in order to apply the other guidance in ASC 606 to a single performance obligation that includes a license and other goods or services.

.02   Leases

The previous topic for leases was ASC 840, while the new topic is ASC 842. The new lease standard came with the issuance of ASU 2016-02, Leases (Subtopic 842). The effective date of the new standard for public business entities was fiscal years beginning after December 15, 2018. The date for other entities was extended with ASU 2019-10 to fiscal years beginning after December 15, 2020, as long as the entity had not issued financial statements with the standard already adopted. ASC 840 is completely superseded as of this writing, so we will refer to ASC 840 as the former standard and ASC 842 as the new standard.

Several ASUs have been issued subsequent to ASU 2016-02 to fine-tune and clarify issues that arose after the issuance and during implementation of ASU 2016-02. For more in-depth information on these clarifying items, the reader is referred to:

- ASU 2018-01, Leases (Topic 842): Land Easement Practical Expedient for Transition to Topic 842
- ASU 2018-11, Leases (Topic 842): Targeted Improvements
- ASU 2018-20, Leases (Topic 842): Narrow-Scope Improvements for Lessors
- ASU 2019-01, Leases (Topic 842): Codification Improvements
- ASU 2021-05, Leases (Topic 842): Lessors—Certain Leases with Variable Lease Payments
- ASU 2021-09, Leases (Topic 842): Discount Rate for Lessees That Are Not Public Business Entities
- ASU 2023-01, Leases (Topic 842): Common Control Arrangements

.02-1 Background

Accounting for leases has historically been a controversial issue. Some leases were recorded on the balance sheet as an obligation and an asset, while others were left off the balance sheet. Although few argued the point that a lease agreement met the requirements to be recorded as a liability, the argument went something like, "Yes, it probably should be a liability. But, if you make us record the liability, we'll also have to record an asset we don't own. It would be misleading to report such an asset as ours on the balance sheet." So certain leases continued to be left off the balance sheet.

Accounting for leases depends on whether it is the lessee reporting or the lessor. Lessor accounting did not change a great deal with the release of the new standard. But lessee accounting did. At least for those leases that were formerly left off the balance sheet.

Under the former lease standard, leases were classified as capital leases or operating leases. If any of the following criteria were met, the lease was capitalized, or shown on the balance sheet. If none of them were met, it was classified as operating:

1. Ownership of the leased asset reverted to the lessee by the end of the lease.
2. The lessee could acquire the leased asset at a bargain purchase price.
3. The present value of minimum future lease payments was equal to or greater than 90 percent of the fair value of the leased asset.

4. The lease term is equal to or greater than 75 percent of the expected useful life of the leased asset.

One can see there is a common theme in these criteria—a focus on the asset. If the lessee got the asset in the end, paid most of the value of the asset, or used the asset for most of its life, then it seemed acceptable to report the asset on the balance sheet, so the liability was also reported. If none of those were true, the argument was that it would be misleading to have an asset on the balance sheet, so no liability was reported either. After a series of what were deemed accounting failures in the early 2000s, not only were new laws implemented, such as Sarbanes-Oxley and Dodd-Frank, but also there was a greater push for transparency; a very strong push to get rid of items referred to as off-balance-sheet financing. This was a large part of the impetus for the new lease standard.

Under the former lease standard, capital leases reported an asset and liability, while operating leases did not. On the income statement, capital leases reported interest expense related to the lease obligation and amortization expense related to the leased asset. Operating leases reported a straight-line rent expense over the term of the lease.

For lessors, leases were classified as sales-type leases, direct financing leases, or operating leases. If any of the four criteria described for the lessee were true and two additional criteria were true, the lease would be either sales-type or direct financing. Those two additional criteria were that the lessor had no significant remaining obligation to perform under the lease and collectability was reasonably assured. Additionally, if there was seller's profit, the lease was a sales-type lease. If not, it was direct financing. Under the new standard, the classifications and accounting are substantially the same for lessors. Arriving at the classification differs slightly, but all else is similar.

.02-2 Lessee Classification

Under the new lease standard, even though all leases, except short-term leases, are reported on the balance sheet, there are still two classifications. Leases are now classified as finance leases or operating leases. If any of the following criteria are met, the lease is a financing lease. If none of them are met, it is classified as operating:

1. Lease transfers ownership of the underlying asset to the lessee by the end of the lease term.
2. The lease grants the lessee an option to purchase the underlying asset that the lessee is reasonably certain to exercise.
3. The lease term is for the major part of the remaining economic life of the asset, unless near the end of the economic life of the lease.

4. The present value of the sum of the lease payments and any residual value guaranteed by the lessee equals or exceeds substantially all of the fair value of the underlying asset.
5. The underlying asset is of such a specialized nature that it is expected to have no alternative use to the lessor at the end of the lease term.

It is immediately evident, except for the addition of the last item, the criteria are pretty much the same as they were previously. One of the FASB's stated goals was to remove the "bright lines" from the old criteria. So "major part" is used instead of 75 percent and "substantially all" is used instead of 90 percent. However, the standard does state that a reasonable approach would be to conclude 75 percent is a major part and 90 percent amounts to substantially all. So, although bright lines are removed, the concepts really have not changed.

The obvious question is, "If all leases except short term leases (12 months or less) are recorded on the balance sheet, why have different classifications?" The answer is the impact on the income statement, as described in the following section.

.02-3 Lessee Accounting

Finance leases and operating leases have the same accounting for the balance sheet. A liability is recorded for the present value of lease payments. An asset is recorded in the same amount plus any initial direct costs and any up-front payments. The asset is called a right-of-use asset. This was primarily done to overcome the argument that the entity does not own an asset so none should be recorded. Accounting concept statements define an asset as something that provides future economic benefit. The right to use an asset does provide future economic benefit, even when the asset is not owned.

Income statement accounting for finance leases is substantially the same as accounting for former capital leases. The asset is amortized over the lease term or the asset's expected useful life, whichever is shorter. The lease obligation is amortized using the effective interest method, with payments reducing principal and recorded as interest expense.

Income statement accounting for operating leases arises from the desire for a consistent expense amount each period, just as in the former operating lease. The challenge is that an operating lease now has an asset and a liability that reduce over time. The reduction of the liability still follows the effective interest method. So, in order to get a straight-line lease expense, the reduction of the asset follows what is essentially the inverse of an accelerated depreciation method. Monthly lease expense is calculated by adding all amounts paid for the lease and dividing that total by the number of months in the lease. A debit to lease expense is recorded in that amount. A credit to cash is recorded for the amount of the payment. A debit to the lease obligation is recorded in accordance with an amortization table prepared according to the effective interest method. The remaining credit is a balancing amount credited to reduce the asset.

.03   Investments in Marketable Securities

The previous topic for marketable securities was ASC 320. The changes to this particular Topic are different from the previous two addressed. While those Updates introduced a new Topic which completely superseded the previous Topic, ASU 2016-01 created a new Topic while just modifying, not superseding, the previous Topic. The previous Topic was ASC 320, *Investments—Debt and Equity Securities*. The revised and new Topics are ASC 320, *Investments—Debt Securities*, and ASC 321, *Investments—Equity Securities*. The effective date of the changes for public business entities was fiscal years beginning after December 15, 2017. The date for other entities was fiscal years beginning after December 15, 2018.

In a nutshell, the previous standard required investments in marketable securities to be classified into one of three categories: Held-to-Maturity, Trading, or Available-for-Sale. Held-to-Maturity Securities could only be investments in debt securities as equity has no maturity date. Those investments would be put into this classification if the entity had the intent AND ability to hold them until they matured. Held-to-Maturity investments were recorded at amortized cost (amortization took place if there was a premium or discount). Trading Securities were those held for short periods of time with the intent to make quick gains (though it sometimes resulted in losses) through the buying and selling, or trading, of those securities. Those securities were recorded at fair value, with unrealized changes in fair value being shown as gains or losses in the income statement. Available-for-Sale Securities included anything that were not classified as one of the other two. Those investments were also recorded at fair value, but unrealized gains and losses were reported as other comprehensive income and did not go directly through the income statement.

The ASU required the separation of the standard into two separate Topics. Debt Securities continue to be accounted for in ASC 320, following the same classifications as previously used. ASC 321 was created for Equity Securities. With that new Topic, all investments in equity securities are accounted for in the same way as trading securities. That is to say, they are reported at fair value, with all unrealized changes in fair value being recognized as unrealized gains or losses in the income statement.

¶7002   Summary of Accounting Standards Updates

The FASB regularly issues amendments to the FASB Codification through Accounting Standards Updates (ASUs). An ASU explains how the FASB has changed U.S. GAAP and the reason for the change and states when the changes will take effect. Below are the summaries of Updates issued during the last few years. Though the descriptions included here are brief, it is hoped there is enough information for the reader to identify if the Update may be applicable so the reader may know if further research in the particular Update is warranted.

.01 Amendments to Remove References to the Concepts Statements

The FASB issued Accounting Standards Update (ASU) No. 2024-02 to remove reference to Concepts Statements, which are not authoritative. In the Board's view, removing all references to Concepts Statements in the guidance will simplify the Codification and draw a distinction between authoritative and nonauthoritative literature.

.02 Scope Application of Profits Interest and Similar Stock Compensation Awards

The FASB issued Accounting Standards Update (ASU) No. 2024-01 to add an illustrative example that includes four fact patterns to demonstrate how an entity should apply the scope guidance in ASC 718-10-15-3 to determine whether a profits interest award should be accounted for in accordance with ASC 718.

.03 Improvements to Income Tax Disclosures

The FASB issued Accounting Standards Update (ASU) No. 2023-09 to require that public business entities disclose specific categories in the rate reconciliation for income taxes and provide additional information for reconciling items that meet a quantitative threshold. More specific, detailed disclosure requirements related to the rate reconciliation are presented in the Update. The Update also requires disclosures related to income taxes paid and other items.

.04 Accounting for and Disclosure of Crypto Assets

The FASB issued Accounting Standards Update (ASU) No. 2023-08 to require entities to subsequently measure assets at fair value, with changes recognized in net income each reporting period, that meet all of the following criteria:

1. Meet the definition of *intangible assets* as defined in the Codification.
2. Do not provide the asset holder with enforceable rights to or claims on underlying goods, services, or other assets.
3. Are created or reside on a distributed ledger based on blockchain or similar technology.
4. Are secured through cryptography.

5. Are fungible.
6. Are not created or issued by the reporting entity or its related parties.

Other presentation and disclosure requirements are also introduced in this Update.

.05   Improvements to Reportable Segment Disclosures

The FASB issued Accounting Standards Update (ASU) No. 2023-07 to improve reportable segment disclosure requirements, primarily through enhanced disclosures about significant expenses that are regularly provided to the chief operating decision maker.

.06   Codification Amendments in Response to the SEC's Disclosure Update and Simplification Initiative

The FASB issued Accounting Standards Update (ASU) No. 2023-06 to modify the disclosure or presentation requirements of a variety of Topics in the Codification, representing clarifications to or technical corrections of the current requirements to better conform to changes made by the SEC.

.07   Recognition and Initial Measurement of Joint Venture Formations

The FASB issued Accounting Standards Update (ASU) No. 2023-05 to reduce diversity in practice by requiring joint ventures to initially measure assets and liabilities using a new basis of accounting upon formation. That new basis will be the fair value, with exceptions to fair value measurement that are consistent with the business combination guidance.

.08   Amendments to SEC Paragraphs Pursuant to SEC Staff Accounting Bulletin No. 121

The FASB issued Accounting Standards Update (ASU) No. 2023-04 to amend the Codification to conform to SAB No. 121 in relation to accounting for obligations to safeguard crypto assets and equity holdings for its platform users.

.09   Amendments to SEC Paragraphs Pursuant to SEC Staff Accounting Bulletin No. 120 and Other Information

The FASB issued Accounting Standards Update (ASU) No. 2023-03 to amend the Codification to conform to SAB No. 120 and other SEC information related to the accounting for expenses or liabilities paid by principal stockholders(s).

.10 Accounting for Investments in Tax Credit Structures Using the Proportional Amortization Method

The FASB issued Accounting Standards Update (ASU) No. 2023-02 to allow reporting entities to consistently account for equity investments made primarily for the purpose of receiving income tax credits and other income tax benefits. ASU 2014-01, Investments—Equity Method and Joint Ventures (Topic 323): Accounting for Investments in Qualified Affordable Housing Projects, introduced the option to apply the proportional amortization method to account for investments made primarily for the purpose of receiving income tax credits and other income tax benefits when certain requirements are met. However, amendments in that Update limited that method to investments in low-income-housing tax credit structures. This Update makes that method available to other structures, as well.

.11 Leases—Common Control Arrangements

The FASB issued Accounting Standards Update (ASU) No. 2023-01 as a result of its Post-Implementation Review process related to leases. The Update requires that entities determine whether a related-party arrangement between entities under common control is a lease. If so, the entity must classify and account for the lease on the same basis as an arrangement with an unrelated party. The Update also requires that leasehold improvements have an amortization period consistent with the shorter of the remaining lease term and the useful life of the improvements.

.12 Reference Rate Reform—Deferral of Sunset Date

The FASB issued Accounting Standards Update (ASU) No. 2022-06 to provide temporary relief during the transition period. The FASB included a sunset provision within Topic 848, *Reference Rate Reform*, based on when London Inter-Bank Offered Rate (LIBOR) would cease being published. When that date was delayed, the sunset date was moved to December 31, 2024.

.13 Insurance—Transition for Sold Contracts

The FASB issued Accounting Standards Update (ASU) No. 2022-05 to require a retrospective transition method as of the beginning of the earliest period presented or the beginning of the prior fiscal year if early application is elected.

.14 Disclosure of Supplier Finance Program Obligations

The FASB issued Accounting Standards Update (ASU) No. 2022-04 to enhance the transparency of supplier finance programs. Supplier finance programs are sometimes referred to as reverse factoring, payables finance, or structured payables arrangements. There has been concern that additional information is needed about such programs.

.15 Fair Value Measurement of Equity Securities Subject to Contractual Sales Restrictions

The FASB issued Accounting Standards Update (ASU) No. 2022-03 to clarify the guidance in Topic 820, *Fair Value Measurement*, when measuring the fair value of an equity security subject to contractual restrictions that prohibit the sale of an equity security, to amend an illustrative example, and to introduce new disclosure requirements.

.16 Troubled Debt Restructurings and Vintage Disclosures

The FASB issued Accounting Standards Update (ASU) No. 2022-02 to eliminate accounting guidance for troubled debt restructurings by creditors in Subtopic 310-40, while enhancing disclosures for certain load refinancings and restructurings by creditors when a borrower is experiencing financial difficulty. In addition, the amendments in this Update require that an entity disclose current-period gross write-offs by year of origination for financing receivables and net investments in leases within the scope of Subtopic 326-20.

.17 Fair Value Hedging—Portfolio Layer Method

The FASB issued Accounting Standards Update (ASU) No. 2022-01 to allow multiple hedged layers to be designated for a single closed portfolio of financial assets or one or more beneficial interests secured by a portfolio of financial instruments so an entity can achieve hedge accounting for hedges of a greater proportion of the interest rate risk inherent in the assets included in the closed portfolio, further aligning hedge accounting with management strategies.

.18 Disclosures by Business Entities about Government Assistance

The FASB issued Accounting Standards Update (ASU) No. 2021-10 primarily in response to the multitude of government assistance programs implemented as a result of the COVID-19 pandemic. The primary requirements are to improve disclosures in order to increase the transparency of transactions with a government accounted for by applying a grant or contribution model by analogy.

.19 Discount Rate for Lessees That Are Not Public Business Entities

The FASB issued Accounting Standards Update (ASU) No. 2021-09, which allows lessees that are not public business entities to elect, as an accounting policy, to use a risk-free rate (currently allowed in ASC Topic 842) election by class of underlying asset, rather than at the entity-wide level. If so elected, disclosure is required.

.20 Accounting for Contract Assets and Contract Liabilities from Contracts with Customers in Business Acquisitions

The FASB issued Accounting Standards Update (ASU) No. 2021-08 to require that an entity (acquirer) recognize and measure contract assets and contract liabilities acquired in a business combination in accordance with ASC Topic 606. At the acquisition date, an acquirer should account for the related revenue contracts as if it had originated the contracts.

.21 Determining the Current Price of an Underlying Share for Equity-Classified Share-Based Awards

The FASB issued Accounting Standards Update (ASU) No. 2021-07, which provides a practical expedient for nonpublic entities to determine the current price input of equity-classified share-based awards issued to both employees and nonemployees using the reasonable application of a reasonable valuation method when fair value is not reasonably determinable.

.22 SEC Update—Presentation of Financial Statements

The FASB issued Accounting Standards Update (ASU) No. 2021-06, which amends SEC portions of ASC Topics 205 and 946 to be consistent with SEC Release No. 33-10786, and ASC Topic 942 to be consistent with SEC Release No. 33-10835. The Update primarily applies to Depository and Lending institutions as well as Investment Companies.

.23 Lessors—Certain Leases with Variable Lease Payments

The FASB issued Accounting Standards Update (ASU) No. 2021-05 to amend classification requirements for lessors to align them with practice under ASC Topic 840. Under this Update, lessors should classify and account for a lease with variable lease payments that do not depend on a reference index or a rate as an operating lease if both of the following criteria are met:

1. The lease would have been classified as a sales-type lease or a direct financing lease in accordance with the classification criteria in paragraphs 842-10-25-2 and 25-3.
2. The lessor would have otherwise recognized a day-one loss.

.24   Issuer's Accounting for Certain Modifications or Exchanges of Freestanding Equity-Classified Written Call Options

The FASB issued Accounting Standards Update (ASU) No. 2021-04 that provides guidance for a modification or an exchange of a freestanding equity classified written call option that is not within the scope of another Topic. A modification should be treated as an exchange of the original instrument for a new instrument. The effect should be measured based on the type of instrument.

.25   Accounting Alternative for Evaluating Triggering Events

The FASB issued Accounting Standards Update (ASU) No. 2021-03 that provides private companies and not-for-profit entities an accounting alternative to perform the goodwill impairment triggering event evaluation as of the end of the reporting period. As a result, affected entities do not need to monitor for goodwill impairment triggering events during the reporting period but, instead, can make the assessment at the end of the reporting period.

.26   Revenue Recognition Practical Expedient for Franchisors

The FASB issued Accounting Standards Update (ASU) No. 2021-02 that introduces a practical expedient to simplify the identification of performance obligations for franchisors that are not public business entities. Pre-opening services provided to a franchisee may be considered distinct from the franchise license if the services are similar to those in a list of items in the ASU.

.27   Scope of Reference Rate Reform

The FASB issued Accounting Standards Update (ASU) No. 2021-01 that provides additional guidance related to reference rate reform (ASC Topic 848). Specifically, certain provisions of Topic 848, if elected by an entity, apply to derivative instruments that use an interest rate for margining, discounting, or contract price alignment that is modified as a result of reference rate reform. The ASU adds background on the discounting transition, clarifies the scope of Topic 848 to capture derivative instruments modified by rate modification, and adds implementation guidance to clarify which optional expedients may be applied to derivative instruments. There is additional guidance related to contract modifications and hedging.

.28   Insurance Effective Date Deferral

The FASB issued Accounting Standards Update (ASU) No. 2020-11 that deferred by one year the effective date of ASU 2018-12, Financial Services—Insurance, as a result of the COVID-19 pandemic.

.29   Codification Improvements

The FASB issued Accounting Standards Update (ASU) No. 2020-10 that makes Codification improvements to consistency by including all disclosure requirements in the disclosure section (Section 50) within each Topic, as well as other varying improvements.

.30   Amendments to SEC Paragraphs

The FASB issued Accounting Standards Update (ASU) No. 2020-09 that amends certain SEC paragraphs pursuant to the release of SEC Release No. 33-10762.

.31   Codification Improvements to Receivables—Nonrefundable Fees and Other Costs

The FASB issued Accounting Standards Update (ASU) No. 2020-08 that clarifies that an entity should reevaluate whether a callable debt security is within the scope of Paragraph 310-20-35-33 for each reporting period.

.32   Presentation and Disclosures by Not-for-Profit Entities for Contributed Nonfinancial Assets

The FASB issued Accounting Standards Update (ASU) No. 2020-07 that provides guidance to not-for-profit entities (NFPs) requiring presentation of contributed nonfinancial assets (often referred to as gifts in kind) as a separate line item in the statement of activities. This ASU also requires disclosure of a disaggregation of contributed nonfinancial assets categorized by type and, for each category, qualitative information about whether the assets were monetized (sold for proceeds then used in the NFP) or utilized and the NFP's policy related to monetization or utilization, any donor-imposed restrictions, and a description of any valuation techniques used, including the principal market (or most advantageous market) used to arrive at a fair value if it is a market prohibited by a donor-imposed restriction.

.33   Debt with Conversion and Other Options

The FASB issued Accounting Standards Update (ASU) No. 2020-06 that simplifies accounting for convertible instruments by removing major separation models required under current U.S. GAAP. Consequently, more convertible debt instruments will be reported as a single liability instrument and more convertible preferred stock as a single equity instrument with no separate accounting for embedded conversion features. The ASU removes certain settlement conditions that are required for equity contracts to qualify for the derivative scope exception, which will permit more equity contracts to qualify for it.

Further, the ASU simplifies the diluted earnings per share (EPS) calculation in certain areas. The ASU applies to public business entities that meet the definition of a Securities and Exchange Commission (SEC) filer, excluding entities eligible to be smaller reporting companies as defined by the SEC, for fiscal years beginning after December 15, 2021, including interim periods within those fiscal years. For all other entities, the standard is effective for fiscal years beginning after December 15, 2023, including interim periods within those fiscal years. Early adoption is permitted.

.34   Revenue from Contracts with Customers and Leases

The FASB issued an Accounting Standards Update (ASU) No. 2020-05 that granted a one-year effective date delay for certain companies and organizations applying the revenue recognition and leases guidance. Early application continues to be permitted.

For leases, the ASU provides an effective date deferral to private companies, private not-for-profit organizations, and public not-for-profit organizations that have not yet issued or made available their financial statements reflecting the adoption of the guidance. It is intended to provide near-term relief for certain entities for whom the leases adoption is imminent.

Under the ASU, private companies and private not-for-profit organizations may apply the new leases standard for fiscal years beginning after December 15, 2021, and to interim periods within fiscal years beginning after December 15, 2022. Public not-for-profit organizations that have not yet issued (or made available to issue) financial statements reflecting the adoption of the leases guidance may apply the standard for fiscal years beginning after December 15, 2019, including interim periods within those fiscal years.

.35   Reference Rate Reform

The FASB issued an Accounting Standards Update (ASU) No. 2020-04 that provides temporary optional guidance to ease the potential burden in accounting for reference rate reform. While LIBOR and other interbank offered rates are widely used benchmark or reference rates in the United States and globally, global capital markets are expected to move away from these rates toward rates that are more observable or transaction based and less susceptible to manipulation.

The new guidance provides optional expedients and exceptions for applying U.S. GAAP to contract modifications and hedging relationships, subject to meeting certain criteria, that reference LIBOR or another reference rate expected to be discontinued.

The ASU is intended to help stakeholders during the global market-wide reference rate transition period. Therefore, it was in effect for a limited time through December 31, 2022.

.36   Codification Improvements to Financial Instruments

The FASB issued an Accounting Standards Update (ASU) No. 2020-03 that makes narrow-scope improvements to various aspects of the financial instruments guidance, including the current expected credit losses (CECL) standard issued in 2016.

The ASU is part of the FASB's ongoing Codification improvement project aimed at clarifying specific areas of accounting guidance to help avoid unintended application. The items addressed in that project generally are not expected to have a significant effect on current accounting practice or create a significant administrative cost for most entities.

"The FASB decided to issue this financial instruments ASU separate from other Codification improvements to increase stakeholder awareness of the changes and to expedite the improvement process," stated FASB Chairman Russell G. Golden. "It addresses areas brought to our attention by stakeholders, and it represents our ongoing commitment to support a successful transition to our standards."

Among its improvements, the ASU clarifies that all nonpublic companies and organizations are required to provide certain fair value option disclosures.

.37   Financial Instruments—Credit Losses, Derivatives and Hedging, and Leases

The FASB issued Accounting Standards Update (ASU) No. 2020-02 that added an SEC paragraph pursuant to the issuance of SEC Staff Accounting Bulletin No. 119 on loan losses to the FASB Codification Topic 326. This ASU also updates the SEC section of the Codification for the change in the effective date of Topic 842. These amendments are effective upon their addition to the FASB Codification.

The FASB issued ASU 2019-11 that requires entities to include expected recoveries of the amortized cost basis previously written off or expected to be written off in the valuation account for purchased financial assets with credit deterioration. In addition, the amendments clarify and improve various aspects of the guidance for an earlier ASU 2016-13.

The FASB issued ASU 2019-10 on credit losses, derivatives and hedging and leases that generally delayed the mandatory effective dates. Application of goodwill impairment test (ASU 2017-04) to calculate credit losses was delayed to December 15, 2022. Hedging is effective for entities other than public business entities for fiscal years beginning after December 15, 2020, and interim periods within fiscal years beginning after December 15, 2021. Early application continues to be allowed.

Because Leases is already effective for public entities and not-for-profit conduit bond obligors, the Board retained the effective date for those entities, including SRCs. The Board also decided to defer the effective date for all other entities by an additional year. Therefore, Leases is effective for all other entities for fiscal years beginning after December 15, 2020, and interim periods within fiscal years beginning after December 15, 2021. Early application continues to be allowed.

In response to those issues and requests to defer certain major Updates not yet effective for all entities, the Board developed a philosophy to extend and simplify how effective dates are staggered between larger public companies (bucket one) and all other entities (bucket two). Those other entities include private companies, smaller public companies, not-for-profit organizations, and employee benefit plans. Under this philosophy, a major Update would first be effective for bucket-one entities, that is, public business entities that are SEC filers, excluding entities eligible to be SRCs under the SEC's definition.

.38   Investment—Equity Method and Joint Ventures

The FASB issued ASU 2020-01 that clarifies the interaction between accounting standards related to equity securities, equity method investments, and certain derivatives. The ASU is based on a consensus of the FASB's Emerging Issues Task Force (EITF).

The new ASU clarifies that a company should consider observable transactions that require a company to either apply or discontinue the equity method of accounting under Topic 323, *Investments—Equity Method and Joint Ventures*, for the purposes of applying the measurement alternative in accordance with Topic 321 immediately before applying or upon discontinuing the equity method. It further clarifies that when determining the accounting for certain forward contracts and purchased options, a company should not consider whether the underlying securities would be accounted for under the equity method or fair value option upon settlement or exercise,

The ASU is expected to reduce diversity in practice and increase comparability of the accounting for these interactions.

.39   Income Tax

The FASB issued Accounting Standards Update (ASU) No. 2019-12 which removes specific exceptions to the general principles in Topic 740 in U.S. Generally Accepted Accounting Principles (U.S. GAAP). It eliminates the need for an organization to analyze whether the following apply in a given period:

- Exception to the incremental approach for intraperiod tax allocation;
- Exceptions to accounting for basis differences when there are ownership changes in foreign investments; and

- Exception in interim period income tax accounting for year-to-date losses that exceed anticipated losses.

The ASU also improves financial statement preparers' application of income tax-related guidance and simplifies U.S. GAAP for:

- Franchise taxes that are partially based on income;
- Transactions with a government that result in a step up in the tax basis of goodwill;
- Separate financial statements of legal entities that are not subject to tax; and
- Enacted changes in tax laws in interim periods.

The ASU is part of the FASB's simplification initiative to make narrow-scope simplifications and improvements to accounting standards through a series of short-term projects.

This checklist is intended to serve as a reference tool to review authoritative standards recently issued or approved by the FASB. The checklist is updated shortly after Codification standards are incorporated into the body of the Codification and no longer the FASB adds content to the Codification. As ASUs and premarked as "Pending Content," they are removed from the checklist via an "editorial and maintenance update"; therefore, not all ASUs appear on our checklist. The concept of "Pending Content" is discussed on page 30 of the "Notice to Constituents" in the Codification.

The FASB issued ASU 2018-05 that amends certain SEC material in Topic 740 for the income tax accounting implications of the Tax Cuts and Jobs Act (Act). The ASU discussed the amounts a company should include in its financial statements when a company issues its financial statements where accounting for certain income tax effects of the Act is not complete for the reporting period which the Act was enacted.

.40   Financial Services—Insurance

The FASB issued Accounting Standards Update (ASU) No. 2019-09 that establishes effective dates for major Updates. The Board decided that, generally, a major Update will first be effective for public business entities that are SEC filers, excluding entities eligible to be SRCs under the SEC's definition. For all other entities, including entities eligible to be SRCs, it is anticipated that the Board will consider requiring an effective date staggered at least two years after the effective date for public business entities that are SEC filers, excluding entities eligible to be SRCs. Generally, it is expected that early application would continue to be permitted for all entities.

The Board decided to change the effective date for Insurance for public business entities that are SEC filers, excluding entities eligible to be SRCs, to be applied for fiscal years beginning after December 15, 2021, including interim periods within those years. The Board also decided to change the effective date for all other entities for fiscal years beginning after December 15, 2023, including interim periods within those fiscal years beginning after December 14, 2024. Early application continues to be allowed for all entities.

The FASB has issued ASU 2018-12 that improves financial reporting for insurance companies that issue long-duration contracts, such as life insurance, disability income, long-term care, and annuities. See ¶21,008.02.

.41   Compensation—Stock Compensation and Revenue from Contracts

The FASB issued Accounting Standards Update (ASU) No. 2019-08 that requires that an entity measure and classify share-based payment awards granted to a customer by applying the guidance in Topic 718. The amount recorded as a reduction of the transaction price is required to be measured on the basis of the grant-date fair value of the share-based payment award in accordance with Topic 718.

.42   Amendment to SEC

The FASB issued Accounting Standards Update (ASU) No. 2019-07 amends various SEC paragraphs pursuant to the issuance of SEC Final Rule Release No. 33-10532, Disclosure Update and Simplification, and Nos. 33-10231 and 33-10442, Investment Company Reporting Modernization. Other miscellaneous updates to agree to the electronic Code of Federal Regulations also have been incorporated.

.43   Not-for-Profit Entities

The FASB issued ASU 2019-03 that modifies the definition of the term collections and require that a collection-holding entity disclose its policy for the use of proceeds from when collection items are deaccessioned or removed from a collection. If a collection-holding entity has a policy that allows proceeds from deaccessioned collection items to be used for direct care, it should disclose its definition of direct care. See ¶10,014.

In 2018, the FASB issued ASU 2018-08 that clarifies and improves the scope and accounting guidance around contributions of cash and other assets received and made by not-for-profit organizations (NFPs) and business enterprises. See ¶10,014.

.44   Stock Compensation

The FASB issued ASU 2018-07 that is intended to reduce cost and complexity and to improve financial reporting for nonemployee share-based payments. The ASU expands the scope of Topic 718, *Compensation—Stock Compensation* (which currently only includes share-based payments to employees), to include share-based payments issued to nonemployees for goods or services. Consequently, the accounting for share-based payments to nonemployees and employees will be substantially aligned. The ASU supersedes Subtopic 505-50, *Equity—Equity-Based Payments to Non-Employees*.

.45   Financial Services—Depository and Lending

The FASB issued ASU 2018-06 that removes outdated guidance related to the Office of the Comptroller of the Currency's Banking Circular 202, Accounting for Net Deferred Tax Charges (Circular 202), in Subtopic 942-740, *Financial Services—Depository and Lending—Income Taxes*, and should have no effect on reporting entities.

.46   Leases

The FASB issued ASU 2019-01 that addresses two lessor implementation issues and also exempts both lessees and lessors from providing certain interim disclosures in the fiscal year in which the company adopts adopting the new leases standard. ASU 2019-01 aligns the guidance for fair value of the underlying asset by lessors that are not manufacturers or dealers in Topic 842 with that of existing guidance. As a result, the fair value of the underlying asset at lease commencement is its cost, reflecting any volume or trade discounts that may apply. However, if there has been a significant lapse of time from the acquisition of the underlying asset and the commencement of the lease, the definition of fair value in Topic 820, *Fair Value Measurement*, should be applied.

.47   Codification

A breakdown of the Topics included in the FASB Accounting Standards Codification™ (ASC), or (Codification), follows:

General Principles
105 – Generally Accepted Accounting Principles

Presentation
205 – Presentation of Financial Statements
210 – Balance Sheet

215 – Statement of Shareholder Equity
220 – Comprehensive Income
225 – Income Statement
230 – Statement of Cash Flows
235 – Notes to Financial Statements
250 – Accounting Changes and Error Corrections
255 – Changing Prices
260 – Earnings per Share
270 – Interim Reporting
272 – Limited Liability Entities
274 – Personal Financial Statements
275 – Risks and Uncertainties
280 – Segment Reporting

Assets
305 – Cash and Cash Equivalents
310 – Receivables
320 – Investments—Debt Securities
321 – Investments—Equity Securities
323 – Investments—Equity Method and Joint Ventures
325 – Investments—Other
330 – Inventory
340 – Other Assets and Deferred Costs
350 – Intangibles—Goodwill and Other
360 – Property, Plant, and Equipment

Liabilities
405 – Liabilities
410 – Asset Retirement and Environmental Obligations
420 – Exit or Disposal Cost Obligations
430 – Deferred Revenue
440 – Commitments
450 – Contingencies
460 – Guarantees
470 – Debt
480 – Distinguishing Liabilities from Equity

Equity
505 – Equity

Revenue
605 – Revenue Recognition (superseded)
606 – Revenue from Contracts with Customers

Expenses
705 – Cost of Sales and Services
710 – Compensation—General
712 – Compensation—Nonretirement Postemployment Benefits
715 – Compensation—Retirement Benefits
718 – Compensation—Stock Compensation
720 – Other Expenses
730 – Research and Development
740 – Income Taxes

Broad Transactions
805 – Business Combinations
808 – Collaborative Arrangements
810 – Consolidation
815 – Derivatives and Hedging
820 – Fair Value Measurements and Disclosures
825 – Financial Instruments
830 – Foreign Currency Matters
835 – Interest
840 – Leases (superseded)
842 – Leases
845 – Nonmonetary Transactions
850 – Related Party Disclosures

Industry
905 – Agriculture
908 – Airlines
910 – Contractors—Construction
912 – Contractors—Federal Government
915 – Development Stage Entities
920 – Entertainment—Broadcasters
922 – Entertainment—Cable Television
924 – Entertainment—Casinos
926 – Entertainment—Films
928 – Entertainment—Music
930 – Extractive Activities—Mining

932 – Extractive Activities—Oil and Gas
940 – Financial Services—Broker and Dealers
942 – Financial Services—Depository and Lending
944 – Financial Services—Insurance
946 – Financial Services—Investment Companies
948 – Financial Services—Mortgage Banking
950 – Financial Services—Title Plant
952 – Franchisors
954 – Health Care Entities
958 – Not-for-Profit Entities
960 – Plan Accounting—Defined Benefit Pension Plans
962 – Plan Accounting—Defined Contribution Pension Plans
965 – Plan Accounting—Health and Welfare Benefit Plans
970 – Real Estate—General
972 – Real Estate—Common Interest Realty Associations
974 – Real Estate—Real Estate Investment Trusts
976 – Real Estate—Retail Land
978 – Real Estate—Time-Sharing Activities
980 – Regulated Operations
985 – Software
995 – U.S. Steamship Entities

.48   Financial Reporting Framework for Small- and Medium-Sized Entities

The Financial Accounting Standards Board (FASB), along with the Private Company Council (PCC), has issued guidance for small and medium-sized businesses (private companies and non-profits), Private Company Decision-Making Framework: A Guide for Evaluating Financial Accounting and Reporting for Private Companies. The guidelines are a long-awaited answer to the request for "small GAAP" to be used by small- and medium sized entities. The International Accounting Standards Board issued guidance for small- and medium-sized entities (SMEs) several years ago.

The position of the AICPA is that as U.S. GAAP has become increasingly complex, to accommodate the needs of larger public corporations and specialized industries, the divergence between the needs of financial statement uses for information about public companies and those needing only basic operating statements to run their businesses more effectively has grown to the point of requiring a more modest standardized financial statement presentation.

In its Financial Reporting Framework for Small and Medium-Sized Entities, the AICPA offers guidance that complies with U.S. GAAP in most general aspects, but eliminates or minimizes some of the reporting requirements that may not serve the users of the financial statements of smaller or non-public corporations.

According to the AICPA, "The framework is intended to serve as a guide for the FASB and the PCC in determining whether and in what circumstances to provide alternative recognition, measurement, disclosure, display, effective date, or transition guidance for private companies reporting under U.S. generally accepted accounting principles (GAAP)."

One significant purpose of the guidance is to allow a private company to select the alternatives within U.S. GAAP for recognition or measurement guidance that it deems appropriate, without having to apply all the alternatives within U.S. GAAP for recognition and measurement.

Based on criteria mutually developed and agreed to with the FASB, the PCC will determine whether exceptions or modifications to existing nongovernmental U.S. Generally Accepted Accounting Principles (U.S. GAAP) are necessary to address the needs of users of private company financial statements. The PCC will identify, deliberate, and vote on any proposed changes, which will be subject to endorsement by the FASB and submitted for public comment before being incorporated into U.S. GAAP. The PCC also will serve as the primary advisory body to the FASB on the appropriate treatment for private companies for items under active consideration on the FASB's technical agenda. Also, according to the news release, "Key Elements of the Private Company Council Responsibilities and Operating Procedures" include:

Agenda Setting. Working jointly, the PCC and the FASB will mutually agree on criteria for determining whether and when exceptions or modifications to U.S. GAAP are warranted for private companies. Using the criteria, the PCC will determine which elements of existing U.S. GAAP to consider for possible exceptions or modifications by a vote of two-thirds of all sitting members, in consultation with the FASB and with input from stakeholders."

To help private companies and their CPAs use the new guidance most effectively, the AICPA issued a "Decision Tool for Adopting an Accounting Framework." The Decision Tool guides the decision process for a company in determining whether it must follow U.S. GAAP, or whether another financial reporting framework (or Other Comprehensive Basis of Accounting) is more appropriate. One important consideration is whether the company operates in an industry for which FASB has prescribed specific guidance. More generally, the decision process considers whether the "accounting framework currently being used by the entity is meeting the needs of financial statement users or whether another framework may better meet those needs." Certain circumstances will dictate that a company must employ traditional U.S. GAAP, for example, the company is planning an IPO.

.49   Private Company Council Framework

On December 23, 2013, the Board and the Private Company Council issued the Private Company Decision-Making Framework: A Guide for Evaluating Financial Accounting and Reporting for Private Companies (the Guide).

The primary purpose of this Guide is to assist the Board and the PCC in determining whether and in what circumstances to provide alternative recognition, measurement, disclosure, display, effective date, and transition guidance for private companies reporting under U.S. GAAP. This Guide provides considerations for the PCC and the Board in making user-relevance and cost-benefit evaluations for private companies under the existing conceptual framework. The Guide is intended to be one of the tools to help the Board and the PCC identify differential information needs of users of public company financial statements and users of private company financial statements and to identify opportunities to reduce the complexity and costs of preparing financial statements in accordance with U.S. GAAP.

¶7003   Older Items of Possible Continuing Interest

Testing Goodwill for Impairment

The FASB has approved changes that will simplify the rules for testing goodwill for impairment. Goodwill impairment occurs when the implied fair value of goodwill in a company's reporting unit declines to an amount that is less than its carrying amount.

Current guidance requires an entity to test goodwill for impairment, at least annually, using a two-step process. In step one of the test, an entity is required to calculate the fair value of a reporting unit and compare the fair value with the carrying amount of the reporting unit, including goodwill. If the fair value of the reporting unit is less than its carrying amount, then the second step of the test must be performed to measure the amount of the impairment loss, if any.

In August 2011, the FASB approved a revised accounting standard intended to simplify how an entity tests goodwill for impairment. The amendments allow an entity to first assess qualitative factors to determine whether it is necessary to perform the two-step quantitative goodwill impairment test. An entity no longer will be required to calculate the fair value of a reporting unit unless the entity determines, based on a qualitative assessment, that it is more likely than not that its fair value is less than its carrying amount. The guidance also includes examples of the types of factors to consider in conducting the qualitative assessment.

Prior to this Board decision, entities were required to test goodwill for impairment, on at least an annual basis, by first comparing the fair value of a reporting unit with its carrying amount, including goodwill. If the fair value of the reporting unit is less than its carrying amount, then the second step of the test is to be performed to measure the amount of impairment loss, if any. The amendments are effective for annual and interim goodwill impairment tests performed for fiscal years beginning after December 15, 2011. Early adoption is permitted.

The amendments approved by the Board reduce complexity and costs by allowing an entity (public or nonpublic) to make a qualitative evaluation about the likelihood of goodwill impairment to determine whether it should calculate the fair value of a reporting unit. Specifically, an entity will have the option of first assessing qualitative factors (events and circumstances) to determine whether it is more likely than not (meaning a likelihood of more than 50 percent) that the fair value of a reporting unit is less than its carrying amount.

If, after considering all relevant events and circumstances, an entity determines it is not more likely than not that the fair value of a reporting unit is less than its carrying amount, then performing the two-step impairment test will be unnecessary. If the entity concludes that the opposite is true, then it would follow the two-step impairment test described above. Under the new guidance, an entity may choose to bypass the qualitative assessment for any reporting unit in any period and proceed directly to performing the first step of the two-step test.

The guidance also expands upon the examples of events and circumstances that an entity should consider between annual impairment tests in determining whether it is more likely than not that the fair value of a reporting unit is less than its carrying amount. Similarly, it will improve the examples of events and circumstances that an entity having a reporting unit with a zero or negative carrying amount will consider in determining whether to measure an impairment loss, if any, under the second step of the goodwill impairment test.

In 2017, ASU 2017-04 was issued to simplify the subsequent measurement of goodwill. The amendments eliminate Step 2 from the goodwill impairment test. An impairment charge should be recognized for the amount by which the carrying amount exceeds the reporting unit's fair value; however, the loss recognized should not exceed the total amount of goodwill allocated to that reporting unit. Also, the income tax effects from any tax-deductible goodwill on the carrying amount of the reporting unit should be considered when measuring the goodwill impairment loss.

The amendments also eliminate the requirements for any reporting unit with a zero or negative carrying amount to perform a qualitative assessment and, if it fails that qualitative test, to perform Step 2 of the goodwill impairment test. But an entity has the option to perform the qualitative assessment for a reporting unit to determine if the quantitative impairment test is necessary. The new rules should be applied prospectively.

Guidance on Liquidation Basis of Accounting

In 2013, the Financial Accounting Standards Board (FASB) issued an Accounting Standards Update (ASU) that improves financial reporting by clarifying when and how public and private companies and not-for-profit organizations should prepare statements using the liquidation basis of accounting. ASU 2013-07, Presentation of Financial Statements (Topic 205): Liquidation Basis of Accounting, is effective for interim and annual reporting periods beginning after December 15, 2013, with early adoption permitted.

Liquidation is the process by which a company converts its assets to cash or other assets and settles its obligations with creditors in anticipation of ceasing all of its activities. An organization in liquidation must prepare its financial statements using a basis of accounting that communicates information to users of those financial statements to enable those users to develop expectations about how much the organization will have available for distribution to investors after disposing of its assets and settling its obligations.

Under the new standard, an organization will be required to prepare its financial statements using the liquidation basis of accounting when liquidation is "imminent." Liquidation is considered imminent when the likelihood is remote that the organization will return from liquidation and either (a) a plan for liquidation is approved by the person or persons with the authority to make such a plan effective and the likelihood is remote that the execution of the plan will be blocked by other parties or (b) a plan for liquidation is being imposed by other forces (for example, involuntary bankruptcy). In cases where a plan for liquidation was specified in the organization's governing documents at inception (for example, limited-life entities), the organization should apply the liquidation basis of accounting only if the approved plan for liquidation differs from the plan for liquidation that was specified in the organization's governing documents.

The Update requires financial statements prepared using the liquidation basis to present relevant information about a company's resources and obligations in liquidation, including the following:

The organization's assets measured at the amount of the expected cash proceeds from liquidation. Included in its presentation of assets should be any items it had not previously recognized under U.S. Generally Accepted Accounting Principles (U.S. GAAP) for entities not in liquidation but that it expects to either sell in liquidation or use in settling liabilities (for example, trademarks).

The organization's liabilities as recognized and measured in accordance with the guidance in other Topics that applies to those liabilities. Importantly, the organization should not anticipate that it will be released from having to pay those liabilities.

Accrual of the costs it expects to incur and the income it expects to earn during liquidation, including any anticipated disposal costs.

The final standard and a FASB in Focus document explaining the standard are available at www.fasb.org.

Accounting for Asset Retirement Obligations

The Board concluded deliberations and unanimously voted to issue Statement No. 143, *Accounting for Asset Retirement Obligations*. Initiated in 1994 as a project to account for the costs of nuclear decommissioning, the Board soon expanded the scope to include similar closure or removal-type costs in other industries. These include oil and gas production facilities, landfills, mines, and environmental cleanups. The existing financial reporting practices had been inconsistent and, in some cases, misleading.

The Standard requires entities to record the fair value of a liability for an asset retirement obligation in the period in which it is incurred. When the liability is initially recorded, the entity capitalizes a cost by increasing the carrying amount of the related long-lived asset. Over time, the liability is accreted to its present value each period, and the capitalized cost is depreciated over the useful life of the related asset. Upon settlement of the liability, an entity either settles the obligation for its recorded amount or incurs a gain or loss upon settlement.

.01   Objective of the Project

The aim of the asset retirement obligations (ARO) project has been to provide accounting requirements for retirement obligations associated with these tangible long-lived assets. The obligations included within the scope of the project are those that an entity cannot avoid as a result of either the acquisition, construction, or normal operation of a long-lived asset.

The obligation must result from a long-lived asset's acquisition, construction, or normal use. The "asset" may be a functional group of assets or a component part of a group of long-lived assets for which there are separable, identifiable asset retirement obligations.

In the case of leased long-lived assets, the standard applies to a lessee's long-lived leased assets accounted for as a capital lease. It applies to the lessor if the lease is an operating lease.

.02   Capitalization

The Board decided that an asset retirement cost should be capitalized as part of the cost of the related long-lived asset. That capitalized asset retirement cost should then be allocated to expense by using a systematic and rational method. An entity is not precluded from using an allocation method that would have the effect of capitalizing and allocating to expense the same amount of cost in the same accounting period.

.03   Requirements

The standard requires:

- Recognition of a long-lived tangible asset retirement obligation liability and an offsetting increase in the amount of the related long-lived asset.
- The obligation be measured at its fair value.
- Allocation of the asset retirement cost in the form of additional depreciation to expense over the related asset's useful life.
- Changes in the amount of the obligation liability subsequent to initial recognition be recognized if they arise from the passage of time and revisions to either the timing or amount of the related estimated cash flows.
- Recognition of an interest-type charge related to the obligation.

.04   Change in Fair Value Methodology

The Board decided that the objective for initial measurement of an ARO liability should be use of the fair value method using a valuation technique, such as expected present value, to estimate fair value.

The methodology to determine fair value under this Standard represents a departure from past practice. The FASB now believes when the timing or amount of estimated cash flow related to an obligation is uncertain and in the absence of quoted market prices in active markets or prices for similar liabilities, fair value should be determined using an expected present value technique.

"Expected present value" refers to the sum of probability-weighted present values in a range of estimated cash flows, all discounted using the same interest rate convention. For purposes of measuring an ARO liability, an entity is required to use a discount rate that equates to a risk-free rate adjusted for the effect of its credit standing (credit-adjusted risk-free rate).

The FASB's traditional present value approach used a single estimate of future cash flows, and the Board still believes the traditional approach is appropriate for measuring the fair value of assets and liabilities with contractual cash flows.

.05   Recognition

An asset retirement obligation must be recognized when three requirements are met:

1. The obligation meets the definition of a liability.
2. A future transfer of assets associated with the obligation is probable.
3. The amount of the liability can be reasonably measured.

In order to meet the definition of a liability—the first test—the three characteristics of a liability must be satisfied:

1. The company has a present duty or responsibility to one or more other entities that entails settlement by probable future transfer or use of assets.
2. The company has little or no discretion to avoid a future transfer of use of assets.
3. An obligating event has already happened.

.06   Obligating Events

The Standard deals with obligations arising under three circumstances:

1. Obligations incurred upon acquisition, construction, or development of an asset.
2. Obligations incurred during the operating life of an asset, either ratably or nonratably.
3. Obligations incurred any time during the life of an asset because of a newly enacted law or statute, or a change in contract provisions, or because an entity has otherwise incurred a duty or responsibility to one or more other entities.

Obligations incurred upon acquisition, construction, or development of an asset should be recognized when the cost of the long-lived asset is recognized. Those incurred during the operating life of an asset should be recognized concurrent with the events creating the obligation.

.07   Subsequent Measurement of an ARO Liability

The Board decided that an entity should be required to use an allocation approach for subsequent measurement of an ARO liability. Under that approach, an entity is not required to remeasure an ARO liability at fair value each period. Instead, it is required to recognize changes in an ARO liability resulting from the passage of time and revisions in cash flow estimates. Those changes are then incorporated into a remeasurement of an ARO liability. The rate used to record accretion of the liability and revisions in cash flow estimates is the credit-adjusted risk-free rate applied when an ARO liability was initially measured.

.08   Disclosures

An entity should disclose the following information in its financial statements:

- A general description of the asset retirement obligations and of the associated long-lived assets.
- The fair value of assets that are legally restricted for purposes of settling asset retirement liabilities.
- If any significant change occurs in the components of an asset retirement obligation, a reconciliation of the beginning and ending aggregate carrying amount of the liability showing separately the changes attributable to:

  - The liability incurred in the current period.
  - The liability settled in the current period.
  - Accretion expense.
  - Revisions in expected cash flows.

Simplification of Inventory Reporting

The FASB's ongoing Simplification Initiative turned to inventory in 2015. In July 2015, the FASB issued ASU 2015-11, Inventory (Topic 330): Simplifying the Measurement of Inventory. While the amendment applies to the most common inventory cost-flow assumption methods, including FIFO (first-in-first-out) and Average Cost, it does not apply to LIFO (last-in-first-out) or the retail inventory method. In applying these inventory cost-flow methods it is assumed the lower of cost and net realizable value has been applied to individual components of inventory.

In so doing, companies are instructed to use the net realizable value of the components of inventory. By this is meant the selling price of inventory items in the ordinary course of business, less estimated costs of completion, disposal and transportation. The net realizable value may be lower than cost for various reasons such as obsolescence, physical damage or deterioration, or price level changes resulting from technological innovation. When it is determined that the cost of inventory is greater than its net realizable value, the difference should be written off in the year the loss occurs. If substantial and unusual inventory losses are determined through subsequent valuations of the inventory existing at the balance sheet date, these losses should be disclosed in the footnotes.

For public companies, these amendments are effective for fiscal years beginning after December 15, 2016, for both annual reports and interim reporting. For nonpublic companies the amendments are also effective for fiscal years beginning after December, 15, 2016, for annual reports, but for interim reporting the amendments apply only after December 15, 2017. The simplified procedure has applicability to special industries including agriculture. The simplifications provided are a further step in the long-running convergence project to align U.S. GAAP more closely with in International Financial Reporting Standards (IFRS), in this case regarding the measurement of inventory.

Elimination of "Extraordinary Item" Classification

Also in the spirit of simplification, in 2015, the FASB eliminated the separate income statement classification "Extraordinary Item(s) Net of Tax" and related earnings-per-share presentation. Previously, U.S. GAAP required organizations to evaluate whether an event or transaction is an extraordinary item and, if it is deemed so, to separately present and disclose the item. However, the concept of extraordinary items was deemed to cause uncertainty because it is unclear when an item should be considered both unusual and infrequent.

The Update removed the income statement presentation extraordinary items but retained the requirement to disclose material items that are unusual in nature or infrequently occurring in the notes to the financial statements. According to the Board, "eliminating the concept will save time and reduce costs for preparers who would not assess whether a particular event or transaction event is extraordinary." The change eliminates Codification Subtopic 225-20, *Income Statement—Extraordinary and Unusual Items*, and is effective for fiscal years beginning after December 15, 2015.

Discontinued Operations

In April 2014, the Financial Accounting Standards Board (FASB) issued guidance that improves U.S. Generally Accepted Accounting Principles (U.S. GAAP) by more faithfully representing when a company or other organization discontinues its operations.

Accounting Standards Update (ASU) No. 2014-08, Presentation of Financial Statements (Topic 205) and Property, Plant, and Equipment (Topic 360): Reporting Discontinued Operations and Disclosures of Disposals of Components of an Entity, changes the criteria for reporting discontinued operations while enhancing disclosures in this area. It also addresses sources of confusion and inconsistent application related to financial reporting of discontinued operations guidance in U.S. GAAP.

According to FASB Chairman Russell G. Golden, "This Update addresses concerns expressed by our stakeholders that too many disposals of assets—including small groups of assets that are recurring in nature—qualify for discontinued operations presentation." The Board anticipates that the Update "will result in more decision-useful financial reporting for investors while eliminating an unnecessary source of cost and complexity for preparers."

Under the guidance, only disposals representing a strategic shift in operations should be presented as discontinued operations. Those strategic shifts should have a major effect on the organization's operations and financial results. Examples include a disposal of a major geographic area, a major line of business, or a major equity method investment.

Additionally, the guidance requires expanded disclosures about discontinued operations that will provide financial statement users with more information about the assets, liabilities, income, and expenses of discontinued operations.

The guidance also requires disclosure of the pretax income attributable to a disposal of a significant part of an organization that does not qualify for discontinued operations reporting. This disclosure will provide users with information about the ongoing trends in a reporting organization's results from continuing operations.

The amendments in this Update enhance convergence between U.S. GAAP and International Financial Reporting Standards (IFRS). Part of the new definition of discontinued operation is based on elements of the definition of discontinued operations in IFRS 5, *Non-Current Assets Held for Sale and Discontinued Operations.*

The standard is effective in the first quarter of 2015 for public organizations with calendar year ends. For most nonpublic organizations, it is effective for annual financial statements with fiscal years beginning on or after December 15, 2014.

CHAPTER 8
Governmental Accounting

¶8000   Overview

The Governmental Accounting Standards Board (GASB) is the independent, private-sector organization that establishes accounting and financial reporting standards for U.S. state and local governments that follow U.S. GAAP. The GASB develops and issues accounting standards through a transparent and inclusive process intended to promote financial reporting that provides useful in-formation to taxpayers, public officials, investors, and others who use financial reports. The Financial Accounting Foundation supports and oversees the GASB. FAF is an independent, private-sector, not-for-profit organization that administers, finance, and appoints the GASB and the Financial Accounting Standards Board (FASB).

Every year the GASB issues statements that amends, improves or clarifies existing applications of U.S. GAAP in government accounting. In 2020, the GASB issued Statements 92 to 97. It also issued guidance on COVID-19 relating to CARES Act and COVID-19 assistance. On June 4, 2021, the GASB released an exposure draft on compensated absences for public comment. The objective of this proposal is to enhance recognition and measurement guidance for compensated absences under a unified model. It would require recognition of a liability if the absence accumulates, is attributable to services rendered, and it is more likely than not to be paid or settled through other means. It would also establish guidance to measure such a liability.

¶8001   Latest GASB Statements

.01   Financial Reporting Model Improvements

GASB Statement No. 103 was issued to improve key components of the financial reporting model to enhance its effectiveness in providing information that is essential for decision making and assessing a government's accountability. It addresses the following areas:

- Management's Discussion and Analysis
- Unusual or Infrequent Items
- Presentation of the Proprietary Fund Statement of Revenues, Expenses, and Changes in Fund Net Position
- Major Component Unit Information
- Budgetary Comparison Information

.02   Certain Risk Disclosures

GASB Statement No. 102 was issued to provide guidance on expanded risk disclosure requirements.

State and local governments face a variety of risks that could negatively affect the level of service they provide or their ability to meet obligations as they come due. Although governments are required to disclose information about their exposure to some of those risks, essential information about other risks that are prevalent among state and local governments is not routinely disclosed because it is not explicitly required. The objective of this Statement is to provide users of government financial statements with essential information about risks related to a government's vulnerabilities due to certain concentrations or constraints.

This Statement defines a *concentration* as a lack of diversity related to an aspect of a significant inflow of resources or outflow of resources. A *constraint* is a limitation imposed on a government by an external party or by formal action of the government's highest level of decision-making authority. Concentrations and constraints may limit a government's ability to acquire resources or control spending.

This Statement requires a government to assess whether a concentration or constraint makes the primary government reporting unit or other reporting units that report a liability for revenue debt vulnerable to the risk of a substantial impact. Additionally, this Statement requires a government to assess whether an event or events associated with a concentration or constraint that could cause the substantial impact have occurred, have begun to occur, or are more likely than not to begin to occur within 12 months of the date the financial statements are issued.

If a government determines that those criteria for disclosure have been met for a concentration or constraint, it should disclose information in notes to financial statements in sufficient detail to enable users of financial statements to understand the nature of the circumstances disclosed and the government's vulnerability to the risk of a substantial impact. The disclosure should include descriptions of the following:

- The concentration or constraint.
- Each event associated with the concentration or constraint that could cause a substantial impact if the event had occurred or had begun to occur prior to the issuance of the financial statements.
- Actions taken by the government prior to the issuance of the financial statements to mitigate the risk.

.03   COVID-19 Guidance on Cares Act and COVID-19 Assistance

The GASB issued staff Technical Bulletin No. 2020-1 (Bulletin), *Accounting and Financial Reporting Issues Related to the Coronavirus Aid, Relief, and Economic Security Act (CARES Act) and Coronavirus Diseases*. The GASB issued the technical guidance as part of its continuing efforts to assist state and local governments during the COVID-19 pandemic.

The Bulletin contains application guidance related to the *Coronavirus Aid, Relief, and Economic Security Act (CARES Act) of 2020* and certain outflows incurred in response to the coronavirus. The Bulletin clarifies the application of existing recognition requirements to resources received from certain programs established by the CARES Act. It also clarifies how existing presentation requirements apply to certain inflows of CARES Act resources and to the unplanned and additional outflows of resources incurred in response to the coronavirus disease.

.04   Compensated Absences

GASB Statement No. 101 was issued to better meet the information needs of financial statement users by updating the recognition and measurement guidance for compensated absences. That objective is achieved by aligning the recognition and measurement guidance under a unified model and by amending certain previously required disclosures.

.05   Accounting Changes and Error Corrections—an amendment of GASB Statement No. 62

GASB Statement No. 100 was issued to enhance accounting and financial reporting requirements for accounting changes and error corrections to provide more understandable, reliable, relevant, consistent, and comparable information for making decisions or assessing accountability.

.06   Deferred Compensation Plans

GASB Statement No. 99 was issued as an omnibus statement to enhance comparability in accounting and financial reporting and to improve the consistency of authoritative literature by addressing (1) practice issues that have been identified during implementation and application of certain GASB statements and (2) accounting financial reporting for financial guarantees.

.07   Deferred Compensation Plans

GASB Statement No. 98 was issued to establish the term *annual comprehensive financial report* and its acronym *ACFR* to replace *comprehensive annual financial report (CAFR)* because stakeholders were concerned that the latter acronym sounds like a profoundly objectionable racial slur.

.08   Deferred Compensation Plans

GASB Statement No. 97 was issued to:

(1) increase consistency and comparability related to the reporting of fiduciary component units in circumstances in which a potential component unit does not have a governing board and the primary government performs the duties that a governing board typically would perform;

(2) mitigate costs associated with the reporting of certain defined contribution pension plans, defined contribution other postemployment benefit (OPEB) plans, and employee benefit plans other than pension plans or OPEB plans (other employee benefit plans) as fiduciary component units in fiduciary fund financial statements; and

(3) enhance the relevance, consistency, and comparability of the accounting and financial reporting for IRC Sec. 457 deferred compensation plans (Section 457 plans) that meet the definition of a pension plan and for benefits provided through those plans.

.09 Subscription-Based Information Technology Arrangements

GASB Statement 96 was issued to provide guidance on the accounting and financial reporting for subscription-based information technology arrangements (SBITAs) for government end users.

This Statement:

(1) defines a SBITA;
(2) establishes that a SBITA results in a right-to-use subscription asset—an intangible asset—and a corresponding subscription liability;
(3) provides the capitalization criteria for outlays other than subscription payments, including implementation costs of a SBITA; and
(4) requires note disclosures regarding a SBITA.

To the extent relevant, the standards for SBITAs are based on the standards established in Statement No. 87, *Leases,* as amended.

.10 Postponements

GASB Statement 95's primary objective was to provide temporary relief to governments and other stakeholders in light of the COVID-19 pandemic. Thus, the effective dates of certain provisions contained in the following pronouncements were postponed by one year:

- Statement No. 83, *Certain Asset Retirement Obligations*
- Statement No. 84, *Fiduciary Activities*
- Statement No. 88, *Certain Disclosures Related to Debt, including Direct Borrowings and Direct Placements*
- Statement No. 89, *Accounting for Interest Cost Incurred before the End of a Construction Period*
- Statement No. 90, *Majority Equity Interests*
- Statement No. 91, *Conduit Debt Obligations*
- Statement No. 92, *Omnibus 2020*
- Statement No. 93, *Replacement of Interbank Offered Rates*
- Implementation Guide No. 2017-3, *Accounting and Financial Reporting for Postemployment Benefits Other Than Pensions (and Certain Issues Related to OPEB Plan Reporting)*
- Implementation Guide No. 2018-1, *Implementation Guidance Update—2018*
- Implementation Guide No. 2019-1, *Implementation Guidance Update—2019*
- Implementation Guide No. 2019-2, *Fiduciary Activities.*

The effective dates of the following pronouncements were postponed by 18 months:

- Statement No. 87, *Leases*
- Implementation Guide No. 2019-3, *Leases*.

.11   Public-Private and Public-Public Partnership Arrangements

GASB Statement 94 was issued to improve financial reporting related to public-private and public-public partnership arrangements (PPPs). This Statement requires that PPPs that meet the definition of a lease apply the guidance in Statement No. 87, *Leases,* as amended, if existing assets of the transferor that are not required to be improved by the operator as part of the PPP arrangement are the only underlying PPP assets and the PPP does not meet the definition of a service concession arrangement (SCA). Further, this Statement provides accounting and financial reporting requirements for all other PPPs: those that either (1) meet the definition of an SCA or (2) are not within the scope of Statement 87, as amended (and as clarified by this Statement).

.12   Replacement of Interbank Offered Rates

GASB Statement 93 addresses accounting and financial reporting implications that result from the replacement of an interbank offered rate (IBOR) by:

- Providing exceptions for certain hedging derivative instruments to the hedge accounting termination provisions when an IBOR is replaced as the reference rate of the hedging derivative instrument's variable payment;
- Clarifying the hedge accounting termination provisions when a hedged item is amended to replace the reference rate;
- Clarifying that the uncertainty related to the continued availability of IBORs does not, by itself, affect the assessment of whether the occurrence of a hedged expected transaction is probable;
- Removing LIBOR as an appropriate benchmark interest rate for the qualitative evaluation of the effectiveness of an interest rate swap;
- Identifying a Secured Overnight Financing Rate and the Effective Federal Funds Rate as appropriate benchmark interest rates for the qualitative evaluation of the effectiveness of an interest rate swap;
- Clarifying the definition of *reference rate,* as it is used in Statement 53, as amended; and
- Providing an exception to the lease modifications guidance in Statement 87, as amended, for certain lease contracts that are amended solely to replace an IBOR as the rate upon which variable payments depend.

.13   Omnibus 2020

GASB Statement 92 was issued to enhance comparability in accounting and financial reporting and to improve the consistency of authoritative literature by addressing practice issues that have been identified during implementation and application of certain GASB Statements. This Statement addresses a variety of topics and includes specific provisions about the following:

- The effective date of Statement No. 87, *Leases,* and Implementation Guide No. 2019-3, *Leases,* for interim financial reports;
- Reporting of intra-entity transfers of assets between a primary government employer and a component unit defined benefit pension plan or defined benefit other postemployment benefit (OPEB) plan;
- The applicability of Statements No. 73, *Accounting and Financial Reporting for Pensions and Related Assets That Are Not within the Scope of GASB Statement 68, and Amendments to Certain Provisions of GASB Statements 67 and 68,* as amended, and No. 74, *Financial Reporting for Postemployment Benefit Plans Other Than Pension Plans,* as amended, to reporting assets accumulated for postemployment benefits;
- The applicability of certain requirements of Statement No. 84, *Fiduciary Activities,* to postemployment benefit arrangements;
- Measurement of liabilities (and assets, if any) related to asset retirement obligations (AROs) in a government acquisition;
- Reporting by public entity risk pools for amounts that are recoverable from reinsurers or excess insurers;
- Reference to nonrecurring fair value measurements of assets or liabilities in authoritative literature; and
- Terminology used to refer to derivative instruments.

¶8002   GASB Statements 88–91

.01   Conduit Debt Obligations

GASB Statement 91 was issued to provide a single method of reporting conduit debt obligations by issuers and eliminate diversity in practice associated with (1) commitments extended by issuers, (2) arrangements associated with conduit debt obligations, and (3) related note disclosures. Thus, this Statement:

- clarifies the existing definition of a conduit debt obligation;
- establishes that a conduit debt obligation is not a liability of the issuer;

- establishes standards for accounting and financial reporting of additional commitments and voluntary commitments extended by issuers and arrangements associated with conduit debt obligations; and
- improves required note disclosures.

All conduit debt obligations involve the issuer making a limited commitment. Some issuers extend additional commitments or voluntary commitments to support debt service in the event the third party is, or will be, unable to do so. This Statement requires issuers to disclose general information about their conduit debt obligations, organized by type of commitment, including the aggregate outstanding principal amount of the issuers' conduit debt obligations and a description of each type of commitment. Issuers that recognize liabilities related to supporting the debt service of conduit debt obligations also should disclose information about the amount recognized and how the liabilities changed during the reporting period.

The requirements of this Statement are effective for reporting periods beginning after December 15, 2020. Earlier application is encouraged.

.02 Majority Equity Interest: Amendment of GASB Statements 14 and 61

GASB Statement 90 was issued to improve the consistency and comparability of reporting a government's majority equity interest in a legally separate organization and to improve the relevance of financial statement information for certain component units. It defines a majority equity interest and specifies that a majority equity interest in a legally separate organization should be reported as an investment if a government's holding of the equity interest meets the definition of an investment. A majority equity interest that meets the definition of an investment should be measured using the equity method, unless it is held by a special-purpose government engaged only in fiduciary activities, a fiduciary fund, or an endowment, including permanent and term endowments, or permanent fund. Those governments and funds should measure the majority equity interest at fair value.

This Statement also requires that a component unit in which a government has a 100 percent equity interest account for its assets, deferred outflows of resources, liabilities, and deferred inflows of resources at acquisition value at the date the government acquired a 100 percent equity interest in the component unit. Transactions presented in flows statements of the component unit in that circumstance should include only transactions that occurred subsequent to the acquisition.

The requirements of this Statement are effective for reporting periods beginning after December 15, 2018. Earlier application is encouraged. The requirements should be applied retroactively, except for the provisions related to (1) reporting a majority equity interest in a component unit and (2) reporting a component unit if the government acquires a 100 percent equity interest. Those provisions should be applied on a prospective basis.

.03   Required Disclosures Related to Debt

GASB Statement 88 aims to improve financial reporting by providing users of financial statements with essential information that currently is not consistently provided. Thus, the Statement requires that additional essential information related to debt be disclosed in notes to financial statements, including unused lines of credit; assets pledged as collateral for the debt; and terms specified in debt agreements related to significant events of default with finance-related consequences, significant termination events with finance-related consequences, and significant subjective acceleration clauses.

In addition, information about resources to liquidate debt and the risks associated with changes in terms associated with debt will be disclosed. As a result, users will have better information to understand the effects of debt on a government's future resource flows.

These requirements are effective for reporting periods beginning after June 15, 2018, but earlier application is encouraged.

.04   Accounting for Interest Cost

GASB Statement 89 aims to enhance the relevance and comparability of information about capital assets and the cost of borrowing for a reporting period and to simplify accounting for interest cost incurred before the end of a construction period. This Statement requires that interest cost incurred before the end of a construction period be recognized as an expense in the period in which the cost is incurred for financial statements prepared using the economic resources measurement focus. As a result, interest cost incurred before the end of a construction period will not be included in the historical cost of a capital asset reported in a business-type activity or enterprise fund.

This Statement also reiterates that in financial statements prepared using the current financial resources measurement focus, interest cost incurred before the end of a construction period should be recognized as an expenditure on a basis consistent with governmental fund accounting principles.

These requirements are effective for reporting periods beginning after December 15, 2019 and should be applied prospectively. Earlier application is however encouraged.

¶8003   GASB Statements 83–87

.01   Leases

GASB Statement 87 supersedes several GASB Statements and amends more for reporting periods beginning after December 15, 2019. Just like in the private sector, the accounting and financial reporting for leases by government was improved. It establishes a single model for lease accounting based on the foundational principle that leases are financings of the right to use an underlying asset. Thus, a lessee is required to recognize a lease liability and an intangible right-to-use lease asset. The lessor, on the other hand, is required to recognize a lease receivable and a deferred inflow of resources. This kind of reporting increases the usefulness of government's financial statements by providing relevant and consistent information about the governments' leasing activities.

.02   Debt Extinguishment

GASB Statement 87 amends portions of some GASB Statements for reporting period beginning after June 15, 2017 on certain debt extinguishment issues. The Statement will improve consistency in accounting and financial reporting for in-substance defeasance of debt and prepaid insurance on debt that is extinguished. Governments are required to include a general description of the transaction in the notes to financial statements in the period of the defeasance. Also, the amount of that debt that remains outstanding at end of the period should be disclosed.

Further, governments that extinguish debt, whether through a legal extinguishment or through an in-substance defeasance, are required to include any remaining prepaid insurance related to the extinguished in the net carrying amount of that debt when calculating the difference between the reacquisition price and the net carrying amount of the debt.

.03   Omnibus 2017

Statement 85 addresses practice issues that have been identified during implementation and application of certain GASB Statements. The requirements of this Statement are effective for reporting periods beginning after June 15, 2017. Following are the topics affected:

1. Blending a component unit when the primary government is a business-type activity that reports in a single column for financial statement presentation;
2. Reporting amounts previously reported as goodwill and "negative" goodwill should not be reported;
3. Classifying real estate held by insurance entities;
4. Measuring certain money market investments and participating interest-earning investment contracts at amortized cost;
5. Timing of the measurement of pension or other postemployment benefits (OPEB) liabilities and expenditures recognized in financial statements prepared using the current financial resources measurement focus;
6. Recognizing on-behalf payments for pensions or OPEB in employer financial statements;
7. Presenting payroll-related measures in required supplementary information for purposes of reporting by OPEB plans and employers that provide OPEB;

8. Classifying employer-paid member contributions for OPEB;
9. Simplifying certain aspects of the alternative measurement method for OPEB; and
10. Accounting and financial reporting for OPEB provided through certain multiple-employer defined benefit OPEB plans.

.04   Fiduciary Activities

Statement 84 was issued to improve guidance regarding the identification of fiduciary activities for accounting and financial reporting purposes and how these activities should be reported, effective for reporting periods beginning after December 15, 2018. Statement 84 establishes the criteria for identifying fiduciary activities of all state and local governments; generally, on:

1. whether a government is controlling the assets of the fiduciary activity and
2. whether the beneficiaries with whom a fiduciary relationship exists.

Separate criteria are added to identify fiduciary component units and pos-templyment benefit arrangements that are fiduciary activities. If an activity meets the criteria, it should be reported in a fiduciary fund in the basic financial statements. Governments that have these activities should present a statement of fiduciary net position and a statement of changes in fiduciary net position. An exception is allowed for a business-type activity that normally expects to hold custodial assets for three months or less.

.05   Certain Asset Retirement Obligations

Statement 83 establishes criteria for determining the timing and pattern of recognition of a liability and a corresponding deferred outflow of resources for certain asset retirement obligations (AROs) and are effective for reporting periods beginning after June 15, 2018. The Statement requires that recognition occur when the liability is both incurred and reasonably estimable. The determination of when the liability is incurred should be based on the occurrence of external laws, regulations, contracts, or court judgments, together with the occurrence of an internal event that obligates a government to perform asset retirement activities.

Laws and regulations may require governments to take specific actions to retire certain tangible capital assets at the end of the useful lives of those capital assets, such as decommissioning nuclear reactors and dismantling and removing sewage treatment plants. Other obligations to retire tangible capital assets may arise from contracts or court judgments. Internal obligating events include the occurrence of contamination, placing into operation a tangible capital asset that is required to be retired, abandoning a tangible capital asset before it is placed into operation, or acquiring a tangible capital asset that has an existing ARO.

¶8004   GASB Statements 78–82 on Pension Issues and Other Reporting Requirements

.01   GASB Statement 82

In March 2016, GASB issued Statement 82 that amends Statements 67, 68 and 73 on pension issues. Specifically, the Statement amends Statements 67 and 68 to require the presentation of covered payroll, rather than that of covered-employee payroll in schedules of required supplementary information. Covered payroll is the payroll on which contributions to a pension plan are based.

The statement also clarifies that a deviation from the guidance in Actuarial Standard of Practice is not considered to be in conformity with the requirements of Statement 67, 68 or 73 for the selection of assumptions used in determining the total pension liability and related measures. The Statement further clarifies that payments made by an employer to satisfy contribution requirements that are identified by the pension plan terms as plan member contribution requirements should be classified as plan member contributions for purposes of Statement 67 and as employee contributions for purposes of Statement 68. It also requires an employer to recognize the expenditures for those amounts in the period for which the contribution is assessed and classified just like similar compensation the employer pays.

.02   GASB Statement 81

Statement 81 was issued to improve accounting and financial reporting for irrevocable split-interest agreements by providing recognition and measurement guidance for situations in which a government is a beneficiary of the agreement. The Statement requires a government that receives resources pursuant to an irrevocable split-interest agreement to recognize assets, liabilities, and deferred inflows of resources at the start of the agreement. The Statement also requires a government to recognize assets representing its beneficial interests in irrevocable split-interest agreements that are administered by a third party, if the government controls the present service capacity of the beneficial interests. The Statement requires a government to recognize revenue when the resources become applicable to the reporting period.

.03   GASB Statement 80

Statement 80 amends the blending requirements for the financial statement presentation of component units of all state and local governments found in Statement 14. The Statement requires blending of a component unit incorporated as a not-for-profit corporation in which the primary government is the sole corporate member.

.04   GASB Statement 79

Statement 79 establishes criteria for an external investment pool to qualify for making the election to measure all of its investments at amortized cost for financial reporting purposes. An external investment pool qualifies for that reporting if it meets all of the following criteria:

1. how the external investment pool transacts with participants;
2. requirements for portfolio maturity, quality, diversification, and liquidity; and
3. calculation and requirements of a shadow price.

An external investment cannot measure all of its investments at amortized cost for financial reporting purposes pool if there is significant noncompliance. Professional judgment should be exercised to determine if certain noncompliance is significant.

.05   GASB Statement 78

Statement 78 amends the scope and applicability of Statement 68 to exclude pensions provided to employees of state or local governmental employers through a cost-sharing multiple-employer defined benefit pension plan that:
1. is not a state or local governmental pension plan,
2. is used to provide defined benefit pensions both to employees of state or local governmental employers and to employees of employers that are not state or local governmental employers, and
3. has no predominant state or local governmental employer (either individually or collectively with other state or local governmental employers that provide pensions through the pension plan).

This Statement establishes requirements for recognition and measurement of pension expense, expenditures, and liabilities, note disclosures and required supplementary information for the excluded pensions.

¶8005   GASB Statements 70–77

.01   GASB Statement 77

In August 2015, GASB issued Statement 77, requiring state and local governments to disclose information about tax abatement agreements. The disclosure requirements in *Tax Abatement Disclosures* require state and local governments for the first time to disclose information about tax abatement agreements and are designed to provide financial statement users with essential information about these agreements and the impact that they have on a government's finances.

Governments often agree to abate or reduce the taxes of individuals and entities to promote economic development, job growth, redevelopment of blighted or underdeveloped areas, and other actions that are beneficial to the government or its citizens. Many state and local governments have tax abatement programs in place and the effects of tax abatements on their financial health and ability to raise revenue can be substantial. However, until now it has been difficult to determine the extent and nature of these effects from financial statements.

Statement 77 requires governments to disclose information about their own tax abatements separately from information about tax abatements that are entered into by other governments and reduce the reporting government's tax revenues. The new disclosures about a government's own tax abatement agreements include:

- The purpose of the tax abatement program
- The tax being abated
- Dollar amount of taxes abated
- Provisions for recapturing abated taxes
- The types of commitments made by tax abatement recipients
- Other commitments made by a government in tax abatement agreements, such as to build infrastructure assets.

.02   GASB Statement 76

In June 2015, the GASB also issued Statement No. 76, *The Hierarchy of Generally Accepted Accounting Principles for State and Local Governments*. The guidance reduces the U.S. GAAP hierarchy to two categories of authoritative U.S. GAAP from the four categories under GASB Statement No. 55, *The Hierarchy of Generally Accepted Accounting Principles for State and Local Governments*. The first category of authoritative U.S. GAAP consists of GASB Statements of Governmental Accounting Standards. The second category comprises GASB Technical Bulletins and Implementation Guides, as well as guidance from the American Institute of Certified Public Accountants that is cleared by the GASB. The Statement also addresses the use of authoritative and nonauthoritative literature in the event that the accounting treatment for a transaction or other event is not specified within a source of authoritative U.S. GAAP.

According to GASB, these changes are intended to improve financial reporting for governments by establishing a framework for the evaluation of accounting guidance that will result in governments applying that guidance with less variation. That will improve the usefulness of financial statement information for making decisions and assessing accountability and enhance the comparability of financial statement information among governments. The Statement also improves implementation guidance by elevating its authoritative status to a level that requires it be exposed for a period of broad public comment prior to issuance, as is done for other GASB pronouncements.

.03   GASB Statement 75

GASB Statement No. 75, *Accounting and Financial Reporting for Postemployment Benefits Other Than Pensions*, addresses reporting by governments that provide OPEB to their employees and for governments that finance OPEB for employees of other governments. The Statement replaces the requirements of GASB Statement No. 45, *Accounting and Financial Reporting by Employers for Postemployment Benefits Other Than Pensions*. Statement 75 requires governments to report a liability on the face of the financial statements for the OPEB that they provide. The provisions in Statement 75 are effective for fiscal years beginning after June 15, 2017. Early application is encouraged.

.04   GASB Statement 74

Also in June 2015, Statement 74 was issued. This statement, *Financial Reporting for Postemployment Benefit Plans Other Than Pension Plans*, addresses reporting by OPEB plans that administer benefits on behalf of governments. Statement 74 addresses reporting by OPEB plans that administer benefits on behalf of governments. Statement 74 replaces GASB Statement 43, *Financial Reporting for Postemployment Benefit Plans Other Than Pension Plans*. Statement 74 addresses the financial reports of defined benefit OPEB plans that are administered through trusts that meet specified criteria. The Statement follows the framework for financial reporting of defined benefit OPEB plans in Statement 45 by requiring a statement of fiduciary net position and a statement of changes in fiduciary net position. The Statement requires more extensive note disclosures and required supplementary information (RSI) related to the measurement of the OPEB liabilities for which assets have been accumulated, including information about the annual money-weighted rates of return on plan investments. Statement 74 also sets forth note disclosure requirements for defined contribution OPEB plans. The provisions in Statement 74 are effective for fiscal years beginning after June 15, 2016.

.05   GASB Statement 73

Statement No. 73, *Accounting and Financial Reporting for Pensions and Related Assets That Are Not within the Scope of GASB Statement 68, and Amendments to Certain Provisions of GASB Statements 67 and 68*, completes the suite of pension standards. Statement 73 establishes requirements for those pensions and pension plans that are not administered through a trust meeting specified criteria (in other words, those not covered by Statements 67 and 68). The requirements in Statement 73 for reporting pensions generally are the same as in Statement 68. However, the lack of a pension plan that is administered through a trust that meets specified criteria is reflected in the measurements. The provisions in Statement 73 are effective for fiscal years beginning after June 15, 2015—except those provisions that address employers and governmental nonemployer contributing entities for pensions that are not within the scope of Statement 68, which are effective for fiscal years beginning after June 15, 2016.

.06   GASB Statement 72

On March 2, 2015, the GASB issued its Statement on fair value measurement and application. GASB Statement No. 72, *Fair Value Measurement and Application*, defines fair value and describes how fair value should be measured, what assets and liabilities should be measured at fair value, and what information about fair value should be disclosed in the notes to the financial statements.

Under the Statement, fair value is defined as the price that would be received to sell an asset or paid to transfer a liability in an orderly transaction between market participants at the measurement date. Investments, which generally are measured at fair value, are defined as a security or other asset that governments hold primarily for the purpose of income or profit and the present service capacity of which are based solely on their ability to generate cash or to be sold to generate cash.

"The Board's new guidance responds to stakeholder requests for greater clarity regarding the fair value standards and for improved consistency and comparability in governments' fair value measurements and disclosures," according to GASB Chairman David A. Vaudt. "The Board believes that requiring governments to provide additional information about how they measure the fair value of their assets and liabilities will increase financial statement users' understanding of the nature of the fair value information they receive and enhance users' ability to make decisions with that information."

The Statement requires disclosure of fair value based on a hierarchy consisting of three categorizes. The categories represent the relative weight accorded the "inputs" to the valuation—the factors used to arrive at the valuation. Level 1 valuations use prices for identical assets or liabilities. Thus, they require quoted prices in an active market, such as bid and ask prices for an actively traded stock. Level 2 valuations involve observable factors presumably permitting others to arrive at the same valuation. For assets or liabilities where there are not identical items but there are similar items, the inputs would correspond to Level 2. Level 3 inputs involve the use of unobservable factors. This implies that different value calculations may result for different observers. Determining the value of commercial real estate would be an example. The method used should recognize and acknowledge the relative risk involved in applying that method. These procedures need not be applied to immaterial items.

Prior to the issuance of Statement 72, state and local governments have been required to disclose how they arrived at their measures of fair value if not based on quoted market prices. Under the new guidance, those disclosures have been expanded to categorize fair values according to their relative reliability and to describe positions held in many alternative investments.

The requirements of this Statement are effective for financial statements for periods beginning after June 15, 2015. Earlier application is encouraged.

.07   GASB Statement 71

GASB Statement No. 71, *Pension Transition for Contributions Made Subsequent to the Measurement Date*, is an amendment of GASB Statement 68 and was issued in November 2013. This Statement addresses the application of the transition provisions of Statement No. 68, *Accounting and Financial Reporting for Pensions*. The issue relates to amounts associated with contributions, if any, made by a state or local government employer or nonemployer contributing entity to a defined benefit pension plan after the measurement date of the government's beginning net pension liability. Statement 68 requires a state or local government employer (or nonemployer contributing entity in a special funding situation) to recognize a net pension liability measured as of a date (the measurement date) no earlier than the end of its prior fiscal year.

.08   GASB Statement 70

GASB Statement No. 70, *Accounting and Financial Reporting for Nonexchange Financial Guarantees,* was issued in April 2013. Some governments extend financial guarantees for the obligations of another government, a not-for-profit entity, or a private entity without directly receiving equal or approximately equal value in exchange (a nonexchange transaction). As a part of this nonexchange financial guarantee, a government commits to indemnify the holder of the obligation if the entity that issued the obligation does not fulfill its payment requirements. Also, some governments issue obligations that are guaranteed by other entities in a nonexchange transaction. The objective of this Statement is to improve accounting and financial reporting by state and local governments that extend and receive nonexchange financial guarantees.

This Statement requires a government that extends a nonexchange financial guarantee to recognize a liability when qualitative factors and historical data, if any, indicate that it is more likely than not that the government will be required to make a payment on the guarantee. The amount of the liability to be recognized should be the discounted present value of the best estimate of the future outflows related to the guarantee expected to be incurred. When there is no best estimate but a range of the estimated future outflows can be established, the amount of the liability to be recognized should be the discounted present value of the minimum amount within the range.

¶8006   GASB Issues Statements No. 67 and No. 68 on Pensions, No. 69, *Government Combinations and Disposals of Government Operations*, and No. 65 and No. 66 on Financial Reporting to Improve Pension Standards

To ensure that GASB pronouncements continue to be of high quality and are in line with the continuously evolving government environment, the GASB periodically reexamines its standards. Reexamination typically takes place after a Statement has been in place and fully implemented for at least five years. Research on the GASB's pension standards, for example, indicated opportunities for significant improvement as well as for other important practice issues for state and local governments.

.01   GASB Issues Statements No. 67 and No. 68 Improve Pension Accounting and Financial Reporting

In June 2012, the Governmental Accounting Standards Board approved two standards that improve the accounting and financial reporting of public employee pensions by state and local governments. Statement No. 68, *Accounting and Financial Reporting for Pensions*, revises and establishes new financial reporting requirements for most governments that provide their employees with pension benefits. Statement No. 67, *Financial Reporting for Pension Plans*, revises existing guidance for the financial reports of most pension plans.

The GASB Chairman explained that these new standards improve the way state and local governments report their pension liabilities and expenses, resulting in a more faithful representation of the full impact of these obligations. He added that among other improvements, net pension liabilities are reported on the balance sheet, providing financial reports that show a clearer picture of the size and nature of the financial obligations to current and former employees for past services rendered.

Pension plans are distinguished for financial reporting purposes in two ways:

1. Plans are classified by:
   a. Whether the income or other benefits that the employee will receive at or after separation from employment are defined by the benefit terms (a defined benefit plan).

b. Whether the pensions an employee will receive will depend only on the contributions to the employee's account, actual earnings on investments of those contributions, and other factors (a defined contribution plan).

2. In addition, defined benefit plans are classified based on the number of governments participating in a particular pension plan and whether assets and obligations are shared among the participating governments. Categories include:

a. Plans where only one employer participates (single employer);

b. Plans in which assets are pooled for investment purposes, but each employer's share of the pooled assets is legally available to pay the benefits of only its employees (agent employer); and

c. Plans in which participating employers pool or share obligations to provide pensions to their employees and plan assets can be used to pay the benefits of employees of any participating employer (cost-sharing employer).

.02   Statement 68 (Employers)

Statement 68 replaces the requirements of Statement No. 27, *Accounting for Pensions by State and Local Governmental Employers,* and Statement No. 50, *Pension Disclosures,* as they relate to governments that provide pensions through pension plans administered as trusts or similar arrangements that meet certain criteria. Under requirements of Statement 68, governments providing defined benefit pensions to:

- Recognize their long-term obligation for pension benefits as a liability for the first time,
- Measure more comprehensively and comparably the annual costs of pension benefits, and
- Enhance accountability and transparency through revised and new note disclosures and required supplementary information (RSI).

Defined Benefit Pension Plans. The Statement requires governments that participate in defined benefit pension plans to report in their statement of net position a net pension liability. The net pension liability is the difference between the total pension liability (the present value of projected benefit payments to employees based on their past service) and the assets (mostly investments reported at fair value) set aside in a trust and restricted to paying benefits to current employees, retirees, and their beneficiaries.

The Statement calls for immediate recognition of more pension expense than is currently required. This includes immediate recognition of annual service cost and interest on the pension liability and immediate recognition of the effect on the net pension liability of changes in benefit terms. Other components of pension expense will be recognized over a closed period that is determined by the average remaining service period of the plan members (both current and former employees, including retirees). These other components include the effects on the net pension liability of:

- Changes in economic and demographic assumptions used to project benefits and
- Differences between those assumptions and actual experience.
- The effects on the net pension liability of differences between expected and actual investment returns will be recognized in pension expense over a closed five-year period.

Statement 68 requires cost-sharing employers to record a liability and expense equal to their proportionate share of the collective net pension liability and expense for the cost-sharing plan. The Statement also will improve the comparability and consistency of how governments calculate the pension liabilities and expense. These changes include:

1. ***Projections of Benefit Payments.*** Projections of benefit payments to employees will be based on the then-existing benefit terms and incorporate projected salary changes and projected service credits (if they are factors in the pension formula), as well as projected automatic postemployment benefit changes (those written into the benefit terms), including automatic cost-of-living-adjustments (COLAs). For the first time, projections also will include ad hoc postemployment benefit changes (those not written into the benefit terms), including ad hoc COLAs, if they are considered to be substantively automatic.
2. ***Discount Rate.*** The rate used to discount projected benefit payments to their present value will be based on a single rate that reflects:
   a. The long-term expected rate of return on plan investments as long as the plan net position is projected under specific conditions to be sufficient to pay pensions of current employees and retirees and the pension plan assets are expected to be invested using a strategy to achieve that return; and
   b. A yield or index rate on tax-exempt 20-year, AA-or-higher rated municipal bonds to the extent that the conditions for use of the long-term expected rate of return are not met.
3. ***Attribution Method.*** Governments will use a single actuarial cost allocation method—"entry age"—with each period's service cost determined as a level percentage of pay.

Note Disclosures and Required Supplementary Information. Statement 68 also requires employers to present more extensive note disclosures and RSI, including:

- Disclosing descriptive information about the types of benefits provided,
- How contributions to the pension plan are determined, and
- Assumptions and methods used to calculate the pension liability.

Single and agent employers will disclose additional information, such as the composition of the employees covered by the benefit terms and the sources of changes in the components of the net pension liability for the current year.

A single or agent employer will present RSI schedules covering the past ten years regarding:

- Sources of changes in the components of the net pension liability,
- Ratios that assist in assessing the magnitude of the net pension liability,
- Comparisons of actual employer contributions to the pension plan with actuarially determined contribution requirements, if an employer has actuarially determined contributions.

Cost-sharing employers also will present the RSI schedule of net pension liability, information about contractually required contributions, and related ratios.

Defined Contribution Pensions. The existing standards for governments that provide defined contribution pensions are largely carried forward in the new Statement. These governments will recognize pension expenses equal to the amount of contributions or credits to employees' accounts, absent forfeited amounts. A pension liability will be recognized for the difference between amounts recognized as expense and actual contributions made to a defined contribution pension plan.

Special Funding Situations. Certain governments are legally responsible for making contributions directly to a pension plan that is used to provide pensions to the employees of another government. For example, a state is legally required to contribute to a pension plan that covers local school districts' teachers. In specific circumstances called special funding situations, the Statement requires governments that are nonemployer contributing entities to recognize in their own financial statements their proportionate share of the other governmental employers' net pension liability and pension expense.

.03   Statement 67 (Plans)

This Statement replaces the requirements of Statement No. 25, *Financial Reporting for Defined Benefit Pension Plans and Note Disclosures for Defined Contribution Plans*, Statement 50 as they relate to pension plans that are administered through trusts or similar arrangements meeting certain criteria. The Statement builds upon the existing framework for financial reports of defined benefit pension plans, which includes:

- A statement of fiduciary net position (the amount held in a trust for paying retirement benefits) and
- A statement of changes in fiduciary net position.

Statement 67 enhances note disclosures and RSI for both defined benefit and defined contribution pension plans. Statement 67 also requires the presentation of new information about annual money-weighted rates of return in the notes to the financial statements and in ten-year RSI schedules.

Effective Dates and Availability. The provisions in Statement 67 are effective for financial statements for periods beginning after June 15, 2013. The provisions in Statement 68 are effective for fiscal years beginning after June 15, 2014. Early application is encouraged for both Statements.

.04   GASB Issues Statement No. 69

In 2013, the Governmental Accounting Standards Board published standards intended to improve accounting and financial reporting for U.S. state and local governments' combinations and disposals of government operations. Government combinations include mergers, acquisitions, and transfers of operations. A disposal of government operations can occur through a transfer to another government or a sale. The pronouncement, which was approved on January 8, 2013, is available to download at no charge on the GASB Web site.

GASB Statement No. 69, *Government Combinations and Disposals of Government Operations,* provides guidance for:

- Determining whether a specific government combination is a government merger, a government acquisition, or a transfer of operations,
- Using carrying values (generally, the amounts recognized in the pre-combination financial statements of the combining governments or operations) to measure the assets, deferred outflows of resources, liabilities, and deferred inflows of resources combined in a government merger or transfer of operations,
- Measuring acquired assets, deferred outflows of resources, liabilities, and deferred inflows of resources based upon their acquisition values in a government acquisition, and
- Reporting the disposal of government operations that have been transferred or sold.

.05   GASB Issues Statements No. 65 and No. 66 Regarding State and Local Governments

The Governmental Accounting Standards Board (GASB) issued two Statements addressing important practice issues for state and local governments on April 2, 2012:

1. Statement No. 66, *Technical Corrections—2012*, enhances the usefulness of financial reports by resolving conflicting accounting and financial reporting guidance that could diminish the consistency of financial reporting.
2. Statement No. 65, *Items Previously Reported as Assets and Liabilities*, clarifies the appropriate reporting of deferred outflows of resources and deferred inflows of resources to ensure consistency in financial reporting.

Statement 66 (Risk). Statement 66 amends Statement No. 10, *Accounting and Financial Reporting for Risk Financing and Related Insurance Issues*, by removing the provision that limits fund-based reporting of a state and local government's risk financing activities to the general fund and the internal service fund type. As a result, governments would base their decisions about governmental fund type usage for risk financing activities on the definitions in Statement No. 54, *Fund Balance Reporting and Governmental Fund Type Definitions*.

This Statement also amends Statement No. 62, *Codification of Accounting and Financial Reporting Guidance Contained in Pre-November 30, 1989 FASB and AICPA Pronouncements*, by modifying the specific guidance on accounting for:

- Operating lease payments that vary from a straight-line basis,
- The difference between the initial investment (purchase price) and the principal amount of a purchased loan or group of loans, and
- Servicing fees related to mortgage loans that are sold when the stated service fee rate differs significantly from a current (normal) servicing fee rate.

These changes would eliminate any uncertainty regarding the application of Statement No. 13, *Accounting for Operating Leases with Scheduled Rent Increases*, and result in guidance that is consistent with the requirements in Statement No. 48, *Sales and Pledges of Receivables and Future Revenues and Intra-Entity Transfers of Assets and Future Revenues*, respectively. Statements No. 48, No. 54, and No. 62 are discussed later in this chapter.

The purpose of Statement No. 66 is to resolve conflicting accounting and financial reporting guidance that could result in inconsistency of financial reporting.

Statement 65 (Financial Statements). GASB Concepts Statement No. 4, *Elements of Financial Statements*, specifies that recognition of deferred outflows and deferred inflows should be limited to those instances specifically identified in authoritative GASB pronouncements. Consequently, guidance was needed to determine which balances being reported as assets and liabilities should actually be reported as deferred outflows of resources or deferred inflows of resources, according to the definitions in Concepts Statement 4. Based on those definitions, Statement 65 *reclassifies* certain items currently being reported as *assets and liabilities* as *deferred outflows of resources and deferred inflows of resources*. In addition, this Statement recognizes certain items currently being reported as assets and liabilities as outflows of resources and inflows of resources.

Thus, this Statement is designed to improve financial reporting by clarifying the appropriate use of the financial statement elements, "Deferred outflows of resources" and "Deferred inflows of resources" to ensure consistency in financial reporting.

The provisions of both Statements are effective for periods beginning after December 15, 2012.

¶8007   GASB Continues to Update and Improve Governmental Accounting and Financial Reporting Standards

After more than a decade operating under the model established in Statement No. 34, the Board continues to reexamine its pronouncements and, when necessary, attempts to improve their effectiveness. The following proposals provide additional information about governmental financial conditions.

.01   GASB Proposal Addresses Financial Guarantees for State and Local Governments

On June 25, 2012, the Governmental Accounting Standards Board issued an Exposure Draft (ED), *Accounting and Financial Reporting for Nonexchange Financial Guarantee Transactions*. The proposal is to provide guidance to state and local governments that offer non-exchange financial guarantees and also for those governments that receive guarantees on their obligations.

A *nonexchange financial guarantee* is a credit enhancement or assurance offered by a guarantor (the government or organization that offers the guarantee) that is provided without receiving consideration of equal value. The guarantor agrees to repay an obligation holder in the event that the debt issuer is not able to fulfill the contractual obligation to make timely payments to the obligation holder. Financial guarantees represent potential claims on a government's resources when it is the guarantor, and a potential reduction of a government's obligations when it is the debt issuer.

The proposed Statement requires a state and local government guarantor that offers a nonexchange financial guarantee to another organization or government to recognize a liability on its financial statements when it is "more likely than not" that the guarantor will actually make a payment to the obligation holders under the agreement. Additionally, the proposed Statement would require:

- A government guarantor to consider qualitative factors when determining if a payment on its guarantee is *more likely than not* to be paid. Such factors may include whether the issuer of the guaranteed obligation is experiencing significant financial difficulty or initiating the process of entering into bankruptcy or financial reorganization.
- An issuer government that is required to repay a guarantor to continue to report a liability unless legally released. When a government is released, the government would recognize revenue as a result of being relieved of the obligation.
- A government guarantor or issuer to disclose information about the amounts and nature of nonexchange financial guarantees.

The increased incidence of financial guarantee arrangements between governments—and their potential to result in payments by the guarantor—prompted the need for consistent recognition and disclosure guidance according to the GASB Chairman. He believes this Statement would enable financial statement users to better understand risk exposures of guarantors from financial guarantees that are issued, and credit enhancements received by state and local government debt issuers. This proposal also would help statement users assess the probability that governments will repay obligation holders.

.02   GASB Proposal Addresses Government Combinations and Disposals of Government Operations

The Governmental Accounting Standards Board (GASB) issued for public comment a proposed Statement that would provide U.S. state and local governments with standards for financial reporting regarding government combinations (mergers, acquisitions, and transfers of operations) and disposals (sales and transfers) of government operations on March 16, 2012. The proposal is contained in its Exposure Draft, *Government Combinations and Disposals of Government Operations.*

The proposed Statement is intended to improve accounting and financial reporting by providing standards for combinations in the governmental environment. Specifically, it requires state and local governments to:

- Identify whether a government combination is a government merger, government acquisition, or a transfer of operations,
- Use carrying values to measure the assets and liabilities combined in a government merger or transfer of operations,
- Measure acquired assets and liabilities based upon their acquisition values in a government acquisition, and
- Provide guidance for government operations that have been transferred or sold.

The proposed Statement would also require disclosures to be made about government combinations and disposals of government operations to enable users of financial statements to evaluate the nature and financial effects of those transactions.

Until now, state and local governments have accounted for mergers and acquisitions by referring to accounting and financial reporting guidance intended for the business environment, the GASB Chairman explained. He added, that based on research and feedback from stakeholders, the GASB decided to propose new guidance tailored to governmental situations and circumstances, to enable financial statement users, preparers, and auditors to evaluate the specific nature and financial effects of those transactions.

.03   GASB Proposal Addresses Financial Projections for Assessing Economic Condition of Governments

On December 6, 2011, the Governmental Accounting Standards Board (GASB) proposed that state and local governments should present five-year projections of cash inflows, cash outflows, and financial obligations that would accompany their financial statements as required supplementary information. The objective of this requirement is to enable taxpayers, bond holders, and other interested parties to better assess a government's financial health.

As a result of research and input from financial statement users, preparers, and auditors, the GASB believes that information outlined in *Preliminary Views, Economic Condition Reporting: Financial Projections* is necessary to assist users in assessing a government's economic condition. Contained in the *Preliminary Views* are:

- Projections of cash inflows and cash outflows, with explanations of the known causes of fluctuations,
- Projections of the financial obligations, including bonds, pensions, other postemployment benefits, and long-term contracts, with explanations of the known causes of fluctuations,
- Projections of annual debt service payments, including principal and interest,
- Narrative discussion of governments' dependencies on other governments to provide its services.

The GASB is considering issuing a Statement because of significant concerns expressed by users of state and local government financial reports regarding the importance of understanding whether governments are on a financially sustainable path. According to the GASB Chairman, the current economic downturn has emphasized what has been known for a long time: information is not always publicly available regarding the financial challenges facing governments.

The GASB proposed that financial projections should be:

- Based on current policy,
- Informed by historical information, and
- Adjusted for known events and conditions that will affect the government's finances during the projection periods.

Governments would be required to present projections for at least the next five fiscal years. The projections would be reported as required supplementary information following the notes to the financial statements.

¶8008   GASB Statements 63 and 64 Address Pressing Issues

In July 2011, the Governmental Accounting Standards Board (GASB) issued two Statements intended to improve governmental financial reporting by:

- Providing taxpayers and others with information about how past transactions will continue to impact a government's financial statements in the future, and
- Clarifying the circumstances in which hedge accounting continues to be applied when a swap counterparty, or related credit support provider, is replaced.

Both Statements No. 63, *Financial Reporting of Deferred Outflows of Resources, Deferred Inflows of Resources, and Net Position,* and No. 64, *Derivative Instruments: Application of Hedge Accounting Termination Provisions* (an amendment of GASB Statement No. 53), address accounting and financial reporting issues requiring attention because of their effects upon other Statements being implemented.

.01   GASB Statement 63

Statement 63 is intended to improve financial reporting by providing citizens and other users of state and local government financial reports with information about how past transactions will continue to impact a government's financial statements in the future.

Statement 63 provides a new statement of net position format to report:

- All assets,
- Deferred outflows of resources,
- Liabilities,
- Deferred inflows of resources, and
- Net position (which is the net residual amount of the other elements).

The Statement requires that deferred outflows of resources and deferred inflows of resources be reported separately from assets and liabilities.

A deferred outflow of resources is a consumption of net assets that is applicable to a future reporting period. An example of a deferred outflow of resources is a government's hedging interest rate swap agreement in which the fair value becomes negative. If the hedge is determined to be effectively offsetting the changes in fair value of the debt, the decrease in the fair value of the derivative instrument would be reported as a liability with a corresponding deferred outflow of resources to reflect the fact that this decrease is not expected to be recognized in investment income in future periods.

A deferred inflow of resources is an acquisition of net assets that is applicable to a future reporting period. An example of a deferred inflow of resources is a service concession arrangement that involves a public toll road. If the government receives an up-front payment from an operator, the revenue associated with that payment will be recognized in future years because the arrangement that generated the up-front payment relates to those periods.

Statement 63 also amends certain provisions of Statement No. 34, *Basic Financial Statements—and Management's Discussion and Analysis—for State and Local Governments*, and related pronouncements to reflect the residual measure in the statement of financial position as net position, rather than net assets. The provisions of Statement 63 became effective for financial statements for periods beginning after December 15, 2011.

.02   GASB Statement 64

GASB Statement No. 64, *Derivative Instruments: Application of Hedge Accounting Termination Provisions* (an amendment of GASB Statement No. 53), will improve financial reporting by state and local governments by clarifying the circumstances in which hedge accounting continues to be applied when a swap counterparty, or a swap counterparty's credit support provider, is replaced.

Statement 64 clarifies that when certain conditions are met, the use of hedge accounting should not be terminated. Those conditions are:

1. The collectability of swap payments is considered to be probable.
2. The replacement of the counterparty or credit support provider meets the criteria of an assignment or in-substance assignment as described in the Statement.
3. The counterparty or counterparty credit support provider (and not the government) has committed the act of default or termination event.

When all of these conditions exist, the GASB believes that the hedging relationship continues and hedge accounting should continue to be applied.

GASB Statement No. 53, *Accounting and Financial Reporting for Derivative Instruments*, provides for the use of hedge accounting for derivatives that are effective hedges. Hedge accounting entails reporting fair value changes of a hedging derivative as either deferred outflows of resources or deferred inflows of resources, rather than recognizing those changes in investment income. When a hedging derivative is terminated, Statement 53 requires that hedge accounting cease and all accumulated deferred amounts be reported in investment income.

As Statement 53 was being implemented, questions had arisen regarding situations in which a government has entered into a hedging interest rate swap or a hedging commodity swap and the swap counterparty (or the swap counterparty's credit support provider) commits or experiences an act of default or a termination event under the swap agreement through no fault of the government. When a swap counterparty (or a swap counterparty's credit support provider) is replaced through an assignment or an in-substance assignment, the GASB concluded that the government's financial position remains unchanged. Statement 64 became effective for periods beginning after June 15, 2011.

¶8009   GASB 62 Helps Practitioners Identify Guidance Applicable to State and Local Governments

The GASB issued Statement No. 62, *Codification of Accounting and Financial Reporting Guidance Contained in Pre-November 30, 1989 FASB and AICPA Pronouncements,* in December 2010. The Statement is intended to improve the usefulness of its Codification by incorporating guidance that previously could be found only in certain Financial Accounting Standards Board (FASB) and American Institute of Certified Public Accountants (AICPA) pronouncements.

The Statement incorporates into the GASB's authoritative literature the applicable guidance previously presented in the following pronouncements issued before November 30, 1989:

1. FASB Statements and Interpretations (APBs)
2. Accounting Principles Board Opinions
3. Accounting Research Bulletins of the AICPA's Committee on Accounting Procedure.

By incorporating and maintaining this guidance in a single source, the Statement reduces the complexity of locating and using authoritative literature needed to prepare state and local government financial reports. It eliminates the need for financial statement preparers and auditors to determine which FASB and AICPA pronouncements apply to state and local governments. The result should be a more consistent application of relevant guidance in their financial statements. Finally, it contributes to the GASB's efforts to codify all sources of U.S. GAAP for state and local governments so that they can be found within a single source.

The requirements of Statement 62 became effective for financial statements for periods beginning after December 15, 2011.

¶8010   GASB No. 61 Updates Reporting Entity Standards

In December 2010, the GASB issued Statement No. 61, *The Financial Reporting Entity: Omnibus.* This Statement is designed to improve financial reporting for governmental entities by amending the requirements of Statements No. 14, *The Financial Reporting Entity,* and No. 34, *Basic Financial Statements—and Management's Discussion and Analysis—for State and Local Governments,* to better meet user needs and address reporting entity issues that have come to light since those Statements were issued in 1991 and 1999, respectively.

The Statement will improve the information presented about the financial reporting entity, which is comprised of a primary government and related entities (component units). The amendments to the criteria for including component units allow users of financial statements to assess the accountability of elected officials of the primary government better by ensuring that the financial reporting entity includes only organizations for which the elected officials are financially accountable or that the government decides would be misleading to exclude.

In addition, the Statement amends the criteria for "blending"—that is, reporting component units as if they were part of the primary government—in certain circumstances. The amendments to the criteria for blending will help ensure that the primary government includes only those component units that are so intertwined with the primary government that they are essentially the same as the primary government, and will clarify which component units have that characteristic.

For primary governments that are business-type activities reporting in a single column (for example, a state university), the new guidance for reporting blended component units will require condensed combining information to be included in the notes to the financial statements, which will allow users to distinguish between the primary government and its component units better.

Lastly, the new requirements for reporting equity interests in component units help to ensure that the primary government's financial statements do not understate financial position. It should also provide for more consistent and understandable display of those equity interests.

The requirements of Statement 61 are effective for financial statements for periods beginning after June 15, 2012. Earlier application is encouraged.

¶8011   GASB Statement No. 60, *Accounting and Financial Reporting for Service Concession Arrangements*

The Governmental Accounting Standards Board issued Statement No. 60, *Accounting and Financial Reporting for Service Concession Arrangements*, in December 2010. Statement 60 addresses how to account for and report service concession arrangements (SCAs), a type of public-private or public-public partnership that state and local governments have begun using more frequently.

Common examples of SCAs include long-term arrangements in which a government (the "transferor") engages a company or another government (the "operator") to operate a major capital asset—such as toll roads, hospitals, and student housing—in return for the right to collect fees from users of the capital asset. In these SCAs, the operator generally makes a large up-front payment to the transferor. Alternatively, the operator may build a new capital asset for the transferor and operate it on the transferor's behalf.

The Statement provides guidance concerning:

- Whether the transferor or the operator should report the capital asset in its financial statements.
- When to recognize up-front payments from an operator as revenue.
- How to record any obligations of the transferor to the operator.
- Governments that are operators in an SCA.

The Statement improves financial reporting by establishing recognition, measurement, and disclosure requirements for SCAs for both transferors and governmental operators. It requires governments to account for and report SCAs in the same manner, which improves the comparability of financial statements. In addition, it is designed to alleviate the confusion that can arise when determining what guidance should be applied in complex circumstances, which previously were not specifically addressed in GASB literature.

The Board stated that feedback received from constituents during the due process was instrumental in developing Statement 60, resulting in requirements they believe will improve the financial reporting of SCAs by state and local governments. By providing specific financial reporting guidance for SCAs entered into by governments, application of the Statement is expected to result in greater clarity and transparency around these emerging types of relationships.

The requirements for Statement 60 became effective for financial statements for periods beginning after December 15, 2011. In general, its provisions are required to be applied retroactively for all periods presented.

¶8012   User Guide Series Updated

The GASB's user guide series, which introduces the financial reports of state and local governments to a broad, nonaccountant audience, has been revised and updated. The *What You Should Know* guides—originally published in 2000–2001—provide a comprehensive, easy-to-read introduction to the annual financial reports of local governments, school districts, and business-type activities, such as utilities, hospitals, and colleges. The titles currently available from the GASB Web site include:

- *An Analyst's Guide to Government Financial Statements—3rd Edition (March 2018)*
- *What You Should Know about Your School District's Finances: A Guide to Financial Statements-3rd Edition (Revised May 2018)*
- *What You Should Know about Your Local Government's Finances: A Guide to Financial Statements-3rd Edition (Revised June 2017)*
- *Government Service Efforts and Accomplishments Performance Reports: A Guide to Understanding (July 2005)*
- *What You Should Know about the Finances of Your Government's Business-Type Activities: A Guide to Financial Statements 2nd Edition (October 2018)*

.01   GASB Analyst Guide to Governmental Financial Statements

Analysts seeking to better understand and navigate state and local governmental financial statements have a beneficial resource. The Governmental Accounting Standards Board published *An Analyst's Guide to Governmental Financial Statements*, third edition, a comprehensive, easy-to-understand primer for:
- investment firms,
- rating agencies,
- institutional investors,
- mutual funds,

- bond agencies, and
- legislative, oversight and research organizations that need financial information about state and local government financial reports.

This guide is a more sophisticated guide aimed at experienced regular users of government financial statements.

The expanded third edition includes:

- 135 annotated examples of financial statement information, including
- Note disclosures,
- Supporting schedules,
- Full sets of financial statements for a state government, municipality, school district, and public university, and
- An example of a complete management's discussion and analysis.

The guide also covers major reporting requirements issued by the GASB since the publication of the original guide in 2001. The new topics covered include:

- Retiree health insurance,
- Fund balance,
- Derivative instruments,
- Deposit and investment risk disclosures, and
- A new statistical section.

As with the first edition, the new guide includes a chapter on the basic tools of analyzing the finances of state and local governments, but with additional attention to:

- Risk,
- Efficiency,
- Retirement benefits,
- Service capacity, and
- Revenue debt analysis.

Analysts tend to be frequent users of governmental financial statements and they rely heavily on the reported financial information for decision-making or assessing accountability, according to the GASB Chairman. This comprehensive guide will help them understand the information that can be found in those financial statements better and will show how basic analytical techniques can be applied to assess financial position, liquidity, long-term solvency, fiscal capacity, and risk exposure, he added.

.02   GASB User Guide to School Districts' Finances Helps Taxpayers Find Answers to Many Questions

Taxpayers learn the answers to many questions in an easy-to-understand guide to school district financial statements published in 2018 by the Governmental Accounting Standards Board (GASB).

What You Should Know about Your School District's Finances: A Guide to Financial Statements, third edition, offers parents, teachers, school board members, educational advocacy groups, and other people who need financial information about public education a comprehensive, easy-to-understand primer on the annual financial reports issued by school districts. The guide includes major reporting requirements issued by the GASB since the publication of the original guide in 2000, in areas that include retiree health insurance and fund balance. The guide includes:

- More than 50 annotated examples of school district financial statements, notes, and schedules,
- A storyline designed to help the reader understand the concepts,
- An introduction to basic financial ratios used to analyze school district finances,
- Helpful boxes and sidebars further exploring issues raised in the text,
- An overview of school district accounting and financial reporting, and
- An exhaustive glossary of terms.

Like other governments, school districts take special care to demonstrate that they are accountable to the public for keeping track of what money is collected and how it is spent, the GASB Chairman explained. He pointed out that the guide helps taxpayers and parents understand what a financial report says. The guide shows how valuable school district financial information is when participating in a variety of important decisions, such as:

- Allocating budget resources among programs;
- Choosing where to send a child to school;
- Buying a house;
- Locating a business;
- Voting in a school board election;
- Voting on a district's annual budget; or
- Buying a school district's bonds.

It may appear that information about state and local financing is not something that an accountant would necessarily be concerned with, however with all the political fervor regarding public school financing, the taxpayer has become very concerned about the distribution of tax monies.

.03   GASB User Guide on Local Government Finances

What You Should Know about Your Local Government's Finances: A Guide to Financial Statements, third edition, is a comprehensive primer on local government annual reports for taxpayers, elected representatives, and other people who need information about cities, counties, towns, and villages.

The guide includes major reporting requirements issued since the publication of the original guide in 2000, in areas that include retiree health insurance and fund balance. The guide includes:

- Annotated examples of more than 50 government financial statements, notes, and schedules,
- A storyline designed to help the reader understand the concepts,
- An introduction to basic financial ratios used to analyze government finances,
- Helpful boxes and sidebars further exploring issues raised in the text,
- An overview of governmental accounting and financial reporting, and
- An exhaustive glossary of terms.

Meeting the needs of taxpayers and other financial statement users is a primary objective of the GASB, according to the board's Chairman. He added that, when users have difficulty understanding the financial statements issued by local governments, the value of that information is diminished. For that reason, the guide is written from the layperson's perspective, without excessive accounting jargon, but with plenty of examples of how to use the information in local government financial reports.

.04   GASB User Guide to Business-Type Activities

What You Should Know about the Finances of Your Business-Type Activities is devoted to the unique features of financial reporting, including the activities that governments operate similar to businesses by charging fees in return for service. These entities include public utilities, airports, public hospitals, and public colleges and universities.

The guide provides detailed overviews of each of the financial statements and other related information and includes:

- Annotated examples of more than 50 government financial statements, notes, and schedules,
- A storyline designed to help the reader understand the concepts,
- An introduction to basic financial ratios used to analyze government finances,
- Helpful boxes and sidebars further exploring issues raised in the text,
- An overview of governmental accounting and financial reporting,
- An exhaustive glossary of terms.

¶8013   GASB Issues Statement No. 59, *Financial Instruments Omnibus*

In June 2010, the GASB issued Statement No. 59, *Financial Instruments Omnibus*. The Statement updates and improves existing standards regarding financial reporting of certain financial instruments and external investment pools. The Statement is effective for financial statements prepared by state and local governments for periods beginning after June 15, 2010, with earlier application encouraged.

"Statement 59 addresses significant practice issues that have arisen when accounting for financial instruments," according to the GASB Chairman. By increasing the consistency of measurements and by providing clarification of existing standards, the Board believes that this guidance will improve financial reporting in ways that benefit both users and preparers of financial reports."

Statement 59 includes the following guidance:

- Emphasizes the applicability of U.S. Securities and Exchange Commission requirements to certain external investment pools—known as 2a7-like pools—to provide users more consistent information on qualifying pools
- Addresses the applicability of Statement No. 53, *Accounting and Financial Reporting for Derivative Instruments*, to certain financial instruments to clarify which financial instruments are within the scope of that pronouncement and to provide greater consistency in financial reporting
- Applies the reporting provisions for interest-earning investment contracts of Statement No. 31, *Accounting and Financial Reporting for Certain Investments and for External Investment Pools*, to unallocated insurance contracts to improve the consistency of reporting by pension and OPEB plans.

¶8014   Statements on OPEB Measurements and Chapter 9 Bankruptcies, Statements No. 57 & 58

The Governmental Accounting Standards Board (GASB) issued Statement No. 57, *OPEB Measurements by Agent Employers and Agent Multiple-Employer Plans*, and Statement No. 58, *Accounting and Financial Reporting for Chapter 9 Bankruptcies*. The Statements are intended to improve consistency in the measurement and financial reporting of other postemployment benefits (OPEB) such as retiree health insurance, and of the effects of municipal bankruptcy.

Statement 57 addresses issues related to measurement of OPEB obligations by certain employers participating in agent multiple-employer OPEB plans. (In agent multiple-employer plans, separate liabilities are calculated and separate asset accounts are kept for each participating government, rather than being administered and accounted for as a single plan as is done in a cost-sharing plan.) Statement 57 amends Statement No. 43, *Financial Reporting for Postemployment Benefit Plans Other Than*

Pension Plans, and Statement No. 45, *Accounting and Financial Reporting by Employers for Postemployment Benefits Other Than Pensions.* Specifically, Statement 57:

- Enables certain agent employers to use the alternative measurement method, a less complex and potentially less expensive alternative to a full actuarial valuation
- Adjusts the requirement that a defined benefit OPEB plan obtain an actuarial valuation, in light of the change allowing more qualifying employers to use the alternative measurement method
- Clarifies that the same frequency and timing of determining OPEB measures are required for both agent multiple-employer plans and their participating employers.

Statement 58 provides guidance for governments that have petitioned for protection from creditors by filing for bankruptcy under Chapter 9 of the United States Bankruptcy Code. It establishes requirements for recognizing and measuring the effects of the bankruptcy process on assets and liabilities, and for classifying changes in those items and related costs.

"The stress that the current economic environment is putting on state and local government resources and the lack of existing financial reporting guidance made it necessary for the GASB to address the financial reporting issues associated with qualified local governments that file for bankruptcy protection under Chapter 9," according to the chairman of the GASB.

The provisions of Statement 57 related to the use and reporting of the alternative measurement method were effective immediately. The provisions related to the frequency and timing of measurements are effective for actuarial valuations first used to report funded status information in OPEB plan financial statements for periods beginning after June 15, 2011. Statement 58 was effective for periods beginning after June 15, 2009. Retroactive application is required for all prior periods presented during which a government was in bankruptcy. Earlier application of both Statements has been encouraged.

¶8015   Suggested Guidelines for Voluntary Reporting of Service Efforts and Accomplishments (SEA) Performance Information

After more than two decades of extensive research and constituent outreach, in June 2010 the GASB issued Suggested Guidelines for Voluntary Reporting, *SEA Performance Information.* The purpose of this document is to provide state and local governments with suggested guidelines intended to provide a common framework for the effective external communication of that body's service efforts and accomplishments (SEA).

The reporting of SEA performance information—indicators of a government's *actual* performance in providing services to its citizens—is a valuable complement to the information currently included in traditional financial statements and is an important method of demonstrating accountability. The Suggested Guidelines are intended to help state and local governments that choose to communicate SEA performance information to citizens, elected officials, and other interested parties to do so effectively.

Regarding the issuance of the Suggested Guidelines document, the chairman of GASB, observed; "The release of the Suggested Guidelines after more than twenty years of research and outreach is an important step toward the reporting of a more complete picture of how well government officials are managing the financial resources that have been entrusted to them. The reporting of SEA performance information better meets the needs of users of governmental financial information by enhancing both accountability and transparency of those governments who choose to report this information."

The Suggested Guidelines include what the GASB has identified as the four essential components of an effective SEA report, the six qualitative characteristics of SEA performance information, and three keys to effective communication.

The four essential components identified are:

1. Purpose and scope: Why is the information being reported and what portion of a government does it relate to?
2. Major goals and objectives: A basis for assessing the degree to which a government has achieved the intended results of its programs and services. What is it the government intends to accomplish?
3. Key measures of SEA performance: Focus should be on the measures most important to readers.
4. Discussion and analysis of results and challenges: An explanation of what has been achieved, what factors affect the level of achievement, and what is planned for addressing the challenges of the future?

The six qualitative characteristics, as set forth in GASB Concepts Statement No. 1, *Objectives of Financial Reporting*, are:

1. Relevance,
2. Understandability,
3. Comparability,
4. Timeliness,

5. Consistency,
6. Reliability.

The three keys to effective communication are:

1. Intended audiences,
2. Multiple levels of reporting, and
3. Forms of communication.

Previous pronouncements leading up to the Guidelines include:

- Suggested Guidelines for Voluntary Reporting, *SEA Performance Information*, in July 2009
- Concepts Statement No. 5, *Service Efforts and Accomplishments Reporting* (An Amendment of GASB Concepts Statement No. 2), in December 2008
- Concepts Statement No. 2, *Service Efforts and Accomplishments Reporting*, in April 1994

¶8016   GASB Issues Statement 56, *Codification of Accounting and Financial Reporting Guidance Contained in the AICPA Statements on Auditing Standards*

The GASB issued Statement No. 56, *Codification of Accounting and Financial Reporting Guidance Contained in the AICPA Statements on Auditing Standards*, in April 2009. This Statement brings accounting and financial reporting guidance from the American Institute of Certified Public Accountants (AICPA) auditing literature into the GASB's accounting and financial reporting literature for state and local governments. Previously this material appeared only in the AICPA literature.

Statement 56 guidance addresses three issues from the AICPA's literature:

- Related party transactions,
- Going concern considerations, and
- Subsequent events.

This Statement brings existing guidance (to the extent appropriate in a governmental environment) without substantive changes into the GASB's body of standards. Statement 56 is part of the GASB's effort to codify all U.S. GAAP for state and local governments so that they derive from a single source. This is intended to make it easier for preparers of state and local government financial statements to identify and apply relevant accounting guidance.

¶8017   GASB Issues Statement No. 55, *The Hierarchy of Generally Accepted Accounting Principles for State and Local Governments*

In April 2009, the Governmental Accounting Standards Board issued GASB Statement No. 55, *The Hierarchy of Generally Accepted Accounting Principles for State and Local Governments*. The Statement incorporates the hierarchy of U.S. Generally Accepted Accounting Principles (U.S. GAAP) for state and local governments into the GASB's authoritative literature. It is intended to make it easier for preparers of state and local government financial statements to identify and apply the "GAAP hierarchy," which consists of sources of accounting principles used in the preparation of financial statements so that they are presented in conformity with U.S. GAAP and the framework for selecting those principles.

¶8018   GASB 54 Improves the Usefulness of Reported Fund Balance Information

The GASB issued Statement No. 54, *Fund Balance Reporting and Governmental Fund Type Definitions*, in March 2009. The Statement is expected to improve the usefulness of information provided to financial report users about fund balance by providing clearer, more structured fund balance classifications, and by clarifying the definitions of existing governmental fund types.

Fund balance—the difference between assets and liabilities in the governmental fund financial statements—constitutes some of the most widely and frequently used information in state and local government financial reports. The GASB developed Statement 54 to address the diversity of practice and the resulting lack of consistency that had evolved in fund balance reporting. To reduce confusion, the new standards establish a hierarchy of fund balance classifications based primarily on the extent to which a government is bound to observe spending constraints imposed upon how resources reported in governmental funds may be used.

For more details on GASB Statement 54, see the discussion in "Governmental Fund Accounting."

¶8019   GASB Issues Statement No. 53, *Accounting and Financial Reporting for Derivative Instruments*

In June 2008, the GASB issued Statement No. 53, *Accounting and Financial Reporting for Derivative Instruments*. It is expected to improve the manner in which state and local governments report information about derivative instruments—financial arrangements used by governments to manage specific risks or make investments—in their financial statements. The Statement specifically requires governments to measure most derivative instruments at fair value in the financial statements prepared using the economic resources measurement focus and the accrual basis of accounting.

The guidance in this Statement also addresses hedge accounting requirements.

¶8020   GASB Issues *Guide to Implementation of Statement 53 on Derivatives*

The GASB issued its *Guide to Implementation of Statement 53 on Derivative Instruments* in April 2009. The purpose of the guide is to assist preparers and auditors of governmental financial statements and those who advise them in implementing the GASB's recently issued standard on accounting and financial reporting for derivative instruments.

The guide provides answers to more than 100 questions on topics relating to the implementation of Statement 53, including:

- Scope and applicability of Statement 53 with special emphasis on the normal purchases and normal sales scope exception;
- Definition of derivative instruments focusing on the distinguishing characteristics of a derivative instrument—settlement factors, leverage, and net settlement;
- Embedded derivative instruments, and when an embedded derivative instrument results in a hybrid instrument;
- Hedge effectiveness criteria, and how to apply the methods of evaluating effectiveness—the consistent critical terms, the synthetic instrument, the dollar-offset, and the regression analysis methods;
- Disclosures; and
- Effective date and transition.

In addition to the illustrations that were included in Statement 53, the journal entries that support the transactions in the illustrations have now been added.

Implementation of Statement 53 began with fiscal years beginning after June 15, 2009.

¶8021   Statement No. 52, *Land and Other Real Estate Held as Investments by Endowments*

The GASB issued Statement No. 52, *Land and Other Real Estate Held as Investments by Endowments*, in November 2007. The statement improves the quality of financial reporting by requiring endowments to report their land and other real estate investments at fair value.

This action creates consistency in reporting among similar entities that exist for the purpose of investing resources to generate income. Previously, state and local government endowments were required to report land and other real estate held as investments at historical cost, which *provides information on investment results only in the year the investments are sold.* However, entities that perform investment functions similar to endowments—including pension plans, other post employment benefit (OPEB) plans, external investment pools, and IRC Sec. 457 deferred compensation plans—have been required to report their land and real estate investments at fair value. Reporting those investments at fair value provides more decision-useful information about their composition, current value, and recent changes in value.

In order to help users of financial statements better evaluate an endowment's investment decisions and performance, Statement 52 requires governments to report the changes in fair value as investment income. It also requires them to disclose the methods and significant assumptions employed to determine fair value, and to provide other information that they currently present for other investments reported at fair value.

¶8022   GASB Issues Technical Bulletin No. 2008-1, *Determining the Annual Required Contribution Adjustment for Postemployment Benefits*

The GASB issued GASB Technical Bulletin No. 2008-1, *Determining the Annual Required Contribution Adjustment for Postemployment Benefits,* in December 2008. This Technical Bulletin clarifies the requirements of GASB Statement No. 27, *Accounting for Pensions by State and Local Governmental Employers,* and Statement No. 45, *Accounting and Financial Reporting by Employers for Postemployment Benefits Other Than Pensions,* for calculating the annual required contribution (ARC) adjustment.

The Technical Bulletin applies to situations in which the actuarial valuation separately identifies the actual amount that is included in the ARC related to the amortization of past employer contribution deficiencies or excess contributions to a pension or other postemployment benefit (OPEB) plan. In response to constituent feedback that questioned the availability of actual amounts, Statements 27 and 45 *required* a procedure for estimating the amount. The new Technical Bulletin encourages use of the actual amount, if known, in place of the estimation procedure for purposes of the ARC adjustment.

For accounting purposes, the portion of the ARC calculation related to past over and underpayments already has been recognized in the financial statements, and an adjustment needs to be made to future ARCs to avoid counting that amount twice. Statements 27 and 45 assume that the amount is not known and, therefore, prescribed a method of estimation that governments are required to use. However, since it has come to the GASB's attention that some actuaries do track that portion of the ARC separately, the purpose of this Technical

Bulletin is to make it clear that governments should base the ARC adjustment on the actual amount when it is known.

¶8023   Standards Nos. 49–51 Provide Additional Base for Meaningful Financial Reporting

The members of the Government Accounting Standards Board are certainly living up to their pledge to review and update their Statements to be sure that all of the citizens and other users of their various financial reports are being supplied with complete and understandable information.

.01   GASB Adopts Statement No. 49, *Pollution Remediation Obligations*

Reflecting its intention to ensure that costs and liabilities not specifically addressed by current governmental accounting standards are included in financial reports, the Board issued GASB Statement 49 in December 2006. The measure requires state and local governments to provide the public with better information about the financial impact of environmental cleanups.

To provide governments with better accounting guidance and consistency, GASB Statement No. 49, *Pollution Remediation Obligations*, identifies the circumstances under which a governmental entity would be required to report a liability related to pollution remediation. According to the Statement, a government would have to estimate its expected outlays for pollution remediation if it knows a site is polluted and any of the following recognition triggers occur:

- Pollution poses an imminent danger to the public or environment and a government has little or no discretion to avoid fixing the problem.
- A government has violated a pollution prevention-related permit or license.
- A regulator has identified (or evidence indicates a regulator will do so) a government as responsible (or potentially responsible) for cleaning up pollution, or for paying all or some of the cost of the clean-up.
- A government is named in a lawsuit (or evidence indicates that it will be) to compel it to address the pollution.
- A government begins to clean up pollution or conducts related remediation activities (or the government legally obligates itself to do so).

Liabilities and expenses would be estimated using an "expected cash flows" measurement technique, which will be employed for the first time by governments. Statement 49 also would require governments to disclose information about their pollution remediation obligations associated with clean-up efforts in the notes to the financial statements.

.02   GASB Issues Statement No. 50, *Pension Disclosures*

In May 2007, the GASB issued Statement No. 50, *Pension Disclosures*, which more closely aligns current pension disclosure requirements for governments with those that governments are beginning to implement for retiree health insurance and other post-employment benefits.

Specifically, GASB Statement 50 amends GASB Statement No. 25, *Financial Reporting for Defined Benefit Pension Plans and Note Disclosures for Defined Contribution Plans*, and Statement No. 27, *Accounting for Pensions by State and Local Governmental Employers*, by requiring:

- Disclosure in the notes to the financial statements of pension plans and certain employer governments of the current funded status of the plan—in other words, the degree to which the actuarial accrued liabilities for benefits are covered by assets that have been set aside to pay the benefits—as of the most recent actuarial valuation date.
- Governments that use the aggregate actuarial cost method to disclose the funded status and present a multi-year schedule of funding progress using the entry age actuarial cost method as a surrogate; these governments previously were not required to provide this information.
- Disclosure by governments participating in multi-employer cost-sharing pension plans of how the contractually required contribution rate is determined.

.03   GASB Issues Standard No. 51 on Intangible Assets

The GASB issued Statement No. 51, *Accounting and Financial Reporting for Intangible Assets*, in July 2007. The Statement provides needed guidance regarding how to identify, account for, and report intangible assets.

The standard characterizes an intangible asset as one that lacks physical substance, is nonfinancial in nature, and has an initial useful life extending beyond a single reporting period. Examples of intangible assets include easements, computer software, water rights, timber rights, patents, and trademarks.

GASB Statement 51 requires that intangible assets be classified as capital assets (except for those explicitly excluded from the scope of the new standard, such as capital leases). Relevant authoritative guidance for capital assets should be applied to these intangible assets.

Statement 51 provides additional guidance that specifically addresses the unique nature of intangible assets, including:

- Requiring that an intangible asset be recognized in the statement of net assets only if it is considered identifiable.

- Establishing a specified-conditions approach to recognizing intangible assets that are internally generated (for example, patents and copyrights).
- Providing guidance on recognizing internally generated computer software.
- Establishing specific guidance for the amortization of intangible assets.

¶8024   GASB Concepts Statement No. 6, *Measurement of Elements of Financial Statements*, and GASB Concepts Statement No. 5, *Service Efforts and Accomplishments Reporting* (An Amendment of GASB Concepts Statement No. 2)

The Governmental Accounting Standards Board issued Concepts Statement No. 6, *Measurement of Elements of Financial Statements*, in March 2014. It establishes two measurement approaches that are used in financial statements, as follows:

- **Initial-Transaction-Date-Based Measurement (Initial Amount)** – The transaction price or amount assigned when an asset was acquired or a liability was incurred, including subsequent modifications to that price or amount that are derived from the amount at which the asset or liability was initially reported.
- **Current-Financial-Statement-Based Measurement (Remeasured Amount)** – The amount assigned when an asset or liability is remeasured as of the financial statement date.

The Statement identifies circumstances in which one measurement attribute is more appropriate than the other. Initial amounts are more appropriate for assets that are used directly in providing services. Remeasured amounts are more appropriate for assets that will be converted to cash (financial assets). Remeasured amounts also are more appropriate for liabilities for which there is uncertainty about the timing and amount of payments.

The Statement also establishes the four measurement attributes used in financial statements, namely, historical cost, fair value, replacement cost, and settlement amount.

The Governmental Accounting Standards Board issued Concepts Statement No. 5, *Service Efforts and Accomplishments Reporting* (an amendment of GASB Concepts Statement No. 2), in December 2008. Statement 5 updates provisions in Concepts Statement 2 to reflect developments that have occurred since Concepts Statement 2 was issued in 1994.

The revisions to Concepts Statement 2 clarify that it is beyond the scope of the GASB to establish the goals and objectives of state and local government services, to develop specific nonfinancial measures or indicators of service performance, or to set benchmarks for service performance. To emphasize this point, Concepts Statement 5 removes an entire section of Concepts Statement 2, titled, "Developing Reporting Standards for SEA Information." Concepts Statement 2 was also amended to update terminology and to modify certain provisions to reflect what has taken place over the past 14 years.

¶8025   GASB Approves Concepts Statement No. 4

GASB approved Concepts Statement No. 4, *Elements of Financial Statements*, defining the basic elements of state and local government financial statements in June 2007. Together, the GASB's Concepts Statements form a conceptual framework that provides a foundation to guide the Board's development of accounting and financial reporting standards.

The Board has defined these fundamental building blocks of financial reporting in order to further develop the basic conceptual foundation for considering the merits of alternative approaches to financial reporting, and to help the GASB develop well-reasoned financial reporting standards. The concept of a *resource*—an item with a present capacity to provide service—is central to the definitions. Accordingly, the new Concepts Statement defines the elements of *statements of financial position* as:

- *Assets*—resources with present service capacity that the government presently controls.
- *Liabilities*—present obligations to sacrifice resources that the government has little or no discretion to avoid.
- A *deferred outflow of resources*—a consumption of net assets by the government that is applicable to a future reporting period.
- A deferred inflow of resources—an acquisition of net assets by the government that is applicable to a future reporting period.
- *Net position*—the residual of all other elements presented in a statement of financial position.

Concepts Statement 4 defines deferred outflows and inflows of resources as distinct financial statement elements for the first time. The Concepts Statement also defines elements of *resource flows statements* as:

- *Outflow of resources*—a consumption of net assets by the government that is applicable to the reporting period.
- *Inflow of resources*—an acquisition of net assets by the government that is applicable to the reporting period.

The GASB is well aware of the importance of establishing a solid conceptual foundation upon which to build their standards. To that end, they have been establishing consistently effective standards, particularly after GASB Statement 34. Definitions of assets, liabilities, and other financial statement elements are cornerstones of that foundation.

Previous Concepts Statements addressed the objectives of financial reporting, service efforts and accomplishments reporting, and communication methods. The Board's next Concepts Statement is expected to address recognition and measurement attributes.

.01   Board Gradually Establishing Concepts Statements

These proposals reflect the Board's ongoing commitment to develop a conceptual framework to guide the Board in its decision making, promote high-quality accounting standards, and make the process for developing those standards more consistent. An improved framework will also aid financial statement preparers and auditors as they evaluate transactions for which there are no existing standards, according to the Board.

- In May 1987, the Board issued Concepts Statement No. 1, *Objectives of Financial Reporting*. (Please see the section on GASB Statement 44 below in this chapter.)
- In April 1994, GASB issued Concepts Statement No. 2, *Service Efforts and Accomplishments Reporting*. (Please see discussion above on relevant project added to agenda.)
- In April 2005, GASB issued Concepts Statement No. 3, *Communication Methods in General Purpose External Financial Reports That Contain Basic Financial Statements*. (See below.)

¶8026   Concepts Statement No. 3 on Communication Methods

In April 2005, GASB issued Concepts Statement No. 3, *Communication Methods in General Purpose External Financial Reports That Contain Basic Financial Statements*. The purpose of the Concepts Statement is to provide a conceptual basis for selecting communication methods to present items of information within the general-purpose external financial reports containing the basic financial statements. These communication methods include:

1. Recognition in basic financial statements.
2. Disclosure in notes to basic financial statements.
3. Presentation as required supplementary information (RSI).
4. Presentation as supplementary information.

The Concepts Statement:

1. Defines the communication methods commonly used in general-purpose external financial reports.
2. Develops criteria for each communication method.
3. Provides a hierarchy for their use.

The definitions, criteria, and hierarchy should help the GASB and preparers of financial reports determine the appropriate methods to use to communicate an item of information. Greater consistency in the communication and reporting methods used by various governmental units should make comparisons more meaningful. This, in turn, should lead to more efficient and effective use of governmental financial reports.

¶8027 GASB Clarifies Guidance on Accounting for Sales and Pledges of Receivables and Future Revenues— Statement No. 48

In September 2006, the Governmental Accounting Standards Board (GASB) issued Statement No. 48, *Sales and Pledges of Receivables and Future Revenues and Intra-Entity Transfers of Assets and Future Revenues*. This Statement establishes criteria that governments will use to ascertain whether certain transactions should be regarded as a sale or a collateralized borrowing. Such transactions are likely to comprise the sale of delinquent taxes, certain mortgages, student loans, or future revenues such as those arising from tobacco settlement agreements.

This Statement also includes a provision that stipulates that governments should not revalue assets that are transferred between financial reporting entity components. Guidance for reporting the effects of such transactions in governmental financial statements have been provided in several standards or, in certain cases, has not been authoritatively addressed. This has resulted in considerable diversity in practice in the manner that such transactions have been reported.

In addition to clarifying guidance on accounting for sales and pledges of receivables and future revenues, the Statement:

- Requires enhanced disclosures pertaining to future revenues that have been pledged or sold
- Provides guidance on sales of receivables and future revenues within the same financial reporting entity.
- Provides guidance on recognizing other assets and liabilities arising from the sale of specific receivables or future revenues.

According to the Board, Statement 48 is intended to clarify accounting by establishing clear criteria for determining whether proceeds received from a given transaction should be reported as revenue or as a liability. In addition, the Standard's enhanced disclosure requirements are expected to improve the usefulness of financial reporting by enabling the public to become better informed about the status of future revenues that may have been pledged or sold.

¶8028   GASB Completes Accounting Standards for Termination Benefits—Statement No. 47

In issuing its Statement No. 47, effective for financial statements covering periods beginning after June 15, 2005, the GASB addresses the issue of the proper accounting for termination benefits. The Statement provides accounting and disclosure benchmarks for state and local governments that offer benefits such as early retirement incentives or severance pay to employees who are involuntarily terminated. Statement 47 specifies when governments should recognize the cost of termination benefits they offer in accrual basis financial statements, Benefits provided for involuntary terminations should be accounted for in the period in which a government becomes obligated to provide benefits to terminated employees, which is not necessarily the same period in which the benefits are actually provided. The cost of such benefits must be recognized when the termination offer is accepted by the employee.

The Statement provides an exception to the general recognition requirements for termination benefits that affect defined benefit postemployment benefits, such as pensions or retiree healthcare. Those termination benefits should be accounted for in the same manner as defined benefit pensions or other postemployment benefits, although any increase in an actuarially accrued liability associated with a termination benefit is required to be disclosed separately. For termination benefits that affect defined benefit postemployment benefits other than pensions, governments should implement Statement 47 simultaneously with Statement No. 45, *Accounting and Financial Reporting by Employers for Postemployment Benefits Other Than Pensions.*

¶8029   GASB Clarifies Reporting of Net Assets— Statement No. 46

The Governmental Accounting Standards Board issued Statement No. 46, *Net Assets Restricted by Enabling Legislation,* as an amendment of GASB Statement 34 in December 2004. The purpose is to determine when net assets have been restricted to a particular use by the passage of enabling legislation and to specify how those net assets should be reported in financial statements when there are changes in the circumstances surrounding that legislation.

A government's net assets should be reported as restricted when the purpose for, or manner in which they can be used, is limited by:

- An external party.
- A constitutional provision.
- Enabling legislation.

Enabling legislation is a specific type of legislation that both authorizes the raising of new resources and imposes legally enforceable limits on how they may be used.

.01   Reasons for Enacting this Standard

Statement 46 is intended to alleviate difficulties in identifying enabling legislation restrictions by clarifying that "legally enforceable" means that an external party "such as citizens, public interest groups, or the judiciary" can compel a government to use resources only for the purposes stipulated by the enabling legislation.

GASB Statement 46 confirms that the determination of legal enforceability is a matter of professional judgment, which may entail reviewing the legislation and determinations made in relation to similar legislation, as well as obtaining the advice of legal counsel. The Statement indicates that governments should review the legal enforceability of enabling legislation restrictions when new enabling legislation has been enacted to replace existing legislation, and when resources are used for purposes not specified by the enabling legislation.

The Statement also requires governments to disclose in the notes to the financial statements the amount of net assets restricted by enabling legislation as of the end of the reporting period.

¶8030   GASB Statement 44, *Economic Condition Reporting: The Statistical Section*

In June 2004, the GASB issued Statement No. 44, *Economic Condition Reporting: The Statistical Section*. This Statement amends the portions of NCGA Statement 1, *Governmental Accounting and Financial Reporting Principles*, that guide the preparation of the statistical section. The new requirements enhance and update the statistical section that accompanies a state or local government's basic financial statements by reflecting the significant changes that have taken place in government finance, including the more comprehensive government-wide financial information required by GASB Statement 34. The added requirements are intended to provide financial statement users with information necessary to assess an entity's financial well-being.

The Board expects to improve the understandability and usefulness of statistical section information by addressing problems identified since the NCGA Statement was issued in 1979:

- Statement 1 presented a list of 15 required schedules with no additional explanation of the nature of the information they were to contain. As a result, some governments prepared their statistical sections differently from others, thus, reducing the usability and comparability of the information.
- The requirements were oriented specifically toward general-purpose local governments, leaving other types of governments with little guidance on adapting the requirements to their particular circumstances. The result has been incomplete and inconsistent application of the standards with little thought to the value of the material to the user or to a basis for comparison with like entities.
- Finally and obviously, the 1979 requirements for the statistical section did not cover the new information governmental bodies are required to present in their financial statements under GASB Statement 34.

The statistical section is made up of schedules presenting the required information. In order to clarify that the requirements are applicable to all types of state and local governmental entities that prepare a statistical section, this Statement establishes the objectives of the statistical section and the five categories of information it is expected to contain:

1. Financial trends information.
2. Revenue capacity information.
3. Debt capacity information.
4. Demographic and economic information.
5. Operating information.

Not only does GASB Statement 44 establish new requirements for the statistical section, but it also attempts to clarify and update some of the previous requirements. The NCGA requirements included a schedule of "miscellaneous statistics." The new Statement specifies that a statistical section should include ten-year trends in three types of operating information: government employment levels, operating statistics, and capital asset information.

This Statement also clarifies certain features of previously required information, such as which governmental funds to include in information about trends in changes in fund balances. It also updates the schedules to include requirements for governments to report the many types of debt they now issue in addition to general obligation bonds that were previously reported. In addition, it replaces prior requirements, which were oriented toward general-purpose local governments. These clearer, more meaningful guidelines can be implemented by any type of governmental body.

With a nod to the average citizen and the less sophisticated investor, the understandability and usefulness of statistical section information is further improved by requiring governments to include notes regarding sources, methodologies, and assumptions, and narrative explanations of:

- The objectives of statistical section information.
- Unfamiliar concepts.
- Relationships between information in the statistical section and elsewhere in the financial report.
- Atypical trends and anomalous data that users would not otherwise understand.

The most significant new information added to the statistical section is the government-wide, accrual-based information required by Statement 34. The statistical section will include ten-year trend information about net assets and changes in net assets. The debt information presented in the statistical section will also be more comprehensive as a result of the requirement to include information from the government-wide financial statements and notes.

It is important to note that the statistical section is a required part of a comprehensive annual financial report (CAFR) if the body does, in fact, present the basic financial statements within a CAFR. Although governments are not required to prepare a statistical section, if they do include one in their basic financial statements, it must now meet the requirements of GASB Statement 44.

Statement 44 is effective for periods beginning after June 15, 2005.

¶8031 GASB Issues Statement 43 to Improve Postemployment Benefit Plan Reporting

In May 2004, the GASB issued Statement No. 43, *Financial Reporting for Postemployment Benefit Plans Other Than Pension Plans.* In addition to pensions, many state and local governmental employers provide other postemployment benefits (OPEB) as part of the total compensation offered to attract and retain the services of qualified employees. OPEB includes postemployment healthcare as well as other forms of postemployment benefits (e.g., life insurance) when provided separately from a pension plan.

GASB Statement 43 establishes uniform financial reporting standards for OPEB plans and supersedes the interim guidance included in Statement No. 26, *Financial Reporting for Postemployment Healthcare Plans Administered by Defined Benefit Pension Plans.* The approach in this Statement generally is consistent with the approach adopted in Statement No. 25, *Financial Reporting for Defined Benefit Pension Plans and Note Disclosures for Defined Contribution Plans,* with modifications to reflect differences between pension plans and OPEB plans.

The Statement covers requirements in financial reports for:

- OPEB trust funds included in the financial reports of plan sponsors or employers.
- The stand-alone financial reports of OPEB plans.
- The public employee retirement systems.
- Third parties that administer retirement systems.
- OPEB funds reported by administrators of multiple-employer OPEB plans, in which the fund used to accumulate assets and pay benefits or premiums when they are due is not a trust fund.

The Board believes that GASB Statement 43 provides a framework for transparent financial reporting by governmental entities that have fiduciary responsibility for OPEB plan assets regarding their stewardship of plan assets, the funded status and funding progress of the plan, and employer contributions to the plan. Very explicit requirements have been specified for the different types of plans that require close attention to the details relating to the financial reporting framework and measurement of the various plans.

To further cover this area, the Board has drafted an additional standard: *Accounting and Financial Reporting by Employers for Postemployment Benefits Other Than Pensions*, issued as GASB Statement 45. Statement 45, referred to as "the related Statement," addresses standards for the measurement, recognition, and display of employers' OPEB expense/expenditures and related liabilities (assets); note disclosures; and, if applicable, required supplementary information (RSI).

The measurement and disclosure requirements of the two Statements (GASBs 43 and 45) are related, and disclosure requirements are coordinated to avoid duplication when an OPEB plan is included as a trust or agency fund in an employer's financial report. In addition, reduced disclosures are acceptable for OPEB trust or agency funds when a stand-alone plan financial report is publicly available and contains all of the information required in this Statement.

.01   Plans Not Administered as Trusts or Equivalent Arrangements

Multiple-employer defined benefit OPEB plans that are not administered as trusts or equivalent arrangements should be reported as agency funds. Any assets accumulated in excess of liabilities to pay premiums or benefits, or for investment or administrative expenses, should be offset by liabilities to participating employers. Required notes to the financial statements include a brief plan description, a summary of significant accounting policies, and information about contributions.

.02   Defined Contribution Plans

Defined contribution plans that provide OPEB are required to follow the requirements for financial reporting by fiduciary funds generally, and by component units that are fiduciary in nature, set forth in Statement 34 and the disclosure requirements set forth in paragraph 41 of Statement 25.

¶8032   GASB 45 Addresses Employer Reporting of OPEB

GASB Statement No. 45, *Accounting and Financial Reporting by Employers for Postemployment Benefits Other Than Pensions*, adopted in August 2004, addresses how state and local governments should account for and report their costs and obligations related to postemployment healthcare and other nonpension benefits. Collectively, these benefits are commonly referred to as *other postemployment benefits*, or *OPEB*.

The statement generally requires that state and local governmental employers account for and report the annual cost of OPEB and the outstanding obligations and commitments related to OPEB in essentially the same manner as they currently do for pensions. Annual OPEB cost for most employers will be based on actuarially determined amounts that, if paid on an ongoing basis, generally would provide sufficient resources to pay benefits as they come due.

¶8033   GASB 42, *Accounting and Financial Reporting for Impairment of Capital Assets and for Insurance Recoveries*

In November 2003, the GASB published Statement No. 42, *Accounting and Financial Reporting for Impairment of Capital Assets and for Insurance Recoveries*, that requires governments to report the effects of capital asset impairment in their financial statements when loss of service utility occurs, rather than as a part of the ongoing depreciation expense or upon disposal of the capital asset. The guidance also enhances comparability of financial statements by requiring all governments to account for insurance recoveries in the same manner.

Because capital assets are long-lived, they are exposed to various risks. Governments are required to evaluate prominent events or changes in circumstances affecting capital assets to determine whether impairment of a capital asset has actually occurred. Events or changes in circumstances that may indicate impairment include:

- Evidence of physical damage
- Enactment or approval of laws or regulations
- Changes in environmental factors

- Technological changes
- Evidence of obsolescence
- Changes in the manner or duration of use of a capital asset
- Construction stoppage.

A capital asset generally should be considered impaired if both the decline in service utility of the capital asset is large in magnitude and the event or change in circumstance is outside the normal life cycle of the capital asset. The statement defines "impairment" as a significant unexpected decline in the service utility of an asset. "Significant" refers to the relative financial impact of the decline in value of the asset. "Unexpected" refers to something that management did not expect when it acquired the asset. The Board has indicated that they are well aware that what is significant for a small entity could have no significance whatsoever for a much larger entity.

Losses are to be reported in accordance with the guidance in pertinent sections of Statement No. 34, *Basic Financial Statements—and Management's Discussion and Analysis—for State and Local Governments*, and Accounting Principles Board Opinion No. 30, *Reporting the Results of Operations—Reporting the Effects of Disposal of a Segment of a Business, and Extraordinary, Unusual and Infrequently Occurring Events and Transactions.*

¶8034   Business-Like Accounting Comes to State and Local Government: GASB 34

The Governmental Accounting Standards Board unanimously adopted the long-awaited comprehensive changes for state and local government financial reporting throughout the country in June 1999. GASB Statement No. 34, *Basic Financial Statements—and Management's Discussion and Analysis—for State and Local Governments*, provides a new look and focus in reporting public finance in the U.S. The Board's action may have been a response to the oft-voiced complaint, "if only they'd run the government more like a business!" Now "they" must, at least from an accounting standpoint. Many big "businesses" and even more mid-size and small "businesses"—states, cities, counties, towns—adding up to a total of 87,000 in 1999, according to the GASB, are adopting the new measures.

.01   The GASB Gains Stature

GASB Statement 34 can certainly be considered the most significant change in the history of governmental accounting and should signal the "coming of age" of the GASB. It represents a dramatic shift in the manner and comprehensiveness in which state and local governments present financial information to the public. When fully implemented, it will create new information and will restructure much of the fund information that governments have presented in the past.

The new requirements were developed to make annual reports more comprehensive and easier to understand and use. Now, anyone with an interest (vested or otherwise) in public finance—citizens, the media, bond raters, creditors, investors, legislators, investment bankers and others—will have readily available information about the respective governmental bodies.

Thousands of preparers, auditors, academics, and users of governmental financial statements participated during a decade and a half in the research, consideration, and deliberations that preceded the publication of Statement 34. Members of various task forces began work on this and related projects as early as 1985.

.02   Provisions of GASB 34

Among the major innovations of Statement 34, governments are required to:

1.   Report on the *overall* state of the government's financial health, not just its individual funds as has been the case.
2.   Provide the most complete information ever made available about the cost of providing services to the citizens.
3.   Prepare an introductory narrative section (the Management's Discussion and Analysis—MD&A) to the basic report analyzing the government's financial performance.
4.   Provide enhanced fund reporting.
5.   Include information about the government's public infrastructure assets. The Statement explains these assets as long-lived assets that are normally stationary and capable of being preserved longer than most capital assets. Bridges, roads, storm sewers, tunnels, drainage systems, dams, lighting systems, and swimming pools are among those mentioned. (This is certainly the most innovative requirement introduced to governmental financial reporting.)

.03   Background Information

The GASB's first Concepts Statement, *Objectives of Financial Reporting*, issued in 1987, identified what the Board believed were the most important objectives of financial reporting by governments. Some of those objectives reaffirm the importance of information that governmental units have historically included in their annual reports. To cover more of the original objectives, the Board felt it necessary to provide for a much broader range of information.

As a result, Statement 34 is a dual-perspective report requiring governmental bodies to retain much of the information they currently report, but also requiring them to go further in revealing their operations. The first perspective focuses on the traditional funds with some additional information required for major funds. The second perspective is government-wide to provide an entirely new look at a government's financial activities.

The Board feels that adding new material will result in reports that accomplish more of the objectives emphasized in the original concepts Statement.

.04 The Time for Accountability Is Now

According to the GASB, state and local governments in the U.S. invest approximately $140–$150 billion annually in the construction, improvement, and rehabilitation of capital assets, including infrastructure assets like bridges, highways, and sewers. Since these expenditures represent more than 10 percent of the monies spent by those governments, it would appear quite natural for them to be accounted for in financial documents readily available to the public.

The majority of this infrastructure investment is financed by borrowing—selling municipal bonds and using the proceeds to pay for construction. (Enter the investor.)

The need for public accountability arises when such sums are spent and when current and future generations are committed to repay such debts. The public should know how much governments spend on infrastructure construction and how much they borrow to finance it. (Enter the taxpayer.)

The public also wants to know if government officials subsequently are caring for the infrastructure they have built with public resources. (Enter the voter.)

Although the need for information about infrastructure should be fairly obvious, the primary instruments for demonstrating fiscal accountability (the government's annual financial statements) have not previously been required to provide this information. The accounting method for preparing state and local government financial statements has focused on short-term financial resources like cash and investments. Infrastructures have been left off the balance sheet and no charge was included on the income statement for the cost of using the infrastructure assets to provide services. Because of the significant share of government spending devoted to capital assets, this has been a major omission. But with the advent of GASB Statement 34, all of that is changing.

.05 Retention of Fund Accounting

Annual reports currently provide information about funds. Most funds are established by governing bodies (such as state legislatures, city councils, or school boards) to show restrictions on the planned use of resources or to measure, *in the short term*, the revenues and expenditures arising from certain activities.

GASB Statement 1 noted that annual reports should allow users to assess a government's accountability by assisting them in determining compliance with finance-related laws, rules, and regulations.

This new Statement requires governments to continue to present financial statements that provide fund information. The focus of these statements has been sharpened to require governments to report information about their major funds, including the general fund. In previous annual reports, fund information was reported in the aggregate by fund type. This often made it difficult for users to assess accountability of any "public servants."

Fund statements continue to measure and report the "operating results" of many funds by measuring cash on hand and other assets that can be easily converted to cash. These statements show the performance, in the short term, of individual funds using the same measures that many governments use when financing their current operations. The Board points out that if a government issues fifteen-year debt to build a school, it does not collect taxes in the first year sufficient to repay the *entire* debt; it levies and collects what is needed to make that year's required payments. On the other hand, when governments charge a fee to users for services—as is done for most water or electric utilities—fund information continues to be based on accrual accounting to ensure all costs of providing services are being measured.

.06 The All-Important Governmental Budget

Showing budgetary compliance is an important component of government's accountability. (At the national level, with which GASB Statement 34 has no connection, of course, THE BUDGET is undoubtedly the most widely recognized financial document.) At the state and local levels, diverse citizen groups, special interest groups, and individuals participate in the process of establishing the original annual operating budgets of the particular body.

Governments will be required to continue to provide budgetary comparison information in their annual reports. An important change that should certainly make the comparison more meaningful is the requirement to add the government's *original* budget to that comparison. Many governments revise their original budgets during the year for various reasons. Requiring governments to report that original document in addition to their *revised* budget adds a new analytical dimension and should increase the usefulness of the budgetary comparison.

.07 Required Supplementary Information

To demonstrate whether resources were obtained and used in accordance with the government's legally adopted budget, RSI should include budgetary comparison schedules for the general fund and for each major special revenue fund that has a legally adopted annual budget.

The budgetary comparison schedules should include:

1. The original budget.
2. The final appropriated budgets for the reporting period.
3. Actual inflows, outflows, and balances, stated on the government's budgetary basis.

As pointed out above, the Statement also requires certain disclosures in RSI for governments that use the modified approach for reporting infrastructure assets and data currently required by earlier Statements.

Presumably, the original budget was the "best thought" of the adopting body at the time. Subsequent "revised" budgets could be the result of political pressures or personal preferences. The GASB concedes that budgetary changes are not necessarily undesirable. However, the Board decided that in the interest of accountability to those who were aware of, and may have made decisions based upon the original budget, inclusion of its contents could deter ill-considered changes. The comparison also gives the user a look at any changes that have been made. The Board suggested that this is an additional method of assessing the governmental body's ability to estimate and manage its general resources—without too many detours.

Thus, the original budget, the final appropriated budgets and the actual inflows, outflows and balances stated on the government's budgetary basis are mandated as required supplemental information (RSI) for the general fund and for each major special revenue fund that has a legally adopted annual budget. Rather than include this information in RSI, a government may elect to report these comparisons in a budgetary comparison statement as part of the basic financial statements.

.08   New Information Is Readily Available

For the first time, government financial managers are required to introduce the financial report by sharing their attitude toward and understanding of the transactions, events, and conditions reflected in the government's report and of the fiscal policies that govern its operations. The required management's discussion and analysis (MD&A) should give the users an easily readable analysis of the government's *financial* performance for the year. Users thus have information they need to help them gauge the government's state of financial health as a result of the year's operations.

Additionally, financial managers themselves are in a better position to provide this analysis because, for the first time, the annual report also includes new government-wide financial statements prepared using accrual accounting for all of the government's activities. Most governmental utilities and private-sector companies use accrual accounting. With GASB Statement 34, state and local governments join most of the rest of the world in using it. The reason for the change is that accrual accounting measures not just current assets and liabilities, but also long-term assets and liabilities (such as capital assets, including infrastructure, and general obligation debt). It also reports all revenues and all costs of providing services each year, not just those received or paid in the current year or soon after year-end. After all, government is an ongoing endeavor; officials elected or appointed come and go.

.09   Users Benefit

These government wide financial statements undoubtedly will help users:

1. Assess the finances of a government in its entirety, including the year's operating results.
2. Determine whether a government's overall financial position improved or deteriorated.
3. Evaluate whether a government's current-year revenues were sufficient to pay for current-year services.
4. Be aware of the cost of providing services to the citizenry.
5. Become cognizant of the way in which a government finances its programs— through user fees and other program revenues, or general tax revenues.
6. Understand the extent to which a government has invested in capital assets, including roads, bridges, and other infrastructure assets.
7. Make better comparisons between governments.

.10   Required Information and Format

GASB Statement 34 sets financial reporting standards for state and local governments, including states, cities, towns, villages, and special-purpose governments such as school districts and public utilities. It establishes that the basic financial statements and required supplementary information for general purpose governments should consist of:

1. *Management's Discussion and Analysis.* MD&A introduces the basic financial statements and provides an analytical overview of the government's financial activities. Although it is required supplementary information and one would expect to find it in the final portion of the report, governments are required to present MD&A *before* the basic financial statements. Presumably the belief is that a clearly written—plain English, perhaps—introduction provides a link between the two perspectives (fund and government-wide) to prepare the reader for a better understanding of the financial statements.
2. *Basic Financial Statements.* The basic financial statements must include:
    a. *Government-wide financial statements*, consisting of a statement of net assets and a statement of activities. Prepared using the economic resources

measurement focus and the accrual basis of accounting, these statements should report all of the assets, liabilities, revenues, expenses, and gains and losses of the government. Each statement should distinguish between the *governmental* and *business-type activities* of the primary government and between the total primary government and the separately presented component units by reporting each in separate columns. (*Fiduciary activities*, with resources not available to finance the government's programs, are not included in the government-wide statements.)

b. *Fund financial statements* consisting of a series of statements that focus on information about the government's major governmental and enterprise funds, including blended component units. Fund financial statements also should report information about a government's fiduciary funds and component units that are fiduciary in nature.

c. *Governmental* fund financial statements (including financial data for the general fund and special revenue, capital projects, debt service, and permanent funds). These are to be prepared using the current financial resources measurement focus and the modified accrual basis of accounting.

d. *Proprietary* fund financial statements (including financial data for enterprise and internal service funds) and *fiduciary* fund financial statements (including financial data for fiduciary funds and similar component units). This group is to be prepared using the economic resources measurement focus and the accrual basis of accounting.

e. *Notes to the financial statements* are notes and explanations that provide information which is *essential* to a user's understanding of the basic financial statements.

3. **Required Supplementary Information (RSI).** In addition to MD&A, this Statement requires *budgetary comparison schedules* to be presented as RSI along with other types of data as required by previous GASB pronouncements. This Statement also requires RSI for governments that use the modified approach for reporting infrastructure assets.

Special-purpose governments engaged in only governmental activities (such as some library districts) or engaged in both governmental and business-type activities (such as some school districts) should normally be reported in the same manner as general purpose governments. Special-purpose governments engaged only in business-type activities (such as utilities) should present the financial statements required for enterprise funds, including MD&A and other RSI.

.11   Content of MD&A

MD&A should provide an objective and easily readable analysis of the government's financial activities based on currently known facts, decisions, or conditions. It should be emphasized that this section is a preparation for the casual reader who is less skilled in reading financial statements as well as for the more experienced "user" to understand fully the implications of the basic report. MD&A should include:

1. Comparisons of the current year to the prior year based on the government-wide information.
2. An analysis of the government's overall financial position and results of operations to assist users in assessing whether that financial position has improved or deteriorated as a result of the year's activities.
3. An analysis of balances and transactions of individual funds and significant budget variances.
4. A description of capital asset and long-term debt activity during the period.
5. A conclusion with a description of currently known facts, decisions, or conditions that could be expected to have a significant effect upon the financial position or results of operations.

.12   Government-Wide Financial Statements

The new annual reports contain much more comprehensive financial information. Government-wide statements now display information about the reporting government as a whole, except for its fiduciary activities. These statements include separate columns for the governmental and business-type activities of the primary government and its component parts. Government-wide statements are prepared using the economic resources measurement focus and the accrual basis of accounting. This latter requirement is a fairly dramatic step forward since heretofore governmental accounting followed only the modified-accrual basis. The statement must include a statement of net assets as well as all of the government's activities, not just those that cover costs by charging a fee for services, as currently required.

Governments should report all *capital assets*, including infrastructure assets, in the government-wide statement of net assets and generally should report depreciation expenses in the statement of activities. Infrastructure assets that are part of a network or subsystem of a network are not required to be depreciated as long as the government manages those assets using an asset management system that has certain characteristics and the government can document that the assets are being preserved approximately at (or above) a condition level established and disclosed by the government in the RSI.

To qualify for a qualified asset management system, the government must:

1. Have an up-to-date inventory of the eligible infrastructure assets.
2. Perform condition assessments of the eligible assets and summarize the results using a measurement scale.

3. Estimate each year the annual amounts necessary to maintain and preserve the assets at the established and disclosed condition level. Condition assessments are to be documented so that they can be replicated. The assessments may be performed by the government itself or by contract with an outside source.

The net assets of a government should be reported in three categories— *invested in capital assets net of related debt, restricted, and unrestricted.* Net assets are considered "restricted" when constraints are placed on their use by:

1. External sources such as creditors, grantors or contributors.
2. Laws or regulations of other governments.
3. Legal or constitutional provisions or enabling legislation.

Permanent endowments or permanent fund principal amounts included in restricted net assets should be displayed in two additional components— *expendable and nonexpendable.*

The government-wide *statement of activities* should be presented in a format that reports expenses minus program revenues, to obtain a measurement of "net (expense) revenue" for each of the government's functions. Program expenses should include all direct expenses. General revenues, such as taxes, and special and extraordinary items should be reported separately to arrive at the change in net assets for the period.

Special and extraordinary items are both significant transactions or other events, either unusual or infrequent, over which management has control. Both types should be reported separately at the bottom of the statement of activities with special items listed prior to any extraordinary items. These types of transactions or events over which a government does not have control should be disclosed in the notes to financial statements.

.13   Fund Financial Statements

To report additional and detailed information about the primary government, separate fund financial statements should be presented for each fund category: governmental, proprietary and fiduciary.

1. *Governmental funds* report on the basic activities of the government, including general fund accounts and special revenue, capital projects, debt service, and permanent funds.
2. *Proprietary funds* cover activities that are generally financed and operated like private businesses such as enterprise (fees charged to outside users) and internal service funds.
3. *Fiduciary funds* include pension and other employee benefit and private purpose trust funds that cannot be used to support the government's own programs.

Required *governmental fund* statements are:

1. A balance sheet.
2. A statement of revenues, expenditures, and changes in fund balances.

Required *proprietary fund* statements are:

1. A statement of net assets.
2. A statement of revenues, expenses, and changes in fund net assets.
3. A statement of cash flows.

To allow users to assess the relationship between fund and government-wide financial statements, governments should present a summary reconciliation to the government-wide financial statements at the bottom of the fund financial statements or in an accompanying schedule.

Each of the fund statements should report separate columns for the *general fund* and for *other major governmental and enterprise funds*.

1. *Major funds* are funds in which revenues, expenditures/expenses, assets, or liabilities (excluding extraordinary items) are at least 10 percent of corresponding totals for all governmental or enterprise funds and at least 5 percent of the aggregate amount for all governmental and enterprise funds. Any other fund may be reported as a major fund if the government's officials consider it to be particularly important to financial statement users.
2. *Nonmajor funds* should be reported in the aggregate in a separate column.
3. *Internal service funds* also should be reported in the aggregate in a separate column on the proprietary fund statements.

Fund balances for governmental funds should also be segregated into *reserved* and *unreserved* categories. Proprietary fund net assets should be reported in the same categories required for the government-wide financial statements. Proprietary fund statements of net assets should distinguish between current and noncurrent assets and liabilities and should display restricted assets.

Proprietary fund statements of revenues, expenses, and changes in fund net assets should distinguish between operating and nonoperating revenues and expenses. These statements should also report capital contributions, contributions to permanent and term endowments, special and extraordinary items, and transfers separately at the bottom of the statement to arrive at the all-inclusive change in fund net assets. Cash flow statements should be prepared using the direct method.

Separate fiduciary fund statements (including component units that are fiduciary in nature) also should be presented as part of the fund financial statements. Fiduciary funds should be used to report assets that are held in a trustee or agency capacity for others and that cannot be used to support the government's own programs.

Required *fiduciary fund* statements are:

1. A statement of fiduciary net assets.
2. A statement of changes in fiduciary net assets.

Interfund activity includes interfund loans, interfund services provided and used, and interfund transfers. This activity should be reported separately in the fund financial statements and generally should be eliminated in the aggregated government-wide financial statements.

.14   Interpretation Relating to Modified Accrual Standards

The Board decided this Interpretation was necessary to shore up usage of modified accrual accounting used in governmental fund accounting retained by GASB Statement 34.

Interpretation 6, *Recognition and Measurement of Certain Liabilities and Expenditures in Governmental Fund Financial Statements*, addresses concerns about the interpretation and application of existing *modified accrual standards*. The purpose of modified accrual accounting is to measure flows of current financial resources in governmental *fund financial statements*.

This Interpretation clarifies the application of existing standards for distinguishing between the portions of certain types of liabilities that should be reported as:

1. Governmental fund liabilities and expenditures.
2. General long-term liabilities of the government.

Statement No. 34, *Basic Financial Statements—and Management's Discussion and Analysis—for State and Local Governments*, carried forward the requirement that governmental fund financial statements be prepared using the existing financial resources measurement focus and the modified accrual basis of accounting. This traditional measurement focus and basis of accounting provides useful information related to a government's fiscal accountability, as part of the new financial reporting model. In addition, the new model provides useful information related to a government's operational accountability, including government-wide financial statements prepared on the *accrual basis* of accounting.

Concerns had been raised, however, about the interpretation and application of *existing modified accrual standards*. These concerns included:

1. Lack of comparability in the application of standards for recognition of certain fund liabilities and expenditures.
2. Perceived subjectivity of some interpretations and applications.
3. Potential circularity of the criteria for recognition of revenues and expenditures.

The objective of Interpretation 6 is to improve the comparability, consistency, and objectivity of financial reporting in governmental fund financial statements by providing a common, internally consistent interpretation of standards in areas where practice differences have occurred or could occur.

The effective date of this Interpretation was designed to coincide with the effective date of Statement 34 for the particular reporting government.

¶8035   GASB 35 Comes to Public Colleges and Universities

After an earlier decision by the Governmental Accounting Standards Board not to require a separate financial reporting model for public colleges and universities in order to make it easier for state and local governments to include these, institutions in their financial statements, the GASB issued a proposal in July 1999 to provide accounting and financial reporting guidance for public colleges and universities in their separately issued financial statements. That proposal became GASB Statement 35.

This Statement amends GASB Statement No. 34, *Basic Financial Statements— and Management's Discussion and Analysis—for State and Local Governments*, to include public colleges and universities within its guidance for general purpose external financial reporting.

It is anticipated that this step will make it easier to compare public institutions and their private counterparts. Such a step had been requested by GASB constituents.

Under the new guidance, public colleges and universities can report their finances as public institutions:

1. Engaged only in business-type activities.
2. Engaged only in governmental activities.
3. Engaged in both governmental and business-type activities.

A public institution is also required to include the following in separately issued financial reports, regardless of whether or not they are legally separate entities:

1. Management's discussion and analysis (MD&A).
2. Basic financial statements, as appropriate for the category of special-purpose government reporting.
3. Notes to the financial statements.
4. Required supplementary information other than MD&A.

The requirements of the Statement are effective in three phases for public institutions that are not part of another reporting entity, beginning with fiscal years beginning after June 15, 2001. All public institutions that are part of (or are component units of) a primary government were required to implement this standard at least by the same time as its primary government, regardless of the phase-in guidance contained in GASB Statement 34.

Public colleges and universities are required to report infrastructure assets as follows:

1. Public institutions that are not part of another primary government and report as either special-purpose governments engaged only in governmental activities or engaged in both governmental and business-type activities must report infrastructure in accordance with the phase-in guidance of GASB Statement 34 beginning with fiscal years ending after June 15, 2005.
2. Public institutions that report as special-purpose governments engaged only in business-type activities are required to report infrastructure upon implementation, without regard to the phase-in periods included in Statement 34.

¶8036   GASB 38, *Certain Financial Statement Note Disclosures*

Statement 38 modifies, adds, and deletes various note disclosure requirements. The requirements cover such areas as:

1. Revenue recognition policies.
2. Actions taken in response to legal violations.
3. Debt service requirements.
4. Variable-rate debt.
5. Receivable and payable balances.
6. Interfund transfers and balances.
7. Short-term debt.

The new requirements are an additional attempt to address the needs of users of financial statements as determined through ongoing Board research. In discussing the benefits to users, the Board considered that with respect to interfund transfers, users of financial statements will, for the first time, be able to trace transfers from the source fund to the receiving fund and to understand why the government uses transfers.

¶8037   GASB 37, *Basic Financial Statements—and Management's Discussion and Analysis—for State and Local Governments: Omnibus—An Amendment of GASB Statements 21 and 34*

GASB Statement 37, which was adopted in June 2001, amends GASB Statement No. 21, *Accounting for Escheat Property,* and GASB Statement No. 34, *Basic Financial Statements—and Management's Discussion and Analysis—for State and Local Governments.*

The amendments to Statement 21 are necessary because of the changes to the fiduciary fund structure required by Statement 34. Generally, escheat property that was previously reported in an *expendable trust fund* should now be reported in a *private-purpose trust fund* under Statement 34. Statement 37 explains the effects of that change.

The amendments to Statement 34 either:

1. Clarify certain provisions that, in retrospect, may not be sufficiently clear for consistent application, or
2. Modify other provisions that the Board believes may have unintended consequences in some circumstances.

The provisions aimed at clarifying previous provisions are not new but may have been unclear or confusing for the user. They include:

1. *Management's Discussion and Analysis (MD&A) requirements—* Governments should confine the topics discussed in MD&A to those listed in Statement 34 rather than consider those topics as "minimum requirements."
2. *Modified approach—*Adopting the modified approach for infrastructure assets that have previously been depreciated is considered a change in an *accounting estimate.* The effect of the change is accounted for prospectively rather than as a restatement of prior periods.
3. *Program revenue classifications—*Fines and forfeitures should be included in the broad *charges for services* category. Also, additional guidance is provided to aid in determining to which function certain program revenues pertain.
4. *Major fund criteria—*Major fund reporting requirements apply to a governmental or enterprise fund if the *same* element (for example, revenues) exceeds *both* the 10 percent *and* 5 percent criteria.

The provisions, which are modifications of the requirements of Statement 34, include:

1. Eliminating the requirement to capitalize construction-period interest for governmental activities.
2. Changing the minimum level of detail required for business-type activities in the statement of activities from *segments* to *different identifiable activities*.

¶8038   GASB 36 on Symmetry Between Recipients and Providers in Accounting for Certain Shared Revenues

GASB Statement 36 amends GASB Statement No. 33, *Accounting and Financial Reporting for Non-exchange Transactions*, which required recipients of shared derived tax or imposed nonexchange revenue to account for it differently from the provider government. This practice could have resulted in the two governments recognizing the sharing at different times.

The Statement provides symmetrical accounting treatment for both the giver and receiver of the shared revenue. Statement 36 eliminates the timing difference by requiring recipients to account for the sharing in the same way as provider governments.

CHAPTER 9
Governmental Fund Accounting

Note: Some information in this chapter may be redundant with Chapter 8. While Chapter 8 is intended to cover the majority of government accounting standards, this chapter primarily focuses on fund accounting. There is, understandably, common information in the two objectives.

¶9000   Overview

The Government Accounting Standards Board (GASB) Statement No. 34, *Basic Financial Statements—and Management's Discussion and Analysis—for State and Local Governments*, established new financial reporting requirements for state and local governments. However, the Statement made it quite clear that these entities are to continue to present financial statements that provide fund information. The focus of these fund statements was sharpened to require governments to report information about their major funds, including the general fund. In current annual reports, fund information is reported in the aggregate by fund type. This has often made it difficult for users to assess accountability.

The GASB points out that fund balance information is of importance to municipal bond analysts, fund taxpayer associations, research organizations, oversight bodies, state, county and local legislators and their staffs, and reporters. Financial statement users examine fund balance information to identify the available liquid resources that can be used to repay long-term debt, reduce property taxes, add new governmental programs, expand existing ones, or enhance the financial position of the government.

¶9001 GASB Issues Statements No. 67 and No. 68 on Pensions and No. 65 and No. 66 on Financial Reporting to Improve Pension Standards

To ensure that GASB pronouncements continue to be of high quality and are in line with the continuously evolving government environment, the GASB periodically reexamines its standards. Reexamination typically takes place after a Statement has been in place and fully implemented for at least five years. Research on the GASB's pension standards, for example, indicated opportunities for significant improvement as well as for other important practice issues for state and local governments.

.01 Issues Statements No. 67 and No. 68 Improve Pension Accounting and Financial Reporting

In June 2012, the Governmental Accounting Standards Board approved two standards that improve the accounting and financial reporting of public employee pensions by state and local governments. Statement No. 68, *Accounting and Financial Reporting for Pensions*, revises and establishes new financial reporting requirements for most governments that provide their employees with pension benefits. Statement No. 67, *Financial Reporting for Pension Plans*, revises existing guidance for the financial reports of most pension plans. In March 2016, GASB issued Statement 82 that amends Statements 67, 68 and 73 on pension issues. The Statement amends Statements 67 and 68 to require the presentation of covered payroll, rather than that of covered-employee payroll in schedules of required supplementary information. See ¶8004.01.

Statement 68 (Employers). Statement 68 replaces the requirements of Statement No. 27, *Accounting for Pensions by State and Local Governmental Employers,* and Statement No. 50, *Pension Disclosures,* as they relate to governments that provide pensions through pension plans administered as trusts or similar arrangements that meet certain criteria. Under requirements of Statement 68, governments providing defined benefit pensions to:

- Recognize their long-term obligation for pension benefits as a liability for the first time,
- Measure more comprehensively and comparably the annual costs of pension benefits, and

- Enhance accountability and transparency through revised and new note disclosures and required supplementary information (RSI).

Statement 67 (Plans). This Statement replaces the requirements of Statement No. 25, *Financial Reporting for Defined Benefit Pension Plans and Note Disclosures for Defined Contribution Plans,* and Statement 50 as they relate to pension plans that are administered through trusts or similar arrangements meeting certain criteria. The Statement builds upon the existing framework for financial reports of defined benefit pension plans, which includes:

- A statement of fiduciary net position (the amount held in a trust for paying retirement benefits) and
- A statement of changes in fiduciary net position.

Statement 67 enhances note disclosures and RSI for both defined benefit and defined contribution pension plans. Statement 67 also requires the presentation of new information about annual money-weighted rates of return in the notes to the financial statements and in ten-year RSI schedules.

Effective Dates and Availability. The provisions in Statement 67 are effective for financial statements for periods beginning after June 15, 2013. The provisions in Statement 68 are effective for fiscal years beginning after June 15, 2014. Earlier application is encouraged for both Statements.

(For further information on Statements No. 67 and No. 68, please see the chapter, "Governmental Accounting.")

.02   GASB Issues Statements No. 65 and No. 66 Regarding State and Local Governments

The Governmental Accounting Standards Board (GASB) issued two Statements addressing important practice issues for state and local governments on April 2, 2012:

1. Statement No. 66, *Technical Corrections—2012,* enhances the usefulness of financial reports by resolving conflicting accounting and financial reporting guidance that could diminish the consistency of financial reporting.
2. Statement No. 65, *Items Previously Reported as Assets and Liabilities,* clarifies the appropriate reporting of deferred outflows of resources and deferred inflows of resources to ensure consistency in financial reporting.

Statement 66 (Risk). Statement 66 amends Statement No. 10, *Accounting and Financial Reporting for Risk Financing and Related Insurance Issues,* by removing the provision that limits fund-based reporting of a state and local government's risk financing activities to the general fund and the internal service fund type. As a result, governments would base their decisions about governmental fund type usage for risk financing activities on the definitions in Statement No. 54, *Fund Balance Reporting and Governmental Fund Type Definitions*.

This Statement also amends Statement No. 62, *Codification of Accounting and Financial Reporting Guidance Contained in Pre-November 30, 1989 FASB and AICPA Pronouncements*, by modifying the specific guidance on accounting for:

- Operating lease payments that vary from a straight-line basis,
- The difference between the initial investment (purchase price) and the principal amount of a purchased loan or group of loans, and
- Servicing fees related to mortgage loans that are sold when the stated service fee rate differs significantly from a current (normal) servicing fee rate.

Statement 65 (Financial Statements). GASB Concepts Statement No. 4, *Elements of Financial Statements*, specifies that recognition of deferred outflows and deferred inflows should be limited to those instances specifically identified in authoritative GASB pronouncements. Consequently, guidance was needed to determine which balances being reported as assets and liabilities should actually be reported as deferred outflows of resources or deferred inflows of resources, according to the definitions in Concepts Statement 4. Based on those definitions, Statement 65 *reclassifies* certain items currently being reported as *assets and liabilities as deferred outflows of resources and deferred inflows of resources*. In addition, this Statement recognizes certain items currently being reported as assets and liabilities as outflows of resources and inflows of resources.

Thus, this Statement is designed to improve financial reporting by clarifying the appropriate use of the financial statement elements, "Deferred outflows of resources" and "Deferred inflows of resources" to ensure consistency in financial reporting.

The provisions of both Statements are effective for periods beginning after December 15, 2012.

(For further information on Statements No. 65 and No. 66, please see the chapter "Governmental Accounting.")

¶9002   GASB 62 Helps Practitioners Identify Guidance Applicable to State and Local Governments

The GASB issued Statement No. 62, *Codification of Accounting and Financial Reporting Guidance Contained in Pre-November 30, 1989 FASB and AICPA Pronouncements*, in December 2010. The Statement is intended to improve the usefulness of its Codification by incorporating guidance that previously could be found only in certain Financial Accounting Standards Board (FASB) and American Institute of Certified Public Accountants (AICPA) pronouncements.

The Statement incorporates into the GASB's authoritative literature the applicable guidance previously presented in the following pronouncements issued before November 30, 1989:

1. FASB Statements and Interpretations (APBs)
2. Accounting Principles Board Opinions
3. Accounting Research Bulletins of the AICPA's Committee on Accounting Procedure.

In addition, GASB 62 supersedes Statement No. 20, *Accounting and Financial Reporting for Proprietary Funds and Other Governmental Entities That Use Proprietary Fund Accounting*. For additional information about this Statement, see the chapter, "Governmental Accounting."

¶9003   GASB 54 Improves the Usefulness of Reported Fund Balance Information

The GASB issued Statement No. 54, *Fund Balance Reporting and Governmental Fund Type Definitions*, in March 2009. The Statement is expected to improve the usefulness of information provided to financial report users about fund balance by providing clearer, more structured fund balance classifications, and by clarifying the definitions of existing governmental fund types. It sets forth clear criteria for the reporting of fund balance so that users of governmental financial statements will receive consistent and easier to understand information that is useful for decision making.

Fund balance—the difference between assets and liabilities in the governmental fund financial statements—constitutes some of the most widely and frequently used information in state and local government financial reports. Diversity of practice in how fund balance has been reported by state and local governments has caused confusion among both preparers and users of financial statements. The Statement addresses these differences by establishing a hierarchy of fund balance classifications primarily based on the extent to which a government is bound to observe spending constraints imposed upon the use of resources reported in governmental fund balances.

Statement 54 distinguishes fund balance between amounts that are considered *nonspendable*, such as fund balance associated with inventories, and "spendable," such as fund balance associated with cash. The spendable category is further broken down based on the relative strength of the constraints that control how specific amounts can be spent. Beginning with the most binding constraints, fund balance amounts will be reported in the following classifications:

- *Restricted*—amounts constrained by external parties, constitutional provision, or enabling legislation
- *Committed*—amounts constrained by a government using its highest level of decision-making authority
- *Assigned*—amounts a government intends to use for a particular purpose
- *Unassigned*—amounts that are not constrained at all will be reported in the general fund.

The Statement also clarifies the definitions of individual governmental fund types. The basic definition of the debt service fund type remains essentially unchanged.

However, the terminology in the definition of the capital project fund type has been clarified to focus on the broader, more consistently understood notion of capital outlays, and to better capture the breadth of capital activities in today's environment.

Statement 54 also provides guidance on the classification of budget stabilization or rainy day funds because of their importance to financial statement users. Stabilization amounts that meet certain criteria are classified as committed or (less commonly) restricted, if imposed externally or by law. Stabilization funds are classified as committed if they are created by a resolution or ordinance that identifies the specific circumstances under which the resources may be expended. Stabilization amounts that are available in emergencies or in periods of revenue shortfalls would not be classified as committed unless the emergency or shortfall condition is specified and of a magnitude to distinguish it from events that occur routinely. Stabilization funds not meeting these conditions are reported as unassigned fund balance in the General Fund.

Fund balance reporting on financial statements is critical to understanding the financial health of state and local governments. According to the GASB, Statement 54 sets forth clear criteria for reporting fund balance so that users of governmental financial statements will receive more consistent and understandable information that is useful for making economic, social, and political decisions, the Board believes.

¶9004   Differences Between Governmental and Commercial Accounting

While both types of entities use double-entry bookkeeping procedures and either cash or accrual methods, and both prepare balance sheets and operating statements, there are many differences between commercial and governmental systems.

Governmental accounting is associated with:

- An absence of a profit;
- Compliance with statutory and/or legal requirements;

- A fundamental difference in the treatment of net worth. Commercial accounting provides accounting for preferred and common stock and retained earnings, with a paid-in capital account where appropriate. Governmental accounting treats "net worth" under account classifications *Reserve for Encumbrances or Unappropriated Surplus*;
- Characteristically, government accounts will include a *Reserve for Contingencies* account since the projected (budgeted) reserve may not materialize as the accounting year progresses.

Governmental Accounting, specifically accounting for state and local governments, is in a transitional stage. These entities have been adding more "business-like" requirements to their financial reporting. At the same time, the government accountant will still need to draw upon his or her knowledge of fund accounting.

.01   GASB Issues White Paper

The Governmental Accounting Standards Board released a white paper emphasizing this point that those who are interested in the financial performance of state and local governments have substantially different information needs than those who follow the financial performance of for-profit entities.

As mentioned above, these different and diverse needs result from basic differences between these types of entities: governments and businesses.

- The primary purpose of governments is to enhance or maintain the well-being of citizens by providing services in accordance with public policy goals.
- In contrast, for-profit business enterprises focus primarily on wealth creation, interacting principally with those segments of society that fulfill their mission of generating a financial return on investment for shareholders.

The white paper cites several other crucial differences that generate user demand for unique information:

- Governments serve a broader group of stakeholders, including taxpayers, citizens, elected representatives, oversight groups, bondholders, and others in the financial community.
- Most government revenues are raised through involuntary taxes rather than a willing exchange of comparable value between two parties in a typical business transaction.
- Monitoring actual compliance with budgeted public policy priorities is central to government public accountability reporting.
- Governments exist longer than for-profit businesses and are not typically subject to bankruptcy and dissolution.

Although investors and creditors are important constituencies of every standards-setting organization, the Governmental Accounting Standards Board's (GASB) conceptual framework also places priority on addressing the informational needs of citizens and elected representatives, two constituencies not identified as users of business enterprise financial statements by the Financial Accounting Standards Board (FASB).

The GASB's financial reporting objectives consider public accountability to be the cornerstone on which all other financial reporting objectives should be built. The Board agrees that investors and creditors are important constituencies of every standards-setting organization, but adds that their conceptual framework also places priority on addressing the informational needs of *citizens and elected representatives*, two constituencies not usually considered to be users of business enterprise financial statements.

Some of the most significant GASB standards that address differences in governmental and business financial reporting include:

- The measurement and recognition of certain types of revenues (for example, taxes and grants),
- The view that capital assets provide services to citizens rather than contribute to future cash flows,
- The use of fund accounting and budgetary reporting to meet public accountability needs,
- The use of accountability principles rather than equity control to define the financial reporting entity,
- The treatment of pensions and other postemployment benefits to allocate cost of services equitably to applicable periods.

The paper points out that the significant differences, and the important role that state and local governments play in the U.S. economy, are the primary reasons that separate accounting and financial reporting standards for governments are needed.

.02   State and Local Governments Employ 18.8 Million Full-Time Equivalent Employees in 2021

In March 2021, state and local governments employed 18.8 million people, a decrease of 4.6 percent from the 2020 figure of 19.7 million. (https//www.census.gov/content/dam/Census/library/publications/2021/econ/aspep-2021_final.pdf)

Local governments—which include counties, cities, townships, special dis-tricts and school districts—accounted for 14.2 million full-time equivalent employees in 2019.

These estimates come from the Census Bureau's Annual Survey of Public Employment and Payroll. The survey shows totals for state and local gov-ernment full-time and part-time employment and details employment by government function at the national and state level.

¶9005   GASB Issues Statement 52, *Land and Other Real Estate Held as Investments by Endowments*

In November 2007, the GASB issued Statement No. 52, *Land and Other Real Estate Held as Investments by Endowments*. The statement improves the quality of financial reporting by requiring endowments to report their land and other real estate investments at fair value, creating consistency in re-porting among similar entities that exist to invest resources for the purpose of generating income.

Prior to the issuance of Statement 52, state and local government endow-ments were required to report land and other real estate held as investments at historical cost, which provides information on investment results *only in the year the investments are sold*. However, entities that perform investment func-tions similar to endowments—including pension plans, other post employment benefit (OPEB) plans, external investment pools, and Internal Revenue Code Section 457 deferred compensation plans—have been required to report their land and real estate investments at fair value. Reporting those investments at fair value provides more decision-useful information about their composition, current value, and recent changes in value.

In order to help users of financial statements better evaluate an endowment's investment decisions and performance, Statement 52 requires governments to report the changes in fair value as investment income. It also requires them to disclose the methods and significant assumptions employed to determine fair value, and to provide other information that they currently present for other investments reported at fair value.

¶9006   GASB Issues Concepts Statement No. 5, *Service Efforts and Accomplishments Reporting* (An Amendment of GASB Concepts Statement No. 2)

The Governmental Accounting Standards Board issued Concepts Statement No. 5, *Service Efforts and Accomplishments Reporting* (an amendment of GASB Concepts Statement No. 2), in December 2008. Concepts Statement 5 up-dates provisions in Concepts Statement 2 to reflect developments that have occurred since Concepts Statement 2 was issued in 1994. The proposed changes are based on the findings of extensive research by the GASB and others and the results of the GASB's monitoring of state and local governments that have been using and reporting service efforts and accomplishments (SEA) performance information.

The reporting of SEA performance information is an important method of demonstrating accountability for the resources raised by a government. SEA reporting provides more decision-useful information about a government's efficiency and effectiveness in providing services to its citizens than can be provided by traditional financial statements. One objective of this updated Concepts Statement is to provide a framework that can inform the GASB as it considers proposed suggested guidelines for voluntary reporting of SEA performance information by state and local governmental entities.

The revisions to Concepts Statement 2 clarify that it is beyond the scope of the GASB to establish the goals and objectives of state and local government services, to develop specific nonfinancial measures or indicators of service performance, or to set benchmarks for service performance. To emphasize this point, Concepts Statement 5 removes an entire section of Concepts Statement 2, titled, "Developing Reporting Standards for SEA Information." Concepts Statement 2 was also amended to update terminology and to modify certain provisions to reflect what has taken place over the past 14 years.

¶9007   Legal Provisions

In governmental accounting, legal provisions relate to budgeting and to the disposition of assets. The preparation and implementation of the projected budget and related accounting procedures are governed by certain legal provisions expressed specifically in legislation (statutory) or restrictions imposed by a nonlegislative (regulatory) authority. The accounting system must have built-in safeguards that expenditures will comply with both types of restrictions. Governmental accounting must also include revenue and expense data which facilitates the preparation of budgets for the future.

As will be seen, certain *funds* are considered less flexible in their accounting treatment. The least flexible type is the one created by a state constitution or by legislation, because the accountant must keep the books as determined by law. The most flexible is the type established by executive authority, since such authority can make changes in a fund without prior legislative approval.

In fund accounting *estimated and actual revenues* and *expenditures* are compared on an ongoing basis, e.g., reviewed by the governing bodies approving the initial budget and the appropriation for the fund. Comparisons reveal the extent to which the "actuals" are in line with the estimates (the budget) and will show significant deviations, if any, during the fiscal year of actual revenues and expenditures from the budgeted amounts.

Assets and liabilities incurred by a fund are similar to those in a commercial enterprise. Asset accounts, for example, will include cash, accounts receivable, etc., while liabilities will show accounts or vouchers payable, notes payable, bonds payable, etc.

A separate *general ledger* must be maintained for each fund related to the governmental entity's budget. Each general ledger has a self-balancing account that brings the revenue and appropriation accounts into balance at the end of the fiscal year.

As a general rule independent auditors will insist on the entity using an *accrual* system, unless the financial authorities for that specific fund can demonstrate that the financial reports would not *materially* differ if a cash accounting system is used.

¶9008   Is Governmental Accounting Complex? No!

While fund accounting is perceived to be complicated, it is not any more difficult than commercial accounting. Why then is it thought to be complicated? The answer is for the same reason that we initially think any totally new and unfamiliar discipline appears difficult—the *terminology* is the culprit. It is well-settled that learning the terminology of a new discipline is 50 percent or more of the learning battle of anything new that one endeavors to learn. Governmental accounting terminology is indeed entirely different from commercial accounting terminology; it has a vocabulary that is totally unique to governmental accounting; no governmental accounting term can be found in any other system of accounting, whether commercial, industrial, or otherwise.

The first step, then, to acquire an understanding of fund accounting procedures is to review and become familiar with the terms. The following list of definitions will enable the user to easily apply the accounting methods for the various types of funds which are covered in the material following the definitions.

¶9009   Terminology

Here is a listing of definitions applicable only to fund accounting:

> **Abatement.** Cancellation of amounts levied or of charges made for services.
>
> **Accrued Assets.** Assets arising from revenues earned but not yet due.
>
> **Accrued Expenses.** Expenses resulting in liabilities which are either due or are not payable until some future time.
>
> **Accrued Revenues.** Levies made or other revenue earned and not collected.
>
> **Allotment Ledger.** A subsidiary ledger which contains an account for each allotment showing the amount allotted, expenditures, encumbrances, the net balance, and other related information.

Appropriation. An authorization granted by the legislative body to make expenditures and to incur obligations for specific purposes.

Appropriation Expenditure. An expenditure chargeable to an appropriation.

Appropriation Ledger. A subsidiary ledger containing an account with each appropriation.

Assessment. The process of making an official valuation of property for the purpose of taxation.

Authority Bonds. Bonds payable from the revenues of a specific public authority.

Betterment. An addition or change made in a fixed asset which prolongs its life or increases its efficiency.

Budget. A plan of financial operation embodying an estimate of proposed expenditures for a given period or purpose, and the proposed means of financing them.

Budgetary Accounts. The accounts necessary to reflect budget operations and condition, such as estimated revenues, appropriations, and encumbrances.

Capital Budget. An improvement program and the methods for the financing.

Clearing Account. An account used to accumulate total charges or credits for the purpose of distributing them among the accounts to which they are allocable, or for the purpose of transferring the net difference to the proper account.

Current Special Assessment. Assessments levied and due during the current fiscal period.

Current Taxes. Taxes levied and becoming due during the current fiscal period—from the time the amount of the tax levy is first established, to the date on which a penalty for nonpayment is attached.

Debt Limit. The maximum amount of gross or net debt legally permitted.

Debt Service Requirement. The amount of money necessary periodically to pay the interest on the outstanding debt and the principal of maturing bonded debt not payable from a sinking fund.

Deficit. The excess of the liabilities of a fund over its assets.

Delinquent Taxes. Taxes remaining unpaid on and after the date on which a penalty for nonpayment is attached.

Direct Debt. The debt which a governmental unit has incurred in its own name, or assumed through the annexation of territory.

Encumbrances. Obligations in the form of purchase orders, contracts, or salary commitments which are chargeable to an appropriation, and for which a part of the appropriation is reserved.

Endowment Fund. A fund whose principal must be maintained inviolate, but whose income may be expended.

Expendable Fund. A fund whose resources, including both principal and earnings, may be expended.

Expenditures. If the fund accounts are kept on the accrual basis, expenditures are the total charges incurred, whether paid or unpaid, including expenses, provision for retirement of debt not reported as a liability of the fund from which retired, and capital outlays.

Franchise. A special privilege granted by a government permitting the continuing use of public property.

Full Faith and Credit. A pledge of the general taxing body for the payment of obligations.

Fund Accounts. All accounts necessary to set forth the financial operations and financial condition of a fund.

Fund Group. A group of related funds.

Governmental Accounting. The preparation, reporting, and interpretation of accounts for governmental bodies.

Grant. A contribution by one governmental unit to another unit.

Gross Bonded Debt. The total amount of direct debt of a governmental unit, represented by outstanding bonds before deduction of sinking fund assets.

Indeterminate Appropriation. An appropriation which is not limited either to any definite period of time, or to any definite amount, or to both time and amount.

Inter-Fund Accounts. Accounts in which transactions between funds are reflected.

Inter-Fund Loans. Loans made by one fund to another fund.

Inter-Fund Transfers. Amounts transferred from one fund to another.

Judgment. An amount to be paid or collected by a governmental unit as the result of a court decision, including a condemnation award in payment for private property taken for public use.

Lapse. As applied to appropriations, this term denotes the automatic termination of an appropriation.

Levy. To impose taxes or special assessments.

Lump-Sum Appropriation. An appropriation made for a stated purpose, or for a named department, without specifying further the amounts that can be spent for specific activities or for particular expenditures.

Municipal. An adjective applying to any governmental unit below or subordinate to the state.

Municipal Corporation. A body or corporate politic established pursuant to state authorization, as evidenced by a charter.

Net Bonded Debt. Gross bonded debt less applicable cash or other assets.

Non-Expendable Fund. A fund the principal, and sometimes the earnings, of which may not be expended.

Non-Operating Income. Income of municipal utilities and other governmental enterprises of a business character, which is not derived from the operation of such enterprise.

Operating Expenses. As used in the accounts of municipal utilities and other governmental enterprises of a business character, the term means the costs necessary to the maintenance of the enterprise, or the rendering of services for which the enterprise is operated.

Operating Revenues. Revenues derived from the operation of municipal utilities or other governmental enterprises of a business character.

Operating Statement. A statement summarizing the financial operations of a municipality.

Ordinance. A bylaw of a municipality enacted by the governing body of the governmental entity.

Overlapping Debt. The proportionate share of the debts of local governmental units, located wholly or in part within the limits of the reporting government, which must be borne by property within such government.

Prepaid Taxes. The deposit of money with a governmental unit on condition that the amount deposited is to be applied against the tax liability of the taxpayer.

Proprietary Accounts. Accounts which show actual financial condition and operations such as actual assets, liabilities, reserves, surplus, revenues, and expenditures as distinguished from budgetary accounts.

Public Authority. A public agency created to perform a single function, which is financed from tolls or fees charged those using the facilities operated by the agency.

Public Trust Fund. A trust fund whose principal, earnings, or both, must be used for a public purpose.

Quasi-Municipal Corporation. An agency established by the state primarily for the purpose of helping the state to carry out its functions.

Refunding Bonds. Bonds issued to retire bonds already outstanding. The refunding bonds may be sold for cash and outstanding bonds redeemed in cash, or the refunding bonds may be exchanged with holders of outstanding bonds.

Related Funds. Funds of a similar character which are brought together for administrative and reporting purposes.

Reserve for Encumbrances. A reserve representing the segregation of surplus to provide for unliquidated encumbrances.

Revenue Bonds. Bonds the principal and interest on which are to be paid solely from earnings, usually the earnings of a municipally owned utility or other public service enterprise.

Revolving Fund. A fund provided to carry out a cycle of operations.

Special Assessment. A compulsory levy made by a local government against certain properties, to defray part or all of the cost of a specific improvement or service, which is presumed to be of general benefit to the public and of special benefit to the owners of such properties.

Special District Bonds. Bonds of a local taxing district, which has been organized for a special purpose—such as road, sewer, and other special districts—to render unique services to the public.

Suspense Account. An account which carries charges or credits temporarily pending the determination of the proper account or accounts to which they are to be posted.

Tax Anticipation Notes. Notes issued in anticipation of collection of taxes, usually retired only from tax collections as they come due.

Tax Levy. An ordinance or resolution by means of which taxes are levied.

Tax Liens. Claims which governmental units have upon properties until taxes levied against them have been paid.

Tax Rate. The amount of tax stated in terms of a unit of the tax base.

Trust Fund. A fund consisting of resources received and held by the governmental unit as trustee, to be expended or invested in accordance with the conditions of the trust.

Unencumbered Appropriation. An appropriation or allotment, or a part thereof, not yet expended or encumbered.

Utility Fund. A fund established to finance the construction, operation, and maintenance of municipally owned utilities.

Warrant. An order drawn by a legislative body, or an officer of a governmental unit, upon its treasurer, directing the treasurer to pay a specified amount to the person named, or to the bearer.

¶9010   Governmental Accounting Systems

.01   Governmental Accounting Standards Board (GASB)

The GASB was established in 1984, under the oversight of the Financial Accounting Foundation which, in turn, oversees the Financial Accounting Standards Board (FASB). Before the establishment of the GASB, the reports of governmental entities were criticized by the accounting community because they could not be interpreted in a manner consistent with the financial reports of private business organizations. The primary purpose of the GASB is to develop standards of reporting for state and local government entities; its organizational and operational structure is similar to that of the FASB, and its objective is to make the combined general purpose financial reports of governmental entities as comparable as possible to those of private business.

As a general rule the GASB will promulgate standards that parallel U.S. GAAP. However, there are instances that require a governmental entity to comply with a state law or regulatory accounting requirement that is in non-compliance with U.S. GAAP. Such reports are classified as *Special Reports or Supplemental Schedules*, which are not a part of the general purpose statements. In these cases, governmental units can publish two sets of statements, one in compliance with legal requirements and one in compliance with U.S. GAAP. (An example of this problem is that it is not uncommon for some governmental entities to be required by law to apply the cash basis of accounting.)

Governmental accounting systems are developed on a *fund basis*. A fund is defined as an independent fiscal and accounting entity with a self-balancing set of accounts recording cash and other resources together with all related liabilities, obligations, reserves, and equities that are segregated for the purpose of carrying on specific activities or attaining specified objectives in accordance with applicable regulations, restrictions, and other statutory and regulatory limitations.

In addition to each fund's transactions within the fund itself, each fund in a governmental unit can have financial transactions with other funds in the same entity. The financial statements must reflect interfund transactions which result from services rendered by one fund to another.

The accrual basis of accounting is recommended for matching revenues and expenditures during a designated period of time which refers specifically to the time when revenues and expenditures are recorded as such in the accounting records.

Governmental revenues should be classified by fund and source. Expenditures should be classified by fund, function, organization unit, activity, character, and principal classes of objectives in accordance with standard recognized classifications. Common terminology and classifications should be used consistently throughout (1) the budget; (2) the accounts; and (3) the financial reports. These three elements of governmental financial administration are inseparable and can be thought of as the "cycle" of governmental financial transactions and final product of the accounting system.

.02   Seven Types of Funds

1. The *General Fund* which accounts for all transactions not accounted for in any other fund.
2. *Special Revenue Fund* which accounts for revenues from specific sources or to finance specific projects.
3. *Debt Service Fund* which accounts for the payment of interest and principal on long-term debt.

4. *Capital Project Fund* which accounts for the receipt and disbursement of funds used for the acquisition of capital facilities.
5. *Enterprise Funds* which account for the financing of services to the public paid for by the users of the services.
6. *Fiduciary Funds: Trust and Agency Funds* which account for assets held by a governmental unit as trustee or agent for individuals, private organizations, or other governmental units.
7. *Internal Service Funds* which account for the financing of special projects and services performed by one governmental entity for an organization unit within the same governmental entity.

The accountant should:

- Maintain complete and adequate files for the initial documentation which established or restricted the fund, together with any special reporting requirements demanded.
- Keep separate detailed books of entry for each fund, separate bank account for that fund, separate identification of all property and securities.
- Under *no* circumstances should assets of separate funds be commingled. Transfers between funds should not be permitted without documentary authorization, and inter-fund receivables and payables should, in contra-effect, be equal and clearly identified, always maintaining the original integrity of each fund.
- Interest accruals, cooperative-share funding (example: government 80 percent —college 20 percent in Work Study Program), expense allowances or allocations—all should be made timely.
- Federal, state and local reporting requirements should be studied, met and reported as due to avoid stringent penalties, interest and possible loss of tax-exempt status. Options may exist regarding the handling of payroll and unemployment taxes; they should be studied and explored for money-saving possibilities.
- Independently audited annual financial statements by fund are usually required both by organizational charter and governmental departments (especially where grant-participation is involved). Publication of the availability of these statements is sometimes mandatory (foundations).
- One area of discussion and dispute is the "compliance" feature of audits involving certain governmental agency grants. Here, the independent auditor is called upon to measure the agency's compliance with certain non-accounting rules, such as eligibility of money-recipients, internal controls and other matters not ordinarily associated with a financial audit. The integrity

of the auditor's financial opinion should never be compromised by peripheral compliance requirements. In most cases, the auditor should qualify any
opinion indicating the results and *extent of tests* made for compliance. The
AICPA, to some extent, has spelled out guidelines for "compliance" opinions in Section 9641 of its "Statements on Auditing Standards."

- Municipal accounting techniques, procedures, format and demands are not
discussed here. Their overall application involves the use of fund accounting.
The main distinction is the entering of the budget—the anticipated revenues and the appropriations thereof—directly on and as part of the books
of account. Progress reports then show how actual compares with anticipated. The estimates are then zeroed out at yearend. The meaning and use
of "encumbrances" should also be understood. Reports for some local subdivisions, such as school boards, usually involve a strict accounting of each
receipt and disbursement, including the detailing of outstanding checks.

Accounting for the General Fund (GF). The General Fund is the type most
frequently used as it accounts for revenues not allocated to specified activities by
law or by contract. Every governmental entity *must* have a General Fund; none
of the other types of funds are required, but are established as needed.

Entries in the GF system originally are made to Estimated Revenues and
Appropriations and simultaneously a debit or credit, whichever is the case, is
recorded in the Fund Balance account. For proper controls the encumbrance
system is used with entries recorded when commitments are made or orders
placed. This procedure has the effect of setting aside the money for the payment
of future purchase orders and payment vouchers. When a purchase is actually
made, the entries to an Encumbrances and Reserve for Encumbrances are reversed and those accounts cleared. (The later expenditure is not always the same
as the encumbrance.) Simultaneously, the actual expenditure is recorded by a
Debit to an Expenditures account and a credit to Vouchers Payable.

Taxes and service charges are budgeted in a Taxes-Receivable—Current Account. The estimated amounts should be recorded after the estimate and posting
of uncollectibles, so the entries are a credit to Revenues and a credit to Estimated
Uncollectible Taxes. When collections are actually received during the fiscal year,
they are recorded with a debit to cash and a credit to Taxes Receivable—Current. Subsequently, it is determined that a certain amount of taxes will become
delinquent as the year progresses. These amounts are recorded in a Taxes Receivable—Delinquent account (debit) and a credit to Taxes Receivable-Current. At
this point an Interest and Penalties account should be opened for fees, penalties
and other charges associated with the collection of delinquent taxes.

Taxes Receivable—Delinquent	xxx	
Estimated Uncollectible Current Taxes	xxx	
Taxes Receivable—Current		xxx
Estimated Uncollectible Delinquent Taxes		xxx
Interest and Penalties	xxx	
Estimated Uncollectible Interest and Penalties		xxx

At the end of the fiscal year, the accounts of the General Fund are closed out. Any differences are recorded for or against the Fund Balance.

Accounting for Special Revenue Funds (SRF). Special Revenue Funds account for revenues obtained via specific taxes or other designated revenue sources. They are usually mandated by statute, charter, or local ordinance to fund specific functions or activities. Examples are parks, museums, highway construction, street maintenance, business licensing.

Revenue Funds resources cannot be used for any purpose other than the purpose for which the bonds were sold.

Journal entries:		
Encumbrances	xxx	
Reserve for Encumbrances		xxx
Reserve for Encumbrances	xxx	
Encumbrances		xxx
Expenditures	xxx	
Vouchers Payable		xxx
Vouchers Payable	xxx	
Cash		xxx

Taxes and service charges are budgeted in a Taxes-Receivable—Current account. The estimated amounts should be recorded after the estimate and posting of uncollectibles, so the entries are a credit to Revenues and a credit to Estimated Uncollectible Taxes; e.g.,

Taxes Receivable—Current	xxx	
Estimated Uncollectible Current Taxes		xxx
Revenues		xxx

When collections are actually received during the fiscal year they are recorded with a debit to Cash and a credit to Taxes Receivable—Current.

Accounting for Debt Service Funds (DSF). Debt Service Fund accounts for the payment of interest and principal on long-term debt resulting from the sale of general obligation bonds. This fund does not include the accounting for special assessments and service debts of governmental enterprises.

There are three types of long-term debt:

- Term or sinking fund bonds.
- Serial bonds.
- Notes and time warrants having a maturity of *more than one year* after issuance.

The first entry in the accounting cycle for a bond fund is to record the bond authorization:

Bonds Authorized—unissued	xxx	
Appropriations		xxx
The bonds are sold:		
Cash	xxx	
Bonds Authorized—unissued		xxx

If the bonds are sold at a premium, a Premium on Bonds account is credited. If sold at a discount, a Discount on Bonds account is debited.

Accounting for the Capital Projects Fund (CPF). Capital Projects Funds are a set of accounts for all resources used to acquire *capital* facilities (except funds financed by special assessment and enterprise funds). There must be Capital Project Funds for each authorized project to ensure that the proceeds of a bond issue, for example, are expended only as authorized. There is also a separate budget for the CPF, usually labeled the Capital Budget.

The accounting process begins with project authorization which is in memorandum form; no entry is necessary. Assuming the project is financed by the proceeds of a bond issue (as most projects are), the proceeds of the borrowing is an entry to the Cash account and a credit to Revenues for the *par value* of the bonds. If the bonds were sold at a premium, there is a credit to a Premium on Bonds account for the amount of the premium. Since U.S. GAAP requires bond premiums to be treated as an adjustment to the interest costs, the premiums are transferred *to* the Debt Service Fund established to service the debt. The entry to record the transfer is:

| Premium on Bonds | xxx | |
| Cash | | xxx |

If the bonds are sold at a discount, the discount is eliminated by a transfer of the amount of the discount *from* the Debt Service Fund *to* the Capital Projects Fund.

Accounting for Enterprise Funds (EF). Enterprise Funds finance self-supporting (not taxpayers') activities of governmental units that render services on a user charge basis to the general public. Common enterprises are water companies, electricity, natural gas, airports, transportation systems, hospitals, port authority, and a variety of recreational facilities.

In most jurisdictions, utilities and other enterprises are required to adopt and operate under budgets in the same manner as non-enterprise operations of governmental units. A budget is essential for control of each enterprise's operating results and to ensure that the resources of one enterprise are not illegally or improperly utilized by another.

The accrual basis of accounting is the required method for Enterprise Funds. As customers are billed, Accounts Receivable accounts are debited and revenue accounts *by sources* are credited.

Four financial statements are required to disclose fully the financial position and results of operations of an Enterprise Fund:

- Balance Sheet
- Revenue and Expenses
- Changes in Financial Position
- Analysis of Changes in Retained Earnings

Accounting for Trust and Agency Funds (TAF). Trust and Agency Funds are similar; the primary difference is that a Trust Fund is usually in existence for a long period of time, even permanently. Both have fiduciary responsibilities for funds and assets that are not owned outright by the funds.

There are two types of Trust Funds, i.e., expendable and nonexpendable funds. The former allows the principal and income to be spent on designated operations, while nonexpendable funds must be preserved intact. Pension and various retirement funds are examples of expendable funds; a loan fund from which loans are made for specific purposes and must be paid back, which requires maintaining the *original amount* of the fund, is a nonexpendable fund.

Trust Funds are operated as required by statutes and governmental regulations established for their existence. Accounting for Trust Funds consists primarily of the proper recording of receipts and disbursements. Additions are credited directly to the Fund Balance account and expenditures charged directly against the Fund Balance.

An Agency Fund can be thought of as sort of a clearinghouse fund established to account for assets received for and paid to others; the main asset is cash which is held only for a brief period of time, so is seldom invested because cash is usually paid out shortly after receipt.

An Agency Fund simplifies the complexities that can result from the use of numerous fund accounting entities; e.g., instances in which a single transaction affects several different funds. All Agency Fund assets are owed to another fund, a person, or an organization. The entries for receipts and disbursements in Agency Funds are easy:

Upon receipt:		
Cash	xxx	
Fund Balance		xxx
Upon disbursement:		
Fund Balance	xxx	
Cash		xxx

Accounting for Intergovernmental Service Funds (ISF). ISF, also referenced as Working Capital Funds and Internal Service Funds, finances and provides accountability for services and commodities provided by a designated agency of a governmental unit to other departments, agencies, etc., of the same governmental entity. Examples are motor pools, centralized garages, central purchasing, storage, facilities, and central printing services.

Funds for the establishment of ISF usually originate from three sources:

- Contributions from another operating fund—e.g., the General Fund or an Enterprise Fund.
- The sale of general obligation bonds.
- Long-term advances from other funds, which are to be repaid over a specific period of time from the earnings of a revolving fund.

As cash is expended for the benefit of other fund-users, the users are charged with the cost of the materials or services furnished by the ISF and the ISF is then reimbursed by interdepartmental cash transfers from the departments of other funds to which materials or services have been furnished.

The accounting for ISF should include all accounts necessary to compile an accurate statement of the outcome of its financial operations, and of its financial position at any given time. These accounts will usually include the fixed assets owned by the fund, accounts for buildings financed from capital

Project Funds, depreciation recorded on fixed assets to obtain an accurate computation of costs and to preclude depletion of the fund's capital. The accrual basis must be used for all ISF accounting, with all charges to departments of various funds billed at the time materials or services are rendered and expenditures are recorded when incurred. Encumbrances may or may not be formally recorded in the books of account; if they are the entries would be:

Encumbrances	xxx	
Reserve for Encumbrances		xxx

If encumbrances are not recorded in the accounts, memorandum records of orders and commitments should be maintained to preclude over-obligation of cash and other fund resources.

When an ISF is established, the entry to be made will depend upon the service the fund is to provide. If the fund's capital is obtained from the General Fund, the entry would be:

Cash	xxx	
Contribution from General Fund		xxx

If a general obligation bond issue is a source of the fund's capital:

Cash	xxx	
Contribution from General Obligation Bonds		xxx

If fund capital is obtained from another fund of the same governmental unit the entry is:

Cash	xxx	
Advance from (name of fund)		xxx

Accounting for the General Fixed Assets Account Group (GFA). The fixed asset accounts are maintained on the basis of original cost, or the estimated cost if the original cost is not available, as in the case of gifts. The appraised value at the time of receipt of the asset is an acceptable valuation. Otherwise, initial costs of fixed assets are obtainable from contracts, purchase vouchers, and other transaction documents generated at the time of acquisition or construction.

Depreciation on fixed assets should not be recorded in the general accounting records. Depreciation charges are computed for unit cost purposes, provided such charges are recorded in memorandum form and do not appear in the fund accounts.

Different from depreciation accounting for commercial enterprises, the depreciation of fixed assets is not recorded as an expense because there is no purpose in doing so. Property records should be kept, however, for each piece of property and equipment owned by the fund. The sum of the cost value of the properties—buildings, improvements, machinery, and equipment—should equal the corresponding balances of those accounts carried in the general ledger.

Accounting for the Long-Term Debt Group (LTD). General Obligation Bonds and other types of long-term debt supported by general revenues are obligations of the governmental unit as a whole, not of any of the entity's constituent funds individually. Additionally, the monies from such debt can be expended on facilities that are used in the operation of several funds. Accordingly, the total of long-term indebtedness backed by the "full faith and credit" of the government should be recorded and accounted for in a separate self-balancing group of accounts titled General Long-Term Debt Group of Accounts. Included in this debt group are general obligation bonds, time warrants, and notes that have a maturity date of *more than one year* from the date of issuance.

Long-term debt is recorded in the self-balancing accounts, so do not affect the liabilities of any other fund. The reason for these accounts is to record a governmental unit's long-term debt at any point in time from the date the debt is incurred until it is finally paid. Under U.S. GAAP the proper valuation for the long-term debt liability is the sum of (1) the present discounted value of the principal payable at the stipulated maturity date in the future and (2) the present discounted value of the periodic interest payments to the maturity date.

The entries to be made at the time the bonds are sold are:

Amounts to be Provided for the Payment of Term Bonds	xxx	
Term Bonds Payable		xxx

The proceeds of the bond issue are entered in a Capital Projects Fund account to be expended as authorized in the Authorized Capital Outlay account.

(Note: Not-for-profit accounting for other than governmental entities uses the accrual basis of accounting—e.g., colleges and universities, voluntary hospitals, health and welfare organizations, and so on.)

¶9011   Objectives of Financial Reporting by Nonbusiness Organizations

The main distinguishing characteristics of nonbusiness organizations include:

1. Receipts of significant amounts of resources from resource providers who do not expect to receive either repayment or economic benefits commensurate with the resources provided.
2. Operating purposes for objectives other than to provide goods or services at a profit.
3. Absence of defined ownership interests that can be sold, transferred, or redeemed, or that convey entitlement to a share of a residual distribution of resources in the event of liquidation of the organization.

These characteristics result in certain types of transactions that are largely, although not entirely, absent in business enterprises, such as contributions and grants, and in the absence of transactions with owners, such as issuing and redeeming stock and paying dividends. General purpose financial reporting by nonbusiness organizations does not attempt to meet all the information needed by those interested parties or to furnish all of the different types of information that financial reporting can provide. It is not intended to meet specialized needs of regulatory bodies, donors or grantors, or others having the authority to obtain the information they need. The most important users in the nonbusiness environment are resource providers, such as members, taxpayers, contributors, and creditors. A full set of financial statements for a period should show:

1. Financial position at the end of the period.
2. Earnings for the period.
3. Comprehensive income for the period.
4. Cash flows during the period.
5. Investments by and distributions to owners during the period.

Financial statements result from simplifying, condensing, and aggregating masses of data. As a result, they convey information that would be obscured if great detail were provided.

CHAPTER 10
Not-for-Profit or Exempt Organizations

¶10,000   Overview

Accounting for organizations such as not-for-profit and exempt organizations (sometimes referred to as nonbusiness organizations) has many of the same characteristics as accounting for for-profit business entities; however, there are also many differences. Among the foremost of these are differing objectives of financial reporting by not-for-profit and exempt entities and tax treatment of such entities.

¶10,001   Recent FASB Updates Related to Not-for-Profit Entities

Following are the Accounting Standards Updates (ASUs) issued by the Financial Accounting Standards Board (FASB) in recent years that are related to not-for-profit entities. Brief summaries are provided here so that the reader may identify any Updates that may be applicable. More detailed guidance may be found in the actual updates on the FASB Web site.

.01   Presentation and Disclosures by Not-for-Profit Entities for Contributed Nonfinancial Assets

The FASB issued Accounting Standards Update (ASU) No. 2020-07 to increase the transparency of contributed nonfinancial assets for not-for-profit entities through enhancements to presentation and disclosure. The amendments require that not-for-profit entities present such assets as a separate line item in the statement of activities, apart from contributions of cash and other financial assets. They also require disclosure of a disaggregation of the amount of such assets by category that depicts the type of asset, as well as qualitative information about whether the assets were monetized or utilized during the reporting period and other related policies and information.

.02   Updating the Definition of Collections

The FASB issued Accounting Standards Update (ASU) No. 2019-03 to align its definition of collections with that used in the American Alliance of Museums' *Code of Ethics for Museums*. The Update modifies the definition of the term collections and requires disclosure of policy for the use of proceeds from when collection items are deaccessioned (removed from a collection).

.03   Clarifying the Scope and the Accounting Guidance for Contributions Received and Contributions Made

The FASB issued Accounting Standards Update (ASU) No. 2018-08 to clarify and improve the scope and the accounting guidance for contributions received and contributions made. The amendments in this Update should assist entities in evaluating whether transactions should be accounted for as contributions (nonreciprocal transactions) or as exchange (reciprocal) transactions and in determining whether a contribution is conditional. Please note that, although contributions is an issue primarily for not-for-profit entities, this Update applies to all entities that receive or make contributions.

.04   Clarifying When a Not-for-Profit Entity That Is a General Partner or a Limited Partner Should Consolidate a For-Profit Limited Partnership or Similar Entity

The FASB issued Accounting Standards Update (ASU) No. 2017-02 to amend consolidation guidance after ASU 2015-02, Consolidation, became effective, superseding previous guidance.

.05   Presentation of Financial Statements of Not-for-Profit Entities

The FASB issued Accounting Standards Update (ASU) No. 2016-14 to make certain improvements that address many, but not all, of the identified issues about then- current financial reporting for not-for-profit organizations. It introduced the broadest range of changes to not-for-profit reporting in a long time. The amendments in this Update are extensive and not detailed here. It is assumed that most readers will have already implemented this guidance. If the reader has any questions about this guidance, the author recommends a thorough reading of the standard.

¶10,002   Organizations that Have Lost Tax-Exempt Status; Help for Revoked Organizations

Each year, the number of tax-exempt organizations increases but so does the number of these organizations that lose their tax exemption. The requirement for small 501(c)(3) organizations is an annual filing of a simple electronic return that requires no accounting or even numbers (Form 990-N). Most small tax-exempt organizations whose annual gross receipts are normally $50,000 or less can file Form 990-N. In spite of this intended simplicity, many of these small organizations lose their exempt status for failing to file these electronic "post cards" for three years. In addition, many organizations that don't qualify for the "post card" return do qualify to file Form 990EZ, a much simplified form of the regular Form 990.

While there is no penalty assessment for filing Form 990-N late, organizations that fail to file required Forms 990, 990-EZ or 990-N for three consecutive years will automatically lose their tax-exempt status. Revocation of the organization's tax-exempt status happens on the filing due date of the third consecutively-missed year.

A small organization may apply for *streamlined retroactive reinstatement* if its exemption has not been previously automatically revoked under IRC Sec. 6033(j), and it must have been eligible to file either Form 990-EZ or Form 990-N for each of the preceding three years in which it failed to file. Action must be taken within 15 months of revocation by completing and submitting an application and including the appropriate user fee and include "Revenue Procedure 2014-11, Streamlined Retroactive Reinstatement" written across the top of the application. See Rev. Proc. 2013-8, 2013-1 I.R.B. 237, sec. 6.07, or its successor.

If an application is approved, the organization will have its tax-exempt status retroactively reinstated and will be deemed to have reasonable cause for its failures to file Form 990-EZ or 990-N, as applicable, for three consecutive years. An organization not eligible for the streamlined retroactive application process described above may still apply for *retroactive reinstatement* within 15 months (or the later of the date of the revocation letter or the date on which the organization's name was posted on the IRS Revocation List) by:

- filing a properly completed and executed paper returns for each of the three years for which the organization was required, and failed, to file annual returns, with "Retroactive Reinstatement" written across the top of each return;
- completing and submitting the application no later than 15 months after the later of the date of the IRS Revocation Letter or the date on which the IRS posted the organization's name on the IRS Revocation List;
- including "Revenue Procedure 2014-11, Retroactive Reinstatement" written across the top of the application;
- including the appropriate fee (see Rev. Proc. 2013-8, Sec. 6.07); *and*
- including the required Reasonable Cause Statement for at least one of the three applicable years, as described below.

If the application is approved, the organization will have its tax-exempt status retroactively reinstated to the date of revocation, and not be subject to penalty under IRC Sec. 6652(c) for failure to file annual returns for three consecutive years (see Rev. Proc. 2014-11, Sec. 5).

Reasonable Cause Statements. To establish reasonable cause, an organization must demonstrate that it exercised ordinary business care and prudence in understanding and attempting to comply with its reporting obligations. The "Reasonable Cause Statement" should include detailed descriptions of all the pertinent facts and circumstances that led to the failure, how and when the failure was discovered, and what steps have been or will be taken to prevent or mitigate future failures. In addition, it must contain an original declaration, dated and signed under penalty of perjury by an official (officer, director, trustee or other) that is authorized to sign for the organization. The specific form and language for this declaration is provided in Sec. 8 of Rev. Proc. 2014-11.

If it has been more than 15 months since the revocation, the organization may still apply for retroactive reinstatement of its tax-exempt status only. The procedures required are described in part 6 of the procedure.

As explained in that section, "An organization that applies for reinstatement of its tax-exempt status more than 15 months from the later of the date of the Revocation Letter or the date on which the IRS posted the organization's name on the Revocation List may have its tax-exempt status retroactively reinstated effective from the Revocation Date only if it satisfies all the requirements of SECTION 5.01 of this revenue procedure, except that it must provide the Reasonable Cause Statement described in SECTION 8.02 of this revenue procedure (in place of the one described in SECTION 8.01) for the requirement described in SECTION 5.01(3)."

If an organization may qualify for this relief, it is recommended that the CPA access and read the procedure in its entirety.

Every year, the IRS announced a number of organizations that have automatically lost their tax-exempt status because they did not file legally required annual reports for three consecutive years. The IRS believes the vast majority of these organizations are defunct, but it also announced special steps to help any existing organizations to apply for reinstatement of their tax-exempt status.

For several years, the IRS has made an extensive effort to inform organizations of the changes in the law through multiple outreach and education avenues, including mailing more than 1 million notices to organizations that had not filed. "During the past several years, the IRS has gone the extra mile to help make tax-exempt groups aware of their legal filing requirement and allow them additional time to file," according to an IRS Commissioner. "Still, we realize there may be some legitimate organizations, especially very small ones, that were unaware of their new filing requirement. We are taking additional steps for these groups to maintain their tax-exempt status without jeopardizing their operations or harming their donors."

¶10,003   Simplified Application Procedures for Small Non-profits

Until 2014, Form 1023, *Application for Recognition of Exemption Under Section 501(c)(3) of the Internal Revenue Code,* was used by non-profit organizations of all sizes. In 2014, the IRS released the new Form 1023-EZ, which provides an abbreviated application process for the review of organizations seeking to obtain recognition of tax-exempt status under IRC Sec. 501(c)(3). The Form 1023-EZ abbreviated process was introduced in response to the IRS's tremendous backlog of Form 1023 applications, due in large part to IRS funding cuts and applications for reinstatement filed as a result of the auto-revocation provision enacted as part of the *Pension Protection Act of 2006.*

Organizations that may use Form 1023-EZ are the same as those who may file the "e-postcard" version of Form 990, discussed above. The Form 1023-EZ application process is available only to nonprofit organizations with anticipated gross receipts of no more than $50,000 for the past three years and which are not projected to exceed this amount for the next three years. In addition, an organization must have total assets that do not exceed $250,000. The form 1023-EZ may only be filed electronically, not in paper form. The associated user fee is $275.

The user fee for Form 1023 remains at $600. The fee for 1023-EZ is $275. Applicants must pay the user fee through Pay.gov when submitting the form. Payment can be made directly from a bank account or by credit/debit card.

The EZ process is unavailable to many types of tax-exempt organizations such as hospitals, schools, supporting organizations, private operating foundations, and limited liability companies. The Form 1023-EZ requests only cursory information from the filing organization, relying heavily on attestations and self-reporting from the organization that it complies with the various requirements of the particular tax-exempt status for which it is seeking recognition.

Because the gross receipts limitation for filing the Form 1023-EZ is the same as for filing a Form 990-N, many of the organizations qualifying for the Form 1023-EZ process will be eligible to file a Form 990-N for their first years of operation, if not longer.

According to a report by the Advisory Committee on Tax Exempt and Government Entities (ACT) 2015, "The Form 1023-EZ received a significant amount of criticism from the nonprofit community. Many grantmakers, state charity officials and others were critical of the IRS taking only a cursory review of a new organization's purposes and activities. For compliance purposes, the IRS selects a statistically valid, random sample (three percent) of the Form 1023-EZ applications filed for a pre-determination review to request additional information to ensure they qualify for the EZ processing. The IRS asks these randomly selected organizations five questions, including information about gross receipts, assets, basis for exemption, copies of articles of incorporation and bylaws, and whether the organization has any transactions with related parties" (Public Meeting, Washington, DC, June 17, 2015).

¶10,004 FASB Not-for-Profit Advisory Committee Recommends Improvements to Financial Reporting

On October 3, 2011, the Not-for-Profit Advisory Committee, an advisory group to the Financial Accounting Standards Board (FASB), recommended changes in accounting rules that would enable not-for-profit organizations to report and explain their finances better to donors and other interested parties.

Key recommendations advanced by the FASB's Not-for Profit Advisory Committee (NAC) include:

- Revisiting current net asset classifications, and how they may be relabeled or redefined, in conjunction with improving how liquidity is portrayed in a not-for-profit's statement of financial position and related notes
- Improving the statements of activities and cash flows to more clearly communicate financial performance
- Creating a framework for not-for-profit directors and managers to provide commentary and analysis about the organization's financial health and operations, somewhat similar to the "Management Discussion and Analysis" provided by publicly traded companies in their annual reports, to help them bring context to their financial story
- Streamlining, where possible, existing not-for-profit-specific disclosure requirements to improve their relevance and clarity.

"The Not-for-Profit Advisory Committee has provided the FASB with focused input about specific areas of improvement for not-for-profit financial reporting, and we commend its members for their thoughtful approach to the issues," according to the FASB Chairman.

Established in October 2009, the NAC is a standing resource group of the FASB. It was created to provide the FASB with input from the nonprofit sector on existing accounting guidance, current and proposed technical agenda projects, and longer-term issues affecting those organizations. The recommendations are based on member discussions at meetings held in September 2010 and February 2011, as well as subsequent work done by three committee subgroups. Those subgroups, consisting of preparers, auditors, and users of nonprofit financial statements, were charged with assessing the effectiveness of the current nonprofit financial reporting model, which dates from the mid-1990s.

"While NAC members largely agree that the basic financial reporting model for not-for-profit organizations is sound, they also believe updates can be made to improve the overall value of a not-for-profit's financial reporting package for users," the NAC chairman and FASB assistant director of nonpublic entities stated. "Some of those proposed improvements have clear linkages with projects already on FASB's agenda, while others would potentially involve entirely new projects."

One recommendation that received unanimous support, he added, was the creation of commentary and analysis framework for managers and directors of not-for-profit organizations to use to tell their financial story more effectively.

Committee members felt strongly that adding this section to financial reports is important in helping not-for-profit organizations in fulfilling the public accountability that is so central to the sector. They cautioned, however, that it should be scalable for smaller not-for-profit organizations.

Along with this NAC recommendation is that of increasing the understandability of financial reports by streamlining certain disclosure requirements specific to not-for-profit organizations. This might include identifying current disclosure requirements that might be better suited for the proposed commentary and analysis section, and is consistent with the FASB's goal of reducing complexity in financial reporting in general and with some of the aims of the FASB's current disclosure framework project in particular.

The recommendation to revisit how net assets are classified in a not-for-profit's financial statements is intended to help to clarify terms that commonly cause confusion, including the definition of an "unrestricted" net asset. This is a critical area for not-for-profits, since net asset classes are used by many credit analysts and other users to determine an organization's liquidity and liquidity risks. The issue of liquidity risk is also being addressed by the FASB in its project on accounting for financial instruments.

Finally, the recommendation to improve how information is aggregated and classified within the statement of activities, and to create better cohesiveness between the financial statements, covers ground being considered by the FASB and IASB in their joint project on financial statement presentation for business enterprises. NAC members agreed that more clearly segregating and defining "operating" versus "nonoperating" activities, for example, would result in greater comparability in financial reporting of not-for-profits.

In addition to the recommendations described above, the NAC identified potential ways to create greater awareness among not-for-profit organizations on ways to improve their financial reporting that are currently permitted by U.S. GAAP.

.01   Presentation of Financial Statements of Not-for-Profit Entities

The FASB issued Accounting Standards Update (ASU) No. 2016-14 that changes how a not-for-profit organization classifies its net assets, as well as the information it presents in financial statements and notes about its liquidity, financial performance, and cash flows.

The ASU requires amended presentation and disclosures to allow not-for-profits to provide more relevant information about their resources (and the changes in those resources) to donors, grantors, creditors, and other users.

These include qualitative and quantitative requirements in the following areas:

- net asset classes;
- investment return;
- expenses;
- liquidity and availability of resources; and
- presentation of operating cash flows.

Not-for-profit organizations that will be affected include charities, foundations, colleges and universities, health care providers, religious organizations, trade associations, and cultural institutions, among others.

The amendments are effective for annual financial statements issued for fiscal years beginning after December 15, 2017, and for interim periods within fiscal years beginning after December 15, 2018. Application to interim financial statements is permitted but not required in the initial year of application. Early application of the amendments is permitted.

.02   Other Recent Updates Related to Not-for-Profit Entities

The FASB issued Accounting Standards Update (ASU) No. 2020-07 that provides guidance to not-for-profit entities (NFPs) requiring presentation of contributed nonfinancial assets (often referred to as gifts in-kind) as a separate line item in the statement of activities. This ASU also requires disclosure of a disaggregation of contributed nonfinancial assets categorized by type and, for each category, qualitative information about whether the assets were monetized (sold for proceeds then used in the NFP) or utilized and the NFP's policy related to monetization or utilization, any donor-imposed restrictions, and a description of any valuation techniques used, including the principal market (or most advantageous market) used to arrive at a fair value if it is a market prohibited by a donor-imposed restriction.

The FASB issued ASU No. 2019-03 that modifies the definition of the term collections and require that a collection-holding entity disclose its policy for the use of proceeds from when collection items are deaccessioned or removed from a collection. If a collection-holding entity has a policy that allows proceeds from deaccessioned collection items to be used for direct care, it should disclose its definition of direct care. See ¶10,014.

The FASB issued ASU No. 2018-08 that clarifies and improves the scope and accounting guidance around contributions of cash and other assets received and made by not-for-profit organizations (NFPs) and business enterprises.

¶10,005   Characteristics of Nonbusiness Organizations

The main distinguishing characteristics of nonbusiness organizations include:

1. Receipts of significant amounts of resources from resource providers who do not expect to receive either repayment or economic benefits commensurate with the resources provided.
2. Operating purposes for objectives other than to provide goods or services at a profit.
3. Absence of defined ownership interests that can be sold, transferred, or redeemed, or that convey entitlement to a share of a residual distribution of resources in the event of liquidation of the organization.

These characteristics result in certain types of transactions that are largely, although not entirely, absent in business enterprises, such as contributions and grants, and in the absence of transactions with owners, such as issuing and redeeming stock and paying dividends. General purpose financial reporting by nonbusiness organizations does not attempt to meet all the information needed by those interested parties or to furnish all of the different types of information that financial reporting can provide. It is not intended to meet specialized needs of regulatory bodies, donors or grantors, or others having the authority to obtain the information they need. The most important users in the nonbusiness environment are resource providers, such as members, tax-payers, contributors, and creditors. A full set of financial statements for a period should show:

1. Financial position at the end of the period.
2. Earnings for the period.
3. Comprehensive income for the period.
4. Cash flows during the period.
5. Investments by and distributions to owners during the period.

Financial statements result from simplifying, condensing, and aggregating masses of data. As a result, they convey information that would be obscured if great detail were provided.

The Financial Accounting Standards Board (FASB) recently issued its Accounting Standards Codification™ (ASC) which includes all Statements on Financial Accounting Standards and Interpretations (SFASs and FINs), Emerging Issues Task Force (EITF) issues, Accounting Principles Board (APB) opinions, American Institute of Certified Public Accountants (AICPA) Statements of Position (SOP) and AICPA Audit Guides and other literature. The codification was issued July 1, 2009 and is effective for all periods ending after September 15, 2009.

As with authoritative financial accounting information generally, the FASB's recent codification of its pronouncements includes a special industry section devoted to not-for-profits. The benefits to users include a more accessible and logically organized starting point for viewing FASB guidance. Below is the topic outline. In the overall FASB Codification™ not-for-profits are one of the specialized industries for which it presents special guidance. Its industry reference number is 958 Not-for-Profit Entities. Under that general heading is the standardized coding for specific topics.

Not-for-Profit Entities FASB Codification 958
    10 – Overall
    20 – Financially Interrelated Entities
    30 – Split-Interest Agreements
    205 – Presentation of Financial Statements
    210 – Balance Sheet
    220 – Income Statement—Reporting Comprehensive Income
    225 – Income Statement
    230 – Statement of Cash Flows
    310 – Receivables
    320 – Investments—Debt Securities
    321 – Investments—Equity Securities
    325 – Investments—Other
    360 – Property, Plant, and Equipment
    405 – Liabilities

450 – Contingencies
470 – Debt
605 – Revenue Recognition
715 – Compensation—Retirement Benefits
720 – Other Expenses
805 – Business Combinations
810 – Consolidation
815 – Derivatives and Hedging
840 – Leases

The Codification may be accessed on the FASB's Web site.

¶10,006   FASB Establishes Not-for-Profit Advisory Committee

The Not-for-Profit Advisory Committee (NAC) was established in October 2009. The NAC is a standing committee that works closely with the FASB in an advisory capacity to ensure that perspectives from the not-for-profit (NFP) sector are effectively communicated to the FASB on a timely basis in connection with the development of financial accounting and reporting standards. The principal responsibilities of the NAC are to:

- Provide focused input and feedback relating to (a) the need for and relative priority of proposed projects, (b) conceptual and practical implication of proposals under development in active projects, (c) practice issues, including implementation issues arising from new standards and potential areas for improvement pertinent to the NFP sector, and (d) longer-term issues important to the NFP sector.
- Assist the FASB and its staff with communication and outreach activities to the NFP sector on recent standards and other existing guidance, current and proposed projects, and longer-term issues. NAC members are encouraged to communicate with the NFP sector, both to educate the sector about the roles of the FASB and the NAC and to encourage the sector to communicate with the FASB on financial reporting matters.
- Advise on other matters for which the FASB may seek guidance.

The NAC consists of 15 to 20 members who demonstrate (a) a keen interest in and knowledge of financial accounting and reporting matters, (b) experience working within the NFP sector, (c) a commitment to improving financial reporting for users of financial statements, and (d) the ability to provide input on a wide variety of financial reporting matters.

The NAC generally meets twice each year, in March and September. Minutes of the meetings may be read on its web page:

https://www.fasb.org/Page/PageContent?PageId=/about-us/advisory-groups/nac/nac-meeting-minutes.html&bcpath=tfff.

The establishment of the NAC solidifies the FASB's commitment to ensuring that the views of the not-for-profit sector are heard in the development of standards. "We anticipate that enhanced participation from not-for-profits will greatly assist the Board in understanding and appropriately considering the issues and needs of the sector, especially insofar as they differ from those of public and private business entities," the chairman of the FASB explained when establishment of the NAC was announced.

¶10,007   FASB Issues Statement No. 164, *Not-for-Profit Entities: Mergers and Acquisitions*

The FASB issued FASB Statement No. 164, *Not-for-Profit Entities: Mergers and Acquisitions*, in May 22, 2009. This Statement is effective for mergers occurring on or after December 15, 2009, and acquisitions for which the acquisition date is on or after the beginning of the first *annual* reporting period beginning on or after December 15, 2009.

The Statement is intended to improve the relevance, representational faithfulness, and comparability of the information that a not-for-profit entity provides in its financial reports about a combination with one or more other not-for-profit entities, businesses, or nonprofit activities. To accomplish that, this Statement establishes principles and requirements for how a not-for-profit entity:

- Determines whether a combination is a merger or an acquisition
- Applies the carryover method in accounting for a merger
- Applies the acquisition method in accounting for an acquisition, including determining which of the combining entities is the acquirer
- Determines what information to disclose to enable users of financial statements to evaluate the nature and financial effects of a merger or an acquisition.

In addition to providing guidance on accounting for both *mergers* of not-for-profit organizations and *acquisitions* by not-for-profit organizations, it provides guidance that assists not-for-profit entities in the application of FASB Statement No. 142, *Goodwill and Other Intangible Assets*, and FASB Statement No. 160, *Noncontrolling Interests in Consolidated Financial Statements*.

The Board decided that a merger of two or more not-for-profit organizations involves the creation of a newly formed entity as of the merger date. In applying the carryover basis of accounting, the merged entity's statement of activities and statement of cash flows for its first period should:

- Reflect the combined amounts of the merging entities' net assets (in total and by classes of net assets) and cash as of the merger date in its opening amounts, and
- Include activity from the merger date through the end of the fiscal period. The opening amounts should be adjusted so that the individual accounting policies of the merging entities conform at the merger date.

¶10,007

Statement 164 provides important information to users of financial statements regarding not-for-profit organizations that have merged or acquired an entity, according to the FASB. Input from users, received during the due process, was useful in creating guidance in an area of accounting that has needed greater clarification, and improvement of the quality of information provided to users of these types of financial reports.

¶10,008   FASB Issues Staff Position FAS 117-1, *Endowments of Not-for-Profit Organizations: Net Asset Classification of Funds Subject to an Enacted Version of the Uniform Prudent Management of Institutional Funds Act, and Enhanced Disclosures for All Endowment Funds*

On August 6, 2008, the Financial Accounting Standards Board (FASB) issued FASB Staff Position (FSP) FAS 117-1, *Endowments of Not-for-Profit Organizations: Net Asset Classification of Funds Subject to an Enacted Version of the Uniform Prudent Management of Institutional Funds Act, and Enhanced Disclosures for All Endowment Funds*. The guidance is intended to improve the quality and consistency of financial reporting of endowments held by not-for-profit organizations.

The FSP addresses issues that are important to the not-for-profit sector, especially organizations with sizeable endowments and the users of their financial statements, such as donors, credit rating agencies, and regulators. To explain the Board's reasoning behind their actions in responding to the Act in this manner, the project manager suggested, "The adoption of the Uniform Prudent Management of Institutional Funds Act of 2006 (UPMIFA) has raised significant questions about the reporting of donor-restricted endowment funds. Moreover, organizations across the country now find themselves subject to increased public scrutiny on how they manage and use their endowments, which in many instances have seen tremendous growth over the past decade."

This FSP *provides guidance* on classifying the net assets (equity) associated with donor-restricted endowment funds held by organizations that are subject to an enacted version of UPMIFA, which serves as a model act for states to modernize their laws governing donor-restricted endowment funds. Approximately 20 states have already done so, and many more are expected to do so over the next few years.

This FSP also requires additional disclosures about endowments (both donor-restricted funds and board-designated funds) for all organizations, including those that are not yet subject to an enacted version of UPMIFA.

The provisions of this FSP are effective for fiscal years ending after December 15, 2008. Early application is permitted, as long as the organization has not previously issued annual financial statements for that fiscal year.

¶10,009 FASB Issues Staff Position FIN 48-3, *Effective Date of FASB Interpretation No. 48 for Certain Nonpublic Enterprises*

The Financial Accounting Standards Board (FASB) issued FASB Staff Position (FSP) FIN 48-3, *Effective Date of FASB Interpretation No. 48 for Certain Nonpublic Enterprises,* on December 30, 2008. The FSP deferred the effective date of FASB Interpretation No. 48, *Accounting for Uncertainty in Income Taxes,* for certain nonpublic enterprises, including nonpublic not-for-profit organizations, for fiscal years beginning after December 15, 2008.

The deferred effective date is intended to give the Board additional time to develop guidance on the application of Interpretation 48 by pass-through entities and not-for-profit organizations. The deferral will also give the Board time to amend the disclosure requirements of Interpretation 48 for nonpublic enterprises.

Nonpublic enterprises that are *eligible* for the deferral are defined in paragraph 289, as amended, of FASB Statement No. 109, *Accounting for Income Taxes.* However, nonpublic consolidated entities of public enterprises that apply U.S. Generally Accepted Accounting Principles (U.S. GAAP) are *not eligible* for the deferral. Also *not eligible* for the deferral are nonpublic enterprises that have applied the recognition, measurement, and disclosure provisions of Interpretation 48 in a full set of annual financial statements issued prior to the issuance of this FSP.

Interpretation 48 is an interpretation of FASB Statement No. 109, *Accounting for Income Taxes,* which increases the relevancy and comparability of financial reporting by clarifying the way companies account for uncertainty in income taxes. It makes recognition and measurement more consistent, as well as offering clear criteria for subsequently recognizing, derecognizing, and measuring such tax positions for financial statement purposes.

The deferred effective date is intended to provide eligible nonpublic enterprises with more time to apply the provisions of Interpretation 48. The Board approved the deferral based on the recommendation of the Private Company Financial Reporting Committee (PCFRC), which observed that there had been confusion among certain entities as to whether Interpretation 48 applied to them.

¶10,010 FASB Staff Position FIN 48-2, *Effective Date of FASB Interpretation No. 48 for Certain Nonpublic Enterprises*

The Financial Accounting Standards Board (FASB) issued FASB Staff Position (FSP) FIN 48-2, *Effective Date of FASB Interpretation, No. 48 for Certain Nonpublic Enterprises* in February 2008. The final FSP incorporates changes made to the original Exposure Draft, and deferred the effective date of FASB

Interpretation 48, *Accounting for Uncertainty in Income Taxes*, for certain nonpublic enterprises, including nonpublic not-for-profit organizations, to the annual financial statements for fiscal years beginning after December 15, 2007.

Interpretation 48 should be applied as of the beginning of an enterprise's fiscal year. This deferral does not apply to nonpublic consolidated entities of public enterprises that apply U.S. generally accepted accounting principles, nor does it apply to nonpublic enterprises that issued a full set of annual financial statements using the recognition, measurement, and disclosure provisions of Interpretation 48 prior to the issuance of this FSP.

Interpretation 48 is an interpretation of FASB Statement No. 109, *Accounting for Income Taxes*, which increases the relevancy and comparability of financial reporting by clarifying the way companies account for uncertainty in income taxes. It makes recognition and measurement more consistent, as well as offering clear criteria for subsequently recognizing, derecognizing, and measuring such tax positions for financial statement purposes.

The deferred effective date was intended to provide eligible nonpublic enterprises with more time to apply the provisions of Interpretation 48. The Board approved the deferral based on the recommendation of the Private Company Financial Reporting Committee (PCFRC), which observed that there had been confusion among certain entities as to whether Interpretation 48 applied to them.

¶10,011 FASB 136, *Transfers of Assets to a Not-for-Profit Organization or Charitable Trust that Raises or Holds Contributions for Others*

FASB Statement 136, issued in June 1999, established standards for transactions in which a donor makes a contribution by transferring assets to a not-for-profit organization or charitable trust—the recipient organization.

The not-for-profit organization accepts the assets from the donor and agrees to do one of the following:

1. Use those assets on behalf of a beneficiary specified by the donor.
2. Transfer those assets to said beneficiary.
3. Transfer the return on investment of those assets to that beneficiary.
4. Transfer both the assets and the return on investments to the specified beneficiary.

It also establishes standards for transactions that take place in a similar manner but are not contributions because the transfers are any of the following:

1. Revocable.
2. Repayable.
3. Reciprocal.

It follows that the Statement requires a recipient organization that is willing to accept cash or other financial assets from a donor and to agree to abide by the stipulations spelled out above in the interest of that specified unaffiliated beneficiary. In doing so, it also agrees to recognize the fair value of those assets as a liability to the specified beneficiary concurrent with recognition of the assets received from the donor.

However, if the donor explicitly grants the recipient organization variance power, or if the recipient organization and the specified beneficiary are financially *interrelated* organizations, the recipient organization is required to recognize the fair value of any assets it receives as a contribution received.

Not-for-profit organizations are financially interrelated if:

1. One organization has the ability to influence the operating and financial decisions of the other.
2. One organization has an ongoing economic interest in the net assets of the other.

The Statement does not establish standards for a trustee's reporting of assets held on behalf of specified beneficiaries, but it does establish standards for a beneficiary's reporting of its rights to assets held in a charitable trust.

Further, it requires that a specified beneficiary recognize its rights to the assets held by a recipient organization as an asset unless the donor has explicitly granted the recipient organization variance power. Those rights are one of the following:

1. An interest in the net assets of the recipient organization.
2. A beneficial interest.
3. A receivable.

If the beneficiary and the recipient organization are financially interrelated organizations, the beneficiary is required to recognize its interest in the net assets of the recipient organization and adjust that interest for its share of the change in net assets of the recipient organization.

If the beneficiary has an unconditional right to receive all or a portion of the specified cash flows from a charitable trust or other identifiable pool of assets, the beneficiary is required to recognize that beneficial interest, measuring and subsequently remeasuring it at fair value, using a valuation technique such as the present value of the estimated expected future cash flows.

If the recipient organization is explicitly granted variance power, the specified beneficiary does not recognize its potential for future distributions from the assets held by the recipient organization. In all other cases, a beneficiary recognizes its rights as a receivable.

FASB 136 covers four conditions under which a transfer of assets to a recipient organization is accounted for as *a liability* by the recipient organization and as *an asset* by the resource provider because the transfer is revocable or reciprocal. The four circumstances occur when:

1. The transfer is subject to the resource provider's unilateral right to redirect the use of the assets to another beneficiary.
2. The transfer is accompanied by the resource provider's conditional promise to give or is otherwise revocable or repayable.
3. The resource provider controls the recipient organization and specifies an unaffiliated beneficiary.
4. The resource provider specifies itself or its affiliate as the beneficiary and the *transfer is not an equity transaction.*
   a. When the transfer is an equity transaction and the resource provider specifies itself as beneficiary, it records an interest in the net assets of the recipient organization (or an increase in a previously recognized interest).
   b. When the resource provider specifies an affiliate as beneficiary, the resource provider records an equity transaction as a separate line item in its statement of activities, and the affiliate named as beneficiary records an interest in the net assets of the recipient organization. The recipient organization records an equity transaction as a separate line item in its statement of activities.

Certain disclosures are required when a not-for-profit organization transfers assets to a recipient organization and specifies itself or its affiliate as the beneficiary or if it includes in its financial statements a ratio of fundraising expenses to amounts raised.

The Statement incorporates without reconsideration the guidance in FASB Interpretation 42, *Accounting for Transfers of Assets in Which a Not-for-Profit Organization Is Granted Variance Power*, and supersedes that Interpretation. (It states that an NPO should be considered both a *donee* and a *donor* when it receives assets from a resource provider, *and* has received explicit unilateral authority to redistribute the assets and income from the assets to a beneficiary.)

FASB 136 became effective for financial statements issued for fiscal periods beginning after December 15, 1999, except for the provisions incorporated from Interpretation 42, which continue to be effective for fiscal years ending after September 15, 1996. Earlier application was encouraged.

¶10,012   IRS Rulings and Legislation Relating to Disclosure

At the same time that the Financial Accounting Standards Board was adopting FASB 136, the Internal Revenue Service was issuing new rulings relating to the availability to the public of financial documents revealing the details of the operations of not-for-profit (or in the parlance of the IRS, *exempt*) organizations. The new regulations increase the disclosure burden of exempt organizations—and their accountants.

These exempt organizations are entities described in IRC Secs. 501(c) and 501(d) of the Internal Revenue Code and exempt from taxation under IRC Sec. 501(a). They include charitable, educational, scientific, literary, and medical organizations, trade and professional associations, sports leagues, social welfare organizations, public radio and television stations, trade and professional associations, social clubs, cemeteries, and fraternal beneficiary societies. The rules do not apply to disclosure requirements of private foundations.

While many smaller exempt organizations (those with less than $25,000 in annual gross receipts) and churches have traditionally been exempted from filing Form 990, the IRS now requires all exempt organizations to at least "check in" by filing an e-post card form with the IRS annually. For 2011 and after, the threshold for small exempt organizations was raised to include those with under $50,000 in gross receipts (from under $25,000). Tax-exempt organizations that fail to satisfy annual filing requirements for three consecutive years automatically lose their tax-exempt status. If an organization loses its exemption, it will have to reapply to regain its tax-exempt status. Any income received between the revocation date and renewed exemption may be taxable.

Compliance with this provision, however, has turned into a problem, as many of these same smaller exempt organizations did not know of this reporting change. Thus, in 2010, the IRS offered something of an amnesty program for organizations that had not filed in the past three years. This one-time filing relief for small exempt organizations that failed to file for three consecutive years ran only through October 15, 2010. The IRS program was designed to allow small exempt organizations to come back into compliance and retain their tax-exempt status even though they failed to file for three consecutive years. This one-time relief benefitted Form 990-N (e-Postcard) and Form 990-EZ filers only. Organizations required to file the Form 990 or the Form 990-PF were not eligible and were automatically revoked if they failed to file for three consecutive years. 990-N filers must file as required by October 15.

.01   Other Disclosure Requirements

Considering the huge sums of money that many of these NPOs handle, it is not surprising that in addition to other FASB Standards discussed later in this chapter, Congress has seen fit to set up some rules relating to disclosure by not-for-profits. Legislation has included the Omnibus Budget Reconciliation Act of 1987 and the Taxpayer Bill of Rights 2, passed in 1996.

The former requires exempt organizations, including public foundations, to provide access for public inspection of their tax exemption applications. It also required that they (other than private foundations) allow public inspection at their principal offices of the last three years' annual reports. The Taxpayer Bill of Rights 2 provided for additional public disclosures which have been finalized in these IRS rulings.

.02   Specific Documents for Inspection

Not only do the most recent rulings specify *what* should be disclosed, but they are very specific about *how* and *where* applicable documents are made available by the exempt organization (other than a private foundation). The most recent addition to the list is Form 990-T filed after August 17, 2006. Form 990-T is the Exempt Organization Business Income Tax Return used to report income from unrelated business income over $1,000.

The documents that must be available upon request for inspection if they apply to the particular organization include:

1. Form 990, *Return of Organization Exempt from Income Tax.*
2. Form 990-T, *Exempt Organization Business Income Tax Return.*
3. Form 990BL, *Information and Initial Excise Tax Return for Black Lung Benefit Trusts and Certain Related Persons.*
4. Form 990EZ, *Short Form Return for Organization Exempt from Income Tax.*
5. Form 1023, *Application for Recognition of Exemption Under Section 501(c) (3) of the Internal Revenue Code.*
6. Form 1024, *Application for Recognition of Exemption Under Section 501(a) for Determination Under Section 120 of the Internal Revenue Code.*
7. Form 1065, *U.S. Partnership Return of Income.*

In addition to the documents themselves, other relevant information must also be made available:

For Form 1023 or 1024, all supporting documents filed by, or on behalf of the organization in connection with that application, as well as any correspondence with the IRS should be available. If the application was filed before July 15, 1987, the organization need not supply the document unless the organization possessed a copy of the application on that date.

For Form 990, 990-EZ, 990-BL or 1065, including all schedules and attachments filed with the IRS, the organization must make available its three most recent returns. However, in the interest of confidentiality, the organization should *not* including the portions of the returns that give the names and addresses of contributors.

The exempt organization must also copy documents, or portions thereof, when requested either in writing or in person.

.03   Procedures

The ruling is quite specific about establishing the various procedures for making these documents available for public inspection.

1. It specifies the amount of fees for copying and postage the organization may charge. The organization may charge a reasonable amount for copying and mailing as long as it does not exceed the IRS fees for copies of documents (currently $1 for the first page and 15 cents for each subsequent page). They can charge for the actual cost of postage.
2. It gives instructions on *where* the documents must be available for inspection. In general, the documents must be made available at the organization's principal office, and at larger regional or district offices.
3. It sets limitations an organization may put on requests for copies of documents. Copies of documents should normally be available upon personal request the same day at the place where the documents are available for inspection. Under unusual circumstances, the organization may respond on the next business day, or on the business day following the day the unusual circumstances occurred, as long as the delay does not exceed 5 business days. Written requests must be honored within 30 days of receipt.
4. It outlines how an organization can avoid having to respond to individual requests for copies. Rather than furnish copies, an organization may put the documents on its Web page or another Web site where there is a database of similar information. Placing the specified documents on the Internet covers the requirement to provide copies, but the organization must still allow public inspection. The regulations specify a number of criteria for posting documents on the Internet.
    a. The documents must be posted so that the public can view, download, and print them in the same format as the original document.
    b. The documents must be accessible without a fee and without having any specialized computer hardware or software.
5. It furnishes guidance to organizations that believe they are the victims of harassment campaigns. If an exempt organization has sufficient cause based on facts and circumstances to believe it is the victim of a harassment campaign, it may take certain steps:
    a. Demonstrate that a group of apparently unreasonable requests aims to disrupt the organization's operations rather than to obtain information.

b. Refuse to respond to those requests.
c. Request the IRS district director for a determination.
d. While a determination is pending, the organization need not respond to the apparently frivolous requests.
e. Comply on a timely basis with any seemingly valid requests.

.04   Noncompliance

The IRS has set rather stiff penalties for noncompliance:

1. An *individual* whose duty it is to make the required disclosures, but fails to comply without reasonable cause with his or her obligations on behalf of the exempt organization is subject to a penalty of $20 per return or exemption application for each day the failure continues. The maximum penalty for failure to disclose is $10,000 per return. No maximum is specified for the exemption application.
2. An exempt *organization* that willfully fails to comply with the requirement to allow public inspection or to provide copies of returns or exemption applications upon proper request is liable for a $5,000 penalty (per return or application).
3. Criminal penalties may be applied to any person or exempt organization that willfully furnishes false or fraudulent information.

¶10,013   FASB Statement 124, *Accounting for Certain Investments Held by Not-for-Profit Organizations*

FASB 124 is another step in the process of bringing reason, conformity, consistency, and comparability in accounting and financial reporting to the world of not-for-profit entities.

This Statement is reminiscent of FASB 115, *Accounting for Certain Investments in Debt and Equity Securities*, to the extent that it covers the same securities; however, accounting treatment for NPOs is markedly different from that applied to for-profit businesses.

.01   Fair Value Requirements

Statement 124 requires that certain equity securities and all investments in debt securities be reported at fair value. The specific equity securities are those with readily determined fair value which are not accounted for by the equity method or as investments in consolidated subsidiaries. Gains and losses are to be reported in the statement of activities. This Statement also requires specific disclosures about all investments, including the return on the investments.

Readily determinable fair value of an equity security is considered to have been met if one of the following criteria applies:

1. Sale prices or bid or asked quotations are available on an SEC registered exchange.
2. Sales prices or bid or asked prices on OTC markets if they are reported by NASDAQ or the National Quotation Bureau.
3. If the equity security is traded only on a foreign market, that market is comparable to one of those given above.
4. If a mutual fund investment, fair value per share or unit has been determined and published as the basis for ongoing transactions.

Although many NPOs have been reporting all of their investments at fair value, it has not been required; therefore, there has been a considerable degree of diversity in the various organizations' accounting and financial reporting. The FASB believes that fair value will give a truer picture of the resources available for the further growth of the program of a not-for-profit organization. In addition, not only the staff and administrators, but also the donors will have improved information to assist them in allocating their efforts and resources.

.02 Accounting Procedures

Application of this Statement may be made in either of two ways:

1. Restating of all financial statements presented for prior years.
2. Recognizing the cumulative effect of the change in the year of adoption.

Accounting and reporting for investments by various types of not-for-profit organizations has heretofore been provided by several AICPA guides. Any guidance in those sources which is inconsistent with the provisions of FASB 124 are superseded by these new requirements in this Statement.

In addition to the accounting principles set forth in this pronouncement, any additional disclosure and accounting requirements not discussed here but included in other Statements may apply to investments held by not-for-profit entities as well as to for-profit companies. They are:

1. FASB 107, *Disclosure about Fair Value of Financial Instruments* (amended).
2. FASB 133, *Accounting for Derivative Instruments and Hedging Activities*.

.03 Disclosure and Reporting

The Statement of Activities for each reporting period for an NPO must include the following specific items:

1. Investment income from dividends, interest, etc.
2. Net gains or losses on investments reported at other than fair value.
3. Net gains or losses on those reported at fair value.
4. Reconciliation of investment return if separated into operating and nonoperating amounts.
5. Description of the policy used to decide what items should be included in determining operating costs.
6. Discussion for so doing if there is a change in that policy.

The Statement of Financial Position for each reporting period for an NPO must include the following:

1. Aggregate carrying amount of investments by major type.
2. Basis on which carrying amounts were determined for investments other than equity securities with readily determinable fair value and all debt securities.
3. Procedures used in determining fair values of investments other than financial instruments if carried at fair value. (Financial instruments are covered by the same requirement in FASB 107.)
4. Aggregate amount of any deficiencies in donor-related funds in which fair value of the assets has fallen below the level necessary to abide by donor stipulation or legal requirements.

For the most recent period, a not-for-profit organization must disclose in the Statement of Financial Position the nature of and carrying amount of any investments that represent a significant concentration of market risk.

¶10,014   FASB Statement 116, *Accounting for Contributions Received and Contributions Made,* and FASB Statement 117, *Financial Statements of Not-for-Profit Organizations*

In the past, differing requirements, or deficient guidelines, have led divergent forms of not-for-profit enterprises to abide by various rulings promulgated for their particular type of organization, to follow lines of least resistance, or merely to perpetuate custom. This was true whether or not the organization or the external users were gaining insightful information from the various accounting and reporting procedures. The new rules supersede any/all inconsistencies or discrepancies with previous guides, announcements, or statements.

Statement 116 has been superseded by ASU No. 2018-08 but an overview is included here for historical purposes. It specifically addressed accounting standards for contributions of cash, assets, services or unconditional promises to provide these at some future time, made or received by any organization, whether it be a not-for-profit or a for-profit business concern:

1. Contributions *received*, including unconditional promises to give, are recognized at fair market value in the period received.
2. Contributions *made*, including unconditional promises to give, are recognized as expenses at fair market value in the period when given.
3. Conditional promises to give (whether received or made) are appropriately recognized when the conditions are substantially met.

This Statement acts to tighten some of the provisions relating to measurement and recognition of volunteer services and their relevancy. It specifies that before these services can be included in revenue, they must create or enhance nonfinancial assets, be of a specialized nature, and be provided by skilled individuals contributing services that would otherwise be purchased. Therefore, the services requiring little skill or training provided by the average volunteer will not be considered as revenue or gains. On the other hand, volunteer work by trained professionals and tradesmen, such as nurses, teachers, carpenters, plumbers may be measured at fair value and recognized in the financial report with explanatory notes describing the value of service rendered to various aspects of particular programs. Recognition of these services must also be deemed to be clearly relevant and clearly measurable. If practicable, the fair value of the ordinary volunteer services contributed but not recognized as revenue should also be disclosed even though not recognized as revenue.

Both Statements 116 and 117 take into consideration three classes of contributions:

1. Permanently restricted net assets.
2. Temporarily restricted net assets.
3. Unrestricted net assets.

Statement 116 also requires accounting for the expiration of donor-imposed restrictions if/when said restrictions expire. It also establishes standards for accounting for disclosures relating to works of art, historical treasures, rare books and manuscripts—collections whether capitalized or not.

To be considered a "collection," the assets must be:

1. For the purpose of public exhibition, education or research, not an investment for financial gain.
2. Conserved, cared for, and remain unencumbered.
3. Protected by an organizational policy requiring that proceeds from the sale of any collection items be used to acquire other items for collections.

¶10,014

An organization is not required to recognize contributions if they are added to collections which meet the above criteria. However, when applying FASB 116, organizations are encouraged to capitalize previously acquired collections retroactively or to capitalize them on a prospective basis. One stipulation is that capitalization of selected collections or items is *not* permitted. If capitalized retroactively, these assets may be stated at their cost, at fair value at the time of acquisition, current cost or current market value.

When collections have been capitalized, additional contributed items are to be recognized as revenue or gains; if the collections have not been capitalized, these items are not recognized. There is, however, additional disclosure information required for them and for collections which have been capitalized prospectively.

1. On the face of the statement of activities, apart from revenues, expenses, gains and losses an organization that has not capitalized must report the cost of items purchased as a decrease in the appropriate class of net assets; or proceeds resulting from the sale of items; or from insurance recoveries as an increase in the appropriate class of net assets.
2. An organization that capitalizes prospectively must report proceeds from sales or insurance recoveries of items not previously capitalized separately.
3. Both those organizations that do not capitalize, or do so prospectively, must describe the collections and their significance, and the accounting conservatorship policies relating to them.
4. They must also describe and report the fair value of items lost or removed from collections for whatever reason.
5. A line in the body of the financial statement must refer directly to the note on collections.

In addition to the accounting functions which these stipulations provide, they would appear to help ensure the integrity of important collections.

FASB 117 has been updated by ASU No. 2016-14 but is included here for historical purposes. The intent and purpose of FASB 117 was to begin to bring a measure of uniformity to the financial statements of NPOs, particularly for the benefit of external users. Emphasis is upon relevance and significance of the information provided, the ease with which it can be understood and interpreted, and the readiness with which financial reports can be compared with those of other not-for-profit entities.

FASB 117 stipulates that three financial statements with appropriate notes be included in all NPO financial reports:

1. Statement of financial position.
2. Statement of activities.
3. Statement of cash flows.

This latter requirement is new for not-for-profit entities and thus amends FASB 95, *Statement of Cash Flows*, in which the requirements had previously applied only to business entities. Statement 117 also *requires* Voluntary Health and Welfare Organizations (*encourages* other NPOs) to prepare an additional financial statement showing expenses in natural classifications as well as the functional classifications required of all NPOs. Organizations may continue to present other financial reports if they have found them to be beneficial in demonstrating the handling of the service aspects of the particular type of NPO.

Most organizations probably found that their accounting and reporting activities had not become more complicated and restrictive, but simplified, and at the same time, more meaningful once the initial changeover had been completed. This is particularly true if the organization carried fund accounting to the extreme and attempted to fit everything into the pattern whether or not this proved to be appropriate or useful. Statement 117 does not tamper with fund accounting *per se* but does require that the emphasis on financial reporting be placed on the entity as a whole. Thus, organizations may continue to prepare their statement of financial position showing fund groups, but the groups must be aggregated into net asset classes.

In line with the aim to give a clear picture of an NPO's liquidity, FASB 117 requires that an organization must break down its net assets into the three classes mentioned above. Further, information about the amounts and/or conditions of the two restricted categories can be made in the statement itself if this is deemed sufficient, or it may be necessary to give detailed explanations in the notes. The latter could be more frequently necessary than not, since the restrictions could range from a wealthy donor's desire to aid a "pet project" to a government grant funding a Congressional bill.

Much of the impetus for these statements was to bring about more readily usable full disclosure. Requirements will now make it more important than ever to distinguish between program and support activities and expenses. FASB 117 separates the latter into three classes:

1. Managements and general.
2. Fund-raising.
3. Membership development.

It is important for the preparer of the financial statement to be reminded that the focus should be on the *service* aspect of the NPO and how well this is being accomplished. Since it is doubtful if this information can be conveyed adequately in the body of the financial statement, the accompanying notes will be of particular relevance.

Below are some important points to keep in mind relating to the purpose of the three basic financial reports of not-for-profit entities.

.01   Statement of Financial Position

- Present assets, liabilities and net asset figures for the organization as a whole.
- Demonstrate credit status, liquidity, ability to meet service and financial obligations, need for outside financial aid.
- Distinguish between permanently restricted assets, temporarily restricted assets, unrestricted assets.
- Disclose donor-imposed restrictions and internally imposed restrictions relating to both time and purpose.

.02   Statement of Activities (Operating Statement for NPOs)

- Report the changes in total net assets (equities).
- Present the changes in each of the three net asset classes (not fund balances): permanently restricted, temporarily restricted, unrestricted.
- Indicate total changes in net assets.
- Disclose expenditures by functional and/or natural classification as required/recommended for a particular type of NPO.

.03   Statement of Cash Flows

- Amends FASB 95 to require *all* NPOs to include a cash flow statement in their external financial reports.
- Present changes in cash and cash equivalents including certain donor-restricted cash used on a long-term basis.
- Present cash flow information utilizing either direct or indirect method.

.04   Accounting Standards Update No. 2018-08

The FASB issued ASU No. 2018-08 that clarifies and improves the scope and accounting guidance around contributions of cash and other assets received and made by not-for-profit organizations (NFPs) and business enterprises. The ASU clarifies and improves current guidance about whether a transfer of assets, or the reduction, settlement, or cancellation of liabilities, is a contribution or an exchange transaction.

It also provides a more robust framework for determining whether a contribution is conditional or unconditional, and for distinguishing a donor-imposed condition from a donor-imposed restriction. The classification affects the timing of contribution revenue and expense recognition.

The amendments in ASU No. 2018-08 should be applied on a modified prospective basis. Retrospective application is permitted. Under a modified prospective basis, in the first set of financial statements following the effective date, the amendments should be applied to agreements that are either:

- Not completed as of the effective date; or
- Entered into after the effective date.

A completed agreement is an agreement for which all the revenue (of a recipient) or expense (of a resource provider) has been recognized before the effective date in accordance with current guidance.

The amendments in ASU No. 2018-08 should be applied only to the portion of revenue or expense that has not yet been recognized before the effective date in accordance with current guidance. No prior-period results should be restated, and there should be no cumulative-effect adjustment to the opening balance of net assets or retained earnings at the beginning of the year of adoption.

.05   Accounting Standards Update No. 2019-03

The FASB issued ASU No. 2019-03 that modifies the definition of the term collections to include items that are sold for the acquisition of new collection items and/or the direct care of existing collections. The amendments also require a collection-holding entity to disclose its policy for the use of proceeds from when collection items are deaccessioned or removed from a collection. Further, if a collection-holding entity has a policy that allows proceeds from deaccessioned collection items to be used for direct care, it should disclose its definition of direct care.

While the amendments apply to all entities that maintain collections, the amendments primarily apply to NFPs. Accounting for collections is an issue for certain NFPs that have collections such as museums, botanical gardens, libraries, aquariums, arboretums, historic sites, planetariums, zoos, art galleries, nature, science, and technology centers, and similar educational, research, and public service organizations.

¶10,015   Helpful IRS Instructional Videos

The Internal Revenue Service launched a program to help exempt organizations and their tax preparers better understand the newly revised Form. They can be found at irsvideos.gov/CharitiesAnd NonProfits and include:

- **Backup Withholding**
- **Car Donations**
- **Did you lose your tax-exempt status? Why it happens and how to fix it?**
- **Exploring the Charities and Nonprofits Webpage**
- **File Error-Free Form 1023 EZ Webinar**
- **File Error-Free Forms 990**
- **Fundraising Guidelines for Charities**
- **TIN Matching Program and other related items.**

.01   What Form to Use

In general, nonprofits are required to file annual returns except for some entities such as a church, a school below college affiliated to a church, certain state institution or governmental unit. If an organization does not file a required return or files late, penalties may be assessed.

Depending on the organization's gross receipts and total assets, the certain Form 990 has to be used as follows:

Gross receipts normally less than $50,000	990-N (postcard)
Gross receipts less than $200,000 and total assets less than $500,000	990-EZ or 990
Gross receipts is or more than $200,000 and total assets is or more than $500,000	990
Private foundation – regardless of financial status	990-PF

Organizations eligible to file the e-Postcard may choose to file a full return. All these returns can now be efiled.

CHAPTER 11
International Standards: Accounting

¶11,000   Overview

International Accounting Standards (IASs) are developed and published by the International Accounting Standards Board (IASB). The IASB is an independent group of experts with an appropriate mix of recent practical experience in setting accounting standards, in preparing, auditing, or using financial reports, and in accounting education. Broad geographical diversity is also required. (IFRS.org)

International Financial Reporting Standards (IFRS) are set by the IFRS Foundation. IFRS Foundation is a not-for-profit, public interest organization established to develop a single set of high-quality, understandable, enforceable and globally accepted accounting standards—IFRSs—and to promote and facilitate adoption of the standards. (IFRS.org)

¶11,001   Recent Developments

IFRS continues to work on the second comprehensive review of the IFRS for SMEs. Deadline to send comments were extended to October 27, 2020, due to the coronavirus (COVID-19) pandemic. Discussions continued through 2022 and into 2023. A final amendment titled, "International Tax Reform - Pillar Two Model Rules – Amendments to the IFRS for SMEs Standard" was published in September 2023 and effective as of January 1, 2023.

The IASB issued two new standards in early 2024:

IFRS 19, Subsidiaries without Public Accountability: Disclosures

IFRS 19 specifies reduced disclosure requirements that an eligible entity is permitted to apply instead of the full disclosure requirements in other IFRS Accounting Standards. Application of IFRS 19 is an option that may be elected and that may later be revoked.

IFRS 18, Presentation and Disclosures in Financial Statements

IFRS 18 replaces IAS 1, *Presentation of Financial Statements.* The objective of IFRS 18 is to set out requirements for the presentation and disclosure of information in general-purpose financial statements to help ensure they provide relevant information that faithfully represents an entity's assets, liabilities, equity, income, and expenses. It applies to all financial statements that are prepared and presented in accordance with IFRS.

The Standard addresses general requirements for financial statements, including what is contained in a complete set of financial statements; aggregation and disaggregation; as well as specific requirements for each specific statement and the notes.

In 2022 and 2023, the IASB issued several small amendments to IFRS as follows:

- Amendments were made to IAS 12 for deferred tax related to assets and liabilities arising from a single transaction.
- Amendments were made to IAS 1, Practice Statement 2, and IAS 8 regarding disclosure of accounting policies and definition of accounting estimates.
- Amendments to the "technology" of the IFRS Accounting Taxonomy, meaning the syntax used to publish and express the content and the taxonomy architecture used. There were no changes in any content.
- Amendments to the initial application of IFRS 17 and IFRS 9, related to comparative information.

In 2021, the IASB issued several small amendments to IFRS as follows:

- Amendments to the definition of accounting estimates in IAS 8.
- Amendments to IAS 1 and IFRS Practice Statement 2 regarding disclosure of accounting policies.
- Amendments to IFRS 17, extension of the temporary exemption from applying IFRS 9 and property, plant and equipment—proceeds before intended use amendments to IFRS 17, IFRS 4, and IAS 16.
- Amendments to provide general improvements and common practice presentation of information in primary financial statements, impacting IFRS 3, IFRS 15, IFRS 16, IFRS 37, IAS 1, IAS 21, IAS 12, IAS 7, IFRS 5, and IAS 33.

¶11,001

- Amendments making general improvements and common practice related to IAS 19, *Employee Benefits*.
- Amendments to IFRS 16, regarding rent concessions related to COVID-19.
- Amendments to IFRS 1 and IAS 12 regarding deferred tax related to assets and liabilities arising from a single transaction.
- Amendments related to initial implementation of IFRS 17 and 9 regarding comparative information.

In 2020, the IASB issued several small amendments to IFRS as follows:

- Amendments to IAS 1 regarding the classification of liabilities as current or non-current.
- Amendments to IFRS 9, IAS 39, and IFRS 7 regarding 2019 interest rate benchmark reform.
- Amendments to IAS 16 regarding the proceeds before intended use of property, plant and equipment.
- Amendments to IFRS 3 regarding the reference to the conceptual framework.
- Amendments to IFRS 37 regarding onerous contracts—cost of fulfilling a contract.
- Amendments to IFRS 16, IFRS 9, IFRS 1 and IAS 41, making annual improvements to IFRS.
- Amendments to IFRS 16 regarding COVID-19-related rent concessions.
- Amendments to IFRS 17 and 4 providing an extension of the temporary exemption of applying IFRS 9.
- Amendments to IFRS 17 impacting several other standards.
- Amendments to IFRS 17 regarding insurance contracts.
- Amendments to IAS 1 regarding the classification of liabilities as current or non-current—deferral of effective date.
- Amendments to IFRS 16 to make further changes to COVID-19-related rent concessions.
- Amendments to IAS 39, IFRS 9, IFRS 7, and IFRS 4 regarding interest rate benchmark reform—phase 2.
- Additional amendments to IAS 39, IFRS 9, IFRS 7, and IFRS 4 regarding interest rate benchmark reform—phase 2.

In 2019, the IASB issued several small amendments to IFRS as follows:

- Amendments to IAS 16, *Property, Plant and Equipment*, to prohibit a company from deducting from the cost of property, plant and equipment amounts received from selling items produced while the company is preparing the asset for its intended use. Instead, a company will recognize such sales proceeds and related cost in profit or loss.

- Amendments to IAS 37, *Provisions, Contingent Liabilities and Contingent Assets,* specifying which costs a company includes when assessing whether a contract will be loss-making.
- Annual Improvements make minor amendments to IFRS 1, *First-time Adoption of International Financial Reporting Standards,* IFRS 9, *Financial Instruments,* IAS 41, *Agriculture,* and the Illustrative Examples accompanying IFRS 16, *Leases.*

In May 2015, the International Accounting Standards Board (IASB) published amendments to its "International Financial Reporting Standard for Small and Medium-sized Entities" (IFRS for SMEs). The amendments are the result of the first comprehensive review of that standard, which was originally issued in 2009. They affect 21 of the 35 sections of the standard (not counting consequential amendments) and the glossary, however, most of the changes are rather minor.

In 2018, the IASB issued the revised Conceptual Framework for Financial Reporting (Conceptual Framework) that underpins IFRS. The Conceptual Framework provides the fundamental concepts of financial reporting that guide the IASB in developing IFRSs. It also helps ensure that IFRSs are conceptually consistent and that similar transactions are treated the same way. This way, the Conceptual Framework and IFRS provide consistent and useful information for investors and others. See ¶11,009.

The vast majority of the changes concern clarifications to the current text and, hence, will not constitute changes to the way entities account for certain transactions and events. For more information, see IFRS for SMEs at ¶11,008.19.

¶11,002   IASB and FASB Agreed on Revenue Recognition

Revenue recognition is the most frequent cause of financial statement restatements. Having clear yet flexible guidance is thus critical. While both IFRS and U.S. GAAP provided its own guidance, each system had recognized limits. IFRS provided limited guidance for some complex transactions while U.S. GAAP's industry-specific guidance could result in diverse treatment for economically similar transactions. One of the stated goals of the new guidance is to improve comparability "across entities, industries, jurisdictions and capital markets." The primary guidance is the issuance of IFRS 15, *Revenue from Contracts with Customers.*

According to the IASB, under the new guidance, "an entity recognizes revenue to depict the transfer of promised goods or services to customers in an amount that reflects the consideration to which the entity expects to be entitled in exchange for those goods and services."

The core principle of the new standard, according to FASB, is for companies to "recognize revenue to depict the transfer of goods or services to customers in amounts that reflect the consideration (that is, payment) to which the company expects to be entitled in exchange for those goods or services." The new standard calls for enhanced disclosures about revenue recognition, providing guidance for transactions that were not previously addressed comprehensively (for example, service revenue and contract modifications).

Generally, the new rules are applicable to all companies in all industries, but with a few exceptions. The new requirements include more extensive disclosure of the specifics of contracts with customers so the readers of the financial statements can better understand how the company is recognizing revenue. Depending on the kinds of customer contracts used, companies need to supply information on the factors related to determining the transaction price as well as information about changes in contracts and obligations for future performance on contracts that remain open at the year-end. The complexities for companies dealing in long-term contracts and contracts involving multiple steps in measuring performance may be significant.

The new guidance has specific impact on revenue generated in connection with performance obligations occurring over time, sales with a right of return, consignment sales, sales with options, the effects of warranty contracts, non-refundable upfront fees, bill-and-hold agreements, repurchase agreements, and customer acceptance.

Both the IASB and the FASB amended their original agreement and postponed the effective date for application of the new standard, *Revenue from Contracts with Customers*, until 2018.

¶11,003   IASB and FASB Mostly Agreed on Lease Accounting Approach

The International Accounting Standards Board (IASB) and the Financial Accounting Standards Board (FASB) agreed in June 2012 to an approach for accounting for lease expenses as part of a project to revise lease accounting in International Financial Reporting Standards (IFRSs) and the U.S. Generally Accepted Accounting Principles (U.S. GAAP).

The boards undertook the leases project to address the widespread concern that many lease obligations currently are not recorded on the balance sheet and that the current accounting for lease transactions does not represent the economics of all lease transaction. Lease standards have been released by both boards.

The boards previously agreed that leases should be recorded on the balance sheet, but differed in the classification and pattern of expenses in the income statement. The IASB decided upon an approach in which most lease contracts would be accounted for using an approach similar to that used previously for capital leases. The FASB decided that some leases would be treated that way but other leases will be accounted for using an approach that results in a straight-line lease expense. See further detailed information in Chapter 6, "Broad Accounting and Reporting Issues."

¶11,004   The Nature of International Accounting

One of the central goals of the movement to unify international accounting practices is the need for financial reporting comparability. Whereas U.S. GAAP seeks meaningful comparison in financial reporting among companies in the same industry, the impetus in international accounting is to avoid reporting that produces different income statement results for the same company during the same period, when the reports are prepared in one country rather than another.

To accommodate relevant differences between countries, one of the principles underlying the desire to unify international accounting practices is to allow reporting flexibility without producing distortion. Since the goal of international accounting, like that of U.S. GAAP accounting, is to produce general-purpose financial statements, it is not necessary to impose a strict standardization. Rather, a coordination or harmonization of reporting that leaves room for legitimate differences but still produces meaningful financial reporting is the desired result.

The Financial Accounting Standards Board (FASB) believes the ideal outcome of cooperative international accounting standard-setting efforts will be the worldwide use of a single set of high-quality accounting standards for both U.S. and cross-border financial reporting. The FASB's objective is to increase the international comparability and the quality of standards used in the United States. Here, domestic firms that are registrants with the Securities and Exchange Commission (SEC) must file financial reports using U.S. GAAP. Foreign firms filing with the SEC can use U.S. GAAP, their home country U.S. GAAP, or international standards. However, if they use their home country U.S. GAAP or international standards, foreign issuers must provide reconciliation to U.S. GAAP. As international standards and U.S. GAAP converge the reconciliation will become easier and involve fewer substantive issues.

In 2002, the FASB and the International Accounting Standards Board (IASB) announced the issuance of a memorandum of understanding, the "Norwalk Agreement." The Agreement was a significant step toward formalizing their commitment to the convergence of U.S. and international accounting standards. At their joint meeting in Norwalk, Connecticut, the FASB and the IASB each acknowledged their commitment to the development of high-quality, compatible accounting standards that can be used for both domestic and cross-border financial reporting. At that meeting, both the FASB and the IASB pledged to use their best efforts to (a) make their existing financial reporting standards fully compatible as soon as practicable and (b) to coordinate their future work programs to ensure that once achieved, compatibility is maintained.

In 2006, a new Memorandum of Understanding was drafted and in 2008, this Memorandum was updated to reflect progress to date and establish priorities. The purpose of the Memorandum was to lay out the steps necessary to complete the convergence process. In 2009, the boards of the two organizations met to set milestone targets for completing the major projects listed in the Memorandum, with an expected completion during 2011. In 2011, the expected completion date was extended until 2012.

¶11,005   2005 Reporting Standards for Listed Public Companies in the EU

Starting January 1, 2005, listed public companies in European Union (EU) were required to report financial results using International Accounting Standards (IASs) and IFRSs. There was a temporary exception for companies that are traded in the United States and use U.S. GAAP and for companies that had issued debt instruments but not equity instruments. Those companies were required to comply with international standards by January 1, 2007.

¶11,006   Exemptions for Small and Medium-Sized Entities

Those responsible for establishing International Accounting Standards recognize the disparity in size between large entities and medium-sized or smaller entities. In the United States, the issue of big GAAP and little GAAP has been around for a long time. The central question regards the relative financial reporting responsibility of entities whose stock is traded on public markets as opposed to privately held entities.

On July 9, 2009, the International Accounting Standards Board (IASB) issued the IFRS for Small and Medium-Sized Entities (IFRS for SMEs). This Standard provides an alternative framework that can be applied by eligible entities in place of the full set of International Financial Reporting Standards (IFRSs) at issue.

The IFRS for SMEs is a self-contained Standard, incorporating accounting principles that are based on full IFRSs but that have been simplified to suit the entities within its scope (known as SMEs). By removing some accounting treatments permitted under full IFRSs, eliminating topics and disclosure requirements that are not generally relevant to SMEs, and simplifying requirements for recognition and measurement, the IFRS for SMEs reduces the volume of accounting requirements applicable to SMEs by more than 90 percent when compared with the full set of IFRSs.

Where financial statements are prepared using the Standard, the basis of presentation note (and, where applicable, the auditor's report) would refer to compliance with the IFRS for SMEs. Many SMEs may find that this internationally recognized "cachet" for their financial statements will improve their access to capital.

The IASB did not set an effective date for the Standard because the decision as to whether to adopt the IFRS for SMEs (and also, therefore, the timing for adoption) is a matter for each jurisdiction.

The complete IFRS for SMEs (together with basis for conclusions, illustrative financial statements, and presentation and disclosure checklist) can be downloaded free from http://go.iasb.org/IFRSforSMEs.

The IASB did a first review of the IFRS for SMEs in 2012, resulting in amendments in May 2015. A second review was started in 2019, with an exposure draft of an amended standard published in September 2022, with an addendum added in March 2024 with comments requested by July 31, 2024.

¶11,007   International Accounting Standards Changes

The International Accounting Standards Board (IASB) adopted the Standards issued by its predecessor body, the International Accounting Standards Committee (IASC). It is now in the process of reviewing and, where necessary, making changes to those standards. Those pronouncements continue to be designated "International Accounting Standards". Following are lists of the IASs to be applied in preparing financial statements, though they are subject to revision. They represent the core group of international standards necessary for cross-border reporting. The IASB employs an annual improvement process to determine which standards need revision and improvement. In April of 2009 it released the results of its most recent improvement project. IASs affected by this round of modifications include numbers IAS 1 (modifying the classification of convertible securities as current or noncurrent), IAS 7 (relating to expenditures on unrecognized assets), IAS 17 (relating to leases of land and buildings), IAS 18 (whether entity is principal or agent), IAS 36 (goodwill impairment), IAS 38 (fair value of intangible assets), and IAS 39 (exemption for business combination contracts, relating to loan repayment penalties and cash flow hedge accounting).

.01   IAS 1, Presentation of Financial Statements

The Standard is applicable for annual periods beginning on or after January 1, 2005. Critical judgments made by management in applying accounting policies must be disclosed (par. IN12). Disclosure is also required for management's assumptions that are important in determining accounting estimates and could cause material adjustment to the carrying amounts of assets and liabilities (par.

IN12) the Standard does not apply to interim financial statements (IAS 34, *Interim Financial Reporting*). The financial statement is to consist of a balance sheet, an income statement, a statement of changes in equity, and a cash flow statement, as well as notes comprising a summary of significant accounting policies, and other explanatory disclosures.

The following specific requirements are mandated:

- Accrual basis accounting.
- Going concern basis.
- Consistent classification schemes from one period to the next.
- Related assets and liabilities are not offset.
- Presentation of comparative information.
- Separate statement of current and noncurrent assets and liabilities.

2011 amendments to IAS 1, *Presentation of Financial Statements,* require companies preparing financial statements in accordance with IFRSs to group together items within Other Comprehensive Income (OCI) that may be reclassified to the profit or loss section of the income statement. The amendments also reaffirm existing requirements that items in OCI and profit or loss should be presented as either a single statement or two consecutive statements.

The definition of "material" was amended to make it easier for companies to make materiality judgments. The amendments clarify the definition of material and how it should be applied. The explanations accompanying the definition have been improved. The new definition is consistent across all IFRS.

The updated definition amends IAS 1 and IAS 8. The changes are effective from January 1, 2020, but companies can decide to apply them.

In 2019, the IASB issued narrow-scope amendments to clarify how to classify debt and other liabilities as current or noncurrent. The objective is to promote consistency in applying the IAS 1 requirements by helping companies determine whether, in the statement of financial position, debt and other liabilities with an uncertain settlement date should be classified as current or non-current. The amendments include clarifying the classification requirements for debt a company might settle by converting it into equity.

The amendments clarify, not change, existing requirements. They are not expected to affect companies' financial statements significantly. However, these amendments could result in companies reclassifying some liabilities from current to non-current, and vice versa. Thus, this could affect a company's loan covenants. So to give companies time to prepare for the amendments, the IASB decided to provide two years to comply.

The amendments are effective for annual periods beginning on or after January 1, 2022.

.02   IAS 2, Inventories

The Standard is applicable for annual periods beginning on or after January 1, 2005. According to IASB the guidance "specifies the requirements for the recognition of inventory as an asset and an expense, the measurement of inventories and disclosures relating to inventories." The cost of inventories, other than those for which specific identification of cost are used, is assigned using first-in, first-out (FIFO) or a weighted average cost flow method. LIFO (last-in, first-out) inventory valuation method sometimes used in the U.S. and elsewhere has been removed (par. IN13). Inventories are measured at the lower of cost or net realizable value. Net realizable value is the estimated selling price in the ordinary course of business less the estimated costs of completion and the estimated costs necessary to sell. The amount of any write-down of inventories to net realizable value is recognized as an expense in the period the write-down or loss occurs.

.03   IAS 7, Cash Flow Statements

Like U.S. GAAP, cash flows are segregated into operating, investing and financing activities. Reporting cash flows allows readers of the financial statements to supplement the income statement and balance sheet perspectives allowing a fuller understanding of the quality of earnings. Operating activities are the primary revenue generating activities of the company—what it does for a living—and their sufficiency for continuing growth, repaying debt and paying dividends are a key consideration in evaluating a company's financial health. Also paralleling U.S. GAAP is the choice to construct the cash flow statement using either the direct or the indirect method, though preference is expressed for the direct method. This Standard "Requires disclosures about the historical changes in cash," according to IASB "and cash equivalents of an entity." Further, the guidance assists "existing and potential investors, lenders and other creditors to assess the ability of the entity to generate cash and cash equivalents and to utilize those cash flows."

On January 2016, IASB issued "Disclosure Initiative, Amendments to IAS 7." The amendments are effective for annual periods beginning on or after January 1, 2017.

The amendments require companies to disclose information about changes in their financing liabilities. The amendments come as a response to requests from investors for information to help them better understand the changes in a company's debt. Thus, the amendments will help investors to evaluate changes in liabilities arising from financing activities, including changes from cash flows and non-cash changes (i.e., foreign exchange gains or losses).

The improvements are part of the IASB's Disclosure Initiative—a portfolio of projects aimed at improving the effectiveness of disclosures in financial reports.

.04 IAS 8, Accounting Policies, Changes in Accounting Estimates, and Errors

This Standard was largely mirrored by U.S. GAAP in FASB 154 as part of the international convergence process. Retrospective application of voluntary changes in accounting policies and retrospective restatement to correct all material prior-period errors are now required. This means a change in accounting policy is applied retrospectively to all periods presented in the financial statements as if the new accounting policy had always been applied.

A material prior-period error is corrected retrospectively in the first set of financial statements after its discovery. The comparative amounts for the prior periods presented in which the error occurred are restated. Before this change IAS 8 contained an alternative for both changes and errors that allowed including the resultant effects in the profit or loss for the current period. When this alternative was applied, comparative information was not amended. Under the improved Standard, comparatives are restated (pars. IN8–IN9). An entity should change an accounting policy only if the change is required by an IFRS or if the change results in the financial statements providing more relevant and reliable information.

The Standard specifies the following hierarchy of guidance, which management uses when selecting accounting policies:

1. Requirements of Standards and Interpretations dealing with similar matters.
2. The definitions, recognition criteria, and measurement concepts for assets, liabilities, income, and expenses in the *Framework for the Preparation and Presentation of Financial Statements*.
3. The most recent pronouncements of other standard-setting bodies that use a similar conceptual framework, other accounting literature, and accepted industry practices, to the extent that these do not conflict with IFRSs and the Framework.

The effect of a change in an *accounting estimate* is recognized prospectively in profit or loss in the period of change and in profit or loss in future periods if the change affects both periods.

The IFRS Foundation has published the *Guide to Selecting and Applying Accounting Policies – IAS 8* to help companies determine their accounting policies when preparing IFRS financial statements.

The Guide explains how to use judgment in applying the IAS 8 requirements, using material and examples that have been discussed by the IASB or the IFRS Interpretations Committee. The Guide uses a three-step process for developing accounting policies and includes illustrative examples at each step to help explain when a company might apply that step:

- Step 1. Consider whether an IFRS specifically applies to the transaction, other event or condition. If yes, the user is directed to apply the IFRS that specifically applies.
- Step 2. Consider whether IFRS deal with similar and related issues. If yes, the user is to apply the IFRS requirements that deal with similar and related issues.
- Step 3. If neither Step 1 nor Step 2 applies, the user is to refer to and consider the applicability of the *IFRS Conceptual Framework for Financial Reporting*.

In addition to providing a graphical representation of the three steps in a flow chart, the Guide provides a detailed explanation of the step and how an entity is to apply it, as well as illustrative examples.

.05   IAS 10, Events after the Reporting Period

The Standard indicates when an entity should adjust its financial statements for events occurring after the reporting period and is applicable for annual periods beginning on or after January 1, 2005. Events after the balance sheet date are those events that occur between the balance sheet date and the date when the financial statements are authorized for issue. The Standard requires an entity to adjust the amounts recognized in the financial statements to reflect adjusting events after the balance sheet date. Adjusting events are those that provide evidence of *conditions that existed at the balance sheet date*. These include, but are not limited to, the settlement of a court case after the balance sheet date that confirms that the entity had a present obligation at the balance sheet date or a customer's filing for bankruptcy thereby confirming the amount of loss at the balance sheet date. Nonadjusting events are not used to adjust the financial statements at the balance sheet date. These are events that occurred after the balance sheet date, but have no reference to the balance-sheet-date values.

.06   IAS 11, Construction Contracts (Superseded by IFRS 15)

This guidance related primarily to revenue recognition for long-term contracts. In May 2014, it was announced that the more comprehensive revenue recognition principles of IFRS 15 would eliminate the need for this specific guidance. IFRS 15 is effective for annual periods beginning on or after January 1, 2017, though earlier application is permitted.

.07   IAS 12, Income Taxes

The Standard requires accounting for the tax consequences of transactions in the same manner as the transactions themselves. A given transaction may result in no income taxes, income taxes payable in the current period or payable in a later period. If in a later period a deferred tax liability is established. A transaction resulting in future deductions establishes a deferred tax asset. Inherent in the recognition of a deferred tax asset or liability is the assumption that the reporting entity expects to recognize the carrying amount of the asset or liability. Deferred tax assets and liabilities are measured at the tax rates that are expected to apply to the period(s) when the asset is realized or the liability settled.

IAS 12 requires an entity to measure the deferred tax relating to an asset depending on whether the entity expects to recover the carrying amount of the asset through use or sale. It can be difficult and subjective to assess whether recovery will be through use or through sale when the asset is measured using the fair value model in IAS 40, *Investment Property*. For this reason, in December of 2010, the rule was amended to provide a practical solution to the problem by introducing a presumption that recovery of the carrying amount will, normally be through sale.

As a result of the amendments, SIC-21, *Income Taxes—Recovery of Revalued Non-Depreciable Assets,* would no longer apply to investment properties carried at fair value. The amendments also incorporate into IAS 12 the remaining guidance previously contained in SIC-21, which is accordingly withdrawn.

In January 2016, IASB issued amendments to IAS 12, *Income Taxes.* The amendments, *Recognition of Deferred Tax Assets for Unrealized Losses (Amendments to IAS 12)*, clarify how to account for deferred tax assets related to debt instruments measured at fair value.

The amendments clarify the requirements on recognition of deferred tax assets for unrealized losses, to address diversity in practice. The amendments are effective for annual periods beginning on or after January 1, 2017. Earlier application is permitted.

.08   IAS 16, Property, Plant, and Equipment

"The principal issues in accounting for property, plant and equipment" according to IASB, "are the recognition of the assets and determination of their carrying amounts, including allocating depreciation and recognizing any impairment losses." The Standard is applicable for annual periods beginning on or after January 1, 2005. An entity is required to measure an item of property, plant, and equipment at fair value when acquired in exchange for a nonmonetary asset or assets, or a combination of monetary and nonmonetary assets. An exception is allowed if the exchange transaction lacks commercial substance (par. IN8).

Property, plant and equipment are initially recognized at cost. Subsequently, the carrying amount is:

- Cost, less accumulated depreciation, and any accumulated impairment losses, or
- Revalued amount, less subsequent accumulated depreciation, and any accumulated impairment losses. The revalued amount is the fair value at the date of revaluation. The choice of measurement is applied consistently to an entire class of property, plant, and equipment. Any revaluation increase is credited directly to the revaluation surplus in equity, unless it reverses a revaluation decrease previously recognized in profit or loss.

This guidance was modified by IFRS 15 with respect to IAS 18.

.09   IAS 17, Leases

The Standard is applicable for annual periods beginning on or after January 1, 2005. Initial direct finance costs for lessors can no longer be charged as expenses as incurred. Rather, they are included in the carrying amount of the leased asset and recognized as an expense over the term of the lease. Manufacturer-dealer lessors recognize costs of this type as an expense when the selling profit is recognized (par. IN12). "The classification of leases is," according to IASB, "based on the extent to which risks and rewards incidental to ownership of a lease asset lie with the lessor or the lessee."

A lease is classified as a finance or operating lease at its inception. Finance leases are those that transfer substantially all of the risks and rewards incident to ownership to the lessee. At the inception of a finance lease, an asset and liability are recognized. The asset is recorded at the lower of the fair value of the leased asset or the present value of the minimum lease payments.

On the books of the lessor, a finance lease is recorded as a receivable at an amount equal to the net investment in the lease. This amount is the present value of the minimum lease payments with any unguaranteed residual value accruing to the lessor. Operating lease income is recognized on a straight-line basis over the lease term.

.10   IAS 18, Revenue (Superseded by IFRS 15)

In May 2014, it was announced that the more comprehensive revenue recognition principles of IFRS 15 would eliminate the need for this specific guidance. IFRS 15 is effective for annual periods beginning on or after January 1, 2017, though earlier application is permitted.

.11   IAS 19, Employee Benefits

"Similarly to the accounting for a defined benefit plan," according to the IASB, "the entity recognizes a liability for the obligation net of the fair value of plan assets, if any." Reliance on judgments and estimates is essential and "the judgments in accounting for short-term employee benefits depend mainly on the uncertainties about the extent of expected future payments, largely because such obligations are measured at the undiscounted amount expected to be paid to settle the obligation."

A 2013 amendment clarified that actuarial gains must be recognized in full in other comprehensive income rather than permitting a choice from among three alternative methods.

.12 IAS 20, Accounting for Government Grants and Disclosure of Government Assistance

This Standard provides guidance for business entities receiving government grants whether in cash or in kind. Government grants are not recognized until there is reasonable assurance that the entity will fulfill the conditions associated with the grant and that the grant will be obtained. Grants fulfilling these conditions and relating to assets are reported on the balance sheet by establishing a deferred income account or by establishing a contra-asset account to be subtracted from the asset associated with the grant.

If a government grant requires repayment it is accounted for in accordance with IAS 8 as a revision of an accounting estimate. Because government grants generally come with strings attached, the disclosure requirement for government grants requires notifying the reader of any unfulfilled conditions or other contingencies attached to the grant.

.13 IAS 21, The Effects of Changes in Foreign Exchange Rates

The Standard is applicable for annual periods beginning on or after January 1, 2005. Capitalization of exchange differences resulting from severe devaluation or depreciation of a currency against which there is no means of hedging is no longer permitted (par. IN10).

A foreign currency transaction is recorded initially in the functional currency (the currency of the primary economic environment in which the entity operates), by applying to the foreign currency amount the spot exchange rate between the functional currency and the foreign currency at the date of the transaction. For practical reasons, a rate that approximates the actual rate at the date of the transaction is often used (e.g., an average weekly or monthly rate).

At each balance sheet date:

1. Foreign currency monetary items are translated using the closing rate.
2. Nonmonetary items that are measured in terms of historical cost in a foreign currency are translated using the exchange rate at the date of the transaction.
3. Nonmonetary items that are measured at fair value in a foreign currency are translated using the exchange rates at the date when the fair value was determined.

When translating a foreign operation for inclusion in the reporting entity's financial statements, assets and liabilities are translated at the closing rate. Income and expenses are translated at exchange rates at the dates of the transactions.

.14 IAS 23, Borrowing Costs

Borrowing costs for the construction or production of assets which require a substantial period of time to get ready for sale or use are the subject of this Standard. Borrowing costs are interest and other costs incurred in connection debt financing. Since the interest and other costs relate to a long-term project they must be capitalized. When substantially all the activities necessary to prepare the asset for sale or use are completed the capitalization of interest ceases.

.15 IAS 24, Related Party Disclosures

The Standard is applicable for annual periods beginning on or after January 1, 2005. The definition of related parties and the disclosure requirement for related parties have both been expanded by adding parties (including joint ventures and postemployment benefit plans) and by requiring the disclosure of transactions, balances, terms and conditions, and details of guarantees (pars. IN8 and IN11–IN13). Entities are also now required to disclose the compensation of key management personnel (par. IN5).

A party is related to an entity if it:

- Directly or indirectly controls, is controlled by, or is under common control with the entity.
- Has significant influence over the entity.
- Has joint control over the entity.
- Is a close member of the family of any individual who controls, or has significant influence or joint control over the entity.
- Is an associate of the entity.
- Is a joint venturer with the entity.
- Is a member of the key management (or close family member) of the entity or its parent.
- Is a postemployment benefit plan for the benefit of employees of the entity, or of any of its related parties.

The Standard prescribes specific disclosure requirements including the nature of the relationships, names of entities, compensation of key management personnel and the nature of the transactions.

.16   IAS 26, Accounting and Reporting by Retirement Benefit Plans

Rather than dealing with the pension obligation of an entity, this Standard states the reporting requirements for retirement benefit plans themselves. For a defined contribution plan the financial statements must show net assets available for benefits. For a defined benefit plan the financial statements must show the net assets available for benefits, the actuarial present value of promised retirement benefits and any excess or deficit between the two. Retirement benefit plan investments are carried at their fair value.

.17   IAS 27, Consolidated and Separate Financial Statements, Replaced by IAS 27, Separate Financial Statements, and IFRS 10, Consolidated Financial Statements

IAS 27 is replaced by IFRS 10, *Consolidated Financial Statements,* and a new IAS 27, *Separate Financial Statements,* takes its place. The new IAS 27 specifies accounting and disclosure requirements for separate presentation of investments in subsidiaries as well as joint ventures and associates. Though in general, an entity that has one or more subsidiaries must present consolidated financial statements, the IASB reports that "in some jurisdictions an entity must present separate financial statements in addition to the consolidated financial statements."

According to the IASB's guidance, "If separate financial statements are prepared, IAS 27 requires investments in subsidiaries, joint ventures and associates to be accounted for either at cost or in accordance with IFRS 9, *Financial Instruments,* or, if appropriate, IFRS 11, *Joint Arrangements.*

The key point of the new IAS 27 is that for separate reporting, the subsidiary or joint venture is treated as an asset invested in by the parent.

.18   IAS 28, Investments in Associates and Joint Ventures

The Standard is applicable for annual periods beginning on or after January 1, 2005. An associate is an entity over which the investor has significant influence and is neither a subsidiary nor an interest in a joint venture. An investment in an associated is generally accounted for using the equity method. However, the equity method is not used when:

- The investment is classified as held for sale in accordance with IFRS 5, *Non-Current Assets Held for Sale and Discontinued Operations*;
- The investor is itself a subsidiary, its owners do not object to the equity method not being applied, and its debt and equity securities are not publicly traded. In this case, the investor's parent must present consolidated financial statement that comply with IFRSs; or

- A holding of 20 percent or more of the voting power (directly or through subsidiaries) indicates significant influence unless it can be clearly demonstrated otherwise. If the holding is less than 20 percent, the investor will be presumed not to have significant influence. Thus, this standard employs the same ownership test, 20 percent or more up to 50 percent, to indicate the use of the equity method is appropriate as APB 18 (now FASB codification ASC 232-10-15).

When financial statements of an associate are used in preparing the financial statements of an investor entity using the equity method of valuation, and the period ended is different from that of the investor, the difference must be no greater than three months (par. IN12). Investors must consider the carrying amount of the investment in the equity of an associate and its other long-term interests in the associate when recognizing its share of losses of that associate (par. IN14).

An investor discontinues the equity method from the date that it ceases to have significant influence over the associate. "Significant influence" is the power to participate in financial and operating policy decisions of the investee, but is not control or joint control over those policies.

In 2016, IASB amended the exposure draft titled, *Effective Date of Amendments to IFRS 10 and IAS 28.* The amendments postpone the date the entities must change some aspects as to how they account for transactions between investors and associates or joint ventures. See ¶11,008.10.

In 2017, the amendments to IAS 28 clarify that companies should account for long-term interests in an associate or joint venture, to which the equity method is not applied, using IFRS 9. The amendments are effective beginning January 1, 2019, with early application permitted.

The IASB has also published an example that illustrates how companies apply the requirements in IFRS 9 and IAS 28 to long-term interests in an associate or joint venture.

.19   IAS 29, Financial Reporting in Hyperinflationary Economies

Economies experiencing hyperinflation present inherent problems for financial reporting. This Standard does not attempt to provide a specific definition of hyperinflation. Rather it supplies a number of symptoms common to hyperinflationary economies. These include the fact that the local population prefers to keep its wealth in non-monetary assets or in a foreign currency judged to be more stable than the local currency.

When the financial statements are restated using a general price index that reflects changes in the purchasing power of the local currency it must be done in a consistent manner.

.20   IAS 31, Interests in Joint Ventures, Replaced by IFRS 11, Joint Arrangements

See IFRS 11 below.

.21   IAS 32, Financial Instruments: Presentation

This Standard deals with the presentation of financial instruments in the financial statements. (IAS 39, *Financial Instruments: Recognition and Measurement*, IFRS 9, *Financial Instruments*, and IFRS 7, *Financial Instruments Disclosure*, deal with recognition, measurement, and disclosure.)

According to the IASB, "For presentation, financial instruments are classified into financial assets, financial liabilities and equity instruments." Though offsetting assets and liabilities is generally prohibited by IFRS, this guidance requires financial assets and financial liabilities to be offset when there exists a legally enforceable right to do so.

.22   IAS 33, Earnings per Share

The Standard is applicable for annual periods beginning on or after January 1, 2005. Additional guidance and illustrative examples have been provided on the following selected complex matters related to earnings per share:

- Contingently issuable shares.
- Potential ordinary shares of subsidiaries, joint ventures or associates.
- Participating equity instruments.
- Written put options.
- Purchased put and call options.
- Mandatorily convertible instruments.

The Standard applies to entities whose ordinary shares are publicly traded or entities in the process of issuing shares to be publicly traded.

Basic earning per share is calculated by dividing profit or loss attributable to ordinary equity holders of the parent entity by the weighted average number of ordinary shares outstanding during the period.

Diluted earnings per share is calculated by adjusting the profit or loss attributable to ordinary equity holders of the parent entity, and the weighted average number of ordinary shares outstanding for the effects of all potentially dilutive shares. Shares are treated as potentially dilutive when their conversion to ordinary shares would decrease earnings per share or increase loss per share from continuing operations. Dilutive shares include options, warrants, convertible instruments, and contingently issuable shares.

In much of this guidance on EPS, both IASB and U.S. GAAP (FASB 128) have been growing closer together. As long as there are differences in revenue and expense recognition, the numerator (company earnings) will differ. At present there are also differences in the denominator caused by different rules on potentially dilutive securities.

.23   IAS 34, Interim Financial Reporting

According to the IASB, this guidance specifies the "minimum content of an interim financial report and prescribes the principles for recognition and measurement in complete or condensed financial statements for an interim period."

Interim financial reporting assumes the reader of the interim report has access to the most recent annual report, and as a result the interim report is presumed to be supplemented by the notes to the prior annual report. The interim statements should thus reference the notes to the most recent annual statement. Similar to U.S. GAAP, this Standard requires the use of the same accounting policies for its interim reports as it uses for its annual reporting. To avoid distortions in interim reporting this may require annualizing certain items.

.24   IAS 36, Impairment of Assets

The Standard is applicable to goodwill and intangible assets acquired in business combinations after March 31, 2004, and to all other assets for annual periods beginning on or after March 31, 2004. IFRS 3, *Business Combinations*, requires goodwill to be tested for impairment annually, or more frequently if events or changes in circumstances indicate a possible impairment. Goodwill impairment is not reversed, nor is goodwill amortized.

The Standard prescribes the procedures that an entity applies to ensure that its assets are carried at no more than their recoverable amount. It does not apply to inventories; assets arising from construction contracts; deferred tax assets, assets arising from employee benefits; financial assets within the scope of IAS 39, *Financial Instruments: Recognition and Measurement*; investment property measured at fair value; biological assets related to agricultural activity; deferred acquisition costs; and intangible assets and noncurrent assets classified as held for sale in accordance with IFRS 5, *Non-Current Assets Held for Sale and Discontinued Operations*.

The recoverable amount of an asset is measured whenever there is an indication that the asset may be impaired, but at least annually. The recoverable amount is determined for an individual asset or the smallest identifiable group of assets that generates cash inflows that are largely independent of the cash inflows from other assets or groups of assets.

An impairment loss, calculated as the carrying amount of an asset less its recoverable amount, is recognized immediately in profit or loss. If the asset is revalued in accordance with another standard, the impairment loss is treated as a revaluation decrease in accordance with that other standard.

An impairment loss recognized in prior periods is reversed if there is a change in the estimates used to determine the asset's recoverable amount since the last impairment loss was recognized. If this has occurred, the carrying amount of the asset is increased to its recoverable amount, but not to exceed the carrying amount of the asset that would have been determined had no impairment loss been recognized in prior years.

Beginning January 1, 2014, this standard is amended to require disclosure of Recoverable Amounts for Non-Financial Assets (clarification of disclosures required).

.25   IAS 37, Provisions, Contingent Liabilities and Contingent Assets

The guidance introduces the term *provision* to name a liability which is uncertain as to amount or timing. Such liabilities should only be recognized in the financial statements when a reliable estimate may be made of the obligation and it represents a present obligation and it is probable that the obligation will require a sacrifice of the company's assets for its settlement. The meaning of *contingent liability* is weaker indicating only a possible obligation. Faced with a contingent liability an entity should not recognize the obligation though it should be disclosed in the footnotes. The conceptual scheme of this IAS is similar to U.S. GAAP but rather than allowing a continuum of contingent liabilities, some of which are recognized and some of which are not, the term *provision* is introduced to name the kinds of probably liabilities that should be recognized.

.26   IAS 38, Intangible Assets

This Standard is applied to the accounting for intangible assets acquired in business combinations after March 31, 2004. IFRS 3, *Business Combinations*, requires goodwill to be tested for impairment annually, or more frequently if events or changes in circumstances indicate a possible impairment. It prohibits the reversal of impairment losses for goodwill as well as prohibiting the amortization of goodwill.

An intangible asset is initially recognized at cost if *all* the following criteria are met:

- The asset is identifiable and controlled by the entity.
- It is probable that future economic benefits that are attributable to the asset will flow to the entity.
- The cost of the asset can be reliably measured.

For an intangible item that does not meet the criteria for recognition as an asset, such as internally generated goodwill, brands, and customer lists, the expenditure is recognized as an expense when incurred.

Subsequent to initial recognition, an intangible asset is carried at one of the following:

- Cost, less any accumulated amortization and any accumulated impairment losses; or
- Revalued amount (only if there is an active market), less any subsequent accumulated amortization and any accumulated impairment losses. The revalued amount is fair value at the date of revaluation and is determined by reference to an active market.

An entity assesses whether the useful life of an intangible asset is finite or indefinite. For assets with finite lives, the asset is amortized on a systematic basis over its useful life. If the life is indefinite, there is no foreseeable limit to the period over which the asset is expected to generate net cash flows, and there is no amortization. This standard forms the basis for IPSAS 31—Intangible Assets in the public sector.

.27   IAS 39 (now IFRS 9), Financial Instruments: Recognition and Measurement

IFRS 9, *Financial Instruments,* replaced IAS 39 which deals with the measurement of financial instruments and with their recognition—when they should be included in the financial statements and how they should be valued. (IAS 32 deals with disclosure and presentation requirements.) The Standard applies to all companies reporting under International Financial Reporting Standards. It requires derivatives to be reported at their fair or market value rather than at cost. This overcomes the problem that the cost of such instruments may be very small in relation to their market value, resulting in distortions when cost is used. The revised Standard now tracks the equivalent U.S. GAAP standard.

The Standard divides financial assets and financial liabilities into five classes with three different accounting treatments; the treatments mirror those for U.S. GAAP, classifying instruments into trading, held to maturity, or available for sale:

1. Trading assets and liabilities, including all derivatives that are not hedges, are measured at fair value. Their gains or losses are recognized currently in profit or loss as they occur.
2. Loans and receivables are accounted for at amortized cost.

3. Held-to-maturity investments are accounted for at amortized cost.
4. Financial liabilities that are not held for trading are amortized using the effective interest method.
5. All other financial assets are ordinarily classified as available for sale and measured at fair value, with all gains and losses taken into equity.

On disposal, gains and losses previously taken into equity are reclassified to profit or loss.

The Standard describes two forms of hedging relationship and their respective accounting treatments:

1. In the case of a fair value hedge, defined as a hedge in which the fair value of the item being hedged changes as market prices change, both the changes in the fair value of the hedging instrument and the hedged item are reported in profit or loss.
2. In a cash flow hedge, one where the cash flows of the item being hedged change as market prices change, the changes in the fair value of the hedging instrument are initially reported in equity and reclassified to profit or loss to match the recognition of the offsetting gains and losses on the hedged transaction.

Another aspect of asset valuation occurs whenever there is evidence of impairment. With respect to when and how losses should be recognized, the Standard clarifies that:

- Impairment should take into account only losses that have already been incurred and not those likely to occur in the future; and
- Impairment losses on available-for-sale assets are reclassified from equity and recognized in profit or loss. For equity investments, objective evidence of impairment may include significant adverse changes in the issuer's market position, or a significant or prolonged decline in the fair value of the investment. This guidance was modified by IFRS 15 with respect to IAS 18.

IAS 39 was superseded by IFRS 9 subject to: (1) the accounting policy choice about whether or not to continue applying the hedge accounting requirements in IAS 39 in accordance with paragraph 7.2.21 or paragraph 6.1.3 of IFRS 9; and (2) the temporary exemption in paragraph 20A of IFRS 4 that provides a temporary exemption to some insurers from applying IFRS 9 until they apply IFRS 17.

.28   IAS 40, Investment Property

The Standard is applicable for annual periods beginning on or after January 1, 2005. Entities are permitted to account for a property interest held under an operating lease as investment property if certain criteria are met and the lessee accounts for the lease as if it were a finance lease and measures the resulting lease at fair value (par. IN5).

Investment property is initially recognized at cost. Subsequently, investment property is carried either at:

- Cost, less accumulated depreciation and any accumulated impairment losses, as prescribed by IAS 16, *Property, Plant, and Equipment*, or
- Fair value. Changes in fair value are recognized immediately in profit or loss.

The investment model is applied consistently to all investment property. However, an entity may choose either the fair value model or the cost model for investment property backing liabilities that pay a return linked directly to the fair value of specified assets including that investment property. This is regardless of the model chosen for all other investment property.

This guidance was modified by IFRS 15 with respect to IAS 18.

.29   IAS 41, Agriculture

This Standard is applicable for periods beginning on or after January 1, 2003. A biological asset is a living animal or plant. The Standard prescribes the accounting treatment, financial statement presentation, and disclosures related to agricultural activity. It applies to biological assets, agricultural produce at the point of harvest, and government grants related to biological assets.

IAS 41 does not apply to:

- Land related to agricultural activity (IAS 16, *Property, Plant and Equipment*).
- Intangible assets related to agricultural activity (IAS 38, *Intangible Assets*).
- The processing of agricultural produce after harvest (IAS 2, *Inventories*).

A biological asset is measured at its fair value less estimated point-of-sale costs, on initial recognition and at each subsequent balance sheet date. Agricultural produce harvested from an entity's biological assets is measured at its fair value less estimated point-of-sale costs at the point of harvest. Point-of-sales costs include commissions, levies, and transfer duties and taxes. A gain or loss arising on initial recognition at fair value less point-of-sale costs and from a change in fair value less point-of-sale costs is included in profit or loss.

An unconditional government grant related to a biological asset is recognized as income when the grant becomes receivable; a conditional government grant is recognized when the conditions attaching to the grant are met.

IAS 41 specifies required disclosures related to agricultural activity.

¶11,008   International Financial Reporting Standards

The IASB publishes its financial reporting standards in a series of pronouncements called International Financial Reporting Standards (IFRSs). It has also adopted the body of Standards issued by its predecessor, the Board of the International Accounting Standards Committee (IASC). Those pronouncements continue to be designated "International Accounting Standards." The IASB employs an annual improvement process to determine which standards need revision and improvement.

.01   IFRS 1, First-Time Adoption of International Financial Reporting Standards

Following recent decisions by several additional jurisdictions to adopt IFRSs, more than more than 140 countries require the use of IFRS for all or most publicly listed companies, with another 13 jurisdictions permitting its use. Thousands of companies worldwide are making a transition in financial reporting by expanding beyond national practices and changing to accounting standards established by the IASB. To help companies make this change as smoothly as possible, and to enable users of company reports to understand the effect of applying a new set of accounting standards, the IASB issued IFRS 1, *First-Time Adoption of International Financial Reporting Standards*, in June 2003. The Standard explains how the transition is made to IFRSs from another basis of accounting.

Through IFRS 1, the IASB has sought to address the demand of investors to have transparent information that is comparable over all periods presented. IFRS 1 is also fashioned to give reporting entities a suitable starting point for their accounting under IFRSs.

IFRS 1 requires an entity to comply with every IASB Standard in force in the first year when the entity first adopts IFRSs. However, after consideration of the cost of full compliance some specific exceptions are permitted (see below.) Under IFRS 1, entities must explain how the transition to IASB Standards affects their reported financial position, financial performance, and cash flow.

IFRS 1 applies to entities whose first IFRS financial statements are for a period beginning on or after July 1, 2009. It also applies to each interim financial report, if any, that the entity presents under IAS 34, *Interim Financial Reporting*, for part of the period covered by its first IFRS financial statements.

Adoption of international reporting standards may not be done piecemeal, an entity must adhere to all requirements as set out in the IFRS. In particular an entity's opening balance sheet must:

- Recognize all assets and liabilities required by IFRSs.
- Not recognize items as assets or liabilities if IFRSs do not permit such recognition.
- Reclassify items that were recognized under previous U.S. GAAP as one type of asset, liability, or component of equity but that should be classified by IFRS as a different type of asset, liability, or component of equity.
- Apply IFRSs in measuring all recognized assets and liabilities. The transition provisions in other IFRSs do not apply to a first-time adopter's transition to IFRSs.

IFRS 1 grants limited exemptions from these requirements in specified areas. Where the cost of complying would be likely to exceed the benefits to users of financial statements. Such exemptions are available for:

- Business combinations.
- Fair value or revaluation as deemed cost for certain noncurrent assets.
- Defined benefit employee benefit plans.
- Cumulative translation differences.
- Compound financial instruments.
- Assets and liabilities of subsidiaries, associates and joint ventures.
- Designation of previously recognized financial instruments.
- Share-based payment transactions.
- Insurance contracts.

The IFRS also prohibits retrospective application of IFRSs in some cases, particularly where retrospective application would require judgments by management about past conditions after the outcome of a particular transaction is already known.

IFRS 1 requires disclosures that explain how the transition from previous U.S. GAAP to IFRSs affected the entity's reported financial position, financial performance, and cash flows.

.02   IFRS 2, Share-Based Payment

"IFRS 2 requires an entity to recognize share-based payment transactions in its financial statements," according to the IASB. "Equity-settled share-based payment transactions are generally those in which shares, share options or other equity instruments are granted to employees or other parties in return for goods or services."

IFRS 2, *Share-Based Payment*, was issued in February 2004 and applies to annual accounting periods beginning on or after January 1, 2005. Its application is retrospectively for liabilities arising from share-based payment transactions existing at the effective date.

The Standard prescribes the financial reporting by an entity when it undertakes a share-based payment transaction. It applies to grants of shares, share options, or other equity instruments made after November 7, 2002, that had not yet vested at the effective date of the IFRS.

When share options are granted to employees, IFRS 2 requires an entity to reflect such payments in its profit or loss and financial position, including expenses associated with share options granted.

The valuation of the transaction for equity-settled, share-based payment transactions with employees (and others providing similar services) is based on the fair value of the equity instruments granted. Fair value is measured at the date of grant. The valuation focuses on the specific terms and conditions of a grant of shares or share options. In general, vesting conditions are not taken into account in the grant date valuation but the number of equity instruments included in the measurement of the transaction amount is adjusted so that, ultimately, the transaction amount is based on the number of equity instruments that vest.

If the terms and conditions of an option or share grant are modified or if a grant is cancelled, repurchased, or replaced with another grant of equity instruments, the IFRS provides guidance. The Standard also contains requirements for equity-settled transactions with parties other than employees and those providing similar services.

For cash-settled transactions, the good or services received and the liability incurred are measured at the fair value of the liability. The liability is re-measured to fair value at each reporting date and at the date of settlement, with changes in fair value recognized in profit or loss.

IFRS 2 also specifies requirements for transactions in which the terms of the arrangement provide either the entity or the supplier of goods or services with a choice of whether the entity settles the transaction in cash (or other assets) or by issuing equity instruments. Disclosure requirements are also specified.

On June 16, 2016, the IASB issued amendments to IFRS 2, *Share-based Payment*, to clarify how to measure certain types of share-based payment transactions.

The amendments, which were developed through the IFRS Interpretations Committee, provide requirements on the accounting for the following:

- effects of vesting and non-vesting conditions on the measurement of cash-settled share-based payments;
- share-based payment transactions with a net settlement feature for withholding tax obligations; and

- modification to the terms and conditions of a share-based payment that changes the classification of the transaction from cash-settled to equity-settled.

The amendments are effective for annual periods beginning on or after January 1, 2018; but earlier application is permitted.

.03   IFRS 3, Business Combinations

This Standard, issued in March 2004, is applicable for business combinations for which the agreement date is on or after March 31, 2004. *It requires the purchase method of accounting and prohibits the pooling method.* The Standard replaces IAS 22, *Business Combinations*.

The Standard prescribes the financial reporting for an entity when involved in a business combination. It "aims to improve the relevance, reliability and comparability of the information about business combinations and their effects," reports the IASB. A business combination is the combining of separate entities or businesses into one reporting unit.

IFRS 3 does *not* apply to:

- Joint ventures.
- Business combinations involving entities or businesses under common control.
- Business combinations involving two or more mutual entities.
- Business combinations in which separate entities or businesses are brought together to form a reporting entity by contract alone without the obtaining of an ownership interest.

All business combinations are required to apply the purchase method of accounting, which views the business combination from the perspective of the acquirer. The acquirer is the combining entity that obtains control of the other combining entities or businesses. This change mirrors a similar reform in U.S. GAAP with the institution of FASB 141, *Business Combinations*.

The new rules require the acquirer to measure the cost of a business combination as the aggregate of:

- The fair values, at the date of exchange, of assets given, liabilities incurred or assumed, and equity instruments issued by the acquirer, in exchange for control of the acquiree.
- Any costs directly attributable to the business combination.

Any adjustment to the cost of the combination that is contingent on future events, is included in the cost of the combination at the acquisition date if the adjustment is probable and can be reliably measured.

The acquiring entity is required to allocate the cost of the business combination by recognizing the acquired entity's identifiable assets, liabilities, and contingent liabilities at their fair value at the date of acquisition. An exception is made for noncurrent assets that are classified as held for sale in accordance with IFRS 5, *Non-Current Assets Held for Sale and Discontinued Operations*. Such assets are recognized at fair value less costs to sell.

Goodwill is recognized as an asset and subsequently carried at cost less any accumulated impairment losses in accordance with IAS 36, *Impairment of Assets*. Goodwill is defined as the excess of the cost over the acquirer's interest in the net fair value of the identifiable assets, liabilities, and contingent liabilities at the date of acquisition. Goodwill and other intangible assets with indefinite useful lives are no longer amortized. Instead, they are to be tested annually for impairment. Reversal of impairment losses, once recognized, is not allowed.

Intangible assets acquired in a combination must be segregated from goodwill if they meet the definition of an asset and their fair value can be separately measured.

If the acquirer's interest in the net fair value of the identifiable assets, liabilities, and contingent liabilities exceeds the cost of the combination (bad will), the acquirer:

- Should reassess the identification and measurement of the acquiree's identifiable assets, liabilities and contingent liabilities and the measurement of the cost of the combination, associating the difference between fair value and cost to specific assets or liabilities where possible.
- Recognize immediately in profit or loss any excess remaining after that reassessment.

This treatment of goodwill closely parallels U.S. GAAP changes in goodwill reporting as set forth in FASB 142.

IFRS 3 specifies the accounting treatment:

- For business combinations that are achieved in stages.
- Where fair values can be determined only provisionally in the period of acquisition.
- Where deferred tax assets are recognized after the accounting for the acquisition is complete.
- For previously recognized goodwill, negative goodwill, and intangible assets.

The disclosure requirements for business combinations and related goodwill issues are also addressed in this Standard.

In 2013, amendments were made to the standard, including the treatment of acquisition-related costs which are generally recognized as expenses (rather than included in goodwill).

.04   IFRS 4, Insurance Contracts

This Standard was issued in March 2004, and is applicable for annual periods beginning on or after January 1, 2005. It prescribes the financial reporting for insurance contracts by any entity that issues such contracts.

It applies to:

- Insurance contracts issued.
- Reinsurance contracts held.
- Financial instruments issued with a discretionary participation feature.

It does *not* apply to:

- Product warranties issued directly by a manufacturer, dealer or retailer (IAS 18, *Revenue*, and IAS 37, *Provisions, Contingent Liabilities, and Contingent Assets*).
- Employers' assets and liabilities under employee benefit plans (IAS 19, *Employee Benefits*) and retirement benefit obligations reported by defined benefit retirement plans (IAS 26, *Accounting and Reporting by Retirement Benefit Plans*).
- Contractual rights or obligations that are contingent on the future use of or right to use a nonfinancial item, as well as lessee's residual value guarantees on finance leases (IAS 17, *Leases*; IAS 18, *Revenue;* and IAS 38, *Intangible Assets*).
- Financial guarantees entered into or retained on transferring financial assets or financial liabilities within the scope of IAS 39.
- Contingent consideration payable or receivable in a business combination (IFRS 3, *Business Combinations*).
- Direct insurance contracts that an entity holds as a policyholder.

IFRS 4 is phase one of the IASB's project on insurance contracts. An entity is temporarily exempt from some requirements of other IFRSs, including the requirement in IAS 8 to consider the Framework in selecting accounting policies for insurance contracts. However, IFRS 4:

- Prohibits the recognition of provisions for possible future claims under insurance contracts that are not in existence at the reporting date (e.g., catastrophe provisions and equalization provisions) as liabilities.
- Requires assessment of the adequacy of recognized insurance liabilities and recognition of any impairment of reinsurance assets.
- Requires an entity to keep insurance liabilities in its balance sheet until they are discharged or cancelled, or expire, and to present insurance liabilities without offsetting them against related reinsurance assets.

An entity may change its accounting policies for insurance contracts only if the result is financial statements that are more relevant and no less reliable, or financial statements that are more reliable and no less relevant. In particular, an entity must not introduce any of the following practices, although it may continue using accounting policies that involve them:

- Measuring insurance liabilities on an undiscounted basis.
- Measuring contractual rights to future investment management fees at an amount that exceeds their fair value as implied by a comparison with current fees charged by other market participants for similar services.
- Using nonuniform accounting policies for the insurance contracts of subsidiaries
- Measuring insurance liabilities with excessive prudence.

There is a rebuttable presumption that an insurer's financial statements will become less relevant and reliable if the presentation introduces an accounting policy that reflects future investment margins in the measurement of insurance contracts. When an insurer changes its accounting policies for insurance liabilities, it may reclassify some or all financial assets as "at fair value through profit or loss."

The Standard also specifies the following:

- An entity need not account for an embedded derivative separately at fair value if the embedded derivative meets the definition of an insurance contract.
- An entity is required to unbundle deposit components of some insurance contracts and account for them separately.
- An entity may apply "shadow accounting" (i.e., account for both realized and unrealized gains or losses on assets in the same way relative to measurement of insurance liabilities).
- Discretionary participation features contained in insurance contracts or financial instruments may be recognized separately from the guaranteed element and classified as a liability or as a separate component of equity.

Disclosure requirements include (1) the amounts in the entity's financial statements that arise from insurance contracts and (2) the amount, timing, and uncertainty of future cash flows from insurance contracts.

This guidance was modified by IFRS 15 with respect to IAS 18.

On September 2016, the IASB issued "Applying IFRS 9 Financial Instruments with IFRS 4 Insurance Contracts" amending IFRS 4. The amendments addressed concerns arising from implementing IFRS 9 before implementing the IFRS 4 replacement standard, IFRS 17. The amendments introduced two approaches:

1. an overlay approach; and
2. a deferral approach.

The amendments:

- gave all companies that issue insurance contracts the option to recognize in other comprehensive income, rather than profit or loss, the volatility that could arise when IFRS 9 was applied before the new insurance contracts Standard was issued; and
- gave companies whose activities are predominantly connected with insurance an optional temporary exemption from applying IFRS 9 until 2021. The entities that defer the application of IFRS 9 continued to apply IAS 39, *Financial Instruments: Recognition and Measurement.*

The amendments to IFRS 4 supplement existing options in IFRS 4 that can already be used to address the temporary volatility.

In 2017, IFRS 4 was replaced by IFRS 17 for fiscal years beginning January 1, 2023. See ¶11,008.17.

.05   IFRS 5, Non-Current Assets Held for Sale and Discontinued Operations

The Standard was applicable for annual periods beginning on or after January 1, 2005. This Standard prescribes the accounting for assets held for sale and the presentation and disclosure of discontinued operations. The measurement provisions of IFRS 5 apply to all noncurrent assets and disposal groups, except for:

- Deferred tax assets (IAS 12, *Income Taxes*).
- Assets arising from employee benefits (IAS 19, *Employee Benefits*).
- Financial assets within the scope of IAS 39, *Financial Instruments: Recognition and Measurement.*
- Noncurrent assets that are accounted for in accordance with the fair value model in IAS 40, *Investment Property.*
- Noncurrent assets that are measured at fair value less estimated point-of-sale costs in accordance with IAS 41, *Agriculture.*
- Contractual rights under insurance contracts as defined in IFRS 4, *Insurance Contracts.*

Assets Held for Sale. An asset held for sale is one available for immediate sale when its sale is highly probable. A noncurrent asset (or disposal group) is classified as held for sale if its carrying amount will be recovered principally through a sale transaction, rather than through continuing use. A noncurrent asset (or group of assets) classified as held for sale is measured at the lower of fair value less costs to sell and its carrying amount.

Any impairment loss on write-down of an asset (or disposal group) to fair value less costs to sell is recognized currently in profit or loss. Any gain on subsequent increase in fair value less costs to sell is also recognized in profit or loss, but not in excess of the cumulative impairment loss already recognized on the asset either in accordance with IFRS 5 or IAS 36, *Impairment of Assets.*

Discontinued Operations. A discontinued operation is a component of an entity that either has been disposed of, or is held for sale. It may be a subsidiary, a major line of business, or geographical area. It will have been a cash-generating unit (or group of cash-generating units) as defined in IAS 36, *Impairment of Assets.*

Disclosures of discontinued operations include:

- Analysis of the post-tax profit or loss into revenue, expenses, pre-tax profit or loss, and the related income tax expense.
- The gain or loss recognized on measurement to fair value less costs to sell or on disposal, and the related income tax expense.
- Net cash flows attributable to operating, investing and financing activities.
- Assets held for sale separately from all other assets.
- Liabilities of a disposal group held for sale separately from all other liabilities.

.06   IFRS 6, Exploration for and Evaluation of Mineral Resources

In December 2004, a reporting standard was issued for the specialized area extractive activities. It is effective for periods beginning on or after January 1, 2006. Industries affected include mining, oil and gas.

.07   IFRS 7, Financial Instruments: Disclosures

In its announcement of IFRS 7 in August 2005, the Board stated its belief that the new guidance will lead to greater transparency about the risks that entities confront from the use of financial instruments. The standard applies to all risks arising from all financial instruments unless an instrument is already covered by a more specific standard. IFRS 7 applies to all entities but the nature and extent of required disclosure will depend on the extent of the entity's use of financial instruments and its exposure to risk.

This guidance, according to IASB, "requires disclosures that enable users to evaluate: the significance of financial instruments for the entity's financial position and performance; and the risks arising from financial instruments to which the entity is exposed and how the entity manages those risks."

.08   IFRS 8, Operating Segments

This Standard requires an entity to report financial information about its reportable segments. Operating segments are reportable when they are components of an entity for which separate financial information is available and that is regularly evaluated by a chief operating decision maker. An important objective of this standard is to reduce differences in segment reporting between IFRSs and U.S. GAAP. Reporting segmented financial data provides information concerning the different types of business activities carried on by the company. Reviewing the operating results in terms of segments allows a better understanding to the entity's performance and a perspective gained from seeing the trees as well as the forest. Identification of segments is based on criteria requiring evaluation of revenues, profits (or losses) or assets to locate significant contributions to the company's overall operations. Both the FASB and the IASB now use the management approach to identify reportable segments, and segment disclosure is required.

.09   IFRS 9, Financial Instruments (Updated)

In July of 2014, IFRS 9 was completed with the addition of new requirements for reporting impairments. In November 2009, the IASB issued IFRS 9, *Financial Instruments*. The standard was the first step in replacing IAS 39, *Financial Instruments: Recognition and Measurement*. The new IFRS employs a single approach to determining whether a financial asset is measured at its amortized cost or fair value. The standard also requires a single impairment method to be used, replacing the multiple methods offered by IAS 39. According to the Board, the new standard improves comparability and makes financial statements easier for investors and others to understand.

In part, the impetus for the change came as a reaction to the global financial crisis. One of the criticisms leveled at earlier guidance involved the incurred loss model employed by IAS 39 which critics complained led to an over-optimistic assessment of investment assets. Under IFRS 9, expected losses on financial assets are to be recognized throughout the life of the asset and not just after a loss event has been identified. In October 2010, the IASB issued requirements on the accounting for financial liabilities. These requirements were added to IFRS 9, *Financial Instruments*, and completed the classification and measurement phase of the IASB's project to replace IAS 39, *Financial Instruments: Recognition and Measurement*.

According to a January 2014 announcement by Sue Lloyd, a member of the IASB, "IFRS 9 will require entities to estimate and account for expected credit losses for all relevant financial assets, starting from when they first lend money or invest in a financial instrument." The guidance requires entities to use all available information in making the determination of impairment. The information to be used will include both historical loss and current information, but also reliable prospective guidance. Further, according to the same IASB board spokesman, "These changes, in the timing of recognition and the consideration of reasonable and supportable forward-looking information, are important changes from existing IFRS, which only allowed impairment losses to be recognized when a loss had been 'incurred'. Even then, only the effect of events that had already occurred could be considered in measuring those impairment losses."

In October 2017, the IASB issued amendments to IFRS 9 that allow companies to measure particular prepayable financial assets with so-called negative compensation at amortized cost or at fair value through other comprehensive income if a specified condition is met, instead of at fair value through profit or loss.

The IFRS Taxonomy will be updated to reflect the new presentation and disclosure requirements introduced by the amendments to IFRS 9. Consequently, the IASB has also published the Proposed IFRS Taxonomy Update, Prepayment Features with Negative Compensation, for public consultation. The amendments are effective beginning January 1, 2019, with early application permitted.

COVID-19. In March 2020, IASB released *IFRS 9 and COVID-19—Accounting for Expected Credit Losses Applying IFRS 9 Financial Instruments in the Light of Current Uncertainty Resulting from the COVID-19 Pandemic.*

The document responds to questions regarding the application of IFRS 9 during this period of enhanced economic uncertainty arising from the COVID-19 pandemic. The document was prepared for educational purposes, highlighting requirements within IFRS 9 that are relevant for companies considering how the pandemic affects their accounting for expected credit losses (ECL). It does not change, remove nor add to, the requirements in IFRS 9. The IASB intends it to support the consistent and robust application of IFRS 9.

The IASB developed IFRS 9 in response to requests by the G20 and others to provide more forward-looking information about loan losses than the predecessor Standard and to give transparent and timely information about changes in credit risk.

The document acknowledges that estimating ECL on financial instruments is challenging in the current circumstances and highlights the importance of companies using all reasonable and supportable information available, historic, current and forward-looking to the extent possible, when determining whether lifetime losses should be recognized on loans and in measuring ECL.

The document also reinforces that IFRS 9 requires judgment in application and does not provide bright lines nor a mechanistic approach in accounting for ECLs. Accordingly, companies may need to adjust their approaches to forecasting and determining when lifetime losses should be recognized to reflect the current environment.

.10   IFRS 10 Consolidated Financial Statements

IFRS 10 replaces IAS 27, *Consolidated and Separate Financial Statements,* and SIC-12, *Consolidation—Special Purpose Entities,* and is effective for annual periods beginning on or after January 1, 2013. When a business is organized as two or more corporations or partnerships with common ownership, the financial statements must be consolidated to report the economic entity's activities and balance sheet as a whole. In October 2012, the standard was amended for investment entities effective January 1, 2014. The concept of control was clarified such that an investor controls an investee when the investor is exposed, or has rights, to variable returns from its involvement with the investee and has the ability to affect those returns through its power over the investee.

In 2016, the IASB amended the exposure draft titled, *Effective Date of Amendments to IFRS 10 and IAS 28.* The amendments postpone the date the entities must change some aspects as to how they account for transactions between investors and associates or joint ventures.

The postponement applies to changes made in September 2014 by the IASB through narrow-scope amendments to IFRS 10, *Consolidated Financial Statements*, and IAS 28, *Investments in Associates and Joint Ventures.* Those changes affect how an entity should determine gain or loss on sale or contribution of assets between an investor and an associate or joint venture in which it invests. The amendments extend the effective date as to when to apply the new provisions to a date to be determined by the IASB. Entities that apply the rules earlier are required to disclose such application.

The IASB postponed the effective date because it is planning a broader review that may result in simplification of accounting for such transactions and of other aspects of accounting for associates and joint ventures.

.11   IFRS 11 Joint Arrangements

IFRS 11 replaces IAS 31, *Interests in Joint Ventures,* and SIC-13, *Jointly Controlled Entities—Non-Monetary Contributions by Venturers,* and is effective for annual periods beginning on or after January 1, 2013. The term joint arrangement refers to contractually enforceable business agreements between two or more parties where the unanimous consent of both (or all) parties is required to effect choices of actions on behalf of the arrangement. Thus, shared control is the key to identifying a joint arrangement.

According to the IASB, joint arrangements may be either joint operations or joint ventures. The difference between these types of joint arrangements has to do with the ownership and direct control of the underlying assets being employed. In the case of a joint venture, the venturers are investors who have rights to the net assets of the arrangement. Joint operators, on the other hand, are the direct owners of the assets and are directly responsible for the liabilities of the arrangement.

.12   IFRS 12, Disclosure of Interests in Other Entities

This standard is effective for periods beginning on or after January 1, 2013. IFRS 12 requires an entity to disclose information that provides investors, lenders, and other creditors with the significant terms and conditions of its interests in other entities to allow those investors or creditors (or potential investors or creditors) to make informed decisions.

The standard applies to subsidiaries, joint arrangements, associations and unconsolidated structured entities. The standard further requires disclosure of the significant judgments and assumptions made when an entity determines whether they do control, jointly control or have significant influence over another entity.

Updated guidance on IFRS 10, 11, and 12. In June 2012, the Board issued "Consolidated Financial Statements, Joint Arrangements and. Disclosure of Interests in Other Entities: Transition Guidance (Amendments to IFRS 10, IFRS 11 and IFRS 12)." The amendments clarify the transition guidance in IFRS 10, Consolidated Financial Statements. The amendments also provide additional transition relief in IFRS 10, IFRS 11, *Joint Arrangements,* and IFRS 12, *Disclosure of Interests in Other Entities,* limiting the requirement to provide adjusted comparative information to only the preceding comparative period. Furthermore, for disclosures related to unconsolidated structured entities, the amendments will remove the requirement to present comparative information for periods before IFRS 12 is first applied. The effective date of the amendments is annual periods beginning on or after January 1, 2013, which is aligned with the effective date of IFRS 10, 11, and 12. In October 2012, the standard was amended for investment entities effective January 1, 2014. The guidance provides disclosure requirements for interests that an entity holds in subsidiaries, joint arrangements, associates and unconsolidated structured entities.

.13   IFRS 13, Fair Value Measurement

IFRS 13 is to be applied for annual reporting periods beginning on or after January 1, 2013. It defines fair value and established a framework for measuring fair value. The definition of fair value relies on the operations of an orderly market for the asset or liability. According to the IASB, "fair value is a market-based measurement, not an entity-specific measurement," emphasizing the importance of objective, empirical data. In the case of liabilities, the Board reports that "their transfer assumes that those items would remain outstanding and that the market participant transferee would be required to fulfill the obligation, or take on the rights and responsibilities, associated with the instrument."

In measuring fair value, the organization must identify the asset or liability that is being measured. If the asset is other than a financial asset, the organization must apply the "highest and best use of the asset" to determine the appropriate market. The fair value of non-financial assets is determined by reference to the asset's highest and best use irrespective of its current use. The highest and best use of an asset must be physically possible, legally permissible and financially feasible.

The guidance further establishes a hierarchy of fair value measures, based on their objectivity and reliability. The highest priority is given to values established by quoted prices on an active market. The lowest priority is given to "unobservable inputs" that reflect "assumptions that market participants would use when pricing the asset or liability."

.14   IFRS 14, Regulatory Deferral Accounts

This guidance affects entities whose prices or rates charged to their customers are subject to rate regulation. These are companies in specific industries where prices or rates are statutorily controlled and subject to change only upon the direction of rate regulator, often a government agency. The purpose of the guidance is to permit first-time adopters of IFRS to coordinate the reporting of certain expenses or income items between how the regulatory agency uses these expense or income items in setting rates and how these expense and income items are reported on their financial statements. Primarily, this will be entities that formerly used U.S. GAAP and in so doing employed cost deferral accounts. An entity is permitted to use this standard only with its first IFRS-based financial statement. Thus, it does not permit entities that had previously been using IFRS to adopt the use of regulatory deferral accounts.

A regulatory deferral account balance is an amount of expense or income that was not required to be recognized as an asset or liability by U.S. GAAP or other standards but that does qualify to be deferred in accordance with this standard because the deferred amount is also used by the rate regulator in setting the regulated price or rate.

.15   IFRS 15, Revenue from Contracts with Customers

As noted at the beginning of this chapter, the convergence on guidance for revenue recognition has been developing over a number of years. Though this guidance is framed in terms of contracts with customers, its intent is general.

In calculating the revenue to be recognized on any contract with a customer the new guidance requires a five-step process.

1. Identify the contracts. This requires that the entity be able to identify each party's rights and the payment terms, and in some cases may require combining separate contracts into a single contract if two or more contracts were entered into with the same customer at the same time. If a contract is modified after the rights and obligations associated with it have been determined, the effect of the modification(s) of those rights and obligations must be reassessed. In some circumstances, the modification of a contract must be treated as a separate contract.

2. Identify any separate performance objectives within the contracts. This requires a specific assessment of the goods or services promised in a contract and whether the contract calls for a distinct good or service or a series of distinct goods or services that have the same pattern of transfer. An entity recognizes revenue when the control of the asset being transferred is obtained by the customer. Control refers to the ability to direct the use of and receive the benefits from that asset. In some cases, the transfer will take place at a clearly designated time while in others it will take place in stages. In the latter case, the revenue is also recognized in stages rather than, for example, at the completion of all the related transfers. Measurement of the progress toward transfer of control may be made by either the input method or the output method.

3. Determine the transaction price. This requires considering all the terms of the contract as well as customary business practices. The transaction price includes the total consideration the entity expects to receive and must be adjusted for the nature and timing of the receipt of the consideration. If the revenue contains a significant financing component, this must be separated out. If the amount to be received is variable, estimates will have to be made about the amount to be received. This variance can be caused by a number of factors including discounts, credits, rebates, incentives, performance bonuses, as well as penalties. The amount that is variable in a contract may be estimated using probability-weighted amounts or the most likely amount from a range of possibilities. As in accounting generally, consistency in the use of a particular method is important.

4. Allocate the transaction price to the separate performance obligations. Once the full transaction price is determined it must be allocated to each of the performance obligation stages already identified. This must be done on a relative stand-alone selling price basis. The stand-alone selling price is that at which the entity would sell the good or service separately; this amount may not be readily available but may have to be inferred from the total contract and the specific conditions of the sale. More than one method is available for determining the stand-alone selling price, including the

adjusted market assessment approach, expected cost plus a margin approach, or a residual approach. If the contract has a variable component, the revenue from this component may be attributed to the whole contract or to a specific part, depending on the terms of the contract.

5.   Recognize revenue when each performance obligation is satisfied.

Additional information is available in Chapter 2, "Income Statement," on revenue and expense as well as Chapter 7, "Actions of the Financial Accounting Standards Board," on actions of the FASB.

In 2015, the IASB issued an amendment to IFRS 15, *Revenue from Contracts with Customers*, deferring the effective date by one year until January 1, 2018.

On April 2016, the IASB issued amendments to IFRS 15 to clarify some requirements and provide additional transitional relief for companies that are implementing IFRS 15. The amendments are effective on the same date as IFRS 15.

The amendments do not change the underlying principles of IFRS 15 but clarify how those principles should be applied. The amendments provided guidance as to how to:

- identify a performance obligation (the promise to transfer a good or a service to a customer) in a contract;
- determine whether a company is a principal (the provider of a good or service) or an agent (responsible for arranging for the good or service to be provided); and
- determine whether the revenue from granting a license should be recognized at a point in time or over time.

The amendments also include two additional reliefs to reduce cost and complexity for a company when it first applies IFRS 15.

.16   IFRS 16, Leases

The IASB issued an amendment to make it easier for lessees to account for COVID-19-related rent concessions such as rent holidays and temporary rent reductions. The amendment exempts lessees from having to consider individual lease contracts to determine whether rent concessions occurring as a direct consequence of the COVID-19 pandemic are lease modifications and allows lessees to account for such rent concessions as if they were not lease modifications.

Requiring lessees to account for a potentially large volume of COVID-19-related rent concessions could be practically difficult, especially in the light of the many challenges stakeholders face during the pandemic. This optional exemption gives timely relief to lessees and enables them to continue providing information about their leases that is useful to investors. The amendment does not affect lessors.

The amendment is effective June 1, 2020 but, to ensure that the relief is available when needed most, lessees can apply the amendment immediately in any financial statements, interim or annual, not yet authorized for issue.

The IASB issued its new lease accounting guidance in IFRS 16, *Leases*. Under the new guidance, lessees will be required to present right-of-use assets and lease liabilities on the balance sheet. This new lease guidance requires that a lessee recognize the following for leases at the commencement date:

- a lease liability, which is a lessee's obligation to make lease payments arising from a lease, measured on a discounted basis; and
- a right-of-use asset, which is an asset that represents the lessee's right to use, or control the use of, a specified asset for the lease term.

IFRS 16 is effective for annual reporting periods beginning on or after January 1, 2019. Earlier application is permitted for entities that apply IFRS 15, *Revenue from Contracts with Customers*, at or before the date of initial application of IFRS 16.

A lessee should apply IFRS 16 to its leases either:

a) retrospectively to each prior reporting period presented applying IAS 8, *Accounting Policies, Changes in Accounting Estimates and Errors*; or

b) retrospectively with the cumulative effect of initially applying IFRS 16 recognized at the date of initial application.

A lessor is not required to make any adjustments on transition for leases in which it is a lessor and should account for those leases applying IFRS 16 from the date of initial application.

.17   IFRS 17, Insurance Contracts

The IASB issued IFRS 17 that replaced IFRS 4. IFRS 17 establishes principles for the recognition, measurement, presentation and disclosure of insurance contracts issued. It also applies to reinsurance contracts and investment contracts with discretionary participation features. The objective of the guidance is to ensure that entities provide relevant information that faithfully represents those contracts. This information gives a basis for users of financial statements to assess the effect that contracts have on the financial position, financial performance and cash flows of an entity. IFRS 17 is effective for fiscal years beginning January 1, 2023. However, early adoption is permitted.

General model approach:

1. Insurance contracts are measured as the sum of fulfilment cash flows (the present value of probability-weighted expected cash flows plus an explicit risk adjustment for insurance risk) and a contractual service margin (the unearned profit from the contract);

2. Profits are recognized over time as insurance services are provided;
3. Losses are recognized immediately when expected; and
4. Insurance contracts are aggregated in groups for measurement.

Premium-allocation approach:

Premium-allocation approach is an alternative approach that reduced implementation costs for simpler contracts such as short-term non-life insurance contracts:

1. Optional for the measurement of contracts for which:
   a. no significant expected changes in estimates before the claims are incurred, or
   b. coverage period is less than a year;
2. Similar outcome of the general model, but no separate identification of unearned profit; and
3. Discounting of liability for incurred claims not required if expected to be settled within 12 months.

Variable fee approach:

1. Only for contracts with direct participation features or investment related services:
   a. policyholder participates in share of clearly identified pool of underlying assets;
   b. company expects to pay policyholder a substantial share of the return from those underlying assets; and
   c. cash flows expect to vary substantially with underlying assets;
2. Measurement of obligation reflects changes in fair value of all underlying items; and
3. Fulfilment cash flow is calculated consistently with the general model.

How changes are handled:

1. Fulfilment cash flows are updated each reporting period;
2. Changes in estimates of future cash flows if related to past coverage go through income, if related to future coverage adjust unearned profit; and
3. The changes in financial market assumptions is an accounting policy election and either flows through current income or is disaggregated between current income and OCI.

How performance is reported:

1. Insurance revenue excludes deposits;
2. Revenue and expense are recognized as earned or incurred;
3. Insurance finance expense is excluded from insurance service results and is presented either fully in current income or between income and OCI, depending on an accounting policy election; and

4. Written premiums are disclosed in the notes.

What should be disclosed:

1. Nature and extent of risks arising;
2. Extent of mitigation of risks arising from reinsurance and participation; and
3. Quantitative data about exposure to credit, market and liquidity risk.

.18 IFRS 18 and 19

See descriptions above under ¶11,001.

.19 IFRS for SMEs

The IFRS for Small and Medium-Sized Entities (SMEs) is a set of high-quality financial reporting principles that is derived from the full set of IFRSs but tailored for the needs and capabilities of non-publicly accountable companies, estimated to account for over 95 per cent of all companies around the world, and users of their financial statements.

The IFRS for SMEs has been widely accepted around the world, with more than 80 jurisdictions having already adopted or planning to adopt the Standard. In some of these jurisdictions the IFRS for SMEs is being used by very small companies with just a few employees. In response to requests from constituents, the IASB has developed guidance both to assist micro-sized entities currently applying the IFRS for SMEs and to make the IFRS for SMEs more accessible for those considering applying it in the future. The guidance supports the IFRS for SMEs and does not constitute a separate Standard for micro-sized entities.

In the first half of 2013, the Study Group reviewed responses to the Request for Information and made recommendations to the Board on possible amendments. During the second half of 2013, responses to the ED were scheduled to be reviewed and recommendations made to the IASB. During the second half of 2013 or first half of 2014, the IASB was expected to publish the final revisions to the IFRS for SMEs. The target effective date for implementation was in 2015.

In July of 2009, the IASB issued guidance for small- and medium-sized entities (SMEs). The Board estimates that 95 percent of businesses fall under this heading. The IFRS contains 230 pages, was developed over five years in consultation with SMEs throughout the world and contains guidance on all major aspects of financial reporting. The IFRS, for example, simplifies the principles for measuring assets, liabilities, income and expenses. The number of required disclosures has been limited as well. The purpose of the IFRA is to simplify the reporting requirements for small and medium-sized businesses.

A number of benefits are expected to accrue from the new guidance. Comparability between companies will be enhanced, costs of compliance will be reduced and overall confidence will be improved in the reporting by SMEs. In addition, SMEs that are growing and may eventually be required to comply with IFRS applicable to larger businesses will have established the reporting groundwork required.

To encourage SMEs to get on board with the new IFRS, the IASC Foundation developed training materials. The anticipated results of this training include a common high-quality reporting capability for SMES worldwide. The IASB has conducted two comprehensive reviews of the IFRS for SMEs to consider whether there is a need for any amendment to the standard. The first review was completed in 2014. The second review was done in 2022. As a result, the FASB published an exposure draft in September 2022 titled *Third Edition of the IFRS for SMEs Accounting Standard*. The results of the review indicated that the standard is generally accomplishing its objectives and the recommended improvements make minor changes and address issues raised by new revenue recognition standards.

In June 2013, the IASB issued guidance to help micro-sized entities apply the IFRS for SMEs.

The guidance has been developed with input from the SME Implementation Group (an advisory body to the IASB). It extracts from the IFRS for SMEs only those requirements that are likely to be necessary for a typical micro-sized entity, without modifying any of the principles for recognizing and measuring assets, liabilities, income and expenses. In a few areas, it also contains further guidance and illustrative examples to help a micro-sized entity apply the principles in the IFRS for SMEs.

The guidance contains cross-references to the IFRS for SMEs for matters not covered by the guidance. Consequently, having applied the guidance, an entity's notes to the financial statements and auditor's report could refer to conformity with the IFRS for SMEs because this guidance does not modify the requirements of the IFRS for SMEs.

In May 2015, the IASB published amendments to its "International Financial Reporting Standard for Small and Medium-sized Entities." The amendments are the result of the first comprehensive review of that standard, which was originally issued in 2009. They affect 21 of the 35 sections of the standard (not counting consequential amendments) and the glossary; however, most of the changes are rather minor. Entities reporting using the IFRS for SMEs are required to apply the amendments for annual periods beginning on or after January 1, 2017. Earlier application is permitted.

The vast majority of the changes concern clarifications to the current text and, hence, will not constitute changes to the way entities account for certain transactions and events. Three amendments are, however, of larger impact.

The Standard now allows an option to use the revaluation model for property, plant and equipment as not allowing this option has been identified as the single biggest impediment to adoption of the IFRS for SMEs in some jurisdictions in which SMEs commonly revalue their property, plant and equipment and/or are required by law to revalue property, plant and equipment; the main recognition and measurement requirements for deferred income tax have been aligned with current requirements in IAS 12, *Income Taxes* (in developing the IFRS for SMEs, the IASB had already anticipated finalization of its proposed changes to IAS 12; however, these changes were never finalized); and the main recognition and measurement requirements for exploration and evaluation assets have been aligned with IFRS 6, *Exploration for and Evaluation of Mineral Resources,* to ensure that the IFRS for SMEs provides the same relief as full IFRSs for these activities.

¶11,009   The IASB Conceptual Framework

The IASB employs a conceptual framework underlying its financial reporting Standards and Interpretations. *The Framework for the Preparation and Presentation of Financial Statements* (the Framework) sets out the concepts that underlie the preparation and presentation of financial statements for external users. The Framework serves to assist the IASB in the development of future International Accounting Standards and in reviewing and evaluating existing standards.

The Framework supports the interests of better reporting through convergence of the IASB with the best accounting practices from around the world. It removed a number of options contained in IASs, whose existence had caused uncertainty and reduced comparability. The completion of these improved standards brings the IASB closer to its commitment to have a platform of high-quality, improved standards.

The primary means of publishing International Financial Reporting Standards is now by electronic format through IASB's subscriber Web site IASB.org.

The Framework specifies:

- The objectives of financial statements.
- The qualitative characteristics used to determine the usefulness of information reported in financial statements.
- The definition, recognition, and measurement of the elements used in preparing financial statements.
- The concepts of capital and capital maintenance.

The Framework endorses the objective of financial statements as general purpose, as does U.S. GAAP. The purpose of financial statements is to provide information about the financial position at a given date, performance during a period, as well as changes in financial position during that period. More specifically, financial statements should provide useful information about an entity's economic resources, financial structure, liquidity, and solvency.

The Framework is based on fundamental assumptions, similar to U.S. GAAP—the use of the accrual basis of accounting and the presumption that an entity is a going concern. Qualitative characteristics of financial statements include: understandability, relevance (including materiality), reliability (faithful representation, substance over form, neutrality, prudence, completeness) and comparability. The elements of financial statements include: financial position (assets, liabilities, equity), performance, income, and expenses.

In 2005, it was announced that the IASB and the FASB had begun a joint project to revisit their conceptual frameworks for financial accounting and reporting. The goal of the joint project are to build on the respective Boards' existing frameworks by refining, updating and converging them to form a common framework to be used by both Boards in formulating new and revising existing accounting standards.

An overriding goal of both the IASB and the FASB is to ground their standards on principles rather than a collection of conventions. The coherency and integrity of a set of financial standards begins with a set of common and agreed-upon fundamental concepts. Using a common framework as a basis for developing a set of financial accounting standards helps insure coherence and internal consistency among the standards.

In developing a conceptual framework, the intention is not only to assist standard setters but also the preparers of financial statements. The IASB and FASB Boards have been pursuing a number of projects that are aimed at achieving short-term convergence on specific issues, as well as several extensive projects aimed at the goal of full convergence. But to achieve the ultimate goal of full convergence of standards it is necessary that the conceptual frameworks first achieve convergence.

The project is simplified by the fact that the existing conceptual frameworks are similar in emphasis. Both stress the need for standards to be useful in:

- Making economic decisions
- Assessing cash flow prospects
- Assessing resources and claims against those resources
- Measuring changes in financial resources

A central issue to be addressed in the course of the project includes providing definitive definitions of such fundamental concepts as asset, liability, equity, revenue recognition, measurement (historical cost, fair value, current cost), and reporting entity.

.01   The 2018 Conceptual Framework

In March 2018, the Board issued 2018 Conceptual Framework. The 2018 Framework includes limited changes to the chapters on the objective of general purpose financial reporting and qualitative characteristics of useful financial information. The FASB did not make corresponding changes to its Statements of Financial Accounting Concepts.

The 2018 Framework fill in the gaps, clarified and updated the 2010 Conceptual Framework. However, it did not fundamentally reconsider all aspects of the 2010 Framework. In developing the 2018 Framework, the Board sought a balance between providing high-level concepts and providing enough detail for the 2018 Framework to be useful to the Board and others. Some stakeholders stated that in some areas, the Board's proposals merely described the factors that the Board would consider in making judgments when developing Standards. The Board, however, did not share their view that the proposals did not examine fundamental concepts and were not sufficiently aspirational. The Board viewed the 2018 Framework as a practical tool to help it to develop Standards. The Board concluded that a Conceptual Framework would not fulfill this role if it described concepts without explaining the factors the Board needs to consider in making judgments when the application of concepts does not lead to a single answer, or leads to conflicting answers.

Further, the Board drew on some concepts developed in recent standard-setting projects. The Board's goal was to reflect the Board's most developed thinking on these matters and not to justify its standard-setting decisions or current practice. The Board did not address the equity method of accounting, the translation of amounts denominated in foreign currency or the restatement of the measuring unit in hyper-inflation. The Board concluded that these issues would best be dealt with if it were to carry out projects to consider revising Standards on these topics.

The revised concepts will guide the Board when it develops or revises Standards. However, changes to the Conceptual Framework will not automatically lead to changes in existing Standards. Accordingly, changes to the Conceptual Framework will have no immediate effect on the financial statements of most reporting entities. Preparers of financial statements could be directly affected by the changes only if they need to use the Conceptual Framework to develop an accounting policy when no Standard applies to a particular transaction or other event or when a Standard allows a choice of accounting policy. The Board also issued the *Amendments to References to the Conceptual Framework in IFRS Standards* to facilitate smoother transition to the 2018 Framework for those entities. Where appropriate, that document replaces references in Standards to the 1989 Framework with references to the 2018 Framework and updates related quotations.

The Board and the IFRS Interpretations Committee will start using the 2018 Framework immediately after it is issued.

¶11,010   Interpretations of International Accounting Standards

The IASC, in 1977, began publishing Interpretations of International Accounting Standards developed by the Standing Interpretations Committee (SICs). This responsibility now falls on the IASB International Financial Reporting Interpretations Committee (IFRIC). Final Interpretations are numbered SIC-1, SIC-2, and so on. Because of the great number of recent changes to the IASs, care should be exercised in consulting the SICs, because they may reflect interpretations that were only reliable until a specific date. Summaries of SICs are available on the IASC Web site for those indicated with an asterisk(*); all those listed without an asterisk are superseded. The SIC numbering was also replaced with a newer series of interpretations by the IFRIC.

The following is a list of the SICs; only those with an * are current, the rest have been superseded:

SIC-1,   *Consistence—Different Cost Formulas for Inventories*

SIC-2,   *Consistence—Capitalization of Borrowing Costs*

SIC-3,   *Elimination of Unrealized Profits and Losses on Transactions with Associates*

SIC-5,   *Classification of Financial Instruments—Contingent Settlement Provisions*

SIC-6,   *Cost of Modifying Existing Software*

SIC-7*,   *Introduction of the Euro*

SIC-8,   *First-Time Application of IASs as the Primary Basis of Accounting*

SIC-9,   *Business Combinations—Classification Either as Acquisitions or Uniting of Interests*

SIC-10*,   *Government Assistance—No Specific Relation to Operating Activities*

SIC-11,   *Foreign Exchange—Capitalization of Losses Resulting from Severe Currency Devaluations*

SIC-12,   *Consolidation—Special-Purpose Entities*

SIC-13,   *Jointly Controlled Entities—Non-Monetary Contributions by Venturers*

SIC-14,   *Property, Plant and Equipment—Compensation for the Impairment or Loss of Items*

SIC-15,   *Operating Leases—Incentives*

SIC-16,   *Presentation of Treasury Shares*

SIC-17,   *Equity—Costs of an Equity Transaction*
SIC-18,   *Consistency—Alternative Methods*
SIC-19,   *Reporting Currency—Measurement and Presentation of Financial Statements Under IAS 21 and IAS 29*
SIC-20,   *Equity Accounting Method—Recognition of Losses*
SIC-21,   *Income Taxes—Recovery of Revalued Non-Depreciable Assets*
SIC-22,   *Business Combinations—Subsequent Adjustment of Fair Values and Goodwill Initially Reported*
SIC-23,   *Property, Plant, and Equipment—Major Inspection or Overhaul Costs*
SIC-24,   *Earnings per Share—Financial Instruments That May Be Settled in Shares*
SIC-25*,   *Income Taxes—Changes in the Tax Status of an Enterprise or its Shareholders*
SIC-26,   *Draft only—never issued—Property, Plant and Equipment – Results of Incidental Operations*
SIC-27,   *Evaluating the Substance of Transactions Involving the Legal Form of a Lease*
SIC-28,   *Business Combinations—Measurement of Shares Issued as Purchase Consideration*
SIC-29*,   *Disclosure—Service Concession Agreements*
SIC-30,   *Reporting Currency—Translation from Measurement Currency to Presentation Currency*
SIC-31,   *Revenue—Barter Transactions Involving Advertising Services*
SIC-32*,   *Intangible Assets—Web Site Costs* (modified in 2014 by IFRS 15 with reference to IAS 11)
SIC-33,   *Consolidation and Equity Method—Potential Voting Rights*

The IASB's International Financial Reporting Interpretations Committee (IFRIC) continues to develop interpretations. Listed here are the active IFRICs except those marked (*) which have been superseded.

IFRIC 1,   *Changes in Existing Decommissioning, Restoration and Similar Liabilities*
IFRIC 2,   *Members' Shares in Co-operative Entities and Similar Instruments*
IFRIC 4*,   *Determining Whether and Arrangement Contains a Lease*
IFRIC 5,   *Rights to Interests Arising from Decommissioning. Restoration and Environmental Rehabilitation Funds*
IFRIC 6,   *Liabilities Arising from Participating in Specific Market—Waste Electrical and Electronic Equipment*
IFRIC 7,   *Applying the Restatement Approach under IAS 29 Financial Reporting in Hyperinflationary Economics*

IFRIC 8*,   *Scope of IFRS 2* (Superseded by IFRS 2)

IFRIC 9,   *Reassessment of Embedded Derivatives*

IFRIC 10,   *Interim Financial Reporting and Impairment*

IFRIC 11*,   *IFRS 2—Group and Treasury Share Transactions*
             (Superseded by IFRS 2)

IFRIC 12,   *Service Concession Arrangements* (modified by IRFS 15 with
             respect to IAS 18)

IFRIC 13*,   *Customer Loyalty Programs* (Superseded by IFRS 15 as of January
             1, 2018)

IFRIC 14,   *IAS 19—The Limit on a Defined Benefit Asset, Minimum Funding
             Requirements and their Interaction*

IFRIC 15*,   *Agreements for the Construction of Real Estate*
             (Superseded by IFRS 15 as of January 1, 2017)

IFRIC 16,   *Hedges of a Net Investment in a Foreign Operation*

IFRIC 17,   *Distributions of Non-cash Assets to Owners*

IFRIC 18*,   *Transfers of Assets from Customers* (Superseded by IFRS 15 as of
             January 1, 2017)

IFRIC 19,   *Extinguishing Financial Liabilities with Equity Instruments*

IFRIC 20,   *Stripping Costs in the Production Phase of a Surface Mine*

IFRIC 21,   *Levies*

IFRIC 22,   *Foreign Currency Transactions and Advance Consideration*

IFRIC 23,   *Uncertainty over Income Tax Treatments*

The International Accounting Standards Board issued IFRIC Interpretation 21, *Levies*, an interpretation on the accounting for levies imposed by governments. The Interpretation had been developed by the IFRS Interpretations Committee ("the Interpretations Committee"), the interpretative body of the IASB.

The Interpretations Committee was asked to consider how an entity should account for liabilities to pay levies imposed by governments, other than income taxes, in its financial statements. The principal question raised was about when the entity should recognize a liability to pay a levy.

IFRIC 21 is an interpretation of IAS 37, *Provisions, Contingent Liabilities and Contingent Assets*. IAS 37 sets out criteria for the recognition of a liability, one of which is the requirement for the entity to have a present obligation as a result of a past event (known as an obligating event). The Interpretation clarifies that the obligating event that gives rise to a liability to pay a levy is the activity described in the relevant legislation that triggers the payment of the levy. IFRIC 21 is effective for annual periods beginning on or after January 1, 2014.

¶11,011   The International Organization of Securities Commissions

According to the International Accounting Standards Committee Foundation, the International Organization of Securities Commissions (IOSCO) is the representative body of the world's securities markets regulators. Members include the Australian Securities and Investments Commission, the French Commission des Operations des Bourse (COB), the Italian Commissione Nazionale per le Societ e la Borsa (CONSOB), the members of the Canadian Securities Administrators (CSA), the UK's Financial Services Authority (FSA) and the United States Securities and Exchange Commission (SEC).

High-quality financial information is vital to the operation of efficient capital markets, and differences in the quality of the accounting policies and their enforcement between countries leads to inefficiencies between markets. IOSCO has been active in encouraging and promoting the improvement and quality of IASs and IFRSs for more than ten years. This commitment was evidenced by the agreement between IASC and IOSCO to work on a program of "core standards," which could be used by publicly listed entities when offering securities in foreign jurisdictions. The Core Standards project resulted in 15 new or revised IASs that were completed in 1999 with the issuance of IAS 39, *Financial Instruments: Recognition and Measurement*. IOSCO spent a year reviewing the results of the project and released a report in May 2000 which recommended to all of its members that they allow multinational issuers to use IASC Standards, as supplemented by reconciliation, disclosure, and interpretation, where necessary, to address outstanding substantive issues at a national or regional level. IASB staff and IOSCO continue to work together to resolve outstanding issues and to identify areas where new IASB Standards are needed. IOSCO representatives sit as observers on the International Financial Reporting Interpretations Committee.

CHAPTER 12

International Standards:
Auditing, Ethics, Public Sector

¶12,000   Overview

As the movement to produce a unified international accounting profession evolved, two authoritative bodies emerged as leaders, the International Federation of Accountants (IFAC) and the International Accounting Standards Board (IASB), formerly the International Accounting Standards Committee (IASC). By 1982, it became obvious to the leadership of the IFAC and the IASC that their particular bailiwicks needed to be clearly established in order to avoid confusion concerning their respective roles. It was agreed that the IASC (now IASB) should be the sole international body to set *financial accounting and reporting standards*. At the same time, IASC agreed to IFAC's role as the worldwide *organization for the accountancy profession*.

Under the umbrella of IFAC, there are four independent standard-setting boards: (1) The International Auditing and Assurance Standards Board® (IAASB®), (2) The International Accounting Education Standards Board™ (IAESB™), (3) The International Ethics Standards Board for Accountants® (IESBA®), and (4) The International Public Sector Accounting Standards Board® (IPSASB®).

The IAASB is an independent standard-setting body that serves the public interest by setting high-quality International Standards for auditing, assurance, and other related Standards, and by facilitating the convergence of international and national auditing and assurance Standards. In doing so, the IAASB enhances the quality and consistency of practice throughout the world and strengthens public confidence in the global auditing and assurance profession.

In January 2015, the IAASB released its new and revised Auditor Reporting standards. In June 2015, the IAASB released its revised International Standard on Auditing™ (ISA™), *Addressing Disclosures in the Audit of Financial Statements*. Additional information on these standards is provided below in Auditing Update.

The IAESB is an independent standard-setting body that serves the public interest by establishing standards in the area of professional accounting education that prescribe technical competence and professional skills, values, ethics, and attitudes.

The IESBA is an independent standard-setting body that serves the public interest by setting robust, internationally appropriate ethics standards, including auditor independence requirements, for professional accountants worldwide. These are compiled in the *Code of Ethics for Professional Accountants™*.

The IPSASB develops International Public Sector Accounting Standards (IPSASs), accrual-based standards used for the preparation of general purpose financial statements by governments and other public sector entities around the world. Through these standards, the IPSASB aims to enhance the quality, consistency, and transparency of public sector financial reporting worldwide. The IPSASB also issues guidance and facilitates the exchange of information among accountants and others who work in the public sector and promotes the acceptance of and international convergence to IPSASs.

In January 2015, the IPSASB published a new standard, IPSAS 33, *First-time Adoption of Accrual Basis IPSASs*. Information on this and other IPSAS is available in The International Federation of Accountants.

¶12,001   The International Federation of Accountants

The Board of the IFAC considered the following to be among the organization's most important tasks:

1. Develop auditing initiatives;
2. Develop guidance and standards relating to education, ethics, management accounting, information technology, and the public sector;

3. Give consideration to such professional issues as accountant's liability and the liberalization of professional services; and
4. Act as primary spokesperson on professional accountancy issues.

Founded in 1977, the International Federation of Accountants with headquarters in New York, now consists of 167 members and associates in 127 countries and jurisdictions, representing approximately 2.5 million accountants in public practice, education, government service, industry, and commerce. Individual accountants are represented through their membership in their national accountancy organization. IFAC emphasizes that the international accountancy profession be considered to have two primary standard-setting bodies: IFAC and the IASC.

Associate members of IFAC are national organizations whose members work in a support role to the accountancy professions and newly formed accountancy bodies that have not yet met the full membership criteria.

Affiliate members of IFAC are international organizations that represent a particular area of interest or a group of professionals who frequently interact with accountants.

There is considerable mutual support for one another's objectives. IFAC member bodies, in addition to their responsibility to promote and use IFAC guidance, are committed to promote and implement IASB pronouncements. There is also regular contact and coordination between the two organizations at the leadership level.

This arrangement has been working successfully. In addition, both organizations appear to believe that it provides, on the one hand, the necessary degree of independence for the IASB Board to set accounting standards, but also ensures the accountancy profession's commitment to help in seeing that these standards are actually implemented in international practice.

IFAC's overall mission is to "serve the public interest, strengthen the worldwide accountancy profession, and contribute to the development of strong international economies by establishing and promoting adherence to high-quality professional standards. The organization realizes that public confidence in financial information is vital to capital market growth and economic development." As a result, in 2002, IFAC began the process of establishing the foundation for major reforms necessary to (re)build trust in the financial reporting process.

This process has continued through the creation of a Monitoring Group, launching of an IFAC Leadership Group, and (in March 2005) the IFAC announced the formation of its Public Interest Oversight Board (PIOB). The Board will oversee the work of IFAC's auditing, ethics and education standard-setting committees. The objective of the board is to ensure that IFAC's standard-setting activities reflect the public interest and are fully transparent to those affected by the standards.

The Monitoring Group (MG) comprises international regulators and representatives of related organizations. The MG will update the Public Oversight Board regarding significant events in the regulatory environment, and among other charges, act as the vehicle for dialogue between regulators and the international accountancy profession.

The IFAC Leadership Group includes the IFAC President, Deputy President, Chief Executive, the Chairs of the IAASB, the Transitional Auditors Committee, the Form of Firms, and up to four other members designated by the IFAC Board. It will work with the MG and address issues related to the regulation of the profession.

In September 2011, two important policy papers were revised and released. Policy Position Paper 1, *Regulation of the Accountancy Profession*, was first issued by IFAC in December 2007. The revised paper includes a new section titled "Current Regulatory Environment." The section highlights the importance of global regulatory convergence, including the adoption and implementation of high-quality standards. It describes recent developments in regulation and makes reference to the Independent Forum of Independent Audit Regulators (IFIAR) Core Principles. Lastly, the revised Policy Position Paper 1 includes a description of what would typically be included in shared regulation of auditing at a national level.

Policy Position Paper 3, *International Standard Setting in the Public Interest*, was issued by IFAC in December 2008. The revised and updated paper describes how current governance arrangements and independent standard-setting boards supported by IFAC operate in the public interest and address the need for legitimacy, transparency, and performance. It further includes discussion of the 2010 Monitoring Group (MG) review.

¶12,002   International Public Sector Accounting Standards

International Public Sector (Governmental) Accounting Standards (IPSASs) set out the requirements for financial reporting by governments and other public sector organizations with the ultimate objective of enhancing the accountability and financial management of governments worldwide. The International Public Sector Accounting Standards Board® (IPSASB®) receives funding from:

1. The World Bank.
2. United Nations Development Program.
3. Asian Development Bank.
4. International Monetary Fund.

Thus far, the Board has developed 32 IPSASs as part of its *comprehensive* Standards Project to assist governments in reporting comparable, relevant, and understandable financial information.

.01   The Public Sector Board (IPSASB)

The International Public Sector Accounting Standards Board® (IPSASB) is charged with servicing the needs of those involved in public sector financial reporting, accounting, and auditing on a worldwide scope. "Public sector" refers to national governments, regional governments (e.g., state, provincial, and territorial), local governments (e.g., city and town) and related governmental entities (e.g., agencies, boards, commissions, and enterprises). The Committee has been given the authority to issue International Public Sector Accounting Standards (IPSASs).

The objective of the Board is to develop programs aimed at improving public sector financial management and accountability, including developing accounting standards and promoting their acceptance.

The problem in international public sector accounting arises from the fact that governments and other public sector entities follow diverse financial reporting practices and, in many countries, there are no authoritative standards for the public sector. In some countries where standards do exist, the body of standards may be either at an early stage of development or limited in application to specific types of entities in the public sector.

The IPSASB issues a range of publications, including Standards, Guidelines, Studies and Occasional Papers. The Standards are the authoritative requirements established by the Board to improve the quality of financial reporting in the public sector around the world.

.02   IPSASB Approves Public Sector Conceptual Framework

In 2014 (September), the International Public Sector Accounting Standards Board® (IPSASB®) announced its approval of the *Conceptual Framework for General Purpose Financial Reporting by Public Sector Entities* (the Conceptual Framework). The Conceptual Framework underpins the development of International Public Sector Accounting Standards (IPSASs) and Recommended Practice Guidelines (RPGs).

The Conceptual Framework establishes the concepts that will guide the IPSASB's approach to standard-setting and guidance. It addresses concepts applicable to both public sector financial statements and a wider set of public sector financial reporting needs. The Conceptual Framework identifies and responds to the key characteristics of the public sector, notably that the primary purpose of most governments and public sector entities is to deliver services to citizens and others. Therefore, the purpose of financial reporting in the public sector is to provide useful information for service recipients and resource providers.

The completed Conceptual Framework was expected to be issued by the end of October 2014. The final four chapters (see below) were approved by the IPSASB during its September meeting. Those four chapters, which address the definition, recognition, and measurement of the "elements" (or building blocks) of financial statements and presentation in General Purpose Financial Reports, join the original four chapters which were issued early in 2013, bringing the entire Conceptual Framework to eight chapters. The development process included eight public consultations with the IPSASB's global constituency.

The Conceptual Framework project has been the key strategic priority for the IPSASB in recent years. Its successful completion allowed the IPSASB to focus on projects to be identified through its public consultation on strategy for 2015 forward and work program for 2015–2019, along with projects already initiated, including social benefits. The Conceptual Framework will provide a solid basis for future standard setting by the IPSASB. The IPSASB will continue to work in the public interest, responding to the global financial reporting needs of governments and other public sector entities as appropriate.

The first four chapters of the Conceptual Framework are:

Chapter 1:   Role and Authority of the Conceptual Framework
Chapter 2:   Objectives and Users of General Purpose Financial Reporting
Chapter 3:   Qualitative Characteristics
Chapter 4:   Reporting Entity

These chapters outline the role of the Conceptual Framework in the IPSAS and RPG development process, identify that the primary users of general purpose financial reports (GPFRs) of public sector entities are service recipients and resource providers, and clarify that the objectives of financial reporting by public sector entities are to provide information useful to users for accountability and decision making purposes. They also identify the qualitative characteristics of, and constraints on, information included in GPFRs and the key characteristics of a public sector reporting entity.

.03   Synopsis of IPSASs

- IPSAS 1—*Presentation of Financial Statements*. This Standard sets out the overall considerations for the presentation of financial statements, guidance for the structure of those statements and minimum requirements for their content under the accrual basis of accounting.
- IPSAS 2—*Cash Flow Statements*. This Standard requires the provision of information about the changes in cash and cash equivalents during the period from operating, investing and financing activities.

- IPSAS 3—*Net Surplus or Deficit for the Period, Fundamental Errors and Changes in Accounting Policies*. This Standard specifies the accounting treatment for changes in accounting estimates, changes in accounting policies, and the correction of fundamental errors; defines extraordinary items; and requires the separate disclosure of certain items in the financial statements.
- IPSAS 4—*The Effect of Changes in Foreign Exchange Rates*. This Standard deals with accounting for foreign currency transactions and foreign operations. It sets the requirements for determining which exchange rate to use for the recognition of certain transactions and balances, and how to recognize in the financial statements the financial effect of changes in exchange rates.
- IPSAS 5—*Borrowing Costs*. This Standard prescribes the accounting treatment for borrowing costs and requires either the immediate expensing of borrowing costs or, as an allowed alternative treatment, the capitalization of borrowing costs that are directly attributable to the acquisition, construction, or production of a qualifying asset.
- IPSAS 6—*Consolidated Financial Statements and Accounting for Controlled Entities*. This Standard requires all controlling entities to prepare consolidated financial statements that consolidate all controlled entities on a line-by-line basis. The Standard also contains a detailed discussion of the concept of control, as it applies in the public sector, and guidance on determining whether control exists for financial reporting purposes.
- IPSAS 7—*Accounting for Investments in Associates*. This Standard requires all investments in associates to be accounted for in the consolidated financial statements using the equity method of accounting. However, when the investment is acquired and held exclusively with a view to its disposal in the near future, the cost method is required.
- IPSAS 8—*Financial Reporting of Interests in Joint Ventures*. This Standard requires proportionate consolidation to be adopted as the benchmark treatment for accounting for such joint ventures entered into by public sector entities. However, IPSAS 8 also permits, as an alternative, joint ventures to be accounted for using the equity method of accounting.
- IPSAS 9—*Revenue from Exchange Transactions*. This Standard establishes the conditions for the recognition of revenue arising from exchange transactions, requires such revenue to be measured at the fair value of the consideration received or receivable, and includes disclosure requirements.
- IPSAS 10—*Financial Reporting in Hyperinflationary Economies*. This Standard describes the characteristics of a hyperinflationary economy and requires financial statements of entities that operate in such economies to be restated.
- IPSAS 11—*Construction Contracts*. This Standard defines construction contracts, establishes requirements for the recognition of revenues and expenses arising from such contracts, and identifies certain disclosure requirements.

- IPSAS 12—*Inventories.* This Standard defines inventories, establishes measurement requirements for inventories (including those inventories held for distribution at no or nominal charge) under the historical cost system and includes disclosure requirements.
- IPSAS 13—*Leases.* This Standard prescribes for both lessees and lessors the appropriate accounting policies and disclosures to apply in relation to finance and operating leases. It includes guidance on the classification of leases, disclosures to be made in the financial statements of lessees and lessors, and accounting for sale and leaseback transactions.
- IPSAS 14—*Events After the Reporting Date.* This Standard prescribes when an entity should adjust its financial statements for events that occur after the reporting date and the disclosures that it should make about other "nonadjusting" events that occur after the reporting date.
- IPSAS 15—*Financial Instruments: Disclosure and Presentation.* This Standard prescribes how financial instruments are to be classified and identifies disclosures to be made in general-purpose financial statements.
- IPSAS 16—*Investment Property.* This Standard prescribes requirements for accounting for investment property, including the initial and subsequent measurement and disclosure of such property by governments and their agencies.
- IPSAS 17—*Property, Plant and Equipment.* This Standard prescribes requirements for the initial recognition and measurement of property, plant, and equipment. It also deals with subsequent measurement, depreciation, and disclosures about these assets. The Standard provides a transitional period to support the orderly implementation of its requirements and allows but does not require heritage assets to be recognized in general-purpose financial statements.
- IPSAS 18—*Segment Reporting.* This Standard establishes principles for reporting financial information about distinguishable activities of a government or other public sector entity appropriate for:
  - Evaluating the entity's past performance in achieving its objectives.
  - Identifying the resources allocated to support the major activities of the entity.
  - Making decisions about the future allocation of resources.
- IPSAS 19—*Provisions, Contingent Liabilities, and Contingent Assets.* The objective of this Standard is to define provisions, contingent liabilities, and contingent assets and to identify the circumstances in which provisions should be recognized, how they should be measured, and the disclosures that should be made about them. The Standard also requires that certain information be disclosed about contingent liabilities and contingent assets in the notes to the financial statements to enable users to understand their nature, timing, and amount.

- IPSAS 20—*Related Party Disclosures.* The objective of this Standard is to require the disclosure of the existence of related party relationships where control exists, and the disclosure of information about transactions between the entity and its related parties in certain circumstances. This information is required for accountability purposes and to facilitate a better understanding of the financial position and performance of the reporting entity. The principal issues in disclosing information about related parties are identifying which parties control or significantly influence the reporting entity, and determining what information should be disclosed about transactions with those parties. These IPSASs are to be applied when the accrual basis of accounting is adopted.

- IPSAS 21—*Impairment of Non-Cash Generating Assets.* The objective of this Standard, issued December 23, 2004, is to prescribe the foundation on which an entity determines whether noncash-generating assets are impaired and, if so, under what conditions a loss should be recognized. Strict guidance on impairment "is a key element in ensuring that property, plant and equipment and certain other assets of public sector entities are not carried at an amount in excess of their service capacity," according to Philippe Adhémar, IPSASB Chair.

  Governments and other public sector entities that prepare general-purpose financial statements under the accrual basis of accounting are the focus of this standard. It requires that an asset not be carried at an amount in excess of its recoverable service amount. If conditions indicate, a determination must be made whether there is an impairment of noncash-generating assets on the balance sheet. If there is such an indication, the entity is required to estimate the recoverable service amount of the asset and to determine whether an impairment loss should be recognized.

  The Standard includes:
    - Definitions of cash-generating assets and impairment.
    - Guidance on identifying an asset that may be impaired.
    - Measuring an asset's recoverable service amount.
    - Measuring an impairment loss.
    - Requirements for the recognition, and reversal of an impairment loss.

- IPSAS 22—*Disclosure of Financial Information About the General Government Sector.* To allow enhanced transparency in financial reporting, this guidance presents information about the presentation of the general government sector in consolidated financial reporting.

- IPSAS 23—*Revenue from Non-Exchange Transactions (Taxes and Transfers).* Describes considerations in recognizing and measuring revenue from non-exchange transactions.

- IPSAS 24—*Presentation of Budget Information in Financial Statements.* Guidance on comparing actual results to budgeted amounts.
- IPSAS 25—*Employee Benefits.* The accounting and disclosure requirement related to employee benefits are prescribed.
- IPSAS 26—*Impairment of Cash Generating Assets.* The guidance sets for procedures an entity should apply to determine whether a cash-generating asset is impaired and when a loss should be recognized from an impairment. Additionally, the guidance indicates the circumstances under which an impairment loss may be reversed.
- IPSAS 27—*Agriculture.* This standard prescribes the accounting treatment and disclosures related to agricultural activity. Agricultural activity is defined as "the management by an entity of the biological transformation of living animals or plants (biological assets) for sale, or for distribution at no charge or for a nominal charge or for conversion into agricultural produce or into additional biological assets."
- IPSAS 28—*Financial Instruments: Presentation Drawn from IAS 32.* This standard establishes principles for presenting financial instruments as liabilities or equity, and for offsetting financial assets and financial liabilities.
- IPSAS 29—*Financial Instruments: Recognition and Measurement.* Drawn primarily from IAS 39, this standard establishes principles for recognizing and measuring financial assets, financial liabilities, and some contracts to buy or sell non-financial items.
- IPSAS 30—*Financial Instruments: Disclosures.* This standard draws on IFRS 7 and requires disclosures for the types of loans described in IPSAS 29. It enables users to evaluate the significance of the financial instruments in the entity's financial position and performance; the nature and extent of risks arising from financial instruments to which the entity is exposed; and how those risks are managed.
- IPSAS 31—*Intangible Assets.* This standard adds some guidance on public sector-specific issues, including intangible heritage assets. Previously there has been no direct guidance to address intangible assets that exist in the public sector. This standard enhances consistency in accounting for intangible assets, while also laying the groundwork for dealing with some of the more complex public sector-specific issues. It is primarily drawn from the IASB IAS 38, *Intangible Assets.* It also contains extracts from the IASB's Standing Interpretations Committee Interpretation 32 (SIC 32), *Intangible Assets—Web Site Costs,* adding application guidance and illustrations that have not yet been incorporated into the IAS.
- IPSAS 32—*Service Concession Arrangements: Grantor.* Service concession arrangements provide a way for governments and other public sector entities to build the infrastructure necessary to maintain and improve critical public

services. Until now, public sector entities have had no international guidance on how to report such transactions.

The Standard addresses the grantor's accounting in such arrangements using an approach that is consistent with that used for the operator's accounting in Interpretation (IFRIC) 12, Service Concession Arrangements, issued by the International Financial Interpretations Committee of the IASB. IPSAS 32 mirrors Interpretation 12 of the International Financial Reporting Interpretations Committee's (IFRIC 12), which sets out the accounting requirements for the private sector operator in a service concession arrangement. Because this Standard deals with the accounting issues of the grantor, this Standard addresses the issues identified in IFRIC 12 from the grantor's point of view.

A service concession arrangement is a contract or other agreement between a grantor and a concession operator. The operator uses the service concession asset to provide a public service on behalf of the grantor for compensation during the period specified in the arrangement.

- IPSAS 33—*First-time Adoption of Accrual Basis IPSASs.* IPSAS 33 grants transitional exemptions to entities adopting accrual basis IPSASs for the first time, providing a major tool to help entities along their journey to implement IPSASs. "With IPSAS 33, the IPSASB has developed a comprehensive standard that provides guidance and exemptions for entities that are transitioning to accrual basis IPSASs," according to IPSASB Chair Andreas Bergmann. "IPSAS 33 meets the needs of both preparers and users of financial statements during the transition period. Its publication is a further incentive for entities to make the decision to apply IPSASs." IPSAS 33 allows first-time adopters three years to recognize specified assets and liabilities. This provision allows sufficient time to develop reliable models for recognizing and measuring assets and liabilities during the transition period.

This new standard addresses situations when reliable historical cost information about assets and liabilities is not available. It also addresses the presentation of comparative information in transitional IPSAS financial statements and an entity's first IPSAS-compliant financial statements.

Using these comprehensive principles will ensure that an entity's first financial statements using accrual basis IPSASs contain high-quality information and can be generated at a cost that does not exceed the benefits.

All Standards have been developed to improve the quality of financial reporting in the public sector worldwide. An important goal is to achieve convergence of these Standards where possible. Additional Standards have been issued, in addition to those summarized above. Following is a list of Standards currently in place:

- IPSAS 1—*Presentation of Financial Statements;*
- IPSAS 3—*Accounting Policies, Changes in Accounting Estimates and Errors;*
- IPSAS 4—*The Effects of Changes in Foreign Exchange Rates;*
- IPSAS 6—*Consolidated and Separate Financial Statements;*
- IPSAS 7—*Investments in Associates;*
- IPSAS 8—*Interests in Joint Ventures;*
- IPSAS 10—*Financial Reporting in Hyperinflationary Economies;*
- IPSAS 12—*Inventories;*
- IPSAS 13—*Leases;*
- IPSAS 14—*Events after the Reporting Date;*
- IPSAS 16—*Investment Property;*
- IPSAS 17—*Property, Plant, and Equipment;*
- IPSAS 19—*Provisions, Contingent Liabilities and Contingent Assets;*
- IPSAS 21—*Impairment of Non-Cash-Generating Assets;*
- IPSAS 22—*Disclosure of Financial Information about the General Government Sector;*
- IPSAS 23—*Revenue from Non-Exchange Transactions (Taxes and Transfers);*
- IPSAS 24—*Presentation of Budget Information in Financial Statements;*
- IPSAS 25—*Employee Benefits;*
- IPSAS 26—*Impairment of Cash-Generating Assets;*
- IPSAS 27—*Agriculture;*
- IPSAS 28—*Financial Instruments: Presentation;*
- IPSAS 29—*Financial Instruments: Recognition and Measurement;*
- IPSAS 30—*Financial Instruments: Disclosures;*
- IPSAS 31—*Intangible Assets;*
- IPSAS 32—*Service Concession Arrangements: Grantor;*
- IPSAS 33—*First-time Adoption of Accrual Basis IPSAS;*
- IPSAS 34—*Separate Financial Statements;*
- IPSAS 35—*Consolidated Financial Statements;*
- IPSAS 36—*Investments in Associates and Joint Ventures;*
- IPSAS 37—*Joint Arrangements;*
- IPSAS 38—*Disclosure of Interests in Other Entities;*
- IPSAS 39—*Employee Benefits* (replacing IPSAS 25);
- IPSAS 40—*Public Sector Combinations;*
- IPSAS 41—*Financial Instruments;*
- IPSAS 42—*Social Benefits;*
- IPSAS 43—*Leases;*
- IPSAS 44—*Non-Current Assets Held for Sale and Discontinued Operations;*
- IPSAS 45—*Property, Plant, and Equipment;*
- IPSAS 46—*Measurement;*
- IPSAS 47—*Revenue; and*
- IPSAS 48—*Transfer Expenses.*

.04 Other Pronouncements

The Public Sector Committee has released Study 14, *Transition to the Accrual Basis of Accounting: Guidance for Governments and Government Entities*. This study identifies key issues to be addressed in the transfer from the cash to the accrual basis of accounting and alternative approaches that can be adopted when implementing the accrual basis in an efficient and effective manner in the public sector.

It also identifies key requirements of IPSASs and other relevant sources of guidance to assist in the transition from the cash basis to the accrual basis. The Committee believes that governments and governmental entities will find Study 14 a useful tool in dealing with complex issues necessary to implement an accrual system. IFAC refers to the study as a "living document" that will be updated periodically as further IPSASs are issued, and additional implementation issues and experiences are identified.

The new study contributes to the ongoing body of guidance being developed by the Public Sector Committee to enhance the accountability and financial management of governments worldwide.

¶12,003 Development of IPSASs

Initially, these Standards (the IPSASs) are being developed through adapting International Accounting Standards issued by the International Accounting Standards Committee (IASC) to a public sector context. In this process, the Committee attempts, wherever possible, to maintain the accounting treatment and original text of the IASs unless there is a significant public sector issue that warrants a departure. The work of the IASC has been turned over to the International Accounting Standards Board and IASs are being updated and revised and supplemented through the issuance of IFRSs.

The Committee is also engaged in projects dealing with:

- Accounting for Development Assistance.
- Accounting for Social Policies of Governments.
- Budget Reporting.
- Harmonization of Government Financial Reporting.
- Revenue from Non-Exchange Transactions.
- Improvements to Existing IPSASs in line with the IASB's General Improvements Project.

In its ongoing work program, the Committee also intends to develop IPSASs dealing with financial reporting issues in the public sector that are either not comprehensively dealt with in existing IASs or for which IASs have not been developed by the IASC (succeeded by IASB).

The Committee is developing a set of IPSASs that will include Standards applying to the accrual basis and a separate IPSAS that will specify the requirements for the cash basis.

To ensure maximum worldwide standards coordination, in developing its standards (IPSASs) the Committee utilizes pronouncements issued by the IASB, national regulatory authorities; professional accounting bodies, and other organizations interested in financial reporting, accounting, and auditing in the public sector.

In the fulfillment of its mission, the IFAC follows the IASB's *Framework for the Preparation and Presentation of Financial Statements.* Thus, most IPSASs are based on IASs. Accordingly, financial statements issued for users who are unable to demand financial information to meet their specific information needs are referred to as *general-purpose financial statements.* When the accrual basis of accounting is used in the preparation of the financial statements, the financial statements are required to include the statement of financial position, the statement of financial performance, the cash flow statement and the statement of changes in net assets/equity. When the cash basis of accounting is used in the preparation of the financial statements, the primary financial statement is the cash flow statement. IPSASs apply to the published financial statements of public sector entities other than Government Business Enterprises.

In addition to preparing general-purpose financial statements, an entity may prepare tailored financial statements to meet the specific needs of governing bodies, the legislature, and other parties who perform an oversight function. Such statements are referred to as *special purpose financial statements.* The Committee encourages the use of IPSASs in the preparation of special purpose financial statements where appropriate.

According to the Committee "some entities in the process of moving from cash accounting to accrual accounting may wish to adopt the requirements of particular accrual-based IPSASs during this process. An entity may voluntarily adopt the relevant disclosure provisions in an accrual-based IPSAS, although its core financial statements will nonetheless be prepared according to the IPSAS dealing with financial reporting under the cash basis of accounting." IPSAS 1, *Presentation of Financial Statements,* requires disclosure of the extent to which the entity has applied any transitional provisions.

Whenever an audit opinion is expressed on public sector financial statements, the same audit principles apply regardless of the nature of the entity, because users of audited financial statements are entitled to a uniform quality of audit performance. Because ISAs set out the basic audit principles and related practices and procedures, they apply to audits of the financial statements of governments and other public sector entities as well. However, the application of certain ISAs may need to be clarified or supplemented to accommodate the public sector circumstances and perspective of individual jurisdictions. The nature of potential matters for clarification or supplementation is identified in the "Public Sector Perspective" included at the end of each ISA.

¶12,004   Auditing Update

In December 2022, the International Auditing and Assurance Standards Board® (IAASB) published the "2021 Handbook of International Quality Control, Auditing, Review, Other Assurance, and Related Services Pronouncements."

In December 2020, the IAASB released International Standards on Quality Management (ISQM) 1 and 2. ISQM 1 is related to quality management for firms that perform audits or reviews of financial statements, or other assurance or related services engagements. ISQM 2 is related to engaging quality reviews.

In January 2015, the IAASB released its new and revised Auditor Reporting standards, designed to significantly enhance auditor's reports for investors and other users of financial statements. "These changes will reinvigorate the audit, as auditors substantively change their behavior and how they communicate about their work," explained Prof. Arnold Schilder, IAASB Chairman. "Informed by extensive research and global outreach to investors, regulators, audit oversight bodies, national standard setters, auditors, preparers of financial statements, audit committee members, and others, the final International Standards on Auditing (ISAs) represent a momentous—and unprecedented—first step. Now, we must study, promote, and plan for the effective implementation of the new and revised standards."

The most notable enhancement is the new requirement for auditors of listed entities' financial statements to communicate "Key Audit Matters"—those matters that the auditor views as most significant, with an explanation of how they were addressed in the audit. The IAASB has also taken steps to increase the auditor's focus on going concern matters, including disclosures in the financial statements, and add more transparency in the auditor's report about the auditor's work. Information about the enhancements to auditor reporting and the ISAs that are affected can be found in the Auditor Reporting Fact Sheet. "The introduction of Key Audit Matters for listed entities is a significant enhancement that will change not only the auditor's report, but more broadly the quality of financial reporting—and therefore the informative value to investors and other key stakeholders," said Linda de Beer, IAASB Consultative Advisory Group (CAG) Chair. "The IAASB CAG, with its diverse membership base, has unanimously supported and encouraged the IAASB's formidable leadership in effecting these changes."

The new and revised Auditor Reporting standards were effective for audits of financial statements for periods ending on or after December 15, 2016.

In June 2015, the IAASB released its revised International Standard on Auditing™ (ISA™), Addressing Disclosures in the Audit of Financial Statements. The revisions to the standards aim to focus auditors more explicitly on disclosures throughout the audit process and drive consistency in auditor behavior in applying the requirements of the ISAs.

As a complement to these revisions, IAASB staff has also developed a publication, Addressing Disclosures in the Audit of Financial Statements, for auditors that describes financial reporting disclosure trends and their possible implications from an audit perspective and highlights how the ISAs as revised guide the auditor in addressing disclosures. This publication is intended to help the consistent, effective, and proper application of the ISAs when addressing disclosures as part of an audit of financial statements, and may be particularly relevant to small and medium practices implementing the changes to the ISAs.

"Addressing the information included in disclosures is an integral part of the audit, regardless of the financial reporting framework under which the financial statements have been prepared," explained Kathleen Healy, IAASB Technical Director. "The IAASB firmly believes these changes to the ISAs will enhance audit quality and are capable of being applied proportionately in audits of entities of all sizes, and in all jurisdictions and sectors."

The revisions to the standards encompass changes to ten ISAs and conforming amendments to five other ISAs. They are effective for audits of financial statements for periods ending on or after December 15, 2016, in line with the effective date for the new and revised Auditor Reporting standards and ISA 720 (Revised), *The Auditor's Responsibilities Relating to Other Information*.

In the March of 2009, the IAASB completed its Clarity Project. The completion of the project was facilitated by the release of the final seven clarified International Standards on Auditing (ISAs). The result of the ambitious project is a set of 36 newly updated and clarified standards for use by auditors worldwide including a new clarified International Standard on Quality Control. The standards are all featured in a new Clarity Center on the IAASB Web site (*www.ifac.org/IAASB*).

The Clarity Project resulted in the issuance of 36 ISAs and one International Standard on Quality Control in a new style that is easier to understand, translate, and implement. In some cases, other major revisions to the content were made as well. The new set of clarified ISAs became effective effect for audits of financial statements for periods beginning on or after December 15, 2009. In practical terms, this means that they would be effective for 2010 year-end audits.

IAASB pronouncements to date include the following International Standards on Auditing (ISAs) (The 36 active standards are listed as well as IASs which were withdrawn, as indicated, for historical reference; inactive standards indicated with *.):

- *ISA 120 (withdrawn 2004).
- ISA 200 (Revised and Redrafted), *Overall Objectives of the Independent Auditor and the Conduct of an Audit in Accordance with International Standards on Auditing.*
- ISA 210 (Redrafted), *Agreeing the Terms of Audit Engagements.*
- ISA 220 (Redrafted), *Quality Control for an Audit of Financial Statements* (revised in 2020).
- ISA 230 (Revised and Redrafted), *Materiality in Planning and Performing an Audit.*
- ISA 240, *The Auditor's Responsibility to Consider Fraud in an Audit of Financial Statements.*
- ISA 250, *Consideration of Laws and Regulations in an Audit of Financial Statements* (redrafted in 2008).
- ISA 260 (Revised 2015), *Communications of Audit Matters with Those Charged with Governance* (conforming amendments effective December 15, 2004).
- ISA 265 (New 2009), *Communicating Deficiencies in Internal Control to Those Charged with Governance and Management.*
- ISA 300 (revised), *Planning an Audit of Financial Statements.*
- *ISA 310 (withdrawn 2004).
- ISA 315, *Understanding the Entity and Its Environment and Assessing the Risks of Material Misstatement.*
- ISA 320 (Revised and Redrafted in 2008), *Audit Documentation.*
- ISA 330, *The Auditor's Procedures in Response to Assessed Risks* (conforming amendments effective June 15, 2006).
- *ISA 400 (withdrawn 2004).
- *ISA 401 (withdrawn 2004).
- ISA 402 (Revised and Redrafted), *Audit Considerations Relating to Entity Using a Service Organization.*
- ISA 450, *Evaluation of Misstatements Identified during the Audit* (revised and redrafted in 2008).
- ISA 500 (Redrafted), *Audit Evidence.*
- ISA 501 (Redrafted), *Audit Evidence—Specific Considerations for Selected Items.*
- ISA 505 (Revised and Redrafted), *External Considerations.*
- ISA 510, *Initial Engagements—Opening Balances* (redrafted in 2008).
- ISA 520 (Redrafted), *Analytical Procedures.*
- ISA 530, *Audit Sampling* (redrafted in 2008).
- ISA 540, *Audit of Accounting Estimates* (revised and redrafted in 2008 and again in 2018 and in 2019).

- *ISA 545 (withdrawn), *Auditing Fair Value Measurements and Disclosures.*
- ISA 550, *Related Parties* (revised and redrafted in 2008).
- ISA 560, *Subsequent Events* (revised and redrafted in 2008).
- ISA 570 (Revised 2015), *Going Concern* (revised and redrafted in 2008).
- IAS 580, *Management Representations.*
- ISA 600, *Using the Work of Another Auditor* (revised 2022).
- ISA 610 (Redrafted), *Using the Work of Internal Auditors.*
- ISA 620 (Redrafted), *Using the Work of an Auditor's Expert.*
- ISA 700 (Revised 2015) (Redrafted 2004), *Forming an Opinion and Reporting on Financial Statements.*
- *ISA 701 (withdrawn), *Modifications to the Independent Auditor's Report.*
- New ISA 701 (2015) deals with the auditor's responsibility to communicate key audit matters (KAM) in the auditor's report. The ISA applies to audits of complete sets of general purpose financial statements of listed entities. It also applies when the auditor is required by law or regulation to communicate KAM for other entities or when the auditor decides to communicate KAM on a voluntary basis. ISA 701 is effective for audits of financial statements for periods ending on or after December 15, 2016.
- ISA 705 (Revised 2015), *Modifications to the Opinion in the Independent Auditor's Report* (revised and redrafted in 2008).
- ISA 706 (Revised 2015), *Emphasis of Matter Paragraphs and Other Matters Paragraphs in the Independent Auditor's Report* (revised and redrafted in 2008).
- ISA 710 (Redrafted), *Comparative Information—Corresponding Figures and Comparative Financial Statements.*
- ISA 720 (Revised 2015), *The Auditor's Responsibilities Relating to Other Information.*
- ISA 800 (Revised and Redrafted), *Special Considerations—Audits of Financial Statements Prepared in Accordance with Special Purpose Frameworks.*
- ISA 805 (Revised and Redrafted), *Special Considerations—Audits of Single Financial Statements and Specific Elements, Accounts or Items of a Financial Statement.*
- ISA 810 (Revised and Redrafted), *Engagements to Report on Summary Financial Statements.*

.01   Discussion of ISA 720 (revised)

ISA 720 (revised), *The Auditor's Responsibilities Relating to Other Information,* aims to clarify and increase the auditor's involvement with "other information"—defined in the standard as financial and non-financial information, other than the audited financial statements, that is included in entities' annual reports. It also includes new requirements related to auditor reporting on other information that complement the changes arising from the IAASB's new and revised Auditor Reporting standards, issued earlier this year.

.02   Discussion of (revised) ISA 705

ISA 705 (revised), *Modifications to the Opinion in the Independent Auditor's Report*, was revised to conform to the enhanced auditor reporting requirements in ISA 700 (revised), *Forming an Opinion and Reporting on Financial Statements*. Changes to this ISA relate primarily to how the form and content of the auditor's report is affected when the auditor expresses a modified opinion. ISA 705 (revised) is effective for audits of financial statements for periods ending on or after December 15, 2016.

.03   Discussion of (revised) ISA 706

ISA 706 (revised), *Emphasis of Matter Paragraphs and Other Matter Paragraphs in the Independent Auditor's Report*, was revised as a result of new ISA 701, *Communicating Key Audit Matters in the Independent Auditor's Report*. ISA 706 (revised) deals with the auditor's responsibility to communicate with those charged with governance in an audit of financial statements. ISA 706 (revised) is effective for audits of financial statements for periods ending on or after December 15, 2016.

.04   Discussion of (revised) ISA 300

The revised ISA 300, *Planning an Audit of Financial Statements*, was released on July 12, 2004, requiring auditors to be more rigorous in the planning of their audits. The revised ISA builds on the new audit risk standards issued in 2003 and requires the auditor to plan audits so that engagements will be performed in an effective manner. The continual nature of planning is emphasized by the standard. It stresses the auditor's responsibility throughout the engagement to be cognizant of unexpected events, changes in conditions, or other circumstances that may lead the auditor to reevaluate the planned audit procedures.

The standard, effective for audits of financial statements for periods beginning on or after December 15, 2004, requires the auditor to establish the overall strategy for the audit that sets the scope, timing, and direction for the audit.

.05   Discussion of (redrafted and revised) ISA 700

International Standard on Auditing (ISA) 700 was issued in revised form on December 28, 2004. It establishes a new form of auditor's report designed to enhance the transparency and comparability of auditor's reports across international borders. The updated standard, *The Independent Auditor's Report on a Complete Set of General Purpose Financial Statements*, sets out a framework to separate audit reporting requirements in connection with an ISA audit from additional supplementary reporting responsibilities required in some jurisdictions.

In those circumstances when an audit is conducted in accordance with both ISAs and the auditing standards of a specific jurisdiction, guidance is provided to the auditor—in particular, on preparing an auditor's report to meet both the report structure required by the national jurisdiction and the requirements of the ISA. According to IAASB Chairman John Kellas, "The European Commission asked the IAASB to look at this project as a matter of urgency to contribute to harmonized audit reporting within the EU. Many EU and other countries require the auditor to report on additional matters to the financial statements, but these requirements differ between countries. Our solution is to require a two-part report: the first deals with the financial statements, and should be essentially the same for all audits conducted in accordance with ISAs; the second deals with any further matters that may be required by local regulations. We thereby require comparability where it matters, while allowing appropriate flexibility to deal with local circumstances."

The new wording for the auditor's report includes:

- Better explanations of the respective responsibilities of management and the auditor;
- An updated description of the audit process to reflect the new IAASB Audit Risk Standards; and
- Clarification of the scope of the auditor's responsibilities with respect to internal control.

The new form of the report is to be applied for auditor's reports dated on or after December 31, 2006. Conforming amendments to other ISAs are applicable for audits of financial statements for periods beginning on or after December 15, 2005. To prevent confusion that might arise if both the old and new forms of report were being used at the same time, the IAASB has not allowed for early application of the new report wording.

In 2015, the standard was revised in conjunction with new and revised Auditor Reporting standards described above. This revised ISA deals with the auditor's responsibility to form an opinion on the financial statements as well as the form and content of the auditor's report issued as a result of an audit of financial statements. This ISA applies to an audit of a complete set of general purpose financial statements. ISA 700 (Revised) is effective for audits of financial statements for periods ending on or after December 15, 2016.

.06   Discussion of ISA 240

Issued in 2004, ISA 240, *The Auditor's Responsibility to Consider Fraud in an Audit of Financial Statements*, is effective for audits of financial statements for periods beginning on or after December 15, 2004. "The purpose of this ISA is to establish basic principles and essential procedures and to provide guidance on the auditor's responsibility to consider fraud in an audit of financial statements." The Standard tracks the U.S. Statement on Auditing Standards (SAS) 99, *Consideration of Fraud in a Financial Statement Audit*. The Standard makes two important preliminary distinctions: between fraud and error, and between fraud resulting from misappropriation of assets and fraud from fraudulent financial reporting. Fraud is distinguished from error primarily on the basis of *intention to defraud*:

> The term "error" refers to an unintentional misstatement in financial statements, including the omission of an amount or a disclosure... The term "fraud" refers to an intentional act by one or more individuals among management [management fraud], those charged with governance, employees [employee fraud], or third parties, involving the use of deception to obtain an unjust or illegal advantage.

The Standard requires the auditor to maintain an attitude of professional skepticism throughout the audit "notwithstanding the auditor's past experience with the entity about the honesty and integrity of management and those charged with governance." It further requires the members of the audit engagement team to "discuss the susceptibility of the entity's financial statements to material misstatement due to fraud."

In designing the audit procedures auditors are required by the Standard to respond to the risk of management override of controls. But "*auditors do not make legal determination of whether fraud has actually occurred.*"

Why Fraud Occurs. ISA 240 points out the importance of understanding why fraud occurs. For example, "fraudulent financial reporting can be caused by the efforts of management to manage earnings." In general terms, the Standard makes reference, without attribution, to the "fraud triangle" concept pioneered by criminologist Donald Cressey. Fraud involves a need, incentive, or pressure. In addition, there must be a perceived opportunity and the ability of the perpetrator to rationalize the need to commit the fraud. In the case of an individual, the need or incentive often involves someone living beyond their means, excess debt, or a drug or gambling problem. Fraudulent financial reporting may be committed because management is being pressured to achieve a certain (and perhaps unrealistic) earnings target. Someone in a position of trust or who knows of specific weaknesses in internal control may, for example, perceive opportunity for fraudulent financial reporting or misappropriation of assets. The process of rationalization consists of contriving reasons why the act of fraud is justified, such as "everyone does it" or "the company owes me a raise."

Management Responsibility. ISA 240 indicates that the primary responsibility for detection and prevention of fraud rests with management. By placing a strong emphasis on fraud prevention, management may reduce opportunities for fraud to take place; by emphasizing fraud deterrence, management could persuade individuals not to commit fraud because of the likelihood of detection and punishment.

Unfortunately, the risk of not detecting *fraud* is higher than the risk of not detecting *error*, "because fraud may involve sophisticated and carefully organized schemes designed to conceal it." In addition, the auditor is less likely to detect fraud perpetrated by management than by employees because management is in a position to directly or indirectly manipulate accounting records and present fraudulent financial information.

In discussing the possibility of audit, the members of the audit team set aside any beliefs that management and those charged with governance are honest and have integrity and must adopt a questioning mind-set. The discussion should take the form of an exchange of ideas and a consideration of the circumstances, known external and internal factors that may create an incentive to commit fraud, and any unusual or unexplained changes in behavior or lifestyle of management or employees that have come to the attention of the engagement team.

Risk Assessment Procedures. The risk assessment procedures to be carried out in the audit include consideration of any unusual or unexpected relationships that have been identified in performing analytic review procedures. In addition, the auditor should make inquiries of "management, internal audit, and others within the entity as appropriate, to determine whether they have knowledge of any actual, suspected, or alleged fraud affecting the entity." The "others" includes those charged with governance, including the board of directors. During the course of the audit, the auditor should also obtain an understanding of the business rationale for significant transactions that are outside of the normal course business for the entity or unusual given the auditor's understanding of the entity and its environment and other information obtained during the audit.

Care should be taken to consider the consequences of performing analytical procedures during the year as well as at year-end. Trends noted during either timeframe should be compared with the other and reconciled if they diverge. It should not be assumed that the year-end results are the only proper data for analysis. Among the reasons for this is that large and unusual amounts of revenue, for example, may be recorded at the end of the year in order to bring significant ratios into normal range. "Determining which particular trends and relationships may indicate a risk of material misstatement due to fraud requires professional judgment." Thus, meta-analytical procedures—analysis of both interim and year-end financial statements against each other as well as against comparable prior periods—are required.

Extent of Auditor's Responsibility. Although the Standard indicates that the auditor is not responsible for making the legal determination that fraud has occurred, paragraph 93 speaks of the auditor identifying fraud in the context of communications with management. "If the auditor has identified a fraud or has obtained information that indicates that a fraud may exist, the auditor should communicate these matters as soon as practicable to the appropriate level of management." This is a stronger statement than the comparable paragraph in U.S. SAS 99.

The Standard requires the auditor to document his or her understanding of the entity and its environment as well as the risks of material misstatement. This should include "The significant decisions reached during the discussion among the engagement team regarding the susceptibility of the entity's financial statements to material misstatement due to fraud; and the identified and assessed risk of material misstatement due to fraud at the financial statement level and at the assertion level."

.07 International Auditing Practice Notes (IAPNs)

International Auditing Practice Note (IAPN) 1000, *Special Considerations in Auditing Financial Instruments*, should be read in conjunction with the Preface to the International Quality Control, Auditing, Review, Other Assurance, and Related Services Pronouncements. IAPNs do not impose additional requirements on auditors beyond those included in the International Standards on Auditing (ISAs), nor do they change the auditor's responsibility to comply with all ISAs relevant to the audit.

IAPNs provide practical assistance to auditors. They are intended to be disseminated by those responsible for national standards, or used in developing corresponding national material. They also provide material that firms can use in developing their training programs and internal guidance.

¶12,005   International Auditing Practice Statements (IAPSs)

Statements in this category provide guidance from the IAASB in specialized areas of auditing.

International Auditing Practice Statements (IAPSs) (* Indicates withdrawn and shown for historical purposes.)

- IAPS 1000, *Inter-Bank Confirmation Procedures*
- IAPS 1004, *The Relationship Between Banking Supervisors and Banks' External Auditors*
- *IAPS 1005 (Withdrawn), *The Special Considerations in the Audit of Small Entities*
- IAPS 1006, *Audits of the Financial Statements of Banks*
- IAPS 1010, *The Consideration of Environmental Matters in the Audit of Financial Statements*

- IAPS 1012, *Auditing Derivative Financial Instruments*
- IAPS 1013, *Electronic Commerce—Effect on the Audit of Financial Statements*
- *IAPS 1014 (Withdrawn), *Reporting by Auditors on Compliance with International Financial Reporting Standards*

International Standards on Assurance Engagements (ISAEs)

- 3000–3399, Applicable to all assurance engagements
- 3400–3699, Subject-specific standards
- 3400, *The Examination of Prospective Financial Information* (Previously ISA 810)
- 3402, *Assurance Reports on Controls at a Service Organization*

International Standard on Review Engagements (ISRE) 2400 (Revised), *Engagements to Review Historical Financial Statements*

Effective date: Reviews of financial statements for periods ending on or after December 31, 2013. These changes were introduced to "enhance the quality and consistency of engagements to review historical financial statements, through revised requirements and guidance addressing the responsibilities, work effort and reporting considerations of practitioners undertaking such engagements."

The project was undertaken in the context of the IAASB's strategic focus to develop standards to address market demand for assurance services other than audits that meet the needs of small- and medium-sized entities (SMEs) and users of their financial information.

IAASB 2012–2014 Strategy and Work Program Sets Auditor Reporting as Top Priority and Highlights Other Relevant Audit and Assurance Initiatives

In 2012, the IAASB released its Strategy and Work Program, 2012–2014. Developed through wide public consultation, it set the direction and priorities for the IAASB's activities over the next three years with a focus on: Supporting global financial stability; Enhancing the role, relevance, and quality of assurance and related services in today's evolving world; and facilitating adoption and implementation of the IAASB's standards.

As the main priority for 2012–2014, the IAASB's Strategy and Work Program identifies the enhancement of auditor reporting standards, a topic that the IAASB will again deliberate intensively at its June 2012 meeting in Edinburgh. The strategy is in keeping with the IAASB's commitment to continue work on a number of its key initiatives related to audit quality, disclosures, review engagements, and assurance engagements, including assurance on greenhouse gas statements. In addition, the IAASB will continue to monitor the adoption and implementation of ISAs globally and focus on standards and initiatives relevant to small- and medium-sized entities. It will also explore appropriate actions stemming from the global financial crisis relating to banking and fair values.

¶12,006   Guidance on Derivatives

The IAPS 10125, *Auditing Derivative Financial Instruments*, provides guidance to the auditor in planning and performing auditing procedures for assertions about derivative financial instruments. The focus of the practice statement is on auditing derivatives held by end users, including banks and other financial sector entities when they are the users.

In addition to addressing auditor responsibilities with respect to assertions about derivatives, the statement also addresses:

1. Responsibility of management and those charged with governance.
2. The key financial risks.
3. Risk assessment and internal control, including the role of internal auditing.
4. Various types of substantive procedures and when they should be used.

¶12,007   Ethics—Revised Code of Ethics Issued

In 2015, changes were made to the Code addressing certain non-assurance services provisions for audit and assurance clients. The changes in the pronouncement enhance the independence provisions in the Code of Ethics for Professional Accountants™ (the Code) by, in particular, no longer permitting auditors to provide certain prohibited non-assurance services to public interest entity (PIE) audit clients in emergency situations, and ensuring that they do not assume management responsibility when providing non-assurance services to audit clients.

The revisions include the removal of provisions that permitted an audit firm to provide certain bookkeeping and taxation services to PIE audit clients in emergency situations, as these were susceptible to being interpreted too generally. In addition, the revised provisions include:

- New and clarified guidance regarding what constitutes management responsibility; and
- Clarified guidance regarding the concept of "routine or mechanical" services relating to the preparation of accounting records and financial statements for audit clients that are not PIEs.

The revisions also include corresponding changes to the Code's non-assurance services provisions with respect to other assurance clients.

The changes are effective April 15, 2016, with early adoption permitted. See the pronouncement below for details.

In July 2009, the International Ethics Standards Board for Accountants (IES-BA) issued a revised Code of Ethics for Professional Accountants. The revised code was effective on January 1, 2011. The new code clarifies requirements for all professional accountants and strengthens the independence requirements of auditors. Some of these changes include:

- Extending the independence requirements for audits of listed entities to all public interest entities
- Extending partner rotation requirements to all key audit partners
- Strengthening independence by modifying requirements when auditors also perform non-assurance services for the same client
- Prohibiting key audit partners from being compensated for selling non-assurance services to audit clients

Although the accountancy profession throughout the world operates in an environment with different cultures and regulatory requirements, it is vital that all accountants share a commitment to a strong code of ethics. The IFAC Code states the fundamental principles that should be observed by professional accountants to meet their responsibility in protecting the public's interests.

The introduction to the Code notes that a distinguishing mark of the accountancy profession is its acceptance of the responsibility to act in the public interest. The organization of the Code includes the fundamental principles of professional ethics including their conceptual framework. Following the statement of general principles the Code provides examples of their application to specific situations noting that is impossible to define every situation that creates ethical concerns for professional accountants.

¶12,008   International Education Standards for Professional Accountants

The Education Committee of the International Federation of Accountants (IFAC) is responsible for establishing educational requirements for all professional accountants. In general, these standards apply to all professional accountants, irrespective of specialty or branch of accounting (auditing, management accounting, financial reporting), area of employment (public sector, public practice, corporate environment).

.01   IES 8, Competence Requirements for Audit Professionals

IES 8 is one of eight standards that address the principles of learning and development for professional accountants. The IESs prescribe good practice in learning and development for professional accountants and should be incorporated into the educational requirements of IFAC's membership body, which is comprised of professional accountancy institutes from around the world. The IESs are also considered relevant to stakeholders interested in the education and development of professional accountants and audit professionals, such as public accounting firms, regulators, and employers.

This is considered a landmark document because it is the first time the Education Committee has developed education requirements for a specific area of the accountancy profession according to the Education Committee Chair. Because of the reliance placed on the audits of financial statements, the committee felt it was vital to provide direction to IFAC member bodies and professional accountants worldwide on the specialized knowledge and skills required to perform competently in the audit field.

The minimum competency requirements for audit professionals include (1) knowledge content, (2) professional skills, (3) professional values, ethics and attitudes, (4) practical experience, (5) continuing professional experience, and (6) assessment of progress in items 1-5 listed. IES 8 prescribes requirements for professional accountants assuming the role of audit professionals and having responsibility for significant judgments in an audit of historical financial information. IFAC member bodies need to establish policies and procedures that will allow members to satisfy the requirements of this IES before they take on the role of an audit professional. The need for specific requirements for audit professionals, according to the IES is the fact that accountants need to specialize, not only to be competitive in the industry, but also in order to be competent professionals. No one professional accountant can master all areas of accountancy. Auditing is one of the recognized professional specialties.

The knowledge content of the audit of historical financial statements should include the best practices of the auditing profession including current issues and developments and International Standards on Auditing (IASs) and International Auditing Practice Statements (IAPSs).

According to the new standard, the professional skills requirement within the development program for auditors should include:

- Identifying and solving problems
- Undertaking technical research
- Gathering and evaluating evidence
- Working effectively in teams
- Presenting, discussing, and defending views effectively through formal, informal, written, and spoken communication

In the advanced development of professional auditors, the standard requires demonstrating professional skepticism, withstanding and resolving conflicts and demonstrating capacity for inquiry, abstract logical thought, and critical analysis.

In specifying the nature of the practical experience required, the IES states that such practical experience would normally be not less than three years, of which at least two years should be spent in the area of audits of historical financial statements under the supervision and guidance of an engagement partner.

The new standard, in addition to establishing guidance for auditors generally, also addresses the need for further specialization within the profession. For example, the IES discusses the need for more specialized development for those doing "transnational audits." These are audits that are or may be relied upon outside the entity s jurisdiction.

Finally, IES 8 gives direction to the measurement of competence in the case of the engagement partner. At this level of the audit, the engagement partner requires the development of additional professional knowledge, professional skills and professional values, ethics and attitudes. Also important at this level are leadership responsibilities and the ability to form conclusions on compliance with applicable independence requirements.

IES 8 was effective from July 1, 2008.

.02   Ensuring Qualifications of New Professional Accountants

A critical area for the accounting profession is ensuring that new entrants to the profession are qualified to meet the responsibilities they will face. To address this challenge, in December 2004 the IFAC Education Committee released International Education Paper (IEP) 3, Assessment Methods, which presents a detailed discussion of assessment techniques to help national accountancy organizations ensure that candidates are appropriately qualified before being admitted to membership of their associations.

According to the IFAC Education Committee the paper is intended to help member bodies meet this obligation and comply with the International Education Standard, IES 6, *Assessment of Professional Capabilities and Competence*, issued in October 2003. Various techniques are used to assess candidates throughout the education process, and many of the member bodies use a wide range of these techniques. The paper is intended to help member bodies consider their current approach to assessment and select techniques which suit their environment and circumstances. It also includes two practical tools: a series of questions designed to assist member bodies when reviewing their assessment methods, and secondly, a list of electronically accessible reference materials available through the Education Committee section of the IFAC Web site.

.03   Developing and Maintaining Professional Values, Ethics, and Attitudes

In a significant move, the International Accounting Education Standards Board issued guidance on the how-tos of imparting ethical development. It is one matter to state the ethical goals and principles of professional accountants; it is another to explain how this can occur. In the first International Education Practice Statement (IEPS 1), issued in October 2007, the IFAC took the first step in providing practical guidance on disseminating ethics education and ensuring the profession's values are internalized by practitioners.

IEPS 1 suggests two possible approaches for developing professional values, ethics and attitudes. The first is referred to as the "topic approach" while the second is the "stage-by-stage approach." In either case the goal is enhancing knowledge in ethics, developing ethical sensitivity, improving ethical judgment and maintaining an ongoing commitment to ethical behavior. These concepts are illustrated in the Statement through an "Ethics Education Continuum."

Enhancing ethical knowledge is accomplished by introducing professionals to ethical and professional standards. Developing ethical sensitivity includes increasing a professional's ability to recognize ethical threats or issues, increasing awareness of alternative courses of action and understanding the effects of alternatives on stakeholders. Improving ethical judgment is designed to assist individuals in applying a considered process for making ethical decisions. Maintaining an ongoing commitment to ethical behavior is accomplished through continuing professional development. Though self-assessment is recognized as one method for effecting ethical improvement, it is strongly suggested that it is not the only nor even the best method.

The Statement also introduces the concept of "ethical courage." This is a recognition of the fact that doing the right thing is not always an easy matter. In situations calling for whistle blowing, for example, it is recognized that the greater good can only be accomplished at great cost to the whistle blower and often other stakeholders as well.

Finally, the Statement concludes with a discussion of the means of implementing ethical development and their relative value. These include:

- Lectures
- Ethics discussions
- Small group and collaborative learning
- Case studies and examples of ethical threats
- Role-play
- Guest speakers and practitioner participation
- E-learning

Enhancing Professional Accounting Education was released in 2014 which covers the release of three revised International Education Standards™ (IESs™) during the year, as well as the board's progress on its adoption and implementation projects and activities to support the revised IESs. The report also summarizes the IAESB's outreach efforts designed to bring greater awareness to its projects and activities.

.04   Prior International Education Standards

From 2003 to 2004, the IFAC issued seven International Education Standards (IESs) intended to promote consistency and convergence in the accounting education process throughout the world. The standards are designed to promote greater global mobility of competent professional accountants and contribute to mutual recognition cooperation among professional accountancy bodies.

The goal of accounting education and practical experience is to produce competent professional accountants capable of making a positive contribution over their lifetimes to the profession and society in which they work.

Increasingly, today's professional accountants need to be technical experts with excellent communication skills; they need to be able to meet the reporting and information needs of the new knowledge economy. At the same time, professional values, ethics and attitudes are integral to being a professional accountant.

IESs for professional accountants are intended to advance the profession of accountancy by establishing benchmarks for the minimum learning requirements of qualified accountants, including education, practical experience, and continuing professional development.

IESs prescribe standards of generally accepted "good practice" in the education and development of professional accountants. These Standards express the benchmarks that member bodies are expected to meet in the preparation and continual development of professional accountants. They establish the essential elements of the content and process of education and development at a level that is aimed at gaining international recognition, acceptance, and application. The gray-letter paragraphs within the Standards are intended to help explain the prescriptions within the black-letter, standard paragraphs.

The pronouncements on education issued by the Education Committee include: (* indicates revised in 2014)

- IES 1, *Entry Requirements to a Program of Professional Accounting Education.*
- *IES 2, Revised in 2014. *Content of Professional Accounting Education Programs* prescribes the learning outcomes for technical competence that aspiring professional accountants are required to demonstrate by the end of Initial Professional Development. Technical competence is the ability to apply professional knowledge to perform role to a defined standard. It is effective from July 1, 2015.
- *IES 3, Revised in 2014. *Professional Skills* prescribes the learning outcomes for professional skills that aspiring professional accountants are required to demonstrate by the end of Initial Professional Development. Professional

skills are the (a) intellectual, (b) interpersonal and communication, (c) personal, and (d) organizational skills that a professional accountant integrates with technical competence and professional values, ethics, and attitudes to demonstrate professional competence. It is effective from July 1, 2015.

- *IES 4, Revised in 2014. *Professional Values, Ethics, and Attitudes* prescribes the learning outcomes for professional values, ethics, and attitudes that aspiring professional accountants are required to demonstrate by the end of Initial Professional Development. Professional values, ethics, and attitudes are defined as the behavior and characteristics that identify professional accountants as members of a profession. These include the ethical principles generally associated with, and considered essential in defining, the distinctive characteristics of professional behavior. It is effective from July 1, 2015.
- IES 5, *Practical Experience Requirements.*
- IES 6, *Assessment of Professional Capabilities and Competence.*
- IES 7, *Continuing Professional Development.*
- IES 8, *Competence Requirements for Audit Professionals.*

The Education Committee has also issued International Education Guideline (IEG) 11, *Information Technology for Professional Accountants.* IESs are an important part of IFAC's overall efforts to ensure high-quality performance by professional accountants worldwide by providing the basis for achieving convergence of technical and practical standards.

All IFAC member bodies are expected to comply with IES, and the Standards are directed primarily at IFAC member bodies rather than individuals. Member bodies are expected to use their best endeavors to:

- Work toward implementation of all IES and other statements developed by the IFAC Education Committee; and
- Incorporate in their education programs the essential elements of the content and process of education on which IES are based or, where responsibility for the education program lies with third parties, persuade those responsible for the educational requirements for the accountancy profession to incorporate the essential elements into that program.

Increased emphasis needs to be placed on a set of professional knowledge, professional skills, and professional values, ethics, and attitudes broad enough to enable adaptation to constant change. Individuals who become professional accountants should have a constant desire to learn and apply what is new.

Accountancy is a profession that plays an important role in all societies. As the world moves toward global market economies, and with investments and operations crossing borders to an ever greater extent, professional accountants need a broad global outlook to understand the context in which businesses and other organizations operate.

Professional education prepares accountants to be able to maintain competence throughout their professional careers. Professional education may be pursued at academic institutions or through the programs of professional bodies or both.

Rapid change has been the main characteristic of the environment in which professional accountants work. Pressures for change are coming from many sources including globalization, information, and communication technologies and the expansion of stakeholder groups, including regulators and oversight boards. Professional accountants are now expected to serve the needs not only of investors and creditors but also the information needs of many other users of financial and nonfinancial information.

Businesses and other organizations are engaging in ever more complex arrangements and transactions:

- Risk management has become more important.
- Information technology continues to advance at a rapid pace.
- The Internet has revolutionized global communications.
- Trade and commerce have become more transnational.
- Privatization has become an increasingly important trend in many countries.
- Legal action has become more usual in many societies, while in others it is the legal framework that defines the profession's responsibilities.
- Concern for the environment and sustainable development has grown.

These trends lead to the need for greater accountability and, as a result, in all cultures demands on the profession are high and continue to rise. It is the profession's capacity to satisfy these demands that determines its value to society.

The overall goal is to produce competent professional accountants by combining the parts of an education program in a suitable fashion. The exact combination of parts may vary as long as this goal is achieved. Different combinations exist in various parts of the world.

In 2013, IES 1, Entry Requirements to Professional Accounting Education Programs, was revised effective July 1, 2014.

IES 1 is intended to protect the public interest by both establishing fair and proportionate entry requirements—which help those individuals considering professional accounting education make appropriate career decisions—and ensuring that requirements for entry to professional accounting education are not misrepresented.

Originally approved in 2004, IES 1 prescribes the principles to be used when setting and communicating educational requirements for entry to professional accounting education programs. Requirements relating to entry to the profession are covered by:

- IES 2, Initial Professional Development—Technical Competence;
- IES 3, Initial Professional Development—Professional Skills;
- IES 4, Initial Professional Development—Professional Values, Ethics, and Attitudes;
- IES 5, Initial Professional Development—Practical Experience; and
- IES 6, Initial Professional Development—Assessment of Professional Competence.

Additionally, the revised standard provides:

- Specification of entry requirements for professional accounting education;
- Explanation for the rationale behind the entry requirements;
- A requirement that excessive barriers to entry are not put in place; and
- A requirement to make relevant information publicly available so that individuals considering a career as a professional accountant can assess their chances of successful completion.

The IAESB has undertaken a project to redraft all eight of its IESs in accordance with the clarity drafting conventions outlined in its 2010-2013 Strategy and Work Plan. Recently, the IAESB released its clarified IES 7, Continuing Professional Development, which identifies the requirements for continuing professional development of professional accountants, and IES 6, Initial Professional Development—Assessment of Professional Competence, which is designed to help IFAC member bodies and other professional accountancy organizations understand the learning and development requirements for assessing professional competence, and their obligations in upholding the standards.

¶12,009   Information Technology Committee (ITC)

This group is charged with keeping the worldwide accounting community abreast of the latest developments and applications relating to information technology (IT). It encourages member bodies to keep up-to-date on available hardware and software and the relationship between IT and the accounting profession.

At a recent international meeting, the committee focused on the use of IT in developing countries and approved a research program and budget. Research will involve determination of the current usage of IT in these countries and identification of the type and level of assistance which would be appropriate in developing economies.

The IFAC *Handbook of International Information Technology Guidelines* includes five Information Technology Guidelines developed by IFAC's IT Committee: *Technology Planning for Business Impact; Managing Information Technology Planning for Business Impact; Managing Security of Information; Acquiring Information Technology;* and *IT Delivery and Support.*

¶12,010   Information Technology—The IFAC Joins the XBRL Consortium

.01   Value of XBRL

The XML-based language automatically and transparently tags each segment of computerized business information with an identification code or marker. These markers remain with the information regardless of how the information is formatted or rearranged by a browser or within software applications.

Before XBRL, no generally accepted format for reporting business data existed. The labor-intensive task of entering and reentering data into computer applications results in substantial costs and the all-too-likely risk of data entry errors. The use of XBRL streamlines this process, potentially lowering costs while helping to ensure the integrity and quality of the data.

With XBRL, once financial information is created and formatted the first time, the data can be rendered in any form; for example:

- A printed financial statement.
- An HTML document.
- A regulatory filing document.
- A raw HML file.
- Credit reports.
- Loan applications.

All of these applications can be created without manually keying information in a second time or reformatting the data.

XBRL does not change existing accounting standards, nor does it require companies to disclose additional information. Instead, it simply enhances the accessibility and usability of the financial information that companies are required to report, according to IFAC.

.02   XBRL Leads to Better Dissemination of Information

By providing easier access to accurate company financial data and more efficient analysis capabilities, XBRL will add value for anyone who creates or accesses an organization's business data. Ultimately, XBRL benefits all users in the financial information supply chain:

- Public and private companies.
- The accounting profession.
- Regulators.
- Analysts.
- The investment community.
- Capital markets.
- Lenders.
- Key third parties—software developers and data aggregators.

IFAC believes that by providing accurate and reliable information, XBRL gives industry leaders access to better information available. Ultimately, it will enable company management to more quickly access information stored in different places within the organization and to move that information both within the company and externally to their shareholders.

With less time spent on translation and data entry, financial advisors and investors, large and small, can devote more time to analysis and can perhaps screen more companies for investment opportunities. This can benefit those companies in the investment community that typically might not make it onto the investor's radar screen.

XBRL should help financial services companies to collect and update information about borrowers, automate reports to regulators and distribute or collect information related to loan portfolio sales and purchases.

Accountancy institutes worldwide consider the development of XBRL as a natural next step in the clarification and development of the fundamental language of business and a vital tool for enhancing the access and breadth of financial information available to the investing public. Additionally, XBRL will help to position accountants as valued knowledge providers and financial advisors for their clients or firms. By helping businesses leverage their use of emerging technologies such as XBRL, accountants can expand their professional opportunities and value in the marketplace, IFAC contends.

¶12,011   Business Planning Guide for SMEs

In August 2011, the Small and Medium Practices (SMP) Committee of the International Federation of Accountants (IFAC) released an updated version of its *Guide to Quality Control for Small- and Medium-Sized Practices* (QC Guide). Intended to help SMPs successfully and cost effectively implement International Standard on Quality Control (ISQC) 1, the third edition of the guide features enhancements to the two sample manuals as well as other refinements for clarity and consistency with ISQC 1.

First released in 2009 and developed with CGA-Canada, the guide contains the requirements set out in the standard in addition to implementation guidance, including discussion material and a case study that can be used as a basis for training. It also contains a range of tools, including checklists and two sample manuals, which have been modified to better illustrate their compatibility with ISQC 1.

"With their limited resources, SMPs may feel burdened by the requirements in ISQC 1. The guide is intended to help mitigate that burden and help SMPs obtain the most benefit from implementing the standard," said SMP Committee Chair Sylvie Voghel. "Effective quality control systems are key to helping ensure SMPs provide their clients with high-quality assurance and related services, which contributes to the quality of the profession overall and our mission to serve the wider public interest."

The updated QC Guide, as well as an article with tips for implementing ISQC 1, can be downloaded free of charge from the SMP Publications and Resources area of IFAC's Web site. See the Translations Database for translations of the guides by member bodies and other organizations. In addition to the guide, the International Center for Small and Medium Practices provides access to numerous free resources from IFAC and our member bodies (see relevant links).

In May 2006, IFAC issued an informational paper entitled "Business Planning Guide: Practical Application for SMEs." The 80-plus-page guide should be a valuable resource for any small or start-up business as it systematically outlines the necessary thought process needed to effectively develop a business plan and an overview of the business and its future. The guide deals with such foundational concepts as the vision and mission statements, corporate values, business goals and objectives as well as risk management and succession planning.

In a section devoted to the organization and organizational structure of a business, the guide outlines the need to present a company's management capabilities and core organizational competencies. A helpful section is devoted to marketing including the crucial processes of identifying a target market and analyzing the competition.

The construction of specific financial statements is clearly outlined including: the income statement, statement of cash flow, and balance sheet. The process of financial budgeting is also discussed.

Perhaps most valuable for many small businesses is the sample business plan and an accompanying business plan checklist presented in the appendix.

PART III

Accounting Procedures

Different areas of accounting follow different procedures and processes. Part III addresses certain procedures related to accountants in management. Specifically, cost accounting and budgeting. It also addresses changes in accounting methods, auditor independence and the audit committee, and financial statement analysis.

CHAPTER 13
Cost Accounting

¶13,000   What Is Cost Accounting?

The cost accounting function in an organization is a system broadly defined in terms of procedures: the gathering, sorting, classifying, resorting, reclassifying, processing (computations), summarizing, reporting and filing of information relevant to a company's costs—largely in the form of data (numbers). It measures all costs associated with doing business and providing a service.

Often, cost accounting is thought of only in terms of manufacturing operations. However, many of the concepts can be useful in other areas of a small business or a service enterprise.

What is the function of a cost accounting system? Primarily, the system accepts disorganized, meaningless raw data (input) from the environment and processes (transforms) the data into understandable form. The information then leaves the system (output) in an organized form of reports required by management to account for the production costs of a business.

Specifically, cost accounting explicitly sets forth data that relate to the costs associated with the business. This includes the assignment of costs to a particular product, process, operation, or service, in the case of a service business.

.01   The Objective of a Cost Accounting System

The primary objective of cost accounting is to provide information management can use to make the decisions necessary for the successful operation of the business. To achieve this objective, the system should be designed to provide information concerning the efficiency and effectiveness of production and service processes. The aim then, is cost reduction and increased profits.

An analysis of accurate cost data is the essence of profit planning:

1. What should be produced?
2. How much should be produced?
3. When does the law of diminishing returns kick in?
4. What price should be charged?
5. Should a particular product be discontinued?
6. Should a new product be given a "break" when dividing overhead?
7. Are costs in line with what they should be?

Management should expect cost reports to show the results of past operations in terms of costs per unit of product, costs per unit of production in each operating department, or costs per unit of service in the case of a service organization. The system should provide immediate feedback information on changes in costs from accounting period to accounting period and on *comparisons of costs with predetermined estimates or norms*. With the proper cost information, management can adjust operations quickly to changing economic and competitive conditions.

.02   Developing a Cost System

The task of developing a cost accounting system is to determine the specific needs of management and the extent to which it is economically feasible to add detailed procedures to a basic system. The system must be easily understood by all individuals in the organization who are involved in the use of control procedures, and it must be flexible in its application. The system should be simple— that is, it must not include procedures that accumulate information that might be interesting but not particularly useful. (A common pitfall is a cost system that, itself, is more expensive than the costs to be saved.) In addition, the cost system must provide useful information in the most efficient manner. *Accurate* accounting records are particularly significant.

The cost accounting system also must be flexible, because businesspeople are often required to adapt their operations to meet changes in:

- The needs and desires of customers.
- Production methods caused by improved technology.
- The economic and social environment in which the business operates.
- Governmental regulations.

Likewise, most business ventures hope to grow and become larger. All business ventures hope to make substantial profits. New cost accounting control requirements will appear as a result of the nature of the growth process. Any system should be planned to meet changing needs with the least possible alteration of the existing system.

Fundamental cost control methods apply to most businesses and include principles applicable to an individual business. The type of production, the number of products manufactured, the size of the business, the types of costs associated with the business and the desires, capabilities and attitudes of the individuals involved in the business will all have a part in determining the structure of the cost control system.

Personnel responsible for the procedures relating to the accounting and control techniques must be constantly aware of the unique characteristics of the particular business.

.03   Alternative Approaches

It is a rare instance that there is just one obviously right answer to any business problem. Certainly, alternative choices for the allocation of an enterprise's limited resource confront the business manager every day. Information for selecting the "right" choice is provided by a cost accounting system:

- Is the product profitable?
- Is the product priced to yield a predetermined profit margin?
- What are the per-unit costs of the product?
- Could it profitably be sold at a lower, more competitive price?
- Should production be expanded, reduced, discontinued?
- Are costs out of line?
- What are the controllable costs?
- What are the uncontrollable costs?

These are only a few items of significant information that are furnished by a well-developed cost accounting system.

¶13,001   Foundation of a Cost Accounting System

What input does a cost accounting system accept? An infinite amount of data within the business environment can be entered into the system. It should be emphasized that the choice of data to be entered is not random. Chance or guesswork are not acceptable determinants of data input. Rather, data selection is performed within a carefully designed framework of the information *needed* to provide the required output (reports), with the framework continually subject to modification by a feedback system. The framework is governed by a set of controls to ensure compliance with the procedures, policies and objectives the system has been designed to carry out.

The elements of the framework for a set of books to track costs are briefly described as follows:

1. The system is for a specific organization and accepts data relating only to that organization.
2. Precautions should be taken against superfluous (and expensive) input.
3. The system accepts information about transactions generated by events that have actually occurred—a purchase, for example.
4. The system accepts information that has numbers assigned to it, with dollars and cents the most common measurement.
5. The system accepts only information that has been predetermined to meet the needs of the users of the information.
6. Information entered into the system should be completely free of bias; only absolutely objective information is acceptable.
7. Information must be verifiable. Verifiability means transactions that are recorded in the same way by two or more qualified personnel acting independently of each other.
8. Information entered into the system must be consistent. Consistency prevents manipulation of data in the accounts and makes the financial information comparable from one period of time to another.

.01   Four Group Classifications

The production activities of most businesses (of any size) can be classified into one of the following four groups:

1. **Jobbing Plants**—Jobbing plants specialize in products that are made to order and therefore not conducive to a repetitive operation. Some examples are machine shops, custom cabinet shops, builders of custom homes, printers and repair shops of all kinds—generally, custom-made products of any kind. Certain service providers, including engineers, architects and various consultants, use some job order techniques to track specific costs of a project (further explanation is given in item 4 below.)
2. **Continuous Processing Plants**—Continuous processing is used for products that are made for inventory and sale at a later date, instead of ordered in advance. The significant aspect of continuous processing is that the production process is a repetitive operation involving sequential steps in the conversion of raw materials into finished products, all the units of which are the same. Mass production techniques apply. Examples are shoe, glass, soap, paper, textile and automobile manufacturers and food processors.
3. **Assembly Plants**—Products are made up of many component parts, either manufactured by the assembler or purchased from other manufacturers. Air-

craft manufacturers are one of the best examples; they subcontract various parts of the aircraft to literally hundreds of subcontractors. Automobile production is an example of both continuous processing and assembling, as many parts for automobiles are purchased from other manufacturing suppliers.

4. **Service Establishments**—Service establishments include businesses that provide various services to the public rather than manufactured products. Medical, legal, accounting, architectural, transportation, food and recreational services are examples of service businesses.

¶13,002   Items for Consideration in Developing Cost Control Systems

Because the cost control problems are different for each of the groups listed above, control and cost procedures must be designed for each type as well as for individual businesses within a group. Certainly not all of the items listed below will apply in every situation; however, careful consideration of this general outline should provide the basis for an effective system for any business.

Cost Accounting System—An Outline

¶13,003   Cost Accounting Terminology for Quick Reference

Following are some brief definitions of various types of costs:

1. Alternative—estimated for decision areas.
2. Controllable—subject to direct control at some level of supervision.
3. Departmental—production and service, for cost distributions.
4. Differential—changes in cost that result from variation in operations.
5. Direct—obviously traceable to a unit of output or a segment of business operations.
6. Discretionary—are avoidable and not essential to an objective.
7. Estimated—are predetermined.
8. Fixed—do not change in the total as the rate of output varies.
9. Future—are expected to be incurred at a later date.
10. Historical—are measured by actual cash payments or their equivalent at the time of outlay.
11. Imputed—never involve cash outlays or appear in financial records. Imputed costs involve a foregoing on the part of the person whose costs are being calculated.
12. Incremental—are the costs that are added or eliminated if segments were expanded or discontinued.

13. Indirect—are not obviously traceable to a unit of output or to a segment of business operations.
14. Joint—exist when from any one unit source, material or process come products having different unit values.
15. Noncontrollable—are not subject to control at some level of supervision.
16. Opportunity—are those for which measurable advantage is foregone as a result of the rejection of alternative uses of resources, whether of materials, labor or facilities.
17. Out of pocket—necessitate cash expenditure.
18. Period—are associated with the income of a time period.
19. Postponable—may be shifted to future period without affecting efficiency.
20. Prime—are labor and material costs that are directly traceable to a unit of output.
21. Product—are associated with units of output.
22. Replacement—are considered for depreciation significance.
23. Standard—are scientifically predetermined.
24. Sunk—are historical and unrecoverable in a given situation.
25. Variable—do change with changes in rate of output.

¶13,004   Historical and Standard Cost Systems

Cost accounting systems vary with the type of cost used—present or future. When present costs are used, the cost system is called an historical or actual cost system. When future costs are used, the cost system is called a standard cost system. In practice, combinations of these costs are used even in actual or standard systems. Where there is an intentional use of both types of costs, it is sometimes referred to as a hybrid cost system.

.01   Actual Cost Systems

Because an actual cost system uses costs already incurred, the system determines costs only after manufacturing operations have been performed. Under this system, the product is charged with the actual cost of materials, the actual cost of labor, and an estimated portion of overhead (overhead costs represent the future cost element in an actual cost system).

.02   Standard Cost Systems

A standard system is based on estimated or predetermined costs. Although both estimated and standard costs are "predetermined" costs, estimated costs are based on average past experience, and standard costs are based on scientific facts that consider past experience and controlled experiments. Arriving at standard costs involves:

- Careful selection of the exact amount of raw material and subassemblies required.
- An engineering study of equipment and manufacturing facilities.
- Time and motion studies.

In either system, adjustment must be made at the financial statement date to the closing inventory so that it is shown at actual cost or reasonably approximate actual cost, or at market if lower.

Also, the inventory must bear its share of the burden of overhead. The exclusion of all overheads from inventory costs does not constitute an accepted accounting procedure.

For interim statements, estimated gross profit rates may be used to determine cost of goods sold during the interim, but this fact must be disclosed.

It must be emphasized that whatever cost accounting method is chosen by a company, its purpose is primarily an internal management tool directed at:

- Controlling costs.
- Setting production goals.
- Measuring efficiencies and variances.
- Providing incentives.
- Identifying production problems.
- Establishing realistic relationships between unit costs, selling prices and gross margins.
- Correcting manufacturing difficulties/errors.

Regardless of costing methods used, U.S. Generally Accepted Accounting Principles (U.S. GAAP) must be followed for the preparation of the financial statements, wherein the valuation must be cost or market, whichever is lower.

In addition, the FIFO or last-in, first-out (LIFO) methods (or the average method) may be used under any cost system. These methods pertain to the assumption of the flow of costs, not to the actual costs themselves. Note that both methods may be used within one inventory, as long as the method is applied to that portion of the inventory consistently from period to period. Disclosures should be made of any change in method.

.03   Elements of Cost

Production costs consist of three elements: direct materials, direct labor, and manufacturing (overhead) expenses. Direct materials are those materials that can be identified with specific units of the product. Direct labor likewise can be identified with specific units of the product. Manufacturing expenses (overhead) are costs (including indirect material or labor) that cannot be identified with specific units of the product. These costs represent expenses for the factory and other facilities that permit the labor to be applied to the materials to manufacture a product. Sometimes, overhead is further subdivided into direct overhead (manufacturing costs, other than for material and direct labor, that specifically apply to production and require no allocation from other expense areas) and indirect overhead (expenses that have been allocated into the manufacturing expense area from other more general areas). For financial statement purposes, overhead should not include selling expenses or general administrative expenses.

.04   Integrating a Cost System

It is not essential to integrate a cost system with the rest of the accounting system, but it is highly desirable. A cost system is actually an extension of the regular system. With an integrated system, entries in the inventory account in the general ledger should represent the sums of figures taken from the cost accounting data. The general-ledger inventory accounts (e.g., finished goods, work in process and raw materials) are the control accounts and they should tie in with the amounts of physical inventories actually on hand. Discrepancies may result from errors, spoilage or thievery.

¶13,005   Job Order or Process Cost Systems

There are distinctions between cost systems other than the use of present or future costs. A job order system compiles costs for a specific quantity of a product as it moves through the production process. This means that material, labor, and overhead costs of a specific number or lot of the product (usually identifiable with a customer's order or a specific quantity being produced for stock) are recorded as the lot moves through the production cycle.

A process system compiles costs as they relate to specific processes or operations for a period of time. To find the unit cost, these figures are averaged for a specified period and spread over the number of units that go through each process. Process costing is used when large numbers of identical products are manufactured, usually in assembly-line fashion.

Keep in mind that actual or estimated costs can be used with either a job order or process cost system.

.01   Benefits and Drawbacks

Whether the job order or process system is used depends on the type of operation. The job order system is rarely used in mass production industries. It is invariably used when products are custom made. Process costing is used when production is in a continuous state of operation, as for baking and making paper, steel, glass, rubber, sugar or chemicals.

Following are some of the relative merits and shortcomings of each method.

ADVANTAGES

Job Order System	Process System
Appropriate for custom-made goods	It is usually only necessary to calculate costs each month
Appropriate for increasing finished goods inventory in desired quantities	A minimum of clerical work is required
Adequate for inventory pricing	
Permits estimation of future costs	If there is only one type of product cost, computation is relatively simple
Satisfies cost-plus contract requisites	

DISADVANTAGES

Job Order System	Process System
Expensive to use—a good deal of clerical work is required	Use of average costs ignores any variance in product cost
Difficult to make sure that all materials are accurately charged to each equivalent	Involves calculating the stage of a specific job in process and the use of units
Difficult to determine cost of goods sold when partial shipments are made before completion	

¶13,006   How to Use Standard Costs

Smith Company manufactures only one product, glubs—a household article made out of a certain type of plastic. Glubs are made from D raw material, which goes through a single process. Glubs are turned out from D material in a fraction of a day. Smith Company has a process-type cost setup integrated with its other financial records. D material is charged to work in process through requisitions based on actual cost. Direct labor is charged to work in process based on payroll. Manufacturing expense is charged to work in process based on the number of payroll hours. Each day, a record of the number of glubs manufactured is kept. This is the responsibility of the production department.

This is the way the Smith Company process cost system operates: Every month, total figures are worked up for raw material, payroll and factory expenses. Each of these figures is then divided by the total number of glubs produced for that month to arrive at a unit cost per glub.

Following is what the unit cost accumulation for the first four months of operation shows (this example assumes no work-in-process inventory and no equivalent units):

UNIT COST PER GLUB MANUFACTURED

	First Month	Second Month	Third Month	Fourth Month	Weighted Average
Material D	$ .94	$ .91	$ .97	$1.10	$ .95
Direct Labor	1.18	1.22	2.00	.70	1.29
Manufacturing Expense	1.22	1.47	2.11	.82	1.42
	$3.34	$3.60	$5.08	$2.62	$3.66

Right now, glubs are being sold at $4.30, and the present profit appears sufficient. T. O. Smith, the president and major stockholder of the corporation, feels that if glubs were sold at $3.30 each, four times as many could be sold. He also reports that he has learned that Glubco, Inc., Smith's competitor, is going to market glubs for $3.60. Smith thinks that $3.30 is a good sales price since the cost records indicate that glubs were manufactured for as low as $2.62 in the fourth month.

Smith Company's accountant says the president is incorrect. He points out that, on the basis of the cost records for six months, the average cost is somewhere in the area of $3.55 to $3.80. Selling glubs for $3.30 would create losses. The factory foreman says that during the third and fourth months there was an error in calculating the number of glubs put into finished goods inventory. From the figures for the fourth month, it appears that the foreman is correct. The unit cost per glub is unusually low. Mr. Smith wants to know the lowest at which he can sell glubs and still make a reasonable profit. The accountant suggests setting up a cost system based on standard costs and the following information is then determined:

1. Purchasing department records indicate that material D should cost no more than 15¢ per pound. (According to the chief engineer, it takes approximately two pounds of D to produce one glub.) The 15¢ figure takes future market conditions into account.
2. A time study of half a dozen workers who produce glubs is made. The average time it takes each of these six workers to produce one glub is one-sixth of an hour. The average hourly wage of these workers is $6.
3. Based on reasonable levels of production for the following year, a departmental manufacturing expense or overhead is estimated to be 100 percent of direct labor.

Based on the preceding determinations, the standard cost per glub is $2.30. It is calculated as follows:

Raw Material D: two pounds at 15¢ per pound	$ .30
Direct Labor: 1/6 hour at $6.00 per hour	1.00
Manufacturing Expense: 100% of direct labor	1.00
Total	2.30

In order to produce glubs at this cost, the following points are agreed upon:

1. When more than 15¢ a pound is paid for raw material D, the excess is to be charged to a special variance account instead of the raw material account. These excesses are to be explained periodically by the purchasing department.
2. Requisitions for raw material D are to be limited to two pounds of D for each glub to be manufactured. If more than two pounds per glub is issued to meet scheduled production, the excess over two pounds is to be charged to a separate variance account. The reason for any excess will also have to be explained.
3. The daily number of direct labor hours spent making glubs is to be multiplied by six. This should equal the number of glubs produced that day. Any discrepancy here is probably due to inefficiency. The number of inefficient hours at the standard $6 rate times the 100 percent manufacturing expense rate is to be charged to a special variance account.
4. Payroll over $6 an hour is to be charged to a variance account. Only $6 an hour is to be charged to the work-in-process account. The factory supervisor will have to explain hourly labor figures over $6 periodically.
5. Departmental variations in the 100 percent of direct labor manufacturing expense burden are to be charged or credited to separate variance accounts. This is what happened each month after this system was instituted:

Variance Accounts	Fifth Month	Sixth Month	Seventh Month	Eight Month	Ninth Month
1. Material D Price	$ 2,100	$ 300	$ 750	$ 0	$ 0
2. Material Usage	19,500	13,000	5,000	500	400
3. Labor Efficiency	8,000	5,050	800	700	300
4. Labor Rate	400	150	(5)	400	100
5. Manufacturing Expense	0	5,000	1,000	300	(100)
	$30,000	$23,500	$ 7,500	$1,900	$ 700
Unit Manufactured	48,000	48,500	48,000	48,000	48,000
Variance per Unit	.63	.49	.16	.04	.01
Standard Unit Cost	2.30	2.30	2.30	2.30	2.30
Actual Cost	$ 2.93	$ 2.79	$ 2.46	$ 2.34	$ 2.31

Where there were variances, this is what was elicited from discussion with the persons responsible for the different variance accounts:

1. The purchase price for raw material D exceeded 15¢ per pound mainly because of the distance of Smith Company from where D is obtained in the South. The head of purchasing feels that D could be purchased for no more than 15¢ if there could be a small office in the South with one assistant who would remain there. It was decided to go ahead and provide the office and the additional employee.

2. The factory supervisor, together with the chief engineer, has been going over the requisitions of raw material D. More D was needed because some of the glubs had air holes in them and were not usable. It seems that the pressure used to extrude them was insufficient. The chief engineer says that he can replace the present air die channels with larger ones so that these defects do not reoccur. The supervisor knew that some glubs were scrapped in the past, but it was not until this switch to standard costs that he knew how much waste there really was.

3. The supervisor and the industrial engineer who performed the time-and-motion study discussed the labor efficiency loss. It was their opinion that:

    a. There were more factory employees than needed to carry out various operations to convert D into finished glubs.

    b. Some employees needed additional training.

    c. Some workers were overskilled for their particular functions.

    d. Other workers were not producing at reasonable levels for some as yet unknown reason.

    Both the supervisor and engineer felt that a training program instructing employees in the efficient use of available tools would increase production. Further, time-and-motion studies on every phase of the production process were initiated.

4. There was not much variance in labor rate, but it was hoped that the training program would release more technically skilled and higher-paid employees for use in the more complicated production steps.

At the end of the seventh month, it was obvious that the steps taken were beginning to pay off. The additional costs incurred in carrying out these steps (for example, the additional employee in purchasing and the southern office) created a manufacturing overhead variance where none had existed before; but the success in other areas outweighed this.

At the end of the ninth month, everyone agreed that the switch to standard costs had exceeded expectations. The new lower production cost would help expand the market for glubs. Smith Company was also in a good competitive position compared with Glubco since it probably could now undersell it.

This illustration shows the advantages of standard costs:

- Control and reduction of costs.
- Promotion and measurement of efficiencies.
- Calculation and setting of selling prices.
- Evaluation of inventories.
- Simplification of cost procedures.

¶13,007   Direct Costing

Another type of cost accounting that is used for internal purposes, but not for financial or tax reporting purposes, is direct costing. This is a method in which only those costs that are a consequence of production of the product are assigned to the product—direct material cost, direct labor cost and only variable manufacturing overhead. All fixed manufacturing costs are treated as expenses of the period.

The methods of recording costs for direct material and direct labor are similar under direct costing and conventional costing. It is in the method of reflecting manufacturing overhead that the systems differ:

1. In conventional costing, only one overhead control account is used.
2. In a direct costing system, overhead costs are classified as fixed or variable.

Two control accounts are used—a direct overhead account and an indirect overhead account. The *direct overhead account* is for variable expenses—those that vary with the volume of production. Under direct costing, direct labor, direct material and overhead costs that vary with production find their way into the inventory. The other manufacturing overhead expenses are charged off currently against income. The important reason behind direct costing is not to value inventories but to segregate expenses.

The *indirect overhead account* is for fixed expenses—those that do not vary with production. These are charged as expenses of the period rather than as costs of the finished product. Research costs, some advertising costs, and costs incurred to keep manufacturing and non-manufacturing facilities ready for use are considered expenses of the period.

.01   The Effect of Direct Costing on Financial Statements

Direct costing, if used on the financial statements (for internal use), would produce the following results:

1. Where the inventory of manufactured goods does not fluctuate from one accounting period to the next, there should be no difference between net income using direct costing or net income using conventional costing.

2. Where the inventory does fluctuate and is increased, net income under direct costing will be lower. This is because fixed overhead costs under direct costing will have been charged to the current period instead of deferred by increasing the value of inventory. Under conventional costing, the value of the ending inventory will have been increased by these fixed overhead costs.

3. Where inventory decreases, net income under direct costing will be higher than conventional costing. The reason is that fixed overhead costs included in the value of the inventory under conventional costing will now increase the cost of goods sold, thereby reducing income.

¶13,008   Summary

When a business enterprise becomes as operationally and financially complex as even most small and medium-sized companies are today, fairly sophisticated control and evaluation techniques must be developed to ensure an adequate level of operational efficiency and financial stability.

The historical essence of cost accounting systems has been the flow of financial resources into, through, and out of the business. It cannot be overemphasized that the ultimate objective of cost accounting is to provide relevant, valid and timely information of the cost of manufactured products or of the cost of services provided by service organizations. It is important to remember that the cost accounting process is a tool, not an end unto itself.

CHAPTER 14
Budgeting for Profit Planning and Budgetary Control

¶14,000   Overview

A budget in its simplest terms is an estimate of future events. A budget is not a purely random guess, but a forecast which is computed from historical data that has been verified and assumed with some degree of credibility. The volume of sales for the following year, for example, may be estimated by using data from past experience, present-day market conditions, buying power of the consumer and other related factors.

Merely preparing the annual budget, then leaving it unaltered for the remainder of the budget period, is not the purpose. Preparation is only the first step. The second step is for management to control the operations of the firm and to adhere to the budget. Budgetary control is the tool of management for carrying out and controlling business operations. It establishes predetermined objectives and provides bases for measuring performance against these objectives. If variations between performance and objective arise, management should alter the situation by either correcting the weakness in performance or modifying the budget. Firms that adopt budgetary control have a better control of operations and are better able to modify them to meet expectations.

In addition to a review of the rolling budgets based on previous years' expenditures and operations, two management tools related to budgeting will also be discussed: break-even analysis (BE) and zero-base budgeting (ZBB).

The objective of break-even analysis is to determine an approximation as close as possible to the changes in costs generated by changes in the volume of production. Determining the BE point is a technique that can be applied to the control of costs, in the evaluation of alternatives, in the allocations of a firm's resources, and in making decisions in virtually every phase of a company's business.

The value to budgeting in break-even analysis is that the approach can be applied to sales, profits, costs, and selling prices, to help make sound decisions for the utilization of idle plant capacity, for proposed advertising expenditures, and for proposed expansion in production levels.

ZBB is a logical process, combining many elements of management. The key components of ZBB are:

1.   Identifying objectives.
2.   Determining value of accomplishing each activity.
3.   Evaluating alternative funding levels.
4.   Establishing priorities.
5.   Evaluating workload and performance measures.

ZBB recognizes that the budgeting process is a management process, a decision-making process, and a driving force.

¶14,001   Types of Budgets

There are two principal types of annual profit budgets: the operating or earnings budget and the financial or cash budget. The earnings budget, as its name implies, is an attempt to forecast the earnings of a company for a future period. To make such forecast, other estimates must be made. Consequently, organizations have sales budgets, production budgets (which include labor budgets, materials budgets, manufacturing expense budgets), capital expenditure budgets, administrative expense budgets, distribution expense budgets and appropriation-type budgets (e.g., advertising, research). The accuracy of each of these budgets determines the accuracy of the earnings forecast.

The cash budget, on the other hand, tries to forecast the utilization of the company's cash resources. It estimates the company's anticipated cash expenditures and resources for a period of operation. Cash budget forecasts, like the earnings forecast, depend heavily on sales forecasts. The amount of sales determines the amount of cash the company has for purposes of its operation.

¶14,002   The Sales Budget

The foundation of the entire budget program is the sales budget. If anticipated sales of a particular product (or project) do not exceed the cost to produce and market it by an amount sufficient to reward the investors and to compensate for the risks involved, the product (project) should not be undertaken. Sales forecasting must be continuous. Conditions change rapidly; in order to direct one's efforts into the most profitable channels, there must be a continuous review and revision of the methods employed.

.01   Forecasting Sales

A sales forecast represents the revenue side of the earnings forecast. It is a prediction as to the sales quantity and sales revenue. Sales forecasts are made for both short and long periods.

Forecasting sales with any degree of accuracy is not an easy task. For example, a firm which estimates sales with the expectation that a patent which it holds will not become obsolete may be disappointed.

In general, the business forecaster has two situations:

1. Those which he or she can to some extent control and
2. Those where conditions created by others can only be observed, recorded, interpreted, and applied to his or her own situation.

A firm that has a monopoly due to an important patent which it owns is an example of a company which controls the situation. Forecasts made by such a company may be very accurate. In most cases, however, a company has no such control. It must attempt to interpret general conditions, the situation in its own industry, and future sales of its particular company before making forecasts.

Making the forecast is the responsibility of the sales manager, who, with the help of the district managers and the individual salespersons, determines the primary sales objectives for the year. Corrections of the forecast are made by the heads of the firm so that sales estimates will better reflect expected economic conditions. Before an estimate of sales is made, there must be a reasonable expectation that the projection is attainable. It must be based on the best evidence available. As conditions change, the forecast is revised.

If a firm desires to sell more than in the past, an analysis of past sales performances must be supplemented by other analyses. Consideration must be given to general business conditions. The effects of political and economic changes throughout the world are quickly reflected on individual business communities. Some of these factors which affect sales are wars, government regulations, and technological developments. This information should be used in appraising the probable effect of these changes on the sales of the firm for the budget period.

.02   Market Analysis

A sales manager needs to know if the firm is getting its full share of potential customer demand as indicated by a market analysis.

The questionnaire is a popular method of reaching consumers, retailers and jobbers. Data collected give the firm valuable information, essential in arriving at a forecast of sales possibilities.

A market analysis at a given time gives a picture of the present and potential consumption of a product. This picture provides only half the significant information. The other half can be obtained by continuing the survey over a period of time to discover market trends.

.03   Pricing Policy

The sales budget is not complete until the firm decides on a practical policy as to what price can be secured for its products. Generally, estimates should be made to conform with the market prices during the budget period.

The next step is to formulate the sales policies of the firm. These policies should be established relative to such considerations as territorial expansion and selection, customer selection, types and quality of products and service, prices, terms of sales, and sales organization and responsibility.

Only after a firm has thoroughly analyzed past sales experience, general business conditions, market potentials, the product to be sold, determined the prices to be charged and formulated its sales policies is it ready to develop the sales program.

.04   Measuring Individual Performance

As a basis for measuring individual performance, a rewarding-merit sales standard could be established. A sales standard is an opinion of the best qualified judgment of performance which may reasonably be achieved under ideal conditions. By comparing this standard with the budget estimate (the figure expected) under normal conditions, management has provided the most important tool of sales control.

An example of how a comparison between the standard and budget estimate may serve as a basis for reward is the following: A saleswoman may be told to produce sales of $150,000 (standard), but the firm may expect her to produce sales of only $125,000 (budget estimate). The saleswoman does not have to be told what the firm's budget figures are. In an endeavor to reach $150,000, she is trying to better what she believes is the budget figure. Depending on how close she comes to the $150,000, the firm may devise a method of rewarding her. It should be kept in mind, however, that the standard should not be set too high, since it may have a reverse effect if the sales personnel feel it is unreachable.

¶14,003   The Production Budget

After the sales budget has been prepared, the next step is to prepare the production budget, which specifies the quantity and timing of production requirements.

While the sales budget is prepared in anticipation of seasonal fluctuations, the production budget endeavors to smooth out the fluctuations and thus make most effective use of productive capacity. This is accomplished by manufacturing for stock over the slow periods and using the stock to cover sales during busy periods.

There are different problems for a firm that sells stock products and one that produces special-order goods. The objective for a stock-order-type firm is to coordinate sales and production to prevent excessive inventories, but at the same time to have enough stock to meet sales. A forecast of production in such a firm should enable the executive to arrange to lay out the factory so as to handle the anticipated volume most conveniently. Production in such a firm must be as evenly distributed as possible over the year. It is uneconomical to manufacture the whole period's requirements within a relatively short time at the beginning of the budget period. This involves unduly heavy capital costs of carrying the large inventory. Also, distributing the work over the entire period spreads the labor costs.

With special-order items, the production department must be prepared at all times to manufacture the goods as soon as possible after receiving the order. Production in this case has to be arranged for the best possible utilization of equipment and labor, so that idle time is reduced to a minimum.

.01   Budgeting Production Costs

Production budgets should be rigid as long as conditions remain the same, but they should be capable of prompt adjustment when circumstances change. For example, if a company operates at 70 percent of capacity in a period and the budget was based on a production volume of 80 percent, the budget is of little use. The budget will have to be altered to show what production costs will be at the 70 percent level. It is prudent when planning production at a particular anticipated percentage level to indicate in the budget the estimates of possible production costs at different levels.

.02   Preparing the Production Budget

The production budget period may vary in length. However, it is common practice among large corporations to use what is known as a "product year." As an example, the automobile industry will usually start with the introduction of new models. The budget year should include at least one complete cycle of operations so that money tied up in raw materials and work-in-process materials may undergo one complete liquidation. Another factor influencing the budget period is the stability of general business conditions. It is more difficult to budget operations during an unstable period, and it is advisable at these times to shorten the budget period.

The production budget should be expressed in terms of physical units. To compute the physical quantities is simple. For example, a simple computation to estimate production required is:

	Units
Estimated sales	250,000
Less opening inventory	150,000
Total requirements	100,000
Add: Closing inventory	100,000
Production required	200,000

Before computing the quantity to be produced, it is necessary to decide quantities to be in the inventory at the end of the period. This decision should be based on factors such as:

1. Adequate inventory to meet sales demands
2. Evenly distributed production to prevent shortage of material and labor
3. Danger of obsolescence
4. High costs of storing large inventories.

Available Facilities. The production program must conform with the plant facilities available and should determine the most economical use of these facilities. The capacity of the plant is measured in two ways: optimum plant capacity and normal plant capacity. All other measurements are in percentages of optimum or normal capacity. Optimum capacity of course, can never actually be attained. There are many unavoidable interruptions, such as waiting for setup of machines; time to repair machines; lack of help, tools, materials; holidays; inefficiency; etc. However, these interruptions should be looked into to determine how they can be minimized.

Management should also consider whether additional equipment is needed just to meet temporary sales demands. Later, such equipment may be idle. The replacement of old machinery with new high-speed equipment should also be considered. A careful study should help determine which step would be more profitable in the long run.

Records for each product showing the manufacturing operations necessary and a record of each machine's capability and capacity, should be maintained. Estimates must be made of material to be used, number of labor hours and quantities of service (power) required for each product. These estimates are called "standards of production performance." The establishment of these standards is an engineering rather than an accounting task. In this respect, these standards are similar to those used in standard cost accounting.

Cost of Production. The following illustrates how cost of production is determined: Assume a concern has a normal capacity of 100 units of product. Current production budget calls for 80 units. Only one product is made; and its production requires two operations, A and B. The standard costs are: variable costs per unit of product, one unit of direct material, $2; operation A (direct labor and overhead), $3; operation B (direct labor and overhead), $5; total $10. Fixed production costs for the budget period are $500, or $5 per unit based on normal capacity. This production cost budget would then be expressed as follows:

Variable cost (80 units @ $10)	$ 800
Fixed costs (80 units @ $5)	400
Costs chargeable to production	1,200
Cost of idle capacity (500 less 400)	100
Total budgeted costs	$1,300

There is a tie-in here between estimated costs, standard costs, and production budgets.

¶14,004   The Labor Budget

The labor budget deals only with direct labor. Indirect labor is included in the manufacturing expense budget. (The manufacturing expense budget includes the group of expenses in addition to indirect labor, expenses such as indirect material, repairs and maintenance, depreciation and insurance.)

The purpose of the labor budget is to ascertain the number and kind of workers needed to execute the production program during the budget period. The labor budget should indicate the necessary worker-hours and the cost of labor required for the manufacture of the products in the quantities shown by the production budget.

.01   Preparation of the Labor Budget

The preparation of a labor budget begins with an estimate of the number of labor hours required for the anticipated quantity of products. Before this can be done, it is necessary to know the quantity of items to be produced, as in the production budget. If the products are uniform and standard labor time allowances have been established, it is just a matter of multiplying the production called for by the standards to determine the labor hours required. If the products are *not* uniform but there is uniformity of operations, it is first necessary to translate production into operation requirements. Operation standards then should be established in terms of worker-or machine-hours to ascertain the quantity of labor required. The next step in preparing the labor budget is to estimate the cost of direct labor. These estimates are computed by multiplying the number of units to be produced by the labor costs per unit. The problem then is to predetermine the unit labor costs. Some of the methods of determining these costs are:

- Day rate system.
- Piece rate system.
- Bonus system.

In firms where standard labor costs have been established for the products manufactured, it is necessary only to multiply the units of the product called for in the production budget by the standard labor costs.

A detailed analysis should frequently be made of the differences between actual and estimated labor costs to determine whether they are justified. An investigation may reveal inefficient workers, wasted time, defective materials, idle time, poor working conditions, high-priced workers, etc. Responsibility must be definitely placed and immediate action taken to correct those factors which are capable of being controlled.

The budgets for direct labor and manufacturing expenses are not complete until schedules of the final estimates are prepared. The form will vary, depending on the needs of the firm. The following is an example of a schedule of estimated direct labor costs where estimates are shown for each department of the firm:

X Corporation
Estimated Direct Labor Costs for the Period 1/1/xx to 12/31/xx

Dept.	Quantity to be Produced	Standard Labor Cost Per Unit	Total Estimated Labor Cost
1	127,600	$ .90	$115,000
2	127,600	1.60	204,000
3	127,600	1.12	143,000
		$3.62	$462,000

¶14,005   Materials Budget

The purpose of the materials budget is to be sure that there are sufficient materials to meet the requirements of the production budget. This budget deals with the purchase of raw materials and finished parts and controls the inventory.

How to estimate the material required depends on the nature of the individual company. A company manufacturing standard articles can estimate fairly accurately the amount of raw materials and the purchases required for the production program. Even where the articles are not standard, there is usually a reliable relationship between the volume of business handled and the requirements for the principal raw materials.

.01   Tie-In to Standard Costs

In the preparation of the material budget, there is a tie-in to standard costs. Here is an example of how purchase requirements are computed:

Quantity required for production	300,000 units
Desired inventory at end of budget period	75,000 units
Total requirements	375,000 units
Less: Inventory at beginning of period	80,000 units
Purchase requirements	295,000 units

The next step is to express material requirements in terms of prices. Some firms establish standard prices based on what are considered normal prices. Differences between standard and actual purchase prices are recorded as price variance.

.02   Factors Affecting Policy

These are:

1.   The time it takes the material to be delivered after the purchase order is issued.
2.   The rate of consumption of material as indicated by the production budget.
3.   The amount of stock that should be on hand to cover possible delays in inventory of raw materials.

On the basis of these factors, the purchasing department working with the production department can establish figures of minimum stocks and order quantities of raw materials and parts for each product handled. Purchases in large quantities are advisable if price advantages can be obtained. Bulk purchases are advisable during periods of rising prices but not during periods of declining prices. The unavoidable time lag between order and delivery of the material is also a reason to buy in advance.

Buying in advance does not necessarily involve immediate delivery. The deliveries may be spread over the budget period in order to coordinate purchases with production and to control inventory. To control inventory, it is desirable to establish minimum and maximum quantities for each material to be carried. The lower limit is the smallest amount which can be carried without risk of production delays. If materials can be obtained quickly, the inventory can be held near the lower limit. The advantage of keeping inventory at this lower limit is that it minimizes the cost of storage and possible obsolescence. If materials cannot be obtained quickly, there is the possibility of a rise in prices, as well as an unforeseen delay in delivery which could hold up production and so it is advisable to carry more than minimum inventory.

.03   Goods in Process

The time it takes for material to enter the factory and emerge as a finished product is frequently much longer than necessary for efficient production. Comparisons with other companies may reveal that a firm allows its goods to remain in process much longer than other firms. Investigations should be made to determine the causes of such delays and formulate remedies. These investigations are usually made in connection with the production budget.

.04   Finished Goods

The budget of finished goods inventory is based on the sales budget. For example, if 100 units of an item are expected to be sold during the budget period, the problem is to determine how much must be kept in stock to support such a sales program. Since it is difficult to determine the exact quantity customers will demand each day, the finished goods inventory must maintain a margin of safety so that satisfactory deliveries can be made. Once this margin is established, the production and purchasing programs can be developed to replenish the stock as needed.

¶14,006   Manufacturing Expense Budget

In preparing the manufacturing expense budget, estimates and probable expenses should be prepared by persons responsible to authorize expenditures. The general responsibility for variable expenses lies with the production manager. But the immediate responsibility for many of these expenses lies with the supervisors of the several departments. Generally, expenses are estimated by those who control them. Each person who prepares a portion of the manufacturing expense budget is furnished with data of prior periods and any plans for the budget period which may affect the amount of expenses. With these data decisions can be made about:

1. Which, if any, present expenses can be eliminated.
2. Probable effect of the sales and production forecasts on those expenses which must be incurred.

No plans for the elimination or reduction of variable expenses should be made unless it is certain that the plan can be enforced.

The responsibility for many fixed manufacturing expenses is with the general executives. Such fixed expenses include long-term leases, pension plans, patents, amortization, salaries of major production executives, etc.

In preparing the budget estimates of manufacturing expenses, a common practice is to use percentages. Each expense is taken as a percent of sales or production costs. For example, if a certain expense is estimated to be 5 percent of sales, this percentage is applied to the sales estimate to obtain the amount of this expense. The fallacy with this method is that all expenses do not vary proportionately with sales or production. A sounder method of estimating manufacturing expenses is to give individual expenses separate treatment.

In estimating the indirect labor expense, it is important to first analyze the expense for the period preceding the budget period. The requirements for additional help, or the possibility of eliminating some of the help, should be considered along with plans for increasing or decreasing any rates of compensation. Detailed schedules should be prepared, showing the nature of each job and the amount to be paid. By summarizing these schedules, an aggregate estimate can be determined.

Indirect materials expense should be estimated by first analyzing the amount consumed in prior periods. This, together with the production budget showing the proposed volume for the budget period, serves as a basis for estimating the quantities of the indirect material requirements. The probable cost of such requirements estimated by the purchasing department is the amount to be shown in the manufacturing expense budget.

Repairs and maintenance estimates are based on past experience data, supplemented by a report on the condition of the present equipment. If any additional equipment is to be installed during the budget period, recognition must be given to the prospect of additional repairs and maintenance charges. Electric power expense is in direct proportion to the production volume. The charges for depreciation of equipment can be estimated with considerable accuracy.

Insurance expense for the budget period is estimated on the basis of the insurance in force charged to production with adjustments made for contemplated changes in equipment, inventories, or coverage of hazard incident to manufacturing.

To budget manufacturing expenses effectively it is important to establish standard overhead rates.

At frequent intervals during the budget period, comparison should be made between the actual expenses in each department and the amount estimated to be spent for actual production during the period. Variations should be investigated and steps taken to correct weaknesses in the production program.

A distinction should be made between controllable and uncontrollable expenses so that the responsibility of individuals can be more closely determined. To facilitate the estimating of expenses, a further distinction is made between fixed and variable expenses. Fixed expenses are those which remain the same regardless of the variations in sales or production. Variable expenses are those which increase or decrease proportionally with changes in volume, sales or production. Maintenance is seldom treated in a separate budget. It is usually regarded as part of the manufacturing expense budget.

Following is an example of a Schedule of Estimated Manufacturing Expenses for each operation of a particular product:

Y Corporation for the Year Ended 12/31/XX

	Total	Operation 1	Operation 2	Operation 3
Variable expenses:				
Indirect materials	$ 20,000	$ 5,000	$ 10,000	$ 5,000
Indirect labor	100,000	10,000	15,000	75,000
Light and power	30,000	5,000	13,000	12,000
Telephone	5,000	3,000	–0–	2,000
Fixed and semi-variable:				
Factory rent	50,000	14,000	18,000	18,000
Superintendence	100,000	30,000	35,000	35,000
Depreciation	100,000	20,000	20,000	60,000
General and administrative expense	50,000	12,000	17,000	21,000
Total	$455,000	$99,000	$168,000	$188,000

After estimates of materials, direct labor and manufacturing expenses have been prepared, a Schedule of Estimated Cost of Production may be prepared as follows:

Z Corporation for the Year Ended 12/31/XX

	Total	Product A	Product B	Product C
Cost Element:				
Materials	$200,000	$ 80,000	$ 50,000	$ 70,000
Labor	340,000	100,000	80,000	160,000
Manufacturing expenses	70,000	30,000	30,000	10,000
Total	$610,000	$210,000	$160,000	$240,000

¶14,007   Capital Expenditures Budget

Since capital expenditures represent a large part of the total investment of a manufacturing concern, the capital expense budget is of great importance. Unwise capital expenditures can seldom be corrected without serious loss to stockholders. The purpose of the capital expenditures budget is to subject such expenditures to careful examination and so avoid mistakes that cannot easily be corrected.

A carefully prepared capital expenditures budget should point out the effect of such expenditures on the cash position of the company and on future earnings. For example, too large a portion of total assets invested in fixed plant and equipment sooner or later may result in an unhealthy financial condition because of the lack of necessary working capital.

.01   Preparation of Capital Expenditures Budget

In preparing the capital expenditures budget, the following information is recorded:

1. The amount of machinery, equipment, etc., on hand at the beginning of the budget period;
2. Additions planned for the period;
3. Withdrawals expected for the period;
4. The amount of machinery, equipment, etc., expected at the end of the budget period.

Consideration should be given to estimates of additions planned for the period. Additions will be justified if they increase the volume of production and earnings, will reduce unit costs, and the money needed can be spared. Consideration should also be given to the percentage of investment for fixed assets as compared with net worth of the firm for a number of years. Various business authorities have realized that an active business enterprise with a tangible net worth between $50,000 and $250,000 should have as a maximum not more than two-thirds of its tangible net worth in fixed assets. Where the tangible net worth is in excess of $250,000, not more than 75 percent of the tangible net worth should be represented by fixed assets. When these percentages are greatly exceeded, annual depreciation charges tend to be too heavy, the net working capital too moderate, and liabilities expand too rapidly for the good health of the business; alternative leasing should be considered.

The capital expenditures budget should include estimates not only for the budget period, but long-range estimates covering a period of many years. The ideal situation occurs when machinery is purchased at a time when prices are low. A long-range capital expenditures budget will indicate what machinery will be of use in the future; then, machinery may be acquired when prices are considered low. Inefficient or obsolete machines can sometimes be made into satisfactory units by rebuilding. If it is estimated that gains derived from rebuilding machinery will exceed the costs, then provision should be made in the capital expenditures budget to incur these expenses. Such expenditures are frequently called betterments and prolong the useful life of the machines. The preparation of detailed and accurate records is an essential part of the capital expenditures budget. The following information should be included in such a record:

1. Description of machines;
2. Date of requisition;
3. Cost for depreciation rate.

From the above information, it is a simple matter to complete the depreciation for the budget period.

As with other budgets, actual expenditures should be compared with the estimates, and any variation should be analyzed. In addition, a statement should be prepared showing the extent to which actual results obtained from the use of certain capital expenditures are in line with expectations. This is particularly important where substantial investments are made in labor-saving equipment, new processes or new machines.

¶14,008   The Cash Budget

The cash budget is a composite reflection of all the operating budgets in terms of cash receipts and disbursements. Its purpose is to determine the cash resources that will be available during the entire budget program so that the company will know in advance whether it can carry out its program without borrowing or obtaining new capital or whether it will need to obtain additional capital from these sources. Thus, the company can arrange in advance for any necessary borrowing, avoiding emergencies and, more important, a cash crisis caused by a shortage.

A knowledgeable financial person goes into the market to borrow money when there is the cheapest rate. The cash budget will tell the manager when there is the need to borrow so he or she can plan accordingly. In a like manner, the manager can foresee when there will be sufficient funds to repay loans.

A cash budget is very important to a firm which does installment selling. Installment selling ties up cash resources, and a careful analysis of estimated future collections is needed to forecast the cash position of the company.

Other purposes of the cash budget are to:

1. Provide for seasonal fluctuations in business which make heavy demands on funds to carry large inventories and receivables,
2. Assist the financial executive in having funds available to meet maturing obligations,
3. Aid in securing credit from commercial banks (a bank is more likely to lend funds for a definite plan that has been prepared, indicating when and how the funds will be repaid), and
4. Indicate the amount of funds available for investments, when available and for what duration.

.01   Preparation of the Cash Budget

The main difference between a cash budget and other budgets is that in the cash budget all estimates are based on the dates when it is expected cash will be received or paid. Other budgets are prepared on the basis of the accrual of the different items (for accrual-basis companies). Therefore, in the cash budget, the budget executive cannot base the estimate of cash receipts directly on the sales budget for the obvious reason that all the cash will not be received from such sales in the same month in which they are billed. This is not true in the case of a business on a strictly cash basis.

Depreciation is another item handled differently in the cash budget. Depreciation is a cost of doing business; it increases expenses and reduces net income for financial reporting purposes. It is not, however, a cash item and is ignored in preparing the cash budget, but the amount paid for a new plant or equipment in a single year or budget period is included in full in the cash budget.

Cash receipts of a typical firm come from cash sales, collections on accounts and notes receivable, interest, dividends, rent, sale of capital assets and loans. The cash sale estimate is taken from the sales budget. The estimate of collections on accounts should be based on the sales budget and company experience in making collections. With concerns whose sales are made largely on account, the collection experience should be ascertained with considerable care. As an illustration, assume the March account sales have actually been collected as follows:

Month	%
March	6.4
April	80.1
May	8.5
June	3.6
Cash Discount Taken	1.1
Bad Debts Loss	.3
Total	100.00

If the same experience is recorded for each month of the year, it is possible to resolve the sales estimates into a collection budget. It is sometimes desirable to develop the experience separately for different classes of customers for different geographical areas. Once these figures are ascertained, they should be tested from time to time.

Cash disbursements in a typical firm are made for payroll, materials, operating expenses, taxes, interest, purchases of equipment, repayment of loans, payment of dividends, and other like items. With a complete operating budget on hand, there is little difficulty in estimating the amount of cash that will be required and when it will be required. Wages and salaries are usually paid in cash and on definite dates. For purchases of material (from the materials budget), the purchasing department can readily indicate the time allowed for payments. Operating expenses must be considered individually. Some items, such as insurance, are prepaid. Others, such as commissions, are accrued. So, cash payments may not coincide with charges on the operating budget.

¶14,009 Zero-Base Budgeting

A different approach to budgeting adopted by some industrial organizations as well as not-for-profit entities and governmental units is appropriately termed *Zero-Base Budgeting*. Whether adopted wholeheartedly on a yearly basis, as a review every few years, or merely as a mind-set tool, its precepts can be of value in the budgeting process.

Expenses for industrial organizations can be divided into two categories:

1. Direct manufacturing expense, for materials, labor, and overhead.
2. Support expense, for everything else.

It is the "everything else" that causes problems at budget time, when, for example, management is beset by rising costs and must decide between decreasing the budgetary allocation for a research and development project or cutting funds for executive development. Traditionally, problems like these boil down to one question: How should the company shift its allocations around? Rather than tinker with their existing budget, many companies have implemented this budgeting method that starts at base-zero.

This approach requires that the company view all of its discretionary activities and priorities afresh, and create a different and hopefully better set of allocations for the ensuring budget year. The base-zero procedure gives management a firm grip on support allocations of all kinds, a procedure for describing all support expense minutely, classifying the alternatives to each, and sorting them all according to their importance and priority.

This technique in budgeting differentiates between the basic and necessary operations and those of a more discretionary character, thus enabling management to focus specific attention on the optional group. The basic steps for effective zero-base budgeting require justification of every dollar spent on discretionary costs, and a prescribed order of approach to the final allocation of funds:

1. Describe each optional activity in a "decision" package.
2. Evaluate and rank these decision packages by cost/benefit analysis.
3. Allocate resources based on this analysis.

.01 Where to Use Zero-Base Budgeting

Zero-base budgeting (ZBB) is best applied to service and support areas of company activity rather than to the basic manufacturing operation. Since a corporation's level of manufacturing activity is determined by its sales volume, the production level, in turn, determines how much the company should spend on labor, materials, and overhead. Hence, there is not the same simple relationship between costs and benefits here as there is in the service and support areas where management can trade off a level of expenditures on a given project against the direct returns on investment. Cost benefit analysis, which is crucial to zero-base budgeting, cannot be applied directly to decisions to increase or decrease expenditures in the manufacturing areas.

The main use of zero-base budgeting occurs when management has discretion to choose between different activities having different direct costs and benefits. Such areas normally include marketing, finance, quality control, personnel, engineering and other non-production areas of company activity.

.02 Decision Package Concept

When implementing ZBB, a company must explain the "decision package concept" to all levels of management and then present guidelines for the individual manager to use in breaking the specific activities into workable packages. Next, higher management must establish a ranking, consolidation and elimination process. The decision package is the document that identifies and describes a specific activity in such a manner that management can:

1. Evaluate and rank that activity against other activities competing for limited resources,
2. Decide whether to approve or disapprove expenditures in that area.

The specifications in each package must provide management with the information needed to evaluate the activity. Included should be:

1. A statement of the goals of the activity,
2. The program by which the goals are to be attained,
3. The benefits expected from the program and methods of determining whether they have been attained,
4. Suggested alternatives to the program,
5. Possible consequences of not approving the package and expenditure of funds, and
6. Designation of personnel required to carry out the program.

There are two basic types of decision packages:

1. Mutually exclusive packages identify alternative means of performing the same function. The best alternative is chosen and the other packages are discarded.
2. Incremental packages reflect different levels of effort that may be expended on a specific function or program. One package, the "base package," may establish a minimum level of activity, and others identify increased activity or expenditure levels.

A logical starting point for determining next year's needs is the current year's operations. Each ground level manager who has the ultimate responsibility takes the area's forecasted expense level for the current year, identifies the activities creating this expense, and calculates the cost for each activity. At this stage, the manager identifies each activity at its current level and method of operation and does not attempt to identify alternatives or increments.

After current operations have been separated into preliminary decision packages, the manager looks at requirements for the upcoming year. To aid in specifying these requirements, upper management should issue a formal set of assumptions on the activity levels, billings, and wage and salary increases for the upcoming year. These formal assumptions provide all managers with uniform benchmarks for estimating purposes.

At the conclusion of the formulation stage, the manager will have identified all of the proposed activities as follows:

1. Business-as-usual packages.
2. Decision packages for other ongoing activities.
3. Decision packages for new activities.

The ranking process forces management to face squarely the most basic decision: How much money is available and where should it be spent to obtain the greatest good? Management arrives at the decisions by listing, and then studying all the packages identified in order of decreasing benefit to the company, and eliminating those of least value.

It is possible for one ranking of decision packages to be obtained for an entire company and judged by its top management. While this one, single ranking would identify the best allocation of resources, ranking and judging the high volume of packages created by describing all of the activities of a large company would result in an unwieldy task for top management.

This problem can be resolved by grouping decision units which may correspond to a budget unit in organizations with detailed cost-center structures, or they can be defined on a project basis.

The initial ranking should occur at the cost-center or project level so that each manager can evaluate the relative importance of the segments and rank the packages accordingly.

The manager at the next level up the ladder then reviews these rankings with the appropriate managers and uses the resulting rankings as guides to produce a single consolidated ranking for all packages presented from below.

At higher levels of a large organization, the expertise necessary to rank packages is best obtained by committee. The committee membership should consist of all managers whose packages are being ranked with their supervisor serving as chairperson.

Each committee produces its consolidated ranking by voting on the decision packages presented by its members. As at the cost-center level, the most beneficial packages are ranked highest and the least important ranked lowest.

It is best to establish the cutoff line at the highest consolidation level first, and then for the lower levels. The most effective way to establish the first cutoff is for management at the highest consolidation level to estimate the expense that will be approved at the top level and then to set the cutoff line far enough below to allow trading off between the divisions whose packages are being ranked.

The ability to achieve a list of ranked packages at any given organization level allows management to evaluate the desirability of various expenditure levels throughout the budgeting process. This ranked list also provides management with a reference point to be used during the year to identify activities to be reduced or expanded if allowable expenditure levels change.

Zero-base budgeting can be a flexible and useful tool in simplifying the budgeting process and in bringing about better resource allocation by forcing meaningful consideration of varying priorities for available funds.

¶14,010   Break-Even Point Analysis

The break-even point (BE) is that amount of sales necessary to yield neither income nor loss. If sales should be less than indicated by the BE point, a loss results. If the total cost of goods sold and other expenses is less than sales, and if this total varied in direct proportion to sales, operations would result in net income. BE analysis is not a budget, in itself, but is an approach in the budgeting process for dealing intelligently with the uncertainty of estimates for future operations that are based on statistical data. Breakeven analysis can be applied to sales, profit, costs, and selling price problems, and it can be used to help make sound decisions for employing idle plant capacity, planning advertising, granting credit, and expanding production. BE is a tool, and a useful one, with which to begin to approach decision problems.

BE Analysis, is an inexpensive method for analyzing the possible effects of decisions. Discounted cash flow techniques require large amounts of data expensive to develop. BE can help with the decision whether or not it is worthwhile to do more intensive, costly analysis.

BE provides a means for designing product specifications, which permits a comparison of different designs and their costs before the specifications for a specific product are accepted as the best choice cost-wise. For example, a new product with an uncertain volume is considered to be feasible if it's made with hand tools rather than with expensive capital equipment. The first method typically has higher variable costs, but lower fixed costs. This often results in a lower breakeven point for the project, and lower risks and potential profits. The fixed capital equipment approach raises the BE, but also raises the risks and profit potential for the manufacturer. BE helps to examine these trade-offs.

An important factor when using BE analysis is the nature of the user's cost structure. Some firms have a flexible labor force and standard cost analysis works well. In other businesses, however, management must treat labor costs differently. Certain skilled workers cannot be laid off when business is slow. BE analysis assumes a realistic definition of costs, both in amount and type. While fixed costs will not change with changes in revenue, variable and semi-variable costs do change with changes in sales, up or down. Product pricing can be significantly aided by using variations of breakeven analysis.

Break-Even Chart. A break-even chart presents a visual representation of sales volume, capacity, or output when expenses and revenues are equal, i.e., a volume level at which income equals expenses. A BE chart provides a projection of the impact of output upon expenses, income, and profits which makes the chart a useful tool for profit planning and control.

The BE chart assumes that selling prices do not change, total fixed expenses remain the same at all levels of output, and variable costs increase or decrease in direct proportion to sales. The N line remains the same regardless of sales volume; the point B on the chart is the total of the fixed and variable expenses on the list on the vertical axis. The area between line M and the fixed expense line N is the amount of variable expenses at different volumes of sales. The area between line M and the horizontal axis represents the total costs at various levels of sales. Line M can be considered a total cost line, since total costs for various volumes of sales can be readily determined from it. This can be done by starting at any point on the horizontal scale and measuring upward to line M and across to the vertical scale.

The income line P starts at zero and extends through point C, which is the point at which total sales and total income are shown on both scales, about $1,200. The profit area lies to the right of break-even point D where the revenue line P crosses the total cost line M. Revenue is greater than costs above— i.e., to the right—of the break-even point D; the loss area is below—i.e., to the left—of the break-even point D.

Break-Even Technique. Break-Even is an inexpensive technique to determine whether or not it would be advisable to do more intensive and costly analysis of a proposed project. It provides a method for designing product specifications. Each design has costs which affect price and marketing feasibility by providing comparison of possible designs before the specifications are frozen by cash commitments. BE serves as a substitute for estimating an unknown factor in making project decisions. In deciding whether to go ahead with a project or to disband it, there are always variables to be considered such as costs, price, demand, and other miscellaneous factors. When most expenses associated with a proposed project can be determined, only two variables need be considered as variable items—profits (cash flow) and demand (sales). Demand is usually more difficult to estimate. By deciding that profit must at least be zero, the BE point, the demand is more easily estimated by determining what sales levels are needed to make the project a worthwhile undertaking. BE provides a way to attack uncertainty, to at least develop marketing targets for desired levels of income. One of the major problems of BE analysis is that no product exists in isolation; there are always alternative uses for an organization's funds. BE analysis helps decision makers to consider not only the value of an individual project, but how it compares to other uses of the funds and facilities.

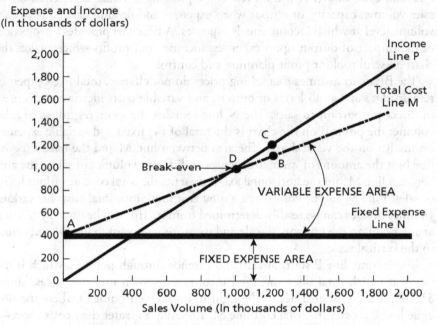

CONVENTIONAL BREAK-EVEN CHART

Another problem is that BE analysis does not permit proper examination of cash flows. In considering financial commitments, the appropriate way to make investment or capital decisions is to consider the value of a proposed project's anticipated cash flows. If the discounted value of the cash flows exceeds the required investment outlay in cash, the project is acceptable. BE analysis makes restrictive assumptions about cost-revenue relationships; it is basically a negative technique defining constraints rather than looking at benefits; it is essentially a static tool for analyzing income and outflow for a single period of time.

The BE technique requires a realistic definition of costs, both in amount and type. A BE approach, therefore, should not be considered a technique to be used to make *final* investment decisions. It is a supplemental tool among the many factors a business decision maker must consider; it is an approach helpful to apply at the beginning of an analysis of a proposed solution of a business problem.

Although a complete and adequate budget may be developed without using a break-even analysis, its use adds to the understanding of estimates as shown in the following example.

Where the total cost of goods sold and other expenses is less than sales and if this total varied in direct proportion to sales, operations would always result in net income. For example, in a company in which the cost of goods sold and expenses amount to $1.80 per unit sold and the sale price is $2, on the first unit there would be net income of 20¢. On a million items, the net income would amount to $200,000.

As a practical matter, the simple example cited above is not realistic. Although some expenses may vary with volume of sales (e.g., salesperson's commissions, traveling expenses, advertising, telephone, delivery costs, postage, supplies, etc.), there are many other types of expenses which are not affected by the variations in sales. These expenses are the fixed expenses. Examples are depreciation, rent, insurance, heat, and so on.

If, going back to the above illustration, it is assumed that fixed costs and expenses amount to $40,000, at least $40,000 of costs and expenses are incurred before even one unit is sold. If a million units are sold, however, income before deducting fixed expenses is $200,000. After fixed expenses, net income is $160,000. So, the income picture goes from a loss of $40,000 (where no units are produced) to a profit of $160,000 (where one million units are produced). Somewhere between these, however, is a point represented by a certain number of units at which there will be neither income nor loss—the break-even point.

.01   How to Compute the Break-Even Point

To determine the break-even point, let S equal the sales at the break-even point. Since sales at this point are equal to the total fixed costs and expenses ($40,000) plus variable costs and expenses ($1.80 per unit or 90 percent of sales):

$$S = \$40,000 + .9S$$
$$S - .9S = \$40,000$$
$$.1S = \$40,000$$
$$S = \$400,000$$

Even the above illustration oversimplifies the problem. It makes the assumption that all costs and expenses can be classified as either fixed or *variable*. However, in actual operations, expenses classified as fixed expenses may become variable where sales increase beyond a certain point, and some variable expenses may not vary in direct proportion to the sales.

Rent expense, for example, may not always be a fixed expense. A substantial increase in sales may create a need for additional showroom or salesroom space or, perhaps, expenses for salesperson's offices, or salesperson's commissions may rise unexpectedly when they have gone above a certain quota.

Then, there are types of hybrid expenses which may be classified as *semi-fixed*. For example, executives' salaries, association dues, subscriptions to periodicals and many other expenses are not in proportion to sales. Another unreality in the above problem is that as sales increase, there is a likelihood that sale prices will decrease because of larger orders. Now let's take a look at another situation:

Net sales		$2,500,000
Costs and expenses:		
Fixed	$ 250,000	
Variable	$1,500,000	1,750,000
Net income		$ 750,000

This company currently has under consideration an investment in a new plant which will cause an increase in its fixed expenses of $200,000.

The present break-even point is as follows:

$$S = \$250,000 + .6S$$
$$S - .6S = \$250,000$$
$$.4S = \$250,000$$
$$S = \$625,000$$

If the company builds the plant, the break-even calculation will be:

$$S = \$450,000 + .6S$$
$$S - .6S = \$450,000$$
$$.4S = \$450,000$$
$$S = \$125,000$$

If the plant expansion is undertaken, then the sales must be increased by $500,000 for the company to maintain its net income of $750,000, as follows:

$$S = \$450,000 + .6S + \$750,000$$
$$S - .6S = \$1,200,000$$
$$.4S = \$1,200,000$$
$$S = \$3,000,000$$
$$\text{Increase} = \$500,000 \ (\$3,000,000 \text{ less } \$2,500,000)$$

The situation can be analyzed using two alternatives. The maximum production with the present plant is 1,500,000 units. At an average sale price of $2 per unit, sales would be $3,000,000. With the new plant, sales are estimated to hit $5,000,000 (2,500,000 units @ $2 per unit).

	Without New Plant	With New Plant
Net Sales	$3,000,000	$5,000,000
Less: Fixed costs and expenses	250,000	450,000
	2,750,000	4,550,000
Less: Variable costs and expenses (60% of sales)	1,800,000	3,000,000
Net income	$ 950,000	$1,550,000

If sales do not increase, the increase in fixed costs and expenses of $200,000 would cut the net income to $550,000. The break-even point will have been boosted $500,000, and the sales will have to be increased by this amount to produce the current $750,000 of income. Alternatively, the net income can be increased by $600,000 if the sales figure is increased by $2,000,000. Although these figures are based on an assumption that all costs and expenses are fixed or variable, the break-even analysis focuses attention on the factors involved in costs and income and provides a basis for consideration of various problems.

CHAPTER 15
Change in Accounting Methods and Consideration of Accounting Periods

¶15,000   Overview

Changes in accounting procedures can take several forms and be prompted by different needs of the organization. For financial accounting as well as for tax accounting, changes require appropriate justification because, in the case of financial accounting, change can lessen comparability of financial statements and, in the case of tax accounting, can lead to a change in tax liability. Changes in accounting include, but are not limited to, changes in methods used to value inventory, changes in estimates regarding assets and liabilities and overall changes of method such as cash method to accrual method. This chapter addresses both the financial reporting of changes as mandated by the FASB and tax reporting of changes under the rules administered by the IRS. Changes in accounting periods are also addressed primarily from the tax accounting standpoint—since it is the tax law that places formidable restrictions on proposed changes in fiscal reporting periods.

The issues related to accounting changes are treated separately for financial accounting and tax accounting because the sources of authority and their diverse goals require very different measures to accomplish similar ends.

From a tax perspective, the IRS considers a change in the timing of the recognition of income or deductions change in method of accounting. Thus, the net is much wider than changing from cash to accrual or FIFO to LIFO. What principle controls the decision to capitalize or expense also constitutes a method of accounting. Such a change generally requires IRS approval, though there are important exceptions. In addition, the use of a "method" of accounting requires the consistent treatment of an item for at least two or more consecutive years. Methods include both those that are permitted and those that are impermissible.

¶15,001   Accounting Method Change for Tangible Property

Accounting and tax procedures are relatively settled regarding when certain costs should be placed on the balance sheet (capitalized) or on the income statement (expensed). But there have always been gray areas as well, especially with respect to items related to inventory and to repairs and maintenance. On December 23, 2011, the IRS issued temporary regulations provided in T.D. 9564 "Capital Expenditures" to clarify and expand the standards in the current regulations under sections 162(a) (trade or business expenses) and 263(a) (capitalization and inclusion in inventory costs of certain expense), and provide some bright-line tests for applying these standards.

In 2013, the IRS and Treasury Department issued the final version of these regulations in T.D. 9636 and T.D. 9689, collectively referred to as the "final tangible property regulations," along with corresponding revenue procedures, issued in 2014 and 2015, on related changes in method of accounting. The final regulations impact a number of code sections relating to expensing and capitalizing costs. Regulation sections modified include sections 1.162-3, 1.162-4, 1.168(i)-1, 1.168(i)-7, 1.168(i)-8, 1.263(a)-1, 1.263(a)-2, and 1.263(a)-3. The final tangible property regulations apply to taxable years beginning on or after January 1, 2014, but also permit a taxpayer to choose to apply them to taxable years beginning on or after January 1, 2012.

In 2014, the IRS modified or rescinded previous several Revenue Procedures interpreting the temporary regulations and issued new ones, the most significant of which are Rev. Proc. 2015-13, 2015-14 and 2015-20. The last of these modifies Rev. Proc. 2015-14 to permit small business taxpayers, defined as a businesses with total assets of less than $10 million or average annual gross receipts of $10 million or less for the prior three taxable years, to make certain tangible property changes in methods of accounting with an adjustment under section 481(a) of the Internal Revenue Code but without filing a Form 3115.

When a business has been using a method of accounting that is now impermissible, it is required to change to the method stipulated by the IRS. Since some of the requirements in the 2014 tangible property regulations differ from the typical practices of most businesses, it will be necessary to formally change to the required method. Though the changes are the same for large or small businesses, the process required is different. Large businesses, those with more than $10 million in annual sales or $10 million in assets will have to complete Form 3115 providing a complete explanation of the changes and detailing their impact on income ("the section 481 adjustment"). Smaller businesses must simply implement the changes and make the requisite adjustments to income to reflect the changes.

Among the information required on Form 3115 are descriptions of the taxpayer's overall method of accounting and then for each specific item to be changed, the current method used and proposed new method.

Expensing elections will primarily benefit small businesses. The regulations offer a safe harbor election allowing a business to deduct expenditures up to $500 ($5,000 if the taxpayer has an applicable financial statement). This is not considered a change in accounting method and so the election can be made on an annual basis. The election is made on the tax return by attaching a statement titled "Section 1.263(a)-1(f) *DeMinimis* Safe Harbor Election."

The regulations also clarify and facilitate the deduction of materials and supplies. The category "materials and supplies" includes tangible property that is either used or consumed and that are not inventory. This includes spare parts, lubricants, fuel and other materials expected to be consumed in the following 12 months. It also includes a unit of property that has a purchase price or production cost of $200 or less. More detailed information on the tangible property regulations is available in the chapter on depreciation.

.01   Filing for Change in Accounting Method

The change in accounting methods listed above require the submission of Form 3115. Two procedures exist under which an applicant may request a change in method of accounting.

1. Automatic change request procedures. Unless otherwise provided in pub-
    lished guidance, the applicant must file under the automatic change request
    procedures if:
    — The change in method of accounting is included in those procedures
       for the requested year of change, and
    — The applicant is within the scope of those procedures for the requested
       year of change.
            The "year of change" is the taxable year for which a change
    in method of accounting is effective, that is, the first taxable year the
    taxpayer uses the proposed method of accounting, even if no affected
    items are taken into account for that year. The year of change is also
    the first taxable year the taxpayer must comply with all the applicable
    provisions.
            A Form 3115 filed under these procedures may be reviewed by
    the IRS and the applicant will be notified if additional information is
    needed or the request is denied. No user fee is required.
            Ordinarily, a taxpayer is required to file a separate Form 3115
    for each change in method of accounting. However, in some cases it is
    required or permitted to file a single Form 3115 for particular concur-
    rent changes in method of accounting.
2. Advance consent request procedures. If the applicant is not within the scope
    of any automatic change request procedures for the requested year of change
    or the accounting method change being requested is not included in those
    procedures for the requested year of change, it may be possible to file under
    the advance consent request procedures. If the requested change is approved,
    the applicant will receive a letter ruling on the requested change. File a sepa-
    rate Form 3115 for each unrelated item or submethod. A user fee is required.

.02   Information for Form 3115

In addition to the other information required on line 12 of Form 3115, the
taxpayer must include the following:

1. The citation to the paragraph of the final tangible property regulations or
    temporary tangible property regulations that provides for the proposed
    method, or methods, of accounting to which the taxpayer is changing (e.g.,
    §1.162-3(a), §1.263(a)-3(i), §1.263(a)-3(k)).
2. If the taxpayer is changing any unit(s) of property under §1.263(a)-3(e) (or
    §1.263(a)-3T(e)) or, in the case of a building, is changing the identification
    of any building structure(s) or building system(s) under §1.263-3(e)(2)
    (or §1.263-3T(e)(2)) for purposes of determining whether amounts are
    deducted as repair and maintenance costs under section §1.162-4 (or
    §1.162-4T) or capitalized as improvement costs under §1.263(a)-3 (or

§1.263(a)-3T), the taxpayer must include a detailed description of the unit(s) of property, building structure(s), or buildings system(s) used under its present method of accounting and a detailed description of the unit(s) of property, building structure(s), and building system(s) under its proposed method of accounting, together with a citation to the paragraph of the final regulation or temporary regulation under which the unit of property is permitted.

.03   Designated Automatic Accounting Method Change Numbers (DCNs)

The IRS has assigned Designated Automatic Accounting Method Change Numbers (DCNs) to specific types of accounting method changes required by the final tangible property regulations. A few common DCNs are listed below with the corresponding accounting change. A complete list may be found in IRS Rev. Proc. 2014-16.

- DCN 184 A change to deducting amounts paid or incurred for repair and maintenance or a change to capitalizing amounts paid or incurred for improvements to tangible property and, if depreciable, to depreciating such property under section 167 or section 168. Includes a change, if any, in the method of identifying the unit of property, or in the case of a building, identifying the building structure or building systems for the purpose of making this change (§§1.162-4, 1.263(a)-3).
- DCN 186 Change to deducting non-incidental materials and supplies when used or consumed (§1.162-3(a)(1), (c)(1)).
- DCN 187 Change to deducting incidental materials and supplies when paid or incurred (§§1.162-3(a)(2), (c)(1)).
- DCN 188 Change to deducting non-incidental rotable and temporary spare parts when disposed of (§1.162-3(a)(3), (c)(2)).
- DCN 192 Change to capitalizing acquisition or production costs and, if depreciable, to depreciating such property under section 167 or section 168 (§1.263(a)-2).

Additional information on the specific requirements for accounting changes required by the "Tangible Property Regulations" may be found in the chapter on depreciation in this volume.

¶15,002   Developments in Treatment of Accounting Changes

The release of FASB 154, *Accounting Changes and Error Corrections,* in 2005 marked a major adjustment in the treatment of changes in accounting principles for financial accounting. This guidance was codified as ASC 250. The change was from the longstanding treatment of a change in accounting principle cumulatively as a separate line item on the income statement to a retrospective approach—requiring the restatement of prior financial statements as if the new principle had been employed in previous reporting periods—and an adjustment to beginning retained earnings of the earliest period being reported to "catch-up" the income or expense difference from prior years.

The FASB issued Statement No. 154 as a replacement of APB Opinion No. 20 and FASB Statement No. 3, in June 2005. The Statement applies to all voluntary changes in accounting principles and dramatically changes the requirements for accounting for and reporting of a change in accounting principles. Opinion 20 previously required that most voluntary changes in accounting principles be recognized by including in net income of the period of the change the cumulative effect of changing to the new accounting principle. Statement 154 requires that a change in method of depreciation, amortization, or depletion for long-lived, nonfinancial assets be accounted for as a change in accounting estimate that is brought about by a change in accounting principle. Opinion 20 previously required that such a change be reported as a change in accounting principle.

A change in accounting principle means a change from one generally accepted accounting principle to another generally accepted accounting principle. Thus, a change from an unacceptable principle to an acceptable one is not a change in principle, but the correction of an error. In addition, the initial adoption of an accounting principle to record or report a new accounting circumstance or to comply with a new accounting pronouncement is not a change in accounting principle. Members of the FASB expressed concern that because such changes are now to be treated as retroactive restatements, that the term *restatement*, already used to refer to changes brought about by the correction of accounting errors and irregularities, would shroud such changes in accounting principle in the same doubt that investors feel when they hear that a company is restating its earnings due to an error.

As the result of a change in accounting principle, certain other items may be directly or indirectly influenced. Deferred taxes, for example, are directly affected by a change in income. Direct changes are treated retrospectively along with the change that caused them. Indirect changes are handled currently. A bonus calculation, based on net income is an example of an indirectly influenced item. Prior periods are not modified for indirect items.

In some circumstances it may be difficult or practically impossible to determine the retrospective effects of a change in accounting principle. If so the change is instituted in the earliest year when its effects can be determined and carried forward from there.

The Board pointed out that this is an example of instances in which the Board concluded that the IASB requirements result in better financial reporting than U.S. GAAP (See IAS 8 in the Chapter, International Standards: Accounting).

Thus, the measure improves financial reporting because its requirements enhance the consistency of financial information between periods, and it also furthers convergence with international standards.

In keeping with the goal of simplifying U.S. GAAP, the Board decided to completely replace Opinion 20 and Statement 3 with one Statement rather than amending both. Therefore, Statement 154 carries forward many provisions of Opinion 20 without change, including:

- The provisions related to the reporting of a change in accounting estimate.
- A change in the reporting entity.
- The correction of an error.

For financial accounting purposes a change in accounting estimate, such as a change in the estimated lives of depreciable assets, is treated prospectively. The change is assumed to be the result of new information or additional experience. In the year the estimate is changed the new estimate is used and no attempt is made to correct past amounts reported. Since an estimate by definition is subject to correction, the change is simply applied in the current year and carried forward. Examples of items subject to estimate that may require revision include obsolete inventory, an allowance for doubtful accounts, periods to be benefited by deferred costs and estimated costs for future warranty agreements.

An example of a change in reporting entity is a change in the subsidiaries that are consolidated in the preparation of consolidated financial statements. In such a case the proper reporting requires the restatement of prior period financial statements that are being presented for comparison with the current year.

The correction of a material error is treated as a prior period adjustment to beginning retained earnings. This includes mathematical errors, errors in applying accounting principles and errors of omission. If more than one year is reported and affected by the error, the prior years are restated to show the corrected numbers.

FASB 154 also carries forward the provisions of FASB 3 that govern reporting accounting changes in interim financial statements.

¶15,003   IRS Automatic Approval Procedures for Accounting Period Changes

An automatic change in accounting method is a convenience for both the taxpayer and the IRS. If the change is one specified in a current Revenue Procedure, Form 3115 still needs to be filed with the return and submitted to the IRS, but the change will be deemed accepted. Described below are Revenue Procedures dealing with changes in accounting method.

.01   Rev. Proc. 2019-43

Rev. Proc. 2019-43 provides the current list of the automatic changes to which the automatic change procedures in Rev. Proc. 2015-13 apply. They are:

(1) **Gross income**—Up-front payments for network upgrades received by utilities (designated change number (DCN) = "91").

(2) **Commodity credit loans**—Treating amounts received as loans (DCN = "1").

(3) **Trade or business expenses**—

- Advances made by a lawyer on behalf of clients (DCN = "2");
- ISO 9000 costs (DCN = "3");
- restaurant or tavern smallwares packages (DCN = "4");
- timber grower fertilization costs (DCN = "86");
- materials and supplies;
- repair and maintenance costs;
- wireline and wireless network asset maintenance allowance and units of property accounting methods (DCNs = "158", "159");
- accounting method for taxpayers in the business of transporting, delivering or selling electricity (DCN = "160");
- accounting method for taxpayers in the business of generating steam or electric power (DCN = "182");
- cable network asset capitalization accounting methods (DCN = "209").

(4) **Bad debts**—

- Change from reserve method to specific charge-off method (DCN = "5");
- conformity election by bank after previous election automatically revoked (DCN = "211").

(5) **Interest expense and amortizable bond premium**—

- Revocation of Code Sec. 171(c) election (DCN = "16");
- change to comply with Code Sec. 163(e)(3) (DCN = "212").

(6) **Depreciation or amortization**—

- Impermissible to permissible method of accounting for depreciation or amortization (DCN = "7");

- permissible to permissible method of accounting for depreciation (DCN = "8");
- sale, lease or financing transactions (DCN = "10");
- change in general asset account treatment due to a change in the use of MACRS property (DCN = "87");
- **change in method of accounting** for depreciation due to a change in the use of MACRS property (DCN = "88");
- depreciation of qualified non-personal use vans and light trucks (DCN = "89";
- impermissible to permissible method of accounting for depreca- tion or amortization for disposed depreciable or amortizable property (DCN = "107");
- tenant construction allowances (DCN = "145");
- safe harbor method of accounting for determining the depreciation of certain tangible assets used by wireless telecommunications carriers (DCN = "157");
- partial dispositions of tangible depreciable assets to which the IRS's adjust- ment pertains (DCN = "198");
- depreciation of leasehold improvements (DCN = "199");
- permissible to permissible method of accounting for depreciation of MACRS property (DCN = "200");
- disposition of a building or structural component (DCN = "205");
- dispositions of tangible depreciable assets (other than a building or its structural components) (DCN = "206");
- dispositions of tangible depreciable assets in a general asset account (DCN = "207");
- depreciation of fiber optic transfer node and fiber optic cable used by a cable system operator (DCN = "210");
- revocation of partial disposition election under the remodel-refresh safe harbor (DCN = "221").

(7) **Research and experimental expenditures**—Changes to a different method or different amortization period (DCN = "17").

(8) **Elective expensing provisions**—Deduction for energy efficient com- mercial buildings (DCN = "152").

(9) **Computer software expenditures** (DCN = "18").

(10) **Start-up and organizational expenditures**—

- Start-up expenditures (DCN = "223");
- organizational expenditures under Code Sec. 248 (new) (DCN = "228");
- organizational expenditures under Code Sec. 709 (new) (DCN = "229").

(11) **Capital expenditures—**

- Package design costs (DCN = "19");
- linepack gas or cushion gas (DCN = "20");
- removal costs (DCN = "21");
- distributor commissions (DCN = "47");
- intangibles (DCN = "78");
- rotable spare parts safe harbor method (DCN = "109");
- repairable and reusable spare parts (DCN = "121");
- tangible property; railroad track structure expenditures (DCN = "213");
- remodel-refresh safe harbor method (DCN = "222").

(12) **Uniform capitalization (UNICAP) methods—**

- Certain UNICAP methods used by resellers and reseller-producers (DCN = "22");
- certain UNICAP methods used by producers and reseller-producers (DCN = "23");
- impact fees (DCN = "25");
- change to capitalizing environmental remediation costs (DCN = "77");
- change in allocating environmental remediation costs (DCN = "92");
- safe harbor methods for certain dealerships of motor vehicles (DCNs = "150", "151");
- change not to apply Code Sec. 263A to one or more plants removed from the list of plants that have a preproductive period in excess of 2 years (DCN = "181");
- change to a reasonable allocation method for self-constructed assets (DCN = "194"); real property acquired through foreclosure (DCN = "195"); sales-based royalties (DCN = "201");
- treatment of sales-based vendor chargebacks under a simplified method (DCN = "202");
- U.S. ratio method (DCN = "214"); depletion (DCN = "215");
- interest capitalization (DCN = "224").

(13) **Losses, expenses and interest with respect to transactions between related taxpayers—**Change to comply with Code Sec. 267 (DCN = "26").

(14) **Deferred compensation—**Deferred compensation (DCN = "28"); grace period contributions (DCN = "29").

(15) **Methods of accounting**—Change in overall method from the cash method to an accrual method (DCNs = "122", "123");

- multi-year insurance policies for multi-year service warranty contracts (DCN = "31");
- change to overall cash method (DCNs = "32", "33");
- nonaccrual-experience method (DCN = "35");
- interest accruals on short-term consumer loans (rule of 78's method) (DCN = "71");
- film producer's treatment of certain creative property costs (DCN = "85");
- deduction of incentive payments to health care providers (DCN = "90");
- change by bank for uncollected interest (DCN = "108");
- change from the cash method to an accrual method for specific items (DCN = "124");
- multi-year service warranty contracts (DCN = "125");
- overall cash method for specified transportation industry taxpayers (DCN = "126");
- change to overall cash/hybrid method for certain banks (DCN = "127");
- change to overall cash method for farmers (DCN = "128");
- nonshareholder contributions to capital under Code Sec. 118 (DCN = "129");
- debt issuance costs (DCN = "148");
- change in utility's treatment of transfers of interties (DCN = "226").

(16) **Taxable year of inclusion**—

- Accrual of interest on nonperforming loans (DCN = "36");
- advance rentals (DCN = "37");
- state or local income or franchise tax refunds (DCN = "38");
- capital cost reduction payments (DCN = "39");
- credit card annual fees (DCN = "81");
- credit card late fees (DCN = "82");
- advance payments (DCNs = "83", "84");
- credit card cash advance fees (DCN = "94");
- retainages (DCNs = "130", "217");
- change in applicable financial statements with respect to recognizing advance payments (DCN = "153").

(17) **Obligations issued at a discount**—U.S. savings bonds (Series E, EE or I) (DCN = "131").
(18) **Prepaid subscription income** (DCN = "132").

(19) **Taxable year incurred—**

- Timing of incurring liabilities for employee compensation (DCNs = "42", "133", "134");
- timing of incurring liabilities for real property taxes, personal property taxes, state income taxes and state franchise taxes (DCN = "43");
- timing of incurring liabilities under a workers' compensation act, tort, breach of contract or violation of law (DCN = "44");
- timing of incurring certain liabilities for payroll taxes (DCNs = "45", "113");
- cooperative advertising (DCN = "46"); timing of incurring certain liabilities for services or insurance (DCN = "106");
- rebates and allowances (DCN = "135");
- ratable accrual of real property taxes (DCN = "149");
- California franchise taxes (DCN = "154");
- gift cards issued as a refund for returned goods (DCN = "156");
- timing of incurring liabilities under the recurring item exception to the economic performance rules (DCN = "161");
- economic performance safe harbor for ratable service contracts (DCN = "220").

(20) **Rent**—Change from an improper method of inclusion of rental income or expense to inclusion in accordance with the rent allocation (DCN = "136").

(21) **Inventories—**

- Cash discounts (DCN = "48");
- estimating inventory shrinkage (DCN = "49");
- small taxpayer exception from requirement to account for inventories (DCNs = "50", "51");
- qualifying volume-related trade discounts (DCN = "53");
- impermissible methods of identification and valuation (DCN = "54");
- core alternative valuation method (DCN = "55");
- replacement cost for automobile dealers' parts inventory (DCN = "63");
- replacement cost for heavy equipment dealers' parts inventory (DCN = "96");
- rotable spare parts (DCN = "110");
- advance trade discount method (DCN = "111");
- permissible methods of identification and valuation (DCN = "137");
- change in the official used vehicle guide utilized in valuing used vehicles (DCN = "138");

- invoiced advertising association costs for new vehicle retail dealerships (DCN = "139");
- rolling average method of accounting for inventories (DCN = "114");
- sales-based vendor chargebacks (DCN = "203");
- changes to the cost complement of the retail inventory method (DCN = "204");
- changes within the retail inventory method (DCN = "225");
- change from currently deducting inventories to permissible methods of identification and valuation of inventories (new) (DCN = "230").

(22) **Last-in, first-out (LIFO) inventories—**

- Change from the LIFO method (DCN = "56");
- determining current-year cost under the LIFO method (DCN = "57");
- alternative LIFO method for retail automobile dealers (DCN = "58");
- used vehicle alternative LIFO method (DCN = "59");
- determining the cost of used vehicles purchased or taken as a trade-in (DCN = "60");
- change to the inventory price index computation (IPIC) method (DCN = "61");
- changes within the IPIC method (DCN = "62");
- changes to the vehicle-pool method (DCN = "112");
- changes within the used vehicle alternative LIFO method (DCN = "140");
- changes to dollar-value pools of manufacturers (DCN = "141").

(23) **Mark-to-market accounting method—**

- Commodities dealers, securities traders and commodities traders electing to use the mark-to-market method (DCN = "64");
- changing method of accounting from the mark-to-market method to a realization method (DCN = "218").

(24) **Bank reserves for bad debts**—Change from the Code Sec. 585 reserve method to the Code Sec. 166 specific charge-off method (DCN = "66").

(25) **Insurance companies—**

- Safe harbor method for premium acquisition expenses (DCN = "67");
- certain **changes in method of accounting** for Code Sec. 833 organizations (DCN = "155");
- change in qualification as life/nonlife insurance company (DCN = "219").

(26) **Discounted unpaid losses**—Composite method for discounting unpaid losses (DCN = "68").

(27) **Real estate mortgage investment conduit (REMIC)**—REMIC inducement fees (DCN = "79").

(28) **Functional currency**—Change in functional currency (DCN = "70").

(29) **Original issue discount**— *De minimis* original issue discount (OID) (DCN = "72"); proportional method of accounting for OID on a pool of credit card receivables (DCN = "183").

(30) **Market discount bonds**—Revocation of Code Sec. 1278(b) election (DCN = "73").

(31) **Short-term obligations**—Interest income on short obligations; stated interest on short-term loans of cash method banks (DCN = "75").

Rev. Proc. 2019-43 is generally effective for Form 3115 filed on or after November 8, 2019, for a year of change ending on or after March 31, 2019. Prior to the effective date for Rev. Proc. 2019-43, the list of automatic changes was included in Rev. Proc. 2018-31.

¶15,004   Significant Tax Changes

Probably the single most important change for the taxpayer was that Form 3115 requesting a change in method may now be filed any time during the year. Other new rules reduce or eliminate many of the complex provisions of the previous procedure including:

1. The Category A and Category B, and Designated A and Designated B have been eliminated.
2. The 90-day window at the *beginning* of an examination has been eliminated.
3. The 30-day window for taxpayers under *continuous examination* has been increased to 90 days.
4. The number of consecutive months the taxpayer is required to be under examination has been reduced from 18 to 12.
5. The definition of "under examination" has been clarified.
6. The consent requirement for taxpayers before an appeals officer or a federal court has been replaced with a notification procedure.
7. The various adjustment periods have been replaced with a single four-year adjustment period for both positive and negative adjustments.
8. Several of the terms and conditions relating to the adjustment have been eliminated.

¶15,005   Change in Method of Accounting Defined

A change in method of accounting includes a change in the overall plan of accounting for gross income or deductions, or a change in the treatment of any material item. A *material item* is any item that involves the proper time for the inclusion of the item in income or the taking of the item as a deduction.

In determining whether a taxpayer's accounting practice for an item involves timing, the relevant question is whether the practice permanently changes the amount of the taxpayer's lifetime income. If the practice does not permanently affect the taxpayer's lifetime income, but does or could change the taxable year in which income is reported, it involves timing and is, therefore, a method of accounting.

Consistency: Although a method of accounting may exist under this definition without a pattern of consistent treatment of an item, a method of accounting is not adopted in most instances without consistent treatment. The treatment of a material item in the same way in determining the gross income or deductions in two or more consecutively filed tax returns, without regard to any change in status of the method as permissible or not permissible, represents consistent treatment of that item. If a taxpayer treats an item properly in the first return that reflects the item, however, it is not necessary for the taxpayer to treat the item consistently in two or more consecutive tax returns to have adopted a method of accounting. If a taxpayer has adopted a method of accounting under the rules, the taxpayer cannot change the method by amending prior income tax returns.

Classification: A change in the classification of an item can constitute a change in the method of accounting if the change has the effect of shifting income from one period to another. A change in method of accounting does not include correction of mathematical or posting errors, or errors in the computation of a tax liability.

¶15,006   Filing Form 3115

Except as otherwise provided, a taxpayer must secure the consent of the Commissioner before changing a method of accounting for federal income tax purposes. In order to obtain the Commissioner's consent for a method change, a taxpayer must file a Form 3115, *Application for Change in Accounting Method* during the taxable year in which the taxpayer wants to make the proposed change.

The Commissioner can prescribe administrative procedures setting forth the limitations, terms, and conditions deemed necessary to permit a taxpayer to obtain consent to change a method of accounting. The terms and conditions the Commissioner can prescribe include the year of change, whether the change is to be made with an adjustment or on a cutoff basis, and the adjustment period.

Unless specifically authorized by the Commissioner, a taxpayer cannot request, or otherwise make, a retroactive change in method, regardless of whether the change is from a permissible or an impermissible method.

.01   Rev. Proc. 2015-13

The IRS updated and revised the procedures to obtain the IRS's consent to change a method of accounting. Rev. Proc. 2015-13 provides both procedures to obtain the:

(1) advance consent of the IRS to change an accounting method, and

(2) automatic consent of the IRS to change an accounting method.

If a taxpayer cannot make an accounting method change under the automatic change procedures, then the taxpayer must use the advance consent procedures. A taxpayer is eligible to request the IRS's consent under the advance consent or non-automatic change procedures if:

(1) on the date the taxpayer files a Form 3115 with the IRS National Office, the taxpayer is not eligible to use the automatic change procedures to make the change; and

(2) the requested year of change is not the final year of the trade or business (but exceptions apply

¶15,007   Method Change with Adjustment

Adjustments necessary to prevent amounts from being duplicated or omitted must be taken into account when the taxpayer's taxable income is computed under a method of accounting different from the method used to compute taxable income of the preceding tax year. When a change in method is applied, income for the taxable year preceding the year of change must be determined under the method of accounting that was then employed. Income for the year of change and the following taxable years must be determined under the new method as if the new method had always been used.

Required adjustments can be taken into account in determining taxable income in the manner and subject to the conditions agreed to by the Commissioner and the taxpayer. In the absence of an agreement, the adjustment is taken into account completely in the year of change, which limits the amount of tax where the adjustment is substantial. However, under the Commissioner's authority to prescribe terms and conditions for changes in method, specific adjustment periods are permitted that are intended to achieve an appropriate balance between mitigating distortions of income that result from accounting method changes and providing appropriate incentives for voluntary compliance.

¶15,008   Method Change Using a Cutoff Method

Certain changes can be made in a method and without an adjustment, using a cutoff method. Under a cutoff method, only the items arising on or after the beginning of the year of change are accounted for under the new method. Certain changes, such as changes in the last-in first-out (LIFO) inventory method, *must* be made using the cutoff method. Any items arising before the year of change or other operative date continue to be accounted for under the taxpayer's former method of accounting. Because no items are duplicated or omitted from income when a cutoff method is used to make a change, no adjustment is necessary.

¶15,009   Initial Method

A taxpayer can generally choose any permitted accounting method when filing the first tax return. IRS approval is not needed for the choice of the method. The method chosen must be used consistently from year to year and clearly show the taxpayer's income. A change in an accounting method includes a change not only in an overall system of accounting, but also in the treatment of any material item. Although an accounting method can exist without treating an item the same all the time, an accounting method is not established for an item, in most cases, unless the item is treated the same every time.

¶15,010   IRS Approval

After a taxpayer's first return has been filed, the taxpayer must get IRS approval to change the accounting method. If the current method clearly shows the income, the IRS will consider the need for consistency when evaluating the reason for changing the method used. The following changes require IRS approval:

1. A change from the cash method to an accrual method or vice versa unless this is an automatic change to an accrual method.
2. A change in the method or basis used to value inventory.
3. A change in the method of figuring depreciation, except certain permitted changes to the straight-line method for property placed in service before 1981.

Approval is not required in the following instances:

1. Correction of a math or posting error.
2. Correction of an error in computing tax liability.
3. An adjustment of any item of income or deduction that does not involve the proper time for including it in income or deducting it.
4. An adjustment in the useful life of a depreciable asset.

¶15,011   Reflections of Income

The important point to remember is that methods of accounting should clearly reflect income on a continuing basis, and that the IRS exercises its discretion and in a manner that generally minimizes distortion of income across taxable years on an annual basis. Therefore, if a taxpayer asks to change from a method of accounting that clearly reflects income, the IRS, in determining whether to consent to the taxpayer's request, will weigh the need for consistency against the taxpayer's reason for desiring to change the method of accounting.

¶15,012   Need for Adjustment

The adjustment period is the applicable period for taking into account an adjustment, whether positive (an increase in income) or negative (a decrease in income), required for the change in method of accounting. Adjustments necessary to prevent amounts from being duplicated or omitted are taken into account when the taxpayer's taxable income is computed under a method of accounting different from the method used to compute taxable income for the preceding taxable year. When there is a change in method of accounting, income for the year preceding the year of change must be determined under the method of accounting that was then employed, and income for the year of change and the following years must be determined under the new method of accounting.

¶15,013   Flexibility for Accrual Basis Taxpayers

In regulations issued in 2004 (Reg. §§1.263(a)-4 and -5), the IRS liberalized the rules for accrual basis taxpayers allowing deduction for certain prepaid expenses, bringing them in line with cash basis deduction rules. However, the rules were buried in the regulations and not widely known or publicized, so the IRS extended the deadline for making the election to change to this alternate method of accounting until the filing of 2005 tax returns in 2006 (Rev. Rul. 2005-9).

When a business using the accrual method incurs an expense—such as an annual casualty insurance premium—during the year, the accrual method generally requires the capitalization of the portion of the premium that extends to the following year, expensing only the portion representing an expense for the current year. Thus, the accrual-basis financial statements will reflect an asset account for prepaid or unexpired insurance. Until this IRS rule change the same treatment would be applicable for tax accounting as well. But this accounting method allows a current deduction of certain prepaid expenses if the benefit received from so doing does not extend past the earlier of 12 months or beyond the end of the following tax year. If the prepayment is made on the last day of the business' fiscal year, therefore, both periods would overlap and end on the same day. In addition to insurance, this method may also be beneficial to businesses in deducting taxes, warranty costs, rebates and refunds, worker's compensation awards, and service contracts.

To qualify for this accounting method for prepaid expenses it is necessary for taxpayers to complete IRS Form 3115 (under Reg. §1.263(a)-4(f)) using "Automatic Change Request 78." The Form 3115 should list each kind of expense for which the change from prepaid to immediate write-off is elected. The completed Form 3115 is attached to the taxpayer's tax return and a copy is also sent to the IRS in Washington D.C. (See Form 3115 instructions.)

As with any accounting method change, it is necessary to compute the amount of any adjustment to current income (under Internal Revenue Code section 481(a)) for beginning balances in prepaid expense accounts. The instructions for Form 3115 should be consulted. (See earlier ¶15,006, Filing Form 3115, and ¶15,007, Method Change with Adjustment.)

A section 481(a) adjustment is the amount necessary to prevent amounts of income or expense from being duplicated or omitted as a result of the taxpayer computing its taxable income for the year of change and thereafter using a different method of accounting as if the different method of accounting had always been used. The section 481(a) adjustment is computed as of the beginning of the year of change. For a change in method of accounting that affects multiple accounts, the taxpayer's section 481(a) adjustment for that change is a net 481(a) adjustment. In computing the net 481(a) adjustment for a change, the taxpayer must take into account all relevant accounts. For example, the net 481(a) adjustment for a change in the proper time for deducting salary bonuses under section 461 reflects any necessary adjustments for amounts of salary bonuses capitalized to inventory under section 263A. The term "section 481(a) adjustment" includes a net section 481(a) adjustment.

The IRS provides the following example to illustrate the process.

"A taxpayer that is not required to use inventories uses the overall cash receipts and disbursements method of accounting and changes to an overall accrual method of accounting. The taxpayer has $120,000 of income earned but not yet received (accounts receivable) and $100,000 of expenses incurred but not yet paid (accounts payable) as of the end of the taxable year preceding the year of change in method of accounting. A positive net section 481(a) adjustment of $20,000 ($120,000 accounts receivable less $100,000 accounts payable) is required as a result of the change in method of accounting."

The same procedure also enables the taxpayer to adopt the "recurring item exception" contained in Reg. §1.461-5. If not previously adopted, this will allow the current accrual and deduction of amounts that are to be paid by the time the tax return is filed or within 8½ months after the business' year-end. The election should indicate which specific expense items constitute recurring items and many or all of these may be the same as for the election relating to prepaid expenses. The flexibility provided by this rule allows businesses to smooth out the deduction of certain recurring expenses without compromising cash flow during a lean year. In the case of the casualty insurance deduction noted earlier, it became possible to accrue the unpaid expense in some years and take a current deduction, or prepay it in other years receiving the same deduction.

It should be noted that accrual basis taxpayers can only take advantage of the prepaid expensing election for expenses which have also met the "economic performance" rules set out in Reg. §1.461-4. Not all expenses can meet the economic performance test just by being paid; generally what is being paid for must also have been received. However, in the case of insurance, taxes, service contracts, awards, rebates or refunds, and worker's compensation award liabilities, economic performance is evidenced by the payment of the expense. On the other hand, rent and interest do not qualify for the economic performance test but can only be deducted by an accrual basis taxpayer with the passage of time.

¶15,014   90-Day and 120-Day Window Periods

A taxpayer under examination cannot file a Form 3115 to request a change in accounting methods except as provided in the 90-day window and 120-day window periods, and the consent of the district director. A taxpayer filing a Form 3115 beyond the time periods provided by the 90-day and 120-day windows will not be granted an extension of time to file except in unusual and compelling circumstances.

A taxpayer can file a Form 3115 during the first 90 days of any taxable year if the taxpayer has been under examination for at least 12 consecutive months as of the first day of the taxable year. The 90-day window is not available if the method of accounting the taxpayer is requesting to change is an issue under consideration at the time the Form 3115 is filed, or is an issue the examining agent has placed in suspense at the time.

A taxpayer requesting a change under the 90-day window must provide a copy of the Form 3115 to the examining agent at the same time the original form is filed with the IRS. The form must contain the name and telephone number of the examining agent, and the taxpayer must attach to the form a separate statement signed by the taxpayer certifying that, to the best of his or her knowledge, the same method of accounting is not an issue under consideration or an issue placed in suspense by the examining agent.

A taxpayer can file a Form 3115 to request a change in accounting method during the 120-day period following the date an examination ends regardless of whether a subsequent examination has commenced. The 120-day window is not available if the method of accounting the taxpayer is requesting to change is an issue under consideration at the time the form is filed or is an issue the examining agent has placed in suspense at the time of the filing.

A taxpayer requesting a change under the 120-day window rule must provide a copy of the Form 3115 to the examining agent for any examination that is in process at the same time the original form is filed with the IRS. The form must contain the name and telephone number of the examining agent, and must have a separate signed statement attached certifying that, to the best of the taxpayer's knowledge, the same method of accounting is not an issue under consideration or an issue placed in suspense by the examining agent.

¶15,015   Under Examination

A taxpayer is "under examination" if the taxpayer has been contacted in any manner by a representative of the IRS for the purpose of scheduling any type of examination of any of its federal income tax returns. If a consolidated return is being examined, each member of the consolidated group will be considered under examination for purposes of the accounting method change requirements.

However, according to the 1997 ruling, on the date a new subsidiary becomes affiliated with a consolidated group, a 90-day window period can be provided within which the parent of the group may request a method change on behalf of the new member, unless the subsidiary itself is already under examination. Previously, if a consolidated group was being examined, each member of the consolidated group was considered under examination regardless of the tax year under examination.

An examination of a taxpayer, or consolidated group of which the taxpayer is a member, is considered to end at the earliest of the date:

1. The taxpayer or consolidated group of which the taxpayer is a member receives a "no-change" letter.
2. The taxpayer or consolidated group of which the taxpayer is a member pays the deficiency—or proposed deficiency.
3. The taxpayer or consolidated group requests consideration by an appeals officer.
4. The taxpayer requests consideration by a federal court.
5. The date on which a deficiency, jeopardy, termination, bankruptcy, or receivership assessment is made.

A taxpayer under examination cannot ask to change an impermissible method of accounting if under examination for the year in which the taxpayer adopted the method, and it was an impermissible method of accounting in the year of adoption. A taxpayer under examination cannot ask to change a method to which it changed without permission if under examination for the year in which the unauthorized change was made. Under any other circumstance, a taxpayer under examination can change an accounting method only if the taxpayer requests the change under the applicable procedures, terms, and conditions set forth in the regulation.

¶15,016   Application Procedures

The IRS can decline to process any Form 3115 filed in situations in which it would not be in the best interest of sound tax administration to permit the requested change. In this regard, the IRS will consider whether the change in method of accounting would clearly and directly interfere with compliance efforts of the IRS to administer the income tax laws.

A change in the method of accounting filed must be made pursuant to the terms and conditions provided in the regulations. The rule notwithstanding, the IRS can determine, based on the unique facts of a particular case, terms and conditions more appropriate for a change different from the changes provided in the regulations.

In processing an application for a change in an accounting method, the IRS will consider all the facts and circumstances, including whether:

1. The method of accounting requested is consistent with the Tax Code regulations, revenue rulings, revenue procedures, and decisions of the United States Supreme Court.
2. The use of the method requested will clearly reflect income.
3. The present method of accounting clearly reflects income.
4. The request meets the need for consistency in the accounting area.
5. The taxpayer's reasons for the change are valid.
6. The tax effect of the adjustment is appropriate.
7. The taxpayer's books and records and financial statements will conform to the proposed method of accounting.
8. The taxpayer previously requested a change in the method of accounting for the same item but did not make the change.

If the taxpayer has changed the method of accounting for the same item within the four taxable years preceding the year of requesting a change for that item, an explanation must be furnished stating why the taxpayer is again requesting a change in the method for the same item. The IRS will consider the explanation in determining whether the subsequent request for change in method will be granted.

¶15,017   Consolidated Groups

Separate methods of accounting can be used by each member of a consolidated group. In considering whether to grant accounting method changes to group members, the IRS will consider the effects of the changes on the income of the group. A parent requesting a change in method on behalf of the consolidated group must submit any information necessary to permit the IRS to evaluate the effect of the requested change on the income of the consolidated group. A Form 3115 must be submitted for each member of the group for which a change in accounting method is requested. A parent can request an identical accounting method change on a single Form 3115 for more than one member of a consolidated group.

¶15,018   Separate Trades or Businesses

When a taxpayer has two or more separate and distinct trades or businesses, a different method of accounting may be used for each trade or business, provided the method of accounting used for each trade or business clearly reflects the overall income of the taxpayer as well as that of each particular trade or business. No trade or business is separate and distinct unless a complete and separate set of books and records is kept for that trade or business. If the reason for maintaining different methods of accounting creates or shifts profits or losses between the trades or businesses of the taxpayer so that income is not clearly reflected, the trades or businesses of the taxpayer are not separate and distinct.

¶15,019   Resolving Timing Issues: Appeals and Counsel Discretion

An appeals officer or counsel for the government may resolve a timing issue when it is in the interest of the government to do so. To reflect the hazards of litigation, they are authorized to resolve a timing issue by changing the taxpayer's method of accounting using compromise terms and conditions or they may use a nonaccounting method change basis using either an alternative-timing or a time-value-of-money resolution.

.01   Requirement to Apply the Law to the Facts

An appeals officer or counsel for the government resolving a timing issue must treat the issue as a change in method of accounting. The law must be applied without taking into account the hazards of litigation when determining the new method of accounting. An appeals officer or government official can change a taxpayer's method of accounting by agreeing to terms and conditions that differ from those applicable to an "examination-initiated" accounting method change.

The appeals officer may compromise on several points:

1. The year of change (by agreeing to a later year of change).
2. The amount of the adjustment (a reduced adjustment).
3. The adjustment period (a longer adjustment period).

If an appeals officer agrees to compromise the *amount* of an adjustment, the agreement must be in writing.

A change in a taxpayer's method of accounting ordinarily will *not defer the year of change* to later than the most recent taxable year under examination on the date of the agreement finalizing the change, and in no event will the year of change be deferred to later than the taxable year that includes the date of the agreement finalizing the change.

.02   Alternative Timing

An appeals officer can resolve a timing issue by not changing the taxpayer's method of accounting, and by the IRS and the taxpayer agreeing to alternative timing for all or some of the items arising during/prior to and during, the taxable years before appeals or a federal court. The resolution of a timing issue on an alternative-timing basis for certain items will not affect the taxpayer's method of accounting for any items not covered by the resolution.

.03   Time-Value-of-Money

An appeals officer or government counsel may resolve a timing issue by not changing the taxpayer's method of accounting, and by the IRS and the taxpayer agreeing that the taxpayer will pay the government a specified amount that approximates the time-value-of-money benefit the taxpayer derived from using its method of accounting for the taxable years before appeals or a federal court. This approach is instead of the method of accounting determined by the appeals officer to be the proper method of accounting. The "specified amount" is reduced by an appropriate factor to reflect the expense of litigation. The specified amount is not interest and cannot be deducted or capitalized under any provision of the law. An appeals officer may use any reasonable manner to compute the specified amount.

.04   Taxpayer's Advantage

As outlined above, these IRS requirements, which are part of the "new" IRS image, cover timing problems that have been resolved by the IRS on a nonaccounting-method change basis. They provide terms and conditions for IRS-initiated changes that are intended to encourage taxpayers to *voluntarily request a change from an impermissible method of accounting* rather than being contacted by an agent for examination. Under this approach, a taxpayer who is contacted for examination and required to change methods of accounting by the IRS generally receives less favorable terms and conditions than if the taxpayer had filed a request to change before being contacted for examination.

The regulations may be consistent with the policy of encouraging prompt voluntary compliance with proper tax accounting principles, but they appear to have some limitations. It is now easier for the taxpayer to change an accounting method, but the IRS ordinarily will not initiate an accounting method change if the change will place the taxpayer in a more favorable position than if the taxpayer had been contacted for examination. An examining agent will not initiate a change from an impermissible method that results in a negative adjustment. If the IRS declines to initiate such an accounting method change, the district director will consent to the taxpayer requesting a voluntary change.

¶15,020   Resolving Timing Issues: Discretion of Examining Agent

An examining agent proposing an adjustment on a timing issue will treat the issue as a change in method of accounting. In changing the taxpayer's method of accounting, the agent will properly apply the law to the facts without taking into account the hazards of litigation when determining the new method of accounting. An examining agent changing a taxpayer's method of accounting will impose an adjustment.

The change can be made using a cutoff method only in rare and unusual circumstances when the examining agent determines that the taxpayer's books and records do not contain sufficient information to compute the adjustment and the adjustment is not susceptible to reasonable estimation. An examining agent changing a taxpayer's method of accounting will effect the change in the earliest taxable year under examination (or, if later, the first taxable year the method is considered impermissible) with a one-year adjustment period.

¶15,021   Method Changes Initiated by the IRS

If a taxpayer does not regularly employ a method of accounting that clearly reflects his or her income, the computation of taxable income must be made in a manner that, in the opinion of the Commissioner, does clearly reflect income. The Commissioner has broad discretion in determining whether a taxpayer's method of accounting clearly reflects income, and the Commissioner's determination must be upheld unless it is clearly unlawful.

The Commissioner has broad discretion in selecting a method of accounting that properly reflects the income of a taxpayer once it has been determined that the taxpayer's method of accounting does not clearly reflect income. The selection can be challenged only upon showing an abuse of discretion by the Commissioner.

The Commissioner has the discretion to change a method of accounting even though the IRS had previously changed the taxpayer to that method if it is determined that the method of accounting does not clearly reflect the taxpayer's income. The discretionary power does not extend to requiring a taxpayer to change from a method of accounting that clearly reflects income to a method that, in the Commissioner's view, more clearly reflects income.

The accounting method of a taxpayer that is under examination, before an appeals office, or before a federal court, can be changed except as otherwise provided in published guidance. The service is generally precluded from changing a taxpayer's method of accounting for an item for prior taxable years if the taxpayer timely files a request to change the method of accounting for the item.

.01   Retroactive Method Change

Although the Commissioner is authorized to consent to a retroactive accounting method change, the taxpayer does not have a right to a retroactive change, regardless of whether the change is from a permissible or impermissible method.

Except under unusual circumstances, if a taxpayer who changes the method of accounting is subsequently required to change or modify that method of accounting, the required change or modification will not be applied retroactively provided that:

1. The taxpayer complied with all the applicable provisions of the consent agreement.
2. There has been no misstatement nor omission of material facts.
3. There has been no change in the material facts on which the consent was based.
4. There has been no change in the applicable law.
5. The taxpayer to whom consent was granted acted in good faith in relying on the consent, and applying the change or modification retroactively would be to the taxpayer's detriment.

.02   New Method Established

An IRS-initiated change that is final establishes a new method of accounting. As a result, a taxpayer is required to use the new method of accounting for the year of change and for all subsequent taxable years unless the taxpayer obtains the consent of the commissioner to change from the new method or the IRS changes the taxpayer from the new method on subsequent examination. As indicated above, the IRS is not precluded from changing a taxpayer from the new method of accounting if the IRS determined that the new method does not clearly reflect the taxpayer's income. A taxpayer who executes a closing agreement finalizing an IRS initiated accounting method change will not be required to change or modify the new method for any taxable year for which a federal income tax return has been filed as of the date of the closing agreement, provided that:

1. The taxpayer has complied with all the applicable provisions of the closing agreement.
2. There has been no taxpayer fraud, malfeasance, or misrepresentation of a material fact.
3. There has been no change in the material facts on which the closing agreement was based.
4. There has been no change in the applicable law on which the closing agreement was based.

.03   Required Change or Modification of New Method

The IRS may require a taxpayer to change or modify the new method in the earliest open taxable year if the taxpayer fails to comply with the applicable provisions of the closing agreement, or upon a showing of taxpayer's fraud, malfeasance, or misrepresentation of a material fact. The taxpayer can be required to change or modify the new method in the earliest open taxable year in which the material facts have changed, and can also be required to change or modify the new method in the earliest open taxable year in which the applicable law has changed. For this purpose, a change in the applicable law includes:

1. A decision of the U.S. Supreme Court.
2. The enactment of legislation.
3. The issuance of temporary or final regulations.
4. The issuance of a revenue ruling, revenue procedure, notice, or other guidance published in the Internal Revenue Bulletin.

Except in rare and unusual circumstances, a retroactive change in applicable law is deemed to occur when one of the events described in the preceding sentence occurs and not when the change in law is effective.

¶15,022   Accounting Periods

Taxable income must be figured on the basis of a tax year. A *tax year* is an annual accounting period for keeping records and reporting income and expenses. The tax years usable are:

1. A calendar year.
2. A fiscal year.

The tax year is adopted in the first year that an income tax return is filed. The tax year must be adopted by the due date, not including extensions, for filing a return for that year. The due date for individual and partnership returns is the 15th day of the 4th month after the end of the tax year. "Individuals" include sole proprietorships, partners, and S corporation shareholders. The due date for filing returns for corporations and S corporations is the 15th day of the 3rd month after the end of the tax year. If the 15th day of the month falls on a Saturday, Sunday, or legal holiday, the due date is the next business day.

.01   Calendar Year

If a calendar year is chosen, the taxpayer must maintain books and records and report income and expenses from January 1 through December 31 of each year. If the first tax return uses the calendar year and the taxpayer later begins business as a sole proprietor, becomes a partner in a partnership, or becomes a shareholder in an S corporation, the calendar year must continue to be used unless the IRS approves a change. Anyone can adopt the calendar year. However, if any of the following apply, the calendar year must be used:

1. The taxpayer does not keep adequate records.
2. The taxpayer has no annual accounting period.
3. The taxpayer's tax year does not qualify as a fiscal year.

.02   Fiscal Year

A fiscal year is 12 consecutive months ending on the last day of any month except December. A 52–53-week tax year is a fiscal year that varies from 52 to 53 weeks. If a fiscal year is adopted, books and records must be maintained, and income and expenses reported using the same tax year.

A 52–53-week tax year may be elected if books and records are kept, and income and expenses are reported on that basis. If this election is chosen, the tax year will be 52 or 53 weeks long, and will always end on the same day of the week. The tax year can end only on the same day of the week that:

1. Last occurs in a particular month.
2. Occurs nearest to the last day of a particular calendar month.

To make the choice, a statement with the following information is attached to the tax return for the 52–53-week tax year:

1. The month in which the new 52–53-week tax year ends.
2. The day of the week on which the tax year always ends.
3. The date the tax year ends. It can be either of the following dates on which the chosen day:
   a. Last occurs in the month in (1).
   b. Occurs nearest to the last day of the month in (1).

When depreciation or amortization is figured, a 52–53-week tax year is considered a year of 12 calendar months unless another practice is consistently used. To determine an effective date, or apply provisions of any law, expressed in terms of tax years beginning, including, or ending on the first or last day of a specified calendar month, a 52–53-week tax year is considered to:

1. Begin on the first day of the calendar month beginning nearest to the first day of the 52–53-week tax year.
2. End on the last day of the calendar month ending nearest to the last day of the 52–53-week tax year.

If the month in which a 52–53-week tax year ends is changed, a return must be filed for the short tax year if it covers more than 6 but less than 359 days. If the short period created by the change is 359 days or more, it should be treated as a full tax year. If the short period created is 6 days or less, it is not a separate tax year. It is to be treated as part of the following year.

A corporation figures tax for a short year under the general rules described for individuals. There is no adjustment for personal exemptions.

.03 Improper Tax Year

A calendar year is a tax year of 12 months that ends on December 31, and a fiscal year is a tax year of 12 months that ends on the last day of any month except December, including a 52–53-week tax year. If business operations start on a day other than the last day of a calendar month and adopt a tax year of exactly 12 months from the date operations began, the taxpayer has adopted an *improper* tax year. The requirements for a calendar or fiscal tax year, including a 52–53-week tax year, have not been met. To change to a proper tax year, one of the following requirements must be met:

1. An amended tax return should be based on a calendar year.
2. IRS approval should be sought to change to a tax year, other than a calendar year.

.04   Business Purpose Tax Year

A business purpose tax year is an accounting period that has a substantial business purpose for its existence.

In considering whether there is a business purpose for a tax year, significant weight is given to tax factors. A prime consideration is whether the change would create a substantial distortion of income. The following are examples of distortions of income:

1. Deferring substantial income or shifting substantial deductions from one year to another to reduce tax liability.
2. Causing a similar deferral or shifting for any other person, such as a partner or shareholder.
3. Creating a short period in which there is a substantial net operating loss.

The following nontax factors, based on convenience for the taxpayer, are generally not sufficient to establish a business purpose for a particular year:

1. Using a particular year for regulatory or financial accounting purposes.
2. Using a particular pattern, such as typically hiring staff during certain times of the year.
3. Using a particular year for administration purposes, such as:
    a. Admission or retirement of partners or shareholders.
    b. Promotion of staff.
    c. Compensation or retirement arrangements with staff, partners, or shareholders.
4. Using a price list, model year, or other item that changes on an annual basis.
5. Deferring income to partners or shareholders.

.05   Natural Business Year

One nontax factor that may be sufficient to establish a business purpose for a tax year is an annual cycle of business, called a "natural business year." A natural business year exists when business has a peak and a nonpeak period. The natural business year is considered to end at or soon after the end of the peak period. A business whose income is steady from month-to-month all year would not have a natural business year as such. A natural business year is considered a substantial business purpose for an entity changing its accounting period. The IRS will ordinarily approve this change unless it results in a substantial deferral of income or another tax advantage.

The IRS provides a procedure for a partnership, an S corporation, or a personal service corporation to retain or automatically change to a natural business year as determined by the 25 percent test. It also allows an S corporation to adopt, retain, or change to a fiscal year that satisfies the "ownership tax year test." The 25 percent test uses the method of accounting used for the tax returns for each year involved. To figure the 25 percent test:

1. The gross sales and services receipts for the most recent 12-month period that includes the last month of the requested fiscal year are totaled for the 12-month period that ends before the filing of the request. Gross sales and services receipts for the last 2 months of that 12-month period are then totaled.
2. The percentage of the receipts for the 2-month period is then determined by dividing the total of the 2-month period by the total for the 12-month period. The percentage should be carried to two decimal places.
3. The percentage following steps 1 and 2 should then be figured for the two 12-month periods just preceding the 12-month period used in 1.

If the percentage determined for each of the three years equals or exceeds 25 percent, the requested fiscal year is the *natural business year*. If the partnership, S corporation, or personal service corporation qualifies for more than one natural business year, the fiscal year producing the higher average of the three percentages is the natural business year. If the partnership, S corporation, or personal service corporation does not have at least 47 months of gross receipts—which may include a predecessor organization's gross receipts—it cannot use this automatic procedure to obtain permission to use a fiscal year.

If the requested tax year is a 52–53-week tax year, the calendar month ending nearest the last day of the 52–53-week tax year is treated as the last month of the requested tax year for purposes of computing the 25 percent test.

An S corporation or corporation electing to be an S corporation qualifies for automatic approval if it meets the ownership tax year test. The test is met if the corporation is adopting, retaining, or changing to a tax year and shareholders holding more than 50 percent of the issued and outstanding shares of stock on the first day of the requested tax year have, or are all changing to, the same tax year.

.06   Change in Tax Year

A tax year change must be approved by the IRS. A current Form 1128 must be filed by the 15th day of the end calendar month after the close of the short tax year to get IRS approval. The *short tax year* begins on the first day after the end of the present tax year and ends on the day before the first day of the new tax year. If the short tax year required to effect a change in tax years is a year in which the taxpayer has a net operating loss (NOL), the NOL must be deducted ratably over a six-year period from the first tax year after the short period.

A husband and wife who have different tax years cannot file a joint return. There is an exception to this rule if their tax years began on the same date and ended on different dates because of the death of either or both. If a husband and wife want to use the same tax year so they can file a joint return, the method of changing a tax year depends on whether they are newly married. A newly married husband and wife with different tax years who wish to file a joint return can change the tax year of one spouse without first getting IRS approval.

The correct user fee must be included, if any. The IRS charges a user fee for certain requests to change an accounting period or method, certain tax rulings, and determination letters. The fee is reduced in certain situations and for certain requests, such as a request for substantially identical rulings for related entities.

.07   Year of Change

While this heading and the one above are similar, the connotation is somewhat different. The year of change is the taxable year for which a change in the method of accounting is effective, that is, the first taxable year the new method is used even if no affected items are taken into account for that year. The year of change is also the first taxable year for taking an adjustment and complying with all the terms and conditions accompanying the change.

.08   Partnership

A partnership must conform its tax year to its partners' tax years unless the partnership can establish a business purpose for a different period. The rules for the required tax year for partnerships are:

1. If one or more partners having the same tax year own a majority interest— more than 5 percent—in partnership profits and capital, the partnership must use the tax year of those partners.
2. If there is no majority interest tax year, the partnership must use the tax year of its principal partners. A principal partner is one who has a 5 percent or more interest in the profits or capital of the partnership.
3. If there is no majority interest tax year and the principal partners do not have the same tax year, the partnership generally must use a tax year that results in the least aggregate deferral of income to the partners.

If a partnership changes to a required tax year because of these rules, the change is considered to be initiated by the partnership with IRS approval. No formal application for change in the tax year is needed. Any partnership that changes to a required tax year must notify the IRS by writing at the top of the first page of its tax return for its first required tax year: *Filed Under Section 806 of the Tax Reform Act of 1986.*

The tax year that results in the least aggregate deferral of income is determined by:

1. Figuring the number of months of deferral for each partner using one partner's tax year. The months of deferral are found by counting the months from the end of that tax year forward to the end of each other partner's tax year.
2. Each partner's months of deferral figured in step (1) are multiplied by that partner's share of interest in the partnership profits for the year used in step (1).
3. The amounts in step (2) are added to get the aggregate (total) deferral for the tax year used in step (1).
4. Steps (1) through (3) are repeated for each partner's tax year that is different from the other partners' years.

The partners' tax year that results in the lowest aggregate—total—number is the tax year that must be used by the partnership. If more than one year qualifies as the tax year that has the least aggregate deferral of income, the partnership can choose any year that qualifies. If one of the tax years that qualifies is the partnership's existing tax year, the partnership must retain that tax year.

.09   S Corporations

If a business meets the requirements of a small business corporation, it can elect to be an S corporation. All S corporations, regardless of when they became an S corporation, must use a *permitted tax year*. A permitted tax year is the calendar year or any other tax year for which the corporation establishes a business purpose.

.10   Personal Service Corporations

A personal service corporation must use a calendar year unless it can establish a business purpose for a different period or it makes a Section 444 election (discussed below). For this purpose, a corporation is a personal service corporation if all of the following conditions are met:

1. The corporation is a C corporation.
2. The corporation's principal activity during the testing period is the performance of personal services.
3. Employee-owners of the corporation perform a substantial part of the services during the testing period.
4. Employee-owners own more than 10 percent of the corporation's stock on the last day of the testing period.

The principal activity of a corporation is considered to be the performance of personal services if, during the testing period, the corporation's compensation costs for personal service activities is more than 50 percent of its total compensation costs.

Generally, the *testing period for a tax year is the prior tax year.* The testing period for the first tax year of a new corporation starts with the first day of the tax year and ends on the earlier of the following dates:

1. The last day of its tax year.
2. The last day of the calendar year in which the tax year begins.

The *performance of personal services* involves any activity in the fields of health, veterinary services, law, engineering, architecture, accounting, actuarial science, performing arts, or certain consulting services.

An employee-owner of a corporation is a person who:

1. Is an employee of the corporation on any day of the testing period.
2. Owns any outstanding stock of the corporation on any day of the testing period.

A further clarification of the definition of an independent contractor by the 1997 Act states, "A person who owns any outstanding stock of the corporation and who performs personal services for or on behalf of the corporation is treated as an *employee* of the corporation. This rule applies even if the legal form of the person's relationship to the corporation is such that the person would be considered an independent contractor for other purposes."

.11   Section 444 Election

A partnership, S corporation, or personal service corporation can elect under Section 444 of the Internal Revenue Code to use a tax year different from its required tax year. Certain restrictions apply to the election. In addition, a partnership or S corporation may have to make a payment for the deferral period. The Section 444 election does not apply to any partnership, S corporation, or personal service corporation that establishes a business purpose for a different period.

A partnership, S corporation, or personal service corporation can make a Section 444 election if it meets all the following requirements:

1. It is not a member of a tiered structure.
2. It has not previously had a Section 444 election in effect.
3. It elects a year that meets the deferral period requirement.

The determination of the *deferral period* depends on whether the partnership, corporation, or personal service corporation is retaining its current tax year or adopting or changing its tax year with a Section 444 election.

A partnership, S corporation, or personal service corporation can make a Section 444 election to *retain* its tax year only if the deferral period of the new tax year is three months or less. The deferral period is the number of months between the beginning of the retained year and the close of the first required tax year.

If the partnership, S corporation, or personal service corporation is *changing* to a tax year other than its required year, the deferral period is the number of months from the end of the new tax year to the end of the required tax year. The IRS will allow a Section 444 election only if the deferral period of the new tax year is less than the shorter of:

1. Three months.
2. The deferral period of the tax year being changed. This is the tax year for which the partnership, S corporation, or personal service corporation wishes to make the Section 444 election.

If the tax year is the same as the required tax year, the deferral period is zero. A Section 444 election is made by filing a form with the IRS by the earlier of:

1. The due date of the income tax return resulting from the 444 election.
2. The 15th day of the 6th month of the tax year for which the election will be effective. For this purpose, the month in which the tax year begins is counted, even if it begins after the first day of that month. The Section 444 election stays in effect until it is terminated. If the election is terminated, another Section 444 election cannot be made for any tax year. The election ends when any of the three corporations does any of the following:
   a. Changes its tax year to a required tax year.
   b. Liquidates.
   c. Willfully fails to comply with the required payments or distributions.
   d. Becomes a member of a tiered structure.

The election also ends if:

1. An S corporation's election is terminated. However, if the S corporation immediately becomes a personal service corporation, it can continue the Section 444 election of the S corporation.
2. A personal service corporation ceases to be a personal service corporation. If the personal service corporation elects to be an S corporation, it can continue the election of the personal service corporation.

.12   Corporations

A new corporation establishes its tax year when it files its first return. A newly reactivated corporation that has been inactive for a number of years is treated as a new taxpayer for the purpose of adopting a tax year. A corporation other than an S corporation, a personal service corporation, or a domestic international sales corporation (C-DISC) can change its tax year without getting IRS approval if all the following conditions are met:

1. It must not have changed its tax year within the 10 calendar years ending with the calendar year in which the short tax year resulting from the change begins.
2. Its short tax year must not be a tax year in which it has a net operating loss.
3. Its taxable income for the whole tax year, if figured on an annual basis, is 80 percent or more of its taxable income for the tax year before the short tax year.
4. If a corporation is one of the following for either the short tax year or the tax year before the short tax year, it must have the same status for both the short tax year and the prior tax year.
    a. Personal holding company.
    b. Foreign personal holding company.
    c. Exempt organization.
    d. Foreign corporation not engaged in a trade or business within the United States.
5. It must not apply to become an S corporation for the tax year that would immediately follow the short tax year required to effect the change.

The corporation must file a statement with the IRS office where it files its tax return. The statement must be filed by the due date for the short tax year required by the change. It must indicate the corporation is changing its annual accounting period, and show that all the preceding conditions have been met. If the corporation does not meet all the conditions because of later adjustments in establishing tax liability, the statement will be considered a timely application to change the corporation's annual accounting period to the tax year indicated in the statement.

The IRS will waive conditions (1) and (5) above, as well as conditions (2) and (3)(c) outlining automatic approval criteria for a corporation that:

1. Meets all the other conditions.
2. Elected to be an S corporation for the tax year beginning January 1, 1997.

3. It must:
   a. Write "Filed" at the top of the forms required.
   b. Write "Attention, Entity Control" on the envelope.
   c. Mail the forms to the IRS where the corporation files its return.

Corporations can automatically change their tax year if it cannot meet the five conditions and has not changed its annual accounting period within 6 calendar years or in any of the calendar years of existence, and if the corporation is *not any of the following*:

1. A member of a partnership.
2. A beneficiary of a trust or an estate.
3. An S corporation.
4. An interest-charging DISC or a foreign sales corporation (FSC).
5. A personal service corporation.
6. A controlled foreign corporation.
7. A cooperative association.
8. Certain tax-exempt organizations.

¶15,023   Changes During the Tax Year

A corporation, other than an S corporation, a personal service corporation, or a domestic international sales corporation (IC-DISC) can change its tax year without getting IRS approval if all the following conditions are met:

1. It must not have changed its tax year within the 10 calendar years in which the short tax year resulting from the change begins.
2. Its short tax year must not be a tax year in which it has a net operating loss (NOL).
3. Its taxable income for the short tax year, when figured on an annual basis, annualized, is 80 percent or more of its taxable income for the tax year before the short tax year.
4. If a corporation is one of the following for either the short tax year or the tax year before the short tax year, it must have the same status for both the short tax and the prior tax year.
5. It must not apply to become an S corporation for the tax year that would immediately follow the short tax year required to effect the change.

The corporation must file a statement with the IRS office where it files its tax return. The statement must be filed by the due date, including extensions, for the short tax year required by the change. It must indicate the corporation is changing its annual accounting period, and that all the preceding conditions have been met.

Certain corporations can *automatically* change their tax year by meeting all the following criteria:

1. It cannot meet the conditions listed earlier.
2. It has not changed its annual accounting period within six calendar years of existence, or in any of the calendar years of existence, if less than six years.

CHAPTER 16
Auditor Independence and the Audit Committee

¶16,000   Overview

The Public Company Accounting Oversight Board (PCAOB) is just one important step toward restoring investor confidence in auditors and, more generally, in the capital markets. The rules regarding independence standards for public company auditors that the Securities and Exchange Commission (SEC) adopted in January 2003 are viewed by the agency as another important step.

The Commission points out that with the accusatory headlines pointing at the accounting profession, it is perceived as no longer acting in a manner that puts investors first. Whether that assertion is true or not really does not matter anymore, according to the SEC. The perception is so strong in the minds of so many people that it has been affecting business activities, investment decisions, and the markets.

¶16,001   Importance of Audit Committee

The emphasis of the rules on auditor independence are aimed at addressing an auditor's independence for the registrant it audits *in both fact and appearance*.

The independence and importance of the independent auditor and audit committee were forcibly emphasized when the Commission adopted rules in 2003, directing the national securities exchanges and national securities associations (self-regulatory organizations) to prohibit the listing of any security of an issuer that is not in compliance with the audit committee requirements established by The Sarbanes-Oxley Act of 2002. These rules and amendments implement the requirements of the Securities Exchange Act of 1934, as added by section 301 of the Sarbanes-Oxley Act.

¶16,002   Requirements for Audit Committee

Under these rules, national securities exchanges and national securities associations are prohibited from listing any security of an issuer that is not in compliance with the following requirements:

- Each member of the audit committee of the issuer must be independent, according to the specified criteria in section 10A(m).
- The audit committee must be directly responsible for the appointment, compensation, retention, and oversight of the work of any registered public accounting firm engaged for the purpose of preparing or issuing an audit report or performing other audit, review, or attest services for the issuer, and the registered public accounting firm must report directly to the audit committee.
- The audit committee must establish procedures for the receipt, retention, and treatment of complaints regarding accounting, internal accounting controls, or auditing matters, including procedures for the confidential, anonymous submission by employees of concerns regarding questionable accounting or auditing matters.
- The audit committee must have the authority to engage independent counsel and other advisors, as it determines necessary to carry out its duties.
- The issuer must provide appropriate funding for the audit committee.

.01   Criteria for Committee Members

The rules established two criteria for audit committee member independence:

1. Audit committee members must be barred from accepting any consulting, advisory, or compensatory fee from the issuer or any subsidiary, other than in the member's capacity as a member of the Board or any Board committee.
2. An audit committee member must not be an affiliated person of the issuer or any subsidiary apart from capacity as a member of the Board or any Board committee.

.02   Specific Rules for Foreign Issuers

The rules apply to both domestic and foreign listed issuers. It is important to note that, based on significant input from, and dialogue with, foreign regulators and foreign issuers and their advisers, several provisions, applicable only to foreign private issuers, have been included that seek to address the special circumstances of particular foreign jurisdictions. These provisions include:

- Allowing nonmanagement employees to serve as audit committee members, consistent with "co-determination" and similar requirements in some countries.
- Permitting shareholders to select or ratify the selection of auditors, also consistent with requirements in many foreign countries.
- Allowing alternative structures, such as boards of auditors, to perform auditor oversight functions where such structures are provided for under local law.
- Addressing the issue of foreign government shareholder representation on audit committees.

The rules also make several updates to the Commission's disclosure requirements regarding audit committees, including updates to the audit committee financial expert disclosure requirements for foreign private issuers.

The release also provides guidance on the provision of nonaudit services by foreign accounting firms, including the treatment of legal services and tax advice. The SEC also stands ready to work with other regulatory bodies on these issues.

¶16,003   Stricter Requirements Regarding Auditor Independence

The SEC adopted amendments to its existing requirements regarding auditor independence to enhance the independence of accountants who audit and review financial statements and prepare attestation reports filed with the SEC. The final rules emphasize the critical role played by audit committees in the financial reporting process and the unique position of audit committees in ensuring auditor independence.

Consistent with the directions in the Sarbanes-Oxley Act, the SEC adopted rules to:

- Revise the Commission's regulations related to the nonaudit services that, if provided to an audit client, would impair an accounting firm's independence.
- Require an issuer's audit committee to preapprove all audit and nonaudit services provided to the issuer by the auditor of an issuer's financial statements.
- Prohibit certain partners on the audit engagement team from providing audit services to the issuer for more than five or seven consecutive years,

depending on the partner's involvement in the audit, except that certain small accounting firms may be exempted from this requirement. The rules provide that firms with fewer than five audit clients and fewer than ten partners may be exempt from the partner rotation and compensation provisions, provided each of these engagements is subject to a special review by the PCAOB at least every three years.

- Prohibit an accounting firm from auditing an issuer's financial statements if certain members of management of that issuer had been members of the accounting firm's audit engagement team within the one-year period preceding the commencement of audit procedures.
- Require that the auditor of an issuer's financial statements report certain matters to the issuer's audit committee, including "critical" accounting policies used by the issuer.
- Require disclosures to investors of information related to audit and nonaudit services provided by, and fees paid to, the auditor of the issuer's financial statements.
- In addition, an accountant would not be independent from an audit client if the audit partner received compensation based on selling engagements to that client for services other than audit, review, and attest services.

These rules also have an impact on foreign accounting firms that conduct audits of foreign subsidiaries and affiliates of U.S. issuers as well as of foreign private issuers. Many of the modifications to the proposed rules, such as those limiting the scope of partner rotation and personnel subject to the "cooling off period," have the added benefit of addressing particular concerns raised about the international implications of these requirements. Additional time is being afforded to foreign accounting firms with respect to compliance with rotation requirements. Guidance on the provision of nonaudit services by foreign accounting firms, including the treatment of legal services and tax services is provided in the final rule.

Keep in mind that the guidelines discussed here are for public reporting entities. Independence related to audits of private companies can be found in the AICPA Code of Professional Conduct, which follows a threats and safeguards model of independence.

¶16,004   Background for Amendments to Auditor Independence

Title II of the Sarbanes-Oxley Act, entitled "Auditor Independence," required the Commission to adopt, by January 26, 2003, final rules under which certain nonaudit services are prohibited, conflict of interest standards are strengthened, auditor partner rotation and second partner review requirements are also strengthened, and the relationship between the independent auditor and the audit committee are clarified and enhanced.

These rules are amendments to current SEC rules regarding auditor independence. The final rules advance the SEC's policy goal of protecting the millions of people who invest in securities markets in reliance on financial statements that are prepared by public companies and other issuers and that, as required by Congress, are audited by independent auditors. The final rules were an attempt at striking a reasonable balance among commenters' differing views about the proposals while achieving the Commission's public policy goals.

As directed by the Sarbanes-Oxley Act, the rules focus on key aspects of auditor independence:

- The provision of certain nonaudit services.
- The unique ability and responsibility of the audit committee to insulate the auditor from the pressures that may be exerted by management.
- The potential conflict of interest that can be created when a former member of the audit engagement team accepts a key management position with the audit client.
- The need for effective communication between the auditor and audit committee.

In addition, under the final rules, an accountant would not be independent from an audit client if any audit partner received compensation based directly on selling engagements to that client for services other than audit, review, and attest services.

.01 Additions to the Securities Exchange Act of 1934

Title II of the Sarbanes-Oxley Act added subsections (g) through (l) to section 10A of the Securities Exchange Act of 1934 as follows:

- Section 201 adds subsection (g), which specifies that a number of nonaudit services are prohibited. Many of these services were previously prohibited by the Commission's independence standards adopted in November 2000 (with some exceptions and qualifications). The rules amend the Commission's existing rules on auditor independence and clarify the meaning and scope of the prohibited services under the Sarbanes-Oxley Act.
- Section 201 also adds subsection (h), which requires that nonaudit services that are *not* prohibited under the Sarbanes-Oxley Act and the Commission's rules be subject to preapproval by the registrant's audit committee. These rules specify the requirements for obtaining such preapproval from the registrant's audit committee.
- Section 202 adds subsection (i), which requires an audit committee to preapprove allowable nonaudit services and specifies certain exceptions to the requirement to obtain preapproval. These rules specify the requirements of

the registrant's audit committee for preapproving nonaudit services by the
auditor of the registrant's financial statements.

- Section 203 adds subsection (j), which establishes mandatory rotation of
the lead partner and the concurring partner every five years. These rules
expand the number of engagement personnel covered by the rotation requirement and clarify the "time out" period.
- Section 204 adds subsection (k), which requires that the auditor report on
a timely basis certain information to the audit committee. In particular, the
Sarbanes-Oxley Act requires that the auditor report to the audit committee
on a timely basis:
  — Alternative accounting treatments that have been discussed with management along with the potential ramifications of using those alternatives.
  — Other written communications provided by the auditor to management,
  including a schedule of unadjusted audit differences. These rules strength-
  en the relationship between the audit committee and the auditor.
- Section 206 adds subsection (l), which addresses certain conflict-of-interest
provisions. The Sarbanes-Oxley Act prohibits an accounting firm from performing audit services for a registrant if certain key members of management have recently been employed in an audit capacity by the audit firm.
These rules clarify which members of management are covered by these
conflict-of-interest rules.
- Under the final rules, an accountant would not be independent of an audit
client if the audit partner received compensation based on selling engagements to that client for services other than audit, review, and attest services.

As noted above, the rules establish and clarify the important roles and responsibilities of registrant audit committees as well as the registrant's independent accountant.

The SEC also adopted a separate rule under the Exchange Act to implement the Sarbanes-Oxley Act and clarify that the rules implementing Title II
of Sarbanes-Oxley not only define conduct that impairs independence but also
constitute separate violations under the Exchange Act. In addition, it adopted
rules (except for the proxy disclosure changes) as part of Regulation S-X, and
placed them among the current auditor independence provisions.

¶16,005   Conflicts of Interest Resulting from Employment Relationships

The Commission's previous rules deem an accounting firm to be not independent with respect to an audit client if a former partner, principal, shareholder,
or professional employee of an accounting firm accepts employment with a client if he or she has a continuing financial interest in the accounting firm or is in

a position to influence the firm's operations or financial policies. The 2003 rules did not change that existing requirement, but they do add other restrictions.

.01   "Cooling Off" Period Provided

In line with section 206 of the Sarbanes-Oxley Act, the SEC added a restriction on employment with audit clients by former employees of the accounting firm. The Act specifies that an accounting firm cannot perform an audit for a registrant if its chief executive officer, controller, chief financial officer, chief accounting officer, or any person serving in an equivalent position for the issuer was employed by that registered independent public accounting firm and *participated in any capacity in the audit* of that issuer during the one-year period preceding the date of the initiation of the audit.

Admittedly, the passage of time is an additional safeguard to reduce the perceived loss of independence for the audit firm caused by the acceptance of employment by specified members of the engagement team with an audit client. However, the SEC believes that the Act is clear that the cooling off period should apply more broadly.

The Commission decided that, when the lead partner, the concurring partner, or any other member of the audit engagement team who provides more than 10 hours of audit, review, or attest services for the issuer accepts a position with the issuer in a "financial reporting oversight role" within the one-year period preceding the commencement of audit procedures for the year that included employment by the issuer of the former member of the audit engagement team, the accounting firm is not independent with respect to that registrant. The rule applies to all members of the audit engagement team unless specifically exempted, as discussed later. (The term "financial reporting oversight role" refers to any individual who has direct responsibility for oversight over those who prepare the registrant's financial statements and related information (e.g., management's discussion and analysis) that are included in filings with the Commission.)

The Commission recognizes that, in certain instances, there are individuals who meet the definition of engagement team members while spending a relatively small amount of time on audit-related matters of the issuer. For example, a staff member may be asked to spend one day of time to observe inventory. Although the input may have been important to resolving specific aspects of the audit, the staff member likely has not had significant interaction with the audit engagement team or management of the issuer. However, it is likely that those who spent more than a de minimis amount of time on the engagement team *did* participate in a meaningful audit capacity. Because of their roles in the engagement, the lead and concurring partner are *always* considered to have participated in a meaningful audit capacity, regardless of the number of hours spent on the engagement. In order to provide useful guidance, the SEC decided that the rule on conflicts of interest resulting from employment relationships should specify that, other than the lead and concurring partner, an individual must provide more than 10 hours of service during the annual audit period as a member of the engagement team to have participated in an audit capacity.

The rules relating to the cooling off period and to employment relationships entered into between members of the audit engagement team also apply to "any person serving in an equivalent position for the issuer."

Few Exemptions Provided. Because the Sarbanes-Oxley Act and the Commission view the auditor independence issue as being vitally important in the effort to regain investor confidence in the veracity of financial statements, few exceptions to the rules have been permitted. They include:

- Those who provided *10 or fewer hours* of audit, review, or attest services.
- Conflicts that are created through merger or acquisition, unless the employment was taken in contemplation of the combination. The individual or the issuer could not be expected to know that his or her employment decision would result in a conflict. Thus, as long as the audit committee is aware of this conflict, the audit firm would continue to be independent under these rules.
- Emergency or unusual circumstances, which should be invoked very rarely. Because in certain foreign jurisdictions, it may be extremely difficult or costly to comply with these requirements, the Commission decided upon an additional exemption. For a company to avail itself of this exemption, the audit committee must determine that doing so is in the best interests of investors.
- Difficulties when there is, potentially, a different applicable date for each member of the engagement team. For that reason, the final rule adopted a uniform date for all members of the engagement team. For purposes of this rule, audit procedures are deemed to have commenced for the current audit engagement period the day after the prior year's periodic annual report (e.g., Form 10-K, 10-KSB, 20-F, or 40-F) is filed with the Commission. The audit engagement period for the current year is deemed to conclude the day the current year's periodic annual report (e.g., Form 10-K, 10-KSB, 20-F, or 40-F) is filed with the Commission.

The Sarbanes-Oxley Act specifies that the cooling off period must be one year. Under Commission rules, the prohibition would require the accounting firm to have completed one annual audit subsequent to when an individual was a member of the audit engagement team. As previously discussed, the measurement period is based upon the dates the issuer filed its annual financial information with the Commission.

With respect to investment companies, the employment of a former audit engagement team member in a financial reporting oversight role at any entity in the same investment company complex during the one-year period after the completion of the last audit would impair the independence of the accounting firm with respect to the audit client. The rule was designed to prevent a former audit engagement team member from taking a position in an investment company complex where he or she could influence the preparation of the financial statements or the conduct of the audit.

The rule recognizes that certain positions exist at an entity in the investment company complex that would be considered financial reporting or oversight positions but that have no direct influence in the financial reporting or operations of an investment company in the investment company complex. In these instances, the SEC believes tailoring the focus of this rule will not harm investor interests.

To provide for orderly transition, the rules are effective only for employment relationships with the issuer that commence after the effective date of the rules.

¶16,006   Scope of Services Provided by Auditors

Section 201(a) of the Sarbanes-Oxley Act added a section to the Securities Exchange Act of 1934. Except as discussed below, this section states that it is unlawful for a registered public accounting firm that performs an audit of an issuer's financial statements (and any person associated with such a firm) to provide to that issuer, contemporaneously with the audit, any nonaudit services, including the nine categories of services set forth in the Act. In addition, the Act states that any nonaudit service, including tax services, that is not described as a prohibited service can be provided by the auditor without impairing the auditor's independence only if the service has been *preapproved* by the issuer's audit committee. The categories of prohibited nonaudit services included in the Act are:

- Bookkeeping or other services related to the accounting records or financial statements of the audit client.
- Financial information systems design and implementation.
- Appraisal or valuation services, fairness opinions, or contribution-in-kind reports.
- Actuarial services.
- Internal audit outsourcing services.
- Management functions or human resources.
- Broker or dealer, investment adviser, or investment banking services.
- Legal services and expert services unrelated to the audit.
- Any other service that the Board determines, by regulation, is impermissible.

The Commission's principles of independence with respect to services provided by auditors are largely predicated on three basic principles, violations of which would impair the auditor's independence. An auditor cannot:

- Function in the role of management.
- Audit his or her own work.
- Serve in an advocacy role for his or her client.

The Commission adopted rules related to the scope of services that independent accountants *can* provide to their audit clients. In adopting these rules, the Commission is clarifying the scope of the prohibited services. The prohibited services contained in these rules apply only to nonaudit services provided by independent accountants to their audit clients. These rules do not limit the scope of nonaudit services provided by an accounting firm to a nonaudit client. Under the Act, the responsibility falls on the audit committee to preapprove all audit and nonaudit services provided by the accountant.

.01 Bookkeeping or Other Services Related to Financial Statement Preparation

Previously, an auditor's independence was impaired if the auditor provided bookkeeping services to an audit client, except in limited situations, such as in an emergency or where the services are provided in a foreign jurisdiction and certain conditions were met. The current rule continues the prohibition on bookkeeping, but the SEC eliminated the limited situations where bookkeeping services could have been provided under the previous rules.

Citing the principle that an auditor cannot audit his or her own work and maintain his or her independence, the SEC pointed out that when an accounting firm provides bookkeeping services for an audit client, the firm may be put in the position of later auditing the accounting firm's own work. If, during an audit, an accountant must audit the bookkeeping work performed by his or her accounting firm, it is questionable that the accountant could (or that a reasonable investor would believe that the accountant could) remain objective and impartial. If the accountant found an error in the bookkeeping, the accountant could well be under pressure not to raise the issue with the client. Raising the issue could jeopardize the firm's contract with the client for bookkeeping services or result in heightened litigation risk for the firm. In addition, keeping the books is a *management function*, which also is prohibited. Therefore, the SEC determined that all bookkeeping services would cause the auditor to lack independence unless it is reasonable to conclude that the results will not be subject to audit procedures. (This proviso applies to all of the services discussed.) The final rules strongly emphasize the responsibility of the accounting firm in making a determination that these services, if provided, will *not* be subject to audit procedures, as further discussed below.

Definition of Bookkeeping or Other Services Used in SEC Rules. The rules utilize the previous definition of bookkeeping or other services, which focuses on the provision of services involving:

- Maintaining or preparing the audit client's accounting records.
- Preparing financial statements that are filed with the Commission or the information that forms the basis of financial statements filed with the Commission.
- Preparing or originating source data underlying the audit client's financial statements.

This definition demonstrates that the concept of bookkeeping and other services is well understood in practice. Accountants are sometimes asked to prepare statutory financial statements for foreign companies, and these are not filed with the SEC. Consistent with the Commission's previous rules, an accountant's independence would be impaired where the accountant prepared the statutory financial statements if those statements form the basis of the financial statements that are filed with the Commission. Under these circumstances, an accountant or accounting firm that has prepared the statutory financial statements of an audit client is put in the position of auditing its own work when auditing the resultant U.S. GAAP financial statements.

With respect to the prohibitions on bookkeeping; financial information systems design and implementation; appraisal, valuation, fairness opinions, or contribution-in-kind reports; actuarial services; and internal audit outsourcing, the rules state that the service may not be provided "unless it is reasonable to conclude that the results of these services will not be subject to audit procedures during an audit of the audit client's financial statements."

As proposed, for bookkeeping, appraisal or valuation, and actuarial services, the provision was "where it is reasonably likely that the results of these services will be subject to audit procedures during an audit of the audit client's financial statements," whereas for the other two services, there was no such wording. The Commission added the new wording to all five services to provide consistency in application. In addition, the change from "reasonably likely..." to "unless it is reasonable to conclude" is intended to narrow the circumstances in which that condition can be invoked to justify the provision of such services.

.02   Financial Information Systems Design and Implementation

Currently, there are certain information technology services that, if provided to an audit client, impair the accountant's independence. The proposed rules identified information technology services that would impair the auditor's independence.

The Commission adopted rules, consistent with previous rules, that prohibit an accounting firm from providing any service related to the audit client's information system. These rules do not preclude an accounting firm from working on hardware or software systems that are unrelated to the audit client's financial statements or accounting records, as long as those services are preapproved by the audit committee.

The rule does prohibit the accountant from designing or implementing a hardware or software system that aggregates source data or generates information that is significant to the financial statements taken as a whole. In this context, information would be "significant" if it is reasonably likely to be material to the financial statements of the audit client. Because materiality determinations may not be complete before financial statements are generated, the audit client and accounting firm by necessity will need to evaluate the general nature of the information as well as system output during the period of the audit engagement. An accountant, for example, would not be independent of an audit client for which it designed an integrated Enterprise Resource Planning or similar system, as the system would serve as the basis for the audit client's financial reporting system.

Designing, implementing, or operating systems affecting the financial statements may place the accountant in a management role, or result in the accountant auditing his or her own work or attesting to the effectiveness of internal control systems designed or implemented by that accountant. This prohibition does not, however, preclude the accountant from evaluating the internal controls of a system as it is being designed, implemented, or operated—either as part of an audit or as part of an attest service—and making recommendations to management. Likewise, the accountant would not be precluded from making recommendations on internal control matters to management or other service providers in conjunction with the design and installation of a system by another service provider.

.03   Appraisal or Valuation Services

The SEC's previous independence rules stated that an accountant is deemed to lack independence when providing appraisal or valuation services, fairness opinions, or contribution-in-kind reports for audit clients. However, the previous rules contained certain exemptions that have been eliminated.

Appraisal and valuation services include a process of valuing assets, both tangible and intangible, or liabilities. They include valuing, among other things, in-process research and development, financial instruments, assets and liabilities acquired in a merger, and real estate. Fairness opinions and contribution-in-kind reports are opinions and reports in which the firm provides its opinion on the adequacy of consideration in a transaction. When it is time to audit the financial statements, it is likely that the accountant would review his or her own work, including key assumptions or variables that underlie an entry in the financial statements. Moreover, if the appraisal methodology involves a projection of future results of operations and cash flows, the accountant who prepares the projection may be unable to evaluate skeptically and without bias the accuracy of that valuation or appraisal. Therefore, the rules prohibit the accountant from providing *any* appraisal service, valuation service, or any service involving a fairness opinion or contribution-in-kind report for an audit client.

The rules do not prohibit an accounting firm from providing such services for non-financial reporting (e.g., transfer pricing studies, cost segregation studies, and other tax-only valuations) purposes. Similarly, the rules do not prohibit an accounting firm from utilizing its own valuation specialist to review the work performed by the audit client itself or an independent, third-party specialist employed by the audit client, provided that specialist (and not the specialist used by the accounting firm) provides the technical expertise that its client used in determining the required amounts recorded in the client's financial statements.

In those instances, the accountant will not be auditing his or her own work, because a third party or the audit client is the source of the financial information subject to the audit. In fact, the quality of the audit may be improved where specialists are utilized in such situations.

Because a strict application of these rules related to contribution-in-kind reports may create conflicts in certain foreign jurisdictions, the SEC will continue to work with other regulatory agencies in solving this type of problem.

.04   Actuarial Services

The previous rules generally barred auditors from providing actuarial services related only to insurance company policy reserves and related accounts. However, the SEC believes that when the accountant provides actuarial services for the client, he or she is placed in a position of auditing his or her own work. Accordingly, the current rules prohibit an accountant from providing an audit client any actuarially oriented advisory service involving the determination of amounts recorded in the financial statements and related accounts for the audit client. It is permissible to assist a client in *understanding* the methods, models, assumptions, and inputs used in computing an amount.

Nevertheless, the Commission believes that it is appropriate to advise the client on the appropriate actuarial methods and assumptions that will be used in the actuarial valuations. It is not appropriate for the accountant to provide the actuarial valuations for the audit client. The rules also provide that the accountant may utilize his or her own actuaries to assist in conducting the audit provided the audit client uses its own actuaries or third-party actuaries to provide management with its actuarial capabilities.

.05   Internal Audit Outsourcing

The previous rules on internal audit outsourcing allowed a company to outsource part of its internal audit function to the independent audit firm subject to certain exemptions. For example, smaller businesses were exempt from the internal audit outsourcing prohibition because there had been concerns about the potentially disproportionate impact on such companies.

Some companies outsource internal audit functions by contracting with an outside source to perform, among other things, all or part of their audits of internal controls. As emphasized by the Committee of Sponsoring Organizations, internal auditors play an important role in evaluating and monitoring a company's internal control system. As a result, some argue that internal auditors are, in effect, part of a company's system of internal accounting control.

Because the external auditor typically will rely, at least to some extent, on the existence of an internal audit function and consider its impact on the internal control system when conducting the audit of the financial statements, the accountant may be placed in the position of auditing his or her firm as part of the internal control system. In other words, if the internal audit function is outsourced to an accountant, the accountant assumes a management responsibility and becomes part of the company's control system.

The rules adopted prohibit the accountant from providing to the audit client internal audit outsourcing services. This prohibition includes any internal audit service that has been outsourced by the audit client and that relates to the audit client's internal accounting controls, financial systems, or financial statements.

When conducting the audit in accordance with generally accepted auditing standards (GAAS) or when providing attest services related to internal controls, the auditor evaluates the company's internal controls and, as a result, may make recommendations for improvements to the controls. Doing so is a part of the accountant's responsibilities under GAAS or applicable attestation standards and therefore does not constitute an internal audit outsourcing engagement.

Along those lines, this prohibition on outsourcing does not preclude engaging the accountant to perform nonrecurring evaluations of discrete items or other programs that are not, in substance, the outsourcing of the internal audit function. For example, the company may engage the accountant, subject to the audit committee preapproval requirements, to conduct "agreed-upon procedures" engagements related to the company's internal controls. It is understood that management takes responsibility for the scope and assertions in those engagements. The prohibition also does not preclude the accountant from performing operational internal audits unrelated to the internal accounting controls, financial systems, or financial statements.

.06   Management Functions

No significant changes were made to the previous rule on management functions. The rules prohibit the accountant from acting, temporarily or permanently, as a director, officer, or employee of an audit client, or performing any decision-making, supervisory, or ongoing monitoring function for the audit client.

However, those types of services in connection with the *assessment* of internal accounting and risk management controls, as well as providing recommendations for improvements, do not impair an accountant's independence. Accountants must gain an understanding of their audit clients' systems of internal controls when conducting an audit in accordance with GAAS. With this insight, accountants often become involved in diagnosing, assessing, and recommending, to audit committees and management, ways in which their audit client's internal controls can be improved or strengthened. The resulting improvements in the audit client's controls not only result in improved financial reporting to investors but also can facilitate the performance of high-quality audits. For these reasons, the rules continue to allow accountants to assess the effectiveness of an audit client's internal controls and to recommend improvements in the design and implementation of internal controls and risk management controls.

Designing and implementing internal accounting and risk management controls is considered to be fundamentally different from obtaining an understanding of the controls and testing the operation of the controls, which is an integral part of any audit of the financial statements of a company. Likewise, design and implementation of these controls involves decision making and therefore is different from *recommending improvements* in the internal accounting and risk management controls of an audit client (which is permissible, if preapproved by the audit committee).

The SEC believes that designing and implementing internal accounting and risk management controls impair the accountant's independence because they place the accountant in the role of management. Conversely, obtaining an understanding of, assessing the effectiveness of, and recommending improvements to the internal accounting and risk management controls are fundamental to the audit process and do not impair the accountant's independence. Furthermore, the accountant may be engaged by the company, subject to the audit committee preapproval requirements, to conduct an agreed-upon procedures engagement related to the company's internal controls or to provide attest services related to the company's internal controls without impairing his or her independence.

.07   Human Resources

The previous rules deemed an accountant to lack independence when performing certain human resources functions. The rules provided that an accountant's independence is impaired with respect to an audit client when the accountant searches for or seeks out prospective candidates for managerial, executive, or director positions; acts as negotiator on the audit client's behalf, such as determining position, status, compensation, fringe benefits, or other conditions of employment; or undertakes reference checks of prospective candidates. Under the current rule, an accountant's independence is also impaired when the accountant engages in psychological testing or other formal testing or evaluation programs, or recommends or advises the audit client to hire a specific candidate for a specific job.

Assisting management in human resource selection or development could place the accountant in the position of having an interest in the success of those employees the accountant has selected, tested, or evaluated.

.08   Broker-Dealer, Investment Adviser, Investment Banking Services

Previous rules deemed an accountant to lack independence when performing brokerage or investment advising services for an audit client. The newer rules add serving as an unregistered broker-dealer to the rules that prohibit serving as a promoter or underwriter, making investment decisions on behalf of the audit client or otherwise having discretionary authority over an audit client's investments, executing a transaction to buy or sell an audit client's investment, or having custody of assets of the audit client. The rule is substantially the same as the Commission's previous rule related to the provision of these types of services to audit clients. However, unregistered broker-dealers are added to the scope of the rules because the nature of the threat to independence is unchanged whether the entity is or is not a registered broker-dealer.

The SEC explains that selling—directly or indirectly—an audit client's securities is incompatible with the accountant's responsibility of assuring the public that the company's financial condition is fairly presented. When an accountant, in any capacity, recommends to anyone (including nonaudit clients) that they buy or sell the securities of an audit client or an affiliate of the audit client, the accountant has an interest in whether those recommendations were correct. That interest could affect the audit of the client whose securities, or whose affiliate's securities, were recommended. These concepts are echoed in the "simple principles" included in the legislative history to the Sarbanes-Oxley Act. In such a situation, if an accountant uncovers an accounting error in a client's financial statements, and the accountant, in an investment adviser capacity, had recommended that client's securities to investment clients, the accountant performing the audit may be reluctant to recommend changes to the client's financial statements if the changes could negatively affect the value of the securities recommended by the accountant to its investment adviser clients.

Broker-dealers often give advice and recommendations on investments and investment strategies. The value of that advice is measured principally by the performance of a customer's securities portfolio. When the customer is an audit client, the accountant has an interest in the value of the audit client's securities portfolio, even as the accountant must determine whether management has properly valued the portfolio as part of an audit. Thus, the accountant would be placed in a position of auditing his or her own work. Furthermore, the accountant is placed in a position of acting as an advocate on behalf of the client.

.09   Legal Services

The previous rule stated that an accountant is deemed to lack independence when he or she provides legal services to an audit client. The SEC believes that a lawyer's core professional obligation is to advance clients' interests. Rules of professional conduct in the U.S. require the lawyer to "represent a client zealously and diligently within the bounds of the law." The lawyer must "take whatever lawful and ethical measures are required to vindicate a client's cause or endeavor...In the exercise of professional judgment, a lawyer should always act in a manner consistent with the best interests of the client."

The Commission maintains that an individual cannot be both a zealous legal advocate for management or the client company, and maintain the objectivity and impartiality that are necessary for an audit. The Supreme Court has also expressed this view. In *United States v. Arthur Young*, the Supreme Court emphasized, "If investors were to view the auditor as an advocate for the corporate client, the value of the audit function itself might well be lost."

The final rule is that an accountant is prohibited from providing to an audit client any service that, under circumstances in which the service is provided, could be provided only by someone licensed, admitted, or otherwise qualified to practice law in the jurisdiction in which the service is provided.

There may be implications for some foreign registrants from this rule. For example, in some jurisdictions it is mandatory that someone licensed to practice law perform tax work, and that an accounting firm providing such services, therefore, would be deemed to be providing legal services. As a general matter, SEC rules are not intended to prohibit foreign accounting firms from providing services that an accounting firm in the United States may provide. In determining whether or not a service would impair the accountant's independence solely because the service is labeled a legal service in a foreign jurisdiction, the Commission will consider whether the provision of the service would be prohibited in the United States as well as in the foreign jurisdiction.

Evaluating and determining whether services are permissible may require a comprehensive analysis of the facts and circumstances. The SEC is aware of these issues, and encourages accounting firms and foreign regulators to consult with the SEC staff to address such issues.

.10   Expert Services

The Sarbanes-Oxley Act includes expert services in the list of nonaudit services an accountant is prohibited from performing for an audit client. As discussed earlier, the legislative history related to expert services is focused on the accountant's role when serving in an advocacy capacity.

Clients retain experts to lend authority to their contentions in various proceedings by virtue of the expert's specialized knowledge and experience. In situations involving advocacy, the provision of expert services by the accountant makes the accountant part of the team that has been assembled to advance or defend the client's interests. The appearance of advocacy created by providing such expert services is sufficient to deem the accountant's independence impaired. The prohibition on providing expert services included in this rule covers engagements that are intended to result in the accounting firm's specialized knowledge, experience, and expertise being used to support the audit client's positions in various adversarial proceedings.

The rules now adopted prohibit an accountant from providing expert opinions or other services to an audit client (or the client's legal representative) to advocate that client's interests in litigation and regulatory or administrative proceedings. For example, under this rule an auditor's independence would be impaired if the auditor were engaged to provide forensic accounting services to the audit client's legal representative in connection with the defense of an investigation by the Commission's Division of Enforcement. An accountant's independence likewise would be impaired if the audit client's legal counsel, in order to acquire the requisite expertise, engaged the accountant to provide such services in connection with a litigation, proceeding, or investigation.

The SEC rules do not, however, preclude an audit committee or its legal counsel from engaging the accountant to perform internal investigations or fact-finding engagements. These types of engagements may include, among others, forensic or other fact-finding work that results in the issuance of a report to the audit client. The involvement by the accountant in this capacity generally requires performing procedures that are consistent with, but more detailed or more comprehensive than, those required by GAAS. Performing such procedures *is consistent* with the role of the independent auditor and should improve audit quality. If, subsequent to the completion of such an engagement, a proceeding or investigation is initiated, the accountant may allow its work product to be utilized by the audit client and its legal counsel without impairing the accountant's independence. The accountant, however, may not then provide additional services, but may provide factual accounts or testimony about the work that had previously been performed.

Therefore, the rules do not prohibit an accountant from assisting the audit committee in fulfilling its responsibilities to conduct its own investigation of a potential accounting impropriety. For example, if the audit committee is concerned about the accuracy of the inventory accounts at a subsidiary, it may engage the auditor to conduct a thorough inspection and analysis of the accounts, the physical inventory, and related matters without impairing the auditor's independence.

The auditors already have obligations under the Exchange Act and GAAS to search for fraud that is material to an issuer's financial statements and to make sure the audit committee and others are informed of their findings. Auditors should conduct these procedures whether they become aware of a potential illegal act as a result of audit, review, or attestation procedures or of the audit committee's expressing concerns about a part of the company's financial reporting system. In these situations, the auditor may conduct the procedures, with the approval of the audit committee, and provide the reports that the auditor deems appropriate. If litigation arises while the auditors are conducting such procedures, the SEC would not consider the completion of these procedures to be prohibited, as long as the auditor remains in control of his or her work. The work may not become subject to the direction or influence of legal counsel for the issuer.

Furthermore, under this rule, an accountant's independence is not considered to be impaired when an accountant provides factual accounts or testimony describing work he or she had previously performed. Nor will it be deemed impaired if the individual explains the positions taken or conclusions reached during the performance of any service provided for the audit client.

.11 Tax Services Permitted

Since the Commission issued its auditor independence proposal, there has been considerable debate regarding whether an accountant's provision of tax services for an audit client can impair the accountant's independence. Tax services are unique among nonaudit services for a variety of reasons. Detailed tax laws must be consistently applied, and the IRS has discretion to audit any tax return. In addition, accounting firms have historically provided a broad range of tax services to their audit clients.

The Commission reiterates its long-standing position that an accounting firm can provide tax services to its audit clients without impairing the firm's independence. Accordingly, accountants may continue to provide tax services such as tax compliance, tax planning, and tax advice to audit clients, subject to the normal audit committee preapproval requirements. However, the rules require registrants to *disclose the amount of fees* paid to the accounting firm for tax services. The rules are consistent with the Act, which states that:

> Merely labeling a service as a "tax service" will not necessarily eliminate its potential to impair independence under Rule 2-01(b). Audit committees and accountants should understand that providing certain tax services to an audit client would, or could, in certain circumstances, impair the independence of the accountant. Specifically, accountants would impair their independence by representing an audit client before a tax court, district court, or federal court of claims. In addition, audit committees also

should carefully scrutinize the retention of an accountant in a transaction initially recommended by the accountant, the sole business purpose of which may be tax avoidance and the tax treatment of which may be not supported in the Internal Revenue Code and related regulations.

At about the time that these rules were being adopted, the Commission had reason to be concerned about having given auditors *any* right to offer tax services to their audit clients. Some very unorthodox and downright illegal shenanigans between major accounting firms and clients regarding tax shelters were being brought to light. Therefore, audit committees should be doubly careful about their preapproval considerations regarding any tax service being provided.

¶16,007   Definition and Extent of Audit Committee

The definition of "audit committee" used in the SEC independence rules is the same as that given in section 205 of the Sarbanes-Oxley Act:

A committee (or equivalent body) established by and amongst the Board of directors of an issuer for the purpose of overseeing the accounting and financial reporting processes of the issuer and audits of the financial statements of the issuer.

The Act further stipulates that if no such committee exists, the audit committee is the entire Board of directors.

The audit committee serves as an important body, acting in the interests of investors to help ensure that the registrant and its accountants fulfill their responsibilities under the securities laws. Because the definition of an audit committee can include the entire Board of directors if no such committee of the Board exists, these rules do not require registrants to establish audit committees. Likewise, the auditor independence rules do not require the committee to be composed of independent members of the Board. Some entities do not have Boards of directors and therefore do not have audit committees. For example, some limited liability companies and limited partnerships that do not have a corporate general partner may not have an oversight body that is the equivalent of an audit committee.

Nevertheless, the Commission is not exempting these entities from the requirements. Such an issuer is expected to scan through each general partner of the successive limited partnerships until a corporate general partner or an individual general partner is reached. With respect to a corporate general partner, the registrant should consider the audit committee of the corporate general partner or to the full Board of directors as fulfilling the role of the audit committee. With respect to an individual general partner, the Commission expects the registrant to consider the individual as fulfilling the role of the audit committee.

The rules, however, do exempt asset-backed issuers and unit investment trusts from this requirement. Because of the nature of the entity, these issuers are subject to substantially different reporting requirements. Most significantly, asset-backed issuers are not required to file financial statements, as are other companies. Similarly, unit investment trusts are not required to provide shareholder reports containing audited financial statements. Such entities are, typically, passively managed pools of assets. Therefore, the requirements related to audit committees in these rules do not apply to such entities.

¶16,008   Retention of Records Relevant to Audits

Rule 2-06 of SEC Regulation S-X implements section 802 of the Sarbanes-Oxley Act. This rule requires that accounting firms retain records relevant to the audits or reviews of issuers' and registered investment companies' financial statements, including workpapers and other documents that form the basis of the audit or review and memoranda, correspondence, communications, other documents, and records (including electronic records) that are created, sent, or received in connection with the audit or review and that contain conclusions, opinions, analyses, or financial data related to the audit or review.

These records must be retained for seven years after the auditor concludes the audit or review of the financial statements, instead of the proposed period of five years from the end of the fiscal period in which an audit or review was concluded. This change coordinated the Commission's rule with the expected auditing standards from the PCAOB that are scheduled to require the retention of audit documentation for seven years.

The rule defines the term "workpapers" to be those documents that record the audit or review procedures performed, the evidence obtained, and the conclusions reached by the auditor. The definition recognizes that the PCAOB may establish auditing standards further defining the term.

The rule also spells out a requirement to keep records that either support the auditor's final conclusions or contain information or data, relating to a significant matter, that is inconsistent with the final conclusions of the auditor on that matter or on the audit or review. The rule also states that the documents and records to be retained include, but are not limited to, those documenting consultations on, or resolutions of, differences in professional judgment.

¶16,009   Disclosure Requirements to Implement the Sarbanes-Oxley Act

The Commission voted to adopt rules implementing sections 406 and 407 of the Sarbanes-Oxley Act of 2002. These rules require public companies to disclose information about corporate codes of ethics and audit committee financial experts. They require a company subject to the reporting requirements of the Securities Exchange Act of 1934 to include the following two new types of disclosures in their Exchange Act filings:

1. Pursuant to section 407, a company will be required to disclose annually whether it has at least one "audit committee financial expert" on its audit committee. If so, the company is to supply the name of said financial expert and whether he or she is independent of management. If the company does not have an audit committee financial expert, it is required to explain why it has no such expert.

2. Pursuant to section 406, a company is required to disclose annually whether the company has adopted a code of ethics for the company's principal executive officer, principal financial officer, principal accounting officer or controller, or persons performing similar functions. If not, the company is required to explain why it has not. The rules also require a company to disclose on a current basis amendments to, and waivers from, the code of ethics relating to any of those officers.

.01   Audit Committee Financial Experts

The rules expand the proposed definition of the term "financial expert" and also substitute the designation "audit committee financial expert" for "financial expert." The rules define "audit committee financial expert" to mean a person who has the following attributes:

- An understanding of financial statements and generally accepted accounting principles.
- An ability to assess the general application of such principles in connection with the accounting for estimates, accruals, and reserves.
- Experience preparing, auditing, analyzing, or evaluating financial statements that present a breadth and level of complexity of accounting issues that are generally comparable to the breadth and complexity of issues that can reasonably be expected to be raised by the registrant's financial statements, or he or she may have experience actively supervising one or more persons engaged in such activities.
- An understanding of internal controls and procedures for financial reporting.
- An understanding of audit committee functions.

A person can acquire such attributes through any one or more of the following means:

- Education and experience as a principal financial officer, principal accounting officer, controller, public accountant, or auditor or experience in one or more positions that involve the performance of similar functions.
- Experience actively supervising a principal financial officer, principal accounting officer, controller, public accountant, auditor, or person performing similar functions or experience overseeing or assessing the performance of companies or public accountants with respect to the preparation, auditing, or evaluation of financial statements.
- Other relevant experience.

An individual must possess all of the attributes listed in the above definition to qualify as an audit committee financial expert.

The rules also provide a safe harbor to make clear that an audit committee financial expert is not to be deemed an "expert" for any purpose, including for purposes of section 11 of the Securities Act of 1933. The designation of a person as an "audit committee financial expert" does not impose any duties, obligations, or liability on the person that are greater than those imposed on such a person as a member of the audit committee in the absence of such designation, nor does it affect the duties, obligations, or liability of any other member of the audit committee or Board of directors.

.02 Codes of Ethics

Under the rules, a company is required to disclose in its annual report whether it has a code of ethics that applies to the company's principal executive officer, principal financial officer, principal accounting officer or controller, or persons performing similar functions. The rules define a code of ethics as written standards that are reasonably necessary to deter wrongdoing and to promote:

- Honest and ethical conduct, including the ethical handling of actual or apparent conflicts of interest between personal and professional relationships.
- Full, fair, accurate, timely, and understandable disclosure in reports and documents that a company files with, or submits to, the Commission and in other public communications made by the company.
- Compliance with applicable governmental laws, rules, and regulations.
- The prompt internal reporting of code violations to an appropriate person or persons identified in the code.
- Accountability for adherence to the code.

A company is required to make available to the public a copy of its code of ethics, or portion of the code that applies to the company's principal executive officer, principal financial officer, principal accounting officer or controller, or persons performing similar functions. The code of ethics may be made available to the public by filing it as an exhibit to its annual report, providing it on the company's Internet Web site, or as otherwise set forth in the final rule.

A company, other than a foreign private issuer or registered investment company, is also required to disclose any changes to, or waivers of, the code of ethics within five business days, to the extent that the change or waiver applies to the company's principal executive officer or senior financial officers. A company can provide this disclosure on Form 8-K or on its Internet Web site. Foreign private issuers and registered investment companies are required to disclose changes to, and waivers of, such codes of ethics in their periodic reports or on their Internet Web sites.

Any change or waiver of the company's code of ethics for senior financial officers, is reported as item 5.05 of Form 8-K. Other specific re-porting disclosures include:

- Item 2.03 Creation of a Direct Financial Obligation or an Obligation under an Off-Balance Sheet Arrangement of a Registrant
- Item 8.01 Other Events (The registrant can use this Item to report events that are not specifically called for by Form 8-K, that the registrant considers to be of importance to security holders.)

¶16,010   The SEC's Rules Governing Independence of Auditors

After extensive prodding and action by the SEC, auditor independence and financial disclosure about audit committees came to the foreground in concerns relating to independence and the openness of the auditing and accounting professions.

The rather lengthy lead time, punctuated by considerable negative pressure from Congress (bipartisan and bicameral), the American Institute of Certified Public Accountants (AICPS), three of the then Big Five firms and the American Bar Association, to single out only a few, ended with the Security and Exchange Commissioners voting unanimously on November 15, 2000, to adopt new rules that modernize the requirements for auditor independence. Obviously, the measures were too little, too late to protect the investors in Enron. Until additional restrictions and guidelines are officially adopted and put in place, the measures adopted at that time are still in effect.

The three areas covered are:

1. Investments by auditors or their family members in audit clients.
2. Employment relationships between auditors or their family members and audit clients.
3. The third area—the scope of services provided by audit firms to their audit clients—has been superseded by the newer rules delineated above.

The new rules reflect the Commission's consideration of comments received on the rules it proposed in June 2000.

.01   Principal Provisions

Significant features of the rules include:

1. Reduction of the number of audit firm employees and their family members whose investments in, or employment with, audit clients would impair an auditor's independence.
2. Identification of certain nonaudit services that, if provided to an audit client, would impair an auditor's independence. (The rules do not extend to services provided to nonaudit clients.)
3. Disclosure in their annual proxy statements of certain information about nonaudit services provided by the company's auditors during the last fiscal year.

.02   Four Principles

A preliminary note to the rules identifies four principles by which to measure an auditor's independence. An accountant is not independent when the accountant:

1. Has a mutual or conflicting interest with the audit client.
2. Audits his or her own firm's work.
3. Functions as management or an employee of the audit client.
4. Acts as an advocate for the audit client.

.03   Financial Relationships

Compared to the previous rules, the newly adopted rules narrow significantly the number of people whose investments trigger independence concerns. Under previous rules, many partners that did not work on the audit of a client, as well as their spouses and families, were restricted from investment in a firm's audit clients. The new rules limit restrictions principally to those who work on the audit or can influence the audit.

.04   Employment Relationships

The employment relationship rules narrow the scope of people within audit firms whose families will be affected by the employment restrictions necessary to maintain independence. The rules also identify the positions in which a person *can* influence the audit client's accounting records or financial statements. These are positions that could impair an auditor's independence if held by a close family member of that auditor.

.05   Business Relationships

Consistent with existing rules, independence will be impaired if the accountant or any covered person has a direct or material indirect business relationship with the audit client, other than providing professional services.

.06   A General Standard for Auditor Independence

This SEC rule is based on the widely endorsed principle that an auditor must be independent both *in fact* and *in appearance*. The new rule specifies that an auditor's independence is impaired either when the accountant is not independent *in fact* or when a "reasonable investor," after considering all relevant facts and circumstances, would conclude that the auditor would not be capable of acting without bias. The reasonable investor standard is a common construct in securities laws.

.07   Affiliate Provisions

When it was first proposed in June 2000, the rule contained a definition of an "affiliate of an accounting firm" that many commenters felt might affect accounting firms' joint ventures with companies that are not their audit clients and the continuation of small firm alliances. These types of relationships traditionally have not been thought to impair an accountant's independence. After considering these comments, the SEC decided that it would continue to analyze these situations under existing guidance.

An "affiliate of an audit client" continues to be defined as any entity that can significantly influence, or is significantly influenced by, the audit client, provided the equity investment is material to the entity or the audit client. "Significant influence" generally is presumed when the investor owns 20 percent or more of the voting stock of the investee. The significant influence test is used because under U.S. GAAP it is the trigger that causes the earnings and losses of one company to be reflected in the financial statements of another company.

.08   Contingent Fee Arrangements

The rules reiterate that an accountant cannot provide any service to an audit client that involves a contingent fee.

.09   Quality Controls

The rules provide a limited exception from independence violations to the accounting firm if certain factors are present:
1.   The individual did not know the circumstances giving rise to his or her violation.
2.   The violation was corrected promptly once the violation became apparent.

3. The firm has quality controls in place that provide reasonable assurance that the firm and its employees maintain their independence.
4. For the largest public accounting firms, the basic controls must include among others:
   a. Written independence policies and procedures.
   b. Automated systems to identify financial relationships that may impair independence.
   c. Training, internal inspection, and testing.
   d. Disciplinary mechanism for enforcement.

.10   Proxy Disclosure Requirement

Companies must disclose in their annual proxy statements the fees for audit, IT consulting, and all other services provided by their auditors during the last fiscal year.

Companies must also state whether the audit committee has considered whether the provision of the nonaudit services is compatible with maintaining the auditor's independence.

Finally, the registrant is required to disclose the percentage hours worked on the audit engagement by persons other than the accountant's full-time employees, if that figure exceeded 50 percent. This requirement is in answer to recent actions taken by some accounting firms to sell their practices to financial services companies. The partners or employees often, in turn, become employees of the financial services firm. The accounting firm then leases assets, namely auditors, back from those companies to complete audit engagements. In such cases, most of the auditors who work on an audit are employed elsewhere without the public, investors, or the client being aware of the situation.

¶16,011   Application of Revised Rules on Auditor Independence

Since the adoption of the Commission's Revised Rules on Auditor Independence, the SEC staff has received questions regarding the implementation and interpretation of the rules. They encourage these questions and related correspondence regarding auditor independence as they do to all of the rulings which may be difficult to interpret.

.01   Frequently Asked Questions

Publications of staff responses to certain questions received are referred to as Frequently Asked Questions (FAQs). Many of the questions are rather technical, referring to a specific item on a specific schedule. Others have a more general and widespread application and give the preparer a better feel for what the SEC staff is looking for in the reports. Following is a sample of the latter variety.

Question 6

Q: Should the fees billed in prior years be disclosed so investors may compare trends in audit, information technology, and other non-audit fees?

A: The rule does not require comparative disclosures. Registrants may include such information voluntarily.

Question 7

Q: In situations where other auditors are involved in the delivery of services, to what extent should the fees from the other auditors be included in the required fee disclosures?

A: Only the fees billed by the principal accountant need to be disclosed. See Question 8 regarding the definition of "principal accountant." If the principal accountant's billings or expected billings include fees for the work performed by others (such as where the principal accountant hires someone else to perform part of the work), then such fees should be included in the fees disclosed for the principal accountant.

In some foreign jurisdictions, a registrant may be required to have a joint audit requiring both accountants to issue an audit report for the same fiscal year. In these circumstances, fees for each accountant should be separately disclosed as they are both "principal accountants."

Question 8

Q: Does the term "principal accountant" in the ruling include associated or affiliated organizations?

A: Yes. "Principal accountant" has the meaning given to it in the auditing literature. In determining what services rendered by the principal accountant must be disclosed, all entities that comprise the accountant, as defined, should be included. This term includes not only the person or entity who furnishes reports or other documents that the registrant files with the Commission, but also all of the person's or entity's departments, divisions, parents, subsidiaries, and associated entities, including those located outside of the United States.

Question 15

Q: Does the restriction on the independent accountant providing legal services to an audit client apply only to litigation services?

A: No. The Commission's rule provides that an auditor's and firm's independence would be impaired if an auditor provides to its audit client a service for which the person providing the service must be admitted to practice before the courts of a U.S. jurisdiction. This standard includes all legal services. The rule does not apply only to appearance in court or solely to litigators. The only circumstances excluded by the rule are those in which local U.S. law allows certain limited activities without admission to the bar (generally confined to advice concerning the law of foreign jurisdictions).

Additionally, as discussed in the adopting release, some firms may be providing legal services outside of the United States to registrants when those services are not precluded by local law and are routine and ministerial or relate to matters that are not material to the consolidated financial statements. Such services raise serious independence concerns under circumstances other than those meeting at least those minimum criteria.

Question 17

Q: The final rule did not define an affiliate of an accounting firm. Does the lack of a definition signal a change in the Commission's approach to this issue?

A: No. The final rule's definition of an "accounting firm" includes the accounting firm's "associated entities." As noted in the adopting release, the Commission used this phrase to reflect the staff's current practice of addressing these questions in light of all relevant facts and circumstances, and of looking to the factors identified in our previous guidance on this subject. Much of this guidance is cited in footnotes of the adopting release. The staff is available for consultations on this issue.

Question 18

Q: Did the final rule change the Commission's guidance with respect to business relationships?

A: No. The final rule is consistent with the Commission's prior guidance on business relationships. The basic standard of the Commission's prior guidance has now been codified in the rule. In addition, as the adopting release notes, much of the Commission's previous guidance has been retained and continues to apply. For example, joint ventures, limited partnerships, investments in supplier or customer companies, certain leasing interest and sales by the accountant of items other than professional services are examples of business relationships that may impair an accountant's independence.

The SEC further explained its position in a letter to an accounting firm. The Commission stated:

"The Commission has recognized that certain situations, including those in which accountants and their audit clients have joined together in a profit-sharing venture, create a unity of interest between the accountant and client. In such cases, both the revenue accruing to each party...and the existence of the relationship itself create a situation in which to some degree the auditor's interest is wedded to that of its client. That interdependence impairs the auditor's independence, irrespective of whether the audit was in fact performed in an objective, critical fashion. Where such a unity of interests exists, there is an appearance that the auditor has lost the objectivity and skepticism necessary to take a critical second look at management's representations in the financial statements. The consequence is a loss of confidence in the integrity of the financial statements."

Question 21

Q: The new rule permits the auditor to continue to provide certain internal audit and financial information systems design and implementation services provided certain criteria are met. Do these criteria for internal audit apply to all internal audit engagements? What are the responsibilities of management pursuant to these criteria?

A: The six criteria for internal audit services apply to all internal audit services the auditor provides to its audit client, including those services related to operational audits or for companies with less than $200 million in assets.

All of the specified criteria must be met for both internal audit and financial information systems design and implementation to ensure that management not only takes responsibility for the services and projects performed by the auditor, but also makes the required management decisions. An audit client that merely signs a letter acknowledging responsibility for the services or project, without actually meeting each of the specified conditions, is not sufficient to ensure the auditor's independence.

¶16,012   The Blue Ribbon Panel's Ten Commandments

Although described as "recommendations," the report of the Blue Ribbon Panel on Improving the Effectiveness of Corporate Audit Committees made it quite clear that not only the average investor but also a distinguished group of those "in the know" had questions about the effectiveness of the "independent" audit process. The group comprising the Panel was formed by the New York Stock Exchange (NYSE) and the National Association of Securities Dealers (NASD or NASDAQ) in September 1998, after the SEC Chairman had publicly expressed grave concern about the "independence" of the audit process. During the deliberations of the group consisting of business, accounting, and securities professionals, testimony was provided by two dozen organizations, including the AICPA, the Financial Executives International, the Independence Standards Board, and the Institute of Management Accountants.

The panel's 71-page report listed ten recommendations for strengthening the independence of the audit committee and increasing its importance and effectiveness. These recommendations were:

1. The NYSE and NASD adopt strict definitions of independence for directors serving on audit committees of listed companies.
2. The NYSE and NASD require larger companies to have audit committees composed entirely of independent directors.

3. The NYSE and NASD require larger companies to have "financially literate" directors on their audit committees.
4. The NYSE and NASD require each company to adopt a formal audit committee charter and to review its adequacy annually.
5. The SEC requires each company to disclose in its proxy statement whether it has adopted an audit committee charter as well as other information.
6. Each NYSE and NASD listed company state in the audit committee charter that the outside auditor is ultimately accountable to the board of directors and the audit committee.
7. All NYSE and NASD listed companies ensure their charters mandate that their audit committee does communicate with the outside auditors about independence issues in accordance with Independent Standards Board regulations.
8. Generally accepted auditing rules require that the outside auditor discuss with the audit committee the quality and suitability, not just the acceptability, of the accounting principles used.
9. The SEC require the annual report include a letter from the audit committee clarifying that it has reviewed the audited financial statements with management as well as performed other tasks.
10. The SEC require the outside auditor to perform an interim review under Statement on Auditing Standards 71, *Interim Financial Information*, before a company files its form 10-Q.

¶16,013   Reviews of Interim Financial Statements

Interim financial statements are an important part of a company's public reporting. Rules dealing with interim reporting are concerned primarily with indicating which rules that apply to the year-end financial statement's preparation apply during the year as well and which are modified. Some adjustments or accruals, for example, are normally made at year end. The rules on interim reporting explain how such procedures should affect financial statements issued during the year.

.01   SEC Rules Relating to the Interim Statement

The Commission's rules require that:

1. Companies' interim financial statements must be reviewed by independent auditors before they are filed on Forms 10-Q or 10-QSB with the Commission.
2. Companies, other than small business issuers filing on small business forms, must supplement their annual financial information with disclosures of selected quarterly financial data under Item 302(a) of Regulation S-K.

3. Companies must disclose in their proxy statements whether the audit com-
    mittee reviewed and discussed certain matters relating to:
    a. The ASB's Statement of Auditing Standards 61 concerning the ac-
        counting methods used in the financial statements.
    b. The Independence Standard Board's Standard 1 (concerning matters that
        may affect the auditor's independence) with management and the auditors.
    c. Possible recommendation to the Board that the audited financial state-
        ments be included in the Annual Report on Form 10-K or 10-KSB for
        filings with the Commission.
4. Companies must disclose in their proxy statements whether the audit com-
    mittee has a written charter, and file a copy of their charter every three years.
5. Companies whose securities are listed on the NYSE or AMEX or are quoted
    on NASDAQ must disclose certain information in their proxy statements
    about any audit committee member who is not "independent." All compa-
    nies must disclose, if they have an audit committee, whether the members
    are "independent." (Independence is defined in the listing standards of the
    NYSE, AMEX, and NASD.)

Under the new rules, timely interim auditor reviews were required beginning
with the first fiscal quarter ended after March 15, 2000. Compliance with the
other new requirements is required in filings after December 15, 2000.

Foreign private issuers are exempt from requirements of the new rules. The
new rules include a "safe harbor" for the disclosures.

.02   Blue Ribbon Reminders

In their final report in August, 2000, the Blue Ribbon Panel on Audit Effectiveness recommended that, among other things audit committees:

1. Obtain annual reports from management assessing the company's internal
    controls.
2. Specify in their charters that the outside auditor is ultimately accountable
    to the board of directors and audit committee.
3. Inquire about time pressures on the auditor.
4. Preapprove nonaudit services provided by the auditor.

.03   Criteria for Gauging Appropriateness

The Panel, more specifically, provided guidance that an audit committee can use to determine the appropriateness of a service. This guidance includes:

1.   Whether the service is being performed principally for the audit committee.
2.   The effects of the service, if any, on audit effectiveness, or on the quality and timeliness of the entity's financial reporting process. For example, what is the effect, if any, upon the technology specialists who ordinarily also provide recurring audit support?
3.   Whether the service would be performed by audit personnel, and if so, whether it will enhance their knowledge of the entity's business and operations.
4.   Whether the role of those performing the service would be inconsistent with the auditor's role (e.g., a role where neutrality, impartiality, and auditor skepticism are likely to be subverted).
5.   Whether the audit firm personnel would be assuming a management role or creating a mutual or conflicting interest with management.
6.   Whether the auditors, in effect, would be "auditing their own numbers."
7.   Whether the project must be started and completed very quickly.
8.   Whether the audit firm has unique expertise in the service.
9.   The size of the fee(s) for the nonaudit service(s).

CHAPTER 17
Financial Statement Analysis

¶17,000   Financial Statement Analysis and Interpretation

Analysis techniques applied to financial statements are of interest to the corporate financial officer of any entity for a number of reasons. For one thing, that particular company's financial statements will be subject to analysis by creditors, credit grantors, and investors. Furthermore, the financial officer will want to analyze the company's statements for internal management use as well as analyze other companies' financial statements for credit purposes and perhaps for investment purposes (where an acquisition is being considered).

The financial statements are a systematic and convenient presentation of the financial position and operating performance of a business entity. The question is: What can be learned by analyzing and interpreting the information available in the statements?

There is much valuable information to be learned, as ratio analysis answers questions concerning the financial facts of a business:

1. U.S. GAAP permits a variety of accounting procedures and practices that significantly affect the results of operation reported in the statements. Statement analysis helps to evaluate the choices of alternative accounting decisions.
2. The statements for a number of successive years can be compared by the use of ratios and unusual trends and changes can be noted.
3. A company's statements can be compared with those of other similar companies in the same industry.
4. Statement analysis is the basis for estimating, or projecting, potential operating results by the development of pro forma statements.
5. The effects of external economic developments on a company's business can be applied to results as shown in the statements.

6. The balance sheet valuations can be related to the operating results disclosed in the income statement, since the balance sheet is the link between successive income statements.
7. Since ratios are index numbers obtained by relating data to each other, they make comparisons more meaningful than using the raw numbers without relating an absolute dollar figure to another statement item.

¶17,001   Four Groups of Ratios

Ratios are usually classified into four groups:

1. *Liquidity Ratios.* Measures of the ability of the enterprise to pay its short-term obligations.
2. *Profitability Ratios.* Measures of the profits (losses) over a specified period of time.
3. *Coverage Ratios.* Measures of the protection for the interest and principal payments to long-term creditors and investors.
4. *Activity Ratios.* Measures of how efficiently the company is employing its assets.

The ratios in the following discussion are those most commonly applied to measure the operating efficiency and profitability of a company. (There are hundreds of possible relationships that can be computed and trends identified.) The discussion includes an explanation of the answers that each ratio provides; each ratio's application to a specific area of a business will be noted.

¶17,002   The Accountant's Responsibility

In evaluating the ratios, the accountant must be mindful that the ratios are simply a measuring tool, not the final answers nor the end in themselves. They are one of the tools for evaluating the *past* performance and providing an indication of the future performance of the company. Ratios are a *control* technique and should be thought of as furnishing management with a "red flag" when a ratio has deviated from an established norm, or average, or predetermined standard.

Accordingly, ratio analysis is meaningless without an *adequate feedback* system by which management is promptly informed of a problem demanding immediate attention and correction.

While accountants are concerned primarily with the *construction* of the financial statements, particularly their technical accuracy and validity, the accountant is also relied upon by the many different users of the statements for assistance in the interpretation of the financial information. The accountant must use experience and technical skill to evaluate information and to contribute to management decisions that will maximize the optimum allocation of an organization's economic resources.

.01   Basic Analysis Techniques

Much of the analytical data obtained from the statements is expressed in terms of ratios and percentages. (Carrying calculations to one decimal place is sufficient for most analysis purposes.) The basic analysis technique is to use these ratios and percentages in either a *horizontal* or *vertical* analysis, or both.

Horizontal Analysis. Here, similar figures from several years' financial statements are compared. For example, it may be useful to run down two years' balance sheets and compare such items as the current assets, plant assets, current liabilities and long-term liabilities on one balance sheet with the similar items on the other and to note the amount and percentage increases or decreases for each item. Of course, the comparison can be for more than two years. A number of years may be used, each year being compared with the base year or the immediate preceding year.

Vertical Analysis. Here, component parts are compared to the totals in a single statement. For example, it can be determined what percentage each item of expense on the income statement is of the total net sales, or, what percentage of the total assets the current assets comprise.

Ratios. Customarily, the *numerator* of the equation is expressed first, then the denominator. For example, fixed assets to equity means fixed assets *divided by* equity. Also, whenever the numerator is the larger figure, there is a tendency to use the word "turnover" for the result.

As indicated above, these techniques are widely used, generally in the course of one analysis.

¶17,003   Balance Sheet Analysis

The significance of the balance sheet is that it shows relationships between classes of assets and liabilities. From long experience, business people have learned that certain relationships indicate the company is in actual or potential trouble or is in good financial shape. For example, these relationships may indicate that the business is short of working capital, is undercapitalized generally, or has a bad balance between short- and long-term debt.

It must be emphasized that there are no fixed rules concerning the relationships. There are wide variations between industries and even within a single industry. It is often more valuable to measure these relationships against the past history of the same company than to use them in comparison with other businesses. If sharp disparities do show, however, it is usually wise not to ignore them. Many of the socalled "excesses" that in the past have led to recessions often show up in the balance sheets of individual companies. The most important balance sheet ratios and their implications for the business are discussed below.

.01   Ratio of Current Assets to Current Liabilities

The *current ratio* is probably the most widely used measure of liquidity (i.e., a company's ability to pay its bills). It measures the ability of the business to meet its current liabilities. The current ratio indicates the extent to which the current liabilities are covered. For example, if current assets total $400,000 and current liabilities are $100,000, the current ratio is 4 to 1.

Good current ratios will range from about 2 to almost 4 to 1. However, the ratio will vary widely in different industries. For example, companies that collect quickly on their accounts and do not have to carry very large inventories can usually operate with a lower current ratio than those companies whose collections are slower and inventories larger.

If current liabilities are subtracted from current assets, the resulting figure is the *working capital* of the company; in other words, the amount of free capital that is immediately available for use in the business. One of the most significant reasons for the failure of small businesses is the lack of working capital, which makes it difficult or impossible for the business to cope with sudden changes in worsening economic conditions. Conversely, lack of a comfortable amount of working capital may prevent a small business from taking advantage of opportunities to expand in a growing economy.

The details of working capital flow are presented in the two-year comparative Statement of Cash Flows, a mandatory part of the financial statements.

An important feature of the ratios to remember is that when both factors are decreased by the same amount, the ratio is increased:

	Old	Change	New
Current Assets	$100,000	$(25,000)	$75,000
Current Liabilities	50,000	(25,000)	25,000
Working Capital	50,000	0	50,000
Ratio	2 to 1		3 to 1

By paying off $25,000 worth of liabilities (depleting Cash), you have increased the ratio from 2 to 1 to 3 to 1. Note that the *dollar* amount of *working capital* remains the same $50,000.

Conversely, should you borrow $50,000 on short-terms (increasing Cash and Current Liabilities), you would *reduce* the ratio to *1½ to 1* ($150,000/ 100,000), again with the dollar amount of working capital remaining at $50,000.

A variation of the current ratio is the *acid test*. This is the ratio of *quick assets* (cash, marketable securities, and accounts receivable) to *current liabilities*. This ratio eliminates the inventory from the calculation, since inventory may not be readily convertible to cash.

.02   Acid-Test Ratio

The current ratio does not disclose the fact that a portion of the current assets may be tied up in slowmoving inventories, which leaves the question of how long it will take to transform the inventories into finished product and how much will be realized on the sale of the merchandise. Elimination of inventories and prepaid expenses from the current assets will give better information for short-term creditors. A *quick* or *acid-test ratio* relates total current liabilities to cash, marketable securities, and receivables. If this total is $150 divided by current liabilities of $100, the acid-test ratio is 1½ to 1, which is low compared to an industry average of 3 to 1. This means a company would have difficulty meeting its short-term obligations and would have to obtain additional current assets from other sources.

.03   Defensive-Interval Ratio

The defensive-interval ratio is computed by dividing defensive assets—cash, marketable securities, and receivables—by projected daily expenditures from operations. This ratio measures the time span a firm can operate with present liquid assets without resorting to revenues from next year's sources. Projected daily expenditures are computed by dividing cost of goods sold plus selling and administrative expenses and other ordinary expenses by 365 days. Assuming a company has a defensive-interval measure of 150 days and an industry average of 75 days, the 150 days provides a company with a high degree of protection, and can offset the weakness indicated by low current and acid-test ratios that a company might have.

.04   Ratio of Current Liabilities to Stockholders' Equity

This ratio measures the relationship between the short-term creditors of the business and the owners. Excessive short-term debt is frequently a danger sign, since it means that the short-term creditors are providing much or all of the company's working capital. If anything happens to concern the short-term creditors, they will demand immediate repayment and create the risk of insolvency. Short-term creditors are most often suppliers of the business, and the company's obligation to them is listed under accounts payable. However, short-term creditors may also include short-term lenders.

A general rule occasionally cited for this ratio is that for a business with a tangible capital and earnings (net worth) of less than $250,000, current liabilities should not exceed two-thirds of this tangible net worth. For companies having a tangible net worth over $250,000, current liabilities should not exceed three-fourths of tangible net worth.

Tangible net worth is used instead of total net worth because intangible assets (such as patents and copyrights) may have no actual market value if the company is forced to offer them in distress selling.

.05   Ratio of Total Liabilities to Stockholders' Equity

The ratio differs from the preceding one in that it includes only long-term liabilities. Since the long-term creditors of a company are normally not in a position to demand immediate payment, as are short-term creditors, this ratio may be moderately greater than the preceding one without creating any danger for the company. However, the ratio should never exceed 100 percent in an industrial company. If it did, this would mean that the company's creditors have a larger stake in the enterprise than the owners themselves. Under such circumstances, it is very likely that credit would not be renewed when the existing debts matured. Utilities and financial companies can operate safely with much higher ratios because more of their liabilities are long-term.

.06   Ratio of Fixed Assets to Stockholders' Equity

The purpose of this ratio is to measure the relationship between fixed and current assets. The ratio is obtained by dividing the book value of the fixed assets by the tangible value of stockholders' equity. A rule sometimes used is that if tangible net worth is under $250,000, fixed assets should not exceed two-thirds of tangible net worth. If tangible net worth is over $250,000, fixed assets should not exceed three-fourths of tangible net worth.

.07   Ratio of Fixed Assets to Long-Term Liabilities

Since long-term notes and bonds are often secured by mortgages on fixed assets, a comparison of the fixed assets with the long-term liabilities reveals what "coverage" the note or bondholders have—that is, how much protection they have for their loans by way of security. Furthermore, where the fixed assets exceed the long-term liabilities by a substantial margin, there is room for borrowing additional long-term funds on the strength of the fixed asset position.

.08   Ratio of Cost of Goods Sold to Inventory—Inventory Turnover

One of the most frequent causes of business failure is lack of inventory control. A firm that is optimistic about future business may build up its inventory to greater than usual amounts. Then, if the expected business does not materialize, the company will be forced to stop further buying and may also have difficulty paying its creditors. In addition, if a company is not selling off its inventory regularly, that item, or part of it, is not really a *current* asset. Additionally, there may be a considerable amount of unsalable inventory included in the total. For all these reasons, a business is interested in knowing how often the inventory "turns over" during the year. In other words, how long will the current inventory be on the shelves, and how soon will it be turned into money?

To find out how often inventory turns over, the average inventory is compared to the cost of goods sold shown on the income statement. (Typically, average is computed by adding opening and closing inventories and dividing the total by two.) For example, if average inventory is $2 million and cost of goods sold adds up to $6 million, during the course of the year, the company has paid for three times the average inventory. Therefore, it can be said that the inventory turned over three times, and at year-end there remained about a four months' supply of inventory on hand.

Because information about cost of goods sold and average inventory may not be readily available in published reports, another way to measure the same results is by using the ratio of net sales to inventory. In this ratio, net sales is substituted for cost of goods sold. Since net sales will always be a larger figure (because it includes the business's profit margin), the resulting inventory turnover will be a higher figure.

How large an inventory should a company carry? That depends upon many factors within a particular business or industry. What may be large or small may vary with the type of business or the time of year. An automobile dealer with a large inventory at the beginning or middle of a model year will be in a strong position. A large inventory at the end of the season places him in a weak financial position.

.09   Ratio of Inventory to Working Capital

This is another ratio to measure over- or under-inventory. Working capital is current assets minus current liabilities. If inventory is too high a proportion of working capital, the business is short on quick assets—cash and accounts receivable. A general rule for this ratio is that businesses of tangible net worth of less than $250,000 should not have an inventory which is more than three-fourths of net working capital. For a business with tangible net worth in excess of $250,000, inventory should not exceed net working capital. The larger-size business can tolerate a condition where there are no quick assets because its larger inventory can be borrowed against; in addition, it presumably has fixed assets which can be mortgaged if necessary.

Inventory as a percentage of current assets may indicate a significant relationship when comparison is made between companies in the same industry, but not between different types of companies because of other variables.

.10   Receivables Turnover

An important consideration for any business is the length of time it takes to collect its accounts receivable. The longer accounts receivable are outstanding, the greater the need for the business to raise working capital from other sources. In addition, a longer collection period increases the risk of bad debts. A general rule for measuring the collection period is that it should not be more than one-third greater than the net selling terms offered by the company. For example, if goods are sold on terms of 30 days net, the average collection period should be about 40 days, though this varies from industry to industry. Special rules apply in the case of installment selling.

Another way of measuring the collection rate of accounts receivable is to divide the net sales from the income statement by the average accounts receivable. This gives the accounts receivable turnover—that is, how many times during the year the average accounts receivable were collected. A comparison with prior years reveals whether the company's collection experience is getting better or worse. The faster the turnover, the more reliable the current and acid-test ratios are for financial analytical purposes.

.11   Asset Turnover

This ratio indicates how efficiently a company utilizes its assets. If the turnover rate is high, the indication is that a company is using its assets efficiently to generate sales. If the turnover ratio is low, a company either has to use its assets more efficiently or dispose of them. The asset turnover ratio is affected by the depreciation method used. If an accelerated method of depreciation is used, the results would be a higher turnover rate than if the straightline method is used, all other factors being equal.

.12   Book Value of the Securities

This figure represents the value of the outstanding securities according to the values shown on the company's books. This may have little relationship to market value—especially in the case of common stock. Profitable companies often show a low net book value but report very substantial earnings. Railroads, on the other hand, may show a high book value for their common stock but have such low or irregular earnings that the stock's market price is much less than the book value. Insurance companies, banks and investment companies are exceptions. Since most of their assets are liquid—cash, accounts receivable, marketable securities—the book value of their common stock may well present a fair approximation of the market value.

Nevertheless, book value is an important test of financial strength. It is computed by simply subtracting all liabilities from total assets. The remaining sum represents the book value of the equity interest in the business. In computing this figure, it is a good idea to include only tangible assets, such as land, machinery and inventory. A patent right or other intangible may be given a large dollar value on the balance sheet, but in the event of liquidation may not be salable at all. The theory underlying the measurement of book value is that it is a good measure of how much cash and credit the company may be able to raise if it comes upon bad times. Book value is usually expressed per share outstanding.

Book value is also an important measure for the bondholders of the company. For them, the value has the significance of telling them how many dollars per bond outstanding the company has in available assets. Since they have a call on the company's assets before either the preferred stockholders or the common stockholders, a substantial book value per bond in excess of the face amount of the bond offers relative assurance of the safety of the bond—assurance that funds will be available to pay off the bonds when they become due. To find the book value of the bonds, add together the total stockholders' equity and the amount of the bonds outstanding.

For example, stockholders' equity totals $5 million. Bonded indebtedness is $2 million. From this $7 million total we subtract $1 million of intangibles. That leaves $6 million of net tangible assets. This represents a coverage of three times the total bond indebtedness, usually a fairly substantial coverage.

¶17,004   Income Statement Analysis

Just as with the balance sheet, most of the figures obtained from the income statement acquire real meaning only by comparison with other figures, either with similar figures of previous years of the same company or with the corresponding figures of other companies in the same or similar business.

For example, comparisons can be made between each significant item of expense and cost and net sales to get a percentage of net sales (vertical analysis) which can then be compared with other companies. Percentages are more meaningful to compare than absolute dollar amounts, since the volume of business done by one company in the same industry may vary substantially from the volume of another company.

Comparison can also be made of each of the significant figures on the income statement with the same figures for prior years (horizontal analysis). Here, too, comparisons of percentages rather than absolute dollar amounts might be more meaningful if the volume of sales has varied substantially from year to year.

Other significant comparisons are covered in the following paragraphs.

.01 Ratio of Long-Term Debt to Equity

This ratio measures the leverage potential of the business; that is, the varying effects which changes in operating profits will have on net profits. The rule is that the higher the debt ratio, the greater will be the effect on the common stock of changes in earnings because of increased interest expenses.

Many security analysts feel that in an industrial company equity should equal at least half the total of all equity and debt outstanding. Railroads and utilities, however, are likely to have more debt (and preferred stock) than common stock because of the heavy investments in fixed assets, much of which is financed by the use of debt and preferred stock.

A stock is considered to have high leverage if the issuing company has a high percentage of bonds and preferred stock outstanding in relation to the amount of common stock. In good years, this will mean that after bond interest and preferred stock dividends are paid, there will be an impressive earnings per share figure because of the small amount of common stock outstanding.

On the other hand, that same high leverage situation could cause real difficulty with even a moderate decline in earnings. Not only would the decline eliminate any dividends for the common stock, but also could even necessitate drawing from accumulated earnings to cover the full interest on its bonds.

.02 Earnings per Share

Probably, the most important ratio used today is the earnings per share (EPS) figure. It is a *mandatory* disclosure on all annual financial (income) statements (for public companies) and mandatory for all interim statements (though unaudited) for public companies. Moreover, the EPS must be broken out separately for extraordinary items. The standards of calculation are quite complex where preferred stock, options and convertibility are involved.

.03 FASB 128, *Earnings per Share*

FASB 128 (FASB ASC paragraph 260-10-45-2) established new standards for computing and presenting earning per share and applies to entities with publicly held common stock or potential common stock.

It simplifies the admittedly complicated methods used for computing earnings per share previously found in APB 15, *Earnings Per Share*, and makes the requirements comparable to international EPS standards (International Accounting Standard 33, *Earnings Per Share*, issued by the International Accounting Standards Committee). In doing this, FASB 128 replaces the presentation of primary EPS with a presentation of basic EPS. It also requires dual presentation of basic and diluted EPS on the face of the income statement for all entities with complex capital structures and requires a reconciliation of the numerator and denominator of the basic EPS computation to the numerator and denominator of the diluted EPS computation.

The two EPS figures required under FASB 128 follow:

1. Basic Earnings per Share is computed by dividing income available to stockholders by the weighted average number of common shares outstanding during the period. Shares issued during the period and shares reacquired during the period should be weighted for the portion of the period they were outstanding. The formula would be: (Net income minus preferred dividends) divided by common stock.
2. Diluted EPS reflects the potential dilution that could occur if securities or other contracts to issue common stock were exercised or converted into common stock or resulted in the issuance of common stock that would then share in the earnings of the entity. It is figured in a similar manner to basic EPS after adjusting the numerator and denominator for the possible dilution. Since it is, therefore, computed in a similar manner to fully diluted EPS under APB 15, it will produce a similar earnings per share figure.

Equity Valuation Unchanged. The new standard did not change U.S. equity valuations because:

1. Even though basic earnings per share show a higher figure than primary earnings per share, informed investors do not use basic earnings per share anyway for companies with complex capital structures because it does not take into account the potential dilutive effect of convertibles, options, warrants, and the like.
2. Most entities' dilutive earnings per share are substantially the same as their fully diluted earnings per share had been.

.04 Sales Growth

The raw element of profit growth is an increase in sales (or revenues when the company's business is services). While merely increasing sales is no guarantee that higher profits will follow, it is usually the first vital step; therefore, in analyzing a company, the sales figures for the past four or five years are important. If they have been rising and there is no reason to believe the company's markets are near the saturation point, it is reasonable to assume that the rise will continue.

When a company's sales have jumped by the acquisition of another firm, it is important to find out if the acquisition was accomplished by the issuance of additional common stock, by the assumption of additional debt, or for cash. If the company was paid for by common stock and if the acquired firm's earnings are the same on a pershare basis as those of the acquiring firm, the profit picture remains exactly as it was before. The additional sales growth is balanced by the *dilution of the equity*—that is, the larger number of shares now sharing in the earnings.

The situation is quite different if the purchase was for cash or in exchange of bonds or preferred stock. Here, no dilution of the common stock has occurred. The entire profits of the new firm (minus the interest which must be paid on the new debt or the interest formerly earned on the cash) benefit the existing shareholders.

In any event, acquisitions of new companies often require a period of consolidation and adjustment, frequently followed by a decreased rate of sales growth.

Consideration should be given to the effect of inflation on sales. A situation can exist where the increase in sales may be caused by the increase in prices. The result may be that unit sales have dropped in relation to the previous year's, but the dollar sales have increased. Comparing unit sales may be a better method of ascertaining the sales increase under certain circumstances.

.05   Computing Operating Profit

A company's costs of operations fall into two groups: *cost of goods sold* and *cost of operations*. The first relates to all the costs of producing the goods or services matched to the revenues produced by those costs. The second includes all other costs not directly associated with the production costs, such as selling and administrative costs (usually called period expenses).

Subtracting both of these groups of costs from sales leaves *operating profit*. Various special costs and special forms of income are then added or subtracted from operating income to get *net income before taxes*. After deducting state and federal income taxes, the final figure (which is commonly used for computing the profit per share) is *net income*. When analyzing a company, however, you will often be most interested in the operating profit figure, since this reflects the real earning capacity of the company.

The best way to look at cost figures is as a percentage of sales. Thus, a company may spend 90 cents out of every dollar in operating costs. We say its cost percentage is 90 percent or, more commonly, its *operating profit margin* is 10 percent. Profit margins vary a great deal among industries, running anywhere from 1 percent to 20 percent of sales; thus, comparisons should not be made between companies in different industries. The trend of the operating profit margin for a particular company, however, will give an excellent picture of how well management is able to control costs. If sales increases are obtained only by cutting prices, this will immediately show as a decrease in the margin of profit. In introducing a new product, it is sometimes necessary to incur special costs to make initial market penetration, but this should be only temporary.

The most used, examined and discussed ratio within a company is the *gross profit ratio*. More significance is probably attached to this ratio than to any other because increases usually indicate improved performance (more sales, more efficient production) and decreases indicate weaknesses (poor selling effort, waste in production, weak inventory controls).

When comparing a company with others in the same field, if the company's profit margin is low by comparison, it signals troubles ahead; if it is high, the company appears to be a worthy competitor.

The terminology in the gross profit percentages is sometimes confusing and misinterpreted, especially when the word "markup" is used. As an example:

	$	%
Sales	$100	100%
Cost of Sales	80	80%
Gross Profit	$20	20%

In conventional usage, there is a 20-percent gross profit or margin on the sale (20/100). However, to determine the *markup*, the cost of sales is the denominator and the gross profit is the numerator (20/80 equals a 25-percent markup).

Starting with gross profit *percentage desired*, to gross 20 percent, what should the selling price be? (The only known factor is cost.)

	%	Known	As calculated
Selling price	100%	?	$150
Cost	80%	$120	120
Gross Profit	20%	?	$30

Selling price is always 100 percent. If cost is $120 and is equal to 80 percent of the selling price (it must be 80 percent because a gross profit of 20 percent was set), divide $120 by 80 percent to get the 100 percent selling price of $150.

.06   Ratio of Net Sales to Stockholders' Equity

A company acquires assets in order to produce sales which yield a profit. If tangible assets yield too few sales, the company is suffering from underselling (the underutilization of its assets). On the other hand, the company may suffer from overtrading (too many sales in proportion to its tangible net worth). In other words, there is too heavy a reliance on borrowed funds to generate sales.

Another way of measuring the effective utilization of assets is to determine the ratio of net sales to total assets (excluding long-term investments).

In either case, comparisons of these ratios with similar ratios of other companies in the same industry can indicate the relative efficiency in utilization of assets of the company being analyzed.

.07   Ratio of Net Sales to Working Capital

This is similar to the preceding ratio, since it measures the relationship between sales and assets. In this case, however, the ratio measures whether the company has sufficient net current assets to support the volume of its sales or, on the other hand, if the capital invested in working capital is working hard enough to produce sales.

.08   Profit Margin on Sales

The profit margin on sales is obtained by dividing net income by net sales for the period. A ratio of 7.5 percent compared to an industry average of 4.6 percent indicates a company is achieving an above-average rate of profits on each sales dollar received.

The profit margin on sales does not indicate how profitable a company is for a given period of time. Only by determining how many times the total assets turned over during a period of time is it possible to ascertain the amount of net income earned on total assets. The rate of return on assets is computed by using net income as the numerator and average total assets as a denominator. An average of 6.2 percent compared to an industry average of 4.9 percent is above the average of an industry and results from a high profit margin on sales.

.09   Rate of Return on Common Stock Equity

This ratio is defined as net income after interest, taxes, and preferred stock dividends (if any) divided by average common stockholders' equity. When the rate of return on common stock equity is higher than the rate of return on total assets, the company is considered to be trading on the equity. Trading on the equity increases a company's financial risk, but it increases a company's earnings.

.10   Dividend Yield

The dividend yield is the cash dividend per share divided by the market price of the stock at the time the yield is determined. This ratio gives the rate of return that an investor will receive at the time on an investment in a stock or bond.

.11   Times Interest Earned

This ratio is computed by dividing income before interest charges and taxes by the interest charge. The ratio indicates the safety of a bondholder's investment. A company that has an interest earned ratio of 5 to 1 shows a significantly safer position for meeting its bond interest obligations than a company with a lower ratio.

¶17,005   Statement of Changes in Stockholders' Equity

This statement presents an equity analysis of changes from year to year in each shareholder's account, records any additional shares issued, foreign currency translation gains/losses, dividends per share (if paid), and retained earnings. This last figure indicates how well the company itself is doing by revealing how much of the profits it can retain to finance further growth opportunities. In an era of corporate raiding and takeovers, management may be wise to be sure that retained earnings are not too high, but are put to good use in increasing total earnings per share for the benefit of current stockholders.

.01   Return on Equity

This ratio is another method of determining earning power. Here, the opening equity (capital stock plus retained earnings, plus or minus any other equity section items) is divided into the net income for the year to give the percentage earned on that year's investment.

.02   Return to Investors

This is a relatively new ratio used mostly by financial publications, primarily for comparison of many companies in similar industries. The opening equity is divided into the sum of the dividends paid plus the market price appreciation of the period. In addition, the ratio is sometimes extended to cover five years, ten years or more.

.03   Dividend Payout Ratio

The *dividend* per common share is divided by the *earnings* per common share to get the *percentage* of dividend payout.

The dividends on common stock will vary with the profitability of the company, but other considerations also affect the percentage of payout:

1. The relative stability of the earnings
2. The need for new capital
3. The directors' judgment concerning the outlook for earnings

4. The general views of management relating to the advisability of:
   a. Plowing back a large part of earnings into the business
   b. Raising additional funds from outside sources.

Dividends on the preferred stock are not subject to a year-to-year fluctuation. If the fixed dividend on *cumulative* preferred stock for any year cannot be met, the payments would accumulate and be paid before any dividends could be declared on the common stock.

¶17,006   Present Value Computation and Application

The procedure of computing interest on principal *and interest on interest* underlies the concept of *compounding*. There are a number of accounting procedures (accounting for bonds, accounts receivable, accounts payable, and leases, for example) to which the compound interest formula (and variations) can be applied:

- The *future value* of a sum of money. If $1,000 (the principal P) is deposited in a bank today, what will be the balance (S) in the account in n years (or *periods*) if the bank accumulates interest at the rate of i percent per year (or *period*)?
- The *present value* of a sum of money due at the end of a period of time. What is the value *today* of the amount owed if $1,000 has to be paid, say to a creditor, n years from today?
- The *future value of an annuity*, which is a series of *equal* payments made at *equal* intervals. If $1,000 a year is deposited for n years, how much will have accumulated at the end of the n-years period if the deposits earn interest at the rate of i percent per year?
- The *present value of an annuity*, which is a series of *equal* payments made at *equal* intervals. If we are to be paid $1,000 a year for n years, how much is this annuity worth today, given i percent rate of interest?

The formula for the future value of a sum of money is the familiar compound interest formula. In the four examples to follow, let:

> S = The future worth of a sum of money invested today.
> P = Principal, or the sum of money that will accumulate to S amount of money.
> i = The rate of interest (r may be substituted).
> n = Number of periods of time.

It is important to understand that a "period of time" is not necessarily one year, even though rates of interest in the United States are always understood to mean the rate for a period of one year. A period can be any length of time (e.g., day, week, month, year, second, minute, hour). Time is a *continuous*, not a *discrete*, function.

With compound interest the total amount accumulated (S in the formula) at the end of one period earns interest during the subsequent period, or "interest on interest." The formula is:

$$S = P(1 + i)^n$$

At this point, it should be emphasized that the user no longer must do the arithmetic. Not only can the problem types be solved by the use of tables, but hand calculators and software programs will perform the computations and give the answers. The user has simply only to enter the numbers that represent the letters in the formula. With respect to the arithmetic, however, three of the variables in the equation are always known quantities; therefore, finding the value of the fourth and *un*known variable follows.

A Word of Caution. Computational errors caused by entering the wrong value for n are not uncommon. If $i = 12\%$ and the compounding period is every six months, n in the formula is 2 (semi-annual) and the interest rate i is 6 percent, the annual rate divided by 2. If the compounding period is quarterly, n is 4 and the interest rate i is 3 percent, the annual rate divided by 4. Thus, since the nominal interest rate is for a one-year period, if more compounding periods are involved the number of these periods = n and the nominal annual interest rate is divided by the number of compounding periods in a year to get the interest rate i needed for the calculation. If the compounding period is daily (as is the case in many financial institutions savings policies), n becomes $i/360$—360 days in the year are applied in this country for interest calculations instead of 365. This is because the smaller the denominator, the bit more interest the *lender* collects. However, if the formula applies to a problem involving U.S. Government bonds, a 365-day year must be assumed because it enables the government to borrow a bit cheaper, relatively.

.01   Annuities

The previous discussion considers the accumulation of interest on a *single* payment, however, the single payment may be invested. *Annuities* apply to problems that involve a series of *equal payments* (or investments or savings) made at *equal intervals* of time. The period of time between payments is called the payment period. The period of time between computation of the interest accumulation is called the *interest-conversion period*. When the payment period exactly equals the interest-conversion period, the annuity is an *ordinary annuity*. The equal payments are termed rents, which are spread over equal periods of time, the first rent payment made at the *start* of the annuity, and the last payment made at the *end* of the annuity.

The *future worth* of the annuity is the sum of the future worth of each of the separate rents. Assuming $100 invested we have $100 at time 1. At time 2, we have the $100 invested that day, plus the $100 invested at time 1, plus the interest earned during the period between time 1 and time 2. At time 3, another $100 is deposited; we now have the $100 deposited that day, the $100 deposited at time 2 plus the interest earned for one period, and the $100 deposited at time 1 plus the interest earned during the period between time 1 and time 2.

The formula for the future worth of an annuity of $1 is:

$$S = \frac{(1 + i)^n - 1}{i}$$

Note that the formula for the accumulation of interest on an ordinary annuity has the same variables as the compounding formula for a single payment.

To obtain S for any amount more than $1, multiply both sides of the equation by the amount invested, by P. In this case, multiply both sides of the equation by 100. As above, the amount for $1 can be found in tables (or by the use of a hand calculator).

The *present worth* of an annuity concerns the same question as the present worth of a single payment for *n years at i rate of interest*. How much would we pay today for an annuity in order to receive a given number of equal payments at equal intervals for a given number of periods in the future?

The formula for $1 is:

$$S = \frac{1 - (1 + i)^{-n}}{i}$$

The method for accounting for the premium or discount on bonds payable are compound interest procedures. The resultant interest charges are the product of the net balance of bonds payable and the effective interest rate at the time the bonds were issued. For bonds issued at a premium, the computed interest charges will *decrease* each year as the bonds approach maturity because the net balance of the liability decreases each year due to the amortization of the premium. Conversely, for bonds issued at a discount, the computed interest charges will *increase* each year as the bonds approach maturity because of the accumulation of the discount. When interest is material, the effective interest method is used to amortize either the premium or the discount (see below).

When interest is not material, straight-line method is used for the amortization of premiums or accumulation of discounts which involves simply dividing the original premium or discount by the number of years until maturity to determine the constant annual amount of amortization or accumulation.

The most frequent application of the above formula for accounting procedures is the present value formula. For example, when a company issues bonds, cash is debited for the proceeds of the bond issue and a liability account is credited for the amount. The entries will be the present value of the bonds. Assume a bond issue sold at a premium, or for more than the typical $1,000 par value, the present value of which we assume to be $1,200. The entries at the time of the sale of the bonds are:

| Cash | $1,200 | |
| Bonds Payable | | $1,200 |

An alternative treatment is permissible by rule:

Cash	$1,200	
Bonds Payable		$1,000 (par)
Premium on Bonds		200

The Premium Account is an adjunct account (an addition) to Bonds Payable. The interest charge each year is computed by multiplying the bond liability *at the end of each year* by the effective rate of interest (see the definition). The adjunct account at the end of each period is debited for the amount of interest which reduces the liability each period. *The interest charge calculation is computed on the reduced amount of the liability that occurs each year as the adjunct account is debited.* At maturity, the Premium Account has a zero balance and the liability will be reduced to the maturity, or face amount (the par value of $1,000) of the bond.

Assume the bond is sold at a $200 *discount*, that is, $200 less than the $1,000 par value. The journal entry is:

Cash	$800	
Bond Discount	200	
Bonds Payable		$1,000

The Bond Discount account is a *contra* account to bonds payable with the liability at time of issue $800. Again, for an amount deposited for the annuity of more than $1, multiply both sides of the equation by that amount. Also, again note the same variables as in the compound interest formula.

PART IV

Niche Accounting

When one thinks of accountants, they usually think of tax professionals or bookkeepers. Perhaps next would be auditors. But there are other areas in which accountants often practice. Some areas do still involve taxes, like practicing before the IRS or exercising power of attorney. But there are also Internet accounting, e-commerce, insurance, expert witness services, sometimes referred to as litigation support, as well as design and implementation of internal controls. Part IV addresses these topics.

CHAPTER 18
Practice Before the IRS and the Power of Attorney

¶18,000 Overview

While anyone may prepare his or her own tax return, and a corporation's accountants may prepare its tax returns, preparing another person's or corporation's tax return for a fee is a different matter. The specific difference results from a determination that an individual is "practicing before the IRS." Just as independent auditors face particular scrutiny when they attest to a company's financial statements, so tax return preparers incur regulation by the IRS when their role with respect to their clients extends beyond mere clerical presentation of income and expenses on a tax return to "practice" before the IRS.

Practice before the IRS comprehends all matters connected with a presentation to the IRS, or any of its officers or employees, relating to a taxpayer's rights, privileges, or liabilities under laws or regulations administered by the IRS. Such presentations include, but are not limited to, preparing documents; filing documents; corresponding and communicating with the IRS; rendering oral and written advice with respect to any entity, transaction, plan or arrangement, or other plan or arrangement having a potential for tax avoidance or evasion; and representing a client at conferences, hearings and meetings.

In recent years, the IRS sought to expand its scope of direct regulation of tax return preparers by broadening the definition of who would be considered to be practicing before the IRS. Currently, the primary scope of regulation covers CPAs, Enrolled Agents, and attorneys. But the IRS has been militating to regulate the majority of tax return prepares who do not fall into one of these three categories. To date this regulation consists in the requirement to obtain an ID number.

In January 2010, the IRS proposed new registration, testing and continuing education of federal tax return preparers, and recommended a number of steps that it planned to implement gradually. At the time, paid tax return preparers had *no registration requirement with the IRS*, but they have been required to sign the returns they prepare and provide either their Social Security Number or a Preparer Tax Identification Number (PTIN). The PTIN had been an optional number a preparer could apply for if they preferred not to disclose their SSN. This IRS plan was scuttled by the courts.

In 2014, as the result of tax preparer lawsuit victories, IRS plans for full-scale regulation of the industry—which were to include mandatory training and testing—were put on hold. Unless Congress eventually authorizes such regulation in the future, it is now a dead issue (except for the PTIN requirement).

The turning point was the IRS loss in the *Loving v. Commissioner* case, holding that the mere preparation of a tax return for pay was not sufficient to constitute "practice before the IRS." As Karen Hawkins, then Director of the Office of Professional Responsibility, clarified, however, that determination is not made on a return-by-return basis but by considering the scope of a preparer's practice. Thus, although a preparer may merely prepare tax returns for some clients, the fact that he or she also represents other clients before the IRS in examinations, means that preparer is covered by the preparer regulations (collectively referred to as Circular 230) and thus falls under the jurisdiction of the Office of Professional Responsibility as one "practicing before the IRS." In addition, Hawkins distinguished between the mere clerical aspect of tax return preparation and the use of judgment in interpreting the tax laws. Thus, the wording of Circular 230 should be read in light of its interpretation by the Office of Professional Responsibility.

Though the regulations constituting Circular 230 were revised in 2010, additional revisions were made in 2014 reflecting the court's ruling in *Loving* and clarifying other issues. Some of these changes are discussed below in section entitled "Clarification and Advice from the Director of the Office of Professional Responsibility."

Among the specific additions in 2014 are 10.31, which prohibits the electronic transfer of a taxpayer's refund to a tax practitioner's account, and 10.35 (replacing old 10.35 that dealt with "covered opinions"), which provides a general standard requiring professional competence in all matters.

¶18,001 PTIN Renewal for All Tax Professionals

What looked like an IRS victory in regulating the tax return preparation industry turned to coal for them after the courts in *Loving v. Commissioner* ruled the IRS had gone beyond the bounds of its authority. Prior to that defeat, the IRS was poised to require not only ID numbers for preparers (PTINs) but mandatory continuing education and qualifying exams. Instead, what was supposed to be required, turned out to be voluntary. For the 2014 tax season, tax preparers were required to have a preparer tax identification number (PTIN) but were not required to undergo mandatory testing or continuing education. As a result, the new Registered Tax Return Preparer (RTRP) designation went by the boards. The annual registration of paid preparers will continue, however.

PTIN renewal and registration for the 2018 filing season began in October of 2017. This timing has held true in subsequent years. Anyone who prepares or assists in preparing federal tax returns for compensation must have a valid PTIN before preparing returns. All enrolled agents must also have a PTIN.

In place of the required program for preparers who are not CPAs, attorneys, or Enrolled Agents, the IRS has substituted a voluntary regimen called the Annual Filing Season Program (AFSP). This program was subsequently challenged by the AICPA. On October 30, 2015, the Federal Circuit Court for Washington D.C. reversed a 2014 Federal District Court ruling dismissing the AICPA's challenge. The case has been resolved with the court rejecting the AICPA's claims. According to the IRS, "the new program aims to recognize the efforts of non-credentialed return preparers who aspire to a higher level of professionalism." The requirements are met by obtaining 18 hours of continuing education, including a six-hour federal tax law refresher course with test. Those who undergo the voluntary training will receive an Annual Filing Season Program – Record of Completion from the IRS. AFSP participants are included in a public database of return preparers. The IRS launched a public education campaign in January 2015 encouraging taxpayers to carefully select return preparers. The Directory of Federal Tax Return Preparers with Credentials and Select Qualifications will include the name, city, state, zip code, and credentials of all attorneys, CPAs, enrolled agents, enrolled retirement plan agents and enrolled actuaries with a valid PTIN, as well as all AFSP – Record of Completion holders.

The change in IRS policy was announced on June 26, 2014, by Commissioner Koskinen. According to the Commissioner, The Voluntary Return Preparer Education Program "is a new program that will help taxpayers by improving the tax know-how and filing season readiness of paid tax return preparers. We intend to have this voluntary education program in place by the beginning of the 2015 filing season. This is part of a broader effort the IRS began a few years ago to achieve a minimum level of competency across the federal tax return preparer community. Taxpayers need to be confident that the preparer they hire knows enough about taxes to help them with their federal income tax returns. That's especially important now, because we have a very complex tax code, and the majority of taxpayers in this country use the help of a paid return preparer to do their taxes each year."

The IRS's concern about prepares is based in part on the fact that "about 60 percent of paid tax return preparers in the U.S. operate without regulation or oversight." According to the IRS Commissioner, "Although many of them do a good job, we have found that others are poorly equipped to assist taxpayers in preparing returns. For that reason, the IRS had started a mandatory program of education and testing for unregulated tax return preparers who did not have professional credentials. But we had to suspend that program because the courts ruled that we didn't have the legal authority to require education and testing. So we're launching a voluntary program as a temporary substitute. It's called the Annual Filing Season Program."

The Commissioner called the program "temporary" because the IRS has been urging Congress to enact a proposal that would give them the authority for mandatory oversight of return preparers. "This voluntary program is not the ideal solution," according to the IRS, "but until legislation is enacted, we still have a responsibility to taxpayers and to our tax system to keep moving forward with our efforts to improve service to taxpayers."

The online PTIN renewal process takes about 15 minutes. Renewed PTINs will be valid for the calendar year. The IRS also has significantly upgraded the PTIN system to make it easier to use and more intuitive.

Preparers who have forgotten their log-in information, password or email address can use online tools to resolve these issues.

Following the IRS's loss in the *Loving* case and the IRS's subsequent announcement of its voluntary preparer program, the "Annual Filing Season Program," the AICPA filed suit on July 15, 2014, challenging the IRS's new rule regulating tax return preparers. In its press release, the AICPA said it "has been a steadfast supporter of the IRS's overall goals of enhancing compliance by tax return preparers and elevating ethical conduct. However, the IRS's new rule regulating tax return preparers is an unlawful exercise of government power. By implementing a purportedly "voluntary" program that is mandatory in effect, the rule is an end-run around *Loving v. IRS*, a federal court ruling which struck down the IRS's earlier attempt to regulate tax return preparers. The IRS simply does not have the authority to proceed with the new rule. By doubling the number of categories of tax return preparers to eight, the rule will also confuse consumers. Worse yet, the new rule will do nothing to address the problem of unethical or fraudulent tax return preparers – which should be a top priority."

"As a result, the AICPA has filed suit in federal court to prevent the IRS from moving ahead with this unjustified and unlawful program. The IRS should withdraw the new rule, consult with stakeholders, and use the tools and data already at its disposal to monitor unethical tax return preparers. At a minimum, the IRS must conduct a legitimate notice-and-comment rulemaking before proceeding." In its suit, the AICPA argues that, "In reality . . . the new rule is de facto mandatory because it creates a strong competitive incentive for unenrolled tax return preparers to comply."

¶18,002 Clarification and Advice from the Director of the Office of Professional Responsibility

Those CPAs and other tax return preparers who have ploughed through the IRS Regulations controlling "practice before the IRS," collectively referred to as Circular 230, are well aware it is not a simple read. For this reason, and also in light of the IRS defeat in the *Loving* case, in June 2015, then Director of the Office of Professional Responsibility, Karen Hawkins, released a two-and-one-half hour webinar explaining in detail the purpose of the regulations, their impact on practitioners and other useful guidance. The purpose of this section is to summarize some of the more salient and practical points noted by the Director. For those interested in viewing the entire webinar it is posted on the IRS Web site and may be found under the "All Webinars" Tab.

One of the most common and contentious areas of tax practice concerns the preparer's relationship to his or her client, which has the dual status of advocate for the client and government-regulated preparer. In the webinar, Director Hawkins points to several key areas that CPAs and other tax return preparers should focus on when walking the line between advocate and regulated preparer. Among these areas are conflicts of interest and the unquestioned acceptance of client representations.

Regarding conflicts of interest, Hawkins points out that while attorneys are trained to spot potential issues of conflict, CPAs are not. It would be more accurate to say that the training CPAs receive on conflicts of interest arises primarily in the area of financial audits rather than tax compliance. As Hawkins explains, conflicts of interest may occur when representing two taxpayers with conflicting interests or when the taxpayer's interests conflict with your interests as a tax preparer. The rules regarding conflicts of interest are found in Circular 230, section 10.29.

Recognizing Conflicts of Interest. As the Director explains, "There are really two triggering points. The first is if you have one client whose interests are directly adverse to another client. Partners are now fighting with one another. You've been representing them in the partnership and now they are disputing something that will essentially implode the partnership. They are directly adverse to one another. . . . It can [also] be true of husbands and wives. The second part of the analysis is a little more challenging. It essentially says that you may not represent a conflicting interest that exists when there is a significant risk that your representation of one client will be materially limited by your representation of another client, a former client, a third party, or . . . your own personal interests. So what does that mean? Well, the responsibilities to the other client is not much different than the direct adversity, except that maybe they are not suing one another. Maybe you have a married couple who has separated and so there is a potential for there to be a significant risk that you're going to be limited in representing husband vis-à-vis the wife."

Further, Hawkins points out, "The one that is most troubling and the one where I think practitioners get themselves into the most trouble is . . . [the conflict with] your own personal interests because this arises probably more than you realize. You prepare tax returns for somebody. The IRS comes in and examines the return. They start asking questions about various entries on the return, some of which you may have advised about, some of which you may have calculated, some of which you may have characterized in some fashion. And you realize that you are going through the examination representing the client which by the way at the initial point in time is no conflict because you have a neutrality of interest. . . . But during the examination suddenly the IRS is focusing on issues that you have some responsibility for them being on the return and you start to temper your responses to the IRS because now you're covering your own self. You're embarrassed, you're afraid of a preparer penalty."

Accepting Client Information at Face Value. The issue of accepting a client's information at face value is another trouble spot according to Karen Hawkins, "The last part of 10.34 is one people think they understand that most of the time they only remember the first part of it. 10.34(d) says that the practitioner may rely in good faith and without verification on client information." The Office of Professional Responsibility interprets this statement quite differently than many practitioners do. It presents a significant challenge to both the ingenuity and professional ethics of practitioners. In particular the challenge is to make a professional determination of the line between what may be taken at face value when offered by the client and what must be questioned or clarified.

As the Director observes, it is true that you don't have to audit your client's information. But, "you can't ignore the implications of other information that you have been given whether by the client or someone else. You can't ignore actual knowledge and you have to make reasonable inquiries if the information you are being given appears to be incorrect or inconsistent or incomplete. So you've got to be thinking about what the client is giving you and saying."

"The other thing about this that's important," according to Hawkins, "is the difference between information or data and actual characterization or decisions. A client comes to you with their tax data where they . . . . tell you they paid $100,000 in alimony. As a matter of 10.34(d) you can accept $100,000. You may want to ask for documentation as a backup. That might be your best practice. If you have no reason to think differently about what the client is telling you maybe it's consistent with prior years or it doesn't appear to be incomplete or incorrect for any reason -- you know they're divorced -- you can accept $100,000. What you cannot accept is the characterization of the 100,000 as alimony. Because that's a legal conclusion. It could be child support, it could be family support. It could be deductible or not deductible. Anybody who's paying it wants to be alimony because deductible. Anybody who's receiving it once to be child support because it's not reportable. Not taxable on the other side. It's your responsibility as part of your due diligence to ask the question that can lead to the characterization issues."

Another example cited by the Director deals with the characterization of income. The client informs you, "I had 50,000 in capital gain last year -- well," says Hawkins, "how do you know capital gain? Maybe some of it was ordinary income. Maybe it is depreciation recapture. You can accept the number in many instances but you cannot accept the characterization. So make the distinction between what is information that your client has that is unique to the client that you can expect to receive from them and trust unless you have some reason not to trust it, versus the determinations that you as the practitioner and the professional need to make about what you're calling that when you put it on the tax return or what you're calling it when you put the deal together, whatever it may be."

New 10.37 Providing Written Advice. Director Hawkins: "The next provision that I'm going to cover is another of the due diligence provisions and this provision is brand-new. There was a 10.37 but this has been rewritten so dramatically that I consider it to be brand-new. It is the due diligence provision for the giving of written advice. Written advice is well settled—anything in writing from a Post-it note to an email to a fax or a letter to a formal opinion. It is all written advice of one sort or another if the tax question has been asked. And the thing I like about 10.37 is it is a very principles-based very practical very flexible provision. So there's no checklist involved. There's nothing that you have to that is black and white, frankly. It's a very amorphous series of reasonableness concepts which is, I think, much more in keeping with ethical concepts. 10.37 says that when you're doing and giving written advice you have to make reasonable efforts to determine the relevant facts, you have to reasonably consider those relevant facts and you have to make reasonable factual and legal assumptions in situations where you don't know actual facts."

Joining Your Client in the Audit Lottery. The Director warns, "You may not rely on representations and statements or agreements or anything else being given to you or told to you if you know or should know that the information is based on incorrect or incomplete or inconsistent representations or assumptions. One of the things that we see in 10.37 tie some of the language from the due diligence provisions into one another. So this concept I already discussed with you when I talked about 10.34d. It is appearing again here. The effort that we made in the latest revision in circular 230 was to try to bring some consistency to the definitions and words we are using. As we move from one provision to the next words would continue to mean the same thing. They mean the same thing here as I discussed in 10.34d. 10.37 goes on to say it's a part of your due diligence and you have to apply the applicable law to the relevant facts. There is part of my discussion with you from 10.22—the general due diligence provision where I talked about round facts and square holes—this is when you are doing written advice. **You may not play audit lottery with your advice** and what I mean by that is you may not give advice that is based on an assumption that whatever the position is will not be found—that the return will not be examined or if it's examined it will be noticed. **These are all versions of audit lottery**. And I know your clients ask you those sorts of things all the time -- what are the odds I'll get caught if, etc. Or what are the odds that the IRS is going to find this if they examine it? What are the odds the IRS is going to examine this if I take this deduction? These are all versions of the client asking you to play audit lottery with them. You are not allowed to do that in the context of your due diligence obligations in giving written advice. You may not take those matters into account."

Forget about Your Email Hold-Harmless Disclaimers. Hawkins: "For those of you . . . [who] still happen to have e-mails that contain that disclaimer and you have forgotten even why it was there or how it started, I am here to tell you not only is it not needed, but I would really appreciate it if you removed at least the beginning phrases that blame the appearance of that disclaimer on your e-mail on the Internal Revenue Service Circular 230, the office of professional responsibility, or Karen Hawkins. We don't have anything to do with that disclaimer anymore. We have rescinded the requirement. If you want to put a disclaimer on your emails of some sort that is entirely up to you that just don't to blame it on the agency or OPR because we no longer think it is unnecessary. In fact I never thought it was necessary."

Judging Your Own Competence (Section 10.35). "You can be competent," the Director explains, "because you have already had experience in a certain way that lets you immediately know what the issues are associated with a particular fact pattern. You can become competent so that you can go into the research, take a class, you can read or you can hire or consult with competence so that you can bring a subject matter expert in, you can call someone you know who is knowledgeable in the particular area on the phone and ask for 30 minutes of their time, whatever it may be. So there are a variety of ways that you can be competent but you don't have to have it all wrapped up into you all the time. None of us are totally competent at all points in time. But we have ways of getting competence. And more importantly, you have to recognize when you are at competence. So that you can either get competent or you can send the client to someone who is. So there is a responsibility here. . . . [Not] only do you need to be competent but you need to recognize your areas of weakness and make sure you are getting your client appropriate representation and advice and some other fashion if they can't come from you."

Expedited Suspension of Practitioners. Final note from Director Hawkins: "Okay so, the next provision I want to tell you about is a new addition to an existing regulation. And 10.82 of Circular 230, the office of professional responsibility is authorized to do what's called expedited suspensions of practitioners who have been adjudicated in some other third-party forum to be unfit to continue to practice. So, these are the sorts of things where a lawyer might lose their license from their state, a CPA might have their CPA certificate revoked by their state, anyone of these or an enrolled agent might be convicted of a tax crime. These are all recited in 10.82 as precursors for our use of this expedited suspension process. And the expedited suspension process proceeds somewhat along the lines that I described of our regular process, just faster. So we are able to move the process and shorten everything that goes on. So there is still an opportunity for a conference, there is still an opportunity to argue your case, there is still an opportunity to argue why we should settle at some other level besides a suspension. So, you have those opportunities. We just give you a very short period of time in which to have them. So that we can move forward."

¶18,003 Paid Tax Preparers Must File Due Diligence Checklist with EITC Claims

One of the most frequent forms of tax refund fraud, other than those involving identity theft, involves Earned Income Tax Credits (EITC). Claiming the credit for taxpayers who do not qualify is a simple way—but still fraudulent—for obtaining or increasing a client's tax refund. The IRS now requires paid tax return preparers to file a due diligence checklist, Form 8867, Paid Preparer's Earned Income Credit Checklist, with any federal return claiming EITC. Tax preparers who do not send Form 8867 with EITC returns are subject to a $500 penalty per return.

The *due diligence* requirement, enacted by Congress over a decade ago, was designed to reduce errors on returns claiming the EITC, most of which are prepared by tax professionals.

The IRS created Form 8867 to help preparers meet the requirement by obtaining eligibility information from their clients. Preparers have been required to keep copies of the form, or comparable documentation, which is subject to review by the IRS. To help ensure compliance with the law and to ensure that eligible taxpayers receive the correct credit amount, effective January 1, 2012, the IRS now requires paid tax preparers to file the Form 8867 with each return claiming the EITC.

According to the IRS, "Only paid preparers have to complete this form. If you were paid to complete a tax return for any taxpayer claiming the earned income credit (EIC), submit this form with the return. If you are a signing tax return preparer electronically filing the return, file the form electronically with the return. If you are a signing tax return preparer not electronically filing the return, give the taxpayer the completed form for filing. If you are a nonsigning tax return preparer, give the signing tax return preparer the completed form in electronic or non-electronic format."

The EITC benefits low-and moderate-income workers and working families and the tax benefit varies by income, family size and filing status. Unlike most deductions and credits, the EITC is refundable—taxpayers can get it even if they owe no tax.

Although as many as one in five eligible taxpayers fail to claim the EITC, some of those who do claim it either compute it incorrectly or are ineligible. The IRS is employing this step as part of its efforts to ensure that the credit actually goes to taxpayers who qualify. As of December 2022, 31 million workers and families received about $64 billion in EITC. The average amount of EITC received nationwide was about $2,043.

¶18,004   Supervised Preparers and Non-1040 Preparers

All tax return preparers must have a PTIN. The suspension by the IRS of its attempt to regulate all tax return preparers by requiring annual training and examinations did not affect its requirement that all paid tax return preparers maintain a PTIN and renew it annually. The fee to renew a PTIN for 2023 is $30.75.

.01 Supervised Preparer Designation

Supervised preparers are individuals who do not sign, and are not required to sign, tax returns as a paid return preparer but are:

- Employed by attorney or CPA firms or
- Employed by other recognized firms that are at least 80 percent owned by attorneys, CPAs, or enrolled agents, and
- Supervised by an attorney, certified public accountant, enrolled agent, enrolled retirement plan agent, or enrolled actuary who signs the returns prepared by the supervised preparer as the paid tax return preparer.

When applying for or renewing a PTIN, supervised preparers must provide the PTIN of their supervisor. The supervisor's PTIN must be a valid and active PTIN. Supervised preparers may not:

- Sign any tax return they prepare or assist in preparing.
- Represent taxpayers before the IRS in any capacity.
- Identify themselves as a registered tax return preparer or a Circular 230 practitioner.

.02 Non-Form 1040 Series Preparer Designation

Non-Form 1040 series preparers are individuals who do not prepare, or assist in the preparation of, any Form 1040 series tax return or claim for refund, except a Form 1040-PR or Form 1040-SS, for compensation.

When applying for or renewing a PTIN, non-Form 1040 series preparers must certify that they do not prepare, or assist in the preparation of, any Form 1040 series tax return or claim for refund, except a Form 1040-PR or Form 1040-SS, for compensation.

Non-Form 1040 series preparers may:

- Sign any tax return they prepare or assist in preparing.

- Represent taxpayers before revenue agents, customer service representatives, or similar officers and employees of the IRS (including the Taxpayer Advocate Service) during an examination if the individual signed the tax return or claim for refund for the taxable year under examination.

Non-Form 1040 series preparers may not:

- Prepare or assist in preparing any Form 1040 series tax return or claim for refund, except a Form 1040-PR or Form 1040-SS, for compensation.
- Identify themselves as a registered tax return preparer or a Circular 230 practitioner.

¶18,005   The Statute of Limitations

It is important for practitioners to understand the statute of limitation rules for tax returns and other tax-related matters. Even though these rules have been in place for many years, subtle changes still occur in their interpretation. In 2015, for example, tagged on to the *Surface Transportation Act of 2015* was a provision making it likely that the six-year statute of limitations (see below) will apply to more taxpayers. The change was a reaction to a 2012 Supreme Court case, *Home Concrete & Supply, LLC*, which took issue with the IRS's interpretation of "omitted income" by making reference to the basis of an asset sold.

A statute of limitations indicates the period of time during which a certain legal action may be taken. After that period has lapsed, the law bars further action. For income tax returns, the basic statute of limitations is three years. The rule means that the IRS is permitted to examine (audit) a tax return for three years from the date it was filed. This is the general rule, to which there are numerous exceptions. One exception deals with returns filed before their original due date. For these returns, the statute of limitations does not begin to run until the due date (without extensions) is passed. If an individual's 1040 return is due on April 18, 2023 for example, and the taxpayer files the return on February 15, 2023, the three-year statute will not commence to run until April 18, 2023. On the other hand, if an individual taxpayer files her return on July 15 (with or without an extension) the three-year statute of limitations will begin to run from July 15 of the year filed. For a return that was never filed, the statute of limitations remains open and the IRS may audit that tax return at any time.

The Six-year Statute of Limitations. If a taxpayer omits to report gross income in excess of 25 percent of the gross income otherwise reported on a tax return, the statute of limitations (using the same conventions noted above regarding early- or late-filed returns) is six years, rather than three. As noted above, the interpretation of this rule (contained in IRC § 6501(e)(1)(A)(i)) has been a source of disagreement between the IRS and taxpayers. According to its plain language, the gross income to be considered appeared to be only the amounts of revenue or gross sales, not the net amount of income as reduced by the basis of the cost of goods sold. In its regulations (Reg. §301.6501(e)-1(a)(1)(iii)), however, the IRS took the position that an understatement of the basis of an asset sold is effectively the same thing as underreporting gross income, since the amount of income subject to tax is affected by both gross revenue and the basis of what was sold. The Supreme Court's *United States v. Home Concrete & Supply, LLC*, had ruled that the IRS's position was incorrect, given the plain wording of the statute, and the court effectively invalidated that portion of the IRS's regulations. But in 2015, Congress, made explicit the principle that an understatement of the basis of an asset, since it impacts taxable income to the same extent as the omission of gross income, will trigger the six-year statute of limitations (assuming the result is an omission of income of more than 25 percent of what was reported on the return). This law change, a part of the *Surface Transportation Act of 2015*, became effective on July 31, 2015. Its effect will not be retroactive.

Extension by Signed Agreement. The most common reason that a taxpayer will extend the statute of limitations is if he is being audited and the auditor request additional time to complete the examination. The extension is granted by signing Form 872.

No Statute of Limitations for Fraud. When a taxpayer commits fraud by intentionally misreporting income or expenses, there is no statute of limitations. If the taxpayer later attempts to amend the fraudulent return by filing an amended return, this action will have no impact on the statute of limitations. Fraud may not be undone by confessing the truth or apologizing, nor by filing a new return.

Statute of Limitations on IRS Collections. The IRS has a ten-year period during which to attempt to collect an assessed tax from a taxpayer. After ten years from the date of the assessment or levy the IRS is barred from any further collection activities. As a practical matter, it may be necessary to call the tolling of the ten-year period to the attention of the IRS to receive a release. It is not an automatic process.

Other Events Extending the Statute of Limitations. There are numerous other events that may extend the statute of limitations. A useful list can be found in the IRS Internal Revenue Manual (IRM) online at Part 25. Special Topics, Chapter 6. Statute of Limitations.

¶18,006   Offers in Compromise

It is not uncommon for a CPA to be confronted with a taxpayer who, for any of a number of reasons, has been unable to pay back taxes owed, although they have filed their tax returns. Depending on the severity of the taxpayer's circumstances, one option is to make an "Offer in Compromise." This is a formal IRS procedure in which the tax owed is weighed against the taxpayer's ultimate ability to pay. The desired result for a taxpayer who is in over his head with the IRS is to come to an agreement to pay a lesser amount in full settlement of the tax debt.

Requesting an offer in compromise requires filing Form 656, Offer in Compromise. The IRS suggests that, "It may be a legitimate option if you can't pay your full tax liability, or doing so creates a financial hardship." Among the facts considered are the following:

- Ability to pay
- Income
- Expenses
- Asset equity
- The taxpayer must not be in an open bankruptcy proceeding
- The taxpayer must be current on filing his or her tax returns
- If the taxpayer is required to make quarterly estimated tax payments, these must be current
- If the taxpayer is a sole proprietor with employees, the payroll tax deposits for the employees must be current
- Doubt as to collectability – taxpayer has insufficient assets and income to pay the full amount.
- Exceptional circumstances – taxpayer owes this amount and has sufficient assets to pay the full amount, but due to exceptional circumstances, requiring full payment would cause an economic hardship or would be unfair and inequitable. Taxpayer must submit a written narrative explaining the exceptional circumstance

The IRS reports, "We generally approve an offer in compromise when the amount offered represents the most we can expect to collect within a reasonable period of time. Explore all other payment options before submitting an offer in compromise. The Offer in Compromise program is not for everyone."

The IRS screening process is quite strict. For a taxpayer to qualify it must be evident to the IRS that based on the taxpayer's income and assets, it is very unlikely that the IRS can expect to receive the full balance due in a timely manner. The application process requires meeting with the client and determining and documenting their monthly budget. The monthly amounts actually paid are generally limited to those specified by the federal government for a given location, referred to as the IRS Collection Financial Standards. The IRS Website offers a pre-qualification electronic worksheet to enable taxpayers or their representatives to see if they may qualify.

The IRS Collection Financial Standards include both national and local standards. The taxpayer's claimed expenses may not exceed these amounts. Standards for food, clothing and other items apply nationwide. Taxpayers are allowed the total National Standards amount for their family size, without questioning the amount actually spent.

National standards have also been established for minimum allowances for out-of-pocket health care expenses. Taxpayers and their dependents are allowed the standard amount on a per person basis, without questioning the amount actually spent.

Maximum allowances for housing and utilities and transportation, (Local Standards), vary by location. In most cases, the taxpayer is allowed the amount actually spent, or the local standard, whichever is less. The IRS provides tables listing the maximum transportation, housing, and utility costs for each of the larger metropolitan regions by county.

In addition to completing Form 656, Offer in Compromise, the taxpayer or his representative will have to complete Form 433-A (OIC), Collection Information Statement for Wage Earners and Self-Employed Individuals. This is a very detailed financial profile that includes the calculation of the taxpayer's equity in assets owned, bank account information, monthly income and sources, monthly expenses, and other information the IRS believes important for its determination.

¶18,007   Expanding the Confidentiality Privilege

The confidentiality protection for communications between a taxpayer and attorney has been expanded to communications involving tax advice between a taxpayer and any *federally authorized tax practitioners*. These tax practitioners include attorneys, certified public accountants, enrolled agents, enrolled actuaries, and certain other individuals allowed to practice before the IRS. This provision became effective for communications occurring after July 21, 1998.

This protection applies only to the advice given to the taxpayer by any of these individuals. Tax advice is considered to be advice in regard to a matter that is within the scope of the practitioner's authority to practice. The confidentiality protection is applied to communications that would be privileged if between the taxpayer and an attorney, and that relate to noncriminal tax matters or to tax proceedings brought in federal court by or against the United States.

This protection of tax advice communications does not apply to certain written communications between a federally authorized tax practitioner and a director, shareholder, officer, employee, agent, or representative of a corporation. It does not apply if the communication involves the promotion of the direct or indirect participation of the corporation in any tax shelter.

¶18,008   Overview of Basic Regulations Governing Practice Before the IRS

The basic regulations became effective July 26, 2002. They modify the general standards of practice affecting those individuals who are eligible to practice before the IRS. The rules require that:

- An enrolled agent maintain records and educational materials regarding his or her satisfaction of the qualifying continuing professional education credit.
- Sponsors of qualifying continuing professional education programs maintain records and educational material concerning these programs and those who attended them. (The collection of this material helps to ensure that individuals enrolled to practice before the IRS are informed of the newest developments in federal tax practice.)
- A practitioner obtain and retain for a reasonable period written consents to representation whenever such representation conflicts with the interests of the practitioner or the interests of another client of the practitioner. The consents are to be obtained after full disclosure of the conflict is provided to each party.
- A practitioner retain for a reasonable period any communication and the list of persons to whom that communication was provided with respect to public dissemination of fee information. (The collection of consents to representation and communications concerning practitioner fees protects the practitioner against claims of impropriety and ensures the integrity of the tax administration system.)
- An agency not conduct or sponsor, and a person not respond to, a collection of information unless it displays a valid control number.
- Books or records relating to a collection of information be retained as long as their contents might become material in the administration of any internal revenue law. Generally, tax returns and tax return information are confidential, as required by 26 U.S.C. 6103.

¶18,009   Practicing Before the IRS

A person is practicing before the IRS if he or she:

1. Communicates with the IRS for a taxpayer regarding taxpayer's rights, privileges, or liabilities under laws and regulations administered by the IRS.
2. Represents a taxpayer at conferences, hearings, or meetings with the IRS.
3. Prepares and files necessary documents with the IRS for a taxpayer.

Just preparing a tax return, furnishing information at the request of the IRS, or appearing as a witness for a taxpayer, does not constitute practicing before the IRS, unless, as noted earlier, the practitioner has other clients who he or she directly represent before the IRS in examinations, conferences, meetings, or hearings before the IRS. According to Karen Hawkins, the Director of the Office of Professional Responsibility, the determination of whether a practitioner is a "mere" tax return preparer or is practicing before the IRS is made by viewing that practitioner's entire tax practice.

.01   IRS Office of Professional Responsibility

The Office of Professional Responsibility (OPR) enforces the regulations governing practice before the IRS. When a final agency decision results in suspension or disbarment of a practitioner or when the practitioner has offered consent to suspension or disbarment and such consent has been accepted by the Director of OPR, the practitioner will not be permitted to practice before the IRS for the period of time imposed by the final agency decision or as agreed to by consent.

"Practice before the Internal Revenue Service" includes all matters connected with a presentation to the IRS or any of its officers or employees relating to a taxpayer's rights, privileges, or liabilities under laws or regulations administered by the IRS.

Such presentations include, but are not limited to:

- Preparing documents,
- Filing documents,
- Corresponding and communicating with the IRS,
- Rendering written advice with respect to any entity, transaction, plan or arrangement, or other plan or arrangement having a potential for tax avoidance or evasion, and
- Representing a client at conferences, hearings and meetings.

OPR issues the following Guidance to individuals who are under suspension or disbarment from practice for the purpose of informing them of specific restrictions these sanctions impose upon their professional conduct and upon the conduct of others with whom they may deal.

Suspended or disbarred individuals may not:

1. Prepare or file documents (including tax returns) or other correspondence with the IRS.
2. Render written advice with respect to any entity, transaction, plan or arrangement, or other plan or arrangement having a potential for tax avoidance or evasion.
3. Represent a client at conferences, hearings, and meetings.
4. Execute waivers, consents, or closing agreements; receive a taxpayer's refund check; or sign a tax return on behalf of a taxpayer.
5. File powers of attorney with the IRS.
6. Accept assistance from another person (or request assistance) or assist another person (or offer assistance) if the assistance relates to a matter constituting practice before the IRS, or enlist another person for the purpose of aiding and abetting practice before the IRS.
7. State or imply that he or she is eligible to practice before the IRS.

Suspended or disbarred individuals may:

1. Represent himself or herself with respect to any matter.
2. Appear before the IRS as a trustee, receiver, guardian, administrator, executor, or other fiduciary if duly qualified/authorized under the law of the relevant jurisdiction.
3. Appear as a witness for the taxpayer.
4. Furnish information at the request of the IRS or any of its officers or employees.
5. Receive information concerning a taxpayer from the IRS pursuant to a valid tax information authorization.

¶18,010   Becoming a Recognized Representative

Any of the following individuals can practice before the IRS. However, any individual who is recognized to practice—a recognized representative—must file a written declaration with the IRS that he or she is qualified and authorized to represent a taxpayer.

Those individuals include:

1. Any attorney who is not currently under suspension or disbarment from practice before the IRS and who is a member in good standing of the bar at the highest court of any state, possession, territory, commonwealth, or in the District of Columbia.
2. Any Certified Public Accountant who is not currently under suspension or disbarment from practice before the IRS and who is qualified to practice as a CPA in any state, possession, territory, commonwealth, or in the District of Columbia.
3. Any enrolled agent.
4. Any individual who is enrolled as an actuary by the Joint Board for the Enrollment of Actuaries. The practice of enrolled actuaries is limited to certain Internal Revenue Code sections that relate to their area of expertise, principally those sections governing employee retirement plans.
5. Any individual other than an attorney, CPA, enrolled agent, or enrolled actuary who prepares a return and signs it as the return preparer is an unenrolled return preparer. Also, any individual who prepares a return and is not required to sign it as the preparer is considered to be an unenrolled preparer.

   These individuals are limited in their practice. They can represent a taxpayer concerning the tax liability only for the year or period covered by the return that he or she prepared. Also, an unenrolled return preparer is permitted to represent taxpayers only before the Examination Division of the IRS and is not permitted to represent taxpayers before the Appeals, Collection, or any other division of the IRS.

Any enrolled retirement plan agent in active status may practice before the IRS. The practice of an enrolled retirement plan agent is limited to certain Internal Revenue Code sections that relate to his area of expertise, principally those sections governing employee retirement plans.

A student attorney who receives permission to practice before the IRS by virtue of his status as a law student under section 10.7(d) of Circular 230 may do so. See *Students in LITCs and STCP under Authorization for Special Appearances* on page 4.

A student CPA who receives permission to practice before the IRS by virtue of his status as a CPA student under section 10.7(d) of Circular 230 may also do so. See *Students in LITCs and STCP under Authorization for Special Appearances* on page 4.

Unenrolled return preparers cannot perform the following activities for another taxpayer:

a.   Sign claims for a refund.

b.   Receive refund checks.

c.   Sign consents to extend the statutory period for assessment for or collection of tax.

d.   Sign closing agreements regarding a tax liability.

e.   Sign waivers of restriction on assessment or collection of a tax deficiency.

6.   Because of their special relationship with a taxpayer, the following unenrolled individuals can represent the specified taxpayers before the IRS, provided they present satisfactory identification and proof of authority to represent.

a.   An individual can represent himself or herself before the IRS and does not have to file a written declaration of qualification and authority.

b.   An individual family member can represent members of his or her immediate family. Family members include a spouse, child, parent, brother, or sister of the individual.

c.   A *bona fide* officer of a corporation (including parents subsidiaries, or affiliated corporation), association, organized group, or, in the course of his or her other official duties, an officer of a governmental unit, agency, or authority can represent the organization of which he or she is an officer.

d.   A trustee, receiver, guardian, personal representative, or executor can represent a trust or estate.

e.   A regular full-time employee can represent his or her employer. An employer can be, but is not limited to, an individual, partnership, corporation (including parents, subsidiaries, or affiliated corporations), association, trust, receivership, guardianship, estate, organized group, governmental unit, agency, or authority.

Note: Unenrolled return preparers generally cannot represent clients before the IRS. However, unenrolled preparers have traditionally been able to deal with the IRS in connection with the returns they prepare. The Circular 230 revisions as originally proposed would have barred unenrolled prepares even from such limited practice. Here again, the IRS had second thoughts. The final revisions do not include that restriction.

Thus, an unenrolled return preparer who prepared the taxpayer's return for a year under examination can now continue to deal with the IRS on behalf of the taxpayer during the examination. However, the new rules make it clear that an unenrolled return preparer cannot represent a taxpayer before any other office of the IRS, including Collection or Appeals; execute closing agreements, claims for refund, or waivers; or otherwise represent taxpayers before the IRS.

An unenrolled individual can represent any individual or entity before IRS personnel who are outside the United States.

.01   Enrolled Retirement Plan Agents

As noted above, in the past only four categories of tax professionals have been eligible to represent clients before the IRS: (1) attorneys, (2) CPAs, (3) enrolled actuaries, and (4) enrolled agents. This meant that many retirement plans whose tax matters are handled by third party administrators or benefits consultants, have representatives who are not eligible to practice before the IRS.

The Circular 230 revisions add an additional category of eligible practitioners entitled *enrolled retirement plan agents*. These individuals are now authorized to handle a variety of retirement plan matters for the various plans they service. Procedures for the qualification of an enrolled retirement plan agent are similar to the current enrolled agent program. In Treasury Department Circular No. 230 (Rev. 4-2008), the Treasury Department granted enrollment as an enrolled retirement plan agent to an applicant who demonstrates special competence in qualified retirement plan matters by written examination administered by, or administered under the oversight of, the Director of the Office of Professional Responsibility and who has not engaged in any conduct that would justify the censure, suspension, or disbarment of any practitioner under the provisions of this part.

As mentioned, enrolled retirement plan agents will be subject to an examination to determine competency, and also to the renewal process and continuing professional education requirements.

.02   Denial of Right to Limited Practice

The IRS Director of Practice, after giving notice and an opportunity for a conference, can deny eligibility for limited practice before the IRS to any unenrolled preparer or other unenrolled individual who has engaged in disreputable conduct. This conduct includes, but is not limited to, the list of items under Disreputable Conduct.

.03   Authorization for Special Appearance

An individual can be authorized to practice before the IRS or represent another person in a particular matter. The prospective representative must request this authorization in writing from the Director of Practice. It is granted only when extremely compelling circumstances exist. If granted, the IRS will issue a letter that details the conditions related to the appearance and the particular tax matter for which the authorization is granted.

The authorization letter should not be confused with a letter from an IRS service center advising an individual that he or she has been assigned a *Centralized Authorization File* number which identifies an assigned representative. The issuance of a number does not indicate that a person is either recognized or authorized to practice before the IRS. It merely confirms that a centralized file for authorizations has been established for the representative under that number.

.04   Who Cannot Practice

Individuals cannot practice before the IRS either because they are not eligible to practice, or because they have lost the privilege as a result of certain actions. The following individuals generally cannot practice before the IRS:

1.   Individuals convicted of any criminal offense under the revenue laws of the U.S.
2.   Individuals convicted of any offense involving dishonesty or breach of trust.
3.   Individuals under disbarment or suspension from practicing as attorneys, CPAs, public accountants, or actuaries in any state, possession, territory, commonwealth, or in the District of Columbia, or before any federal court, or any body or board of any federal agency.
4.   Individuals who are disbarred or suspended from practice before the IRS because they refuse or have refused to comply with the regulations governing practice before the IRS.

¶18,011   Methods of Enrollment

The Director of Practice can grant an enrollment to practice before the IRS to an applicant who has demonstrated special competence in tax matters by passing a written examination. Enrollment also can be granted to an applicant who qualifies because of past service and technical experience in the IRS. In either case certain application forms must be filed. An applicant must never have engaged in any conduct that would justify suspension or disbarment by the IRS.

An *enrollment card* will be issued to each individual whose application is approved. The individual is enrolled until the expiration date shown on the enrollment card. To continue practicing beyond the expiration date, the individual must request renewal of the enrollment.

.01 New Provisions for the Special Enrollment Examination

Thomson Prometric, a global testing firm, was selected in 2006 by the IRS to develop and administer a computer-based version of the Special Enrollment Examination (SEE).

In general, passing the Special Enrollment Examination enables an individual to become an enrolled agent through demonstrating special competence in tax matters. An Enrolled Agent is a person who has earned the privilege of practicing before the IRS. Enrolled agents, like attorneys and certified public accountants (CPAs), can represent taxpayers in both examinations and collection matters. Those who pass the SEE also undergo an additional background check before enrollment.

The revised exam consists of three parts:

- Part 1 – Individuals
- Part 2 – Businesses
- Part 3 – Representation, Practice and Procedures

Each part of the exam will have about 100 questions, but candidates will not be required to take all parts in one sitting. Candidates will take the examination at a computer terminal at approximately 300 testing centers operated by Thomson Prometric. Previously, the IRS offered testing at about 90 locations.

.02 Renewal of Enrollment

One condition for renewal of enrollment is that the enrolled agent complete a minimum number of hours of continuing professional education (CPE) in programs comprising current subject matter in federal taxation or federal-tax-related matters. It incorporates a system of rolling renewals for enrollment. The year in which enrolled agents will be required to apply for renewal of enrollment will vary based on the last digit of the enrolled agent's social security number. This change is made in order to balance the workflow involved in processing renewals.

The final regulations clarify that enrollment and the renewal of enrollment of *actuaries* is also governed by the regulations of the Joint Board for the Enrollment of Actuaries.

.03   Unenrolled Practice

The final regulations preserve the scope of unenrolled practice as it has existed and make only nonsubstantive changes in nomenclature that are necessitated by the organizational restructuring of the IRS.

.04   Expansion of Issues Authorized for the Enrolled Actuary

The regulations also expanded the list of issues with respect to which an *enrolled actuary* is authorized to represent a taxpayer in limited practice before the IRS. The list is expanded to include issues involving:

- Treatment of funded welfare benefits.
- Transfers of excess pension assets to retiree health accounts.
- Tax on nondeductible contributions to qualified employer plans.
- Taxes with respect to funded welfare benefit plans.
- Tax on reversion of qualified plan assets to employer.

¶18,012   Rules of Practice

An attorney, CPA, enrolled agent, or enrolled actuary authorized to practice before the IRS who is referred to as a practitioner has the duty to perform certain acts and is restricted from performing other acts. Any practitioner who does not comply with the rules of practice or engages in disreputable conduct is subject to disciplinary action. Also, unenrolled preparers must comply with most of these rules of practice and conduct to exercise the privilege of limited practice before the IRS.

Practitioners must promptly submit records or information requested by officers or employees of the IRS. When the IRS requests information concerning possible violations of the regulations by other parties, the practitioner must provide it and be prepared to testify in disbarment or suspension proceedings. A practitioner can be exempt from these rules if he or she believes in good faith and on reasonable grounds that the information requested is privileged or that the request is of doubtful legality.

A practitioner who knows that his or her client has not complied with the revenue laws, or has made an error in or omission from any return, document, affidavit, or other required paper has the responsibility to advise the client promptly of the noncompliance error or omission.

.01   Required Due Diligence

A practitioner must exercise due diligence when performing the following duties:

1. Preparing or assisting in the preparation, approving, and filing of returns, documents, affidavits, and other papers relating to IRS matters.
2. Determining the correctness of oral or written representations made by him or her to the Department of the Treasury.
3. Determining the correctness of oral or written presentations made by him or her to clients with reference to any matter administered by the IRS.

.02   Restrictions

Practitioners are restricted from engaging in certain practices:

1. A practitioner must not unreasonably delay the prompt disposition of any matter before the IRS.
2. A practitioner must not knowingly, directly or indirectly, employ or accept assistance from any person who is under disbarment or suspension from practice before the IRS.
3. He or she must not accept employment as an associate, correspondent, or subagent from, or share fees with, any person under disbarment or suspension by the IRS.
4. He or she must not accept assistance from any former government employee where provisions of these regulations or any federal law would be violated.
5. If a practitioner is a notary public and is employed as counsel, attorney, or agent in a matter before the IRS, or has a material interest in the matter, he or she must not engage in any notary activities relative to that matter.
6. A partner of an officer or employee of the executive branch of the U.S. Government, or of an independent agency of the U.S. or of the District of Columbia, cannot represent anyone in a matter before the IRS in which the officer or employee has or had a personal or substantial interest as a government employee. There are similar and additional restrictions on former government employees.

.03   Disreputable Conduct

Disreputable conduct by a practitioner includes such things as:

1. Committing any criminal offense under the revenue laws, or committing any offense involving dishonesty or breach of trust.
2. Knowingly giving or participating in the giving of false or misleading information in connection with federal tax matters.

3. Willful failure to file a tax return, evading or attempting to evade any federal tax or payment, or participating in such actions.
4. Misappropriating, or failing properly and promptly remit funds received from clients for payment of taxes.
5. Directly or indirectly attempting to influence the official action of IRS employees by the use of threats, false accusations, duress, or coercion, or by offering gifts, favors, or any special inducements.
6. Being disbarred or suspended by the District of Columbia or by any state, possession, territory, commonwealth, or any federal court, or any body or board of any federal agency.
7. Knowingly aiding and abetting another person to practice before the IRS during a period of suspension, disbarment, or ineligibility, or maintaining a partnership so that a suspended or disbarred person can continue to practice before the IRS.
8. Contemptuous conduct in connection with practice before the IRS, including the use of abusive language, making false accusations and statements, or circulating or publishing malicious or libelous matter.
9. Giving a false opinion knowingly, or recklessly, or through gross incompetence, or following a pattern of providing incompetent opinions in questions arising under the federal tax laws.
10. Soliciting employment by prohibited means.

¶18,013   Information to be Furnished

A practitioner is required to respond promptly to a proper and lawful request for records and information, unless the practitioner believes in good faith and on reasonable grounds that the records or information are privileged. The right and ability of practitioners to resist efforts that the practitioner believes to be of doubtful legality is preserved.

As a result, the practitioner must provide information regarding the identity of persons the practitioner reasonably believes may have possession or control of requested documents. The requirement applies only when requested records or information are not in the possession or control of the practitioner or the practitioner's client. The practitioner's duty is limited only to making reasonable inquiry of the practitioner's client and there exists no obligation on the practitioner to make inquiry of any other person or to independently verify information provided by a client.

¶18,014   Knowledge of Client's Omission

IRS Circular 230 has historically required a practitioner to advise a client promptly of any noncompliance, error, or omission. The regulations modify this preexisting duty by simply requiring that, in addition to notifying the client of the fact of the noncompliance, error, or omission, the practitioner advise the client of the consequences as provided under the Code and regulations of the noncompliance, error, or omission. This change requires practitioners to provide information that taxpayers who consult tax professionals typically *expect to receive.*

.01   Diligence as to Accuracy

A practitioner is presumed to have exercised due diligence if the practitioner relies on the work product of another person and the practitioner uses reasonable care in engaging, supervising, training, and evaluating such person, taking proper account of the relationship between the practitioner and the person. It is expected that practitioners will use common sense and experience in guiding their conduct under this section. The section applies both in the *context of a firm* and in circumstances involving a practitioner's engagement of an *outside practitioner.*

For example, in circumstances in which a practitioner must hire another practitioner for a specialized or complicated matter, the practitioner's duty under the section will be more focused on the reasonable care taken in the engagement of the specialist. Supervising and training are not part of a practitioner's engagement of a specialist. Conversely, in the context of a firm, the section's application will focus more on supervising and training, if there is an issue with regard to a supervisory practitioner's reliance on a subordinate.

¶18,015   Contingent Fees

Contingent fees for the preparation of tax returns have long been banned. The Department of the Treasury and the IRS *remain concerned* regarding the use of contingent fees and intend to give the matter further consideration.

The revisions as originally proposed would have imposed a total ban on charging clients contingent fees. However, the final revisions (2007) are not that restrictive. The IRS relented after considering complaints that a ban on contingent fees could prevent taxpayers from pursuing legitimate tax claims.

The final rules permit a practitioner to charge a contingent fee for services rendered in connection with the IRS examination of, or challenge, to:

- An original tax return, or
- An amended return or claim for refund or credit where the amended return or claim for refund or credit was filed within 120 days of the taxpayer's receiving a written notice of the examination or challenge to the original tax return.

The final regulations also permit the use of contingent fees for interest and penalty reviews and judicial proceedings arising under the IRC.

Other contingent fee arrangements are banned under the 2007 rules. However, to avoid any adverse impact on pending transactions, the ban applies only to fee arrangements entered into after March 26, 2008.

¶18,016   Return of Client's Records

At the request of the taxpayer, the tax preparer is required to return the client's original tax records. This section is restricted to the extent that the client's records are necessary for the client to comply with his or her federal tax obligations. Further, the term "records of the client" is defined to exclude such items as returns or other documents prepared by the practitioner that the practitioner is withholding pending the client's payment of fees for those documents. These changes are incorporated to protect practitioners from being disadvantaged or compromised by clients seeking to obtain an unfair advantage under this section.

In consideration of various state laws that may permit liens on a client's records in favor of practitioners during the course of fee disputes, the regulations provide that a practitioner must return only those records that must be attached to the client's return if a fee dispute has triggered an applicable state lien provision. The practitioner, however, must provide the client access to review and copy any of the records retained by the practitioner under law that are necessary for the client to comply with federal tax obligations.

¶18,017   Renewal of Enrollment for Actuaries

An individual who is enrolled as an actuary by the Joint Board for the Enrollment of Actuaries may practice before the IRS. The practice of enrolled actuaries is limited to certain Internal Revenue Code sections that relate to their area of expertise, principally those sections governing employee retirement plans.

¶18,018   The Power of Attorney

A power of attorney is a taxpayer's written authorization for an individual to act for him or her in tax matters. If the authorization is not limited, the individual can generally perform all acts that a taxpayer can perform. The authority granted to an unenrolled preparer cannot exceed that shown under the special rules of limited practice.

Any representative, other than an unenrolled preparer, can usually perform the following acts:

1. Represent the taxpayer before any office of the IRS.
2. Record the interview.

3. Sign an offer or a waiver of restriction on assessment or collection of a tax deficiency, or a waiver of notice of disallowance of claim for credit or refunds.
4. Sign a consent to extend the statutory time period for assessment or collection of a tax.
5. Sign a closing agreement.
6. Receive, but not endorse or cash, a refund check drawn on the U.S. Treasury. The taxpayer must specifically sign a form showing the name of the individual designated to receive the refund check.

The representative named under a power of attorney is not permitted to sign the taxpayer's income tax return unless the signature is permitted under the Internal Revenue Code and the related regulations of the Tax Regulations. The taxpayer can authorize this in the taxpayer's power of attorney.

The regulation permits a representative to sign a client's income tax return if the client is unable to make the return for any of the following reasons:

1. Disease or injury.
2. Continuous absence from the United States for a period of at least 60 days prior to the date required by law for filing the return.
3. Other good cause if specific permission is requested of and granted by the IRS.

If a taxpayer wants a representative to receive a refund check, the taxpayer must specifically so authorize it in the power of attorney. However, if the representative is an income tax return preparer, the representative cannot be authorized to endorse or otherwise cash the client's check related to income taxes. This is also true if the refund is electronically deposited in the preparer's account.

The appointed representative can substitute a representative or delegate authority to a new representative only if this is specifically authorized under the power of attorney. A power of attorney is generally terminated if the client becomes incapacitated or incompetent. The power of attorney can continue, however, in the case of the taxpayer's incapacity or incompetency if the taxpayer had previously authorized that it be continued.

.01   When a Power of Attorney Is Required

A taxpayer should submit a power of attorney when he or she wants to authorize an individual to represent him or her before the IRS, whether or not the representative performs any of the other acts discussed earlier. A power of attorney is most often required when a taxpayer wants to authorize another individual to perform at least one of the following acts on his or her behalf:

1. Represent the taxpayer at a conference with the IRS.
2. Prepare and file a written response to the IRS.

A taxpayer can appoint an unenrolled return preparer as his or her representative. The preparer can represent the taxpayer only before revenue agents and examining officers. Also, the preparer can represent a taxpayer concerning his or her tax liability only for the period covered by a return prepared by the preparer.

The IRS will accept a non-IRS power of attorney, but a transmittal form must be attached in order for the power of attorney to be entered into the *Centralized Authorization File*. If a power of attorney document other than the required transmittal form is used, it must contain the following information:

1. The taxpayer's name and mailing address, Social Security number, and/or employer identification number.
2. An employee plan number, if applicable.
3. The name and mailing address of the taxpayer's representative.
4. The types of tax involved.
5. The federal tax form number.
6. The specific years or periods involved.
7. For estate tax matters, the decedent's date of death.
8. A clear expression of the taxpayer's intention concerning the scope of authority granted to his or her representative.
9. The taxpayer's signature and date.

The taxpayer must also attach to the non-IRS power of attorney a signed and dated statement made by the taxpayer's representative. This statement, which is referred to as the *Declaration of Representative* is included with the transmittal form filed.

.02   Filing a Power of Attorney

The power of attorney is filed with each IRS office with which the taxpayer deals. If the power of attorney is filed for a matter currently pending before an office of the IRS, it should be filed with that office. Otherwise, the power should be filed with the service center where the related return was, or will be, filed.

.03   Third-Party Designee

The authority given to a designee was expanded in 2004 and is now revocable. Designees are now able to exchange information with the IRS. They may also request and receive written tax information relating to the tax return, including copies of notices, correspondence, and account transcripts. The designee may be any individual (including a spouse), corporation, firm, organization, or partnership. To name a designee, the taxpayer should check the Yes box in the Third-Party Designee area of the return. This new provision results in change regarding when a power of attorney is not required as indicated below.

.04   When a Power of Attorney Is Not Required

A power of attorney is not required in some situations when dealing with the IRS, such as when:

- Providing information to the IRS.
- Authorizing the disclosure of tax return information through Form 21.
- Allowing the IRS to discuss return information with a third-party designee.
- Allowing a tax matters partner or person (TMP) to perform acts for the partnership.
- Allowing the IRS to discuss return information with a fiduciary.
- Representing a taxpayer through a nonwritten consent.
- You are merely providing information to the IRS at the request of the IRS.

.05   Tax Matters Partner or Person (TMP)

A TMP is authorized by law to perform various acts on behalf of a partnership or Subchapter S corporation. This includes the power to delegate authority to represent the TMP and to sign documents in that capacity, but certain acts performed by the TMP cannot be delegated.

.06   Fiduciary

A fiduciary, trustee, executor, administrator, receiver, or guardian stands in the position of the taxpayer and acts as the taxpayer. Therefore, a fiduciary does not act as a representative and should not file a power of attorney. A fiduciary should file Form 56, *Notice Concerning Fiduciary Relationship*, to notify the IRS of the fiduciary relationship.

.07   Completed Documents

A power of attorney will be recognized after Form 56 is received, reviewed, and determined by the IRS to contain the required information. However, until a power of attorney is entered into the Centralized Authorized File (CAF), IRS personnel, other than the individual to whom the form is submitted, may be unaware of the authority of the taxpayer's representative and request an additional copy.

When the IRS receives a complete and valid power of attorney, the IRS will take action to recognize the representative. This involves processing the document into the CAF system. The power of attorney is not considered valid until all required information is entered on the document. The individual named as representative will not be recognized to practice before the IRS until the document is complete and accepted by the IRS.

In most instances, the recognition involves processing the document by recording the information on the CAF which enables the IRS to automatically direct copies of mailings to an authorized representative and to instantly recognize the scope of authority granted.

After the power of attorney is filed, the IRS will recognize the taxpayer's representative. However, if it appears the representative is responsible for unreasonably delaying or hindering the prompt disposition of an IRS matter by failing to furnish, after repeated requests, nonprivileged information, the IRS can bypass the representative and contact the taxpayer directly.

.08   Revoking a Power of Attorney

If a taxpayer wants to revoke an existing power of attorney and does not want to name a new representative, there are two ways to do it:

- By sending a *revocation copy* of a previous appointment form to each office of the IRS where forms were originally filed.
- By sending a *revocation statement* to the service center where a return was filed that was covered by the power of attorney.

Unless a taxpayer wants to revoke a power of attorney for which no form was filed, a letter can be written requesting the revocation with a copy of the power of attorney to be revoked. The letter should be signed and dated and sent to each office of the IRS where the taxpayer originally filed the non-IRS power of attorney.

Unless a taxpayer specifies otherwise, a newly filed power of attorney concerning the same matter will revoke a previously filed power of attorney, but not a previously filed tax authorization. A newly filed tax information authorization will revoke a previously filed tax authorization concerning the same matter, but will not revoke a power of attorney concerning that matter.

CHAPTER 19
Internet Accounting

¶19,000   Overview

With anything new, many and varied practices spring up. Some variations are a result of different people attempting to explain a similar situation in as logical a manner as possible. Other variations have arisen as a result of less fair-minded individuals attempting to show a situation to the best advantage for themselves. Or it may be that the variations stem from mere ineptitude to downright chicanery.

This phenomenon is as true of Internet business accounting practices as it is of any other innovation. Who better to try to bring order to a rather chaotic state of development than the Chief Accountant's Office of the Security and Exchange Commission (SEC)?

The SEC's stated purpose is to protect the investor. How companies recognize revenue for the goods and services they offer and, in turn, how this appears on their financial report have become increasingly important issues.

¶19,001   Internet Accounting Issues

Thus, it was that in 1999, the SEC's Chief Accountant's Office sent a letter to the FASB suggesting that the Emerging Issues Task Force (EITF) look into/suggest solutions to issues arising in the "new" Internet businesses. It is doubtful that anyone in the office at that time realized the *extent* to which Internet usage would increase, and thus influence Internet business and the need for specific Internet accounting rules and regulations.

From its inception, the Internet has promised to transform how business is done. With changing business practices comes the potential for changing accounting requirements. The first step in evolving or modifying prior accounting practices is to identify problem areas—issues where normal accounting practices overlaid on Internet businesses produce results that are or may be misleading for investors and other users of a company's financial statements.

Attached to the 1999 letter to the FASB's Director of Research and Technical Activities was a list of 20 accounting issues developed by the SEC staff. The list included those issues they believed warranted consideration by a standard-setting body with suggested priority levels for addressing each of the issues (priority levels 1-3). However, they expected that all of the issues should eventually be addressed.

These 20 problems are:

1. Gross versus net revenue reporting
2. Bartering for advertising
3. Transactions with retailers
4. Shipping and handling costs
5. Heavy discounts
6. Service outages
7. Definition of software
8. Web site development costs
9. Revenue recognition
10. Hosting arrangements
11. Customer Web site access
12. Advertising over time
13. Point and loyalty arrangements
14. Long-term contractual rights
15. Up-front fees
16. Customer base costs
17. Equity conversions
18. Segments
19. Expense classification
20. Coupons

¶19,002   Targeted Areas in Accounting for Internet Activities

The list comprises accounting on issues the SEC staff had dealt with in registrant filings, as well as issues identified through input from accounting firms. One or more of the following applies to all of these issues:

1. There appeared to be a diversity in practice.
2. The situation did not appear to be addressed in then-existing accounting literature.
3. The SEC staff was concerned that the developing practice could be inappropriate under U.S. Generally Accepted Accounting Principles (U.S. GAAP).

Some of the issues arose because of the new business models used in Internet operations, while others are issues that also existed in businesses with no Internet operations. It was pointed out that advertising partnerships, coupon and rebate programs, and complex equity instruments, while perhaps more common in Internet businesses, were in use long before the Internet. As a general rule, the SEC staff believes that Internet companies engaging in transactions that are similar to transactions entered into by traditional companies should follow the already established accounting models for those transactions.

The SEC believed that all of the issues discussed deserved further consideration by the accounting and financial reporting community. Each issue represented an area in which investors benefit from improved financial information and consistency as a result of providing additional guidance on the issue. In order to maximize the benefits of providing such guidance, the Commission believed it was important that guidance address not only recognition and measurement questions but also classification and disclosures.

For each issue, the SEC staff added comments regarding the issue, and an assessment of the priority for addressing the issue.

¶19,003   Quality Accounting Needed

After careful consideration of the "call to accountability" letter from the SEC's Chief Accountant, it would appear that the Task Force (and the SEC, for that matter) really believed that the new economy was not so much in need of "new accounting," as of *quality* accounting. Basically, the EITF had resolved many of the issues by reference to interpretations and guidance found in existing accounting pronouncements. Regardless of the rather complex list of perceived abuses and inconsistencies referred to, the solutions did not appear to require radical changes to traditional accounting models.

Please note that each EITF Consensus, as with all other pre-codification FASB Standards, has been superseded and put into Topics in the Accounting Standards Codification™ (ASC).

While the issues listed are still important considerations to be addressed, accounting standards at that time and since that time have included Internet accounting issues as they have been issued or amended. For example, the revenue recognition issues raised in the list, are all accounted for in accordance with ASC Topic 606, along with nearly all other revenue recognition in nearly all industries. Therefore, this chapter will address "internet accounting issues for beginners."

A large number of people are starting and running Internet businesses these days. Many are good at what they do but may or may not have any accounting experience. Therefore, we believe it could be useful to cover basic accounting considerations for this type of business.

¶19,004   Accounting Issues for Internet Small Businesses

Doing business on the Internet is generally referred to as ecommerce. There are a variety of ways to make money through the Internet, so a very large number of people are using these earning methods. Following are some things to keep in mind while working to make money using these resources:

.01   Accounting Overview

Every business has activities and transactions that help it fulfill its objectives. At its most basic level, accounting is nothing more than recording those activities and transactions in a numerical format and then using those numbers to report the entity's performance to interested parties. That reporting is helpful for outside users of the financial information so they can make good, well-informed decisions about the entity. For example, a bank may decide whether or not to give the company a loan. Investors may consider putting money into the company in hopes of a strong return on that investment. Donors may provide funding to a non-profit organization based on its financial performance, in addition to supporting its mission. Financial reporting is also very useful for internal users of financial information. It is critical to help management better run the business. The following sections will focus largely on the usefulness of information for management, though they are also applicable to reporting for external users of accounting information.

.02   Accounting Methods

The two primary accounting methods are cash basis accounting and accrual accounting. A nonpublic company can generally use either method.

Cash basis accounting

Cash basis accounting is a method of accounting that measures the transfer of cash. When the cash basis of accounting is used, there is generally only one statement used. It is generally titled Statement of Cash Receipts and Disbursements, or something similar. When cash comes in, revenue is recognized. When cash goes out, expenses are recognized. Not much to it! Cash basis accounting is generally the simplest accounting method. However, it generally does not provide as much information as the accrual method, addressed next.

Accrual accounting

Accrual accounting, unlike cash basis accounting, measures a transaction when funds are earned or expenses are incurred, not when payment changes hands.

The accrual method is more frequently used by large companies, and it may require more specialized accounting knowledge and a more hands-on approach to account management than the cash basis method does.

This method gives a more accurate picture of a company's financial situation, but it is also more complex than cash basis accounting. Accrual basis accounting is the method required by U.S. Generally Accepted Accounting Principles (U.S. GAAP).

Although accrual accounting can provide a more accurate picture of your business's long-term financial picture, it has the potential to mislead business owners about the current state of their accounts. For example, a coffee-table maker would "earn" $800 as soon as she finished her table, but her business bank account might still be empty.

.03   Common Accounts

Chapter 1, "Balance Sheet," goes into detail about most of the balance sheet accounts and Chapter 2, "Income Statement," goes over the accounts on the income statement. As a quick overview, the most common asset accounts on the balance sheet are cash, accounts receivable, inventory, and fixed assets. Liability accounts on the balance sheet are accounts payable, accrued expenses, and debt. Equity accounts on the balance sheet may be stock, additional paid-in capital, and retained earnings. Income statement accounts are usually revenue, cost of goods sold, operating expenses, gains and losses, and income taxes. For more detail, see Chapters 1 and 2.

.04   Important Information for Small Business Owners

Owners of small businesses are generally also the management of the business. So these sections will use the terms "owners" and "managers" somewhat interchangeably. In order to manage a business well, there are certain things that are important to track. Perhaps the most important thing for a small business owner to stay on top of is cash flows. It has been said that "cash is king" in running a business, especially a small business. Management needs to be sure they will bring in enough money, timely enough, to meet their financial obligations, such as payroll, rent, utilities, and other necessary costs. Because small businesses seldom have excess cash, a common question might be, "Can I collect receivables quickly enough to allow me to pay my accounts payable and payroll on time?" With that in mind, it is very important for management to track cash flows. Nearly as important as tracking cash flows is the ability to project cash flows. An old joke is to say, "I still have checks in my checkbook, so I can still spend money." Almost as unwarranted an idea is to assume that cash in one's bank account means there is money to spend. Management needs to be aware of upcoming cash requirements before making spending decisions. That is why tracking and projecting cash flows is so important. Financial statements generally include a statement of cash flows.

Management should also be tracking and projecting earnings and expenditures. While similar to cash flows, the timing often differs. The difference between cash and accrual accounting methods is discussed above. A company may earn income but not yet receive it. It may incur expenses but not yet pay for them. Taken in conjunction with cash flows, profits and losses help management make better business decisions. One of the common financial statements is an income statement, also called a profit and loss statement.

In addition to knowing how much cash a company has, and the related current and projected cash flows, it is important to know what other assets and liabilities a company has. Assets are resources that provide future benefits to a company. Liabilities represent future obligations of a company. Knowing amounts like accounts receivable and accounts payable are crucial for management to understand the company's financial position. Assets, liabilities, and equity are shown on a company's balance sheet.

.05 Bookkeeping

Bookkeeping is the process through which accounting generally takes place. It is the process of recording transactions, activities, and events in numerical format into a system that provides financial statements with useful information for internal and external users to help them in decision making. Bookkeeping nearly always makes use of some type of accounting software. For this process to be effective, it is important for a company to have processes and internal controls in place to ensure the creation of source documents when transactions take place. Source documents may consist of invoices, receipts, timesheets, payroll reports, bills, etc. Those source documents are then used to enter accounting information into the software, which then processes it into the financial statements.

.06 Budgeting

Part of the usefulness of financial statements is to assist users of the information to project possible financial information for the future. The income statement, or profit and loss statement, is most often used to make those projections. This process is often referred to as budgeting. Primarily using historical financial information, management prepares a budget of expected future revenue and expenses. Such a budget can help guide management in setting priorities and determining plans for the use of their funds in the future. In addition to income statement budgeting, management will often prepare cash flow budgets.

As previously mentioned, cash flows generally differ in timing from recognition of revenue and expenses. Having separate budgets for each can be very helpful.

.07   Tax Issues

Taxes are often a key factor in many business decisions. It is important, especially for a small business, to do everything possible to legally reduce the amount spent on taxes. Income taxes—federal, state, and local—are a primary concern, but an entity needs to also consider employment taxes, property taxes, and possibly other kinds of tax obligations. Taxes generally consist of complex technical issues and are generally best handled by finding and paying a professional with training and experience in taxes.

CHAPTER 20
E-Commerce

¶20,000   Overview

E-commerce is an important facet of personal and business activities today. Considering the impressive growth in retail sales as shown by the retail e-commerce figures below, it is fairly obvious that many are finding that buying online is the way to go.

It is forecasted that e-commerce sales, with Asia-Pacific quickly overcoming North America as the largest e-commerce market, are expected to surpass $8 trillion worldwide by the end of 2027. Total retail e-commerce sales worldwide in 2023 were $5.8 trillion, with U.S. e-commerce sales of $1.16 trillion in 2023, while China had $3.02 trillion in 2023.

In the United States, we are expecting 333.5 million online shoppers in 2029; that is expected to be about 90 percent of the entire country's population! Currently, over 80 percent of Americans have shopped online, and 25 percent of Americans shop online at least once per month. The majority (around 59 percent) of these shoppers bought clothing items, and 47 percent bought their first item on Amazon. But Americans are not the only ones who shop online. People from all over the world shopped as well. According to dash.app, the countries with the leading e-commerce revenues are: China ($3,023 billion), USA ($1,163 billion), UK ($195 billion), Japan ($193 billion), South Korea ($147 billion), India ($118 billion), Germany

($97 billion), Indonesia ($97 billion), Canada ($83 billion), and France ($79 billion).

¶20,001 M-Commerce Makes Its Presence Known

The development of m-commerce may very well follow the path of exponential growth previously experienced by the e-commerce surge, according to a project manager at an e-commerce and m-commerce research and consulting firm. He feels that the optimum time for online retailers to start developing a mobile strategy has actually passed. Those who have already invested in the mobile channel are poised to benefit the most from marketing their mobile presence to early adopters, and the exponential revenue growth rates that will follow.

But just what exactly is m-commerce? M-commerce, or mobile commerce, is the selling and purchasing of goods and/or services on handheld (mobile) devices like cell phones, smart phones, and personal digital assistants (PDAs). Unlike e-commerce, m-commerce allows the user to access the Internet without needing to find a place to plug in.

The technology behind m-commerce is based on a wireless application protocol (WAP), an application environment, and a set of communication protocols for wireless devices designed to enable manufacturer-, vendor-, and technology-independent access to the Internet and advanced telephonic services.

In 2023, the number of mobile subscriptions was 8.9 billion, up from 8.6 billion in 2022 and 7.9 billion in 2018.

Many mobile Web users are mobile-only, i.e., they do not, or very rarely, use a desktop, laptop or tablet to access the Web. Even in the United States, 25 percent of mobile Web users are mobile-only. These users tend to be under 25 years of age.

.01 Mobile Strategies for Business—And More

Considering mobile use in a more serious vein, one survey, conducted by Adobe Systems Incorporated and released to the media on August 12, 2010, found four key areas of focus for businesses' mobile strategies: promotions, commerce, product information and branding. Seventy-five percent of respondents named promotions as the core of their mobile strategy, validating the mobile channel as an important method to drive traffic and support multi-channel commerce.

Multi-channel shoppers tend to purchase more; therefore, companies must effectively engage customers by delivering consistent, rich experiences across all channels, including mobile, to maintain and fuel current double-digit e-commerce industry growth rates.

The survey results demonstrated the opportunities that exist for companies to leverage rich visualization features to improve their emerging mobile presences and drive cross-channel sales. Mobile user experience findings from the survey point to full-screen image zoom and videos as the most important way to browse or display products on mobile devices, specifically:

- More than 55 percent of respondents cited full-screen image zoom and videos as indispensable viewing features for driving conversion.
- In addition, 96 percent of respondents asserted the most effective visual merchandising features were catalogs & brochures, alternative images, and zoom & pan.
- While only 18 percent of respondents currently utilize rich visual merchandising features for mobile commerce, up to 81 percent of respondents cited plans to develop these features, thus implying richer mobile experiences would be created and offered over the next 12 months.

However, mobile usage for business is not limited to merchandising. In order of importance, the key drivers are money transfer, location-based services, mobile search, mobile browsing, mobile health monitoring, mobile payment, near-field-communication services, mobile advertising, instant messaging, and mobile music. Although the order fluctuates and the list varies somewhat, depending on the source, in Q2 2024, the top used apps appear to be Amazon, Temu, and Shein. Other apps mentioned are Walmart, Fetch, Nike, Etsy, Bloomingdales, Capital One, Crate and Barrell, and more.

¶20,002   Economic Effect of E-Commerce Sales

E-commerce sales are sales of goods and services in which an order is placed by the buyer, or price and terms of sale are negotiated over an Internet, extranet, Electronic Data Interchange (EDI) network, electronic mail, or other online system. Payment may or may not be made online.

.01   Quarterly Retail E-Commerce Sales 1st Quarter 2024

The Census Bureau of the Department of Commerce announced that the estimate of U.S. retail e-commerce sales for the first quarter of 2024, adjusted for seasonal variation, but not for price changes, was $289.2 billion, an increase of 2.1 percent (±0.7%) from the fourth quarter of 2023.

.02   Survey Description

Retail e-commerce sales are estimated from the same sample used for the Monthly Retail Trade Survey (MRTS) to estimate preliminary and final U.S. retail sales. Advance U.S. retail sales are estimated from a subsample of the MRTS sample that is not of adequate size to measure changes in retail e-commerce sales.

A stratified simple random sampling method is used to select approximately 12,500 retail firms whose sales are then weighted and benchmarked to represent the complete universe of over two million retail firms. The MRTS sample is probability based and represents all employer firms engaged in retail activities as defined by the North American Industry Classification System (NAICS). Coverage includes all retailers whether or not they are engaged in e-commerce.

The MRTS sample is updated on an ongoing basis to account for new retail employer businesses (including those selling via the Internet), business deaths, and other changes to the retail business universe. Firms are asked each month to report e-commerce sales separately. For each month of the quarter, data for nonresponding sampling units are imputed from responding sampling units falling within the same kind of business and sales size category. Responding firms account for approximately 72 percent of the e-commerce sales estimate and about 70 percent of the estimate of U.S. retail sales for any quarter.

For each month of the quarter, estimates are obtained by summing weighted sales (either reported or imputed). The monthly estimates are benchmarked to prior annual survey estimates. Estimates for the quarter are obtained by summing the monthly benchmarked estimates. The estimate for the most recent quarter is a preliminary estimate. Therefore, the estimate is subject to revision. Data users who create their own estimates using data from this report should cite the Census Bureau as the source of the input data only.

¶20,003   Ease in Shopping is Important to Internet Customers

E-retailing remains the fastest growing sector in the U.S. retail industry, reaching sales exceeding $1 trillion in 2023, and expected to reach $1.2 trillion in the United States in 2024 and $6.3 trillion globally. Internet retailers across the board have been making a sizable investment in new e-commerce solutions and services by setting the following goals:

- Having quality, varied competitive products.
- Being easy to navigate without too many "clicks" to find the desired item.
- Having simple direction to make it easy to shop and settle the account.

To accomplish these goals, Web retailers have been:

- Building new Web sites and redesigning existing ones.
- Installing state-of-the-art e-commerce platforms.
- Refining their digital marketing strategies.
- Integrating their multi-channel systems.

The technological tools and third-party services aimed at improving Web-based retailing are becoming ever more sophisticated and relevant to resolving real-world challenges in Internet retailing. The vendors offering these technologies and services continue to increase and strengthen their market positions.

¶20,004   The Internet Crime Complaint Center (IC3)

The Internet Crime Complaint Center (IC3) hit its high water mark on May 10, 2014, when its 3 millionth consumer Internet crime complaint was received. The total loss in dollars in claims registered in the five years ending 2023 is $37.4 billion. According to the 2023 Internet Crime Report, the IC3 received 3.79 million consumer complaints in the last five years ending 2023.

In 2023, IC3 received a total of 880,418 complaints with reported losses of $12.5 billion. The most prevalent crime types reported were Phishing/Spoofing (by far!), Personal Data Breach, and Non-Payment/Non-Delivery. The top three crime types with the highest reported losses were Investment – losses of nearly $4.6 billion, business e-mail compromise (BEC) – losses of nearly $3 billion , and tech support – losses of nearly $1 billion.

Established in 2000, the IC3 is a partnership between the Federal Bureau of Investigation (FBI) and the National White Collar Crime Center (NW3C) and serves as a means to receive Internet related criminal complaints and to further research, develop, and refer the criminal complaints to federal, state, local, or international law enforcement and/or regulatory agencies for any investigation they deem to be appropriate. The IC3 serves the broader law enforcement community to include federal, as well as state, local, and international agencies, which are combating Internet crime and, in many cases, participating in Cyber Crime Task Forces.

Since its inception, the IC3 has received complaints crossing the spectrum of cyber crime matters, to include online fraud in its many forms including:

- Online fraud (in its many forms),
- Intellectual property rights (IPR) matters,
- Computer intrusions (hacking),
- Economic espionage (theft of trade secrets),
- Child pornography,
- International money laundering,
- Identity theft,
- Online extortion, and
- A growing list of additional criminal and civil matters.

Through a number of technological advancements, IC3 has streamlined the way it processes and refers victim complaints to law enforcement. In 2004, IC3 developed Automatch, an automated internal complaint grouping and analytical search tool. The design of Automatch is based on an assessment of the IC3 partnership aimed at defining a joint workflow for the project partners with different service requirements.

IC3 IT staff continually review and update Automatch to meet the needs of analysts who build cases for law enforcement worldwide gathering all related information based on commonalities in the IC3 data. In 2009, NW3C developed the state-of-the-art Internet Complaint Search and Investigation System (ICSIS), which fosters seamless collaboration among law enforcement from multiple jurisdictions. Expert IC3 analysts also provide key analytical and case support.

.01   Fighting Internet Crime at All Levels

The *Internet Crime Complaint Center* (IC3) gives the victims of cybercrime a convenient and easy-to-use reporting mechanism that alerts authorities of suspected criminal or civil violations. For law enforcement and regulatory agencies at the local, state, and federal level, IC3 provides a central referral mechanism for complaints involving Internet-related crimes. For affected members of industry, IC3 can leverage both intelligence and subject matter expert resources to identify and craft an aggressive, proactive approach to combating cybercrime.

.02   NWC3 Combats Internet and High Tech Crime

The National White Collar Crime Center (NW3C) provides support services to state and local law enforcement for the prevention, investigation, and prosecution of high-tech and economic crime. The organization partners with other appropriate entities in addressing homeland security initiatives, as they relate to economic and high-tech crimes.

NW3C is a congressionally funded, non-profit corporation whose membership primarily comprises law enforcement agencies, state regulatory bodies with criminal investigative authority, and state and local prosecution offices. While NW3C has no investigative authority itself, its job is to help these law enforcement agencies better understand and utilize tools to combat economic and high-tech crime.

.03   Filing a Complaint with the IC3

The IC3 accepts online Internet crime complaints from either the actual victim or from a third party to the complainant. The following information should be provided when filing a complaint:

- Complainant name.
- Complainant mailing address.
- Complainant telephone number.
- The name, address, telephone number, and Web address, if available, of the individual or organization allegedly perpetrating the fraud.
- Specific details on how, why, and when the alleged fraud took place.
- Any other relevant information necessary to support the complaint.

¶20,005   IC3 2023 Annual Report on Internet Crime

Rankings of the types of crimes reported in the IC3 2023 Annual Report have not changed significantly over the last five years. Phishing/Vishing/Smishing/Pharming is still far and away the most frequent Internet crime perpetuated.

.01   Common Internet Crime Schemes

Some common Internet Crime schemes as reported in the 2023 Internet Crime Report are listed below.

Advanced Fee. An individual pays money to someone in anticipation of receiving something of greater value in return, but instead, receives significantly less than expected or nothing.

Business Email Compromise (BEC). BEC is a scam targeting businesses or individuals working with suppliers and/or businesses regularly performing wire transfer payments. These sophisticated scams are carried out by fraudsters by compromising email accounts and other forms of communication such as phone numbers and virtual meeting applications, through social engineering or computer intrusion techniques to conduct unauthorized transfer of funds.

Botnet. A botnet is a group of two or more computers controlled and updated remotely for an illegal purchase such as a Distributed Denial of Service or Telephony Denial of Service attack or other nefarious activity.

Confidence/Romance. An individual believes they are in a relationship (family, friendly, or romantic) and are tricked into sending money, personal and financial information, or items of value to the perpetrator or to launder money or items to assist the perpetrator. This includes the Grandparent's Scheme and any scheme in which the perpetrator preys on the targeted individual's "heartstrings."

Credit Card Fraud/Check Fraud. Credit card fraud is a wide-ranging term for theft and fraud committed using a credit card or any similar payment mechanism (ACH, EFT, recurring charge, etc.) as a fraudulent source of funds in a transaction.

Crimes Against Children. Anything related to the exploitation of children, including child abuse.

Data Breach. A data breach in the cyber context is the use of a computer intrusion to acquire confidential or secured information. This does not include computer intrusions targeting personally owned computers, systems, devices, or personal accounts such as social media or financial accounts.

Employment. An individual believes they are legitimately employed and loses money, or launders money/items during the course of their employment.

Extortion. Unlawful extraction of money or property through intimidation or undue exercise of authority. It may include threats of physical harm, criminal prosecution, or public exposure.

Government Impersonation. A government official is impersonated in an attempt to collect money.

Harassment/Stalking. Repeated words, conduct, or action that serve no legitimate purpose and are directed at a specific person to annoy, alarm, or distress that person. Engaging in a course of conduct directed at a specific person that would cause a reasonable person to fear for his/her safety or the safety of others or suffer substantial emotional distress.

Identity Theft. Someone wrongfully obtains and uses personally identifiable information in some way that involves fraud or deception, typically for economic gain.

Investment. Deceptive practice that induces investors to make purchases based on false information. These scams usually offer those targeted large returns with minimal risk. (Retirement, 401K, Ponzi, Pyramid, etc.).

IPR/Copyright and Counterfeit. The illegal theft and use of others' ideas, inventions, and creative expressions – what's called intellectual property – everything from trade secrets and proprietary products and parts to movies, music, and software.

Lottery/Sweepstakes/Inheritance. An individual is contacted about winning a lottery or sweepstakes they never entered, or to collect on an inheritance from an unknown relative.

Malware. Software or code intended to damage, disable, or capable of copying itself onto a computer and/or computer systems to have a detrimental effect or destroy data.

Non-Payment/Non-Delivery. Goods or services are shipped, and payment is never rendered (nonpayment). Payment is sent, and goods or services are never received, or are of lesser quality (non-delivery).

Overpayment. An individual is sent a payment/commission and is instructed to keep a portion of the payment and send the remainder to another individual or business.

Personal Data Breach. A leak/spill of personal data which is released from a secure location to an untrusted environment. Also, a security incident in which an individual's sensitive, protected, or confidential data is copied, transmitted, viewed, stolen, or used by an unauthorized individual.

Phishing/Spoofing. The use of unsolicited email, text messages, and telephone calls purportedly from a legitimate company requesting personal, financial, and/or login credentials.

Ransomware. A type of malicious software designed to block access to a computer system until money is paid.

Real Estate. Loss of funds from a real estate investment or fraud involving rental or timeshare property.

SIM Swap. The use of unsophisticated social engineering techniques against mobile service providers to transfer a victim's phone service to a mobile device in the criminal's possession.

Tech Support. Subject posing as technical or customer support/service.

Threats of Violence. An expression of an intention to inflict pain, injury, self-harm, or death not in the context of extortion.

¶20,006   E-Business Accounting Principles and Criteria

Management is responsible for the attainment of the enterprise's objectives *in accordance with the business strategy it has defined*. If an e-business system is used for this purpose, it is important that those in management make appropriate arrangements to manage the ensuing risks. An enterprise's e-business strategy, as an integral part of the information technology (IT) strategy, ordinarily includes consideration of *all aspects of business risks, including IT risks*. Consequently:

1.   Management assesses IT risks with respect to information reliability.
2.   Information reliability, in turn, depends on IT system reliability.
3.   IT system reliability depends on IT controls.

It is important that management implements IT controls that operate effectively to help ensure that an IT system performs reliably. Information generated by an IT system will be reliable where that system is capable of operating without material error, fault, or failure during a specified period. This also applies to accounting information. The following *principles* may be used to evaluate whether processed accounting information is reliable:

1.   Principles for accounting information security.
2.   Principles for appropriate accounting information processing.

The reliability of accounting information relating to the entire e-business process is increased if the accounting system satisfies both accounting information security principles and the principles for appropriate accounting information processing.

The principles for appropriate accounting information processing are fulfilled where the e-business system and the entire IT system safeguards comply with the following general criteria for the input, processing, output and storage of information and data about e-business transactions:

1.   Completeness.
2.   Accuracy.
3.   Timeliness.
4.   Assessability.
5.   Order.
6.   Inalterability (logging of alterations).

The *completeness* criterion refers to the extent and scope of processed e-business transactions—that is, the recipient of transactions determines that all transactions are input completely into the e-business system. Each transaction should be individually identifiable and recorded separately. The completeness of the recorded entries should be demonstrably preserved throughout processing and for the duration of the retention period.

In accordance with the *accuracy* criterion, processed information should accurately reflect e-business transactions—that is, recorded transactions should reflect the actual events and circumstances in conformity with the applicable financial reporting framework.

Under the *timeliness* criterion, e-business transactions should be recorded on a timely basis—that is, as soon as possible after the transaction has occurred. When time elapses between the occurrence of a transaction and its recording, further appropriate action may become necessary to determine completeness and accuracy of the entry recorded.

Under the criterion of *assessability*, each item and disclosure in the financial statements should be verifiable in that it can be traced back to individual entries in the books and records and to the original source documents that support that entry. Furthermore, the criterion of assessability implies that an expert third party should be able to gain an insight into the transactions and position of the enterprise within a reasonable period of time.

To meet the *order* criteria, accounting entries in an accounting system should be organized in both chronological order (a journal function) and by nature (by type of asset, liability, revenue or expense—a ledger function). Transactions and their recording should be identifiable and capable of conversion into human-readable format in a reasonable period of time.

In accordance with the criterion of *inalterability*, no entry or record may be changed after the posting date so that its original content can no longer be identified, unless the change to the original content can be identified by means of a log of such alterations. Therefore, alterations of entries or records should be made in a way that both the original content and the fact that changes have been made are evident or can be made evident. For program-generated or program-controlled entries (automated or recurring vouchers), changes to the underlying data used to generate and control accounting entries would also be recorded. This applies, in particular, to the logging of modifications of settings relevant to accounting or the parameterization of software and the recording of changes to master data.

Before accepting a transaction for processing, it would be useful to verify the following:

1. That all transaction details have been entered by the customer.
2. The authenticity of the customer.

3.   The availability of the products or services to be supplied.
4.   The reasonableness of the order, for example, to identify an unusually large quantity resulting from an input error, or to identify erroneous duplicate orders.
5.   The pricing structure applied, including delivery costs, where appropriate.
6.   The method of payment or credit worthiness of the customer.
7.   The non-repudiability of the transaction in that its author cannot later deny having entered into it.

In an e-business process, it is often not possible to provide evidence of transactions by way of conventional vouchers. Despite this fact, transactions should continue to be supported by appropriate documentary evidence (i.e., the source document entry function).

¶20,007   Taxing Problems

What of the tax accountant? The accounting for e-commerce required organizations to review policies and procedures. Accounting concerns such as recording multiple tax payments, which might not be an issue in a paper-based trading environment, quickly became major concerns. Other tax concerns have continued to develop.

.01   The Streamlined Sales and Use Tax Agreement

Under 1992's *Quill v. North Dakota (Quill)*, the U.S. Supreme Court ruled that retailers are required to collect sales tax from out-of-state customers only if they have a physical presence such as a store, warehouse or office in the customer's state. The court held that the 45 state and 7,600 local sales tax systems across the nation were too complicated for a retailer to know how much tax to collect. The Court said Congress has the authority to allow states to require remote sellers to collect tax.

The Streamlined Sales and Use Tax Agreement is, to some extent, a response to this Supreme Court Ruling. The purpose of the Agreement is to simplify and modernize sales and use tax administration in order to substantially reduce the burden of tax compliance. The Agreement focuses on improving sales and use tax administration systems for all sellers and for all types of commerce through all of the following:

- State level administration of sales and use tax collections.
- Uniformity in the state and local tax bases.
- Uniformity of major tax base definitions.
- Central, electronic registration system for all member states.

- Simplification of state and local tax rates.
- Uniform sourcing rules for all taxable transactions.
- Simplified administration of exemptions.
- Simplified tax returns.
- Simplification of tax remittances.
- Protection of consumer privacy.

In June 2018, based on a Supreme Court review of a South Dakota bill, the Court ruled on a 5-4 decision that the physical presence aspect of *Quill* was "unsound and incorrect" with the state of current technology, and overturned *Quill*. As a consequence of this and other related events, most online retailers now collect and submit sales taxes.

.02   Taxation of Items Purchased Online

In a news release on September 12, 2012, the California State Board of Equalization declared that "internet shopping was never tax-free." Prior to this date, items purchased from online or mail order retailers were not tax-free, because, since 1935, consumers have owed use tax on untaxed purchases made from out-of-state retailers.

Use tax is the equivalent of sales tax and applies to purchases from retailers who are not required to report and pay sales tax in a given state—and most states have use tax laws. Residents of these states who purchase items from out-of-state retailers that do not collect sales tax are required to pay the use tax directly to the state. This rarely happens, as most residents are unaware these laws exist.

In California, the new law, which took effect on September 15, 2012, requires out-of-state retailers to collect the tax when they make the sale, rather than requiring taxpayers to report the tax on their own.

.03   Taxation of International E-Commerce Sales

An online merchant selling to international customers must pay careful attention to the tax implications of those sales. In general, once a company crosses a certain threshold of activity in a foreign country, the company becomes subject to income tax in that foreign country. In many cases, a company must have a "permanent establishment" in the foreign country before that country will subject the company to income tax on the company's business profits from that country. Thus, for example, an American online vendor of digitally or physically delivered products that does not have equipment or personnel located in Japan generally would not be subject to Japanese income tax on its sales. However, there are important exceptions to this general rule. Some payments from customers in a foreign country may be subject to withholding tax by the foreign country (e.g., if the foreign country determines that the payments are "royalties" or other payments subject to withholding).

Electronically delivered goods should be treated like any other sale to a foreign customer. It generally is the responsibility of customer/importers to declare their purchase and pay any taxes. Tax and tariff information on a country-by-country basis is available, or a Commercial Specialist in the targeted country offers more information.

In addition, a foreign country may impose other types of taxes, such as value-added tax (VAT), on sales into its jurisdiction. For example, as of July 1, 2003, the EU member states began taxing sales of electronically supplied products and services by non-EU firms to nonbusiness customers located in the EU. Non-EU providers of electronically supplied products and services are now required to register with a tax authority in a member state and collect and remit VAT based on the VAT rate of the member state in which their customer is located. More information on online taxation can be obtained from the Department of Commerce.

.04   Laws and Issues—E-Business & E-Commerce

The IRS reviews and updates tax rules and reminders related to e-business and e-commerce for small businesses or individuals on a regular basis. It is particularly this segment who may not have a clear picture of Internet and/or foreign tax liabilities.

Internet Sales are Taxable. Misinformation about laws such as the prohibition of the taxation of Internet access (Internet Tax Freedom Act) and limiting sales tax on interstate sales have led some to believe incorrectly that Internet sales income is not subject to income tax.

An online business may be subject to liabilities for income tax, self-employment tax, employment tax, or excise tax. The sales may result in capital gains, nondeductible personal losses, or ordinary business income.

Income from Abroad is Taxable. There have been recent reports about the interest of the IRS in taxpayers with offshore bank accounts. The IRS's interest, however, extends beyond offshore bank accounts. Worldwide income including income from foreign customers must be reported on a U.S. tax return. Civil and criminal penalties may apply for not reporting all taxable income, including income from overseas business transactions whether for a company or an individual.

A U.S. citizen or resident alien must report income from all sources within and outside of the U.S. This is true whether or not a Form W-2 Wage and Tax Statement, a Form 1099 (Information Return) or the foreign equivalents has been received. (See Publication 525, Taxable and Nontaxable Income, for more information.)

Home Office Deduction. If a portion of an individual's home is used for online business, it may be possible to take a home office deduction. In order to deduct expenses related to the business use of the home, it must be used for a "bona fide" business and meet other specific requirements. Even then, the deduction may be limited. To qualify to claim expenses for the business use of a home, both of the following tests must be met:

1. Use of the business part of the home must be:
   a. Exclusive,
   b. Regular, and
   c. For trade or business, and
2. The business part of the home must be one of the following:
   a. The principal place of business,
   b. A place where customers are met and dealt with in the normal course of the trade or business, or
   c. A separate structure used in connection with the trade or business.

Consequences for Evading Taxes on Foreign Source Income. Substantial civil and criminal penalties may apply if all taxable income from domestic and foreign sources is not properly reported or properly disclosed, in Part III of Schedule B and on Form TD F 90-22.1.

¶20,008   Cautions for E-Communication Web Site Use

With the Internet now playing an increasingly important role in investing and financial reporting, the Securities and Exchange Commission Private Securities Litigation Reform Act of 1995 may be cited frequently. It is important that companies be aware of pitfalls that could lead to a new wave of litigation.

Following are several cautions that could reduce the legal risks from electronic disclosures, particularly those associated with company Web sites:

1. Meaningful, obvious, clearly worded cautionary disclaimers must accompany any and all "forward-looking" statements.
2. Some of these forward-looking statements may appear in varied guises: transcripts of speeches, press conferences, and quotes should be treated as written disclosures and must include an appropriate written disclaimer situated as closely as possible to the statement.

3.   A full set of financial statements and notes should always be included. "Selected" portions, summations, "fractured" financial statements, even a complete set without the footnotes, could be an invitation for litigation.

4.   A company should not commit to update disclosures and should include on its Web site disclaimers regarding the absence of any obligation to do so. However, the site should be monitored very closely for any information that is outdated or misleading.

5.   Management should be wary of any "selectivity" relating to analysts. Do not frame, inline, or link to analysts' sites or include analysts' comments on the company's site. If a list of analysts covering the company is provided, the names of *all* analysts must be included, not just those with favorable comments.

6.   Probably the most cogent advice relating to "chat rooms" (for the company as well as the investor) has come from the chairman of the SEC in a much publicized speech:

     "Chat rooms, which increasingly have become a source of information and misinformation for many investors, have been compared to a high-tech version of morning gossip or advice at the company water cooler. But, at least you knew your co-workers at the water cooler. For the future sake of this medium, I encourage investors to take what they see over chat rooms— not with a grain of salt—but with a rock of salt."

     Obviously, it is in the best interest of the company to establish well-defined policies for employee participation in chat room discussions about their jobs and their organization.

7.   Keeping in mind the seemingly never-ending abilities of the "hackers" to access a mainframe and compromise a Web site, it is paramount that there should be continuing reevaluation of a system's security measures.

¶20,009   Glossary of Terms

This glossary provides common definitions of some of the terms in contacts with clients or e-business vendors. Some of the definitions have been simplified for conciseness and ease of understanding. We are all familiar with many of the terms, although we would be hard-pressed actually to define them, thus:

Affiliate Programs. Cooperative arrangements that involve providing a link to another Web site in exchange for a commission on purchases made by users following that link to the other Web site.

Access Provider. An intermediary remote computer system through which a user may then connect to the Internet.

Acrobat Reader. A software application from Adobe that provides the formatted display of documents in portable document format (see PDF).

Applet. A JAVA program designed to perform a specific task within a larger program. Applets may be embedded and run from within another application such as a Web page.

Applications Programming Interface. A program or data mapping mechanism that allows separate applications to work together by mapping data in one application to the format required in another application.

Application Service Provider (ASP). An organization that provides software applications over the Internet. A common example is an Internet Service provider (ISP).

ADSL. See Asymmetric Digital Subscriber Line.

ASP. See Application Service Provider.

Asymmetric Digital Subscriber Line (ADSL). A dedicated connection to the Internet that is suitable for individual and small business use. It is quicker for downloads than for uploads.

Authentication (authorization). The process a computer used to "verify" a user attempting to access the computer. Authentication may include user names, passwords, encryption, digital security certificates and signatures and other forms of security checking prior to allowing access to a computer, Web site, systems, files or data.

Auto-Responder. A feature of some e-mail programs that can be set to provide an automatic response to incoming messages. It is frequently used by business to acknowledge the receipt of a customer's messages and to provide a timeframe for the response. It is also used by individual employees to send a response to messages when they are out of the office.

Backbone. A top-level, high-speed connection to the Internet that serves as a major access point for ISPs and major users of the Internet (e.g., large business).

Bandwidth. The amount of information that can be carried through a communication system in a set time.

Banner. A graphical display, usually an ad, that is displayed on a Web page.

Bit. A single binary value, either 0 or 1, used to store data or provide instructions to a computer. Bits are collected in multiples, called bytes.

Bookmarks/Favorites. A list of Web pages visited and to which one will likely return that are created by Internet browsers, such as Netscape and Internet Explorer. These bookmarks are direct links to the Web page.

Browser. A user interface program that allows access to the Internet. The most well-known browsers are Internet Explorer and Netscape Navigator.

Business Intelligence (BI). Organizing, searching, analyzing and reporting trends or business specific information from data contained in Web sites, business applications and/or databases.

Business Process Reengineering (BPR). Analysis and reengineering of specific business processes and management systems to eliminate redundancy and non-value-added steps and to improve efficiency and performance.

Certificates. A security mechanism used in Internet communications to ensure that the Web site and data or communications conducted with it are trusted and secure.

C-Commerce (Collaborative Commerce). Technology-enabled business interactions among anyone involved in a business process, including internal employees, suppliers, business partners and customers.

The Cloud. A secure online venue for data storage allowing backup of files from physical storage devices such as external hard drives and USB flash drives.

Contact Center. A component of customer relationship management (CRM), that is a centralized support center for all customer contact channels, including phone, e-mail, Internet, fax, mail or other forms of communication between customers and their providers of goods or services.

Cookie. A small text file that is put on users' hard drives when they visit a Web page so that other Web pages can remember certain information about the user.

Customer Relationship Management (CRM). An organizational strategy to maximize revenue, profitability and brand loyalty by focusing business processes and information analysis around customer intelligence. Key investment in technologies that connect internal business systems with external customer-facing systems to improve response to customer demands and related product, revenue and profitability mixes.

Database Management System (DBMS). Software that enables systematic data storage and retrieval in a repeatable mechanism to create, update and report on large amounts of data.

Data Mining. Sorting and analyzing trends or meaningful patterns across large amounts of data.

Digital Signature. A code that can be attached to a transmission (e.g., e-mail message, order request) that authenticates the sender.

Domain Name. A name designated to represent a location on the Internet, such as the address for a Web site.

Domain Name Server (DNS). A server that associates a number (an Internet Protocol, or IP address) with a text-based domain name.

DNS. See Domain Name System.

E-Business. All activities conducted by a business over the Internet.

E-Commerce. The procurement and distribution of goods and services over the Internet using digital technology.

EDI. Electronic Data Interchange is the transfer of data using networks, such as the Internet.

E-Marketplace. An online marketplace where buyers and sellers can exchange goods and services. Normally relates to business-to-business transactions.

Electronic Data Interchange. The exchange of documents in standardized electronic form between parties in an automated manner directly from one party's computer system to an application in another.

Encryption. The encoding of a message or electronic transmission to prevent unauthorized access.

Enterprise Resource Planning (ERP). Large-scale business software applications that support key management functions of the enterprise, such as financial, manufacturing, human resources, procurement, customer relationship management and other key business processes.

Favorites. See Bookmarks.

FAQ. See Frequently Asked Questions.

Firewall. Hardware and software used to prevent unauthorized access to a computer or network.

Frequently Asked Questions (FAQs). A list of answers to commonly asked questions, especially on a Web site.

GIF. See Graphics Interchange Format.

Graphical User Interface (GUI). A graphical tool that allows users to access the features and functionalities of a software application. On the Web, it refers to the parts of the Web site the users actually see, and would not include the back end software such as the database and programs that power the site.

Graphics Interchange Format (GIF). One of the two most common formats for graphics on the Web (the other being JPEG).

Hyperlink. A highlighted link or graphic within a hypertext document or Web page that will take the user to another place within the same Web page or to another Web site or page.

IC3. The Internet Crime Complaint Center was established as a partnership between the Federal Bureau of Investigation (FBI) and the National White Collar Crime Center (NW3C) to serve as a means to receive Internet related criminal complaints and to further research, develop, and refer the criminal complaints to appropriate agencies.

Intranet. A secure network within a company accessible only by internal users of the company network. Intranets are protected by firewalls and other security mechanisms that prevent unsecure parties from accessing internal data.

Java. A programming language developed by SUN Microsystems that has been widely adopted for developing Internet applications.

JPEG. A compression format used for Internet graphics or images.

Knowledge Management (KM). An organizational strategy to use technology to capture, organize, access and manage the "knowledge" assets of a business. The deployment of "content management" systems to provide storage, search, retrieval and use of information assets across collaborative groups of people within an organization.

LAN (Local Area Network). A computer network established within a specific area, such as a university or business headquarters. LANs were developed to facilitate the exchange and sharing of data, software, printers, and storage within an organization.

M-Commerce. Any transaction, involving the transfer of ownership or rights to use goods and services, which is initiated and/or completed by using mobile access to computer-mediated networks with the help of an electronic device.

Middleware. Software applications that support integration of different data, programs, databases, and Web sites across or between multiple computer systems.

NW3C. National White Collar Crime Center provides a nationwide support system for law enforcement and regulatory agencies involved in the prevention, investigation and prosecution of economic and high-tech crime.

PDF (Portable Document Format). A file format created by Adobe that delivers and displays an entire document with text and complex graphics in a single readable file.

PDA (Personal Digital Assistant). Any small, mobile, handheld device that creates, stores and retrieves data. Many PDAs may also connect to the Internet through wireless technology for sending and retrieving data such as e-mail.

Pharming. A hacker's attack aiming to redirect a Web site's traffic to another bogus Web site. Pharming can be conducted either by changing the hosts file on a victim's computer or by exploitation of a vulnerability in software.

Phishing. The act of acquiring *private* or sensitive *data* from personal *computers* for use in fraudulent *activities*. Phishing is usually done by sending emails that seem to appear to come from credible *sources* which require *users* to put in personal data such as a *credit card* number or *social security number*. This *information* is then transmitted to the *hacker* and utilized to commit *acts* of *fraud*.

Permission Marketing. Involves persuading customers to physically request that marketing information be sent to them (sometimes called opt-in marketing).

Personalization. Individual user's ability to configure their own preferences for information selection and display on their access pages to a Web site or application.

POP (Post Office Protocol or Point Of Presence). Refers to one common way that e-mail software gets mail from a mail server. Point of presence usually refers to the locations where a dial-up connection to a mail server is available.

Portal. A Web site used as a primary starting point to get to other Web sites. It often refers to search directories such as Yahoo and Search engines such as Google.

Search Directory. A human-compiled directory of information on the Web sorted under meaningful categories (e.g., Yahoo, About, open directory).

Search Engine. A computer program that automatically seeks out Web sites, creates an index of these sites and then allows you to search the index (e.g., Altavista, Alltheweb, Hotbot).

Secure Sockets Layer (SSL). A communication protocol developed to securely transmit data on the Internet. Data is encrypted prior to being transferred over SSL to its destination. Many Web sites support SSL to confidentially process user information, such as credit card payments.

Service-Level Agreement (SLA). An agreement between an ASP and a user that describes the level of service expected throughout the duration of the contract.

SLA. See Service-Level Agreement.

SPAM. A term used to describe unsolicited and unwanted messages sent to an e-mail address or to an online discussion group.

Splash Page. An initial Web page that is used to capture the user's attention and is usually a lead-in to the home page.

Spoofing. A technique whereby a subject pretends to be someone else's email or Web site. This is typically done by copying the Web content of a legitimate company onto a Web site of the subject's own creation. Instead of actually typing in the legitimate business's Uniform Resource Locator (URL), the victim is given a hyperlink, usually in an email, that directs the victim to the fraudulent site. Spoofing is done to further perpetrate other schemes, including identity theft and auction fraud.

Structured Query Language (SQL). A standard programming language use for updating and retrieving data from a database.

SSL. See Secure Sockets Layer.

Stickiness. A term used to describe the ability of a Web site to keep users on the site. Usually measured by the average length of time visitors spend on a Web site.

Supply Chain Management (SCM). Business processes and technology-based applications that support the process of planning, producing, ordering, stocking, delivering and supporting goods, services and information from a supplier to a customer.

T1 (also T3). High-speed, high-bandwidth, dedicated connections to the Internet. T1 offers 20 times the bandwidth of a 56K modem. A T3 connection is made up of 28 T1 lines.

24/7. Refers to services offered 24 hours a day, 7 days a week.

Telephony. A general term applied to any type of voice communication as opposed to data communication.

Traffic. Refers to the amount of visitors that a Web site receives.

Transition Logs. Reports designed to create an audit trail for each online transaction and its terminal of origin, time, user, and details.

URL. See Uniform Resource Locator.

Uniform Resource Locator (URL). Another way of describing a Web page address. When a URL is entered into a Web browser, it will be bring the user to that site.

Viral Marketing. Involves using the customer as a sales person to encourage others to use a product/service.

WAN (Wide Area Network). A computer network established across an expanded area, such as between hospital sites, city utilities sites, or multiple corporate subsidiaries. Several local area networks (LANs) can be interconnected into a WAN.

WAP. Wireless Application Protocol allows users to access information instantly and securely via handheld wireless devices.

Web site. Generally, a set of Web pages all located within the same URL.

World Wide Web (or WWW or the Web). A series of hypertext markup language (HTML) documents all connected using the Internet.

www. See World Wide Web.

Workflow Management. Supports the ability to define specific business rules or data events that are automatically routed to users and managers for review or action.

¶20,010   An E-Business Checklist

Keys to the success of any project include executive support and constant communication. Usually a steering committee of executives is established to report regularly on a project. This allows project decisions to be made quickly. Any business policy or business process change requires this. "Quickly" is often important because usually any decision that delays a project adds costs to the project.

Using this checklist could assist in developing successful project policies.

Is there an executive who can serve as a project liaison with senior management?
☐ yes ☐ no

Is there a cross-departmental team of both business and Information Technology users assigned to the implementation of the project?
☐ yes ☐ no

Are the business objectives of both the organization and the project clearly identified and agreed upon?
☐ yes ☐ no

Are business and information managers fully aware of the plans and strategies of the organization?
☐ yes ☐ no

What benefits and improvements can be expected from this project, and how will they be measured?

_____

_____

_____

Which business processes will be improved, and how will customers benefit?

_____

_____

_____

Are the people involved in the project development and implementation capable and reliable?
☐ yes ☐ no

Are there sufficient resources to implement the new project while adequately supporting the old system?
☐ yes ☐ no

Has the total cost of the project been identified and estimated, including staffing, training, and any external consulting that may be required?
☐ yes ☐ no

Has a detailed business case, supported by resource and technical plans, been prepared along with a proper project proposal?
☐ yes ☐ no

Can the implementation of the project be "phased" in stages to deliver incremental early successes as opposed to the "big bang" approach in which success is not identified until the entire project is complete?
☐ yes ☐ no

Is there an experienced project leader dedicated full time to the management of the teams, tasks, and external consultants on a daily basis?
☐ yes ☐ no

Have effective means of communicating developments and progress to all staff members been put in place?
☐ yes ☐ no

Have the role, responsibilities and time commitment of the people involved been clearly set out and accepted by them?

☐ yes ☐ no

Are information and communication strategies and systems reviewed frequently?

☐ yes ☐ no

Is it possible to benchmark the business and information systems against those of the company's peers and competitors?

☐ yes ☐ no

Does the project help achieve the strategic objectives of the business?

☐ yes ☐ no

CHAPTER 21
Insurance Accounting

¶21,000   Overview

As unlikely as it would have appeared in another time, there is actually a Federal Insurance Office (FIO) in the Treasury Department as mandated by Title V of the Dodd-Frank Wall Street Reform and Consumer Protection Act. For the first time, Congress created a federal agency charged with monitoring and, to some extent, regulating, the insurance industry, which until that legislation has been entirely within the purview of the individual states.

The FIO has made strides in getting organized in several areas as discussed below. Committees have been formed, are being formed, and the FIO is joining others. A professional staff has been accumulated by the Director, who has been busy explaining the activities and accomplishments of the FIO to Congressional committees and insurance organizations.

FIO has been issuing annual reports on the insurance industry since 2013. It has also issued other reports, such as those covering Terrorism Risk Insurance, in 2020 and 2021. Although FIO has myriad responsibilities, including providing insurance sector expertise to the Financial Stability Oversight Council, FIO's immediate predominant focus is on international issues, involving key bilateral relationships and critical international initiatives. FIO provides the United States with a sophisticated, experienced and authoritative voice on international insurance matters. Given the current fast-paced development of international insurance supervisory standards, and the explosive growth of premium volume in emerging markets, FIO's participation and engagement arrives at an opportune moment for U.S-based insurance consumers and industry.

¶21,001   The Role of the Federal Insurance Office

The FIO advises the Secretary of the Treasury on major domestic and prudential international insurance policy issues. This includes:

1. The FIO Director serves as a non-voting member of the Financial Stability Oversight Council (FSOC) in an advisory capacity. The FIO has the authority to recommend to the FSOC that FSOC designate an insurer (including affiliates) to be an entity subject to regulation as a nonbank financial company supervised by the Board of Governors of the Federal Reserve.
2. The FIO monitors all aspects of the insurance industry, including identifying issues or gaps in the regulation of insurers that could contribute to a systemic crisis in the insurance industry or the U.S. financial system.
3. The Director also plays a role in authorizing the resolution of any insurance companies subject to regulation as a nonbank financial company.
4. The FIO coordinates and develops Federal policy on prudential aspects of international insurance matters, including representing the United States, as appropriate, in the International Association of Insurance Supervisors (or a successor entity), and assisting the Secretary of the Treasury (with the United States Trade Representative) in negotiating certain written bilateral or multilateral agreements regarding prudential insurance measures with respect to the business of insurance or reinsurance. The Office assists the Director in determining whether State insurance measures are preempted by such agreement or agreements.
5. The FIO monitors the extent to which traditionally underserved communities and consumers, minorities, and low- and moderate- income persons have access to affordable insurance products regarding all lines of insurance, except health insurance.
6. The FIO assists the Secretary of the Treasury and other officials in administering the Terrorism Risk Insurance Program.
7. The FIO also performs such other related duties and authorities as may be assigned to it by the Secretary of the Treasury.

In carrying out these functions, the Office may:

- Receive and collect data and information on and from the insurance industry and insurers,
- Enter into information-sharing agreements,
- Analyze and disseminate data and information, and
- Issue reports regarding all lines of insurance except health insurance,
- Certain types of long-term care insurance, and
- Crop insurance.

¶21,002   International Association of Insurance Supervisors (IAIS)

In an appearance before a Congressional committee, the Director of the FIO pointed out that the Dodd-Frank Act established the FIO to coordinate federal efforts and develop federal policy on prudential aspects of international insurance matters, including representing the U.S., as appropriate, in the International Association of Insurance Supervisors (IAIS), and assisting the Secretary of the Treasury in negotiating covered agreements.

This established for the first time an office within the U.S. government that participates in and represents the collective interests of the United States on international prudential insurance matters. FIO became a full member of the IAIS on October 1, 2011, and joined the IAIS Executive Committee on February 24, 2012.

The IAIS, which includes insurance supervisors and regulators from 140 countries, has two primary objectives:

1. To promote effective and globally consistent supervision of the insurance industry in order to develop and maintain fair, safe, and stable insurance markets for the benefit and protection of policyholders; and
2. To contribute to global financial stability.

.01   IAIS—Common Framework for the Supervision of Internationally Active Insurance Groups

FIO has been engaged in the IAIS effort to develop a common framework, or "ComFrame," for the supervision of internationally active insurance groups. The objectives of ComFrame are to:

1. Develop methods of operating group-wide supervision of internationally active insurance groups;
2. Establish a comprehensive framework for supervisors to address group-wide activities and risks and also set grounds for better supervisory cooperation; and,
3. Foster global convergence of supervisory approaches and measures.

ComFrame confronts the difficult task of establishing a common translation of different regulatory systems that:

- Evaluate capital adequacy differently,
- Employ unique accounting approaches,
- Evaluate and weigh risks differently, and/or
- Utilize varied approaches to regulation of insurers' investments.

These differences often render the work of the ConFrame subcommittees complex and challenging. While recognizing these hurdles, FIO supports the objectives of the ComFrame initiative as critical to the increasingly global nature of insurance markets across jurisdictions.

.02   IAIS—Financial Stability Committee

The IAIS, in cooperation with the Financial Stability Board (FSB), is developing the methodology and indicators to identify global systemically important insurers (GSIIs). The IAIS Executive Committee assigned this important task to its Financial Stability Committee (FSC), and FIO has participated in the FSC's work since July 2011. FIO has developed solid working relationships with its counterparts on the FSC, and is working to ensure this process will align with the criteria, methodology and timing of the Council's process for designating systemically important nonbank financial institutions. The IAIS plans to finalize the criteria and methodology and use this methodology to produce, early in the second quarter of 2013, an initial list of insurers considered of global systemic importance. This timeline, slower than originally envisioned, which has been approved by the FSB Steering Committee, allows more time for development by IAIS experts, and aligns with plans applicable to the Council process.

¶21,003   Federal Advisory Committee on Insurance

In May 2011, the Treasury Department determined that it was in the public interest to establish the Federal Advisory Committee on Insurance (FACI). A charter for the Committee had been prepared and was to be filed in the Federal Registrar.

The purpose of FACI is to present advice and recommendations to the Federal Insurance Office (FIO) to assist the Office in carrying out its duties and authorities.

.01   The Structure of the Federal Advisory Committee on Insurance

The creation of FACI was one in a series of steps that Treasury is taking to establish the new Federal Insurance Office (FIO) created under the Dodd-Frank Wall Street Reform and Consumer Protection Act.

The Committee is to provide advice to the FIO and the Treasury Department, including to the FIO Director in the Director's role of a member of the

Financial Stability Oversight Council (FSOC). Through the Committee, the FIO and the Treasury will benefit from the deep knowledge and regulatory experience of state and tribal insurance regulators, as well as the perspective of industry experts, academics, and other stakeholders and affected constituencies. These views will be offered directly to the Director of the FIO on a regular basis. There exists no other source within the Federal government that could serve this function.

The FACI is to be a continuing advisory committee with an initial two-year term, subject to two-year re-authorizations.

.02   Objective, Scope and Description of the Committee

The FACI is expected to provide its advice, recommendations, analysis, and information directly to the FIO. The FIO may also share the FACI advice and recommendations with the Secretary of the Treasury or other Treasury officials. The FIO may share information with the FACI as the Director determines to be helpful in allowing the FACI to carry out its role.

Members are:

- Selected by the Department from persons with expertise in the area of insurance,
- Appointed to serve a two-year term,
- Drawn from State and Tribal insurance regulators and/or officials, industry experts, and
- Others who possess relevant expertise and/or who are familiar with or representative of affected constituencies.

Appointments are to be made with the objective of creating a diverse and balanced body with a variety of interests, backgrounds, and viewpoints represented. The FACI is to be made up of not more than 15 members.

The Committee is chaired by a member selected by the FIO and Treasury officials and serves a two-year period before renewal or termination. It will meet periodically, generally four times per year, in Washington, DC.

¶21,004   Federal Insurance Office Requests Comments on Global Reinsurance Market

In June 2012, the U.S. Treasury Department's Federal Insurance Office (FIO) issued a notice requesting public comments on the global reinsurance market and the regulation of reinsurance. Comments were requested to assist the FIO in completing its report to Congress on the global reinsurance market, as required under the Dodd-Frank Act. Since that time, FIO has had similar activities related to natural catastrophe insurance, affordability of auto insurance, risk-sharing mechanisms, and other related issues.

The FIO is tasked with monitoring the insurance industry and gathering information, including "identifying issues or gaps in the regulation of insurers that could contribute to a systemic crisis in the insurance industry or the United States financial system. Dodd-Frank requires that the FIO issue several reports to Congress on the insurance industry, including a report on "the breadth and scope of the global reinsurance market and the critical role such market plays in supporting insurance in the United States."

¶21,005   Federal Insurance Office

With passage of the Dodd-Frank Wall Street Reform and Consumer Protection Act, the Federal Insurance Office (FIO) provides the federal government for the first time with dedicated expertise regarding the insurance industry. The Office is expected to monitor the insurance industry, including identifying gaps or issues in the regulation of insurance that could contribute to a systemic crisis in the insurance industry or the United States financial system, according to an official in the Treasury Department.

Among the Federal Insurance Office's principal functions are the authority to:

- Monitor the insurance industry, including identifying regulatory loopholes that may expose the financial system to systemic risk in the insurance industry or the U.S. financial system;
- Ensure access for underserved communities, minorities and certain other groups to affordable insurance products in all lines of insurance, except health insurance;
- Report to Congress on domestic and international reinsurance markets, investigating ways to modernize and improve insurance regulation in the United States;
- Declare state insurance laws preempted by international agreements regarding insurance regulation;
- Consult with the states (including state insurance regulators) regarding insurance matters of national importance and prudential insurance matters of international importance;
- Develop federal policy on prudential aspects of international insurance matters, including representing the United States, as appropriate, in the International Association of Insurance Supervisors (or a successor entity) and assisting the Secretary in negotiating covered agreements; and
- Assist the Secretary in administering the Terrorism Insurance Program established in the Treasury Department.

The Director is appointed by the Secretary of the Treasury. Although the Treasury Secretary has had the authority to negotiate for increased access to foreign markets for U.S. insurers and reinsurers, and to prevent discrimination against foreign insurers and reinsurers by state regulatory bodies, this authority arguably has been eclipsed by the overall lack of federal regulation of the insurance sector. Congress has now granted the Treasury Department further authority to preempt state law in negotiating international agreements with foreign countries.

Despite conferring considerable powers on the FIO, Congress has left state-based insurance regulation largely intact. The legislation does not grant the FIO or the Treasury Department general supervisory or regulatory authority over the business of insurance, but rather aims to streamline state regulation with uniform national and international insurance regulations and standards. The legislation represents a relatively narrow, but significant, entry of the federal government into insurance regulation.

¶21,006   Financial Stability Oversight Council

As established under the Dodd-Frank Act, the Financial Stability Oversight Council (FSOC) provides, comprehensive monitoring to ensure the stability of the nation's financial system. The Council is charged with identifying threats to the financial stability of the United States; promoting market discipline; and responding to emerging risks to the stability of the United States.

The Council, made up of nine federal financial agencies and an independent insurance member, and five nonvoting members is charged with identifying and responding to emerging risks throughout the financial system, including the designation of systemically significant firms. The Council is chaired by the Treasury Secretary. (The Council's first quarterly meeting was held in October 2010.)

Lawmakers had previously agreed to add two nonvoting members to a new Financial Services Oversight Council, which would regulate risks to the U.S. financial system. There would be one representative each from the FIO and from state insurance regulators.

The state presence may come from the Treasury Department having asked the NAIC for a representative, an official of NAIC explained. "If you're going to have an oversight council that is going to be looking at the overall financial sector, insurance is an important segment."

Upon enactment, the Council was authorized to approve a Federal Reserve decision to require a large, complex company to divest some of its holdings if it posed a grave threat to the financial stability of the United States.

¶21,007   Contracts Summary of Decisions Reached to Date

On October 18, 2012, the IASB and the FASB elected to go over important background material before beginning deliberations of issues raised in response to IASB's Exposure Draft, *Insurance Contracts,* and FASB's *Preliminary Views on Insurance Contracts.*

The background material included:
1. A proposed timetable in which the IASB was to have completed the process of replacing IAS 39 with IFRS 9, and for the FASB to have completed the proposed guidance by 2011.
2. A summary of the reasons for the Boards' decision to develop a standard on insurance contracts as well as the proposed measurement model.
3. A summary of feedback received during various outreach activities during the comment period and the overview of the main issues raised.

The IASB and FASB are also continuing their joint discussion of the accounting for insurance contracts, focusing on how an entity would present premiums, claims, non-claims fulfillment costs, and acquisition costs in the statement of comprehensive income.

.01   Project Plan

The FASB discussed how to proceed with this project in light of the feedback it has received from stakeholders through comment letters on the FASB's Discussion Paper and related outreach activities.

The FASB decided to continue this project, affirming the objective of developing standards of accounting for insurance contracts that would improve existing U.S. Generally Accepted Accounting Principles (U.S. GAAP) and converge with International Financial Reporting Standards (IFRSs). The FASB will pursue those objectives by deliberating the issues in this project jointly with the IASB.

.02   Project Objective

The objective of this joint IASB/FASB insurance contracts project was to develop common, high-quality guidance that would:
- Address recognition,
- Measurement,
- Presentation, and
- Disclosure requirements for insurance contracts (including reinsurance), even if the contracts are not issued by an insurance entity.

Specifically, the project was intended to improve, simplify, and converge the financial reporting requirements for insurance contracts and to provide investors with decision-useful information.

.03   IASB Targets Re-exposure of Insurance Contracts Proposal

The International Accounting Standards Board (IASB) met on September 26, 2012, to continue its discussions on proposals for insurance contracts accounting. After extensive deliberations and exposure drafts, the IASB issued IFRS 17, *Insurance Contracts*, in May 2017. Since that time there have been amendments to IFRS 17, primarily to assist entities to implement the Standard while not unduly disrupting implementation or diminishing the usefulness of the information provided by applying IFRS 17.

The key principles in IFRS 17 are that an entity:

- Identifies as insurance contracts those contracts under which the entity accepts significant insurance risk from another party (the policyholder) by agreeing to compensate the policyholder if a specified uncertain future event (the insured event) adversely affects the policyholder;
- Separates specified embedded derivatives, distinct investment components and distinct performance obligations from the insurance contracts;
- Divides the contracts into groups that it will recognize and measure;
- Recognizes and measures groups of insurance contracts at:
  — A risk-adjusted present value of the future cash flows (the fulfilment cash flows) that incorporates all of the available information about the fulfilment cash flows in a way that is consistent with observable market information; plus (if this value is a liability) or minus (if this value is an asset)
  — An amount representing the unearned profit in the group of contracts (the contractual service margin);
- Recognizes the profit from a group of insurance contracts over the period the entity provides insurance contract services, and as the entity is released from risk. If a group of contracts is or becomes loss-making, an entity recognizes the loss immediately;
- Presents separately insurance revenue (that excludes the receipt of any investment component), insurance service expenses (that exclude the repayment of any investment components) and insurance finance income or expenses; and
- Discloses information to enable users of financial statements to assess the effect that contracts within the scope of IFRS 17 have on the financial position, financial performance and cash flows of the entity.

IFRS 17 includes an optional simplified measurement approach, or premium allocation approach, for simpler insurance contracts.

¶21,008   FASB Accounting Standards Updates

The following Accounting Updates have been issued related to accounting issues for entities in the insurance and health care fields.

.01   ASU No. 2022-05—Financial Services—Insurance (Topic 944): Transition for Sold Contracts

The FASB issued ASU No. 2022-05 to reduce implementation costs and complexity associated with ASU No. 2018-12, described below. The amendments allow an insurance entity to make an accounting policy election on a transaction-by-transaction basis. An insurance entity may elect to exclude contracts that meet certain criteria from applying the amendments in ASU No. 2018-12.

.02   ASU No. 2020-11, Financial Services—Insurance (Topic 944): Effective Date and Early Application, and 2019-09—Financial Services—Insurance (Topic 944): Effective Date, and ASU No. 2018-12, Financial Services—Insurance (Topic 944): Targeted Improvements to the Accounting for Long-Duration Contracts

The FASB issued ASU No. 2020-11 to defer the effective date of ASU No. 2018-12 by an additional year over the deferral made by ASU No. 2019-09.

The FASB issued ASU No. 2019-09 to defer the effective date of ASU No. 2018-12 by one year for all entities.

The FASB issued ASU No. 2018-12, which improves financial reporting for insurance companies that issue long-duration contracts, such as life insurance, disability income, long-term care, and annuities. The ASU improved area of financial reporting by:

- requiring updated assumptions for liability measurement. Assumptions used to measure the liability for traditional insurance contracts, typically determined at contract inception, are now reviewed and updated, if necessary, at least annually, with the net effect recorded in net income;
- standardizing the liability discount rate. The liability discount rate will be a standardized, market-observable discount rate, with the effect of rate changes recorded in other comprehensive income;
- providing greater consistency in measurement of market risk benefits. The two previous measurement models have been reduced to one measurement model (i.e., fair value), resulting in greater uniformity across similar market-based benefits and better alignment with the fair value measurement of derivatives used to hedge capital market risk;
- simplifying amortization of deferred acquisition costs. Previous earnings-based amortization methods have been replaced with a more level amortization basis; and

- requiring enhanced disclosures. They include rollforwards and information about significant assumptions and the effects of changes in those assumptions.

.03   ASU No. 2015-09, Financial Services—Insurance (Topic 944): Disclosures about Short-Duration Contracts

The FASB issued ASU No. 2015-09 that requires insurance entities to disclose for annual reporting periods specified information about the liability for unpaid claims and claim adjustment expenses.

.04   ASU No. 2010-26, Financial Services—Insurance (Topic 944): Accounting for Costs Associated with Acquiring or Renewing Insurance Contracts (a consensus of the FASB Emerging Issues Task Force)

The objective of ASU No. 2010-26, issued by the FASB in October 2010, is to address diversity in practice regarding the interpretation of which costs relating to the acquisition of new or renewal insurance contracts qualify for deferral. The current definition of acquisition costs in the Master Glossary of the FASB Accounting Standards Codification™ is "costs that vary with and are primarily related to the acquisition of insurance contracts." Costs that meet that definition are typically recognized as assets and are commonly referred to as *deferred acquisition costs*.

Deferred acquisition costs are amortized over time using amortization methods dependent upon the nature of the underlying insurance product (that is, proportional to revenues, based on a contract's estimated gross profit, or based on a contract's estimated gross margin). Other costs that do not vary with and are not primarily related to the acquisition of new and renewal insurance contracts—such as those relating to investment management, general administration, and policy maintenance—are charged to expense as incurred.

As a result of the diversity in practice relating to the interpretation of which costs qualify as deferrable acquisition costs within the insurance industry, certain stakeholders initially raised the question of whether advertising costs meet the definition of acquisition costs. However, interpretation of the phrase *vary with and are primarily related* to raises a broader conceptual issue that also applies to other types of costs; therefore, application of the amendments in this Update are not limited to advertising costs.

¶21,009   NAIC Adopts Standard Valuation Model Legislation

Members of the National Association of Insurance Commissioners (NAIC) took steps to update the regulation of life insurance and annuity products on September 23, 2009. At the Executive/Plenary session of its Fall National Meeting, NAIC members adopted changes to the Standard Valuation Model Law that, when enacted by state legislatures, is designed to improve the way life insurers calculate the reserves held to protect consumer's financial interests in insurance products. Currently, insurance reserves are calculated using static formulas that are not always optimal when matching risks to reserves.

The organization has adopted a new *principles-based approach* that uses risk analysis techniques such as modeling and simulation to capture the various risks inherent in establishing adequate reserves. As a result, regulators are replacing static formulas with more modern tools to protect the insurance consumer.

Changes in the Standard Valuation Model Law are closely associated with changes in the Valuation Manual used by regulatory actuaries to verify the accuracy and adequacy of the reserves being held by insurers. These measures are expected to add important consumer protections to safeguard consumers' investments in life insurance products.

The Valuation Manual provides specific guidance for each product to make sure the life insurer is holding the correct amount in reserve to meet its obligations to policyholders.

¶21,010   IRS Insurance Fraud Program

Criminal Investigation's (CI) Insurance Fraud Program addresses criminal tax and money laundering violations relative to insurance claims and fraud perpetrated against insurance companies. Insurance fraud is either internal or external in nature and covers a wide variety of schemes.

Internal fraud schemes include:

- Agent/Broker premium diversion,
- Reinsurance fraud,
- Rented asset schemes,
- Many other forms of fraud.

External fraud schemes include:

- Phony insurance companies,
- Offshore/unlicensed Internet companies,
- Staged auto accidents, and
- Viatical and senior settlement fraud.

Rented assets schemes involve companies that pay an up-front fee to borrow assets and then, sometimes without the knowledge of the real owners, list them on their balance sheet. Reinsurance is the process in which insurance companies offset all or a part of their risk through other insurance companies. Fraud in this area involves non-existent reinsurance companies or moving illegally obtained insurance premiums offshore through transactions disguised as payments to a reinsurance company. Automobile fraud rings, assisted by corrupt doctors and attorneys continue to be a major source of false insurance claims.

Viatical settlements involve the purchase of life insurance policies, or their benefits, at a discounted rate from a terminally ill person. The beneficial interests in the insurance policies purchased are sold or assigned to an investor. A viatical investor receives the full benefits when the ill person dies. Viatical fraud is a major form of insurance fraud. Investors are promised guarantees that have no basis and in some instances have no underlying insurance policy securing their investment. Fraud involving senior settlements is also becoming more prevalent. Senior settlements follow the basic premise of viatical settlements but involve senior citizen insurance policies.

Criminal Investigation is an active participant in the National Association of Insurance Commissioners (NAIC) which is comprised of state insurance commissioners and regulators, fraud bureaus, and industry specialists. The goal of this cooperative effort is to bar unscrupulous brokers and adjusters from the insurance industry. One of NAIC's benefits to law enforcement is its database of fraudulent activity within the industry. The NAIC has established a Web site that allows each state to post emerging schemes and significant investigations.

To address international issues within the insurance industry effectively, CI has maintained its affiliation with the International Association of Insurance Fraud Agencies. This association brings together insurance companies throughout the world. Their focus is to identify and combat fraud in the insurance industry through international cooperation.

¶21,011   Financial Accounting Standards Board Statements Prior to the Accounting Standards Codification (ASC) that Cover Accounting and Reporting by Insurance Enterprises

Five statements apply to insurance entities. These have now been codified into the ASC. The basic document is SFAS 60, *Accounting and Reporting by Insurance Enterprises*. It has been amended and amplified by the three other statements in the following discussions.

.01   SFAS 60, Accounting and Reporting by Insurance Enterprises

In June 1982, the Financial Accounting Standards Board extracted the specialized principles and practices from the AICPA insurance-industry-related Guides and Statements of Position to produce Standard No. 60, *Accounting and Reporting by Insurance Enterprises*. It established financial accounting and reporting standards for insurance enterprises other than mutual life insurance enterprises, assessment enterprises, and fraternal benefit societies.

The Statement classified insurance contracts as short-duration or long-duration contracts. Long-duration contracts include contracts, such as:

- Whole-life.
- Guaranteed renewable term life.
- Endowment.
- Annuity.
- Title insurance contracts that are expected to remain in force for an extended period.

All other insurance contracts are considered short-duration contracts and include most property and liability insurance contracts.

Premiums from short-duration contracts ordinarily are recognized as revenue during the period of the contract in proportion to the amount of insurance protection provided. Claim costs, including estimates of costs for claims relating to insured events that have occurred but have not been reported to the insurer, are recognized when insured events occur.

Premiums from long-duration contracts are recognized as revenue when due from policyholders. The present value of estimated future policy benefits to be paid to or on behalf of policyholders less the present value of estimated future net premiums to be collected from policyholders are accrued when premium revenue is recognized. Those estimates are based on assumptions applicable at the time the insurance contracts are made, including:

- Estimates of expected investment yields.
- Mortality.
- Morbidity.
- Terminations.
- Expenses.

Claim costs are recognized when insured events occur.

Costs that vary with and are primarily related to the acquisition of insurance contracts (acquisition costs) are capitalized and charged to expense in proportion to premium revenue recognized.

Investments are reported as follows:

- Common and nonredeemable preferred stocks at market.
- Bonds and redeemable preferred stocks at amortized cost.
- Mortgage loans at outstanding principal or amortized cost.
- Real estate at depreciated cost.

Realized investment gains and losses are reported in the income statement below operating income and net of applicable income taxes. Unrealized investment gains and losses, net of applicable income taxes, are included in stockholders' (policyholders') equity.

.02   SFAS 97, Accounting and Reporting by Insurance Enterprises for Certain Long-Duration Contracts and for Realized Gains and Losses from the Sale of Investments

FASB Statement 97 amended Statement 60 by concluding that the accounting methods required by Statement 60 are not appropriate for insurance contracts in which the insurer can vary amounts charged or credited to the policyholder's account or the policyholder can vary the amount of premium paid.

The Statement outlines the accounting methods for three different classifications of long-duration life and annuity products. These classifications are:

1.   Universal life-type policies.
2.   Limited payment policies.
3.   Policies not covering significant mortality or morbidity risks.

Universal Life-Type Policies. Universal life-type policies must utilize a retrospective deposit method. The liability for this type of policy will be equal to the gross account balances before deduction of surrender charges. Revenues reported will be made up of charges assessed against the policy for mortality, expenses, and surrenders. These charges are presumed to be earned in the period during which they were assessed; however, charges, such as front-end fees, for example, assessed a limited number of times are deferred as unearned revenue.

Limited-Payment Policies. Limited-payment policies consist of life insurance and annuity policies with fixed and guaranteed terms having premiums that are payable over a period shorter than the period during which benefits are paid. The premiums for this type of policy are reported as revenues (reserves are computed in accordance with rulings set forth in Statement 60). However, the accumulated profit, formerly shown as a percentage of premiums, is deferred. The amount of coverage must be related to life insurance in force or expected future annuity benefit payments.

Policies Not Covering Significant Mortality or Morbidity Risk. Policies not covering significant mortality or morbidity risks, such as *guaranteed investment contracts* (GICs) and some types of annuities, are shown as interest-bearing or other financial instruments, rather than as insurance contracts. Therefore, the accounting for these policies would show the account balance as a liability, and premiums as deposits rather than as revenues. Deferred acquisition costs would primarily be amortized in relation to future interest margins.

Policies including accident and health insurance not falling under one of these three classifications remain within the requirements of Statement 60.

Statement 97 also requires that property/casualty and stock life insurance companies must provide one-step income statements for realized investment gains or losses instead of the currently required two-step statement. The latter shows operating income after taxes but before net realized investment gains or losses. The one-step income statement presents realized investment gains or losses on a pretax basis with revenues, investment income, and expenses to show income before taxes.

.03   SFAS 113, Accounting and Reporting for Reinsurance of Short-Duration and Long-Duration Contracts

FASB Statement 113, *Accounting and Reporting for Reinsurance of Short-Duration and Long-Duration Contracts*, amends FASB Statement 60, *Accounting and Reporting by Insurance Companies*, and was effective for fiscal years starting after December 15, 1992. This rule eliminated the former practice of reporting assets and liabilities related to insurance contracts net of the effects of reinsurance. Statement 60, which is the basic document dealing with specialized insurance accounting and reporting practices, had continued the statutory accounting practice of offsetting reinsurance assets and liabilities. However, this procedure is now considered inconsistent with the generally accepted criteria for offsetting. Under this rule, the practice is eliminated for general-purpose financial statements.

Beginning in 1993, reinsurance receivables and prepaid reinsurance premiums are reported as assets. Reinsurance receivables include amounts related to (a) claims incurred but not reported and (b) liabilities for future policy benefits. Estimated reinsurance receivables are recognized in a manner consistent with the related liabilities.

Statement 113 set up a method of determining whether a specific contract qualified for reinsurance accounting. The accounting standard revolves around determination of whether the reinsurance is long-duration or short-duration, and, if short-duration, whether it is prospective or retroactive insurance. A contract must result in a reasonable possibility that the reinsurer may realize a significant loss from assuming insurance risk, or the contract does not qualify for reinsurance accounting, but must be accounted for as a deposit. All reinsurance contracts prohibit the reinsurance from recognizing immediately a gain if there remains a chance of liability to the policyholder by the ceding enterprise.

To further clarify the financial picture, the reinsurer is required to provide footnote disclosures explaining all facets of the terms, nature, purpose, and effect of ceded reinsurance transactions. In addition, disclosures of concentrations of credit risk associated with reinsurance receivables and prepaid premiums are also required under the provisions of FASB 105, *Disclosures of Information About Financial Instruments with Off-Balance-Sheet Risk and Financial Instruments with Concentrations of Credit Risk.*

.04 SFAS 120, Accounting and Reporting by Mutual Life Insurance Enterprises and by Insurance Enterprises for Certain Long-Duration Participating Contracts

SFAS 120 is the result of considerable cooperation between the Financial Accounting Standards Board and the American Institute of CPAs to provide guidance in accounting, reporting, and disclosure procedures to mutual life insurance companies. Prior to the enactment of this standard and those rulings cited below, these companies reported financial information to their creditors and policyholders primarily following the statutory provisions of various state insurance regulatory bodies. The companies are now to report insurance and reinsurance activities according to U.S. Generally Accepted Accounting principles (U.S. GAAP).

The thrust of this Statement is to apply the provisions of SFAS 60, *Accounting and Reporting by Insurance Enterprises*, SFAS 97, *Accounting and Reporting by Insurance Enterprises for Certain Long-Duration Contracts and for Realized Gains and Losses from the Sale of Investments*, and SFAS113, *Accounting and Reporting for Reinsurance of Short-Duration and Long-Duration Contracts*, to mutual life insurance enterprises, assessment enterprises and to fraternal benefit societies. Certain participating life insurance contracts of those same enterprises have also been addressed in the AICPA's Statement of Position 95-1, *Accounting for Certain Activities of Mutual Life Insurance Enterprises*.

The three earlier FASB Statements had specifically exempted mutual life insurance enterprises from their requirements. FASB Interpretation 40, *Applicability of Generally Accepted Accounting Principles to Mutual Life Insurance and Other Enterprises*, did not address or change the exemption of mutual life insurance companies from these Statements. Interpretation 40 had been scheduled to become effective earlier but the date was changed to permit simultaneous application with SFAS 120 and SOP 95-1.

.05 SFAS 163, Accounting for Financial Guarantee Insurance Contracts

In May 2008, the FASB issued Statement No. 163, *Accounting for Financial Guarantee Insurance Contracts*. The standard clarifies how Statement No. 60, *Accounting and Reporting by Insurance Enterprises*, applies to financial guarantee insurance contracts issued by insurance enterprises, including the recognition and measurement of premium revenue and claim liabilities. It also requires expanded disclosures about financial guarantee insurance contracts.

By issuing Statement 163, the FASB took a major step toward ending inconsistencies in practice that have made it difficult for investors to receive comparable information about an insurance enterprise's claim liabilities, according to the FASB. Its issuance is particularly timely in light of recent concerns about the financial health of financial guarantee insurers, and should help bring about much needed transparency and comparability to financial statements of insurance enterprises.

The accounting and disclosure requirements of SFAS 163 are intended to improve the comparability and quality of information provided to users of financial statements by creating consistency, for example, in the measurement and recognition of claim liabilities. Statement 163 requires that an insurance enterprise recognize a claim liability prior to an event of default (insured event) when there is evidence that credit deterioration has occurred in an insured financial obligation.

It also requires disclosure about:

- Risk-management activities used by an insurance enterprise to evaluate credit deterioration in its insured financial obligations, and
- An insurance enterprise's surveillance or watch list.

CHAPTER 22
Expert Witness

¶22,000   Overview

With the plethora of high profile legal cases which have inundated the news in the last few years, we've all become trial experts. After being briefed on a variety of cases, we're aware of all the legal terms—and ramifications.

But of a less spectacular nature has been the steady increase of experts in more dignified, straightforward, less publicized cases; in fact, to the lay person, these are often downright boring. However, to the accountant who has found his niche as an "expert witness," they are not only fascinating, but can be quite remunerative. (After all, it was accounting that finally put Al Capone behind bars.) Many accountants are discovering they can increase business, gain public awareness, and enjoy using their special knowledge and experience as expert witnesses. Their financial knowledge and ability to follow a paper trail of figures gives them importance as investigators as well as witnesses in complicated court cases involving financial dealings. There can also be pitfalls along the way.

The need for the accountant as an "expert witness" has increased proportionately with the growing complexity of business affairs. For a number of years, the courts had permitted a rather liberal use of experts in trials; however, the days of relative immunity from prosecution of the expert witness seem to have ended as litigation threatened to become a national pastime. Obviously, the more lawsuits, the more losers. And the loser has to take it out on someone. (That loser may be the opposing party—or it could be the accountant's client.) Why not go after that expert who caused all the trouble? And his firm, too!

¶22,001   Engagement Letter

Therein lies the raison d'etre of a well thought-out, carefully constructed engagement agreement containing buffers against both parties. This agreement needs, at the minimum, to spell out carefully:

1. What the accountant has agreed to do.
2. What information the client *must* make available to the expert witness to enable him or her to investigate the evidence and reach an opinion.
3. Lines of effective communication with both the client(s) and the attorney(s).
4. What the client can expect if the accountant is *required* to reveal on the stand any and all information on which his opinion is based.
5. That the attorney *must* keep the accountant informed in a timely fashion of any and all legal requirements such as filing times, submission of written documents, when any graphic presentations are due, and the like.

The corollary of this is, of course, that the accountant needs to guarantee to do or not do several things of concern to the client and/or attorney. If the accountant feels that he may not "fit the bill" as an expert witness in a case, he must not accept the engagement. The accountant must:

1. Possess the necessary qualifications and background.
2. Be cognizant of the accounting profession's technical and ethical standards applicable to litigation services, specifically those applying to expert witnesses.
3. Schedule adequate time and opportunity to investigate the case thoroughly.
4. Be prepared to furnish testimony in a forceful, confident manner.
5. Be prepared to defend a position "properly taken" in a polite, matter-of-fact manner in cross-examination.
6. Keep foremost in mind that the objective is to aid the client and attorney in winning the case, but *not* at the cost of the accountant's integrity.
7. Remember that the expert witness is *not* a client advocate, but an advocate of the accountant's own opinion and point of view.
8. Be positive that there can be no taint of conflict of interest that could be detrimental to the case.
9. Steer away from any engagement where there could be a possibility of divulging privileged information.

10. Withdraw as expeditiously as possible if there are any doubts about the litigation in question.
11. Adhere to the strategy of the lawyer, but here again, *not* at the expense of the accountant's integrity.

¶22,002 Prep Time

Preparing for the first trial may be the most difficult part of joining the growing number of accountants entering the expert witness niche. This is the time when the accountant, if he's been lucky or hasn't served on a jury, really becomes familiar with the down-to-earth aspects of the judicial system.

There's nothing like familiarity in developing confidence and ease of presentation; therefore, preparation should include:

1. Becoming familiar with the general rules governing real-life courtroom procedure in the locale where the testimony will be given.
2. A visit to a court, preferably one where there is a trial being held involving an accountant expert witness. In metropolitan areas, this should be relatively easy.
3. When apprised of the specific court assignment of the case, the accountant should visit the particular judge's courtroom to observe his attitude and demeanor.
4. Role playing. This activity is recommended for all sorts of therapy, where it may or may not work, but it definitely works in a situation like this. (The attorneys had to play out their role for moot court in law school. Why not the accountant turning expert witness?) Partners, staff and/or family members make great critics—as well as actors in this courtroom drama. Even a full-length mirror can ask questions and talk back.

¶22,003 Definition of an Expert Witness

The courts uniformly agree that the accountant possesses the qualifications of an expert witness on any subject matter falling within the scope of his experience, training, and education.

There are perhaps as many definitions of an "expert witness" as there are statutes, judges, and writers concerned with testimony. The following definition of an expert witness is designed to cover all aspect of "expert" definitions (without any whereases or wherefores): *A witness is an expert witness and is qualified to give expert testimony if the judge finds that to perceive, know, or understand the matter concerning which the witness is to testify requires special knowledge, skill, experience, training, and/or education, and that the witness has the requisite special knowledge, skill, experience, training, and/or education deemed necessary and appropriate.*

If the opposing party offers any objection to the use of an expert's testimony, the accountant's special knowledge, skill, experience, training, or education must be shown before the witness may testify as an expert. Regardless, this information should be made known to the court. A witness's special knowledge, skill, training, or education may be shown by his own testimony, but it will probably "set" better with the jury if the lawyer elicits the pertinent information from the witness relating to his or her education, experience, and specialized knowledge.

Since the basic requirement of an expert witness is that the witness possess the ability to interpret, analyze, and evaluate the significant facts on a question concerning which just a judge or a judge and jury need assistance to resolve, it is imperative that they be aware of the accountant's background. This expertise must be demonstrated in a positive but unassuming manner to be effective. No one likes a braggart.

The courts have uniformly accepted the accountant as an expert. In the majority of cases, the primary and most significant criteria in guidance of a trial court's determination of qualifications of an expert witness are based on occupational experience. Equally significant is the judicial recognition of the special knowledge acquired by an accountant relating to a particular industry, trade, occupation, or profession to qualify her as an expert on particular business and trade practices and on other factors relating to costs and gross profit margins.

In actual practice, it is rare that the trial court will refuse to permit the witness to testify as an expert because he is insufficiently qualified. Rather, any weakness or deficiency will show up in the quality and impact of the testimony rather than its admissibility.

Therefore, it is imperative that an accountant be very cautious about accepting an assignment that may be beyond his or her area of expertise.

¶22,004   *Daubert* and Federal Rule of Evidence 702

The rules behind the admissibility of scientific or expert testimony in Federal Courts prior to *Daubert* were based on relevancy and the *Frye* test. The latter was based on a 1923 case involving the admissibility of evidence from a polygraph or "deception" test. The court decided, "the systolic blood pressure deception test has not yet gained such standing and scientific recognition among physiological and psychological authorities as would justify the courts in admitting expert testimony deduced from the discovery, development, and experiments thus far made."

In *Daubert*, the U.S. Supreme Court ruled that the 1923 Frye test was superseded by the 1975 Federal Rules of Evidence. specifically Rule 702. Testimony by Experts. Rule 702 originally stated (in its entirety),

"If scientific, technical, or other specialized knowledge will assist the trier of fact to understand the evidence or determine a fact in issue, a witness

qualified as an expert by knowledge, skill, experience, training, or education, may testify thereto in the form of an opinion or otherwise."

By 2008, this stipulation had been added to Rule 702, "or otherwise, if (1)
the testimony is based upon sufficient facts or data, (2) the testimony is the
product of reliable principles and methods, and (3) the witness has applied the
principles and methods reliably to the facts of the case."

The Supreme Court clarified in the *Daubert* case that trial judges are "gate-
keepers" who may prevent dubious scientific testimony from being introduced
at trial. The eight concurring judges went further to extend substantial discretion to admit or exclude expert testimony to *all* areas, not just scientific ones.
Thus, the gatekeeping obligation of judges imposed in *Daubert* applies to any
"expert" testimony. The judge may inquire into the particular methodology
used. If the evidence appears to be questionable or unreliable, the judge at his
or her discretion may exclude the testimony.

¶22,005   Function of the Expert Witness

The function of the expert witness is to form an opinion or inference on matters
when individuals in the normal course of affairs would probably not be able to
do so. Therefore, an expert witness is needed in any case where by reason of his
special knowledge, the expert is able to form a valid opinion on the facts while
the man on the street would—or should—not.

Courts vary in their conception of when the expert is needed. Some courts
maintain that expert testimony is admissible only when the subject matter is beyond the common experience of the ordinary juror who would then be unable
to reach an informed opinion or draw a valid inference from the facts. In effect,
they apply a "strict" test of necessity. More often, the determination is made on
the basis of whether this testimony would be of "assistance" to the judge or jury.

¶22,006   Basis of Investigation

In his investigation preparatory to giving testimony, an expert may rely upon
various sources. He may:

1. Rely on known facts if such facts are material to the inquiry.
2. Obtain information gained from a demonstrably reliable source.

     This could include previous audit reports, certified financial state-
     ments, books and records of the business—even though they were not kept
     by the expert witness—or demonstrable customs and practices within the
     business or industry of the client for whom the expert is testifying.

3. If the expert has firsthand knowledge of the situation, inferences or opinions may be stated directly. However, care should be taken to be absolutely sure that the practitioner states fully the facts relied upon, the reliable source, and the permissibility of the basis upon which an opinion was founded. Otherwise, the testimony will do more harm than good. If a judge and/or jury become aware of even one instance in which the accountant has slipped up, his expertise will henceforth be open to question.

In addition, the expert witness must have a thorough knowledge of the substantive issue in the case. The investigation and subsequent conclusion may be incomplete and unrelated to the issue if he either has not been informed properly of the particulars in a case, or has not done his homework thoroughly. It is also necessary that he know the issues of the case so that he can anticipate and respond promptly and forcefully to cross-examination and avoid answers that are incomplete, confusing, and irrelevant. In other words, the expert must be made privy to all relevant facts in the case as well as to the direction of the lawyer's attack or counterattack.

The "need to know" policy should not be carried so far that the accountant appears "in the dark" or at best ill-informed. Therefore, it is important for the accountant to ascertain whether the attorney is willing to work closely with the "expert witness." If the accountant finds it impossible to work in good faith with a particular attorney or law firm, he should withdraw from the case, if possible, or at least refuse to work with that individual or firm in the future. Failure to be aware of or to consider all of the facts not only diminishes the value of the expert's testimony to the case but quite often leaves the expert vulnerable to attack on cross-examination. Not only can the accountant become surprised and confused by the additional facts, but the image as an expert will be damaged in the minds of the judge and jury. The individual's credibility and reputation could be severely damaged.

¶22,007   Exhibits

It is almost mandatory that the expert witness prepare, or have prepared, some type of exhibit for several obvious reasons, not the least of which is the fact that very few individuals can make any sense of numbers from just *hearing* them. Oversize charts, graphs, schedules, diagrams—whatever aids the court in visualizing the accountant's findings—can be useful in focusing their attention. Visual aids not only help the expert witness explain his conclusions but they can have a greater impact on the judge and jury. *If* these graphics can be presented in an interesting, imaginative way, they might also tend to lessen the tedium of often very dry facts and figures.

This "demonstrative evidence" (in the parlance of the court) must not appear to be a way of "lecturing" to the judge and jury. At the same time, these are not people preparing for the CPA exam. The visual materials must present readily understood, clearly identifiable steps the accountant took in arriving at opinions and conclusions—not just a jumble of numbers.

It may be appropriate to provide copies of the material to the judge and the members of the jury so that they can use both eyes and ears to follow the testimony of the expert. Even then, it is probably better to have too little information on a graph or schedule than too much.

¶22,008 Understandable Testimony

Expert testimony is valuable only when it is understood by the judge and jury. The expert must be able to explain and defend her opinion in language reasonably understood by the layman. Everyone complains about "legalese." What about "accountantese"? It should always be kept in mind that the very reason the expert is testifying is that the subject matter is beyond the common knowledge and experience of the average juror.

A common error committed by the accounting expert is to use technical language in testimony without offering an explanation of its meaning.

Terms like *earnings per share*, *stockholder's equity*, and *retained earnings* may have a nice ring to them. However, if the testimony must necessarily involve technical accounting terms and concepts of this caliber, they must be defined and explained in a clear and simple manner.

¶22,009 Cross-Examination

An accountant testifying as an expert may be cross-examined to the same extent as any other witness.

Therefore, the expert should assume that his opinion will be rigorously challenged on cross-examination. The fact that the subject matter is being litigated indicates conflicting theories or facts upon which an opinion may be based. In order to preserve the value and effectiveness of testimony given as an expert, the witness should anticipate what may be brought up in cross-examination. Thorough preparation, awareness of other aspects of a case, anticipation of where the "attack" may come will all aid in the individual's holding up well in this phase of a court appearance. Now is the time when the opposing counsel will attempt to discredit the expert witness concerning qualifications, knowledge of the subject matter, the validity of the source of relevant information, and the basis for arriving at the stated opinion and conclusions.

It is important for the accountant to remember that this is the lawyer's job. Since the purpose of cross-examination is to diminish or destroy the expert's conclusions, the lawyer may be argumentative, supercilious, and aggressive in an attempt to catch the witness off balance—to make the expert react too quickly and speak before thinking. Instead, this is the time when remaining courteous, unemotional, and firmly convinced of the correctness of previous statements pays off.

One of the techniques used in cross-examination is to show a contradiction or omission of facts upon which the expert founded an opinion. For this reason, it is essential that the expert make a thorough investigation, have knowledge of all relevant theories and material facts, and be prepared to support that opinion rationally on cross-examination. If the expert has adequately prepared, she can reasonably anticipate any weak or questionable aspects of the testimony and be ready to cope with them quickly and spontaneously on cross-examination.

¶22,010   Rebuttal

Rebuttal testimony provides the opposing party with an opportunity to introduce evidence that refutes the prior evidence of the other side in the case. The opposing side may decide to offer in rebuttal its own expert to directly refute the testimony of the original expert. Rebuttal testimony may not go beyond the scope of the original evidence. In other words, a party may not introduce new evidence but is limited to a direct rebuttal of prior evidence. However, there is still plenty of opportunity for accounting expert witness No. 2 to question the validity of the original expert's assumptions, opinions, and conclusions concerning alternative ways of looking at a situation.

If the original expert has considered and discussed the cause for litigation from every possible angle, the impact of a rebuttal expert witness who attempts to base opinion on opposing theories and facts has basically been forestalled, because that ground has already been covered, and discarded.

¶22,011   Legal Matters

What are these weighty matters which the expert witness is going to investigate, form opinions concerning, testify to, be cross-examined about or offer rebuttal to? As might be expected, there may even be a "mini-niche" within this niche where the accountant could decide to specialize. Among the more likely spots are:

1. Tax cases-civil, criminal, fraud—both state and federal. It is difficult to imagine a tax case that does not involve accounting problems. Attorneys for both the government and the taxpayer can be expected to have a general knowledge of accounting principles, but they have other responsibilities in the case. Enter the practitioner investigator and witness to refute the charge of "willful attempt to evade taxes," or just an assertion of deficiency in tax payments.

2. Divorce cases. In states with community property laws, this can become extremely involved in tracing and determining which funds are community property, separate property, proceeds from separate property, commingled funds, and separate funds of various descriptions.
3. Probate proceedings. Wills, state inheritance taxes, and federal estate taxes in states with community property laws also often need testimony from investigative accountants. In fact, the distinction between separate and community property is often crucial in figuring the amount of state inheritance and federal estate taxes owed.
4. Partnership dissolution and/or valuation of partnership interest. The accountant is frequently employed as an expert to prepare a partnership accounting of a dissolved partnership. Following is a sampling of the items that will come to the attention of the accountant in preparing her report for submission to the court:
   a. Contractual agreements among the partners expressly providing for a partnership accounting for capital or profits.
   b. Capital contributions reflected in the partnership agreement, additional loans, and restrictions or limitations on the right of a partner to withdraw the profits or capital.
   c. Present fair market value (FMV) of property previously contributed by a partner.
   d. Allocation of profits and losses for the current year in accordance with the partnership agreement.
5. Corporate suits brought by shareholders; corporate fraud cases. These involve not only large corporations, but also very small ones that have been inundated in the flood of litigation in the U.S.

The accountant must, obviously, have an understanding of the pertinent substantive law before being competent to undertake an investigation of the facts and testify as an expert witness—giving an opinion and conclusions concerning a legal as well as a financial matter.

It becomes fairly obvious that the neophyte expert witness needs to do some investigating to determine just what laws apply to the niche he has chosen to delve into. The particular state laws are undoubtedly the place to begin the investigation since each will be somewhat different—some more than others.

CHAPTER 23
Internal Controls for Small Businesses

¶23,000   Overview

There are many definitions of a small business. The most commonly accepted one is the U.S. Department of Commerce classification of an enterprise of fewer than 500 employees as a small business concern. Using this definition, there are millions of non-agricultural small business establishments in the United States. In an operational sense, a small business can be defined as one that is too small to have its own internal auditors or too small to successfully segregate the various accounting functions to achieve a reliable set of internal controls. When such a business must be audited, it is then necessary for the CPAs to perform additional work to replace a reliance on the company's internal controls.

In a small business organization of only a few people, little reliance can be placed on internal controls involving a segregation of duties, as it is among several persons in a large organization. However, that is no excuse for ignoring the importance of some degree of internal controls. Limited personnel who perform more than one related function and are associated with the handling of a company's money should trigger an assessment of the need for the establishment of at least a modified control system. In this chapter we look at a number of areas where even the smallest business can take some precautions. Our approach in this discussion is to touch on both possible control procedures and on the possible consequences of weak or nonexistent controls in terms of embezzlement or other kinds of employee fraud.

A plan of organization that provides at least a limited segregation of functional responsibilities within the constraint of a small staff should be developed. In a small business, the segregation is not so much between employees as between the owner and employees. An alert and able owner can provide about as much control as the segregation of duties does in a large organization. Just as critical as establishing such controls is following them 100 percent of the time.

The owner of a small business usually is the key person in its management. Unlike in a large organization, in the small business, the owner represents one of the effective components of a control system—that of personal observation. Principally, the owner can personally focus attention on selective areas of the business, such as reconciling the bank statement—one of the prime areas of control for a manager with limited time and staff. However, even if the owner himself or herself is not inclined to do a formal bank reconciliation to check an employee's work, it is possible to engage the services of a temporary accounting agency or an outside CPA to perform the reconciliation periodically or even once a year. The additional cost may be well worth it, as too many times the most trusted employee also turns out to be the one in the best position to relieve the company of some of its cash or other assets.

The selection of a few areas for control is an important step. A tendency to over-control must be avoided in order to prevent a negative cost benefit allocation of time and expense. There is no need to control pencils and paper clips; the effort should be directed toward areas where the risk of error and material loss are greatest. Careful evaluation can uncover areas over which no control is exercised, but that are significant enough for procedures to be established for their control.

Over and over, those who investigate why controls break down stress that it starts with the attitude of those at the top. In the case of a small business, the attitude evidenced by the owner(s) is critical. If the owner(s) displays real concerns that procedures always be followed, even if it is a small business, this sends an important message to employees. Though it may seem unnecessary to some in a small business, having written procedures in place that are used and maintained is also important. Employees should feel that their work is important enough to require periodic monitoring. But once the owner(s) sends a signal to the employees that rules are meant to be broken and that close is good enough, this attitude will soon permeate the organization and its accounting functions.

.01 COSO Internal Control Framework

The Committee of Sponsoring Organizations (COSO) was formed by five major professional organizations (American Institute of Certified Public Accountants (AICPA), American Accounting Association (AAA), Financial Executives International (FEI), Institute of Internal Auditors (IIA), and Institute of Management Accountants (IMA)). COSO was formed to sponsor the National Commission on Fraudulent Financial Reporting, also known as the Treadway Commission (James C. Treadway, Jr. was the original chair of the Commission). This Commission was to study the causal factors that can lead to fraudulent financial reporting and was to develop recommendations as a result of the study.

In 1992, COSO developed a framework known as the "Internal Control—Integrated Framework" to help companies across all industries and sizes measure the effectiveness of their internal control structures. This framework identified five components of internal controls, which were Control Environment, Risk Assessment, Control Activities, Information & Communication, and Monitoring Activities. All components are critical to an effective design and implementation of internal controls. In 2013, COSO instituted new guidelines. The five components did not change but 17 principles were added that fall within those five original components. These added principles provide more detailed guidance for companies to design and implement and assess effectiveness of their internal controls.

While all five components of the internal control framework are important, accountants tend to focus on the Control Activities component, which provides for more detailed controls at the account level, whereas the other components tend to be more at the entity level. The remainder of this chapter provides guidance to primarily assist in the design and implementation of control activities.

¶23,001 Red Flags for Accountants

Before we describe specific controls for particular accounts, it is helpful to review a list of red flags for accountants. Because the internal controls in a small business are generally unreliable, it is especially important for both the outside CPA and the controller or inside accountant to be aware of red flags that may indicate a problem with the accounting records or with the business.

.01 Red Flags for the Accounting Records:

- Frequent duplicate payment of bills
- Second or third party endorsements of company checks

- Payment of bills for condominium fees, florist or jewelry shops, personal credit card bills
- Business checks made payable to cash
- Frequent transfers of funds between business accounts or between personal accounts of the owners and the business
- Checks written in round amounts to unknown vendors
- Checks written out of sequence
- Requests from owners to manipulate accounting records, enter journal entries at year-end for round numbers and holding off on billing or paying bills as regularly scheduled

.02   Red Flags for the Health or Illegality of a Business

An accountant whose work is narrowly focused on the day-to-day activities of the company—balancing the bank accounts, reconciling accounts receivables and keeping up with payables—may overlook certain issues of potential concern about the business itself. The nature of the business as portrayed by the owners and as envisioned by the accountant may differ from the true nature of the business. There are enough front businesses operating that seek the trappings of legitimacy, including an outside CPA, that indicators of certain illegal activities should not be ignored:

- Frequent checks payable from one bank to another bank
- A large number of bank accounts for no apparent reason, with continuous activity between the accounts.
- Low bank balances with frequent bounced checks
- Owners checking with the bank daily to determine the balances in various accounts
- Payments to non-employees who performed no known services
- Owners cashing checks made out to the business
- Personal expenses of the owners paid from the business
- Large currency transactions, especially when the business is not primarily involved in cash sales (including home builders and car dealers or jewelry stores).
- Frequent deviations from stated or written company policy regarding banking activities
- The "tone" of management regarding internal controls
- Funds transfers to international bank secrecy locations such as the Cayman Islands, Israel or the Bahamas.
- Funds transfers to international money laundering or drug locations such as Mexico, the Channel Islands or Antigua
- Frequent deposits of bundled folding money
- Payments to fictitious corporations or shell businesses
- Payment of bills with certified checks

¶23,002   Internal Control for Inventories

It is obvious that merchandising and manufacturing companies in particular need to keep a complete, secure inventory of goods held for sale. Management is responsible for determining and maintaining the proper level of goods in inventory because:

1. If inventory is too low, sales opportunities may be missed.
2. If inventory is too large, the business pays unnecessarily high costs for storing, insuring and providing security. As a result, the company's cash flow becomes one sided—cash drains out to purchase inventory, but cash does not flow in from sales.

Merchandising companies classify all goods available for sale in one inventory category. Manufacturing companies generally use three inventory categories: finished goods, work-in-process and raw materials and supplies. This chapter emphasizes inventory for manufacturing companies, but many of the principles and practices also apply to merchandising companies.

Following is a discussion of internal control procedures that can be used in conjunction with different types of inventories: goods for resale, finished goods, materials and work in process.

.01   Inventories of Merchandise Purchased for Resale and Supplies

The departments involved in internal control in merchandise and supplies inventories are purchasing, sales, receiving, accounts receivable, and accounts payable. The following controls should be implemented:

1. The purchasing department approves the purchase orders for merchandise to be bought. In a small company, the owner or manager may be the one to approve these purchase orders, which should be sequentially numbered and traced to final destination.
2. After okays from the purchasing manager have been received, requests for price quotations are usually sent out. These requests should go to various sources, and the company quoting the lowest price will be the one from which the purchases are made, unless there is some overriding consideration.
3. In the selling department, an updated individual quantity record for each type of unit is kept on perpetual inventory stock cards. It is usually the responsibility of inventory clerks to keep these cards up to date:
   a. The number of units of merchandise ordered is entered on the inventory stock cards by one clerk.
   b. The number actually received is entered from the receiving list by a different clerk.

    c.   The number sold or used is recorded by still another clerk from sales lists or salesperson's orders.

         These stock cards indicate the need for reorders. They should be checked against a purchase requisition by the manager of the selling department or other person in control of the merchandise stock. In a business too small to have a separate selling department, the owner or manager should perform these functions.

         After the number of units ordered, received and issued have been recorded on the inventory cards, the balance represents the number of units actually on hand. A well-rounded perpetual card system usually includes detailed unit costs for ready computation under the LIFO, FIFO or average method.

4.   In the receiving department, the receiving clerk should not be allowed to see purchase order records or purchase requisitions. Receiving reports are checked against the perpetual inventory stock records and a notation is made on these stock record cards indicating the date, order number, and quantity received.

         Even where a business is too small to have a perpetual inventory, a receiving report should be made. It should then be checked against the purchase orders and a notation as to the day and quantity received made on those purchase orders.

5.   In the accounts payable department, the receiving report is checked against the merchandise stock record, then sent to the accounts payable department, where it is verified against the seller's invoice. The purchasing agent should have approved the price on the seller's invoice before that invoice was sent to the accounts payable department.

         A clerk in the accounts payable department should verify all extension totals on the invoice. If the vendor's invoice and receiving report are in agreement, the invoice is then entered into a purchase journal or voucher register for future payment. Any discrepancy between quantity received and quantity on the seller's invoice will necessitate holding up payment until an adjustment is made by the seller.

.02   Finished Goods Inventories

The departments involved in internal control of finished goods inventories are manufacturing, cost accounting, accounts receivable and sales. The following controls should be implemented:

1.   It is necessary to ascertain the quantity of units completed from the production record and transferred to the shipping department or warehouse. The daily report of finished goods units transferred to the shipping department or warehouse indicates the number of finished units available to the sales department.

2. The unit cost of finished goods delivered to the sales department must be computed. This information is obtained from the unit cost sheet (for a process cost accounting system) or from the job-order cost card (in a job-order cost accounting system). (For more information see the chapter, "Change in Accounting Methods and Consideration of Accounting Periods".)

3. Finished goods inventory cards should be set up. For each item, the following should be recorded:
   a. The quantity received at the warehouse.
   b. The quantity shipped on orders.
   c. The balance remaining at specified unit costs. The number of finished goods units in the warehouse or stockroom should tie in with this finished goods inventory file.

4. Periodically, a physical count of the finished goods inventory is required. It should tie in with the finished goods inventory file.

.03   Raw Materials and Supplies Inventories

The departments involved in internal control for raw materials and supplies inventory are stores, purchasing, accounts payable, and manufacturing. The following controls should be implemented:

1. In the stores department, the storekeeper must safeguard the raw materials and supplies inventories—both physically and by accounting control. No raw materials or supplies can leave without a stores requisition. Quantity control at minimum levels is also the responsibility of the storekeeper. The storekeeper should maintain a stores record for each item, listing:
   a. The maximum and minimum quantities.
   b. Quantity ordered and number.
   c. Quantity received.
   d. Quantity issued.
   e. Balance on hand.

   When stores cards show minimum quantities, a stores ledger clerk pulls those cards from the file to make sure that materials or supplies are ordered to cover minimum needs. Quantities shown on the stores record should be verified by making an actual count of the stores items that are to be ordered. A purchase requisition is then filled out from the stores records. The quantity of each item ordered is approved by the storekeeper who knows the average monthly consumption of each item.

   The ordering of special equipment by department heads also goes through the storeroom after having the necessary executive approval. The purchase requisition is then forwarded to the purchasing agent.

In the stores department, a receiving report is prepared in triplicate by the receiving clerk:

a. One copy goes to the stores ledger clerk.
b. The second is sent to the accounts payable department.
c. The third is kept by the receiving clerk.

The receiving clerk puts the stores items in proper places within the storeroom after preparing the receiving report. Ideally, location numbers are used to facilitate ready accessing.

The stores ledger clerk gets a copy of the receiving report and makes a record of the quantity and the order number on the stores ledger card affected by the items received.

2. In the purchasing department, the purchase agent places the order for the quantity needed on the quantity requisition. If the agent feels the quantity ordered is excessive, he or she may look into the storekeeper's purchase requisition. The next step is to request price quotations from various supply companies. The order should normally be placed with the lowest bidder. The purchase agent also verifies the prices on the seller's invoices by comparing them to the price quotations.

3. In the accounts payable department, no bill should be approved for payment until:

a. Materials ordered have actually been received.
b. Materials have been inspected and are in good condition.
c. The prices of the seller's invoice match the quotations.

4. In the manufacturing department, different individuals have authority to sign stores requisitions to withdraw materials from the storeroom. Usually, a foreman prepares a stores requisition when raw materials or supplies are needed in any of the manufacturing departments. This requisition contains:

a. The account name and number.
b. The department name and number.
c. The job order number.
d. The quantity of material issued.
e. The stores item name and classification symbol.
f. The name of the person to withdraw materials from the storeroom.
g. The unit price of the item and the total cost of items withdrawn from the storeroom.

.04   Work-in-Process Inventory

The departments involved in internal control of work-in-process inventories are manufacturing and cost accounting. The following controls should be implemented:

1. In the manufacturing department, stores requisitions are prepared by shop foremen for materials that are to be charged to the work-in-process in-

ventory account. Quantities of materials are obtained from engineering or administrative departments. Specifications for raw materials are usually shown on a bill of materials (a list of different items required to complete an order). The stores requisition will specify:

a. Quantity.
b. Price.
c. Cost of each item of raw material requisitioned.
d. Job order number.

Time tickets are prepared by the workers and approved by a foreman in the department in which work is performed before it is charged to the work-in-process inventory account. Each labor operation may have a standard time for performing a certain operation, as predetermined by the engineering department. There may also be a predetermined standard wage rate, determined by the head of the manufacturing department and known by the payroll department.

The cost accounting department is responsible for the amount of manufacturing expense charged to the work-in-process inventory account.

2. In the cost department:

a. Raw material cost is computed from sales requisitions.
b. Direct labor costs are obtained from time tickets.
c. Manufacturing expense is estimated from prevailing overhead rates.

Internal control methods for the work-in-process inventory account depend on whether the firm has a process cost accounting or job-order cost accounting system.

The chief point of internal control for work-in-process inventories is computing costs. Product costs are analyzed by operations, departments and cost elements. This permits measurement of the cost of products at different stages of completion. The number of partly finished units when multiplied by a cost at a particular stage should come close to the value in the work-in-process inventory account.

.05 Taking Count—The Physical Inventory

The two most significant factors of inventory control are knowing what should be on hand based on paper controls and then verifying what actually is on hand from a physical count. As with all other controls, in a small business the owner(s) must instill in the employees undertaking the physical count how critical it is to the success of the business. Sample counts by employees should be checked by the owner(s) and spot checks made to ensure that all sections of the inventory have been counted. The accuracy of the inventory affects the owner's ability to know if the company is profitable and this will affect the company's ability to obtain financing if needed.

The Perpetual System—Knowing What Should Be on Hand. In many firms, not enough effort and emphasis are put into the timely keeping of detailed perpetual inventory stock records, the most basic control available. The nature and extent of the records to maintain vary from company to company, but at the least, there should be a constantly updated record of the units handled. The "ins" and "outs" are posted, showing the new morning's balance on hand, or rather, the balance that *should* be on hand. If expanded to the fullest, the system would also include:

1. Unit costs of acquisitions (in manufacturing, detailed material, labor and overhead costs assigned).
2. Unit sales deleted at cost (based on the company's flow-of-cost assumption of LIFO, FIFO or average costs).
3. Balance on hand extended at cost.
4. Back-order positions, write-downs, destructions and, most important, locations in the storage area (by location number or description) are shown on the individual record.
5. The total sales income for that particular unit shown on the individual record and displaying unit gross profits.

Retail stores using the gross profit method of valuing inventories usually maintain controls over entire departments, or sections of departments rather than by individual units. Extended values are at retail, showing markups and markdowns as well as bulk cost figures.

The general-ledger summary inventory asset account should (where the system provides cost-flowing movement) always tie in to the total of the subsidiary perpetual system (at least monthly). They should be matched as often as possible and all differences traced to eliminate any weaknesses in the system. The point is—know what should be on hand!

The Physical Count—Verifying What Is Actually on Hand. At least once a year, a physical count of the entire inventory should be taken, usually as of the balance sheet date. Management, not the auditor, is responsible for taking this physical inventory. The auditor is only an observer of methods, count and valuation. Personnel may help establish the system of counting, the tags to use, the methods of ensuring a full count, the cut-off procedures and the pricing. The auditor should observe the process to be satisfied about the reasonability of the total value acceptable for attestation.

The method of tagging, counting, weighing or measuring, locating and recounting—the assignment of personnel—all the procedures should be set in advance and followed (unless properly authorized changes develop).

As to the nitty-gritty of an actual inventory count, considerations include:

1. Particular items should be counted by employees who do not have custody of the items.
2. Supervisors should be responsible for assigning each employee to a specific set of inventory tasks.
3. Employees who help take inventory are responsible for verifying the contents of any and all containers and storage places, including boxes, barrels, tubs and closets.
4. Prenumbered tally sheets are provided to all employees involved in actually taking the inventory.
5. The tally sheets provide evidence to support reported inventory levels and show exactly who is responsible for the information they include.
6. Access to inventory should be limited until the physical inventory is completed.
7. If any items are scheduled for shipping during a physical inventory, they should be segregated and not included in the count.
8. If shipments are received during a physical inventory, they also should be segregated and counted separately.
9. After the regular counting, a supervisor should verify that all items have been counted and that none has been counted twice.

The auditor should become familiar with the nature of the products handled, the terminology, the packaging, the principles of measurement and all of the precautions have been taken before the actual process is scheduled. Such education in the client's processes should not be obtained at the sacrifice of counting-time.

The auditor is concerned with the final evaluation of that physical inventory. The perpetual records, as such, and errors therein are not a necessary part of the audit process, though weaknesses should be commented upon in the management letter.

However, a history of *accurate* internal control of inventory can substantially reduce the extent of testing by the auditor. When it can be expected that variations from perpetual inventories will be small and within tolerable limits, the auditor may choose to use statistical random sampling in testing either an immediately prior physical count or in counting only those items *drawn by the auditor* (without advance notice) for random selection.

If the sample then indicates an unacceptable rate of error, the auditor may request another (or full) physical count, or may, with management's consent, adjust the overall value of the inventory to an amount indicated by the sample, with management required to investigate the error in the ensuing fiscal year. When an effective perpetual inventory control is in use, management usually cycle-counts the inventory. This may occur once or several times during the year. Unscheduled testing of bits and pieces throughout the year will keep everyone aware of attention given to the inventory; however, it must be covered entirely at least annually.

There are often *portions* of an inventory that would require more time and effort for the physical count than the relative merit of those portions warrants. Such items may be reasonably estimated (with joint approval of management and auditor), based on such elements as:

1. Last year's value.
2. Movement during the year.
3. Space occupied.
4. Weight.
5. Sales and purchases, using an estimated gross profit method.

The accuracy of a physical inventory even with the most sophisticated computerized system, may always be in doubt if there is no perpetual record for comparison. *A perpetual inventory is meaningless unless tested periodically to a physical count.* A history of accurate perpetual records can be justification for an auditor's using statistical sampling for year-end evaluation. Moreover, management itself can use statistical sampling techniques for cycle-counting. Tie-in to the general-ledger asset account should be made regularly by management. The financial statement value of the inventory must be at *cost* or *market*, whichever is lower. Standards are unacceptable, unless approximating cost.

¶23,003 Internal Control for Expenses

Each of the various types of expenses requires special internal control procedures. These procedures are covered in the following paragraphs.

.01 Manufacturing Expenses

The departments involved in internal control of manufacturing expenses are factory production, factory service and accounts payable. The following controls should be implemented:

1. In the manufacturing service and producing department, small tools that are not constantly being used should be kept in the tool room. Each worker requiring such tools can be given metal checks, each stamped with a personal number. The tool room attendant will release a tool to a worker in exchange for a metal check bearing the worker's number. The check is retained in the tool room until the tool is returned, at which time the check is returned.

    The department supervisor has the responsibility of approving a requisition for a new tool when one wears out.
2. Charges for freight and shipping on incoming supplies should be charged to the account to which the supplies are charged. Copies of the freight or

shipping bills should be attached to supply invoices. Supplies inventory is, therefore, charged for these freight and shipping charges instead of an expense account.

3. Numerous types of shop supplies, such as brooms, oil, waste, solder, wire, are part of the raw materials and supplies inventory. They should be kept in the storeroom and issued only by a stores requisition, signed by an authorized individual. The individual who indicates the need for such supplies (usually a supervisor) should indicate the job order number or departmental expense account number to which the material is to be charged on the stores requisition.

4. Workers categorized as indirect laborers should have an identification number when they work in a specific department. A time clock card should be kept and verified by a supervisor or timekeeper.

.02 Selling Expenses

The departments involved for internal control of selling expenses are sales and accounts payable. The following controls should be implemented:

1. Salespersons' salaries should be okayed by the sales department manager before a summary is sent to the payroll department. The basis for the summary is the salesperson's daily report. Commissions earned are verified from duplicate sales invoices mailed to the customer. These are computed in the sales department and approved by the sales department manager.

2. To prevent padding of travel expenses, many companies allow flat rates or maximum amounts for each day of the week. Unusual amounts should require an explanation from the salesperson.

3. The office manager retains control over outgoing mail and postage. A mail clerk usually affixes the postage. Control of postage expenses involves limiting the number of office workers who have access to stamps or a postage meter.

4. Telephone expenses can be controlled by maintaining a record of all outgoing calls. Long distance calls should be reported indicating the party making the call and where the call is going. From the long distance call record, telephone expenses are distributed by departments.

5. Subscriptions to publications and dues of various organizations and professional societies should be approved by the sales manager before a voucher is prepared.

6. All bills approved by the sales manager are sent to the accounting department for payment.

.03 Administrative Expenses

The departments involved in internal control of administrative expenses are administrative and accounts payable. Internal control for administrative expenses is very similar to that for the sales department. Bills for administrative expense items should be approved by an administrative department executive before they are sent to the accounts payable department for payment.

.04   Financial and Other Expenses

In corporations that have special departments to control financial problems in the company, a treasury department or similar department will handle expenses in the nature of interest and discount and dividends and may even supervise handling of cash. The financial department may also have the responsibility for authorizing credit extended to customers.

The departments involved in internal control for factory payrolls are timekeeping, payroll, accounts payable and the particular manufacturing division. The following controls should be implemented:

1. A credit manager in the financial department should have the responsibility for approving sales orders above a specific amount. The manager should be in constant touch with the accounts receivable department to determine whether or not a customer has been regular in payments. The treasurer has the responsibility for authorizing bad debt write-offs. The write-off itself should be made by someone in the accounts receivable department on the authority of the financial department executive—not the sales manager.
2. The financial department executive or office manager approves expenditures such as interest and bank discounts, office expenses and supplies. After approval of these items, invoices are sent to the accounts payable department.

.05   Salaries and Wages

The departments involved in internal control for factory payrolls are timekeeping, payroll, accounts payable, and the particular manufacturing division. The following controls should be implemented:

1. In the timekeeping department, each worker is given an identifying number that will serve to identify his or her department. A badge with this number serves as identification when presence within the factory is checked each day.
2. It is the duty of a time clerk to check the presence of each worker once or twice a day, every day. This is to eliminate the possibility of one person punching the time clock for another who is absent. Absences are noted in a time book. These are then checked against the employee's time ticket, time clock card, or payroll sheet at the end of each specific pay period.

3. Care should be taken to prevent one worker punching another worker's time clock card. The time clock card indicates the number of hours the worker is present each day in the plant and can be used to verify either daily or weekly the hours shown on daily time tickets.

4. In the manufacturing department, a time ticket that lists the worker's name, number of hours worked on different jobs and labor operations, and total hours worked is prepared. It must be approved by the foreman of the department in which the work is performed.

5. In the payroll department, time tickets are verified against the time clock cards and the timekeeper's time clock book. The time ticket is then given to a clerk who inserts the hourly or piecework rate of each worker. Another clerk computes the earnings. The time tickets are then used for working up the payroll sheet. The time tickets are sent to the cost accounting department to prepare a payroll distribution sheet. The payroll sheet becomes the record by which the worker is paid. After the payroll sheet has been completely okayed, it is sent to the accounts payable department for payment. Payment to each worker, either by check or cash, should be receipted. In the accounts payable department, the payroll sheet serves as the basis for payment.

.06   Office Payroll

The following controls should be implemented for the office payroll:

1. In the sales department, the sales manager approves the daily sales reports. From these reports, a record of the salesperson's days is prepared. The record is sent to the payroll department after approval by the sales manager. The manager in the sales department also approves the records of work performed by the sales office force before sending it to the payroll department.

2. In the administrative department, the office manager approves time worked by the office force and then sends it to the payroll department. Salaries of top executives are often placed on a special payroll. Their salaries are usually known by the paymaster who prepares their checks and sends them directly to the executives' offices.

3. The treasurer or financial department office manager similarly approves the work performed by the clerical personnel in his or her department.

4. Upon receiving these authorized reports from the various departments, the paymaster sets them up on a payroll sheet and after computing the applicable salary for each office worker, takes all applicable deductions and indicates a net salary for each employee.

5. In the accounts payable department, payment for these office workers' salaries is prepared from the payroll sheets.

.07   Other Procedures for Payroll

In addition to the above regular procedures, certain periodic checks of payroll activity should be made by the owner(s) of a small business. In some small businesses the owner(s) may insist on signing all checks; but in many, this task is delegated to the employee paying the bills, who is often the one reconciling the bank accounts. For this reason it is important for the owner(s) to review the list of vendors periodically looking for unfamiliar names or post office box addresses. It is also advisable to cross check the addresses of the vendors with those of the employees. It is not difficult for a clever employee to set up a phony vendor to be paid each month for some undisclosed service.

Though part of the payables procedure as well, it is important to review one month's activity closely looking for duplicate payments of the same bill. It is possible for an employee to discover that the duplicate payment will be refunded by the vendor in the form of the vendor's check which the employee can easily steal undetected and cash or deposit in his or her own account. This procedure has the same effect as if the employee wrote a check to him or herself, except that since the refund check is unexpected by the owner (though the employee will be expecting it), chances of detection are much lower.

Because some small businesses can have a growing number of employees on the payroll, at some point the owner(s) may no longer know each employee's name. When this occurs it is important for the owner(s) to periodically review the payroll checks before they are issued looking for unfamiliar names and questioning supervisors or others as to what the employee does. Additionally, the list of payroll checks being issued should be scanned for the names of employees who no longer work at the company. It has occurred often enough that checks made out to former employees are negotiated by current employees, that the owner(s) must be on guard for this type of fraud.

¶23,004   Internal Control for Cash

Where currency is available, internal control is most necessary. Incoming checks may be used in manipulating accounts receivable and must be controlled. Accounts receivable control becomes part of cash control, and vice versa. Cash disbursements and petty cash also need special internal controls. Details follow.

.01   Cash Receipts

The departments involved in internal control of cash receipts are selling, treasury or cashier's and accounts receivable. The following controls should be implemented:

1. In the selling department, cash sales should be recorded in a register. A numbered sales slip should be made up for each sale. These slips should be used in numerical order.
2. In the cashier's department, an employee should count the cash at the end of the day. Except for a small amount left to make change, all cash should be removed. The total daily cash receipts should be recorded on slips and placed in the same pouch as the cash itself. The pouch should then be turned over to a clerk (a different employee from the one who counted the cash in the register) who will make out a bank deposit slip. Still another clerk in the cashier's department should read the cash register totals of the day or remove the cash sales slips.

   The cash removed from the register must agree with the tape and the total of cash slips, which are numbered sequentially (all numbers must have been accounted for). The sales readings are then compared with the amount of cash removed from the registers by the cashier. Small discrepancies are charged to a cash short or over account. Larger discrepancies call for an explanation.
3. In the accounts receivable department, incoming mail should be opened by a bonded clerk. All checks, currency, and money orders are listed by this clerk on a cash-received record. The cash-received record lists date of receipt, name of sender and amount. The record and totals are then sent to the accounts receivable department to be properly applied to the customers' accounts. The cash is sent to the cashier's office and subsequently given to the deposit clerk.
4. In the accounts receivable department, the record of cash received is used to credit customers' accounts. This record then goes to the general accounting department where it is compared with daily deposit slips of cash received from customers before it is entered on the books.

.02 Cash Disbursements

The departments involved in the internal control of cash disbursements are accounts payable and voucher.

In the accounts payable department, purchase of any item must have prior approval from the authorized person in charge of the department in which the expenditure originates before it comes to the accounts payable department. Where a voucher system is in operation, vouchers are prepared for each expenditure. Information on the voucher matches that shown on the seller's invoice. Vouchers are entered in the voucher register after having been approved by the head of the voucher department and then placed in a pending file for future payments.

.03   Petty Cash

The departments involved in the internal control of petty cash are selling, administrative or others in which there is a need for such petty cash funds, and accounts payable.

In any department where it is necessary to have a petty cash fund, at least two individuals should have the responsibility for handling petty cash. One individual inspects and approves the item for payment. The other has charge of the petty cash fund and pays the vouchers as they are presented. Each petty cash voucher should list the date, amount paid and name of the account to be charged. A bill or other receipt, if there is one, should be attached to the voucher. The employee who controls the petty cash fund should compare the receipts attached to the petty cash vouchers with the vouchers.

When the petty cash fund needs reimbursement, the person controlling the fund totals those petty cash vouchers which have been paid out and presents them to the accounts payable department. This department then arranges for the necessary reimbursement.

.04   Accounts Receivable

The departments responsible for internal control of accounts receivable are accounts receivable and sales.

Copies of sales slips from the sales department are used to charge customers' accounts. Copies of any credits due customers come from the sales department. These records are sent to the accounts receivable department, where, if possible, one clerk should have the responsibility for entering only debits to customers' accounts and another for posting credits, such as for returned merchandise or receipt of a note. Still a third employee should enter the credit in the customer's account for cash received.

Sending statements at the end of each month is a good way to check the accuracy of the customer's accounts.

.05   Notes Receivable

The departments responsible for internal control of notes receivable are treasury and accounts receivable.

In the treasury department, a record of notes held from customers is maintained. A record is then sent to the accounts receivable division where a clerk makes the proper credits. A copy is sent to the general accounting department to reflect the charge to the control account—notes receivable. The treasurer keeps the notes until maturity date or until discounted with the bank. A subsidiary note register should be kept if the company receives a large number of such notes.

.06   Cash and Bank Reconciliations

Cash is the lifeblood of the company. It is the center upon which the whole circle of business activity pivots. Here is the reservoir through which all flows—in and out. Preferably more of the former.

It is surprising to find that tests of cash receipts and cash disbursements are usually limited by management (through intermediaries) to monthly bank reconciliations. Nothing is more effective than unannounced, non-routine, spot tests of the cash-handling procedures (for that matter, *any* business procedure) by the highest authority within the company. Think of the impact made on an employee who *knows* there may be an impromptu test by the president of the company—at any time! Imagine the psychological impact if this is done periodically, but irregularly. Such tests of the application of payments on account—receivables and payables—encourage peak, honest, performance.

Bank reconciliations by and of themselves cannot stand alone as proof of cash authenticity. They prove only the activity within that one period and serve to lend to prior reconciliations substantiation of then-listed outstanding checks. The current reconciliation is technically unproved until the outstanding checks and uncredited deposits in transit appear.

Reconciliations should be tested by someone other than the original preparer.

Block-proofs of cash should also be used occasionally to test an entire year's transactions. Here, all deposits are matched to all receipts recorded (in total); and all recorded disbursements are matched to total bank charges for cleared checks and minor items, with consideration given to opening and closing transit items.

The theory behind the mechanics of the bank reconciliation is to update the bank figures (on a worksheet) to reflect all transit items that have not yet cleared the bank, as follows:

Bank shows a balance of	$ 10,500	
Add deposits in transit	2,000	
	12,500	
Less checks outstanding (itemized)	600	
Adjusted bank balance	$ 11,900	
Balance per books shows	$ 11,909	
Difference	$ 9	(more on books)

Having taken the preliminary steps of determining the deposits in transit (by checking the bank credits against recorded receipts) and the outstanding checks (by checking off all returned canceled checks against the listing of those issued or carried over), a remaining difference of $9 is noted.

In the following order, the most expedient ways to find this difference are to:

1.   Look at the bank statement for any bank charge not yet recorded in the general ledger.
2.   Look at the books for any $9 debit (or combination) on the books and not on the statement.
3.   Match the bank's opening pickup balance to the closing one on the last statement to determine whether the $9 is indicative of a transposition. Specifically,
     a.   Match deposits to receipts recorded.
     b.   Check general-ledger footings and subtraction.
     c.   Check summary postings into the general ledger from the original source.
     d.   Check footings in the books of original entry (receipts, disbursements and general journal).
4.   Having exhausted the above possibilities and still not having found the difference, check the face amount of each check to the amount charged by the bank (each check is canceled with a clearance date).
5.   Now match the listing of the check to the actual check. (Steps 4 and 5 are interchangeable).
6.   Not yet? Prove the bank's additions.
7.   If still elusive, it probably has been missed above or a transposition error has been made in listing transit checks or deposits; or, it may be an error made last month that was missed.

¶23,005   File Maintenance

How costly is the time wasted in frustrating searches for misfiled data, when initial precautions and firm rules might have assured quick access to, and retrieval of, needed documents by competent, authorized personnel. One of the most important, yet least emphasized, facets of the business enterprise is the establishment and proper maintenance of an effective, accurate filing system. Following are some suggestions for doing just that:

1.   Establish firm rules for filing.
2.   Provide adequate accessible filing space for current files.
3.   Pinpoint responsibilities for filing and accessing files.
4.   Follow legal requirements for record retention.
5.   Establish an annual policy of removing outdated files.
6.   Utilize flow charts when appropriate.
7.   Have sufficient copies of documents (e.g., purchase orders, sales shipping papers, and all papers) ultimately tied to a sales or vendor's invoice, to allow for a complete numerical file of each document.

A List of File Categories. File maintenance embraces all of the following:

1. Sales invoices to customers—both alphabetic and numeric files.
2. Vendor invoices—alphabetic, sometimes with copy of paid voucher check or numbered voucher. Some firms keep invoices segregated in an unpaid file until paid.
3. Canceled checks—kept by month in reconciled batches. Do not intermingle different batches.
4. Correspondence files—for customers, vendors, others.
5. Permanent files—organizational information, legal documents, leases, minutes and deeds. These are usually kept in fireproof areas and accessibility is limited.
6. Other:
   a. Tax files.
   b. Payroll and personnel files.
   c. Backup for journal entries.
   d. Investment files—security transactions.
   e. Petty cash voucher files.
   f. Purchasing department files—such as supplies and bids (costs).
   g. Credit department files.
   h. Prior years' books of entry.
   i. Data from subsidiary companies owned.
   j. Advertising programs, literature.

Computer Files—Considerations. Computer files present some unique problems that should be given special consideration. At a minimum, it is important to:

1. Have security protection—access, codes, permanent tapes or disks of programs and updated balance files for accounts receivables, payables, general ledger, payrolls. Keep enough of these changing files for reruns or accumulation runs, as needed for emergencies.
2. Keep hard copy until sure replacement hard copy is accurate, or as necessary for continuous file.
3. Be prepared for manual emergency work, if the computer goes down suddenly.
4. Pinpoint responsibility for keeping logs right through storage, updating software, and general housekeeping functions.

The checklists that follow have been developed as an economic and simplified guide for the responsible person in a small business to conduct periodic internal audits for the implementation and continuous review of the activities in the various areas of the business.

Too many companies give little if any thought to fraud prevention until after the fact. Then, any plan is a reaction to a specific situation rather than well-thought-out proactive steps and procedures to prevent misappropriation in any form from taking place in the future. Here, if not earlier, the accountant can come to the rescue with a skeleton plan that can be fleshed out with input from the owner and managers. Even this plan should be reconsidered periodically.

From these checklists, which include the significant areas of any business, can be selected those areas most important to the individual user. While a small business does not need accounting controls as sophisticated and expensive as those of a large company, neither can a small business be lax and informal with respect to procedures that can prevent possible mismanagement of assets or even embezzlement or fraud. The checklists indicate procedures that can lead to a suitable system.

.01   Internal Controls Checklists for Small Business Entities

The following checklists provided in Forms 23-1 through 23-9 should help management keep tabs on what is and is not being done to prevent fraud and to foster efficiency. These forms are available at *download.cchcpelink.com/ADB.docx*. (After selecting the areas that are considered to be necessary for some degree of control, the user can refer back to sections in this chapter for additional detail about each checklist deemed appropriate for the particular enterprise.)

Form 23-1				
General Internal Control Checklist				
	N/A	**Yes**	**No**	**Action or Remarks**
1. Are accounting records kept up to date and balanced monthly?				
2. Is a standard chart of accounts with descriptive titles in use?				
3. Are adequate and timely reports prepared to ensure control of operations? a. Daily reports? b. Monthly financial statements? c. Ratio analysis, such as cost of goods sold or gross profit? d. Comparison of actual results with budget? e. Cash and other projections?				
4. Do the owner/directors take an active interest in the financial affairs and reports available?				
5. Are personal expenses kept separate from business expenses?				
6. Are employees who are in a position of trust bonded?				
7. Are the director and employees required to take annual vacations, and are their duties covered by another?				
8. Are monthly bank reconciliations reviewed by the owner and director?				
9. Do employees appear to be adequately trained and technically competent?				
10. Are job descriptions prepared and updated regularly to reflect current thinking?				
11. Are volunteers properly trained and supervised?				
12. Is there appropriate separation of duties?				
13. Are minutes up to date and complete?				
14. Are authorized signatories for bank accounts designated with due diligence?				
15. Are account reconciliations performed regularly by personnel independent of the bank account?				
16. Are bank statements received directly by the person doing the bank reconciliation?				
17. Are the reconciliations reviewed by a qualified appropriate independent person?				
18. Is there a built-in system of checks and balances?				
19. Are governmental reporting requirements being complied with in a timely manner?				

	N/A	Yes	No	Action or Remarks
Form 23-2 **Accounts Receivable and Sales Checklist**				
1. Are work orders, sales orders, shipping documents and invoices prenumbered and controlled?				
2. Would the existing system disclose any shipments being made without recording a sale (such as for sales on consignment and samples)?				
3. Is a credit check approved by owner?				
4. Are sales invoices reviewed for accuracy of price, terms, extensions and footings?				
5. Is an aged trial balance prepared monthly, reconciled to the general ledger and reviewed by the owner?				
6. Are monthly statements: a. Reviewed by owner? b. Mailed to all accounts? Does each account have a permanently assigned "account number"? c. Are zero and credit balance statements mailed?				
7. Are write-offs, credit memos and special terms approved by the owner and directors?				
8. Is there sufficient separation of the receipts function and the application of payments to the accounts receivable?				
9. Are notes and other receivables under separate control?				
10. If there are any pledges receivable: a. Are they properly recorded? b. Is there collection follow-up?				
11. Is there a collections method in place either in-house or by a reputable agency?				
12. Is a schedule of late charge fees in place?				
13. Is there a schedule of charges for bounced checks?				

Form 23-3 Cash Receipts Checklist				
	N/A	**Yes**	**No**	**Action or Remarks**
1. Does the accounting system provide means to identify, classify, record and report cash transactions?				
2. Is mail opened by director or owner or someone other than the bookkeeper?				
3. Are receipts copied with payment and listed prior to turning them over to the bookkeeper?				
4. Are they subsequently traced to the cash receipts journal?				
5. Does the client have adequate documentation of cash receipts?				
6. Are checks immediately endorsed "for deposit only" and deposited promptly and intact?				
7. Are over-the-counter receipts controlled, as by cash register and prenumbered receipts?				
8. Are these reviewed by owner or director?				
9. Is there a follow-up policy established to collect on bounced checks?				
10. Are over-the-counter cash receipts compared against register tapes and a count of sales tickets?				
11. Does the bank confirm deposits directly to someone independent of the cash deposit function?				
12. Does the bank alert the cash manager to incoming wires? Are they recorded properly?				
13. Are cash receipts managed according to policy?				

Form 23-4 Inventories Checklist				
	N/A	Yes	No	Action or Remarks
1. Are perpetual inventories maintained?				
2. Are they verified periodically by someone not normally in charge of inventories?				
3. Where perpetual records are not in use: a. Are periodic physical counts taken by responsible employees? b. Is owner exercising control by review of gross profit margins?				
4. Are physical facilities organized to discourage pilferage by employees and others?				
5. Are policies established to ensure all employee purchases are approved by a manager? And properly logged?				
6. Are off-premises inventories controlled?				
7. Is customer's merchandise on the premises physically segregated and under accounting control?				
8. Are inventories reviewed periodically for old, obsolete, or overstocked items?				

	N/A	Yes	No	Action or Remarks
Form 23-5				
Accounts Payable, Purchases and Disbursements Checklist				
1. Are prenumbered purchase orders used and are these approved by the owner or director?				
2. Are competitive bids required above prescribed limits?				
3. Are payments made from original invoices?				
4. Are supplier statements compared with recorded liabilities?				
5. Are all disbursements made by prenumbered checks and accounted for by someone independent of the disbursement function?				
6. Is the owner's or director's signature required on all checks? a. Does owner or director sign checks only when they are accompanied by original supporting documentation? b. Is the documentation adequately canceled to prevent reuse? c. Do the persons responsible for the expenditure sign "ok to pay"? d. Is the computer set to note the date and amount of the last payment on scheduled payments (e.g., phone and utilities bills) so that variations in billing are apparent?				
7. Is there evidence that the following items have been checked before invoices are paid? a. Prices, trade discounts and sales tax? b. Receipt of goods or services?				
8. Are voided checks properly redeposited and stored?				
9. Is the disbursement officer independent of the accounting function?				
10. Is there a petty cash fund with one person responsible for its security and disbursement?				
11. Are vouchers used for petty cash disbursement?				
12. Are periodic reconciliations of the petty cash fund conducted by someone independent of the function?				
13. Is the size of the petty cash fund appropriate for its anticipated use?				

Form 23-6				
Investments Checklist				
	N/A	Yes	No	Action or Remarks
1. Is access to certificates, notes and other investment documents carefully spelled out and appropriately monitored?				
2. Is the physical possession of investment securities appropriately safeguarded?				
3. Is there a formalized investment policy?				
4. Is income from investments accounted for monthly?				
5. Is there effective utilization of temporary excess funds?				
6. Are investment securities of the type specified by management policy?				
7. Do the investment maturities fit the current cash flow plan?				
8. Do the returns of the portfolio warrant the risks?				
9. Are brokers' statements reconciled to the general ledger and the investments ledger by someone independent of the function?				
10. Are brokerage confirmations sent directly to someone independent of the investment function?				
11. Are periodic inventory counts made of the securities portfolio?				

12. In case of not-for-profit organizations:
  a. Is dual control exercised over certificates?
  b. Is there a written investment policy?
  c. Does the board approve sales and purchases?
  d. Is the return on investment checked periodically by the board?				

Form 23-7				
Property, Plant and Equipment Checklist				
	N/A	**Yes**	**No**	**Action or Remarks**
1. Are there detailed and updated records to support general-ledger totals for assets and accumulated depreciation?				
2. Are the owner or directors acquainted with assets owned?				
3. Is approval required for sale or acquisition of assets?				
4. Are there physical safeguards against theft or loss of small tools and other highly portable equipment?				
5. Is there a policy distinguishing capital and expense items?				
6. Is there a policy regarding security of building and well-being of employees?				

Form 23-8				
Insurance Checklist				
	N/A	**Yes**	**No**	**Action or Remarks**
1. Is insurance maintained in all major cases and is this coverage reviewed periodically by a qualified individual?				
2. Is insurance coverage adapted to needs of the specific type of organization?				
3. Are insurance claims checked carefully?				
4. Fidelity bonding helps to limit the loss on fraud; however, is there an understanding of just what the insurance covers and when to file claims?				

Form 23-9 Payroll Checklist				
	N/A	Yes	No	Action or Remarks
1. Is owner or director acquainted with with all employees and does he or she approve all new hires and changes of pay rates?				
2. Is there a folder for each employee containing full documentation, including an employment application W4, authorizations for deductions and signed employee handbook.				
3. Are there controls to prevent the payroll from being inflated without the knowledge of owner or director by fictitious employees, padded hours or inappropriate overtime?				
4. Does the owner or director sign all payroll checks and approve all state taxes and IRS deposits?				
5. If payroll is prepared by a bank or service bureau, does the owner or director of the company periodically review each check and related journals prior to distribution to employees?				
6. Are voided checks properly redeposited and stored?				
7. Is the payroll bank reconciliation balanced by someone other than the preparer?				
8. Is the payroll paid from a separate bank account?				
9. Is someone responsible for keeping current on change in payroll tax code laws?				
10. Is someone in charge of "scheduling" eligibility for and payment of simplified employee pensions (SEPs)?				

PART V

SEC Accounting and Oversight

The Financial Accounting Standards Board (FASB) sets accounting standards in the United States. FASB standards are applicable to all non-governmental organizations. Public companies must also adhere to standards set by the Securities and Exchange Commission (SEC), which has statutory (by law) authority to set standards for public companies. A background of the SEC and overview of some standards set and related laws is provided in Part V, as well as those of the Public Company Accounting Oversight Board (PCAOB), created by the Sarbanes-Oxley Act to provide oversight for auditors of public companies.

CHAPTER 24

The Securities and Exchange Commission—Organization and the Acts

¶24,000   Overview

In a confusing and contentious regulatory environment, it is more important than ever before to understand the role, rules, and regulations of our regulatory bodies. The Securities and Exchange Commission has been in the news constantly and is a source of great curiosity to the public at large. Both public accounting professionals and their clients can enhance their understanding of current affairs by knowing what the SEC can—and cannot—do. This is particularly important now as we are in a period of constant very public negative events attached to the securities industry. What the SEC and the Financial Industry Regulatory Authority (FINRA) can and cannot do about these issues needs detailed clarification.

In the late 1920s, there was widespread speculation in the stock market. When the market crashed in 1929, the public demanded protective action by their legislators. Congressional committees held hearings into all phases of the securities industry, investment banking, and commercial banking activities prior to the market crash. As a result of these hearings, eight Federal statutes were enacted between 1933 and 1940 (with a ninth in 1970), bringing the securities markets and the securities business under federal jurisdiction. These laws are referenced as the "truth in securities" statutes. They include the Securities Act of 1933, the Securities Exchange Act of 1934, the Public Utility Holding Company Act of 1935, the Maloney Amendment to the Securities Exchange Act of 1934, and the Federal Bankruptcy Code. Also included are the Trustee Indenture Act of 1939, the Investment Company Act of 1940, the Investment Advisers Act of 1940, the Securities Investor Protection Act (SPIC) of 1970, and the Securities Act Amendments of 1975.

One of the latest tools employed by the SEC in securing compliance with its rules was instituted in 2011: rewarding whistleblowers. The SEC's whistleblower program authorized by the Dodd-Frank Act rewards high-quality, original information that results in an SEC enforcement action with sanctions exceeding $1 million. A large award was made by the SEC's whistleblower program in October 2013 when it paid more than $14 million to a whistleblower whose information led to an enforcement action that recovered substantial investor funds. Subsequently, a payout of $50 million was made in June 2020 and $114 million (the largest to date) was paid out in October 2020. Whistleblower awards can range from 10 percent to 30 percent of the money collected in a case. Payments to whistleblowers are made from a separate fund previously established by the Dodd-Frank Act and do not come from the agency's annual appropriations or reduce amounts paid to harmed investors. By law, the SEC must protect the confidentiality of whistleblowers and cannot disclose any information that might directly or indirectly reveal a whistleblower's identity. For more information about the whistleblower program and how to report a tip, see Appendix J on the Whistleblower Program in this volume and visit *www.sec.gov/whistleblower*.

In March 2015, the SEC adopted rules to facilitate smaller companies' access to capital thereby providing investors with more investment choices. The new rules update and expand Regulation A, an existing exemption from registration for smaller issuers of securities. The rules are mandated by Title IV of the *Jumpstart Our Business Startups (JOBS) Ac*t. The updated exemption will enable smaller companies to offer and sell up to $50 million of securities in a 12-month period, subject to eligibility, disclosure and reporting requirements. More information is available in this chapter in ¶24,005, Registration.

¶24,001   SEC Addresses: Headquarters and Regional and District Offices

SEC Headquarters

100 F Street, NE
Washington, DC 20549

Various phone numbers depending on need. See sec.gov/contact-information/sec-directory for more information.

New York Regional Office

100 Pearl St., Suite 20-100
New York, NY 10004-2616
(212) 336-1100
e-mail: *newyork@sec.gov*

State jurisdiction: New York,
New Jersey

Boston Regional Office

33 Arch Street, 24th Floor
Boston, MA 02110
(617) 573-8900
e-mail: *boston@sec.gov*

State jurisdiction: Connecticut,
Maine, Massachusetts, New
Hampshire, Vermont, Rhode Island

Philadelphia Regional Office

1617 JFK Boulevard, Suite 520
Philadelphia, PA 19103
(215) 597-3100
e-mail: *philadelphia@sec.gov*

State jurisdiction: Delaware,
Maryland, Pennsylvania, Virginia,
West Virginia, District of Columbia

Miami Regional Office

801 Brickell Ave., Suite 1950
Miami, FL 33131
(305) 982-6300
e-mail: *miami@sec.gov*

State jurisdiction: Florida,
Mississippi, Louisiana, U.S. Virgin
Islands, Puerto Rico

Atlanta Regional Office

950 East Paces Ferry, N.E. Ste 900
Atlanta, GA 30326
(404) 842-7600
e-mail: *atlanta@sec.gov*

State jurisdiction: Georgia,
North Carolina, South Carolina,
Tennessee, Alabama

Chicago Regional Office

175 W. Jackson Boulevard, Suite 900
Chicago, IL 60604
(312) 353-7390
e-mail: *chicago@sec.gov*

State jurisdiction: Illinois, Indiana,
Iowa, Kentucky, Michigan,
Minnesota, Missouri, Ohio,
Wisconsin

Denver Regional Office

1961 Stout Street, Suite 1700
Denver, CO 80294
(303) 844-1000
e-mail: *denver@sec.gov*

State jurisdiction: Colorado, Kansas, Nebraska, New Mexico, North Dakota, South Dakota, Wyoming

Fort Worth Regional Office

801 Cherry Street, Unit 18
Fort Worth, TX 76102
(817) 978-3821
e-mail: *dfw@sec.gov*

State jurisdiction: Texas, Oklahoma, Arkansas, Kansas (except for the exam program which is administered by the Denver Regional Office)

Salt Lake Regional Office

351 S. West Temple St., Suite 6100
Salt Lake City, UT 84101

(801) 524-5796
e-mail: *saltlake@sec.gov*

State jurisdiction: Utah

Los Angeles Regional Office

444 South Flower Street, Suite 900
Los Angeles, CA 90070
(323) 965-3998
e-mail: *losangeles@sec.gov*

State jurisdiction: Arizona, Hawaii, Guam, Nevada, Southern California (zip codes 93599 and below, except for 93200–93299)

San Francisco Regional Office

44 Montgomery Street, Suite 2800
San Francisco, CA 94104
(415) 705-2500
e-mail: *sanfrancisco@sec.gov*

State jurisdiction: Washington, Oregon, Alaska, Montana, Idaho, Northern California (zip codes 93600 and up plus 93200–93299)

¶24,002 The Securities and Exchange Commission

The Commission is composed of five members: a Chairman and four Commissioners. Commission members are appointed by the President, with the advice and consent of the Senate, for five-year terms. The Chairman is designated by the President. Terms are staggered; one expires on June 5th of every year. Not more than three members can be of the same political party.

Under the direction of the Chairman and Commissioners, the SEC staff ensures that publicly held entities, broker-dealers in securities, investment companies and advisers, and other participants in the securities markets comply with federal securities laws. These laws are designed to facilitate informed investment analyses and decisions by the investment public, primarily by ensuring adequate disclosure of material significant information. Conformance with federal securities laws and regulations does not imply merit of securities. If information essential to informed investment analysis is properly disclosed, the

Commission cannot bar the sale of securities which analysis may show to be of questionable value. Investors, not the Commission, must make the ultimate judgment of the worth of securities offered for sale. Emphatically, there are no judgments, endorsements, or qualifications of any offered security. Also, there are no guarantees or insurances or whatever as we see with bank or some other financial services products.

The Commission's staff is composed of lawyers, accountants, financial analysts and examiners, engineers, investigators, economists, and other professionals. The staff is divided into divisions and offices, including eleven regional and district offices, each directed by officials appointed by the Chairman.

¶24,003   Glossary of Security and Exchange Commission Terminology

The Securities and Exchange Commission in Article 1, Rule 1-02, Title 17, Code of Federal Regulations (which is Accounting Regulation S-X), defines the meaning of terms used by the SEC in its Accounting Rules and Regulations. Also, many of the terms are defined as they appear in the Securities Act of 1933, the Securities Exchange Act of 1934, in Regulations S-K and D, and in the various Forms which publicly held corporations must file periodically with the SEC.

Occasionally, the Commission will use a term in a rule which in context will have a meaning somewhat different from its commonly understood meaning. Many of the definitions as they are written in the statutes and accounting regulations are lengthy and legalistic in style. The objective here is to "delegalize" the "legalese" in the interests both of clarity and brevity. The definitions are not, therefore, verbatim as developed by the Commission.

> ***Accountant's Report.*** In regard to financial statements, a document in which an independent public accountant or certified public accountant indicates the scope of the audit (or examination) which has been made and sets forth an opinion regarding the financial statements taken as a whole, or an assertion to the effect that an overall opinion cannot be expressed. When an overall opinion cannot be expressed, the reasons therefore should be stated.
>
> ***Accounting Principle, Change In.*** Results from changing one acceptable principle to another principle. A change in practice, or in the method of applying an accounting principle, or practice, is also considered a change in accounting principle.
>
> ***Affiliate.*** One that directly or indirectly, through one or more intermediaries, controls or is controlled by, or is under common control with, the person specified (see **Person** below).

Amicus Curiae ("Friend of the Court"). An SEC advisory upon request of a court which assists a court in the interpretation of some matter concerning a securities law or accounting regulation.

Amount. When used to reference securities means:
  a. The principal amount of a debt obligation if "amount" relates to evidence of indebtedness.
  b. The number of shares if "amount" relates to shares.
  c. The number of units if "amount" relates to any other type of securities.

Application for Listing. A detailed questionnaire filed with a national securities exchange providing information concerning the corporation's history and current status.

Assets Subject to Lien. Assets mortgaged, pledged, or otherwise subject to lien, and the approximate amounts of each.

Associate. When used to indicate a relationship with any person (see **Person** below), any corporation or organization, any trust or other estate, and any relative or spouse of such person, or any relative of such spouse.

Audit (or examination). When used in regard to financial statements, an examination of the statements by an accountant in accordance with generally accepted auditing standards for the purpose of expressing an opinion.

Audit Committee. A special committee of the board composed of directors who are *not* (if possible) officers of the company. The SEC wants the Audit Committee to assume the responsibility for arranging the details of the audit. In addition, an audit committee's major responsibilities include dealing with the company's financial reports, its external audit, and the company's system of internal accounting control and internal audit. The duties and responsibilities of audit committee members should be reasonably specific, but broad enough to allow the committee to pursue matters believed to have important accounting, reporting and auditing consequences.

Balance Sheet. Includes statements of assets and liabilities as well as statements of net assets unless the context clearly indicates the contrary.

Bank Holding Company. A person who is engaged, either directly or indirectly, primarily in the business of owning securities of one or more banks for the purpose, and with the effect of exercising control.

Blue Sky Laws. Terminology for State securities laws.

Broker. A person in the business of buying and selling securities, for a commission, on behalf of other parties.

Call. (See **Option** below.)

Censure. A formal reprimand by the SEC for improper professional behavior by a party to a filing.

Certificate. A document of an independent public accountant, or independent certified public accountant, that is dated, reasonably comprehensive as to the scope of the audit made, and states clearly the opinion of the accountant in respect to the financial statements and the accounting principles and procedures followed by the registrant (see **Registrant** below).

Certification. It is the accountant's responsibility to make a reasonably unqualified certification of the financial statements. It is important for the auditor to incorporate in the certificate an adequate explanation of the scope (see **Scope** below) of the audit.

Certified. When used in regard to financial statements, examined and reported upon with an opinion expressed by an independent public or certified public accountant.

Certiorari, Writ of. An order issued by a superior court directing an inferior court to deliver its record for review.

Chapter X Bankruptcy. Voluntary or involuntary reorganization of a corporation with publicly held securities.

Chapter XI Bankruptcy. Deals with individuals, partnerships and with corporations whose securities are not publicly held. Affects only voluntary arrangements of unsecured debts.

Charter. Includes articles of incorporation, declarations of trust, articles of association or partnership, or any similar instrument, as amended, affecting the organization of an incorporated or unincorporated person.

Civil Actions. Involves the private rights and remedies of the parties to a suit; actions arising out of a contract.

Class of Securities. A group of similar securities that give shareholders similar rights.

Closed-End Investment Company. A corporation in the business of investing its funds in securities of other corporations for income and profit. Investors wishing to "cash out" of the investment company do so by selling their shares on the open market, as with any other stock.

Closing Date. Effective date (see **Effective Date** below) of a registration statement.

Comment Letters. (See **Deficiency Letter** below.)

Common Equity. Any class of common stock or an equivalent interest, including but not limited to a unit of beneficial interest in a trust or a limited partnership interest.

Compensating Balance. Restricted deposits of a borrower required by banks to be maintained against short-term loans. A portion of any demand, time, or certificate of deposit, maintained by a corporation, or by any person on behalf of the corporation, which constitutes support for existing borrowing arrangements of the corporation, or any other person, with a lending institution. Such arrangements include both outstanding borrowings and the assurance of future credit availability.

Consent Action. Issued when a person agrees to the terms of an SEC disciplinary action without admitting to the allegations in the complaint.

Consolidated Statements. Include the operating results of a corporation's subsidiary(ies) with inter-company transactions eliminated.

Control (including the terms "controlling," "controlled by," "under common control with"). The possession, direct or indirect, of the power to direct or cause the direction of the management and policies of a person, whether through the ownership of voting shares, by contract, or otherwise.

Cooling-Off Period. The period between the filing and effective date (see **Effective Date** below) of a registration statement.

Criminal Action. Suits initiated for the alleged violation of a public law.

Dealer. A person in the business of buying and selling securities for his or her own account.

Deficiency Letter. A letter from the SEC to the registrant setting forth the needed corrections and amendments to the issuing corporations' registration statement.

Delisting. Permanent removal of a listed security from a national securities exchange.

Depositary Share. A security evidenced by an American Depositary Receipt that represents a foreign security or a multiple of or fraction thereof deposited with a depositary.

Development Stage Company. A company is considered to be in the development stage if it is devoting substantially all of its efforts to establishing a new business and either of the following conditions exists.

    a.   Planned principal operations have not commenced.

    b.   Planned principal operations have commenced, but there has been no significant revenue therefrom.

Disbarment. Permanent removal of a professional's privilege to represent clients before the SEC.

Disclosure. The identification of accounting policies and principles that materially affect the determination of financial position, changes in financial position, and results of operations.

Domiciled Corporation. A corporation doing business in the state in which its corporate charter was guaranteed.

Due Diligence Meeting. A meeting of all parties in the preparation of a registration statement to assure that a high degree of care in investigation and independent verification of the company's representations has been made.

Effective Date. The twentieth (20th) day after the filing date of a registration statement or amendment unless the Commission shortens or extends that time period.

Employee. Any employee, general partner, or consultant or advisor, insurance agents who are exclusive agents of the registrant, its subsidiaries or parents. It also includes former employees as well as executors, administrators or beneficiaries of the estates of deceased employees, guardians or members of a committee for incompetent former employees, or similar persons duly authorized by law to administer the estate or assets of former employees.

Equity Security. Any stock or similar security; or any security convertible, with or without consideration, into such a security, or carrying any warrant or right to subscribe to or purchase such a security, or any such warrant or right.

Examination. (See **Audit** above.)

Exchange. An organized association providing a market place for bringing together buyers and sellers of securities through brokers.

Exempt Security. One that is not required to be registered with the SEC.

Exempt Transaction. A transaction in securities that does not require registration with the SEC.

Expert. Any specialist, accountant, attorney, engineer, appraiser, etc., who participates in the preparation of a registration statement. Broadly, any signatory to the registration statement is assumed to be an expert.

Fifty-Percent-Owned-Person. A person whose outstanding voting shares are approximately 50 percent owned by another specified person directly, or indirectly, through one or more intermediaries.

Filing. The process of completing and submitting a registration statement to the SEC.

Filing Date. The date a registration statement is received by the SEC.

Financial Statement. Includes all notes to the statements and all related schedules.

Fiscal Year. The annual accounting period or, if no closing date has been adopted, the calendar year ending on December 31.

Float. The difference on a bank's ledger and a depositor's books caused by presentation of checks and deposits in transit.

Footnote. Appended to financial statements as supplemental information for specific items in a statement.

Foreign Currency. Any currency other than the currency used by the enterprise in its financial statements.

Forms. Statements of standards with which registration statements and other filings must comply. Essentially, SEC forms are a set of instructions to guide the registrant in the preparation of the SEC reports to be filed; the forms are not required to be precisely copied.

Form S-1. A registration statement (see **Registration Statement** below) is filed on Form S-1 for companies issuing securities to the public. This form incorporates specified standards for financial statements and auditor's report.

Form 8-K. A report which is filed only when a reportable event occurs which may have a significant effect on the future of a company and on the value of its securities. Form 8-K must be filed not later than 15 days after the date on which the specified event occurs.

Form 10-K. The annual report to the SEC which covers substantially all of the information required in Form S-1. Form 10-K is due 90 days after a company's December 31 fiscal year, or by March 31 of each year.

Form 10-Q. A quarterly report containing *unaudited* financial statements. If certain types of events occur during the period, they must be reported on the Form. The 10-Q is due 45 days after the end of the first three fiscal quarters.

Going Private. The term commonly used to describe those transactions having as their objective the complete termination or substantial reduction of public ownership of an equity's securities.

Going Public. Registering a new issue of securities with the SEC. *Going public* is closely related to the process of applying for listed status on one or more of the exchanges, or registering for trading in the over-the-counter market.

Indemnification Provision. An agreement protecting one party from liability arising from the occurrence of an unforeseeable event.

Independent Accountants (CPA). Accountants who certify financial statements filed with the SEC. Accountants must maintain strict independence of attitude and judgment in planning and conducting and audit and in expressing an opinion on financial statements. The SEC will not recognize any public accountant or certified public accountant that is not independent.

Information Statement. A statement on any pending corporate matters furnished by the registrant to every shareholder who is entitled to vote when a proxy is not solicited.

Initial Margin Percentage. The percentage of the purchase price (or the percentage of a short sale; see **Short Selling** below), that an investor must deposit with his/her broker in compliance with Federal Reserve Board margin requirements.

Injunction. A court order directing a person to stop alleged violations of a securities law or regulation.

Insurance Holding Company. A person who is engaged, either directly or indirectly, primarily in the business of owning securities of one or more insurance companies for the purpose, and with the effect, of exercising control.

Integrated Disclosure System (IDS). An extensive revision of the mandatory business and financial disclosure requirements applicable to publicly-held companies. It establishes a uniform and integrated disclosure system under the securities laws. The IDS adopted major changes in its disclosure systems under the Securities Act of 1933, and the Securities Exchange Act of 1934. The changes include amendments to Forms 10-K and 10-Q, amendments to the proxy rules, amendments to Regulation S-K which governs the non-financial statement disclosure rules (see **Regulation S-K** below), uniform financial statement instructions, a general revision of Regulation S-X which governs the form, content, and requirements of financial statements (see **Regulation S-X** below), and a new simplified form for the registration of securities issued in business combinations.

Issuer. Any corporation that sells a security in a public offering.

Letter-of-Consent. Written permission from participating experts to include their names and signatures in a registration statement.

Line-of-Business Reporting. Registrants must report financial information regarding segments of their operations. The SEC does not define the term "line-of-business." Rather, the responsibility of determining meaningful segments that reflect the particular company's operations and organizational concepts is the responsibility of management. No more than ten classes of business are required to be reported.

Listed Status. Condition under which a security has been accepted by an exchange for full trading privileges. As long as a corporation remains listed on an exchange, it must file periodic reports to its stockholders.

Listing. A corporation applying to list its securities on an exchange must file a registration statement and a copy of the application for listing with the SEC.

Majority-Owned Subsidiary. A subsidiary more than 50 percent of whose outstanding voting shares is owned by its parent and/or the parent's other majority-owned subsidiaries.

Managing Underwriter. Underwriter(s) who, by contract or otherwise, deals with the registrant; organizes the selling effort; receives some benefit directly or indirectly in which all other underwriters similarly situated do not share in proportion to their respective interests in the underwriting; or represents any other underwriters in such matters as maintaining the records of the distribution, arranging the allotments of securities offered or arranging for appropriate stabilization activities, if any.

Margin Call. The demand by a broker that an investor deposit additional cash (or acceptable collateral) for securities purchased on credit when the price of the securities declines to a value below the minimum shareholder's equity required by the stock exchange.

Material. Information regarding any subject that limits the information required to those matters about which an average prudent investor ought reasonably to be informed.

Mutual Fund. Not legal terminology. It is a financial term commonly used in street jargon to mean an open-end investment company (see **Open-End Investment Company** below) as defined in the Investment Company Act of 1940.

National Association of Securities Dealers, Inc. (NASD). An association of brokers/dealers who are in the business of trading over-the-counter securities.

Net Sales. Income or loss from continuing operations before extraordinary items and cumulative effect of a change in accounting principle.

New York Stock Exchange (and Regional Exchanges). An association organized to provide physical, mechanical, and logistical facilities for the purchase and sale of securities by investors through brokers and dealers.

No-Action Letter. The SEC's written reply to a corporate issuer of securities stating its position regarding a specific filing matter.

Notification. Filing with the SEC the terms of an offering of securities that are exempt from registration.

Offering Date. The date a new security can be offered to the public.

Open-End Investment Company. A corporation in the business of investing its funds in securities of other corporations for income and profit. An open-end company continuously offers new shares for sales and redeems shares previously issued to investors who want to cash out.

Opinion. A required statement in the certification that the auditor believes the audit correctly reflects the organization's financial condition and results of operation.

Option. The contractual privilege of purchasing a security (Call) for a specified price, or delivering a security (Put) at a specified price.

Over-the-Counter Securities. Corporate and government securities that are not listed for trading on a national stock exchange.

Parent. A "parent" of a specified person(s) is an affiliate controlling such person(s) directly or indirectly through one or more intermediaries.

Pension Plan. An arrangement whereby a company undertakes to provide its retired employees with benefits that can be determined or estimated in advance.

Person. An individual, corporation, partnership, association, joint-stock company, business trust, or unincorporated organization.

Predecessor. A person from whom another person acquired the major portion of the business and assets in a single succession or in a series of related successions. In each succession the acquiring person acquired the major portion of the business and assets of the acquired person.

Prefiling Conference. A meeting of corporate officers and experts outlining the SEC requirements for the filing of a registration statement. Occasionally an SEC staff member will attend.

Previously Filed or Reported. Previously filed with, or reported in a definitive proxy statement or information statement, or a registration statement. Information contained in any such document will be assumed to have been previously filed with the exchange.

Principal Holder of Equity Securities. Used in respect of a registrant or other person named in a particular statement or report, a holder of record or a known beneficial owner of more than 10 percent of any class of securities of the registrant or other person, respectively, and of the date of the related balance sheet filed.

Promoter. Any person who, acting alone or in conjunction with one or more other persons, directly or indirectly takes initiative in founding and organizing the business or enterprise of an issuer. Any person is a promoter who, in connection with the founding and organizing of the business or enterprise of an issuer, directly or indirectly receives in consideration of services or property, or both services and property, 10 percent or more of any class of securities of the issuer or 10 percent or more of the proceeds from the sale of any class of securities. However, a person who receives such securities or proceeds either solely as underwriting commissions or solely in consideration of property shall not be deemed a promoter within the meaning of this paragraph if such person does not otherwise take part in founding and organizing the enterprise.

Prospectus. Document consisting of Part 1 of the registration statement filed with the SEC by the issuing corporation that must be delivered to all purchasers of newly issued securities.

Proxy. A power of attorney whereby a stockholder authorizes another person, or group of persons, to act (vote) for that stockholder at a shareholders' meeting.

Proxy Statement. Information furnished in conjunction with a formal solicitation in the proxy for the power to vote a stockholder's shares.

Put. (See **Option** above.)

Red-Herring Prospectus. Preliminary prospectus with a statement (in red ink) on each page indicating that the security described has not become effective, that the information is subject to correction and change without notice, and is not an offer to buy or sell that security.

Refusal. SEC action prohibiting a filing (see **Filing** above) from becoming effective.

Regional Exchanges. (See **New York Stock Exchange** above.)

Registrant. An issuer of securities for which an application, a report, or a registration statement has been filed.

Registration. Act of filing with the SEC the required information concerning the issuing corporation and the security to be issued.

Registration Statement. The document filed with the SEC containing legal, commercial, technical, and financial information concerning a new security issue.

Regulation S-K. An authoritative statement of disclosure standards under all securities acts. Regulation S-K establishes the standards of disclosure for non-financial information not included in financial statements, footnotes or schedules.

Regulation S-X. The principal document reporting for financial statements, footnotes and schedules' standards under all securities acts. No filing can be made without reference to Regulation S-X. It integrates all accounting requirements prior to February 21, 1940, into a single regulation.

Related Party. One that can exercise control or significant influence over the management and/or operating policies of another party, to the extent that one of the parties may be prevented from fully pursuing its own separate interests. Related parties consist of all affiliates of an enterprise, including its management and their immediate families, its principal owners and their immediate families, its investments accounted for by the equity method, beneficial employee trusts that are managed by the management of the enterprise, and any party that may, or does, deal with the enterprise and has ownership of, control over, or can significantly influence the management or operating policies of another party to the extent that an arms-length transaction may not be achieved. Transactions between related parties are generally accounted for on the same basis as if the parties were not related, unless the substance of the transaction is not arm's length. Substance over form is an important consideration when accounting for transactions involving related parties.

Replacement Cost. The lowest amount that would have to be paid in the normal course of business to obtain a new asset of equivalent operating or productive capability.

Restricted Security. Private offering of an issue that cannot be resold to the public without prior registration. Also called "investment letter" securities for the letter that the purchaser of such securities must submit to the SEC stating that the securities are being acquired for investment purposes, not for immediate resale.

Right. Provides current security holders the privilege of participating on a pro rata basis in a new offering of securities.

Roll-Up Transaction. Any transaction or series of transactions that, directly or indirectly through acquisition or otherwise, involves the combination or reorganization of one or more partnerships. The term includes the offer or sale of securities by a successor entity, whether newly formed or previously existing, to one or more limited partners of the partnership to be combined or reorganized, or the acquisition of the successor entity's securities by the partnerships being combined or reorganized.

Rules of Practice. Establishes standards of conduct for professionals practicing before the SEC.

Sale. Every contract of sale, disposition, or offer of a security for value (see **Security** below).

Schedule. Detailed financial information presented in a form prescribed by the SEC in Regulation S-X.

Scienter. Intent to deceive, manipulate, or defraud. Requires proof that defendant knew of material misstatements or omissions; that defendant acted willfully and knowingly.

Scope (of an Audit). A complete, detailed audit. The auditor includes in the certificate an adequate explanation of the extent of the audit.

Securities Act of 1933. Requires the disclosure of financial data for issues not exempted from registration and prohibits fraudulent acts and misrepresentations and omission of material (see **Material** above) facts in the issue of securities.

Securities Exchange Act of 1934 (The Exchange Act). Covers the regulation of stock market activities and the public trading of securities. The regulations covered are the disclosure of significant financial data, the regulation of securities market practices and operation, and control of credit (margin requirements) extended for the purchase and short sales of securities.

Security. Any instrument representing a debt obligation, an equity interest in a corporation, or any instrument commonly known as a security. In the Securities Act, security is defined to include by name or description many documents in which there is common trading for investment or speculation. Some, such as notes, bonds and stocks, are standardized and the name alone carries well settled meaning. Others are of a more variable character and were necessarily designated by more descriptive terms, such as transferable share, investment contract, and in general any interest or instrument commonly known as a security.

Selling Group. Several broker/dealers who distribute a new issue of securities at retail.

Share. A share of stock in a corporation or unit of interest in an unincorporated person.

Short-Selling. Selling a security that is not owned with the expectation of buying that specific security later at a lower market price.

Significant Subsidiary. A subsidiary (including its subsidiaries) in which the registrant's (and its other subsidiaries') investments in and advances to exceed 10 percent of the total assets of the registrant and its subsidiaries consolidated as of the end of the most recently completed fiscal year. For a proposed business combination to be accounted for as a pooling of interests, this requirement is also met when the number of common shares exchanged by the registrant exceeds 10 percent of its total common shares outstanding at the date the combination is initiated, or the registrant's (and its other subsidiaries') proportionate share of the total assets, after intercompany eliminations, of the subsidiary exceeds 10 percent of the total assets of the registrant and its subsidiaries consolidated as of the end of the most recently completed fiscal year.

Small Business Issuer. An entity that (a) has revenues of less than $25,000,000; (b) is a U.S. or Canadian issuer; (c) is not an investment company; (d) if a majority-owned subsidiary, the parent corporation is also a small business issuer.

Solicitation. Any request for a proxy or other similar communication to security holders.

Sponsor. The person proposing the roll-up transaction. (See **Roll-Up Transaction** above.)

Spread. The difference between the price paid for a security by the underwriter and the selling price of that security.

Stockholders' Meeting, Regular. The annual meeting of stockholders for the election of directors and for action on other corporate matters.

Stockholders' Meeting, Special. A meeting in which only specified items can be considered.

Stop Order. An SEC order stopping the issue or listing of a security on a stock exchange.

Subsidiary. An affiliate controlled by a specified person directly, or indirectly, through one or more intermediaries.

Substantial Authoritative Support. FASB principles, standards and practices published in Statements and Interpretations, AICPA Accounting Research Bulletins, and AICPA Opinions, except to the extent altered, amended, supplemented, revoked or superseded by an FASB Statement.

Succession. The direct acquisition of the assets comprising a going business, whether by merger, consolidation, or other direct transfer. This term does not include the acquisition of control of a business unless followed by the direct acquisition of its assets.

Successor. The surviving entity after completion of the roll-up transaction, or the entity whose securities are being offered or sold to, or acquired by, limited partners of the partnerships or the limited partnerships to be combined or reorganized.

Summary Prospectus. A prospectus containing specific items of information which subsequently will be included in the registration statement.

Suspension. An SEC order temporarily prohibiting the trading of a security on the stock exchange, usually invoked by the SEC when a news release is pending which may cause a disorderly market in that security. Trading is usually resumed shortly after the information has been publicly disseminated.

Totally Held Subsidiary. A subsidiary substantially all of whose outstanding securities are owned by its parent and/or the parent's other totally held subsidiaries. The subsidiary is not indebted to any person other than its parent and/or the parent's other totally held subsidiaries in an amount which is material in relation to the particular subsidiary, excepting indebtedness incurred in the ordinary course of business which is not overdue and which matures within one year from the date of its creation, whether evidenced by securities or not.

Underwriter. (See **Managing Underwriter** above.)

Unlisted Trading Privileges. A security issue authorized by the SEC for trading on an exchange without requiring the corporation to complete a formal listing application.

Voting Securities. Securities whose holders are presently entitled to vote for the election of directors.

Warrant. A security that grants the holder the right to purchase a specific number of shares of the security to which the warrant is attached at a specified price and usually within a stated period of time.

Wholly-Owned Subsidiary. A subsidiary substantially all of whose outstanding voting securities are owned by its parent and/or the parent's other wholly-owned subsidiaries.

¶24,004   Securities Act of 1933

The *truth in securities* law has two main objectives:

- To require that investors are provided with material information concerning securities offered for sale to the public.
- To prevent misrepresentation, deceit, and other fault in the sale of securities.

The primary means of accomplishing these objectives is by requiring full disclosure of financial information by registering offerings and sales of securities. Securities transactions subject to registration are mostly offerings of debt and equity securities issued by corporations, limited partnerships, trusts and other issuers. Federal and certain other government debt securities are not. Certain securities and transactions qualify for exemptions from registration provisions. They are included in the discussion that follows.

¶24,005   Registration

Registration is intended to provide adequate and accurate disclosure of material facts concerning the company and the securities it proposes to sell. This enables investors to make a thorough appraisal of the merits of the securities and exercise informed judgment in determining whether or not to purchase them. There are, however, no fundamental or technical research or other comment function to their work. Indeed, there are no subjective contents to anything they issue – they regurgitate information in a prescribed format for the investor to examine.

Registration requires, but does not guarantee, the accuracy of the facts represented in the registration statement and prospectus. However, the law does prohibit false and misleading statements under penalty of fine, imprisonment, or both. Investors who purchases securities and suffer losses have important recovery rights under the law if they can prove that there was incomplete or inaccurate disclosure of material facts in the registration statement or prospectus. If such misstatements are proven, the following could be liable for investor losses sustained in the securities purchase:

- The issuing company.
- Its responsible directors and officers.
- The underwriters.
- The controlling interests.
- The sellers of the securities.
- Others that are affiliated with the securities of the issuer.

Registration of securities does not preclude the sale of stock in risky, poorly managed, or unprofitable companies. Nor does the Commission *approve or disapprove* securities on their merits; and it is unlawful to represent otherwise in the sale of securities. The only standard which must be met when registering securities is adequate and accurate *disclosure* of required material facts concerning the company and the securities it proposes to sell. The fairness of the terms, the issuing company's prospects for successful operation, and other factors affecting the merits of investing in the securities have no bearing on the question of whether or not securities can be qualified for registration.

.01   The Registration Process

To facilitate registration by different types of enterprises, the Commission has special forms that vary in their disclosure requirements, but generally provide essential facts while minimizing the burden and expense of complying with the law. In general, registration forms call for disclosure of information such as:

- Description of the registrant's properties and business.
- Description of the significant provisions of the security to be offered for sale and its relationship to the registrant's other capital securities.
- Information about the management of the registrant.
- Financial statements certified by independent public accountants.

Registration statements become public immediately upon filing with the SEC. After the registration statement is filed, securities can be *offered* orally or by summaries of the information in the registration statement, but it is unlawful to *sell* the securities until the *effective date* which is on the 20th day after filing the registration statement, or on the 20th day after filing the last amendment, if any. The SEC can issue a *stop order* to refuse or suspend the effectiveness of the statement if the Commission concludes that material deficiencies in a registration statement appear to result from a deliberate attempt to conceal or mislead. A stop order is not a permanent prohibition to the effectiveness of the registration statement, or to the sale of the securities, and can be lifted and the statement declared effective when amendments are filed correcting the statement in accordance with the requirements in the stop order decision.

There are exemptions to the registration requirements:

- Private offerings to a limited number of persons or institutions who have access to the kind of information that registration would disclose and who do not propose to redistribute the securities.
- Offerings restricted to residents of the state in which the issuing company is organized and doing business.
- Securities of municipal, state, federal and other governmental instrumentalities, such as charitable institutions and banks.
- Offerings not exceeding certain specified amounts made in compliance with regulations of the Commission.
- Offerings of small business investment companies made in accordance with the rules and regulations of the Commission.

Regardless of whether or not the securities are exempt from registration, anti-fraud provisions apply to all sales of securities involving interstate commerce or the mails.

The small business exemption from registration—known as Regulation A—provides that offerings of securities under $5 million can be exempt from full registration, subject to conditions the SEC prescribes to protect investors. Certain Canadian and domestic companies are permitted to make exempt offerings. Regulation A is a longstanding exemption from registration. The unregistered public offerings of up to $5 million of securities, including no more than $1.5 million of securities offered by security-holders of the company is measured during any 12-month period. In recent years, Regulation A offerings have been relatively rare in comparison to offerings conducted in reliance on other Securities Act exemptions or on a registered basis.

In March 2015, the SEC adopted rules to facilitate smaller companies' access to capital thereby providing investors with more investment choices. The new rules, referred to as Regulation A+, update and expand Regulation A. The rules are mandated by Title IV of the *Jumpstart Our Business Startups (JOBS) Act*. The updated exemption will enable smaller companies to offer and sell up to $50 million of securities in a 12-month period, subject to eligibility, disclosure and reporting requirements.

"These new rules provide an effective, workable path to raising capital that also provides strong investor protections," according to SEC Chair Mary Jo White. "It is important for the Commission to continue to look for ways that our rules can facilitate capital-raising by smaller companies."

The final rules, of Regulation A+, provide for two tiers of offerings: Tier 1, for offerings of securities of up to $20 million in a 12-month period, with not more than $6 million in offers by selling security-holders that are affiliates of the issuer; and Tier 2, for offerings of securities of up to $50 million in a 12-month period, with not more than $15 million in offers by selling security-holders that are affiliates of the issuer. Both Tiers are subject to certain basic requirements while Tier 2 offerings are also subject to additional disclosure and ongoing reporting requirements.

The final rules also provide for the preemption of state securities law registration and qualification requirements for securities offered or sold to "qualified purchasers" in Tier 2 offerings. Tier 1 offerings will be subject to federal and state registration and qualification requirements, and issuers may take advantage of the coordinated review program developed by the North American Securities Administrators Association (NASAA).

Exhibit: General Form for Registration of Securities

UNITED STATES
SECURITIES AND EXCHANGE COMMISSION
Washington, D.C. 20549

FORM 10
GENERAL FORM FOR REGISTRATION OF SECURITIES
Pursuant to Section 12(b) or (g) of The Securities Exchange Act of 1934

(Exact name of registrant as specified in its charter)

(State or other jurisdiction of incorporation or organization) (I.R.S. Employer Identification No.)

(Address of principal executive offices) (Zip Code)

Registrant's telephone number, including area code _____

Securities to be registered pursuant to Section 12(b) of the Act:

Title of each class to be so registered	Name of each exchange on which each class is to be registered

Securities to be registered pursuant to Section 12(g) of the Act:

(Title of class)

(Title of class)

INFORMATION REQUIRED IN REGISTRATION STATEMENT

Item 1. Business.

Furnish the information required by Item 101 of Regulation S-K (§ 229.101 of this chapter).

Item 2. Financial Information.

Furnish the information required by Items 301 and 303 of Regulation S-K (§§ 229.301 and 229.303 of this chapter).

Item 3. Properties.

Furnish the information required by Item 102 of Regulation S-K (§ 229.102 of this chapter).

Item 4. Security Ownership of Certain Beneficial Owners and Management.

Furnish the information required by Item 403 of Regulation S-K (§ 229.403 of this chapter).

Item 5. Directors and Executive Officers.

Furnish the information required by Item 401 of Regulation S-K (§ 229.401 of this chapter).

Item 6. Executive Compensation.

Furnish the information required by Item 402 of Regulation S-K (§ 229.402 of this chapter).

Item 7. Certain Relationships and Related Transactions.

Furnish the information required by Item 404 of Regulation S-K (§ 229.404 of this chapter).

Item 8. Legal Proceedings.

Furnish the information required by Item 103 of Regulation S-K (§ 229.103 of this chapter).

Item 9. Market Price of and Dividends on the Registrant's Common Equity and Related Stockholder Matters.

Furnish the information required by Item 201 of Regulation S-K (§ 229.201 of this chapter).

Item 10. Recent Sales of Unregistered Securities.

Furnish the information required by Item 701 of Regulation S-K (§ 229.701 of this chapter).

Item 11. Description of Registrant's Securities to be Registered.

Furnish the information required by Item 202 of Regulation S-K (§ 229.202 of this chapter).

Item 12. Indemnification of Directors and Officers.

Furnish the information required by Item 702 of Regulation S-K (§ 229.702 of this chapter).

Item 13. Financial Statements and Supplementary Data.

Furnish all financial statements required by Regulation S-X and the supplementary financial information required by Item 302 of Regulation S-K (§ 229.302 of this chapter).

Item 14. Changes in and Disagreements with Accountants on Accounting and Financial Disclosure.

Furnish the information required by Item 304 of Regulation S-K (§ 229.304 of this chapter).

Item 15. Financial Statements and Exhibits.

(a) List separately all financial statements filed as part of the registration statement.

(b) Furnish the exhibits required by Item 601 of Regulation S-K (§ 229.601 of this chapter).

SIGNATURES

Pursuant to the requirements of Section 12 of the Securities Exchange Act of 1934, the registrant has duly caused this registration statement to be signed on its behalf by the undersigned, thereunto duly authorized.

_____
(Registrant)

Date_____   _____
(Signature)*

*Print name and title of the signing officer under his signature.

GENERAL INSTRUCTIONS

A. Rule as to Use of Form 10.

Form 10 shall be used for registration pursuant to Section 12(b) or (g) of the Securities Exchange Act of 1934 of classes of securities of issuers for which no other form is prescribed.

B. Application of General Rules and Regulations.

    a.   The General Rules and Regulations under the Act contain certain general requirements which are applicable to registration on any form. These general requirements should be carefully read and observed in the preparation and filing of registration statements on this form.

    b.   Particular attention is directed to Regulation 12B [17 CFR 240.12b-1–240.12b-36] which contains general requirements regarding matters such as the kind and size of paper to be used, the legibility of the registration statement, the information to be given whenever the title of securities is required to be stated, and the filing of the registration statement. The definitions contained in Rule 12b-2 [17 CFR 240.12b-2] should be especially noted.

C. Preparation of Registration Statement.

    a.   This form is not to be used as a blank form to be filled in, but only as a guide in the preparation of the registration statement on paper meeting the requirements of Rule 12b-12 [17 CFR 240.12b-12]. The registration statement shall contain the item numbers and captions, but the text of the items may be omitted. The answers to the items shall be prepared in the manner specified in Rule 12b-13 [17 CFR 240.12b-13].

    b.   Unless otherwise stated, the information required shall be given as of a date reasonably close to the date of filing the registration statement.

    c.   Attention is directed to Rule 12b-20 [17 CFR 240.12b-20] which states: "In addition to the information expressly required to be included in a statement or report, there shall be added such further material information, if any, as may be necessary to make the required statements, in light of the circumstances under which they are made, not misleading."

D. Signature and Filing of Registration Statement.

Three complete copies of the registration statement, including financial statements, exhibits and all other papers and documents filed as a part thereof, and five additional copies which need not include exhibits, shall be filed with the Commission. At least one complete copy of the registration statement, including financial statements, exhibits and all other papers and documents filed as a part thereof, shall be filed with each exchange on which any class of securities is to be registered. At least one complete copy of the registration statement filed with the Commission and one such copy filed with each exchange shall be manually signed. Copies not manually signed shall bear typed or printed signatures.

E. Omission of information Regarding Foreign Subsidiaries.

Information required by any item or other requirement of this form with respect to any foreign subsidiary may be omitted to the extent that the required disclosure would be detrimental to the registrant. However, financial statements, otherwise required, shall not be omitted pursuant to this instruction. Where information is omitted pursuant to this instruction, a statement shall be made that such information has been omitted and the names of the subsidiaries involved shall be separately furnished to the Commission. The Commission may, in its discretion, call for justification that the required disclosure would be detrimental.

F. Incorporation by Reference.

Attention is directed to Rule 12b-23 [17 CFR 240.12b-23] which provides for the incorporation by reference of information contained in certain documents in answer or partial answer to any item of a registration statement.

¶24,006   Securities Exchange Act of 1934

The 1934 Act extends the disclosure doctrine of investor protection to securities that are listed and registered for public trading on U.S. national securities exchanges. In 1964, the SEC was authorized by Congress to include disclosure and reporting requirements to equity securities in the over-the-counter market. The object of the 1934 Act is to ensure *fair and orderly securities markets* by prohibiting certain types of activities and by setting forth rules regarding the operation of the markets and the participants.

Companies wanting to have their securities registered and listed or publicly traded on an exchange must file a registration application with the exchange and the SEC. Companies whose equity securities are traded over-the-counter must file a similar registration form. SEC rules prescribe the content of registration statements and require certified financial statements. After a company's securities have become registered, annual and other periodic reports to update information contained in the original registration statement must be filed.

The 1934 Act governs the solicitation of proxies (votes) from holders of registered securities, both listed and over-the-counter, for the election of directors and for approval of other corporate action. All material facts concerning matters on which shareholders are asked to vote must be disclosed. In 1970, Congress amended the Exchange Act to extend its reporting and disclosure provisions to situations where control of a company is sought through a tender offer to other planned stock acquisitions of over five percent of a company's equity securities by direct purchase or by a tender offer. Disclosure provisions are supplemented by other provisions to help ensure investor protection in tender offers.

¶24,007 Insider Trading

Insider trader prohibitions are designed to curb misuse of material confidential information not available to the general public. Examples of such misuse are buying or selling securities to make profits or avoid losses based on material nonpublic information, or by telling others of the information before such information is generally available to all shareholders. The *Insider Trading Sanctions Act of 1984* allows imposing fines up to three times to profit gained or losses avoided by use of material nonpublic information. "Insider Trading" is a term that enjoys great journalistic currency; however, most of what is described as insider trading is absolutely not insider trading. Insider Trading is an insidious crime that is immensely difficult to prove and consequently carries enormous punishment once conviction is secured. All officers and directors of a company and beneficial owners of more than ten percent of its registered equity securities must file an initial report with the SEC and with the exchange on which the stock is listed, showing their holdings of each of the company's equity securities. Thereafter, they must file reports for any month during which there was any change in those holdings, and any profits obtained by them from purchases and sales, or sales and purchases, of such equity securities within any six-month period can be recovered by the company or by any security holder on its behalf. Insiders are also prohibited from making short sales of their company's equity securities.

¶24,008 Security and Exchange Commission Issues Report on Brokerage Firms' Handling of Confidential Information

In September 2012, the Securities and Exchange Commission issued a staff report intended to help broker-dealers safeguard confidential information from misuse, such as insider trading. The report by the Office of Compliance Inspections and Examinations (OCIE) describes strengths and weaknesses identified in examinations into how broker-dealers keep material nonpublic information from being misused.

According to the director of the OCIE, the report is designed to help broker-dealers assess the effectiveness of their controls over sensitive information. The report illustrates the types of conflicts of interest that may arise between a broker-dealer's obligations to clients that provide confidential information for business purposes and the potential misuse of such information for insider trading or other improper ends. It also describes various methods that broker-dealers use to identify and effectively manage such conflicts, including information barriers that limit the flow of sensitive information, the director concluded.

Conflicts of interest and other issues of concern raised by the report include:

- A significant amount of informal, undocumented interaction occurs between groups that have material nonpublic information and internal and external groups with sales and trading responsibilities that might profit from the misuse of such material nonpublic information
- At some broker-dealers, a senior executive might have access to material nonpublic information from one business unit while overseeing a different unit that could potentially profit from misuse of that information, with few if any restrictions or monitoring to prevent such misuse
- Some broker-dealers did not have risk controls to address certain business units that possess material nonpublic information such as sales, trading or research personnel who receive confidential information for business purposes; institutional and retail customers or asset management affiliates with access to material nonpublic information, or firm personnel who receive information through business activities outside of investment banking, such as participation in bankruptcy committees or through employees serving on the boards of directors of public companies.

The report also highlights effective practices that examiners observed at some broker-dealers, such as:

- Broker-dealers sometimes adopt processes that differentiate between types of material nonpublic information based on the nature of the information or where it originated. In some cases, broker-dealers create tailored "exception" reports that take into account the different characteristics of the information
- Some broker-dealers expand reviews for potential misuse of confidential information to include trading in credit default swaps, equity or total return swaps, loans, components of pooled securities such as unit investment trusts and exchange traded funds, warrants, and bond options
- Broker-dealers often consider electronic sources of confidential information and instituted monitoring to identify which employees have accessed the information
- Broker-dealers often monitor access rights for key cards and computer networks to confirm that only authorized personnel have access to sensitive areas.

The types of issues identified in this report may be helpful to firms as they review their conflict of interest risk management programs. In particular, in any review of information barriers control programs, broker-dealers should be alert to changes in business practices and available compliance tools. It should be pointed out that the plupart of these issues result from a certain laxity or sloppiness, not from any real or intended malfeasance.

¶24,009 Margin Trading

The 1934 Act authorizes the Board of Governors of the Federal Reserve System to set limits on the amount of credit which can be extended for the purpose of purchasing or carrying securities. The objective is to restrict excessive use of credit in the securities markets. While the credit restrictions are set by the Board of Governors, investigation and enforcement is the responsibility of the SEC. This is of particular importance in an era that has been and for the foreseeable future will remain a time of record low interest rates.

¶24,010 Division of Corporation Finance

Corporation Finance has the overall responsibility of ensuring that disclosure requirements are met by publicly held companies registered with the SEC. Its work includes: reviewing registration statements for new securities; proxy material and annual reports the Commission requires from publicly held companies; documents concerning tender offers, and mergers and acquisitions in general.

This Division renders administrative interpretations to the public of the Securities Act and the Securities Exchange Act, and to prospective registrants, and others. It is also responsible for certain statutes and regulations pertaining to small businesses and for the Trust Indenture Act of 1939. Applications for qualification of trust indentures are examined for compliance with the applicable requirements of the law and the Commission's rules. Corporation Finance works closely with the Office of the Chief Accountant in drafting rules and regulations which prescribe requirements for financial statements.

¶24,011 Truth in Securities Laws

The objectives of the laws are twofold. First is the protection of investors and the public against fraudulent acts and practices in the purchase and sale of securities. The second objective is to regulate trading in the national securities markets. For example:

- "To provide full and fair disclosure of the character of securities sold in interstate and foreign commerce and through the mails, and to prevent fraud in the sale thereof, and for other purposes." (Securities Act of 1933.)
- "To provide for the regulation of securities exchanges and the over-the-counter markets operating in interstate and foreign commerce and through the mails, to prevent inequitable and unfair practices on such exchanges and markets, and for other purposes." (Securities Exchange Act of 1934.)
- "To provide for the registration and regulation of investment companies and investment advisers, and for other purposes." (Investment Company Act of 1940 and the Investment Advisers Act of 1940.)

¶24,012   Development of Disclosure: 1933 and 1934 Acts

Two separate disclosure systems developed under the two principal securities laws. Generally, the Securities Act of 1933 regulates the *initial* public distribution of securities. The disclosure system developed under the 1933 Act emphasizes the comprehensive information about the issuer, because it was developed primarily for companies going public for the *first time* and about which the public had very little information or even none.

The Securities Exchange Act of 1934 regulates the trading of securities in *publicly held companies* which are traded both on the exchanges and in the over-the-counter markets. The dual disclosure system developed under the 1933 and 1934 Acts deals primarily with the form and content of financial and business data in the annual reports to the SEC and to shareholders, and concerns proxy statements as well as the dissemination of interim data. The emphasis of this disclosure system is on periodic information concerning issuers already known to security holders, and the purpose is to keep the data up-to-date.

The dual system generated a large number of registration and periodic reporting forms, each with its own set of instructions. Many publicly-held companies filed numerous registration statements and distributed related reports to the public containing the same information produced several times in slightly different forms, repeating much information that was already available within the financial community. This relates to the compliance functions the companies are obligated to operate under.

In addition, the audited primary financial statements prepared in conformity with U.S. GAAP that were included in the annual reports to shareholders, were not explicitly covered by the very detailed disclosure requirements in S-X. These mandated the form and content of the audited primary financial statements that were included in documents filed with the SEC and in prospectuses. However, since the financial statements had to be in conformity with U.S. GAAP there were no essential differences between the two.

Financial statements that conformed to S-X included numerous additional technical disclosures to satisfy the needs of professional financial analysts and the SEC staff. Uniform financial disclosure requirements for virtually all documents covered by either the 1933 or the 1934 Acts as well as for nonfinancial disclosures under the 1934 Act and for a major portion of those required under the 1933 Act have been formulated. To reach the objective, where identical disclosures are included both in documents filed with the Commission and distributed to security holders in prospectuses, proxy statements and annual reports, the Commission has two basic regulations. These are Regulation S-X (see the chapter, "Auditor Independence and the Audit Committee.") which covers the requirements for audited primary financial statements, and Regulation S-K which covers most of the other business, analytical, and unaudited financial disclosures.

Regulation S-K covers analytical and unaudited supplementary financial disclosures under the 1934 Act and most disclosures under the 1933 Act. One of the key requirements in Regulation S-K is the *Management's Discussion and Analysis of Financial Condition and Results of Operations.* The discussion must cover the three years presented in the audited financials and treat not only results of operations, but also financial condition and changes in financial condition. Although the requirement is for three years, the SEC suggests that when trends are being discussed, references to five years of selected financial data are appropriate.

The discussion and analysis is filed under the Securities Acts, as well as included in all annual reports and prospectuses. Accordingly, companies should document the adequacy of their systems and procedures for analyzing past results to be sure that there is an adequate and reliable information base for the management discussion and analysis, including decisions as to scope and content. Since future plans and expectations, such as capital expenditure commitments, are important in formulating management's discussion and analysis, it may be prudent to reappraise internal financial forecasting procedures periodically.

Although forward-looking information is not mandated, the specifically required information is such that financial analysts will be able to work out a forecast of future operating results. As practice develops, managements may find it preferable simply to include formal financial forecasts and comply with the safe harbor rules, rather than rely solely on the forecasts analysts will make based on data presumed to be reliable.

Form S-15. When a company acquires a business that is relatively minor when compared to the acquiring company, a process that was difficult because of the complexity and cost of registration requirements is greatly simplified by the use of Form S-15 for the registration requirements. Form S-15 enables an issuer to provide an abbreviated prospectus accompanied by the issuer's latest annual report to shareholders instead of larger documents. This procedure is limited to cases where the acquiring company's key financial indices as specified in the regulations are not affected by more than 10 percent by the acquired company, and where State law applicable to the merger does not require a vote by the security holders of the company being acquired. There are other restrictions, however, and it is likely this simplified procedure will be most usable for mergers where the company to be acquired is closely-held and will not become a significant part of the combined company.

Three copies of Form S-15 must be filed with the SEC. One copy must be signed manually by an officer of the registrant, or by counsel, or by any other authorized person. The name and title of the person signing Form S-15 should be typed or printed under that person's signature.

¶24,013   Synopsis: The Securities Act of 1933

In 1933, the first Federal legislative act designed to regulate the securities business on an interstate basis was passed. Its expressed purpose was:

"To provide full and fair disclosure of the character of securities . . . and to prevent frauds in the sale thereof, and for other purposes." There are four things to note:

- It related to newly-issued securities, not to those already in the hands of the public.
- It called for full and fair disclosure of all the facts necessary for an intelligent appraisal of the value of a security.
- It was designed to prevent fraud in the sale of securities.
- This legislation led to the Securities Exchange Act of 1934 establishing the Securities and Exchange Commission which would administer both acts.

There are 26 sections to the Act:

Section 1. "This title may be cited as the Securities Act of 1933." Various court decisions have very liberally interpreted the meaning of "securities" as covered by the Act. One decision contains the following: ". . . that this statute was not a penal statute but was a remedial enactment. . . . A remedial enactment is one that seeks to give a remedy for an ill. It is to be liberally construed so that its purpose may be realized." (*SEC v. Starmont*, 31 F. Supp. 264 (E.D. Wash. 1939).)

Section 2. Definitions. This section defines many of the terms used throughout the other sections of the Act. Importantly, it contains definitions of "security," "person," "sale," "offer to sell," and "prospectus," among many others. Several important Rules of the SEC are directly derived from this section, including Rule 134 (discussed in Section 5).

Section 3. Exempted Securities. Some securities, such as those issued or guaranteed by the United States, are exempted from the provisions of the Act.

Section 4. Exempted Transactions. Describes the transactions for which Section 5 does not apply.

Section 5. Prohibitions Relating to Intrastate Commerce and the Mails. It is unlawful to offer any security for sale "by any means or instruments of transportation or communication in interstate commerce or of the mails," unless a registration statement is in effect as to that security. It also prohibits the transportation by any means of interstate commerce or the mails of such a security for the purpose of sale or delivery after sale.

This Section further requires that any security that is registered cannot be sold without prior or concurrent delivery of an effective prospectus that meets the requirements of Section 10(a) of the Act.

There have been two important Rules promulgated by the SEC under this Section. The first, Rule 134, defines the types of advertising and of letters or other communications that can be used without prior or concurrent delivery of a prospectus. This Rule is frequently violated in letter form and also in telephone conversations. SEC Release 3844 of October 8, 1957, shows the importance of delivering a prospectus either before or at the same time that an attempt to sell is made. This Release states that a prospectus is defined to include any notice, circular, advertisement, letter, or communication, written or by radio or by television, which offers any security for sale except that any communication sent or given after the effective date of a registration statement shall not be deemed a prospectus if, prior to or at the same time with such a communication, a written prospectus meeting the requirements of Section 10 of the Act was sent or given.

Thus, any letter that gives more information than that allowed by Rule 134 becomes itself a prospectus, unless it is preceded or accompanied by the actual prospectus. A letter prospectus is in violation of Section 5 since it could not possibly comply with the requirements of Section 10.

The second, Rule 433, deals with the so-called "red-herring" prospectus which cannot be used as an offer to sell, but merely to disseminate information prior to the delivery of a regular prospectus which does offer the security for sale.

Section 6. Registration of Securities and Signing of Registration Statement. This Section details what securities may be registered and how such registration is to be done.

Section 7. Information Required on Registration Statement. This Section gives the SEC broad powers in regulating what must appear in a registration statement. In part, the section reads:

"Any such registration statement shall contain such other information, and be accompanied by such other documents, as the Commission may by rules or regulations require as being necessary or appropriate in the public interest or for the protection of investors."

Section 8. Taking Effect of Registration Statements and Amendments Thereto. Registration statements normally become effective on the twentieth day after filing, under this section. However, the SEC is empowered to determine whether or not the statement complies with the Act as to completeness and may refuse to allow the statement to become effective unless amended. If it appears to the SEC that untrue statements have been included, the Commission may issue a stop order.

Section 9. Court Review of Orders. As with any other act of Congress, provision is made so that any person who is aggrieved by an order of the administrative body (in this case the SEC) may obtain a review of the order in the Federal courts.

Section 10. Information Required in Prospectus. A prospectus must contain the same information as that contained in the registration statement. In addition, the SEC is given the authority to define the requirements for any additional material which that body considers necessary in the public interest. "Red herring" requirements and the manner of use of this type of preliminary prospectus are also detailed in this Section.

Note the application of Rule 134, discussed under Section 5, with respect to an "incomplete" prospectus.

One part of the Section, 10(3), relates to the length of time a prospectus may be used (that is, be considered an effective prospectus).

Under this Section of the Act, the SEC issued Rule 425, which requires the statement at the bottom of the first page of all prospectuses "These securities have not been approved or disapproved by the Securities and Exchange Commission nor has the commission passed upon the accuracy or adequacy of this prospectus. Any representation to the contrary is a criminal offense."

Section 11. Civil Liabilities on Account of False Registration Statement. Anyone directly connected with a company or signing the registration statement is subject to suit at law or in equity should the registration statement contain an untrue statement or fail to include a material fact necessary to make the statement not misleading.

Section 12. Civil Liabilities. If any person offers to sell or does sell a security in violation of Section 5, or uses any fraudulent means to sell a security, he or she is liable to civil suit for damages. This liability is in addition to any criminal liability arising under the Act.

Section 13. Limitation of Actions. Specified are the time limits within which civil suits may be instituted under Sections 11 and 12.

Section 14. Contrary Stipulations Void. Any provision in the sale of a security that binds the purchaser to waive the provisions of this Act or of the rules and regulations of the SEC is void. In other words, no one buying a security can relieve the seller from complying with the Act and with the rules issued under the Act.

Section 15. Liability of Controlling Persons. A dealer or broker is liable under Section 11 or 12.

Section 16. Additional Remedies. "The rights and remedies provided by this title (the Act) shall be in addition to any and all other rights and remedies that may exist at law or in equity."

Section 17. Fraudulent Interstate Transactions. As interpreted by the SEC, this section might be referred to as a "catch-all" section.

(a) "It shall be unlawful for any person in the offer or sale of any securities by the use of any means or instruments of transportation or communication in interstate commerce or by the use of the mails, directly or indirectly.

1. to employ any device, scheme or artifice to defraud, or
2. to obtain money or property by means of any untrue statement of a material fact or any omission to state a material fact necessary in order to make the statements made, in the light of the circumstances under which they were made, not misleading, or
3. to engage in any transaction, practice or course of business that operates or would operate as a fraud or deceit upon the purchaser."

Internet, television, and radio have been included by the SEC as "communication in interstate commerce" because it is impossible to control their area of reception.

While Section 17(a) refers only to the criminal courts in the term "unlawful," a court decision makes it clear that civil liability, in addition to criminal liability is incurred by violation of the section.

Court decisions also implement and amplify the language of the Act itself, with respect to the phrase "or by use of the mails." It would appear that Section 17 only applies to interstate mailings. However, the courts have ruled that if one used the mails *within one State* on an *intrastate* offering, and violated any provision in Section 17(a), that person is as guilty as if he or she had mailed across a state line.

Subparagraph (b) of Section 17 makes it illegal for anyone to publish descriptions of securities when the publisher is paid for such publicity, without also publishing the fact that compensation has been, or will be, received.

Section 17(c) makes the Section applicable to those securities exempted under Section 3. In other words, fraud is fraud whether in connection with exempt or other securities.

Section 18. State Control of Securities. "Nothing in this title (the Act) shall affect the jurisdiction of the Securities Commission . . . of any State . . . ." In other words, all the provisions of the Federal act *and* all the laws of the State in which business is being conducted must be complied with.

Section 19. Special Powers of Commission. The Commission has the authority to make, amend, and rescind such rules and regulations as may be necessary to carry out the provisions of the Act. Commissioners or their representatives are also empowered to subpoena witnesses and to administer oaths.

Section 20. Injunctions and Prosecution of Offenses. The SEC is empowered to make investigations and to bring criminal actions at law against persons deemed to have violated the Act. The wording of the section is interesting in that it gives the Commission power to act "whenever it shall appear ... that the provisions of this title (the Act) ... have been *or are about to be* violated...."

Section 21. Hearings by Commission. "All hearings shall be public and may be held before the Commission or an officer or officers of the Commission designated by it, and appropriate records shall be kept."

Section 22. Jurisdiction of Offenses and Suits. Jurisdiction of offenses and violations and certain rules in connection with them, are defined in this section. Jurisdiction is given to the District Courts of the United States, the U.S. Court of any Territory, and the U.S. District Court of the District of Columbia.

Section 23. Unlawful Representations. The fact that the registration statement for a security has been filed or is in effect does not mean that the statement is true and accurate, or that the Commission has in any way passed upon the merits of the security. It is unlawful to make any representations to the contrary.

In short, the words in the registration statement (*and* the prospectus) have been made under the penalties of fraud. The registrants are liable, even though the Commission has not certified the truth and accuracy of the statements or of the worth of the security.

Section 24. Penalties. "Any person who willfully violates any of the provisions of this title (the Act), or the rules and regulations promulgated by the Commission under authority thereof ... shall upon conviction be fined not more than $10,000.00 or imprisoned not more than five years, or both."

Section 25. Jurisdiction of Other Government Agencies Over Securities. Nothing in the Act shall relieve any person from submitting to other U.S. Government supervisory units information required by any provision of law.

Section 26. Separability of Provisions. If any one section of the Act is invalidated, such findings will not affect other sections.

Schedule A. Sets forth the requirements for the registration of securities.

Schedule B. Sets for the registration requirements for securities issued by a foreign government or political subdivision thereof.

¶24,014   Synopsis: The Securities Exchange Act of 1934

The Securities Act of 1933 protects investors in the purchase of newly-issued securities. The Securities Exchange Act of 1934 concerns the regulation of trading in already issued securities.

The stated purpose of the 1934 Act is "to provide for the regulation of securities exchanges and of over-the-counter markets operating in interstate and foreign commerce and through the mails, to prevent inequitable and unfair practices on such exchanges and markets, and for other purposes."

The Act has been of importance in prohibiting abuses and manipulations through its creation of the SEC and later of the self-regulatory National Association of Securities Dealers, Inc.

The Act has 34 sections:

Section 1. Short Title. "This Act may be cited as the Securities Exchange Act of 1934."

Section 2. Necessity of Regulation. Citing that transactions in securities are affected with a national public interest, this section states that it is necessary to regulate and control such transactions and other matters in order to protect interstate commerce, the national credit, the Federal taxing power, to protect and make more effective the national banking system and Federal Reserve System, and to insure the maintenance of fair and honest markets in such transactions.

Parts of Sections 2(3) and 2(4) explain the effects of "rigged" markets and manipulative practices:

Section 2(3). Frequently, the prices of securities on such exchanges and markets are susceptible to manipulation and control, and the dissemination of such prices gives rise to excessive speculation, resulting in sudden and unreasonable fluctuations in the prices of securities which (a) cause alternately unreasonable expansion and unreasonable contraction of the volume of credit available for trade, transportation, and industry in interstate commerce ... (c) prevent the fair valuation of collateral for bank loans and/or obstruct the effective operation of the national banking system and Federal Reserve System.

Section 2(4). "National emergencies, which produce widespread unemployment and the dislocation of trade, transportation, and industry, and which burden interstate commerce and adversely affect the general welfare, are precipitated, intensified, and prolonged by manipulation and sudden and unreasonable fluctuations of security prices and by excessive speculation on such exchanges and markets, and to meet such emergencies the Federal Government is put to such great expense as to burden the national credit."

Section 3. Definitions. In addition to defining 38 technical terms used in the Act, this Section gave the Securities Exchange Commission and the Federal Reserve System the authority to define technical, trade, and accounting terms so long as such definitions are not inconsistent with the provisions of the Act itself.

Section 4. This Section established the Securities and Exchange Commission. Prior to the Commissioners' taking office, the Securities Act of 1933 was administered by the Federal Trade Commission.

Section 5. Transactions on Unregistered Exchanges. Under this Section, it became illegal for transactions to be effected by brokers, dealers, or exchanges on an exchange unless the exchange was registered under Section 6 of the Act.

Section 6. Registration of Exchanges. Combined with Section 5, this Section sets forth the requirements for exchanges to be registered and the method of registration. Exchanges file their rules and regulations with the SEC and must agree to take disciplinary action against any member who violates the Act or violates any of the rules and regulations issued by the SEC under the Act.

Section 7. Margin Requirements. The Board of Governors of the Federal Reserve System is given the power to set margin requirements for any securities, which requirements may be changed from time to time at the discretion of the Board. Under this authority, the Board issued Regulation T and Regulation U. Regulation T governs the extension and maintenance of credit by brokers, dealers, and members of national securities exchanges. Regulation U governs loans by banks for the purpose of purchasing or carrying stocks registered on a national securities exchange.

Section 8. Restrictions on Borrowing. In four parts, this Section (a) details from whom brokers or dealers may borrow money on listed securities, (b) lays the foundation for the SEC's "net capital rule," (c) deals with pledging and commingling of customers' securities, and (d) states no broker or dealer may lend or arrange for the lending of any securities carried for the account of a customer without the written consent of the customer.

Section 9. Prohibition Against Manipulation. Both this Section and Section 10 deal with manipulative practices that are intended to make money for those in the Securities business at the expense of the general public.

Section 9 makes it unlawful to do certain things that constitute manipulation, such as: (a) creating a false or misleading appearance of active trading in a security, (b) giving of information to potential investors as to the likelihood of a rise or fall in price solely for the purpose of causing the market price to react to purchases or sales by such potential investors, (c) making false or misleading statements about a security, (d) "pegging" or "fixing" prices, (e) improper use of puts, calls, straddles, or other options to buy or sell. Transactions in which there is no real change in ownership are also specifically prohibited.

Section 10. Regulation of Manipulative and Deceptive Devices. Section 10 first forbids the use of short sales or stop-loss orders that violate any rules or regulations the Commission may set to protect investors. Its wording, then, becomes much more inclusive than Section 9 or the first part of Section 10, since it forbids in general "any manipulative or deceptive device or contrivance...."

Section 11. Trading by Members of Exchanges, Brokers, and Dealers. Authority is given to the Commission to set rules and regulations as to floor trading by members, brokers, or dealers for their own accounts and to prevent excessive trading off the floor of the exchanges. A part of this Section deals with the roles of the odd-lot dealers and the specialist on the floor of the exchange. Further, the Section places a limitation on certain customer credit extension in connection with underwritings.

Section 11A. National Market System for Securities; Securities Information Processors. Concerns the planning, developing, operating, or regulating of a national market system.

Section 12. Registration Requirements for Securities. It is unlawful for any broker or dealer to effect transactions in a security or a national securities exchange unless a registration statement is effective for that security. Information stating how such registration is to be accomplished is given here. The SEC is given authority to allow trading on one exchange in securities that are listed on another exchange (such securities are said to have "unlisted trading privileges").

Section 13. Reports. All companies whose securities are listed on a national securities exchange must file reports at such intervals and in such form as the SEC may require. The purpose of requiring such reports was to ensure that enough information was available on any company to enable an investor to make an intelligent decision concerning the worth of its securities.

Section 14. Proxies. Paragraph (a) of this Section gives the SEC the authority to make rules and regulations as to the solicitation of proxies and makes it illegal to solicit proxies other than in accord with such rules and regulations. Several rules have been issued under this Section which detail the manner in which proxies may be solicited and the information that must be given to shareholders whose proxies are being solicited. All of these rules are designated to ensure that the recipient of a proxy solicitation will understand what it is that he or she is being asked to sign and to give enough background on the matter in question so that the shareholder can make an intelligent decision about how to vote.

Paragraph (b) relates to the giving of proxies by broker or dealers in connection with securities held for the accounts of customers. It is standard practice for broker/dealers to vote proxies for shares held in their names for customers directly in accord with the wishes of the customers themselves.

Section 15. Over-The-Counter Markets. It is mandatory that all brokers and dealers who deal in the over-the-counter market (on other than an intrastate basis) be registered with the SEC. Further, the Section states that registration will be in accord with rules and regulations issued by the Commission. "Intrastate" means that the broker or dealer deals in intrastate securities as well as doing business only within his state. Here, as elsewhere in the Act, the "use of mails," even if within one State, places the user under the Act.

Section 15 also defines the grounds for denial of registration, for suspension, or for revocation of registration. Basically, these grounds are:

1. Making false or misleading statements in the application for registration.
2. Having been convicted within the last ten years of a felony or misdemeanor involving the purchase or sale of any security or arising out of the business of a broker or dealer.
3. Being enjoined by a court from engaging in the securities business.
4. Having willfully violated any of the provisions of the 1933 Act or of the 1934 Act. (After passage of the Investment Advisers Act of 1940 and the

Investment Company Act of 1940, violation of those Acts also became grounds for suspension or revocation.)

Sections 9 and 10 dealt with manipulation with respect to securities listed on a national exchange. Section 15 adds a prohibition against over-the-counter manipulation as defined by the Commission. Some of the practices that have been so defined are:

1. Excessive prices that are not fairly related to the market.
2. False representations to customers.
3. Taking of secret profits.
4. Failure to disclose control of a market.
5. Creating false impression of activity by dummy sales.
6. "Churning," or unnecessary purchases and sales in a customer's account.

Another important rule of the SEC under Section 15 seeks to protect investors by forbidding certain practices in connection with pledging or commingling of securities held for the accounts of customers. This rule specifically applies to over-the-counter broker/dealers; a similar rule, under Section 8, applies to broker/dealers who are members of or do business through members of a national exchange.

Section 15A. Registration of National Securities Associations. Aided by the Maloney Act of 1938, which amended the original Act by adding this Section, the formation of associations, such as the National Association of Securities Dealers, was authorized.

Section 15B. Concerns municipal securities dealers and transactions in municipal securities.

Section 15(c)(3) requires financial responsibility on the part of broker/ dealers.

Sections 12 and 13 deal with registration and report requirements for listed securities. Section 15(d) is a corresponding list of requirements with respect to unlisted securities.

Section 16. Directors, Officers, and Principal Stockholders. Requires statements of ownership of stocks by "insiders" and other related information.

Section 17. Accounts and Records. Not only does this Section require that all brokers and dealers maintain records in accord with such rules and regulations as the SEC may set forth, but it also authorizes the SEC to make examinations of any broker's or dealer's accounts, correspondence, memoranda, papers, books, and other records whenever the Commission deems it in the public interest. Rules and regulations issued by the SEC under this Section state the types of records that must be kept. In practice, an SEC examiner may walk into a broker/dealer's office and ask that all files and books be opened for inspection. Under the law, no broker/dealer may refuse the examiner access to any and all correspondence and records. A broker/dealer can have his or her registration suspended or revoked by failure to keep copies of all correspondence or to keep books and records as required by the SEC.

Section 17A. Settlement of Securities Transactions. Concerns the clearance and settlement of securities transactions, transfer of ownership, and safeguarding of securities and funds. Congress directed the SEC to facilitate the establishment of a national system for securities clearings.

Section 18. Liability for Misleading Statements. In a rather unusual statement of law, this Section makes a person both criminally and civilly liable for any misleading statements made in connection with the requirements of Section 15 of this Act.

Section 19. Registration, Responsibilities, and Oversight of Self-Regulatory Organizations. The SEC has the power to suspend for 12 months or revoke the registration of any national securities exchange or of any security, if the Commission is of the opinion that such action is necessary or appropriate for the protection of investors. Further, authority is granted the SEC to suspend or expel from an exchange any member or officer who has violated any of the provisions of this Act.

Other provisions of this Section give the SEC broad powers in supervising the rules of national securities exchanges, which the Commission may require to be changed or amended. In other words, the SEC supervises the members of an exchange through the exchange itself as well as on an individual basis.

Section 20. Liabilities of Controlling Persons. In effect, this Section states that if A commits an illegal act under the direction of B, who controls A, then both A and B are equally liable under the law. Section 20 also makes it illegal for any "controlling person" to "hinder, delay, or obstruct" the filing of any information required by the SEC under this Act.

Section 21. Investigations; Injunctions and Prosecution. In the Securities Act of 1933, Sections 19 and 20 gave the SEC special powers in the areas of investigation, subpoenaing of witnesses, prosecutions of offenses and the like. Section 21 of this Act is similar in its provisions.

Section 22. Hearings. It is interesting to note the difference in wording with respect to hearings in the 1933 Act and in this Act. Section 21 of the 1933 Act states that "All hearings *shall* be public...." Section 22 of the 1934 Act states "Hearings *may* be public...."

Section 23. Rules and Regulations. Power to make rules and regulations under this Act is specifically given the SEC and the Board of Governors of the Federal Reserve System by this Section. Both bodies are required to make annual reports to Congress.

Section 24. Public Availability of Information. To protect those required to file under this Act, this Section makes it possible for certain information, such as trade secrets, to be made confidential and not a matter of public record. This Section also forbids any member or employee of the Commission to use information that is not public for personal benefit.

Section 25. Court Review of Orders and Rules. Like Section 9 of the 1933 Act, this Section reserves final judgment on any issue to the courts, rather than to the Commission itself.

Section 26. Unlawful Representations. It is unlawful to make any representation to the effect that the SEC or the Federal Reserve Board has passed on the merits of any issue. Also, the failure of either body to take action against any person cannot be construed to mean that that person is not in violation of the law.

Section 27. Jurisdiction of Offenses and Suits. Jurisdiction of violations of this Act is given to the district courts of the United States.

Section 28. Effect on Existing Law. "The rights and remedies provided by this title (the Act) shall be in addition to any and all other rights and remedies that may exist in law or at equity…." The Section also leaves jurisdiction of offenses against a State law with the State.

Section 29. Validity of Contracts. No one can avoid compliance with the provisions of this Act by getting someone else to waive the requirements in any contract. Any contract that seeks to avoid the provisions of this Act are automatically void.

Section 30. Foreign Securities Exchange. It is unlawful to deal in securities whose issuers are within the jurisdiction of the United States on a foreign exchange in any manner other than that in which dealing in such securities would have to be handled in this country. In other words, the laws of the U.S. exchanges cannot be circumvented by placing business through a foreign exchange.

Section 31. Transaction Fees. Each national securities exchange is required to pay an annual fee to the Commission.

Section 32. Penalties. Individuals may be fined a maximum of $1,000,000 or sentenced to a maximum term of imprisonment of ten years, or both, for violations of the Act.

Section 33. Separability of Provisions. An escape section that states that if any one section of the Act is found to be invalid, such findings shall have no effect on the other sections.

Section 34. Effective Date, July 1, 1934.

¶24,015   Public Utility Holding Company Act of 1935

Interstate holding companies engaged through subsidiaries in the electric utility business or in the retail distribution of natural or manufactured gas are subject to regulation under the Act. These systems must register with the SEC and file initial and periodic reports. Detailed information concerning the organization, financial structure, and operations of the holding company and its subsidiaries is contained in these reports. If a holding company or its subsidiary meets certain specifications, the Commission can exempt it from part or all of the duties and obligations otherwise imposed by statute. Holding companies are subject to SEC regulations on matters such as structure of the system, acquisitions, combinations, and issues and sales of securities.

The most important provisions of the Act are the requirements for physical integration and corporation simplification of holding company systems. Integration standards restrict a holding company's operations to an *integrated utility system*. An integrated system is defined as one:

1. Capable of economical operation as a single coordinated system.
2. Confined to a single area or region in one or more states.
3. Not so large that it negates the advantages of localized management, efficient operation, and effective regulation.

The original structure and continued existence of any company in a holding company system must not necessarily complicate the corporate structure of the system or result in the distribution of voting power inequitably among security holders of the system.

The SEC can determine what action, if any, must be taken by registered holding companies and their subsidiaries to comply with Act requirements. The SEC can apply to federal courts for orders compelling compliance with Commission directives.

.01 Acquisitions

To be authorized by the SEC, the acquisition of securities and utility assets by holding companies and their subsidiaries must meet the following standards:

1. The acquisition must not tend toward interlocking relations or concentrating control to an extent detrimental to investors or the public interest.
2. Any consideration paid for the acquisition, including fees, commissions, and remuneration, must not be unreasonable.
3. The acquisition must not complicate the capital structure of the holding company systems or have a detrimental effect on system functions.
4. The acquisition must tend toward economical and efficient development of an integrated public utility system.

.02 Issuance and Sale of Securities

Proposed security issues by any holding company must be analyzed and evaluated by the SEC staff and approved by the Commission to ensure that the issues meet the following tests under prescribed standards of the law:

1. The security must be reasonably adapted to the security structure of the issuer, and of other companies in the same holding company system.
2. The security must be reasonably adapted to the earning power of the company.
3. The proposed issue must be necessary and appropriate to the economical and efficient operation of the company's business.
4. The fees, commissions, and other remuneration paid in connection with the issue must not be unreasonable.
5. The terms and conditions of the issue or sale of the security must not be detrimental to the public or investor interest.

Other provisions of the Act concern regulating dividend payments, inter-company loans, solicitations of proxies, consents and other authorizations, and insider trading.

¶24,016   Trust Indenture Act of 1939

This Act applies to bonds, debentures, notes, and similar debt securities offered for public sale and issued under trust indentures with more than $7.5 million of securities outstanding at any one time. Even though such securities are registered under the Securities Act, they cannot be offered for sale to the public unless the trust indenture conforms to statutory standards of this Act. Designed to safeguard the rights and interests of the investors, the Act also:

1. Prohibits the indenture trustee from conflicting interests which might interfere with exercising its duties on behalf of the securities purchasers.
2. Requires the trustee to be a corporation with minimum combined capital and surplus.
3. Imposes high standards of conduct and responsibility on the trustee.
4. Precludes, in the event of default, preferential collection of certain claims owing to the trustee by the issuer.
5. Provides that the issuer supply to the trustee evidence of compliance with indenture terms and conditions.
6. Requires the trustee to provide reports and notices to security holders.

Other provisions of the Act prohibit impairing the security holders' right to sue individually for principal and interest, except under certain circumstances. It also requires maintaining a list of security holders for their use in communicating with each other regarding their rights as security holders.

In 1987, the Commission sent a legislative proposal to Congress which would modernize procedures under the Act to meet the public's need in view of novel debt instruments and modern financing techniques. This legislative proposal was adopted and enacted into law in 1990. This law proved quite prescient as debt securities, for better or for worse, have only become more complicated with the passage of time.

¶24,017   Investment Advisers Act of 1940

This law establishes a pattern of regulating investment advisers. In some respects, it has provisions similar to the Securities Exchange Act provisions governing the conduct of brokers and dealers. This Act requires that persons or firms compensated for advising others about securities investment must register with the SEC and conform to the statutory standards designed to protect investors.

The Commission can deny, suspend, or revoke investment adviser registrations if, after notice and hearings, it finds that grounds for a statutory disqualification exist and that the action is in the public interest. Grounds for disqualification include conviction for certain financial crimes or securities law violations, injunctions based on such activities, conviction for violating the mail fraud statute, willfully filing false reports with the SEC, and willfully violating the Advisers Act, the Securities Act, the Securities Exchange Act, the Investment Company Act, or the rules of the Municipal Securities Rulemaking Board. The SEC can recommend criminal prosecution by the Department of Justice for violations of the laws, fraudulent misconduct or willful violation of Commission rules.

The law contains antifraud provisions and empowers the Commission to adopt rules defining fraudulent, deceptive, or manipulative acts and practices. It requires that investment advisers:

1. Disclose the nature of their interest in transactions executed for their clients.
2. Maintain books and records according to SEC rules.
3. Make books and records available to the SEC for inspections.

¶24,018   Trust Investment Company Act of 1940

Activities of companies engaged primarily in investing, reinvesting, and trading in securities, and whose own securities are offered to the public, are subject to statutory prohibitions and to SEC regulations under this Act. Public offerings of investment company securities must be registered under the Securities Act of 1933. It is important that investors understand that the SEC does not supervise the investment activities of these companies and that regulation by the Commission does not imply safety of investment in them.

In addition to the registration requirement for investment companies, the law requires that they disclose their financial condition and investment policies to provide investors complete information about their activities. This Act also:

1. Prohibits investment companies from substantially changing the nature of their business or investment policies without stockholder approval.
2. Prohibits persons guilty of securities fraud from serving as officers and directors.
3. Prevents underwriters, investment bankers, or brokers from constituting more than a minority of the directors of the companies.
4. Requires that management contracts and material changes be submitted to security holders for their approval.
5. Prohibits transactions between companies and their directors, officers, or affiliated companies or persons, except when approved by the SEC.
6. Forbids investment companies to issue senior securities except under specific conditions and upon specified terms.
7. Prohibits pyramiding of such companies and cross-ownership of their securities.

Other provisions of the Act involve advisory fees, nonconformance of an adviser's fiduciary duty, sales and repurchases of securities issued by investment companies, exchange offers, and other activities of investment companies, including special provisions for periodic payment plans and face-amount certificate companies.

Investment companies must register securities under the Securities Act, and also must file periodic reports and are subject to the SEC proxy and insider trading rules.

¶24,019   Corporation Reorganization

Reorganization proceedings in the U.S. Courts under Chapter 11 of the Bankruptcy Code are begun by a debtor voluntarily, or by its creditors. Federal bankruptcy law allows a debtor in reorganization to continue operating under the court's protection while the debtor attempts to rehabilitate its business and work out a plan to pay its debts. If a debtor corporation has publicly issued securities outstanding, the reorganization process may raise many issues that materially affect the rights of public investors.

Chapter 11 authorizes the SEC to appear in any reorganization case and to present its views on any issue. Although Chapter 11 applies to all types of business reorganizations, the SEC generally limits its participation to proceedings involving significant public investor interest, i.e., protecting public investors holding the debtor's securities, and participating in legal and policy issues of concern to public investors. The SEC also continues to address matters of traditional Commission expertise and interest relating to securities. When appropriate, the SEC comments on the adequacy of reorganization plan disclosure statements and participates where there is a Commission law enforcement interest.

Under Chapter 11, the debtor, official committees, and institutional creditors negotiate the terms of a reorganization plan. The court can confirm a reorganization plan if it is accepted by creditors for:

1. At least two-thirds of the amounts of allowed claims.
2. More than one-half the number of allowed claims.
3. At least two-thirds in amount of the allowed shareholder interest.

The principal safeguard for public investors is the requirement that a disclosure statement containing adequate information be transmitted by the debtor or plan proponent in connection with soliciting votes on the plan. In addition, reorganization plans involving publicly-held debt usually provide for issuing new securities to creditors and shareholders which are exempt from registration under Section 5 of the Securities Act of 1933.

CHAPTER 25
The Securities and Exchange Commission—Materiality

¶25,000   Overview

The Securities and Exchange Commission staff seems to always be thinking about *materiality*. One of the concerns being mentioned is the iron curtain versus rollover issue. Not all materiality problems were considered or solved by the SEC's Staff Accounting Bulletin (SAB) No. 99, *Materiality*. The SEC staff believes that more guidance may be needed in this particular area as well as others. The Commission has given a considerable amount of thought to the issue over the last year or so. The Commission has not completed the analysis, but is planning to do so in the near future. As with any undertaking dealing with amorphous concepts like materiality there will be some difficult issues to consider.

On March 9, 2022, Paul Munter, then Acting Chief Accountant at the SEC, issued a statement titled "Assessing Materiality: Focusing on the Reasonable Investor When Evaluating Errors." Although not authoritative, it provides good insight into the SEC's current position on materiality. He referred to the Supreme Court's statement that a fact is material if there is: "a substantial likelihood that the … fact would have been viewed by the reasonable investor as having significantly altered the 'total mix' of information made available." He addressed the colloquial "Big R" restatement and "little r" restatement. Big R refers to a restatement of prior-period financial statements. Little r refers to an adjustment not material to the prior-period financial statement but is material to the current financial statements so the adjustment to the prior-year information is only done in the current-year comparative financial information. The important point of both such errors is that they should be transparently disclosed to investors.

Mr. Munter addressed an increased need for objectivity in the assessment of qualitative factors. Although total restatements declined each year from 2013 to 2020, little r restatements as a percentage of total restatements increased from about 35 percent in 2005 to 76 percent in 2020. So the SEC is monitoring this and other restatement trends to understand the nature and prevalence of accounting errors and how they are corrected.

Mr. Munter also addressed accounting errors and internal control over financial reporting, and other auditor considerations.

On March 7, 2024, the SEC Investor Advisor Committee held a panel discussion related to several items, including SAB 99 and issues related to materiality. The general consensus was that SAB 99 has stood the test of time and is a solid foundation. However, additional comments supported the first paragraph and identified some concerns with SAB 99 and the concept of materiality. There is an issue related to issues being ignored because they are deemed immaterial but then become material over time. It was suggested that identifying such issues and addressing them before they become material could significantly enhance financial reporting. Also, it was suggested that it could be helpful to investors for entities to be required to disclose their policies and approaches to materiality. Ongoing discussion is expected to take place.

¶25,001   SEC Considering Problems Relating to Materiality

The SEC's Staff Accounting Bulletin No. 99 includes significant discussion of how materiality should be evaluated and provides detailed guidance in some areas, but it has not resolved all of the issues regarding materiality evaluations. Members of the staff believe that, to some extent, it has had the effect of causing confusion about how quantitative and qualitative considerations on materiality should be analyzed. It has been pointed out that some of the most difficult discussions are those having to do with the evaluation of materiality of errors. The staff has given careful consideration to that and other problems, including the following.

.01   Areas to Consider in Evaluation of Materiality of Errors

It is important to remember that accounting for something in a way that is not consistent with U.S. GAAP is still an error, regardless of whether the item is material. That is, just because an item is small does not mean that no accounting standards apply to it. It just means that accounting for it incorrectly does not materially misstate the financial statements.

Before a registrant decides not to apply specific requirements of U.S. GAAP because of materiality, the registrant and its auditors have an obligation to appropriately evaluate whether the impact of not applying that required guidance is material, as discussed in SAB Topic 1.M. That evaluation should be documented and completed for each reported financial period. The registrant's methodology for determining the quantitative impact of not applying the required guidance must allow the registrant and its auditor to reliably measure the difference for each reported financial period. If the pool of transactions to which the relevant accounting guidance has not been applied is not homogenous or varies from period to period, a sampling technique will most likely not allow the registrant and its auditor to reliably measure the impact of not applying U.S. GAAP.

Registrants need to keep in mind that, just like every other area of financial reporting, the initial conclusion about whether an error is material is the company's to make. Management should not merely ask its auditors whether an error must be corrected. Instead, an analysis should be done, considering all relevant qualitative and quantitative factors, to support a conclusion about whether the error represents a material misstatement, alone or in combination with other errors. Only after the registrant has reached a conclusion as to the materiality of an item should an auditor do so. The importance in every possible regard of disclosure at every opportunity cannot be exaggerated.

The SEC staff has asked that management not outsource the decision to the Commission. Too often SEC staff gets submissions from registrants seeking concurrence with not restating for an error based on materiality before they attempt to analysis why the error should not be considered material. In some cases, the submission has indicated that neither the registrant nor the auditors had yet reached a conclusion. The SEC explains that the Commission is not in a position to do the analysis. Commission personnel do not know as much about the entity's situation as management and the auditors do. However, the SEC will provide opinions on materiality considerations after the company and its auditors have completed their analyses. At best, this appears to be asking the SEC to do the registrant's and/or auditor's work; at worst, buck-passing.

The staff is considering an aspect of materiality analyses that is rarely talked about: the so-called income statement versus balance sheet approach question.

1. The *income statement method* of evaluating materiality, which is also called the *current-period or rollover method*, considers as an error the amounts recorded in the current period income statement that should not have been.
2. The *balance sheet method*, which is also called the *cumulative* or *iron curtain method*, considers as an error the total effect of all amounts that have been recorded in the company's books during the current or prior periods.

.02   Difference Between Iron Curtain and Rollover Methods

A simple example demonstrates the difference between these two methods: if a company increases a reserve $10 more than necessary each year for three years, the rollover method treats the error as being $10 in each year, whereas the iron curtain method treats the error as $10 in the first year, $20 in the second, and $30 in the third.

Assume that $10 would be immaterial to all periods, but $30 would be material. Under the rollover method, there is never a material error, unless the company wants to reverse the accrual in the fourth year, because doing so would put $30 out of period. So, under the rollover method, eliminating the overaccrual becomes a material error. Under the iron curtain method, the error would need to be corrected in year three, as it became material that year.

Auditing standards briefly mention this debate in a footnote, noting only that "The measurement of the effect, if any, on the current period's financial statements of misstatements uncorrected in prior periods involves accounting considerations and is therefore not addressed in this section." Because the debate is an accounting one, not an auditing one, a problem arises. Unfortunately, accounting literature does not deal with this at all.

The SEC believes that auditors generally believe the iron curtain method is the preferable method in most situations. For various reasons, both methods are used in practice and have been accepted by auditors and regulators. This is often considered to be a policy election, and the fact that the accounting literature does not specify which method to use appears to support acceptability of both methods. However, a company seldom, if ever discloses—in its summary of accounting policies or elsewhere—which method it uses to evaluate errors and why. To do so would, of course, be a welcomed gesture toward greater transparency.

¶25,002   Possible Direction of New Guidance

Previous initiatives to provide guidance on which method should be selected for particular situations have been made, with no substantive progress. Recent events have the SEC thinking that the time has come to provide more guidance in this area. Although there are no plans ready to provide that guidance immediately, representatives of the Agency have been bringing up the topic of materiality in speeches and round tables, and specifically discussing the iron curtain and rollover methods. With the issuance of Staff Accounting Bulletin 108, the SEC requires both the Iron Curtain and Rollover methods.

¶25,003   SEC Staff Accounting Bulletin 99

The Securities and Exchange Staff Accounting Bulletin (SAB) 99, *Materiality*, issued in August 1999, delineates the staff's views concerning reliance on certain quantitative benchmarks to assess materiality in preparing financial statements and performing audits of those financial statements. The SEC has decided that the practice of adopting an arbitrary margin of error is inappropriate. SAB 99 concludes that misstatements are not immaterial simply because they fall beneath a numerical threshold.

The SEC is quick to point out that statements in the staff accounting bulletins are not rules or interpretations of the Commission, nor are they published as bearing the Commission's official approval. However, they do represent interpretations and practices followed by the Division of Corporation Finance and the Office of the Chief Accountant in *administering the disclosure requirements of the federal securities laws.* To put it bluntly, anyone ignoring this SAB, is putting himself, herself and/or their company at risk: this new materiality test is the standard the SEC will use for enforcement purposes.

It should be emphasized that SAB 99 does not constitute a new approach to the consideration of "materiality," but is an attempt to "shore up" the definition of the concept and in so doing reemphasize the Commission's foremost goal—the protection of the investor. Therefore, it provides guidance in applying materiality thresholds to the *preparation of financial statements filed with the Commission and the performance of audits of those financial statements.*

.01   Misusing the "Rule of Thumb"

The SEC staff has been cognizant of the fact that many registrants gradually adopted as "rules of thumb" a 5 percent quantitative margin of error in preparing their financial statements, and that auditors also have used these thresholds in their evaluation of whether items might be considered material to users of a registrant's financial statements. One rule of thumb in particular suggests that the *misstatement* or *omission* of an item that falls under a 5omission of an item that falls under a 5 percent threshold is not material in the absence of particularly "egregious circumstances, such as self-dealing or misappropriation by senior management." (In this SAB, "misstatement" or "omission" refers to a financial statement assertion that would not be in conformity with U.S. GAAP.)

The staff reminds registrants and the auditors of their financial statements that exclusive reliance on this or any percentage or numerical threshold has no basis in the *accounting literature* or the *law*.

The use of a percentage as a numerical threshold, such as 5 percent, may provide the basis for a *preliminary* assumption that, without considering all relevant circumstances, a deviation of less than the specified percentage with respect to a particular item on the registrant's financial statements is unlikely to be material. The staff has no objection to such a "rule of thumb" as an *initial* step in assessing materiality. But the bulletin cautions that quantifying the magnitude of a misstatement in percentage terms can be only the beginning of an analysis of materiality; it cannot be used as a substitute for a *full analysis* of all relevant considerations.

¶25,004   Defining Materiality

Materiality concerns the significance of an item to users of a registrant's financial statements. A matter is "material" if there is a substantial likelihood that a reasonable person would consider it important. Early in its existence, the Financial Accounting Standards Board made this clear. In its Statement of Financial Accounting Concepts 2, the FASB stated the essence of the concept of materiality as follows: *The omission or misstatement of an item in a financial report is material if, in the light of surrounding circumstances, the magnitude of the item is such that it is probable that the judgment of a reasonable person relying upon the report would have been changed or influenced by the inclusion or correction of the item.*

This Statement is almost identical to that expressed by the courts in interpreting the federal securities laws. In 1976, the Supreme Court held that a fact is material if there is "a substantial likelihood that the fact would have been viewed by the reasonable investor as having significantly altered the 'total mix' of information made available."

Thus, we see that an assessment of materiality requires that the facts be considered in the context of the "surrounding circumstances," according to accounting literature, or the "total mix" of information, in the opinion of the Supreme Court.

¶25,005   Qualitative and Quantitative Factors Are Important

In the context of a misstatement of a financial statement item, while the "total mix" includes the *size* in numerical or percentage terms of the misstatement, it also includes the *factual context* in which the user of financial statements appraises the financial statement item. Therefore, financial management and the auditor must consider both "quantitative" and "qualitative" factors in assessing an item's materiality. Court decisions, Commission rules and enforcement actions, and accounting and auditing literature have all considered "qualitative" factors in various contexts.

The FASB has repeatedly emphasized that materiality cannot be reduced to a numerical formula. In FASB Statement 2, the FASB noted that some commenters had urged it to promulgate quantitative materiality guides for use in various situations. The FASB decided against a blanket approach as representing only a "minority view" and went on to explain, "The predominant view is that materiality judgments can properly be made only by those who have all the facts."

According to FASB 2, an additional factor in making materiality judgments revolves around the *degree of precision* that can be attained in *estimating* the judgment item. The amount of deviation that is considered immaterial may increase as the attainable degree of precision decreases. As an example, the SAB points out that *accounts payable* usually can be estimated more accurately than can *contingent liabilities* arising from litigation or threats of it. Therefore, a deviation considered to be material in figuring accounts payable may be quite trivial when considering contingent liabilities.

¶25,006   FASB Considerations and Opinion

The FASB's present position is that no general standards of materiality can be formulated to take into account all the considerations that enter into an experienced human judgment. The Board noted that, in certain limited circumstances, the SEC and other authoritative bodies have issued quantitative materiality guidance, citing as examples guidelines ranging from 1 to 10 percent with respect to a variety of disclosures. They looked at contradictory studies: one showing a lack of uniformity among auditors on materiality judgments; another suggesting widespread use of a "rule of thumb" of 5 to 10 percent of net income. They also considered whether an evaluation of materiality could be based solely on anticipating the market's reaction to accounting information.

In the end, the FASB rejected any simplified approach to discharging "the onerous duty of making materiality decisions" in favor of an approach that takes into account *all relevant considerations*. In so doing, it made clear that, "Magnitude by itself, without regard to the nature of the item and the circumstances in which the judgment has to be made, will not generally be a sufficient basis for a materiality judgment."

The FASB's definition of materiality and related information may be found in Statement of Financial Accounting Concepts No. 8, Chapter 3, *Qualitative Characteristics of Useful Financial Information.*

¶25,007   Small Figures May Cause Big Misstatements

Evaluation of materiality requires a registrant and its auditor to consider all the relevant circumstances, and the staff believes that there are numerous circumstances in which misstatements below five percent could well be material. As does the SEC Chairman who pointed out that given the attitude of investors in the stock market today, *everything* matters when "...missing an earnings projection by a penny can result in a loss of millions of dollars in market capitalization."

SAB 99 takes into consideration this concern that *qualitative factors* may cause misstatements of quantitatively extremely small amounts to be material. Thus, the bulletin, in effect, cautions the auditor that as a result of the interaction of quantitative and qualitative considerations in materiality judgments, misstatements of relatively small amounts that come to the auditor's attention *could* have a material effect upon the financial statements. Among those considerations that may well render material a quantitatively small misstatement of a financial statement item are whether the misstatement:

1. Results from an item capable of precise measurement or from an estimate and, if so, the degree of imprecision inherent in the estimate.
2. Masks a change in earnings or other trends.
3. Hides a failure to meet analysts' consensus expectations for the enterprise.
4. Actually changes a loss into income or vice versa.
5. Concerns a *segment* or other portion of the registrant's business that has been identified as playing a *significant role* in the registrant's operations or profitability.
6. Affects the registrant's compliance with regulatory requirements.
7. Affects the registrant's compliance with loan covenants or other contractual requirements.
8. Has the effect of increasing management's compensation, for example, by satisfying requirements for the award of bonuses or other forms of incentive compensation.
9. Involves concealment of an unlawful transaction.
10. Aims toward smoothing earnings artificially to give a false impression of stability.

The bulletin does not claim this to be an exhaustive list of the circumstances that may affect the materiality of a quantitatively small misstatement, but it certainly makes the decision process a little more exhausting than merely adhering to some predetermined "percentage."

¶25,008   Other Considerations

Other factors and situations may bring to question the materiality of a quantitatively small misstatement of a financial statement item:

1. The demonstrated volatility of the price of a registrant's securities in response to certain types of disclosures may provide guidance as to whether *investors* regard quantitatively small misstatements as material.

2. Consideration of potential market reaction to disclosure of a misstatement is by itself "too blunt an instrument to be depended on" in considering whether a fact is material. However, when management or the independent auditor expects (based, for example, on a pattern of market performance) that a known misstatement *may* result in a significant positive or negative market reaction, that expected reaction should be taken into account when considering whether a misstatement is material.

Even if management does not expect a significant market reaction, a misstatement still may be material and should be evaluated under the criteria discussed in this SAB.

¶25,009   "Managed" Earnings—Here, There, and Everywhere

For the reasons noted above, the staff believes that a registrant and the auditors of its financial statements should *not* assume that even small intentional misstatements in financial statements—for example, those pursuant to actions to "manage" earnings—are immaterial. (Intentional management of earnings and intentional misstatements, as used in SAB 99, do not include insignificant errors and omissions that may occur in systems and recurring processes in the normal course of business.)

While the *intent* of management does not render a misstatement material, it may provide significant evidence of materiality. The evidence may be particularly revealing when management has intentionally misstated items in the financial statements to "manage" reported earnings.

In such an instance, management has presumably done so believing that the resulting amounts and trends *would be significant* to users of the registrant's financial statements. Or have the earnings been "managed" just enough to meet or marginally exceed the expectations of securities analysts who appear to be very significant players in today's volatile markets?

SAB 99 mentions that assessment of materiality should occur not only in annual financial reports, but also during the preparation of each quarterly or interim financial statement. After all, savvy investors and even less well informed ones are known to research these statements.

.01   Consider the Investor

The staff believes that investors generally would regard as significant a management practice to overstate or understate earnings up to an amount just short of a percentage threshold in order to "manage" earnings. Investors presumably also would regard with a jaundiced eye an accounting practice that, in essence, rendered all earnings figures subject to a management-directed margin of misstatement.

The materiality of a misstatement may be judged based upon where it appears in the financial statements. For example, if a misstatement involves a segment of the registrant's operations, in assessing materiality of a misstatement to the financial statements taken as a whole, registrants and their auditors should consider:

1. The *size* of the misstatement.
2. The *significance* of that particular segment information to the financial statements as a whole.

A misstatement of the revenue and operating profit of a relatively small segment which management indicates is important to the future profitability of the entity is more likely to be material to investors than a misstatement in a segment that management has not identified as especially important. In assessing the materiality of misstatements in segment information, as with materiality generally, situations may arise in practice where the auditor will conclude that a matter relating to segment information is *qualitatively material* even though, in his or her judgment, it is *quantitatively immaterial* to the financial statements as a whole.

¶25,010   Aggregating and Netting Misstatements

In determining whether multiple misstatements cause the financial statements to be materially misstated, registrants and the auditors of their financial statements should consider the effect of each misstatement separately, and in the aggregate.

Obviously, the concept of materiality takes into consideration that some information, whether viewed individually or as a part of the whole report, may be required for fair presentation of financial statements in conformity with U.S. GAAP in one context or the other. Furthermore, it is necessary to evaluate misstatements in light of quantitative and qualitative factors. It is also necessary to consider whether the following can materially misstate the financial statements taken as a whole:

1. Individual line item amounts
2. Subtotals
3. Totals

This requires consideration of:

1. The significance of an item to a particular type of business enterprise; for example, inventories to a manufacturing company. (An adjustment to inventory seen as immaterial to pretax or net income could be material to the financial statements because it could affect a working capital ratio or cause the registrant to be in default of a loan covenant.)

2. The pervasiveness of the misstatement—whether it affects the presentation of numerous financial statement items.
3. The effect of the misstatement on the financial statements taken as a whole.

Accountants and auditors should consider whether each misstatement is material, regardless of its effect when combined with other misstatements. The literature notes that the analysis should consider whether the misstatement of "individual amounts" causes a material misstatement of the financial statements taken as a whole. As with materiality generally, this analysis requires consideration of both quantitative and qualitative factors.

If the misstatement of an individual amount causes the financial statements as a whole to be materially misstated, that effect cannot be eliminated by other misstatements whose effect may be to diminish the impact of the misstatement on other financial statement items.

Quantitative materiality assessments often are made by comparing adjustments to revenues, gross profit, pretax and net income, total assets, stockholders' equity, or individual line items in the financial statements. The particular items in the financial statements to be considered as a basis for the materiality determination depend on the proposed adjustment to be made and other factors, such as those identified in this SAB. For example, an adjustment to inventory that is immaterial to pretax income or net income may be material to the financial statements because it may affect a working capital ratio or cause the registrant to be in default of loan covenants.

.01 Aggregation May Lead to Aggravation

If a registrant's revenues are a material financial statement item and if they are materially overstated, the financial statements taken as a whole will be materially misleading even if the effect on earnings is completely offset by an equivalent overstatement of expenses. Even though *one misstatement* of an individual amount may not cause the financial statements taken as a whole to be materially misstated, it may nonetheless, when *aggregated with other misstatements*, render the financial statements taken as a whole to be materially misleading.

Registrants and the auditors of their financial statements should consider the effect of the misstatement on *subtotals* or *totals*. The auditor should aggregate all misstatements that affect each subtotal or total and consider whether the misstatements in the aggregate affect the subtotal or total in a way that causes the registrant's financial statements taken as a whole to be materially misleading.

The staff believes that, in considering the aggregate effect of multiple misstatements on a subtotal or total, accountants and auditors should exercise particular care when considering misstatement of an estimated amount with a misstatement of an item capable of precise measurement. As noted above, *assessments of materiality should never be purely mechanical;* given the imprecision inherent in estimates, there is by definition a corresponding imprecision in the aggregation of misstatements involving estimates with those that do not involve an estimate.

Registrants and auditors also should consider the effect of misstatements from prior periods on the current financial statements. For example, the auditing literature states that matters underlying adjustments proposed by the auditor but not recorded by the entity could potentially cause future financial statements to be materially misstated, even though the auditor has concluded that the adjustments are not material to the current financial statements. This may particularly be the case where immaterial misstatements recur in several years and the cumulative effect becomes material in the current year.

¶25,011   Intentional Immaterial Misstatements

The SEC reemphasizes their caution that a registrant may *not* make intentional immaterial misstatements in its financial statements. A registrant's management may never intentionally make adjustments to various financial statement items in a manner inconsistent with U.S. GAAP.

In any accounting period in which such actions might be taken, it could be that none of the individual adjustments would be considered material, nor would the aggregate effect on the financial statements taken as a whole be material *for the period*.

The adjustments could even be considered irrelevant; however, at the same time, they could actually be unlawful. In the books and records provisions under the Exchange Act, even if misstatements are immaterial, registrants must comply with the law. Under these provisions, each registrant with securities registered pursuant to the Act, or required to file reports pursuant to it, must:

1. Make and keep books, records, and accounts, which, in *reasonable detail*, accurately, and fairly reflect the transactions and dispositions of assets of the registrant.
2. Maintain internal accounting controls that are sufficient to provide *reasonable assurances* that, among other things, transactions are recorded as necessary to permit the preparation of financial statements in conformity with U.S. GAAP.

FASB Statements of Financial Accounting Standards generally include the statement: "The provisions of this Statement need not be applied to immaterial items." This SAB does not countermand that provision of the Statements. However, it does vanquish the 5 percent of net income quantitative test often applied in the past. The SEC admits that, in theory, this language in the FASBs is subject to interpretation that a registrant may intentionally record immaterial items in a manner that would unquestionably be contrary to U.S. GAAP if the misstatement were considered material. It should be carefully noted, however, that the staff believes the FASB did not intend such a conclusion. Regardless, some companies have in the past apparently interpreted the sentence in just that fashion. They evidently felt they could ignore certain immaterial transactions and misapply U.S. GAAP to so-called immaterial transactions with impunity. No more!

Both the U.S. Code and the Securities Exchange Act indicate that criminal liability may be imposed if a person knowingly circumvents or knowingly fails to implement a system of internal accounting controls or knowingly falsifies books, records, or accounts. This should make it perfectly clear that any degree of "cooking the books," setting up "cookie jar reserves," "managing," or otherwise obfuscating may result in violations of the securities laws.

¶25,012   The Prudent Man Concept

In this context, determinations of what constitutes "reasonable assurance" and "reasonable detail" are based not on a "materiality" analysis but on the level of detail and degree of assurance that would satisfy *prudent* officials in the conduct of their own affairs. The books and records provisions of the Exchange Act, in which this is developed, originally were passed as part of the Foreign Corrupt Practices Act (FCPA). In the conference committee report regarding the 1988 amendments to the FCPA, the report stated, "The conference committee adopted the prudent man qualification in order to clarify that the current standard does not connote an unrealistic degree of exactitude or precision. The concept of reasonableness contemplates the weighing of a number of relevant factors, including the costs of compliance."

¶25,013   "Reasonableness" Should Not Be Unreasonable

The SEC staff is well aware of the fact that there is little authoritative guidance regarding the "reasonableness" standard in the Exchange Act. A principal statement of the Commission's policy in this area was set forth in a 1981 address by the SEC Chairman who noted that, like materiality, "reasonableness" is not an "absolute standard of exactitude for corporate records."

Unlike materiality, however, "reasonableness" is not solely a measure of the significance of a financial statement item to investors. "Reasonableness," here reflects a judgment as to whether an issuer's failure to correct a known misstatement brings into question the purposes underlying the accounting provisions of the Exchange Act. In assessing whether a misstatement results in a violation of a registrant's obligation to keep books and records that are accurate "in reasonable detail," registrants and their auditors should consider, in addition to the factors discussed above concerning an evaluation of a misstatement's potential materiality, the following factors:

1. *The significance of the misstatement.* Though the staff does not believe that registrants need to make in-depth determination of significance regarding all immaterial items, it is "reasonable" to treat misstatements whose effects are clearly inconsequential differently from possibly more significant ones.

2. *How the misstatement arose.* It is undoubtedly never "reasonable" for registrants to record misstatements or not to correct known misstatements, even immaterial ones, as part of an ongoing effort directed by or known to senior management for the purposes of "managing" earnings. On the other hand, insignificant misstatements that arise from the operation of systems or recurring processes in the normal course of business generally will not cause a registrant's books to be inaccurate "in reasonable detail."

   To carry it a step further, the SEC appears to be emphasizing the caution that criminal penalties *will be imposed* where acts of commission or omission in keeping books or records or administering accounting controls *are deliberately aimed at* falsification, or circumvention of the accounting controls set forth in the Exchange Act. (This would also include the deliberate falsification of books and records and other conduct calculated to evade the *internal accounting controls requirement* which is about to come under close scrutiny by the Commission. See below.)

3. *The cost of correcting the misstatement.* The books and records provisions of the Exchange Act do not require registrants to make major expenditures to correct small misstatements. (To put it succinctly, thousands of dollars should ordinarily not be spent conserving hundreds.) Conversely, where there is little cost or delay involved in correcting a misstatement, failure to do so is unlikely to be "reasonable."

4. *The clarity of authoritative accounting guidance with respect to the misstatement.* In instances where reasonable individuals could differ about the appropriate accounting treatment of a financial statement item, a failure to correct it may not render the registrant's financial statements inaccurate "in reasonable detail." On the other hand, when there is little basis for reasonable disagreement, the case for leaving a misstatement uncorrected is decidedly weaker.

The SEC acknowledges that there may be additional indicators of "reasonableness" that registrants, their accountants and auditors may take into consideration. Because the judgment is seldom unanimous, the staff will be inclined to continue to defer to judgments that "allow a business, acting in good faith, to comply with the Act's accounting provisions in an innovative and cost-effective way."

¶25,014   The Auditor's Response to Intentional Misstatements

The Exchange Act requires auditors to consider several courses of action when discovering an illegal act which is defined as "…an act or omission that violates any law, or any rule or regulation having the force of law."

The statute specifies among other things that:

1. These obligations are triggered regardless of whether or not the illegal acts are considered to have a material effect upon the financial statements of the issuer.
2. The auditor is required to inform the appropriate level of management of an illegal act unless it is clearly "inconsequential."
3. When an auditor discovers an intentional misstatement of immaterial items in a registrant's financial statements which violates the Exchange Act and thus is an illegal act, the auditor must take steps to see that the registrant's audit committee is "adequately informed" about the illegal act. (Since the provisions of the Act are triggered regardless of whether an illegal act has a material effect on the registrant's financial statements, when the illegal act is a misstatement in the registrant's financial statements, the auditor is required to report that illegal act to the audit committee irrespective of any "netting" of the misstatements with other financial statement items.)

Auditors who become aware of intentional misstatements may also be required to:

1. Reevaluate the degree of audit risk involved in the audit engagement.
2. Determine whether to revise the nature, timing, and extent of audit procedures accordingly.
3. Consider whether to resign.

Cases of intentional misstatements may serve as a signal of the existence of reportable conditions or material weaknesses in the registrant's system of internal accounting control that should have been designed to detect and deter improper accounting and financial reporting.

.01   Management's Role

As stated by the National Commission on Fraudulent Financial Reporting (also known as the Treadway Commission) in its 1987 report, the *tone* set by top management, the corporate environment, or the culture within which financial reporting occurs is the most important factor contributing to the integrity of the financial reporting process. Even if there is an in-depth set of written rules and procedures, if this tone is lax or permissive, fraudulent financial reporting is more likely to occur.

Here again, it is up to the auditor to report to a registrant's audit committee any *reportable conditions or material weaknesses* in a registrant's system of internal accounting control that he or she uncovers in the course of the examination of the registrant's financial statements.

.02   Materiality in Professional Standards

In 2019, the AICPA's Auditing Standards Board (ASB) issued Statement on Auditing Standards (SAS) No. 138, *Amendments to the Description of the Concept of Materiality*, and Statement on Standards for Attestation Engagements (SSAE) No. 20 of the same title. These statements align the materiality concepts discussed in AICPA Professional Standards with the descriptions of materiality used by the U.S. judicial system, the PCAOB, the SEC, and FASB.

¶25,015   U.S. GAAP Takes Precedence Over Industry Practice

It has been argued that registrants should be permitted to continue to follow an *industry* accounting practice even though that practice is—or has become—inconsistent with authoritative accounting literature. Such a situation might occur:

1.   If a practice is developed when there are few transactions.
2.   The accounting results are clearly inconsequential.
3.   That particular industry practice never changed despite a subsequent growth in the number or materiality of such transactions.

Regardless of how or why the practice had developed, this may not be considered a valid argument for its continued use. Authoritative literature *always* takes precedence over industry practice that is contrary to U.S. GAAP.

.01   Determining Appropriate Accounting Treatment

As pointed out above, SAB 99 is not intended to change current law or guidance in the accounting or auditing literature. This SAB and the authoritative accounting literature cannot specifically address all of the novel and complex business transactions and events that may occur. Accordingly, registrants may at times account for, and make disclosures about these transactions and events based on analogies to similar situations or other factors.

The SEC staff may not, however, always be convinced that a registrant's determination is the most appropriate under the circumstances. When disagreements occur after a transaction or an event has been reported, the consequences may be severe for registrants, auditors, and, most important, for the *users of financial statements* who have a right to expect consistent accounting and reporting for, and disclosure of, similar transactions and events.

The SEC, therefore, encourages registrants, their accountants and auditors to discuss on a timely basis with the staff proposed accounting treatments for, and disclosures about, transactions or events not specifically covered by the existing accounting literature. This caution should also apply in instances where there is any question in the mind of any of the entity's "team" concerning the appropriateness of a particular procedure. In more forceful terms, "Don't let creative accounting get you or your firm into trouble." Tell the truth.

¶25,016   SEC Adopts Standards for Risk Management and Operations of Clearing Agencies

The Securities and Exchange Commission adopted a rule in October 2012, that establishes standards for how registered clearing agencies should manage their risks and run their operations.

Clearing agencies generally act as middlemen to the parties in a securities transaction. They play a critical role in the securities markets by ensuring that transactions settle on time and on the agreed-upon terms.

The rule was adopted in accordance with the Securities Exchange Act of 1934 and the Dodd-Frank Wall Street Reform and Consumer Protection Act. The Dodd Frank Act provides the SEC with additional authority to establish standards for clearing agencies, including for those clearing agencies that clear security-based swaps.

These new rules are designed to ensure that clearing agencies will be able to fulfill their responsibilities in the multi-trillion dollar derivatives market as well as more traditional securities markets, according to SEC Chairman. The rules are part of a broader effort to put in place an entirely new regulatory regime intended to mitigate systemic risks that emerged during the financial crisis.

The new rule requires registered clearing agencies that provide central counterparty services to maintain certain standards with respect to risk management and operations. Among other things, the rules set standards with respect to:

- Measurement and management of credit exposures,
- Margin requirements,
- Financial resources, and
- Margin model validation.

The rule also establishes certain recordkeeping and financial disclosure requirements for all registered clearing agencies as well as several new operational standards for these entities.

The new rule 17Ad-22 became effective 60 days after the date of publication in the Federal Register.

.01 Background

A clearing agency generally acts as a middleman between the parties to a transaction, and when acting as a central counterparty it assumes the risk should there be a default. When structured and operated appropriately, such a clearing agency can provide such benefits as improving the management of counterparty risk and reducing outstanding exposures through multilateral netting of trades.

Because of the integral role that clearing agencies play in the securities markets, Congress directed the SEC to oversee these entities.

.02 Risk Management Standards for Central Counterparties

Under the final rule, a registered clearing agency that performs central counterparty services is required to establish, implement, maintain and enforce written policies and procedures reasonably designed to:

- Measure its credit exposures to its participants at least once a day.
- Use margin requirements to limit its credit exposures to participants using risk-based models and parameters, to be reviewed at least monthly.
- Maintain sufficient financial resources to withstand, at a minimum, a default by the participant family to which it has the largest exposure in extreme but plausible market conditions (and a default by the two participant families to which it has the largest exposures for security-based swap clearing agencies).
- Provide for an annual model validation by a qualified person who is free from influence from the persons responsible for the development or operation of the models being validated.

.03 Membership Standards for Central Counterparties

The final rule also requires a registered clearing agency that performs central counterparty services to establish, implement, maintain, and enforce written policies and procedures reasonably designed to:

- Provide the opportunity to obtain membership in the clearing agency for persons who are not dealers or security-based swap dealers on fair and reasonable terms.

- Have membership standards that do not require participants to maintain a minimum size portfolio or minimum transaction volume.
- Provide a person that maintains net capital equal to or greater than $50 million with the ability to obtain membership provided that the person is able to comply with other reasonable membership standards, with net capital requirements being scalable in relation to the risks posed by such person's activities to the clearing agency.

.04   Recordkeeping and Financial Disclosure by Registered Clearing Agencies

Under the final rule, registered clearing agencies that perform central counterparty services are required to calculate and maintain a record of the financial resources that would be needed in the event of a participant default. Clearing agencies must perform the calculation quarterly or at any time upon the SEC's request.

In addition, the final rule will require each registered clearing agency to post on its Web site its annual audited financial statements within 60 days after the end of its fiscal year.

.05   Other Standards for Clearance and Settlement Processes

The final rules also require each registered clearing agency to (as applicable):

- Have rules and procedures that provide for a well-founded, transparent and enforceable legal framework.
- Require participants to have sufficient financial resources and robust operational capacity to meet obligations arising from participation and publicly disclose the clearing agency's participation requirements.
- Hold assets in a manner whereby risk of loss or delay is minimized and assets are invested in instruments with minimal credit, market and liquidity risks.
- Identify sources of operational risk and minimize them through the development of appropriate systems, controls and procedures.
- Employ money settlement arrangements that eliminate or strictly limit settlement bank risks and require funds transfers to the clearing agency to be final when effected.
- Be cost-effective in meeting the requirements of participants while maintaining safe and secure operations.
- Evaluate risks involved with any link arrangements and ensure they are managed prudently.
- Have governance arrangements that are clear and transparent and promote the effectiveness of risk management.
- Provide market participants with sufficient information for them to identify and evaluate the risks and costs associated with the clearing agency's services.

- Immobilize and dematerialize stock certificates and transfer them by book entry to the greatest extent possible.
- Make key aspects of its default procedures publicly available and establish default procedures that ensure timely action to contain losses and liquidity pressures.
- Ensure settlement no later than the end of the settlement day and require intraday or real-time finality where necessary to reduce risks.
- Eliminate principal risk by linking securities transfers to funds transfers to achieve delivery versus payment.
- Institute risk controls to address participants' failure to settle when the clearing agency performs central securities depository services and extends intraday credit.
- State to participants the clearing agency's obligations with respect to physical delivery risks and identify and manage associated risks.

CHAPTER 26
The Sarbanes-Oxley Act of 2002

¶26,000   Overview

The passage of the Sarbanes-Oxley Act in 2002 marked an important turning point for accountants. The accounting profession, which had considered itself self-regulated to that point, was now under the direct regulation of federal law, at least for auditors. Although the ethics rules promulgated by the AICPA had stressed the importance of independence in fact and appearance, Sarbanes-Oxley specified a number of rules to help ensure that independence became a reality. New rules regulated the board of directors and its audit committee, proscribed specific non-audit activities, and required the employment of a code of ethics.

In this chapter, we describe provisions of the law and update changes and developments since its inception. Further information on auditor independence and the audit committee is contained in Chapter 16, "Auditor Independence and the Audit Committee."

Although Sarbanes-Oxley became law in 2002, its implementation and authority continue to meet challenges. For example, the decision of the U.S. Supreme Court on June 28, 2010, stated that the provision permitting the Securities and Exchange Commission to remove a member of the Public Company Accounting Oversight Board (PCAOB) only "for good cause" did indeed violates the Constitution's separation of powers. In effect, this gave the SEC the power to remove board members at will, but left intact the rest of the Sarbanes-Oxley law governing the Board. Even more than that, in effect it validated the entire Act and its past and future actions.

An important part of that future action was determined by the Dodd-Frank Wall Street Reform and Consumer Protection Act which solved the problem of whether or not smaller companies should be required to comply with Section 404(b) of the Sarbanes-Oxley Act. The Dodd-Frank Act added Section 404(c), which provides that the auditor attestation requirement of Section 404(b) will permanently apply only to accelerated filers and large accelerated filers, as detailed below.

¶26,001   SEC Adopts Amendments to Rules and Forms

On September 21, 2010, the Securities and Exchange Commission made it all very official by adopting amendments to conform to provisions in the Dodd-Frank Act:

The Commission is adopting amendments to its rules and forms to conform them to new Section 404(c) of the Sarbanes-Oxley Act, as added by Section 989G of the Dodd-Frank Act. Section 404(c) provides that Section 404(b) of the Sarbanes-Oxley Act shall not apply with respect to any audit report prepared for an issuer that is neither an accelerated filer nor a large accelerated filer as defined in Rule 12b-29 under the Exchange Act. Prior to enactment of the Dodd-Frank Act, a non-accelerated filer would have been required, under existing Commission rules, to include an attestation report of its registered public accounting firm on internal control over financial reporting in the filer's annual report filed with the Commission for fiscal years ending on or after June 15, 2010.

To conform the Commission's rules to Section 404(c) of the Sarbanes-Oxley Act, these amendments remove the requirement for a non-accelerated filer to include in its annual report an attestation report of the filer's registered public accounting firm. The Commission is adopting a conforming change to the rules concerning management's disclosure in the annual report regarding inclusion of an attestation report to provide that the disclosure only applies if an attestation report is included. The Commission is also making a conforming change to Rule 2-02(f) of Regulation S-X to clarify that an auditor of a non-accelerated filer need not include in its audit report an assessment of the issuer's internal control over financial reporting.

All issuers, including non-accelerated filers, continue to be subject to the requirements of Section 404(a) of the Sarbanes-Oxley Act. Section 404(a) and its implementing rules require that an issuer's annual report include a report of management on the issuer's internal control over financial reporting.

NOTE: Although the term "non-accelerated filer" is not defined in Commission rules, it is used to refer to a reporting company that does not meet the definition of either an "accelerated filer" or a "large accelerated filer" under Exchange Act Rule 12b-2. Under Exchange Act Rule 12b-2, an accelerated filer is an issuer that "had an aggregate worldwide market value of the voting and non-voting common equity held by its non-affiliates of $75 million or more, but less than $700 million, as of the last business day of the issuer's most recently completed second fiscal quarter" and a large accelerated filer is an issuer that "had an aggregate worldwide market value of the voting and non-voting common equity held by its non-affiliates of $700 million or more, as of the last business day of the issuer's most recently completed second fiscal quarter". In addition, for both definitions, the issuer needs to have been subject to reporting requirements for at least 12 calendar months, have filed at least one annual report, and not be eligible to use the requirements for smaller reporting companies for its annual and quarterly reports.

¶26,002 Dodd-Frank Requires Two Studies About Section 404 Compliance

The Dodd-Frank Wall Street Reform and Consumer Protection Act mandates a study of the costs and benefits resulting from compliance with Sarbanes-Oxley. The SEC is required to report to Congress within nine months how to reduce the time and costs for the audit of internal control over financial reporting even further for companies in the market cap range of $75 million to $250 million. Congress wants to know if companies in that range would be more inclined to list their initial public offerings on U.S. exchanges if the audit requirements were either reduced or removed entirely.

The Dodd-Frank Act also requires that within three years, the Government Accountability Office conduct a study and report on how the 404(b) exemption may affect the number of restatements, the cost of capital, and influence investor confidence. In addition Congress is interested in further guidance on the costs and benefits of voluntary compliance with the audit of internal controls and whether exempted companies should be required to disclose to investors that they are not providing a 404(b) audit report.

¶26,003   Answering the Call for Action to Help Small Companies

Not only did the PCAOB and Securities and Exchange Commission take their responsibility seriously to help companies interpret Section 404 of Sarbanes-Oxley in a way that would save both time and money, they very actively took measures to rectify the situation. With rumblings about Congress being urged to amend, negate, modify Sarbanes-Oxley, they took major steps to make Section 404 less costly, without lessening its ability to protect the investor.

The SEC provided interpretive guidance for management, and the PCAOB did not amend, but replaced AS2 with a much improved Auditing Standard No. 5, *An Audit of Internal Control Over Financial Reporting That is Integrated With An Audit of Financial Statements*. Among its salient points:

1. Auditing Standard No. 5 is less prescriptive.
2. Auditing Standard No. 5 makes the audit scalable—it can change to fit the size and complexity of any company.
3. Auditing Standard No. 5 directs auditors to focus on what matters most—and eliminates unnecessary procedures from the audit.
4. Finally, Auditing Standard No. 5 includes a principles-based approach to determining when and to what extent the auditor can use the work of others.

A press release announcing the approval of Auditing Standard No. 5 stated, "The Commission expects the new auditing standard, in combination with the Commission's new management guidance, will make Section 404 audits and management evaluations more risk-based and scalable to company size and complexity."

In June 2008, the SEC announced receipt of Office of Management and Budget (OMB) approval to proceed with data collection for a study of the costs and benefits of Section 404 implementation. The study focused on the consequences for smaller companies and the effects of the Section 404 auditor attestation requirements. (For a discussion of the actions taken by the SEC and the PCAOB, as well as the provisions of AS5, see Chapter 27, "Public Company Accounting Oversight Board.")

Any business organization that does not have an established system of fraud control and other internal controls in place should have one; any organization that does have such a policy should review and update it periodically. If the system has developed haphazardly—reactively rather than proactively—it probably needs a thorough overhaul.

Enron is not the only cataclysmic event that has spurred change, reform, legislation and a closer look at business practices in general and accounting and auditing practices in particular. Other occurrences have also resulted in an attempt to bring honesty and increased productivity to the business world.

Action was taken in response to the series of savings and loan failures and spectacular frauds during and after the Watergate era. Increased emphasis was placed on improving the quality of financial reporting through *business ethics*, effective *internal controls*, and *corporate governance*. Concentrated effort was made to correct the existing situation and to prevent future fiascoes. In the latter attempt, the effort appears to have failed spectacularly.

More recently, Section 404 of the Sarbanes-Oxley Act of 2002 requires public companies (those required to register with the SEC) to include with their annual report to the Securities and Exchange Commission a separate assessment report, indicating the effectiveness of the company's internal controls. The report to the SEC is further required to be attested to and separately reported on by the external auditors for the company. Each annual report must contain a report stating the responsibility of management for establishing and maintaining an adequate internal control structure and procedures for financial reporting.

The report by management on its internal control is required to disclose the criteria against which its internal control effectiveness has been measured. The general industry standard used as a measurement criterion is the Committee on Sponsoring Organizations (COSO) framework discussed below. The assessment of internal control effectiveness is to be made as of the end of the fiscal year being reported on and any changes in internal control that have occurred during the year should also be indicated.

In May 2007, the Board adopted Auditing Standard No. 5, *An Audit of Internal Control Over Financial Reporting That Is Integrated with An Audit of Financial Statements*, to replace its previous internal control auditing standard, Auditing Standard No. 2. The Board also adopted the related Rule 3525, *Audit Committee Pre-Approval of Non-Audit Services Related to Internal Control Over Financial Reporting*, and conforming amendments to certain of the Board's other auditing standards.

This auditing standard is principles-based. It is designed to increase the likelihood that material weaknesses in internal control will be found before they result in material misstatement of a company's financial statements, and, at the same time, eliminate procedures that are unnecessary. The final standard also focuses the auditor on the procedures necessary to perform a high quality audit that is tailored to the company's facts and circumstances. The Board worked closely with the Securities and Exchange Commission to coordinate Auditing Standard No. 5 with the guidance to public company management the SEC had approved earlier.

The internal control reporting requirements of the Sarbanes Oxley Act are a key reason that the reliability and accuracy of financial reporting has improved over the past few years, according to the Board. They feel that the new auditing standard, by focusing the auditor's attention on those matters that are most important to effective internal control, presents another significant opportunity to strengthen the financial reporting process.

The Standard, along with Rule 3525, and the conforming amendments, are required for all audits of internal control for fiscal years ending on or after November 15, 2007. (For further discussion of internal control, see Chapter 27, "Public Company Accounting Oversight Board."

¶26,004 Background and History

The Committee of Sponsoring Organizations was formed in 1985 to establish and support the National Commission on Fraudulent Financial Reporting. The National Commission was organized as an independent private-sector initiative to study the causal factors that can lead to fraudulent financial reporting. It developed recommendations for public companies and their independent auditors, for the Securities and Exchange Commission (SEC) and other regulators and for educational institutions.

The National Commission (otherwise referred to as the "Treadway Commission," in honor of its first chairman, a former Commissioner of the SEC) was jointly sponsored by the five major U.S. financial professional associations:

1. The American Institute of Certified Public Accountants (AICPA).
2. The American Accounting Association (AAA).
3. The Institute of Internal Auditors (IIA).
4. The Institute of Management Accountants (IMA).
5. The Financial Executives Institute (FEI).

However, it was wholly independent of each of the sponsoring organizations and contained representatives from industry, public accounting, investment firms and the New York Stock Exchange.

.01 The COSO Framework for Internal Control

The COSO sponsored the development and publication of *Internal Control— Integrated Framework*, which provides the COSO model. The model outlines a sound basis for establishing internal control systems and for determining their effectiveness in practice. It does not attempt to reinvent internal controls but to define them in broader terms and to provide a framework for describing and evaluating the effectiveness of internal controls within a control environment.

The COSO basis for internal controls is widely accepted:

1. It has been incorporated into U.S. Generally Accepted Accounting Principles (U.S. GAAP) with the adoption of *Statement on Auditing Standards No. 78* by the AICPA.

2. The COSO framework has also been adopted by the financial services industry in response to the Federal Deposit Insurance Improvement Act requirements for assessing internal controls.
3. The Office of Management and Budget (OMB) Circular A-123, "Management Accountability and Control," of June 21, 1995, provides the requirements for assessing controls under COSO. OMB Circular A-123 uses the term "management control" to cover all aspects of internal control over an agency's operations (operational, financial and compliance).
4. The General Accounting Office (GAO) standards provide the measure of quality against which controls in operation are assessed, and the COSO model is the model accepted by GAO.
5. Many large and small companies use the framework as the basis for their internal control procedure, as does the Small Business Administration.

.02   Components of Internal Control

The COSO determined that a comprehensive assessment of risk and improved internal controls were necessary to manage business risk effectively. The standards and guidance developed by the committee are referred to as the COSO Internal Control Framework. According to COSO, internal control consists of five interrelated components:

1. *The control environment.* The control environment, as established by the head of the organization and senior managers, sets the tone and influences the control consciousness of employees. Control environment factors include integrity and ethical values, employee competence, leadership philosophy and style, and assignment of authority and responsibility.
2. *Risk assessment.* Risk assessment is the identification and analysis of relevant risks to the achievement of the organization's objectives. It forms the basis for determining how risks should be managed.
3. *Control activities.* Control activities are the policies and procedures that help to ensure that management directives are carried out. They also help to ensure that necessary actions are taken to address any risks to the achievement of the organization's objectives.
4. *Information and communication.* Information and communication systems enable the organization's managers and employees to capture and exchange the information needed to conduct, manage and control its operations.
5. *Monitoring.* The entire process must be monitored to assess the quality of the internal control system's performance over time. Ongoing monitoring occurs in the course of operations:
   a. As part of regular management and supervisory activities.
   b. For employee performance of their duties.

Separate periodic evaluations assess the effectiveness of the internal control process and the ongoing monitoring procedures.

.03   The COSO Definition of Internal Control

Internal control is a process, effected by an entity's board of directors, management and other personnel, designed to provide reasonable assurance regarding:

1. Effectiveness and efficiency of operations.
2. Reliability of financial reporting.
3. Compliance with applicable laws and regulations.

.04   Key Concepts Considered by COSO

Following are those key concepts assumed by COSO's model and framework:

1. Internal control is a *process*. It is a means to an end, not an end in itself.
2. Internal control is effected by *people*—it is not merely policy manuals and forms, but people at every level of an organization.
3. Internal control can be expected to provide only *reasonable assurance*, not absolute assurance, to an entity's management and board.
4. Internal control is geared to the achievement of *objectives* in one or more separate but overlapping categories.

.05   Birth of Sarbanes-Oxley and the PCAOB

Under pressure from accounting scandals at Enron, Congress reached an agreement with lightning speed on legislation to overhaul the rules governing the accounting profession. With the time constraint of the August congressional recess forcing their hand, House and Senate members hammered out a compromise on reform legislation in less than a week and reached an accord on July 24, 2002. The compromise called for the creation of an independent Accounting Oversight Board governed by the Securities and Exchange Commission (SEC).

Despite pressure to tone down the language and requirements of the Sarbanes-sponsored Senate bill, which placed stringent limits on the consulting services that audit firms can provide to public company audit clients, the strictures prevailed. Moreover, the act included House measures on stiffer criminal penalties for corporate crimes.

Adoption of the legislation marked a drastic shift for the accounting profession, which has, thus far, been self-regulated. The legislation makes control of the accounting profession similar to that of the brokerage industry's regulation under the NASD.

The bill places a federal government bureaucracy at the helm of accounting regulation. It is hoped that this new oversight structure will renew the faith the public had in auditors and the financial statements that they helped prepare. On the other hand, it will take a little while to see how closely the SEC and the Oversight Board itself follow the dictates of the law.

The American Institute of Certified Public Accountants (AICPA) noted that the changes demanded by the legislation would be dramatic and challenging for the accounting profession. The AICPA has pledged to work cooperatively with firms engaged in conducting public company audits in adapting to changes mandated by the new legislation. One immediate problem facing the AICPA is the appropriate role of its SEC Practice Section, within the framework of the new oversight board. At this juncture, it is a little difficult to foresee fully just what the role of the AICPA, Financial Accounting Standards Board (FASB), and other professional and standard-setting organizations may be.

An official of the SEC, speaking before a group of accountants at the end of January 2003, remarked that the past two weeks had been "…the busiest two weeks of rulemaking in the history of the Commission." He stated his belief that to restore the honor and credibility of the accounting profession, all participants must focus on one thing—doing what is best for investors.

These are still busy rulemaking activities going on with little indication that they will stop soon. Many feel that the rulemaking has gone too far, too fast. On the other hand, many supporters of SOX and the PCAOB applaud the progress that has been made in placing some limits and controls upon corporations and management for the benefit of the investor.

¶26,005   Focusing on Investors

Several of the initiatives under way at the SEC addressed the issue of focusing on investors. Much of this activity was generated by the passage of the Sarbanes-Oxley Act. In that time, the Commission adopted nine final rules implementing both the legislative mandates of the Act and, in some cases, additional reforms that the Commission and Commission staff deemed necessary to advance the interests of investors. Those rules relate to:

1. CEO and CFO certifications.
2. Pro forma financial information.
3. Codes of ethics for senior executives.
4. Financial experts on audit committees.
5. Trading during pension fund blackout periods.
6. Disclosure of material off-balance-sheet transactions.
7. Retention of audit records.
8. Independence standards for public company auditors.
9. Standards of conduct for attorneys.

.01   Importance to the Accounting Profession

Three of these initiatives undertaken by the SEC that are believed to have the potential for having the most significant effect upon the accounting profession are:

1. The establishment of the Public Company Accounting Oversight Board.
2. The adoption of new independence standards for public company auditors.
3. The efforts under way to improve the accounting standard-setting process and bring about international convergence of accounting standards.

The list of rules noted above indicates that the Act requires significant reform in all aspects of financial reporting and the disclosure system. The status of both registrants and auditors has been changed drastically. Other members of the capital market system, including investment bankers, analysts, and attorneys will now also operate under new and more stringent regulation.

.02   Sarbanes-Oxley More Than a List of Specifics

Details of the Act follow, but the Commission considers that the underlying themes are relatively simple, straightforward, and intended to restore market credibility. They include some old-fashioned truths about life in general as well as warnings for avoiding trouble in the corporate world:

- Each person must accept responsibility for his or her own behavior.
- Being an accomplice to, or ignoring, a bad deed may be the same as doing the bad deed.
- Those who carry out bad deeds shall be punished.
- Appearance counts.

¶26,006   Types of Services Considered Unlawful

The big accomplishment was to bring to fruition what the SEC and FASB had been trying to accomplish (with little success) before all the scandals came to light. Accounting firms are now barred from providing:

1. Bookkeeping or other services related to the accounting records or financial statements of public company audit clients.
2. Financial information systems design and implementation services.
3. Appraisal or valuation services, fairness opinions, or contribution-in-kind reports.
4. Actuarial services.
5. Internal audit outsourcing services.
6. Management functions or human resources.
7. Broker or dealer, investment advisor, or investment banking services.

8. Legal services and expert services unrelated to the audit.
9. Any other service that the Board determines, by regulation, is impermissible.

However, the Board does have the power to grant exceptions. Under certain conditions, some services may be performed if prior approval has been sought and granted. A similar measure in the House bill would have barred only consulting on system implementation and internal audits for audit clients. There are those who feel that Congress did not need to set hard and fast rules regarding independence and non-audit services. Some knowledgeable commenters consider those are matters better attended to by an expert regulatory body. On the other hand, if such matters are actually spelled out, obfuscation might not prevail.

The final legislation took the tougher measures proposed by the House on penalties for corporate crimes. A new securities fraud section was established to handle white-collar crime. Conviction carries a maximum penalty of a 25-year prison term, and penalties for mail and wire fraud are increased to 20 years.

¶26,007   The Public Company Accounting Oversight Board (PCAOB)

The Oversight Board has the power to:

1. Establish auditing.
2. Set up quality control.
3. Draft ethics and independence standards for public company auditors.
4. Investigate and discipline accountants.
5. Apply oversight of foreign firms that audit the financial statements of companies under U.S. securities laws.

Because the measure was passed so quickly and powered by such emotional fervor, there may be even more need for "technical corrections" than the many that are necessary for even the most routine legislation. The first of these corrections, Public Law 108-44, the *Accountant, Compliance, and Enforcement Staffing Act of 2003* was enacted and signed into law July 3, 2003. The purpose of this change is to "provide for the protection of investors, increase confidence in the capital markets system, and fully implement the Sarbanes-Oxley Act of 2002 by streamlining the hiring process for certain employment positions in the Securities and Exchange Commission." Board membership qualifications and constraints include the following:

1. The Board is made up of five financially literate members who are appointed for five-year terms.
2. Two of the members must be or have been CPAs.
3. The remaining three *must not be and cannot have been* CPAs.

4. The Chair may be held by one of the CPA members, provided that he or she has not been engaged as a practicing CPA for five years.
5. The Board's members are to serve on a full-time basis.
6. No member may, concurrent with service on the Board, share in any of the profits of, or receive payments from, a public accounting firm, other than "fixed continuing payments," such as retirement payments.
7. Members of the Board are appointed by the SEC after consultation with the Chairman of the Federal Reserve Board and the Secretary of the Treasury.
8. Members may be removed by the SEC "for good cause."

Yes, there they are, the three little words that carried a lawsuit all the way to a decision by the U.S. Supreme Court that in effect validated the entire Sarbanes-Oxley Act and the Private Company Accounting Oversight Board.

Yes, those little words had to be deleted, but otherwise everything remained as it was and business proceeded as usual.

.01   Responsibilities of the Board Related to Auditing Standards

The Oversight Board is expected to:

1. Cooperate on an ongoing basis with designated professional groups of accountants and any advisory groups convened in connection with setting auditing standards. Although the Board can, to the extent that it deems appropriate, adopt standards proposed by those groups, the *Board will have authority to amend, modify, repeal, and reject any standards suggested by the groups.* The Board is to report on these standard-setting activities to the Commission annually.
2. Require registered public accounting firms to "prepare, and maintain for a period of not less than seven years, audit work papers, and other information related to any audit report, in sufficient detail to support the conclusions reached in such report."
3. Require a second partner in public accounting firms to review and approve audit reports that registered accounting firms must adopt related to quality control standards.
4. Adopt an audit standard to implement the internal control review required by the act. This standard must require that the auditor evaluate whether the internal control structure and procedures include records that:
   a. Accurately and fairly reflect the transactions of the issuer.
   b. Provide reasonable assurance that the transactions are recorded in a manner that will permit the preparation of financial statements in accordance with U.S. GAAP.
   c. Include a description of any material weaknesses in the internal controls of the particular firm.

.02 Mandatory Registration and Other Oversight Functions

The Board will be responsible for:

1. Registering public accounting firms. In order to audit a public company, a public accounting firm must register with the Board. The Board is empowered to collect a registration fee and an annual fee from each registered public accounting firm in amounts that are "sufficient" to recover the costs of processing and reviewing applications and annual reports.

   The Board is required to establish a reasonable annual accounting support fee in an amount necessary or appropriate to maintain the Board. This fee will be assessed on issuers only.

   The registration requirement also applies to foreign accounting firms that audit a U.S. company. This would include foreign firms that perform some audit work, such as in a foreign subsidiary of a U.S. company that is relied on by the primary auditor.

2. Establishing (or adopting, by rule) auditing, quality control, ethics, independence, and other *standards* relating to the preparation of audit reports for issuers.

3. Conducting inspections of accounting firms. Annual quality reviews (inspections) must be conducted for firms that audit more than 100 issues; all other inspections must be conducted every three years. The SEC or the Board may order a special inspection of any firm at any time.

4. Conducting investigations and disciplinary proceedings and imposing appropriate sanctions. All documents and information prepared or received by the Board are treated as confidential and privileged as an evidentiary matter in any proceeding in any federal or state court or administrative agency, unless they are presented in connection with a public proceeding or released in connection with a disciplinary action. However, all such documents and information can be made available to the SEC, the U.S. Attorney General, and other federal and appropriate state agencies. Disciplinary hearings will be closed unless the Board orders that they be public, for good cause, and with the consent of the parties. Sanctions can be imposed by the Board upon a firm if it fails to supervise, within reason, any associated person with regard to auditing or quality control standards, or otherwise. No sanctions report will be made available to the public unless and until stays pending appeal have been lifted.

5. Performing such other duties or functions as necessary or appropriate.

6. Enforcing compliance with the act, the rules of the Board, professional standards, and the securities laws relating to the preparation and issuance of audit reports and the obligations and liabilities of accountants with respect to them.

7. Setting the budget and managing the operations of the Board and the staff of the Board.

¶26,008   SEC Oversight of the PCAOB

The Securities and Exchange Commission:

1. Has oversight and enforcement authority over the Board.
2. Can give the Board additional responsibilities, other than those specified in the Act.
3. May require the Board to keep certain records.
4. Has the power to inspect the Board itself, in the same manner as it can with regard to self-regulatory organizations, such as the NASD.
5. Is to treat the Board as if it were a registered securities association; that is, a self-regulatory organization.
6. Requires that the Board file proposed rules and rule changes with the SEC and may approve, reject, or amend such rules.
7. Requires that the Board notify the SEC of pending investigations involving potential violations of the securities laws and coordinate its investigation with the SEC Division of Enforcement, as necessary, to protect an ongoing SEC investigation.
8. May, by order, censure or impose limitations on the activities, functions, and operations of the Board if it finds that the Board has violated the act or the securities laws. The same applies if the Board has failed to ensure the compliance of accounting firms, with applicable rules, without reasonable justification.
9. Requires that the Board must notify the SEC when it imposes any "final sanction" on any accounting firm or associated person. The Board's findings and sanctions are subject to review by the SEC. The SEC may enhance, modify, cancel, reduce, or require remission of such sanction.

.01   SEC Announces Committee to Advise Small Public Companies

In its role as overseer, the Securities and Exchange Commission in December 2004 announced the establishment of an advisory committee to assist in examining the impact of the Sarbanes-Oxley Act, as well as other aspects of the federal securities laws affecting smaller public companies.

Two cochairs were appointed to head the committee, which will be known as the Securities and Exchange Commission Advisory Committee on Smaller Public Companies. Its areas of inquiry are:

▪ Frameworks for internal control over financial reporting applicable to smaller public companies, methods for management's assessment of such internal control, and standards for auditing such internal control.
▪ Corporate disclosure and reporting requirements and federally imposed corporate governance requirements for smaller public companies, includ-

ing differing regulatory requirements based on market capitalization, or other measurements of size or market characteristics.

- Accounting standards and financial reporting requirements applicable to smaller public companies.
- The process, requirements, and exemptions relating to offerings of securities by smaller companies, particularly public offerings.

The Advisory Committee is charged with considering the impact of the Sarbanes-Oxley Act of 2002 in each of these areas. The SEC will direct the committee to conduct its work with a view of protecting investors, considering whether the costs imposed by the current securities regulatory system for smaller public companies are proportionate to the benefits, identifying methods of minimizing costs and maximizing benefits, and facilitating capital formation by smaller companies. The Chairman also stated the Commission expects the committee to provide recommendations about where and how the Commission should draw lines to scale regulatory treatment for companies based on size.

SEC Appoints Members of Advisory Committee. In March 2005, the SEC Chairman appointed the 19 additional members of the Commission's Advisory Committee on Smaller Public Companies to bring the total number of members of the Advisory Committee to 21. At that time, the Chairman also announced that representatives of three groups, the Public Company Accounting Oversight Board, the Financial Accounting Standards Board, and the North American Securities Administrators Association, had accepted invitations to become official observers of the committee.

The SEC established the advisory committee to examine the impact of the Sarbanes-Oxley Act and other aspects of the federal securities laws on smaller companies. The Commission stated that that Sarbanes-Oxley Act had already benefited America's investors enormously and would spur further improvements in the securities markets.

The role of the advisory committee is to advise the SEC on how best to ensure that the costs of regulation for smaller companies under the Act and other securities laws are commensurate with the benefits. The appointments to the Advisory Committee are intended to ensure that the Commission receives input on these issues from a broad range of market participants, including individuals from diverse industries, geographical areas, professions, and categories of smaller companies and investors. Selection of members took into consideration the varied interests to be represented and a fair balance of points of view.

¶26,009   Accounting Standards

The SEC is authorized to recognize, as generally accepted, any accounting principles established by a standard-setting body that meets the bill's criteria, which include requirements that the body:

1.   Be a private entity.
2.   Be governed by a board of trustees (or equivalent body), the majority of whom are not, nor have been, associated with a public accounting firm for the past two years.
3.   Be funded in a manner similar to the Board.
4.   Have adopted procedures to ensure prompt consideration of changes to accounting principles by a majority vote.
5.   Consider, when adopting standards, the need to keep them current and the extent to which international convergence of standards is necessary or appropriate.

¶26,010   Public Company Audit Committees

The audit committee of the issuers plays an important part in overseeing many of the provisions of the Sarbanes-Oxley Act.

.01   Qualifications and Responsibilities

Each member of the audit committee must be a member of the board of directors of the issuer and otherwise be independent. "Independent" is defined as not receiving (other than for service on the board) any consulting, advisory, or other compensatory fee from the issuer. In addition, no member may be an "affiliated" person of the issuer or of any of his or her subsidiaries. However, the SEC may make exemptions for certain individuals *on a case-by-case basis*. The SEC is expected to announce rules to require issuers to disclose whether at least one member of its audit committee is a "financial expert."

Each issuer must provide appropriate funding to the audit committee to allow the committee to carry out its responsibilities. The audit committee of an issuer, in turn, is directly responsible for the appointment, compensation, and oversight of the work of any registered public accounting firm employed by that issuer. The audit committee must also establish procedures for receiving, retaining, and handling complaints received by the issuer regarding accounting, internal controls, and auditing. In addition, the committee must engage independent counsel or other advisors that it determines necessary to carry out its duties.

.02   Auditor Reports to Audit Committees

The accounting firm must report to the audit committee all critical accounting policies and practices to be used and any alternative disclosures and treatments of financial information within U.S. GAAP that have been discussed with management, along with the ramifications of their use and the treatment preferred by the firm. Other nonaudit services, including tax services, require preapproval by the audit committee on a case-by-case basis and must be disclosed to investors in periodic reports.

¶26,011 Management Assessment of Internal Controls

The Sarbanes-Oxley Act requires that each annual report of an issuer contain an internal control report, which is to state the responsibility of management for establishing and maintaining an adequate internal control structure and procedures for financial reporting. It also must contain an assessment, as of the end of the issuer's fiscal year, of the effectiveness of the internal control structure and procedures of the issuer for financial reporting. Each issuer's auditor must attest to, and report on, the assessment made by the management of the issuer. An attestation made under this section must be in accordance with standards for attestation engagements issued or adopted by the Board. An attestation engagement may not be the subject of a separate engagement.

The legislation directs the SEC to require each issuer to disclose whether it has adopted a code of ethics for its senior financial officers and the contents of that code. It directs the SEC to revise its regulations concerning prompt disclosure on Form 8-K to require immediate disclosure "of any change in, or waiver of," an issuer's code of ethics.

¶26,012 Financial Report Requirements in the Act

Nothing is more important to a business entity, large or small, its creditors, investors, even its employees and rank-and-file officers and directors than a true and honest financial report. When ranking officers do not play by the rules (however flawed the rules) and skew that report to their own advantage, all and sundry suffer in the final analysis.

Much of the Sarbanes-Oxley Act is drafted to attempt to improve the quality and reliability of these reports.

Each financial report must be prepared in accordance with U.S. GAAP and must "reflect all material correcting adjustments ... that have been identified by a registered accounting firm..." In addition, each annual and quarterly financial report is required to disclose all material off-balance-sheet transactions and any other relationships with unconsolidated entities that may have a material current or future effect on the financial condition of the issuer.

The SEC is expected to issue rules providing that pro forma financial information must be presented in such a manner that it does not contain an untrue statement or omit a material fact that, by its omission, would make the pro forma financial information misleading.

Officer and Director Penalties. If an issuer is required to prepare a restatement owing to *material noncompliance* with financial reporting requirements, the chief executive officer and the chief financial officer are required to reimburse the issuer for any bonus or other incentive-or equity-based compensation received during the 12 months following the issuance or filing of the non-compliant document. They must also reimburse the issuer for any profits realized from the sale of securities of the issuer during that period.

In any action brought by the SEC for violation of the securities laws, federal courts are authorized to "grant any equitable relief that may be appropriate or necessary *for the benefit of investors.*"

Improper Influence on Conduct of Audits. It shall be unlawful for any officer or director of an issuer to take any action to fraudulently influence, coerce, manipulate, or mislead any auditor engaged in the performance of an audit for the purpose of rendering the financial statements materially misleading.

Corporate Responsibility for Financial Reports. The CEO and CFO of each issuer are ordered to prepare a statement to accompany the audit report to certify the "appropriateness of the financial statements and disclosures contained in the periodic report, and that those financial statements and disclosures fairly present, in all material respects, the operations and financial condition of the issuer." In particular, section 301 of the Act (*Corporate Responsibility for Financial Reports*) requires each annual or quarterly report filed to contain a statement that:

1. The signing officer has reviewed the report;
2. Based on the officer's knowledge, the report does not contain any untrue statement of a material fact or omit to state a material fact necessary in order to make the statements made, in light of the circumstances under which such statements were made, not misleading;
3. Based on such officer's knowledge, the financial statements and other financial information included in the report fairly present in all material respects the financial condition and results of operation of the issuer as of, and for, the periods presented in the report;
4. The signing officers:
    a. Are responsible for establishing and maintaining internal controls;
    b. Have designed such internal controls to ensure that material information relating to the issuer and its consolidated subsidiaries is made known to such officer by others within those entities, particularly during the period in which the periodic reports are being prepared;
    c. Have evaluated the effectiveness of the issuer's internal controls as of a date within 90 days prior to the report;

   d.   Have presented in the report their conclusions about the effectiveness of their internal controls based on their evaluations as of that date;

   e.   Have disclosed to the issuer's auditors and the audit committee of the board of directors (or persons fulfilling the equivalent function):

     (1) All significant deficiencies in the design or operation of internal controls that could adversely affect the issuer's ability to record, process, summarize, and report financial data and have identified for the issuer's auditors any material weaknesses in internal controls; and

     (2) Any fraud, whether or not material, that involves management or other employees who had a significant role in the issuer's internal controls; and

   f.   Have indicated in the report whether or not there were significant changes in internal control or in other factors that could significantly affect internal controls subsequent to the date of their evaluation, including any corrective actions with regard to significant deficiencies and material weaknesses.

In response to questions about the actual implementation of the requirements of the corporate responsibility statements, the SEC has issued, in question and answer format, a number of clarifications. Many relate to highly technical issues while the following have general import.

Question 12: If the same individual is both the principal executive officer and principal financial officer, must he or she sign two certifications?

Answer: The individual may provide one certification and provide both titles underneath the signature.

Question 13: A CEO resigned after the end of the quarter but before the filing of the upcoming Form 10-Q. The company appointed a new CEO prior to the filing. Who signs the certification?

Answer: The new CEO, because he or she is the principal executive officer at the time of filing.

Question 15: An issuer currently does not have a CEO/CFO. Who must execute the certifications required by Rules 13a-14 and 15d-14?

Answer: as set forth in paragraph (a) of Rules 13a-14, where an issuer does not have a CEO/CFO, the person or persons performing similar functions must execute the required certification.

A violation of this section must be knowing and intentional to give rise to liability.

¶26,013   SEC Involvement in the Act

Not only is a new Board created by the Sarbanes-Oxley Act, but the Securities and Exchange Commission is given control of it, additional oversight assignments, study problems, and added funds and labor power to accomplish the job. Throughout this chapter, the SEC figures prominently in new and revised rules and regulations. Following are some additional areas of the Commission's role in the new legislation. Among the provisions is a section that empowers the SEC to prohibit a person from serving as an officer or director of a public company if the person has committed securities fraud. This, and many of the other measures, would seem to be iteration of provisions that have been in place, but they need to be emphasized.

.01   Study and Report on Special-Purpose Entities

The Commission is to study off-balance-sheet disclosures to determine (1) the extent of such transactions (including assets, liabilities, leases, losses and the use of special purpose entities) and (2) whether generally accepted accounting rules result in financial statements of issuers reflecting the economics of such off-balance-sheet transactions to investors in a transparent fashion. The Commission is to make a report containing its recommendations to Congress.

.02   Miscellaneous Assignments

Various sections of the legislation include the requirements placed on firms and their officers and the specifically assigned oversight tasks to the Commission. Among them are:

1. A direction that the SEC require each issuer to disclose whether it has adopted a code of ethics for its senior financial officers and the contents of that code. The SEC is also directed to revise its regulations concerning prompt disclosure on Form 8-K that requires immediate disclosure of any change in, or waiver of, an issuer's code of ethics.
2. The expectation that the SEC will issue rules providing that pro forma financial information must be presented in such a manner that it does not contain an untrue statement or omit to state a *material fact* that, by its omission, would make the pro forma financial information misleading. (Many firms that have rather straightforward financial reports have managed to produce questionable pro forma information and have defined materiality rather loosely.)

.03 Officer and Director Penalties

The SEC is empowered to issue an order to prohibit, conditionally or unconditionally, permanently or temporarily, any person who has violated section 10(b) of the 1934 Act from acting as an officer or director of an issuer if the SEC has found that such person's conduct demonstrates unfitness to serve as an officer or director of any such issuer:

(Section 10: It shall be unlawful for any person, directly or indirectly, by the use of any means or instrumentality of interstate commerce or of the mails, or of any facility of any national securities exchange—[b] To use or employ, in connection with the purchase or sale of any security registered on a national securities exchange or any security not so registered, or any securities-based swap agreement (as defined in section in the Gramm-Leach-Bliley Act), any manipulative or deceptive device or contrivance in contravention of such rules and regulations as the Commission may prescribe as necessary or appropriate in the public interest or for the protection of investors.)

.04 Appearance and Practice Before the Commission

The SEC may censure any person or temporarily bar or deny any person the right to appear or practice before the SEC if the person does not possess the requisite qualifications to represent others, lacks character or integrity, or has willfully violated federal securities laws.

.05 Rules of Professional Responsibility for Attorneys

The SEC is required to establish rules setting minimum standards for professional conduct for attorneys practicing before it.

.06 Study and Report

The SEC is ordered to conduct a study of "securities professionals" (public accountants, public accounting firms, investment bankers, investment advisors, brokers, dealers, and attorneys) who have been found to have aided and abetted a violation of federal securities laws.

.07 Temporary Freeze Authority

The SEC is authorized to freeze an extraordinary payment to any director, officer, partner, controlling person, agent, or employee of a company during an investigation of possible violations of securities laws.

¶26,014   Measures Relating to Corporate Officers

Because many of the problems facing corporations and the stock market at present result from actions by ranking corporate officers, a number of provisions in this legislation deal directly with corporate governance and related matters:

1. *Prohibition of insider trades during pension fund black-out periods.* The Act prohibits the purchase or sale of stock by officers and directors and other insiders during black-out periods. Any profits resulting from sales in violation of this section "shall inure to and be recoverable by the issuer." If the issuer fails to bring suit or prosecute diligently, a suit to recover such profit may be instituted by "the owner of any security of the issuer."

2. *Prohibition of personal loans to executives.* Generally, it will be unlawful for an issuer to extend credit to any director or executive officer. Consumer credit companies may make home improvement and consumer credit loans and issue credit cards to its directors and executive officers, if it is done in the *ordinary course of business* on the same terms and conditions made to the general public.

3. *Timely disclosures.* Issuers must disclose information on material changes in the financial condition or operations of the issuer on a rapid and current basis. Directors, officers, and 10 percent owners must report designated transactions by the end of the second business day following the day on which the transaction was executed.

4. *Conflicts of interest.* The CEO, Controller, CFO, Chief Accounting Officer, or person in an equivalent position cannot have been employed by the company's audit firm during the one-year period preceding the audit.

5. *Audit partner rotation.* The lead audit or coordinating partner and the reviewing partner must rotate off of the audit every five years.

6. *Tampering with an official proceeding.* The Act makes it a crime for any person to corruptly alter, destroy, mutilate, or conceal any document with the intent to impair the object's integrity or availability for use in an official proceeding or to otherwise obstruct, influence or impede any official proceeding. Perpetrators are liable for up to 20 years in prison and a fine.

7. *Sense of Congress regarding corporate tax returns.* It is the sense of Congress that the federal income tax return of a corporation should be signed by the chief executive officer of such corporation.

¶26,015   Amendments to the Sarbanes Senate Bill

Rather than rely on other laws to punish those who dispose of evidence, shred documents, and otherwise attempt to impede investigations, Congress has spelled out the crime and punishment in amendments to the Sarbanes-Oxley Act.

.01   The Corporate and Criminal Fraud Accountability Act of 2002

It is a felony to knowingly destroy or create documents to "impede, obstruct or influence" any existing or contemplated federal investigation. Auditors are required to maintain all audit or review work papers for five years.

The statute of limitations on securities fraud claims is extended to the earlier of five years from the fraud or two years after the fraud was discovered, from three years and one year, respectively.

Employees of issuers and accounting firms are extended whistle-blower protection that would prohibit the employer from taking certain actions against employees who lawfully disclose private employer information to, among others, parties in a judicial proceeding involving a fraud claim. Whistle-blowers are also granted a remedy of special damages and attorney's fees.

A new crime for securities fraud has penalties of fines and up to 10 years of imprisonment.

.02   White-Collar Crime Penalty Enhancement Act of 2002

The provisions include a long list of penalties that have increased the time of imprisonment and amount of fines for specified crimes as follows:

1. The maximum penalty for mail and wire fraud is increased from 5 to 10 years.
2. Tampering with a record or otherwise impeding any official proceeding is classified as a crime.
3. The SEC is given authority to seek a court freeze of extraordinary payments to directors, officers, partners, controlling persons, and agents of employees.
4. The U.S. Sentencing Commission is to review sentencing guidelines for securities and accounting fraud.
5. The SEC may prohibit anyone convicted of securities fraud from being an officer or director of any publicly traded company.
6. Financial Statements filed with the SEC must be certified by the CEO and CFO.
7. The certification must state that the financial statements and disclosures fully comply with provisions of the Securities Exchange Act and that they fairly present, in all material respects, the operations and financial condition of the issuer.
8. Maximum penalties for willful and knowing violations of this section are a fine of not more than $500,000 and/or imprisonment of up to five years.

¶26,016   SEC's Relationship with the FASB

The federal securities laws set forth the Commission's broad authority and responsibility to prescribe the methods to be followed in the preparation of accounts and the form and content of financial statements to be filed under those laws, as well as its responsibility to ensure that investors are furnished with other information necessary for investment decisions. To assist it in meeting this responsibility, the Commission historically has looked to private sector standard-setting bodies designated by the accounting profession to develop accounting principles and standards. At the time of the FASB's formation in 1973, the Commission reexamined its policy and formally recognized pronouncements of the FASB that establish and amend accounting principles and standards as "authoritative" in the absence of any contrary determination by the Commission. The SEC concluded at that time that the expertise and resources the private sector could offer to the process of setting accounting standards would be beneficial to investors.

The Sarbanes-Oxley Act amends section 19 of the Securities Act of 1933 to establish criteria that must be met in order for the work product of an accounting standard-setting body to be recognized as "generally accepted." A new subsection indicates that, in carrying out its authority under the Securities Exchange Act of 1934, the Commission may recognize as "generally accepted" for purposes of the federal securities laws any accounting principles established by a standard-setting body that:

- Is organized as a private entity.
- Has, for administrative and operational purposes, a board of trustees serving in the public interest, the majority of whom are not, concurrent with their service on such board, and have not been during the two-year period preceding such service, associated persons of any registered public accounting firm.
- Is funded as provided by the Sarbanes-Oxley Act.
- Has adopted procedures to ensure prompt consideration, by majority vote of its members, of changes to accounting principles necessary to reflect emerging accounting issues and changing business practices.
- Considers, in adopting accounting principles, the need to keep standards current in order to reflect changes in the business environment, the extent to which international convergence on high-quality accounting standards is necessary or appropriate in the public interest and for the protection of investors.

    Representatives of the FASB and FAF requested that "[t]he FASB ... continue to be the designated organization in the private sector for establishing standards of financial accounting and reporting." In reaffirming the FASB's position, the SEC pointed out that the Act does not restrict the Commission's ability to develop accounting principles on its own, nor does it limit the number of private-sector bodies the Commission may recognize.

.01   Qualification and Recognition of the FASB

In assessing compliance with the provisions of section 108, the SEC evaluated the organizational structure, operations, and procedures of both the FAF and the FASB.

The FAF is composed of independent trustees and is responsible for overseeing, funding, and appointing members of the Board, as well as selecting members of an advisory body. The Commission was informed that the majority of the FAF trustees is not, and has not been during the two-year period preceding their service on the FAF, associated with a public accounting firm. Based on their past relationship with the FAF, the SEC believes that the FAF serves the public interest. Accordingly, the FAF meets the applicable criteria in Section 108 of the Sarbanes-Oxley Act for the board of trustees of a recognized private sector accounting standard setter.

The Board is responsible for promulgating financial accounting and reporting standards. It currently has seven members who have expertise in accounting and financial reporting. Members generally are appointed for five-year terms and can be reappointed to one additional term. Board members are full-time employees of the FAF.

.02   Commission Oversight of FASB Activities

Whereas the SEC consistently has looked to the private sector to set accounting standards, the securities laws, including the Sarbanes-Oxley Act, clearly provide the SEC with authority to set accounting standards for public companies and other entities that file financial statements with the Commission. In addition, recognition of standards set by a private sector standard-setting body as "generally accepted" is only appropriate under Section 108 of the Sarbanes-Oxley Act if, among other things, the Commission determines that the private-sector body "has the capacity to assist the Commission in fulfilling the requirements of ... the Securities Exchange Act ... because, at a minimum, the standard setting body is capable of improving the accuracy and effectiveness of financial reporting and the protection of investors under the securities laws." As previously noted, Section 108 also emphasizes the Commission's responsibility to determine that the standard-setting body:

- Has "procedures to ensure prompt consideration ... of changes to accounting principles necessary to reflect emerging accounting issues and changing business practices."
- Considers the need to amend standards "to reflect changes in the business environment."
- Considers, to the extent necessary or appropriate, international convergence of accounting standards.

Given the Commission's responsibilities under the securities laws and specific responsibilities under the Sarbanes-Oxley Act to make findings regarding the procedures, capabilities, activities, and results of any designated accounting standards-setting body, the SEC believes that:

- The FAF and FASB should give the SEC timely notice of, and discuss with it, the FAF's intention to appoint a new member of the FAF or FASB. The FAF makes the final determinations regarding the selection of FASB and FAF members. However, to fulfill its statutory responsibilities, the SEC provides the FAF with its views, and expects that they will continue to be taken into consideration in making the final selection. The SEC, FAF, and FASB share the belief that the qualifications and appropriateness of each member of the FAF and the FASB are critical if the FASB is to continue to be a premier private sector standards-setting body.
- The FASB, in its role of "assist[ing] the Commission in fulfilling the requirements of the Securities Exchange Act," should provide timely guidance to public companies, accounting firms, regulators, and others on accounting issues that the Commission considers to be of immediate significance to investors. The Commission and its staff, however, do not prohibit the FASB from also addressing other topics and do not dictate the direction or outcome of specific FASB projects so long as the conclusions reached by the FASB are *in the interest of investor protection.*

The SEC staff will continue to refer issues to the FASB or one of its affiliated organizations when those issues may call for new, amendments to, or formal interpretations of, accounting standards. The FASB is expected to address such issues in a timely manner. On occasions when the FASB determines that consideration of the issue is inadvisable or that the issue cannot be resolved within the time frame acceptable to the SEC, it is expected that the Board will notify the Commission or its staff promptly, provide its views regarding an appropriate resolution of the issue, and work with the Commission to ensure the protection of investors from misleading or inadequate accounting or disclosures.

One such affiliated organization is the Emerging Issues Task Force (EITF), which comprises approximately 13 members who serve, generally without compensation, on a part-time basis. EITF members are partners in large, medium-sized, and small accounting firms; business executives; financial analysts and other users of financial statements; and academics. Upon ratification of an EITF consensus by the FASB, the consensus is published as part of the EITF's minutes and may be relied upon by SEC registrants and others in the preparation of financial statements that purport to conform to generally accepted accounting principles.

- Because the SEC and FASB share the common goal of providing investors with the disclosure of meaningful financial information, the Commission anticipates continuation of the collegial working relationship with
the FASB. It expects that, when requested to do so, the FASB will make
information and staff reasonably available to facilitate the understanding
and implementation of a particular FASB standard.

The SEC and its staff intend to work with the FAF and the FASB to ensure
that proper oversight procedures and policies are in place to allow the SEC to
assess whether the FASB continues to meet the characteristics of an accounting
standard setter that are discussed in the Sarbanes-Oxley Act.

.03 Key FASB Initiatives

As noted earlier, the SEC has treated FASB accounting standards as authoritative since 1973. In order for U.S. accounting standards to remain relevant and
to continue to improve, however, the Commission expects the FASB to:

- Consider, in adopting accounting principles, the extent to which international convergence on high-quality accounting standards is necessary or appropriate in the public interest and for the protection of investors, including consideration of moving toward greater reliance on principles-based
accounting standards (rather than specifics) whenever it is reasonable to do
so. The SEC expects that, during its deliberations of any accounting issue,
the FASB will carefully consider international accounting and financial reporting standards that cover that same issue. This has been done in the past
and increasingly so in recent years as it becomes clear that it is, indeed, a
global economy.
- Take reasonable steps to continue to improve the timeliness with which it
completes its projects while satisfying appropriate public notice and comment requirements.
- Continue to be objective in its decision making and to weigh carefully the
views of its constituents and the expected benefits and perceived costs of
each standard.

.04 FASB's Independence

Although effective oversight of the FASB's activities is necessary in order for
the Commission to carry out its responsibilities under the securities laws,
the SEC continues to recognize the importance of the FASB's independence.
Therefore, the Commission's determination is that the FASB should continue

its role as the preeminent accounting standard setter in the private sector. In performing this role, the SEC feels that the Board must use independent judgment in setting standards and should not be constrained in its exploration and discussion of issues. This is necessary to ensure that the standards developed are free from bias and have the maximum credibility in the business and investing communities.

.05   Conclusion of the Commission

Based on available information, the SEC has reached several conclusions. The organizational structure, operating activities, and procedures of the FAF and FASB were deemed to meet the criteria in Section 108 of the Sarbanes-Oxley Act. As mentioned, one of the statutory criteria is that the recognized accounting body be funded as provided in Section 109 of the Act. These funding provisions replace the FAF's funding responsibilities; the FAF will continue to be responsible for the fee requests, including establishing the FASB's budget for review by the Commission each year. The SEC stated that it is providing the endorsement of the FASB so that it can begin to work with the Public Company Accounting Oversight Board to implement these funding mechanisms. The recognition of the FASB by the SEC is in anticipation of, and with the expectation that, this funding will be forthcoming in the near term. There has been a great deal of discussion concerning the source of this funding.

The FASB has the capacity to assist the Commission in fulfilling the requirements of the Securities Act of 1933 and of the Securities Exchange Act of 1934 and is capable of improving both the accuracy and effectiveness of financial reporting and the protection of investors under the securities laws. The FASB does not act alone, but receives input relating to standard setting and interpretation from, among other sources, a standing advisory body, the Financial Accounting Standards Advisory Council (FASAC), which is composed of members from the accounting and business communities, academia, and professional organizations. All share an interest in fostering quality financial reporting and disclosure. FASAC's primary mission is to advise the FASB on its projects and agenda. In addition, the FASB has established a User Advisory Council (UAC) to assist the FASB in raising awareness of how investors and investment professionals, equity and credit analysts, and rating agencies use financial information. The FASB has recruited more than 40 professionals, representing a variety of investment and analytical disciplines, to participate on the UAC. Council meetings will concentrate on major Board projects that could significantly change financial information currently available to users. Early meetings have covered a range of issues including accounting for financial instruments, revenue recognition, and pension accounting.

The standards set by the FASB should be recognized as "generally accepted" under Section 108 of the Sarbanes-Oxley Act. (At the same time, the Sarbanes-Oxley Act states, "Nothing in this Act, … shall be construed to impair or limit the authority of the Commission to establish accounting principles or standards for purposes of enforcement of the securities laws.")

As required under the securities laws, including the Sarbanes-Oxley Act, the Commission will monitor the FASB's procedures, qualifications, capabilities, activities, and results, as well as the FAF's and FASB's ongoing compliance with the expectations and views expressed in this policy statement.

The SEC will issue an appropriate revision of this policy statement if it determines that the FAF or FASB no longer meets the statutory criteria or expectations discussed in the policy statement, or if it is otherwise necessary or appropriate to do so. The occasions when the Commission has not accepted a particular FASB standard have been extremely rare because of its past and continuing recognition and support of the Board's independence. The Commission and its staff do not prohibit the FASB from addressing a particular topic and do not dictate the direction or outcome of specific FASB projects provided that the conclusions reached by the FASB are in the interest of investor protection.

¶26,017 SEC Adopts Attorney Conduct Rule Under Sarbanes-Oxley Act

In January 2003, the SEC adopted final rules to implement Section 307 of the Sarbanes-Oxley Act by setting "standards of professional conduct for attorneys appearing and practicing before the Commission in any way in the representation of issuers."

In addition, the Commission approved an extension of the comment period on the "noisy withdrawal" provisions of the original proposed rule and publication for comment of an alternative proposal to it. There was much concern expressed regarding the effects of the original "noisy withdrawal" proposal. The American Bar Association was particularly concerned about several issues, including the client confidentiality aspects of the provisions.

On November 6, 2002, the Commission voted to propose the new standards of professional conduct. That proposal more specifically defined the role and activities of a lawyer who is *appearing and practicing before the Commission* in the representation of an issuer. Attorneys were required to report evidence of a material violation "up the ladder" within an issuer. In addition, under certain circumstances, these provisions permitted or required attorneys to effect a so-called "noisy withdrawal"—that is, to withdraw from representing an issuer and notify the Commission that they have withdrawn for professional reasons.

.01   Provisions of the Rule

The rules adopted by the Commission:

- Require an attorney to report evidence of a material violation, determined according to an objective standard, "up the ladder" within the issuer to the chief legal counsel or the chief executive officer of the company or the equivalent.
- Require an attorney, if the chief legal counsel or the chief executive officer of the company does not respond appropriately to the evidence, to report the evidence to the audit committee, another committee of independent directors, or the full board of directors.
- Clarify that the rules cover attorneys who are providing legal services to an issuer, who have an attorney-client relationship with the issuer, and who are aware that documents they are preparing or assisting in preparing will be filed with or submitted to the Commission.
- Provide that foreign attorneys who are not admitted in the United States and who do not advise clients regarding U.S. law would *not* be covered by the rule, whereas foreign attorneys who provide legal advice regarding law would be covered to the extent they are appearing and practicing before the Commission unless they provide that advice in conjunction with U.S. counsel.
- Allow an issuer to establish a "qualified legal compliance committee" (QLCC) as an alternative procedure for reporting evidence of a material violation. Such a QLCC would consist of at least one member of the issuer's audit committee (or an equivalent committee of independent directors) and two or more independent board members, and would have the responsibility, among other things, to recommend that an issuer implement an appropriate response to evidence of a material violation. One way in which an attorney could satisfy the rule's reporting obligation is by reporting evidence of a material violation to the issuer's QLCC.
- Allow an attorney, without the consent of an issuer client, to reveal confidential information related to his or her representation to the extent the attorney reasonably believes it is necessary in order to:
  - Prevent the issuer from committing a material violation likely to cause substantial financial injury to the financial interests or property of the issuer or investors.
  - Prevent the issuer from committing an illegal act.
  - Rectify the consequences of a material violation or illegal act in which the attorney's services have been used.

- State that these Commission rules govern in the event the rules conflict with state law, but will not preempt the ability of a state to impose *more rigorous* obligations on attorneys that are not counter to the SEC rules.
- Affirmatively state that the rules do not create a private cause of action and that authority to enforce compliance with the rules is vested exclusively with the Commission.

.02   Definition Modified

Further, the final rules modify the definition of the term "evidence of a material violation," which defines the trigger for an attorney's obligation to report up the ladder within an issuer's ranks. The revised definition confirms that the SEC intends an *objective* triggering standard, rather than a *subjective* one.

This "trigger" must involve credible evidence, based on which it would be unreasonable, under the circumstances, for a prudent and competent attorney not to conclude that it is reasonably likely that a material violation *has occurred, is ongoing, or is about to occur.*

CHAPTER 27

Public Company Accounting Oversight Board

¶27,000   Overview

In March 2015, the Public Company Accounting Oversight Board (PCAOB) approved the reorganization of its auditing standards to help users navigate the standards more easily. The Board adopted amendments to its rules and standards to implement a topical system that integrates the existing interim and PCAOB-issued auditing standards. "The standards will be organized by topics that generally follow the flow of the audit process, making their use easier and more efficient for auditors," according to then PCAOB Chairman James R. Doty.

Under the reorganization, the individual standards will be grouped into the following topical categories:

- General Auditing Standards: standards on broad auditing principles, concepts, activities, and communications
- Audit Procedures: standards for planning and performing audit procedures and for obtaining audit evidence
- Auditor Reporting: standards for auditors' reports
- Matters Relating to Filings Under Federal Securities Laws: standards on certain auditor responsibilities relating to U.S. Securities and Exchange Commission (SEC) filings for securities offerings and reviews of interim financial information
- Other Matters Associated with Audits: standards for other work performed in conjunction with an audit

These amendments also remove references to superseded standards and inoperative language and references. They do not impose new requirements on auditors or change the substance of the requirements for performing and reporting on audits under PCAOB standards.

All amendments to PCAOB standards adopted by the Board are submitted to the SEC for approval. The effective date for these amendments, following SEC approval, was December 31, 2016. The SEC gave its approval on September 17, 2015 (see Release No. 34-75935).

In July 2015, the PCAOB announced settled disciplinary orders against seven audit firms and seven individuals for violating Auditing Standard (AS) No. 7, Engagement Quality Review, and other requirements.

"PCAOB rules require engagement quality reviews, which serve as important safeguards against erroneous or insufficiently supported audit opinions," said James R. Doty, PCAOB Chairman. "Investors rightly expect the PCAOB to hold accountable auditors who fail to adhere to these requirements."

According to the Board's orders, in five of the seven cases, firms permitted clients to use their audit reports without having an engagement quality reviewer provide a concurring approval of issuance of the report. The CPA firms are located in New York, New Jersey, Illinois, California, Georgia and Texas. The investigations that resulted in the settlements originated with information obtained through the Board's inspection program.

In December 2023, the PCAOB outlined their priorities for 2024 inspections in a PCAOB staff report, noting the following overall business risk considerations:

- Persistent high interest rates, tightening of credit availability, and/or inflationary challenges.
- Disruptions in the supply chain and rising costs.
- Business models that are significantly impacted by rapidly changing technology.
- Geopolitical conflicts.
- Financial statements that include areas with a higher inherent risk of fraud, estimates involving complex models or processes, and/or presentation and disclosures that may be impacted by complexities in the public company's activities.

Activities related to prioritized sectors/industries noted were:

- Continue emphasis on selecting audits of companies engaging in merger and acquisition activities or business combinations.
- Continue emphasis on selecting audits of broker-dealers that file compliance reports and others that provide customers with various investment opportunities, such as introducing brokers.
- Continue to select non-traditional audit areas to inspect.
- Continue emphasis on:
  — Financial sector,
  — Information technology, and
  — Other.

Inspections considerations include:

- Challenges and recurring deficiencies observed in inspections of broker-dealers
- Recurring deficiencies
- Evaluating audit evidence
- Understanding the company and its environment
- Use of other auditors
- Going concern
- Critical audit matters (CAMs)
- Digital assets
- Cybersecurity
- Use of data and technology

In June 2010, the U.S. Supreme Court issued its decision in the constitutional lawsuit challenging the PCAOB, affirming in part and reversing in part the judgment of the Court of Appeals in favor of the PCAOB.

The suit, *Free Enterprise Fund v. PCAOB*, originally filed in 2006, charged the creation and operation of the PCAOB under the Sarbanes-Oxley Act of 2002 was unconstitutional because it did not permit adequate control of the PCAOB by the U.S. president.

The Supreme Court held that the Sarbanes-Oxley Act's provisions making PCAOB Board members removable by the SEC only for good cause were inconsistent with the Constitution's separation of powers. Because the Court severed these provisions from the Act, however, no legislation was necessary to bring the Board's structure within constitutional requirements.

PCAOB Board members will now be removable by the SEC at will, rather than only for good cause. All other aspects of the SEC's oversight, the structure of the PCAOB and its programs are unaffected by the Court's decision. As a result, all PCAOB programs will continue to operate as usual, including registration, inspection, enforcement, and standard-setting. Furthermore, the opinion does not call into question any action taken by the PCAOB since its inception.

The PCAOB was created 10 years ago by the Sarbanes-Oxley Act, ending more than 100 years of auditor self-regulation and reminding auditors that it is their duty under the law to serve, first and foremost, the interests of the investors.

¶27,001   Recent Updates to PCAOB Auditing Standards

.01   New Quality Control Standard

In May 2024, the PCAOB adopted a new quality control standard with a risk-based approach designed to drive continuous improvement in audit quality. The standard requires firms to identify their risks and design a quality control (QC) system to guard against those risks. This replaces a set of standards issued by the accounting profession before the PCAOB was created.

Firms that perform audits of public companies or SEC-registered brokers and dealers are required to implement and operate the QC system they design, monitor the system, and take remedial actions where policies and procedures are not operating effectively, creating a continuous feedback loop for improvement. The firms must annually evaluate their QC systems and report the results of the evaluation to the PCAOB on a new Form QC. Firms that audit more than 100 issuers annually are required to establish an external oversight function for the QC system.

.02   New Standard on General Responsibilities of the Auditor

The PCAOB adopted a new auditing standard in May 2024, AS 1000, *General Responsibilities of the Auditor in Conducting an Audit,* along with related amendments to other PCAOB Standards. The amendments from this standard will:

- Modernize, clarify, and streamline the general principles and responsibilities of auditors and provide a more logical presentation, which should enhance the useability of the standards by making them easier to read, understand, and apply.
- Clarify the auditor's responsibility to evaluate whether the financial statements are "presented fairly."
- Clarify the engagement partner's due professional care responsibilities by adding specificity to certain audit performance principles set out in the standards.
- Accelerate the documentation completion date by reducing the maximum period for the auditor to assemble a complete and final set of audit documentation from 45 days to 14 days.
- Clarify an auditor's professional skepticism extends to other information that is obtained to comply with PCAOB standards and rules.

.03   New Standard Modernizing Auditors' Use of Confirmation

In September 2023, the PCAOB adopted a new standard to strengthen and modernize the requirements for the auditor's use of confirmation. The new standard reflects changes in technology, communications, and business practices since the interim standard was first adopted by the PCAOB in 2003 after being issued by the AICPA in 1991.

.04   Audits with Other Auditors

The PCAOB filed a proposal with the SEC which was issued as Release No. 34-95488; File No. PCAOB-2022-001, dated August 12, 2022. It was an Order Granting Approval of Amendments to Auditing Standards Governing the Planning and Supervision of Audits Involving Other Auditors and Dividing Responsibility for the Audit with Another Accounting Firm. The Release modifies many different audit standards but primarily rescinds Auditing Standard (AS) 1205, Part of the Audit Performed by Other Independent Auditors, and adopts AS 1206, Dividing Responsibility for the Audit with Another Accounting Firm.

The amendments are intended to improve the PCAOB's standards principally by (i) applying a risk-based supervisory approach to the lead auditor's oversight of other auditors whose work the lead auditor assumes responsibility for, and (ii) requiring that the lead auditor perform certain procedures when planning and supervising an audit that involves other auditors. In summary, the amendments:

- Require that the engagement partner determine whether their firm's participation in the audit is sufficient for the firm to carry out the responsibilities of a lead auditor and report as such. The amendments include considerations for the engagement partner to use in making this determination and require that the audit's engagement quality reviewer review the determination.

- Require that the lead auditor, when determining the engagement's compliance with independence and ethics requirements, understand the other auditor's knowledge of those requirements and experience in applying them. The lead auditor is required to obtain and review written affirmations regarding the other auditor's policies and procedures related to those requirements and regarding its compliance with the requirements, and a description of certain auditor-client relationships related to independence. In addition, the amendments require the sharing of information about changes in circumstances and the updating of affirmations and descriptions in light of those changes.

- Require that the lead auditor understand the knowledge, skill, and ability of other auditors' engagement team members who assist the lead auditor with planning and supervision, and obtain a written affirmation from the other auditor that its engagement team members possess the knowledge, skill, and ability to perform assigned tasks.

- Require that the lead auditor supervise other auditors under the Board's standard on audit supervision and inform the other auditors about the scope of their work, identified risks of material misstatement, and certain other key matters. The amendments also require that the lead auditor and other auditors communicate about the audit procedures to be performed, and any changes needed to the procedures. In addition, the lead auditor is required to obtain and review a written affirmation from the other auditors about their performance of work in accordance with the lead auditor's instructions, and to direct the other auditors to provide certain documentation about their work.

- Provide that, in multi-tiered audits, a first other auditor may assist the lead auditor in performing certain required procedures with respect to second other auditors.

.05 Auditing Accounting Estimates, Including Fair Value Measurements

The PCAOB has issued an amendment to AS 2501, Auditing Accounting Estimates, Including Fair Value Measurements. The amendment was issued as PCAOB Release No. 2018-005, with SEC Action taken in Release No. 34-86269 in 2018 and 2019, respectively. The new standard replaces three existing standards by establishing a single standard that sets forth a uniform, risk-based approach. It emphasizes that auditors need to apply professional skepticism, including addressing potential management bias, when auditing accounting estimates. It also provides more direction on addressing certain aspects unique to auditing fair values of financial instruments, including the use of pricing information from third parties such as pricing services and brokers or dealers. In addition to amending AS 2501, it supersedes AS 2502 and AS 2503. The standard is effective for audits of fiscal years ending on or after December 15, 2020.

.06 Auditor's Use of the Work of Specialists

The PCAOB issued an amendment that retitled and replaced AS 1210, Using the Work of a Specialist, as AS 1210, Using the Work of an Auditor-Engaged Specialist; and amended AS 1105, Audit Evidence, and AS 1201, Supervision of the Audit Engagement. The amendment was issued as PCAOB Release No. 2018-006, with SEC Action taken in Release No. 34-86270 in 2018 and 2019, respectively. The new standard strengthens the requirements for evaluating the work of a company's specialist, whether employed or engaged by the company. It is designed to increase audit attention in areas where a specialist is used and to align applicable requirements with the PCAOB's risk assessment standards. It also applies a supervisory approach to both auditor-employed and auditor-engaged specialists.

.07 Auditor Reporting

The PCAOB issued a standard that amended AS 3101, The Auditor's Report on an Audit of Financial Statements When the Auditor Expresses an Unqualified Opinion. The new standard had been issued as PCAOB Release No. 2017-001, with SEC Action taken in Release No. 34-81916 in 2017. The new standard retained the pass/fail opinion of the existing auditor's report, but made significant changes to the auditor's report, including communication of critical audit matters, disclosure of auditor tenure, and other improvements to the auditor's report. Critical audit matters (CAMs) are matters communicated or required to be communicated to the audit committee and that relate to accounts or disclosures that are material to the financial statements; and involved especially challenging, subjective, or complex auditor judgment. Specific information about CAMs must now be included in an auditor's report. Disclosure of auditor tenure requires the year in which the auditor began serving consecutively as the company's auditor. Other improvements include a statement that the auditor is required to be independent, changes to certain standardized language in the auditor's report, and changes to the standardized form of the auditor's report.

.08 Form AP, Auditor Reporting of Certain Audit Participants

The PCAOB issued a standard that includes new rules and amendments to auditing standards that require audit firms to disclose the names of each audit engagement partner as well as the names of other audit firms that participated in each audit. The new standard had been issued as PCAOB Release No. 2015-008, with SEC Action taken in Release No. 34-77787 in 2015 and 2016, respectively.

Under these rules, auditors are required to file a new PCAOB Form AP, *Auditor Reporting of Certain Audit Participants*, for each issuer audit to disclose:

- the name of the engagement partner;
- the names, locations, and extent of participation of other accounting firms that took part in the audit, if their work constituted 5 percent or more of the total audit hours; and
- the number and aggregate extent of participation of all other accounting firms that took part in the audit whose individual participation was less than 5 percent of the total audit hours.

The standard filing deadline for Form AP is 35 days after the date the auditor's report is first included in a document filed with the SEC. For initial public offerings, the Form AP must be filed ten days after the auditor's report is first included in a document filed with the SEC.

.09   Other Projects and Resources

The PCAOB is conducting research and engaging in outreach activities related to Data and Technology, Audit Evidence, Quality Control, and Other Auditors. In addition, the PCAOB Web site (pcaobus.org) has other beneficial resources, such as implementation guidance related to the standards of the PCAOB, as well as Staff Audit Practice Alerts that highlight new, emerging, or otherwise noteworthy circumstances that may affect how auditors conduct audits under the existing requirements of PCAOB standards and relevant laws. There are also Staff Questions and Answers that set forth the staff's opinions on issues related to implementation of PCAOB standards.

¶27,002   Updates to Legacy Auditing Standards

.01   PCAOB Adopts Auditing Standard No. 18, Related Parties

In June 2014, the PCAOB adopted Auditing Standard No. 18, Related Parties, and amendments to other auditing standards to strengthen auditor performance requirements in three critical areas of the audit: related party transactions, significant unusual transactions, and a company's financial relationships and transactions with its executive officers.

The Board took this action because these transactions and relationships could pose increased risk of material misstatement in company financial statements. The Board determined that its existing requirements in these critical areas do not contain sufficient required procedures and are not sufficiently risk-based.

"The new auditing standard and amendments we adopted address transactions and relationships that have been contributing factors in a number of financial reporting frauds," said James R. Doty, PCAOB Chairman. "Subjecting these areas to enhanced auditor scrutiny may help avert corporate failures and avoid harm to investors," he added.

Auditing Standard No. 18, Related Parties, requires specific audit procedures for the auditor's evaluation of a company's identification of, accounting for, and disclosure of transactions and relationships between a company and its related parties. The new standard supersedes the Board's interim auditing standard, AU Section 334, Related Parties.

The amendments regarding significant unusual transactions include specific audit procedures that are designed to improve the auditor's identification and evaluation of such transactions, and to enhance the auditor's understanding of their business purposes.

Other amendments to PCAOB auditing standards include, among other things, specific audit procedures requiring the auditor to obtain, during the risk assessment process, an understanding of a company's financial relationships and transactions with its executive officers.

.02   Auditing Standard No. 17

The PCAOB adopted Auditing Standard No. 17, *Auditing Supplemental Information Accompanying Audited Financial Statements*, and it is effective for audits of fiscal years ending on or after June 1, 2014. This standard, in its Introductory section states that: "This standard sets forth the auditor's responsibilities when the auditor of the company's financial statements is engaged to perform audit procedures and report on supplemental information that accompanies financial statements audited pursuant to Public Company Accounting Oversight Board ("PCAOB") standards."

.03   PCAOB Adopts Auditing Standard No. 16, Communications with Audit Committees, and Amendments to Other PCAOB Standards

The PCAOB adopted Auditing Standard No. 16, *Communications with Audit Committees*, and amendments to other PCAOB standards, on August 15, 2012.

The standard establishes requirements that enhance the relevance and timeliness of the communications between the auditor and the audit committee, and is intended to foster constructive dialogue between the two on significant audit and financial statement matters.

According to the PCAOB Chairman, open lines of communication between auditors and audit committees improve the quality of audits, and the final standard enhances the quality and relevance of those communications.

The Board initially proposed the standard on March 29, 2010, and reproposed it on December 20, 2011. The proposed standard was revised in response to comments received in comment letters and at a roundtable on September 21, 2010.

The PCAOB Chief Auditor and Director of Professional Standards explains that the standard on communications with audit committees will improve audit quality. It emphasizes effective two-way communication on matters of great importance to the audit and the financial statements, such as:

- Significant risks,
- Critical accounting estimates,
- Difficult or contentious matters,
- Significant unusual transactions, and
- Going concern.

The standard supersedes the Board's interim auditing standards AU Section 310, Appointment of the Independent Auditor, and AU Section 380, Communication with Audit Committees, and amends other PCAOB standards.

All new auditing standards and amendments to PCAOB standards adopted by the Board are submitted to the SEC for approval. The new standard and related amendments, if approved by the SEC, are effective for public company audits of fiscal periods after December 15, 2012. Under the Jumpstart Our Business Startups Act of 2012, the standard and related amendments will apply to audits of "emerging growth companies" if the SEC makes a determination called for under that Act.

The SEC adopted the standard on December 17, 2012, as announced by the Board. Auditing Standard No. 16, Communications with Audit Committees, and amendments to other PCAOB standards are effective for public company audits of fiscal periods beginning on or after December 15, 2012. Additionally, the SEC determined that the standard and related amendments will apply to audits of "emerging growth companies" under the Jumpstart Our Business Startups Act of 2012.

"AS 16 supports the critical role of auditors and audit committees in financial reporting," said PCAOB Chairman James R. Doty in a PCAOP news release. "The standard moves the auditor's communication with the audit committee away from compliance checklists, and decisively in the direction of meaningful, effective interchange."

The standard establishes requirements that enhance the relevance and timeliness of the communications between the auditor and the audit committee, and is intended to foster constructive dialogue between the two on significant audit and financial statement matters.

The standard supersedes the Board's interim auditing standards AU Section 310, Appointment of the Independent Auditor, and AU Section 380, Communication with Audit Committees, and amends other PCAOB standards.

¶27,003   PCAOB Scholarship Program and Academic Recipients

The PCAOB announced on June 15, 2012, the colleges and universities that would participate in the PCAOB Scholarship Program for that upcoming academic year.

For the 2023-2024 academic year, the PCAOB awarded 369 merit-based scholarships to students of $10,000 each. The scholarships are awarded to only one student at each of the recipient colleges and universities.

The PCAOB Chairman stated that he is pleased that this scholarship program allows the PCAOB and the academic community to work together to encourage the best and the brightest students to choose auditing as a career path.

The Sarbanes-Oxley Act of 2002 provides that funds generated from the collection of monetary penalties imposed by the PCAOB are to be used to fund a merit scholarship program for students in accredited accounting degree programs. The PCAOB Scholarship Program was created to identify eligible students for scholarships and award funds through the students' educational institutions.

.01   Requirements for Qualification

Students may be eligible for PCAOB scholarships if they are enrolled in an accounting degree program at an accredited participating, nominating institution. To qualify, students must do the following:

- Be enrolled in a bachelor's or master's degree program in accounting.
- Demonstrate interest and aptitude in accounting and auditing.
- Demonstrate high ethical standards.
- Not be a PCAOB employee or a child or spouse of a PCAOB employee.

The PCAOB scholarship program is merit-based but educational institutions are encouraged to give consideration to students from populations that have been historically underrepresented in the accounting profession.

¶27,004   PCAOB Issues Report on the Interim Inspection Program for Broker and Dealer Auditors

The PCAOB released its first report on the progress of the interim inspection program for auditors of brokers and dealers, on August 20, 2012. The report provides an overview of the program and the audit deficiencies identified in the initial group of inspected audits of brokers and dealers.

In this first look, carried out over a five-month period from October 2011 to February 2012, PCAOB inspectors reviewed 10 audit firms covering portions of 23 audits of brokers and dealers registered with the SEC. Deficiencies were discovered in all of the audits inspected.

The audits inspected were required to be conducted under generally accepted auditing standards issued by the AICPA, and not under PCAOB standards.

While the results of these initial inspections cannot be generalized to all securities broker and dealer audits and represent only a small portion of the inspections planned for the interim program, the nature and extent of the findings are of concern to the Board according to the PCAOB Chairman.

The report, entitled, "Report on the Progress of the Interim Inspection Program Related to Audits of Brokers and Dealers," describes deficiencies observed in the following areas:

- Audit procedures related to the computations of customer reserve and net capital requirements,
- Audits of financial statements, and
- Auditor independence.

All registered firms that issue audit reports for SEC-registered brokers and dealers should consider whether the audit deficiencies described in this report might be present in audits they currently perform, and should take appropriate action to prevent or correct any such deficiencies identified.

Of the firms that were audited:

- Three of the ten firms were already subject to PCAOB inspection because they audited public companies.
- Seven were newly subject to inspection under the interim inspection program.

The audits and firms selected were not representative of all broker and dealer audits, or all auditors for SEC-registered brokers and dealers.

The interim inspection program:

- Consists of reviewing approximately 100 audit firms covering portions of more than 170 audits of brokers and dealers through 2013.
- Is designed to cover a cross-section of audits of SEC-registered brokers and dealers.
- Will continue until new rules for a permanent program are adopted and become effective.

The program has two purposes:

1. It enables the Board to assess the compliance of registered firms and their associated persons conducting audits of brokers and dealers with the Sarbanes-Oxley Act, Board and SEC rules, and professional standards.
2. It informs the Board's eventual determinations about the scope and elements of a permanent inspection program.

¶27,005   PCAOB Interim Inspection Program for Broker-Dealer Audits and Broker and Dealer Funding Rules

The PCAOB adopted certain rules on June 14, 2011, to implement provisions of the Dodd-Frank Wall Street Reform and Consumer Protection Act related to audits of securities brokers and dealers.

Specifically, the Board adopted:

- A temporary rule to establish an interim inspection program for registered public accounting firms' audits of brokers and dealers.
- Rules for assessing and collecting a portion of its accounting support fee from brokers and dealers to fund PCAOB oversight of audits of brokers and dealers, consistent with the Dodd-Frank Act.
- Certain amendments to existing funding rules for issuers.

"The Board's actions today are an important step in oversight of the audits of brokers and dealers," the PCAOB Chairman stated. "The interim inspection program will allow the Board to gain a better understanding of how PCAOB can provide meaningful investor protection, consistent with our intent to avoid imposing unnecessary burdens on smaller auditors and broker-dealers.

"And I believe the amendments to the Board's funding rules provide an efficient mechanism to fund the PCAOB's oversight without imposing unwarranted costs and administrative burdens on smaller brokers and dealers," he added.

.01   Interim Inspection Program

The Dodd-Frank Act authorized the Board to establish, by rule, a program of inspection of auditors of brokers and dealers. The law leaves to the Board, subject to the approval of the SEC, which was granted in August 2011, important questions concerning the scope of the program and the frequency of inspections, including whether to differentiate among categories of brokers and dealers and whether to exclude from the inspection program any categories of auditors. The temporary rule adopted by the Board provides for an interim inspection program while the Board considers the scope and other elements of a permanent inspection program.

Under the temporary rule, the Board will begin to inspect auditors of brokers and dealers and identify and address with the registered firms any significant issues in those audits. The Board also expects that insights gained through the interim program will inform the eventual determination of the scope and elements of a permanent program. The Board expects to propose rules governing the scope and elements of a permanent program in 2013.

During the interim program, the Board will provide public reports on the progress of the interim program and significant issues identified. In the absence of unusual circumstances, however, the Board will not issue firm-specific inspection reports before inspection work is performed under the permanent program and will not issue firm-specific inspection reports on any firms that are eventually excluded from the scope of the permanent program.

The temporary rule does not change anything about the rules or standards that govern audits of broker-dealers. As the SEC has previously explained, its rules continue to require those audits to be carried out under GAAS, or generally accepted auditing standards.

.02   Funding Provisions

Section 109 of the Sarbanes-Oxley Act, as originally enacted, provided that funds to cover the PCAOB annual budget, less registration and annual fees paid by registered public accounting firms, would be collected from issuers and brokers and dealers based on each issuer's relative average monthly equity market capitalization. The amount due from issuers is referred to as the accounting support fee.

¶27,006   PCAOB Publishes Staff Audit Practice Alert

Staff Audit Practice Alerts are published by the PCAOB to highlight new, emerging, or otherwise noteworthy circumstances that may affect how auditors conduct audits under the existing requirements of PCAOB standards and relevant laws.

.01   Matters Related to Auditing Revenue from Contracts with Customers

Staff Audit Practice Alert No. 15, *Matters Related to Auditing Revenue from Contracts with Customers*, highlights PCAOB requirements and other considerations for audits of a company's implementation of the new revenue accounting standard. See ¶7001.01. These are:

- transition disclosures and transition adjustments;
- internal control over financial reporting;
- fraud risks;
- revenue recognition; and
- disclosures.

¶27,007   PCAOB Affected by Dodd-Frank Wall Street Reform and Consumer Protection Act

Enactment of the Dodd-Frank Wall Street Reform and Consumer Protection Act in July 2010 facilitates the PCAOB's ability to share information with foreign auditor oversight authorities and gives them expanded responsibilities for the audits of SEC-registered securities broker-dealers.

.01   Right to Share Information with Foreign Oversight Bodies

While the Sarbanes-Oxley Act of 2002 protects the PCAOB's inspection and investigative processes from public disclosure, it permits the Board, in certain circumstances, to share information with federal and state authorities. However, at the time the Sarbanes-Oxley Act was enacted, very few other countries had audit oversight bodies and, therefore, there was no provision in the Sarbanes-Oxley Act authorizing the PCAOB to share information with foreign authorities. Since that time, many countries have established or are in the process of establishing audit oversight bodies. The Dodd-Frank Act allows the Board, under certain circumstances, to share information with such foreign auditor oversight authorities.

.02   Oversight of Broker-Dealer Auditors

Dodd-Frank expands the PCAOB's inspections, enforcement, and standard-setting authority to include auditors of brokers-dealers. Those auditors had previously been required to register with the Board, but, until now, had not been subject to any other Board authority. This legislation had a significant effect on our work, the acting chairman of the PCAOB explained at a meeting of the Standing Advisory Group. There are currently about 3,400 SEC-registered broker-dealers, a decrease of 41 firms from 2020 and 1,432 firms from 2017. In the past two years, over 500 additional audit firms registered with the Board because they conduct audits of broker-dealers, and of course many previously-registered firms are also involved in that work.

¶27,008 Ethics and Independence Rule Concerning Communications with Audit Committees and Amendment to Tax Services Rule

In April 2008, the Board adopted Rule 3526, *Communication with Audit Committees Concerning Independence*, to enhance communication between audit committees and registered firms regarding the firm's independence. Rule 3526 requires a registered public accounting firm, before accepting an initial engagement pursuant to the standards of the PCAOB, to describe in writing to the audit committee all relationships between the firm or any of its affiliates and the issuer or persons in a financial reporting oversight role at the issuer that may reasonably be thought to bear on the firm's independence. Registered firms are required to discuss with the audit committee the potential effects of any such relationships on the firm's independence. Rule 3526 requires firms to make a similar communication annually for continuing engagements. Rule 3526 supersedes the Board's interim independence requirement, Independence Standards Board Standard No. 1, *Independence Discussions with Audit Committees*, and two related interpretations.

The Board also adopted an amendment to Rule 3523, *Tax Services for Persons in Financial Reporting Oversight Roles*. The amendment excludes from the scope of the rule, tax services provided during the portion of the audit period that precedes the beginning of the professional engagement period. As originally adopted by the Board, the rule provided that a registered public accounting firm is not independent of its audit client if it, or any of its affiliates, provides any tax service to a person in a financial reporting oversight role, or an immediate family member of such a person during the audit and professional engagement period. The Board determined that providing tax services to such a person during the portion of the audit period preceding the beginning of the professional engagement period does not necessarily impair a firm's independence.

The two actions taken touch on the crucial area of auditor independence, which the PCAOB strongly supports as a key component to audit quality. Rule 3526, in particular, reflects the critical role of the audit committee under the Sarbanes-Oxley Act. The PCAOB understands the importance of audit committee members obtaining the information they need to assess the independence of prospective or current auditors, according to the PCAOB. By adopting the amendment to Rule 3523, together with the strengthened responsibility for the auditor to communicate critical information about auditor independence to the audit committee, the Board reduced the likelihood that a company's choice of auditor will be unnecessarily restricted.

Rule 3526 along with two related interpretations and an amendment to Rule 3523 were approved by the SEC on August 22, 2008.

¶27,009   PCAOB Issues Release Concerning its Inspection Process

The PCAOB issued a release on August 2, 2012, to provide information to audit committees about its inspection process and the meaning of reported inspection results. The goal is to equip audit committees of public company boards of directors to engage in more meaningful discussion with PCAOB-registered audit firms about the results of inspections.

The release provides information about the meaning and significance of PCAOB inspection findings in the context of engagement reviews, and quality control reviews. The release also suggests some specific approaches that an audit committee might consider for initiating or enhancing inspection-related discussions with an audit firm.

"The Board encourages registered public accounting firms to communicate openly, candidly, and effectively with audit committees about the results of PCAOB inspections, including discussing the problematic aspects of otherwise nonpublic information," the PCAOB Chairman stated.

The release highlights certain areas of inquiry that audit committees may wish to address with their auditors. These include, for example:

- Whether the audit overseen by the audit committee was selected by the PCAOB for an inspection and whether any findings were made;
- Potentially relevant inspection findings on other audits performed by the firm;
- The firm's response to PCAOB findings; and
- The firm's remedial efforts in light of any quality control deficiencies that may have been identified by the PCAOB.

An audit firm's candid discussion of any problems identified in the PCAOB inspection can be useful to an audit committee in carrying out its responsibility for oversight of the audit engagement. "This will help audit committees approach those discussions with an understanding of the Board's perspective on important aspects of the process," Chairman Doty added.

¶27,010   Varied Responsibilities Assigned to the PCAOB

The Sarbanes-Oxley Act established the PCAOB, to be organized as a nonprofit corporation, with SEC administration and oversight. The PCAOB's mission is to oversee the audits of public companies and related matters. Its more specific tasks as described in the Act include:

- *Auditor registration.* All auditors of public companies must register with the PCAOB, identify public audit clients, identify all accountants associated with those clients, list fees earned for audit and nonaudit services, explain their audit quality control procedures, and identify all criminal, civil, administrative, and disciplinary proceedings against the firm or any of its associated persons in connection with an audit.
- *Inspection of CPA firms.* The PCAOB must inspect all CPA firms that audit public companies to assess compliance with the law, SEC regulations, rules established by the PCAOB, and professional standards. Firms that audit more than 100 public companies will be inspected annually. Firms that audit 100 or fewer public companies must be inspected at least once every three years. If violations are found, the PCAOB must take disciplinary action.
- *Audit, quality control, ethics, and independence standards.* The PCAOB must adopt audit, quality control, ethics, and independence standards. In doing so, the PCAOB may look to standards established by recognized professional organizations such as the AICPA.
- *Quality control.* The PCAOB's quality control standards must require that registered firms properly supervise all work, monitor compliance with ethics and independence rules, and establish internal systems for consultation, professional development, and client acceptance and retention.
- *Restrictions on services to audit clients.* The Act restricts consulting work that auditors can do for their audit clients. The PCAOB may enumerate additional prohibited services to those covered in the Act.

¶27,011   Discussion of Inspection of U.S. and Non-U.S. Firms

Below is a historical description of early efforts and obstacles faxed by the PCAOB. The most recent update to this information is as of December 15, 2022, when the PCAOB secured complete access to inspect and investigate Chinese firms for the first time. In passing the Holding Foreign Companies Accountable Act of 2020 (HFCAA), the U.S. Congress sent a clear message that access to U.S. capital markets is a privilege and not a right. As a result of the HFCAA, the PCAOB was able to secure access in the People's Republic of China (PRC). This was followed by the PCAOB posting its first-ever inspection reports for audit firms located in mainland China and Hong Kong in May 2023.

Currently, there are more than 1,600 public firms registered with the PCAOB, including U.S. and non-U.S. firms.

The Board conducts regular, periodic inspections of hundreds of those firms, but not all of them. It should not be assumed or expected that a firm registered with the PCAOB is, or necessarily will be, inspected by the PCAOB.

The Sarbanes-Oxley Act authorizes the PCAOB to inspect registered firms for the purpose of assessing compliance with certain laws, rules, and professional standards in connection with a firm's audit work for clients that are "issuers" as that term is defined in the Act. Many PCAOB-registered firms perform no such work, and the work they do perform is not within the scope of the PCAOB's statutory responsibility and authority to assess. The PCAOB does not inspect those firms.

Firms that perform no issuer audit work might register with the PCAOB for a variety of reasons. The Securities Exchange Act of 1934, as amended by the Sarbanes-Oxley Act, requires financial statements filed by a registered broker-dealer to be certified by a PCAOB-registered firm, even if, as is typically the case, the broker-dealer is not an issuer. Some regulators also have adopted rules requiring persons subject to their jurisdiction to use PCAOB-registered firms for specified services unrelated to audits of issuers. In addition, firms that currently do not work on issuer audits might register with the PCAOB just to be in a better position to compete for future business for which registration is required.

The PCAOB regularly inspects those firms that issue audit reports stating an opinion on the financial statements of issuers. There are currently more than 1,600 public accounting firms registered with the PCAOB. In general, the PCAOB inspects each firm in this category either annually or triennially, depending upon whether the firm provides audit reports for more than 100 issuers (annual inspection) or 100 or fewer issuers (triennial inspection). At any time, the PCAOB might also inspect any other registered firm that plays a role in the audit of an issuer, and the PCAOB has begun a practice of inspecting some firms in that category each year.

¶27,012   Audit Standard Setting

With regard to standard setting, the first question was whether the Board would set its own standards or adopt standards recommended by an advisory group. Regardless of that decision, any new rules would require SEC approval. Effectively ending the era of self-regulation for the public accounting and auditing industry, the PCAOB unanimously voted to review the existing auditing standards and to write new ones. This, in effect, replaces the Auditing Standards Board

(ASB) of the AICPA as the highest authority for standard-setting guidance of public companies. The Sarbanes-Oxley Act had allowed the PCAOB the option of delegating that authority to an industry group such as the ASB, but the PCAOB decided to accept the responsibility of developing its own guidance. Accounting, investment, and financial experts were asked to assist in developing the new auditing standards.

In the interim—or transition period—the SEC issued an order that the adoption of interim professional standards be consistent with the requirements of the Act and the federal securities laws. These interim professional standards were considered necessary for use in connection with the audits of public companies and for the protection of investors.

Under the Sarbanes-Oxley Act, the PCAOB's duties include the establishment of auditing, quality control, ethics, independence, and other standards relating to public company audits. In connection with this standard-setting responsibility, Section 103 of the Act provides that the PCAOB may adopt any portion of any statement of auditing standards or other professional standards that the PCAOB determines satisfy the requirements of the Act and that were proposed by one or more professional groups of accountants as initial or transitional standards, to the extent the PCAOB determines necessary. This section of the Act also provides that any such initial or transitional standards must be separately approved by the Commission at the time it makes the determination required by the Act, without regard to the procedures that otherwise would apply to Commission approval of PCAOB rules.

On April 16, 2003, the Board adopted some pre-existing standards as interim standards to be used on an initial, transitional basis. PCAOB Rules 3200T, 3300T, 3400T, 3500T, and 3600T describe the standards that the Board adopted and required registered public accounting firms and their associated persons to comply with as the interim standards to the extent *not superseded or amended by the Board*. If any one of the new Standards addresses a subject matter that also is addressed in the interim standards, the affected portion of the interim standard should be considered superseded or effectively amended.

The Board also has made certain conforming amendments to the interim standards to reflect the effect of the adoption of PCAOB standards. The present electronic version of the interim standards reflects those amendments. If and when the interim standards are used, it is the responsibility of the CPA firm and its associated persons (and anyone else using the interim standards) to determine whether a particular interim standard has been superseded or amended.

The Board cautions that the electronic version of the interim standards may be updated from time to time to correct typographical or other technical errors.

Within a year and one-half, five final standards were issued that take precedence over at least some provisions of these interim standards:

- Auditing Standard No. 1 modifies the auditor's report.
- Auditing Standard No. 2 superseded by Auditing Standard No. 5.
- Auditing Standard No. 3 sets forth the rules for audit documentation.
- Rule 3100 dictates auditor compliance with PCAOB Professional Practice Standards.
- Rule 3101 deals with certain terms used in the Auditing and Professional Practice Standards.

The three PCAOB Auditing Standards supersede the applicable sections of temporary rules and the two Rules relate to them. Another measure, Auditing Standard No. 4 was added in 2006.

.01   Auditing Standard No. 1

Effective February 5, 2004, PCAOB Auditing Standard No. 1, *References in Auditors' Reports to Standards of the Public Company Accounting Oversight Board*, required that auditors' reports on audits and other engagements relating to public companies include a reference stating that the engagement was performed *in accordance with the standards of the PCAOB*. This replaces previous reference to generally accepted auditing standards (GAAS). Therefore, auditors are to *cease referring to GAAS in audit reports* relating to financial statements of issuers of public companies and instead refer to "standards of the Public Company Accounting Oversight Board (United States)." However, it should be noted that the Standard is applicable *only* to auditors' engagements that are governed by PCAOB rules.

PCAOB Rule 3100 requires registered public accounting firms and their associated persons to comply with the applicable auditing and related professional practice standard established or adopted by the PCAOB. Because of this, according to the SEC, and because the PCAOB has adopted interim standards incorporating generally accepted auditing standards, references to GAAS *and* standards established by the AICPA are now *superseded*.

As noted, Auditing Standard No. 1 requires that an auditor's report issued in connection with any engagement performed in accordance with the auditing and related professional practice standards of the PCAOB state that it was performed in accordance with "the standards of the Public Company Accounting Oversight Board (United States)." According to the SEC, given the possible confusion between Commission rules and staff guidance references in the federal securities laws, on the one hand, and the PCAOB's rules, on the other, the Commission decided some guidance was necessary. Therefore, they published interpretive guidance based upon comments and queries received prior to their approval of the Standard. With that approval, references in SEC rules and staff guidance and in the federal securities laws to GAAS or to specific standards under GAAS, as they relate to issuers, should be understood to mean the standards of the PCAOB plus any applicable rules of the Commission.

Although the PCAOB has indicated that Auditing Standard No. 1 supersedes references to GAAS, U.S. GAAP, "auditing standards generally accepted in the United States of America," and "standards established by the AICPA," this Standard *does not* supersede other SEC rules or regulations.

- **Rule 3200T, Interim Auditing Standards.** In connection with the preparation or issuance of any audit report, a registered public accounting firm and its associated persons must comply with generally accepted auditing standards, as described in the AICPA Auditing Standards Board's (ASB's) Statement of Auditing Standards (SAS) 95 (AU 150) and as in existence on April 16, 2003.

   Public accounting firms were not required to be registered with the Board until October 23, 2003. The Board intended that the Interim Auditing Standards apply to public accounting firms that would be required to be registered after the mandatory registration date and to associated persons of those firms, as if those firms had already registered.

- **Rule 3300T, Interim Attestation Standards.** In connection with an engagement described in the ASB's Statements on Standards for Attestation Engagements (SSAE), and related to the preparation or issuance of audit reports for issuers, a registered public accounting firm and its associated persons must comply with these standards and related interpretations and Statements of Position in existence on April 16, 2003.

- **Rule 3400T, Interim Quality Control Standards.** A registered public accounting firm and its associated persons should comply with quality control standards as described in the ASB's Statements on Quality Control Standards (SQCSs) and in existence on April 16, 2003, and with the AICPA SEC Practice Section's Requirements of Membership in existence on April 16, 2003.

- **Rule 3500T, Interim Ethics Standards.** In connection with the preparation or issuance of any audit report, a registered public accounting firm and its associated persons are to comply with ethics standards as described in the AICPA's Code of Professional Conduct Rule 102 and interpretations and rulings in existence on April 16, 2003.

- **Rule 3600T, Interim Independence Standards.** In connection with the preparation or issuance of any audit report, a registered public accounting firm and its associated persons are required to comply with independence standards as described in the AICPA's Code of Professional Conduct Rule 101 and interpretations and rulings in existence on April 16, 2003, as well as with Standards 1, 2, and 3 and Interpretations 99-1, 00-1, and 00-2 of the Independence Standards Board. (The Board's Interim Independence Standards do not supersede the Commission's auditor independence rules. Therefore, to the extent that a provision of the Commission's rule is more restrictive or less restrictive than the Board's Interim Independence Standards, a registered public accounting firm must comply with the more restrictive rule.)

Each of the interim standards described would remain in effect until modified or superseded either by PCAOB action approved by the Commission as provided in the Act or by Commission action pursuant to its independent authority under the federal securities laws and those rules and regulations.

.02   Auditing Standard No. 2

Auditing Standard No. 2 has been superseded by Auditing Standard No. 5 for audits of fiscal years ending on or after November 15, 2007.

.03   Auditing Standard No. 3

In August 2004, the SEC approved PCAOB Auditing Standard No. 3, *Audit Documentation*, which requires registered public accounting firms to prepare and maintain, for at least seven years, audit documentation in sufficient detail to support the conclusions reached in the auditor's report. The Standard also imposes unconditional responsibility on the principal auditor to obtain certain audit documentation from another auditor (who, although not named in the audit report, has performed part of the audit work used by the principal auditor) prior to the audit report release date. The Standard was effective for fiscal years ending on or after November 15, 2004, for all engagements conducted in accordance with PCAOB standards (audits of financial statements, audits of internal control over financial reporting and reviews of interim financial information).

At the same time that it approved the proposed Auditing Standard No. 3, the SEC also approved an Amendment to Interim Auditing Standards—AU Section 543, *Part of Audit Performed by Other Independent Auditors*. (This measure is discussed below.)

Auditing Standard No. 3 establishes general requirements for documentation the auditor should prepare and retain in connection with engagements conducted pursuant to the standards of the PCAOB. Such engagements include:

- An audit of financial statements.
- An audit of internal control over financial reporting.
- A review of interim financial information.

This standard does not replace specific documentation requirements of other standards of the PCAOB.

Documentation Requirement. The auditor must prepare audit documentation in connection with each engagement conducted pursuant to the standards of the PCAOB. Audit documentation should be prepared in sufficient detail to provide a clear understanding of its purpose, source, and the conclusions reached. Also, the documentation should be appropriately organized to provide a clear link to the significant findings or issues. Examples of audit documentation include memoranda, confirmations, correspondence, schedules, audit programs, and letters of representation. Audit documentation may be in the form of paper, electronic files, or other media.

Because audit documentation is the written record that provides support for the representations in the auditor's report, it should:

1. Demonstrate that the engagement complied with the standards of the PCAOB.
2. Support the basis for the auditor's conclusions concerning every relevant financial statement assertion.
3. Demonstrate that the underlying accounting records agreed or reconciled with the financial statements.

Steps to be Followed in Documentation. The auditor must document the procedures performed, evidence obtained, and conclusions reached with respect to relevant financial statement assertions. Audit documentation must clearly demonstrate that the work was in fact performed. This documentation requirement applies to the work of all those who participate in the engagement as well as to the work of specialists the auditor uses as evidential matter in evaluating relevant financial statement assertions. Audit documentation must contain sufficient information to enable an experienced auditor, having no previous connection with the engagement to:

1. Understand the nature, timing, extent, and results of the procedures performed, evidence obtained, and conclusions reached.

2. Determine who performed the work and the date such work was completed as well as the person who reviewed the work and the date of such review.

.04   Auditing Standard No. 4

In February 2006, Auditing Standard No. 4, *Reporting on Whether a Previously Reported Material Weakness Continues to Exist*, was approved by the SEC. This Standard establishes requirements that apply when an auditor is engaged to report on whether a material weakness in internal control over financial reporting has been eliminated. AS 4 institutes a stand-alone engagement that is entirely voluntary, performed only at the company's request after the company, has disclosed a material weakness.

Like other attestation service, an auditor's report under this Standard is based on an evaluation of management's statement that the material weakness has been eliminated. Management is required to present a written report that will accompany the auditor's report that contains specified elements. Unlike an auditor's report on internal control over financial reporting, in which the assessment is required to be as of the date of the annual financial statements, an auditor's report on whether a material weakness continues to exist may be as of any date set by management.

That date represents management's belief that that is the day the material weakness no longer exists. They also believe that the company has adequately assessed the effectiveness of the specified controls that address the material weakness. The auditor's opinion relates to the existence of a specifically identified material weakness as of a specified date.

To establish the narrow focus of this engagement clearly, AS 4:

- Requires the auditor's report to describe the material weakness.
- Identify all of the specified controls that management asserts address the material weakness.
- Identify the stated control objective achieved by these controls.
- Include language to emphasize that the auditor has not performed procedures sufficient to reach conclusions about the effectiveness of any other controls or provided an opinion regarding the effectiveness of internal control over financial reporting overall.

Because of the narrow focus of this engagement, qualified opinions are not permitted—the auditor's opinion as to whether a previously reported material weakness continues to exist may be expressed as either "the material weakness exists" or "the material weakness no longer exists."

.05   Auditing Standard No. 5

In May 2007, the Board adopted Auditing Standard No. 5, *An Audit of Internal Control Over Financial Reporting That Is Integrated with An Audit of Financial Statements*, to replace its previous internal control auditing standard, Auditing Standard No. 2. The Board also adopted the related Rule 3525, *Audit Committee Pre-Approval of Non-Audit Services Related to Internal Control Over Financial Reporting*, and conforming amendments to certain of the Board's other auditing standards.

This auditing standard is principles-based. It is designed to increase the likelihood that material weaknesses in internal control will be found before they result in material misstatement of a company's financial statements, and, at the same time, eliminate procedures that are unnecessary. The final standard also focuses the auditor on the procedures necessary to perform a high quality audit that is tailored to the company's facts and circumstances. The Board worked closely with the SEC to coordinate Auditing Standard No. 5 with the guidance to public company management the SEC approved this month.

The internal control reporting requirements of the Sarbanes-Oxley Act are a key reason that the reliability and accuracy of financial reporting has improved over the past few years, according to the Board. They feel that the new auditing standard, by focusing the auditor's attention on those matters that are most important to effective internal control, presents another significant opportunity to strengthen the financial reporting process.

The Standard, along with Rule 3525, and the conforming amendments, are required for all audits of internal control for fiscal years ending on or after November 15, 2007.

.06   Auditing Standard No. 6

Auditing Standard No. 6, *Evaluating Consistency of Financial Statements*, and an accompanying set of amendments to the Board's interim auditing standards were adopted in January 2008.

The Board adopted the standard and amendments in light of the Financial Accounting Standards Board's (FASB) issuance of Statement of Financial Accounting Standards No. 154, *Accounting Changes and Error Corrections*, and impending issuance of Statement of Financial Accounting Standards, *The Hierarchy of Generally Accepted Accounting Principles*.

This standard and related amendments update the auditor's responsibilities to evaluate and report on the consistency of a company's financial statements and align the auditor's responsibilities with FASB Statement 154.

Auditing Standard No. 6 also improves the auditor reporting requirements by clarifying that the auditor's report should indicate whether an adjustment to previously issued financial statements results from a change in accounting principle or the correction of a misstatement.

The Board also removed the hierarchy of U.S. Generally Accepted Accounting Principles (U.S. GAAP) from its interim auditing standards. The U.S. GAAP hierarchy identifies the sources of accounting principles and the framework for selecting principles to be used in preparing financial statements. The Board believes that the U.S. GAAP hierarchy is more appropriately located in the accounting standards. Because the FASB intends to incorporate the hierarchy in the accounting standards, it no longer will be needed in the auditing standards. The Board has coordinated with the FASB and understands that the FASB intends to coincide the effective date of its U.S. GAAP hierarchy standard with that of the PCAOB.

Auditing Standard No. 6 is expected improve the quality of the auditor's reporting on items that affect the consistency of financial statements, such as a company's adoption of new accounting principle or its correction of a material misstatement, according to the PCAOB.

.07   Auditing Standard No. 7 on Engagement Quality Review Approved by SEC

The PCAOB announced in January 2010 that the SEC approved Auditing Standard No. 7, *Engagement Quality Review (EQR)*. The standard is effective for engagement quality reviews of audits and interim reviews for fiscal years that began on or after December 15, 2009.

Accordingly, for interim reviews of public companies that file financial reports on a calendar-year basis, the EQR standard was applicable beginning with the quarter ending March 31, 2010. The EQR standard was adopted by the PCAOB on July 28, 2009.

The EQR standard provides a framework for the engagement quality reviewer to evaluate objectively the significant judgments made, and related conclusions reached by the engagement team in forming an overall conclusion about the engagement.

The EQR standard focuses the engagement quality reviewer's attention on the *areas that are most likely to contain a significant engagement deficiency* and increases the likelihood of identifying and correcting those deficiencies before the audit report is issued. This standard goes a long way in clarifying the process.

The PCAOB believes this standard should improve the reliability of audited financial statements by increasing the likelihood that reviewers will identify significant engagement deficiencies before audit reports are issued to the investing public.

The Sarbanes-Oxley Act directs the PCAOB, among other things, to set standards for public company audits, including a requirement for each registered public accounting firm to "provide a concurring or second partner review and approval of [each] audit report (and other related information), and concurring approval in its issuance by a qualified person (as prescribed by the Board) associated with the public accounting firm, other than the person in charge of the audit, or by an independent reviewer (as prescribed by the Board)."

The PCAOB published staff questions and answers in February 2010 to help auditors implement, and the Board's staff administer, the Board's standards. The statements contained in the staff questions and answers are not rules of the Board, nor have they been approved by the Board.

¶27,013   Investor Advisory Group

The PCAOB formed Investor Advisory Group (IAG) to aid the Board in carrying out its responsibilities and hear from investors on a broad range of issues affecting investor protection through the oversight of registered audit firms.

The PCAOB established this Group to inform the Board on matters that affect the investor community. The Board will look to the advisory group to provide high level comment to assist the Board in fulfilling the PCAOB mission. The Board's mission, as mandated by the Sarbanes-Oxley Act of 2002, is to protect the interests of investors by ensuring the preparation of informative, accurate, and independent audit reports.

The purpose of the advisory group is to provide a forum for the Board to obtain the views of, and advice from, the broader investor community on matters affecting investors and the work of the PCAOB. Since its inception, the Board has benefited from the views of the investor community informally. With the establishment of the Investor Advisory Group, the Board now has the opportunity to hear from investors on a regular basis.

Members of the IAG are selected by the Board at its sole discretion to serve a three-year term. Prospective members will be selected from nominations, including self-nominations, received from any person or organization. They represent a broad spectrum of the investment community, as well as individuals who have demonstrated history of commitment to investor protection.

Topics the IAG has discussed include:

- Audit firm transparency,
- Going concern and related global initiatives, and
- Fraudulent financial reporting.

Although IAG Members may be employed or otherwise affiliated with other organizations, IAG Members will serve in their personal capacities and not as representatives of particular employers. They are subject to certain sections of the Board's Ethics Code, as provided in PCAOB Rule 3700, Advisory Group.

The Board has determined that the Chairman of the Board will designate one of the Board members to serve as the Chair of the IAG. The Chair of the IAG will not be considered one of the Members. The Chair will approve the agenda for all IAG meetings. The Chair will be responsible for preparing the meeting agenda, organizing and overseeing meetings, conference calls and related activities, and acting as the general liaison to his colleagues on the Board.

The IAG shall hold one- or two-day semi-annual meetings. Other meetings may be held at the discretion of the Chair. At the discretion of the Chair, the IAG's meetings or portions thereof may be open to the public.

¶27,014   Office of Internal Oversight and Performance Assurance

In early 2004, the PCAOB created the Office of Internal Oversight and Performance Assurance (IOPA) to provide internal examination of the programs and operations of the PCAOB and, in so doing, help ensure the efficiency, effectiveness and integrity of those activities.

IOPA conducts performance reviews and real-time quality assurance of PCAOB functions and programs. IOPA's role at the PCAOB is similar to that of an Inspector General in a government agency.

Specifically, IOPA conducts annual and special reviews and inquiries, to help ensure that the PCAOB:

- Identifies and appropriately addresses risks to the integrity and effectiveness of its programs and operations.
- Identifies and implements opportunities to improve the effectiveness or efficiency of those programs and operations.
- Reports material and relevant financial and operating information, including performance and financial information, in a fair, complete, reliable and timely manner to the public, Congress and the SEC.
- Complies with applicable laws, regulations, and policies, and encourages and enforces such compliance by PCAOB employees.
- Appropriately safeguards and uses resources in an efficient manner.
- Conducts its programs and operations so as to protect and promote the public interest in the integrity of audits.

One of the PCAOB's strategic goals is to operate in a manner that recognizes its public mission and responsibility to exercise careful stewardship over its resources. To further this goal, IOPA conducts performance reviews and real-time quality assurance of PCAOB functions and programs. This will often include recommendations to enhance Board operations.

PART VI

Investments

Though investment guidance is generally provided by finance professionals, rather than accountants, accountants are often asked for assistance or counsel in investing activities. Guidance in some of those areas are provided here in Part VI.

CHAPTER 28
Equity Strategies

¶28,000 Overview

Because of the widespread nature of investment by clients, the CPA/personal financial specialist (PFS) must learn and know about equities, debt and other investment vehicles. In the 1950s, only wealthy people owned stocks and bonds. Now, most clients have investment portfolios. For the CPA, there is a sea of certification and licensing possibilities that are available on both a state and federal level to address these needs.

The AICPA will develop a variety of resources to help credential-holding practitioners provide services to their clients and employers. The NAC will coordinate its activities with the executive committees of each underlying discipline to achieve an integrated approach to help members succeed in their specialty areas.

Financial Industry Regulatory Authority (FINRA) administers all licenses for the Securities and Exchange Commission (SEC). However, even if the CPA elects not to pursue a PFS designation or any of the various financial services licenses, he or she had best be familiar with stocks, bonds, and their corresponding mutual funds—if only from the standpoint of self-defense!

¶28,001 What the Different Types of Stock Investments Offer

When the CPA/PFS discusses the types of stock investments that are available to the client, he or she must first look at what can be done for the client—the professional must define the parameters for measuring results. Results in the stock arena are measured in three ways: growth, income, and total return. These measures in turn must be assessed in the context of relative volatility or risk.

To make the best choice for the client, the CPA/PFS must know what these three goals mean and what they have to offer the client as an investor. Each offers something different:

- Growth increases net worth.
- Income is cash flow to the shareholder.
- Total return is a combination of both growth and income.

Examining each type of investor and providing an example of each may help matching a particular investor with the appropriate stocks.

.01   The Growth Investor

Growth investors typically are those with an ongoing need to increase their net worth and are willing to accept some risk and volatility to accomplish this goal. A growth-oriented investor tends to be either middle class or wealthy. If the investor is wealthy, watching growth stocks is an enjoyable experience. If an investor is of moderate means, seeing a measurable increase year after year in net worth is exhilarating. However, the median investor must be more circumspect in choosing stock, because money is often illiquid and cannot be easily replaced. These investors should look back to when they had very little and should continue looking forward to when they will need a lot. The CPA/PFS needs to help median investors keep their feet firmly on the ground. They have little margin for error, especially when their time considerations are factored into the equation.

Growth stocks are what equity investments are all about. When they perform well, the world is seen through the snappiest rose-tinted glasses. For example, Mary Sue is an administrative manager working at a large computer sales company and makes $35,000 per year. She receives $10,000 per year from her widowed mother to put away for her children's education and often is able to supplement that with a portion of her annual bonus of $5,000 to $15,000. What kind of stocks should she buy for her children? Growth stocks. They have no need for current income, as they are students in school, but their needs for college are almost limitless. Mary Sue's plan of action should be to research and select industries she feels will provide real growth during her children's school years and start a portfolio of the industry leaders in her chosen groups. She can consider as many industry groups as she wants, define her parameters, and start narrowing down her choices. With several good candidates, she then chooses stocks and proceeds to invest her money. She does not have to make perfect choices, but she should look for some research consensus about her selections.

.02   The Income Investor

An income stock is not as glamorous as a growth stock, but it performs a noble function. It is very kind to one's standard of living because it generates a usable cash flow, cushions downturns in growth stocks, and provides a supplement to fixed income investments that neither increase dividends as earnings increase nor have the potential for even modest growth while tracking inflation.

Aunt Sally is a representative income stock investor. During the Carter era, she was happy to roll over short-and intermediate-term fixed income instruments, such as Certificates of Deposit and Treasury Bills, but now the yield advantage of those investments is ancient history. Sally must turn to stocks because the inflation of the ensuing years has eroded the purchasing power of her remaining fixed income investments and she simply has to have more cash flow. For a number of reasons, stocks with big dividends are the answer. She is not happy about buying stock, but the advantages from an income standpoint far outweigh the risks.

The following are reasons for moving to a stock income portfolio:

- Income stocks pay higher yields than comparable fixed income investments because stock investments are more risky than bond investments—the yields are higher because there is no set rate or income for a set rate of time.
- Historically, successful income stocks tend to increase their dividends—a real plus for the income investor. As time and inflation marches on, the investor receives more and more dividends, which hopefully keep pace with her need for more income.
- The growth component inherent in stock investing cannot be ignored—if the value of the stocks appreciate, and should the need arise, some of the stock can be liquidated to generate cash for Sally. Her profits can then be used to pay her obligations.

.03   The Total Return Investor

Total return stocks are the best of both worlds—growth increases net worth and income generates cash flow to supplement other income. It is prototypical money management because the growth and income stocks complement each other and are a balancing factor that is required by many investors. Most people have both net worth and income-sensitive concerns.

Phil is looking forward to retirement in several years. He has almost enough to live on happily in retirement, but he is worried about having to dip into his principle later in life. He is more than a little concerned about the future of Social Security, and whether his pension plan, which does not have cost-of-living adjustments, will be sufficient for future living expenses. Phil needs everything stock investment has to offer—growth and income.

Phil can afford to be moderately aggressive because he is well established for life. But he has to watch his balance. If he generates some decent dividend income before he needs it, he can use his cash flow to address his upcoming requirements later in life. He needs help in seeking out the highest-quality total return stocks the industry provides and starting to build positions in them now.

¶28,002   Value and Growth Stock Investing

Both value and growth have strengths and weaknesses. There are no perfect solutions for investment, or there would be only a few investments from which to choose. Fortunately, there are plenty of investments available to earn the client's money. Three basic characteristics of value and growth help summarize their styles:

1. Value focuses on past performance to determine what is undervalued; growth is very forward looking to project anticipated earnings momentum.
2. Value opportunities are created by the predictably bad behavior of investors; growth opportunities depend on corporate management to make the right decisions to fulfill expectations.
3. Value focuses on out-of-favor basic industries that are staples of society; growth looks at glamour industries for explosive returns.
4. Value is often generated by the short-sightedness of investors. Studies have shown that markets frequently overreact to recent bad news resulting in over-selling stocks beyond otherwise supportable values. Such stocks, if the source of the bad news was overblown, tend to outperform the market in subsequent years.

The CPA/PFS can work through stocks' realistic possibility of increase based on these parameters. This exercise will narrow the field and offer direction toward attainable goals as clients choose to buy stock.

.01   Value Stock Investing

A traditional solution for a bear market is for the CPA/PFS to look for relative value every time the investor makes a securities purchase. The difficulty lies in defining "value." The answer is to buy a quality stock that has rising earnings prospects; that is, it is selling at a discount to itself, its industry group, or the market. This applies to individual stocks, groups, or even markets.

Several examples of value investing follow:

- A stock has had bad earnings because of a one-time charge against earnings for a write-off. Ignoring long-term excellent prospects, institutional investors sell the stock and in one week the stock is off 20 percent. The stock is an A rated equity by Standard & Poor's, analysts still like its long-term appreciation potential, and the stock's 2 percent dividend is perceived as secure. For value and fundamental analytical reasons, the CPA/PFS selects it and the client buys it.

- A group of software stocks has lagged the market. Every time the group starts to rally, one of the companies announces bad earnings, has some negative event, or runs afoul of regulatory agencies. Because the CPA/PFS decides the product the group provides is essential to the United States, he or she picks several of the best stocks in the group, and clients buy them.
- A country has settled its differences with its neighbors and a new government has taken power thanks to supervised elections. The new leaders embrace capitalism wholeheartedly and immediately move to privatize (sell to the public through a stock offering) the telephone company of this emerging nation. Clients buy the stock on the offering. They consider the telephone company a proxy for the whole country, whose prospects the CPA/PFS analyzes and likes. The CPA/PFS considers this an index for the country's fledgling market and concludes that it will take off during this period of enlightened rule.

Much can go wrong, which is why there are always contrary convictions. Because there is a case for three hypothetical investments, playing devil's advocate helps explain when not to make these investments. These are the cases for not investing in any of the preceding three choices:

1. The client decides not to buy the stock. The CPA/PFS decides not to endorse the stock because of its 20 percent drop in one week. They are not totally confident of the company's long-term prospects, because no analyst expected this write-off. What bad news will the next announcement bring?
2. The client decides against investing in stocks in this underperforming software group. A chain is only as strong as its weakest link. The CPA/ PFS cannot decide whether it is profit margins, management, or the cost of financing, but there is something wrong.
3. The client decides to look at another country for foreign investment. The new government seems open to U.S. involvement, but what if they receive all this cash and nationalizes its telephone company again? Even if the government is stable, emerging markets regularly collapse and close for months on end.

Investors must constantly evaluate the risk-to-reward parameters of value stocks. If they are engaged in direct investment, they must continually draw conclusions on examples like these. If the clients have managed money or mutual funds, the portfolio manager is responsible for making these decisions.

.02   Growth Stock Investing

If value investing and all it entails seems too demanding, perhaps the investor is better suited to investing for growth. Growth stocks show great earnings momentum. They are concentrated in the glamour stocks that are all household names, rather than in the fallen angels of esoteric industries that are impossible to understand.

Following are some pithy investment ideas for growth stocks:

- Buy USA! In a risk-averse world, the only safe place to invest money is in the United States. Here is where the earnings are. Every other country is subject to high risk, and why assume more risk than the minimum needed to take the investors where they want to go?
- Buy technology! In a post-industrial society, all that matters is information services. Brains are more important than brawn, and technology is where the brains are. Who cares about the last three years—it will all work out over time.

Once again, as with value investing, what can go wrong? The answer is plenty. Look at the other side of the coin:

- Buy foreign! Many foreign markets have outperformed the U.S. markets. They will continue to do so as long as they continue to develop at the extraordinary rate of growth they have demonstrated for the past decade.
- Forget about technology! The margins in the high-tech industries have shrunk to such an extent that it is impossible to accurately forecast earnings for any of these companies. The technology area soon will be left with only nine or ten companies. The rest will vanish.

¶28,003   High-Quality versus Low-Quality Stocks

If the investor would rather not juggle value versus growth, another stock strategy is selecting high-quality versus low-quality stocks. Low-quality stocks in theory provide significantly greater returns over time because the investor assumes more risk. Unfortunately, this approach can be disappointing. Sometimes, low-quality stocks, when price/earnings ratios are compared, trade at a premium to quality. Therefore, investors have a good chance of losing significantly more money than they can make because they have paid for the privilege of assuming more risk. That is a lose-lose proposition if ever there was one. If the investors have bought low-quality stock, when the high-and low-quality stocks start to trade in line again, the investors may lose in another way. Their low-quality stocks come back to the mean, in addition to underperforming the good-quality stocks. From a commonsense standpoint, most people cannot address such issues because most people simply do not have several dozen (let alone hundreds) of stock positions. The primary benefit of understanding high-quality versus low-quality stock is to gain an understanding of which types of mutual funds to invest in either inside of or outside of a self-directed retirement plan. Although value and growth questions are not too much of an issue with fund choices, most conservative stock funds are of high quality, and most speculative stock funds are of low quality. When it is time for the CPA/PFS to vote with the client's money, the CPA/PFS and clients must choose the quality with which they feel most comfortable.

Fortunately, over longer periods of time, growth stocks and value stocks alternate leadership positions in the market, lending to the wisdom of diversifying across both categories of investments.

¶28,004 Small, Middle, and Large Capitalization Stocks

The CPA/PFS could take a totally different tack and decide to concentrate on selecting weightings between small, mid, and large capitalization stocks. Such stocks define the size of a company. Small capitalization stocks are stocks of up to $10 billion in market capitalization (number of outstanding shares of common stock multiplies by market price), mid caps are up to $100 billion, and large caps can be as much as $500 billion in value of outstanding shares. The larger the capitalization, the larger the trading volume and the better the liquidity. Larger capitalization stocks have more research and media coverage than do small caps. However, small and mid cap stocks traditionally have greater gain potential. It is possible to make a modest investment and have a sizable windfall profit within a few years' time in these less-well-known stocks.

Small cap stocks have historically outperformed large cap stocks, but during certain periods, large cap stocks have survived better than small cap stocks. Some calculate that the earnings streams of small cap are more dependable than large cap because their revenues are not dependent on foreign countries for income. In some corrections, the entire episode seemed to be generated by foreign markets. However, the thought of concentrating on small cap stocks can be dangerous. The professional knows that most small and mid cap stocks are over-the-counter stocks. The NASDAQ, where these stocks are traded, suffered drastic losses during the early years of this century.

¶28,005 Controlling Risk through Diversification

What do the institutional money managers responsible for managing multibillion dollar portfolios and funds do with money? The best lessons in the investment world come from success stories. Modern money management, despite many well-publicized fiascoes, is doing a better job of generating profits and managing risk for clients. Investors can learn a lot from what is applicable to the retail stock portfolio. In the past few years, money managers have attempted to "style invest," which is rotating between value and growth. However, the attempt to correctly time switching between value and growth is only marginally less frustrating than trying to define the styles themselves. Understanding what they are trying to do has clear benefits to stock investors because money management issues are a macrocosm of everything individual investors are trying to accomplish.

Style switchers try to invest in the up cycle of whichever style—value or growth—is outperforming the other. For example, if there is a perception that blue chip basic industry stocks have hit their peak, managers switch over to explosive growth, small capitalization, over-the-counter stocks. When value outperforms, growth underperforms—there is a cycle to that performance. There is a reversal and growth outperforms value. The managers then reverse direction and sell their small caps and go back to the large caps. Market timing is anything but neutral—it is totally subjective, because investors are completely dependent on the manager's insights to switch styles. This method is not foolproof. Sometimes, the waxing and waning of value and growth only reveals itself in hindsight.

CHAPTER 29
Advanced Equity Strategies

¶29,000   Overview

Although initial public offerings (IPOs) decreased rapidly in number in the wake of the turmoil over the accounting scandals at the turn of the century and frequently fell below the initial selling price, indications are that this is changing. Analysts and financial professionals are predicting that IPOs worth considering will be appearing in the near future. It is absolutely necessary that the responsible CPA/personal financial specialist (PFS) be aware of this activity and other aggressive equity strategies. The lively interest in stock concepts will continue as long as the equity arena continues to attract money from almost every class of active securities investor.

¶29,001   Initial Public Offerings

It is difficult for the individual investor to be the early bird on an IPO. However, although the majority of shares usually go to mutual funds and other institutions, that does not mean they all do. Therefore, if the client wants to give it a try, there are right and wrong ways to go about it. The CPA/PFS must understand the IPO process. An IPO is the first time a company raises money from the public by issuing its stock. In order to do so, the company goes to an investment banking firm to discuss, establish, and complete the process of selling its stock. The investment bank appraises the value of the company, figures out how many shares to sell and at what price, and then buys the stock from the company and sells it. After the company receives money from the investment bank, it is out of the loop.

The stock is then sold through a selling syndicate. The company receives X amount of money, the investment banking firm sells it at X plus its markup, and the selling syndicate marks it up still more for sale to the public. Although the investor pays no direct stock commissions to buy IPOs, there is plenty of "selling concession" built into the price of any offering. The benefit for the investor is the opportunity to invest in new companies that they hope will become the Microsofts and Intels of the future. The results can be somewhat different and much more complicated, but finding tomorrow's hot stock is what IPOs are all about.

.01 Entering the IPO Fray

As mentioned, there is a right way and a wrong way to approach the IPO market. For the client to profit, the CPA/PFS must follow the "rules of engagement":

1. *Learn the IPO game.* The company must need money or it would not be going public. This is not necessarily bad, however, the client does not want to invest money in some executive branch's estate planning exercise, in a company whose board thinks earnings have peaked, or in a company that is desperate to expand or buy new property simply to maintain market share. The CPA/PFS should perform the necessary research to identify the company's reasons for going public.
2. *Select the right broker.* New issue trading is a specialty and clients benefit from hiring an expert for this activity. A broker should be able to show the CPA/PFS which IPOs have been allocated stock, in what volume, where the stock has gone, and how the various underwritings did.
3. *Open the account at a large wirehouse brokerage office.* Big wirehouse deals have tended to outperform their smaller counterparts' performances in this area. Discount brokerages rarely participate in any worthwhile deals.
4. *Spread around the accounts.* If clients have enough assets, deposit them at all the big wirehouses and do some business with all of them. The more professional relationships the CPA/PFS has, the more apt the clients are to be in the right place at the right time to purchase IPO stock.
5. *Remember, the best clients have the opportunity to buy the most stock.* IPO participation often takes on highly political sales-driven overtones. Brokerage clients are repaid for previous business with their firm's IPO allocations.

6. *Collect prospectuses and research choices.* Earnings of new issues average falling 20 percent to 30 percent in the year following a stock offering.
7. *Put in an indication of interest (IOI) as fast as possible.* If clients think they want a stock, ask immediately—too soon is better than too late. The client can always pull an order before the deal is released. Prospectuses are often impossible to understand, especially because so many new issues are either high-tech or biotech stocks. In whatever order the CPA/PFS prefers, he or she will often have to rely on either gut instinct or the investment professional.
8. *Avoid pressure sales.* Securities are sold rather than bought: rather than actively buy securities for themselves, conventional retail brokerage clients are shown products by their brokers and choose their investments from what they are shown. If someone is trying hard to persuade the client to buy something, the client probably does not want it.
9. *Stick to the plan.* The CPA/PFS should be careful to invest in what the client wants and be very cautious about investing in anything else.
10. *Flip new issues.* "Flipping" new issues is the technique of buying an IPO and immediately selling it into the market. The client realizes an immediate gain or loss and goes onto the next deal immediately. This is what many institutions do with new issues and perhaps so should the clients. Most new issues tend to track down in price and volume over a period of time as their fundamentals deteriorate. See point 1 above.

If the CPA/PFS and client really like a stock and yet cannot buy the stock on the IPO, he or she should buy it later in the open market. IPOs that do well usually continue to do well for some time, so subsequent investors tend to do well, too. Half the new deals close down from their opening price at the end of their first trading day. Often, the stocks are cyclical (rise fast in good times; decline fast in bad) and, as previously discussed, are at or near a peak in their cycle.

Good clients of large wirehouses rarely get burned by IPOs. It pays to be a good client (an active fee-generating market participant) in the new issue arena. Many IPOs never receive research coverage from the large wirehouses, the stocks drift off in price and volume, and the companies' images are permanently damaged. Brokers are very careful to avoid such deals, but the CPA/PFS would be hard put to determine this alone. Salespeople tend to know quickly which issues are hot and which issues are bad investments.

.02 Investment Banking Today: The IPO Scene

At this point, any resemblance between investment banking relationships today and the banking relationships of yesteryear is virtually coincidental. There is an industry-wide problem of too many bankers courting too few clients. In an era of corporate consolidations, as opposed to expansions, this problem can only worsen. The unhappy byproduct of all this is a lowering of banking standards and parameters when faced with the necessity to "do deals." Particularly as investment banking relates to smaller companies, this courtship ritual can easily prove fatal. The successful, new, publicly owned company has employees whose expertise in their specialty is unquestioned, but their knowledge of business is nonexistent. These companies may have complete contempt for "bean counters," except as the bean counters relate to their own personal beans. The owners succumb completely to the untoward advances of the various investment bankers that come calling. They select the banker who makes them feel the best about themselves and start down the road to what often becomes a disastrous union.

Although this all sounds pretty pessimistic, there are some distinct benefits to the investor who understands this process. Everyone hears about and remembers the highly successful IPOs; everyone hears about and ignores the failures. The nature of the American investor is to be optimistic. Given the past few years of stock market performance, American investors are not as optimistic as they were, but hope springs eternal. Therefore, the investor should be aware that sometimes things could go very wrong with an investment. The CPA/PFS who studies and learns from these negative episodes may be in a better position to avoid such failures.

Although in hindsight it is almost impossible to decide who is to blame for the thousands of IPOs that have failed over the years, it is a somewhat easier task to discover what went wrong. The investor can be "on guard" and watch for the telltale signs of problems. Armed with knowledge about stock liquidity, research coverage, and trading volume, the CPA/PFS can help clients either avoid or escape such offerings with minimal damage.

It is safe to say that almost no company going public really understands the machinations of Wall Street, but certainly may understand these machinations once the deal is complete. Because of the company's justified enthusiasm, it is often caught up in a process that has no relationship with the quality of what has come before it. The employee's abilities, the company's products, and its future—all are swept aside by the normal desire to quantify the business it has created. The business sections of local papers are riddled with stories about the founders and board members of "fallen angels" and "orphans" that still have excellent products, good management, and fine futures. However, all this is tainted by the fact that the stock has become a "single-digit midget" since its much-ballyhooed regional offering.

What happened? The companies experienced too much, too soon from a securities standpoint and simply fell apart. Whether an earnings issue, a product issue, or an accounting issue, it does not matter. What does matter, however, is that, in the stock market, "down" is usually "out" for small capitalization companies.

From the point of view of the retail investor, it is most important for the CPA/PFS to watch for the slightest suggestion that IPO earnings may disappoint. There are numerous small deals that have immediate liquidity problems because they never earn research coverage from national, regional, or even local brokerage firms. For example, XYZ Technology comes to market; the deal is a success, trading up to $15 from its IPO price of $12. Everyone is happy…for the moment. No brokerage firm picks up research coverage of XYZ Technology. Although assured by its bankers that its stock would be a popular issue with analysts, the opposite proves to be the case. The issue receives several months of unnecessary price support—unnecessary because it is trading above its offering price—but even the tout services do not pick up the stock. Worse yet, XYZ Technology is about to end its softest sales quarter and realizes it will have to announce a decline in revenues and earnings for the quarter. When XYZ was still a private company, this issue did not matter because everyone inside the company knew this happened every year or so. The public shareholders, however, are not so understanding, nor are they as sanguine about XYZ Technology's future. The stock, in a week, goes from $14 to $5, perhaps on its way to zero.

When the public sees the largest capitalization, most well-known companies announce the probability of lower earnings (usually, after the market close), the market responds immediately on the next day's opening, and the response is harsh.

Factor in the response of such negative news with high tech and biotech stocks, remembering that most IPOs are small to mid cap high tech and biotech companies, and the offerings have the makings of some real disasters.

.03   Conclusion on IPOs

To conclude the discussion of IPOs, 5 percent to 10 percent of the price of an IPO pays for fees. If the CPA/PFS is of the opinion that the deal has run its course at the current price, he or she should sell. There is too much excess built into the price of any deal to wait. The CPA/PFS must keep careful track of all public discussions of the deals before, during, and after their release. The Internet can be invaluable here. If there is a lot of negative publicity from legitimate sources, or if there is a suggestion that a price may be lowered to improve its appeal, the client's IOI should be pulled immediately, as this indicates an impending disaster. Conversely, if the broker calls and says the price range on a deal has been raised, the CPA/PFS should thank him or her and anticipate a nice lunch together—on the client, as the stock is probably a winner. If the CPA/PFS notices an investment banker consistently in litigation over deals, particularly with former banking clients, he or she should not participate in the banker's deals—in investment banking, where there is smoke, there is often fire.

¶29,002 Foreign Stocks

Conventional wisdom, a term that often proves to be an oxymoron, says that some foreign exposure in equities is necessary in all accounts because of an eventual return of inflation and the high performance of some overseas equity markets. Factually, 60 percent of the world's equity assets are nondomestic, but only 15 percent of domestic investment is foreign. For example, John Doe participates in only 15-percent ownership in foreign stocks here, although 60 percent of the world's equity is in foreign investment and available for John Doe to buy. By equity size alone, some foreign stock exposure should have the effect of hedging a domestic stock portfolio, because often what makes U.S. markets go down has the opposite effect abroad. Although this is not uniformly the case, there is some valid historic precedent for such belief. As seen time and again, moderation is often the key to success, in any areas of investment.

Also, there is a belief that foreign exposure can enhance the overall return of a stock portfolio while insuring against domestic market volatility. Foreign stocks are attractive from a diversification standpoint. There is more out there left untouched by many investors because they either do not want what they do not know or they cautiously want what is familiar to them.

The primary risk of investment in foreign equity markets is currency exposure. Foreign exchange rates come into play as investors buy foreign-currency-denominated securities with U.S. dollars and reconvert back to U.S. dollars from foreign currency dividends or sale proceeds. If the dollar weakens in relation to a foreign stock's currency, the investors make money; if the dollar strengthens in relation to a foreign stock's currency, the investors lose. For example, investors buy XYZ foreign stock here; the stock continues to rise in its home country, but here the dollar becomes stronger and stronger. The stock simply does not go up in price. In the opposite case, a stock remains flat in its home country, but its currency strengthens in relationship to the dollar—the domestic shareholder sees his or her investment go up in price.

Another foreign investment concern is the actual costs of buying and selling foreign securities in their markets. Some foreign markets have huge buy/sell costs. Of course, time zone constraints, money settlement problems, and the always present issue of liquidity can all cause problems.

Most retail investors make foreign securities purchases in the form of mutual fund choices. The costs of foreign investment are still there, although greatly reduced by volume fund purchases. There are so many foreign funds, both closed and open ended, that there is not a single market, vehicle, or strategy that a person cannot invest in through mutual funds. In the mutual fund arena it is important to distinguish between foreign funds and international funds. Foreign funds invest in other-than-U.S. stocks while international funds may own

U.S. stocks as well as foreign equities. Also, as will be explained more fully, funds owning international corporations tend to blunt the distinction between domestic and foreign investing.

Mutual funds will always mirror the best and worst of any investment plan. They facilitate diversification for an investor—but that is the very nature of mutual funds, not just foreign stock ones. Investors can probably have a higher than usual return and lower than usual risk (volatility) portfolio with some foreign exposure. However, in times of extreme and dramatic domestic downside stress, the foreign markets react accordingly to the downside, often even to a degree in excess of domestic corrections. In addition, these markets tend to stabilize more slowly.

¶29,003   Emerging Markets

Emerging markets, quite simply, are markets in countries whose output of goods and services falls below the average per capita output of goods and services for the world. Above average countries are considered developed. If a country does not exceed the average production of the world, it is an emerging nation economically, regardless of its age or history. Emerging markets are the most aggressive growth and value areas in the equity universe. The greatest opportunities and the greatest risk are in the global emerging markets. Geographically, investment is spread through Latin America, emerging Asia, emerging Europe, and South Africa. As with generic foreign investment, if domestic markets continue to do better, a very selective posture should be assumed with emerging markets investment.

The historic tendency is for emerging markets to underperform U.S. markets when the U.S. is outperforming other markets. However, emerging markets tend to outperform the established, mature foreign markets when U.S. markets are under performing globally. Therefore, when U.S. markets are doing well, they tend to outperform all foreign investment, but when foreign markets are doing well relative to U.S., the emerging markets tend to do the best of all.

When considering the matter of investing in foreign markets, significant issues of risk must be addressed by the individual investor:

- Is the market liquid? Some countries have constant liquidity problems that should dissuade all but the most determined investors. However, there are some countries absolutely determined to present the maximum liquidity they can generate in hopes of attracting "serious money" investment from well-developed countries and their investors.
- Does the country present an investor-friendly profile to the world? This issue is linked to the question of liquidity and hinges on whether the country is open-minded about and willing to encourage international investment.

If a country is hostile to capitalism, there is no reason to invest there. Conversely, if a country has laws friendly to investment and securities regulations supporting the privatizing of its industrial and utility companies, why not take a look?

- Does a country have the capability of harnessing its aspirations? All the material and natural resources in the world are worthless if no one can mine, drill, or harvest them and there is nobody there who can develop a local use for them.
- Will opening up a country to investment benefit or brutalize its nascent markets? Anyone can make a strong case for either view in any country—it is the job of investors to sort out each country's potential prior to investment.

As time goes by and these markets mature, their dependency upon U.S. market performance should diminish. "Decoupling" will be accomplished as managers take a bottom-up approach to looking at individual companies. More and more of these companies will then find themselves in the country and regional fund trading here in the U.S. They will have increased liquidity as they become more familiar to domestic investors, both retail and institutional. However, investors cannot forget that, uniformly, these countries are characterized by nonstandard methods of accounting and reporting, a lack of market regulation, and currency risks. Any of these factors can quickly eliminate any profits or diversification benefits that might be gained from the stocks.

For the domestic retail investor who is determined to invest in emerging markets, there are two reasonable ways to participate in these markets:

1. Invest in America—Buy domestic stocks that earn a large percentage of their profits in countries or regions that captivate the investor. The client can own direct participation in the economies of these countries and regions without direct involvement with their markets.
2. Buy the mutual funds of the countries or regions that the CPA/PFS and client select. In particular, the close-ended funds are often covered by the big wirehouses and, therefore, are managed with care. Although the specialty funds often generate enormous losses, the expertise of a manager can generate more success than clients might on their own.

¶29,004   Convertible Bonds

For investors who are concerned about the stock market, convertible bonds and convertible preferred stock can be the perfect hybrid investment. They can be perfect for modest or indirect stock or bond exposure, because convertibles are a true hybrid fixed income and equity product.

Like everything in securities, there are two sides to every story. Convertible securities are generally issued as debt securities, but when certain price conditions are met, they can be converted into equity securities. Proponents of convertibles like the bonds because, if a stock rises, the bonds can be converted into that stock. In addition, convertibles typically generate much higher income than do comparable stocks. Naysayers on convertibles consider them the worst of both debt and equity investments—the yields never approach straight debt yields and the appreciation never approaches straight equity appreciation.

Converts are true "total return" vehicles, with the strengths and weaknesses inherent in total return investments per se. The individual receives the yield that the bond or preferred stock pays, plus the predetermined amount of appreciation built into the bond if it is achieved by the issuer's common stock. Because the convertible instruments are issued at a convertible price 20 percent or 25 percent or so above the then current price of the stock, they do not participate dollar for dollar as the stock appreciates. However, they can gain 60 percent to 70 percent of upside, yet appear to have only 30 percent to 40 percent of downside stock market risk. They tend to trade like bonds in bad stock market periods and like stock during good stock market times. This seeming irrationality makes perfect sense when one considers that converts are hybrid products of debt and equity.

.01   Picking Convertible Securities

The traditional issuer of convertibles is usually a small-or mid-capitalization company with extraordinary growth and the presumed capability of sustaining this growth. These bonds are rarely particularly seasoned. Best estimates suggest that convertibles of rising market stars last three to five years before they are converted en masse to equities and cease to exist.

Most investors are best off selecting an appropriate mutual fund or money manager for investment in convertible securities. The primary benefits of mutual fund investment and money management for the investor are the usual ones inherent to mutual fund investment and money managers per se—professional management, diversification, and relief from responsibility. Furthermore, there are elements of significance attached to convertible investment that make the alternative, individual issue selection difficult for the retail investor:

1. *Rating issues.* The usual convertible issuer is rated below investment grade (BBB). Not only are retail investors incapable of learning about or understanding the nuances of lower-quality debt, but often they cannot buy junk debt directly. Junk debt is a small segment of the domestic bond market and convertible debt is a small segment of junk debt. Therefore, there are genuine inventory problems that are too great a hurdle for even the most determined investor to overcome.

2. *Timeliness of portfolio management.* Because of the volatility of the under-
    lying stocks of most convertible issues, the buy-and-hold investor takes a
    decided back seat in this area of investment. The convertible issues are con-
    stantly changing their natures in the face of complex issues related to their
    highly specialized market. For example, because of the comparatively small
    size of this market, there is a strong tendency (particularly to the downside)
    to overreact temporarily to news that immediately relates to major issues or
    issuers (especially technology or biotech).
3. *New issue securities.* Because most new issue convertible debt is priced at
    or near par, they do not have the peculiar premiums and discounts with
    which many seasoned issues trade. These premiums and discounts are re-
    flections of the trading price of the convertible securities underlying equity
    prices—successful stocks have premium convertibles, unsuccessful stocks
    have discount convertibles. The retail client cannot normally expect to par-
    ticipate in the new issue convertibles, because they often carry sizable bond
    investment minimums.
4. *Portfolio turnover.* For many reasons (e.g., calls, rating changes, equity
    behavior, and mergers and acquisitions), convertible portfolios' turnover
    of securities tends to be both rapid and significant. This extreme activity
    makes the services of a mutual fund or money manager much more desir-
    able for the more practical retail investor who cannot make the necessary
    time commitment to keep pace with the price and market activity.
5. *Convertible preferred stock.* Convertible preferred stock is a hybrid invest-
    ment of a hybrid investment. These are hard for anyone to understand—
    and there are many kinds, with varying levels of liquidity. They are a retail
    "made for packaging" product.

¶29,005   Micro-Capitalization Stocks

"Micro-capitalization stocks" are often fancy words for "penny stocks." Many
small-cap specialists have had to ratchet up their limits of what constitutes
"small" as the market has moved upward. Formerly, $250 million was the up-
per limit—it may now be $1 billion.

As mutual fund managers who specialize in micro-caps are forced to step up to
the plate with larger capitalization limits, the issue of concern is the extent to which
these portfolios still mirror the principles with which they were created. Even though
the managers may actually remain consistent in their investment philosophies, the
makeup of their fund portfolios may change dramatically. This would happen as the
securities within the fund grow or reflect higher capitalization limits, thus putting
managers in the awkward position of drifting away from their stated style.

All concerns notwithstanding, the micro-cap stock, perhaps as a function
of terminology and "language inflation," has taken on a life of its own and

an identity of the old small cap stock. These stocks are currently perceived as corporations of $250 million capitalization and less, sometimes $500 million, sometimes and $100 million. They account for 5,000 or so companies, which constitute 70 percent to 80 percent of the publicly traded stocks in the U.S.

Every investor who owns stocks is interested in micro-cap stocks, because they are the penny stocks that can increase in value a hundred-or even a thousandfold. However, the stocks are invariably thinly traded, the markets and the market makers are often nonprofessionals, and the cost of "doing business" is very high. Nevertheless, long-term, micro-capitalization stocks have outperformed large capitalization stocks. Research sources are available from the mutual fund rating services. For the direct investment oriented, the investor can often talk directly to the highest level of management in a micro-cap company.

There are about 50 mutual funds that invest in micro-caps, and their results are often astonishing. Up and down years of 50 percent are not uncommon. If ever there is an area where the fund manager provides added value, it is in the area of micro-cap portfolio management. Even with all the research available, most investors would benefit from the mutual fund vehicle for this type of security. Happily, there are a number of micro-cap funds that enjoy the highest mutual fund ratings available from the various rating services.

¶29,006   Exchange-Traded Funds

January 29, 1993, saw the premier of the S&P Depository Receipts, Trust Series 1, the first Exchange-Traded Fund (ETF). The investment world changed forever that day. Nobody could have even vaguely predicted the growth of ETFs through the succeeding decade and a half. Their growth is more than double the growth of index mutual funds.

More than 100 new ETFs were introduced in 2008 in what has become an endless stream of new vehicles. In 2009, that stream had become 593 portfolios or series of registered open-end investment companies operating as ETFs.

On January 13, 2009, the Securities and Exchange Commission (SEC) adopted amendments to Form N-1A used by mutual funds to register under the Investment Company Act of 1940 and to offer their securities under the Securities Act of 1933. in order to enhance the disclosures that are provided to mutual fund investors. Of particular interest to readers of this chapter is the fact that the Commission is adopting additional amendments that are specifically intended to result in the disclosure of more useful information to investors who purchase shares of exchange-traded funds on national securities exchanges.

The amendments to Form N-1A include enhanced disclosure requirements focused on retail investors who buy ETF shares in the secondary market, as opposed to financial institutions that purchase creation units directly from the fund. ETF-specific amendments to Form N-1A, including some that are specific to ETFs with creation units of at least 25,000 shares, are addressed in the following items:

- Item 1: Front and Back Cover.
- Item 3: Costs, Fees and Turnover.
- Item 6: Purchase and Redemption Information.
- Item 11: Shareholder Information.

The SEC proposed several amendments to Form N-1A to accommodate the use of the form by ETFs. Most ETFs are organized and registered as open-end funds. Unlike traditional mutual funds, however, they sell and redeem individual shares ("ETF shares") only in large aggregations called "creation units" to certain financial institutions. ETFs register offerings and sales of ETF shares under the Securities Act and list their shares for trading under the Securities Exchange Act of 1934 ("Exchange Act"). As with any listed security, investors trade ETF shares at market prices.

The proposed amendments for ETF prospectuses were designed to meet the needs of investors (including retail investors) who purchase ETF shares in secondary market transactions rather than financial institutions that purchase creation units directly from the ETF. The SEC adopted the proposed amendments for ETF prospectuses with changes to respond to issues raised by commenters on the summary prospectus proposing release and the ETF proposing release.

The SEC amended Form N-1A to eliminate the requirement that ETF prospectuses disclose information on how to buy and redeem shares directly from the ETF because it is not relevant to investors who are secondary market purchasers of ETF shares. The Commission proposed to require ETF prospectuses to state the number of shares contained in a creation unit (*i.e.*, the aggregate number of shares an ETF will issue or the number it is necessary to redeem from the ETF). The prospectus would also state that individual shares can only be bought and sold on the secondary market through a broker-dealer, and that shareholders may pay more than net asset value ("NAV") when they buy ETF shares and receive less than NAV when they sell shares because shares are bought and sold at current market prices.

The Summary Prospectus Rules require all ETFs, regardless of creation unit size, to disclose information in their prospectuses regarding the extent and frequency with which market prices of fund shares have tracked the fund's net asset value (NAV). The premium/discount is also required to appear in the fund's annual reports.

Another provision is that an ETF may omit disclosure of this prospectus and annual report if the fund provides the information on its website and discloses in its prospectus or annual report an Internet address where investors can locate the information.

In general, the amendments require key information to appear in plain English in a standardized order at the front of the mutual fund statutory prospectus. The SEC also is adopting rule amendments that permit a person to satisfy its mutual fund prospectus delivery obligations under Section 5(b)(2) of the Securities Act by sending or giving the key information directly to investors in the form of a summary prospectus and providing the statutory prospectus on an Internet Web site. Upon an investor's request, mutual funds also must send the statutory prospectus to the investor. These amendments are intended to improve mutual fund disclosure by providing investors with key information in plain English in a clear and concise format, while enhancing the means of delivering more detailed information to investors.

ETFs are a minimal cost security that can be used to create any kind of index the investor can conceive, and they are totally tax efficient for the investor. There are myriad nonsecurity asset classes from which to select. Every securities sector known—domestic, international, or global. Furthermore, any asset allocation model no matter how complex can be quickly realized with ETFs. They can be as broad based or as fine-tuned a matrix as an investor desires. Indeed, only a couple dozen ETFs are broad based, household name index products—the remainder are all narrowly defined specialists funds. Hence, they are often diverse in content, but within a very small niche.

There are no managers of traditional ETFs but there are now enhanced, managed ETFs. Therefore, whether an investor prefers passive or active management of an index, there is probably a vehicle to fit the bill.

While all traditional indexes are represented, it cannot be over emphasized that there are numerous specialty indexes that are tied to many uncommon concepts.

There are, of course, long ETFs, but recently long/short, short, and leveraged ETFs have also been added. As a consequence, there is very little a manager can do with bushels, baskets, or bundled securities that are not available packaged as an ETF. This has very significant ramifications from both a liquidity and a facilitation standpoint because, on a modest scale, the sophisticated efforts of a large scale money manager can be replicated by anyone who wants to try sophisticated strategies "on their own."

For example, there are social consciousness, equal weight, and divided growth ETFs. There are ETFs that attempt to index and measure most hard assets and most collectible assets.

While ETFs are used in many tax deferred accounts, and some 401k platforms now include only ETFs in their menus with no traditional mutual funds, ETFs can be of particular value for tax liability efficiency. While most investment advisors are conscious of the need to use investment vehicles that are as tax efficient as possible, some may not be as prone as they might be to search for the most suitable ones for accomplishing these goals.

Traditional mutual funds are decidedly inefficient tax vehicles. Everyone knows this and there is nothing to be done about it given the structure of open ended mutual funds. Indexes do not approach the trading activity that managed funds have. Also, the investor controls the trading of an ETF, whereas they have no control over what a traditional fund manager does. If an investor wants to realize a gain or a loss, they sell their ETF. If they don't want to realize a gain or a loss, they don't sell their ETF. It is that simple. The exact size of the gain or loss is managed, too—by the investor—whereas the investor has no say with a traditional mutual fund.

Also, more specifically, ETFs can be used to avoid wash sales. If a stock situation does not work out and there is a desire to harvest a loss, an ETF index fund in the specific area of the stock sold can be purchased without creating a wash sale, but the sector position is still maintained.

ETFs are also immediately liquid throughout the trading day, which is totally unlike the traditional mutual fund that can only be transacted "blind" during the course of the day because the net asset value (price) is not calculated until after the close of the trading day.

The only downside of ETFs is the opportunity for abuse inherent in any trading type vehicle. ETFs are an absolute bonanza for their managers, brokers, marketers, and the financial services industry per se, but they can be used and abused by the public like any other investment vehicle. The rate of turnover of the most liquid ETFs is 2500 percent per year, according to best estimates, and it is easy to conclude that many of those trades are closed on the loss side of the ledger. Be that as it may, the ETF is a vehicle that has arrived within the last 15 years and is most certainly here to stay. It is for many purposes a better mousetrap. It behooves every conscientious financial advisor to learn and understand all they can about the expanding ETF universe.

In addition to ETF's, Exchange Traded Notes (ETNs) exist as a vehicle to track a strategy or index. The difference between ETF's and ETN's is that ETN's are debt (other than equity) securities of their issuers and are rated by credit agencies just like any other debt. They may have an advantage in terms of specificity for various commodities, currency, assets, and strategies, but that is hard to prove. They have the same tax advantages ETF's have. Indeed, they may be even better because they often make no distributions of either income or gains. Tax liability (if it exists) is recognized at the time of sale or maturity.

¶29,007   Structured Investment Products

There are several types of structured investments that investors should be familiar with. The most important aspect of structured investment products is that they are designed to meet some clearly defined investment objective that can be quantified in a very simple investment format. The return is a function of whatever assets are contained in the product and their performance. There are no practical limits on the type of assets contained in structured investment products—equity, debt, commodities, domestic, foreign, global—anything.

What is common to all of them is one or more of the key features and key benefits of the products. The primary feature is market participation in all manners of markets and strategies that are not normally available to conventional retail clients.

Some of that market participation in structured investment products is enhanced participations with the possibility of outperforming the markets the products are attached to. Commonly, this out performance is a byproduct of investment in options, futures, and other leveraged products.

Somewhat related to enhanced participation in equity growth is that some structured investment products offer enhanced income. Favorable rates of interest are created by leverage, forfeit of capital gains, and market volatility.

However, even market volatility may be mitigated in the structured investment products. Some offer partial or even full principal protection at the expiration of the holding period.

The benefits are very easy to describe and understand. The structured investment product is a model of simplicity that any reasonably savvy investor can understand. They are very flexible and this is clearly substantiated by the extraordinary variety of the markets, viewpoints, and strategies contained and implemented in structured investment products.

Related to this, they are products of great diversity. There are no asset classes unrepresented by structured investment products. Furthermore, in these various products, both aggressive and conservative risk/return profiles are utilized in all the different asset classes.

Lastly, there are distinct tax advantages related to single security characteristics of structured investment products. They are consolidations of legal, operational, financial, and portfolio matters under one security that dramatically enhances control of the products.

¶29,008   Accelerated Return Notes

Accelerated Return Notes (ARNs) are usually unsecured senior debt of their issuers. They are created to offer investors a multiple, typically 2x or 3x, upside with a cap, but retain one for one downside, sometimes with a downside cap.

They are of greatest value in a market of flat or modest return in their normal form. However, there are also bearish ARNs for a moderately declining market perception.

They are a short-term vehicle with terms of anywhere from 9 to 24 months. Although they are debt vehicles, there are no periodic interest payments. Typically, they are released at an offering price of $10 per unit. They are often issued as shares and are exchange traded. Once again, although most are bullish, there are also bearish views ETNs.

The opportunity for enhanced returns is their primary investment feature, as said at usually a 2x or 3x multiple with one to one downside. However, there are other advantages to consider for potential investment. Their duration (9–24 months, as noted above) can facilitate hedges and other strategies for a long-term standpoint portfolio. Hence, they create an absolute time value for an investment. While initially there were only a few ARN strategies marketed, there is now a wide variety of index, stock, commodity, currency, and asset classes in our and other markets.

¶29,009 Hedge Funds

Hedge funds are here to stay. Despite 2008 meltdowns and a very hostile press, the fact of the matter is that many institutional investors will own little else.

There is an infinite variety of funds and an almost equally infinite variety of funds within individual funds of a given style.

It is important to be familiar with the characteristics of hedge funds and know a bit about the different styles and strategies of the hedge fund vehicle.

The primary perceived virtue of hedge funds is the absence of regulation. Very, very few individual investors in the domestic investing universe can qualify as individuals to buy hedge funds. There are very high income, net worth, and minimum participation requirements. Lack of regulation translates into more open portfolio management, flexibility of fees, less disclosure of investments, and avoidance of myriad rules attendant to conventional mutual funds.

"Hedge Fund" does not mean hedge fund anymore. Hedging can be a part of a hedge fund strategy, but it by no means is either the driving or the major tenet of hedge funds. It's just a name—nothing more for a wide variety of lightly regulated, aggressive, active investment vehicles. They are, then, legal entities with some sort of investment structure (or, structures) that employ a strategy (or, strategies) that is designed to make large amounts of money in as short a time as possible. They do not operate as U.S. registered investment companies, so in no way should they be confused with mutual funds. Indeed, they operate in almost total anonymity even given what reporting they are required to do. Nobody can seem to even figure out how many there are and how much capital they control. Their contribution to the market's collapse in 2008 is therefore a matter of huge dispute because of the illusive nature and moving target aspect of the genre. As if this were not confusing enough, there are so many funds of hedge funds now that quantification in any context is nearly impossible.

For example, the performance characteristics are (as easily imagined) thoroughly elusive. They are presumed (because of a lack of regulation) to outperform normal mutual funds; they are perceived to be less volatile than mutual funds, and they are supposed to be less correlated with traditional markets. This is impossible to quantify, but easy to surmise.

What is impossible to ignore is that they are the most expensive securities vehicle ever created. They are only for wealthy retail and institutional investors who can afford the risks associated with the generation of these rewards and should only be embarked upon with the clear understanding that every penny of the client's investment can and might be lost.

¶29,010   Alternative Investments

With the collapse of traditional stock and bond investments in 2008, it is a safe assumption to believe that the broadly defined area of alternative investment will generate more activity rather that less. A good reason for this is that the traditional strengths of stocks and bonds—liquidity, daily valuation, diversity, global characteristics, transparent costs, and more fly out the window when money is being vaporized on a daily basis with no reasonable expectation of a rapid recovery. While this is not to say that stocks and bonds have permanently lost their appeal, it certainly is valid to say that investors are open to looking at a lot more alternative investments than they were during the 2002–2007 period when traditional markets appeared to be impervious to sustained declines. It appeared that a rising tide raised many ships (most notably, commodities), but that turned out to be sadly incorrect. By late 2008, it was widely believed in the financial services industry that there were only two positions secure in the industry—cash and fetal. And even cash had its tremors when a money market fund "broke the buck" and had to be shut down before federal insurance supported the product.

While there is no way to discuss with expertise or even detail the possibilities out in the open, it may be of value to mention them and then know what might be considered by clients looking for "something different."

The majority of them that are not brokerage products relate to what may be broadly defined as collectibles. Well, anything can be described as a collectible, one way or another. However, without holding up to ridicule any of them, it is certainly true that some have a more developed and longer history, and hence a more rational price structure historically than others.

Of course, what instantly comes to mind is art. While art certainly has volatile market periods and requires great expertise (and luck!) in selection, it appears true that it tends to hold and increase value over time for the investors who know it well. Art collection is also not an activity confined to the wealthiest and is something that with educated and honest guidance can increase in value significantly for the people who invest in it.

In addition, the most traditional of collectibles like stamps, coins, china, crystal, and such can be lucrative. Related areas like antiques, musical instruments, and other functional items can also yield significant profit.

Without belaboring the point, they can all under some standards be described as equity oriented investments with growth potential. It behooves anyone advising people about investments to be cognizant of these markets and be able to discuss them coherently with their clients.

¶29,011   Real Estate Investment Trusts

REITs are real estate investments that are publically traded. Their primary utility is as an income vehicle for the investor and a tax avoidance vehicle for the issuer.

REITs are tax vehicles for the companies that issue them. The investor in the REIT assumes the tax consequence of their income and capital gains distributions. Companies can retain only a small part of the income or gains, usually no more than 10 percent. They are very similar to closed-end mutual funds in that they are traded daily like stocks. They are also like pass-through securities because they distribute materially all of their income as often as these distributions are scheduled. Also, like closed-end funds, there are hundreds of them. REITs tend to be primarily hybrids (both income and gains), but there are some that distribute only income and some that distribute only capital gains.

Like closed-end mutual funds, REITs have a net asset value (NAV) that they can trade at, or at a discount, or at a premium. Over the last two years, post 4th quarter of 2008 and 1st quarter of 2009, some REITs traded at huge discounts (40–80 percent) to their perceived NAV. However, with real estate values plunging, it is very difficult to arrive at a fair NAV for many of these securities. Great care should be used in the selection process of REITs. When reputable, recognized analysts classify many REITs as speculative or high risk, believe them! While the income from REITs has averaged 5–8 percent as a class per year for many years, the NAV fluctuates in a dramatically more volatile manner.

¶29,012   Options

There are many books with highly developed strategies and programs for options activities. Those are available at any bookstore for investors that want expert detailed advice.

For the average investor, what is necessary to know is simple because what options require for most investors is merely that they are familiar with their existence. Despite all the publicity attached to options trading, the fact of the matter is that very, very few individual investors ever do them.

Most options and options activities center around options on equity securities. They have been used for speculation, income, and hedging for decades. They are available on every significant domestic stock at a wide variety of prices and expirations.

In addition, there are equity options on the indexes made up of the individual stocks. They are an opportunity to utilize specific index values and specific expiration dates leveraged so that the actual cost is dramatically less than ETF's might be.

In addition to equity options, there are other types of options. One variety is debt options. They are options based on rates, yields, and prices of debt securities. Treasury securities are of course the most common options available.

In addition, there are foreign currency options. They are commonly used to hedge currency with or speculate about currency movement. Because the markets for foreign currencies are often very different than our own, there are some characteristics and risks associated with currency options that are specific to them and must be considered before investing. Without going into detail, there are dollar-denominated, cross-rate, and cash-settled foreign currency options—all similar but all with significant differences.

¶29,013   Transparency Necessary for All Investment Products

The most significant aspect of creating transparency is its absolute necessity for facilitating whatever new regulations may be put in place to cover the newer product as well as older ones. And new regulations there will continue to be in response to the 2008 financial crisis and panic. If regulators cannot see the truth about the products, there is no way to implement any manner of controls regardless of how strict, well intentioned, or accepted the laws may be.

For example, from a negative standpoint, NYU's Stern School of Business recently completed a study of hedge fund management due diligence reports on 444 funds prepared between 2003 and 2008. The examination was not encouraging. Twenty percent misrepresented factual contents in their reports. They exaggerated assets under management, personal histories of managers, regulatory histories, and performance. The distortions were significant in size, material in their effects, and too large to be simple mistakes. The fact that some of them were due to an ignorance of the existing laws or their own internal compliance certainly is no comforting excuse. Many of the funds were quite large and had a multi-decade track record, so NYU was not studying infant, fly-by-night, nor obscure funds.

Another problem area is the arena of structured products. After the 2008 debacle, the financial services industry is at this juncture attempting to do all it can to simply keep structured products viable as investment vehicles. The SEC has constantly addressed the concept of investor protection, but many structured products have proven so toxic that buy side investors may have walked away from them forever. What had been hailed as innovative products created by brilliant financial minds are incomprehensible even to their creators.

Two facts related to recent products, however, are encouraging. One, most of them have been simple in nature. The esoteric products of yore are probably gone forever. Vanilla may be a dull ice cream, but "plain vanilla" investments often work best. Two, there is a commensurate transparency to these offerings that was sorely lacking before. Whether this is due to their plain vanilla aspect, regulatory pressure, or an attempt to make the deals more marketable remains to be seen.

There have been a variety of studies done since the NYU study and the results are mixed. Some show marked improvement since that time but there are still challenges to be addressed.

FASB determination to create a more accurate mark to the market and other fair value measures will help stabilize existing issues and create a more orderly market going forward.

It is in the area of risk that transparency issues must be addressed. To have a company go broke because of off-balance sheet investments that nobody appears to know how to price is Orwellian. Assets quickly become liabilities as supposed equity investments turned into sorrowful debt instruments leveraged beyond normal calculation. The question that must be addressed going forward is whether *regulation coupled with cooperative transparency* is enough to mitigate the horrors perpetrated by losses created by systemic risk run amok. Let's face it—no institution is "too big to fail," but the question arose whether they should be permitted to. The answer in 20/20 hindsight is absolutely not. Lehmann Brothers should not have been allowed to fail. The notion that their failure would ultimately affect the entire world was 100 percent correct.

The solution to all this will take years to unfold. The near term concern is that the current administration is spread out too far and wide with such limited resources and manpower that almost any kind of reform will be diluted, ineffectual, and too late.

To conclude, many of the broader issues of transparency will be addressed by solving the questions of capital reserves. Capital is in reserve form used to limit surprise losses from sources that do not generate liabilities or need repayment. During the period preceded by the crisis, financial entities had gigantic credit financed investments without sufficient capital to shore up losses. As the losses mounted, more money was lost than the firms had to cover them. Despite rapid fire sales of new common stock, not enough capital was raised to mitigate the losses. Many believe larger resources and more stringent regulation will prevent future similar disasters. Conversely, some believe a too wide pendulum swing would frustrate legitimate and necessary growth. Only time will tell what the proper course should be.

CHAPTER 30
Debt Securities

¶30,000   The Role Bonds Play in Asset Allocation

There are several reasons to accept the notion of diversification among stocks, bonds, and cash. Historically, bonds are prone to less risk and less return than stocks. Recent years have occasionally seen bonds outperform stocks; but, historically, this is the exception. From a diversification and asset allocation viewpoint, what makes investing in both classes of securities so useful is that, when one goes down, the other often goes up. Therefore, in a volatile or bearish market, either in equity or debt, the most dramatic swings in portfolio value can be mitigated by diversification. The reason most people own bonds in a balanced portfolio is to provide solace when the stock market goes down.

The fact that corrections until the past few years have been sharp, brief, and followed by rapid recovery does not refute the theory of diversification. It means that diversification, in hindsight, has not been necessary—lately. However, as the public has experienced in a recent, extended bear market (which the boomer generation and younger investors had never experienced before), bonds regained their prestige and luster by virtue of their income and relative stability. Because their virtues are somewhat subtle, investors easily missed their importance.

Two general categories of risk are systematic and unsystematic risk. The first type includes risks such as the general fluctuation of interest rates that cannot be reduced by diversifying a portfolio—since the entire portfolio is affected. Other types of risk considered systematic include reinvestment rate risk, purchasing power risk, market risk, exchange rate risk, and political risk. Unsystematic risk, also called diversifiable risk, includes risks specific to individual businesses or industries. These risks may be controlled by diversifying the investments in an investor's portfolio. This category includes business risk, financial risk, default risk, credit risk, liquidity risk, call risk, event risk, and prepayment risk.

¶30,001   Bond Risks

Risks associated with bonds may be divided into two groups. The first are those facing the market as a whole and therefore not curable by diversifying among bonds. These risks, called systematic risks, cause bonds as a whole, as opposed to individual bonds, to move in tandem—the market moves in response to them. Some of the more basic systematic bond risks follow:

- *Interest rate risk*—the possibility of lost potential income caused by rates rising during the holding period of a lesser paying instrument. The bondholder owns bonds at 6 percent and as rates rise, bonds of a similar type pay 8 percent.
- *Inflation risk*—the lost value of money due to inflation. The bondholder owns a fixed income portfolio that pays $30,000 per year income, but the purchasing power continues to drop as inflation continues to erode purchasing power.
- *Currency risk*—the money lost because foreign-currency-denominated bonds and their income payout drops as the dollar becomes stronger. A foreign bond pays 10 percent in its own currency, but its currency is so weak versus the dollar that the bondholder realizes a yield of only 3 percent after currency exchange.
- *Political or geo-political risk*—the possibility of an international incident, for example, having an overall positive or negative effect on the bond market.
- *Legislative risk*—the possibility that the bondholder will lose money because regulatory, tax, or other legislation will negatively affect the holdings. The government declares private purpose municipal debt no longer tax exempt—a 3-percent tax-exempt bond is now generating fully taxable income in a taxable environment that pays twice as much.

In addition there are other risks unique to a specific bond issue. These risks, called unsystematic risk, are partially overcome by diversifying among bonds.

- *Due diligence risk*—the possibility that an issue is rated improperly and will default with no warning. A county historically issuing AA and AAA debt defaults after declaring bankruptcy. The holdings in that county are of little value, less liquidity, and no longer pay interest payments.

- *Default risk*—the possibility that the issuer will not pay back. A corporation goes out of business and the bondholders are left with worthless bonds and consequently no interest payments forthcoming.
- *Event risk*—lost money because of a catastrophic event attached to the bond issuer. The bondholder owns hospital bonds and the hospital closes indefinitely after earthquake damage.
- *Call risk*—the possibility that a bond will be redeemed or called-in before its stated due date.

¶30,002   How to Select Bonds

All investors attempt to outsmart compelling obstacles to make correct investment choices. To avoid the risks mentioned and to take bond selection into the realm of logic and reason in order to offset those risks, the CPA/PFS should assess the extent to which the bond investments are exposed to these risks. This involves studying analysts' comments about the bonds and subscribing to the monthly Standard & Poor's or Moody's or other corporate bond guides. Bond ratings are attempts to determine default risk. A typical bond rating comment is full of various balance sheet and financial statement numbers translated into a series of ratios that are explained and interpreted by the analyst preparatory to articulating an opinion. The CPA/PFS then uses this information to determine the risks and judge portfolio appropriateness.

¶30,003   Fixed Income Analysts and Fixed Income Markets

The fixed income analyst is an individual who rates bonds and suggests investment strategies. Investors want increasingly more sophisticated products that perform at high rates of return. The financial officers of the issuers and the banking firms want the analysts to help with origination, trading, sales, and investment decisions. The issues themselves are difficult to understand and evaluate. The generalists of yesterday are gone, replaced by gifted specialists trained in sophisticated quantitative research. If investors are unclear about which bonds to select for their investment portfolio, an income analyst can help tremendously—bonds have their own language and the CPA/PFS and his or her clients are advised to ask for help. As of now, credit rating services are the best place for the CPA/PFS to find facts on bonds; these facts on bonds will help the CPA/PFS decide whether the client should invest in them. The CPA/PFS looks at the various publications of the major bond rating services to determine the level of rating considered an acceptable minimum and then buys bonds at or above that rating.

¶30,004   Credit Rating Services

Credit-rating services are all private firms. They are not government agencies with legislative power behind them, yet (and this is the source of some problems) their opinions are legislated into the operating rules of many public enti-ties, both here and abroad. For example, rating service opinions determine how many public funds are invested. The rating services exert tremendous pressure and wield tremendous power through their examinations. The problem is this: credit rating services comment upon issuer default risk, and, like personal credit reports, these comments assume a life far beyond their actual area of expertise. Credit rating services have repeatedly cautioned that no one should rely on their opinions for any-more than what they are—credit ratings.

¶30,005   Different Types of Bonds

From an asset allocation standpoint, the CPA/PFS should focus on the same diversity mode that is used for stocks.

.01   U.S. Treasury Securities

The safest debt investments for someone who cannot afford to lose money are U.S. Treasury securities, which are backed by the full faith and credit of the U.S. gov-ernment. The most popular vehicles for investment are 3-, 6-, 9-, and 12-month Treasury bills issued at a discount in $1,000 denominations. The accretion from the discounted purchase price to the face value is interest income. Those who have a longer time horizon often invest in 2-, 3-, or 5-year Treasury notes. There are also 10-and 30-year notes and bonds, but neither is primarily a retail investment vehicle. The investor pays no state or local taxes on any Treasury issue.

.02   Certificates of Deposit

Insured Certificates of Deposit (CDs) are similar to U.S. Treasury securities in that the Federal Deposit Insurance Corporation (FDIC) has the full faith and credit of the U.S. government. CDs of two years' maturity or less have been popular with investors for years. CDs often have lower rates than Trea-suries of comparable maturity, though, and the taxpayer pays state and local taxes on them. Because the banks do not necessarily want money from inves-tors (remember, to them, CDs are a liability), they are not often promoted as an attractive product. Although they are insured up to $100,000, most short-term income vehicles are very safe, so the investor may have no need for FDIC insurance. The highest CD rates are usually available through bro-kered CDs, so it is worth talking to a broker about CDs and other short-and intermediate-term income investments. For example, the brokerages also sell retail deposit notes (RTNs) and medium-term notes (MTNs), many of which pay monthly. The RTNs also have FDIC insurance. Certificates of deposit are subject to the income reporting requirements of original issue discount bonds (see below). That is, if the duration of the CD is more than one year, a cash basis owner is still required to report interest income although no cash payments have been received.

.03   Money Market Funds

From a practical standpoint, most people's short-or intermediate-term cash investment needs are best served by money market funds. There is minimal risk attached to these funds. Investors who are risk adverse can invest in money market funds available in Treasury, government, insured, and/or tax-free formats. In addition, for somewhat longer maturities, in the area of a year or so, there are an assortment of both open-ended and closed-ended money fund and intermediate-term mutual fund clones and spin-offs. However, they are definitely not actual money market funds because their net asset value can vary—occasionally widely.

.04   Zero Coupon Bonds

Wild and woolly bond products can generate stock-like gains, or losses, because of their volatility. The most widely used and least understood bond vehicle is the zero coupon bond. Many college savings accounts, which are very serious money, are full of them, because these accounts generally have a longer time horizon and because the accrued but unpaid interest income is sheltered in these accounts as it is in IRAs and profit sharing plans. Among the characteristics of these bonds are the following:

- The long maturities are volatile.
- They have standard deviation that cannot be identified with conservative investment.
- There is not a penny of cash flow between origination and maturity.
- The deep discount they are issued at is de facto leverage.
- When things go wrong with the bond market, they go unbelievably wrong with zero coupon bonds.
- They produce taxable income without corresponding cash payments.

With no cash flow and the pseudo-leverage, zeros in a bear market works against the holder to an extent far greater than coupon issues, precisely because there is no cash flow to mitigate declining value. Of course, this reverses itself in a bull market, because there is no cash flow coming out of zeros for which to find a home. Therefore, because the investor has no reinvestment responsibilities in a low interest environment, the zero coupon investments go up further and faster than any other debt type. Investors want cash flow in a bear market because they invest at a high rate. They do not want cash flow in a bull market because they are investing at low rates. Interest rate risk is extremely high on zeros—a long-term zero can lose 20 percent to 30 percent of its value with a 1-percent rise in rates, depending on its maturity, issuer, and the prevailing rate. They are, for the adventurous, one of the great, pure interest-rate trading plays, in the form of the U.S. Treasury strips. There is absolutely no risk other than interest rate sensitivity risk, because none of the other types of risk apply to a direct obligation of the government. Many packaged zero coupon products can have standard deviations of 30, 40, even 50 percent.

Zero coupon bonds purchased from the original issuer generate a form of income called original issue discount (OID). If the bonds are held by an individual outside a tax sheltering vehicle (such as an IRA or college savings account) the bond will generate annual taxable interest income, OID, without any corresponding cash interest payments. Inside an IRA or other tax sheltering investment vehicle the cashless income is still reported but its effects are mitigated. The owner of a zero coupon bond needs to add the OID income reported each year to the basis of the obligation so that upon redemption there is no gain or loss.

.05   Foreign Debt

Another often used but rarely understood investment item is foreign debt. Most carry some varying level of currency risk, unless they are dollar denominated, in which case, their income stream is paid in dollars. Many carry political risk, although plenty of countries' stability is not an issue. There is a reasonable concern of political unrest in a lot of countries, but the chances of currency problems are far greater. With the dollar in a steady downtrend the past few years, many foreign bond bets dependent upon dollar weakness have made vast sums of money.

A continued weak dollar could make quality foreign bond investing attractive for the domestic investor, retail or institutional. As international bond yields go up and divorce in interest rate parity with U.S. rates, there is very great impetus to pay a premium to acquire more risk. If the risk is hedged, the expense of hedging the risk is so modest that the investor can end up with much more money than would be received from relatively passive domestic investment. This investment can be inexpensive and have modest risk to gain higher returns when compared to less adventurous domestic investments.

When international debt return advantage is uncertain relative to domestic debt, investors are almost forced out of high-quality foreign debt. Then, if trying to significantly outperform a domestic debt index, they are led into the more problematic distressed debt. From an asset allocation standpoint, purely as a strategic activity, many institutions insist on foreign debt. However, as a retail investor, unless the investor has a huge portfolio, one can basically forget about direct investment. An average investor cannot invest directly in international bonds as cheaply or as easily as he or she can in stocks. There are dozens of stock exchange listed foreign companies, but no debt. The bond buying costs are significant and the liquidity is always an issue.

It is hard to make much of a case for direct investment in sovereign foreign debt, Brady bonds, or overseas junk bonds because there is never a level playing field for retail investors. There are so many risks and they are of such significant magnitude that it is hard to make much of a case for funds, either. Some of the biggest fund problems immediately relate to foreign income funds. A straight international debt sector fund has too much standard deviation for too little potential return and the managers are tightly restricted by the legislated style of the fund.

.06   Junk Bonds

What about homebred junk? It is very easy to make a good case for almost any investor owning some "high yield domestic debt," as junk is more properly termed. Junk bonds are those rated BB or lower by a recognized rating service. In well-managed, highly diversified funds, they are powerful investment vehicles almost anyone can own. Although the area has been tainted by notoriety, it deserves a fresh look from a new perspective.

Junk bonds are a tremendous enhancement for income-oriented portfolios in a low-interest environment. They usually pay significantly more than Treasuries or high-quality corporate debt. Furthermore, junk bonds are a good diversification tool. They generate income as a debt instrument (of course, because they are junk, they have the biggest coupons). When the bond market declines, junk bonds tend to behave more like stocks (they are allied with the equity of their companies rather than with conventional debt products). Not only do they not decline as much as high quality debt, they are sometimes less volatile than Treasuries of comparable maturity.

Performance in high yield is a function of security selection, diversification, and risk management. The ability to predict credit upgrades is the focus of a lot of this expertise—one needs to know a lot about credits or a lot about math to do well in this area. With these standards in mind, a well-regarded junk bond mutual fund is the best vehicle for this investment for the retail investor. The diversification includes different issuers, issues, maturities, credits, and industries. They can also buy the private placements of junk debts. They can drastically reduce costs (bonds cost a lot more than stocks), demand "equity kickers" (i.e., stock inducements to buy bonds) from issuers, enhance returns with leverage, and quickly respond to market and credit analysis issues.

Only 20 percent of the deals are rated B or lower, as compared to 65 percent 15 years ago. Liquidity is more adequate, as many issues have decent balance sheets, good cash flow, and viable and successful franchises. So why not buy the debt? Most of the current era problems relate to accounting event risks that nobody can predict but that are certainly going to crop up occasionally—this is still junk debt, after all. But now a one-time "notable event" is the norm for an issuer, rather than terminal default, and once the problem is solved, the risk is gone, and the debt begins to trade toward par with other issues in its sector of the market.

Fund managers can evaluate and process information of this type best, so the client essentially hires a fund manager when the CPA/PFS selects a fund for the expertise of the fund manager. A case can be made for timeliness in junk debt management, which eliminates the conventional investor from the picture. An average investor simply has no time to devote to active securities management. Good fund managers have access to far more information (company, research, and rating) than the average investor ever would. In fact, they can go straight to the "horse's mouth," if the need arises. Whereas most income funds are for people who have time or cash restraints, in the area of junk, a manager can provide genuine value added for the investor, large or small. Many institutional investors buy funds that normally shun the fund industry as a matter of principle. In addition, the diversification necessary in a portfolio of this nature is beyond almost any investor (not to mention that some junk debt comes in minimum orders of $5 million). A junk bond fund manager has something to do that cannot realistically be done by the client, so these services are quite beneficial for those who want junk.

Distressed Junk Bonds. Special situations with distressed bonds are the province of the professional money manager. Distressed bonds cause major valuation and transaction cost problems because, although an investor pays perceived bargain prices for bad deals, the investor can still end up losing all the money. No one ever lost all their money paying too much for high-quality deals, but they have often lost everything buying bad deals cheaply. As stated, transaction costs are always significant in bonds because they cost so much more than stocks. By definition, distressed junk bonds require tricky evaluation above and beyond normal debt issues. Distressed junk is not a popular investment vehicle, so information is usually difficult to obtain, pricing is inefficient, and risk evaluation is extraordinarily difficult. The same logic regarding junk bond funds applies in spades to distressed junk bonds.

Looking for a junk fund is a difficult task. What a professional can do is rely upon the mutual fund rating services to reveal certain important facts about returns, risk, and consistency. The ideal junk bond fund is very similar to a balanced fund or total return fund—income and growth are both components of the return. These funds have averaged about 8 percent to 10 percent per year for the last decade or so, and the investor should expect the same return from a junk fund.

More of the return will be from income and less of it will be gain than that of a balanced or total return fund. At times, as discussed, the junk market acts like an equity market, so gains have to show in fund performance distributions, or the manager is not doing the job. In addition, for the increased risk, there should be demonstrably more cash flow than in a comparable high-quality corporate or government mutual fund. If not, why bother with the extra risk? That is, unless there are big capital gains distributions. A moderate cash flow may indicate a rise in credit quality in the fund or large investments in distressed securities. Both conditions and suitability are important for the CPA/PFS to assess. The evaluator may want junk to be junky or may want nothing to do with distressed debt. Do not prejudge a situation like relatively modest cash flow without finding out why it exists and what is at the root of the condition. Parenthetically, the CPA/PFS cannot assume that the highest yielding junk fund is the best one, because, until the he or she finds out where the money is coming from, there is no clue as to what the fund is doing. The fund may be passing back a lot of principal, it may generate huge gains on concentrated speculative positions—the professional has to find out for him- or herself, with or without the help of an investment or securities professional.

The CPA/PFS should find funds that are at or slightly above their index, especially in regard to income (cash flow from interest and dividends). It is important to see a stable return with stable net asset value. In addition, extreme volatility in high-yield bond funds would suggest really low-rated and distressed debt, which is fine for some of the fund assets. Currently, about two-thirds of junk is rated BB, the remaining third is B. Many funds are two-thirds B and one-third BB, so investors have to pay close attention to portfolio weight before selecting a fund. Although it is true that no one can control what returns are, an investor certainly can control what risk is assumed. There is no reason to accept any more risk than predetermined return expectations require.

Risk in Junk Bonds. There are three types of risk in junk:

1. *Interest rate risk.* This is the risk that market rates will go up and the investor will have less income than prevailing bonds, and then the value of the bonds will go down accordingly to meet the income levels of the new debt.
2. *Stock risk.* The stock market is subject to tremendous volatility in the speculative and high-risk stock areas. It is the speculative and high-risk areas, which represent the issuers of junk debt.
3. *High-yield debt risk.* High-yield debt comes in and goes out of fashion and prominence independent of what goes on in other markets. The risk is owning junk bonds or junk bond funds as they go out of fashion and their liquidity dries up. A lot of the go-go junk bond mutual funds of the 1970s

and 1980s had to be absorbed into other funds because net asset values disappeared—often at great loss of income and principal to shareholders.

Interest rate risk is completely normal to all debt. The stock risk is because junk trades with equities and is open to the same risks as the stock market. Finally, there are some aspects of junk, which are idiosyncratic to junk, and they impose their own risks on the market.

.07   Strategic Income Fund

The best way to answer the question of what strategic income funds are is to make the statement, "All of the above." They are the "open season on anything" funds of the debt world. Obviously, there are some position limits, but these funds are nowhere near as constrained as conventional income funds. Strategic income funds are similar to both the balanced/total return funds and the junk bond funds. They often have double-digit returns from a combination of income and gain. Because they participate in a variety of debt and equity markets, both domestically and internationally, they fit perfectly into a passive asset allocation framework dedicated to income.

The diversity of the fund format incurs a very high level of operating costs, so high expense ratios should be no surprise. If the CPAs/PFSs can understand plain vanilla debt or debt funds, they can understand the mutual fund rating service reports on these funds. It is important to find which fund has an investment philosophy similar to that of the CPAs/PFSs and their clients by reviewing a fund's:

1. *Research stance.* Which securities does it like and which securities do they not like?
2. *Asset allocation.* What mix of debt, equity, and cash does it normally employ?
3. *Market weightings.* Where does it put money?
4. *Economic, social, and political focus.* Does it have an ax to grind? What does it believe in and is it compatible with the view of the universe held by the CPAs/PFSs and their clients?

The goal of most of these funds is to provide maximum income with minimum volatility. They generate maximum income by having unlimited access to any income vehicles; they generate minimal volatility because of their ability to diversify across all income investments. The primary areas of investment are U.S. government debt, foreign debt of all classes, and domestic junk bonds. The managers also look at the emerging markets, domestic and foreign stocks with high dividends, domestic and foreign preferred stock, and all grades of domestic debt. All of the funds tend to be "custom blends," thus apple-to-apple comparisons between funds are impossible. Once again, this means the professional has to look at philosophy rather than numbers when doing homework. Low-risk strategic income funds generate less income than high-risk funds, so the CPA/PFS cannot simply pick the highest yielding fund and think the job is done. The indexes used for strategic funds are so hypothetical that they apply to no funds in the strategic fund universe other than by coincidence.

.08   Tax-Free Municipal Bonds

There are some specific matters related to bonds with which every experienced investor should be familiar. Municipal bonds are bonds that carry no federal tax liability for interest payments. They are usually free of taxes in the states from which they are issued. Some states do not tax municipal interest if it is from another state and accept any municipal interest of any state as free from their taxes. Furthermore, some cities that have income taxes exempt the interest payments from their municipal debt from tax liability. Finally, Puerto Rico and a few other territories issue bonds whose interest payments are exempt from tax liability in all states.

The rate of return is adjusted for the fact that there are no tax consequences. The CPA/PFS must calculate whether tax-free or fully taxable debt is best for the client. (As a happy medium, there is never any state or local tax on Treasury obligations.)

There are investment rules that are peculiar to tax-free debt. In addition, some rules that are generic to all bond investment apply more specifically in some cases or somewhat differently in other cases to tax-free debt. Generally, anything that happens to an issuer of a financial nature is of interest to investors. Issuers are state, county, municipal, or other taxing authorities.

CPAs/PFSs should learn about municipal bonds before clients buy any. Furthermore, the CPA/PFS should learn about all the bonds their clients are buying. If the client decides to invest in municipal bonds for tax-free income, the professional must decide whether to invest in individual bonds or mutual funds and address price and default risk. Price risk is usually a function of the maturity of the bonds. The longer the maturity, as already seen, the more apt the bonds are to be volatile in a lively interest rate scenario. Default risk for municipal debt is an extensive list, but not as common an event.

Minimizing Common Default Risks. Some of the common default risks are:

- *Natural disasters.* Earthquakes, fires, floods, hurricanes, and tornadoes.
- *Fiscal mismanagement.* Profligate spending or poor money management.
- *Taxing authority regulations.* Changes that effect issuers or investors.
- *Revenue declines.* Inability to pay income or principal when due.

- *Infrastructure problems.* Problems with everything from sewers to the mayor's mansion.
- *Specific project failures.* Failure to meet deadlines, failure to complete projects, failure of project as a revenue source.

To minimize common default risks and other non-market-related risks, the investor can simply select insured bonds. Bond insurance and how it works will be discussed in more, but for current purposes, suffice it to say that the insurance is a valuable retail investor feature that mitigates the covered risks. The costs to the issuer and thus to the investor are minimal. Municipal debt insurance works—for issuer and investor.

The retail investor must be careful not to become entranced by the tax-free nature of municipal debt. The CPA/PFS who prepares taxes can calculate whether taxable or tax-free debt yields the most to the client. The tax issue is not significant intrinsically—what matters is what income is brought to the bottom line. As a rule of thumb, if the client is in a high tax bracket, more is earned from municipal debt. If the client is in a low or medium tax bracket, even after the CPA/PFS allows for a tax liability, more may be earned from taxable corporate or government bonds. Most everything depends upon the interest rate spread between taxable and tax exempt income. Currently, tax-free bonds are appropriate relative to Treasuries for taxpayers in all but the lowest brackets. The reason for this is that some municipals yield more than Treasury securities do.

.09 Income Tax Aspects of Municipal Bonds

Although municipal bonds are generally tax free, this refers to the income tax effect of their interest payments. The sale of a municipal bond still results in a taxable capital gain or loss and municipal bonds held in an estate are still subject to estate tax or if given, subject to gift tax.

A municipal bond purchased on a secondary market (as opposed to the original issuer) after April 30, 1993, may have a market discount. A market discount arises when the value of a bond decreases after its issue date, generally because of an increase in interest rates. Market discount is the amount of the stated redemption price of a bond at its maturity that is more than your basis in the bond immediately after its acquisition. In such a situation, if the bond is held to maturity, it will pay the bondholder back its face amount. In so doing the bondholder receives back not only his or her original investment but the difference between the discounted price paid and the face amount. What is the taxable character of this difference? It is not additional tax-free income. When you buy a market discount bond, you can choose to accrue (on a daily basis) the market discount over the period you own the bond and include it in your income currently as taxable interest income. As you accrue the discount and record the amount in taxable income, you are simultaneously increasing your basis in the bond. If the bond is subsequently redeemed for is face value you will have no gain or loss. If this is not done then any gain resulting when the bond is disposed of (up to the amount of the market discount) is treated as ordinary income (not capital gain). These market discount rules apply to taxable bonds as well but the effect there is less dramatic because the bondholder is not assuming all income from the bond is tax-exempt. There the difference is one of converting the accretion from the discounted basis to the face amount as ordinary income (whether done ratably or at the time of sale or redemption) rather than treating as capital gain.

Certain municipal bonds may produce income subject to alternative minimum tax. These bonds, referred to as private activity bonds, are debt instruments where more than 10 percent of the proceeds of the issue was used for a private business or 10 percent of the principle or interest is secured by private business property. Interest received on privative activity bonds issued after August 7, 1986, is generally a "tax preference item" for calculation of alternative minimum tax although the interest is otherwise tax-exempt like other municipal bonds.

The original issue discount (OID) on tax-exempt state or local municipal bonds is also tax-exempt. Interest on federally guaranteed state or local tax-exempt bonds issued after 1983 is generally taxable.

.10   Municipal Bond Mutual Funds

Many investors avoid the issue of individual bond selection by investing in a municipal bond mutual fund. There are four basic types of municipal funds:

1. *State and federal tax-free bond funds.* These single-state funds are the most common type of fund. They have the name of a state somewhere in their title, thus delineating the contents of and stated potential investors for that fund.
2. *State and federal tax-free high-yield bond funds.* High yield comes to the municipal arena. These funds invariably have mostly investment-grade paper, but lower and not-rated paper exceeds the limits imposed on conventional funds. Although there are certainly more risks associated with these funds, they are usually the stellar performers of their respective fund group and generally enjoy astronomically high ratings and regard by fund rating services.
3. *State and federal tax-free insured bond fund.* Funds that are almost exclusively insured paper. They are at the opposite end of the spectrum from the high-yield funds and all but the most reactionary would consider them very safe. They generally have comparatively low yields and are regularly criticized by the rating services as unnecessary from a safety standpoint and an overprotection from risk.

4. *State and federal tax-free money market and intermediate bond funds.* Short- and intermediate-term paper makes up these funds. These funds can have anything from one month's to several years' duration. They earn high marks for safety of principal and stability of net asset value.

5. *Federal tax-free funds, called "national" or "general" tax-free funds.* If they are owned in a state where there is a state income tax, they are often fully taxable interest-bearing vehicles for that state (but still not federally). Except for the amount of the total income generated by that state, which is still tax-free, the fund income is subject to state income tax. These funds can have all 50 states and the various territories represented in their portfolio.

The state and federal funds are usually concentrated in the long-term debt of their issuer, characteristically 10 to 30 years. The insured funds have the same timeframe, as do the high-yield funds. High-yield tax-free funds are very similar to their taxable corporate counterparts. The "high-yield" component relates to:

- *Lower ratings.* Under BBB paper makes up a large percentage of the fund's assets. BBB and above are investment grade, "bank-quality" paper; all other ratings are junk.
- *Less favorable call and refunding provisions.* This is call risk and refunding provision risk exposure that limits dependability of income.
- *Secondary or junior debt.* This is debt subordinate to senior debt of issuers that are perceived as unstable.
- *Special situations.* This is debt issued to cover the more problematic aspects of municipal issuance.
- *Non-rated debt.* Debt sold directly to the fund without rating.

Municipal debt is so credit sensitive that, as a total return item, high-yield muni funds often do not outperform conventional funds. Insured funds, however, almost always under perform their uninsured counterparts. Should investors want insured municipals, their interests are best served by directly investing in those bonds.

Like most insurers, muni insurers do not insure any entity that needs insurance. They have no time for higher-risk issuers—they are poor credit risks. The representative issuer who gets insurance is an issuer of A or AA credit quality. The insured debt is automatically upgraded to AAA—because it is insured. The issue is generally sold at one-tenth or two-tenths of a percent lower yield than comparable uninsured issues of the same maturity. It is a very cheap price for the retail investor to pay for this feature. Some financial advisors stopped recommending to their individual clients anything but insured debt all the way back in the early 1980s. The retail muni investor is most impressed with safety, liquidity, and stability, all of which are immeasurably enhanced by municipal insurance.

¶30,006   Debt Maturities

The issue that every investor talks about the most is maturity. There are several levels of maturity: short term is up to one year, intermediate term is one to five years, and long term is six or more years.

An endless debate concentrates on short-term versus long-term risk. Long-term risk relates to price risk; income risk applies to short-term issues. Normally, short-term debt pays less than long-term debt. When interest rates are low, most investors are best served by investing in intermediate-and long-term debt. However, there is not a single uncertainty related to debt maturities that diversification cannot help. From an asset allocation standpoint, whether debt maturity is short, intermediate, or long term, all deserve a place in the investor's portfolio and are beneficial for the achievement of fixed income goals. They will play off against each other as time goes by and soften the blow of the errors— errors that everyone makes, no matter how well laid their plans. Specific asset allocation between short, intermediate, and long term are up to the CPAs/PFSs and their clients. There is a place for short-, intermediate-, and long-term debt, but it is all determined by the needs of the individual investor. Factors related to risk, age, income needs, credits, and comfort level are part of the equation.

Extending maturities often does not result in generating more income for the fixed income investor. Therefore, benefits to the investor may be marginal. However, extending maturity does address several negative issues for the fixed income investor. First, if short-term rates decline and they have nothing but cash, the chances are very good that intermediate and long-term rates will also decline.

If the investor prefers capital preservation and liquidity, which basically describes a short-term income vehicle investor, an asset allocation shift of money to longer maturities may be unsatisfactory both because of time of maturity and size of dollar commitment. However, many investors falsely exaggerate their need for capital preservation and liquidity. Although it may be true that investors are intimidated by long-term bonds or mutual funds, it is equally true that, from an income orientation, they only hurt themselves by not investing in long-term bonds or mutual funds. Somehow, some way, these investors must truthfully assess their need for liquidity and inability to accept principal fluctuation or they will be unable to realize the benefits available to them from a traditional fixed income investment.

Current income investors are much more pragmatic about maturities, although they can error through aggressive investments. Some income investors chase yield and own only the most long-term debt available. These investors can be carried away with income stream and disregard the multitude of risks they assume grasping for all that income. Owning too many large positions in long-term debt is not really a problem in an era where all municipal and corporate debt is skewed in favor of the issuer (not in favor of the investor) from a call "protection" standpoint. All municipal and corporate debt seems to be called away well before its time. However, large positions of low-rated debt and equity certainly can be a problem. The reason for this is risk and its relationship to the individual investor's risk profile. Across asset classes, assuming great credit risk in both junk debt and high-dividend payout, low-quality stocks is inappropriate financial planning, money management, and asset allocation. The most beneficial risk level to the investor is one that has been created by a balanced portfolio. The CPA/PFS must look for a balance.

Capital appreciation investors are similar to total return investors, but in the bond arena. They seek to manage capital gains, but they want coupon income, too. The exception is traders who assume positions in zero coupon bonds. Since there is no cash flow (but interest continues to accrete passively onto the bond), these investors are actively seeking only capital gains. The conventional capital appreciation investor is trying to capitalize on perceived future changes in interest rates, asset value variances, and yield curve differences.

¶30,007   Par, Premium, or Discount Bonds

Another issue is whether to invest in par ($1,000 per bond), premium (priced above par), or discount (priced below par) bonds. In the recent past, investors who bought premium debt have locked in attractive yields compared to discount and par bonds with similar maturities. With premium bonds, the cash flow from having a larger coupon causes the price to be higher, to compensate for the bigger coupon cash flow. All bonds pay off at par, unless they are called or refunded at a premium, so all that premium normally disappears. However, increased income more than makes up for the lost premium. Premium bonds are relatively defensive in nature, because in a bull market they tend to lag the performance of lower coupon issues because of "reinvestment" risk. The bondholders have more income to find a home for if they own large coupon, premium issues. However, in a bear market, when interest rates rise and bond values decline, the large coupon buoys the premium bond relative to par and discount issues. Whether rates go up, down, or sideways, from a capital preservation standpoint, premium bonds are less volatile than par or discount issues. Simply put:

- Premium bonds are for maximum cash flow, cost the most money, and go down less in a bad market.
- Discount bonds have the least cash flow, cost the least money, but go up the most in a good market.

- Par bonds are the happy medium. They cost $1,000 per bond, which is their face value and value at maturity, generate income exactly at the rate of the current environment, and behave as the market behaves because they represent the market at the time of their issuance, because their coupon is "current."

Note that in the case of premium bonds, producing greater cash flow is the result of paying a higher price for the bond. The overall economic effect may thus only be receiving more cash because of parting with more cash.

If you buy a bond at a discount when interest has been defaulted or when the interest has accrued but has not been paid, the transaction is described as trading the bond "flat." When you receive the defaulted or unpaid interest it is not taxable income to you as it was accounted for in the purchase price. When you receive the payment of the unpaid or defaulted interest it is a return of capital and it reduces your basis in the bond. Interest that accrues after the date of purchase is taxable to the purchaser.

¶30,008 Bond Calls

Calls in the past few years of gradually declining interest rates have become a major bond investment. Calls are provisions in bond covenants, which allows the issuer to retire a bond and pay back the investor before the bond matures. Investors, however, earn a higher yield on callable bonds as compared to noncallable bonds. They pay more as a payment for uncertainty about the life of the bond. A noncallable bond has a set maturity date that cannot be altered by calls or refunding.

Bonds are called for several reasons:

- To reduce financing costs and retire or reissue at a lower rate of interest. An issuer is flush and pays off its debt or, at least, refinances it at a lower rate of interest.
- To change cash flow. An issuer receives a better return on its money by paying off debt rather than investing it.
- To replace with different investment vehicle, turning bonds into preferred stock, private placements, or some other loan vehicle.
- To change duration—exchange long-term debt for shorter-term debt.

¶30,009 Bond Ladders

Probably the most misunderstood and least utilized damage control strategy for calls and other problems is bond laddering. Bond ladders extend through various maturities as a diversification tool. The investor starts with an equally or near equally weighted series of maturities. Some examples would be:

- 1, 2, 3, 4, and 5 years.
- 1, 3, and 5 years.
- 1, 3, 5, and 10 years.

As each issue matures, the CPA/PFS and client reinvest at the longest maturity in the series and continue to "roll out" (extend to the longest maturity) at the same or similar maturity. Ladders are useful for various reasons. Ladders are more flexible than single-maturity portfolios. If liquidity needs surface, there is always a part of the portfolio near maturity and therefore trading near par, so price risk concerns are minimal. If the client needs money and owns a note maturing in seven months, he or she can sell it very near par with no loss of principal, unless there is a major problem. In addition, because of continued income stream and regular principal distributions, the ladder strategy amounts to dollar cost averaging. The investor gets the level of income associated with all the levels of maturity the CPA/PFS and client select. The client's income is somewhere near the median maturity of the portfolio weighting. Interest rate fluctuations have minimal significance. There is no rate chasing with the fixed ladder format. There is no need to predict rates or second-guess economic developments. The CPA/PFS has covered all the bases. Ladders can structure income and principal needs precisely. An investor can set up a five-year college savings plan, for example, with a ladder lasting five years and then scale in maturities to correspond with each September financing. Zero coupon bond ladders are used constantly for this purpose.

Practically, what the investor accomplishes with a ladder is a hedge strategy. The investor combines short-term liquidity with long-term returns and avoids the worst extremes of each. There is always something that can go wrong with any investment, but there is not much that can go wrong with a bond ladder. The investor can miss out on gains in a bull market, but the strategy is supposed to be used to avoid market issues—down and up. If the CPA/PFS is inattentive to the ratings or calls of the portfolio, a mistake here and there leading to premature return of principal or loss of it or income through default can certainly spoil the ladder. Nonetheless, it does not make sense to ladder bonds laden with call provisions and poor rating. If that is what the client wants, he or she should simply select a strategic income fund that corresponds with investment needs.

¶30,010   Bond Mutual Fund Ladders

Regarding funds, funds can be used to create a passive ladder by asset allocation between money market, intermediate-term, and long-term income funds. Because many laddered funds are available, the CPA/PFS need only carefully examine the information reports from the mutual fund rating service to select the one that best suits the client. What is interesting with funds, whether laddered by using several funds or one internally laddered by its manager, is an income comparison with directly owned bonds. Bonds are much more expensive than stocks to buy. So, if the professional can isolate funds with low expense ratios and 12b-1 fees, the client might come out well ahead of buying own bonds alone. However, there is no such thing as a set dividend from a mutual fund. The dividends can be changed at the whim of the fund family's board of directors—even the fund managers and traders are often not consulted. Funds will eventually reflect the interest rate environment of the client's portfolio. In the interim, the strategy works very well because the manager addresses call and credit risks with far more expertise than the nonprofessional. Even given compensating fund expenses, fund managers can also buy bonds at far cheaper prices than retail investors.

¶30,011   Duration

Duration is an attempt to quantify various aspects of current bond performance to predict future performance. It addresses such issues as why long-term debt is more volatile than short-term debt and why low-coupon issues are more volatile to the downside than high-coupon issues. It is similar to stock beta in that it measures volatility, but it is more oriented toward future performance than past.

Duration determines the investor's breakeven point on a bond. It takes into consideration maturity, coupon, yield, and call. It is a technique utilized by investors to compare sensitivity to the interest rate environment of various bonds. The hope is that CPAs/PFSs will use duration to make bond investing more simple, safe, and profitable for their clients.

Duration is a number that tells how long it will take the income and principal payments of a bond to pay back the original investment on that bond. For example, the investor buys a 30-year Treasury bond for $1,000. The bond has a 5-percent coupon, so the client receives $50 per year ($25 per semiannual payment) in interest payments for 30 years. At the end of 40 payments (20 years), the investor has broken even. The duration, then, is 20 years. The larger the interest payment, the shorter the duration. If an investor selects a 15-percent coupon nonrated junk bond with a 20-year maturity, he or she would receive $75 per 6-month payment, $150 per year, and have a break even of 14 payments or seven years. Therefore, the 20-year junk bond (assuming it does not default) duration is seven years.

The CPA/PFS can use duration to evaluate both bonds and mutual funds. Duration is multiplied times interest rate fluctuation to find the expected volatility response to a change in rates. For example, if rates drop 1 percent, then the 30-year Treasury example above will go up about 20 percent in value. On the other hand, if rates go up one-half percent, because values react inversely to rate fluctuations, the 30-year Treasury will drop approximately 10 percent in value.

The CPA/PFS can do the same calculation for mutual funds, too. The information sheets from the mutual fund rating service give duration figures for funds, although it is more accurate to contact fund families with all choices to learn the current duration of the portfolio if the CPA/PFS and client are making a new investment. As an example, a mutual fund with a duration of 10 years would fall 5 percent in value if there were a half-point drop in rates, exactly like with an individual bond.

As anyone can gather, nothing has longer duration than a zero coupon bond, because there is no cash flow until it pays off at maturity. A 30-year Treasury strip will rise 30 percent in value if interest rates drop 1 percent, which is why these securities are a rate speculator's dream product. No coupon issue would ever perform even close to that. Alas, if rates rise 1 percent, a 30-year Treasury strip's value can drop 30 percent, too.

How can the CPA/PFS use duration as a technique for successful retail debt investment? If the CPA/PFS and client believe in declining interest rates long term, the client should invest in long-duration debt. If the CPA/PFS and client believe the trend is the opposite direction, the client should invest in short-duration debt. Essentially, duration is a tool that forces the investor to take a stand on rates and inflation. Although speculators love to take stands, nobody likens that behavior to plain vanilla debt investment. Plain vanilla investors like market-neutral stances. Much of the appeal of ladders is to avoid the pitfalls of duration. The examples are intentionally somewhat extreme to accentuate the vivid reality of duration.

There are many ways to calculate duration and many variables, such as call provisions and future value dollar calculations, to muddy the duration formulas. The CPA/PFS must always remember that:

- Duration changes with calls or prerefunding.
- A larger coupon means shorter duration and less volatility.
- Duration does not consider credit quality or other unrelated risk issues.

The CPA/PFS now knows that bonds range from ownership of simple debt instruments to extraordinarily complex products. Like many concepts and ideas that seem to flourish only in ivory towers, the climb to learn what makes bonds important investments reveals something both simple and profound. Bonds are loaded with depths of usefulness for every investor. There are plenty of reasons the debt markets continue to dwarf the stock markets in size. The CPA/PFS asset allocation plan has surged with their strength the last few years.

CHAPTER 31
Demystifying Funds

¶31,000   Overview

Everybody loves mutual funds. The average mutual fund investor is a Baby Boomer 44 years old, married, employed, with investments in three different funds in two different mutual fund families. The household income is $100,000 per year. In addition, the average fund owner knows absolutely nothing about what he or she owns.

The basic cause of confusion regarding mutual funds is the rapid growth and expansion of this nation's, and the entire investment world's, reliance upon this vehicle. The mutual fund vehicle is asked to be both the savior and the scapegoat for the investing public.

Approximately 116,000,000 people, representing 68.7 million U.S. households, own funds. The primary source of this meteoric rise in numbers is retirement plan assets. The shift from corporate-managed pension plans to self-directed retirement vehicles opened an ever-widening gate for the novice investor. Today, it is rarely the company's responsibility for planning successful employee pensions; usually, it is financially naive employees responsible for selecting successful investments for themselves. This has given new meaning to the term "dartboard investing."

¶31,001   The Mutual Fund Industry

Wall Street is as fond of mutual funds as are investors. From a traditional investment banking standpoint, issuer products have been largely stocks or bonds.

Furthermore, most of the attention was concentrated on the institutional investors, who would buy most of the stocks or bonds in a banking issue for their own use—investment, pension plans, cash flow needs, or whatever. In recent years, however, mutual funds (overwhelmingly directed toward the retail investor) have assumed a larger and larger slice of the investment banker pie. Not surprisingly, Wall Street pays attention.

Both open-ended and closed-ended mutual funds have generated enormous banking fees and enjoyed enthusiastic acceptance with investors. "Enthusiastic acceptance" describes a huge asset shift—and assets mean a lot to Wall Street. Of late, the most institutionally driven of investment banking firms have signed mutual fund distribution contracts with the large retail wire houses and discount brokerage firms. This is a revenue expanding and gathering activity for both.

Today, the retail investor directly owns half of all U.S. financial assets and will acquire more as savings and retirement investment expands and grows. Much of this money resides in mutual fund investments. The scramble is still unfolding regarding how this class will grow and best be harnessed by both institutions and investors.

Another measure of the fund industry's success is its seemingly daily consolidation. Mutual fund families are on a merger course that rivals the consolidation mania of the rest of the financial services industry itself. As the families consolidate, so do the funds. Happily, all this appears beneficial for the investor, too, because the investor has more funds to choose from within the expanded family groups.

To summarize, mutual fund management is a primary source of income to the financial services industry. That income is largely impervious to market fluctuations because funds need management in bad years as well as good years. Long-term investing is simply that: there will be both up and down cycles. It is the overall, long-term, extended holding period (5–10-year) return that is important to the investor because the long time frame is where the benefits lie—not short term. The investor, once again, pays fees no matter what goes on with the markets.

¶31,002   What You Buy Is What You Get

On the other hand, investors can get quite a bit for what they pay. The average mutual fund investor owns $25,000 worth of funds. Almost 80 percent of those funds are selected with the help of an investment professional. There are three basic types of funds: stock, bonds and money market funds. Three-quarters of all fund owners own stock funds, half own bond funds, and half own money market funds. Almost all owners own two or three of the three types of funds.

Half are comfortable with risk, a quarter are somewhat speculatively inclined, and almost 10 percent are either totally risk adverse or totally high risk oriented, putting them at either extreme of the investor bell curve. Each investor's fee facilitates finding each investor the correct fit.

How do the mutual fund investors get what they pay for? Probably only a small percentage of fund investors understand diversification and asset allocation. Consequently, most investors in mutual funds don't know what they own. Only a fraction of investors could ever hope to duplicate their fund performance on their own. Quite simply this is what they pay for—high returns from investments they may know nothing about and have no input in selecting. This represents an enormous opportunity for the CPA/PFS to add value.

¶31,003   What Are Mutual Funds?

What are these behemoths we call mutual funds? They're everyone who wants to commingle their money to work more aggressively to increase their wealth. They prefer to do it with a collectively huge sum of money rather than individually with a small amount of money. The benefit to the investor is that a small amount of money makes an investor part-owner in fabulous wealth that is invested for them according to a prospectus plan.

For the most part, they are pooled assets historically created for two types of investors. These investors were people with little time or with moderate amounts of money—as little as $100. Like most antiquated investment rules, these investor profiles have expanded with time, but the rules still apply to the most representative types of mutual fund shareholders, those with little time and moderate amounts of money. These pooled assets make investing easier because, once the investor designates a fund type, the mutual fund management company assumes responsibility for everything else. The selection, diversification, buying and selling—all are the direct responsibility of the manager.

If the manager has selected correctly, funds can perform extremely efficiently. Consequently, people with a lot of money invest in funds for the extraordinary level of performance they can enjoy. Many of the investment banking firm mutual funds were created for this group. A mutual fund can own hundreds or even thousands of individual issues. This makes the whole process cost-effective. Purchases in bigger blocks generate fewer fees. In addition, some investors who enjoy spending time studying investments spend it examining and rating different funds. They do this because mutual fund investment can be a cost-efficient way to diversify assets. Most funds have diversification above and beyond almost any investor's dreams.

There is a major disadvantage to all of this. By delegating responsibility to a manager, the investor loses control over the investment and, thus, his or her money. The investor's choice is confined to buying and selling the fund. Many investors view security selection as a sport. It is important for the CPA to rein in this activity.

Direct stock and bond investment costs end as soon as the client buys the security; mutual fund fees are ongoing. Fund fees only rarely are tied to returns. In other words, fees are rarely dictated by performance. Usually, they are fixed, regardless of how the market or how the funds behave. With high turnover (of assets in the fund) and increasingly modest disclosure requirements (of activity generated within the mutual fund), interested investors often have no idea (other than asset class) what they own or what they have earned.

To top it off, the primary fund support document, the prospectus, may be difficult to understand. However, recent prospectus requirements were cut and edited to modest-sized disclosure documents by the Securities and Exchange Commission's Rule on the "Profile" disclosure option. Another SEC Rule mandates the use of "Plain English" for disclosure documents. (Both SEC Rules are explained in other chapters.)

Not all funds have these various disadvantages. Furthermore, many have them to a lesser extent than their more confusing or complicated mutual fund rivals. It is true that some mutual funds' portfolio guidelines are almost impossible to understand. Incredibly enough, however, mutual fund companies are regularly rated, based on the reporting documents to shareholders and their shareholder relations departments. But their portfolio guidelines never win awards for clarity.

¶31,004   Open-Ended and Closed-Ended Mutual Funds

There are two types of mutual funds: open ended and closed ended. By far the most common, popular and largest are open ended, so-called because they can continue to take in new money every trading day, thus creating new shares that represent a pro rata portion (the investor's share of the pot) of the fund's assets. Open-ended funds are listed in the mutual fund section of the business section of the newspaper, fund family by fund family. They are priced by their net asset value (total net value of the fund divided by the number of shares in the fund) at the close of the trading day. There are no fluctuating quotes during the course of the market day.

Closed-ended funds, on the other hand, trade throughout the day on an exchange the same way stocks do—their prices fluctuate during the course of the day and are listed and quoted daily under their proper exchange listing. Closed-ended funds are always listed under the exchange quotes (in alphabetical order) of the exchange on which they are listed (usually the New York Stock Exchange and American Stock Exchange). They are not priced by their net asset value the way open-ended funds are. The two can vary widely—market (price) value and underlying asset value. Most closed-ended funds sell at either a premium (above) or a discount (below) to their underlying net asset value. Net asset value is total fund assets remaining after total fund liabilities, such as trading fees and margin interest, have been subtracted. XYZ Fund owns $125,000,000 of stock (after all liabilities are subtracted from fund assets) and there are 10,000,000 shares outstanding. Therefore, the net asset value is $12.50 ($125,000,000 ÷ 10,000,000 shares = $12.50).

Closed-ended funds tend to be a bit more esoteric as investment items than open-ended funds because little about them is as cut-and-dried as open-ended funds. Discounts to (prices below) their net asset value are much more common than premiums (prices above), so people tend to assume there is something wrong with closed-ended funds per se. Many of the funds are made up of foreign, illiquid, or small capitalization securities; therefore, many investors are wary of investing in something they are unfamiliar with and do not understand. Closed-ended funds often employ leveraging (borrowing) to enhance cash flow, gains or total return—many clients want nothing to do with leveraged securities purchases in any form and should avoid closed-end funds altogether.

¶31,005 Mutual Fund Sales Costs

Far more popular than worrying about closed-ended funds and their investment practices is the issue of mutual fund costs. A large library could be filled with the book, magazine, newspaper, TV and radio coverage of mutual fund costs. They all so thoroughly contradict one another and come to such contrary conclusions that, other than as a cure for insomnia, they may be collectively without value. As an introduction to mutual fund costs, the CPA/PFS must remember there are no free lunches in the mutual fund industry. Mutual fund companies are not philanthropic entities. They are in the business of making money for themselves and their clients. If they don't, they don't survive.

.01 Definitions of Sales Fees of Mutual Funds

The issue of cost arises because there is a multiplicity of pricing matrixes for the same or very similar products. The sales fees of mutual funds are called "loads." There are front-ended loads, no-loads, back-ended (trailing) loads, and level-load funds. In addition, there are internal charges, called 12(b)-1 fees and management fees, which serve to further muddy the waters. Enumerated, stated and defined are all the loads:

1. *Load*—the different types of sales charges associated with open-ended mutual fund purchases.
2. *Front-ended load*—up-front pay for the purchase.

3. ***No-load***—no direct purchase or sell costs are associated with investment. However, there are internal fees (to make up for no direct sales charges), which can be considerable.
4. ***Back-ended (trailing) load***—a fee is attached if the fund is liquidated within a stated time period that declines at stated intervals, usually yearly, as ownership continues.
5. ***Level-load***—a combination of front-ended and back-ended (trailing) load in which a reduced front-ended charge is paid upon purchase and a reduced back-ended (trailing) load is paid if the investment is liquidated early in holding period.
6. ***Internal charges***—fees paid within the fund itself for the ongoing expenses of the fund.
7. ***12(b)-1 fees***—fees charged to fund assets for mutual fund advertising and sales.
8. ***Management fees***—administrative and trading costs charged to the fund assets.

.02   The Significance of Fund Costs

To an investor, these charges are at best inconsequential and at worst blinding. At one end of the spectrum, there are investors who ignore the costs of a product and simply invest passively, regardless of the price. At the other end, are investors who ignore every characteristic of a fund except its costs. The realistic approach lies somewhere between the two extremes. The consequence of mutual fund costs is significant because of the nature of mutual fund investing itself. A single year of sales and related fees may not seem like much, but mutual fund investment is perceived as a long-term commitment. With time (as these fees never go away), the costs of a fund are clearly significant, because they affect fund performance. The more sophisticated a fund's investment mission, the more sizable are their fees. There are no super expensive plain-vanilla index funds; there are no bargain-basement leveraged, international, multi-sector commodities pools. Often, then, but not always, the investors pay for what they get. However, it is a mistake to assume that the highest fees necessarily guarantee the investor the best manager or performance. The highest fees simply provide the investor with the most costly securities—much of the time.

High costs generate virulent controversy because investors do not like to pay them and, as already stated, the costs do not go away. It is incorrect to assume that someone who attacks mutual fund fees is simply a crank unwilling to pay fair value for services rendered. Studies suggest that, when mutual funds perform above the average of income funds, their success is directly related to modest costs. Conversely, these studies suggest that, when funds perform below the average, they lose too much return to the cost of the fees. Internal fees rarely scale down as funds grow in size; some studies suggest that fees tend to go up as funds do better! So, one is at a loss to determine exactly what is fair. "Fair" pricing structure in mutual funds may be impossible to define, but everyone is well advised to pay attention to all of these costs.

.03 How Mutual Fund Costs Affect Performance

Less subjectively, it can be said that a lot of effort has been expended trying to answer questions about mutual fund costs and almost all of that effort focuses on performance. How do costs affect performance? Respected research offers conflicting data. One company that researches, evaluates, and comments on mutual funds, has concluded that, over the long run (10 years), fund returns are not influenced by the type of sales charges a fund family uses. This company perceives the real issue to be whether investors receive fair value for whatever expense they generate determining their mutual fund selections. The company addresses investor need by looking at:

1. What the investor can expect from a fund.
2. Products offered by the different fund families—by segregating all the various types of funds and defining them in plain English.
3. Value added by the fund family—by determining the role played in various fund classes and types by managers, trading costs and management fees.

Of mutual fund sales, 25 to 30 percent are no-load. Much of the no-load sales are in defined contribution retirement plans, an area that load-fund families are aggressively targeting. More and more investors feel the need to consult professional advice and are unwilling to go the investment route solo with direct-marketed (not broker-sold) mutual funds. Supporting the point, more and more direct-marketed fund families have sprouted broker-marketed fund subsidiaries, often with different names. Broker-sold funds, through the CPA/personal financial specialist (PFS) may be less risky than direct-marketed funds for the novice investor. The financial advisor can help select the clients' fund choices and provide them with research and documentation. Most investors cannot confidently or wisely select mutual funds on their own.

Even more confusing, a financial journal has concluded that no-load mutual fund investors made more money than load investors, but that their superior results came from more aggressive investment. The problem with this conclusion is that it does not:

1. Address the suitability of the specific mutual fund for the investor.
2. Take into consideration the goals set by the individual investor.
3. Consider how asset allocation was able to offset market upsets to the good or detriment of the fund.

It is difficult to congratulate an investor group on performance achieved as a happy by-product of ignorance of their own investment profile. On the other hand, if professional advisors tend to defer to a conservative investment posture to police clients "for their own good," the clients must wonder what is going on. Until the mid-1990s, pension plan investment tended to be biased toward capital preservation and low volatility.

Hindsight demonstrates in this instance that professional advice that is too conservative is fully as undesirable as the opposite stance. It can be very difficult for the CPA to ascertain a clear picture of how a mutual fund is doing in relation to individual client's needs.

.04   Conclusions About Mutual Fund Costs

It should be clear that cost problems in the mutual fund industry are not going away. Perhaps most inequitable is the fact that all of the costs in all of the sale configurations are borne by the investors. The investor pays for everything. Almost no fund fees are tied to the performance of the mutual fund. Consequently, the investor reads all about the gains of mutual funds but has no familiarity with the costs incurred by the fund itself. Many assumptions are made about mutual funds because the investor believes that they all behave the same as the other funds of their class and variety. They do not.

For a moment, the CPA should look at the conventional buying and selling of securities. One of the most incorrect statements made about the financial services entities that sell securities is that the industry does not care whether the market goes up or down. The conventional belief is that, buying or selling, the client has to pay a commission, so the broker makes out no matter what. Well, that's just plain silly. What is true is that the money managers who manage mutual funds often do not share the responsibility for good or bad results with mutual fund shareholders the way they do with other financial commitments. To say managers are neither rewarded for good performance nor penalized for bad is incorrect and an exaggeration. They receive better bonuses if all goes well; they are fired if things do not. However, the fund companies themselves receive the same fees regardless of the results. While it is true clients exit poor performing funds, their money tends to remain with the same mutual fund family—they simply switch to a better-performing fund within that family. The fund company still gets their fees.

Direct-sales clients can come and go as they please because they pay no direct sales fees to inhibit their departure; however, broker-sold fund families have better retention because sales regulatory principles that govern broker practices discourage switching between fund families. One would be hard put to determine which is the better practice.

.05   So... What's the Answer?

The SEC requires mutual fund families to share in gains and assume responsibilities in losses if a performance-based fee program is implemented. Over an extended holding period, the fees might be the same with or without a performance-based fee program. To determine that would require still another industry study. One would suspect that the gigantic fund families (as they continue to consolidate) would not really care much. However, smaller companies with specialized funds would experience significant revenue volatility. Particularly acute would be problems that a prolonged downturn in their markets would create because these companies would lose assets. For example, any specialty fund loses money under management when its area of specialization falls out of favor.

.06   The Answer Is...

Like so many seemingly simple investment questions, there are sadly no simple answers. The global investment public continues to rely on the mutual fund industry to manage assets; therefore, the way that industry is compensated will be scrutinized. Who knows what will come of it?

Costs are more relevant an issue to the investor than ever before with their shift toward allocating capital to equity funds. The reason for this is that the cost of equity funds so grossly exceeds that of debt funds. All debt funds charge about the same amount of money to do the same thing, which is why they all tend to have about the same yield. This is anything but the case with equity funds. In a bull market, the return on successful equity funds is so high that most clients cannot see the costs that they are paying to own the funds. This is not a good situation, because it creates opportunities for shareholder abuse. However, in a bear market, every client is aware of where every penny (that they do not receive) goes. Hence, fund fees and sales charge abuses are less apt to be a problem. The issue of costs with income funds (which generate a cash flow to the client as opposed to growth, as with an equity fund) is largely self-policed in a low interest rate environment. Excessive costs eliminate yield, which is the reason most investors buy debt funds. Thus, costs tend to remain low or investors do not invest in the fund. If costs are high, they eat up the yield and investors select a different fund for their income.

¶31,006   Stock Mutual Funds

Again, in an equity bull market, performance can conceal a multitude of sins, let alone bury internal costs. Until 1994, a terrible year for both equity and debt securities, stock and bond fund cash flows were about equal. By 2000, the net inflow to bond funds became essentially zero. Equities account for nearly 40 percent of all household financial assets, much of them contained in mutual funds concentrating in equities. The retail investor has, for several years, been a net seller of directly owned equities.

Interestingly, from a performance standpoint, most equity mutual funds, if compared to the Standard & Poor's 500 Index, do not do well. The S&P 500 is the accepted measurement and usual index for equity performance measurement. Large equity funds have a difficult time beating their index (once again, usually, but by no means always, the S&P 500). Some of the index funds have a hard time duplicating the performance of their index.

.01   What's an Investor to Do?

A head-banging exercise in equity fund investment futility is to try to pick funds with the aid of mass media periodical rankings. None of these publications agrees on much of anything and their choices are often atrocious performers, even if their selection is not entirely capricious. They do seem to try, and yet routinely fail. So, the CPA/PFS and client can go ahead and read periodical rankings, but they must keep in mind the lack of reliability.

.02   Special and Sector Equity Funds

While nobody can begin to sort out magazine fund rankings, what is true is that if such specialized sectors as real asset funds, emerging economy funds, socially responsible funds, or other esoteric types suit the client's fancy, the CPA should learn a lot about how to evaluate funds. Nothing out there can help very much. Many of these funds are completely uncharacteristic and capricious in their investment styles. They often have abominable performance by any standard of measurement and are despised by the rating services. The financial planner is going to have to take down and tear apart each fund one by one to glean any uniqueness or value for the client. They are often bad investments.

.03   Equity Funds: Costs and Conclusions

To conclude remarks on equity funds, the CPA and client cannot afford to ignore investment costs. The most common measurement of costs is expense ratios. They are a statement of costs expressed as a percentage of assets. For example, if the net asset value of a fund is $25.00 and the expenses total 50 cents, then 2 percent of the assets go to expenses. The expense ratios vary from less than 1 percent to as much as 10 percent in growth-oriented mutual funds. Once again, there is no correlation, good or bad, between expenses and performance over time. However, a "study of studies" suggests that:

1. Large capitalization fund performance is affected negatively by large fees.
2. Small capitalization stock fund performance is related positively to high expense ratios.

3. There is no correlation between costs and global fund performance. There-fore, it cannot be that the more esoteric the investment, the more money needs to be spent on the funds.

With equity mutual funds, there is really only one way to find a correlation between costs and performance. The solution is to take a long list of stock funds, break down what their expenses are allotted to, and determine whether any particular expense correlates with either positive or negative performance. Nobody wants to be the one to try to do it, though. Can anyone imagine calling a variety of privately owned investment companies to ask them for a list of their expenses, broken down item by item, for each fund? "Go fish!"

¶31,007   Bond Funds

A bond fund is a mutual fund made up almost entirely, but by no means exclusively, of bonds. There are numerous income-generating securities that can end up in a bond fund—from simple money market instruments to the sophisticated synthetics or derivatives. Their primary purpose is to generate a cash flow the investor can use for immediate spending.

Bond fund costs, happily, are clearer and easier to understand than equity fund costs. Since bond funds tend to be specialized and simple to categorize, they are easier than stock funds to evaluate. Bond funds, in brief, usually under perform their indexes, especially on a risk-adjusted, post-expense basis. In a low-interest-rate environment, the only way a manager can perform at or above his or her index is to increase his risk significantly (on a relative basis to that index and to funds like it).

In addition, the manager can try to enhance the return with strategies that few individual investors would ever consider, let alone try to do or be able to understand, on their own. At the most elementary level, very few individuals use margin to buy bonds on credit, either for income or gain. At its most sophisticated, money managers have sizable commitments to synthetically created securities, derivatives of conventional bonds, uncommon option and futures strategies… the list is endless.

While the aggressive management of bond funds is not categorically bad (investors do, after all, pay a fund manager to do better than they think they can do on their own), the investment public has seen some mind-boggling bond fund disasters over the last 20 years CNBC reported that 2022 was the worst-ever year for U.S. Bonds. Many of these misfortunes arose because a fund manager failed to realize exceptional returns for his or her shareholders. Although it is ludicrous to say fund managers' errors were made in an effort to offset large expenses, this strategy did play a role in these fiascoes. For example, common sense dictates that if a manager of anything—mutual fund or fast food restaurant—has large expenses, the manager tries to do the best he or she can to cover expenses.

.01   Bond and Other Income Fund Costs

One service has claimed that risks and high expense ratios in income funds go hand in hand, especially large 12(b)-1 fees. Bond fund promotion costs through 12(b)-1 fees are so large that the effects on yield are perceptible. Evidently, aside from assuming more credit risk, expensive funds have longer duration (more volatility), use margin (leveraged purchases) and employ options and futures strategies (high risk) more often. Another of the largest managers of income funds was accused for years of buying premium bonds in its income funds only to beef up yields to cover enormous advertising costs. Of course, premiums disappear as bonds approach par value at maturity, so a lot of money just disappears from net asset value—but cash flow stays higher in the meantime.

How much of all this quibbling becomes "chicken and egg" controversy is arguable. The 12(b)-1 fees are so controversial and confusing that one can safely predict an eventual legislated end to their existence. The consumer is confused by the blend of internal sales, management and distribution fees, and logic suggests that these fees in their current form cannot last much longer. Full disclosure of costs would mitigate most of the problems attached to mutual fund fees.

.02   Junk Bond Funds

Before addressing fund selection, there are a few special types of bond funds the financial planner should understand. Even in an equity-obsessed universe, these income funds generate a large amount of press coverage and should be understood by the financial advisor. The most notorious of all bond vehicles, in or out of a mutual fund, are junk bonds. Junk bonds are lower-rated debt that is not investment or "bank quality" debt—which must be rated BBB or better. Despite the general antipathy generated by the sector, the fact remains that junk (or high-yield bonds, to be less pejorative) generates large cash flow and excellent total return. It took a while, after Michael Milken, but lower-rated debt has returned to the generally high level of performance conventionally associated with this investment before the junk market collapse.

Junk bonds historically have returned about 50 percent more than Treasury bonds. In a time when few companies default, where there is little inflation and the economy usually chugs along quite nicely, the risks of lower-rated debt (particularly diversified in a large mutual fund investment pool) seems well worth the risk to many investors. Of particular note is that, as more companies continue to turn their performance around for the better, credit upgrades resulting from these turnarounds can only enhance the value of junk bond portfolios. An example would be all the debt issued to fund the growth and development of the major high-tech companies. When the companies were created in the 1960s and 1970s, those that were able to issue debt were rated very low. However, as some of these companies became large capitalization companies of immense value, their debt was upgraded accordingly and traded in line with the higher-quality debt to which they became comparable.

.03 Global Bond Funds

Global bond funds enjoy reputations similar to junk bond funds. Most countries have debt that is rated below investment grade. Many countries enjoy decent ratings simply because their debt is guaranteed or backed by the U.S. government. Thanks to the collapse of short-term multimarket income funds several years ago (when much foreign debt either defaulted or dropped like a stone as the dollar strengthened), many clients respond to the mention of global bond funds with genuine loathing. The reason for this antipathy is that the short-term multimarket income funds fell apart never to recover, and they generated legal proceedings that continue to this day.

Global bond funds are sophisticated investments with multiple risks that are rather difficult to understand. Without an elaborate discussion of bond fund risks, suffice it to say that if global debt is a client's interest rate vehicle of choice, the CPA/PFS must do some homework preparatory to selecting a fund and investing the client's hard-earned money in it.

The CPA must learn about those countries that a "chosen" fund invests in. It would be unwise under any circumstances to invest in countries the client does not like. On the other hand, it would be interesting for the client to invest in countries that he or she does like. The CPA must always remember—debt securities are loans; hence, loans should be made to countries clients want to lend their money to, because that is exactly what they are doing. Then, it is important to examine the nature of the fund's currency exposure—do they own mostly dollar-denominated securities? Or are they all tied up with a lot of soft currency paper? As has been discussed, the CPA should determine whether the fund's expense ratio is consistent with the costs of implementing the investment strategy stated in its prospectus. For example, a plain vanilla fund without leverage or advanced trading strategies should have significantly lower expenses than one with sophisticated futures, options, currency and derivative plays.

.04 Emerging Markets Bond Funds

Closely aligned to global bond fund investing are emerging markets bond fund investing. While global funds can invest in domestic and foreign debt from highest to lowest quality, emerging market bond funds invest only the debt of developing nations. The debt of emerging nations by definition is often of highest credit risk, illiquid and tied to currencies that are not traded on global markets. The fact that these currencies are often pegged to the dollar helps stabilize them, but the risks attached to these countries can quickly eliminate this advantage. It is safe to say that most emerging nation debt funds trade like high-risk equity funds with an income kicker (in the form of cash flow) attached to them. The emerging debt fund group is a vehicle designed to generate a huge cash flow, but certainly things go wrong. Every kind of risk can apply to a greater or lesser extent to emerging market debt.

.05   Insured Municipal Bond Funds

The last bond fund the CPA should learn about is the insured municipal bond fund. Many investors become very concerned with municipal bond fund problems—problems they think owning an insured fund will cure. What they want is so many layers of protection that they ignore the fact that they may give up more income than their concern justifies. For example, if a person wants insured debt, he or she should invest in direct ownership of individual issues. Then, the investor will have fixed cash flow and fixed maturity, which do not exist in funds.

Now, to be totally contradictory, if there are high-yield (lower-rated) mutual funds of a state, the CPA should examine these offerings. The default risk of municipal debt is slight. Funds managers have mind-numbing diversity to consider in any single state's municipal funds; there are hundreds of issuers and thousands of issues. A good municipal fund manager might generate very high yields for the client unconstrained by conventional rating.

.06   Bond Funds and Risk

Bond funds have significant risk. The types of risk associated with income-oriented investment that directly apply to income mutual funds follow:

Interest Rate Risk. There's not a thing anyone can do about interest rates, unless they are on the Federal Reserve Board. If the CPA and the client are afraid of rates rising and eroding the value of a fund position, they should switch into the fund family's money market fund or intermediate term bond fund. Rate issues generate much less significant principal risk in intermediate-term maturities than in long-term ones. Of course, for all practical purposes, principal is not at risk in a money market fund, regardless of rate fluctuations.

Credit Risk. If the CPA and client do not like lower-rated debt because of a fear of default, the client should not own any lower-rated debt, period. The incremental return is not worth the fact that the client will never stop worrying about his or her position.

Sector Risk. Sector risks are very real. Most single state municipal funds are very responsive to their state's financial well-being. However, the municipal markets are comparatively stable, state to state, because they operate in fairly benign isolation and suffer from a chronic supply shortage of bonds. On the other hand, with most high-risk global, junk or emerging market funds, an investor must exercise great restraint, from an asset allocation standpoint. High yield seduces many investors with visions of chunks of cash flow dancing in their heads into overcommitting assets. Concentrated positions in low-rated and high-risk securities makes no sense in income-oriented investments—to place 25 percent of your principal at risk to generate 4 percent more income per year is hardly sound money management. Junk funds are good for income enhancement, but the client cannot overcommit to them. Murphy's Law is fully operative with greedy income investors. They are always punished.

Style Risk. The CPA/PFS must be well-versed in leverage, options and futures strategies, derivatives and foreign exchange risk before employing these strategies to invest the clients' money in funds. Also, the financial advisor must read the prospectuses and quarterly reports of all these funds to determine which employ risk or risk management strategies and to attempt to learn exactly how they affect the performance of the funds.

CHAPTER 32
Mutual Funds

¶32,000   Overview

On June 30, 2009, in response to the credit crisis's impact on money market funds, the SEC issued a comprehensive set of proposals to strengthen the money market fund regulatory regime. The proposals focused on tightening the credit quality, maturity, and liquidity standards for money market funds to better protect investors and make money market funds more resilient to risks in the short-term securities markets. In addition, the proposals would require money market funds to stress test their portfolios and report their portfolio holdings each month to permit investors and regulators to better assess their risk characteristics.

A money market fund is a type of mutual fund that is required by law to invest in low-risk securities. Typically these funds invest in government securities, certificates of deposit, commercial paper of companies, or other highly liquid and low-risk securities. They attempt to keep their net asset value (NAV) at a constant $1.00 per share—only the yield goes up and down. But a money market's per share NAV may fall below $1.00 if the investments perform poorly. While investor losses in money markets have been rare, they are possible, and did happen in this case for only the second time ever. Unlike a "money market deposit account" at a bank, money market funds are not federally insured.

The proposals also seek to facilitate an orderly liquidation of any money market fund that has "broken the buck" (re-priced its securities below $1.00 per share) by requiring funds to have the capability to process trades at prices other than $1.00 and permitting them to suspend redemptions in order to distribute assets in an orderly manner. In addition, the SEC requested comment on whether more fundamental changes may be warranted, such as converting money market funds to a floating rate net asset value, in order to better protect investors from abuses and runs on the funds.

In addition, on June 18, 2009, the SEC and the Department of Labor held a joint hearing on target date funds. Target date funds and other similar investment options are investment products that allocate their investments among various asset classes and automatically shift that allocation to more conservative investments as a "target" date approaches. These funds have become popular, with growth in target date fund assets likely to continue since these funds can be default investments in 401(k) retirement plans under the Pension Protection Act of 2006. Target date funds, however, have produced some troubling investment results. The average loss in 2022 among 143 funds with a 2025 retirement date was 10.38 percent. In addition, varying strategies among these funds produced widely varying results, as returns of 2025 target date funds ranged from minus 4.33 percent to minus 12.98 percent.

The SEC Chairman stated that the SEC staff had also been asked to prepare a recommendation on rule 12b-1, which permits mutual funds to use fund assets to compensate broker-dealers and other intermediaries for distribution and servicing expenses. These fees, with their bureaucratic sounding name and sometimes unclear purpose, are not well understood by investors. Despite this, in 2008, aggregate rule 12b-1 fees amounted to more than $13 billion. It is essential, therefore, that the SEC conduct a comprehensive re-examination of rule 12b-1 and the fees collected pursuant to the rule. If issues relating to these fees undermine investor interests, then we at the SEC have an obligation to adjust our regulations.

On July 12, 2023, the SEC adopted amendments to certain rules that govern money market funds under the Investment Company Act of 1940.

The amendments increase minimum liquidity requirements for money market funds to provide a more substantial liquidity buffer in the event of rapid redemptions. The amendments also remove provisions in the current rule that permit a money market fund to suspend redemptions temporarily through a gate and allow money market funds to impose liquidity fees if their weekly liquid assets fall below a certain threshold. These changes are designed to reduce the risk of investor runs on money market funds during periods of market stress.

To address concerns about redemption costs and liquidity, the amendments require institutional prime and institutional tax-exempt money market funds to impose liquidity fees when a fund experiences daily net redemptions that exceed five percent of net assets, unless the fund's liquidity costs are de minimis. In addition, the amendments require any nongovernment money market fund to impose a discretionary liquidity fee if the fund board determines that a fee is in the best interest of the fund. These amendments are designed to protect remaining share-holders from dilution and to more fairly allocate costs so that redeeming share-holders bear the costs of redeeming from the fund when liquidity in underlying short-term funding markets is costly.

"Money market funds – nearly $6 trillion in size today – provide millions of Americans with a deposit alternative to traditional bank accounts," said SEC Chair Gary Gensler. "Money market funds, though, have a potential structural liquidity mismatch. As a result, when markets enter times of stress, some investors – fearing dilution or illiquidity – may try to escape the bear. This can lead to large amounts of rapid redemptions. Left unchecked, such stress can undermine these critical funds. I support this adoption because it will enhance these funds' resiliency and ability to protect against dilution. Taken together, the rules will make money market funds more resilient, liquid, and transparent, including in times of stress. That benefits investors."

Separately, the amendments also modify certain reporting forms that are applicable to money market funds and large private liquidity funds advisers.

The rule amendments became effective 60 days after publication in the Federal Register (August 3, 2023) with a tiered transition period for funds to comply with the amendments. The reporting form amendments became effective June 11, 2024.

¶32,001   Enhanced Disclosure and New Prospectus Delivery Option for Registered Open-End Management Investment Companies

On January 13, 2009, the Securities and Exchange Commission (SEC) adopted amendments to Form N-1A used by mutual funds to register under the Investment Company Act of 1940 and to offer their securities under the Securities Act of 1933 in order to enhance the disclosures that are provided to mutual fund investors. The amendments require key information to appear in plain English in a standardized order at the front of the mutual fund statutory prospectus.

The Commission is also adopting rule amendments that permit a person to satisfy its mutual fund prospectus delivery obligations under Section 5(b)(2) of the Securities Act by sending or giving the key information directly to investors in the form of a summary prospectus and providing the statutory prospectus on an Internet Web site. Upon an investor's request, mutual funds are also required to send the statutory prospectus to the investor. These amendments are intended to improve mutual fund disclosure by providing investors with key information in plain English in a clear and concise format, while enhancing the means of delivering more detailed information to investors. Finally, the SEC adopted additional amendments that are intended to result in the disclosure of more useful information to investors that purchase shares of exchange-traded funds on national securities exchanges.

.01   Amendment to Form N-1A and Related Rules

The amendments to Form N-1A and related rules include the following:

- Requires each mutual fund statutory prospectus to include a summary section that lists certain specified information about the fund covered by the prospectus;
- Amends certain disclosure requirements for exchange-traded funds (ETF) that register as open-end funds on Form N-1A; and
- Allows a fund to satisfy its prospectus delivery requirements by providing to investors a summary prospectus, which is composed of the summary section of the statutory prospectus.

The amendments were effective on March 31, 2009. Compliance is mandatory on or after January 1, 2010 for initial registrations and post-effective amendments that add a new series or provide annual updates. Compliance is mandatory for other post-effective amendments filed on or after January 1, 2011. A fund may elect to comply with the new form requirements at any time after the effective date. It is important to note that because the post-effective amendments using the new format must be filed under Rule 485(a) under the 1933 Act, they are, therefore, not effective for at least 60 days.

There have been several additional amendments in subsequent years, including the addition of item 27A in 2022 including concise discussions of fund expenses, performance, and portfolio holdings. The SEC's stated goal is to ensure that shareholders receive information more narrowly tailored to their specific investments and to reduce the complexity of the disclosures. The form was

often more than 100 pages. It may now be as short as three pages. Go to www.
sec.gov/files/form-n-1a.pdf to see the most recent version of the form.

.02   Specific Requirements for Summary Section of Prospectus

Amended Form N-1A requires each statutory prospectus to include, at the beginning, a summary section that contains, in plain English and in a prescribed
numerical order, certain required disclosures. Registrants are not permitted to
omit any of the prescribed disclosures or include any additional information
that is not otherwise required. Furthermore, nothing other than the cover page
and the table of contents may precede the summary section.

The SEC believes that a standardized summary section will enhance investor understanding and the ability to compare funds. Information included in the summary
section need not be repeated elsewhere in the prospectus. While a fund may continue
to include information in the prospectus that is not required, a fund may not include
any such additional information in the summary section of the prospectus.

Although the amendments do not include a specific page limit for the summary portion of a statutory prospectus, the SEC stated, "it is our intent that
funds prepare a concise summary (on the order of three or four pages) that will
provide key information."

The following disclosures are required to be included in the summary portion of each statutory prospectus:

- Investment objectives;
- Costs;
- Principal investment strategies, risks, and performance;
- Investment advisers and portfolio managers;
- Brief purchase and sale and tax information; and
- Financial intermediary compensation.

These items will appear in this prescribed order.

.03   Small Entities Subject to the Rule

For purposes of the Regulatory Flexibility Act, an investment company is a
small entity if it, together with other investment companies in the same group
of related investment companies, has net assets of $50 million or less as of the
end of its most recent fiscal year. Approximately 312 mutual funds registered
on Form N-1A meet this definition. Of the approximately 866 registered open-
end investment companies that are ETFs, 54 are small entities.

The Commission believes at the present time that special compliance or
reporting requirements for small entities, or an exemption from coverage for
small entities, would not be appropriate or consistent with investor protection.

We believe that the amendments to Form N-1A will provide investors with enhanced disclosure regarding funds. This enhanced disclosure will allow investors to better assess their investment decisions.

¶32,002   SEC Enhanced Disclosure and New Prospectus Delivery Rule

On January 13, 2009, the Commission adopted a final rule for an improved mutual fund disclosure framework that was originally proposed in November 2007. This improved disclosure framework is intended to provide investors with information that is easier to use and more readily accessible, while retaining the comprehensive quality of the information that is available today. The foundation of the improved disclosure framework is the provision to all investors of streamlined and user-friendly information that is key to an investment decision.

To implement the new disclosure framework, the SEC adopted amendments to Form N-1A that require every prospectus to include a summary section at the front of the prospectus, consisting of key information about the fund, including investment objectives and strategies, risks, costs, and performance. There is also a new option for satisfying prospectus delivery obligations with respect to mutual fund securities under the Securities Act. Under the option, key information is sent or given to investors in the form of a summary prospectus ("Summary Prospectus"), and the statutory prospectus will be provided on an Internet Web site. Funds that select this option will also be required to send the statutory prospectus to the investor upon request.

In addition, the Commission is adopting amendments to Form N-1A relating to exchange-traded funds (ETFs) that are proposed in a separate release in March 2008. These amendments are intended to result in the disclosure of more useful information to investors who purchase shares of exchange-traded funds on national securities exchanges.

Numerous commentators have suggested that investment information that is key to an investment decision should be provided in a streamlined document with other more detailed information provided elsewhere. Furthermore, recent investor surveys indicate that investors prefer to receive information in concise, user-friendly formats.

The SEC adopted amendments to Form N-1A that require every prospectus to include a summary section at the front of the prospectus, consisting of key information about the fund, including investment objectives and strategies, risks, costs, and performance. This key information is required to be presented in plain English in a standardized order. The intent is that this information will be presented succinctly, in three or four pages, at the front of the prospectus.

.01   Background

Millions of individual Americans invest in shares of open-end management investment companies ("mutual funds"), relying on mutual funds for their retirement, their children's education, and their other basic financial needs. These investors face a difficult task in choosing among the more than 8,700 available mutual funds. Fund prospectuses, which have been criticized by investor advocates, representatives of the fund industry, and others as being too long and complicated, often prove difficult for investors to use efficiently in comparing their many choices. Current Commission rules require mutual fund prospectuses to contain key information about investment objectives, risks, and expenses that, while important to investors, can be difficult for investors to extract. Prospectuses are often long, both because they contain a wealth of detailed information, as per SEC requirements, and because prospectuses for multiple funds are often combined in a single document. Too frequently, the language of prospectuses is complex and legalistic, and the presentation formats make little use of graphic design techniques that would contribute to readability.

A new option is also being adopted for satisfying prospectus delivery obligations with respect to mutual fund securities under the Securities Act. Under the option, key information will be sent or given to investors in the form of a Summary Prospectus, and the statutory prospectus will be provided on an Internet Web site. Upon an investor's request, funds will also be required to send the statutory prospectus to the investor. The intent in providing this option is that funds take full advantage of the Internet's search and retrieval capabilities in order to enhance the provision of information to mutual fund investors.

This disclosure framework has the potential to revolutionize the provision of information to the millions of investors who rely on mutual funds for their most basic financial needs. It is intended to help investors who are overwhelmed by the choices among thousands of available funds described in lengthy and legalistic documents to access readily key information that is important to an informed investment decision. At the same time, by harnessing the power of technology to deliver information in better, more useable formats, the disclosure framework can help those investors, their intermediaries, third-party analysts, the financial press, and others to locate and compare facts and data from the wealth of more detailed disclosures that are available.

In addition, effective February 28, 2010, the SEC adopted rules amendments that enhanced information provided in connection with proxy solicitations and in other reports filed with the Commission. The amendments required registrants to make new or revised disclosures about: compensation policies and practices that present material risks to the company; stock and option awards of executives and directors; director and nominee qualifications and legal proceedings; board leadership structure; the board's role in risk oversight; and potential conflicts of interest of compensation consultants that advise companies and their boards of directors. The amendments to these disclosure rules were applicable to proxy and information statements, annual reports and registration statements under the Securities Exchange Act of 1934, and registration statements under the Securities Act of 1933 as well as the Investment Company Act of 1940. The requirement to disclose shareholder voting is transferred from Forms 10-Q and 10-K to Form 8-K.

¶32,003   Funds Reaction to Widespread Scandal

By 2006, the chairman of a fund family must be independent of that fund family. In addition, three-fourths of the board of directors must be independent, too, by 2006. The SEC passed the new rules, briefly outlined below.

There are several hundred thousand employees of the mutual fund industry. Obviously, some of them were unconcerned with the trust the investment community had placed in their actions. However, some of the specific concerns are yet to have a clear case made for the propriety or impropriety of their existence. Market timing, for example, has yet to be proven to be an infringement on shareholder value and rights.

The SEC effort, nevertheless, has been quite rapid, determined, and fair in an attempt to restore confidence to a beleaguered investment public. Whereas the level of compliance and self-regulation of the mutual fund industry are open to question, the fact of the matter is that some media representatives may underestimate the level of disclosure of the fund industry and/or the ability of investors to determine their own investment choices accurately.

What certainly does matter is that the mutual fund vehicle is a universal vehicle and the CPA/PFS must be very familiar and current with the fund industry to understand and help realize their clients' interests and goals.

.01   Disclosure Regarding Approval of Investment Advisory Contracts

In June 2004 and subsequent years, the SEC voted to adopt amendments to its rules and forms that are designed to improve the disclosure that mutual funds and other registered management investment companies provide their shareholders concerning the basis for the fund board's approval of an investment advisory contract. The amendments are intended to encourage fund boards to consider investment advisory contracts more carefully and to encourage investors to consider more carefully *the costs and value of the services* rendered by the fund's investment adviser.

The amendments required fund shareholder reports to discuss, in reasonable detail, the material factors and the conclusions with respect to these factors that formed the basis for the board of directors' approval of advisory contracts during the most recent fiscal half-year. Because fund shareholder reports contain disclosure with respect to *all* advisory contracts approved by the board, the amendments removed the existing requirement for disclosure in the Statement of Additional Information.

The amendments do not basically change the rules discussed in this chapter, but they include the following enhancements to the existing disclosure requirements in fund proxy statements that parallel the disclosure in fund shareholder reports:

1. *Selection of Adviser and Approval of Advisory Fee.* The amendments clarify that the fund must discuss both the board's selection of the investment adviser and its approval of amounts to be paid under the advisory contract.
2. *Specific Factors.* The fund is required to include a discussion of:
   a. The nature, extent, and quality of the services to be provided by the investment adviser;
   b. The investment performance of the fund and the investment adviser;
   c. Costs of the services to be provided and profits to be realized by the investment adviser and its affiliates from the relationship with the fund;
   d. The extent to which economies of scale would be realized as the fund grows; and
   e. Whether fee levels reflect these economies of scale for the benefit of fund investors.
3. *Comparison of Fees and Services Provided by Adviser.* The fund's discussion is required to indicate whether the board relied upon comparisons of the services to be rendered and the amounts to be paid under the contract with those under other investment advisory contracts, such as contracts of the same and other investment advisers with other registered investment companies or other types of clients (e.g., pension funds and other institutional investors).

.02 Investment Company Governance

The Commission also voted to adopt amendments designed to improve the governance of investment companies (funds) and the independence of fund directors. These amendments are the latest in a series of reforms the Commission is adopting to solve problems that have made media headlines relating to the mismanagement of mutual funds.

The SEC pointed out that mutual fund boards of directors play an important role in protecting fund investors. They have overall responsibility for the fund and they oversee the activities of the fund adviser and negotiate the terms of the advisory contract, including the amount of the advisory fees and other fund expenses. Certain exemptive rules under the Investment Company Act require the oversight and approval of the independent directors if the fund engages in transactions with the fund manager and other affiliates, which transactions can involve inherent conflicts of interest between the fund and its managers. The Commission adopted the following amendments to these rules, to further the independence and effectiveness of the fund's independent directors in overseeing or approving these transactions:

- *Independent Composition of the Board.* Independent directors will be required to constitute at least 75 percent of the fund's board. An exception to this 75 percent requirement will allow fund boards with three directors to have all but one director be independent. This requirement is designed to strengthen the presence of independent directors and improve their ability to negotiate lower advisory fees and other important matters on behalf of the fund.
- *Independent Chairman.* The board will be required to appoint a chairman who is an independent director. The board's chairman typically controls the board's agenda and can have a strong influence on the board's deliberations.
- *Annual Self-Assessment.* The board will be required to assess its own effectiveness at least once a year. Its assessment must include consideration of the board's committee structure and the number of funds on whose boards the directors serve.
- *Separate Meetings of Independent Directors.* The *independent* directors will be required to meet in separate sessions at least once a quarter. This requirement could provide independent directors the opportunity for candid discussions about management's performance and could help improve collegiality.
- *Independent Director Staff.* The fund will be required to authorize the independent directors to hire their own staff. This requirement is designed to help independent directors deal with matters on which they need outside assistance.

¶32,004   Kinds of Distributions

There are several kinds of distributions that a shareholder can receive from a mutual fund. They include:
1. Ordinary dividends.
2. Capital gain distributions.
3. Exempt-interest dividends.
4. Return of capital (nontaxable) distribution.

.01   Tax-Exempt Mutual Fund

Distributions from a tax-exempt mutual fund—one that invests primarily in tax-exempt securities—can consist of ordinary dividends, capital gains distributions, undistributed capital gains, or return of capital like any other mutual fund. These contributions follow the same rules as a regular mutual fund. Distributions designated as exempt-interest dividends are not taxable.

A mutual fund may pay exempt-interest dividends to its shareholders if it meets certain requirements. These dividends are paid from tax-exempt interest earned by the fund. Since the exempt-interest dividends keep their tax-exempt character, the taxpayer does not have to include them in income, but may need to report them on his or her return. The mutual fund will send the taxpayer a statement within 60 days after the close of its tax year showing the amount of exempt-interest dividends. Although exempt-interest dividends are not taxable, they must be reported on the tax return if one is required to be filed. This is an information reporting requirement and does not convert tax-exempt interest to taxable interest.

.02   Return of Capital

A distribution that is not out of earnings and profits is a return of the investment, or capital, in the mutual fund. The return of capital distributions are not taxed as ordinary dividends and are sometimes called tax-free dividends or nontaxable distributions that may be fully or partly taxable as capital gains.

A return of capital distribution reduces the basis in the shares. The basis cannot be reduced below zero. If the basis is reduced to zero, the taxpayer must report the return of capital distribution on the tax return as a capital gain. The distribution is taxable if, when added to all returns of capital distribution received in past years, it is more than the basis in the shares. Whether it is a long-term or short-term capital gain depends on how long the shares had been held.

.03   Reinvestment of Distributions

Most mutual funds permit shareholders to automatically reinvest distributions, including dividends and capital gains, in more shares in the fund. Instead of receiving cash, distributions are used to purchase additional shares. The reinvested amounts must be reported to the IRS in the same way as if the reinvestment were received in cash. Reinvested ordinary dividends and capital gains distributions must be reported as income; reinvested exempt-interest dividends are not reported as income.

¶32,005   Foreign Tax Deduction or Credit

Some mutual funds invest in foreign securities or other instruments. A mutual fund may choose to allow an investor to claim a deduction or credit for the taxes the fund paid to a foreign country or U.S. possession. The notice to the fund's investors will include their share of the foreign taxes paid to each foreign country or possession, and the part of the dividend derived from sources in each country or possession.

¶32,006   Basis

The basis in shares of a regulated investment company (mutual fund) is generally figured in the same way as the basis of other stock. The cost basis of purchased mutual fund shares often includes a sales fee, also known as a *load charge*. In certain cases, the entire amount of a load charge incurred after October 3, 1989, cannot be added to the cost basis, if the load charge gives the purchaser a reinvestment right.

.01   Commissions and Load Charges

The fees and charges paid to acquire or redeem shares of a mutual fund are not tax deductible. They are usually added to the cost of the shares and increase the basis. A fee paid to redeem the shares is usually a reduction in the redemption price (sales price) in the case of mutual funds.

.02   Keeping Track of the Basis

The investor in mutual funds should keep careful track of his or her basis because the basis is needed to figure any gain or loss on the shares when they are sold, exchanged, or redeemed. When mutual fund shares are bought or sold, the confirmation statements should be kept to show the price paid for the shares, and the price received for the shares when sold. If the shares are acquired by gift or inheritance, the investor needs information that is different from that in a confirmation statement for figuring the basis of those shares. The basis of shares of a mutual fund is important to know in figuring a gain or loss, with the basis dependent upon how the shares are acquired.

.03   Shares Acquired by Inheritance

If mutual funds shares are inherited shares, the basis is the fair market value (FMV) at the date of the decedent's death, or at the alternate valuation date, if chosen for estate tax purposes. In community property states, each spouse is considered to own half the estate. If one spouse dies and at least half of the community interest is includable in the decedent's gross estate, the FMV of the community property at the date of death becomes the basis of both halves of the property.

.04   Adjusted Basis

After mutual fund shares are acquired, adjustments may need to be made to the basis. The adjusted basis of stock is the original basis, increased or reduced. The basis is increased in a fund by 65 percent of any undistributed capital gain that is included in the taxpayer's income. This has the effect of increasing the basis by the difference between the amount of gain included in income and the credit claimed for the tax considered paid on that income. The mutual fund reports the amount of undistributed capital gain.

.05   Reduction of the Basis

The basis must be reduced in the fund by any return of capital distributions received from the fund. The basis is not reduced for distributions that are exempt-interest dividends.

¶32,007   Sales, Exchanges and Redemptions

When mutual fund shares are sold, exchanged, or redeemed, the investor will usually have a taxable gain or deductible loss. This includes shares in a tax-exempt mutual fund. The amount of the gain or loss is the difference between the adjusted basis in the shares and the amount realized from the sale, exchange, or redemption.

Gains and losses are figured on the disposition of shares by comparing the amount realized with the adjusted basis of the owner's shares. If the amount realized is more than the adjusted basis of the shares, a gain results; if the amount realized is less than the adjusted basis of the shares, a loss results. The amount received from a disposition of mutual fund shares is the money and value of any property received for the shares disposed of, minus expenses of sale such as redemption fees, sales commissions, sales charges, or exit fees.

The exchange of one fund for another fund is a taxable exchange, regardless of whether shares in one fund are exchanged for shares in another fund that has the same distributor or underwriter without paying a sales charge. Any gain or loss on the investment in the original shares as a capital gain or loss must be reported in the year in which the exchange occurs. Service charges or fees paid in connection with an exchange can be added to the cost of the shares acquired. Mutual funds and brokers must report to the IRS the proceeds from sales, exchanges, or redemptions. The broker must give each customer a written statement with the information by January 31 of the year following the calendar year the transaction occurred. The broker must be given a correct taxpayer identification number (TIN); a social security number is acceptable as a TIN.

.01   Identifying the Shares Sold

When mutual fund shares are disposed of, the investor must determine which shares were sold and the basis of those shares. If the shares were acquired all on the same day and for the same price, figuring their basis is not difficult; however, for shares that are acquired at various times, in various quantities, and at various prices, determining the cost basis can be a difficult process. Two methods can be used to figure the basis, the cost basis, or the average basis.

Under the cost basis one of the following methods can be chosen:

1. Specific share identification.
2. First-in first-out (FIFO).

If the shares sold can be definitely identified, the adjusted basis of those particular shares can be used to figure a gain or loss. The shares can be adequately identified, even if bought in different lots at various prices and times, if:

1. The buyer specifies to the broker or other agent the particular shares to be sold or transferred at the time of the sale or transfer.
2. The buyer receives confirmation of the specification from his or her broker in writing within a reasonable time.

The confirmation by the mutual fund must state that the seller instructed the broker to sell particular shares. The owner of the shares has to be able to prove the basis of the specified shares at the time of sale or transfer.

If the shares were acquired at different times or at different prices, and the seller cannot identify which shares were sold, the basis of the shares acquired initially (first-in, first-out) is used as the basis of the shares sold. Therefore, the oldest shares still available are considered sold first. An adequate record should be kept of each purchase and any dispositions of the shares, until all shares purchased at the same time have been disposed of completely.

.02   Average Basis

The average basis can be used to figure a gain or loss when all or part of the number of shares in a regulated investment company are sold. This choice can be made only if acquired at various times and prices, and the shares were left on deposit in an account handled by a custodian or agent who acquires or redeems those shares. The investor may be able to find the average basis of the shares from information provided by the fund. Once the average basis is used, it must continue to be used for all accounts in the same fund. However, a different method can be used for the shares in other funds.

To figure average basis, one of the following methods can be used:

1. Single-category method.
2. Double-category method.

Single-Category Method. In the single-category method, the average cost is found of all shares owned at the time of each disposition, regardless of how long the shares were owned. Shares acquired with reinvested dividends or capital gains distributions must be included. Even if only one category is used to compute the basis, it is possible to have short-term or long-term gains or losses. To determine the holding period, the shares disposed of are considered to be those acquired first. The following steps are used to compute the basis of shares sold:

1. The cost of all shares owned is added.
2. The result of Step 1 is divided by the number of shares owned. This gives the *average basis* per share.
3. The result of Step 2 is multiplied by the number of shares sold. This gives the basis of the shares sold.

The basis of the shares determined under average basis is the basis of all the shares in the account at the time of each sale. If no shares were acquired or sold since the last sale, the basis of the remaining shares at the time of the next sale is the same as the basis of the shares sold in the last sale.

Double-Category Method. In the double-category method, all shares in an account at the time of each disposition are divided into two categories: short-term and long-term. The adjusted basis of each share in a category is the total adjusted basis of all shares in that category at the time of disposition, divided by the total shares in the category.

The investor can specify to the custodian or agent handling the account from which category the shares are to be sold or transferred. The custodian or agent must confirm in writing the seller's specification. If the investor does not specify or receive confirmation, the shares sold must first be charged against the long-term category and then any remaining shares sold against the short-term category.

When a share has been held for more than one year, it must be transferred from the short-term category to the long-term category. When the change is made, the basis of a transferred share is its actual cost or adjusted basis; if some of the shares in the short-term category have been disposed of, its basis falls under the average basis method. The average basis of the undisposed shares would be figured at the time of the most recent disposition from this category.

.03   Holding Period

When mutual fund shares are disposed of, the holding period must be determined. The period starts by using the trade date—the *trade date* is the date on which the holder of the shares bought or sold the mutual fund shares. Most mutual funds will show the trade date on confirmation statements of the purchases and sales.

¶32,008   Investment Expenses

The expenses of producing taxable investment income on a *nonpublicly* offered mutual fund during the year are generally deductible expenses; these include counseling and advice, legal and accounting fees, and investment newsletters. These are deductible as miscellaneous itemized deductions to the extent that they exceed 2 percent of adjusted gross income. Interest paid on money to buy or carry investment property is also deductible.

A nonpublicly offered mutual fund is one that:

1.   Is not continuously offered pursuant to a public offering.
2.   Is not regularly traded on an established securities market.
3.   Is not held by at least 500 persons at all times during the tax year.

Generally, mutual funds are *publicly* offered funds. Expenses of publicly offered mutual funds are not treated as miscellaneous itemized deductions because these mutual funds report only the net amount of investment income after the investor's share of the investment expenses has been deducted.

Expenses on the shares of nonpublicly offered mutual funds can be claimed as a miscellaneous itemized deduction subject to the 2 percent limit.

Expenses cannot be deducted for the collection or production of exempt-interest dividends. Expenses must be allocated if they were for both taxable and tax-exempt income. One accepted method for allocating expenses is to divide them in the same proportion that the tax-exempt income from the mutual fund is to the total income from the fund.

The amount that can be deducted as investment interest expense must be limited in two different ways. First, the interest cannot be deducted for the expenses borrowed to buy or carry shares in a mutual fund that distributes only tax-exempt dividends. Second, investment interest is limited by the amount of investment income. Deductions for interest expense are limited to the amount of net investment income. Net investment is figured by subtracting investment expenses other than interest from investment income. Investment income includes gross income derived from property held for investment, such as interest, dividends, annuities, and royalties. It does not include net capital gains derived from disposing of investment property, or capital gains distributions from mutual fund shares. Investment interest that cannot be deducted because of the 2 percent limit can be carried forward to the next tax year, provided that net investment income exceeds investment interest in the later year.

¶32,009 Background of SEC Final Rules and Amendments on Independent Fund Advisors

Mutual funds are organized as corporations, trusts or limited partnerships under state laws and thus are owned by their shareholders, beneficiaries or partners.

Like other types of corporations, trusts or partnerships, a mutual fund must be operated for the benefit of its owners. However, unlike most business organizations, mutual funds are typically organized and operated by an investment adviser who is responsible for the day-to-day operations of the fund. In most cases, the investment adviser is separate and distinct from the fund it advises, with primary responsibility and loyalty to its own shareholders.

Therefore, the "external management" of mutual funds presents inherent conflicts of interest and potential for abuses that the Investment Company Act and the Securities and Exchange Commission (SEC) have addressed in different ways.

One of the ways that the Act addresses conflicts between advisers and funds is by giving mutual fund boards of directors, and in particular the disinterested directors, an important role in fund governance. In relying upon fund boards to represent fund investors and protect their interests, Congress avoided the more detailed regulatory provisions that characterize other regulatory schemes for collective investments.

The SEC has similarly relied extensively on independent directors in rules that exempt funds from provisions of the Investment Company Act.

.01 SEC Study of Role of Independent Directors

The SEC pointed out that millions of Americans had been investing in mutual funds, which experienced a tremendous growth in popularity over the previous 20 years. In 1999 and 2000, because of that growth and the growing reliance on independent directors to protect fund investors, the SEC felt compelled to study:

1. The governance of investment companies.
2. The role of independent directors.
3. SEC rules that rely on oversight by independent directors.
4. The information that funds are required to provide to shareholders about their independent directors.

They held a roundtable discussion at which independent directors, investor advocates, executives of fund advisers, academics and experienced legal counsel offered a variety of perspectives and suggestions. After evaluating the ideas and suggestions offered by roundtable participants, the SEC proposed a package of rule and form amendments that were designed to:

1. Reaffirm the important role that independent directors play in protecting fund investors.
2. Strengthen their hand in dealing with fund management.
3. Reinforce their independence.
4. Provide investors with better information to assess the independence of directors.

In addition to input from the roundtable, in response to their usual policy of requesting comments to proposed rule changes, amendments and additions, the SEC received 142 comment letters on the proposals, including 86 letters from independent directors.

Commenters generally supported the efforts to enhance the independence and effectiveness of fund directors, although many offered recommendations for improving portions of the proposals. Many of these letters were taken into consideration in formulating the final rules and amendments.

.02   Early Results of Study

The SEC believes that the efforts to improve the governance of mutual funds on behalf of mutual fund investors began to have effect even before the final adoption. The roundtable discussions and proposed rules provoked a great deal of discussion among directors, advisers, counsel, and investors about governance practices and policies. After the roundtable, an advisory group organized by the Investment Company Institute (ICI) made recommendations regarding fund governance in a "best practices" report.

Many boards adopted the recommendations set forth in the ICI Advisory Group Report. Some groups of independent directors hired independent counsel for the first time. Director nomination and selection procedures have been revised.

During the next year, Commissioners and members of the staff began meeting with independent directors and sharing ideas and concerns regarding the governance of mutual funds. A former SEC chairman established the Mutual Fund Directors Education Council, a broad-based group of persons interested in fund governance and operations. Their main purpose is to foster the development of educational activities designed to promote the efficiency, independence, and accountability of independent fund directors.

The American Bar Association formed a task force to examine the role of counsel to independent directors, and the task force released a report offering guidance to counsel and fund directors regarding standards of independence for counsel, and guidelines for reducing potential conflicts of interest (ABA Task Force Report).

All of these initiatives have focused attention on the important role of independent directors, and their importance in promoting and protecting the interests of fund shareholders.

¶32,010   The SEC Adopts Final Rules and Amendments on Fund Governance

In January 2001, the SEC adopted amendments to certain exemptive rules under the Investment Company Act of 1940 relating to investment company governance based upon changes that were proposed in October 1999. Many of the proposed rule and form amendments were basically those initially proposed. However, the final amendments, summarized below, contain several modifications made as a result of suggestions made during the comment period. In line with the original proposals, the rule and form changes cover three areas:

1. Rule amendments relating to directors.
2. Conditions for reliance on certain exemptive rules.
3. Changes in disclosure requirements.

These amendments are designed to enhance the independence and effectiveness of boards of directors of investment companies and to better enable investors to assess the independence of those directors.

¶32,011   The Role of Independent Directors of Investment Companies

The SEC's first order of business was adopting amendments to require (for funds relying on these "certain exemptive rules") that:

1. Independent directors constitute a majority of the fund's board of directors.
2. Independent directors select and nominate other independent directors.
3. Any legal counsel for the fund's independent directors is an independent legal counsel—that is, he or she does not also represent the fund's management or close affiliates.

The three new conditions are generally the same as had been proposed, though some clarifications and modifications were made. Specifics of these items are discussed in some detail below.

.01   Independent Directors Constitute Majority of Fund's Board

Rather than the 40 percent previously required by the Investment Company Act of 1940, the Commission adopted a simple majority independence requirement. They had originally proposed a two-thirds supermajority requirement, but adopted the simple majority in response to public comments.

According to the adopting release, a majority independence requirement will permit, under state law, the independent directors to have a strong influence on fund management. It should enable them to represent shareholders better by being in a stronger position to elect officers, call meetings and solicit proxies.

To allow funds time to implement this provision, compliance is required after July 1, 2002.

In connection with this new requirement, the Commission also adopted a new rule that suspends the board composition requirement *temporarily* in the event of the death, disqualification or bona fide resignation of a director. The final rule provides that if the remaining directors can fill the vacant board position, the suspension is for 90 days; if a shareholder vote is required, the suspension is for 150 days. This time period begins to run when the fund no longer meets the board composition requirement, even if the fund is not yet aware of its non-compliance. The effective date for this specific rule was February 15, 2001.

.02   Independent Directors Select, Nominate Other Independent Directors

This rule amendment was adopted substantially as proposed. The adopting release clarifies that a fund's adviser may be involved in the nomination process. The independent directors must maintain control of the nomination process; however, the adviser may suggest candidates at the independent directors' invitation and provide administrative assistance in the selection and nomination process.

The self-nomination requirement is not intended to supplant or limit the ability of shareholders under state law to nominate directors. At the same time, the involvement of shareholders or the adviser does not excuse the independent directors from their responsibility to canvass, recruit, interview and solicit candidates.

The self-nomination requirement is prospective only. Current independent directors who were selected through a different process may continue to serve as independent directors but—beginning after July 1, 2002—all *new* independent directors must be researched, recruited, considered and formally named by the existing independent directors.

.03   Legal Counsel for Independent Directors Must Be an "Independent Legal Counsel"

This rule's conditions were modified in response to the large number of comments the SEC received relative to it. The proposal defined "independent legal counsel" in narrow terms. Many commenters felt that this explicit definition of "independent" could have unintended negative results:

1.   Discouraging the independent directors from even consider selecting their own counsel.
2.   Limiting the pool of eligible counsel unnecessarily.

3. In some instances, possibly forcing independent directors to terminate longstanding relationships with counsel.

In line with the final rule, as well as with the proposal, independent directors are not required to have counsel. However, if they do, that counsel must be an "independent legal counsel," as determined by the independent directors. A "person"—the lawyer, his or her firm and partners and employees—is considered an independent legal counsel if the independent directors:

1. Determine that any representation of the fund's investment adviser, principal underwriter, administrator or their control persons during the past two fiscal years is or was "sufficiently limited" that it is unlikely to adversely affect the professional judgment of the person in providing legal representation.
2. Have obtained sufficient background information from the counsel for them to determine at that time that any relationship is, indeed, "sufficiently limited." The legal counsel must update the independent directors promptly on any relevant information if the counsel begins or materially increases his or her representation of a management organization or control person.

Directors may rely on information provided by counsel for these decisions.

The final rule requires that the independent directors determine whether a person is an independent legal counsel at least annually. The basis for the determination must be recorded in the board's meeting minutes. If the board receives information from counsel concerning his or her representation of a management organization or a control person, the fund can continue to rely on the relevant exemptive rules for up to three months. This period should provide sufficient time for the independent directors to make a new determination about the counsel's independence under the circumstances or, on the other hand, to hire a new independent legal counsel.

The SEC states that in making the determination of whether counsel is an independent legal counsel, the judgment of the independent directors must be *reasonable* and should take into consideration all relevant factors in evaluating whether the conflicting representations are sufficiently limited. For example, the independent directors should consider such factors as:

1. Is the representation current and ongoing?
2. Does it involve a minor or substantial matter?
3. Does it involve the fund, the adviser, or an affiliate, and if an affiliate, what is the nature and extent of the affiliation?
4. The duration of the conflicting representation.
5. The importance of the representation to counsel and his firm, including the extent to which counsel relies on that representation economically.

6. Does it involve work related to mutual funds?
7. Whether or not the individual who will serve as legal counsel was or is involved in the representation. (In the opinion of the SEC, this would exclude a lawyer from simultaneously representing the fund's adviser and independent directors in connection with such matters as the negotiation of the advisory contract or distribution plan or other *key areas* of conflict between the fund and its adviser.)

Compliance with the independent legal counsel provision also became effective July 1, 2002.

¶32,012   Amendments to Exemptive Rules to Enhance Director Independence and Effectiveness

In amending the 10 rules to exempt funds and their affiliates from certain prohibitions of the Act, the SEC added conditions to the Exemptive Rules to require that, for funds relying upon those rules, the independence and effectiveness of independent directors must be guaranteed. The efforts in that direction have been discussed above.

The SEC pointed out that some commenters questioned the need to amend the rules, because each rule already requires independent directors to approve separately some of the fund's activities under the rule. In truth, these rules were selected because they require the independent judgment and scrutiny of the independent directors in overseeing activities that are beneficial to funds and investors *but involve inherent conflicts of interest between the funds and their managers.* The amendments are designed to increase the ability of independent directors to perform their important responsibilities under each of these rules.

.01   Amendments to Exemptive Rules

The 10 rules exempting funds and their affiliates from certain stipulations of the Investment Company Act make the following actions possible:
1. Permission for funds to purchase securities in a primary offering when an affiliated broker-dealer is a member of the underwriting syndicate.
2. Permission to use fund assets to pay distribution expenses.
3. Permission for fund boards to approve interim advisory contracts without shareholder approval.
4. Permission for securities transactions to take place between a fund and another client of the fund's adviser.
5. Permission for mergers between certain affiliated funds.
6. Permission for funds and their affiliates to purchase joint liability insurance policies.

7. Specific conditions under which funds may pay commissions to affiliated brokers in connection with the sale of securities on an exchange.
8. Permission for funds to maintain joint insured bonds.
9. Permission for funds to issue multiple classes of voting stock.
10. Permission for the operation of interval funds by enabling closed-end funds to repurchase their shares from investors.

¶32,013   Additional Rule Changes

Other rule changes affecting independent directors and their qualification duties and responsibilities have been adopted, including:

.01   Joint Insurance Policies

A rule of the Investment Company Act has been amended so that funds may now purchase joint "errors and omissions" insurance policies for their officers and directors, but *only* if the policy does not exclude:

1. Bona fide claims brought against any independent director by a co-insured.
2. Claims brought by a co-insured in which the fund is a co-defendant with an independent director.

.02   Independent Audit Committees

The SEC also adopted a rule exempting funds from the Act's requirement that shareholders vote on the selection of the fund's independent public accountant if the fund has an audit committee composed *wholly* of independent directors.

The rule permits continuing oversight of the fund's accounting and auditing processes by an independent audit committee instead of the shareholder vote. Commenters agreed that the shareholder ratification had become largely perfunctory and that an independent audit committee could exercise more meaningful oversight.

Consistent with the proposed rule, the final rule provides that a fund is exempt from having to seek shareholder approval if:

1. The fund establishes an audit committee composed solely of independent directors to oversee the fund's accounting and auditing processes.
2. The fund's board of directors adopts an audit committee charter setting forth the committee's structure, duties, powers, and methods of operation or sets out similar provisions in the fund's charter or bylaws.
3. The fund maintains a copy of such an audit committee charter. Some commenters questioned whether the proposed rule would require the audit

committee to supervise a fund's day-to-day management and operations. The rule does not require, nor was it intended, that an audit committee perform daily management or supervision of a fund's operations.

The effective date for this particular rule was February 15, 2001.

.03   Qualification as an Independent Director

A new rule conditionally exempts individuals from being disqualified from serving as independent directors because they invest in index funds that hold shares of the fund's adviser or underwriter or their controlling persons. The rule as *proposed* would have applied only if the value of securities issued by the adviser or controlling person did not exceed 5 percent of the value of any index tracked by the index fund. The SEC has *modified the final rule* to provide relief if a fund's investment objective is to replicate the performance of one or more "broad-based" indices. The effective date for this rule was February 15, 2001.

In addition, the SEC has rescinded a rule that provides relief from a section of the Investment Company Act defining when a fund director is considered to be independent. The SEC had proposed amending the rule to permit a somewhat higher percentage of a fund's independent directors be affiliated with registered broker-dealers, under certain circumstances. The enactment of the Gramm-Leach-Bliley Act amended the Act to establish new standards for determining independence under the same circumstances, thus making the proposed amendments redundant. The rescission became effective on May 12, 2001.

.04   Recordkeeping Requirements

The rule was amended to require funds to preserve for at least six years any record of:

1. The initial determination that a director qualifies as an independent director.
2. Each subsequent determination of whether the director continues to qualify as an independent director.
3. The determination that any person who is acting as legal counsel to the independent directors is an independent legal counsel.

These requirements are designed to permit the SEC's staff to monitor a fund's assessment of director independence. Compliance with this requirement was required after July 1, 2002.

¶32,014   Disclosure Requirements

As is to be expected the SEC has adopted rule and form changes that will require funds to *disclose additional director information* beyond that currently available in a fund's statement of additional information (SAI) and proxy statements. The amendments were adopted with several modifications to tailor them more closely to the goal of providing shareholders with better information without overburdening directors.

.01   Basic Information About Fund Directors

The Commission adopted requirements that basic information about the identity and experience of directors should be outlined in tabular form and included in the fund's annual report to shareholders, the SAI, and any proxy statement for the election of directors. Specifically, the table must disclose detailed information about each and every director:

1. Name, address, and age.
2. Current positions held with the fund.
3. Term of office and length of time served.
4. Principal occupations during the past five years.
5. Number of portfolios overseen within the fund complex (as opposed to the current requirement to disclose the number of registered investment companies overseen).
6. Other directorships held outside the fund complex.
7. The relationship, events, or transactions that make each "interested" director an "interested person" of the fund.

The annual report is required also to include a statement that the SAI has additional information about the directors that is available without charge upon request.

.02   Ownership of Equity Securities in Fund Complex

The proposed requirement to disclose the amount of equity securities of funds in a fund complex owned by each fund director was adopted with certain modifications, as described below.

Disclosure of Amount Owned. The SEC responded to comments that fund disclosure of the dollar amount of directors' fund holdings was not necessary to demonstrate alignment of directors' interests with those of shareholders and would impinge on directors' privacy. The provision adopted requires disclosure of a director's holdings of fund securities using specified dollar ranges rather than an exact dollar amount. Commenters considered the exact amount impinged too greatly upon the director's privacy. The rule incorporates the following dollar ranges: none; 0–$10,000; $10,001–$50,000; $50,001–$100,000; over $100,000.

Beneficial Ownership. The SEC received a number of comments requesting clarification about the types of director holdings that would be disclosed under the proposal. Based on these comments, the Commission reevaluated the proposal to require disclosure of securities owned beneficially and of record by each director.

Under the original proposal, beneficial ownership would have been determined in accordance with a rule of the Exchange Act, which focuses on a person's voting and investment power. In view of the objective of providing information about the alignment of directors' and shareholders' interests, they believe that disclosure of record holdings should not be required and that the focus of beneficial ownership should be on whether a director's economic interests are tied to the securities rather than on his or her ability to exert voting power or to dispose of the securities.

As a result, disclosure of director holdings will be required only in those instances where the director's economic interests are tied to the securities and will not be triggered solely by his or her ability to exert voting power or to dispose of the securities.

Disclosure of Ownership of Funds Within the Same Family of Investment Companies. The proposal that directors disclose their aggregate holdings in a fund complex was modified to require disclosure of:

1. Each director's ownership in every fund that he oversees.
2. Each director's aggregate ownership of all funds that he oversees within a fund family.

The ownership in specific funds demonstrates a director's alignment of interests with shareholders. The SEC realized that a director may have legitimate reasons for not having shares of a specific fund in his or her portfolio; however, the adopting release states that the requirement to disclose aggregate ownership should help to negate any inference that otherwise could be made about why a director has chosen not to own shares of a particular fund.

To determine a director's holdings in a fund complex, the SEC agreed with public comments that the proposed definition of fund complex was too broad. Instead, the Commission adopted a more specific definition of "family of investment companies," to include only funds that have the same investment adviser or principal underwriter and actually publicize themselves to investors as related companies for purposes of investment and investor services.

The equity ownership information must be included in the SAI and any proxy statement relating to the election of directors. For the proxy statement, the equity ownership information must be provided as of the most recent practicable date, as proposed, in order to ensure that shareholders receive up-to-date information when they are asked to vote to elect directors.

For the SAI, the SEC modified the proposal to require that the equity ownership information be provided as of the end of the last completed calendar year. They believe that this modified time period requirement facilitates our goal that investors receive equity ownership information to evaluate whether directors' interests are aligned with their own and imposes less of a burden on directors, especially those who serve multiple funds with staggered fiscal years.

Conflicts of Interest. Consistent with the proposal, fund SAIs and proxy statements will be required to disclose three types of circumstances that, according to the adopting release, could affect the allegiance of fund directors to shareholders. These are the positions, interests and transactions and relationships of directors and their immediate family members with the fund and persons related to the fund. The proposal was modified in several significant respects in response to comments that it was too broad.

Persons Covered. The final rule excludes "interested" directors from the conflict of interest disclosure requirements in both the SAI and proxy statement.

In addition, the SEC narrowed the scope of "immediate family members" covered by the disclosure requirements to a director's spouse, children *residing in the director's household,* including step and adoptive children and dependents of the director. The SEC concluded that these are family members from whom directors can reasonably be expected to obtain the required information. Thus, in contrast to the proposal, the final disclosure requirements do not apply to the director's parents, siblings, children not residing with the director or in-laws.

On the other hand, the SEC did not go to the extent of adopting a suggestion made by some commenters to limit disclosure about positions, interests and transactions and relationships of a director's family members to those about which the director has actual knowledge.

The SEC excluded administrators from the persons related to the fund that are covered by the requirements. This exclusion is limited to administrators that are not affiliated with the fund's adviser or principal underwriter. Entities (including administrators) that control, are controlled by or are under common control with the adviser or principal underwriter will be covered by the disclosure requirements.

Despite these modifications narrowing the disclosure requirements, the adopting release strongly suggests examining any circumstances that could *potentially impair* the independence of independent directors, regardless of whether or not such circumstances are actually spelled out in the SEC's disclosure requirements.

Threshold Amounts. The SEC adopted a $60,000 threshold for disclosure of interests, transactions and relationships. For this provision, it is necessary for a director's interest to be aggregated with those of his immediate family members.

The adopting release warns funds that the $60,000 threshold should not be equated with materiality. The statement is made that "a transaction between a director and a fund's adviser may constitute a material conflict of interest with the fund or its shareholders that is required to be disclosed, regardless of the amount involved, if the terms and conditions of the transaction are not comparable to those that would have been negotiated at 'arm's length' in similar circumstances."

Time Periods. The SEC also modified some of the proposed time periods for disclosure of conflicts of interest in the proxy statement and SAI. In the proxy statement, disclosure of positions and interests of directors and their immediate family members is required, as proposed, for a five-year period. Disclosure of material transactions and relationships must be provided from the beginning of the last two completed fiscal years. In the SAI, disclosure of positions and interests of directors and their immediate family members, as well as disclosure of material transactions and relationships is required for the two most recently completed calendar years, rather than fiscal years.

Routine, Retail Transactions and Relationships. The adopting release clarifies that the exception from the disclosure requirements for routine, retail transactions and relationships, such as credit card or bank or brokerage accounts (unless the director is accorded special treatment), extends to residential mortgages and insurance policies as well as other routine transactions not specifically enumerated.

The Board's Role in Fund Governance. The SEC has adopted, as proposed, disclosure requirements in the proxy rules and SAI relating to board committees. Funds must identify each standing committee of the board in both the SAI and any proxy statement for the election of directors. Funds also are required to provide:

1. A concise statement of the functions of each committee.
2. Names of the members of the committee.
3. Information regarding the number of committee meetings held during the last fiscal year.
4. An indication of whether the nominating committee would consider nominees recommended by fund shareholders; if so, procedures for submitting recommendations should be provided.

Approval of the Advisory Contract. Funds must also disclose in the SAI the board's basis for approving an existing advisory contract. In response to comments that this disclosure would become "boilerplate," the adopting release specifies that boilerplate language is not adequate; funds are required to provide appropriate detail regarding the board's basis for approving an existing advisory contract, including the particular factors forming the basis for this determination.

Separate Disclosure. Funds must present all disclosure for *independent directors* separately from disclosure for *interested directors* in the SAI, proxy statements for the election of directors and annual reports to shareholders. The SEC felt this would aid shareholders in understanding information about directors and in evaluating the effectiveness of independent directors to oversee fund operations.

Compliance Date for Disclosure Amendments. All new registration statements and post-effective amendments that are annual updates to effective registration statements, proxy statements for the election of directors and reports to shareholders filed on or after January 31, 2002, must comply with the disclosure amendments. Based on the comments, the SEC felt that this would provide funds with sufficient time to make the necessary changes to disclosure documents.

CHAPTER 33
Reverse Mortgages

¶33,000   Overview

HUD's stated mission is "to create strong, sustainable, inclusive communities and quality affordable homes for all. HUD is working to strengthen the housing market to bolster the economy and protect consumers; meet the need for quality affordable rental homes; utilize housing as a platform for improving quality of life; build inclusive and sustainable communities free from discrimination; and transform the way HUD does business."

Although application for reverse mortgage has been on a downward trend the past three years, it is thought that this trend will reverse as home values are beginning to increase in some areas. Also, they are seen as a means to finance elderly care costs that continue to rise over time.

The loan limit for reverse mortgages insured by the Federal Housing Administration is $625,500.

¶33,001   Grant to Help Seniors Evaluate Options to Age in Place

On December 23, 2010, the National Council on Aging (NCOA) received $2.53 million from the U.S. Department of Housing & Urban Development (HUD) to continue counseling older homeowners on the benefits and risks of reverse mortgages through NCOA's National Reverse Mortgage Counseling Services (RMCS) Network. This effort is being conducted in partnership with the Administration on Aging (AoA).

NCOA is one of five HUD-approved Counseling Intermediaries that provide mandated counseling nationwide to older adults who are considering a reverse mortgage. A reverse mortgage allows homeowners aged 62+ to convert a portion of their home equity into cash while they continue to live at home for as long as they want.

"As Boomers retire, many will look for solutions to help them remain economically secure and in their own homes," according to the CEO for NCOA. "Unbiased counseling is essential to keeping them informed about their options when considering a reverse mortgage."

In only four years, the ranks of seniors at risk of outliving their resources increased by nearly 2 million households. Using the Senior Financial Stability Index, economic insecurity among senior households increased by one-third, rising from 27 percent to 36 percent from 2004 to 2008. This steady and dramatic increase was in progress even before the full force of the recession hit.

NCOA will use part of the $2.53 million HUD grant to assist Area Agencies on Aging (AAAs) and state Aging and Disability Resource Centers (ADRCs) to develop reverse mortgage counseling strategies as part of their overall services and supports for seniors in their area.

Additional funds will be used to support reverse mortgage counseling mandates approved by HUD in September 2010. The first requires that all HUD-approved reverse mortgage counselors provide their clients with NCOA's 28-page consumer booklet, *Use Your Home to Stay at Home*™. Free copies can be downloaded at *www.ncoa.org/reversemortgagecounseling* in English or Spanish.

The second mandate requires all reverse mortgage counselors to complete a budget review with clients using NCOA's Financial Interview Tool (FIT). The tool helps prospective borrowers consider both immediate financial needs and long-term challenges that could make it difficult to stay at home and benefit from a reverse mortgage.

Finally, all reverse mortgage counselors must complete a BenefitsCheckUp° screening for all clients who have incomes below 200 percent of the federal poverty level. NCOA's BenefitsCheckUp° (*www.BenefitsCheckUp.org*) is the nation's most comprehensive web-based service to screen for benefits for seniors with limited income and resources. It includes details on more than 2,000 public and private programs to help seniors pay for food, medicine, utilities, and more. Reverse mortgages saw a surge in popularity during the financial crisis of 2007-2009. Between September and December 2010, reverse mortgage counselors completed 15,467 BenefitsCheckUp® screenings and identified unclaimed benefits valued at almost $76 million annually for older adults. Many face an economic crisis caused by the coronavirus pandemic and may consider a reverse mortgage as a result. According to the Government Accountability Office (GAO), defaults increased from 2% in 2014 to 18% in 2018, mostly due to borrowers failing to meet occupancy requirements or to pay property taxes and insurance. So, although reverse mortgages can be used as financial tools to allow older homeowners to stay in their homes, they come with risks.

¶33,002   HUD's Reverse Mortgage Option

The Federal Housing Administration (FHA) announced a modified version of its *Home Equity Conversion Mortgage* (HECM) product in September 2010. The HECM loan is a reverse mortgage insured by the federal government. It allows older homeowners to tap into their equity to cover living expenses and health care costs while continuing to live in their home without having to make the mortgage payments that are required with a traditional mortgage or equity loan.

FHA designed *HECM Saver* as a second reverse mortgage option for the purpose of lowering upfront loan closing costs for homeowners who want to borrow a smaller amount than the amount that would be available with a HECM Standard loan. This option was available for all HECM case numbers assigned on or after October 4, 2010.

"Despite the popularity of our HECM loan product, we have noted concerns that some senior citizens find that our fees are too high for them," according to an FHA Commissioner. "In response, we created *HECM Saver* which will provide seniors with a reverse mortgage option that significantly lowers costs by almost eliminating the upfront Mortgage Insurance Premium (MIP) that is required under the standard HECM option."

HECM Saver will have an upfront premium of only .01 percent of the property's value. Under the HECM Standard option, the upfront premium will remain at 2 percent. The MIP for both *HECM Saver* and HECM Standard will be charged monthly at an annual rate of 1.25 percent of the outstanding loan balance.

The reduction in upfront fees will be accomplished while substantially lowering the risk to the FHA insurance fund because the principal limit or amount of money available to a borrower under the *HECM Saver* program will be reduced. Borrowers will receive approximately 10 to 18 percent less under the *HECM Saver* option, than they would receive under HECM Standard.

HECM borrowers may opt to receive funds as a lump sum at loan origination, establish a line of credit or request fixed monthly payments that are disbursed for as long as they continue to live in the home. Funds are advanced to the borrower and interest accrues, but the outstanding amount does not have to be repaid until the borrower dies, leaves the home or sells the property. At that time, if the balance due on the loan exceeds the value of the home, FHA insurance pays the difference.

.01   FHA Mortgagee Letter

The letter sent to all approved mortgagees and all HUD-Approved Counseling Agencies on September 21, 2010, not only announced the second option for a HECM Mortgage Program but also discussed features of each.

This Mortgagee Letter provides policy guidance for HECM Saver and HECM Standard by describing:

- The amount of initial and monthly MIP due to the Secretary;
- The availability of all existing program features for both options;
- How to calculate initial MIP due on HECM refinance transactions;
- How to access new principal limit factor (PLF) tables;
- Changes to FHA Connection; and
- How to manage pipeline loans.

This Mortgagee Letter also reiterates HUD's long standing policy of requiring mortgagees to adapt the legal documents as necessary to ensure compliance with the program requirements

HECM Saver and HECM Standard are available for:

- All HECM transaction types (traditional, purchase and refinance);
- All five payment plans (tenure, term, line of credit, modified tenure and modified term);
- All interest rate indices (Constant Maturity Rate and London Interbank Offered Rate);
- Adjustable rate mortgages (monthly and annual); and
- Fixed interest rate mortgages.

As the result of Public Law 111-229, signed by the President on August 12, 2010, HUD is authorized to adjust the amount of the annual mortgage insurance premiums through Federal Register Notice or Mortgagee Letter. Consistent with this statutory authority, this Mortgagee Letter makes this adjustment. The revised annual mortgage insurance premiums announced in this Mortgagee Letter are applicable in lieu of those currently provided in 24 CFR part 206. Through rulemaking to be subsequently undertaken, HUD will conform its HECM regulations to reflect this adjustment.

¶33,003   Counseling Guidelines Require Non-Borrowing Spouse To Be Present

Changes to HECM counseling protocol were announced on August 29, 2011, by the Department of Housing and Urban Development, which now requires that all owners shown on the property deed as well as any non-borrowing spouse must personally receive counseling.

Additionally, the HECM Saver has been added as one of the options counselors will present to clients and when a Power of Attorney is present, the name of the Attorney-In-Fact will be entered at the top of the certificate along with the name of the homeowner.

Other changes include the replacement of Agency Tax ID Number with Agency Housing Counseling System ID number.

A lawsuit filed by AARP against HUD presented several reverse mortgage borrowers who faced foreclosure, including one plaintiff who had lost his home after his name was removed from title during the process of the reverse mortgage. Prior to this guidance, non-borrowing spouses were not required to receive counseling.

¶33,004   Retirees Face Rising Financial Pressures

This generation of retirees may be more accustomed to living with debt than previous ones. After all, they have lived with credit card debt while paying their mortgage. Why not let that "savings account" now make life easier for them? Beyond that, some are already running into financial hardship resulting from the lessening of pension benefits, increased healthcare costs, homeowners' insurance, real estate taxes, and the ever-rising cost of living in general. These expenses are making it more difficult for seniors to remain in their home at the same time that there is pressure by the government to cut back benefits on Social Security, Medicare and Medicaid, and corporate pensions are disappearing rapidly. On the other hand, it may not be a matter of need, at all, but of making some wish or dream come true. Not all members of this generation of retirees appear to be as emotionally attached to the old homestead as previous generations; some view it as a financial instrument capable of enhancing the quality of their retirement. Most importantly, however, it is a way to access an asset at a time when cash flow is all-important.

With the new increased limit in place for HECM reverse mortgages, a senior home owner aged 75 and above with a home worth more than $625,500 can get around $420,000, but they could get only $280,000 before the loan limit increase. This can be very important for senior home owners who have properties with high values and existing mortgages with balances where the traditional reverse mortgage was not enough.

The increased limit is applicable for all areas with no differences between high-cost or low cost areas. The limit increase is applicable nationally. The changes are expected to flood the reverse mortgage market. For now, this allows more elderly families to borrow enough money from a reverse mortgage to save their home from foreclosure. "Our hope was that by raising the limit, more homeowners facing foreclosure and living in higher-valued homes might be able to take out a reverse mortgage and keep their homes," according to the Director of the Reverse Mortgage Education Project for the AARP Foundation.

.01 Financial Planners See Future for Reverse Mortgages

As some see it, reverse mortgages—in new variations—are destined to become increasingly popular with Boomers possibly being more comfortable with accepting debt in old age than today's seniors. Evidently financial planners appear to believe this to be true. Planners speaking at advertising seminars on the product have suggested that in the future reverse mortgage will be as normal as a 30-year fixed one. One lender envisions a future in which reverse mortgages may be seamlessly linked with the conventional variety. The suggestion is that a loan might start off as a traditional mortgage. Years later, when the note is finally paid off, it isn't burnt or thrown out, but automatically moves into reverse. The borrower has paid off the mortgage, is retiring, and now takes out some of the equity to enhance that retirement. They can access as much as, or as little as they want when they want and pay back as the occasion arises.

.02 Caution: Could Be Risky Business

If handled properly, a reverse mortgage can be an effective way for seniors to reduce living costs or pay off expenses. But the product's potential risks have left some government officials unnerved. In a June speech, the Comptroller of the Currency expressed a degree of concern about reverse mortgages because of some of the similarities he saw to the risks of subprime mortgages:

- A vulnerable customer class;
- Complex product features that can be difficult to explain;
- Product features that can be susceptible to deceptive marketing;
- Nontraditional, asset-based underwriting;
- The potential for skewed incentives for key distributors of the product.

Another problem he noted was that unlike other mortgage products, reverse mortgages do not have a requirement for associated taxes and insurance costs to be escrowed—or set aside in a separate account—to ensure payment. As a result, it's up to the reverse mortgage borrower to budget enough cash to cover these costs. In his speech, the Comptroller called on HUD to address this issue. Escrows for reverse mortgages "seem to make good sense from both the consumer's and the lender's perspective because of the significant home-loss risk that flows from nonpayment of taxes and insurance," he said.

¶33,005   FHA Issues Guidance for Reverse Mortgage Borrowers and Lenders

The Federal Housing Administration (FHA) today released guidance to homeowners and lenders that use the reverse mortgage or Home Equity Conversion Mortgage (HECM) program and are dealing with outstanding property taxes and unpaid hazard insurance premiums. FHA's guidance is intended to assist elderly borrowers who have neglected to pay these expenses and may face foreclosure.

"We understand that some senior citizens have not paid their taxes or insurance for some time and may be at risk of losing their home," according to an FHA Commissioner. "Today's guidance is designed to establish a clear framework that protects both the homeowner and the lender who participate in our reverse mortgage program."

.01   FHA Insurance Fund at Risk

HUD regulations allow lenders to make tax and insurance payments on behalf of their elderly clients from the borrower's available mortgage funds. However, once those resources are exhausted, the lender must advance funds to protect FHA's interest and obtain reimbursement from the borrower.

Over time, however, these unpaid debts and lender advances have resulted in an untenable situation that could put the FHA Insurance Fund at risk and result in foreclosure proceedings against delinquent seniors. While the guidance issued today is intended to help elderly homeowners avoid foreclosure, lenders may have no choice if these defaults are not cured.

FHA's *Mortgagee Letter* applies to all HECM loans where the lender/servicer advanced corporate funds to satisfy an unpaid property charge on behalf of the borrower. It reminds lenders that foreclosure is to be a last resort when dealing with their elderly clients. It also includes sample letters that lenders may use to make certain borrowers understand that property tax and hazard insurance are required expenses that must be paid even though the homeowners owe nothing on their mortgage loan.

.02   Reporting Requirements for Lender/Servicers

When a borrower fails to pay a property charge, the loan is deemed to be out of compliance with the provisions of the mortgage and FHA considers the loan to be delinquent. Lenders/servicers, however, must work with the borrower to try to bring the loan current at the earliest possible point. It is only after all loss mitigation strategies have been exhausted that the lender may submit a "due and payable" request to FHA.

Today's Mortgagee Letter precisely defines the process and reporting requirements lender/servicers must follow to collect unpaid property charges from HECM borrowers. FHA is strongly encouraging HECM borrowers who have outstanding property charges to work closely with loan servicers and approved housing counselors who can provide free assistance to help them resolve the situation and avoid any foreclosure action.

Meanwhile, the U.S. Department of Housing and Urban Development (HUD) is providing nearly $3 million to housing counseling agencies to specifically help reverse mortgage borrowers facing this issue. Counselors will help elderly homeowners work with their servicer to create repayment plans that cure the outstanding balance. If keeping the home is no longer an option, the counselors will help the borrower transition to alternative housing.

Under this new guidance, lenders must send letters to borrowers:

- Who recently missed a property charge payment,
- Who had an unpaid property charge balance for an extended period, and
- With a significant unpaid property charge balance.

.03   Preventative Measures and Consumer Protections

To avoid problems with unpaid property charges, FHA recently enhanced the HECM program's pre-closing counseling requirements. Counselors must now place a greater focus on educating borrowers on how important it is that they fulfill the terms of the mortgage, including the requirement that borrowers make timely tax and insurance payments. In addition, counselors now employ a new financial tool which helps identify potential budget shortfalls. Finally, HUD will shortly publish a proposed rule that adds more preventative measures and consumer protections to the existing HECM.

¶33,006   FTC Issues New Rule Strengthening Consumer Protections Against Deceptive Mortgage Advertisements

A Federal Trade Commission (FTC) rule adopted in July 2011 strengthens consumer protections by banning deceptive claims about consumer mortgages in advertising or other types of commercial communications. The rule is designed to create a level playing field for legitimate businesses to compete in the marketplace.

Congress directed the FTC to initiate a rulemaking proceeding on mortgage loans in the Omnibus Appropriations Act of 2009, as clarified by the Credit

Card Act of 2009. As a first step, on June 1, 2009, the FTC issued an *advance notice of proposed rulemaking* seeking public comment on whether certain mortgage acts and practices were unfair or deceptive. In September 2010, the agency issued a proposed rule that would ban deceptive mortgage advertising practices and sought further public comment about its costs and benefits, including whether any alternatives would adequately protect consumers at a lower cost.

The Final rule is substantially the same as the proposed rule. It applies to all entities within the FTC's jurisdiction that advertise mortgages—mortgage lenders, brokers, and servicers; real estate agents and brokers; advertising agencies; home builders; lead generators; rate aggregators; and others. The rule, however, does not cover banks, thrifts, federal credit unions, and other entities that are outside the Commission's jurisdiction.

The rule lists 19 examples of prohibited deceptive claims, including misrepresentations about the:

- Existence, nature, or amount of fees or costs to the consumer associated with the mortgage;
- Terms, amounts, payments, or other requirements relating to taxes or insurance associated with the mortgage;
- Variability of interest, payments, or other terms of the mortgage;
- Type of mortgage offered;
- Source of an advertisement or other commercial communication; and
- Consumer's ability or likelihood of obtaining a refinancing or modification of a mortgage or any of its terms.

Section 5 of the FTC Act generally prohibits advertisers from making false or misleading claims. The rule parallels this legal principle and will allow the FTC to seek appropriate relief (including civil penalties) against those who engage in deceptive mortgage advertising. The Consumer Financial Protection Bureau (CFPB) and state law enforcement authorities also may bring actions to enforce the rule. On July 21, 2011, the Commission's rulemaking authority for the rule transfers to the CFPB, but the FTC, the CFPB, and the states all will have authority to enforce the rule.

¶33,007   Not Just Low Income Individuals Tapping into Equity in Home

The mortgage industry foresees a strong growth ahead for reverse mortgages amid a demographic shift to senior citizens as Baby Boomers approach retirement age. Currently over 20 million people are older than 65. Of these, 77 percent are homeowners and 84 percent of them own their home free and clear. Best of all, 85 percent of senior homeowners want to remain in their home according to an American Association of Retired Persons (AARP) study.

Reverse mortgage loans are not appropriate for everyone. However, anecdotal evidence suggests that seniors of all income levels are cashing in on their home by using reverse mortgages for many different reasons. For many older home-owners, reverse mortgages provide the extra dollars that let them stay securely in their homes throughout retirement, help pay for home repairs and improve-ments, give gifts to their children and grandchildren or to continue their own education or provide funds for their children's or grandchildren's educations.

For others, the funds from a reverse mortgage are being used to pay taxes, support health care needs such as prescription drugs and medical care, includ-ing care at home or in funding long term care expenses.

And for a growing group of seniors, reverse mortgages provide a means to live more comfortably and pursue their dreams. For example, the funds have been used to buy, not just a second car, but also a second home, or an airplane, a boat, or other recreational vehicle. Others have been taking that dream vacation to see the Parthenon, the pyramid at Giza or to cruise the Mediterranean, the South Seas Islands, or even around the world. Since they are not special purpose loans, they can be used for anything.

¶33,008   Homeowners Eligible for a Reverse Mortgage

To be eligible for a HUD reverse mortgage, HUD's Federal Housing Admin-istration (FHA) requires that the borrowers be homeowners, 62 years of age or older; own their home outright, or have a low mortgage balance that can be paid off at the closing with proceeds from the reverse loan; not be delinquent on any federal debt; and must live in the home. They are further required to receive consumer information from HUD-approved counseling sources prior to obtaining the loan.

The total amount of cash accessible depends on the borrower's age, the value of the home, and interest rates. Homeowners in their early or mid-60s can most likely borrow around 50 percent of what their home is worth, and an 80-year-old can probably borrow about 70 percent. Since lenders scrutinize the house—rather than the borrower—as the source of repayment for the loan, it doesn't matter what a borrower's credit history is as long as he or she doesn't owe the government taxes or is not behind on an FHA mortgage, but that may be a cause for concern because, as noted earlier, the borrower is responsible for insurance, property taxes, and also upkeep of the property.

Reverse mortgage loan advances are not taxable, and generally do not affect Social Security or Medicare benefits. The owner retains title to the property and is not required to make monthly repayments. The loan must be repaid when the last surviving borrower dies, sells the home, or no longer lives in the home as a principal residence. In the HECM program, a borrower can live in a nursing home or other medical facility for up to 12 months before the loan becomes due and payable. By contacting HUD, it is possible to obtain the name and telephone number of a HUD-approved counseling agency and a list of FHA approved lenders within the appropriate area.

¶33,009   Types of Reverse Mortgages

A "reverse" mortgage, also referred to as a home-equity conversion loan, as opposed to a straight home equity loan, is just what it sounds like—the reverse of a conventional or "forward" mortgage—the one that everyone looked forward to burning.

There are three basic types of reverse mortgages:

- Single-purpose reverse mortgages, which are offered by some state and local government agencies and nonprofit organizations.
- Federally-insured reverse mortgages, which are known as Home Equity Conversion Mortgages (HECMs), and are backed by the U.S. Department of Housing and Urban Development (HUD). A lending institution such as a mortgage lender, bank, credit union or savings and loan association funds the loan.
- Proprietary reverse mortgages, which are private loans that are backed by the companies that develop them.

Since the HECMs and proprietary reverse mortgages are both handled by profit making organizations, they are more expensive than single purpose ones. On the other hand, they are readily available, have no income or medical requirements, and can be used for almost any purpose. According to HUD, last year volume in FHA HECMs increased by 77 percent with many of the top players in the reverse mortgage market booking huge volume increases.

The single-purpose reverse mortgage, when available, can be used for a particular purpose specified by a government or nonprofit lender. These loans are usually offered at very low costs for individuals with low or moderate incomes to pay for home repairs, improvements, or property taxes, for example. The biggest problem here appears to be that the need exceeds available resources. Most of the programs have a two or three year waiting list.

¶33,010   Loan Payment Options

Reverse-mortgage borrowers can take their money in a lump sum, and HUD lists five partial payment options:

- Tenure—equal monthly payments as long as at least one borrower lives in and continues to occupy the property as a principal residence.
- Term—equal monthly payments for a fixed period of months selected.

- Line of Credit—unscheduled payments or installments, at times and in amounts of borrower's choosing until the line of credit is exhausted.
- Modified Tenure—combination of line of credit with monthly payments for as along as the borrower remains in the home.
- Modified Term—combination of line of credit with monthly payments for a fixed period of months selected by the borrower.

It is important to be aware of the fact that homeowners whose circumstances change can restructure their payment options for a fee of $20.

¶33,011   Basis for Size of Loan

The amount that an individual can obtain on a reverse mortgage is based on the age of the youngest owner, current interest rates, the appraised value of the property, the location of that property, and the stability of the local real estate market.

Generally, the older a borrower, the larger the percentage of the home's value that can be borrowed. The lender arranges a professional appraisal to establish the lending value of the property. The general condition of the property is taken into consideration.

As noted above, the older borrower may expect a larger amount when seeking a reverse mortgage. Each piece of property represents a finite amount of equity. If this equity is released over a shorter period, it will generate larger individual payments, as there are fewer to make. Reverse mortgage lenders base their calculations on the life expectancy projections of the borrower(s).

¶33,012   Property Eligible for a Reverse Mortgage

The standard single family one-unit home is the most likely property to be considered. Others include two to four unit dwelling with the owner(s) occupying one unit. (Eligible property must be the borrowers primary residence.) HUD approved condominiums and manufactured homes that meet FHA requirements are also eligible. It is wise to check with the lender before going too far in the process to be sure that the unit is eligible. Most mobile homes are not eligible, but firmly grounded units may qualify. Cooperative units are usually not considered for a reverse mortgage, but here again—check with the lender.

¶33,013   Consumer Protection Measures

As is true when anything a little different or unusual gains a lot of attention, the scam artists are soon there to add a few twists to the process. Because there has been little history of using reverse mortgages as financial planning tools to supplement retirement incomes, few are conversant with the advantages or the pitfalls. The consensus appears to be that this lack of knowledge applies not only to the general public and the mortgage industry, but to financial planners as well. For this reason, the family's trusted CPA, whether a Personal Financial Specialist (PFS), or not, should be prepared to advise those clients who may consider a reverse mortgage. Several measures have been provided to help protect the consumer. Foremost is a requirement in several states and for all FHA federally insured reverse mortgages that individual(s) seeking a reverse mortgage must agree to a counseling session with an independent government approved agency.

See discussion above of a Federal Reserve proposal for enhanced consumer protections and disclosures for home mortgage transactions, as well as the Federal Trade Commission's proposed rule to ban deceptive mortgage ads.

Other consumer protection includes:

- Since a reverse mortgage is a nonrecourse loan, the borrower and/or his estate is liable only for the amount of the loan plus accrued interest if the property is worth less than that amount when the account is settled. On the other hand, at that time, any additional value of the property belongs to the borrower or the estate.
- Most plans carry mortgage insurance guarantees so that the borrower will continue to receive money if the lender goes out of business or defaults for any reason whatsoever.
- Interest rates on adjustable loans are capped so that they will never rise above a specific level.
- Comprehensive disclosures concerning all terms of the loan are required.
- Title to the property is always retained by the borrower(s).
- There is no prepayment penalty, and borrowers can change their minds up to 72 hours after signing the papers.

Along these same lines, an article in the Atlanta Federal Reserve publication, suggests that when they are feasible, reverse mortgages can serve as a tool to combat predatory lending practices that have targeted low-income elderly households. Unlike home equity loans, reverse mortgages are now structured to protect elderly homeowners against foreclosure and other predatory practices. The article points to the requirement mentioned above referring to the fact that reverse mortgage programs require pre-approval counseling for potential applicants to determine if the product is appropriate for them. Counseling, which is usually conducted by nonprofit consumer credit organizations, provides seniors with an opportunity to assess their overall financial circumstances and apply for other assistance if they need/qualify for it. Figures show that 202,795 clients received mortgage refinance and reverse mortgage counseling in fiscal year 2008.

PART VII

Tax Matters

The general public nearly always associates the title CPA (Certified Public Accountant) with tax preparation. Although CPAs practice in many other areas, tax services continue to be a primary focus. Part VII covers various tax matters.

CHAPTER 34
Recent Tax Changes

¶34,000   Overview

There has been relatively little activity in new tax legislation, especially when compared to the flurry of tax laws issued during the COVID-19 pandemic years. With a divided Congress on Capitol Hill and other issues dominating the debate, tax legislation is less of a focus than it was in late 2022, when Congress passed and the President signed into law the Inflation Reduction Act, which contained a number of important and complex tax changes affecting corporations and individuals, including a new 15-percent minimum tax on book income, a particularly important development given its similarity in name, but not operations, with separate work at the Organisation for Economic Co-operation and Development (OECD) to create a global minimum tax (Pillar Two) and to address the increasing digitization of the economy (Pillar One). However, many other tax policy proposals, like the new Section 174 R&D rules, were not addressed in a post-election Lame Duck session at the end of the year, and Congress is struggling to find a way to address those. We also need to begin to think about the major tax policy challenges that must be addressed soon, given how much of 2017's Tax Cuts and Jobs Act is scheduled to expire at the end of 2025.

The Consolidated Appropriations Act, 2024, provides appropriations for several federal departments and agencies. It also extends several expiring programs and authorities, including various public health programs. It includes six appropriations bills:

- the Military Construction, Veterans Affairs, and Related Agencies Appropriations Act, 2024;
- the Agriculture, Rural Development, Food and Drug Administration, and Related Agencies Appropriations Act, 2024;
- the Commerce, Justice, Science, and Related Agencies Appropriations Act, 2024;
- the Energy and Water Development and Related Agencies Appropriations Act, 2024;
- the Department of the Interior, Environment, and Related Agencies Appropriations Act, 2024; and
- the Transportation, Housing and Urban Development, and Related Agencies Appropriations Act, 2024.

The act also modifies the Compacts of Free Association that govern the relationship between the United States and the Republic of the Marshall Islands, the Federated States of Micronesia, and the Republic of Palau.

Later on January 31, 2024, the House passed the Tax Relief for American Families and Workers Act of 2024. The bill provides for increases in the child tax credit, delays the requirement to deduct research and experimentation expenditures over a five-year period, extends 100-percent bonus depreciation through 2025, and increases the Section 179 deduction limitation, among other business-friendly provisions. As of the date of this writing, the bill has still not passed in the Senate. It was originally expected to pass easily, but it is now questionable whether it will pass at all.

Earlier but still recent federal tax legislation includes the SECURE 2.0 Act, enacted as part of the Consolidated Appropriations Act, 2023, in December 2022; the Inflation Reduction Act and the Creating Helpful Incentives to Produce Semiconductors and Science Act (CHIPS Act), both enacted in August 2022; and the Infrastructure Investment and Jobs Act, enacted in November 2021.

The SECURE 2.0 Act mostly has to do with retirement, impacting contributions and withdrawals, and other areas. One interesting component is that, starting in 2024, employers will be able to "match" employee student loan payments with matching payments to a retirement account, giving workers an extra incentive to save while paying off educational loans. The Inflation Reduction Act contains spending provisions for the environment, healthcare, energy infrastructure, and domestic manufacturing, as well as a number of tax provisions. The CHIPS Act is designed to boost U.S. competitiveness, innovation, and national security. It aims to catalyze investments in domestic semiconductor manufacturing capacity.

A great deal of effort went into attempts to make drastic tax law changes during most of 2021 and into 2022. However, most of those efforts were unsuccessful. In spite of no major overriding new tax laws, however, there have been numerous changes related primarily to individual income taxes. These changes include the widening of tax brackets, as well as changes in the child tax credit and a number of other credits, long-term capital gains tax rates, required minimum distributions from retirement savings, unemployment income taxability, charitable contributions, 1099-K rules, a 100 percent meal tax deduction, and employer incentives and payroll credits for small businesses. Following are descriptions of major tax law passed before that time.

On March 11, 2021, President Biden signed the American Rescue Plan Act of 2021 (ARPA) into law. The $1.9 trillion package was intended to combat the COVID-19 pandemic, including the public health and economic impacts. ARPA included $65.1 billion in direct, flexible aid to every county in America, based on the county share of the U.S. population. It also provided state and local fiscal recovery funds, assistance to individuals and families, education and childcare, health, transportation, and other programs.

At the end of 2022, the Consolidated Appropriations Act, 2023, became law. Except for the year, it bears the same name as similar Acts in 2022, 2021, and 2020. The 2023 Act includes funding for a range of domestic and foreign policy priorities, including support for Ukraine, defense spending, and aid for regions affected by natural disasters. It also includes provisions related to health care, electoral reform, and restrictions on the use of the social media app Tik-Tok. The 2022 Act included $13.6 billion in aid to Ukraine as part of the United States' response to the 2022 Russian invasion of Ukraine. It also included a reauthorization of the Violence Against Women Act. It included a ban on the use of any maps by the U.S. Department of State and its foreign operations that "inaccurately" depict Taiwan as part of China. It amended the definition of the term "tobacco product" and included $4.5 million to fund the White House internship program. The 2021 Act provided extensions of many expiring deductions, credits, extensions and expansions of certain tax relief provisions. It included $600 advance payments of a tax credit per taxpayer ($1,200 for married filing jointly) plus $600 for each qualifying child. It phased out starting at $75,000 of modified adjusted gross income ($112,500 for heads of household and $150,000 for married filing jointly). It also provided an extension of the ability for businesses to deduct 100 percent of certain meal expenses. It included a clarification that personal protective equipment was a deductible expense for qualified teachers as part of the $250 qualified educator tax deduction. It provided an extension of the $300 deduction for cash charitable contributions when the taxpayer claimed the standard deduction. For 2021, the deduction was increased to $600 for joint filers. It also clarified that gross income would not include any amount from forgiveness of a Paycheck Protection Program loan and that expenses paid with those loans were fully deductible, even when the loan is forgiven.

Last minute legislation happened before the end of 2019. The SECURE Act was a government bill enacted on December 20, 2019, which funded the government through September 20, 2020. But it also included significant changes to laws affecting retirement accounts, hence the name SECURE (Setting Up for Retirement Enhancement Act). It also included extenders, disaster tax relief and a lot more.

The SECURE 2.0 Act was part of the Consolidated Appropriations Act, 2023, described above, with more details provided below.

Throughout 2019 and 2020, the IRS released a lot of guidance on implementation of the Tax Cuts and Jobs Act (TCJA), particularly on qualified business income (QBI), bonus depreciation and opportunity zones.

Earlier in 2019, the President signed into the law the Taxpayer First Act of 2019, an IRS reform legislation intended to broadly redesign the IRS for the first time in over 20 years. The Taxpayer First Act aims for a taxpayer-friendly IRS.

In early 2020, two laws were enacted to address the pandemic caused by the spread of coronavirus (COVID-19), which rattled the financial markets, closed most businesses and schools and canceled major public events across the country. The first one called the Families First Coronavirus Response Act moved the tax day to July 15, required employers with fewer than 500 employees to provide paid sick leaves to employees who are forced to stay home and tax credits will be given to employers to compensate for the paid leaves.

The second bill was the CARES Act meant to support the economy during the pandemic. As unemployment skyrocketed like never before, airlines barely flying, rents get unpaid, and employers lacked funds to pay their employers, the President signed a $2.2 trillion bill. Almost everyone received a benefit from this Act one way or another.

This chapter draws attention to a number of changes having the most general significance. Certain highly specialized and technical issues are beyond the scope of this overview. The remainder of this overview provides a summary of changes affecting a large number of taxpayers, both individual and corporate.

¶34,001   Extenders

The Consolidated Appropriations Act of 2020 extended several expiring provisions for both individuals and businesses; resurrected some expired ones and made them retroactive to 2018 and extending them through the end of 2020.

The Consolidated Appropriations Acts in subsequent years, including 2024, further extended provisions. These include the following:

A. Individuals:
    a. Medical and Dental Expense Deductions. The threshold was dropped from 10 percent to 7.5 percent of adjusted gross income (AGI);
    b. Above-the-line deduction for tuition and fees;
    c. Mortgage insurance premium as deductible qualified resident interest; and
    d. Exclusion of qualified principal residence indebtedness from gross income.

B. Businesses:
    a. Classification of certain racehorses as three-year property;
    b. Allowance of a seven-year recovery period for motorsports entertainment complexes;
    c. Accelerated depreciation for business property on an Indian reservation;
    d. Special expensing rules for film, television, and live theatrical performances;
    e. New markets tax credit;
    f. Incentives for investments in empowerment zones;
    g. Credit for employers providing paid family and medical leave;
    h. Look-thru rule for controlled foreign corporations; and
    i. Provisions to incentivize the production of beer, wine and distilled spirits.

C. Energy Credits
    a. Carbon dioxide sequestration credit;
    b. Credit for energy production from certain solar fuel cell or wind property;
    c. Credits for nonbusiness energy property;
    d. Qualified fuel cell vehicles;
    e. Alternative fuel vehicle refueling property;
    f. Energy efficient commercial buildings; and
    g. Incentives for biodiesel and renewable diesel.

¶34,002 Retirement Plans

The Consolidated Appropriations Act of 2020 also included the SECURE Act, which changed 401(k) plans and the IRA landscape and added a new pooled multiple-employer plan. The SECURE Act 2.0, part of the Consolidated Appropriations Act of 2023, further changed items related to retirement. The impacts of both Acts are included below.

The SECURE 2.0 Act expanded coverage and increased retirement savings by expanding automatic enrollment in retirement plans, modifying credit for small employer pension plan startup costs, providing a saver's match and promoting it, modifying pooled employer plans and multiple-employer plans, providing higher catch-up limits on IRA contributions, and several other modifications, some of which are described below.

.01 IRA Changes

The new laws changed the IRA landscape by:

a. delaying the start for the required minimum distributions (RMDs) to age 72, and to age 73 beginning January 1, 2023, and to age 75 beginning January 1, 2033;
b. Removing the restriction to contribute from 70½ years old and up; and
c. Shortening the distribution period for non-spouse inherited IRAs to a ten-year maximum.

.02 401(k) Changes

Changes to 401(k) plans were also introduced primarily to encourage taxpayers to save more for retirement. These are:

a. Requiring plans to offer participation to long-term, part-time employees;
b. Permitting plans to adopt qualified birth or adoption distributions;
c. Encouraging auto-enrollment by increasing the cap;
d. Adding new tax credit for small employers using auto-enrollment plans; and
e. Streamlined the safe harbor for non-elective contributions.

.03 Other Changes for Individuals

There were several changes affecting the individuals. These are:

a. Permitting qualified birth or adoption distributions up to $5,000 that would be exempt from the early-withdrawal penalty; and
b. Counting taxable non-tuition fellowships and stipends and nontaxable "difficulty of care payments" earned by home healthcare workers as compensation for purposes of retirement plan contributions.

.04 Changes for Employers

The new law also encouraged small employers to offer retirement plans to employees by making plans affordable and less complicated. The changes include:

a. Small employers are allowed to band together to create a pooled multiple employer plans;
b. Employers are encouraged to steer employees toward lifetime annuities;

c. Allowing plans administrative flexibility, including relief for "close" plans;

d. New annual disclosure requirements;

e. Providing a safe harbor for plan sponsors in the selection of an annuity provider; and

f. Qualified defined contribution plans, 403(b) plans, and governmental 457(b) plans are now able to make direct trustee-to-trustee transfers to other employer-sponsored retirement plans or IRAs of lifetime income investments or distributions of a lifetime income investment in the form of a qualified plan distribution annuity.

.05   Plan Administration Changes

Several administrative changes were adopted that will provide flexibility for employees and will reduce costs for employer sponsors. These are:

a. Plans adopted by the filing due date (including extensions) of the tax return for the tax year may treat the plan as having been adopted as of the last day of the tax year;

b. Defined contribution plans, with the same trustee, the same named fiduciary under ERISA, and the same administrator, using the same plan year, and providing the same investments or investment options to participants and beneficiaries may file a consolidated Form 5500;

c. The nondiscrimination rules with respect to closed defined benefit plans to permit existing participants to continue to accrue benefits are modified to protect the benefits for older, longer-service employees as they near retirement;

d. The use of credit cards or similar arrangements to draw down on plan loans is prohibited so that plan loans are not used for routine or small purchases;

e. If an employer terminates a 403(b) custodial account, the distribution effectuating the termination may be the distribution of an individual custodial account in-kind to a participant or beneficiary;

f. Individuals who may be covered by plans maintained by church-controlled organizations include:

1. duly ordained, commissioned, or licensed ministers, regardless of the source of compensation; employees of a tax-exempt organization controlled by or associated with a church or a convention or association of churches; and

2. certain employees after separation from service with a church, a convention or association of churches, or an organization described above; and

g. Community newspapers are given funding relief for community news-paper plan sponsors by:

1. increasing the interest rate to calculate those funding obligations; and
2. providing a longer amortization period of 30 years from seven years.

¶34,003   Coronavirus Tax Relief

In early 2020, the world was beset with the virus that has affected millions of people. In the United States, the coronavirus (a.k.a. COVID-19) spread so fast that most states declared a state of emergency and addressed the situation in different ways. Many governors ordered a stay at home at varying degrees. On March 13, 2020, the President declared a national emergency. The President then signed the Families First Coronavirus Response Act on March 18, 2020.

To augment the first stimulus bill, the President signed the Coronavirus Aid, Relief, and Economic Security Act (a.k.a. CARES Act) on March 27, 2020. The two bills provide extensive relief for medical professionals, first responders, in-dividuals, industries, small businesses and employers affected by the pandemic.

Primarily as a result of the pandemic, the Consolidated Appropriations Act (CAA) was signed into law on December 28, 2020. It included a second stimu-lus payment, as well as allowing a deferral of payroll taxes for individuals and ad-ditional deductions for teachers. For businesses, it also included a second round of Paycheck Protection Program (PPP) loans, which are generally forgiven upon meeting certain requirements. PPP loan forgiveness is not considered taxable income for federal purposes, even though the related expenses are tax deductible. Businesses must use caution, however, because many states do recognize the PPP loan forgiveness as taxable income for state income tax purposes. The CAA also modified tax deductibility of meals expenses. Whereas only 50 percent of meal expenses have historically been deductible, for tax years 2021 and 2022, 100 per-cent of meals are deductible. Presumably, this is an attempt to encourage people to return to restaurants in order to help boost that section of the economy.

.01   Tax Return Deadline Postponed

The tax filing deadline for 2021 taxes was April 18, 2022, for most taxpayers. In the previous year, as a result of the coronavirus (COVID-19) crisis, the due date for individuals, estates, and trusts for filing federal income tax returns and federal income tax payments otherwise due on April 15, 2020, was extended to July 15, 2020. Similarly, the due date for filing a federal gift tax return and paying gift or generation-skipping transfer (GST) tax was extended to July 15, 2020. The extension was automatic, and taxpayers did not need to file any form or call the IRS. Penalties, interest, and additions to tax for failure to file the returns or pay the taxes did not accrue until July 16, 2020.

.02   Stimulus Checks

Recovery Rebate Credits for tax year 2020 were refunded in advance through Economic Impact Payments (popularly called stimulus checks) of up to $1,200 per eligible individual plus $500 for a qualifying child. Almost everyone except dependents and nonresident aliens was eligible, but the credit was phased out for higher-income taxpayers.

Credit amounts and phase-outs. The maximum credit is:

- $1,200 for each eligible individual (so $2,400 for two eligible individuals who file a joint return), plus
- $500 for each qualifying child

The maximum credit amount is reduced (but not below zero) by 5 percent of AGI that exceeds:

- $150,000 if married filing jointly—so the $2,400 credit phases out completely at $198,000
- $112,500 if filing as head of household—so the $1,200 credit phases out completely at $136,500
- $75,000 if filing as single or married filing separately—so the $1,200 credit phases out completely at $99,000.

.03   Retirement Plans

The 10-percent additional tax is waived for any qualified coronavirus-related distributions from a retirement plan. Further, eligible individuals who take such distributions can include them in gross income over a three-year span and have three years to repay the amount. To qualify as a "coronavirus-related distribution," the distribution should be made on or after March 27, 2020, and before December 31, 2020. In addition, it should be made to an individual:

- who is diagnosed with the virus SARS-CoV-2 or with coronavirus disease 2019 (COVID-19) by a test approved by the Centers for Disease Control and Prevention (CDC);
- whose spouse or dependent is diagnosed with such virus or disease by such a test, or
- who experiences adverse financial consequences as a result the coronavirus.

Further, the threshold limit on loans from an employer-sponsored retire-ment plan for a qualified individual affected by the coronavirus is increased to the lesser of $100,000 or 100 percent of the present value (but not less than $10,000) of the plan participant's benefits under the plan. In addition, if a qualified individual has a loan repayment due date after March 27, 2020, and before December 31, 2020, on an outstanding loan, the payment due date is delayed one year. Any subsequent repayments with respect to the loan will be adjusted accordingly and the five-year period for repayment is disregarded.

The required minimum distribution (RMD) requirements for 2020 gener-ally applicable to retirement plans are suspended.

If the participant dies before minimum distributions have begun, and the entire remaining interest must be distributed within five years of the partici-pant's death, then 2020 is excluded from the five-year period.

.04   Net Operating Losses

Any net operating losses (NOLs) arising in a tax year beginning after Decem-ber 31, 2017, and before January 1, 2021, might be carried back five years in response to the COVID-19 (coronavirus) crisis unless the carryback period is waived.

.05   Payroll Credit

An employer can claim a refundable payroll tax credit for 50 percent of wages paid during the COVID-19 crisis if:
  (1) business operations were suspended due to a COVID-19-related shut-down order, or
  (2) gross receipts declined by more than 50 percent as compared to the same quarter in the prior year.

For eligible employers with 100 or fewer full-time employees, all employee wages qualify for this employee retention credit. For eligible employers with more than 100 full-time employees, only wages paid to employees when they are not providing services due to the COVID-19-related circumstances will qualify. The credit applies to the first $10,000 of compensation (including health benefits) paid to an eligible employee from March 13, 2020, through December 31, 2020.

.06   Employee Retention Credit

Certain employers can claim a refundable employee retention credit for each calendar quarter for which the credit is allowed, for either:

- the *employer's portion* of the Old-Age, Survivors, and Disability Insurance (OASDI); or
- the *employer's portion* of the Railroad Retirement Tax Act (RRTA) Tier 1 tax attributable to the 6.2-percent OASDI tax rate.

The amount of the credit is equal to 50 percent of the qualified wages paid by the eligible employer for that calendar quarter. For each employee, an eligible employer can claim a credit for up to $10,000 of qualified wages paid. The employee retention credit applies only to wages paid after March 12, 2020, and before January 1, 2021.

.07   Paid Leave

Eligible employers may receive a refundable payroll credit for required paid sick leave or family leave paid to an employee who cannot work due to COVID-19. The sick leave credit is for leave paid to an employee who is quarantined, has been advised to self-quarantine, has coronavirus symptoms and is seeking a medical diagnosis, or is caring for someone with coronavirus or for a child whose school or care facility is closed or whose care provider is unavailable. The family leave credit is for leave paid to an employee who is caring for a child whose school or care facility is closed, or whose care provider is unavailable. The credits have per-day and maximum dollar limits for each employee. The credits are available for wages paid for the period that begins on April 1, 2020, and ends on December 31, 2020.

.08   Paycheck Protection Program

The Paycheck Protection Program (PPP) is a loan made available through the Small Business Administration (SBA) to help small businesses pay payroll costs, mortgages, rent, and utilities during the COVID-19 crisis. All payments of principal, interest, and fees under the loans are deferred for a period of time. The loans may be forgiven if used for payroll costs, mortgage or rent obligations, and certain utility payments incurred between February 15, 2020, and December 31, 2020. The amount forgiven is excluded from gross income of the eligible recipient and not considered cancellation of debt income for federal income tax purposes. However, states have taken different positions so the reader should research applicable state law to determine if it is taxable or not at the state level. The loans are 100 percent guaranteed by the SBA.

.09   Emergency Relief Loans

The Treasury Department is authorized to make loans, loan guarantees, and other investments in the aggregate of up to $500 billion to provide liquidity to eligible businesses, states, and municipalities related to losses incurred as a result of the COVID-19 (coronavirus) crisis. Any emergency relief loan made by or guaranteed by the Treasury Department under the program is treated as debt for federal tax purposes.

¶34,004   Expired and Expiring Tax Provisions

The Consolidated Appropriations Act of 2020 signed on December 18, 2019 resurrected most of the extenders that expired which the Bipartisan Budget Act (P.L. 115-123) that was signed on February 9, 2018 extended.

All of 2018 and nearly all of 2019 extenders passed with no action to extend the provisions. The extenders that were resurrected were made retroactive to 2018 and extended them through the end of 2020. These were:

- exclusion from gross income of discharge of qualified principal residence indebtedness;
- mortgage insurance premiums treated as qualified residence interest;
- above-the-line deduction for qualified tuition and related expenses;
- Indian employment tax credit;
- railroad track maintenance credit;
- mine rescue team training credit;
- classification of certain race horses as three-year property;
- seven-year recovery period for motorsports entertainment complexes;
- accelerated depreciation for business property on an Indian reservation;
- election to expense mine safety equipment;
- special expensing rules for certain productions;
- deduction allowable with respect to income attributable to domestic production activities in Puerto Rico;
- special rule relating to qualified timber gain;
- empowerment zone tax incentives;
- American Samoa economic development credit;
- credit for nonbusiness energy property;
- credit for nonresidential energy property (extended through 2021 and modified);
- credit for new qualified fuel cell motor vehicles;
- credit for alternative fuel vehicle refueling property;
- credit for two-wheeled plug-in electric vehicles;
- second generation biofuel producer credit;
- biodiesel and renewable diesel incentives;
- production of credit for Indian coal facilities (extended to a 12-year period);
- credits with respect to facilities producing energy from certain renewable resources;
- credit for energy-efficient new homes;

- energy credit (extended through 2021 and modified);
- special allowance for second generation biofuel plant property;
- energy efficient commercial buildings deduction;
- special rule for sales or dispositions to implement FERC or state electric restructuring policy for qualified electric utilities;
- excise tax credits relating to alternative fuels;
- oil spill liability trust fund financing rate;
- temporary increase in limit on cover over rum excise taxes to Puerto Rico and the Virgin Islands;
- waiver of limitations with respect to excluding from gross income amounts received by wrongfully incarcerated individuals (extended through December 18, 2018); and
- carbon dioxide sequestration credit (enhanced, modified and generally extended through 2023).

Protecting Americans from Tax Hikes Act of 2015 (PATH Act) made over 20 key tax provisions permanent, including the research tax credit, and enhanced IRC §179 expensing. It also extends other provisions, including bonus depreciation, for five years; and revives many others for two years. Many extenders have been enhanced.

The **PATH Act** made the following provisions permanent:

- IRC §179 expensing
- Research and development (R&D) tax credit
- 100 percent gain exclusion on qualified small business stock held for more than five years by non-corporate taxpayers
- Five-year recognition period for built-in gain following conversion from a C to an S corporation
- 15-year straight-line cost recovery for qualified lease-hold improvements, restaurant property and retail improvements
- Employer wage credit for employees who are active duty members of the uniformed services
- Treatment of certain dividends of regulated investment companies (RICs)
- The subpart F exception for active financing income
- Charitable deductions for the contribution of food inventory
- Tax treatment of certain payments to controlling exempt organizations
- Basis adjustment in stock when an S corporation makes charitable contributions of property
- Minimum low-income housing tax credit for non-federally subsidized buildings
- Military housing allowance exclusion in determining a low-income tenant
- RIC qualified investment entity treatment under FIRPTA

Five-year extensions for businesses. The following provisions were extended through 2020:

- Bonus depreciation
- Work Opportunity Tax Credit (WOTC)
- New markets tax credits
- Look-through treatment for payments of dividends, interest, rents, and royalties between related controlled foreign corporations under the foreign personal holding company rules

The following provisions for individuals were made permanent:

- The $250 above-the-line deduction for teachers' out-of-pocket classroom expenses.
- The itemized deduction of state sales tax as an alternative to deducting state income tax.
- American Opportunity Tax Credit for $2,500.
- The purchase of computer equipment and technology with a distribution from an IRC §529 plan is permanently considered a qualified expense.
- Child tax credit, available up to $1,000 for qualifying dependents under age 17, may be refundable to the extent of 15 percent of the taxpayer's earned income in excess of $3,000.
- Parity among transit benefits.
- The rule permitting individuals who have reached 70½ and are required to make distributions from their IRA, to make direct distributions to charities that qualify as their distributions (IRC §408(d)).
- Contributions of capital gain real property for conservation purposes.

¶34,005   Gray Areas in Recent Cases

.01   The Emerging Medical Marijuana Business

Because over 38 states, three territories, and the District of Columbia have now legalized the medical use, and 21 states have legalized the recreational use of marijuana, and the trend is expected to continue, it is important for accountants to be aware of certain tax matters related to the legal sale of marijuana. First, it should be noted that even though a state legalizes the sale of marijuana for medical purposes, or as a few states have recently done, for recreational purposes, this does not impact the federal law or the IRS treatment of these businesses. Under federal law, marijuana is still labeled a controlled substance. The Internal Revenue Code contains a provision, Section 280E, which impacts businesses "trafficking in controlled substances." The point of this code section is to disallow the deduction for all ordinary and necessary business expenses, and permit the deduction only of the cost of goods sold.

In a Tax Court case, *Martin Olive v. Comm.,* 139 TC 19 (2012), the court upheld the IRS's determination, following the audit of a legal marijuana distributor in California, that the business' income was much larger than reported on its tax return. This was partly the result of disallowing the business' ordinary and necessary operating expenses. The court thus upheld the fact that even though what the business was doing was legal under California state law, it was nonetheless not legal under federal law.

Eventually, either the federal law will be changed or this or a similar case will wind up at the Supreme Court to settle this conflict between state and federal law, as recently occurred with the federal Defense of Marriage Act.

Another practical problem faced by marijuana businesses occurs when they attempt to comply with federal law requiring the electronic deposit of payroll taxes. An IRS Chief Counsel Memorandum (January 9, 2014 Mitchel S. Hyman, Senior Technician Reviewer, Branch 3) addresses at least some aspects of this problem. Banks may be understandably reluctant to open accounts for these businesses due to their heavily-regulated status, concerns with money laundering and the fact that the proceeds are from the sale a federally-controlled substance. However, the IRS requires payroll tax deposits to be made electronically, which requires the cooperation of a bank or other agency with this capability. As an accommodation to this conundrum the IRS considers the "walk-up cash method" involving a third party to be acceptable.

The question posed in the memorandum was "Whether payment of taxes through a walk-up cash method is authorized under I.R.C. §§6311and/or 6302, without the need for new regulations?" According to the advice, "One goal of the proposed method [walk-up cash] is to allow individuals without bank accounts or credit or debit cards to pay their income taxes through electronic transfers."

Accordingly, "a walk-up cash payment method, which allows a taxpayer to pay cash so that a third party processor will electronically transfer funds to pay the tax to the IRS, is permissible under I.R.C. §6302 and existing regulations, provided the Service sets forth the payment process in published guidance, publications, forms, or instructions. The only difference between this type of payment and a more common electronic payment of individual income taxes is that the payment is transmitted from a third party's account rather than a personal bank account of the taxpayer. The third-party payment is nonetheless a voluntary remittance by an electronic fund transfer, and so is authorized by the regulation."

.02 Passive Activity Taxation

The area of exposure to the tax on investment income that may draw the most attention from taxpayers and the IRS is income from passive business activities. This is the case because what constitutes an activity is, to some extent, under the taxpayer's control. Business activities that may be passive when considered by themselves (because the taxpayer does not materially participate), may be aggregated or grouped with other activities to attempt to produce an activity that is overall active, and therefore not subject to the tax. The IRS Regulations specify the criteria, however, so not every grouping attempt will be successful.

For individuals, the gross income and gains from passive business activities and rental activities are included in the definition of net investment income. A passive business activity is one in which the taxpayer does not materially participate. A taxpayer materially participates in an activity if he or she works on a "regular, continuous and substantial basis in operations" (IRC §469(h)(1)). If a taxpayer does not materially participate, income and losses are passive, which means generally that the income is subject to the new 3.8 percent tax and that any losses are not deductible except against other passive activity income.

As the IRS notes, "Material participation is time sensitive." A taxpayer materially participates in an activity only if he or she meets any one of the seven material participation tests in Reg. §1.469-5T(a). Whether a taxpayer materially participates is determined each year, and what was a passive activity in one year may be an active activity in the next.

While material participation is the key concept for determining whether a taxpayer's relationship to a business activity is active or passive, this test does not apply to the following activities: (1) Rentals, which are generally passive, whether or not the taxpayer materially participates (with exceptions, of course). Rental real estate interests of real estate professionals are one exception. (See Reg. §1.469-9(e)(1).) Another exception relates to rentals for periods of less than seven days. (2) Working interests in oil and gas activities are exempt from the passive loss limitations. If a taxpayer's liability is not limited, the taxpayer has a "working interest." (3) Income from a partnership or S Corporation that trades in stocks, bonds or securities for the accounts of the partners or shareholders is non-passive. Income or losses, even from a limited partnership interest, may be deducted as non-passive. (See Reg. §1.469-1T(e)(6)).

A key to understanding the passive vs. active business activity determination is the meaning of an activity. Reg. §1.469-4 provides the definition of an activity.

A trade or business activity is an activity that:

- Involves the conduct of a trade or business (within the meaning of IRC §162) (profit motive is the key);
- Is conducted in anticipation of starting a trade or business; or
- Involves research & development expenditures that would be deductible under IRC §174.

A critical point is that related businesses that form an economic unit may be treated as a single "activity". Whether something is an activity is not determined by its existence as a separate taxable business entity. (See Reg. §§1.469-4(c) and 1.469-4(d)(4)). On the other hand, one taxable business entity may contain more than one business activity, and on the other hand, separate business entities may be combined.

By grouping related businesses as a single activity, the taxpayer can more easily meet the 500-hour test for material participation.

The Seven Tests. Material participation is the key determination. A trade or businesses is a passive activity if the taxpayer does not materially participate. The taxpayer materially participates if (and only if) he or she meets one of the following seven tests provided in Reg. §1.469-5T(a).

1. The taxpayer works 500 hours or more during the year in the activity.
2. The taxpayer does substantially all the work in the activity.
3. The taxpayer works more than 100 hours in the activity during the year and no one else works more than the taxpayer.
4. The activity is a significant participation activity (SPA), and the sum of SPAs in which the taxpayer works 100-500 hours exceeds 500 hours for the year.
5. The taxpayer materially participated in the activity in any five of the prior ten years.
6. The activity is a personal service activity and the taxpayer materially participated in that activity in any three prior years.
7. Based on all of the facts and circumstances, the taxpayer participates in the activity on a regular, continuous, and substantial basis during such year. However, this test only applies if the taxpayer works at least 100 hours in the activity, no one else works more hours than the taxpayer in the activity, and no one else receives compensation for managing the activity.

If a taxpayer is the owner of a partnership that owns another partnership, the material participation test is made on the basis of his or her direct ownership of the first partnership. The same rule applies with other groupings of pass-through entities.

If the taxpayer participates more than 500 hours during the year in a business, income or loss from the activity will be non-passive. Participation of both spouses is counted, but participation by the children or employees is not.

Participation in operations must be regular, continuous, and substantial. The taxpayer should determine whether the quantity of time documented is reasonable in light of other obligations, such as a regular full-time job.

The taxpayer is considered to perform substantially all of the work if he or she does most of the work required to operate the business in question. If so, the income is not passive.

If a taxpayer participates in an activity for more than 100 hours and no other individual participates more than the taxpayer (including any employee or non-owner), income or losses from the activity are non-passive.

The term *significant participation activity* is unique to Reg. §1.469-5T. If the sum of the taxpayer's time in all significant participation activities (SPAs) is more than 500 hours for the year, then income or losses from the businesses are non-passive. For each significant participation activity (SPA), the regulations require:

- The taxpayer to participate more than 100 hours during the year.
- The activity must be a business, i.e. it cannot be a rental or investment activity.
- The business must be a passive activity.

A significant participation passive activity is any trade or business activity in which you participated for more than 100 hours during the tax year but did not materially participate.

If your gross income from all significant participation passive activities is more than your deductions from those activities, a part of your net income from each significant participation passive activity is treated as nonpassive income.

Thus, if the taxpayer works more than 500 hours in the business, it is not a significant participation activity (SPA) as 500 hours is one of the qualifying tests for material participation. Similarly, if the taxpayer does most of the work in the business, it cannot be a significant participation activity (SPA) as Reg. §1.469-5T(a)(2) holds that performing substantially all the work qualifies for material participation.

An activity is non-passive if the taxpayer would have been treated as materially participating in any five of the previous ten years (whether or not consecutive). This test usually applies when a taxpayer "retires from material participation" but maintains an ownership interest in the activity.

If a taxpayer materially participated for any three prior taxable years in a personal service activity the current year income or loss will be treated as non-passive. It does not matter whether those three prior taxable years were consecutive.

The facts and circumstances test may apply if none of the other tests is met. This test does not apply unless the taxpayer worked more than 100 hours a year. Furthermore, the taxpayer's time spent managing will not count if:

- Any person received compensation for managing the activity; and
- Any person spent more hours than the taxpayer managing the activity.

Indicators that the taxpayer did not materially participate:

- The taxpayer was not compensated for services. Most individuals do not work significant hours without expecting wage or commissions.
- The taxpayer's residence is hundreds of miles from the activity.
- The taxpayer has a W-2 wage job requiring 40+ hours a week for which he or she receives significant compensation.
- The taxpayer has numerous other investments, rentals, business activities, or hobbies that absorb significant amounts of time.
- There is paid on-site management/foreman/supervisor and/or employees who provide day-to-day oversight and care of the operations.
- The taxpayer is elderly or has health issues.
- The majority of the hours claimed are for work that does not materially impact operations.
- Business operations would continue uninterrupted if the taxpayer did not perform the services claimed.

Limited Partners. Section 469(h)(2) presumes that limited partner interests are per se passive, and losses are therefore not deductible unless the taxpayer has passive income reported on the return.

There are three exceptions to the limited partner passive taint (Reg. §1.469-4(d)(5)):

- The taxpayer works 500 hours or more in the trade or business activity.
- The taxpayer materially participated in the activity in any five of the prior ten years.
- The activity is a personal service activity and the taxpayer materially participated in that activity in any three prior years.

If a taxpayer holds both a general and a limited partnership interest all year, he may use any one of the seven tests to qualify for material participation.

The courts have repeatedly taken a dim view of self-serving guesstimates of time. Likewise, taxpayers attempting to convert investment income into active income, if the taxpayer-investor claims to be in the full-time business of investing, have generally been disallowed by the courts. The Supreme Court's tests in its *Groetzinger* decision should be consulted. Groetzinger was a full-time gambler who convinced the court that he was in the trade or business of gambling.

Investor-type activities do not count unless the taxpayer is directly involved in day-to-day management or operations. Reg. §1.469-5T(f)(2)(ii)(B) provides that the following types of activities do not count unless the taxpayer is directly involved on a day-to-day basis in management or operations:

- Studying or reviewing financial statements or reports.
- Preparing or compiling summaries or analyses for the individual's own use.
- Monitoring finances or operations in a non-managerial capacity.

Also, travel time and being "on-call" are not considered in calculating the time.

As the IRS audit guide points out, if the taxpayer has not provided both services performed and hours attributable to those services, he does not meet the record-keeping requirements of IRC §469.

Grouping Activities. If related businesses form an appropriate economic unit, entities may be grouped as a single activity, making it easier to meet the 500-hour test. The taxpayer needs to show he materially participates in the grouped activity as a whole. A sole proprietorship (Schedule C or F), C or S Corporation, partnership or LLC may be grouped into one single activity if the businesses form an appropriate economic unit. (See Reg. §1.469-4).

An "activity" is not constrained by entity lines. If the taxpayer spends 500 hours among the grouped businesses, even though in different entities, he materially participates in all. The entire 500+ hours could be spent all in one business entity or could be spread among several related entities.

It is important to note that Reg. §1.469-4(a) only provides for grouping of businesses (or rentals). Businesses generally may not be grouped with rentals. Land or buildings held for investment may not be grouped. And, of course, no personal activity or portfolio activity belongs in the grouping.

It is possible that several different activities may exist within a single entity. Example: two unrelated businesses or a business and a rental activity within a single partnership.

Five Factors. Reg. §1.469-4 provides a facts and circumstances approach to determine whether two or more activities form an appropriate economic unit for the measurement of gain or loss. Five factors in Reg. §1.469-4(c)(1) are given significant weight:

1. Similarities and differences in the types of businesses.
2. Extent of common control.

3. Extent of common ownership.
4. Geographical location.
5. Interdependencies between or among the activities.

Not all factors are necessary.

Rentals. Reg. §1.469-4(d)(1) prohibits grouping a rental activity with a trade or business unless:

- Either is insubstantial in relation to the other; OR,
- The owner has the same proportionate interest in the rental as in the business.

Grouping real property and personal property rentals is also prohibited unless the personal property is provided in connection with the real property.

Limited Partners. A limited partnership interest (or limited entrepreneur) generally may be grouped with other activities which form an appropriate economic unit. However, a limited partnership interest in any of the following types of businesses may not be grouped with another business unless it is the same type of business and the two form an appropriate economic unit:

- Motion picture films or videotapes
- Farming
- Leasing IRC §1245 property (personal property)
- Exploring for or exploiting oil and gas
- Exploring for or exploiting geothermal deposits

C Corporations. A personal service corporation or closely held C Corporation may be part of the grouping that forms an appropriate economic unit.

Partnerships and S Corporations. If an entity contains more than one business or rental activity, it must group or separate activities. Once the entity groups its activities, the investor may group those activities with each other, with activities he conducts himself or with activities conducted through other entities – as long as the grouped businesses form an economic unit, i.e., they are integrated interrelated activities. (See Reg. §1.469-4(d)(5)).

Consistency Requirement. Reg. §1.469-4(e) imposes a consistency requirement. Once the taxpayer has selected his grouping, he must use that same grouping in future years unless the original group is clearing inappropriate or there is a material change in facts and circumstances. As noted, an exception to this rule was provided for 2013 that permitted a one-time re-grouping of activities.

A decision not to group, i.e., to treat each activity separately, is a grouping decision. This decision generally should have been made starting in 1994, when Reg. §1.469-4 was finalized or, if subsequent to that date, at the time the activity was first reflected on a return. A taxpayer cannot pick and choose each year what his grouping is. The taxpayer must maintain the grouping he originally chose under the consistency rules in Reg. §1.469-4(e).

Anti-Abuse Provision. The anti-abuse provision in Reg. §1.469-4(f) permits the Commissioner (examiner) to regroup businesses if:

1. The taxpayer's grouping is not an appropriate economic unit; and
2. One of the primary purposes of the taxpayer's grouping is to circumvent the underlying purposes of IRC §469.

Examples. To illustrate, the regulations provide an example in Reg. §1.469-4(f)(2). In this example, a limited partnership (formed by five doctors, each of whom were limited partners) produced net income. Because it formed an economic unit with the doctors' practices and the purpose was to circumvent IRC §469, the Government could group the two businesses as a single activity, with the result that income from the partnership was deemed non-passive.

Another example is provided by a medical doctor in *William J. Dunn v. Comm.*, TC Memo 2010-198. In this case a doctor, who had a pilot's license and owned an airplane in a single-member LLC, attempted to convert the primarily personal use of the airplane to business use by grouping the airplane with a series of real estate investments he controlled through an S Corporation.

These arrangements were the result of planning by a CPA firm specializing in the business use of airplanes. The S Corporation was said to provide management services for four properties, including an apartment in Ormond Beach, Florida; a condominium in Key Largo, Florida; an unimproved parcel of land in Lake Mary, Florida; and a condominium in Telluride, Colorado. An outside management company was hired to rent or maintain the apartments and condos, calling to question what management services were being provided by the S Corporation.

Dr. Dunn attempted to group these activities, along with activities of his medical practice, in such a way as to produce the maximum non-passive loss. The doctor claimed that "all [his] activities—including his medical professional activities, his medical research activities, his real estate investment activities, and the ownership and use of airplanes—should be regarded as a 'single activity' for purposes of section 469." In particular he desired to group his employment activity with the airplane activity (single-member LLC reported on Schedule C) and the rental activities (of the S Corporation reported on Schedule E). The doctor's contention with respect to the airplane was that roughly two-thirds of its use was in connection with his employment as a doctor or in connection with managing his real estate investments. An IRS examination of his records disclosed that there was no business being conducted with respect to the airplane. Instead, the airplane consistently generated losses which the doctor deducted as non-passive losses help offset his W-2 income as a doctor.

The IRS reclassified the claimed losses as passive, effectively disallowing their deduction in the year at question. The court agreed with the IRS that the airplane activity losses were generated without any business purpose, thus precluding the grouping of that activity with others. The airplane losses were non-deductible either as passive losses or because they are losses from an activity not conducted with a profit motive. The court ruled that the doctor had failed to supply evidence of the business purpose of any of the flights.

The court also agreed with the IRS that the rental properties generated non-deductible passive losses. Management activities essential to showing the doctor's involvement with the rentals had been delegated to independent management companies, meaning that the doctor's involvement was minimal. The IRS argued that, whether or not these rental activities are deemed per se passive, all the taxpayer's activities were in fact passive because the taxpayer failed to materially participate in them.

The court recited the regulations stating that, Generally, "[o]ne or more trade or business activities or rental activities may be treated as a single activity if the activities constitute an appropriate economic unit for the measurement of gain or loss for purposes of section 469" (Reg. §1.469-4(c)(1)). As an exception to this general rule, however, an activity involving the rental of real property and an activity of the rental of personal property generally may not be treated as a single activity (Reg. §1.469-4(d)(2)).

Compounding the doctor's problems in this case, the court found that his medical research activities did not constitute a trade or business, making them ineligible for grouping with his other activities.

With respect to the doctor's employment by his medical practice, the court noted that "being an employee may be a trade or business" (citing *Putoma Corp. v. Comm,* 66 T.C. 652, 673 (1976)). However, in order to group the trade or business activity of being an employee with other the other activities, the doctor would have had to have shown that the grouped activities constituted an "appropriate economic unit," for which there are five tests. These test involve determining (1) similarities and differences in types of trades or businesses, (2) the extent of common control, (3) the extent of common ownership, (4) geographical location, and (5) interdependencies between or among the activities (for example, the extent to which the activities purchase or sell goods between or among themselves, involve products or services that are normally provided together, have the same customers, have the same employees, or are accounted for with a single set of books and records). (See Reg. §1.469-4(c)(2).) In response, the court noted that there was no connection demonstrated between any of the activities, not even between the doctor's medical practice and his research activities. Since the doctor's personal residence was nearby his medical practice, it was not possible to show any need for the airplane. The doctor tried to argue that the use of the airplane in connection with non-medical activities saved time, making more of his time available for his medical practice. The court rejected this argument, noting that any such connection involving time allocation "does not suffice to make his various activities an 'appropriate economic unit.'"

.03   Tax Clarification for Same-Sex Marriage Reporting

On June 26, 2015, the United States Supreme Court (5-4) settled the question of same-sex marriage for all 50 states by declaring that the Fourteenth Amendment requires states to license a marriage between two people of the same sex. "It follows that the Court also must hold—and it now does hold—that there is no lawful basis for a State to refuse to recognize a lawful same-sex marriage performed in another State on the ground of its same-sex character." All state laws and court decisions banning same-sex marriage are now invalid.

In the years leading up to this decision, most states had lined up on one side of the issue or the other, with some states enacting constitutional amendments defining a marriage as between a man and a woman.

In its explanation of the importance of marriage and its historical evolution the Court cited authorities as diverse as Confucius, Cicero, and Alexis de Tocqueville, as well as its earlier cases setting the foundation. It noted that "marriage was once viewed as an arrangement by the couple's parents based on political, religious, and financial concern." As the notions of personal freedom and autonomy expanded, the Court observed, the parameters of marriage followed. "The nature of injustice," according to the Court, "is that we may not always see it in our own times. The generations that wrote and ratified the Bill of Rights and the Fourteenth Amendment did not presume to know the extent of freedom in all of its dimensions, and so they entrusted to future generations a charter protecting the right of all persons to enjoy liberty as we learn its meaning. When new insight reveals discord between the Constitution's central protections and a received legal stricture, a claim to liberty must be addressed." One such area, affecting at least half the population concerned the rights of women in marriage. "Under the centuries-old doctrine of coverture, a married man and woman were treated by the State as a single, male-dominated legal entity. . . . As women gained legal, political, and property rights, and as society began to understand that women have their own equal dignity, the law of coverture was abandoned."

Three cases in particular were cited as leading directly to the *Obergefell* decision. Justice Kennedy wrote, "Applying these established tenets, the Court has long held the right to marry is protected by the Constitution. In *Loving v. Virginia*, 388 U.S. 1, 12 (1967), which invalidated bans on interracial unions, a unanimous Court held marriage is "one of the vital personal rights essential to the orderly pursuit of happiness by free men." The Court reaffirmed that holding in *Zablocki v. Redhail*, 434 U.S. 374, 384 (1978), which held the right to marry was burdened by a law prohibiting fathers who were behind on child support from marrying. The Court again applied this principle in *Turner v. Safley*, 482 U.S. 78, 95 (1987), which held the right to marry was abridged by regulations limiting the privilege of prison inmates to marry."

The Court supported its conclusion with four premises grounded in its understanding of the importance of marriage and of the U.S. Constitution. 1) "the right to personal choice regarding marriage is inherent in the concept of individual autonomy"; 2) "the right to marry is fundamental because it supports a two-person union unlike any other in its importance to the committed individuals"; 3) "the right to marry . . . safeguards children and families and thus draws meaning from related rights of childrearing, procreation, and education": and, 4) "this Court's cases and the Nation's traditions make clear that marriage is a keystone of our social order."

Historical Context. In 2013, the Supreme Court, in *Windsor*, ruled that the federal Defense of Marriage Act (DOMA) violated the equal protection clause of the Fifth Amendment of the Constitution. This meant that same-sex couples who were legally married in states that permitted same-sex marriage, should have their marriages recognized by the federal government. DOMA, since 1996, had precluded same-sex couples, who were married under state law, to claim the rights of a married couple with respect to federal laws and regulations. In particular, DOMA precluded a married same-sex couple from filing a joint federal income tax return. After the Court's ruling, this will no longer be the case. For same-sex couples legally married in a state that permits same-sex marriage, the couple would be able to file a tax return as married-filing-jointly for both federal and state tax purposes (assuming they are residents of the state in which they were married).

¶34,006 Depreciation and Amortization

.01   Section 179 Expensing

The IRC §179 dollar limitation is increased to $1.16 million for 2023 and $1.22 million for 2024 and the investment limitation is increased to $2.89 million in 2023 and $3.05 million in 2024. The definition of qualified real property eligible for expensing is redefined to include improvements to the interior of any nonresidential real property, i.e. qualified improvement property," as well as roofs, heating, ventilation, and air-conditioning property, fire protection and alarm systems, and security systems installed on such property. The exclusion from expensing for property used in connecting with lodging facilities, such as residential rental property, is eliminated. The IRC §179 expensing limit on certain heavy vehicles is $26,200 for 2023 and $30,500 for 2024.

.02   100% Bonus Depreciation

The Tax Cuts and Jobs Act increased the bonus depreciation rate to 100 percent for property acquired and placed in service after September 27, 2017 and before January 1, 2023. The rate phases down thereafter. For 2023, first-year bonus depreciation is 80 percent of the purchase price. It falls to 60 percent in 2024, 40 percent in 2025, and 20 percent in 2026. In 2027, the program will cease to exist. Any amount not deducted as bonus depreciation will still be claimed over the remaining useful life of the asset. Used property and films, television shows, and theatrical productions are eligible for bonus depreciation. Property used by rate-regulated utilities and property of certain motor vehicle, boat, and farm machinery retail and lease businesses that use floor financing indebtedness is excluded from bonus depreciation.

Bonus depreciation provision was extended for five years through 2019. For 2012 through 2017, the 50 percent bonus depreciation was available for businesses purchasing new personal property; 40 percent in 2018, and 30 percent in 2019. Thus, a machine purchased new for $50,000 could be depreciated by 50 percent, and the balance, if any, depreciated according to the normal rules for MACRS depreciation. If a company plans to take IRC §179 depreciation, this is computed before the 100 percent or 50 percent first-year depreciation.

The 100 percent or 50 percent bonus depreciation is not an election but like regular MACRS depreciation is automatic unless an affirmative election is made with the IRS not to claim the bonus depreciation. This causes a potential trap for taxpayers who neglect to take the first-year depreciation. When the asset in question is eventually disposed of, the IRS will apply the allowed or allowable test to determine the proper basis for computing gain or loss. The allowable depreciation will include both the proper amount of MACRS cost recovery and the available 100 percent or 50 percent first-year depreciation. Thus failure to elect out of the 100 percent or 50 percent depreciation means the IRS will assume the depreciation was still allowable and will be used to reduce an asset's basis as if it had been claimed—increasing the resulting gain or minimizing the resulting loss. If a taxpayer elects out of the bonus depreciation this is done for a whole class of property (for example, five-year property) not on an item by item basis. Thus, special care should be exercised if the bonus depreciation is not desired.

Bonus depreciation also extends to new cars used in business. Though depreciation on automobiles has been restricted for a number of years, a taxpayer is allowed to add $8,000 to the amount of the first-year depreciation.

The annual limits on depreciation deductions for "luxury cars" are almost quadrupled for property placed in service after 2017. The IRS will need to issue a safe harbor in order to allow taxpayers to claim depreciation after the first year a vehicle is placed in service if the 100 percent bonus depreciation deduction is claimed.

¶34,007   Corporations

.01   Brother-Sister Controlled Group—Modified Definition Has Broader Reach

Pairs or groups of small C corporations owned and controlled by five or fewer shareholders have been subject to possible restriction on the use of separate tax brackets, separate exemptions for alternative minimum tax, and separate accumulated earnings credits. This provision of the tax law is intended to prevent corporations from manipulating the corporate graduated tax rates by operating in controlled groups.

The effect of the law is to broaden the reach of the brother-sister rules. If five or fewer individuals (estates or trusts) own more than 50 percent of the combined voting power or more than 50 percent of the total value of two or more corporations' stock, they are now considered related even if the there is no 80 percent common ownership, as under prior law. This will mean that more corporations with overlapping ownership are required to share tax brackets, AMT exemptions and accumulated earnings retention limits. Pairs or groups of corporations with five or fewer shareholders (individuals, estates, or trusts) that had formerly escaped classification as a brother-sister controlled group by failing the 80 percent common ownership test should now retest their status using only the more than 50 percent common ownership test.

To illustrate this change, consider the following example.

	Corporation 1	Corporation 2	Identical
Shareholder A	30%	40%	30%
Shareholder B	40%	30%	30%
Shareholder C	30%	0%	0%
Shareholder D	0%	30%	0%
> 50% identical ownership test			60%
80% common ownership test	70%	70%	

Five or fewer individuals own corporations 1 and 2. In addition they share 60 percent identical ownership because Shareholders A and B each own at least 30 percent of both corporations. Under the new law the two corporations are part of a brother-sister controlled group. However, the two corporations fail the 80 percent common ownership test, which required the ownership of the individuals controlling greater than 50 percent of the stock to also own 80 percent or more of the two corporations. Under the old law, the two corporations would have failed the 80 percent test and not been classified as brother-sister controlled corporations. The result: tax planning that aimed to limit commonly owned corporations from being taxed as brother-sister corporations may no longer work. All such groups of interrelated corporations should now be reevaluated applying this less stringent test.

.02   Limitation on Deduction of Business Interest

The deduction of business interest is limited for any tax year beginning after 2017 to the sum of the taxpayer's business interest income, floor plan financing, and 30 percent of adjusted taxable income. The limitation generally applies to all taxpayers, but does not apply for small businesses with average gross receipts of $25 million or less (adjusted for inflation). Any disallowed interest generally may be carried forward indefinitely. In the case of a partnership or S corporation, the deduction limitation applies at the entity level, except that disallowed interest of the entity is allocated to each partner or shareholder as excess business interest.

.03   Net Operating Losses

Net operating losses (NOLs) may no longer be carried back but may be carried forward indefinitely. However, the five-year carryback period for farming losses is reduced to two years and a two-year carryback and 20-year carryforward period is retained for insurance companies other than life insurance companies. A net operating loss may only reduce 80 percent of taxable income in a carryback or carryforward tax year. The taxable income limitation does not apply to non-life insurance companies.

.04   Alternative Minimum Tax

The alternative minimum tax (AMT) for corporations has been repealed beginning after 2017. Any unused minimum tax credit of a corporation may be used to offset regular tax liability for any tax year. In addition, a portion of unused minimum tax credit is refundable in 2018 through 2021. The refundable portion is 50 percent (100 percent in 2021 and subsequently) of any excess minimum tax for the year over any credit allowable against regular tax for that year.

.05 Changes in Corporate Tax

The Tax Cuts and Jobs Act eliminated the graduated corporate structure and imposed flat 21-percent rate on corporation's taxable income for tax years beginning after December 31, 2017. The lower corporate tax rate will peg domestic corporations in a position to compete globally and may increase international investments in the United States. The lower corporate tax rate can lead to economic growth and jobs creation. However, those really small corporations whose taxable income is not more than $50,000 and was previously taxed at 15 percent will end up paying more at the new 21 percent rate. On the other hand, stockholders of S Corporations who will be taxed at higher individual tax rates can take advantage of the qualified business income deduction (a.k.a. passthrough deduction) that will allow them to deduct up to 20 percent of the passthrough's income.

.06 Business Provisions

The Tax Cuts and Jobs Act made a lot of changes for the businesses in general. First and foremost is the lowering of the corporate income tax rate to a 21-percent flat rate by eliminating the graduated rate structure for tax years beginning after December 31, 2017.

The deduction of business interest is limited for any tax year beginning after 2017 to the sum of the taxpayer's business interest income, floor plan financing, and 30 percent of adjusted taxable income. The limitation generally applies to all taxpayers, but does not apply for small businesses with average gross receipts of $25 million or less (adjusted for inflation). Any disallowed interest generally may be carried forward indefinitely. In the case of a partnership or S corporation, the deduction limitation applies at the entity level, except that disallowed interest of the entity is allocated to each partner or shareholder as excess business interest.

Excess business losses of noncorporate taxpayers are not allowed for tax years beginning in 2018 through 2025. Any disallowed excess business loss is treated as a NOL carryover to the following tax year. However, the passive activity loss rules apply before application of the excess business loss rules

Research and experimental expenditures paid or accrued after 2021 generally must be amortized ratably over five years. Any amount paid or incurred in connection with the development of any software is treated as a research or experimental expenditure for. A 15-year amortization period applies to research or experimental expenditures attributable to foreign research.

Business expense deductions are eliminated for some entertainment costs and commuting benefits after 2017 and for some employer-provided meal expenses after 2025. Further, employers are prohibited from deducting achievement awards that are given in cash, cash equivalents, gift cards, gift coupons, gift certificates, vacations, meals, lodging, tickets to theater or sporting events, stocks, bonds, other securities or similar items.

For purposes of the limitation on the deduction for employee compensation paid by publicly held corporations, the definition of covered employee is expanded to include both the principal executive officer and the principal financial officer, as well as the other three most highly compensated employees. Employees who are covered employees after December 31, 2016, remain as covered employees for all future tax years. The exclusions from the limitation for commission-based and performance-based compensation was repealed. However, eligible employers are entitled to claim a credit for paid family and medical leave equal to 12.5 percent of wages paid to qualifying employees during any period in which such employees are on family and medical leave (FML) provided that the rate of payment is 50 percent of the wages normally paid to the employee. The credit was part of the general business credit and only available for wages paid in tax years beginning after December 31, 2017, and before January 1, 2020.

Businesses may not deduct fines and penalties incurred due to the violation of a law (or the investigation of a violation) if a government (or similar entity) is a complainant or investigator. Exceptions to this rule are certain cases where the payment was compensation for damages, compliance with the law, paid to satisfy a court order where the government is not a party, or paid for taxes due. The deduction for local lobbying expenses by a taxpayer as an ordinary and necessary business is repealed for expenses paid after December 22, 2017.

.07   Corporate Tax Inversions

A number of former U.S. corporations have recently moved their corporate headquarter oversees. When well-known corporations became involved in either looking into or actually moving to another country, some members of the U.S. Congress began to take note and the news media followed. The idea of relocating to another country to save on taxes is not new, and in the past it might have involved a shell corporation formed in a tax haven. But Congress saw fit to end that practice and so it is now much more complex. Current inversions are primarily to countries in Europe or to Canada and involve joining forces with a substantial business already operating the foreign country. The issue affects multinational corporations incorporated and headquartered in the U.S. Like U.S. citizens, these corporations are taxable on their international income. The result of the U.S. system is a potential double taxation of income, once by the U.S. and again by the foreign jurisdiction where the income was earned. To ameliorate the double taxation, U.S. tax law provides a credit against U.S. income tax for taxes already paid or accrued on the same income in a foreign state (foreign tax credit). Unfortunately, the foreign tax credit rules are often complex, and in spite of their theoretical benefit, U.S. companies may still be disadvantaged by incurring a higher effective tax rate than their foreign competitors. This is the major complaint by U.S. corporations: that they cannot compete as effectively with foreign companies.

To illustrate the problem, consider a U.S. corporation generating income in a foreign country with a 20 percent corporate tax rate. The income generated in this country will first be taxed by the foreign country and then again by the U.S. at 35 percent. The U.S. foreign tax credit may offset the 20 percent foreign tax paid, but the additional 15 percent tax (35%-20%) will still be due to the U.S. treasury, maintaining the 35 percent rate. The existence of tax treaties with foreign countries may complicate the matter, however, as the treaty provisions may override some aspects of the Internal Revenue Code.

In addition to lower corporate tax rates in other countries, a major reason for considering a tax inversion is the number of foreign countries that tax only a company's income earned within their territorial boundaries, rather than taxing a company's worldwide income, as the U.S. does. Unlike many countries, the U.S. tax code taxes domestic corporations on their global income, including income from operations in the U.S. and income generated in other countries. The Internal Revenue Code already contains provisions intended as disincentives for corporate inversions. Section 367—"Foreign corporations," for one, was enacted to prevent use of the non-recognition provisions in sub-chapter C (the tax-free reorganization provisions) to avoid taxation on the transfer of property by and to controlled foreign corporations in transactions which would otherwise be covered by those non-recognition provisions. It does so by providing, in the situations that it covers, that the entity will not be considered to be a corporation for the purposes of IRC §§332, 351, 354, 356, and 361. Since the provisions of these code sections are available only to corporations, the non-recognition provisions would not apply. Section 367 has two broad purposes: 1) To prevent the tax free removal of appreciated stock, assets, or other property from U.S. tax jurisdiction, and 2) To preserve the ability to impose U.S. income tax currently, or at a later time, on the accumulated E&P of certain foreign corporations.

Section 367(a) is intended to prevent U.S. persons from avoiding U.S. tax by transferring appreciated property to a foreign corporation in a tax-free organization or reorganization, and then selling the appreciated property outside the tax jurisdiction of the United States. Section 367(b) is principally concerned with monitoring the earnings and profits of a controlled foreign corporation. It provides that in the case of any exchange described in IRC §§332, 351, 354, 355, 356 and 361 in connection with which there is no transfer of property described in IRC §367(a)(1), a foreign corporation shall be considered to be a corporation except to the extent provided in regulations prescribed by the

Secretary which are necessary or appropriate to prevent the avoidance of federal income taxes (source: Internal Revenue Manual).

IRC §7874. "Rules relating to expatriated entities and their foreign parents" imposes a tax on inversion gain of expatriated entities. The term "inversion gain" means the income or gain recognized by reason of the transfer during the applicable period of stock or other properties by an expatriated entity, and any income received or accrued during the applicable period by reason of a license of any property by an expatriated entity: (1) as part of the acquisition described in subsection (a)(2)(B)(i), or (2) after such acquisition if the transfer or license is to a foreign related person.

¶34,008   Individuals

.01   New Tax Rates and AMT

While the Tax Cuts and Jobs Act reduced the tax rates for individuals and in-creased basic standard deduction, it took away or reduced several tax-saving deductions and suspended personal and dependency exemptions, for 2018 through 2025 tax years.

The individual income tax rates are 10, 12, 22, 24, 32, 35, and 37 percent. The AMT exemption amounts in 2024 are $133,300 for married individuals filing jointly, and $85,700 for unmarried. The phaseout thresholds are also tem-porarily increased to $1,218,700 if married filing jointly or surviving spouse and $609,350 for all other individuals.

.02   Shared Responsibility Payment

Effective for months beginning after December 31, 2018, the amount owed by any taxpayer under the individual health insurance mandate "shared responsi-bility payment" for lack of minimum essential health insurance for themselves and their dependents is zero. In other words, the penalty for not having health insurance coverage will not be imposed.

.03   Basic Standard Deduction

The basic standard deduction amounts (adjusted annually for inflation) in 2024 were increased to:

- $14,600 for single individuals and married individuals filing separately;
- $21,900 for heads of household; and
- $29,200 for married individuals filing jointly (including surviving spouses).

The basic standard deduction amounts (adjusted annually for inflation) in 2023 were increased to:

- $13,850 for single individuals and married individuals filing separately;
- $20,800 for heads of household; and
- $27,700 for married individuals filing jointly (including surviving spouses).

.04   Itemized Deductions

An individual cannot deduct foreign real property taxes, but itemized deduction for state and local property taxes, income taxes, and general sales taxes paid or accrued in the tax year is capped at $10,000 ($5,000 for married taxpayer filing a separate return). Further, the itemized deduction for personal casualty and theft losses is limited to those attributable to a federally declared disaster. Also, the deduction for moving expenses is temporarily repealed while the exclusion for qualified moving expense reimbursements is suspended; which means that these reimbursements will be taxable.

The itemized deduction for home mortgage interest is limited to interest paid or accrued on acquisition debt and not on home equity debt. The maximum amount that may be treated as acquisition debt is also reduced to $750,000 ($375,000 if married filing separately) for any acquisition debt incurred after December 15, 2017. The maximum amount that may be treated as acquisition debt remains $1 million ($500,000 if married filing separately) for any acquisition debt incurred with respect to the taxpayer's principal residence on or before December 15, 2017.

The $1 million ($500,000 if married filing separately) dollar limit will also continue to apply to a taxpayer who entered into a binding written contract before December 15, 2017, to close on the purchase of a principal residence before January 1, 2018, so long as the residence was purchased before April 1, 2018. Similarly, the higher limit continues to apply to any debt incurred after December 15, 2017, to refinance existing acquisition debt on the taxpayer's principal residence to the extent the amount of the debt resulting from the refinancing does not exceed the amount of the refinanced debt. Thus, the maximum dollar amount that may be treated as acquisition debt on the taxpayer's principal residence will not decrease by reason of a refinancing. The exception for refinancing existing acquisition will not apply after:

(1) the expiration of the term of the original debt; or

(2) the earlier of the expiration of the first refinancing of the debt or 30 years after the date of the first refinancing.

Further, the threshold to claim an itemized deduction for unreimbursed expenses paid for the medical care is reduced to 7.5 percent of adjusted gross income (AGI) for all taxpayers for tax years beginning after December 31, 2016. The reduced threshold applies for both regular tax and alternative minimum tax purposes.

Also, gambling losses were temporarily expanded to include other expenses incurred by the individual in connection with the conduct of that individual's gambling activities for tax years 2018 to 2025; such as expenses incurred in travelling to and from a casino. But these expenses remained to be deducted only to the extent of gambling winnings.

However, the phaseout or overall limitation on itemized deductions is temporarily repealed applicable to tax years beginning after December 31, 2017, and before January 1, 2026.

.05   Capital Gains Rate

Short-term capital gains are taxed the same as ordinary income. For the 2024 tax year, net capital gains and qualified dividends are taxed at zero percent for joint filers or surviving spouses with taxable income below $89,250, heads of households with taxable income below $59,750, and unmarried taxpayers and married taxpayers filing separately with taxable income below $44,625. The rate is 15 percent for joint filers or surviving spouses with taxable income below $553,850, heads of households with taxable income below $523,050, unmarried taxpayers with taxable income below $492,300, and married taxpayers filing separately with taxable income below $276,900. Taxpayers with taxable income equal to or exceeding these "breakpoints" are subject to a 20-percent tax on net capital gains and qualified dividend income. The amounts are adjusted annually for inflation.

.06   Dependency Exemptions and Child Tax Credit

The Tax Cuts and Jobs Act temporarily repealed the deduction for personal and dependency exemptions for tax years 2018 through 2025. However, the child tax credit is temporarily expanded after 2017 by increasing the credit amount for each qualifying child to $2,000, increasing the phaseout threshold to $400,000 if married filing jointly ($200,000 for other taxpayers), and providing a $500 nonrefundable credit for each dependent who is not a qualifying child. The refundable portion of the credit (additional child tax credit) is limited to $1,500 per qualifying child, but is indexed for inflation, and the earned income threshold is reduced to $2,500. A qualifying child's Social Security number is required to receive the nonrefundable or refundable portion of the credit.

.07   Qualified Tuition Program

The Tax Cuts and Jobs Act expanded IRC §529 or qualified tuition plans to allow distribution for elementary and secondary tuition. However, such distributions are limited to $10,000 per year per student, and not per account. The provision for distribution incurred while the beneficiary is in college remained the same.

Further, individuals are allowed to roll over amounts from 529s to an Achieving a Better Life Experience (ABLE) account if the ABLE account is owned by the same designated beneficiary of the 529 or a member of the designated beneficiary's family before January 1, 2026. Under certain circumstances, the contribution limitation to ABLE accounts is increased for contributions made by the designated beneficiary before January 1, 2026. ABLE programs are established by a state, its instrumentality or an agency to encourage individuals and families to save funds to assist a disabled individual in paying qualified disability expenses through a tax-favored savings account. Except for rollover contributions, the aggregate annual contributions to a single ABLE account cannot exceed the inflation-adjusted annual gift tax exclusion amount ($15,000 in 2018 through 2021, $16,000 in 2022, $17,000 in 2023 and $18,000 in 2024).

.08 Cash Charitable Contributions

The Tax Cuts and Jobs Act temporarily increased the income-based percentage limit from 50 percent to 60 percent for an individual taxpayer's cash charitable contributions to public charities, private foundations other than nonoperating private foundations, and certain governmental units (i.e., "50 percent organizations"). The 60-percent contribution base limit applies to qualifying cash contributions made in any tax year beginning after December 31, 2017, and before January 1, 2026. The individual may carry forward for five years any qualifying cash contributions that exceed the 60-percent ceiling for the tax year of the contribution.

.09 Moving Expenses

The Tax Cuts and Jobs Act temporarily repealed the deduction for moving expenses for tax years 2018 through 2025. However, the special rules for a member of the Armed Forces to deduct moving expenses and exclude in-kind moving expenses, and reimbursements or allowances, continues to apply during these tax years.

.10 Supreme Court Rules on Inherited IRAs in Bankruptcy

Retirement plans including IRAs are exempt from the reach of creditors when an individual declares bankruptcy. But what about an IRA that has been inherited? According to the Supreme Court in *Clark v. Rameker*, "In ordinary usage, to speak of a person's "retirement funds" implies that the funds are currently in an account set aside for retirement, not that they were set aside for that purpose at some prior date by an entirely different person. Under petitioners' contrary logic, if an individual withdraws money from a traditional IRA and gives it to a friend who then deposits it into a checking account, that money should be forever deemed "retirement funds" because it was originally set aside for retirement. That is plainly incorrect." Thus the investments in an inherited IRA lose their status as "retirement funds" and are subject to creditor's claims. Additional information on this topic is contained in Chapter 35, "Insolvency, Debt Forgiveness and Bankruptcy."

.11   Uniform Definition of Child: "Qualifying Child"

Various provisions of the Internal Revenue Code dealing with children have been subsumed under a new uniform definition of a child. Previously different definitions of child were applied for different purposes. The new definition of a qualifying child applies, for example, to children in determining:

- The dependency exemption.
- The child tax credit.
- Head-of-household status.
- Earned income credit.
- The dependent care credit.
    The tests for a qualifying child include:

- Relationship.
- Domicile.
- Age.

For the dependency exemption, for example, this streamlines the prior five-test determination:

- Relationship for qualifying child: daughter, son, stepdaughter, stepson, sister, brother, stepsister, stepbrother, half-sister, half-brother, or a descendent of one of these individuals (grandchild, niece, nephew). The relationship test is also met for an adopted child or an authorized foster child.
- The child is qualifying only if he or she had the same principal place of abode as the taxpayer for more than one-half of the taxable year.
- A qualifying child must be under age 19—unless he or she is a full-time student—in which case the child must be less than age 24. A disabled child, however, is exempt from the age requirement. The age requirement for the child tax credit remains at under age 17 and under age 13 for the dependent care credit.

The new rules incorporate the realities of many contemporary domestic relations. As a result, it was necessary to establish a number of tie-breaking rules in which a child might be considered a qualifying child by more than one adult in the household. These rules hold as follows:

- If more than one adult could otherwise claim a qualifying child, a parent trumps the other(s).
- If both parents are living apart and could claim the qualifying child, the one with whom the child lived the longer period during the year predominates. Should the child have lived with both parents for an equal period of time, the parent with the greater AGI is allowed to claim the qualifying child.
- If two nonparents could each claim the qualifying child, the one with the highest AGI prevails.

As a result of these changes, the law no longer automatically awards the exemption for a child of divorced parents to the custodial parent. The new law adds, as one test for claiming the exemption, the specific wording of the divorce decree awarding the exemption to the noncustodial parent. Without this wording the noncustodial parent may not claim the child; with the wording, the noncustodial parent is entitled to the exemption if the support, residency and other requirements of IRC §152(e)(1) are met.

This chart may help to simplify the new dependency rules.

	Qualifying Child	Qualifying Relative or Member of Household
Relationship	Son, daughter, stepson, stepdaughter, brother, sister, stepbrother, stepsister, half brother, half sister or a descendent of one of these, for example, grandchildren, nephews, nieces, (not cousins), adopted child, foster child (with exceptions). Note: Because more than one taxpayer may qualify to claim a given child, tie breaking rules allow first priority to a parent, then to the parent with most days of custody for the year, then higher AGIs have priority over lower AGIs.	A relative need not be member of the household; a member of household need not be relative, but must live in the household for the entire year. In addition to the relatives listed under *qualifying* child are added: father, mother, stepfather, stepmother, uncle, aunt, son-in-law, daughter-in-law, father-in-law, mother-in-law, brother-in-law, sister-in-law, grandfather, grandmother—relationships formed by marriage continue after divorce (exception for ex-spouse one-year rule). A cousin is not a relative and would have to qualify as member of household.
Age	Must be under age 19 or, if full time student, under age 24 (exception for disabled child).	Only important for child of taxpayer who must be under age 19 or under 24 if full-time student because the income requirement is waived (may earn any amount). A child over these ages may still qualify as relative or member of household but is subject to the income test.
Support	No specific support calculation—but must live in home of taxpayer claiming child as a dependent for more than half the year. For a taxpayer to claim the child it is not necessary to prove they provided more than half of the support. But if the child is self-supporting (where the child supplies more than half of his or her own support) the child does not qualify.	The taxpayer claiming the dependent must provide more than half of the support for the individual. Amounts earned by the individual but saved are not counted in determining support. Support includes payments for room and board, insurance, and capital goods used only by the dependent.

Domicile	Must have same principal place of abode as the taxpayer for more than half of the year. Temporary absences for education or illness do not count against the half year residency.	If not a relative, must live in the taxpayer's house for the entire year.
Joint return	A married qualifying child may not file a joint return with a spouse. An exception is made if the couple owes no tax, is not required to file a return, and is only filing to receive a refund of withheld taxes.	A married qualifying child may not file a joint return with a spouse. An exception is made if the couple owes no tax, is not required to file a return, and is only filing to receive a refund of withheld taxes.
Gross income	No gross income test—unless child is self-supporting, in which case he or she is not a qualifying child. See Support above.	May not exceed amount of personal exemption except for children under 19 or children who are full time students and under age 24.
Citizenship or residence	Must be U.S. citizen, U.S. resident, or a resident of Mexico or Canada for some part of the year. Exception for adopted child who need not meet the general rule above is his or her principal place of abode is with a U.S. citizen.	Must be U.S. citizen, U.S. resident, or a resident of Mexico or Canada for some part of the year. Exception for adopted child who need not meet the general rule above if his or her principal place of abode is with a U.S. citizen.

Relationships created by marriage, except spouse, are not terminated by divorce. This means, for example, that a stepchild or a mother-in-law created by marriage retains this relationship to the taxpayer even after a divorce of the couple who created the relationship.

.12   The Affordable Care Act

Individuals must obtain minimum essential health care insurance coverage. The failure to do so will be penalized by an additional amount of tax assessed on the individual's Form 1040. For taxpayers not purchasing health insurance coverage, a monthly penalty will be assessed. The amount of the penalty will depend on a number of factors including the taxpayer's income and the number of months for which coverage was not purchased. However, effective for months beginning after December 31, 2018, the amount owed by any taxpayer under the individual health insurance mandate "shared responsibility payment" for lack of minimum essential health insurance for themselves and their dependents is zero.

¶34,009   Noncorporate Taxpayers

.01   Qualified Business Income Deduction

Noncorporate taxpayers may deduct up to 20 percent of domestic qualified business income from a partnership, S corporation, or sole proprietorship. A similar deduction is allowed for specified agricultural or horticultural cooperatives. A limitation based on wages paid, or on wages paid plus a capital element, is phased in for taxpayers with taxable income above a threshold amount. The deduction is not allowed for certain service trades or businesses, but this disallowance is phased in for lower income taxpayers. The deduction applies to tax years 2018 through 2025.

¶34,010   Recent IRS Changes

.01   Mileage Allowance

The IRS announced the automobile mileage rate for 2024. Business mileage, which includes an allowance for depreciation and the cost of fuel and repairs, is set at 67 cents a mile. As an alternative, the taxpayer may determine the actual costs of operating the car for the year. In either case, they are required to keep a record of their business mileage as well as the total miles driven. For medical, the rate is set at 21 cents per mile in 2024. For charitable mileage, the rate is still the statutory 14 cents per mile, which has not changed in quite a few years.

.02   Injured Spouse and Innocent Spouse

When a couple files a joint tax return, they agree to be jointly and severally responsible for any tax due. Because of this, the IRS can seek to collect any tax due from either or both spouses, even if the income that produced the tax was generated by only one of the spouses. When the IRS seeks to collect taxes from one spouse that were generated by the income of the other spouse, for example, for unreported income, there is potential help for the aggrieved spouses referred to as "innocent spouse relief." In the flip-side of the situation, there are times when the couple is due a tax refund, but it is seized by the IRS in payment of some tax or other government-controlled debt. This may give rise to "injured spouse relief."

Often against the advice of their CPAs, individuals prefer to receive a tax refund rather than make a tax payment, though this involves an interest-free loan to the government. Some couples who file joint tax returns allocate their refunds to determine what amount represents each spouse's portion. In some instances, when one spouse has a legally-enforceable debt for child support or a student loan, for example, the IRS may seize all or a part of the joint refund in settlement of the debt. According to the IRS, "You may be an injured spouse if you file a joint tax return and all or part of your portion of the overpayment was, or is expected to be, applied (offset) to your spouse's legally enforceable past-due federal tax, state income tax, state Unemployment compensation debts, child or spousal support, or a federal nontax debt, such as a student loan." To protect a refund that is in jeopardy of being seized to fulfill your spouse's obligation, file Form 8379, advises the IRS, "when you become aware that all or part of your share of an overpayment was, or is expected to be, applied (offset) against your spouse's legally enforceable past-due obligations. You must file Form 8379 for each year you meet this condition and want your portion of any offset refunded." Form 8379 is filed by the injured spouse on a jointly filed tax return when the joint overpayment was (or is expected to be) applied (offset) to a past-due obligation of the other spouse. By filing Form 8379, the injured spouse may be able to get back his or her share of the joint refund.

.03   Meals and Entertainment 50 Percent Disallowance Clarified

The IRS regulations under IRC §274 were finalized clarifying an important issue. The rule itself did not change, only 50 percent of meal and entertainment costs may be deducted. What was clarified is the result when there is a chain of payments, one reimbursing another for meals and entertainment costs. The rule that applies is that the final payer is the one who may only deduct 50 percent of the cost. For example, assume a CPA is in travel status on an out-of-town audit and incurs costs for meals and entertainment. Her company has an accountable plan and the CPA itemizes the specific meal and entertainment costs on her expense report and is reimbursed for these costs. The CPA firm, in turn bills these costs as itemized to the audit client; that is, in its bill to the audit client, the CPA firm segregates the hours charged for the audit from the costs reimbursed to its employees for meals and entertainment. In this situation, the audit client is the final payer, and since it is paying for meals and entertainment costs of its auditors, it may only deduct 50 percent of these costs.

However, the Tax Cuts and Jobs Act, eliminated deductions for most entertainment expenses beginning in 2018. Further, it also eliminated the deduction for amounts paid by employer for meals that are excludable from an employee's income because they are provided to employees and their spouses and dependents for the employer's convenience and on the employer's business premises; or food, beverage, and facility expenses for meals that are de minimis fringe benefit. However, an employer may continue to deduct 50 percent of its expenses for food, beverages, and related facilities that are furnished on its business premises primarily for its employees, such as a cafeteria or executive dining room.

As another result of the COVID-19 pandemic, there was an enhanced business meal deduction. The pandemic caused severe financial difficulty for restaurants because they had so many fewer patrons during that period. In order to provide incentive for increased use of restaurants, for 2021 and 2022 only, businesses could deduct the full cost of business-related food and beverages purchased from a restaurant.

.04   The Six-year Statute of Limitations Clarified

If a taxpayer omits gross income in excess of 25 percent of the gross income other-wise reported on a tax return, the statute of limitations is six years rather than the normal three. The interpretation of this rule (contained in IRC §6501(e)(1)(A) (i)) has been a source of disagreement between the IRS and taxpayers. According to its plain language, the gross income to be considered appeared to be only the amounts of revenue or gross sales, not the net amount of income as reduced by the basis of the cost of goods sold. In its regulations (Reg. §301.6501(e)-1(a)(1)(iii)), however, the IRS took the position that an understatement of the basis of an asset sold is effectively the same thing as underreporting gross income, since the amount of income subject to tax is affected by both gross revenue and the basis of what was sold. The Supreme Court's *United States v. Home Concrete & Supply, LLC*, had ruled that the IRS's position was incorrect, given the plain wording of the statute, and the court effectively invalidated that portion of the IRS's regula-tions. But in July 2015, Congress made explicit the principle that an understate-ment of the basis of an asset, since it impacts taxable income to the same extent as the omission of gross income, will trigger the six-year statute of limitations (as-suming the result is an omission of income of more than 25 percent of what was reported on the return). The new law states "An understatement of gross income by reason of an overstatement of unrecovered cost or other basis is an omission from gross income." This law change, a part of the *Surface Transportation Act of 2015*, became effective on July 31, 2015. Its effect will not be retroactive. For Congress, this is effectively a broadening of the tax base, as more taxpayers are exposed to examination for a longer period of time. The change, as noted, was a reaction to a 2012 Supreme Court case, *Home Concrete & Supply, LLC*, which took issue with the IRS's interpretation of "omitted income" by making reference to the basis of an asset sold.

.05   IRS Treatment of Virtual Currencies including Bitcoin

During the past several years, virtual currencies—and especially Bitcoin—have become a topic of interest to investors and taxpayers and to the IRS. Some of the touted advantages of virtual currency—difficulty in tracing transaction, anonymity, lack of government reporting and oversight—are also sources of concern for law enforcement. From money laundering to fraud to tax evasion, the potential illegal uses of virtual currencies were quickly recognized. In 2014, the IRS issued a notice providing answers to frequently asked questions (FAQs) on virtual currency, such as Bitcoin. These FAQs provide basic information on the U.S. federal tax implications of transactions in, or transactions that use, virtual currency.

According to the IRS, "In some environments, virtual currency operates like "real" currency—i.e., the coin and paper money of the United States or of any other country that is designated as legal tender, circulates, and is customarily used and accepted as a medium of exchange in the country of issuance—but it does not have legal tender status in any jurisdiction."

"Virtual currency that has an equivalent value in real currency, or that acts as a substitute for real currency, is referred to as "convertible" virtual currency. Bitcoin is one example of a convertible virtual currency. Bitcoin can be digitally traded between users and can be purchased for, or exchanged into, U.S. dollars, Euros, and other real or virtual currencies."

The IRS has taken the position that virtual currency is treated as property for U.S. federal tax purposes. General tax principles that apply to property transactions apply to transactions using virtual currency.

"Among other things, this means that:

- Wages paid to employees using virtual currency are taxable to the employee, must be reported by an employer on a Form W-2, and are subject to federal income tax withholding and payroll taxes.
- Payments using virtual currency made to independent contractors and other service providers are taxable and self-employment tax rules generally apply. Normally, payers must issue Form 1099.
- The character of gain or loss from the sale or exchange of virtual currency depends on whether the virtual currency is a capital asset in the hands of the taxpayer.
- A payment made using virtual currency is subject to information reporting to the same extent as any other payment made in property."

Following is the IRS guidance in the form of questions and answers (abridged).

Q-1: How is virtual currency treated for federal tax purposes?

A-1: For federal tax purposes, virtual currency is treated as property. General tax principles applicable to property transactions apply to transactions using virtual currency.

Q-2: Is virtual currency treated as currency for purposes of determining whether a transaction results in foreign currency gain or loss under U.S. federal tax laws?

A-2: No. Under currently applicable law, virtual currency is not treated as currency that could generate foreign currency gain or loss for U.S. federal tax purposes.

Q-3: Must a taxpayer who receives virtual currency as payment for goods or services include in computing gross income the fair market value of the virtual currency?

A-3: Yes. A taxpayer who receives virtual currency as payment for goods or services must, in computing gross income, include the fair market value of the virtual currency measured in U.S. dollars, as of the date that the virtual currency was received.

Q-4: What is the basis of virtual currency received as payment for goods or services in Q&A-3?

A-4: The basis of virtual currency that a taxpayer receives as payment for goods or services in Q&A-3 is the fair market value of the virtual currency in U.S. dollars as of the date of receipt.

Q-5: How is the fair market value of virtual currency determined?

A-5: For U.S. tax purposes, transactions using virtual currency must be reported in U.S. dollars. Therefore, taxpayers will be required to determine the fair market value of virtual currency in U.S. dollars as of the date of payment or receipt. If a virtual currency is listed on an exchange and the exchange rate is established by market supply and demand, the fair market value of the virtual currency is determined by converting the virtual currency into U.S. dollars (or into another real currency which in turn can be converted into U.S. dollars) at the exchange rate, in a reasonable manner that is consistently applied.

Q-6: Does a taxpayer have gain or loss upon an exchange of virtual currency for other property?

A-6: Yes. If the fair market value of property received in exchange for virtual currency exceeds the taxpayer's adjusted basis of the virtual currency, the taxpayer has taxable gain. The taxpayer has a loss if the fair market value of the property received is less than the adjusted basis of the virtual currency. See Publication 544, Sales and Other Dispositions of Assets, for information about the tax treatment of sales and exchanges, such as whether a loss is deductible.

Q-7: What type of gain or loss does a taxpayer realize on the sale or exchange of virtual currency?

A-7: The character of the gain or loss generally depends on whether the virtual currency is a capital asset in the hands of the taxpayer. A taxpayer generally realizes capital gain or loss on the sale or exchange of virtual currency that is a capital asset in the hands of the taxpayer. For example, stocks, bonds, and other investment property are generally capital assets. A taxpayer generally realizes ordinary gain or loss on the sale or exchange of virtual currency that is not a capital asset in the hands of the taxpayer. Inventory and other property held mainly for sale to customers in a trade or business are examples of property that is not a capital asset.

Q-8: Does a taxpayer who "mines" virtual currency (for example, uses computer resources to validate Bitcoin transactions and maintain the public Bitcoin transaction ledger) realize gross income upon receipt of the virtual currency resulting from those activities?

A-8: Yes, when a taxpayer successfully "mines" virtual currency, the fair market value of the virtual currency as of the date of receipt is includible in gross income.

Q-9: Is an individual who "mines" virtual currency as a trade or business subject to self-employment tax on the income derived from those activities?

A-9: If a taxpayer's "mining" of virtual currency constitutes a trade or business, and the "mining" activity is not undertaken by the taxpayer as an employee, the net earnings from self-employment (generally, gross income derived from carrying on a trade or business less allowable deductions) resulting from those activities constitute self-employment income and are subject to the self-employment tax.

Q-10: Does virtual currency received by an independent contractor for performing services constitute self-employment income?

A-10: Yes. Generally, self-employment income includes all gross income derived by an individual from any trade or business carried on by the individual as other than an employee. Consequently, the fair market value of virtual currency received for services performed as an independent contractor, measured in U.S. dollars as of the date of receipt, constitutes self-employment income and is subject to the self-employment tax.

Q-11: Does virtual currency paid by an employer as remuneration for services constitute wages for employment tax purposes?

A-11: Yes. Generally, the medium in which remuneration for services is paid is immaterial to the determination of whether the remuneration constitutes wages for employment tax purposes. Consequently, the fair market value of virtual currency paid as wages is subject to federal income tax withholding, Federal

Insurance Contributions Act (FICA) tax, and Federal Unemployment Tax Act (FUTA) tax and must be reported on Form W-2, Wage and Tax Statement.

Q-12: Is a payment made using virtual currency subject to information reporting?

A-12: A payment made using virtual currency is subject to information reporting to the same extent as any other payment made in property. For example, a person who in the course of a trade or business makes a payment of fixed and determinable income using virtual currency with a value of $600 or more to a U.S. non-exempt recipient in a taxable year is required to report the payment to the IRS and to the payee. Examples of payments of fixed and determinable income include rent, salaries, wages, premiums, annuities, and compensation.

Q-13: Is a person who in the course of a trade or business makes a payment using virtual currency worth $600 or more to an independent contractor for performing services required to file an information return with the IRS?

A-13: Generally, a person who in the course of a trade or business makes a payment of $600 or more in a taxable year to an independent contractor for the performance of services is required to report that payment to the IRS and to the payee on Form 1099-MISC, Miscellaneous Income. Payments of virtual currency required to be reported on Form 1099-MISC should be reported using the fair market value of the virtual currency in U.S. dollars as of the date of payment. The payment recipient may have income even if the recipient does not receive a Form 1099-MISC.

Q-14: Are payments made using virtual currency subject to backup withholding?

A-14: Payments made using virtual currency are subject to backup withholding to the same extent as other payments made in property. Therefore, payors making reportable payments using virtual currency must solicit a taxpayer identification number (TIN) from the payee. The payor must backup withhold from the payment if a TIN is not obtained prior to payment or if the payor receives notification from the IRS that backup withholding is required.

Q-15: Are there IRS information reporting requirements for a person who settles payments made in virtual currency on behalf of merchants that accept virtual currency from their customers?

A-15: Yes, if certain requirements are met. In general, a third party that contracts with a substantial number of unrelated merchants to settle payments between the merchants and their customers is a third party settlement organization (TPSO).

A TPSO is required to report payments made to a merchant on a Form 1099-K, Payment Card and Third Party Network Transactions, if, for the calendar year, both (1) the number of transactions settled for the merchant exceeds 200, and (2) the gross amount of payments made to the merchant exceeds $20,000. When completing Boxes 1, 3, and 5a-1 on the Form 1099-K, transactions where the TPSO settles payments made with virtual currency are aggregated with transactions where the TPSO settles payments made with real currency to determine the total amounts to be reported in those boxes. When determining whether the transactions are reportable, the value of the virtual currency is the fair market value of the virtual currency in U.S. dollars on the date of payment.

.06 IRS Offshore Voluntary Disclosure Program

The IRS Offshore Voluntary Disclosure Program is closed as of September 28, 2018, although, according to the IRS Web site, the Voluntary Disclosure Practice is a longstanding practice of IRS Criminal Investigation. A voluntary disclosure will not automatically guarantee immunity from prosecution; however, a voluntary disclosure may result in prosecution not being recommended.

CHAPTER 35
Insolvency, Debt Forgiveness and Bankruptcy

¶35,000 Insolvency and Debt Forgiveness

Although residential real estate markets have been consistently growing, the downturn in the residential real estate market that began in 2006, followed by the recession and related increase in unemployment, brought the issues of insolvency and debt forgiveness income to the forefront for many people. Whether because of first or second mortgages, home equity loans or credit card debt, many individuals face potential tax problems brought about by debt reduction or debt forgiveness. For individuals experiencing these problems, it is likely the tax consequences are among the last things they consider. For a homeowner trying to stay in his or her home, financing and the ability to make house payments, not tax questions are at the forefront.

The housing bubble has been blamed on the ease with which too many people were granted too much credit. From cars to credit cards to homes, the years leading up to the recession saw a leveraging-up process that is continuing to unwind since its peak. As a result of too much debt, many people have sought refuge in bankruptcy, which is the major topic of this chapter. However, partly because of the large number of people involved and also because of government urging, there has been a great deal of restructuring of debt accomplished outside of bankruptcy. The banking sector, for example, has undertaken a number of adjustments to the terms of mortgages, involving altering the payment terms, and, in some cases, forgiving a portion of the mortgage. The credit card business has also seen customers default on their payments which, in many cases, has resulted in writing off the debt and for the consumer, cancellation of debt income (COD).

This section of the chapter addresses various situations facing consumers as taxpayers with respect to actual or potential cancellation of debt income. The tax code treats forgiveness of debt, as a general rule, as income. Numerous exceptions have been carved out, some of which are discussed here, including taxpayers who are insolvent or who have filed for bankruptcy.

The general tax rule states that if a debt for which you are personally liable (recourse debt) is canceled or forgiven, the amount of debt for which you are no longer responsible is included in your income for tax reporting. A debt includes any indebtedness for which you are liable or which attaches to property owned by you. Fortunately, for many taxpayers, one or more exceptions apply, reducing or eliminating the tax bite otherwise adding insult to injury.

If a financial institution such as a bank or credit union cancels or forgives a debt of $600 or more, they are required to issue the taxpayer a Form 1099-C, Cancellation of Debt. The amount of the canceled debt is shown in box 2. Unless the taxpayer meets one of the exceptions, the amount of the canceled debt is ordinary income and must be included in the taxpayer's gross income.

In addition to loan principal, a Form 1099-C may also report interest forgiven which may also be included in the amount of canceled debt in box 2. When this occurs, the interest portion included in box 2 is shown separately in box 3 so the taxpayer can identify how much is principal and how much is interest. The reporting of interest forgiven or cancelled does not automatically signal that this amount is taxable income. This determination may depend on the nature of the interest, specifically whether it would have been deductible when paid.

If the interest when paid would not have been deductible, such as interest on a personal loan or credit card interest, it should be included in the taxpayer's income according to the IRS.

If the forgiven interest reported on Form 1099-C would have been deductible, for example on a business loan or home mortgage, it is not included in taxable income and thus you should subtract the amount in box 3 of Form 1099-C from the amount in box 2, leaving only the principal.

The discussion and explanation in the remainder of this section assumes the taxpayer has not filed for bankruptcy. The primary topics addressed are 1) qualified principal residence indebtedness, 2) relief from credit card or other consumer debt, 3) abandonment of personal residence, 4) the insolvency exceptions, 5) mortgage loan modifications and 6) purchase-money debt reductions. Following these topics is a general discussion of tax aspects of bankruptcy.

.01   Qualified Principal Residence Indebtedness

Qualified principal residence indebtedness discharged before January 1, 2018, is excludable from income. The Bipartisan Budget Act of 2018 amended the Code to exclude qualified principal residence indebtedness that is discharged after December 31, 2015, under an arrangement that is entered into in writing before January 1, 2018.

The Mortgage Debt Relief Act of 2007 generally allowed taxpayers to exclude income from the discharge of debt on their principal residence. Debt reduced through mortgage restructuring, as well as mortgage debt forgiven in connection with a foreclosure, qualifies for the relief.

This provision applied to debt forgiven in calendar years 2007 through 2017. Up to $2 million of forgiven debt is eligible for this exclusion ($1 million if married filing separately). The exclusion did not apply if the discharge is due to services performed for the lender or any other reason not directly related to a decline in the home's value or the taxpayer's financial condition.

A taxpayer can exclude canceled debt from income if it is *qualified principal residence indebtedness*. Qualified principal residence indebtedness is debt incurred in acquiring, constructing, or substantially improving a principal residence and which is secured by a principal residence. Thus, the provision does not apply to secondary or vacation homes or investment real estate. Qualified principal residence indebtedness can also include debt that results from refinancing the original debt secured by your principal residence but only to the extent the amount of new debt does not exceed the amount of the refinanced debt. That is, if a mortgage that otherwise qualifies as qualified principal residence indebtedness is refinanced for a larger balance than the amount owed at the time of the refinancing, the excess obtained will not receive the preferential debt cancellation treatment, only the amount refinancing the then existing balance on the mortgage.

Example. In 2002, Lucy purchased a principal residence for $315,000. Lucy made a down payment of $15,000 and took out a $300,000 first mortgage for the balance of the purchase price. The loan was secured by the principal residence. A principal residence is the home where you ordinarily live most of the time. You can have only one principal residence at any one time. In 2003, Lucy took out a second mortgage in the amount of $50,000 that she used to add a swimming pool to her home.

In 2008, when the outstanding principal of her first and second mortgage loans was $325,000 (she had paid off $25,000 of the original first and second mortgages), Lucy refinanced the two loans into one in the amount of $400,000. The FMV of the principal residence at the time of the refinancing was $430,000. Lucy used the additional $75,000 debt ($400,000 new mortgage loan minus $325,000 outstanding principal balances of on first and second mortgages immediately before the refinancing) to pay off personal credit cards and to purchase a new car.

After the refinancing, Lucy's qualified principal residence indebtedness is limited to $325,000, the amount or her acquisition indebtedness that remained at the time of the refinancing, plus the amount of the second mortgage used to make substantial improvements. The maximum amount you can treat as qualified principal residence indebtedness is $2 million ($1 million if married filing separately). In addition, canceled qualified principal residence indebtedness may not be excluded from income if the cancellation was in exchange for services performed for the lender or on account of any other factor not directly related to a decline in the value of your residence or to your financial condition.

If, as in the above example, only a part of a loan is qualified principal residence indebtedness ($325,000 of the $400,000 borrowed), the exclusion from income does not apply to the amount exceeding the qualified principal residence indebtedness ($75,000 in the example). Thus, if Lucy's lender later forgave $100,000 of her mortgage balance because of the house value decline, the first $75,000 would not be excluded from income as qualified principal residence indebtedness, only $25,000. Consider the following example.

Example. In 2004, Bret purchased a principal residence for $880,000 putting $80,000 down and applying a jumbo mortgage of $800,000 to complete the purchase. Bret is personally liable for the first mortgage, which is therefore considered recourse debt. In 2006, when the FMV of the property was $1,000,000, Bret refinanced the debt, paying off the $740,000 existing balance on his first mortgage ($800,000 original balance less principal paid down since 2004) and thereby obtaining an additional $110,000 for a total first (refinanced) mortgage of $850,000. The additional $110,000 received in the refinancing was used to pay off his credit cards and to buy a new car.

In 2007, Bret's employer downsized its workforce and he was laid off. Since the refinancing in 2006 and the layoff in 2007, Bret's residence had declined in value to from $1,000,000 to only $725,000. Based on Bret's circumstances, the lender agreed to forgive $125,000 of the $850,000 debt. Because non-qualified principal residence indebtedness is considered forgiven first by the IRS's ordering rules, Bret can exclude only $15,000 of the canceled debt from his income, ($125,000 canceled debt minus the $110,000 amount of the debt that was not qualified principal residence indebtedness as a result of the refinancing). Bret must include the remaining $110,000 of canceled debt in ordinary income on his tax return for the year, unless another exception, such as insolvency or bankruptcy applies.

IRS Form 982 is used to report the portion of any cancelled debt that qualifies as qualified principal residence indebtedness. In addition, if the taxpayer continues to own their residence after a cancellation of qualified principal residence indebtedness, he or she must reduce the basis in the residence by the amount excluded, thereby increasing the potential gain or reducing the potential loss resulting from a later sale.

This exclusion does not apply to a cancellation of debt in a Title 11 bankruptcy (Chapters 7, 11, 12, 13). If the taxpayer was insolvent immediately before the debt cancellation, he or she may be able to apply the insolvency exclusion rather than the qualified principal residence indebtedness exclusion (see below).

.02   Personal Auto Indebtedness Cancelled

If an individual purchases a car on credit and the car is later repossessed because the loan payments were not made on time, the result may produce forgiveness of debt income. However, while there is no specific exclusion for this kind of income, as there is for personal residence indebtedness, the taxpayer may be able to avoid including part or all of the forgiven debt in income if they were insolvent at the time of the repossession. The following illustration covers both the inclusion of forgiven debt and the exclusion available to an insolvent taxpayer.

Example. Luka purchased a new car in 2005 at a total cost of $12,000. She put $2,000 down and financed the balance ($10,000). Luka was personally liable for the debt. In 2008, when the balance due on the car loan was $8,500, Luka lost her job and was unable to keep up the car payments. At the time the lender repossessed Luka's car, it was worth $7,000 ($1,500 less than the balance due). The portion of the loan that was exchanged for the car, $7,000, is not considered forgiveness of debt since the lender received an asset of equal value. However, if the lender forgives the remaining balance of the loan, $1,500, there is no consideration provided and therefore this portion of the original $8,500 loan is considered forgiven. As a result, Luka would have taxable income of $1,500 from the repossession and loan cancellation. She will therefore receive a Form 1099-C from the lender showing forgiven debt of $1,500 in box 2 and in box 7 the $7,000 fair market value of the car repossessed will be reported.

If, however, Luka is insolvent at the time of the car's repossession and the debt cancellation, an exclusionary rule applies. Based on this rule, if Luka's liabilities exceeded her assets by at least $1,500, this amount of insolvency may be applied causing the forgiven debt to be excluded from her gross income. A corresponding reduction in the basis of her other assets must be made, however. For purposes of the insolvency test the fair market value of Luka's assets is used.

When measuring insolvency, assets include the value of everything the taxpayer owns, including assets that serve as collateral for debt and exempt assets which are beyond the reach of creditors under the law. An example of the latter is a taxpayer's pension plan or other retirement account. Liabilities include: the entire amount of recourse debts, and the amount of nonrecourse debt that is not in excess of the FMV of the property that is security for the debt.

Thus, if in addition to the car Luka owned furniture with a FMV of $4,000 this amount would be used to determine insolvency by comparing it with her total liabilities. Assuming that her only other liability at the time of the car's repossession consisted of $10,000 of credit card debt, her insolvency would be determined as the total debt ($8,500 car loan plus $10,000 credit card debt = $18,500) less the FMV of the car ($7,000) plus the FMV of the furniture ($4,000) or $7,500. Since this amount of insolvency is greater than the amount of debt forgiven ($1,500) the total amount of the debt may be excluded from cancellation of debt income. If on the other hand, if the taxpayer's amount of insolvency were less than the amount of debt cancelled, only the amount of forgiven debt up to the balance of the insolvency can be excluded from income. In this case, if Luka's liabilities exceeded her assets by only $1,000 before the debt cancellation, only $1,000 of the cancelled debt could be excluded from income and the remaining $500 would be included as taxable income.

.03   Credit Card Debt Cancellation

When credit card debt is cancelled or forgiven outside of bankruptcy, similar rules apply. If the taxpayer is solvent at the time of the cancellation, the result is taxable income from cancellation of debt. If the taxpayer is insolvent, the extent of the insolvency controls how much of the cancelled debt may be excluded from income. Consider an example.

Example. In 2008, the bank released Jenkins from his obligation to pay his personal credit card debt in the amount of $5,000. Jenkins would therefore receive a Form 1099-C from his credit card lender showing canceled debt of $5,000 in box 2. If solvent, he has income of $5,000. If Jenkins is insolvent the amount of insolvency must be determined. Assume his total liabilities immediately before the cancellation were $15,000 and the FMV of his total assets immediately before the cancellation were $7,000. This means that immediately before the cancellation, Jenkins was insolvent to the extent of $8,000 ($15,000 total liabilities minus $7,000 FMV of his total assets). Because the amount by which Jenkins was insolvent immediately before the cancellation exceeds the amount of his debt canceled, Jenkins can exclude the entire $5,000 canceled debt from income.

As in the earlier example, if the extent of the insolvency was less than $5,000, part of the cancelled credit card debt would have to be included in Jenkins's income. Form 982 is used for reporting cancelled debt which is not taxable, as in the case of insolvency.

.04   Student Loans Discharge

The Tax Cuts and Jobs Act temporarily expanded the exclusion of discharge of debt income for student loans due to student's death or total and permanent disability if discharged from December 31, 2017, and before January 1, 2026. Loans eligible for this exclusion are loans made by:
- the United States or its instrumentality or agency;
- a state or its political subdivision;
- certain tax-exempt public benefit corporations that control a state, county, or municipal hospital and whose employees have been deemed to be public employees under state law;

- an educational organization that originally received the funds from which the loan was made from the United States, a state, or a tax-exempt public benefit corporation; or
- private education loans.

.05   Abandonments

Homeowners who abandon their homes—some apparently leaving the keys on the counter and walking out—may incur a loss on the abandonment, but this loss is personal and therefore nondeductible. The act of abandonment is considered a disposition, a triggering tax event. The amount of the loss is equal to the property's basis at the time it is abandoned. A property is considered abandoned when the owner(s) voluntarily and permanently gives up use and possession of the property with the intention of ending their ownership in the property and without arranging to transfer the ownership to any other party.

The rate of abandoned homes has increased recently due to the decline in housing values. Some homeowners, unable to keep up with their mortgage payments and realizing that the balance of the mortgage was now greater than the fair market value of the home have decided that abandoning the property is the appropriate solution. If the abandoned home is security for a mortgage, and the homeowner is personally liable for the mortgage, abandoning the home does not automatically cancel the mortgage. The homeowner remains liable until some finality is achieved with respect to the mortgage. If the mortgage that was secured by the abandoned property is later cancelled by the lender, the former homeowner incurs forgiveness of debt income. This income is separate from the non-deductible loss on the abandonment and the two are not simply offset. The income must be reported unless an exception such as insolvency applies.

.06   Mortgage Loan Modifications

In some situations, homeowners have found themselves owning homes for which the outstanding mortgage balance is greater than the fair market value of the home (they are "upside down"). Some have been able to negotiate a reduction in the principal balance of their mortgage with the lender, allowing them to stay in their homes. These loan modifications are referred to as "work-outs." In such loan modifications, the lender will issue a Form 1099-C indicating the amount of the loan cancellation, which is considered forgiven debt. Whether the taxpayer must pay tax on this forgiven debt or not depends on the same principles discussed above. If the homeowners are insolvent, they may be able to avoid paying tax on part or all of the forgiven debt based on the extent of their insolvency. The amount of mortgage forgiven may also qualify as principal residence indebtedness. Here, as noted, care must be taken to determine whether all or only a part of the homeowner's mortgage is qualified principal residence indebtedness. If the original mortgage used to purchase the home was refinanced, for example, it must be determined if the refinancing was for the exact amount of the balance of the original mortgage at the time of the refinancing, or whether there was a "cash-out" wherein the homeowner borrowed more money in the process of the refinancing than the amount needed to pay off the original mortgage. In a situation where this occurred, the amount of any loan modification later effected by the lender is considered to have applied first to the amount of any "cash-out" before applying to the qualified principal residence indebtedness. Thus, to the extent of any excess borrowings at the time of the refinancing, the forgiven debt resulting from the loan modifications is cancellation of debt income and not excludable from income as qualified personal residence indebtedness.

.07 Purchase-Money Debt

Another important exception to cancellation of debt income results from the seller financing the purchase, referred to as purchase-money debt. If a house is purchased from the builder, for example, and the builder is owed the mortgage, a later adjustment to the amount of the mortgage is considered a reduction in the sales price of the home rather than forgiveness of debt.

Other special exclusions apply to qualified real property business debt, qualified Midwest disaster area debt and certain farm debt.

.08 Qualified Real Property Business Debt

In many contexts in the tax law, a distinction is drawn between business and non-business. Appending the term business to an activity connotes at least a profit motive and generally a level of taxpayer involvement. While section 162 permits the deduction of expenses in a business, section 212 permits a deduction of the same expenses though they are "for the production and collection of income" rather than for a business endeavor. For individuals this can affect where the items are deducted (for AGI or from AGI). Limiting the discussion to real estate, a hotel, because of the level of services provided, is a generally a business rather than merely an investment. An apartment building, on the other hand, is normally treated as an investment rather than a business, unless the level of services provided comes closer to what one might receive in a hotel.

In addition to taxpayers who are in bankruptcy or who are insolvent, §108(a)(1)(D) provides relief from recognizing cancellation of debt income "in the case of a taxpayer other than a C corporation [if] the indebtedness discharged is qualified real property business indebtedness." The latter phrase is defined in § 108(a)(3). "The term 'qualified real property business indebtedness' means indebtedness which—(A) was incurred or assumed by the taxpayer in connection with real property used in a trade or business and is secured by such real property, (B) was incurred or assumed before January 1, 1993, or if incurred or assumed on or after such date, is qualified acquisition indebtedness, and (C) with respect to which such taxpayer makes an election to have this paragraph apply."

In so defining qualified real property business indebtedness, congress sought to differentiate such debt from both qualified farm indebtedness, already covered by §108(a)(1)(C), and to exclude indebtedness where the taxpayer could qualify for the insolvency provision of § 108(a)(1)(B). The purpose of this subsection was to deal with situations where a taxpayer was not bankrupt or insolvent, but because the real estate market had declined, the amount of a taxpayer's debt exceeded the value of his or her business real estate that secures the debt. But this still leaves open the question of determining what the term "business" is intended to add to the description. For example, how much activity is necessary to convert an activity from an investment to a business? In several cases involving foreign owners of apartment buildings in the U.S., the courts found that the owners were not in business because they had hired management companies to take care of any business activities of the properties, and thus the owners were only investors.

In Chief Counsel Advice 200919035, the IRS states that, "Whether it's residential or non residential [real estate] is irrelevant." Instead, the purpose of the subsection is to distinguish between personal use and business use property (CCA 200919035). Thus, rental property can qualify for §108(a)(1)(C) relief, not only property "used in business" in the strict sense.

¶35,001   Inherited IRA in Bankruptcy

The status of "retirement funds" has significance in many contexts, including bankruptcy. In 2014, the Supreme Court heard the case of *Clark et ux. v. Rameker, Trustee, et al.* (certiorari to the United States Court of Appeals for the Seventh Circuit, No. 13-299) involving the question of the status of the funds received in an inherited IRA. Are they still "retirement funds" or does their status change upon the death of the owner of the IRA? To the recipient of the IRA it can make a great deal of difference. The decision of the Court in upholding the Seventh Circuit was that the funds in the IRA lose their status as "retirement funds."

The opinion of the Court was delivered by Justice Sotomayor. "When an individual files for bankruptcy, she may exempt particular categories of assets from the bankruptcy estate. One such category includes certain 'retirement funds.' 11 U. S. C. §522(b)(3)(C). The question presented is whether funds contained in an inherited individual retirement account (IRA) qualify as 'retirement funds' within the meaning of this bankruptcy exemption. We hold that they do not." The Court continued by stating, "the Bankruptcy Code does not define 'retirement funds,' so we give the term its ordinary meaning."

"Allowing debtors to protect funds held in traditional and Roth IRAs comports with this purpose by helping to ensure that debtors will be able to meet their basic needs during their retirement years. At the same time, the legal limitations on traditional and Roth IRAs ensure that debtors who hold such accounts (but who have not yet reached retirement age) do not enjoy a cash windfall by virtue of the exemption—such debtors are instead required to wait until age 59½ before they may withdraw the funds penalty-free. The same cannot be said of an inherited IRA. For if an individual is allowed to exempt an inherited IRA from her bankruptcy estate, nothing about the inherited IRA's legal characteristics would prevent (or even discourage) the individual from using the entire balance of the account on a vacation home or sports car immediately after her bankruptcy proceedings are complete. Allowing that kind of exemption would convert the Bankruptcy Code's purposes of preserving debtors' ability to meet their basic needs and ensuring that they have a 'fresh start.'

"When an individual debtor files a bankruptcy petition, her 'legal or equitable interests . . . in property' become part of the bankruptcy estate. §541(a)(1). 'To help the debtor obtain a fresh start,' however, the Bankruptcy Code allows debtors to exempt from the estate limited interests in certain kinds of property. *Rousey v. Jacoway*, 544 U. S. 320, 325 (2005). The exemption at issue in this case allows debtors to protect 'retirement funds to the extent those funds are in a fund or account that is exempt from taxation under section 401, 403, 408, 408A, 414, 457, or 501(a) of the Internal Revenue Code.' §§522(b)(3)(C), (d)(12). The enumerated sections of the Internal Revenue Code cover many types of accounts, three of which are relevant here."

The Court's opinion continued, "Inherited IRAs do not operate like ordinary IRAs. Unlike with a traditional or Roth IRA, an individual may withdraw funds from an inherited IRA at any time, without paying a tax penalty. §72(t)(2)(A)(ii). Indeed, the owner of an inherited IRA not only may but must withdraw its funds: The owner must either withdraw the entire balance in the account within five years of the original owner's death or take minimum distributions on an annual basis. See §§408(a)(6), 401(a)(9)(B); 26 CFR §1.408–8 (2013) (Q–1 and A–1(a) incorporating §1.401(a)(9)–3 (Q–1 and A–1(a))). And unlike with a traditional or Roth IRA, the owner of an inherited IRA may never make contributions to the account. 26 U. S. C. §219(d)(4)."

¶35,002   Types of Bankruptcies

The remainder of this chapter covers basic principles of bankruptcy and federal income tax aspects of a bankruptcy filing for corporations, partnerships, and for individuals. The discussion does not provide detailed coverage of the tax rules for complex corporate bankruptcy reorganizations or other highly technical and legal aspects of business and individual bankruptcy proceedings. Competent professional advice should be obtained for the highly complex bankruptcy law.

Bankruptcy proceedings begin with a decision by the attorney for the debtor regarding the appropriate "Chapter" under which a petition for bankruptcy is filed with the U.S. Bankruptcy Court. The filing of the petition produces a stop to the collection activities of the creditors (*automatic stay*) and creates a bankruptcy estate, consisting of all the assets of the person or business filing the bankruptcy petition.

The various chapters by which bankruptcies are referred are chapters of the *Bankruptcy Code*, Title 11 of the U.S. Code. Chapter 7, for example, deals with bankruptcies requiring liquidation of the debtor's assets and satisfaction of liabilities with the proceeds. In such cases an individual's assets and debts are turned over to a *bankruptcy trustee* who, under the guidance of a plan of liquidation and with the supervision of the Bankruptcy Court judge, disposes of the assets and makes equitable payment to the creditors. In this most drastic form of bankruptcy, the debtor is generally allowed to exempt specific items based on federal or state law. These items vary in kind and value from state to state but often include the debtor's homestead and certain personal property. One function of such a proceeding, as in all bankruptcy matters, is to protect the debtor from further collection efforts by the creditors and to see that creditors are paid according to their rights under the law rather than in terms of their size or the aggressiveness of their collection efforts.

Bankruptcy cases originally filed under one chapter of the Bankruptcy Code may be converted to another chapter if there is a need to do so and the requirements for such conversion are met. Thus, a case originally filed under Chapter 7 may be converted to Chapter 11, 12, or 13. Chapter 11 bankruptcies are reorganizations of a debtor's financial affairs effected in such a way as to use the debtor's existing assets to generate revenue to pay the creditors—but not necessarily the original amounts owed nor in compliance with the original terms of the debts when incurred.

Corporations as well as individuals may file for bankruptcy protection under Chapter 11—for individuals it is sometimes referred to as the "rich man's bankruptcy." In the case of a corporation or other business, the daily operations of the business may be taken over by a bankruptcy trustee or in other cases left in the hands of the owners or management, referred to *debtor-in-possession*. Bankruptcies may be voluntary, in which case they are initiated by the debtor, or involuntary, in which case they are filed by a group of creditors.

Under whichever chapter of the Bankruptcy Code a petition for bankruptcy is filed, the process is overseen and under the jurisdiction of the U.S. Bankruptcy Court. In each case as well, a trustee carries out the necessary mechanics of the proceeding, and both the creditors' and debtor's rights regarding the bankruptcy are enforced.

Creditors' claims are categorized in a hierarchical scheme beginning with priority claims, listed here in descending priority order:

1. Payroll (trust fund) taxes.
2. Court-ordered child care and maintenance payments and administrative expenses of the bankruptcy estate.
3. Secured debt (creditor has lien against debtor's assets).
4. Unsecured debt, which is further subdivided.

Chapter 12 bankruptcies deal with the adjustments of debts of a family farmer with regular annual income. A case originally filed under Chapter 12 may be converted to Chapter 7. Like Chapter 11, Chapter 12 does not involve a liquidation of assets but rather the continuation of a business and structured payment of its debts. Under such a plan future earnings of the farmer are allocated for payment of debt in a manner overseen by the trustee and the court.

Chapter 13 bankruptcy is an adjustment of debts of an individual with regular income (wage earner, self-employed or retiree with pension or other regular income). Eligibility includes a limit on the amount of unsecured debt (that is not contingent or in dispute), which may not exceed $100,000. Like Chapters 11 and 12, future income is allocated, via a plan overseen by a trustee of the court, to the payment of debts over a specified period up to five years. If the debtor is self-employed, the business is the source of future income and is continued under the supervision of the court. A case originally filed under Chapter 13 may be converted to Chapter 7 for liquidation of the bankruptcy estate or Chapter 11 if unsecured debt exceeds $100,000.

For a number of years Congress has been aware of the increasing number of bankruptcy filings and specific abuses of the system, but not until 2005 was it able to complete a package of reforms that became law on April 20, 2005, when President Bush signed the Bankruptcy Abuse Prevention and Consumer Protection Act.

¶35,003   2005 Bankruptcy Abuse Prevention and Consumer Protection Act

The 2005 law is intended to fight abuses to the bankruptcy process, and it focuses attention on the intent and timing of transactions entered into by individual debtors before their filing for bankruptcy as well as abuses caused by the same debtors repeatedly filing for protection under the bankruptcy laws.

.01   Mandatory Credit Counseling and Debtor Education

Within 180 days prior to filing for bankruptcy protection, an individual debtor must receive credit and budget counseling from an approved (by the U.S.

bankruptcy trustee) nonprofit credit counseling agency. Upon completion of the counseling, the debtor is required to file with the Bankruptcy Court a certificate from the credit counseling agency describing the services provided along with the debt management plan developed as the result of such counseling. This provision applies to Chapter 7, 11, 12, and 13 filings. A requirement for the approval of nonprofit credit counseling agencies is that they provide their services for a fee that is not contingent on the debtor's ability to pay. Exceptions are provided to these rules in the case of emergencies and for debtors who are incapacitated or disabled.

In the case of a Chapter 13 filing the court will not grant the discharge of debt until the debtor has also completed a course in personal financial management as approved by the Bankruptcy Trustee.

.02 Production of Tax Returns and Other Documents

Among petition filing requirements for individual debtors seeking bankruptcy protection are the following:

- Recent pay stubs—"copies of all payment advices or other evidence of payment received within 60 days before the filing."
- A calculation of net monthly income remaining after essential expenses are paid—referred to as *current monthly income.*
- Evidence that the debtor was given an informational notice required by the law.
- A calculation of reasonably anticipated increases in income or expenses during the 12-month period following the date of the filing of the petition.
- Current federal, state, and local income tax returns and, in the case of Chapter 13 filings, evidence that all applicable tax returns that were due within the preceding four years were filed with the appropriate taxing body.
- A Chapter 13 plan will not be confirmed until the debtor certifies that all postpetition domestic support obligations (child support and maintenance) are current. Past due domestic support obligations owed directly to a family member are classified as *priority claims* and must be paid in full; such obligations paid to a government agency may be paid in less than the full amount due.

.03 Means Testing for Chapter 7 Bankruptcy

The individual debtor's "state median income" is an important threshold for qualifying under Chapter 7. This is the median income in the debtor's state of residence as reflected in U.S. Census Bureau data. In the case of debtors whose income exceeds this amount, abuse of the bankruptcy system is presumed, and the trustee or any creditor may bring a motion to dismiss the bankruptcy proceeding.

The calculation of the threshold involves a five-year (60-month) calculation that effectively compares the debtor's condition to that of a Chapter 13 filer.

The calculation of the debtor's income begins with a determination of one month's current gross income (for example, take-home pay) based on a look-back to the most recent six-month period. This income excludes Social Security Act payments and certain payments to victims of war crimes or payments to victims of international or domestic terrorism. From this income is subtracted 1/60 of the secured debt payments scheduled during the following 60 months. From this remainder is subtracted the equivalent of one month's priority debts (the total amount of priority payments due in the next five years, divided by 60).

The amount of monthly expenses allowed by the IRS in its offers-in-compromise and other delinquent tax payment negotiations (living expenses not including debt payments) is then subtracted, along with the monthly amount of certain other allowed expenses (for example: payments for the care of an elderly, chronically ill, or disabled household member). If the debtor's actual monthly expenses are less than the IRS allowance, the lower actual amount is used.

If the remainder (the *current monthly income*) is less than $100, the Chapter 7 case may go forward; there is no automatic presumption of abuse. If the current monthly (net) income is $100 or more per month (after above deductions), the debtor is presumed abusive and the case may be dismissed or, with the consent of the debtor, converted to a Chapter 11 or 13 bankruptcy. The new law provides that such Chapter 13 cases will generally involve a five-year debt payment plan and require annual financial statements to be prepared and filed with the U.S. Bankruptcy Court or trustee.

An exception to the above abuse presumption (current monthly income of more than $100) exists if the debtor's unsecured debt exceeds $24,000 and the remaining net income after deducting the items listed above is sufficient to pay 25 percent of this unsecured debt during a five-year period.

If the current monthly (net) income after allowed deductions is $150 or more, abuse is presumed unless the debtor has more than $36,000 of unsecured debt. And if the current monthly (net) income is $166.67 ($2,000 per year or, for five years, $10,000) then abuse is presumed unless the unsecured debt is greater than $39,998.40. The finding of abuse is a presumption and may be rebutted; but the presumption of abuse is grounds for the Court's dismissal of the bankruptcy case.

If the debtor's income is less than the state median, the Court may still determine abuse, but the creditors no longer have standing to file a motion for dismissal. Abuse can be alleged for a number of separate reasons, including previous recent bankruptcy filings, fraudulent asset conveyances, bad faith in presenting or failing to present documentation, or incurring debt for luxury items shortly before filing. Under prior law fraud was presumed if a debtor charged on a credit card luxury goods of $1,225 or more shortly before filing for bankruptcy; the current law reduces the presumption threshold to $500. A similar adjustment is made with cash advances from a credit card where the presumed fraud limit is reduced from $1,225 to $750.

The yardstick used for determining the debtor's income for testing against the state's median income is the National Standards and Local Standards issued by the IRS for the area in which the debtor lives. Allowed in the calculation of monthly expenses are amounts for health and disability insurance, as well as payments to a health savings account. In contrast to the otherwise Spartan levels of IRS sanctioned expenses, the new law also allows the debtor's monthly costs to include "actual expenses for each dependent child less than 18 years of age, not to exceed $1,500 per year per child, to attend a private or public elementary or secondary school."

Other expenses deductible in arriving at the current monthly income include:

- Certain additional home energy costs.
- Expenses of administering a Chapter 13 plan.
- Certain expenses for protection from family violence.
- 1/60 of all secured debt and priority debt due in the succeeding five years.

An exception is provided to the means test if the debtor is a disabled veteran if the debt "occurred primarily during a period during which he or she was on active duty or performing a homeland defense activity." No discharge is allowed under the law of fraudulent taxes in Chapter 11 or 13 cases and certain student loans are also barred from discharge.

Median state income will be determined from U.S. Census Bureau data adjusted for increases in the Consumer Price Index (CPI). The data will reflect the size of the family unit. In a joint filing for bankruptcy, both spouses' income is included in the determination. It appears that the means test, applying U.S. Census Bureau data for gross annual income and Internal Revenue Service data for monthly allowed expenses—resulting in a net income—will require considerable coordination in applying the triggering thresholds for presumed abuse (such as the greater than $100 current monthly income). Either the allowed IRS expenses must be annualized and grossed-up to arrive at annual gross income, or the gross income will have to be converted to monthly net income by applying the IRS allowed deductions.

In addition to the formal means test applied to determine abuse on the part of the debtors, abuse and consequent dismissal of Chapter 7 cases may also result from a finding by the U.S. trustee, bankruptcy administrator, or Court that the debtor filed for bankruptcy in bad faith.

.04   Time Between Debt Discharges

Preempting the Biblical admonition to forgive our debtors every seven years, the law, in the case of Chapter 7 bankruptcy filings, extends the period for new filings to eight years if the debtor has previously received a discharge of debt in a Chapter 7 or Chapter 11 case. (Prior law specified six years.) For debtors filing under Chapter 13, who had previously filed under Chapter 7, 11, or 12, the waiting period to file a new petition is now four years; if the previous filing was under Chapter 13, the waiting period is two years. Limited exceptions are provided.

.05   Homestead Limitations

A controversial area of bankruptcy law is the state *homestead exemption*. This is the value of the debtor's equity in his or her personal residence, which amount varies greatly from one state to another. The state homestead exemption protects the debtor's interest in his or her personal residence from creditor claims. Although federal bankruptcy law generally allows state homestead exemptions for the debtor's state of residence, the law places limits on the amount of the exemption in certain cases. Under the law, if a debtor has increased the value of his or her home's equity—the amount qualifying for state homestead exemption—by more than $125,000 during the 1,215 days prior to the bankruptcy filing, the amount greater than $125,000 is excluded from the state exemption amount.

In addition, if the debtor has been convicted of a felony or owes a debt from the violation of federal or state securities laws or racketeering or fiduciary fraud or crimes or intentional torts causing serious bodily injury or death during the five years preceding the bankruptcy filing, a limit of $125,000 is placed on the amount of homestead exemption available to the debtor. An exception is made if the homestead is "reasonably necessary for the support of the debtor and any dependent of the debtor"—for example, a family farm.

.06   Limitations on an Automatic Stay

To curb the abuse of frequent bankruptcy filings, through which abusers gain the benefit of the automatic stay from collections, the new law stipulates that for any Chapter 7, 11, or 13 case filed within one year of the dismissal of an earlier case, generally the automatic stay for the new filing will terminate after 30 days. An exception is provided if the debtor can establish that the new case is filed in good faith. If a second filing occurs within a one-year period, the automatic stay will not take affect at all.

.07   Limitation on Items Available for Discharge

Certain items of debt—most notably income taxes but including debt induced by fraud, embezzlement, or breach of fiduciary duty—have traditionally been beyond the scope of discharge. The 2005 law expanded this list of items to include student loans, debt for certain luxury purchases and cash advances (described above), debt incurred in violation of securities fraud laws (this provision is effective retroactively to July 30, 2002—the effective date of the Sarbanes-Oxley Act) and certain homestead exemption amounts. In addition, to discourage debtors from shopping for the states with the largest exemptions, the law specifies that the debtor's state of residence for exemption purposes is the state in which the debtor resided for the 730 days prior to filing.

.08   Exclusion from Bankruptcy Estate Property

The assets in the bankruptcy estate are those that may be used to liquidate the debtor's liabilities. Certain items, like the amount of the homestead exemption, fall outside this category. To assets that may not be used for discharging debt, the law adds amounts deposited to an educational retirement account more than 365 days prior to the bankruptcy filing. These amounts are set aside to pay for the education of a child or grandchild of the debtor. The amount contributed prior to the 365 days may not be more than $5,000.

.09   Disclosures Under an Open-End Credit Plan

Attacking the causes of consumer credit problems from the perspective of consumer education, the law establishes a series of consumer warnings to appear on the consumer's bill. "In the case of an open end credit plan that requires a minimum monthly payment of not more than 4 percent of the balance on which finance charges are accruing, the following statement, located on the front of the billing statement, disclosed clearly and conspicuously: 'Minimum Payment Warning: Making only the minimum payment will increase the interest you pay and the time it takes to repay your balance. For example, making only the typical 2-percent minimum monthly payment on a balance of $1,000 at an interest rate of 17 percent would take 88 months to repay the balance in full. For an estimate of the time it would take to repay our balance, making only minimum payments, call this toll-free number: XXXXXX.' (the blank space to be filled in by the creditor.)"

A similar minimum payment warning is also required for open-end credit plans that require a minimum monthly payment of more than 4 percent. In certain cases the toll-free number will be a number at the Federal Trade Commission.

.10   Tax Deductibility of Interest on Home Mortgage

Deductibility of interest on a home mortgage is generally only limited if the acquisition debt exceeds $1 million. The bankruptcy law places a further limit on deductibility of home mortgage interest if the mortgage exceeds the fair market value of the personal residence. The rule stipulates that "in any case in which the extension of credit exceeds the fair market value (as defined under the Internal Revenue Code of 1986) of the dwelling, the interest on the portion of the credit extension that is greater than the fair market value of the dwelling is not tax deductible for Federal income tax purposes." The Truth in Lending Act includes a requirement that advertisements relating to home mortgage lending include a warning that interest on the balance of the mortgage in excess of fair market value is not tax deductible.

.11   Pro-Creditor Provisions

If the changes described so far are seen as negatives for debtors, the glass is definitely half-full for creditors. Sprinkled through the above changes limiting the abusive actions of debtors are pro-creditor provisions. Creditors have increased powers to move for the dismissal of a bankruptcy filing. The rules limiting the ability of debtors to repeatedly file for bankruptcy, thus enjoying the benefits of the automatic stay on collections, give more control to creditors. The antifraud provisions and the presumption of abuse by debtors whose income exceeds their state median income are further evidence of the benefits accruing to business from the new law.

.12   New CPA Practice Area

According to the law, 0.4 percent of individual Chapters 7 and 13 cases will be selected randomly for audit, as well as other cases "which reflect greater than average variances from the statistical norm of the district in which the schedules were filed." Such variances include higher income or greater expenses than the statistical norm for that district. The audits are to be conducted by Certified Public Accountants or Licensed Accountants. Specific auditing standards are to be developed for use in these audits. CPAs interested in more information about such work should contact the U.S. Attorney General's office, which has been directed to develop the applicable audit standards.

¶35,004   Federal Tax Aspects of Bankruptcy

Bankruptcy proceedings begin with the filing of a petition with the U.S. Bankruptcy Court. The filing of the petition creates a bankruptcy estate, which consists of all the assets (with certain exceptions) of the person filing the bankruptcy petition.

Note: A *person* in the tax law is an individual, a trust, estate, partnership, association, company, corporation, an officer or employee of a corporation, a member or employee of a partnership who is under a duty to surrender the property or rights to property to discharge the obligation.

Just as a separate taxpayer is created upon the death of a taxpayer, the taxpayer's estate, a separate taxable entity is created when a petition is filed by an individual under Chapter 7 or Chapter 11 of the Bankruptcy Code—the bankruptcy estate. The tax obligations of the person filing a bankruptcy petition, the debtor, vary depending on the bankruptcy chapter under which the petition is filed.

.01   Individuals in Chapter 7 or Chapter 11 Proceedings

For an individual debtor who files for bankruptcy under Chapter 7 or Chapter 11 of the Bankruptcy Code, a separate estate is created consisting of property that belonged to the debtor before the filing date. This bankruptcy estate is a new taxable entity, completely separate from the debtor as an individual taxpayer. The estate, under a Chapter 7 proceeding, is represented by a trustee. The trustee is appointed by the U.S. Bankruptcy Court to administer the estate and liquidate the *nonexempt assets* of the debtor. In a Chapter 11 case either the debtor remains in control of the assets as a debtor-in-possession or the bankruptcy court will appoint a trustee who will take control of the assets.

.02   The Bankruptcy Estate

The individual debtor must file income tax returns during the period of the bankruptcy proceedings; the income, deductions, or credits belonging to the separate bankruptcy estate should not be included. Also, the debts canceled because of bankruptcy should not be included in the debtor's income; as explained below, the bankruptcy estate must reduce certain losses, credits, and the basis in property, to the extent of these items by the amount of canceled debt. The debtor has the option of ending the tax year on the date before the bankruptcy petition is filed. This allows the tax due on the short-period return to be a claim on the bankruptcy estate.

If a bankruptcy case begins, but is later dismissed by the bankruptcy court, the estate is not treated as a separate entity and the debtor is treated as if the bankruptcy petitions had never been filed. When this occurs, the debtor files an amended return (Form 1040X) to replace any returns previously filed that should include items of income, deductions, or credits that were or would have been reported by the bankruptcy estate on its returns and were not reported on individual returns previously filed.

.03   Transfer of Assets to the Estate

All of the debtor's legal and equitable interests initially become property of the estate, and certain property can subsequently become exempt from the estate. A transfer, other than by sale or exchange of an asset from the debtor to the bankruptcy estate, is not treated as a disposition for income tax purposes. This means that the transfer does not result in gain or loss, recapture of deductions or credits, or acceleration of income or deductions. The transfer of an installment obligation, for example, to the estate would not accelerate gain under the rules for reporting installment sales. When the bankruptcy estate is terminated, the debtor is treated the same as the estate was regarding any assets transferred back to the debtor.

The Bankruptcy Abuse Prevention and Consumer Protection Act of 2005 added to the items included in the estate, in the case of Chapter 11 filings, all property that "the debtor acquires after the commencement of the case but before the case is closed, dismissed, or converted" as well as "earnings from services performed by the debtor after the commencement of the case but before the case is closed, dismissed, or converted."

The individual debtor cannot carry back any net operating loss or credit carryback from a year ending after the bankruptcy case has begun to any tax year ending before the case began. The estate, however, can carry the loss back to offset any prebankruptcy income.

.04 Election to End the Tax Year

If an individual debtor has assets, other than those exempt from the bankruptcy estate, the debtor can choose to end his or her tax year on the day before the filing of the bankruptcy case. Then the tax year is divided into two short tax years of fewer than 12 months each. The first year ends on the day before the filing date, and the second year begins with the filing date and ends on the date the tax year normally ends. Once made this choice cannot be changed. Any income tax liability for the first short tax year becomes an allowable claim arising before bankruptcy against the bankruptcy estate. If the tax liability is not paid in the bankruptcy proceeding, the liability is not canceled because it can be collected from the debtor as an individual. If the debtor does not choose to end the tax year, then no part of his or her tax liability for the year in which bankruptcy proceedings began can be collected from the estate.

If married, the debtor's spouse can also join in the choice to end the tax year, only if the two file a joint return for the first short tax year. These choices must be made by the due date for filing the return for the first short tax year. Once the choice is made, it cannot be revoked for the first year, but the choice does not mean that they must file a joint return for the second short tax year.

If the debtor's spouse files for bankruptcy later in the same year, he or she can also choose to end his or her tax year, regardless of whether he or she joined in the choice to end the debtor's tax years. Because each of the two has a separate bankruptcy estate, one or the other of them can have three short tax years in the same calendar year. If the debtor's spouse had joined in his or her choice, or if the debtor had not made the choice to end his/her tax year, the debtor can join in his or her spouse's choice. But if the debtor had made an election and his or her spouse did not join in the election, the debtor cannot join in the spouse's later election. This is because the debtor and spouse, having different tax years, could not file a joint return for a year ending on the date before the spouse's filing of bankruptcy.

.05   Employer Identification Number

The trustee or the debtor-in-possession must obtain an employer identification number (EIN) for a bankruptcy estate if the estate must file any form, statement, or document with the IRS. The trustee uses the EIN on any tax return filed for the bankruptcy estate including estimated tax returns. The Social Security number of the individual debtor cannot be used as the EIN for the bankruptcy estate.

.06   Determination of the Estate's Tax

The gross income of the bankruptcy estate includes any of the debtor's gross income to which the estate is entitled under the bankruptcy law. The estate's gross income also includes any income the estate is entitled to and receives or accrues after the beginning of the bankruptcy case. Gross income of the bankruptcy estate does not include amounts received or accrued by the debtor before the bankruptcy petition date.

The bankruptcy estate can deduct or take as a credit any expenses it pays or incurs, the same way that the debtor would have deducted or credited them had he or she continued in the same trade, business, or activity and actually paid or accrued the expenses. Allowable expenses include administrative expenses, such as attorney's fees and court costs.

The bankruptcy estate figures its taxable income the same way as individuals figure their taxable income. The estate can take one personal exemption and either individual itemized deductions, or the basic standard deduction for a married individual filing a separate return. The estate cannot take the higher standard deduction allowed for married persons filing separately who are 65 or older, or blind. The estate uses the rates for a married individual filing separately to figure the tax on its taxable income.

Bankruptcy law determines which of the debtor's assets become part of the bankruptcy estate. These assets are treated the same in the estate's hands as they were in the debtor's hands.

When the bankruptcy estate is terminated, any resulting transfer other than by sale or exchange of the estate's assets back to the debtor is not treated as a disposition. The transfer does not result in gain or loss, recapture of deductions or credits, or acceleration of income or deductions to the estate.

.07 Determination of Tax—Corporations

A bankrupt corporation—or a receiver, bankruptcy trustee, or assignee having possession of, or holding title to, substantially all the property or business of the corporation—files a Form 1120 for the tax year. After the return is filed, the Internal Revenue Service can redetermine the tax liability shown on the return. When the administrative remedies with the Service have been exhausted, any remaining tax issues can be litigated either in the bankruptcy court or in the U.S. Tax Court.

The trustee of the bankruptcy estate can request a determination of any unpaid liability of the estate for the taxes incurred during the administration of the case by the filing of a tax return and a request for such a determination with the IRS. Unless the return is fraudulent or contains a material misrepresentation, the trustee, the debtor, and any successor to the debtor are discharged from liability for the taxes upon payment of the taxes:

- As determined by the IRS.
- As determined by the bankruptcy court, after the completion of the IRS examination.
- As shown on the return if the IRS does not notify the trustee within 60 days after the request for the determination that the return has been selected for examination.
- As shown on the return, if the IRS does not complete the examination and notify the trustee of any tax due within 180 days after the request or any additional time permitted by the bankruptcy court.

To request a prompt determination of any unpaid tax liability of the estate, the trustee must file a written application for the determination with the IRS District Director for the district in which the bankruptcy case is pending. The application must be submitted in duplicated executed under the penalties of perjury. The trustee must submit with the application an exact copy of the return(s) filed by the trustee with the IRS for a completed tax period, and a statement of the name and location of the office where the return was filed. On the envelope must be written: *Do Not Open in Mail Room*.

The IRS examination agent will notify the trustee within 60 days from receipt of the application whether the return filed by the trustee has been selected for examination or has been accepted as filed. If the return is selected for examination, it will be examined as soon as possible. The examination function will notify the trustee of any tax due within 180 days from receipt of the application, or within any additional time permitted by the bankruptcy court.

.08   Discharge of Unpaid Tax

Debts are divided into two categories: dischargeable and nondischargeable. *Dischargeable debts* are those that the debtor is no longer personally liable to pay after the bankruptcy proceedings are concluded. *Nondischargeable debts* are those that are not canceled because of the bankruptcy proceedings. The debtor remains personally liable for their payment.

There is no discharge for the individual debtor at the termination of a bankruptcy case for taxes for which no return, a late return, or a fraudulent return was filed. Claims against the debtor for other taxes predating the bankruptcy petition by more than three years can be discharged. If the IRS has a lien on the debtor property, the property can be seized to collect discharged tax debts.

If the debtor completes all payments under a Chapter 13 debt adjustment plan for an individual with regular income, the court can grant a discharge of debts, including priority debts (described above). If the debtor fails to complete all payments under the plan, the taxes are not discharged although the court can grant a discharge of other debts in limited circumstances.

If a debt is canceled or forgiven, other than as a gift or bequest, the debtor must include the canceled amount in gross income for tax purposes. A debt includes any indebtedness for which the debtor is liable or which attaches to property the debtor holds. However, a canceled debt should not be included in gross income if any of the following situations applies:

- The cancellation takes place in a bankruptcy case under the U.S. Bankruptcy Code.
- The cancellation takes place when the debtor is insolvent.
- The canceled debt is qualified farm debt incurred in operating a farm.
- The canceled debt is qualified real property business indebtedness, i.e., debt connected with business real property.

If a cancellation of debt occurs in a Chapter 11 bankruptcy case, the bankruptcy exclusion takes precedence over the insolvency, qualified farm debt, or qualified real property business indebtedness exclusions. To the extent that the taxpayer is insolvent, the insolvency exclusion takes precedence over qualified term debt or qualified real property business indebtedness exclusions.

A bankruptcy case is a case under Chapter 11 of the U.S. Code, but only if the debtor is under the jurisdiction of the court and the cancellation of the debt is granted by the court or occurs as a result of a plan approved by the court. None of the debt canceled in a bankruptcy case is included in the debtor's gross income in the year canceled. Instead, certain losses, credits, and basis of property must be reduced by the amount of excluded income, but not below zero. These losses, credits, and basis in property are called *tax attributes*.

A debtor is insolvent when and to the extent that his or her liabilities exceed the fair market value of the debtor's assets. The liabilities and the fair market value of assets are determined immediately before the cancellation of a debt to determine whether the debtor is insolvent and the amount by which he or she is insolvent. Gross income debt canceled when insolvent is excluded, but only up to the amount of the insolvency. The amount excluded must be used to reduce certain tax attributes.

.09   Tax Attributes

Certain deduction and credit carryovers and elections that the debtor made in earlier years are taken over by the bankruptcy estate when the petition is filed. These include carryovers of deductions, losses, and credits, the debtor's method of accounting, and the basis and holding period of assets, referred to as tax attributes.

When the estate is terminated, the debtor assumes any remaining tax attributes that were taken over by the estate as well as any attributes arising during the administration of the estate. The bankruptcy estate's income tax returns are open upon written request for inspection by the individual debtor. The disclosure is necessary so that the debtor can properly figure the amount and nature of the tax attributes, if any, that the debtor must assume when the bankruptcy estate is terminated. In addition, the debtor's income tax returns for the year the bankruptcy case begins and for earlier years are open to inspection by or disclosure to the bankruptcy estate's trustee.

.10   Reduction of Tax Attributes

If a debtor excludes canceled debt from income because it is canceled in a bankruptcy case or during insolvency, he or she must use the excluded amount to reduce certain tax attributes. Tax attributes include the basis of certain assets and the losses and credits listed below. By reducing these tax attributes, taxes on the canceled debt are in part postponed instead of being entirely forgiven. This prevents an excessive tax benefit arising from the debt cancellation.

If a separate bankruptcy estate was created, the trustee or debtor-in-possession must reduce the estate's attributes by the canceled debt, but not below zero.

The amount of canceled debt is used to reduce the tax attributes in the order listed below. However, the debtor can choose to use all or a part of the amount of canceled debt to first reduce the basis of depreciable property before reducing the other tax attributes.

Reduction of tax attributes is managed in the sequence described next.

Net Operating Loss. NOLs are handled in this order:

1. Any net operating loss for the tax year in which the debt cancellation takes place.
2. Any net operating loss carryover to that tax year.

General Business Credit Carryovers. Any carryovers to or from the tax year of the debt cancellation of amounts used to determine the general business credit are reduced.

Minimum Tax Credit. Any minimum tax credit that is available at the beginning of the tax year following the tax year of the debt cancellation is reduced. This only applies to debt canceled in tax years beginning after 1993.

Capital Losses. Any net capital loss for the tax year of the debt cancellation, and any capital loss carryover to that year are reduced.

Basis. The basis (see the discussion below) of the debtor's property is reduced. This reduction applies to the basis of both depreciable and nondepreciable property.

Passive Activity Loss and Credit Carryovers. Reduce any passive activity loss or credit carryover from the tax year of the debt cancellation. This applies to debt canceled in tax years beginning after 1993.

Foreign Tax Credit. Any carryover to or from the tax year of the debt cancellation of an amount used to determine the foreign tax credit or the Puerto Rico and other possessions' tax credits is reduced.

Except for the credit carryovers, the tax attributes are reduced one dollar for each one dollar of canceled debt that is excluded from income. The credit carryovers are reduced by 33 ½ cents for each dollar of canceled debt that is excluded from income. The required reductions in tax attributes are to be made after figuring the tax for the year of the debt cancellation. In reducing net operating losses and capital losses, the loss for the tax year of the debt cancellation is reduced first, and then any loss carryover to that year in the order in which the carryovers are taken into account for the tax year of the debt cancellation.

In an individual bankruptcy under Chapter 7 (liquidation) or Chapter 11 (reorganization) of the U.S. Code, the required reduction of tax attributes must be made to the attributes of the bankruptcy estate, a separate taxable entity resulting from the filing of the case. Also, the trustee of the bankruptcy estate must make the choice of whether to reduce the basis of depreciable property first before reducing other tax attributes.

.11   Basis Reduction

If any amount of the debt cancellation is used to reduce the basis of assets, the following rules apply to the extent indicated.

The reduction in basis is to be made at the beginning of the tax years following the tax year of the debt cancellation. The reduction applies to property held at that time.

Bankruptcy and Insolvency Reduction Limit. The reduction in basis because of canceled debt in bankruptcy or in insolvency cannot be more than the total basis of property held immediately after the debt cancellation, minus the total liabilities immediately after the cancellation. This limit does not apply if an election is made to reduce basis before reducing other attributes.

Exempt Property Under Chapter 11. If debt is canceled in a bankruptcy case under Chapter 11, no reduction is made in basis for property that the debtor treats as exempt property.

Election to Reduce Basis First. The estate in the case of an individual bankruptcy under Chapter 7 or 11 can choose to reduce the basis or depreciable property before reducing any other tax attributes. This reduction of the basis of depreciable property cannot be more than the total basis of depreciable property held at the beginning of the tax year following the tax year of the debt cancellation.

Depreciable property means any property subject to depreciation, but only if a reduction of the basis will reduce the amount of depreciation or amortization otherwise allowable for the period immediately following the basis reduction. The debtor may choose to treat as depreciable property any real property that is stock in trade or is held primarily for sale to customers in the ordinary course of trade or business. The debtor must make this choice on the tax return for the tax year of the debt cancellation, and once the choice is made, he or she can only revoke it with IRS approval. If the debtor establishes reasonable cause, he or she can make the choice with an amended return or claim for refund or credit.

An election should be made to reduce the basis of depreciable property before reducing other tax attributes as well as the election to treat real property inventory as appreciable property. If any basis in property is reduced and is later sold or otherwise disposed of again, the part of the gain that is attributable to this basis reduction is taxable as ordinary income. The ordinary income part can be figured by treating the amount of the basis reduction as a depreciation deduction. A determination is made of what would have been straight-line depreciation as though there had been no basis reduction for debt cancellation.

.12   Attribute Carryovers

The bankruptcy estate must treat its tax attributes the same way that the debtor would have treated them. These items must be determined as of the first day of the debtor's tax year in which the bankruptcy case begins. The bankruptcy estate gets the following tax attributes from the debtor.

1. Net operating carryovers.
2. Carryovers of excess charitable contributions.
3. Recovery of tax benefit items.
4. Credit carryovers.
5. Capital loss carryovers.
6. Basis, holding period, and character of assets.
7. Method of accounting.
8. Passive activity loss and credit carryovers.
9. Unused at-risk deductions.
10. Other tax attributes as provided in regulations.

Certain tax attributes of the estate must be reduced by any excluded income from cancellation of debt occurring in a bankruptcy proceeding. If the bankruptcy estate has any tax attributes at the time it is terminated, they are assumed by the debtor.

.13   Bankruptcy Court Jurisdiction

The bankruptcy court has authority to determine the amount or legality of any tax imposed on the debtor for the estate, including any fine, penalty, or addition to the tax, whether or not the tax was previously assessed or paid.

The bankruptcy court does not have authority to determine the amount or legality of a tax, fine, penalty, or addition to taxes contested before and finally decided by a court administrative tribunal of competent jurisdiction before the date of filing the bankruptcy petition. Also, the bankruptcy court does not have authority to decide the right of the bankruptcy estate for a tax refund until the trustee of the estate properly requests the refund from the IRS and either the Service determined the refund or 120 days pass after the date of the request.

If the debtor has already claimed a refund or credit for an overpayment of taxes on a properly filed return or claim for refund, the trustee can rely on that claim. Otherwise, if the credit or refund was not claimed by the debtor, the trustee can make the request by filing the appropriate original or amended return or form with the District Director in the district in which the bankruptcy case is pending. For overpayment of taxes of the bankruptcy estate incurred during the administration of the case, the trustee can use a properly executed tax return form as a claim for refund or credit.

The IRS examination agent, if requested by the trustee or debtor-in-possession, examines the appropriate amended return, claim, or original return filed by the trustee on an expedited basis, and completes the examination and notify the trustee of its decision within 120 days from the date of filing of the claim.

.14   Employment Tax

The trustee or debtor-in-possession in a Chapter 11 case must withhold income and Social Security taxes and file employment tax returns for any wages paid by the trustee or debtor, including wage claims paid as administrative expenses. Until these employment taxes are deposited as required by the IRS, they should be set apart in a separate bank account to ensure that funds are available to satisfy the liability. If the employment taxes are not paid as required, the trustee can be held personally liable for payment of the taxes.

The trustee has the duty to prepare and file Form W-2, "Wage and Tax Statement," in connection with wage claims paid by the trustee, regardless of whether the claims accrued before or during bankruptcy. If the debtor fails to prepare and file Form W-2 for wages paid before bankruptcy, the trustee should instruct the employees to file an IRS Form 4852, Substitute for Form W-2.

The debtor's income tax returns for the year the bankruptcy case begins and for earlier years are, upon written request, open to inspection by or disclosure to the trustee. If the bankruptcy case was not voluntary, disclosure cannot be made before the bankruptcy court has entered an order for relief, unless the court rules the disclosure is needed for determining whether relief should be ordered.

.15   Statute of Limitations for Collection

In a Chapter 11 bankruptcy case, the period of limitations for collection of taxes—10 years after assessment—is suspended for the period during which the IRS is prohibited from assessing or collecting, plus six months thereafter.

.16   Passive and At-Risk Activities

For bankruptcy cases beginning on or after November 9, 1992, passive activity carryover losses and credits and unused at-risk deductions are treated as tax attributes that the debtor passes to the bankruptcy estate and the estate passes back to the debtor when the estate terminates. Transfers to the debtor, other than by sale or exchange, of interests in passive or at-risk activities are treated as exchanges that are not taxable. These transfers include the return of exempt property to the debtor and the abandonment of estate property to the debtor.

If a bankruptcy case begins before November 9, 1992, and ends on or after that date, the debtor and the trustee for an individual Chapter 7 case and the debtor-in-possession for a Chapter 11 case can elect to have these provisions apply. In a Chapter 7 case, the election is made jointly by the debtor and the trustee of the bankruptcy estate. In a Chapter 11 case, the election is incorporated in the bankruptcy plan.

The bankruptcy estate is allowed a deduction for administrative expenses and any fees or charges assessed to it. These expenses are deductible as itemized deductions subject to the 2 percent floor on the miscellaneous itemized deductions. Administrative expenses attributable to the conduct of a trade or business by the bankruptcy estate or the production of the estate's rents or royalties are deductible in arriving at adjusted gross income.

The expenses are subject to disallowance under other provisions of the Internal Revenue Code, such as disallowing certain capital expenditures, taxes, or expenses relating to tax-exempt interest. These expenses can only be deducted by the estate, never by the debtor.

If the administrative expenses of the bankruptcy estate are more than its gross income for the tax year, the excess amount can be carried back three years and forward seven years. The amounts can only be carried back or forward to a tax year of the estate, never to the debtor's tax year. The excess amount to be carried back or forward is treated like a net operating loss and must first be carried back to the earliest year possible.

The bankruptcy estate can change its accounting period tax year once without getting IRS approval. This allows the trustee of the estate to close the estate tax year early, before the expected termination of the estate. The trustee can then file a return for the first short tax year to a quick determination of the estates tax liability. If the bankruptcy estate itself has a net operating loss, separate from any losses passing to the estate from the debtor under the attribute carryover rules, the bankruptcy estate can carry the loss back not only to its own earlier tax years but also to the debtor's tax years before the year the bankruptcy case began. The estate can also carry back excess credits, such as the business credit, to the prebankruptcy years.

CHAPTER 36

Depreciation

¶36,000 Overview

Depreciation is an accounting and tax convention used to write-off the cost or other basis of long-lived assets, generally over more than one year. In the case of financial accounting, the purpose of depreciation is to match the expense of the assets against the revenue generated by their use on the income statement and to reflect wear and tear, age, deterioration, and obsolescence on the balance sheet. In the case of tax depreciation, it is a statutory method of expensing the basis of assets and is an integral part of the federal government's fiscal policy. This chapter primarily addresses tax basis depreciation. For book depreciation, see ¶1006.02. Though the basic rules covering tax depreciation have been in place since 1986, the status of two forms of accelerated depreciation, one elective and the other automatic, have been the subject of continual revision in recent years as part of a Congressional response to economic conditions. The mechanics of these two forms of accelerated depreciation, referred to as Section 179 and first-year bonus depreciation are explained below.

¶36,001 Types of Property

To determine if property may produce a depreciation deduction, the property must be used in business or for the production of income and classified as either tangible or intangible.

Tangible property is property that can be seen or touched. There are two main types of tangible property, real property, such as land, buildings, and generally anything built or constructed on land, growing on land, or attached to the land;

and personal property including cars, trucks, machinery, furniture, equipment and anything that is not real property.

Intangible property is generally any property that has value but cannot be seen or touched. It includes items such as computer software, copyrights, franchises, patents, trademarks, and trade names. Generally, if the cost of intangible property is to be written off over a number of years the straight line method of amortization is used. It allows for the same amount of amortization each year.

In general, only the owner using the property for business or for producing income may claim depreciation or amortization.

Only property meeting all the following requirements may be depreciated.

1. It must be used in business or held to produce income.
2. It must be expected to last more than one year. In other words, it must have a useful life that extends substantially beyond the year it is placed in service.
3. It must be something that wears out, decays, gets used up, becomes obsolete, or loses its value from natural or economic causes.

¶36,002   What Cannot Be Depreciated

Property placed in service and disposed of in the same year may not be depreciated. Inventory and assets held for sale may not be depreciated.

.01   Tangible Property

The following are types of tangible property that cannot be depreciated, even though they are used in business or held to produce income:

1. The cost of land may not be depreciated because land does not wear out, become obsolete, or get used up. The cost of land generally includes the cost of clearing, grading, planting, and landscaping, because these expenses are all part of the cost of the land itself.
2. Inventory is any property held primarily for sale to customers in the ordinary course of business and may not be depreciated.
3. Generally, containers are part of inventory and cannot be depreciated.
4. Leased property may be depreciated only if the incidents of ownership for the property are retained. Leased property to use in business or for the production of income cannot be depreciated because the incidents of ownership are not retained. A lessor generally can depreciate its cost even if the lessee has agreed to preserve, replace, renew, and maintain the property. However, if the lease provides that the lessee is to maintain the property and return to the lessor the same property or its equivalent in value at the expiration of the lease in as good condition and value as when leased, the cost of the property may not be depreciated.

"Incidents of ownership" include the legal title, the legal obligation to pay for it, the responsibility to pay its maintenance and operating expenses, the duty to pay any taxes and the risk of loss if the property is destroyed, condemned, or diminishes in value through obsolescence or exhaustion.

5. Generally, a deduction for depreciation may not be taken on a term interest in property created or acquired after July 27, 1989, for any period during which the remainder interest is held, directly or indirectly, by a person related to the owner.

.02 Intangible Property

The depreciation of intangible property is referred to as amortization. Intangible assets, including goodwill and going-concern value, franchises (except sports franchises), trade names and trademarks, copyrights, patents, and covenants not to compete may be amortized over a 15-year period for tax purposes. This rule applies only to assets acquired in connection with the purchase of a business in the case of goodwill, covenants not to compete, copyrights, and patents. Note: for financial reporting purposes FASB No. 142 discontinued the amortization of goodwill. Other intangible assets may be amortizable if they have determinable lives.

¶36,003 Special Timing Considerations

.01 When Depreciation Begins and Ends

Property may be depreciated when it is placed in service for use in a trade or business or for the production of income. It is no longer depreciable when the cost has been fully recovered or other basis or when it is retired from service, whichever happens first.

For depreciation purposes, property is placed in service when it is ready and available for a specific use, whether in a trade or business, for the production of income, a tax-exempt activity, or a personal activity. Even if the property is not being used, it is in service when it is ready and available for its specific use. This last point was reaffirmed by the courts in 2015. The U.S. District Court in *Stine LLC v. U.S.* ruled that a building was placed in service when it was ready to occupy, not, as the IRS contended, when the doors were finally opened for business.

Property permanently withdrawn from use in trade or business or from use in the production of income is considered retired from service and is no longer depreciable. Property can be retired either when sold or exchanged, when it is abandoned or when it is destroyed.

.02   Bonus Depreciation for New Property

The Tax Cuts and Jobs Act increased the 50-percent bonus depreciation rate to 100 percent for property acquired and placed in service after September 27, 2017, and before January 1, 2023. The rate phases down thereafter. Property used by rate-regulated utilities, and property of certain motor vehicle, boat, and farm machinery retail and lease businesses that use floor financing indebtedness, is excluded from bonus depreciation. In general, the bonus depreciation percentage rates are as follows:

- 100 percent for property placed in service after September 27, 2017, and before January 1, 2023;
- 80 percent for property placed in service after December 31, 2022, and before January 1, 2024;
- 60 percent for property placed in service after December 31, 2023, and before January 1, 2025;
- 40 percent for property placed in service after December 31, 2024, and before January 1, 2026;
- 20 percent for property placed in service after December 31, 2025, and before January 1, 2027; and
- 0 percent (bonus expires) for property placed in service after December 31, 2026;

In 2015, bonus or first-year depreciation was extended for five years. Beginning in 2008, in response to worsening economic conditions, Congress instituted a special 50 percent bonus depreciation for new tangible property. The amount was increased to 100 percent for 2011 and then returned to 50 percent for 2012 to 2017. The bonus rate is reduced from 50 percent to 40 for property placed in service in 2018 and to 30 percent for property placed in service in 2019. The same law made permanent the Section 179 expensing limit at $500,000 with a $2 million overall investment limit before phaseout; both amounts are indexed for inflation beginning in 2016. See amounts for 2024 below.

The 100 percent or 50 percent bonus depreciation is not an election but like regular MACRS depreciation is automatic unless an affirmative election is made with the IRS not to claim the bonus depreciation. This causes a potential trap for taxpayers who neglect to take the first-year depreciation. When the asset in question is eventually disposed of, the IRS will apply the allowed or allowable test to determine the proper basis for computing gain or loss. The allowable depreciation will include both the proper amount of MACRS cost recovery and the available 100 percent or 50 percent first-year depreciation. Thus, failure to elect out of the 100 percent or 50 percent depreciation means the IRS will assume the depreciation was still allowable and will be used to reduce an asset's basis as if it had been claimed—increasing the resulting gain or minimizing the resulting loss. If a taxpayer elects out of the bonus depreciation this is done for a whole class of property (for example, five-year property) not on an item by item basis. Thus, special care should be exercised if the bonus depreciation is not desired.

.03   Allowed or Allowable Rule

The IRS applies a special convention to overcome the fact that the statute of limitations on auditing tax returns is generally three years, while fixed assets are depreciated over periods of three, five, seven, ten and up to 39 years. The convention has the unfortunate name of the "allowed or allowable rule." Depreciation is *allowed* in the amount you deducted on your tax return, whether or not this was the correct amount. The amount *allowable* is the amount the law allows. When depreciable property is sold its original cost or basis is reduced by depreciation, arriving at its book value or adjusted basis. This amount is used to compute any gain or loss on the sale. For each year the asset was depreciated, you are required to use the *larger* (greater) of the allowed or the allowable amount of depreciation when computing the basis of the asset sold. This will ensure that if you took too much depreciation you cannot later claim only the amount allowed by law when computing the gain. It also means that if you took no depreciation or too little, it will be assumed you took the correct amount when determining the basis of the asset sold. This system ensures you will pay tax on the maximum gain, providing the greatest amount of tax to the U.S. Treasury.

¶36,004   Using the Section 179 Deduction

The Section 179 deduction is a means of recovering the cost of property through a current deduction rather than through depreciation. Section 179 of the Internal Revenue Code allows for the deduction of all or part of the cost of certain qualifying property in the year it is placed in service. This would be done instead of recovering the cost by taking depreciation deductions over a specified recovery period. However, there are limits on the amount that can be deducted in a year.

.01   What Costs Can and Cannot Be Deducted

The Section 179 deduction may be used for the cost of qualifying property acquired for use in trade or business, but not for the cost of property held only for the production of income (rental, investment).

Only the cost of property acquired by purchase for use in business qualifies for the Section 179 deduction. The cost of property acquired from a related person or group may not qualify.

If an asset is purchased with cash and a trade-in, a Section 179 deduction can be claimed based only on the amount of cash paid. The Section 179 deduction does not include the adjusted basis of the trade-in used in the purchase.

.02   Qualifying Property

Property qualifying for the Section 179 deduction is depreciable property and includes the following.

1. Tangible personal property.
2. Other tangible property (except buildings and their structural components) used as:
   a. An integral part of manufacturing, production, or extraction or of furnishing transportation, communications, electricity, gas, water, or sewage disposal services,
   b. A research facility used in connection with any of the activities in above, or
   c. A facility used in connection with any of the activities for the bulk storage of fungible commodities.
3. Single purpose agricultural (livestock) or horticultural structures.
4. Storage facilities (except buildings and their structural components) used in connection with distributing petroleum or any primary product of petroleum.

Generally, a Section 179 deduction may not be claimed based on the cost of leased property or real estate. However, a Section 179 deduction may be claimed based on the cost of the following:

1. Property manufactured or produced and leased to others.
2. Property purchased and leased to others if both of the following apply.
   a. The term of the lease (including options to renew) is less than half of the property's class life.
   b. For the first 12 months after the property is transferred to the lessee, the total business deductions allowed on the property (other than rent and reimbursed amounts) is more than 15 percent of the rental income from the property.

The Tax Cuts and Jobs Act increased Section 179 dollar limitation to $1 million and the investment limitation to $2.5 million for tax years beginning after 2017. The definition of qualified real property eligible for expensing is redefined to include improvements to the interior of any nonresidential real property ("qualified improvement property"), as well as roofs, heating, ventilation, and air-conditioning property, fire protection and alarm systems, and security systems installed on such property. The exclusion from expensing for tangible personal property used in connection with lodging facilities (such as residential rental property) is eliminated. The $25,000 Section 179 expensing limit on certain heavy vehicles is adjusted for inflation after 2018.

Qualified leasehold improvement property is a category of interior improvements to nonresidential real estate, made pursuant to a lease. Excluded are elevators and escalators among others. Qualified restaurant property is defined as improvements to a building if more than 50 percent of the building's space is allocated to restaurant activities. Qualified retail improvement property is improvements made to the interior of a nonresidential retail building. Elevators and escalators are excluded.

.03 Partial Business Use

When property is used for both business and nonbusiness purposes, the Section 179 deduction may be used if the property is used more than 50 percent for business in the year it was placed in service. The part of the cost of the property that is for business use is the cost of the property multiplied by the percentage of business use. The result is the business cost.

.04 Nonqualifying Property

Generally, the Section 179 deduction cannot be claimed on the cost of any of the following.

1. Property held only for the production of income (rental, investment).
2. Real property, including buildings and their structural components.
3. Property acquired from certain groups or persons.
4. Air conditioning or heating units.
5. Certain property used predominantly outside the U.S.
6. Property used predominantly to furnish lodging or in connection with the furnishing of lodging.
7. Property used by certain tax-exempt organizations.
8. Property used by governmental units.
9. Property used by foreign persons or entities.
10. Certain property leased to others by a noncorporate lessor.

.05 Electing the Deduction

The Section 179 deduction is not automatic. An individual must elect to take a Section 179 deduction. For purposes of the Section 179 deduction, property is considered placed in service in the year it is first made ready and available for a specific use. If property is placed in service in a use that does not qualify it for the Section 179 deduction, it cannot later qualify in another year even if it is changed to business use. Records must be kept that show the specific identification of each piece of qualifying Section 179 property. These records must show how the property was acquired, the person it was acquired from and when it was placed in service.

.06   How to Figure the Deduction

The total cost a business can elect to deduct under Section 179 is $1,220,000 in 2024. This maximum dollar limit applies to each taxpayer, not to each business. A taxpayer who is the owner of an interest(s) in a pass-through entity such as an S corporation, partnership or limited liability company, must aggregate pass-through Section 179 amounts from these entities and subject them to the limitations at the taxpayer level. The full amount does not have to be claimed. A percentage of the business cost of qualifying property may be deducted under Section 179. Then it may be possible to depreciate any difference in the cost not deducted under Section 179. If more than one item of qualifying property is acquired and placed in service during the same year, it is possible to divide the deduction among the items in any way, as long as the total deduction is not more than the limits.

If there is only one item of qualifying property and it does not cost more than the dollar limit, the deduction is limited to the lesser of the following.

1.   An individual's taxable income from trade or business.
2.   The cost of the item.

The Section 179 deduction must be figured before figuring the 100 percent bonus deduction or regular MACRS depreciation deduction, but must be deducted after the bonus and MACRS depreciation to ensure the effectiveness of the income limitation (Section 179 expense may not produce a NOL). The amount deducted under Section 179 must be subtracted from the business/investment cost of the qualifying property. The result is called the unadjusted basis and is the amount used to figure any depreciation deduction.

.07   Deduction Limits

The Section 179 deduction cannot be more than the business cost of the qualifying property. In addition, the following limits must be applied to the Section 179 deduction:

1.   Maximum dollar limit. The total cost of Section 179 property that can be elected for deduction cannot be more than the amounts listed above.
2.   Investment limit. If the cost of the qualifying Section 179 property placed in service in a year is over $3,050,000, the maximum dollar limit for each dollar over that amount must be reduced (but not below zero). The inflation-adjusted limitation for the 2024 tax year is $3,050,000.
3.   Taxable income limit. The total cost that can be deducted each year is limited to the taxable income from the active conduct of any trade or business dur-

ing the year. Generally, an individual is considered to be actively conducting a trade or business if he or she meaningfully participates in the management or operations of the trade or business. When computing this income limit, the order of the components of the depreciation deduction is important. First deduct regular MACRS depreciation, then bonus depreciation, and last deduct Section 179 depreciation. This will ensure that no more than the allowable amount of Section 179 depreciation will be permitted to zero out the income but not produce (or increase) a net operating loss (NOL).

.08   When Costs Are Capitalized

Whether an asset must be depreciated and using what method is a key question whenever tangible property is acquired. In situations where an existing asset is either improved or repaired important questions arise about the proper treatment of those costs. In particular, should they be capitalized and depreciated or expensed. The IRS finalized its regulations clarifying the rules for deducting or capitalizing expenditures to tangible property "Tangible Property Regulations" in September 2013 and they became effective on January 1, 2014. These regulations finalized a project initiated in 2006 to clarify this always-contentious area of tax law. The regulations under Sections 162 and 263 are extensive with many useful examples. When costs are incurred to improve an existing asset, those costs are generally capitalized. In its regulations (Reg. §1.263(a)-1) the IRS states its starting position which is that any amount paid for new buildings or for permanent improvements or betterments made to increase the value of property or paid to restore the property should be capitalized unless there is a rule that permits it to be expensed. This is consistent with the tax maxim that deductions are a matter of legislative grace: nothing may be deducted unless a specific provision says it can. In particular, deductible business expenses must be ordinary and necessary and those are terms of art, crafted by numerous court decisions.

In many cases the judgment as to the effect of a cost's future benefits is difficult to make. At what point in a building's roof repair, for example, are the costs considered a normal repair and expensed, or the costs are extensive enough that they must be added to the cost of the building and depreciated? While the general rules have not changed, the IRS has tried to give clarity to some of the terms used in describing the type of costs that should be capitalized, including betterment, restoration, rehabilitation, and improvement. For costs that may be expensed, the IRS gives examples of repairs and routine maintenance.

The regulations (Reg. §1.263(a)-1) provide the following examples of capital expenditure:

1.   An amount paid to acquire or produce a unit of real or personal tangible property. See Reg. §1.263(a)-2.
2.   An amount paid to improve a unit of real or personal tangible property. See Reg. §1.263(a)-3.
3.   An amount paid to acquire or create intangibles. See Reg. §1.263(a)-4.
4.   An amount paid or incurred to facilitate an acquisition of a trade or business, a change in capital structure of a business entity, and certain other transactions. See Reg. §1.263(a)-5.

Definitions of key terms are also provided in these regulations.

One feature of these regulations that should draw the attention of accountants is the introduction of *de minimis* rules, permitting automatic expensing if certain conditions are met. The *de minimis* rules are found at Reg. §1.263(a)-1(f) and provide the following conditions when costs incurred to acquire or produce a unit of real estate or personal property may be expensed (though it would otherwise be capitalized):

- The taxpayer has an "applicable financial statement," defined generally to mean an audited financial statement—audited by a CPA—and accompanied by the CPA's opinion (though it is not specified whether it must be an unqualified opinion or may be a qualified or some lesser opinion; the regulation uses the anachronistic term "certified" audit). Specifically mentioned are audited financial statements that are required to be filed with the SEC. But for non-public companies it includes audited financial statements required for credit purposes, or used for reporting to shareholders, or any other "substantial non-tax purpose."
- In addition, the company must have a written policy for non-tax purposes, specifying a threshold cost, above which items are capitalized and below which they are expensed.
- The amounts expensed on the tax return must also have been expensed on the taxpayer's audited financial statements in accordance with the written statement's criteria.
- The final requirement stipulates two dollar amounts as limits for when an item may be expensed. The *de minimis* expensing exception applies to the aggregate amount expensed for the year under this exception if that amount is equal to or less than the greater of two amounts. The first is less than or equal to 0.1 percent of the taxpayer's gross receipts for the taxable year, as determined for tax purposes. (Practitioners should note that gross receipts for tax purposes is not the same as gross income. Reg. §1.61-(3)(a) defines gross income as sales minus cost of goods sold.) The 0.1 percent limit applies to gross receipts and not gross income. The second is 2 percent of the taxpayer's total depreciation and amortiza-

tion expense for the taxable year as determined in its applicable financial statement. So the aggregate amount expensed under the *de minimis* exception must be equal to or less than either 0.1 percent of gross receipts or 2 percent of total depreciation and amortization expense, whichever of those two amounts is greater.

The IRS provides these additional examples of capital expenditures, which include amounts paid:

- to acquire or create interests in land, such as easements, life estates, mineral interests, timber rights, zoning variances, or other interests in land.
- under an agreement between bondholders or shareholders of a corporation to be used in a reorganization of the corporation or voluntary contributions by shareholders to the capital of the corporation for any corporate purpose.
- by a holding company to carry out a guaranty of dividends at a specified rate on the stock of a subsidiary corporation for the purpose of securing new capital for the subsidiary and increasing the value of its stockholdings in the subsidiary. This amount must be added to the cost of the stock in the subsidiary.
- to sell property.

The regulations present numerous examples that should be consulted if there is a question regarding a specific transaction. Following is Example 14 from Reg. §1.263-3, illustrating the application of the rules to the purchase of office equipment and laptop computers.

Example. "N provides consulting services to its customers. In Year 1, N pays amounts to purchase 50 laptop computers. Each laptop computer is a unit of property under Reg. §1.263(a)-3(e), costs $400, and has an economic useful life of more than 12 months. Also in Year 1, N purchases 50 office chairs to be used by its employees. Each office chair is a unit of property that costs $100. N has an applicable financial statement (as defined in Reg. §1.263(a)-1(f)(4)) and N has a written accounting policy at the beginning Year 1 to expense amounts paid for units of property costing $500 or less. N treats amounts paid for property costing $500 or less as an expense on its applicable financial statement in Year 1. (ii) The laptop computers are not materials or supplies under paragraph (c) of this section. Therefore, the amounts N pays for the computers must generally be capitalized under Reg. §1.263(a)-2(d) as amounts paid for the acquisition of tangible property. The office chairs are materials and supplies under paragraph (c)(1)(iv) of this section. Thus, under paragraph (a)(1) of this section, the amounts paid for the office chairs are deductible in the taxable year in which they are first used in N's business. However, under paragraph (f) of this section, if N properly elects to apply the *de minimis* safe harbor under Reg. §1.263(a)-1(f) to amounts paid in Year 1, then N must apply the *de minimis* safe harbor under Reg. §1.263(a)-1(f) to amounts paid for the computers and the office chairs, rather than treat the office chairs as the costs of materials and supplies under Reg. §1.162-3. Under the *de minimis* safe harbor, N may not capitalize the amounts paid for the computers under Reg. §1.263(a)-2 nor treat the office chairs as materials and supplies under Reg. §1.162-3. Instead, in accordance with Reg. §1.263(a)-1(f)(3)(iv), under Reg. §1.162-1, N may deduct the amounts paid for the computers and the office chairs in the taxable year paid."

Another area where the IRS attempted to shed more light is on the meaning of a "unit of property." The general rule is that a taxpayer must capitalize costs that improve a unit of property. An example of a unit of property is building systems such as elevators, plumbing systems, HVAC systems, and other structural components, as well as the building structure itself. The regulations provide numerous specific examples that can be helpful in determining the proper accounting treatment. This topic is covered in more detail later in this chapter in the section on cost segregation studies. Additional information is also provided in Chapter 38, "Business Use of a Home," on determining the basis of an asset.

Additional expensing elections will benefit small businesses (those with less than $10 million in assets or $10 million in annual sales). The regulations offer a safe harbor election allowing a business to deduct expenditures up to $500 ($5,000 if the taxpayer has an applicable, e.g. "audited," financial statement). This is not considered a change in accounting method and so the election can be made on an annual basis. The election is made on the tax return by attaching a statement titled "Section 1.263(a)-1(f) *De Minimis* Safe Harbor Election."

The regulations also clarify and facilitate the deduction of materials and supplies. The category "materials and supplies" includes tangible property that is either used or consumed and that is not inventory. This includes spare parts, lubricants, fuel and other materials expected to be consumed in the following 12 months. It also includes a unit of property that has a purchase price or production cost of $200 or less.

When applying these regulations, the CPA must determine whether the method applied constitutes a change of accounting method or coincides with the method traditionally used by the taxpayer. In most cases it is assumed that any change will be a change in accounting method. This will be a case-by-case determination. When a change in procedure constitutes a change in accounting method, a Form 3115, Application for Change in Accounting Method, is generally required. Its preparation will typically require the computation of a Section 481 adjustment. Fortunately, for small businesses—those with assets less than $10 million or annual sales of less than $10 million—the IRS made an exception and no Form 3115 is needed (see below).

A change in accounting method produces a "section 481 adjustment." The Section 481(a) adjustment takes into account how the company treated certain expenditures in years before the effective date of the change in accounting methods to avoid duplication or omission of amounts in taxable income. A taxpayer that changes a method of accounting must apply the provisions of Section 481, which accounts for how the taxpayer treated the items being changed in prior years to avoid duplication of deductions or omission of income. To avoid duplication or omission, taxpayers must follow the rules of Sections 446(e) and 481 when applying the final tangible property regulations. For detailed instructions for filing applications for changes in methods of accounting under the tangibles regulations, see Rev. Proc. 2015-13 and sections 6.37-6.40 and 10.11 of Rev. Proc. 2015-14. This volume also contains a chapter on changes in accounting methods, providing general guidance and background information.

Rev. Proc. 2015-14 provides detailed guidance on the accounting method changes related to:

Tangible property (sec. 10.11)
Removal costs (sec. 10.03)
Disposition of building or structural component (sec. 6.33)
Disposition of tangible depreciable assets (other than buildings) (sec. 6.39)

It also provides tables of Designated Automatic Accounting Method Change Numbers (DCNs) to be used on Form 3115 to notify the IRS of the specific nature of the change. The IRS has assigned Designated Automatic Accounting Method Change Numbers (DCNs) to specific types of accounting method changes required by the final tangible property regulations. A few common DCNs are provided in the chapter on changes in accounting methods. A complete list may be found in Rev. Proc. 2014-16.

Rev. Proc. 2015-13 provides the general procedures for requesting a change in accounting method. The IRS has indicated it will give automatic consent to changes that comply with the new regulations. For larger businesses, this will require filing Form 3115.

Generally, a company will receive automatic consent to change a method of accounting by completing and filing Form 3115, Application for Change in Accounting Method, and including it with its timely-filed original federal tax return for the year of change. A duplicate copy of Form 3115 must also be mailed to Ogden, Utah at the address indicated in the instructions. The Form 3115 will identify the taxpayer, describe the methods that are being changed, identify the type of property involved in the change, and include a Section 481(a) adjustment, if applicable.

Small Business Exception. In February 2015, the IRS responded to concern from the small business community and tax preparers by offering simplified rules for small businesses including sole proprietors, with assets totaling less than $10 million or average annual gross receipts totaling $10 million or less for the three preceding years. Details are in Rev. Proc. 2015-20, posted on *IRS.gov*.

A change in the taxpayer's policies regarding capitalizing or expensing to comply with the new regulations is considered a change in accounting method. The new procedure allows small businesses to change a method of accounting under the final tangible property regulations on a prospective basis for the first taxable year beginning on or after January 1, 2014. Rev. Proc. 2015-20 modifies certain procedures provided in Rev. Proc. 2015-14 to permit small business tax-payers to make changes in methods of accounting with a Section 481(a) adjust-ment that takes into account only amounts paid or incurred, and dispositions, in taxable years beginning on or after January 1, 2014. This modification means that, effectively, small business taxpayers making these changes in method of ac-counting for the first taxable year that begins on or after January 1, 2014, may elect to make the change on a cut-off basis.

The IRS also waived the requirement to complete and file a Form 3115, Application for Change in Accounting Method, applicable to small business taxpayers that choose to use this simplified procedure.

One trade-off from using this simplified method for small business is the loss of any protection in the case of an IRS audit. Thus, for taxpayers desir-ing some defense against the uncertainty that the IRS may disagree with their characterization of the change in accounting method it may still be advisable to file Form 3115.

The AICPA, which had lobbied for changes for small businesses, released the following statement. "We welcome the news that the IRS has . . . issued relief to small business owners from application of the repair regs. The AICPA and the state CPA societies have made numerous requests on behalf of our members and their small business clients for this relief over several months. We appreciate that the IRS understood how burdensome the regulations are for small business and acted to provide relief for 2014 and future year tax returns."

¶36,005   The Modified Accelerated Cost Recovery System (MACRS)

The Modified Accelerated Cost Recovery System (MACRS) consists of two sys-tems that determine how to depreciate property. The main system is called the General Depreciation System (GDS) and the second system is called the Alter-native Depreciation System (ADS).

The main difference between the two systems is that ADS generally provides for a longer recovery period and uses only the straight line method of depreciation to figure a deduction. Unless specifically required by law to use ADS, GDS is generally used to figure a depreciation deduction.

Both systems simplify the way to figure the deduction by providing three preset conventions. These conventions determine the number of months for which depreciation may be claimed both in the year the property is placed in service, and in the year in which the property is disposed of. The conventions are as follows:

1. Mid-month convention. Used for all nonresidential real property and residential rental property. The property is treated for tax purposes as if use began or ended in the middle of the month.
2. Mid-quarter convention. Used if the basis of property placed in service during the last three months of the tax year is more than 40 percent of the total bases of all property placed in service for the entire year (excluding nonresidential real property, residential rental property, Section 179 property and property placed in service and disposed of in the same year). The property is treated for tax purposes as if use began or ended in the middle of the quarter.
3. Half-year convention. Used for all other property. The property is treated for tax purposes as if use began or ended in the middle of the year.

MACRS provides four methods of figuring depreciation on property:

a. The 200 percent declining balance method over a GDS recovery period.
b. The 150 percent declining balance method over a GDS recovery period.
c. The straight line method over a GDS recovery period.
d. The straight line method over an ADS recovery period.

.01   What to Depreciate Under MACRS

MACRS applies to most tangible depreciable property placed in service after 1986. MACRS must be used to depreciate all real property acquired before 1987 that has been changed from personal use to a business or income-producing use after 1986.

.02   Knowing Which System to Use

Most tangible depreciable property falls within the *general* rule of MACRS, which is also called the General Depreciation System (GDS). Because GDS permits use of the declining balance method over a shorter recovery period, the deduction is greater in the earlier years.

However, there are specifications for the use of each system.

Both GDS and ADS have pre-established class lives for most property. Under GDS, most property is assigned to eight property classes based on these class lives. These property classes provide the number of years over which the cost of an item in a class may be recovered.

Some examples of this:

- Three-year property. Any race horse over two years old when placed in service.
- Any other horse over 12 years old when placed in service.
- Five-year property. Automobiles, taxis, buses, and trucks; computers and peripheral equipment; some office machinery; breeding cattle and dairy cattle.

However, ADS must be used for the following property:

1. Any tangible property used predominantly outside the U.S. during the year.
2. Any tax-exempt use property.
3. Any tax-exempt bond-financed property.
4. Any property used predominantly in a farming business and placed in service during any tax year in which the individual makes an election not to apply the uniform capitalization rules to certain farming costs.
5. Any imported property covered by an executive order of the President of the United States.

.03 What Cannot Be Depreciated Under MACRS

MACRS cannot be used to depreciate the following property:

1. Intangible property.
2. Any motion picture film or video tape.
3. Any sound recording.
4. Certain real and personal property placed in service before 1987.

Any property that can be properly depreciated under a method of depreciation not based on a term of years may be excluded from MACRS.

Property Placed in Service Before 1987. There are special rules that prevent the use of MACRS for property placed in service by anyone (for any purpose) before 1987 (before August 1, 1986, if MACRS was elected). These rules apply to both personal and real property. However, the rules for personal property are more restrictive. And although there are some exceptions to these rules, they do offer a basic guideline from which to work.

Personal Property. MACRS may not be used for most personal property acquired after 1986 (after July 31, 1986, if MACRS was elected) if any of the following apply:

1. The individual or a relative owned or used the property in 1986.
2. The property was acquired from a person who owned it in 1986 and as part of the transaction the user of the property did not change.
3. The property was leased to a person (or someone related to this person) who owned or used the property in 1986.
4. The property was acquired in a transaction in which:
   a. The user of the property did not change, and
   b. The property was not MACRS property in the hands of the person from whom the individual acquired it because of (2) or (3).

Real Property. MACRS may not be used for certain real property. This includes real property acquired after 1986 (after July 31, 1986, if MACRS was elected) if any of the following apply:

1. The individual or a relative owned the property in 1986.
2. The property was leased back to the person (or someone related to this person) who owned the property in 1986.
3. The property was acquired in a transaction in which some of the individual's gain or loss was not recognized. MACRS applies only to that part of the basis in the acquired property that represents cash paid or unlike property given up. It does not apply to the substituted portion of the basis.

Certain Nontaxable Transfers of Property. MACRS does not apply to property involved in certain nontaxable transfers. This applies to property used before 1987 and transferred after 1986 to a corporation or partnership if its basis is determined by reference to the basis in the hands of the transferor or distributor. If MACRS was elected, it also applies to property used before August 1, 1986, and transferred after July 31, 1986, to a corporation or partnership if its basis is determined by reference to the basis in the hands of the transferor or distributor.

The nontaxable transfers covered by this rule include the following:

1. A distribution in complete liquidation of a subsidiary.
2. A transfer to a corporation controlled by the transferor.
3. An exchange of property solely for corporate stock or securities in a reorganization.
4. A contribution of property to a partnership in exchange for a partnership interest.
5. A partnership distribution of property to a partner.

.04   Election to Exclude Property from MACRS

If property is depreciated under a method not based on a term of years, such as the unit-of-production method, that property may be excluded from MACRS.

.05   Use of Standard Mileage Rate

If the standard mileage rate, 67 cents a mile for 2024, is used to figure a tax deduction for a business automobile, it is treated as having made an election to exclude the automobile from MACRS. However, the mileage rate is considered to include a depreciation component that reduces the vehicle's basis year by year. When the vehicle is sold or traded this reduced basis is used to compute any gain or loss.

.06   How to Figure the Deduction

Once it is determined that the property may be depreciated under MACRS and whether it falls under GDS or ADS, the following information must be known about the property.

1. Its basis. Generally, this refers to the cost plus amounts paid for items such as sales tax, freight, installation, and testing.
2. Its property class and recovery period. This refers to the member of years over which the cost "basis" of the property is recovered.
3. The date it was placed in service. This refers to the date the item was actually first used—not when it was purchased.
4. Which convention to use—mid-month, mid-quarter, or half-year.
5. Which depreciation method to use:
   a. GDS or ADS.
   b. Which class the property is in.
   c. What type of property it is.

¶36,006   Dispositions

A disposition is the permanent withdrawal of property from use in a trade or business or in the production of income. A withdrawal can be made by sale, exchange, retirement, abandonment, involuntary conversion, or destruction. Generally, gain or loss on the disposition of property is recognized by a sale. However, nonrecognition rules may allow for postponement of some gain.

If property is disposed of before the end of its recovery period, it is called an early disposition. If that property is depreciated under MACRS, a depreciation deduction for the year of disposition is allowed. The depreciation deduction is determined for the year of disposition.

With the exception of gain on the disposition of residential rental and nonresidential real property, all gain on the disposition of property depreciated under MACRS is included in income as ordinary income, up to the amount of previously allowed depreciation deducted for the property. There is no recapture for residential rental and nonresidential real property.

¶36,007   General Asset Accounts

It is possible to group separate properties into one or more general asset accounts. They then can be depreciated as a single item of property. Each account can include only property with similar characteristics, such as asset class and recovery period. Some property cannot be included in a general asset account. There are additional rules for passenger automobiles, disposing of property, converting property to personal use, and property that generates foreign source income.

Once a general asset account is established, the amount of depreciation for each account is achieved by using the depreciation method, recovery period, and convention that applies to the property in the account. For each general asset account, the depreciation allowance is recorded in a separate depreciation reserve account.

Property used in both a trade or business (or for the production of income) and in a personal activity in the year in which it was first placed in service may not be in a general asset account.

.01   How to Group Property in General Asset Accounts

Each general asset account must include only property placed in service in the same year and that has the following in common:

1. Asset class.
2. Recovery period.
3. Depreciation method.
4. Convention.

The following rules also apply when establishing a general asset account:

1. No asset class. Property without an asset class, but with the same depreciation method, recovery period, and convention, placed in service in the same year, can be grouped into the same general asset account.
2. Mid-quarter convention. Property subject to the mid-quarter convention can only be grouped into a general asset account with property that is placed in service in the same quarter.
3. Mid-month convention. Property subject to the mid-month convention can only be grouped into a general asset account with property that is placed in service in the same month.
4. Passenger automobiles. Passenger automobiles subject to the limits on passenger automobile depreciation must be grouped into a separate general asset account.

.02   Dispositions and Conversions

Property in a general asset account is considered disposed of when any of the following occurs:

1. It is permanently withdrawn from use in trade or business or from the production of income.
2. It is transferred to a supplies, scrap, or similar account.
3. It is sold, exchanged, retired, physically abandoned, or destroyed.

Note the following:

1. The retirement of a structural component of real property is not a disposal.
2. The unadjusted depreciable basis and the depreciation reserve of the general asset account are not affected by the disposition of property from the general asset account.
3. Any property changed to personal use must be removed from the general asset account.

Unadjusted Depreciable Basis. The unadjusted depreciable basis of an item of property in a general asset account is the same amount used to figure gain on the sale of the property, but it is figured without taking into account any depreciation taken in earlier years. The unadjusted depreciable basis of a general asset account is the total of the unadjusted depreciable bases of all of the property in the account.

Adjusted Depreciable Basis. The adjusted depreciable basis of a general asset account is the unadjusted depreciable basis of the account minus any allowed or allowable depreciation based on the account.

Disposition of Remaining Property. If all or the last item of property is disposed of in a general asset account, the adjusted depreciable basis of the general asset account can be recovered. Under this rule, the general asset account ends and the amount of gain or loss for the general asset account is figured by comparing the adjusted depreciable basis of the general asset account with the amount realized. If the amount realized is more than the adjusted depreciable basis, the difference is a gain. If it is less, the difference is a loss. If there is a gain, the amount that is subject to recapture as ordinary income is limited.

Change to Personal Use. An item of property in a general asset account becomes ineligible for general asset account treatment if it is used in a personal activity. Once the property has been converted to personal use, it is removed from the general asset account as of the first day of the year in which the change in use occurs and make the appropriate adjustments are made.

¶36,008   Cost Segregation Studies

Cost segregation has become increasingly valuable, as depreciation write-off periods for commercial real estate have been repeatedly lengthened because of tax law changes. Initially, depreciable lives were lengthened from 15 to 18 years, then to 19 years, subsequently to 31.5 years, and finally, to 39 years for commercial property (or 27.5 years for residential property) as a result of the Revenue Reconciliation Act of 1993. Although a long-term depreciable life of 39 years is appropriate for assets such as buildings, it is not appropriate for assets that can be properly classified with shorter depreciable lives.

Examples of these include land improvements as outlined in asset class #00.3 under Rev. Proc. 87-56 and tangible personal property such as machinery/equipment, furniture and fixtures, as well as related components such as utilities, dedicated HVAC, and plumbing or electrical lines directly related to the particular type of machinery or equipment. Reclassification of assets as tangible personal property will result in depreciation periods of five or seven years, depending on the industry classification in which the business operates, whereas reclassification to land improvements will result in a depreciation period of 15 years. For example, businesses that are in the professional services or retail field would fall under asset class #57.0, Distributive Trade or Services, and be classified as tangible personal property with a depreciable life of five years.

.01   Benefits of Cost Segregation Studies

Cost segregation studies (CSSs) have been an underused method of reducing current tax liabilities and improving the economic returns to owners of commercial properties. A *cost segregation study* is a total review of all costs associated with the acquisition or construction of a building. These studies require the use of tax experts and engineers who specialize in this area and are familiar with IRS requirements. These specialists can help to maximize the returns on commercial property investment and facilitate informed decisions that address the unique requirements of a specific piece of property. The purpose is to identify and classify the costs as either real or personal property so that the personal property items can be depreciated on an accelerated basis.

Thus, the time value of the property owner's money prevails. For example, if a property owner was able to carve out $100,000 of assets from a 39-year period to a five-year period, the difference in year one along would be an increase tax deduction (via depreciation) of $17,500 (39-year depreciation schedule approximately $2,500 versus $20,000 if under a five year life. The property owner will get the deduction over 39 years or $2,500 per year, whereas the cost segregation study will enable the complete write-off of the $100,000 asset in five years.

The next best thing to not paying taxes is deferring the payment of taxes. Thus, the process identifies personal property assets that often get buried or grouped together within the real property asset.

It becomes obvious that many property owners can benefit from a cost segregation study. A CSS appears to be the answer for owners and investors who have been searching for ways to increase the current tax benefits from owning or investing in real estate. Both commercial and residential property can benefit from one, but in general, the more elaborate and costly the property, the greater the tax benefit.

.02   Commercial Property Suitable for a CSS

Properties that readily lend themselves to the benefits of a cost segregation study, because they typically contain a significant amount of shorter-life assets, include:

- Apartments.
- Golf courses.
- Nursing homes.
- Parking lots.
- Hotels, motels, and casinos.
- Restaurants.
- Hospitals and medical facilities and offices.
- Warehouses and distribution centers.
- Manufacturing and industrial plants.
- Shopping centers.
- Senior living facilities.
- Grocery stores.
- Office and retail facilities.
- Car dealerships.
- Maintenance/service centers.
- Large distribution facilities.
- Data centers.
- Owner-occupied office buildings.
- For-profit health care and assisted living facilities.

Although almost every type of real estate can benefit from a CSS, certain types of property yield the highest tax saving benefits. Those properties include specialty-use buildings, such as medical facilities, manufacturing facilities, and high-end office buildings, to name a few. Warehouses and industrial properties tend to yield lower benefits, while residential garden apartments come some place between.

.03   Property Eligible for Cost Segregation

Construction-related soft costs have historically been lumped together as part of real property. However, by performing a cost segregation study, these soft costs can be allocated on a pro rata basis to various components as discovered within the cost segregation analysis. Some examples include architect/engineer fees, permits, capitalized interest, and the contractor's overhead and profit. The result is a faster write-off of costs previously included as real property. The amount of the benefits from performing a CSS will, of course, vary depending upon the type of property, the cost of the property, and the year it was placed in service. CSSs can be performed on the following:

- New buildings presently under construction.
- Purchases of existing properties.
- Existing buildings undergoing major renovation, remodeling, restoration, or expansion.
- Office/facility leasehold improvements and "fit-outs."
- Post-1986 real estate construction, building acquisitions or improvements where no cost segregation study was performed (even though the statute of limitations previously closed on the property construction/acquisition year).

In addition, Rev. Proc. 2004-11 permits companies that have *claimed less than the allowable depreciation* to claim the omitted amount over a one-year period on a going-forward basis. Furthermore, the segregated components continue to be depreciated over shorter lives going forward. Savings derived from these studies flow directly to the bottom line in tax deferred savings and cash flow. This omitted amount, often referred to as the "catch-up deduction," is reported as a Section 481(a) adjustment that is an accounting method change and reported via Form 3115. (See *Brookshire Holdings*—a case that states that this is not an accounting method change.)

This filing procedure is an automatic approval by the IRS with no filing fees. It must be filed separately with the IRS in Washington, D.C., with a copy to be attached to the tax return of the entity that owns the real estate. The Form 3115 must be filed on the earlier of the due dates including extensions of the company's tax return or the date the company files its tax return.

.04   Questions to Be Answered by the Client Before Undertaking a CSS

After considering these lists, some of the obvious questions for the CPA to ask the client include:

1. Do you have considerable depreciable real property?
2. Do you have a newly constructed building?
3. Have you recently purchased a building?
4. Are you planning a major renovation or expansion?
5. Have you purchased, constructed, or expanded real estate holdings any time after 1986?
6. Is the cost of the building at least $1,000,000?
7. Do you expect to retain your real estate holdings for at least the next three or four years?

A positive answer to any of these questions should indicate that the client could probably benefit from accelerating tax depreciation on their real estate holdings.

.05   Legal Background for Cost Segregation Studies

Engineering-based cost segregation studies to classify depreciation have become an accepted standard approved by the IRS. Recent revenue rulings and procedures and a landmark court case make it possible to realize significant tax savings through accelerating the depreciation of real property costs. The Service has also published a *Cost Segregation Audit Techniques Guide (ATG)*, which gives very thorough instructions for conducting and/or scrutinizing a CSS. The IRS explains that the lack of consistency in cost segregation studies and the absence of bright-line tests for distinguishing property have both contributed to the difficulties related to cost segregation. The Service adds that the purpose of this ATG is to:

- Provide the basis for a better understanding of cost segregation studies.
- Provide a detailed outline and description of the examination steps that will facilitate the audit process.
- Minimize the burden on taxpayers, practitioners, and IRS examiners alike.

.06   Methodologies Used in Preparing Cost Segregation Studies

The following is a list of the methodologies described in the IRS Guide. Each approach is described in some detail. The attributes and potential drawbacks are also discussed.

The IRS notes that other methodologies may be used, but that most are merely derivatives of these:

- Detailed Engineering Approach from Actual Cost Records.
- Detailed Engineering Cost Estimate Approach.
- Survey or Letter Approach.
- Residual Estimation Approach.

- Sampling or Modeling Approach.
- "Rule of Thumb" Approach.

.07   Detailed Engineering Approach from Actual Cost Records

The detailed engineering approach from actual cost records, or *detailed cost approach*, is the ideal approach for conducting a cost segregation study. It uses costs from contemporaneous construction and accounting records. In general, it is the most methodical and accurate approach, relying on solid documentation and minimal estimation. Construction-based documentation, such as blueprints, specifications, contracts, job reports, change orders, payment requests, and invoices, is used to determine unit costs. The use of actual cost records contributes to the overall accuracy of cost allocations, although issues may still arise as to the classification of specific assets. This approach is generally applied only to new construction, for which detailed cost records are available. But, ideally, the cost segregation study can begin before construction of a new building to take advantage of more tax planning.

For used or acquired property and for new projects for which original construction documents are not available, an alternative approach (e.g., the second approach, *detailed engineering cost estimate approach*) may be more appropriate.

The detailed cost approach typically includes the following activities:

1. Identify the specific project/assets that will be analyzed.
2. Obtain a complete listing of all project costs and substantiate the total project costs.
3. Inspect the facility to determine the nature of the project and its intended use.
4. Photograph specific property items for reference. Request previous site photographs that illustrate the construction progress as well as the condition of the property before the project began.
5. Review "as-built" blueprints, specifications, contracts, bid documents, contractor pay requests, and other construction documentation.
6. Identify and assign specific project items to property classes (e.g., land, land improvements, building, equipment, furniture and fixtures, and other items of tangible personal property).
7. Prepare quantitative "take-offs" for all materials and use payment records to compute unit costs.
8. Apply unit costs to each project component to determine its total cost. Reconcile total costs obtained from quantitative take-offs to total actual costs.
9. Allocate indirect costs, such as architectural fees, engineering fees, and permits, to appropriate assets.
10. Group project items with similar class lives and placed-in-service dates to compute depreciation.

The detailed cost approach is the most time consuming method and generally provides the most accurate cost allocations. The IRS explains that the discussion in each approach takes a closer look at the main components and attributes of each of the six methodologies discussed in the Guide. They point out to the examiners that these are the steps normally taken in the *preparation* of a cost segregation study. The examiners' responsibility is to review the steps taken in each study that comes before them, and evaluate the accuracy of that study.

.08 Pros and Cons of Cost Segregation Studies

The resulting benefits of accelerated depreciation from a CSS can include:

- Eligibility to receive sales/use tax benefits.
- Property tax relief and other credits and incentives.
- Reduced current income taxes.
- Improved current cash flow.
- Improved internal rate of return on investment.
- Potential recapture of overpayments of sales tax (resulting from exemptions, which might have been overlooked prior to the segregation of assets).

As indicated earlier, a CSS is a systematic process of identifying and segregating the components of commercial property and associated costs according to their depreciable lives. Too often, all assets are lumped into a long-term depreciation account using a 39-year, straight-line method, thereby substantially reducing their current economic benefits. The CSS may identify between 5 and 50 percent of assets that qualify to depreciate over a 5-, 7-, or 15-year life.

A study accelerates tax deductions and the time-value of money generated by current tax savings. That tax deduction is worth significantly more today than it will be in the future. Although the savings from a cost segregation study vary depending on the type and cost of the property and the year placed in service, if expectations are realistic going into the undertaking, a CSS, usually results in considerable current tax savings.

.09 Example of Savings Resulting from Study

Following is an example of a study completed by a company that specializes in conducting cost segregation studies with/for CPA firms.

For a 19-story office retail property acquired in 2004, containing approximately 300,000 square feet, located on a two-acre site at a cost basis of $35 million, a properly conducted CSS could provide an estimated benefit as follows:

- For years 2004–2007, additional tax depreciation of approximately $3.3 million in addition to what would have been received without a cost segregation study.
- For years 2004–2007, tax deferred savings (including both federal and state at a combined rate of 42 percent) of approximately $1.4 million.

.10   Levels of Service Offered to CPAs

A company that specializes in these studies offers various service levels to CPA firms:

1. The company will cobrand or private label a service or study.
2. The company may partner with a CPA firm just to provide the engineer breakouts with the cost segregation engineer expertise. The CPA firm will complete the report to their client.
3. The CPA may refer the cost segregation company to his or her clients and the company will work directly with the CPA's clients.

Many CPA firms see the value added service as a way to provide unconventional services that competitors might not consider providing.

An active cost segregation company may also conduct educational (promotional) seminars and deal directly with end users of commercial real estate. They take into consideration the advantage of having the full complement of professionals on their payroll to provide a turnkey service.

A relatively small number of CPA firms provide this service to their real estate clients. There are other firms whose particular niche is to partner with accounting firms to conduct these studies for CPAs and their clients. These companies often employ the non-CPA or engineer type professionals that have the background and training not only in the construction in commercial real estate, but the experience in reading, interpreting of blueprints along with the knowledge of estimating project costs in all construction divisions. Most of these professionals also have a working knowledge of the national industry average costing manuals.

.11   Results Worth the Trouble

Even though the CSS is a relatively new procedure, it has generated millions of dollars in current federal and state income tax savings for owners of real estate. But it is not a quick-and-easy savings method. On the contrary, conducting the CSS can be fairly expensive, time consuming (four to six weeks) and complicated. Because of the nature of the study, it is obvious that a single CPA, even a tax expert, cannot expect to conduct a study without a team.

However, it is often the CPA who suggests consideration of a CSS to the client. A team for a study requires a tax expert with an intimate knowledge of the IRC, the relevant tax cases, and a network of resources to maximize the benefits for the accounting phase. The real estate/construction phase may include architects, structural experts, contractors, and/or engineers. As outlined above, even though a CSS may appear to be a complicated process, it is invariably worth the time, effort, and cost.

CHAPTER 37

Asset Valuation for Tax Purposes

¶37,000   Overview

Basis is the adjusted amount of an investment (equity) in property for tax purposes. The basis of property is used not only to figure depreciation but also amortization, depletion, and casualty losses. Further, it is also used to figure gain or loss on the sale or other disposition of property such as a like-kind exchange or involuntary conversion. It is important to keep accurate records of all items that affect the basis of property so that these computations can be made quickly and accurately.

This discussion is divided into three sections:

1. Cost Basis.
2. Adjusted Basis.
3. Basis Other Than Cost.

The basis of property bought is usually its cost. It may also be necessary to capitalize (add to basis) certain other costs related to buying or producing the property.

The original basis in property is adjusted (increased or decreased) by certain events. If improvements are made to the property, the basis is increased. If deductions are taken for depreciation or casualty losses, the basis is reduced.

Basis in some assets cannot be determined by cost. This includes property received as a gift or inheritance. It also applies to property received in a nontaxable exchange and in certain other circumstances.

¶37,001   Cost Basis of Assets

The basis of property bought is usually its cost. The cost is the amount paid in cash, debt obligations, other property, or services. Cost also includes amounts paid for the following items:

1. Sales tax.
2. Freight.
3. Installation and testing.
4. Excise taxes.
5. Legal and accounting fees (when they must be capitalized).
6. Revenue stamps.
7. Recording fees.
8. Real estate taxes (if assumed for the seller).

Certain other costs related to buying or producing property may have to be capitalized.

For property bought on any time-payment plan that charges little or no interest, the basis of that property is the stated purchase price, minus the amount considered to be unstated interest. There generally is unstated interest if the interest rate is less than the applicable federal rate. When a trade or business is purchased, this generally includes all assets used in the business operations, such as land, buildings, and machinery. The price is spread among the various assets, including any Section 197 intangibles such as goodwill.

In 2013, the IRS issued final regulations dealing with the important question of capitalizing and expensing costs. These regulations are commonly referred to as the tangible property regulations. For specific issues related to questions of capitalization, the reader is referred to chapter 36 on depreciation—especially the section on when costs are capitalized—and to chapter 15 on changes in accounting methods.

.01   Stocks and Bonds

The basis of stocks or bonds bought is generally the purchase price plus any costs of purchase, such as commissions and recording or transfer fees. If a person gets stocks or bonds other than by purchase, the basis is usually determined by the fair market value (FMV) on a certain date or the previous owner's adjusted basis (in the case of a gift). Adjustments to the basis of stocks for certain events that occur after purchase will be necessary. Common examples include allocating the basis of stocks after a stock split or stock dividend or in the case of a wash sale. A wash sale occurs when a stock is sold at a loss but the same stock is bought or sold within 30 days before or after the sale. In that case the loss on the original sale is disallowed. However, the amount of the disallowed loss is allocated to the basis of the new (replacement) stock thereby reducing any future gain or increasing any future loss by the amount of the loss disallowed.

When it is possible to identify the shares of stock or the bonds sold, their basis is the cost or other basis of the particular shares of those stocks or the particular bonds. If someone buys and sells securities at various times in varying quantities, and no one can identify the shares sold, the basis of the securities is the basis of the securities acquired first.

For mutual fund shares acquired at different times and prices, it is appropriate to use an average basis.

.02   Real Property

In a purchase of real property, certain fees and other expenses become part of the cost basis in the property.

If the purchaser pays the real estate taxes the seller owed on real property bought, and the seller did not reimburse the buyer, those taxes are part of the basis. The buyer cannot deduct them as taxes.

If a buyer reimburses the seller for taxes the seller paid, the buyer can usually deduct that amount as an expense in the year of purchase. That amount is not included in the basis of the property.

If the buyer did not reimburse the seller, the buyer must reduce the basis by the amount of those taxes.

Settlement Costs. A buyer can include in the basis of property the settlement fees and closing costs that are for buying the property. A buyer cannot include fees and costs for getting a loan on the property. (A fee for buying property is a cost that must be paid even if the buyer bought the property for cash.)

The following items are some of the settlement fees or closing costs buyers *can* include in the basis of the property:

1. Abstract fees (abstract of title fees).
2. Charges for installing utility services.
3. Legal fees (including title search and preparation of the sales contract and deed).
4. Recording fees.
5. Surveys.
6. Transfer taxes.
7. Owner's title insurance.
8. Any amounts the seller owes that the buyer agrees to pay, such as back taxes or interest, recording or mortgage fees, charges for improvements or repairs, and sales commissions.

Settlement costs do not include amounts placed in escrow for the future payment of items such as taxes and insurance.

The following items are some settlement fees and closing costs a buyer *cannot* include in the basis of the property:

1. Fire insurance premiums.
2. Rent for occupancy of the property before closing.
3. Charges for utilities or other services related to occupancy of the property before closing.
4. Charges connected with getting a loan. The following are examples of these charges:
   a. Points (discount points, loan origination fees).
   b. Mortgage insurance premiums.
   c. Loan assumption fees.
   d. Cost of a credit report.
   e. Fees for an appraisal required by a lender.
5. Fees for refinancing a mortgage.

If these costs relate to business property, items (1) through (3) are deductible as business expenses. Items (4) and (5) must be capitalized as costs of getting a loan and can be deducted over the period of the loan.

Points and Mortgages. If a buyer pays points to obtain a loan (including a mortgage, second mortgage, line of credit, or a home equity loan), the points are not added to the basis of the related property. Generally, a buyer can deduct the points over the term of the loan.

Special rules may apply to points the buyer and the seller pay when obtaining a mortgage on the purchase of a main home. If certain requirements are met, the buyer can deduct the points in full for the year in which they are paid. The basis of the home is reduced by any seller-paid points.

If a person buys property and assumes (or buys subject to) an existing mortgage on the property, the basis includes the amount the buyer pays for the property plus the amount to be paid on the mortgage.

If an individual builds property or has assets built, the expenses for this construction are part of the basis. Some of these expenses include the following items:

1. The cost of land.
2. The cost of labor and materials.
3. Architect's fees.
4. Building permit charges.
5. Payments to contractors.
6. Payments for rental equipment.
7. Inspection fees.

In addition, if the owner of a business uses employees, material, and equipment to build an asset, the basis would also include the following costs:

1. Employee wages paid for the construction work.
2. Depreciation on equipment owned while it is used in the construction.
3. Operating and maintenance costs for equipment used in the construction.
4. The cost of business supplies and materials used in the construction.

These expenses may not be deducted. They must be capitalized; therefore, they are included in the asset's basis. On the other hand, it is necessary to reduce the basis by any work opportunity credit, welfare-to-work credit, Indian employment credit, or empowerment zone employment credit allowable on the wages paid in constructing an asset. The value of the owner's own labor, or any other labor not paid for, is not to be included in the basis of any property constructed.

.03   Business Assets

If property is purchased to use in a business, the basis is usually its actual cost. If the owner constructs, creates, or otherwise produces property, the costs must be capitalized as the basis. In certain circumstances, the project may be subject to the uniform capitalization rules.

Costs to Capitalize or Expense. A central question of accounting, that has always plagued accountants, is whether certain costs must be capitalized or whether they may be expensed. At what point in a building's roof repair, for example, are the costs considered a normal repair and expensed, or the costs are extensive enough that they must be added to the cost of the building and depreciated? Expensing produces better tax results which is why taxpayers favor it and the IRS says, "Not so fast." In an attempt to bring some needed clarity to the question of capitalize or expense, the IRS has replaced previously issued temporary regulations with final regulations.

The IRS finalized its regulations clarifying the rules for deducting or capitalizing expenditures to tangible property "Tangible Property Regulations" in September 2013 and they became effective on January 1, 2014. The regulations under sections 162 and 263 are extensive with many useful examples. When costs are incurred to improve an existing asset, those costs are generally capitalized. In its regulations (Reg. §1.263(a)-1) the IRS states its starting position which is that any amount paid for new buildings or for permanent improvements or betterments made to increase the value of property or paid to restore the property should be capitalized unless there is a rule that permits it to be expensed. This is consistent with the tax maxim that deductions are a matter of legislative grace: nothing may be deducted unless a specific provision says it can. In particular, deductible business expenses must be ordinary and necessary and those are terms of art, crafted by numerous court decisions.

For a more complete description of the rules and changes implemented by the final tangible property regulations, see chapter 36 on depreciation, especially the section on when costs are capitalized. In addition, if a current procedure is found to be at odds with new IRS requirements the reader may find chapter 15 on changes in accounting methods a helpful reference as well.

Uniform Capitalization Rules. The uniform capitalization rules specify the costs added to basis in certain circumstances. Uniform capitalization rules must be used when any of the following applies to a trade, business, or any activity carried on for profit:

1. Production of real or tangible personal property for use in the business or activity.
2. Production of real or tangible personal property for sale to customers.
3. Acquisition of property for resale.

Property is produced when it is constructed, built, installed, manufactured, developed, improved, created, raised, or grown. Property produced for someone under a contract is treated as produced by that person up to the amount paid or costs incurred for the property.

Tangible personal property includes films, sound recordings, video tapes, books, or similar property.

Under the uniform capitalization rules, a person must capitalize all direct costs and an allocable part of most indirect costs incurred due to production or resale activities.

The following are not subject to the uniform capitalization rules:

1. Property someone produces that he or she does not use in trade, business, or activity conducted for profit.
2. Qualified creative expenses paid or incurred as a freelance (self-employed) writer, photographer, or artist that are otherwise deductible on the freelancer's tax return.
3. Property someone produced under a long-term contract, except for certain home construction contracts.
4. Research and experimental expenses allowable as a deduction under Section 174 of the Internal Revenue Code.
5. Costs for personal property acquired for resale if the current (or predecessor's) average annual gross receipts for the three previous tax years do not exceed $10 million.

Intangible Assets. Intangible assets include goodwill, patents, copyrights, trademarks, trade names, and franchises. The basis of an intangible asset is usually the cost to buy or create it.

The basis of a *patent* is the cost of development, such as research and experimental expenditures, drawings, working models, and attorneys' and governmental fees. If research and experimental expenditures are deducted as current business expenses, they cannot be included in the basis of the patent. The value of the inventor's time spent on an invention is not part of the basis.

For an author, the basis of a *copyright* will usually be the cost of getting the copyright plus copyright fees, attorneys' fees, clerical assistance, and the cost of plates that remain in the author's possession.

The value of the author's time, or any other person's time that was not paid for, is not included.

The purchase price of a *franchise, trademark,* or *trade name* is the basis unless the payments can be deducted as a business expense.

.04   Allocating the Basis

When multiple assets are purchased for a lump sum, the amount paid is allocated among the assets received. This allocation is used to figure the basis for depreciation and gain or loss on a later disposition of any of these assets.

The buyer and the seller may agree to a specific allocation of the purchase price among the multiple assets in the sales contract of a lump-sum sale. If this allocation is based on the value of each asset, and the buyer and the seller have adverse tax interests, the allocation generally will be accepted.

Acquisition of a Trade or Business. In the acquisition of a trade or business, the purchase price is allocated to the various assets acquired.

For asset acquisitions occurring *after* January 5, 2000, the allocation must be made among the following assets in proportion to (but not more than) their fair market value (FMV) on the purchase date, in the following order:

1. Certificates of deposit, U.S. Government securities, foreign currency, and actively traded personal property, including stock and securities.
2. Accounts receivable, mortgages, and credit card receivables that arose in the ordinary course of business.
3. Property of a kind that would properly be included in inventory if on hand at the end of the tax year, and property held by the tax-payer primarily for sale to customers in the ordinary course of business.
4. All other assets except Section 197 intangibles, goodwill, and going concern value.

5.   Section 197 intangibles, except goodwill, and going concern value.
6.   Goodwill and going concern value (whether or not they qualify as Section 197 intangibles).

The buyer and seller may enter into a written agreement as to the allocation of any consideration or the FMV of any of the assets. This agreement is binding on both parties unless the IRS determines the amounts are not appropriate.

Both the buyer and seller involved in the sale of business assets must report to the IRS the allocation of the sales price among Section 197 intangibles and the other business assets.

In the case of the sale of an on-going non-publicly traded corporation's assets, the IRS requires both the buyer and seller of the business to file a Form 8594, Asset Acquisition Statement Under Section 1060. The completed form is attached to the tax return for Form 1040, 1041, 1065, 1120, or 1120S when there is a transfer of a group of assets that make up a trade or business and the purchaser's basis in the assets determined by the amount paid for the assets. The form requires allocating the purchase price among the assets based on a prescribed asset class scheme. This procedure allocates the basis of the purchase price to readily identifiable such as cash at face value following a 7 class allocation process. Moving from most identifiable to least, class 7 includes goodwill, whose value is allocated on a residual basis.

Land and Buildings. When a purchaser obtains buildings and the land on which they stand for a lump sum, the basis of the property is allocated among the land and the buildings to figure the depreciation allowable on the buildings.

The basis of each asset is obtained by multiplying the lump sum by a fraction. The numerator is the FMV of that asset, and the denominator is the FMV of the whole property at the time of purchase. If there is uncertainty about the FMV of the land and buildings, the basis can be allocated based on their assessed values for real estate tax purposes.

Demolition costs, and other losses incurred for the demolition of any building, are added to the basis of the land on which the demolished building was located. The costs may not be claimed as a current deduction.

A modification of a building will not be treated as a demolition if the following conditions are satisfied:

1.   75 percent or more of the existing external walls of the building are retained in place as internal or external walls.
2.   75 percent or more of the existing internal structural framework of the building is retained in place.

If the building is a certified historic structure, the modification must also be part of a certified rehabilitation.

If these conditions are met, the costs of the modifications are added to the basis of the building.

Subdivided Lots. If a tract of land is purchased and subdivided, the basis for *each* lot must be determined. This is necessary because the gain or loss must be figured on the sale of each individual lot. As a result, the entire cost in the tract is not recovered until all of the lots have been sold.

To determine the basis of an individual lot, multiply the total cost of the tract by a fraction. The numerator is the FMV of the lot, and the denominator is the FMV of the entire tract.

If a developer sells subdivided lots before the development work is completed, it is possible (with IRS consent) to include, in the basis of the properties sold, an allocation of the estimated future cost for common improvements.

In addition, in many real estate development projects, the city or other local government requires the developer to set aside part of the land for a water-retention area or a park. In such cases care must be taken to allocate a reasonable amount of the purchase price of the project as well as cite work costs to these items that will remain behind after all the lots are sold.

¶37,002   Adjusted Basis of Property

Before figuring gain or loss on a sale, exchange, or other disposition of property, or figuring allowable depreciation, depletion, or amortization, it is usually necessary to make certain adjustments to the basis of the property. The result of these adjustments to the basis is the adjusted basis.

.01   Increases to Basis

The basis of any property is increased by all items properly added to a capital account. These include the cost of any improvements having a useful life of more than one year.

Rehabilitation expenses also increase basis. However, any rehabilitation credit allowed for these expenses must be subtracted before adding them to the basis. If any of the credit must be recaptured, the basis is increased by the recapture amount.

Separate accounts must be kept for additions or improvements to business property. Also, the basis of each modification is depreciated according to the depreciation rules that would apply to the underlying property, had they been placed in service at the same time as the addition or improvement.

The following items increase the basis of property:

1. The cost of extending utility service lines to the property.
2. Legal fees, such as the cost of defending and perfecting title.
3. Legal fees for obtaining a decrease in an assessment levied against property to pay for local improvements.
4. Zoning costs.
5. The capitalized value of a redeemable ground rent.

Assessments for Local Improvements. The basis of property is increased by assessments for items such as paving roads and building ditches that increase the value of the property. They may not be deducted as taxes. However, charges for maintenance, repairs, or interest charges related to the improvements can be deducted as taxes.

Deducting versus Capitalizing Costs. Costs that can be deducted as current expenses are not added to the basis. Amounts paid for incidental repairs or maintenance that are deductible as business expenses cannot be added to the basis. However, certain other costs can be either deducted or capitalized. If they are capitalized, they are included in the basis. If they are deducted, they are not included.

The costs that can be either deducted or capitalized include the following:

- Carrying charges, such as interest and taxes, that someone pays to own property, except those carrying charges that must be capitalized under the uniform capitalization rules (discussed earlier).
- Research and experimentation costs.
- Intangible drilling and development costs for oil, gas, and geothermal wells.
- Exploration costs for new mineral deposits.
- Mining development costs for a new mineral deposit.
- Costs of establishing, maintaining, or increasing the circulation of a newspaper or other periodical.
- Cost of removing architectural and transportation barriers for people with disabilities and the elderly. If someone claims the disabled access credit, they must reduce the amount deducted or capitalize by the amount of the credit.

.02   Decreases to Basis

The following items reduce the basis of property:

- Section 179 deductions.
- Deduction for clean-fuel vehicles and refueling property.

- Nontaxable corporate distributions.
- Deductions previously allowed (or allowable) for amortization, depreciation, and depletion.
- Exclusion of subsidies for energy conservation measures.
- Credit for qualified electric vehicles.
- Postponed gain from sale of home.
- Investment credit (part or all) taken.
- Casualty and theft losses and insurance reimbursements.
- Certain canceled debt excluded from income.
- Rebates received from a manufacturer or seller.
- Easements.
- Tax credit or refund for buying a diesel-powered highway vehicle.
- Adoption tax benefits.

A few of the more timely of these items are discussed below.

Environmental Considerations. If a deduction is taken for *clean-fuel vehicles or clean-fuel vehicle refueling property*, the basis is decreased by the amount of the deduction. Any subsidy received from a public utility company for the purchase or installation of an *energy conservation measure* for a dwelling unit can be excluded from gross income. The basis of the property for which the subsidy was received is reduced by the excluded amount.

Depreciation. The IRS employs an "allowed or allowable" rule for determining the basis of property when sold. The purpose of this rule is to prevent taxpayers who may have taken too much depreciation on an asset while it was in use, from re-computing the depreciation to the correct amount when the property is sold. The basis of property is decreased by the depreciation that was deducted, or could have been deducted, on tax returns under the method of depreciation chosen. If less depreciation was taken than could have been taken, the basis should be decreased by that amount. If no depreciation deduction was made, the basis is reduced by the full amount permitted. If more was deducted than should have been, the basis is decreased by the amount equal to the depreciation that should have been deducted, plus the part of the excess depreciation deducted that actually reduced the tax liability for the year. In decreasing the basis for depreciation, the amount deducted on the tax returns as depreciation, and any depreciation capitalized under the uniform capitalization rules, must be included.

¶37,003   Basis Other than Cost

There are many instances in which cost *cannot be used* as basis. In these cases, FMV or the adjusted basis of property may be used. Adjusted basis is discussed above; FMV is discussed in this section.

Fair market value (FMV) is the price at which property would change hands between a buyer and a seller, neither having to buy or sell, and both having reasonable knowledge of all necessary facts. Sales of similar property on or about the same date may be helpful in figuring the property's FMV.

.01   Property Received for Services

If someone receives property for services, the property's FMV should be included in income. The amount included in income becomes the basis. If the services were performed for a price agreed upon beforehand, it will be accepted as the FMV of the property if there is no evidence to the contrary. This is the case, for example, where a partner is admitted to a partnership and receives a capital account in exchange for management or other services.

Bargain Purchases. A bargain purchase is a purchase of an item for less than its FMV. If, as compensation for services, someone purchases goods or other property at less than FMV, the difference between the purchase price and the property's FMV is included in income. The basis in the property is its FMV (the purchase price plus the amount included in income).

If the difference between the purchase price and the FMV represents a qualified employee discount, the difference should not be included in income. However, the basis in the property is still its FMV.

.02   Taxable Exchanges

A taxable exchange is one in which the gain is taxable or the loss is deductible. A taxable gain or deductible loss is also known as a recognized gain or loss. If someone receives property in exchange for other property in a taxable exchange, the basis of the property received is usually its FMV at the time of the exchange. A taxable exchange occurs when a taxpayer receives cash or gets property not similar or related in use to the property exchanged.

.03   Involuntary Conversions

If property is received as a result of an involuntary conversion, such as a casualty, theft, or condemnation, the basis of the replacement property is figured using the basis of the converted property.

If replacement property is similar or related in service or use to the converted property, the replacement property's basis is the old property's basis on the date of the conversion. However, the following adjustments should be made:

1. Decrease the basis by the following:
    a.   Any loss recognized on the conversion.
    b.   Any money received that is not spent on similar property.
2. Increase the basis by the following:
    a.   Any gain recognized on the conversion.
    b.   Any cost of acquiring the replacement property.

Money or property not similar or related in service or use to the converted property may be received. If the recipient buys replacement property similar or related in service or use to the converted property, the basis of the new property is its cost decreased by the gain not recognized on the conversion.

If more than one piece of replacement property is purchased, the basis is allocated among the properties based on their respective costs. There are time limits on replacing property in an involuntary conversion situation that vary depending on the circumstances of the conversion. In general a taxpayer has two years from the end of the year in which their property was converted to acquire replacement property with the proceeds received from the conversion.

.04   Partnership Basis Adjustments

The unique nature of partnerships affects the basis of assets owned by a partnership in certain situations. The most common basis adjustment results from a new partner purchasing an ownership interest of a selling partner. In such a case, especially with real estate partnerships, it frequently occurs that the purchase price paid for the partnership interest is greater than the basis of the underlying assets within the partnership (inside basis). In such a case the partnership may elect, under IRC 754, to adjust the basis of the underlying assets representing the new partner's share of the assets to equal the purchase price of the partnership interest. Assume, for example, that a partnership has four equal partners and it owns one building with a fair market value of $1 million and an adjusted basis of $800,000. One of the partner's sells his interest to a new partner for $250,000 (one fourth of the fair market value of the building). Without a basis adjustment, the new partner would have paid $250,000 for a $200,000 share of the basis of the partnership's building. If the basis adjustment is made by the partnership, the new partner will have a full $250,000 share of the underlying assets and the partner's depreciation allocation will reflect depreciation on the added $50,000.

.05   Like-Kind Exchanges

The exchange of property for the same kind of property is the most common type of nontaxable exchange. To qualify as a like-kind exchange, both the property transferred and the property received must be held by the transferor for business or investment purposes. There must also be an exchange of like-kind property. For real estate, like-kind is a generic concept and even raw land can be exchanged for land with a building on it. In the case of personal property the rules are much more stringent. Here like-kind refers to the same depreciation class (5-year property, for example) as well as the property's use. Care should be taken to research personal property exchanges to ensure the acquired property is really of a like kind with the property disposed of.

The basis of the property received is the same as the basis of the property given up. Exchange expenses are generally closing costs. They may include such items as brokerage commissions, attorney fees, and deed preparation fees. They should be added to the basis of the like-kind property received.

Related Persons. If a like-kind exchange takes place directly or indirectly between related persons and either party disposes of the property within two years after the exchange, the exchange no longer qualifies for like-kind exchange treatment. Each person must report any gain or loss not recognized on the original exchange. Each person reports it on the tax return filed for the year in which the later disposition occurs. If this rule applies, the basis of the property received in the original exchange will be its fair market value.

These rules generally do not apply to the following kinds of property dispositions:

1. Dispositions due to the death of either related person.
2. Involuntary conversions.
3. Dispositions in which neither the original exchange nor the subsequent disposition had as a main purpose the avoidance of federal income tax.

Generally, related persons are ancestors, lineal descendants, brothers and sisters (whole or half), and spouses. Other "related" persons may, for example, include two corporations, an individual and a corporation, a grantor and a fiduciary, or other business arrangements.

Partially Nontaxable Exchange. A partially nontaxable exchange is an exchange in which someone receives unlike property or money in addition to like property. The basis of the property received is the same as the basis of the property given up, with the following adjustments:

1. Decrease the basis by the following amounts:
   a. Any money received.
   b. Any loss recognized on the exchange.
2. Increase the basis by the following amounts:
   a. Any additional costs incurred.
   b. Any gain recognized on the exchange.

If the other party to the exchange assumes the liabilities, the debt assumption is treated as money received in the exchange.

Partial Business Use of Property. If someone has property used partly for business and partly for personal use, and exchanges it in a nontaxable exchange for property to be used wholly or partly in their business, the basis of the property received is figured as if two properties had been exchanged. The first is an exchange of like-kind property. The second is personal-use property on which gain is recognized and loss is not recognized.

The adjusted basis in the property should first be figured as if someone transferred two separate properties. The adjusted basis of each part of the property is figured by taking into account any adjustments to basis. The depreciation taken or that could have taken is deducted from the adjusted basis of the business part. The amount realized for the property should then be figured and allocated to the business and nonbusiness parts of the property.

The business part of the property may be exchanged tax-free. However, any gain must be recognized from the exchange of the nonbusiness part. The taxpayer is deemed to have received, in exchange for the nonbusiness part, an amount equal to its FMV on the date of the exchange. The basis of the property acquired is the total basis of the property transferred (adjusted to the date of the exchange), increased by any gain recognized on the nonbusiness part.

If the nonbusiness part of the property transferred is the main home, it may be possible to exclude from income all or a portion of the gain on that part.

.06 Property Transferred from a Spouse

The basis of property transferred to a spouse or transferred in trust for one's benefit by a spouse (or former spouse if the transfer is incident to divorce) is the same as the spouse's adjusted basis. However, the basis must be adjusted for any gain recognized by the spouse or former spouse on property transferred in trust. This rule applies only to a transfer of property in trust in which the liabilities assumed, plus the liabilities to which the property is subject, are more than the adjusted basis of the property transferred.

If the property transferred is a series E, series EE, or series I U.S. Savings Bond, the transferor must include in income the interest accrued to the date of transfer. The basis in the bond immediately after the transfer is equal to the transferor's basis increased by the interest income includable in the transferor's income. The transferor must, at the time of the transfer, turn over the records necessary to determine the adjusted basis and holding period of the property as of the date of transfer.

.07   Inherited Property

The basis in property inherited from a decedent is generally one of the following:

1. The FMV of the property at the date of the individual's death.
2. The FMV on the alternate valuation date (six months later), if the personal representative for the estate chooses to use alternate valuation.
3. The value under the special-use valuation method for real property used in farming or other closely held business, if chosen for estate tax purposes.
4. The decedent's adjusted basis in land to the extent of the value that is excluded from the decedent's taxable estate as a qualified conservation easement.

If a federal estate tax return does not have to be filed, the basis in the inherited property is its appraised value at the date of death for state inheritance or transmission taxes.

Appreciated Property. The above rule does not apply to appreciated property received from a decedent if a taxpayer or spouse originally gave the property to the decedent within one year before the decedent's death. The basis in this property is the same as the decedent's adjusted basis in the property immediately before his or her death, rather than its FMV.

Appreciated property is any property whose FMV on the day it was given to the decedent is more than its adjusted basis.

.08   Community Property

In community property states (Arizona, California, Idaho, Louisiana, Nevada, New Mexico, Texas, Washington, and Wisconsin), husband and wife are each considered to own half the community property. When either spouse dies, the total value of the community property, even the part belonging to the surviving spouse, generally becomes the basis of the entire property.

For this rule to apply, at least half the value of the community property interest must be includable in the decedent's gross estate, whether or not the estate must file a return.

.09   Farm or Closely Held Business

Under certain conditions, when a person dies, the executor or personal representative of that person's estate may choose to value the qualified real property on other than its FMV. In that-case, the executor or personal representative values the qualified real property based on its use as a farm or its use in a closely held business. If the executor or personal representative chooses this method of valuation for estate tax purposes, that value is the basis of the property for the heirs. The qualified heirs should be able to get the necessary value from the executor or personal representative of the estate.

If a qualified heir received special-use valuation property, the basis in the property is the estate's or trust's basis in that property immediately before the distribution. The basis is increased by any gain recognized by the estate or trust because of post-death appreciation. Post-death appreciation is the property's FMV on the date of distribution minus the property's FMV either on the date of the individual's death or the alternate valuation date. All FMVs should be figured without regard to the special-use valuation.

It is possible to elect to increase the basis in special-use valuation property if it becomes subject to the additional estate tax. This tax is assessed if, within ten years after the death of the decedent, the property is transferred to a person who is not a member of the family, or the property stops being used as a farm or in a closely held business.

.10   Property Changed to Business or Rental Use

When property held for personal use is changed to business use or to produce rent, its basis for depreciation must be figured. An example of changing property held for personal use to business use would be renting out a former main home.

The basis for depreciation is the lesser of the following amounts:

1. The FMV of the property on the date of the change.
2. The adjusted basis on the date of the change.

If the property is later sold or disposed of, the basis of the property used will depend upon whether gain or loss occurred. The basis for figuring a gain is the adjusted basis when the property is sold. Figuring the basis for a loss starts with the smaller of the adjusted basis or the FMV of the property at the time of the change to business or rental use. This amount is then adjusted for the period after the change in the property's use to arrive at a basis for loss.

CHAPTER 38

Business Use of a Home

¶38,000   Overview

Now, with email and wireless connections—and with voice mail the industry standard—not only is it hard to tell where anyone is… but also, the public perception of someone who works from home has gone from "hardly working" to "smart businessperson." The home office means that the client is not paying for an upscale office, a receptionist, a parking valet, or even a water cooler. The client is paying for time and product.

On airplanes now, the only limit to the work time is the life of the computer battery, and even this is no longer an issue, as many airlines offer electrical outlets on seat armrests. The home office has taken to the sky!

¶38,001   Claiming the Deduction

Claiming the deduction for business use of the home may include deductions involving a house, apartment, condominium, mobile home, or boat. As pointed out later, it may include an unattached garage, studio, barn, or greenhouse;

however, it does not include any part of the property used exclusively as a hotel or inn. In this chapter are:

1. The requirements for qualifying to deduct expenses for the business use of the home (including special rules for storing inventory or product samples).
2. Types of expenses that can be deducted.
3. How to figure the deduction (including depreciation of the home).
4. Special rules for day-care providers.
5. Deducting expenses for furniture and equipment used in the business.
6. Records that should be kept.

The rules in this chapter apply to individuals, trusts, estates, partnerships, and S corporations. They do not apply to corporations (other than S corporations). There are no special rules for the business use of a home by a partner or S corporation shareholder.

¶38,002   Principal Place of Business

Rules that went into effect in 1999 make it easier to claim a deduction for the business use of a home. Under these rules, many taxpayers may qualify to claim the deduction, even though they had never qualified before. The following information explains these rules.

Under these latest rules for deducting expenses for the business use of a home, it is easier for a home office to qualify as the principal place of business. Under the old rules, a taxpayer had to consider the relative importance of the activities carried out at each business location when determining if a home was the principal place of business. The place where the taxpayer conducted the most important activities was the place where meetings were held with clients, customers, or patients, or the location where goods or services were delivered. Performing administrative or management duties in the home office was considered less important.

Before 1999, an outside salesperson's home office did not qualify as a principal place of business. The place where he or she met with customers to explain available products and take orders was considered more important than the home office where administrative duties were conducted. Beginning in 1999, however, a home office qualifies as a principal place of business for deducting expenses for the use of it:

1. If the home office is used exclusively for administration or management activities of a trade or business.
2. If the taxpayer has no other fixed location for conducting substantial administrative or management activities relating to a trade or business.

There are many activities that are administrative or managerial in nature. Some of these activities are:

1. Billing customers, clients, or patients.
2. Keeping books and records.
3. Ordering supplies.
4. Setting up appointments.
5. Forwarding orders or writing reports.

The following administrative or management activities performed at other locations will *not* disqualify a home office as a principal place of business:

1. When others conduct a taxpayer's administrative or management activities at locations other than the home.
2. The conduct of administrative or management activities at places that are not fixed locations of a business, such as in a car or a hotel room.
3. The taxpayer occasionally conducts minimal administrative or management activities at a fixed location outside of the home.
4. The taxpayer conducts substantial *non*administrative or *non*management business at a fixed location outside the home.
5. Suitable space to conduct administrative or management activities is available outside the home office, but a home office is used for those activities instead.

¶38,003   Other Criteria for Determining Place of Business

If the newer rules do not appear to cover the taxpayer's particular situation, the older rules may give an indication of other aspects when considering deductions for business use of the home.

It is permissible to have more than one business location, including a home, for a single trade or business. To qualify to deduct the expenses for the business use of a home, the home must be a principal place of business of that trade or business. To determine the principal place of business, all of the facts and circumstances must be considered. If, after considering the business locations, one cannot be identified as a principal place of business, then home office expenses cannot be deducted. The two primary factors to consider are:

1. The relative importance of the activities performed at each location.
2. The time spent at each location.

To determine whether a home is the principal place of business, the taxpayer must consider the relative importance of the activities carried out at each business location. The relative importance of the activities performed at each business location is determined by the basic characteristics of the business. If the business requires that meetings or conferences be held with clients or patients, or that goods or services be delivered to a customer, then the place where contacts are made must be given great weight in determining where the most important activities are performed.

If the relative importance of the activities does not clearly establish the principal place of business, such as when to deliver goods or services at both the office, in the home, and elsewhere, then the time spent at each location is important. Comparison should be made of the time spent on business at the home office with the time spent at other locations.

¶38,004   Separate Structures

Expenses can be deducted for a separate free-standing structure, such as a studio, garage, or barn, if the structure is used exclusively and regularly for the business. The structure does not have to be the principal place of business, or a place where patients, clients or customers are met.

¶38,005   Figuring the Deduction

Once it has been determined that the "home office" does qualify for a deduction, the next step is determining how much the taxpayer can deduct. Certain expenses related to the business use of a home can be deducted, but deductions are limited by the following:

1. Percentage of the home used for business, i.e., the business percentage.
2. Deduction limit.

To find the *business percentage*, the taxpayer must compare the size of the part of the home used for business to the entire house. The resulting percentage is used to separate the business part of the expenses from the expenses for operating the entire home. Any reasonable method to determine the business percentage can be used. Two commonly used methods are:

1. Dividing the square foot area of the "business space" by the total area of the home.
2. Dividing the number of rooms used for business by the total number of rooms in the home. This method can be used if the rooms in the home are all about the same size.

Beginning with 2013 tax returns the IRS permits a simplified method for calculating the amount of deduction. Just as for automobiles, there is a choice between a standard mileage rate and computing the actual expenses, so now with a home office, the taxpayer can select to compute the deduction at the rate of $5 per square feet (up to 300 square feet) or add up all the actual expenses and multiply by a percentage. It is advised that tax preparers initially compute the deduction under both methods to get an idea if the simplicity of claiming $5 per square foot is outweighed by a significant loss in the amount of the deduction. Use of the new $5 per square foot method means that the house will not be depreciated and that upon its eventual sale, no depreciation recapture will be required. The simplified method is claimed by checking the appropriate box on Schedule C.

In using the simplified method, it should be kept in mind that all of the usual requirements described in this chapter apply (exclusive use of the area, for example). For taxpayers who itemized deductions for home mortgage interest and real estate taxes, and used a portion of these expenses in computing their home mortgage deduction, there is good news. In using the simplified method, it is not necessary to reduce the $5 per square feet by any amount related to the mortgage interest and real estate taxes. In other words, the full amounts of the home mortgage interest and real estate tax deductions—which would be deductible whether or not the taxpayer claimed a home office deduction—are still fully deductible even if the taxpayer switches to the $5 per square foot method.

If the home office is used for only part of the year, it is necessary to calculate an average monthly square footage in order to apply the $5 per square foot method. Thus, a taxpayer using a 400 square foot office for only three months of the year will have the equivalent 100 square feet to multiply by the $5.

¶38,006   Deduction Limit

If gross income from the business use of a home equals or exceeds the total business expenses (including depreciation), all of the business expenses can be deducted. If the gross income from that use is less than the total business expenses, the deduction for certain expenses for the business use is limited. The deduction of otherwise nondeductible expenses, such as insurance, utilities, and depreciation (with depreciation taken last), allocable to business is limited to the gross income from the business use of the home minus the sum of the following:

1. The business part of expenses that could be deducted even if the home was not used for business (such as mortgage interest, real estate taxes, and casualty and theft losses).
2. The business expenses that relate to the business activity in the home (for example, salaries or supplies), but not to the use of the home itself.

A self-employed individual may not include in (2) above the deduction for half of the self-employment tax.

If deductions are greater than the current year's limit, it is possible to carry over the excess to the next year. Any carryover is subject to the gross income limit from the business use of the home for the next tax year. The amount carried over will be allowable only up to the taxpayer's gross income in the next tax year from the business in which the deduction arose whether the individual lives in that particular house or home during that year or not.

¶38,007   Assorted Use Tests

To qualify under the *regular use test*, a specific area of the home must be used for business on a continuing basis. The regular-use test is not met if the business use of the area is only occasional, even if that area is not used for any other purpose.

To qualify under the *trade or business use* test requires that part of a home be used in connection with a trade or business. If part of the home is used for some other profit-seeking activity that is not a trade or business, a deduction cannot be taken for a business use.

A taxpayer who is an employee must qualify under the *convenience-of-the-employer* test. If an employer provides suitable work space for administrative management activities, this fact must be considered in determining whether this test is met. Even if expenses qualify for a deduction for the business use of a home, the deduction may be limited. If the employee's gross income from the business use of a home is less than the employee's total business expenses, the deduction for some of the expenses—utilities, insurance, depreciation, for example—is limited.

¶38,008   Exclusive Use

To qualify under the *exclusive use* test, a specific area of a home must be used only for a trade or business. The area used for business can be a room or other separately identifiable space. The space does not need to be marked off by a permanent partition. If the home area in question is used both for business and personal purposes, it does not meet the requirements of the exclusive use test rule.

The exclusive use test does not have to be met if space is used for the *storage of inventory or product samples*, or for a *day-care facility*. When part of a home is used for the storage of inventory or product samples, the following 5 tests must all be met:

1. The inventory or product samples are kept for use in a trade or business.
2. The trade or business is a wholesale or retail selling of products.
3. The home is the only fixed location of a trade or business.
4. The storage space must be used on a regular basis.
5. The space is an identifiably separate space suitable for storage.

¶38,009   Part-Year Use

Expenses for the business use of a home *may not* be incurred during any part of the year it was not being used for business purposes. Only those expenses for the portion of the year in which it was actually used for business may be used in figuring the allowable deduction.

¶38,010   Day-Care Facility

If space in the home is used on a regular basis for providing day care, it may be possible to deduct the business expenses for that part of the home even though the same space is used for nonbusiness purposes. To qualify for this exception to the exclusive use rule, the following requirements must be met:

1. The space must be used in the trade or business of providing day care for children, persons 65 or older, or persons who are physically or mentally unable to care for themselves.
2. The taxpayer must have applied for, been granted or be exempt from having a license certification registration, or approval as a day-care center or as a family or group day-care home under state law. An individual does not meet this requirement if an application was rejected or license or other authorization was revoked.

If a part of the home is regularly used for day care, it is necessary to figure the percentage of that part which is used for day care, as explained above under *business percentage.* All the allocable expenses subject to the deduction limit, as explained earlier, may be deducted for that part used exclusively for day care. If the use of part of the home as a day-care facility is regular, but not exclusive, it is necessary to figure what part of available time it is actually used for business.

A room that is available for use throughout each business day and that is regularly used in the business is considered to be used for day care throughout each business day. It is not necessary to keep records to show the specific hours the area was used for business. The area may be used occasionally for personal reasons; however, a room used only occasionally for business does not qualify for the deduction.

To find that part of the available time the home is actually used for business, the total business-use time is compared to the total time that part of the home can be used for all purposes. The comparison may be based upon the hours of business use in a week with the number of hours in a week (168), or the hours of business use for the tax year with the number of hours in the tax year.

.01 Meal Allowance

If food is provided for a day-care business, the expense is not included as a cost of using the home for business. It is a separate deduction on the tax-payer's Schedule C (Form 1040). The cost of food consumed by the taxpayer or his or her family may not be deducted. However, 100 percent of the cost of food consumed by the day-care recipients and generally only 50 percent of the cost of food consumed by employees can be deducted. However, 100 percent of the cost of food consumed by employees can be deducted if its value can be excluded from their wages as a de minimis fringe benefit. The value of meals provided to employees on business premises is generally de minimis if more than half of these employees are provided the meals for the taxpayer's convenience.

If cost of food for the day-care business is deducted, a separate record (with receipts) must be maintained of the family's food costs. Reimbursements received from a sponsor under the Child and Adult Food Care Program of the Department of Agriculture are taxable only to the extent they exceed expenses for food for eligible children. If reimbursements are more than expenses for food, the difference is shown as income in Part I of Schedule C. If food expenses are greater than the reimbursements, the difference is shown as an expense in Part V of Schedule C. Alternatively, day care providers may choose to use a standardized rate to claim the deduction for meals provided to children in their care instead of keeping detailed records and receipts of food purchased for use in their business. The rates follow the USDA Child and Adult Food Care Program.

¶38,011 Business Furniture and Equipment

Depreciation and Section 179 deductions may be used for furniture and equipment that an employee uses in his or her home for business or work. These deductions are available whether or not the individual qualifies to deduct expenses for the business use of a home. Following are explanations of the different rules for:

1. Listed property.
2. Property bought for business use.
3. Personal property converted to business use.

.01 Listed Property

Special rules apply to certain types of property, called listed property, used in the home. Listed property includes any property of a type generally used for entertainment, recreation, and amusement (including photographic, phonographic, communication, and video recording equipment). But "listed property" also includes cell phones, computers and related equipment.

Listed property bought and placed in service since 1998 must be used more than 50 percent for business (including work as an employee) to be claimed as a Section 179 deduction or an accelerated depreciation deduction. If the business use of listed property is 50 percent or less, a Section 179 deduction cannot be taken and the property must be depreciated using the Alternate Depreciation System (ADS) (straight-line method). Listed property meets the more-than-50%-use test for any tax year if its qualified business use is more than 50 percent of its total use. Allocation among its various uses must be made for the use of any item of listed property used for more than one purpose during the tax year. The *percentage of investment use may not be used* as part of the percentage of qualified business use to meet the more-than-50%-use test. However, the taxpayer should use the combined total of business and investment use to figure the depreciation deduction for the property.

If an employee uses his or her own listed property (or listed rented property) for work as an employee, the property is business-use property only if both of the following requirements are met:

1. The use is for the convenience of the employer.
2. The use is required as a condition of employment.

"As a condition of employment" means that the use of the property is *necessary* for proper performance of work. Whether the use of the property is required for this purpose depends on all the facts and circumstances. The employer does not have to tell the employee specifically to have a computer for use in the home, nor is a statement by the employer to that effect sufficient.

If, in a year after placing an item of listed property in service, the taxpayer fails to meet the more-than-50%-use test for that item of property, he or she may be required to do both of the following:

1. Figure depreciation, beginning with the year the property is no longer used more than 50 percent for business, using the straight-line method.
2. Figure any excess depreciation and Section 179 deduction on the property and add it to:
   a. Gross income.
   b. The adjusted basis of the property.

It is not possible to take any depreciation of the Section 179 deduction for the use of listed property unless business/investment use can be proved with adequate records or sufficient evidence to support the individual's own statements. To meet the adequate records requirement, the taxpayer must maintain an account book, diary, log, statement of expense, trip sheet, or similar record or other documentary evidence that is sufficient to establish business/investment use.

.02   Property Bought for Business Use

The taxpayer who has bought certain property to use in his or her business can do any one of the following (subject to the limits discussed below):

1. Elect a Section 179 deduction for the full cost of the property.
2. Take part of the cost as a Section 179 deduction.
3. Depreciate the full cost of the property.

.03   Section 179 Deduction

A Section 179 deduction can generally be claimed on depreciable tangible personal property bought for use in the active conduct of business. The taxpayer can choose how much (subject to the limit) of the cost to deduct under Section 179 and how much to depreciate. The amount of immediate write-off available changes annually but is $1.16 million for 2023 and was $1.08 million for 2022. The Section 179 deduction can be spread over several items of property in any way selected as long as the total does not exceed the maximum allowable. However, the taxpayer cannot take a Section 179 deduction for the basis of the business part of the home or other real estate.

.04   Section 179 Deduction Limits

The Section 179 deduction cannot be more than the business cost of the qualifying property. In addition, the following limits apply when figuring a Section 179 deduction:

1. Maximum dollar limit.
2. Investment limit.
3. Taxable income limit.

If the cost of qualifying Section 179 property placed in service in a year is more than $2,890,000, the dollar limit must be reduced dollar for dollar. The deduction is subject to the following further limitations and conditions:

1. If the taxpayer places more than $2,890,000 of qualified property in service during the year, the amount is reduced dollar for dollar by the amount exceeding $2,890,000.
2. Taxpayers may now file an amended return to revoke or change an earlier Section 179 election.
3. The expensing election is now applicable to off-the-shelf computer software.

4. The full expensing election is no longer available for sport utility vehicles (SUVs) with a gross weight exceeding 6,000 pounds; for these vehicles it is limited to $26,200.

Existing rules concerning the kind of property eligible, the income limitations, and the carryover of unused depreciation remain in effect as under prior law.

The total cost that can be deducted each tax year is subject to the total *taxable income limit*. This is figured on the income from the active conduct of all trade or business activities, including wages, during the tax year. The taxable income for this purpose is figured in the usual way, but without regard to all of the following:

1. The Section 179 deduction.
2. The self-employment tax deduction.
3. Any net operating loss carryback or carryforward.

Thus, all expenses, including regular MACRS depreciation are first deducted and then the Section 179 depreciation may be used to zero-out the company's income but not to produce a net loss.

.05   Telephone and Internet Service

While it is possible to allocate utility costs such as electricity and gas to a home office based on the square feet of the office, other costs may be allocated on another basis. The long-standing rule for deducting the costs of a phone (land line) requires there be at least two phone lines, the first one always personal and the second presumptively for business. For a taxpayer with only one land line no allocation of that cost is permitted by the IRS. Thus, it is only the cost of a second land line (or additional lines) that may be deducted if the line is used for business.

Cell phones are treated differently. The Tax Court has ruled that a taxpayer may use a cell phone for business even if the cost of the phone is part of a family plan (*Kaminsski*, TC Summary Opinion 2015-7). But again, the existence of more than one cell phone is critical.

The Court has also characterized Internet access expenses as utility expenses (*Verma v. Commissioner*, T.C. Memo. 2001-132). Strict substantiation—as with listed property—therefore does not apply, and the Court may estimate a taxpayer's deductible expenses provided that the Court has a reasonable evidentiary basis for making an estimate (following the Cohan rule).

¶38,012   Depreciation

Form 4562 is used to claim a deduction for depreciation. It does not include any costs deducted in Part I (Section 179 deduction).

Most business property used in a home office is either five-year or seven-year property under MACRS.

1. Five-year property includes computers and peripheral equipment, type-writers, calculators, adding machines, and copiers.
2. Seven-year property includes office furniture and equipment such as desks, files, and safes.

Under MACRS, the half-year convention is generally used, which allows deduction of a half-year of depreciation in the first year the property is used in the business. If more than 40 percent of the depreciable property was placed in service during the last three months of the tax year, the mid-quarter convention must be used instead of the half-year convention.

¶38,013   Personal Property Converted to Business Use

If property is used in the home office that was used previously for personal pur-poses, a Section 179 deduction cannot be taken for the property, but it can be depreciated. The method of depreciation depends upon when the property was first used for personal purposes. When property was formerly used personally and is now converted to business use, for example, office furniture or a com-puter, the basis used for depreciation is the lower of the asset's cost or other basis and its fair market value at the time it is converted to business use.

¶38,014   Additional First-Year Depreciation

The sluggish recovery from the recession and the desire for increased business spending led Congress to implement an ultra-accelerated depreciation regimen beginning in 2008. Depending on the year—between 2008 and 2017—busi-nesses were allowed to write off either half or the full cost of new personal prop-erty placed in service. For property acquired and placed in service during 2022, taxpayers could take a 100-percent bonus first-year depreciation. In 2023, first-year bonus depreciation is 80 percent of the purchase price, and 60 percent in 2024, 40 percent in 2025, 20 percent in 2026, and none thereafter. To qualify for this first-year depreciation, property must be new personal property (origi-nal use) and not real estate.

CHAPTER 39
Limited Liability Companies

¶39,000   Overview

One of the most important decisions an accountant may advise a client about is the structure of a new business—the choice of entity. In the past, the analysis required a comparison of the advantages and disadvantages of a taxable corporation, an S corporation, a partnership, or a sole proprietorship. To this mix has been added the limited liability company (LLC). An LLC, if so elected, is taxed in the same manner as a partnership for federal income tax purposes. However, the owners may also elect to have the LLC taxed as an S corporation, a taxable corporation (C corporation) or a sole proprietorship. The advantage of an LLC over a partnership is the fact that the owners, referred to as members, are shielded from personal liability for the business' debts and liabilities. LLC members are liable only for their capital contributions. A general partner is not afforded this protection.

An LLC offers the tax flexibility of a partnership with the personal liability protection of a corporation. It also provides options for management, allowing members either to participate directly in the management of the business or to designate certain members or nonmembers as managers.

In part, the demand for a new entity grew out of the restrictive nature of S corporations as vehicles for small business. These corporations were originally designed as a hybrid between a regular C (tax-paying) corporation and a partnership. However, in drafting the rules for S corporations, Congress limited the number of shareholders to 100 (originally 10), placed restrictions on classes of stock, prescribed the type of taxpayers who could own stock, controlled the relative amounts that can be distributed to shareholders, and introduced other restrictions and limitations as well as special taxes. The S corporation hybridization thus produced a very high-strung tax entity. In response, beginning with Wyoming in 1977, all 50 states have passed statutes creating LLCs as an alternative. For many small businesses that form LLCs, however, a serious disadvantage is the requirement to pay Self-Employment (SE) tax (15.2%) on their share of income. As a result, some LLCs have elected to be taxed as S Corporations to eliminate their exposure to SE tax. However, the extent to which all members of an LLC are subject to SE tax has remained controversial. This is due in part to the fact that limited partners in a limited partnership are not required to pay the SE tax. This has led some accountants to ask: What about minority members of an LLC who perform no services? Or what about an allocation of an LLC member's income between earnings from services and earnings that are a return on capital? This would make only the service earnings subject to SE tax. Congress has not definitively ruled on this issue. Taxpayers and the IRS have their own opinions.

¶39,001   Advantages of LLCs over S Corporations

LLCs offer many advantages over S corporations, sixteen of which are discussed below:

1. *Type of ownership.* Owners (members) may be individuals, partnerships, C corporations, S corporations, trusts or estates (there is no restriction on the type of tax entity that may own an interest). Whereas, only individuals, estates, S corporations owning 100 percent of their stock, and certain trusts may own S corporations. They may not be owned by C (taxable) Corporations or partnerships. In addition, only citizens or residents of the U.S. may own an S corporation.

2. *Number of owners.* There is no limit on the number of owners for an LLC. S corporations are limited to 100 shareholders; if they exceed that number, their status as an S corporation is terminated.
3. *Special allocations.* Like partnerships, LLCs are allowed to make special allocations of a member's share of income, deduction, gain, loss, or credit items, as long as such allocations have economic substance (are not done primarily for tax reasons). S corporations are allowed to allocate only separately stated items on a per-day, per-share basis.
4. *Basis adjustments.* Like partnerships, LLCs may elect to adjust the basis of assets to reflect changes in ownership. This election, which is not available to S corporations, allows new owners to benefit from additional depreciation deductions resulting from the appreciation of assets reflected in the purchase price.
5. *Basis from debt.* Members of an LLC, like partners in a partnership, may be permitted to include in the calculation of their individual ownership basis (outside basis), their share of the LLC's debt, if they have personally guaranteed the debt. This may allow for the deduction of a loss that exceeds the basis of the assets contributed to the LLC by a member. S corporation shareholders include only the amount of debt personally loaned to the corporation in the calculation of their shareholder basis. Thus, S corporation shareholders may not use the S corporation's debt to allow deductions for losses generated by the S corporation, even if they are personally liable.
6. *Special taxes.* LLCs are not subject to any special taxes. S corporations are subject to a built-in gains tax (Internal Revenue Code [IRC] Section 1374) upon disposing of an appreciated asset held less than ten years (assuming the S corporation converted from a former C corporation). [Note: Ten years was temporarily reduced to seven years for 2010.]
7. *Partnership rules apply.* One of the greatest advantages of an LLC is that the rules of partnership taxation apply. Although LLCs are not covered by specific code sections in the Internal Revenue Code, their taxation is identical to partnerships, assuming they have elected to be treated in that manner. This confers on them the flexibility of partnership taxation.
8. *S corporation termination.* S corporations are subject to inadvertent termination of their tax status if they fail to comply with the ongoing eligibility requirements. Specifically, the election may be terminated by the IRS for having more than 100 shareholders, issuing more than one class of stock, having a foreign (nonresident, noncitizen) shareholder, having a corporate shareholder, or having a nonresident shareholder. LLCs are terminated in accordance with their controlling member agreements (analogous to a partnership agreement) or state law. The partnership rule that terminates a partnership when more than 50 percent of its ownership is sold, also applies to LLCs, however.

9. *Cash distributions to members.* LLCs offer more flexibility when it comes to distributions to members than do S corporations. LLCs place no limits on the amounts or timing of distributions to members. By contrast, S corporation distributions that are preferential or not based on shareholder ownership percentages (pro rata) may be construed by the IRS as evidence of more than one class of stock.

10. *Fringe benefits.* Fringe benefits provided to LLC members may be treated as guaranteed payments, and are therefore deductible by the LLC. Such benefits include medical insurance, group-term life insurance, and similar items. In the case of S corporations, a deduction for fringe benefits is allowed only for those shareholders owning 2 percent or less of the company's stock.

11. *Transfer of appreciated assets.* The transfer of appreciated assets to an LLC may be accomplished without the recognition of gain. LLCs are not subject to the requirements of IRC Section 351 that applies to S corporations. Shareholders of an S corporation failing to qualify under IRC Section 351 must recognize gain on the difference between the basis of assets they contribute and the fair market value of the stock they receive if the 80 percent control requirement of IRC Section 368(c) is not met. The IRC Section 351 requirement is ownership of at least 80 percent of the S corporation's stock by those transferring the assets.

12. *Transfer of liabilities.* The transfer of assets with related liabilities is generally not a problem for LLCs, as the liabilities adjust the basis of the LLC members' ownership interest (outside basis). In contrast, S corporation shareholders transferring assets with liabilities in excess of the basis of the assets will recognize a gain on the difference.

13. *Distribution of appreciated assets.* The distribution of appreciated assets to the members of an LLC generally does not produce gain for the LLC or its members. Corporations, including S corporations, however, are required to recognize the gain on appreciated property distributed to shareholders, although the gain is passed through to the S corporation shareholders (IRC Sections 311 and 336).

14. *Former status.* S corporations that were formerly C corporations and have retained earnings and profits are subject to special rules regarding distributions to shareholders. While the amount of the Accumulated Adjustment Account (AAA) may be distributed tax free to shareholders, distributions in excess of that amount may be deemed distributions of former C corporation Earnings and Profits, which are taxable as dividends. In addition, S corporations are subject to potential personal holding company income tax and risk termination of their S corporation elections if they generate a certain amount of passive income over a three-year period. LLCs have no such

restrictions. Finally, though an S corporation may terminate its S corporation election and revert to C corporation status, the shareholders have only one year to distribute any balance in the AAA to the shareholders tax-free. After one year, the balance in the AAA is terminated and the shareholders are taxed on distributions based on the C corporation rules. If the corporation later re-elects to become an S corporation (after the five-year waiting period, for example) the former balance in the former AAA account is not restored, it was lost forever after one year from the termination of the previous S corporation status.

15. *Liquidation.* In contrast to S corporations, LLCs are not required to recognize gain on appreciated assets upon liquidation.

16. *Guaranteed payments.* Unique to partnerships and LLCs are payments from the partnership or LLC to a member for services or capital. The payments are deductible by the LLC and reportable as income by the member. In contrast to a member draw that has no tax result to the member, except to reduce his or her basis in the LLC interest, a guaranteed payment does not affect the member's basis. This is because distribution is cancelled out, as it is included in income. Guaranteed payments provide flexibility in compensating LLC members. This provision is not available to S corporations.

¶39,002 Disadvantages of LLCs Compared to S Corporations

The main disadvantages of LLCs as compared to S corporations follow:

- *Payroll taxes.* The S corporation's income taxed to its shareholders is not subject to self-employment Tax. Income earned by an LLC resulting from the efforts of its members is subject to self-employment tax. This provides an advantage to S corporation shareholders who may take part of the company's profits as salary, subject to Social Security, and part as S corporation distributions, which are *not* subject to self-employment or other payroll taxes.

- *Continuity of life.* The sale of S corporation stock does not dissolve the corporate entity (although the sale of more than 50 percent can result in revocation if the new majority owner affirmatively refuses to consent to election). Sale of more than 50 percent of an LLC interest dissolves the LLC (in accordance with partnership accounting rules and state law).

- *Untested waters.* Because state statutes regarding LLCs are not uniform and there is not yet a history of litigation and judicial rulings on their operation, some taxpayers have hesitated to use LLCs, especially in interstate commerce or when members are residents of different states. Third parties, such as banks may show reluctance to deal with an LLC until the legal status is more secure. As states adopt uniform LLC statutes and allow registration of foreign (from other states) LLCs, this problem should be resolved. Activities such as real estate holdings and exploitation of natural resources may use LLCs with little concern for these problems.

- *Family income splitting.* In attempts to split income among family members, the gift of the stock of an S corporation is more likely to be respected by the IRS than a similar gift of an LLC interest.

¶39,003   Terminology

An understanding of LLCs can be aided by becoming familiar with the terms used to describe them. The following list of definitions will allow the accountant to better advise a client in choosing an entity that best represents the structure of a new business:

Articles of organization. The agreement forming the LLC and setting out its operating procedures.

Capital account. Each member has a capital account on the books of the LLC. To determine the value of a capital account, a member's capital sharing ratio is multiplied by the net asset value of the LLC (fair market value of assets less liabilities). This represents the amount a member would receive upon liquidation of the LLC.

Disregarded entity. The term applied by the IRS for one-member LLCs electing to be taxed as sole proprietorships.

Inside basis. The LLC's tax basis in its assets for depreciation purpose.

K-1. The annual reporting form received by each member of the LLC (assuming the LLC has elected to be taxed as a partnership and not as a corporation).

Manager. Refers to a person who, alone or together with others, is vested with the continuing exclusive authority to make management decisions necessary to conduct the business for which the LLC was formed.

Members. The owners of an LLC are referred to as *members* rather than as partners or shareholders. Members may be assigned different roles in the organization with some handling management responsibilities and others serving only as investors.

Outside basis. The basis of an LLC member in his or her ownership position.

Profit and loss sharing ratios. Each member is assigned a percentage of the profits and losses of the LLC. The percentage may be changed by amending the operating agreement.

Separately stated items. The items of income, deduction, gain, loss, or credit that are allocated to each member in accordance with the operating agreement.

Single-member LLC. An LLC formed under state law with only one owner.

Special allocation. The operating agreement may specify that specific separately stated items be allocated in other than the profit and loss sharing ratios.

¶39,004   Formation of an LLC

An LLC is formed by the operation of state law. The first step is to draft *articles of organization* or a *certificate of formation*. This document, like articles of incorporation or a partnership agreement, sets out the basic ground rules for the organization. LLCs may be formed as new entities or they may emerge from the conversion or merger of already existing entities.

The articles of organization state the business purpose of the entity, its duration, the requirements for transfer of an interest, and the nature of management. In drafting the document, the goal is to maintain the limited legal liability of the owners while distinguishing the organization from a corporation. Until the "check the box" entity classification regulations promulgated by the IRS in 1996, there was significant concern and discussion regarding the avoidance of the following corporate characteristics: unlimited duration, free transferability of ownership interests, or centralization of management. The 1996 IRS rules allow LLCs to be taxed as partnerships or corporations at the election of the owners. The IRS developed Form 8832, *Entity Classification Election*, allowing taxpayers to check a box indicating what kind of taxable entity they elect to be. (Reg. §§301.7701-1–3.) The default for an LLC with two or more members is a partnership. For a single member LLC the default is a sole proprietorship. If the LLC wishes to be taxed as a corporation this form should be filed with the IRS within 75 days of the LLC's formation. If this deadline is passed, the IRS has provided relief, if the form is filed with the taxpayer's first tax return (see "LLC Developments and Cautions"). It is possible to change the election in a later year. All states also allow one-member LLCs that are described later.

.01   Contribution of Assets

Contributions of property to an LLC (upon formation or later) generally result in no tax consequences to the contributing member or the LLC at the time of contribution. The LLC takes over the tax basis of the contributing member.

A member contributing appreciated property (fair market value in excess of tax basis), however, is allocated the precontribution gain or loss, to be recognized later when the property is sold. When the LLC sells the nondepreciable property, the built-in portion of the gain or loss is allocated first to the contributing partner before being allocated in accordance with the income and loss-sharing percentages of the articles of organization. For depreciable property, the Regulations (§1.704-3) allow alternative methods of determining the precontribution gain. The assets are depreciated for book (capital account) and tax to reflect the differences in their basis.

Illustration 39-1. Contribution of Assets

The articles of organization for the Fred-Bob Limited Liability Company call for all profits and losses to be allocated equally to the members, unless otherwise required by law. At the start of the company, Fred contributed 25 acres of land he had purchased for $25,000 ten years ago. At contribution the land is worth $100,000. Bob contributed cash of $100,000. The LLC uses the cash to develop a nine-hole golf course. Two years later, the golf course is completed and sold for $300,000. Each member receives $150,000 and the LLC is dissolved. How much gain is allocated to each member?

1. Total gain = $175,000 (sales price $300,000 minus basis $125,000)
2. Less: Fred's precontribution gain = $75,000 (fair market value of land $100,000 at contribution less basis $25,000)
3. Allocate balance of gain, $100,000 equally to Fred and Bob per articles of organization
4. Result = Fred's total gain is $125,000 and Bob's $50,000

.02   Accounting Methods, Tax Year, and Elections of LLCs

The partnership accounting rules are applied to LLCs. An LLC is allowed to use the cash method, accrual method, or a hybrid accounting method that clearly reflects its income. However, with the exception of small LLCs, if one or more of its members (owners) is a corporation required to use the accrual method, it must use the accrual method as well.

The tax year of an LLC is controlled by the partnership rules; it must use the year of its principle members. Generally, if the members are individuals, the LLC will have a calendar year. Exceptions are available for natural business years or business purpose.

Like partnerships, LLCs are allowed an election to step up the basis of a pro rata share of its property to reflect the purchase price a new member pays to buy the interest of an existing member. In the case of real estate investment, for example, this increases the depreciation deduction for the new member relative to the other members (see "Basis Step-Up Rules for Purchased LLC Interests").

Elections of other accounting methods such as inventory flow assumptions, depreciation method, and long-term contracts follow general tax rules set out in the Internal Revenue Code. An unincorporated business having two or more owners may elect to be taxed for federal income tax purposes as a corporation or as a partnership (Form 8832). Thus, an LLC has the option of how it is taxed. Unless the LLC wishes to be taxed as a corporation the form is not filed.

Organization costs are amortized over 180 months except that up to $5,000 may qualify as an immediate deduction.

.03   Allocation of Income, Deductions, Gain, Loss and Credits

For start-up businesses, the use of an LLC provides definite advantages over a taxable corporation or an S corporation. The LLC form allows special allocations of income, deductions, gains, losses, and credits tailored to the individual investors (subject to economic reality checks). In particular, this may be beneficial with businesses incurring significant initial R&D expenses. To the extent that these costs qualify, a loss produced by their deduction may be passed through to the members, offsetting their individual income.

¶39,005   Ordering Rules for Deduction of Losses

A member's basis in the LLC is determined at the end of the tax year and includes all increases (including income) and decreases (including distributions)—*except losses*. The deductibility of losses is determined last. Losses are only deductible up to the amount of a member's basis. Losses are allocated to basis last (distributions and changes in liabilities have already been taken into account). This increases the chances of losses being disallowed (though they may be carried over to future years).

¶39,006   Separately Stated Items

The separately stated items are those items of income or deduction, gain, loss, or credit that could affect the computation of one member's personal income tax differently from another member's. The list of separately stated items for LLCs is identical to that of partnerships or S corporations:

- Capital gains and losses—long term.
- Capital gains and losses—short term.
- IRC section 1231 gains and losses.
- Charitable contributions.
- Portfolio income (interest and dividends).
- Expenses related to portfolio income.
- Section 179 immediate expensing.
- Items specially allocated—specific items controlled by the operating agreement and differing from the profit or loss sharing ratios.
- Alternative Minimum Tax (AMT) preference items.
- Passive activity items—including rental income and expenses.
- Investment interest expense.

- Intangible drilling costs.
- Taxes paid to foreign countries.
- Tax-exempt income (increases member's basis).
- Nonbusiness and personal (nondeductible) items (decrease member's basis).

¶39,007　Distribution of Assets

Generally no gain or loss is recognized by the LLC or the member to whom assets are distributed. An exception occurs when the cash and marketable securities distribution is greater than the basis of the member in his or her LLC membership interest. The property distributed to the member retains the same tax basis it had to the LLC. When an LLC is liquidated, each member must receive assets with a fair market value equal to the member's capital account. A member with a negative capital account is required to restore the balance to zero. If the articles of organization guarantee specific distributions upon liquidation, *regardless of the capital account balance*, the allocation will not have economic effect.

¶39,008　Compliance Issues

A multimember LLC must file IRS Form 1065 to report the LLC's income and the members' shares of income or loss as well as the members' shares of separately stated items. Single-member LLCs that have elected to be taxed as sole proprietorships report their activity on Schedule C of the owner's Form 1040. If Form 8832, *Entity Classification Election*, is being filed, it should be filed within 75 days of the formation of the entity. If this deadline is passed, it should be attached to the federal tax or information return of the entity for the taxable year for which the election is made (see "LLC Developments and Cautions").

¶39,009　Capital Account Versus Basis

Members of LLCs are required to maintain a record of their ownership basis in the LLC (outside basis). This balance frequently differs from their capital account that is maintained on the LLC's books.

The member's basis in his or her ownership position is computed at least annually and consists of the prior year's ending basis *plus*:

- The basis of additional property contributed to the LLC during the year.
- Income (including tax exempt income) and gains (including capital gains) generated by the LLC and passed through to the member.
- Fair market value of services provided to the LLC in exchange for additional capital ownership.
- Any increase in the member's share of the LLC's liabilities.

Minus:

- Distributions from the LLC to the member.
- Losses and deductions (including nondeductible items) passed through to the member.
- The member's share of any reduction in the LLC's liabilities.

As with partnership accounting, the (book/accounting) capital accounts of the LLC members reflect the fair market value of their ownership interest in the LLC, whereas the basis in their LLC interest is used to compute gain or loss upon sale or other disposition of the interest.

A distribution (draw) cannot reduce the member's basis below zero. There-fore, a distribution in excess of basis produces a capital gain to the member. A reduction in a member's share of liabilities is treated as a distribution and has the same result as a cash distribution.

¶39,010   Assets Contributed to the LLC

Assets contributed to an LLC by a member carry over the property's basis in the hands of the member. The holding period of capital and IRC section 1231 assets contributed continues the member's holding period as well. In the case of ordinary income property, such as inventory, the holding period for the LLC begins upon contribution. Capital gain property with a built-in loss (the basis exceeded the fair market value on the date of contribution) must be held by the LLC for five years before its sale will result in an ordinary loss.

The method and life used to depreciate property before its contribution carry over and are used by the LLC. No section 179 deduction is allowed on contrib-uted property. If the property contributed was not used in a trade or business prior to its contribution, its basis for depreciation is the lower of its original cost or its fair market value on the date of contribution.

¶39,011   Basis Step-Up Rules for Purchased LLC Interests

When an LLC interest is purchased, there is often a difference between the pur-chase price and the LLC's proportionate share of basis in its assets (inside basis). This is particularly common in real estate LLCs. An election is available to step-up (or down) the basis of the portion of the assets that represent the purchasing member's interest in those assets (IRC sections 754, 743, and 734). The assets are stepped-up to the new member's basis in the LLC. Depreciable assets are, thereby, stepped up to their fair market value, and depreciation deductions are increased *only with respect to the new member*. Additional accounting records are required to keep track of the depreciation for the new member as well as for the old, but if the difference between the old LLC basis and the purchase price of the LLC interest is significant, it can be worth the additional effort.

¶39,012   Debt Allocation—Recourse Versus Nonrecourse

The amount of debt allocated to a member of an LLC affects his or her basis in that individual's ownership interest. The distinction between recourse and nonrecourse debt affects partnership accounting because general partners are personally liable for recourse debt. However, different rules apply to determine the amount of the debt allocated to a partner, depending upon whether it is recourse or nonrecourse debt.

Debt for which individual partners are personally responsible is recourse debt. In the case of recourse debt, the IRS prescribes a *constructive liquidation scenario*, which generally allocates an amount of debt to each partner that corresponds to his or her personal liability to the partnership were it to liquidate. See Illustration 39-2 below.

Debt for which no individual partner is personally liable is nonrecourse. Nonrecourse debt is allocated in stages depending upon the existence in the partnership (LLC) of minimum gain, precontribution gain and the wording of the operating agreement.

Because members of an LLC are protected from liability for the LLC's debt, all debt is nonrecourse, unless a member has agreed to be personally liable. Nonrecourse debt increases member basis but not necessarily the amount at-risk.

Illustration 39-2: Nonrecourse Debt Allocation

Level 1 :   Amount of nonrecourse debt
                }
                Section 704(b)   } = minimum gain
                } (allocate per agreement)

Level 2:   Fair market value of property on date of contribution
                }
                Section 704(c)   } = precontribution gain
                } (specific allocation)

Level 3:   Tax basis of property on date of contribution
                }
                } = allocation [based on
                } (profit sharing percent)

Minimum gain. If the amount of nonrecourse debt exceeded the fair market value of the assets on the date of contribution, a minimum gain was created.

Calculation of the minimum gain assumes, hypothetically, that the lender is to foreclose on the property securing the debt (IRC Section 704(b)).

If the property were foreclosed and the amount of LLC nonrecourse debt is in excess of the book basis (accounting/capital account basis/fair market value on date of contribution) of the property, the excess of the nonrecourse debt over the book basis is referred to as the minimum gain, and its allocation is in accordance with the LLC articles of organization.

If the property has been contributed to the LLC and the contributing member's tax basis in the property was less than the nonrecourse debt encumbering the property at the date of contribution, and less than its fair market value, an additional allocation of nonrecourse debt is made.

The amount of fair market value that was in excess of the contributing member's basis is allocated to that member. (This gain amount is the *built-in gain*, or *precontribution gain*.) (IRC Section 704(c))

The balance of the nonrecourse debt (the amount up to the tax basis of the property when it was contributed) is allocated to the members using their profit sharing ratio.

¶39,013   At-Risk Limits

LLCs are covered by the same restrictive limits as individuals, partnerships, and S corporations when it comes to the at-risk limits of IRC section 465. Losses passed through to the members by the LLC are deductible by the members only to the extent they *are* at economic risk of loss. The allocation of basis from LLC debt does not guarantee that a member will be able to deduct losses generated by the LLC. Unused losses may be carried forward by members and deducted later when the LLC generates income.

Planning can improve the ability of a member to deduct losses. An important step in this process involves the aggregation of at-risk activities. If a loss business and a profitable one operated by the LLC can be combined into one activity for at-risk purposes, the loss can offset the profit, and the net will be passed through to the members. If the two businesses are treated as separate activities, however, the profit will pass through separately to the member as well as the loss, and the loss may not be deductible.

¶39,014   Limited Liability Partnerships

In place of LLCs for professional services—doctors, dentists, attorneys, architects, accountants—states allow the formation of Limited Liability Partnerships.

These afford general liability protection for a business in the same manner as professional corporations, but thus do not protect the individual owners from liability for their own malpractice or the malpractice of those whom they directly supervise. However, the limited liability generally extends protection to each individual owner against the malpractice of the other owners.

.01   Tax Matters Partner

An LLC electing to be taxed as a partnership files Form 1065 and is requested to name a *tax matters partner*, designated to deal with the IRS on behalf of the partnership. For purposes of naming a tax matters partner on behalf of an LLC, the IRS will allow only a member-manager of the LLC to be so named. In a partnership, only a general partner may serve as a tax matters partner.

¶39,015   One-Member LLCs

All states allow the formation of one-member LLCs. These entities provide the owner with the personal liability protections of an LLC under state law but they are taxed either as a sole proprietor or a corporation for federal income tax purposes, including the choice of being taxed as an S Corporation if a further election is made with the IRS. The default of a one-member LLC is a sole proprietorship and if the owner desires corporate taxation, the owner makes this choice by filing IRS Form 8832 and checking the appropriate box. Form 8832 should be filed within 75 days of formation or be attached to the federal tax return of the entity (or individual) for the taxable year for which the election is made. If the owner does not elect to be taxed as a corporation the IRS refers to him or her as a *disregarded entity*. The owner completes 1040 form Schedule C (for a business) or Schedule E (for a real estate rental operation) and SE for other sole proprietorships.

In the past, sole proprietors seeking legal liability protection under state law were required to incorporate their business to gain this protection. As a result of forming a corporation, whether a taxable C corporation or a flow-through S corporation, the business incurs the additional accounting and paperwork required to file a federal income tax return for the business. In most cases this also requires quarterly payroll tax filing as well, for the owner's salary. The single-member LLC avoids the necessity of additional accounting and tax filing while providing the desired liability protection. Some states do impose an entity tax on single-member LLCs.

¶39,016   LLC Electing To Be Taxed as S Corporation

To come full circle in a discussion of the advantages and disadvantages of an LLC as opposed to an S Corporation, is to examine the reasons that some LLCs elect to be taxed as S Corporations. As noted earlier, LLCs have a number of choices with respect to their tax status with the IRS. Single member LLCs may be taxed as sole proprietors or may elect to be taxed as corporations. Once taxed as corporations they can make the further election to be taxed as S Corporations. The same is true for two or more member LLCs, within the 100 shareholder limit of S Corporation status. The primary advantage of so doing is to reduce the bite of Self-employment tax (Social Security taxes).

An LLC, like a partnership, distributes its earned income to its members (partners) who are subject to Self-employment tax on their share. Self-employment tax is the equivalent of both the employee's and the employer's share of Social Security. Distributions of an S Corporation's income, on the contrary, are not self-employment income. Shareholders of an S Corporation pay Social Security taxes only on their wages. For this reason, some LLCs, especially if they believe all their income is not the result of the owners' personal efforts, decide that electing to be taxed as an S Corporation is more beneficial than being taxed as a partnership and paying Self-Employment tax on all the company's earnings. However, just as any S Corporation must be prepared to justify to the IRS the reasonableness of the owners' salaries—that they are not arbitrarily set too low to avoid Self-Employment tax—an LLC that elects to be taxed as an S Corporation is subject to the same restrictions.

¶39,017   Conversion to an LLC

The owners of a corporation, including an S corporation, desiring to convert the corporation to an LLC are faced with the prospect of first liquidating the corporation and thereby incurring double taxation—first at the corporate level—and then on the distribution of assets to the shareholder. There is no direct reorganization statute that allows a tax-free conversion of a corporation to an LLC. By contrast, the conversion of a partnership or a sole proprietorship to an LLC is straightforward and can be accomplished without generating taxable income. However, state law may hold the members personally liable for the debts of the former entity.

¶39,018   LLC Developments and Cautions

.01   Members Can Avoid Liability for Unpaid Payroll Taxes

Businesses that find themselves strapped for cash sometimes hold back payments of withheld income, FICA, and Medicare taxes (trust fund taxes) to the IRS. This has always been a dangerous maneuver because the IRS has the authority to collect these taxes from the individual(s) involved in the decision to place other creditors ahead of the IRS (referred to as the "responsible person," IRC Section

6672). The result is referred to as the 100 percent penalty—the IRS collects up to 100 percent of the withheld payroll taxes from the responsible person. The responsible person has sometimes been the comptroller or the controlling share-holders of a small business. In addition, the IRS can collect withheld payroll taxes from the general partners of a partnership. However, in Rev. Rul. 2004-41, the IRS indicated that it cannot collect delinquent withheld payroll taxes from a member of an LLC—unless, of course, the member is also found to be a respon-sible person—the one with authority to withhold payment from the IRS. LLC members not directly involved in such decisions therefore receive protection not accorded the partners of a general partnership.

.02   Built-in Loss Rules Tightened to Curb Abuse of Duplicate Loss Deductions

Contributions of property to partnerships by partners can produce built-in losses if the partner's basis of the property contributed exceeds its fair market value. The transfer of a partnership interest involving a substantial built-in loss (defined as basis exceeding fair market value by more than $250,000) now re-quires a mandatory IRC Section 743 basis adjustment reducing the property's basis to the partnership to its fair market value, thus preventing loss recognition when the property is sold.

.03   AICPA Issues LLC Practice Bulletin

To aid practitioners in the preparation of financial statements for LLCs the AICPA issued Practice Bulletin 14, *Accounting and Reporting by Limited Li-ability Companies and Limited Liability Partnerships* in April 1995. The bulletin addresses issues of disclosure and presentation. According to the AICPA, "A complete set of LLC financial statements should include a statement of finan-cial position as of the end of the reporting period, a statement of operations for the period, a statement of cash flows for the period, and accompanying notes to the financial statements."

.04   Form 8832, Entity Classification Election

The IRS has provided relief for LLCs that fail to file the Form 8832, *Entity Classification Election*, within 75 days of the entity's formation. IRS Rev. Proc. 2002-59 specifies procedures for filing the form by the due date of the LLC's first federal income tax return (not including extensions). Owners failing to comply with government filing requirements risk personal liability for obliga-tions of the LLC. If the LLC status is not properly maintained in accordance with state law, it may be disregarded by the IRS. Most states require an annual filing and fee. This is true of corporations as well.

Other cautions include:

- The at-risk loss rules apply to members of LLCs and may limit the deduction of losses by a member.
- The passive activity loss limits apply to members of LLCs and may limit the deduction of losses on passive rental activities.
- The Alternative Minimum Tax (AMT) adjustments and preferences generated by an LLC flow through to the individual members and are combined with their personal AMT items.
- The Internal Revenue Code contains rules defining tax shelters. If an LLC is classified as a tax shelter, specific restrictions apply, including the inability of the LLC to use the cash method of accounting.
- When an LLC interest is being sold, the kinds of assets held by the company should be analyzed. Although in general the sale will produce a capital gain to the seller, certain assets will convert part or all of the gain to ordinary income. The kinds of assets causing this result are referred to as *hot assets* and include unrealized receivables and inventory.

CHAPTER 40

Independent Contractor or Employee?

¶40,000   Overview

Whether a person is an employee or independent contractor has been an area of uncertainty for many years. In August 1996, during the 104th Congress, changing and strengthening the "safe harbor" provisions were enacted as part of the Small Business Jobs Protection Act. The changes allow small businesses to rely on previous IRS actions and determinations to avoid reclassification of independent contractors as employees. The legislation does, however, still leave open the key question of what exactly is an independent contractor.

In February 2011, the IRS developed new training materials for tax examiners handling worker classification cases—that is, whether a worker should be classified as an employee or an independent contractor. At various meetings with small business owners, sponsored by the IRS, participants identified worker classification as a major concern. To address this concern, all IRS examiners handling worker classification cases are to receive additional training to ensure that workers are properly classified.

For federal tax purposes, this is an important distinction. Worker classification affects the payment of federal income tax, social security and Medicare taxes, and the filing of tax returns. Classification may affect a worker's eligibility for social security and Medicare, employer provided benefits and other tax responsibilities.

¶40,001   Voluntary Worker Classification Settlement Program

The Internal Revenue Service launched a program in September 2011 to enable employers to resolve past worker classification issues and achieve certainty under the tax law at a low cost by voluntarily reclassifying their workers.

This program allows employers the opportunity to get into compliance by making a minimal payment covering past payroll tax obligations rather than waiting for an IRS audit.

This is part of a larger "Fresh Start" initiative at the IRS to help taxpayers and businesses address their tax responsibilities without inflicting too many hardships.

"This settlement program provides certainty and relief to employers in an important area," an IRS Commissioner commented. "This is part of a wider effort to help taxpayers and businesses to help give them a fresh start with their tax obligations."

The Voluntary Classification Settlement Program (VCSP) is designed to increase tax compliance and reduce the burden for employers by providing greater certainty for employers, workers and the government. Under the program, eligible employers can obtain substantial relief from federal payroll taxes they may have owed for the past, if they prospectively treat workers as employees. The VCSP is available to many businesses, tax-exempt organizations and government entities that currently erroneously treat their workers or a class or group of workers as nonemployees or independent contractors, and now want to correctly treat these workers as employees.

To be eligible, an applicant must:

- Consistently have treated the workers in the past as nonemployees.
- Have filed all required Forms 1099 for the workers for the previous three years.
- Not currently be under audit by the IRS, the Department of Labor or a state agency concerning the classification of these workers.
- Not currently be under audit by the Department of Labor or a state agency concerning the classification of these workers.

Interested employers can apply for the program by filing Form 8952, Application for Voluntary Classification Settlement Program, at least 60 days before the employer wants to begin treating the workers as employees.

An employer accepted into VCSP must agree to prospectively treat the class or classes of workers as employees for future tax periods. In exchange, the employer:

- Will pay 10 percent of the employment tax liability that may have been due on compensation paid to the workers for the most recent tax year, determined under the reduced rates of section 3509(a) of the Internal Revenue Code.

- Will not be liable for any interest and penalties on the amount; and
- Will not be subject to an employment tax audit with respect to the worker classification of the workers being reclassified under the VCSP for prior years.

In addition, as part of the VCSP program, the employer must agree to extend the period of limitations on assessment of employment taxes for three years for the first, second and third calendar years beginning after the date on which the employer has agreed under the VCSP closing agreement to begin treating the workers as employees.

During 2013, the IRS expanded VCSP, paving the way for more taxpayers to take advantage of this low-cost option for achieving certainty under the law by reclassifying their workers as employees for future tax periods.

The IRS is modifying several eligibility requirements, thus making it possible for many more interested employers, especially larger ones, to apply for this program. Thus far, according to the IRS, nearly 1,000 employers have applied for the VCSP, which provides partial relief from federal payroll taxes for eligible employers who are treating their workers or a class or group of workers as independent contractors or other nonemployees and now want to treat them as employees. Businesses, tax-exempt organizations and government entities may qualify.

Under the revamped program, employers under IRS audit, other than an employment tax audit, can qualify for the VCSP. Furthermore, employers accepted into the program will no longer be subject to a special six-year statute of limitations, rather than the usual three years that normally applies to payroll taxes. These and other permanent modifications to the program are described in Announcement 2012-45 and in questions and answers, posted on IRS.gov.

On its website, the IRS has posted 24 questions and answers to help employers determine if they qualify for this program and how it will impact them.

¶40,002   Determining Who Is an Employee and Who Is an Independent Contractor

Before it is possible to treat payments made for services, it is necessary to know the business relationship that exists between the employer and the person performing the services. The person performing the services may be:

1. An independent contractor.
2. A common-law employee.
3. A statutory employee.
4. A statutory nonemployee.

These four categories are discussed below. A later section points out the differences between an independent contractor and an employee. If an individual who is not an employee under the common-law rules is employed by a business, generally it is not necessary to withhold federal income tax from that individual's pay. However, in some cases the employer may be required to withhold under backup withholding requirements on these payments.

.01   Independent Contractors vs. Employee

People such as doctors, dentists, veterinarians, lawyers, accountants, contractors, subcontractors, public stenographers, or auctioneers who are in an independent trade, business, or profession in which they offer their services to the general public are generally independent contractors.

The determining factor is the employer's right to control the manner and means of accomplishing a desired result. If that right of control exists for the payer, it is an employer-employee relationship.

Such instructions can establish employer control:

- how, when, or where to do the work
- what tools or equipment to use
- what assistants to hire to help with the work
- where to purchase supplies and services

If an employer-employee relationship exists, the worker is not an independent contractor and his or her earnings are generally not subject to Self-Employment Tax, however, may be subject to Social Security and Medicare tax, and income tax withholding.

An individual is an independent contractor if the employer has the right to control or direct *only* the result of the work and not what will be done and how it will be done.

Some guidelines that may suggest an employer-independent contractor relationship:

- worker is not reimbursed for some or all business expenses.
- worker can realize a profit or incur a loss.
- worker may have significant investment in his or her work.
- worker has control over purchase of supplies, outside services, tools and equipment.

An independent contract will be subject to Self-Employment Tax.

.02 Common-Law Employees

Under common-law rules, anyone who performs services for an entity is an employee if the employer can control what will be done and how it will be done. This is so even when the employee is given freedom of action. What matters is that the employer has the right to control the details of the services performed.

If there is an employer-employee relationship, it makes no difference how it is labeled. The substance of the relationship, not the label, governs the worker's status. Nor does it matter whether the individual is employed full or part time.

For employment tax purposes, no distinction is made between classes of employees. Superintendents, managers, and other supervisory personnel are all employees. An officer of a corporation is generally an employee; however, an officer who performs no services or only minor services, and neither receives nor is entitled to receive any pay, is not considered an employee. A director of a corporation is not an employee with respect to services performed as a director.

It is generally necessary to withhold and pay income, Social Security, and Medicare taxes on wages paid to common-law employees. However, the wages of certain employees may be exempt from one or more of these taxes.

Leased Employees. Under certain circumstances, a corporation furnishing workers to various professional people and firms is the employer of those workers for employment tax purposes. For example, a professional service corporation may provide the services of secretaries, nurses, and other similarly trained workers to its subscribers.

The service corporation enters into contracts with the subscribers under which the subscribers specify the services to be provided and the fee to be paid to the service corporation for each individual furnished. The service corporation has the right to control and direct the worker's services for the subscriber, including the right to discharge or reassign the worker. The service corporation hires the workers, controls the payment of their wages, provides them with unemployment insurance and other benefits, and is the employer for employment tax purposes.

.03 Statutory Employees

If workers are independent contractors under the common law rules, such workers may nevertheless be treated as employees by statute ("statutory employees") for certain employment tax purposes if they fall within any one of the following four categories and meet the three conditions described under Social Security and Medicare taxes, below. The four categories are:

1. A driver who distributes beverages (other than milk) or meat, vegetable, fruit, or bakery products, or one who picks up and delivers laundry or dry cleaning, if the driver is the entity's agent or is paid on commission.

2.   A full-time life insurance sales agent whose principal business activity is selling life insurance, annuity contracts, or both, primarily for one life insurance company.
3.   An individual who works at home on materials or goods that are supplied and that must be returned to a business establishment, if the business also furnishes specifications for the work to be done.
4.   A full-time traveling or city salesperson who works on the entity's behalf and turns in orders to the business from wholesalers, retailers, contractors, or operators of hotels, restaurants, or other similar establishments. The goods sold must be merchandise for resale or supplies for use in the buyer's business operation. The work performed must be the salesperson's principal business activity.

Social Security and Medicare Taxes. Social Security and Medicare taxes must be withheld from the wages of statutory employees if all three of the following conditions apply:

1.   The service contract states or implies that substantially all the services are to be performed personally by them,
2.   They do not have a substantial investment in the equipment and property used to perform the services (other than an investment in transportation facilities), and
3.   The services are performed on a continuing basis for the same payer.

The Federal Unemployment Tax Act (FUTA) and Income Tax. For FUTA tax, the term employee means the same as it does for Social Security and Medicare taxes, except that it does not include statutory employees in categories 2 and 3 above. Thus, any individual who is an employee under category 1 or 4 is also an employee for FUTA tax purposes and subject to FUTA tax.

Income taxes are not to be withheld from the wages of statutory employees.

.04   Statutory Nonemployees

There are two categories of statutory nonemployees: direct sellers and licensed real estate agents. They are treated as self-employed for all federal tax purposes, including income and employment taxes, if:

1.   Substantially all payments for their services as direct sellers or real estate agents are directly related to sales or other output rather than to the number of hours worked.
2.   Their services are performed under a written contract providing that they will not be treated as employees for federal tax purposes.

Direct Sellers. Direct sellers include persons falling within any of these three groups:

1. Persons engaged in selling (or soliciting the sale of) consumer products in the home or place of business other than in a permanent retail establishment.
2. Persons engaged in selling (or soliciting the sale of) consumer products to any buyer on a buy-sell basis, a deposit-commission basis, or any similar basis prescribed by regulations, for resale in the home or at a place of business other than in a permanent retail establishment.
3. Persons engaged in the trade or business of delivering or distributing newspapers or shopping news (including any services directly related to such delivery or distribution).

Direct selling includes activities of individuals who attempt to increase direct sales activities of their direct sellers and who earn income based on the productivity of their direct sellers. Such activities include providing motivation and encouragement; imparting skills, knowledge or experience; and recruiting.

¶40,003   Worker Classification

With the exception of statutory employees, work classification is based upon a common law standard for determining whether the worker is an independent contractor or employee. That standard essentially asks whether the business has the right to *direct and control the worker*. The courts have traditionally looked to a variety of evidentiary facts in applying this standard, and the IRS has adopted those facts to assist in classifying workers.

¶40,004   Accountant's Concern?

When conducting an audit, the auditor needs to assist taxpayers in identifying all of the evidence relative to their business relationships with workers. Many taxpayers may not be aware of what information is needed to make a correct determination of worker classification. Others have turned a blind eye. This is especially true of small business owners who may not be aware of the relief available under Section 530 of the Revenue Act of 1978, resulting from worker reclassification. An auditor's examination should actively consider Section 530 during an examination, including furnishing taxpayers with a summary of Section 530 at the beginning of an examination.

Essentially, an accountant's responsibility is similar to an IRS tax examiner's responsibility as set forth by the Treasury Department that states:

"The examiner has a responsibility to the taxpayer and to the government to determine the correct tax liability and to maintain a fair and impartial attitude in all matters relating to the examination. The fair and impartial attitude of an examiner aids in increasing voluntary compliance. An examiner must approach each examination with an objective point of view."

¶40,005   Section 530 Relief Requirements

A business has been selected for an employment tax examination to determine whether certain workers were correctly treated as independent contractors. However, the employer will not owe employment taxes for those workers if the employer meets the relief requirements described below. If the employer does not meet these relief requirements, the IRS will need to determine whether the workers are, in fact, independent contractors or employees and whether employment taxes are actually owed for those workers.

To receive relief from paying employment taxes, three requirements must be met: reasonable basis, substantive consistency and reporting consistency.

.01   Reasonable Basis

To establish a reasonable basis for not treating the workers as employees, an employer must show that:

1. It reasonably relied on a court case about federal taxes or a ruling issued by the IRS.
2. The business was audited by the IRS at a time when similar workers were treated as independent contractors and the IRS did not reclassify those workers as employees.
3. Workers were treated as independent contractors because that was how a significant segment of that particular industry treated similar workers.
4. The employer relied on some other reasonable basis—for example, on the advice of a business lawyer or accountant who knew the facts about the particular business and that industry.

The employer does not have a *reasonable basis* for treating the workers as independent contractors and therefore will not meet the relief requirements if his or her decision was not made on the basis of one of these criteria.

.02   Substantive Consistency

In addition, the employer (and any predecessor business) must have treated the workers, and any similar workers, as independent contractors. If similar workers were treated as employees, this relief provision is not available.

.03   Reporting Consistency

Form 1099-MISC must have been filed for each worker, unless the worker earned less than $600. Relief is not available for any year in which the required Forms 1099-MISC were not filed. If they were filed for some workers but not others, relief is not available for the workers for whom they were not filed.

¶40,006   The Decision: Employee or Independent Contractor?

An employer must generally withhold income taxes, withhold and pay Social Security and Medicare taxes, and pay unemployment tax on wages paid to an *employee*. An employer does not generally have to withhold or pay any taxes on payments to *independent contractors*. This is the important distinction.

To determine whether an individual is an employee or an independent contractor under the common law, the relationship of the worker and the business must be examined. All evidence of control and independence must be considered. In any employee–independent contractor determination, all information that provides evidence of the degree of control and the degree of independence must be considered.

¶40,007   Primary Categories

Officially termed the *worker classification issue*, the focus is centered on three main areas that the IRS has concluded are primary categories of evidence to draw a distinction between an employee and an independent contractor. The essence of the distinction is whether or not the employer has the right to direct and control the worker. The three areas are:

1. Behavioral control.
2. Financial control.
3. Relationship of the parties.

Those three areas provide evidence that substantiates the right to direct or control the details and means by which the worker performs the required services. Training is important in this context. Significant are such workplace developments as evaluation systems and concern for customer security in conjunction with business identification. All relevant information must be considered and weighed to determine whether a worker is an independent contractor or an employee.

Virtually every business will impose on workers, whether contractors or employees, some form of instruction. How else would a worker know what he or she is supposed to do, what duties to perform? This fact alone, however, is not sufficient evidence to determine a worker's status. As with every relevant fact, the problem is to determine whether the employer has retained the right to control the *details* of a worker's performance, or instead has given up the business's right to control those details. Accordingly, the weight of evidence in any case depends on the *degree* to which instructions apply with respect to *how the job gets done rather than to the end result.*

.01   Behavioral Control

Behavioral control concerns whether there is a right to direct or control how the worker performs the specific task for which he or she is engaged. Instructions and training are the main factors in considering the degree of behavioral control.

An employee is generally subject to the business's instructions about when, where, and how to work. Following are types of instructions about how to do work:

1.   When and where to do the work.
2.   What tools or equipment to use.
3.   What workers to hire or to assist with the work.
4.   Where to purchase supplies and services.
5.   What work must be performed by a specified individual.
6.   What order or sequence to follow.

The degree of instruction depends on the scope of instructions, the extent to which the business retains the right to control the worker's compliance with the instructions, and the effect on the worker in the event of noncompliance. All these provide useful clues for identifying whether the business keeps control over the manner and means of work performance, or only over a particular product or service. The more detailed the instructions are that the worker is required to follow, the more control the business exerts over the worker, and the more likely the business retains the right to control the methods by which the worker performs the work. Absence of detail in instructions reflects less control.

Although the presence and extent of instructions is important in reaching a conclusion as to whether a business retains the right to direct and control the methods by which a worker performs a job, it is also important to consider the weight to be given those instructions if they are imposed by the business only in compliance with governmental or governing body regulations. If a business requires its workers to comply with established, municipal building codes related to construction, for example, the fact that such rules are imposed by the business should be given little weight in determining the worker's status. However, if the business develops more stringent guidelines for a worker in addition to those imposed by a third party, more weight should be given to these instructions in determining whether the business has retained the right to control the worker.

The nature of a worker's occupation also affects the degree of direction and control necessary to determine worker status. Highly trained professionals such as doctors, accountants, lawyers, engineers, or computer specialists may require very little, if any, training and instruction on how to perform their services for a particular business. In fact, it may be impossible for the business to instruct the worker on how to perform the services because it may lack the essential knowledge and skills to do so. Generally, professional workers who are engaged in the pursuit of an independent trade, business, or profession in which they offer their services to the public are independent contractors, not employees. In analyzing the status of professional workers, evidence of control or autonomy with respect to the financial details of how the task is performed tends to be especially important, as does evidence concerning the relationship of the parties.

An employment relationship can also exist when the work can be done with a minimal amount of direction and control, such as work done by a store clerk, or gas station attendant. The absence of a *need* to control should not be confused with the absence of the *right* to control. The right to control as an incident of employment requires only such supervision as the nature of the work requires. The key fact to consider is whether the business retains the *right* to direct and control the worker, regardless of whether the business actually exercises that right.

Evaluation systems are used by virtually all businesses to monitor the quality of work performed by workers, whether independent contractors or employees. In analyzing whether a business's evaluation system provides evidence of the right to control work performance, or the absence of such a right, an auditor should look for evidence of how the evaluation system may influence the worker's behavior in performing the details of the job.

If an evaluation system measures compliance with performance standards concerning the details of how the work is to be performed, the system and its enforcement are evidence of control over the worker's behavior. However, not all businesses have developed formal performance standards or evaluation systems. This is especially true of smaller businesses.

Training is the established means of explaining detailed methods and procedures to be used in performing a task. Periodic or ongoing training provided by a business about procedures to be followed and methods to be used indicates that the business wants the services performed in a particular manner. This type of training is strong evidence of an employer-employee relationship.

.02   Financial Control

Financial control concerns the facts which illustrate whether there is a *right* to direct or control how the worker's activities are conducted.

Factors to be considered are the business aspects of the worker's activities; significant investment, if any; unreimbursed expenses; services available to the relevant market; method of payment; and opportunity for profit or loss. These factors can be thought of as bearing on the issue of whether the recipient has the right to direct and control the means and details of the business aspects of how the worker performs services.

A significant investment is evidence that an independent contractor relationship may exist. It should be stressed that a significant investment is not necessary for an independent contractor. Some types of work simply do not require large expenditures. Even if large expenditures, such as costly equipment, are required, an independent contractor may rent the equipment needed at fair rental value. There are no precise dollar limits that must be met in order to have a significant investment. The size of the worker's investment and the risk borne by the worker are not diminished merely because the seller or lessor receives the benefit of the worker's services.

The extent to which a worker chooses to incur expenses and costs impacts his or her opportunity for profit or loss. This constitutes evidence that the worker has the right to direct and control the financial aspects of the business operations. Although not every independent contractor needs to make a significant investment, almost every independent contractor will incur an array of business expenses either in the form of direct expenditures or in the form of fees for pro rata portions of one or several expenses. Businesses often pay business or travel expenses for their employees. Independent contractors' expenses may also be reimbursed. An independent contractor can contract for direct reimbursement of certain expenses, or can seek to establish contract prices that will reimburse the contractor for these expenses. Attention should center on *unreimbursed* expenses, which better distinguish independent contractors and employees, inasmuch as independent contractors are more likely to have unreimbursed expenses. If expenses are unreimbursed, then the opportunity for profit or loss exists. Fixed ongoing costs that are incurred regardless of whether work is currently being performed are especially important. However, employees may also incur unreimbursed expenses in connection with the services they perform for their businesses. Relatively minor expenses incurred by a worker, or more significant expenses that are customarily borne by an employee in a particular line of business, would generally not indicate an independent contractor relationship.

An independent contractor is generally free to seek out business opportunities, as independent contractors' income depends on doing so successfully. As a result, independent contractors often advertise, maintain a visible business location, and are available to work for the relevant market. An independent contractor with special skills may be contacted by word of mouth and referrals without the need for advertising. An independent contractor who has negotiated a long-term contract may find advertising equally unnecessary, and may be unavailable to work for others for the duration of a contract. Other independent contractors may find that a visible business location does not generate sufficient business to justify the expense. Therefore, the absence of these activities is a neutral fact.

The method of payment can be helpful in determining whether the worker has the opportunity for profit or loss. A worker who is compensated on an hourly, daily, weekly, or similar basis is guaranteed a return for labor. This is generally evidence of an employer-employee relationship, even when the wage or salary is accompanied by a commission. In some lines of business, such as law, it is typical to pay independent contractors on an hourly basis. Performance of a task for a flat fee is generally evidence of an independent contractor relationship, especially if the worker incurs the expenses of performing the services. A commission-based worker can be either an independent contractor or employee. The worker's status will depend on the worker's ability to realize a profit or incur a loss as a result of services rendered.

The ability to realize a profit or incur a loss is probably the strongest evidence that a worker controls the business aspects of services rendered.

Also to be considered is whether the worker is free to make business decisions that affect his profit or loss. If the worker is making decisions that affect the bottom line, the worker likely has the ability to realize profit or loss. It is sometimes thought that because a worker can receive more money working longer hours or receive less money by working less, he has the ability to incur a profit or loss. This type of income variation, however, is also consistent with employer status and does not distinguish employees from independent contractors.

Not all financial control facts need be present for the worker to have the ability to realize profit or loss. For example, a worker who is paid on a straight commission basis, makes business decisions, and has unreimbursed business expenses, likely would have the ability to realize a profit or loss, even if the worker does not have a significant investment and does not market her services.

.03   Relationship of the Parties

There are other facts that recent court decisions consider relevant in determining worker status. Most of these facts reflect how the worker and the business perceive the relationship to each other. It is much more difficult to link the facts in this category directly to the right to direct and control *how* work is to be performed than the categories discussed above. The relationship of the parties is important because it reflects the parties' *intent* concerning control. Courts often look at the intent of the parties because the intent is most often stated in their contractual relationship. A written agreement describing the worker as an independent contractor is viewed as evidence of the parties' intent that a worker is an independent contractor. However, a contractual designation, in and of itself, is not sufficient evidence for determining worker status. The facts and circumstances under which a worker performs services determine a worker's status. The *substance* of a relationship, not a label, governs the worker's status. The contract may be relevant in ascertaining methods of compensation, expenses that will be incurred, and rights and obligations of each party with respect to *how* work is to be performed. In addition, if it is difficult, if not impossible, to decide whether a worker is an independent contractor, the intent of the parties, as reflected in the contractual designation, is an effective way to resolve the issue.

Questions sometimes arise concerning whether a worker who creates a corporation through which to perform services can be an employee of a business that engages the corporation. If the corporate formalities are properly followed, and at least one nontax business purpose exists, the corporate form is generally recognized for both state law and federal law, including federal tax purposes. Disregarding the corporate entity is generally an extraordinary remedy, applied by most courts only in cases of clear abuse, so the worker will usually not be treated as an employee of the business, but as an employee of the corporation. (It should be noted that the fact that a worker receives payment for services from a business through the worker's corporation does not automatically require a finding of independent contractor status with respect to those services.)

Employee Benefits. Providing a worker with employee benefits has traditionally been linked with employee status and, therefore, can be an important factor in deciding an independent contractor-employee relationship. If a worker receives employee benefits, such as paid vacation days, paid sick days, health insurance, life or disability insurance, or a pension, this constitutes some evidence of employee status. The evidence is strongest if the worker is provided with employee benefits under a tax-qualified retirement plan, 403(b) annuity, or cafeteria plan, because by statute, these benefits can be provided to employees only. If an individual is excluded from a benefit plan because the worker is not considered an employee by the business, this is relevant though not conclusive in determining the worker's status as an independent contractor. If the worker is excluded on some other grounds, the exclusion is irrelevant in determining whether the worker is an independent contractor or an employee. This is because none of these employee benefits is required to be provided to employees. Many workers whose status as bona fide employees is unquestioned receive no employee benefits, as there is no requirement that all workers be covered.

Termination Rights. The circumstances under which a business or a worker can terminate their relationship have traditionally been considered useful evidence bearing on the status the parties intended the worker to have. However, in order to determine whether the facts are relevant to the worker's status, the impact of modern business practices and legal standards governing worker termination must be considered. A business's ability to terminate the work relationship at will, without penalty, provides a highly effective method to control the details of how work is performed, and indicates employee status. On the other hand, in the traditional independent contractor relationship, the business could terminate the relationship only if the worker failed to provide the intended service, which indicates the parties' intent that the business does not have the right to control how the work was performed. In practice, businesses rarely have complete flexibility in discharging an employee. The business may be liable for pay in lieu of notice, severance pay, "golden parachutes," or other forms of compensation when it discharges an employee. In addition, the reasons for which a business can terminate an employee may be limited, whether by law, by contract, or by its own practices.

A worker's ability to terminate work at will was traditionally considered to illustrate that the worker merely provided labor and tended to indicate an employer-employee relationship. In contrast, if the worker terminated work, and the business could refuse payment or sue for nonperformance, this indicated the business's interest in receiving the contracted product or service, which tended to indicate an independent contractor relationship. In practice, however, independent contractors can enter into short-term contracts for which nonperformance remedies are inappropriate; or they may negotiate limits on their liability for nonperformance. Typical examples are professionals, such as doctors and attorneys, who can terminate their contractual relationship without penalty.

Businesses can successfully sue employees for substantial damages resulting from their failure to perform the services for which they were engaged. As a result, the presence or absence of limits on workers' ability to terminate the relationship, by themselves, no longer constitutes useful evidence in determining worker status. A business's ability to refuse payment for unsatisfactory work continues to be characteristic of an independent contractor relationship.

Permanent/Indefinite Relationship. The existence of a permanent relationship between the worker and the business is relevant evidence in determining whether there is an employer-employee relationship. If a business engages a worker with the expectation that the relationship will continue indefinitely, rather than for a specific project or period, it is a factor that is generally considered evidence of an intent to create an employment relationship.

A relationship that is created with the expectation that it will be indefinite should not be confused with a long-term relationship. A long-term relationship may exist between a business and either an independent contractor or an employee. The relationship between the business and an independent contractor can be long-term for several reasons:

1. The contract may be a long-term contract.
2. Contacts can be renewed regularly due to superior service, competitive costs, or lack of alternative service providers.

A business can also have a relationship with an employee that is long-term, but not indefinite. This could occur if temporary employment contracts are renewed, or if a long-term, but not indefinite, employment contract is entered into. As a result, a relationship that is long-term, but not indefinite, is a neutral fact that should be disregarded.

A temporary relationship is a neutral fact that should be disregarded. An independent contractor will typically have a temporary relationship with a business, but so too will employees engaged on a seasonal project, or on an "as needed" basis. The services performed by the worker, and the extent to which those services are a key aspect of the regular business of the company, are germane. In considering this, it should be remembered that the fact that a service is desirable, necessary, or even essential to a business does not mean that the service provider is an employee. The work of an attorney or paralegal is part of the regular business of a law firm. If a law firm hires an attorney or paralegal, it is likely that the law firm will present the work as its own. As a result, there is an increased probability that the law firm will direct or control the activities. However, further facts should be examined to see whether there is evidence of the *right* to direct or control before a conclusion is reached that these workers are employees. It is possible that the work performed is part of the principal business of the law firm, yet it has hired workers who are outside specialists and may be independent contractors.

¶40,008   Checklist

The 20 factors indicating whether an individual is an employee or an independent contractor follow:

1. *Instructions.* An employee must comply with instructions about when, where, and how to work. Even if no instructions are given, the control factor is present if the employer *has the right* to control how the work results are achieved.
2. *Training.* An employee may be trained to perform services in a particular manner. Independent contractors ordinarily use their own methods and receive no training from the purchasers of their services.
3. *Integration.* An employee's services are usually integrated into the business operations because the services are important to the success or continuation of the business. This shows that the employee is subject to direction and control.

4. *Services Are Rendered Personally.* An employee renders services personally. This shows that the employer is interested in the methods as well as the results.
5. *Hiring Assistants.* An employee works for an employer who hires, supervises, and pays workers. An independent contractor can hire, supervise, and pay assistants under a contract that requires their contractor to provide materials and labor and to be responsible only for the result.
6. *Continuing Relationship.* An employee generally has a continuing relationship that may exist even if work is performed at recurring although irregular intervals.
7. *Set Hours of Work.* An employee usually has set hours of work established by an employer. Independent contractors generally can set their own work hours.
8. *Full-Time Required.* An employee may be required to work or be available full-time. This indicates control by the employer. An independent contractor can work when and for whom he or she chooses.
9. *Work Done on Premises.* An employee usually works on the premises of an employer, or works on a route or at a location designated by an employer.
10. *Order or Sequence Set.* An employee may be required to perform services in the order or sequence set by an employer. This shows that the employee is subject to direction and control, in contrast to the independent contractor who determines the order and sequence in which the work is performed.
11. *Reports.* An employee may be required to submit reports to an employer, which shows that the employer maintains a degree of control.
12. *Payments.* An employee generally is paid by the hour, week, or month. An independent contractor is usually paid by the job or on a straight commission. An independent contractor is paid by the job, which can include periodic payments based upon a percentage of job completed. Payment can be based on the number of hours needed to do the job times an hourly wage. The payment method should be determined before the job is undertaken.
13. *Expenses.* An employee's business and travel expenses are generally paid by an employer. This shows that the employee is subject to regulation and control.
14. *Tools and Materials.* An employee is normally furnished significant tools, materials, and other equipment by an employer.
15. *Investment.* An independent contractor has a significant investment in the facilities used in performing services for someone else.
16. *Profit or Loss Possibilities.* Independent contractors should be able to make a profit or a loss. Employees can not suffer a loss. Five circumstances show that a profit or loss is possible:
    — The independent contractor hires, directs, and pays assistants.
    — The independent contractor has his or her own office, equipment, materials, or facilities.
    — The independent contractor has continuing and recurring liabilities.

— The independent contractor has agreed to perform specific jobs for prices agreed upon in advance.

— The independent contractor's services affect his or her own business reputation.

17. *Works for More than One Person or Firm.* An independent contractor is generally free to provide services to two or more unrelated persons or firms at the same time.

18. *Services Available to the Public.* Independent contractors make their services available to the general public by one or more of the following:

— Having an office and assistants.

— Having business signs.

— Having a business license.

— Listing their services in a business directory.

— Advertising their services.

19. *Right to Fire.* An employee can be fired by an employer. An independent contractor cannot be fired as long as results are produced that meet the specifications of the contract.

20. *Right to Quit.* An employee can quit a job at any time without incurring liability. An independent contractor usually agrees to complete a specific job and is responsible for its satisfactory completion, or legally is obligated to make good for failure to complete it.

¶40,009   Emphasis on Categories

Since the publication of the training manual for IRS personnel on worker classification, there has been less reliance upon the common law standard or the list of 20 factors. The three categories (behavioral control, financial control, and relationship of the parties) are relied upon more heavily for the determination. However, it is wise to consider all aspects of the arrangement. In fact, the IRS cautions, "In each case, it is very important to consider all the facts—no single fact provides the answer."

¶40,010   "Economic Reality" Test

The Department of Labor (DOL) published a fact sheet aimed at helping to solve the employee/independent contractor dilemma. It points out that employment relationship under the Fair Labor Standards Act (FLSA) must be distinguished from a strictly contractual one and may be somewhat different from standards used by other agencies. The sheet states, "Such a relationship must exist for any provision of the Act to apply to any person engaged in work, which may otherwise be subject to the Act." In the application of the FLSA, an employee, as distinguished from a person who is engaged in a business of his or her own, is one who, as a matter of economic reality, follows the usual path of an employee and is dependent on the business he or she serves. Thus, the employer-employee relationship under the FLSA is tested by "economic reality" rather than "technical concepts." It is *not* determined by the common law standards previously discussed.

As has become fairly evident through the years, even the U.S. Supreme Court has indicated on several occasions that the Court does not consider a single rule or test for determining whether an individual is an independent contractor or an employee for purposes of the FLSA, the IRS, state agencies, or any other path followed by a particular case. The Court has held that it is the *total activity or situation*, which controls the determination. Many of these factors are discussed above, but in summary, those the Court has considered significant are:

- The extent to which the services rendered provide an integral part of the principal's business.
- The permanency of the relationship.
- The amount of the alleged contractor's investment in facilities and equipment.
- The nature and degree of control by the principal party over the manner in which the work is performed.
- The worker's opportunities for profit and loss determined by the hiring party or the worker's own managerial skill.
- The amount of initiative, judgment, foresight, or skill in open market competition with others required for the success of the claimed independent contractor.
- The degree of independent business organization and operation.

Certain factors are considered immaterial in determining whether there is an employment relationship. Included among conditions considered to have *no* bearing on determinations as to whether there is an employment relationship or not are:

- The absence of a formal employment agreement.
- Whether an alleged independent contractor is licensed by a state or local governmental body.
- The time or mode of payment.
- The place where work is performed.

The last condition can pose problems. In these times of flexible hours and workplaces, people who perform work at their own home are often improperly considered to be independent contractors. The Act covers such homeworkers as employees and they are entitled to all benefits of the law if they meet those requirements that are material in the determination.

The employer is responsible for the following when it has been determined that an employer-employee relationship does exist and the employee is engaged in work that is subject to the FLSA:

- The employee must be paid at least the federal minimum wage.
- Usually, time and one-half must be paid for time worked over 40 hours per week.
- Child labor laws regulating the employment of minors under the age of 18 must be observed.
- Specific record-keeping requirements must be followed.

¶40,011   Procedures for Processing Employment Tax Cases

It is not only the employer who considers the independent contractor/employee situation a morass. At one point in the ongoing attempts to decipher the complex tax code tax lawyers, CPAs and corporate tax officers came up with a list of high priority suggestions for simplifying the tax situation: drop the minimum tax; standardize the rules on classifying workers as employees or independent contractors; clarify the eight tax incentives for education.

This addition to the Internal Revenue Code may not help in the worker classification process, but it does provide Tax Court review rights.

The Taxpayer Relief Act of 1997 (TRA'97) created Section 7436 of the Internal Revenue Code, which provides Tax Court review rights concerning certain employment tax determinations.

Code Notice 98-43 provides information about how taxpayers can petition for Tax Court review of employment tax determinations under the provision that became effective August 5, 1997. Attached to this notice as Exhibit 1 is a "Notice of Determination Concerning Worker Classification Under Section 7436."

With respect to taxpayers whose workers are the subject of an employment tax determination as to whether they are independent contractors, or, in fact, employees, the attached Notice of Determination addressed to a taxpayer will constitute the "determination" that is a prerequisite to invoking the Tax Court's jurisdiction.

The new Section of the Code contains the following provisions:

1. The Tax Court has the jurisdiction to review determinations by the IRS that workers are employees for purposes of Subtitle C of the Code.
2. And that the organization for which services are performed is not entitled to relief from employment taxes under Section 530 of the Revenue Act of 1978.
3. The determination must involve an actual controversy relating to independent contractor/employee status.
4. The determination is made as part of an examination of worker classification.

Section 7436 can be conducted pursuant to the Tax Court's simplified procedures for small tax cases set forth in the new Section of the Code and Rule 295 of the Tax Court's Rules of Practice and Procedure. Currently, taxpayers can elect, with the concurrence of the Tax Court, to use these simplified procedures if the amount of employment taxes placed in dispute resulting from workers being designated as independent contractors is $50,000 or less for each calendar quarter involved.

.01   Issues to Which Section 7436 Applies

Section 7436(a) provides the Tax Court with jurisdiction to review the IRS's determinations that one or more individuals performing services for the taxpayer are employees of the taxpayer, not independent contractors, for purposes of Subtitle C of the Code, or that the taxpayer is not entitled to relief under Section 530 with respect to such individuals.

Thus, Section 7436(a) does not:

1. Provide the Tax Court with jurisdiction to determine any amount of employment tax or penalties.
2. Provide the Tax Court with jurisdiction to review other employment tax issues.
3. Apply to employment-related issues not arising under Subtitle C, such as the classification of individuals with respect to pension plan coverage or the proper treatment of individual income tax deductions.

Additionally, insofar as Section 7436(a) only confers jurisdiction upon the Tax Court to review determinations that are made by the IRS as part of an employment tax examination, other IRS determinations that are not made as part of an examination, including those that are made in the context of private letter rulings or Form SS-8, "Determination of Employee Work Status for Purposes of Federal Employment Taxes and Income Tax Withholding," are not subject to review by the Tax Court under this provision.

The IRS will issue a Notice of Determination only after the IRS has determined both that:

1. One or more individuals performing services for the taxpayer are employees for purposes of Subtitle C.
2. The taxpayer is not entitled to relief under Section 530. This will provide taxpayers with the opportunity to resolve both issues in one judicial determination.

.02   Taxpayers Eligible to Seek Review

Section 7436(b) provides that a pleading seeking Tax Court review of the IRS's determination can be filed only by "the person for whom the services are performed."

Thus, workers may not seek review of the IRS's determinations under these provisions. In addition, because there must be an actual controversy, review may not be sought by a third party who has not been determined by the IRS to be the employer.

.03   Notice of Determination

The IRS will inform taxpayers of a determination by sending the taxpayer a Notice of Determination by certified or registered mail. The Notice of Determination will advise taxpayers of the opportunity to seek Tax Court review, and it provides information on how to do so. Attached to the notice will be a schedule showing each kind of tax with its proposed employment tax adjustment for the specific taxpayer by calendar quarter.

This schedule will be provided to enable the taxpayer to determine eligibility to elect use of the small tax case procedures under Section 7436(c). Currently, the small tax case procedures may be available if the amount of employment taxes in dispute is $50,000 or less for each calendar quarter involved.

In most cases, a taxpayer who receives a Notice of Determination will have previously received a "thirty-day letter," which the IRS sends to taxpayers in unagreed examination cases. The thirty-day letter lists the proposed employment tax adjustments to be made and describes the taxpayer's right either to agree to the proposed employment tax adjustments or, alternatively, to protest the proposed adjustments to the Appeals Division within thirty days of the date of the letter.

If the taxpayer does not respond to the thirty-day letter by agreeing to the proposed adjustments or, alternatively, by filing a protest with the Appeals Division, the taxpayer will receive, by certified or registered mail, a Notice of Determination. Under normal procedures, if the taxpayer does not respond to the thirty-day letter, the taxpayer should generally expect to receive the notice within 60 days after expiration of the thirty-day period beginning with the date on the thirty-day letter. If no notice is received during this period, the taxpayer may wish to contact the local Internal Revenue Service office to check on the status of the case.

If the taxpayer responds to the thirty-day letter by filing a protest with the Appeals Division (or if the case proceeds to Appeals by way of the employment tax early referral procedures), and the worker classification and Section 530 issues are not settled on an agreed basis in the Appeals Division, the taxpayer will then receive a Notice of Determination.

Taxpayers are encouraged to resolve cases in nondocketed status by requesting use of the early referral procedures in appropriate cases.

.04   Prerequisite for Seeking Review

Because a Notice of Determination constitutes the IRS's determination of worker classification, it is a jurisdictional prerequisite for seeking Tax Court review of the IRS's determinations regarding classification of the worker as an independent contractor or an employee, and Section 530 issues (see above). Tax Court proceedings seeking review of these determinations cannot begin prior to issuance of the notice.

.05 Time of Filing

Section 7436(b)(2) provides that a taxpayer's petition for review must be filed with the Tax Court before the 91st day after the IRS mails its Notice of Determination to the taxpayer by certified or registered mail. If the taxpayer discusses the case with the IRS during the period before the 91st day following the mailing of the notice, the discussion will not extend the period in which the taxpayer may file a petition with the Tax Court.

A taxpayer who does not file a Tax Court petition within the allotted time retains the right to seek judicial review of the employment tax determinations by paying the tax and filing a claim for refund, as required by the Code. If the claim for refund is denied, the taxpayer may file a refund suit in district court or the Court of Federal Claims.

.06 Appeals Jurisdiction

Cases docketed in the U.S. Tax Court will be referred by District Counsel to the Appeals Division of the IRS for consideration of settlement unless the Notice of Determination was issued by Appeals. Cases in which Appeals issued such a Notice of Determination may be referred to them unless District Counsel determines that there is little likelihood that a settlement of all or a part of the case can be achieved in a reasonable period of time. Appeals will have sole settlement authority over docketed cases referred to them until the case is returned to District Counsel.

.07 Suspension of the Statute of Limitations

The ruling provides that the suspension of the limitations period for assessment in Section 6503(a) of the Code applies in the same manner as though a notice of deficiency had been issued. Thus, the mailing of the Notice of Determination by certified or registered mail will suspend the statute of limitations for assessment of taxes attributable to the worker classification and Section 530 issues. Generally, the statute of limitations for assessment of taxes attributable to these issues is suspended for the 90-day period during which the taxpayer can begin a suit in Tax Court, plus an additional 60 days thereafter.

Moreover, if the taxpayer does file a timely petition in the Tax Court, the statute of limitations for assessment of taxes attributable to the issues will be suspended during the Tax Court proceedings, and for 60 days after the decision becomes final.

.08   Restrictions on Assessment

This same ruling provides that the restrictions on assessment in Section 6213 of the Code apply in the same manner as if a notice had been issued. Thus, the IRS is precluded from assessing the taxes prior to expiration of the 90-day period during which the taxpayer can file a timely Tax Court petition.

If he or she does file, this generally precludes the IRS from assessing the taxes until the decision of the Tax Court has become final. If the taxpayer does not file a timely Tax Court petition before the 91st day after the Notice of Determination was mailed, the employment taxes attributable to the workers described in the Notice of Determination can then be assessed.

.09   Agreed Settlements

If the taxpayer wishes to settle the employment issues on an agreed basis before issuance of a Notice of Determination, the taxpayer must formally waive the restrictions on assessment. This will generally be accomplished by execution of an agreed settlement that contains the following language: "I understand that, by signing this agreement, I am waiving the restrictions on assessment provided in Sections 7436(d) and 6213(a) of the Internal Revenue Code of 1986."

The IRS will not assess employment taxes attributable to those issues unless either a Notice of Determination has been issued to the taxpayer and the 90-day period for filing a Tax Court petition has expired or, alternatively, the taxpayer has waived the restrictions on assessment.

If the IRS erroneously makes an assessment of taxes attributable to those issues without first either issuing a Notice of Determination or obtaining a waiver of restrictions on assessment, the taxpayer is entitled to an automatic abatement of the assessment. However, once any such procedural defects are corrected, the IRS can reassess the employment taxes to the same extent as if the abated assessment had not occurred.

Section 1454 of the Tax Relief Act (TRA) of 1997 was effective as of August 5, 1997. Thus, assessments that were made prior to the August 5, 1997 effective date of the Act are not subject to this legislation or the procedures discussed above. All employment tax examinations involving worker classification and/ or Section 530 issues that were pending as of August 5, 1997, became subject to the legislation.

CHAPTER 41
Tip Income

¶41,000   Overview

What's the big deal? Although it is impossible to be certain, estimates range from $1 billion to $12 billion a year in unreported, untaxed tip income, that is what. Reporting all tip income has always been required by law. When the significant extent to which taxpayers were ignoring the law became evident, the IRS stepped up the emphasis on the requirements for both employee and employer to report tip income.

While the traditional requirements of tip reporting are covered later in the chapter, we begin with an overview of more streamlined procedures that have helped produce greater tip reporting compliance. These rules involve safe harbors and simplifying assumptions, agreements between employees and their employers, and between employers and the IRS. These procedures and agreements have brought uniformity and better compliance rates than the traditional tip reporting rules, which left the job primarily to the employee.

One challenge for an employer is to determine from the four formalized tip reporting programs which is best suited for its type of business. This will depend on numerous factors including the number of employees, the percentage of sales that are reported on credit cards, the willingness of employees to sign an agreement with their employer and the motivation of the employer to avoid time-consuming and expensive audit procedures carried on by the IRS.

Since the Tip Rate Determination/Education Program (TRD/EP), was introduced, voluntary compliance has significantly increased.

The Internal Revenue Service (IRS) points out that the TRD/EP has proven to be a winner for employers, employees, and the IRS. It reduces taxpayer burden and increases compliance. The Service hopes that more industries and employees will take advantage of the program.

¶41,001   IRS Guidance on FICA Taxes on Tips

In July 2012, the IRS supplied guidance in the form of questions and answers on FICA taxes on tips. Rev. Rul. 2012-18 is designed to clarify and update previous guidelines. The guidance supersedes Rev. Rul. 95-7.

Excluded from FICA reporting (but included in income reporting) are tips received in any medium other than cash. This includes in-kind tips such as passes or tickets to sporting events.

The law requires every employee who receives tips that are wages, to report all those tips in a written statement furnished to the employer by the tenth day of the month following the month of receipt by the employee. Unreported tips received by an employee are deemed to be paid to the employee when actually received by the employee.

The employer's characterization of a payment as a "tip" is not determinative of its proper characterization. For example, an employer may characterize a payment as a tip, when in fact the payment is a service charge. Thus, a fixed charge imposed by a banquet hall that is distributed to the employees who render services is a service change and not a tip. Thus, it is still income, but it is not included in FICA wages. A true tip is a payment made by a customer free from compulsion and with full discretion as to the amount. If it is a tip, it is not subject to negotiation by the employer's policy.

The IRS emphasizes that, "All cash tips received by a employee are wages for FICA tax purposes and, therefore, must be reported to the employer unless the cash tips received by the employee during a single calendar month while working for the employer total less than $20."

If an employee fails to report all or his or her cash tips to the employer, the employee is still responsible for the employee's half of the FICA on those tips. The employer is not, initially, responsible for its share of the FICA on the unreported tips. However, once the unreported tips are discovered by the IRS, the IRS will give notice to the employer and the employer's share will become due as well.

Internal Revenue Bulletin 2023-6, released February 6, 2023, contains notice of a proposed revenue procedure establishing the Service Industry Tip Compliance Agreement (SITCA) program. SITCA is a voluntary tip reporting program between the IRS and employers in the service industry (excluding gaming) that is designed to enhance tax compliance through the use of agreements instead of traditional audit techniques. It is intended to replace TRAC, TRDA, and EmTRAC, described below. A participating employer would be required to establish annually that each of its participating covered establishments satisfied a minimum reported tips requirement with respect to its tipped employees. In calculating the annual estimated amount of all cash tips, the covered establishment would use three rates established by the IRS: the SITCA Minimum Charge Tip Percentage, the Cash Differential, and the Stiff Rate, each defined in the proposal. Comments were to be received by May 7, 2023.

¶41,002   Expiration of Simplified Tip Reporting

In Rev. Proc. 2011-51, 2011-44 IRB 669 (October 27, 2011), the IRS announced the expiration of the Attributed Tip Income Program (ATIP). The program that simplifies the recordkeeping burden for reporting tip income in the food and beverage industry was extended only until December 31, 2011. The discussion of this program is presented here for reference and in the event the IRS decides to restore ATIP in the future.

The ATIP was first announced in 2006 in Rev. Proc. 2006-30. The program, which was originally set to expire December 31, 2009, was previously extended to December 31, 2011, under Rev. Proc. 2009-53.

ATIP expands the existing IRS tip reporting and education program by offering employers in the food and beverage industry another option for reporting tip income. ATIP reduces industry recordkeeping burdens, has simple enrollment requirements and promotes reporting tips on federal income tax returns.

ATIP provides benefits to employers and employees similar to those offered under previous tip reporting agreements; however, it does not require employers to meet with the IRS to determine tip rates or eligibility. Employers are not required to sign an agreement with the IRS to participate. Like other tip reporting programs, participation by employers and their employees is voluntary.

Employers who participate in ATIP report the tip income of employees based on a formula that uses a percentage of gross receipts, which are generally attributed among employees based on the practices of the restaurant.

Both employers and employees should find this program beneficial at the same time that the IRS gains as a result of an increase in reported tip income.

Employers receive significant benefits by participating in ATIP as follows:

- The IRS will not initiate an "employer-only" 3121(q) examination during the period the employer participates in ATIP.
- Tip reporting is simplified and in many cases employers will not have to receive and process tip records from participating employees.
- Enrollment is simple. There are no one-on-one meetings with the IRS and no agreements to sign. Employers elect participation in ATIP by checking the designated box on Form 8027, Employer's Annual Information Return of Tip Income and Allocated Tips.

Participating employees are not required to keep a daily tip log or other tip records. They also benefit from ATIP because:

- The IRS will not initiate a tip examination during the period the employer and employee participate in ATIP.
- The improved income reporting procedures could help employees qualify for loans or other financing.
- Employees who work for a participating employer can easily elect to participate in ATIP by signing an agreement with their employer to have their tip income computed under the program and reported as wages.

The IRS also expects to benefit from the program by:

- Promoting tax compliance by both employers and employees with the Internal Revenue Code.
- Reducing disputes on audit.
- Reducing filing and recordkeeping burdens.

Some general requirements for participating restaurants:

- The employer annually elects to participate in ATIP and uses the prescribed methodology for reporting tips by filing Form 8027 and checks the ATIP participation box. Simplified filing is provided for small establishments not required to file Form 8027.
- Employer's establishment must have at least 20 percent of gross receipts as charged receipts that reflect a charged tip.
- At least 75 percent of tipped employees must agree to participate in the program. This test must be met annually.
- Employer reports attributed tips on Employees' Forms W-2 and pays taxes using the formula tip rate.
- The formula tip rate is the charged tip rate minus two percent—the two percent takes into account a lower cash tip rate.
- The charged tip rate is based on information from the establishment's Form 8027.

¶41,003   Tip Rate Determination/Education Program

The TRD/EP was first promoted in the gaming industry (casino industry) in Las Vegas, Nevada, and has spread to the food and beverage industry. Other industries whose employees receive tips include beauty parlors, barber shops, nail salons, taxi companies, and pizza delivery establishments.

The Tip Rate Determination/Education Program created in 1993 is a national program used in all states. The employer has the option to enter into one of two arrangements under this program: the Tip Rate Determination Agreement (TRDA) or the Tip Reporting Alternative Commitment (TRAC) created in June 1995.

With the introduction of the new programs, four options became available for tip reporting:

1. Tip Rate Determination Agreement.
2. Tip Reporting Alternative Commitment.
3. The status quo—the old basic method following the requirements listed below without any "formal" agreement.
4. Examination of Tip Income Reporting.

Under the Tip Rate Determination/Education Program, the employer may enter into either the TRDA or TRAC arrangement. The IRS will assist applicants in understanding and meeting the requirements for participation. Many similarities exist between the two new alternatives, but there are some differences. Following is a descriptive list of the requirements for each, particularly in reference to the food and beverage industry.

.01 TRDA

1. Requires the IRS to work with the establishment to arrive at a tip rate for the various restaurant occupations.
2. Requires the employee to enter into a Tipped Employee Participation Agreement (TEPA) with the employer.
3. Requires the employer to get 75 percent of the employees to sign TEPAs and report at or above the determined rate.
4. Provides that if employees fail to report at or above the determined rate, the employer will provide the names of those employees, their social security numbers, job classification, sales, hours worked, and amount of tips reported.
5. Has no specific education requirement relating to legal responsibility to report tips under the agreement.
6. Participation assures the employer that prior periods will not be examined during the period that the TRDA is in effect.
7. Results in the mailing of a notice and demand to employer for the employer's portion of FICA taxes on unreported tips determined for the six-month period used to set the tip rate(s).
8. Prevents employer (only) assessments during the period that the agreement is in effect.

.02 TRAC

1. Does not require that a tip rate be established, but it does require the employer to:
   a. Establish a procedure where a directly tipped employee is provided (no less than monthly) a written statement of charged tips attributed to the employee.

b.   Implement a procedure for the employee to verify or correct any statement of attributed tips.

c.   Adopt a method where an indirectly tipped employee reports his or her tips (no less than monthly). This could include a statement prepared by the employer and verified or corrected by the employee.

d.   Establish a procedure where a written statement is prepared and processed (no less than monthly) reflecting all cash tips attributable to sales of the directly tipped employee.

2.   Does not require an agreement between the employee and the employer.

3.   Affects all (100 percent) of the employees.

4.   Includes a commitment by the employer to educate and reeducate quarterly all directly and indirectly tipped employees and new hires of their statutory requirement to report all tips to their employer.

5.   Participation assures the employer that prior periods will not be examined during the period that the agreement is in effect.

6.   Prevents employer (only) assessments during the period that the agreement is in effect.

7.   Assures that employers comply with all tax reporting, filing, and payment obligations.

8.   Requires employers to maintain and make available records to the IRS.

9.   Emphasizes that employees earning $20 or more a month in tips must report them to the employer.

In return, the IRS generally will not perform a tip examination on employers complying with the TRAC guidelines. In contrast, an establishment whose employees underreport their tips could be liable for back FICA taxes.

The approach has helped lead to increased tip reporting, but the IRS believes there is still ample room for improvement.

TRAC Agreement Revised. The IRS has been working cooperatively with the restaurant industry in response to industry concerns regarding some aspects of the TRAC program. In late 1999, the IRS took steps to reduce the administrative burdens of restaurant operators by making changes in the regulations:

1.   The IRS will no longer revoke TRAC agreements in cases where employers make a good-faith effort at following the guidelines but employees still fail to report tips. Instead of pursuing the employers in such situations, the IRS will focus on the employees who are not in compliance with tip reporting.

2.   Another change involves restaurants with locations in different IRS Districts. Under the new plan, the restaurant's headquarter operations will work directly with their local IRS office on TRAC issues. This streamlined approach will be simpler and more straightforward than the old system,

where different locations of a company had to deal with different people in different IRS Districts.

The IRS has now extended TRD/EP to continue without a sunset date. With the indefinite extension of the tip program, the IRS will administer existing tip agreements without the need for employers to re-sign agreements.

.03 Instituting the Program

To enter into one of the arrangements, an employer should submit an application letter to the area IRS Chief, Examination/Compliance Division, Attn: Tip Coordinator. The Tip Coordinator can provide a letter format as well as extensive information on the two separate arrangements.

All employers with establishments where tipping is customary should review their operations. Then, if it is determined that there is or has been an under-reporting of tips, the employer should apply for one of the two arrangements under the TRD/EP. Employers currently with the TRDA in effect may revoke the arrangement and simultaneously enter into a TRAC.

The particular advantage to the employer who adopts one of these programs is that no subsequent tip examination is imposed as long as terms of the arrangement have been met and all tips have been reported.

.04 Special Tip Reporting Rules for Large Restaurants

Special rules are established for larger restaurants and other food and beverage establishments. "Large" in this context refers to restaurants with more than ten employees. In addition, large food or beverage establishments must meet the following criteria:

- Tipping is customary.
- Food or beverage is provided and consumed on the premises.
- In the preceding calendar year, the average number of hours worked by all employees on a typical business day was more than 80.

Establishments meeting the above criteria must satisfy additional tip reporting rules under the IRC §6053(c)(4):

- Allocate tips if total tips reported by employees are less than 8 percent of gross receipts (excludes carry-out sales, receipts with a service charge added of more than 10 percent and state or local taxes).
- Report tip allocations on W-2 forms (for each employee who did not meet his or her share of the 8 percent).
- File Form 8027, *Employer's Annual Information Return of Tip Income and Allocated Tips*, to the IRS by the last day in February of the following year.

¶41,004   Employer Tip Reporting Alternative Commitment Program (EmTRAC)

The IRS developed the EmTRAC Agreement program in response to employers in the food and beverage industry who expressed an interest in designing their own TRAC programs. These agreements are available to employers in this industry in which employees receive both cash and charged tips. The EmTRAC program retains many of the provisions of the TRAC agreement, including:

- The employer must establish an educational program that emphasizes that the law requires employees to report to their employer all of their cash and charged tips.
- Education must be furnished immediately for newly hired employees and quarterly for existing employees.
- The employer must establish tip reporting procedures under which a written or electronic statement is prepared and processed on a regular basis (no less than monthly), reflecting all tips for services attributable to each employee.

The employer may have one, or many places of business. For purposes of the program, each place of business is called an establishment. If an employer has more than one establishment, it can choose which establishments to include in its EmTRAC program.

.01   Specific Requirements of the Program

The EmTRAC program provides an employer with considerable latitude in designing its educational program and tip reporting procedures, which the employer may combine. For example, a point-of-sale tip reporting system could meet both of these requirements, because the employee is reminded of the tip reporting requirement at the end of each sale and because the reporting occurs at the end of each sale.

The employer must agree:

- To comply with the requirements for filing all required federal tax returns and paying and depositing all federal taxes.
- To maintain the following records for at least four years after the April 14 following the calendar year to which the records relate:
    - Gross receipts subject to tipping.
    - Charge receipts showing charged tips.
- Upon the request of the IRS, to make the following quarterly totals available, by establishment, for statistical samplings of its establishments:

— Gross receipts subject to tipping.
— Charge receipts showing charged tips.
— Total charged tips.
— Total tips reported.

The IRS agrees:

- Not to initiate any tip examinations of the employer or an establishment included in the EmTRAC for any period for which the EmTRAC program is in effect, except in relation to a tip examination of one or more employees or former employees of the employer or an establishment.
- To base any section 3121(q) notice and demand issued to the employer or an establishment included in the EmTRAC and relating to any period during which the EmTRAC program is in effect solely on amounts reflected on:
  — Form 4137, *Social Security and Medicare Tax on Unreported Tip Income*, filed by an employee with his or her Form 1040, or
  — Form 885-T, *Adjustment of Social Security Tax on Tip Income Not Reported to Employer*, prepared at the conclusion of an employee tip examination.
- Not to evaluate the employer for compliance with the provisions of its EmTRAC program for the first two calendar quarters for which the EmTRAC program is effective.

Both parties agree that, for purposes of the EmTRAC program, a compliance review is not treated as an examination or an inspection of books of account or records, and an inspection of books of account or records pursuant to a tip examination is not an inspection of books or records for purposes of IRC §7605(b), and is not a prior audit for purposes of section 530 of the Revenue Act of 1978.

The effective date of an EmTRAC program is the first day of the quarter beginning on or after the date the IRS signs an approval letter.

An employer may at any time terminate its EmTRAC program either completely or with respect to one or more establishments. The IRS may terminate its approval with respect to the EmTRAC program or a specific establishment or establishments, only if:

- The IRS determines that the employer or establishment(s) has failed to comply with the required provisions.
- The IRS pursues an administrative or judicial action relating to the employer, an establishment included in the EmTRAC, or any other related party to the employer's EmTRAC program.

Generally, any termination is effective the first day of the first calendar quarter after the terminating party notifies the other party in writing. If the employer has an existing TRAC agreement or TRDA covering one or more establishments included in the employer's EmTRAC program, the existing TRAC agreement or TRDA will terminate with respect to that establishment or those establishments upon the approval of the employer's EmTRAC program.

.02   Procedures for Requesting Approval

The employer must request approval of its EmTRAC program. For this purpose, the Service has developed a pro forma letter that an employer must use to request approval of its EmTRAC program. The letter requests approval of the employer's EmTRAC program and states that the employer will comply with the provisions set forth in the letter and in the information above. A copy of the approval request letter can be obtained by mail by contacting the tip coordinator in any local IRS office or by calling (202) 622-5532.

.03   Procedures for Approving Requests

After receiving the approval request letter, the IRS will review the employer's program. If the program meets the necessary requirements, the IRS will send the employer an approval letter specifying the effective date of the employer's EmTRAC program.

If the IRS determines that the employer's EmTRAC program fails to meet all the requirements, it will contact the employer and offer assistance in working out a program that will meet both the employer's needs and the IRS requirements.

Upon request to the local tip coordinator or the EmTRAC Coordinator, the IRS will assist any employer in establishing, maintaining, or improving its educational program or tip reporting procedures.

The Commissioner of Internal Revenue may terminate all EmTRAC programs at any time following a significant statutory change in the FICA taxation of tips.

In 2004, the Service announced an indefinite extension of the Tip Rate Determination and Education Program since by then, the program had helped in almost doubling the reporting of tip income. Now, the successful program will continue without a sunset date.

.04   Wage Reduction under "Tip Credit" Rule

The Fair Labor Standards Act (FLSA), also commonly known as the federal wage and hour law, provides directives for employers on how much to pay their employees for both regular and overtime hours. The act requires employers to pay employees who are not otherwise exempt as follows:

- Regular wages must be paid at least the federal minimum wage of $7.25 an hour or the state minimum wage, whichever is higher.
- Overtime wages must be paid at one and one-half the regular rate of pay for each hour worked exceeding 40 hours a week.

One benefit under the FLSA is that restaurant owners are allowed to pay tipped employees less than the federal minimum wage as long as the difference is made up from tips. This wage reduction is known as a "tip credit." Restaurant owners may pay tipped employees a reduced federal minimum wage rate of $2.13, which may vary by state. However, this approach increases an employer's responsibilities when dealing with tipped employees:

- Tipped employees must be informed in writing that they are paid a reduced rate. Otherwise, the employer may be liable to pay them the full minimum wage rate.
- If hourly wages plus tips do not equal minimum wage for regular or over-time hours, the employer must make up the difference.
- Because not all states follow the federal law, the employer should check with the particular state's Department of Labor for rules on both minimum wage requirements and maximum tip credit amounts.

¶41,005   Gaming Industry Tip Compliance Agreement Program

The Gaming Industry Tip Compliance Agreement Program (GITCA Program), Rev. Proc. 2007-32, is designed to promote compliance by gaming industry employers and employees with the provisions of the Internal Revenue Code relating to tip income and to reduce disputes under section 3121(q).

The original program was established by Rev. Proc. 2003-35 in May 2003. It provides an updated model Gaming Industry Tip Compliance Agreement for use by the IRS and gaming industry employers. The new model agreement has been revised to enhance administration of the GITCA Program by both the employers and the Service and to facilitate and promote the use of current financial information technology in the tip reporting process.

.01   Cooperative Effort

Under the GITCA Program, a gaming industry employer and the IRS work together to reach a Gaming Industry Tip Compliance Agreement that:

- Establishes minimum tip rates for tipped employees in specified occupational categories,
- Prescribes a threshold level of participation by the employer's employees, and
- Reduces compliance burdens for the employer and enforcement burdens for the Service.

With the consent of the IRS, all employers operating a gaming establishment may participate in the GITCA Program. Either the Service or an employer may suggest the employer's potential participation in the program. The Service's decision to refuse participation by any employer in this program is not subject to review.

.02   Basic Conditions of a GITCA Program

1. To participate in this program, an employer must execute a Gaming Industry Tip Compliance Agreement. The Agreement will conform to all requirements of this revenue procedure and will use the form appended to this revenue procedure as Exhibit 1.
2. An executed Gaming Industry Tip Compliance Agreement supersedes all existing tip compliance agreements between an employer and the Service. A gaming industry employer under any existing tip compliance agreement with the Service, including a Tip Rate Determination Agreement, may request to change to a Gaming Industry Tip Compliance Agreement.
3. In general, Gaming Industry Tip Compliance Agreements are for a term of three years. For new properties and for properties that do not have a prior agreement with the IRS; however, the initial term of the Agreement may be for a shorter period.
4. All Gaming Industry Tip Compliance Agreements may be renewed for additional terms of up to three years, in accordance with Section IX of the model Gaming Industry Tip Compliance Agreement. Beginning not later than six months prior to the termination date of a Gaming Industry Tip Compliance Agreement, the Service and the employer will commence discussions as to any appropriate revisions to the agreement, including any appropriate revisions to the tip rates described in Section VIII of the model Gaming Industry Tip Compliance Agreement. In the event that the Service and the employer have not reached final agreement on the terms and conditions of a renewal agreement, the parties may, by mutual agreement, extend the existing agreement for an appropriate time in order to finalize and execute a renewal agreement.
5. Decisions regarding renewal of a Gaming Industry Tip Compliance Agreement are not subject to review.

.03   Compliance with Section 6053

An employer who complies with the reporting requirements of Section V of its Gaming Industry Tip Compliance Agreement, and participating employees of the employer who report in accordance with the agreement, will be deemed to be in compliance with the reporting requirements of IRC §6053 for the taxable periods during which the agreement remains in effect.

.04   Effective Date and Effect on Other Documents

Rev. Proc. 2007-32 is effective May 2, 2007. Rev. Proc. 2003-35 is superseded. All Gaming Industry Tip Compliance Agreements executed pursuant to Rev. Proc. 2003-35 will remain in effect until the expiration date set forth in that Agreement, unless superseded by the execution of a Gaming Industry Tip Compliance Agreement under Section 4.02 of this Revenue Procedure.

.05   Indian Tribal Gaming

The Office of Indian Tribal Governments, under the Tax Exempt and Governmental Entities Operating Division (TEGE), serves as the coordinating office for all federal tax administration needs with Indian tribal governments, which includes tax administration in connection with Indian tribal gaming.

There are 566 federally recognized tribes across the country. There are 310 gaming facilities within these tribal units, approximately 65 percent of which have occupations where significant tipping occurs. The remaining 35 percent consist principally of bingo or video lottery terminals, and do not lend themselves to having tipped employees.

Between entities where agreements are in place, and entities where compliance actions are currently underway, tip reporting compliance is being addressed with nearly 90 percent of the applicable customer base. The IRS expects to reach 100 percent and will then focus primarily on maintaining compliance in the tip reporting area.

¶41,006   Basic Rules Relating to Tip Income Reporting

The following discussion concerns how tip income is taxed and how it should be reported to the IRS on the federal income tax return. The employees of food and beverage companies are the main subjects of this review; the record keeping rules and other information also apply to other workers who receive tips.

As pointed out earlier, all tips that are received by employees are taxable income and are subject to federal income taxes. Employees must include in gross income all tips received directly from customers, and tips from charge customers paid to the employer, who must pay them to the employee. In addition, cash tips of $20 or more that an employee receives in a month while working for any one employer are subject to withholding of income tax, social security retirement tax, and Medicare tax. The same rule applies to non-cash tips, such as passes or tickets to sporting events given in lieu of cash. The employee should report tips to the employer in order to determine the correct amount of these taxes. IRS Form 4070 is used to report tip activity.

Tips and other pay are used to determine the amount of social security benefits that an employee receives when he or she retires, becomes disabled, or dies. Noncash tips are not counted as wages for social security purposes. Future Social Security Administration (SSA) benefits can be figured correctly only if the SSA has the correct information. To make sure that an employee has received credit for all his or her earnings, the employee should request a statement of earnings from the SSA at least every other year. The SSA will send the person a statement that should be carefully checked to be sure it includes all of the employee's earnings.

Every large food and beverage business must report to the IRS any tips allocated to the employees. Generally, tips must be allocated to be paid by employees when the total tips reported to an employer by employees are less than 8 percent of the establishment's food and beverage sales of that employee. This necessitates the employer and employees keeping accurate records of the employee's tip income.

.01   Daily Tip Record

The employee must keep a daily tip record so he or she can:

1. Report tips accurately to the employer.
2. Report tips accurately on a tax return.
3. Prove tip income if the taxpayer's return is ever questioned.

There are two ways to keep a daily tip record:

1. The employee can keep a daily "tip diary."
2. The employee should keep copies of documents that show the tips, such as restaurant bills and credit card charge slips.

The employee can start record keeping by writing his or her name, the employer's name, and the name of the business if it is different from the employer's name. Each workday, the employee should write and date the following information in a tip diary.

1. Cash tips received directly from customers or other employees.
2. Tips from credit card charge customers that the employer pays the employee.
3. The value of any noncash tips received, such as tickets, passes, or other items of value.
4. The amount of tips the employee paid out to other employees through tip pools, tip splitting, or other arrangements, and the names of the employees to whom tips were paid.

.02 Reporting Tips to the Employer

The employee must report tips to the employer so that:

1. The employer can withhold federal income tax, social security taxes, and Medicare taxes.
2. The employer can report the correct amount of the employee's earnings to the Social Security Administration. This will affect the employee's benefits when the employee retires or becomes disabled, or the family's benefits upon the employee's death.

.03 What Tips to Report

Only cash, check, or credit card tips should be reported to the employer, not in-kind tips such as passes or tickets to sporting events. If the total tips for any one month from any one job are less than $20, they should not be reported to the employer. The value of any noncash tips, such as tickets or passes, is not reported to the employer because the employee does not have to pay social security and Medicare taxes on these tips. The employee will, however, report them on his or her individual tax return. The following information should be written on the report to be given to the employer:

1. Name, address, and social security number.
2. The employer's name, address, and business name if it is different from the employer's name.
3. The month, or the dates of any shorter period, in which the tips are received.
4. The total amount of tips the employee received.

The employee must sign and date the report and give it to the employer. The employee should keep a copy of the report for his or her personal records. The report is to be completed each month and given to the employer by the tenth of the next month.

.04   Employer Records for Tip Allocation

Large food and beverage establishments are required to report certain additional information about tips to the IRS. To make sure that employees are reporting tips correctly, employers must keep records to verify amounts reported by employees. Certain employers must allocate tips if the percentage of tips reported by employees falls below a required minimum percentage of gross sales. To allocate tips means to assign an additional amount as tips to each employee whose reported tips are below the required percentage. The rules apply to premises in which:

1. Food and beverages are provided for consumption on the premises.
2. Tipping is customary.
3. The employer normally employed more than ten people on a typical business day during the preceding calendar year.

Tip allocation rules do not apply to food and beverage establishments where tipping is not customary such as:

1. A cafeteria or fast food restaurant.
2. A restaurant that adds a service charge of 10 percent or more to 95 percent or more of its food and beverage sales.
3. Food and beverage establishments located outside the United States.

The rules apply only if the total amount of tips reported by all tipped employees to the employer is less than 8 percent, or some lower acceptable percentage of the establishment's total food or beverage sales, with some adjustments. If reported tips total less than 8 percent of total sales, the employer must allocate the difference between 8 percent of total sales, or some lower acceptable percentage approved by the IRS, and the amount of tips reported by all tipped employees. The employer will exclude carryout sales, state and local taxes, and sales with a service charge of 10 percent or more when figuring total sales.

Usually, the employer will allocate to all affected employees their share of tips every payroll period. However, the employer should not withhold any taxes from the allocated amount. No allocation will be made to the employee if the employee reports tips at least equal to the employee's share of 8 percent of the establishment's total food and beverage sales.

.05   Penalty for Not Reporting Tips

If the employee does not report tips to his or her employer as required, the employee can be subject to a penalty equal to 50 percent of the social security and Medicare taxes owed. The penalty amount is in addition to the taxes owed.

The penalty can be avoided if the employee can show reasonable cause for not reporting the tips to the employer. A statement should be attached to the tax return explaining why the tips were not reported to the employer. If an employee's regular pay is not enough for the employer to withhold all the taxes owed on the regular pay plus reported tips, the employee can give the employer money to pay the rest of the taxes, up to the close of the calendar year.

If the employee does not give the employer enough money, the employer will apply the regular pay and any money given by the employee in the following order:

1. All taxes on the employee's regular pay.
2. Social security and Medicare taxes on the reported tips.
3. Federal, state, and local income taxes on the reported tips.

Any taxes that remain unpaid can be collected by the employer from the employee's next paycheck. If withholding taxes remain uncollected at the end of the year, the employee must make an estimated tax payment. To report these taxes, a return must be filed even if the employee would not otherwise have to file. If the employer could not collect all the social security and Medicare taxes owed on the tips reported to the employer, the uncollected taxes must be shown by the employer on a Form W-2. The employee must then also report these uncollected taxes on his or her return.

¶41,007 Tip Rates

Depending on the Occupational Category and the employer's business practices, tips can be *measured* in different ways:

1. *Actual tips* generally apply to Employees in Occupational Categories (O.C.) where pooling of tips is common. The tips are pooled during a shift and the total is split among the employees of the O.C. who worked the shift.
2. *Tip rates* generally apply to employees in O.C. where pooling of tips is not common. The rate may be a percentage of sales, a dollar amount, or other accurate basis of measurement per hour or shift, a dollar amount per drink served, a dollar amount per working hour, or other accurate measurement.

.01 Methods for Determining Tip Rates

The employer will determine tip rates for the O.C. based on information available to the employer, historical information provided by the IRS representative, and U.S. Generally Accepted Accounting Principles (U.S. GAAP). The rates will specify whether the tips are received as a percentage of sales, a dollar amount per hour or shift, a dollar amount per drink served, a dollar amount per dealing hour in a casino, or on another basis.

.02   Initial Tip Rate

The initial tip rate for each O.C. is shown where pool and split tips methods are used by the employees.

¶41,008   Annual Review

The employer will review annually, on a calendar-year basis, changes in the tip rates assigned to its O.C. In connection with the review, the employer can review its O.C. The initial rates for each O.C. will apply to the first full calendar year of the review.

.01   Employer Submission

If the employer believes that a revision of one or more rates or O.C. is appropriate, the employer will submit proposed revisions to the IRS representative by September 30. If the employer fails to submit a proposed rate revision by September 30 of the taxable year, the employee will be treated as having submitted the rate in effect for the current year.

.02   Internal Revenue Service Review

The IRS representative will review the proposed rates and notify the employer in writing of the approval or disapproval by November 30. If the IRS representative does not approve one or more proposed rates, the existing rate or rates will be continued until no later than the last day of the following February.

The effective date of revised rates and O.C. will become effective on the later of January 1 of the calendar year, or on the first day of the month following the date the employer and the IRS representative agree upon a revised rate. The IRS representative can examine a participating employee's tip income for any period if an employee reports tips at a rate less than the tip rate for the employee's occupational category.

These amounts must be an additional tax on the employee's tax return. The employee may have uncollected taxes if his or her regular pay was not enough for the employer to withhold all the taxes the taxpayer owed, but did not give the employer enough money to pay the rest of the taxes. The employee must report these uncollected taxes on a return.

¶41,009   Allocated Tips

Allocated tips are tips that the employer assigned to an employee in addition to the tips the employee reported to the employer for the year. The employer will have done this only if the employee worked in a restaurant, cocktail lounge, or similar business that must allocate tips to employees, and the reported tips were less than the employee's share of 8 percent of food and drink sales. If allocated tips are shown on a return, and if social security and Medicare taxes were not withheld from the allocated tips, these taxes must be reported as additional tax on a return.

.01   Allocation Formula

The allocation can be done either under a formula agreed to by both the employer and the employees or, if they cannot reach an agreement, under a formula prescribed by IRS regulations. The allocation formula in the regulations provides that tip allocations are made only to directly tipped employees. If tips are received directly from customers, the employees are directly tipped employees, even if the tips are turned over to a tip pool. Waiters, waitresses, and bartenders are usually considered directly tipped employees. If tips are not normally received directly from customers, the employee is an indirectly tipped employee. Examples are busboys, service bartenders, and cooks. If an employee receives tips both directly and indirectly through tip splitting or tip pooling, the employee is treated as a directly tipped employee.

If customers of the establishment tip less than 8 percent on average, either the employee or a majority of the directly tipped employees can petition to have the allocation percentage reduced from 8 percent. This petition is made to the IRS representative for the IRS district in which the establishment is located. The percentage cannot be reduced below 2 percent.

A fee is required to have the IRS consider a petition to lower the tip allocation percentage. The fee must be paid by check or money order made out to the IRS. (The user fee amount for 2022 and 2023 is $275; the IRS representative in the taxpayer's area will know if this amount has changed.)

The employees' petition to lower the allocation percentage must be in writing, and must contain enough information to allow the IRS representative to estimate with reasonable accuracy the establishment's actual tip rate. This information might include the changed tip rate, type of establishment, menu prices, location, hours of operation, amount of self-service required, and whether the customer receives the check from the server or pays the server for the meal. If the employer possesses any relevant information, the employer must provide it to the district upon request of the employees or the IRS representative.

The employees' petition must be consented to by more than one-half of the directly tipped employees working for the establishment at the time the petition is filed. If the petition covers more than one establishment, it must be consented to by more than one-half of the total number of directly tipped employees of the covered establishments. The petition must state the total number of directly tipped employees of the establishment(s) and the number of directly tipped employees consenting to the petition.

The petition may cover two or more establishments if the employees have made a good faith determination that the tip wages are essentially the same and if the establishments are:

1. Owned by the same employer.
2. Essentially the same type of business.
3. In the same IRS region.

A petition that covers two or more establishments must include the names and locations of the establishments and must be sent to the IRS representative for the district in which the greatest number of covered establishments are located. If there is an equal number of covered establishments in two or more districts, the employees can choose which district to petition. Employees who file a petition must promptly notify their employer of the petition. The employer must then promptly furnish the IRS representative with an annual information return form showing the tip income and allocated tips filed for the establishment for the three immediately preceding calendar years.

The employer will report the amount of tips allocated to employees on the employees' Form W-2 separately from wages and reported tips. The employer bases withholding only on wages and reported tips. The employer should not withhold income, social security, and Medicare taxes from the allocated amount. Any incorrectly withheld taxes should be refunded to the employee by the employer.

If an employee leaves a job before the end of the calendar year and requests an early Form W-2, the employer does not have to include a tip allocation on the Form W-2. However, the employer can show the actual allocated amount if it is known, or show an estimated allocation. In January of the following year, the employer must provide Form W-2 if the early Form W-2 showed no allocation and the employer later determined that an allocation was required, or if the estimated allocation shown was wrong by more than 5 percent of the actual allocation.

If an employee does not have adequate records for his or her actual tips, the employee must include the allocated tips shown on the Form W-2 as additional tip income on the tax return. If the employee has records, allocated tips should not be shown on the employee's return. Additional tip income is included only if those records show more tips received than the amount reported to the employer.

CHAPTER 42

The Legal Environment of Accounting—Federal Law and Cases Impacting Accountants

¶42,000   Overview

This chapter highlights significant federal legislation and court cases that impact the legal environment in which accountants operate.

¶42,001   Dodd-Frank Wall Street Reform and Consumer Protection Act

The Dodd-Frank Act was passed in 2010 to enhance the Commodity Futures Trading Commission's (CTFC) regulatory authority to oversee the more than $400 trillion swaps market. It primarily addresses issues in the financial institutions industry but can have a significant impact on accounting and auditing.

The Dodd-Frank Act required the CFTC to conduct a number of studies and reports on a wide variety of issues that affect the derivatives market. The Act brings comprehensive reform to the regulation of swaps. They were not regulated previously and were at the center of the 2008 financial crisis. The Act authorizes the CTFC to:

- Regulate swap dealers
  - List provisionally registered swap dealers.
  - Swap dealers will be subject to capital and margin requirements to lower risk in the system.

- Dealers will be required to meet robust business conduct standards to lower risk and promote market integrity.
- Dealers will be required to meet recordkeeping and reporting requirements so that regulators can police the markets.
- Increase transparency and improve pricing in the derivatives marketplace
  - Instead of trading out of sight of the public, standardized derivatives will be required to be traded on regulated exchanges or swap execution facilities.
  - Transparent trading of swaps will increase competition and bring better pricing to the marketplace. This will lower costs for businesses and consumers.
- Lower risk to the American public
  - Standardized derivatives will be moved into central clearinghouses to lower risk in the financial system.
  - Clearinghouses act as middlemen between two parties to a transaction and take on the risk that one counterparty may default on its obligations.
  - Clearinghouses have lowered risk in the futures marketplace since the 1890s. The Dodd-Frank Act brings this crucial market innovation to the swaps marketplace.

42,002   Sarbanes-Oxley Act—Restrictions on Non-Audit Functions Provided by Auditors

Since 2002, the Sarbanes-Oxley Act (section 201) has placed limitations on the ancillary services that an audit firm may perform for its audit clients. The SEC was responsible for implementing and clarifying these rules. These restrictions were a reaction to what many people saw as the problem of one-stop shopping for all accounting services. Since auditors in particular are required to be independent from their clients, both in appearance and in fact, the coziness of some CPA-client relationships was seen as pushing the envelope. The related activities which auditors were previously performing for their audit clients, but which are now proscribed, are listed and briefly described below. For a more extensive explanation, see Chapter 16, "Auditor Independence and the Audit Committee."

- Bookkeeping or other services related to the accounting records or financial statements of the audit client.
- Maintaining or preparing the audit client's accounting records.
- Preparing financial statements that are filed with the Commission or the information that forms the basis of financial statements filed with the Commission.
- Preparing or originating source data underlying the audit client's financial statements.
- Financial information systems design and implementation.

- Appraisal or valuation services, fairness opinions, or contribution-in-kind reports.
- Actuarial services.
- Internal audit outsourcing services.
- Management functions or human resources.
- Broker or dealer, investment adviser, or investment banking services.
- Legal services and expert services unrelated to the audit.
- Any other service that the Board determines, by regulation, is impermissible.

Tax services are permitted and any of the above services is permitted to non-audit clients.

See Chapter 16, "Auditor Independence and the Audit Committee," and Chapter 26, "The Sarbanes-Oxley Act of 2002," for more information on the Sarbanes-Oxley Act.

¶42,003   The Corporate and Criminal Fraud Accountability Act of 2002

It is a felony to knowingly destroy or create documents to "impede, obstruct or influence" any existing or contemplated federal investigation. Auditors are required to maintain all audit or review work papers for five years.

The statute of limitations on securities fraud claims is extended to the earlier of five years from the fraud or two years after the fraud was discovered, from three years and one year, respectively.

Employees of issuers and accounting firms are extended whistle-blower protection that would prohibit the employer from taking certain actions against employees who lawfully disclose private employer information to, among others, parties in a judicial proceeding involving a fraud claim. Whistle-blowers are also granted a remedy of special damages and attorney's fees.

A crime for securities fraud has penalties of fines and up to 10 years of imprisonment.

.01   White-Collar Crime Penalty Enhancement Act of 2002

The provisions include a long list of penalties that have increased the time of imprisonment and amount of fines for specified crimes as follows:

- The maximum penalty for mail and wire fraud is increased from five to ten years.
- Tampering with a record or otherwise impeding any official proceeding is classified as a crime.
- The SEC is given authority to seek a court freeze of extraordinary payments to directors, officers, partners, controlling persons, and agents of employees.

- The U.S. Sentencing Commission is to review sentencing guidelines for securities and accounting fraud.
- The SEC may prohibit anyone convicted of securities fraud from being an officer or director of any publicly traded company.
- Financial statements filed with the SEC must be certified by the CEO and CFO.
- The certification must state that the financial statements and disclosures fully comply with provisions of the Securities Exchange Act and that they fairly present, in all material respects, the operations and financial condition of the issuer.
- Maximum penalties for willful and knowing violations of this section are a fine of not more than $500,000 and/or imprisonment of up to five years.

¶42,004   Money Laundering

The compliance work provided by CPAs and other accountants for their clients includes government reporting in addition to income tax returns and, in the case of public companies, reporting to the SEC. In particular, accountants are charged with advising and fulfilling other reporting requests such as those involving potential money laundering and reporting foreign bank accounts.

One of the tools used in the federal government's battle against money laundering is IRC §6050I's reporting requirement for cash received in a trade or business if the amount exceeds $10,000. Subject to certain exceptions and clarifications discussed below, the general rule of §6050I requires the recipient of such payments to report the amounts and payees to the IRS within 15 days using IRS Form 8300, "Report of Cash Payments Over $10,000 Received in a Trade or Business."

In the Regulations and elsewhere the IRS provides examples showing when the cash reporting requirements are applicable to any organization, taxable or tax-exempt. The following stipulate specific ground rules and definitions for the application of the rules.

- The receipt of cash required to be reported includes currency (folding money and coins) of the U.S. *or any other country* (Reg. §1.6050I-1(c)(1)).
- Cash reporting does not apply to the receipt of a personal check.

To be considered cash, payments received in the form of money orders, travelers checks, bank drafts, cashier's checks, bank checks or treasurer's checks (herein after referred to alternatively as money orders or financial instruments), if the amount of the instrument is *less than* $10,000, must meet one of two conditions (Reg. §1.6050I-1(c)(1)(ii)(B)). First, to be characterized as cash, the financial instrument must have been received in a *designated reporting transaction*—defined as a retail sale—involving either (1) consumer durables, or (2) collectibles or (3) travel and entertainment activities (Reg. §1.6050I-1(c)(1)). Alternately, the receipt of a money order (or other like financial instrument) is considered cash "in any transaction in which the recipient knows that such instrument is being used in an attempt to avoid the reporting of the transaction" (Reg. §1.6050I-1(c)(1) (B)(ii)) to the IRS, otherwise referred to as a *suspicious transaction.*

For the purpose of determining if money orders are cash, a *consumer durable* is an item of "tangible personal property of a type that is suitable under ordinary usage for personal consumption or use," having an expected useful life of at least one year, and with a sales price of more than $10,000 (IRC §6050I(c)(2)). Examples include cars, furniture, boats, antiques, art works, motorcycles and jewelry.

If payments received include a combination of money orders with a face value of less than $10,000 (each) and cash, the total exceeding $10,000, the receipt is reportable (Reg. §1.6050I-1(c)(1)(ii)(B)).

.01   Illustrative Examples

Application of the ground rules and definitions is illustrated by the Service through questions and answers. Though the direct connection between the particular examples and the operations of charitable organizations may not obvious in some cases, the underlying principles of application may still be instructive, as they clarify when the cash reporting rules do or do not apply.

Q-1). If several items are purchased at the same time and paid for in cash, and though none of the items is sold individually for more than $10,000, the total of the items is greater than $10,000, does the cash reporting requirement apply?

Yes. Here the Regulations state that the "transaction" is the underlying event precipitating the payer's transfer of cash to the recipient (Reg. §1.6050I-1(c)(7)(3)). "Transactions include (but are not limited to) a sale of goods or services and may not be divided into multiple transactions to avoid reporting under Section 6050I of the Code (TAM 200501016)." Caution on the part of a taxpayer would thus dictate that when more than $10,000 in cash is received for several items of personal property purchased at the same time the sales should be aggregated as one transaction.

Q-2). Does the same principle apply when what is essentially one cash transaction is paid for in two or more separate payments?

Yes. Multiple payments related to the same transaction are aggregated to measure whether the total exceeds $10,000 (Reg. §1.6050I-1(b)). The question was posed to the IRS in the context of a customer purchasing several items of furniture, no one of which exceeded $10,000, but collectively the amount of cash paid was greater than $10,000 and the cash was paid at two or more times. According to the IRS, "The reporting requirements of section 6050I apply when a single customer purchases multiple items of personal property at the same time and pays for the purchase via a series of cash payments totaling in excess of $10,000" (TAM 200501016).

Here two separate issues are involved. The first is the aggregation of payments for a single transaction when the total cash received exceeds $10,000. This occurs, for example, when the customer puts $5,000 cash down on the purchase of $12,000 of furniture, paying the balance in cash upon delivery. The store's responsibility is clear in such a case; it must aggregate and report both payments as one. The second issue is the aggregation multiple items purchased for cash as one transaction explained in A-1 (Reg. §1.6050I-1(c)(7)(3)).

Q-3). Can the cash reporting requirements be avoided if an individual who buys goods or services, signs a note or purchases items on account rather than paying cash, but later liquidates the debt using cash in excess of $10,000?

The IRS says no. When a loan—made in the course of a trade or business—is repaid in cash exceeding $10,000 the recipient is required to file Form 8300. This applies to the payment of a "preexisting debt, a contribution to a custodial account, trust or escrow arrangements or the reimbursement of expenses" (Reg. §1.6050I-1(c)(7)).

Q-4). Is cash in excess of $10,000 received by one person, including an agent, for the account of a second, considered a reportable transaction by the first person? For example, when a collection agency collects cash which is applied to the accounts receivable of another trade or business, is the collection agency required to report the cash?

The Regulations say yes (Reg. §1.6050I-1(a)(2) and (3)).

What about delivery companies that collect COD payments at the point of delivery? Are they required to report cash receipts in excess of $10,000, even though the delivery company is simply the conduit for the underlying transaction between the customer and the business where the item was purchased?

According to the IRS, the answer is again yes. The service states, "If a driver receives more than $10,000 in currency (and coin), the receipt is clearly reportable under section 1.6050I-1 without regard to whether it was received in a designated reporting transaction (TAM 9718003)." The guidance goes on to clarify that if the payment received is comprised partly of cash of less than $10,000 and the balance in money orders (or other financial instruments) of less than $10,000 each, the delivery company must combine the cash with the money orders (as explained earlier) and report the total on Form 8300, if the total is greater than $10,000.

Q-5). How is the distinction between a retail business and a wholesale business drawn for purposes of determining whether a money order (or other financial instrument) less than $10,000, constitutes cash?

The IRS illustrates the difference with examples of retail and wholesale automobile auctions. Since the focus of the distinction between cash reporting requirements for retail as opposed to wholesale customers using money orders, turns on whether the money order is considered cash, the Service uses the example of a sale by a retail auto auction to a customer who pays a total of $25,000 in the form of 50 $500 money orders. This is a transaction requiring reporting (Chief Counsel Advice 200211046). On the other hand, when the same transaction occurs in the context of a wholesale auto auction, the result is different. Since the basis for the reporting requirement—a designated reporting transaction—is a retail sale, the fact that this is a wholesale transaction removes the money orders from the category of cash. However, the wholesale auto auction would still report the receipt of cash (currency or coin) in excess of $10,000.

In addition, reporting is required—even by the wholesale auto auction—if the recipient believes the payment of more than $10,000 in money orders (or other financial instruments)—each with a face value of less than $10,000—constitutes a suspicious transaction (Chief Counsel Advice 200211046). This could occur, for example, where the customer initially tells the auto action that he intends to pay in cash in excess of $10,000. Since the auction house is required to file Form 8300 in such an instance, the auctioneer requests the customer's Social Security number. As a result of this turn of events, the customer informs the auto auction that he has changed his mind and will pay with money orders. The customer then produces a series of $500 money orders totaling the purchase price of the car. Since this change in the form of payment could reasonably be construed as an attempt to avoid the cash reporting requirements of §6050I, it constitutes a suspicious transaction (Chief Counsel Advice 200152047). The result would be the same if the initial offer of cash was replaced with an offer to pay with a check or by some other means. Even though the payment by check is not a reportable cash transaction, a suspicious transaction is one "in which it appears that a person is attempting to cause Form 8300 not to be filed, or to file a false or incomplete form or there is an indication of illegal activity" (Chief Counsel Advice 200152047).

Q-6). In analyzing the meaning of *cash receipt*, what is the locus of *receipt*? What is meant by recipient? (Reg. §1.6050I-1(c)(8)). If a department store has many cashiers, for example, and a customer makes purchases from several different cashiers during a day, where the total cash tendered exceeds $10,000 but no individual cashier receives more than $10,000. Is the cashier or the store the recipient?

In answering the question the IRS says it depends on the particular facts of the case. The Regulations state that "each store, division, branch, department, headquarters, or office ('branch') (regardless of physical location) comprising a portion of a person's trade or business shall for purposes of this section be deemed a separate recipient." (Reg. §1.6050I-1(c)(8)(i)). In an analogous situation, where an individual places pari-mutuel wagers at separate racetrack betting windows, the separate cash wagers—in spite of the fact that they collectively exceed $10,000 in cash—are not assumed to be received by the racetrack but rather by each separate betting window (Reg. §1.6050I-1(c)(8)(iii)(2); TAM 200501016, 1/7/2005). Each window is a separate recipient as the racetrack does not maintain an account for each patron.

On the other hand, a branch (or individual cashier) that receives cash payments is *not* a separate recipient if the branch has reason to know the identity of the payer making cash payments to other branches (Reg. §1.6050I-1(c)(8)(ii)). Thus, if the customer is specifically identified by the store as she makes her purchases from several cashiers, and as a result the purchases are reflected in her account with the store, the IRS holds the store responsible to aggregate the individual cash payments although paid to separate cashiers (or branches) (TAM 200501016). Must a company's right hand have to know what its left hand is doing? It depends.

Q-7). Does payment to a racetrack in the form of a winning ticket plus cash totaling more than $10,000 constitute a reportable transaction?

The Service says no. The winning ticket is not cash, nor is it a financial instrument like a money order. The ticket may only be used at the racetrack and has no general standing as currency (Chief Counsel Advice 200012047).

¶42,005   The Foreign Corrupt Practices Act (FCPA)

Investigations by the Securities and Exchange Commission in the mid-1970s showed that more than 400 U.S. companies admitted making questionable or outright illegal payments in excess of $300 million to foreign government officials, politicians and political parties.

When the Foreign Corrupt Practices Act (FCPA) was enacted by Congress in 1977, the act was characterized by the American Bar Association as the most extensive application of federal law to the regulation of business since the passage of the 1933 and 1934 Securities Acts. As a matter of fact, the FCPA is an amendment to the 1934 Securities Exchange Act and is generally administered by the SEC.

One reason for the significance of this statutory requirement is that it represents the first time, historically, that the U.S. Congress legislated an accounting rule. U.S. GAAP, of course, have always been developed and promulgated by private-sector authorities—the AICPA, the Financial Accounting Standards Board (FASB), the AAA and other authoritative sources. However, indications at present are that this may not hold true in the future.

.01   Importance of the Act to the Accounting Profession

Primarily as a result of the enactment of the FCPA, internal accounting controls have become a significant point of concern for corporate management, the public accounting profession and the Securities and Exchange Commission.

Section 102 of the FCPA titled "Accounting Standards" specifies that all corporations required to file with the SEC must "Make and keep books, records, and accounts, which, in reasonable detail, accurately and fairly reflect the transactions and dispositions of the assets of the issuer."

.02   The Accountant's Responsibility

Again, the significance of the act is the explicit statutory recognition by the federal government given to accounting controls and control systems. The accountant's responsibility is to plan a system that constantly monitors for errors, irregularities, malfeasance, embezzlement and fraudulent manipulation of the accounts. The accountant is, in fact, the monitor who must continually evaluate the effectiveness of the system and monitor compliance with the requirements of the statute. This, of course, also includes compliance with U.S. GAAP, because the statute explicitly includes U.S. GAAP in the wording of the act.

That the statutory requirement applies to publicly held corporations led, initially, to the misunderstanding that it is of no concern to public accountants who are not involved in auditing public corporations. But auditors must be mindful of the Statement on Auditing Procedure No. 1, which applies to the scope of the examination of *all companies*, whether public or private corporations, partnerships or other forms of business organizations. This Statement specifically references creditors, for example, who are a primary user of financial statements and to whom an auditor has a potential liability for materially misleading financial statements accompanying applications for credit to financial institutions, regardless of honest error or fraudulent intent.

.03   Compliance Problems

What can an accountant do to ascertain compliance with the 1977 act? Because neither the act nor the professional literature actually specifies criteria for evaluating a system's adequacy or materiality levels, compliance can be demonstrated by an intent to comply. This makes it difficult for management, directors, independent auditors, and legal counsel to be sure of compliance with the act as far as the government is concerned.

The following suggestions may be helpful both to the accountant and to management for establishing intent to comply. There should be:

- Records of memos and minutes of meetings held by management, the board of directors and the audit committee (if there is no audit committee, one should be instituted) concerning internal accounting control concepts. The discussions should include legal counsel, internal auditors and independent auditors.
- Statements for the record of intention to comply.

- A record of all company meetings with the accounting personnel and internal audit staff held to ensure that they understand the importance of compliance and are capable of monitoring compliance.
- A written program for continuing review and evaluation of the accounting controls system.
- Letters from the independent auditors stating that no material weaknesses in internal accounting controls were discovered during the audit or that suggested needed improvements have in fact been made. If necessary, the independent auditors' comments should also include other deficiencies discovered during the audit. Management's written plans to correct these deficiencies should be included.
- A record of periodic review and approval of the evaluation of the system by senior management, the audit committee and the board of directors.
- Instructional manuals for the development of methods and techniques for describing, testing and evaluating internal controls.
- Training programs conducted for internal auditors and other company personnel responsible for internal controls.
- Changes in internal controls to overcome identified deficiencies that are initiated and documented.
- A formal written code of conduct appropriately communicated and monitored. (Note: the SEC regards a corporate written code of conduct as imperative. At the same time, a non-listed corporation might find that such a written code is even more important as a protection in case of litigation.)
- Documentation that compliance testing was done by direct visual observations during the period being audited.

.04   1988 Amendment to the FCPA

The basic act was amended in 1988 to spell out and clarify certain provisions of the act. As more and more small businesses became involved in world trade, it became essential for persons doing business overseas to understand fully the FCPA and its implications. It is an extremely important law that can result in grave consequences for those who disregard it. This law criminalizes certain conduct by or on behalf of U.S. entities doing business abroad. There are two basic parts of this law:

Anti-bribery provisions, which prohibit the payment of bribes to foreign officials to obtain business. This measure applies to *all* entities, *not* just listed companies. (See below.)

Accounting provisions, which require *public* companies to maintain accurate books and records, and an *adequate internal accounting control system.* The accounting rules apply only to companies that are required to report financial information under the Securities laws. These accounting and recordkeeping rules are broad and should be thoroughly understood.

.05   Anti-Bribery Provisions of the FCPA

Under the FCPA, a "U.S. person" is precluded from providing certain things to a "foreign official" to get that foreign official to behave contrary to the obligations of his or her position. Specifically, the FCPA prohibits any U.S. person from corruptly proposing or giving money or other things of value to a foreign official, an official of a foreign political party, a candidate for foreign political office, or a foreign political party for the purposes of:

- Influencing any act or decision of such foreign official in his official capacity.
- Inducing such foreign official "to do or omit to do" any act in violation of a lawful duty of such official.
- Inducing such official to use his or her influence with a foreign government or instrumentality thereof to affect or influence any governmental act or decision.
- Securing any improper advantage.

.06   Accounting Provisions: Financial Policies and Internal Control

The FCPA states that corporations filing with the SEC are required to keep an accurate accounting of all financial transactions, including payment of commissions, consulting fees, service fees, facilitating payments and gratuities. All financial transactions must be characterized accurately in company financial records. Mislabeled or hidden transactions can result in liability for the company under the accounting provisions of the FCPA.

A company's *finance policies* and *internal controls* must ensure that all such transactions are properly and fully recorded. Therefore, it is mandatory that appropriate contracts govern international relationships and that all terms and conditions regarding payment under those contracts are clearly spelled out.

The statute requires publicly held companies to develop and maintain a system of internal accounting controls sufficient to ensure:

- That transactions are executed in accordance with management's general or specific authorization.
- That transactions are recorded as necessary to permit preparation of financial statements in conformity with U.S. GAAP or any other criteria applicable to such statements.
- That the system maintains accountability for assets.
- That access to assets is permitted only in accordance with management's general or specific authorization.

- That the recorded accountability for assets is compared with existing assets at reasonable intervals, with appropriate action taken with respect to any difference.

The Role of the Auditor. The significance of the act, insofar as auditors are concerned, is the explicit statutory recognition given to accounting controls. The auditor's objective is to plan the examination to search for errors or irregularities that would have a material effect on the financial statements and to use skill and care in the examination of the client's internal control system. Although the independent auditor is not part of a company's internal accounting control system, the auditor must evaluate the effectiveness and monitor compliance of internal accounting control systems.

.07   Further Discussion of the Anti-Bribery Provisions

Because the scope of the FCPA is very broad, additional discussion of the anti-bribery provisions seems appropriate. It is important to keep in mind that the act covers not only large public companies but essentially any person residing in the United States as well as businesses incorporated in the United States or those that have their principal place of business in the United States. While the original intent of the law was to cut off large bribery-type payments to foreign officials, *any business, large or small,* that exports a product outside of the United States should be aware of the law.

According to the FCPA, covered companies, their employees and agents are prohibited from making, authorizing or promising payments or gifts of money or anything of value corruptly. In other words, no person may make a payment or gift to influence the recipient in any official act, such as failing to perform an official duty. Nor can any person give a gift to induce an individual to use his or her influence with his or her government or business for the entity's business benefit. (The prohibitions apply when the recipient is a foreign official, a foreign political party, a party official, a candidate for a foreign political office or any individual who will transmit some or all of the payment or gift to an illegal recipient.) Payments for seemingly *routine* matters—for example, expediting a shipment or speed up issuance of a permit—*may* violate the FCPA.

The Department of Justice has established a Foreign Corrupt Practices Act Opinion Procedure from which any U.S. company or national may request a statement from the Department's present enforcement policy in relation to anti-bribery provisions of the FCPA regarding a proposed business arrangement or action.

Although the Department of Commerce has no enforcement role regarding the FCPA, it supplies general guidance to U.S. exporters who have questions about the FCPA and about international developments concerning the FCPA.

.08 Relevant Definitions

A *U.S. person* is defined as:

- Domestic concerns (i.e., U.S. citizens, residents, business entities organized under the laws of any U.S. state or territory, and business entities with their principal place of business in the United States).
- Issuers of stock traded on a stock exchange.
- Officers, directors, employees, agents, and stockholders of domestic concerns.

A *foreign official* is considered to be:

- Any officer or employee of a foreign government or instrumentality thereof or any person acting in an official capacity for or on behalf of any such government or instrumentality.
- Officers and employees of state-owned enterprises.
- Political parties and candidates.
- Officers or employees of public international organizations such as the United Nations.

.09 Sanctions for Violating the FCPA

The consequences for a violation of the FCPA are severe, both for a company and for individuals.

Fines and penalties for violations of the *anti-bribery provisions* are as follows:

- Maximum criminal fine for a business entity is $2 million.
- Maximum criminal fine for individuals is $100,000. Maximum imprisonment term is five years.
- Civil penalty of $10,000 may also be imposed.

A fine imposed on a corporate employee or representative may not be paid directly or indirectly by the corporation.

For violations of the *accounting provisions*, there is no criminal liability, except the FCPA specifically criminalizes conduct by persons who knowingly circumvent a system of internal accounting controls or who knowingly falsify books and records. Fines and penalties are as follows:

- Fines for individuals up to $1 million; imprisonment for up to 10 years or both.
- Fines for corporations may be up to $2.5 million.

.10 FCPA Red Flags

The following types of activities may involve FCPA violations:

- Money or property passed through a consultant or representative to a public official to obtain certain government actions.
- Use of consultants or representatives who are closely connected intermediaries with the government or a political party of the country in which the corporation is doing business.
- Gifts or gratuities to government officials or political party officials, candidates for public office, or their families.
- Extravagant entertaining of government officials or party leaders or their families.
- Indirect payments to government officials or their families.
- Use of company facilities by such government officials.
- Negative information (flawed background) is discovered as part of due diligence.
- A representative refuses to make FCPA-related certification.
- A request for unusually large commissions, retainers, or other fees.
- An unusual method of payment or payment in a third country proposed by representative.
- Retention of a contingent fee representative when procurement decision is imminent.

.11 1998 Amendment to the FCPA

In 1998, the International Anti-Bribery and Fair Competition Act of 1998 amended the FCPA to implement the Organization for Economic Cooperation and Development (OECD) Convention on Combating Bribery of Foreign Public Officials in International Business Transactions. The 1998 amendments:

- Clarify that the act applies to payments to obtain any "improper advantage."
- Assert nationality jurisdiction over U.S. companies and nationals that take any act in furtherance of a bribe, even in the absence of an interstate commerce nexus.
- Expand the definition of foreign officials to include officials of *international public organizations*.
- Provide for criminal liability over *foreign companies and nationals* that take any act in furtherance of a bribe *within the territory of the United States*.
- Eliminate a *disparity in penalties* between U.S. nationals and non-U.S. nationals employed by or acting as agents of U.S. companies.

.12 Preventing Non-Compliance

Any entity exporting products or services or preparing to export, must make sure that all employees and agents understand the requirements of the FCPA.

To emphasize the importance of abiding by the provisions of the FCPA, a business should establish written policy statements concerning proper conduct. It would be appropriate for those policy statements to address not only bribery of foreign officials but also officials in the U.S.

Individuals responsible for the actual exporting activities, especially those that may come in direct contact with foreign officials or appoint local representatives who will do so, should be especially aware of the FCPA rules. The policy should also stipulate that employees should not accept any gifts or payments that could be interpreted as intent to persuade the company to act in a certain way.

¶42,006   Racketeer Influenced and Corrupt Organization Act (RICO)

In 1970 when Congress passed the Racketeer Influenced and Corrupt Organization Act, it was aimed primarily at business organizations involved in racketeering activities. Until 1993, it was not clear whether an outside auditor who audited a company found to have engaged in racketeering activities could also be held liable for the law's triple (treble) damages and the recovery of legal fees.

Racketeering involves crimes against individuals, businesses or the government including fraud, bribery, loan sharking, extortion, counterfeiting, selling protection, illegal gambling as part of a questionable or totally illegal business. Businesses involved in trafficking in illegal drugs and prostitution may also fall under the heading of rackets. Money laundering is often associated with racketeering activities when there is a need to cover up the original illicit sources. The term racket refers to an illegal activity and one purpose of RICO was to bring certain criminal activity under federal jurisdiction if there was a pattern of activity and it involved crossing state lines or the use of the U.S. Postal Service.

Criminal organizations that engage in racketeering often operate legitimate businesses as well, for instance licensed gaming establishments, towing services, junk yards, board-up services, liquor stores and restaurants and bars in order to provide cover for their rackets. Certain labor organizations have been involved in racketeering activities and even white-collar crimes can fall into this category. In order to gain the "cooperation" of the police or local government officials, racketeering often involves bribery, blackmail, or extortion.

Initially the concept behind RICO was to deal at the federal level with crimes systematically carried out by organized criminal groups. Later, attempts were made, sometimes successfully, to apply the definition of racketeering more broadly. Some accounting firms were charged with RICO violations when the companies they audited had committed fraud. The reasoning was that if an auditor provided a company with an unqualified ("clean") opinion on its financial statements, but later it was determined that the financial statements involved a fraud on the investors or others users of the statements, the accountants must be dragged in as parties to the fraud.

In 1993, the United States Supreme Court decided in *Reves v. Ernst & Young* that merely auditing a client company was not enough to involve RICO. The Court narrowed the scope of lawsuits that can be brought against accountants and accounting firms under RICO. In the case, the Supreme Court held that before liability would attach because of RICO, it must be established that accountants had participated or assisted in the management or decision making at the company that led up to the fraud. Since public accounting firms generally don't involve themselves to the extent required in the management decisions of their clients, this Supreme Court decision was good news for the accounting profession. However, the E & Y case also stands as a reminder to auditors to maintain their independence and even when consulting on matters relating to the audit, to keep a safe distance from management.

¶42,007   IRS Circular 230

In its Circular 230, the IRS sets out its expectations and requirements for practicing before the IRS. The regulation does not apply to all tax preparers but specifically to those who would represent taxpayers before the IRS in an audit or examination and later in an administrative appeal of the audit findings. Those primarily controlled by Circular 230 are attorneys, CPAs and Enrolled Agents.

Until 2011, anyone could prepare a tax return for another taxpayer and the industry was generally unregulated. Beginning in 2011, the first steps were taken to begin the regulation process by requiring tax return preparers to pay an annual fee of $64.25 and obtain a Preparer Tax Identification Number (PTIN).

Future IRS plans for tax return preparers include examinations for non-CPAs, Attorneys or Enrolled Agents as well as required continuing professional education for those otherwise not required to obtain such training by their profession. These changes are coming from the IRS's Department of Practice which is the IRS branch that oversees tax return preparers. These changes are in response to unqualified and rogue tax return preparers causing problems for the system.

As a starting point, the courts have had to determine what constitutes a tax return.

- An unsigned return is not considered a return.
- A return reporting only zeros on the lines for income is not considered a return.
- A return filed by someone claiming to be a citizen of one of the states but not a citizen of the United States, and thus exempt from the income tax is not considered a tax return.
- A return claiming that wages are not subject to income tax since the dollar was removed from the gold standard in 1933 is not considered a return.
- A return claiming that wages are not income because an amount of labor exchanged for an equal amount of money results in no gain is not considered a return (labor theory of value).

- A return claiming that paying income taxes is a violation of the Thirteenth Amendment (abolished slavery) because it requires taxpayers to work for the government without compensation is not considered a return.
- A return claiming that paying taxes that go for war is a violation of the taxpayer's religious freedom if the taxpayer's religious beliefs oppose war, is not a tax return.

These kinds of non-returns are collectively referred to as protestor claims and subject to a $5,000 frivolous return penalty.

In 2008, the U.S. Justice Department established the Tax Defier Initiative, which seeks to prosecute taxpayers who "spout rhetoric" about the income tax system being illegal or that paying taxes are voluntary or encouraging others not to file tax returns. This was the program that put Wesley Snipes in prison.

If a taxpayer does not file a tax return, the IRS is permitted to file a return for them (IRC §6020) which is referred to as a substitute for return. The IRS prepared return is considered a return for most purposes (it allows the IRS to assess and collect tax, for example) but the return is not considered a "return" for starting the statute of limitations on assessment and collection.

.01   Specific IRS Circular 230 Rules

- If you prepare a return for someone else and charge them, you must sign the return or face a penalty.
- You must also put your Social Security number on the return—this allows the IRS to sort returns by preparers, looking for patterns of errors.
- Starting in 2011, you must also include your PTIN on the return.

Circular 230 defines "practice before the IRS." This refers to representing someone else at an IRS audit or appeal. Only the following individuals are permitted to represent someone else:

- CPAs
- Attorneys
- Enrolled Agents

Thus a preparer is not automatically allowed to represent a taxpayer in an IRS audit or appeal. There are exceptions to this rule, including the following:

- Anyone can represent him or herself.
- An employee represents his or her employer.
- An officer of a corporation may represent the corporation.
- Family members, under specific conditions, may represent other family members
- A partner may represent the partnership.

The rules of Circular 230 restrict a practitioner's conduct in a number of ways:

- Tax preparers may be penalized by the IRS for preparing tax returns negligently. Negligence includes not applying standards accepted in the industry.
- Tax preparation does not require interrogating the client, but does involve pursuing logical implications of available data. The *Brockhouse* case described below illustrates this process.
- A tax preparer may not charge a contingent fee for preparing a tax return. A contingent fee is one based on the amount of tax paid—for example, the larger the refund, the greater the fee for the tax preparer (as a percentage).
- A contingent fee may be charged in connection with an audit or amended return.
- When an error is discovered on a prior year tax return, Circular 230 prescribes the following actions by the tax return preparer:
  - Notify client of the error.
  - Explain consequences of filing or not filing an amended tax return to correct the error.
  - Tax return preparer should not take it upon him or herself to prepare an amended return without client's ok.
  - A tax preparer should not notify the IRS of the error.
- Sanctions by the IRS—CPAs, attorneys and enrolled agents may be barred from practicing before the IRS for:
  - Ignoring requests by the IRS for information.
  - Delaying the IRS.
  - Use of disbarred practitioners.
  - Conflicts of interest (preparing separate returns for both husband and wife following a divorce).
  - Charging contingent fees–for an original return.
  - A client's records may not be "held hostage" if the client doesn't pay the accountant's fee.
- Advertising must not be misleading.
- A tax preparer should not negotiate refund checks.

Though not mentioned in Circular 230, tax practitioners must be careful not to get involved in practicing the law without a license. For example, a tax practitioner (non-attorney) should not prepare a will or partnership agreement for a client.

The degree of reliance that may be placed by a CPA or other tax preparer, regulated by Circular 230, on information provided by the client is also described.

It is strongly recommended that anyone preparing tax returns for others read the rules of Circular 230, especially regarding the reliance on a taxpayer's records and the degree of professional skepticism required of a tax return preparer.

¶42,008 Cases

.01 Tax Preparers and the Brockhouse case

Tax preparers are subject to a number of IRS penalties including the IRC §6694 negligence preparer penalty. Since 1984, tax preparers have been on notice that they must do more than merely compile a client's tax return from information provided by the client. This has also been clear from IRS Circular 230 which provides the rules for tax preparers. But the IRS's guidance provides only general rules, and does not provide specific examples. In the *Brockhouse* case (*Brockhouse v. U.S.*, 749 F.2d 1248, 1984), the U.S. Seventh Circuit Court of Appeals took issue with one accountant, but thereby surprised many others.

The case was brought to the Appeals Court on the issue of whether a tax return preparer should be assessed a negligence penalty, when the preparer understates income tax liability of his or her client because he or she relied solely on information supplied to him or her by the taxpayers. At the conclusion of its audit of his client, the IRS assessed a penalty against appellant John Brockhouse who had prepared the tax return. Pursuant to Section 6694(c), the appellant paid 15 percent of the penalty and sued for a refund.

The case involved a certified public accountant and his preparation of a client's tax return in 1979. The CPA prepared the client's corporate income tax return for its fiscal year ended February 28, 1979. He used a trial balance prepared by the corporation's bookkeeper. The trial balance showed loans to the corporation from its sole owner and from a bank. It also showed that the corporation had made payments for interest expense; however, it did not show whether any of the interest had been paid to the sole shareholder.

The CPA also prepared the 1978 Form 1040 income tax return for the corporation's owner and his wife. The CPA had sent a tax organizer (data questionnaire) to each of his individual income tax clients. The clients were either to complete and return the questionnaire or to use it as a guide in collecting the information necessary to prepare the return. The Client in question chose not to complete a questionnaire. Rather, the information was supplied by his corporation's business manager or bookkeeper. The information was then entered on input sheets of an outside computer service. The CPA reviewed the sheets and compared them with the information supplied and the information shown on the clients' 1977 return. There were no items shown on the 1977 return that were not accounted for in the 1978 return. The CPA signed the 1978 return and sent it to the client for signature and filing. The appellant never inquired whether any of the interest expense shown on the corporate trial balance sheet had been paid to the client.

In May 1980, an IRS agent began an examination of the corporate return. The agent requested an analysis of the corporation's interest expense account.

The CPA went to the corporation's offices and examined the general ledger and disbursements journal. From this, he learned that the corporation had paid interest to its sole shareholder, his 1040 client. The CPA promptly brought the omission to the attention of the IRS agent.

The corporation had paid its sole owner interest income in the amount of $15,291.20. The owner had not reported the income on his 1978 joint return. This resulted in an underpayment of federal income taxes in the amount of $10,538.76.

The IRS assessed a $100 tax preparer penalty against the CPA. Pursuant to Section 6694(c), the appellant paid $15 and filed a claim for refund. The refund was disallowed, and he filed suit in district court. Although the penalty itself was not that large, the accountant's reputation and the degree of responsibility borne by a tax preparer were at stake.

The district court denied the refund. It found that the appellant was negligent in omitting interest income from the return. The court found that he knew that the corporation had borrowed money from its owner and also that it had made interest payments. The court held that under these circumstances, a reasonable, prudent person would have made inquiries to determine whether any interest was paid to the corporation's owner. The court held that CPA was negligent in failing to obtain a completed data questionnaire from his 1040 client. Finally, the court relied on the factors listed in Rev. Proc. 80-40, which deals with liability under Section 6694(a), to hold that the CPA had negligently disregarded a tax rule or regulation and thus was liable for the penalty.

On appeal, the CPA argued that Section 6694(a) does not apply to a tax return preparer's negligence in gathering facts from the taxpayer. He believed that Section 6694(a) only applies where a preparer negligently misapplies a rule or regulation to a known item, and that where the preparer does not know of an item, he is not required to make inquiries or verify data. The CPA maintained that even if Section 6694(a) does apply to a negligent failure to gather facts, his actions in this case were not negligent.

Section 6694(a) allows a penalty of $100 to be assessed against an income tax return preparer whose negligent disregard of rules or regulations results in an understatement of tax liability. The preparer has the burden of proving the absence of negligence. Section 6694 was one of several provisions added by the *Tax Reform Act of 1976* to regulate income tax return preparers. Congress generally was concerned with deterring abusive practices by preparers. Prior to 1976, preparers were subject only to criminal penalties for willfully aiding or assisting in the preparation of a fraudulent return. Although Congress was concerned with abuses by commercial preparers—those who are not accountants or lawyers—it determined that regulation of all preparers was appropriate. Section 6694 was added primarily to deter preparers from engaging in negligent or fraudulent practices designed to understate tax liability. However, Congress did not limit the applicability of Section 6694(a) to situations involving disregard of rules or regulations applicable to the facts as provided by the taxpayer. Rather, Section 6694(a) applies generally to "negligent disregard." The court therefore held that a tax preparer negligently disregards a rule or regulation under Section 6694(a) if his or her negligent failure to inquire into information provided by the taxpayer results in the filing of a return that violates a rule or regulation.

To determine whether a tax preparer's actions constitute negligence under Section 6694(a), the court reasoned that it must first determine the applicable standard of care. According to the court, negligence in this context is a lack of due care or failure to do what a reasonable and ordinarily prudent person would do under the circumstances. The regulation under Section 6694(b), relating to willful disregard of rules or regulations, expressly provides that a preparer may not rely without verification on information supplied by the taxpayer if that information appears incomplete or incorrect. The regulation under Section 6694(a) does not contain such an express provision, but it does provide that a preparer is not negligent if he or she "exercises due diligence in an effort to apply the rules and regulations to the information given" to him or her. This due diligence requirement means that a preparer must act as a reasonable, prudent person with respect to the information supplied to the preparer. Accordingly the court held that if the information supplied would lead a reasonable, prudent preparer to seek additional information, it is negligent not to do so. A reasonable, prudent preparer would inquire as to additional information where it is apparent that the information supplied was incorrect or incomplete and it is simple to collect the necessary additional information.

The court found this standard of care to be consistent with congressional intent. For a preparer to ignore the implications of information furnished, the court reasoned, where the error is apparent and simple to correct would be an abusive practice. The court also noted that the IRS has interpreted Section 6694(a) to apply to situations where the preparer has reason to know that the information supplied is incomplete or incorrect. (See Rev. Rul. 80-265, 1980-2 C.B. 378.) Further, according to the court, although the preparer is not required to audit information, "the preparer may not ignore the implications of information furnished to the preparer."

Finally, the court in *Brockhouse* wrote that a prudent preparer would have inquired about interest payments on the loans rather than ignoring the implications of the information furnished. The CPA's negligent failure to inquire led him to disregard the applicability of Section 61, which provides that gross income includes interest income. Thus, the court held the CPA liable under Section 6694(a).

.02   Auditor Liabilities to Third Parties

In the wake of an audit failure—the failure of the auditors to adequately warn readers of a company's financial statements of an impending problem—law suits are often brought against auditors by third parties. The extent of an auditor's responsibility to third parties is a contentious issue.

.03   *Ultramares Corp. v. Touche*

This 1931 case against the auditing firm Touche, Niven & Co. was brought by a third party to the audit, a factoring company Ultramares. The factoring company had extended credit to Stern & Co. based on the audited financial statements and opinion of Touche. Following the bankruptcy filing of Stern & Co., Ultramares took the then unusual step of suing the auditors for negligence. After reviewing the facts, the court ruled that Touche had not acted negligently. The precedent set by the case was the court's acknowledgment that a company's audit is not a private matter between the auditor and the client, but affects third parties who relied on the audit and permits them to sue for damages.

The finding of the court in *Ultramares* was upheld in a subsequent case, *State Street Trust Co. v. Ernst* (278 N.Y. 105, 15 N.E 2d 415 (1938)). In the latter case the court stated that auditors "may be liable to third parties, even where there is lacking deliberate or active fraud…A representation certified as true to the knowledge of the accountants when knowledge there is none, is a reckless misstatement, or an opinion based upon grounds so flimsy…In other words, heedlessness and reckless disregard of consequences may take the place of deliberate intention."

Depending on the state in which the lawsuit is brought, the standing of a third party to sue the auditors may vary. In *Credit Alliance v. Arthur Andersen*, a 1985 case, the court made it clear that especially when the auditors know that a third party is relying on their audit and the third party has been identified to the auditors ahead of time and the auditors had acknowledged this third party reliance in some way, the third party is certainly in a position to sue the auditors for negligence. Depending on the circumstances of the case and the state, a third party may also be in a position to sue for gross negligence or fraud.

¶42,009   IRS Access to QuickBooks and Similar Accounting Software

Changes in the law often follow innovations in technology. Before the age of computers, accounting books and records meant paper documents. Now books and records include data files stored on a computer's hard drive or in cloud. This distinction is important during an IRS examination. The Internal Revenue Code Section at issue is §7602(a), which speaks of "books, papers, records, and other data." The significance of this fact became more important for accountants with the issuance of a new IRS Chief Counsel Advice (CCA 201146017) at the end of 2011. This IRS guidance pulls together the rulings from a number of recent court cases illustrating what "books and records" means to the IRS when it makes a request for these records to the taxpayer or her representative.

The IRS ruling and a number of the court cases cited by the IRS involved QuickBooks and similar accounting software; this means that CPAs and other accountants working with small business clients—not just large firms with their own IT departments—need to know not only how to use the accounting software, but also know what they can and can't do with the computer records when a client is audited. One problem the IRS ruling poses for accountants who handle their clients' IRS audits is that the IRS may request the computer files themselves, not merely a printout of the general ledger. Once the IRS obtains the QuickBooks (or other similar accounting software), agents are instructed by the Internal Revenue Manual (IRM 25.5.4.3) to make a copy of the files, in the event the taxpayer or its representative asks that the records to be returned. Once the IRS has the computer files, it is possible for agents to look at the details for the year(s) under audit—but also, potentially, at earlier or later years—because those records will normally be recorded as part of the QuickBooks files.

In addition, and perhaps a more serious concern, the IRS will also have access to the computer's "metadata files." Metadata is defined as the information stored by the computer that describes "how, when, and by whom a particular item or set of electronic information was collected, created, accessed, modified, and formatted" (IRS CCA). This information can be useful to the IRS for determining, for example, "the original date a transaction was entered in the electronic records, the dates of any changes to the entries, and the user name of the person who made the entries." This information, according to the IRS, "tends to support or undermine the credibility of the entries in the business records." The IRS guidance states that, "So long as the information in the metadata 'may be relevant,' within the broad meaning of I.R.C. §7602(a)(2) ["Examination of books and witnesses"], to a proper purpose for which the examination is being conducted, such as ascertaining the correctness of the return, the Service may properly summon the taxpayer's original electronic data files containing the unaltered metadata."

In addition, "the Service may summon information, including metadata, concerning transactions and events that occurred before and after the periods under examination so long as that information 'may be relevant,' within the meaning of I.R.C. §7602(a)(2), to the issues arising in the examination of the taxable periods at issue."

Among the data included in "books, papers, records, and other data" is tax preparation software containing a series of coded instruction enabling a computer to generate a taxpayer's tax return. In requesting such records, the IRS must only show that looking at how the software calculated the tax will "illuminate any aspect of the return." In measuring the relevance of tax data, the courts apply a test asking whether the information "might throw light upon the correctness of the return," which encompasses a wide range of data. In the 1984 *Arthur Young* case (465 U.S. 805), the U.S. Supreme Court observed that the relevance standard of Section 7602(a) is far broader than the federal rules of evidence. According to the IRS, it was Congress's "express intention to allow the IRS to obtain items of even potential relevance to an ongoing investigation, without reference to its admissibility."

Additionally, the IRS reports that it has the "authority to summon the taxpayer's original electronic data files from the taxpayer's accountant when the accountant possesses the records, whether or not the accountant recorded the entries of the business transactions into the file." One defense the law permits against such an IRS summons is if the IRS already has the information. But here, if the IRS only has an electronic copy of the accounting records, but the copy does not contain the metadata, the IRS is still entitled to request the original with the metadata.

The facts of a 2006 bankruptcy court case help illustrate the concerns accountants face when dealing with client's electronic accounting records. In *U.S. v. Krause* (2007), the taxpayer was seeking to have in excess of $3 million in tax debts discharged by the court. The IRS had ascertained that the taxpayer controlled "a vast network of trusts, business concerns, and possible offshore entities" that were not directly owned by the taxpayer, but nevertheless were under his control. Since records of his financial activities were maintained on his computers, the IRS requested a laptop and a desktop computer from the debtor. The IRS discovered, however, that shortly before turning the computers over to the IRS, the taxpayer had installed GhostSurf software on these computers, which he used to "permanently wipe or purge sensitive files and e-mails from both hard drives." The bankruptcy trustee charged that the files that were destroyed may have contained evidence that was important to the case, such as indications of control of the numerous trusts and other entities.

Testimony of an expert claimed that GhostSurf "wipes files by searching the hard drive for files that Windows 'no longer knows about' because they have been previously deleted, and writing data over those locations with random data to obscure it from un-deleting. Once the files are overwritten in this fashion, an undelete utility cannot recover them." This is an example of what the court referred to as "spoliation." According to the court, "spoliation is defined as the destruction or significant alteration of evidence, or the failure to preserve property for another's use as evidence in pending to reasonably foreseeable litigation."

In the *Krause* case, the court determined that the taxpayer/debtor had willfully destroyed electronic evidence of his financial holdings by using GhostSurf to alter the QuickBooks files on his computers shortly before turning the computers over to the IRS. As a result of analyzing all the evidence and in light of the taxpayer/debtor's obstructionist actions with respect to his financial records, the court determined that the various trusts and other entities that Krause claimed not to own, were indeed his property and as such must be turned over to the trustee in the Chapter 7 bankruptcy proceeding.

In dealing with the IRS and with clients who use Quickbooks or other similar accounting software, accountants must be cognizant of crossing a line when attempting to limit the IRS's access to the client's data files. Commercial programs are available, such as QB Audit Disclosure, which will allow you to partition or restrict QuickBooks files to, "provide selective data for the time period required and no more." The marketing for these programs claims that, "by divulging only limited financial information to third parties you avoid the risk of revealing sensitive information." Care should be taken in limiting the IRS's access to specific data, however, so as not to obstruct their investigation or destroy critical records (recalling Arthur Anderson's infamous paper shredding incident).

CHAPTER 43
The Finances of a Higher Education

¶43,000   Overview

Education-related tax breaks come in three varieties—deductions, credits, and income exclusions—each with its limitations and restrictions. Some can be used together; some are mutually exclusive. Some change incrementally each year; some the government changes arbitrarily. Some are federal; some are state.

Confused? Just imagine what the client is thinking... and join the club. Take the state-offered College 529 plans. With a multitude of plans sold nationwide by individual states, they include an ever-changing array of state tax implications, a wide range of fees, and everything from an average portfolio with conservative returns to high-risk mutual fund investments. It's a jungle out there.

Federally, the IRS delineates education-related adjustments to income. The guidelines are fairly clear. However, which to use, when and whether it is possible to use multiple adjustments, is not.

There are dozens of Internet Web sites that compare and contrast many of these college plans, showing up-to-the minute changes and excellent definitions of each plan. As always, reader beware. Web sites are for educational purposes only and usually present one side of a discussion.

The cost of higher education, or its affordability, is affected by fraud. Students and their parents should be wary, for example, of operators and their websites promising to find anyone a scholarship who is willing to pay a non-refundable fee of $150 to $500 or more. The Department of Education warns, "Avoid scams while searching for scholarships, filling out the FAFSA®, and giving personal information to schools and lenders." Federal tax credits have been a lucrative sources of fraudulent revenue in recent years. In 2015, the Treasury Inspector General for Tax Administration (TIGTA) issued a report, "Billions of Dollars in Potentially Erroneous Education Credits Continue to Be Claimed for Ineligible Students and Institutions." While not all of the erroneously claimed credits are fraudulent, refundable tax credits have historically proven an easy mark for those seeking fast cash. In its report the TIGTA "estimates that more than 3.6 million taxpayers (claiming more than 3.8 million students) received more than $5.6 billion in potentially erroneous credits." In a breakdown of these statistics, TIGTA reports that, "More than 2 million taxpayers received more than $3.2 billion in education credits for students with no Form 1098-T, Tuition Statement." This is the statement that colleges and universities send to the IRS and to students indicating the amount of tuition paid. In addition, the report discloses that, "More than 1.6 million taxpayers received approximately $2.5 billion in education credits for students attending ineligible institutions." Other ineligible students included prisoners, less than half-time students and students who did not attend any educational institution.

Alarming to the accounting profession, the TIGTA report notes that, "Paid tax return preparers continue to prepare a significant number of returns with questionable education credit claims. More than 1.7 million (49 percent) of the 3.6 million taxpayers with questionable education credits claims we identified were prepared by a tax return preparer." While it may be easy to blame the IRS for lax administration of education tax credits, it should be recalled that the IRS has requested Congressional assistance in regulating tax rogue return preparers to no avail. In addition, as TIGTA notes, "The IRS can use the Form 1098-T to verify that a student claiming an education credit attended an eligible educational institution or attended for the required period of time. However, these forms are not available at the time tax returns are filed."

¶43,001   Building American Skills Through Community Colleges

News of record college debt levels has prompted a national discussion of the problems related to financing this unique and valuable cost. Estimates vary, but a consensus indicates that the total outstanding college debt exceeds $1 trillion. This amount is shared by 40 million people, for an average of $25,000 each. For years increasing tuition costs have out-paced the official national inflation figures. Public universities have struggled to find new sources of funds as many states have decreased their tax-supported contributions.

The need for enough income to make large monthly payments may discourage some graduates from starting a new job-creating business or entering teaching or another lower-paying public service career. As one step in dealing with this problem, President Obama in 2015 announced a plan to make community college more affordable—free. Time will tell.

The community college initiative announced by the White House in 2015, sets out the rationale and strategy for encouraging more students to seek college education by reducing the cost of at least the first two years. An outline of the White House program is provided below.

"In an increasingly competitive world economy, America's economic strength depends upon the education and skills of its workers. In the coming years, jobs requiring at least an associate degree are projected to grow twice as fast as those requiring no college experience. To meet this need, President Obama set two national goals: by 2020, America will once again have the highest proportion of college graduates in the world, and community colleges will produce an additional 5 million graduates."

"As the largest part of the nation's higher education system, community colleges enroll more than 6 million students and are growing rapidly. They feature affordable tuition, open admission policies, flexible course schedules, and convenient locations. Community Colleges are particularly important for students who are older, working, or need remedial classes. Community colleges work with businesses, industry and government to create tailored training programs to meet economic needs like nursing, health information technology, advanced manufacturing, and green jobs."

"President Obama proposed the American Graduation Initiative to invest in community colleges and help American workers get the skills and credentials they need to succeed. The Health Care and Education Reconciliation Act includes $2 billion over four years for community college and career training. These resources will help community colleges and other institutions develop, improve, and provide education and training, suitable for workers who are eligible for trade adjustment assistance. The initiative will be housed at the Department of Labor and implemented in close cooperation with the Department of Education. With these resources, community colleges across the country could:

- Work with businesses: Colleges could build partnerships with businesses and the workforce investment system to create career pathways through which workers will earn new credentials and promotions through step-by-step, worksite education programs that build essential skills. Colleges will work closely with employers to design training that is relevant to the local labor market and likely to lead to employment and careers.
- Create education partnerships: Colleges could work with other educational institutions to expand course offerings and promote the transfer of credit among colleges.
- Teach basic skills: Colleges could improve remedial and adult education programs, accelerating students' progress and integrating developmental classes into academic and vocational classes.
- Meet students' needs: Colleges could offer their students more than just a course catalog through comprehensive, personalized services to help them plan their careers, stay in school, and graduate.
- Develop online courses: Colleges could create open online course materials such as interactive tutors, simulations, and multimedia software that can help students learn more, and learn better, in less time.

This program would complement President Obama's broader agenda for higher education, including nearly doubling funding for Pell grants over three years and tripling the largest college tax credit, now known as the American Opportunity Tax Credit. At this time of economic hardship and uncertainty, the Administration's agenda will build the highly skilled workforce that is crucial for success in the 21st century."

¶43,002   Plain Writing Act Compliance Report

From website tracking, it is clear that the vast majority of interest in information published by the United States Department of Education is for federal student aid. Clarity and accuracy are essential in these communications to ensure that all potential applicants for aid, and those who advise them, such as guidance and career counselors, comprehend correctly what is needed to qualify and apply for student aid.

In response to The Plain Writing Act of 2010, the Federal Student Aid (FSA) Office has majorly revamped its website to make it friendlier to visitors. FSA reorganized and rewrote the content of its website to improve clarity and accessibility, launching the new site on July 15, 2012. *https://studentaid.ed.gov/sa/* FSA also shortened and simplified *Funding Your Education: The Guide to Federal*

Student Aid, in line with the Plain Writing precepts. *Funding Your Education,* which addresses the basics that readers, especially high school seniors, want to know about how to afford postsecondary education, is available both in a printed form and online.

In addition to providing background information on the myriad of programs, the guide spells out requirements for grant applicants in each case. To increase the ability of users to navigate through this lengthy, complex material, the guide has undergone significant changes, primarily in terms of organization. The table of contents is now comprehensive, and there are new indexes to enable quicker, easier searches by several routes, including program title, subject, education level and more.

The Department distributes its printed publications through ED Pubs, a warehouse the public can access via phone, email, fax, and snail mail. In the last year of availability of printed copies. ED Pubs received orders for more than 24 million copies of publications. The 10 most requested publications were about federal student aid, for a total of 15 million copies. Since 2018, hard copies are no longer available. Resources are now available electronically.

¶43,003   Net Price Calculator Requirement

In accordance with the *Higher Education Opportunity Act of 2008* (HEOA), by October 29, 2011, each postsecondary institution that participates in Title IV federal student aid programs must post a net price calculator on its website that uses institutional data to provide estimated net price information to current and prospective students and their families based on a student's individual circumstances. The net price calculator is required for all Title IV institutions that enroll full-time, first-time degree- or certificate-seeking undergraduate students.

Institutions use the U.S. Department of Education's Net Price Calculator template or develop their own customized calculator that includes, at a minimum, the same elements as the Department's template. See *http://nces.ed.gov/collegenavigator/* National Center for Education Statistics.

.01   U.S. Department of Education Net Price Calculator Template

The Department's template is made up of two components:

1. the institutional data maintenance application and
2. the user application.

In the first component, institutions input the following data:

1. Price of attendance
2. Median amounts of grant and scholarship aid awarded to, and accepted by, first-time, full-time degree/certificate-seeking students by Expected Family Contribution (EFC) range

In the second component, users are asked nine questions to establish the following:

1. Their dependency status
2. Their estimated cost of attendance
3. Approximated EFC

The template uses a "look-up" table populated with data from the Free Application for Federal Student Aid (FAFSA) applications database to identify a median EFC. Median EFC is then matched with the median grant and scholarship aid amount entered by the institution for the corresponding EFC range to determine the student's estimated amount of total grant aid. Estimated net price is calculated by subtracting estimated total grant aid from the estimated total price of attendance.

¶43,004   PCAOB Announces Scholarship Program and Academic Recipients

The Public Company Accounting Oversight Board announced on July 6, 2011, the inauguration of the PCAOB Scholarship Program.

Under the Sarbanes-Oxley Act of 2002, monetary penalties imposed by the PCAOB must be used to fund merit scholarships for students in accredited accounting degree programs. The Board has established the PCAOB Scholarship Program to provide a source of funding to encourage outstanding undergraduate and graduate students to pursue a career in auditing.

For the 2020-2021 academic year, the PCAOB announced 234 recipients of $10,000 merit scholarships intended to encourage students to pursue a career in auditing. Each of the students-recipients is from a different college or university.

"We are grateful to Congress for allowing us to bring the PCAOB and the academic community closer together with this scholarship program that will provide a source of funding to encourage outstanding students to pursue a career in auditing. We hope to inspire future thought leaders in auditing for the benefit of investors," the PCAOB Chairman stated.

The Sarbanes-Oxley Act of 2002 provides that funds generated from the collection of monetary penalties imposed by the PCAOB must be used to fund a merit scholarship program for students in accredited accounting degree programs. The PCAOB Scholarship Program, therefore, has been created to identify eligible students for scholarships and to award funds through the students' educational institutions.

.01   Scholarship Program Administration

The PCAOB has selected ACT, Inc. (ACT) of Iowa City, Iowa, to administer and manage the program on behalf of the PCAOB, including contacting eligible educational institutions, providing customer service, and disbursing funds. On an annual basis, the PCAOB will select, with the help of ACT, educational institutions and invite them to nominate an eligible student as a recipient of the PCAOB Scholarship. The scholarships are one-time awards that will be paid directly to the educational institution for eligible expenses such as tuition, fees, books, and supplies. Recipients will receive written notification of their selection as well as notification when the funds have been provided to the school.

.02   Selection of Nominating Institutions

Accredited U.S. colleges and universities that award bachelor's or master's degrees in accounting and report the number of degrees awarded using the Integrated Postsecondary Education Data System (excluding on-line colleges and universities) are eligible to be selected to nominate students for the scholarships. Eligible institutions will be divided into two groups:

- Group A includes the one hundred institutions with the highest total of master's degrees in accounting conferred during the preceding five academic years.
- Group B contains all other institutions that offer bachelor's and master's degrees in accounting.

The PCAOB, with ACT's help, will select institutions to provide student nominations by using a statistical selection process that follows protocols for fairness and impartiality. Seventy-five percent of the scholarships will go to students attending institutions in Group A and 25 percent will be awarded to students who attend institutions in Group B. Schools selected as nominating institutions in a given year will not be considered for selection for the next five years or until all institutions in the respective group have been selected, whichever occurs first.

.03   Student Eligibility Criteria

Students may be eligible for scholarships if they are enrolled in an accredited accounting degree program and attend a participating, nominating institution. Students eligible to receive a PCAOB scholarship must:

- Be enrolled in a bachelor's or master's degree program in accounting.
- Demonstrate interest and aptitude in accounting and auditing.
- Demonstrate high ethical standards.
- Not be a PCAOB employee or a child or spouse of a PCAOB employee.

The PCAOB scholarship program is merit-based but educational institutions are encouraged to give consideration to students from populations that have been historically underrepresented in the accounting profession.

¶43,005   Health Care and Education Reconciliation Act of 2010

On March 30, 2010, President Obama signed the Health Care and Education Reconciliation Act of 2010 (HCERA) (Public Law 111-152), the combined vehicle for reforms to federal financial aid and amendments to the national health care reform bill, that among other major provisions, makes significant changes to the Federal student aid programs authorized by Title IV of the Higher Education Act of 1965, as amended (the HEA).

HCERA also includes provisions from the Student Aid and Fiscal Responsibility Act (SAFRA), which the House had passed in September 2009. The original SAFRA legislation ended the role of private lenders in issuing federal student loans, a change projected to save $87 billion over 10 years by eliminating subsidies to private lenders and making the federal government the sole initiator of federal student loans. The savings from this reform were to be used to create and strengthen several programs designed to improve postsecondary access and success, as well as to establish a grant program for early care and education and to renovate public school facilities.

Between September and March, however, SAFRA's revenue estimate dropped from $87 billion to $61 billion. In addition, congressional leaders allocated $10 billion to reduce the budget deficit, and another $9 billion to help the combined legislation meet the budget reconciliation requirement of a net reduction in federal spending. As a result, the House cut several provisions of SAFRA from the final legislation. Another provision was added to fund grants to community colleges through the Trade Adjustment Assistance (TAA) program. Following are key provisions of HCERA affecting training and postsecondary education.

.01   Indexing of Pell Grants

The HCERA investment in the Pell Grant is $36 billion. This includes $13.5 billion to fund a shortfall in the program resulting from increased demand for financial aid. It is the single biggest source of free money for low-income students (generally, students from families earning less than $50,000 a year).

Amounts can change yearly. For the 2021–22 award year (July 1, 2021, to June 30, 2022), the maximum award is $6,495, slightly up from the 2019–20 award year which is $6,195. The amount you get, though, will depend on

- your financial need,
- your cost of attendance,
- your status as a full-time or part-time student, and
- your plans to attend school for a full academic year or less.

You may not receive Federal Pell Grant funds from more than one school at a time.

The maximum Pell Grant amount will increase each year according to the Consumer Price Index + one percent. This provision was implemented to combat inflation and will significantly expand the amount of financial aid that can be accessed via the Pell Grant.

The expectation is that 820,000 more Pell Grants will be provided by 2020.

.02   Federal Supplemental Educational Opportunity Grant (FSEOG)

The Federal Supplemental Educational Opportunity Grant (FSEOG) program is administered directly by the *financial aid office* at each participating school and is therefore called "campus-based" aid. Not all schools participate. Check with your school's financial aid office to find out if the school offers the FSEOG. You can receive between $100 and $4,000 a year, depending on your financial need, when you apply, the amount of other aid you get, and the availability of funds at your school. Each participating school receives a certain amount of FSEOG funds each year from the U.S. Department of Education's office of Federal Student Aid. Once the full amount of the school's FSEOG funds has been awarded to students, no more FSEOG awards can be made for that year. This system works differently from the *Federal Pell Grant* Program, which provides funds to every eligible student.

So, make sure you apply for federal student aid as early as you can. Each school sets its own deadlines for campus-based funds. You can find a school's deadline on its website or by asking someone in its financial a aid office. If you're eligible, your school will credit your student account, pay you directly, or combine these methods. Your school must disburse (pay out) funds at least once per term (semester, trimester, or quarter). Schools that do not use semesters, trimesters, or quarters must disburse funds at least twice per *academic year*.

.03   Grants to Black Colleges and Universities and Minority-Serving Institutions

The legislation provides $255 million to minority-serving institutions annually through 2020 and thereafter. Of the total grant:

- $100 million is allocated to Hispanic-serving institutions;
- $100 million is allocated to historically black colleges and universities and predominantly black institutions; and
- $55 million is allocated to other minority serving institutions, including tribal colleges and institutions that serve Alaska Natives, Native Hawaiians, Asian-Americans, Native Pacific Islanders, and nontribal Native Americans.

¶43,006   American Opportunity Tax Credit

Under the *American Recovery and Reinvestment Act* (ARRA), more parents and students can qualify for a tax credit, the American Opportunity Tax Credit (AOTC), to pay for college expenses.

AOTC, which originally modified the existing Hope credit and set to expire after 2017, was made permanent in 2015 by the PATH Act. AOTC made the benefit available to a broader range of taxpayers, including many with higher incomes and those who owe no tax. Unlike the other education tax credits, the American opportunity tax credit includes expenses for course-related books, supplies and equipment that are not necessarily paid to the educational institution. It also differs from the Hope scholarship credit because it allows the credit to be claimed for four years of post-secondary education instead of two.

Many of those eligible qualify for the maximum annual credit of $2,500 per student.

The full credit is available to individuals whose modified adjusted gross income is $80,000 or less, or $160,000 or less for married couples filing a joint return. The credit is phased out for taxpayers with incomes above these levels. These income limits are higher than under the Hope and lifetime learning credits. Forty percent of the credit may be refundable even if the taxpayer owes no tax. Claiming this credit precludes also claiming the Lifetime Learning Credit (below) for that year for that student. The $2,500 maximum credit is calculated based on 100 percent of the first $2,000 of qualified expenses plus 25 percent of the next $2,000. The first 40 percent of the qualified credit is refundable, up to $1,000.

¶43,007   Penalty-free IRA Distributions

For taxpayers under the age of 59½, a 10 percent penalty is generally imposed on distributions from IRAs. But if a distribution is made from an IRA for qualified higher education expenses the penalty can be avoided. For purposes of avoiding the 10 percent addition, the education expenses include tuition, fees, books, supplies, and equipment required for enrollment or attendance at an eligible educational institution. They also include expenses for special-needs services incurred by or for special-needs students in connection with their enrollment or attendance. In addition, if the student is at least a half-time student, room and board are qualified education expenses. The education expenses must be for a qualified educational institution.

At least part of the distribution itself may be subject to tax. Generally, if the taxable part of the distribution is less than or equal to the adjusted qualified education expenses, none of the distribution is subject to the additional tax. The IRS provides specific examples on its website. If the taxable part of the distribution is more than the adjusted qualified education expenses, only the excess is subject to the additional tax.

If the taxpayer received an early distribution from an IRA, it must be reported on Form 1040, line 15b (Form 1040NR, line 16b). If the taxpayer qualifies for an exception for qualified higher education expenses, they must file Form 5329 to show how much, if any, of the early distribution is subject to the 10 percent additional tax. See the Instructions for Form 5329, Part I, for help in completing the form and entering the results on Form 1040 or 1040NR.

¶43,008   Lifetime Learning Credit

The lifetime learning credit helps parents and students pay for post-secondary education.

For the tax year, an individual may be able to claim a lifetime learning credit of up to $2,000 for qualified education expenses paid for all students enrolled in eligible educational institutions. There is no limit on the number of years the lifetime learning credit can be claimed for each student. However, a taxpayer cannot claim both the American Opportunity Tax Credit and lifetime learning credits for the same student in one year. Thus, the lifetime learning credit may be particularly helpful to graduate students, students who are only taking one course and those who are not pursuing a degree.

An individual who is eligible to claim the lifetime learning credit and is also eligible to claim the American Opportunity Tax Credit for the same student in the same year, may choose to claim either credit, but not both.

If qualified education expenses are paid for more than one student in the same year, it is possible to choose to take credits on a per-student, per-year basis. This means that, for example, the American Opportunity Tax Credit may be claimed for one student and the Lifetime Learning Credit claimed for another student in the same year.

The Lifetime Learning Credit is non-refundable but is available for an unlimited number of years. The AGI limits for eligibility are $58,000 - $68,000 for single or head of household and $116,000 - $136,000 for married couples filing jointly for 2019. An eligible student does not need to be pursuing a program leading to a degree or other recognized educational credential. The student may be enrolled in only one class to qualify. Thus, this credit is beneficial for adults returning to college or those taking an occasional course.

¶43,009   Student Loan Income Based Repayment (IBR)

Income Based Repayment (IBR) is a repayment plan for the major types of federal loans made to students. It was proposed as part of the College Cost Reduction and Access Act of 2007 and became effective July 1, 2009. Under IBR, the required monthly payment is capped at an amount that is intended to be affordable based on income and family size. The recipient is eligible for IBR if the monthly repayment amount under IBR will be less than the monthly amount calculated under a 10-year standard repayment plan.

All Stafford, Grad PLUS, and Consolidation Loans made under either the Direct Loan or Federal Family Education Loan programs are eligible to be included in the program. Non-federal loans, loans currently in default, and Parent PLUS Loans are not eligible for the income-based repayment plan.

Many borrowers will find they have a monthly payment under income-based repayment that is less than 10 percent of their gross income. This includes single borrowers with less than $50,000 in income and married borrowers with two children who have less than $100,000 in income.

Under HCERA, student borrowers will qualify for IBR if the borrower's standard repayment exceeds 10 percent of discretionary income (reduced from 15 percent), and the income-based repayment amount is lowered to 10 percent of the borrower's discretionary income. (Discretionary income is the amount of the borrower's AGI that exceeds 150 percent of the poverty line for the borrower's family size.) The loans will be forgiven entirely after 20 years, instead of 25 years, or the loans will be forgiven after 10 years if the individual is in public service, such as teaching, nursing or serving in the military. These changes are effective for *new* borrowers of *new* loans made on or after July 1, 2014.

.01   Eligible for IBR

IBR helps people whose federal student loan debt is high relative to income and family size. As of September 2012, students are able to apply using the U.S. Department of Education's IBR calculator to estimate qualification. The calculator looks at income, family size, and state of residence to calculate an IBR monthly payment amount. If that amount is lower than the monthly payment currently being made on eligible loans under a 10-year standard repayment plan, then the student is eligible to repay loans under IBR.

If a joint federal tax return is filed, both spouses' incomes are used to calculate an IBR monthly payment amount. If married, and both have IBR-eligible loans, the eligible loan debt is combined when determining eligibility. If the combined monthly amount under IBR is lower than the combined monthly amount currently paid under a 10-year standard repayment plan, the couple is eligible for IBR.

¶43,010   Tuition and Fees Deduction

The law permits a before-AGI deduction for up to $4,000 referred to as the Tuition and Fees Deduction (IRC Sec. 222). This rule made it possible to deduct qualified education expenses paid during the year for an individual, the individual's spouse and dependents. It was not possible to claim this deduction if the filing status is married filing separately or if another person can claim an exemption for that individual as a dependent on his or her tax return.

Generally, it was possible to claim the tuition and fees deduction if the taxpayer met all three of the following requirements:

- Pays qualified education expenses of higher education.
- Pays the education expenses for an eligible student.
- The eligible student is the taxpayer, the taxpayer's spouse, or a dependent for whom the taxpayer claims an exemption.

.01   Student Loan Interest Deduction

Generally, personal interest paid, other than certain mortgage interest, is not deductible on a tax return. However, if the modified adjusted gross income (MAGI) is less than $85,000 ($170,000 if filing a joint return), there is a special deduction allowed for paying interest on a student loan (also known as an education loan) used for higher education. The deduction starts to phase out at $70,000 ($140,000 for joint filers). Student loan interest is interest paid during the year on a qualified student loan. It includes both required and voluntary interest payments.

For most taxpayers, MAGI is the adjusted gross income as figured on their federal income tax return before subtracting any deduction for student loan interest. This deduction can reduce the amount of income subject to tax by up to $2,500.

The student loan interest deduction is taken as an adjustment to income (for AGI deduction). This means this deduction can be claimed even without itemizing deductions on **Schedule A** (Form 1040).

.02   Qualified Student Loan

This is a loan taken out solely to pay qualified education expenses (defined later) that were:

- For the taxpayer, his or her spouse, or a person who was a dependent when taking out the loan.
- Paid or incurred within a reasonable period of time before or after taking out the loan.
- For education provided during an academic period for an eligible student.

Loans from the following sources are not qualified student loans:

- A related person.
- A qualified employer plan.

.03   Qualified Education Expenses

For purposes of the student loan interest deduction, these expenses are the total costs of attending an eligible educational institution, including graduate school. They include amounts paid for the following items:

- Tuition and fees.
- Room and board.
- Books, supplies and equipment.
- Other necessary expenses (such as transportation).

The cost of room and board qualifies only to the extent that it is not more than the greater of:

- The allowance for room and board, as determined by the eligible educational institution, that was included in the cost of attendance (for federal financial aid purposes) for a particular academic period and living arrangement of the student, or
- The actual amount charged if the student is residing in housing owned or operated by the eligible educational institution.

¶43,011   Business Deduction for Work-Related Education

A self-employed individual can deduct expenses for qualifying work-related education directly from self-employment income. This may reduce the amount of income subject to both income tax and self-employment tax.

Work-related education expenses may also qualify for other tax benefits, such as the American Opportunity and Lifetime Learning credits.

To claim a business deduction for work-related education, a person must:

- Be working.
- Itemize deductions on Schedule A (Form 1040 or 1040NR) if an employee.
- File Schedule C (Form 1040), Schedule C-EZ (Form 1040), or Schedule F (Form 1040) if self-employed.
- Have expenses for education that meet the requirements discussed under *Qualifying Work-Related Education*, below.

.01   Qualifying Work-Related Education

The costs of qualifying work-related education can be deducted as business expenses. This is education that meets at least one of the following two tests:

- The education is required by the employer or the law to keep the present salary, status or job. The required education must serve a bona fide business purpose of the employer.
- The education maintains or improves skills needed in the present position.

However, even if the education meets one or both of the above tests, it is not qualifying work-related education if it:

- Is needed to meet the *minimum educational requirements* of that particular trade or business or
- Is part of a program of study that will qualify the employee for a new trade or business.

The costs of qualifying work-related education can be deducted as a business expense even if the education could lead to a degree. But if the degree is in a field different from the employee's current employment, it may be determined that the education was undertaken to qualify for a new profession and therefore not deductible. On many occasions the courts have been asked to rule whether the education undertaken was to maintain the employee's current employment or qualify the taxpayer for a new career. For example, accountants undertaking CPA review courses in preparation to take the CPA exam have been ruled to be making a career change and the course fees were therefore not deductible. Pursuit of an MBA has commonly been permitted as a deductible education expense.

.02   Education Required by Employer or by Law

Education needed to meet the minimum educational requirements for a person's present trade or business is not qualifying work-related education. Once having met the minimum educational requirements for the job, the employer or the law may require additional education. This additional education *is* qualifying work-related education if all three of the following requirements are met:

- It is required to keep the present salary, status or job.
- The requirement serves a business purpose of the employer.
- The education is not part of a program that will qualify a worker for a new trade or business.

When a worker acquires more education than the employer or the law requires, the additional education can be qualifying work-related education only if it maintains or improves skills required in the individual's present work.

.03   Education to Maintain or Improve Skills

If additional education is not required by the employer or the law, it can be qualifying work-related education only if it maintains or improves skills needed in the worker's present work. This could include refresher courses, courses on current developments, and academic or vocational courses.

¶43,012   529 Plans

529 Plans are investment vehicles designed to help families pay for future expenses associated with college or other qualified post-secondary training. Though contributions to a 529 plan are not deductible, these plans offer other tax advantages and are named after Section 529 of the Internal Revenue Code. All 50 states and the District of Columbia sponsor at least one type of 529 plan.

As tax-free college savings plans and prepaid tuition programs, these 529 or "qualified tuition programs" have since 1996 become a popular way for parents and other family members to save for a child's college education. 529 plan distributions are tax-free as long as they are used to pay qualified higher education expenses for a designated beneficiary. Qualified expenses include tuition, required fees, books, supplies, equipment and special needs services. With the expiration of the American Opportunity Tax Credit, it is no longer possible to withdraw tax free funds to pay for some educational costs including computers and internet access.

For someone who is at least a half-time student, room and board also qualify. Although contributions to 529 plans are not deductible, there is also no income limit for contributors. However, see below for other limitations.

529 plans allow distribution of not more than $10,000 in tuition expenses incurred during the tax year for designated beneficiaries enrolled at a public, private, or religious *elementary* or *secondary* school.

Contribution Limitations. Contributions cannot exceed the amount necessary to provide for the qualified education expenses of the beneficiary. *Contributors* should be aware of potential gift tax issues if the amount contributed by any one contributor during a year to a given beneficiary, together with other gifts to that beneficiary, is greater than $15,000. For information on a special rule that applies to contributions to 529 plans, see the instructions for **Form 709**, United States Gift (and Generation-Skipping Transfer) Tax Return. If the balance accruing in the plan is not expended on tuition and related education expenses, a prorated portion of the excess will be taxable when withdrawn.

Advantages of a 529 plan. There are advantages of 529 plans. Earnings are not subject to federal tax when used for eligible college expenses. Earnings are often not subject to state tax. States may offer other incentives to in-state participants. There are no income restrictions on individual contributors. Contributions are only limited by the qualified education expenses of the beneficiary. It is possible to change the beneficiary of a plan if the new beneficiary is in the same family. An individual can open a plan benefiting anyone: a relative, a friend or even himself. The plan owner or custodian controls the funds until withdrawal, not the beneficiary.

How 529 Plans Are Structured. There are two basic types of 529 plans— prepaid tuition plans and savings plans. A prepaid tuition plan enables a family to pay for future tuition now in current dollars and prices. A savings plan enables a family to accumulate funds in a tax-advantaged way for future tuition costs. A 529 plan can be established and maintained by a state, state agency, or an eligible educational institution. Each 529 plan is somewhat unique. Some state-sponsored plans offer incentives to in-state participants, such as state income-tax deductions or credits. Each 529 plan has one custodian and one beneficiary. A student or future student can be the beneficiary of more than one 529 plan.

States sponsor 529 plans that allow taxpayers either to prepay or to contribute to an account for paying a student's qualified higher education expenses. Similarly, colleges and groups of colleges sponsor 529 plans that allow them to prepay a student's qualified education expenses.

¶43,013   Coverdell Education Savings Accounts

A Coverdell Education Savings Account (ESA) is an account created as an incentive to help parents and students save for education expenses.

There is no limit on the number of separate Coverdell ESAs that can be established for a designated beneficiary. However, total contributions for the beneficiary in any year cannot be more than $2,000, no matter how many accounts have been established. A beneficiary is someone who is under age 18 or is a special needs beneficiary.

Contributions to a Coverdell ESA are not deductible, but amounts deposited in the account grow tax free until distributed. The beneficiary will not owe tax on the distributions if they are less than a beneficiary's qualified education expenses at an eligible institution. This benefit applies to qualified higher education expenses as well as to qualified elementary and secondary education expenses.

Here are some things to remember about Distributions from Coverdell Accounts:

- Distributions are tax-free as long as they are used for qualified education expenses, such as tuition and fees, required books, supplies and equipment and qualified expenses for room and board.
- There is no tax on distributions if they are for enrollment or attendance at an eligible educational institution. This includes any public, private or religious school that provides elementary or secondary education as determined under state law. Eligible institutions also include any college, university, vocational school or other postsecondary educational institution eligible to participate in a student aid program administered by the Department of Education. Virtually all accredited public, nonprofit, and proprietary (privately owned profit-making) postsecondary institutions are eligible.
- The Hope and lifetime learning credits can be claimed in the same year the beneficiary takes a tax-free distribution from a Coverdell ESA, as long as the same expenses are not used for both benefits.
- If the distribution exceeds qualified education expenses, a portion will be taxable to the beneficiary and will usually be subject to an additional 10 percent tax. Exceptions to the additional 10 percent tax include the death or disability of the beneficiary or if the beneficiary receives a qualified scholarship.

The modified adjusted gross income (MAGI) of the person contributing to the account may not be more than $110,000 ($220,000 if filing a joint return). For most taxpayers, MAGI is the adjusted gross income as figured on their federal income tax return.

If there is a balance in the Coverdell ESA when the beneficiary reaches age 30, it must generally be distributed within 30 days. The portion representing earnings on the account will be taxable and subject to the additional 10 percent tax. The beneficiary may avoid these taxes by rolling over the full balance to another Coverdell ESA for another family member. For more details, see IRS Publication 970, Tax Benefits for Higher Education (at *IRS.gov*) or call 800-TAX-FORM (800-829-3676).

¶43,014 Scholarships and Fellowships

A scholarship is generally an amount paid or allowed to, or for the benefit of, a student at an educational institution to aid in the pursuit of studies. The student may be either an undergraduate or a graduate. A fellowship is generally an amount paid for the benefit of an individual to aid in the pursuit of study or research. Generally, whether the amount is tax-free or taxable depends on the expense paid with the amount and whether the individual is a degree candidate.

A scholarship or fellowship is tax free only if the recipient meets the following conditions:

- Is a candidate for a degree at an eligible educational institution.
- The scholarship or fellowship is used to pay qualified education expenses.

.01 Qualified Education Expenses

For purposes of tax-free scholarships and fellowships, these are expenses for:

- Tuition and fees required to enroll at or to attend an eligible educational institution.
- Course-related expenses, such as fees, books, supplies, and equipment that are required for the courses at the eligible educational institution. These items must be required of all students in that course of instruction.

However, in order for these to be qualified education expenses, the terms of the scholarship or fellowship cannot require that it be used for other purposes, such as room and board, or specify that it cannot be used for tuition or course-related expenses.

.02 Expenses That Don't Qualify

Qualified education expenses do not include the cost of:

- Room and board.
- Travel.
- Research.
- Clerical help.
- Equipment and other expenses that are not required for enrollment in or attendance at an eligible educational institution.

This is true even if the fee must be paid to the institution as a condition of enrollment or attendance. Scholarship or fellowship amounts used to pay these costs are taxable.

For more information, see IRS Pub. 970.

.03 Exclusions from Income

Certain educational assistance benefits may be excluded from income. That means there is no tax to pay on them. However, it also means that none of the tax-free education expenses can be used as the basis for any other deduction or credit, including the Hope credit and the lifetime learning credit.

.04   Employer-Provided Educational Assistance

Up to $5,250 of educational assistance benefits received from an employer under an educational assistance program can be excluded each year. This means the employer *should not include* those benefits with wages, tips, and other compensation shown in box 1 of the employee's Form W-2. These education expenses are not eligible for the tax credits or deductions described above.

.05   Educational Assistance Program

To qualify as an educational assistance program, the plan must be written and must meet certain other requirements. The employer can tell employees whether there is a qualified program in effect at the workplace.

.06   Educational Assistance Benefits

Tax-free educational assistance benefits include payments for tuition, fees and similar expenses, books, supplies, and equipment. The payments may be for either undergraduate- or graduate-level courses. The payments do not have to be for work-related courses. Educational assistance benefits do not include payments for the following items:

- Meals, lodging, or transportation.
- Tools or supplies (other than textbooks) that the student can keep after completing the course of instruction.
- Courses involving sports, games, or hobbies unless they:
  - Have a reasonable relationship to the business of the employer, or
  - Are required as part of a degree program.

.07   Benefits over $5,250

If the employer pays more than $5,250 for educational benefits for an employee during the year, the recipient must generally pay tax on the amount over $5,250. The employer should include in wages (Form W-2, box 1) the amount that must be included in income.

.08   Working Condition Fringe Benefit

However, if the benefits over $5,250 also qualify as a working condition fringe benefit, the employer does not have to include them in wages. A working condition fringe benefit is a benefit, which had the employee, paid for it, it could be deducted as an employee business expense.

¶43,015   Varied Methods of Loan Deferment, Forgiveness, Cancellations, or Consolidation

Forgiveness of debt, whether in full or in part, is generally taxable and must be included in on the taxpayer's return. There are numerous exceptions to this rule, however. Some of these exceptions pertain to educational loans.

The types of assistance are student loan cancellation and student loan repayment assistance.

.01   Loan Discharge (Cancellation)

It's possible to have a student loan debt discharged (canceled) or reduced, but only under certain specific circumstances:

- The recipient dies or becomes totally and permanently disabled.
- The school closed before the recipient could complete the program.
- For FFEL and Direct Stafford Loans only: The school owes the lender a refund, forged the recipient's signature on a promissory note, or certified a loan for the recipient even though that individual did not have the ability to benefit from the coursework.
- The individual works in certain designated public school service professions (including teaching in a low-income school).
- The individual files for bankruptcy. (This cancellation is rare and occurs only if a bankruptcy court rules that repayment would cause undue hardship.)

.02   Cancellation and Deferment Options for Teachers

For a teacher serving in a low-income or subject-matter shortage area, it may be possible to cancel or defer payment of a student loans. Those with a loan from the Federal Perkins Loan Program, a Stafford Loan on or after October 1, 1998, a FFEL or Direct Stafford Loan or a Paul Douglas Teacher Scholarship should check to see if there are options available for them.

.03   Loan Forgiveness for Public Service Employees

In 2007, Congress created the Public Service Loan Forgiveness Program to encourage individuals to enter and continue to work full-time in public service jobs. Under this program, borrowers may qualify for forgiveness of the remaining balance due on their eligible federal student loans after they have made 120 payments on those loans under certain repayment plans while employed full time by certain public service employers. Only loans received under the William D. Ford Federal Direct Loan (Direct Loan) Program are eligible for PSLF.

.04   Loan Consolidations

Borrowers who have loans in the Direct Loan program, the FFEL program, or loans purchased by the Department under ECASLA may consolidate those loans into a Direct Consolidation loan between July 1, 2010 and July 1, 2011. The borrower must have at least one loan in each of two of the three categories named, and have not yet entered repayment on at least one of those loans. NASFAA advocated for the return of in-school consolidation to deal with borrower repayment issues in regards to FFELP, ECASLA, and Direct Loans.

¶43,016   Regional Domestic Exchange Programs

Regional exchange programs that allow out-of-state students to pay in-state or discounted tuition are not widely used and many students could benefit from knowing about the existence of these programs. For some it would open a broader group of colleges and universities from which to choose. For all it would mean the savings of several thousand dollars.

Most of the participating schools are public, but there are some private ones, also. That highlights the most important point: little if anything appears to be "set in stone." The four regional programs described below differ widely; even their requirements seem to change from year to year. There seem to be reciprocal arrangements of all kinds that receive little publicity. Therefore, it's up to the individual to check with a knowledgeable college counselor or directly with the school of choice to see if there is an opportunity to lower the tuition. Everyone knows to check on scholarships, grants, loans, credits, and tax breaks, but few are aware of a tuition discount.

Admissions requirements and eligibility vary greatly, but none appears to be tied to financial need. Some students can get the discount only if they are pursuing a specific major. Other programs automatically give students a discount if they are admitted to a particular university from an eligible state.

.01   Academic Common Market in the South

America's first interstate compact for education, the Southern Regional Education Board is a nonprofit, nonpartisan organization that helps government and education leaders in its 16 member states work together to advance education and improve the social and economic life of the region. Member states include: Alabama, Arkansas, Delaware, Florida, Georgia, Kentucky, Louisiana, Maryland, Mississippi, North Carolina, Oklahoma, South Carolina, Tennessee, Texas, Virginia and West Virginia.

For more than 50 years, the SREB Academic Common Market has enabled students to pursue out-of-state college majors at discounted tuition rates, through agreements among the states and colleges and universities. More than 1,400 undergraduate and graduate degree programs are available in the 16 SREB states.

To qualify the applicant must:

- Be a resident of one of the 16 SREB states.
- Select a program eligible for residents of the home state.
- Complete the admission process at the institution offering the eligible Academic Common Market program.
- Certify residency in one of the home states.

In some ways, the Academic Common Market has the strictest qualifications: some SREB states limit participation to graduate programs and/or students are eligible only if they are pursuing a specific major listed in the program's catalog. These majors are fairly specialized. Examples of majors include wireless engineering, education of the deaf, and public-health administration. However, SREB students get the biggest discount: All pay in-state tuition while those in other regions usually pay 150 percent of in-state tuition, or sometimes more.

.02   Western Undergraduate Exchange in the West

WUE (pronounced "woo-wee") is the Western Undergraduate Exchange, a program of the Western Interstate Commission for Higher Education (WICHE). Through WUE, students in western states may enroll in more than 140 two-year and four-year college institutions in member WUE states at a reduced tuition level: 150 percent of the institution's regular resident tuition. The program began in 1987 and all WICHE states have now signed the agreement.

A copy of each state's signed WUE agreement is available for review. Students from all WICHE member states are eligible to request the WUE tuition discount. Schools that participate in the Western Undergraduate Exchange are often more liberal with discounts on an individual basis.

Virtually all undergraduate fields are available to WUE students at participating colleges and universities. Some institutions have opened their entire curriculum on a space-available or first-come, first-serve basis; others offer only designated programs.

WICHE states include: Alaska, Arizona, California, Colorado, Hawaii, Idaho, Montana, Nevada, New Mexico, North Dakota, Oregon, South Dakota, Utah, Washington, Wyoming.

.03   New England Board of Higher Education Regional Student Program

The New England Board of Higher Education's Regional Student Program (RSP) provides New England residents with a tuition break when they study certain majors—not available at public colleges in their home state—at public colleges and universities in other New England states. The RSP tuition rate reflects a significant break on a college's out-of-state tuition rate. It is usually 150 percent of the college's in-state tuition.

All 78 public colleges and universities in New England participate in the Regional Student Program. Together, these two-year and four-year higher education institutions offer more than 700 academic programs at reduced tuition to out-of-state New England residents.

Programs are available through the RSP at all academic levels: associate, bachelor's, master's, certificate or advanced graduate study, doctoral and first-professional. These majors are approved each year by the participating institutions and listed in the annual RSP catalog.

When a degree program is offered through the RSP at both an in-state and out-of-state two-year public college, and the out-of-state college is closer to the student's legal residence, the student may apply for RSP status at that college. The Nearer-to-Legal-Residence Option also applies to residents and four-year state colleges in Connecticut, Massachusetts, Rhode Island, and Vermont. It does not apply to the state universities—University of Connecticut, Maine, Massachusetts, New Hampshire, Rhode Island and Vermont.

.04   Midwest Student Exchange Program

MHEC helps improve access to postsecondary education through the Midwest Student Exchange Program (MSEP). Since 1994, the MSEP has provided more affordable opportunities for students to attend out-of-state institutions. The MSEP serves as the Midwest's largest multi-state tuition reciprocity program. MSEP is not a scholarship.

Over 140 colleges and universities in Illinois, Indiana, Kansas, Michigan, Minnesota, Missouri, Nebraska, North Dakota and Wisconsin have opened their doors to each other's citizens at more affordable rates. Although the Midwestern Higher Education Compact is composed of twelve Midwestern states, the MSEP is a voluntary program (as are all MHEC programs) and only eight of the twelve states participate. Iowa, South Dakota, and Ohio do not participate in MSEP at this time.

Through the MSEP, public institutions agree to charge students no more than 150 percent of the in-state resident tuition rate for specific programs; private institutions offer a 10 percent reduction on their tuition rates. You must be enrolling as a non-resident student at a participating MSEP campus to receive the discount.

Actual savings through the program will vary from institution to institution depending upon the tuition rates. Participating students will typically realize savings between $500 and $3,000 annually.

Note: The Illinois Board of Higher Education formally endorsed MSEP in December 2006, but the program did not go into effect until individual Illinois institutions elected to participate. Current MSEP institutions will began offering MSEP rates to all Illinois students admitted under MSEP after August 15, 2011. Campuses in all participating states are not required to "grandfather" in students admitted prior to this date.

.05   Other Tuition Program Arrangements

The tuition arrangements appear not to stop with the four large geographically based programs. In addition to the programs listed above, the following states have their own two-state exchange programs: Wisconsin and Minnesota; California and Nevada; and Indiana and Illinois.

The University of Cincinnati offers in-state tuition to the residents of eight Kentucky counties. A number of individual schools also offer tuition discounts that are not considered scholarships. Morehead State University, Morehead, Kentucky, offers a Tuition Assistance Grant of up to $2,000 for out-of-state students who qualify.

There are also several groups that organize cultural exchange and study abroad scholarships throughout the world for qualified applicants.

CHAPTER 44
Taxpayer Rights

¶44,000   Overview

The National Taxpayer Advocate is required by statute to submit two annual reports to the House Committee on Ways and Means and the Senate Committee on Finance. The statute requires these reports to be submitted directly to the Committees without any prior review or comment from the Commissioner of Internal Revenue, the Secretary of the Treasury, the IRS Oversight Board, any other officer or employee of the Department of the Treasury, or the Office of Management and Budget.

One report is submitted mid-year and must identify the objectives of the Office of the Taxpayer Advocate for the fiscal year beginning in that calendar year. The other report, due on December 31 of each year, must identify at least 20 of the most serious problems encountered by taxpayers, discuss the ten tax issues most frequently litigated in the courts, and make administrative and legislative recommendations to resolve taxpayer problems.

¶44,001   Taxpayer Bill of Rights

Former National Taxpayer Advocate Nina E. Olson emphasized the protection of taxpayer rights in tax administration. In her 2007 Annual Report to Congress, and in later reports, she proposed a new Taxpayer Bill of Rights. On June 10, 2014, the IRS formally adopted the Advocate's proposal, to renew the focus on protecting the rights of taxpayers in all of their dealings with the IRS. This document groups the dozens of existing rights in the Internal Revenue Code into ten fundamental rights, and makes these rights clear, understandable, and accessible for taxpayers and IRS employees alike. The rights are published on the IRS Web site and presented in eight languages: English, Chinese (Traditional), Chinese (Simplified), Haitian Creole, Korean, Russian, Spanish, and Vietnamese.

1. The Right to Be Informed, including clear explanations of the laws and IRS procedures. Taxpayers have the right to be informed of IRS decisions about their tax accounts and to receive clear explanations of the outcomes.
2. The Right to Quality Service, including the right to receive clear and easily understandable communications from the IRS, and to speak to a supervisor about inadequate service.
3. The Right to Pay No More than the Correct Amount of Tax, including the right to have the IRS apply all tax payments properly.
4. The Right to Challenge the IRS's Position and Be Heard, which allows taxpayers to provide additional documentation in response to formal IRS actions.
5. The Right to Appeal an IRS Decision in an Independent Forum and to receive a written response regarding the Office of Appeals' decision.
6. The Right to Finality which includes the right to know when the IRS has finished an audit and to know the maximum amount of time they have to challenge the IRS's position.
7. The Right to Privacy and including an expectation that the IRS will be no more intrusive than necessary.
8. The Right to Confidentiality including the right to expect appropriate action will be taken against employees, return preparers, and others who wrongfully use or disclose taxpayer return information.
9. The Right to Retain Representation including the right to seek assistance from a Low Income Taxpayer Clinic if they cannot afford representation.
10. The Right to a Fair and Just Tax System including receiving assistance from the Taxpayer Advocate Service if they are experiencing financial difficulty or if the IRS has not resolved their tax issues properly and timely through its normal channels.

.01 Minimum Standards for Tax Return Preparers

In the absence of congressional action, the IRS in 2010 began to implement preparer standards on its own. In 2015, the U.S. Court of Appeals for the District of Columbia affirmed a lower court decision concluding that the IRS exceeded its rulemaking authority in acting without a statutory grant of authority. Then, the IRS announced that lacking the authority to continue its mandatory credentialing program, it will implement a voluntary program. TAS recommended that Congress pass legislation authorizing the IRS to reinstitute the program it had implemented prior to the U.S. Court of Appeals decision.

The minimum standards for return preparers are important to protect taxpayers from incompetent or unscrupulous preparers. More than 140 million individual taxpayers each year file tax returns, and well over half use return preparers. Yet there are currently no standards for hanging out a shingle and preparing returns, and there is considerable evidence that many preparers lack the knowledge and ability to prepare accurate tax returns.

Significantly, according to the 2023 Taxpayer Advocate's report, over 75% of taxpayers who claim the Earned Income Tax Credit (EITC) use unregulated preparers to prepare their returns. Because these taxpayers are low income, the report says they often turn to pawn shops, used car dealers, and check-cashing outlets for return preparation assistance. Without meaningful standards, Olson wrote, "we will continue to subject these low income taxpayers to the actions of incompetent or unscrupulous preparers and we will be unlikely to make progress in reducing the EITC noncompliance rate to an acceptable level, thus harming the public fisc."

Olson reiterates her longstanding recommendation that a meaningful preparer standards program must contain four components: (1) registration to promote accountability; (2) a one-time "entrance" examination to ensure basic competency in return preparation; (3) continuing education courses to ensure preparers keep up to date with the many frequent tax-law changes; and (4) a taxpayer education campaign to help guide taxpayers to credentialed practitioners (i.e., CPAs, attorneys, and Enrolled Agents) or preparers who have satisfied the above requirements.

.02   Tax Fraud

Nina Olson, the IRS National Taxpayer Advocate, testified before the Senate in 2006 that "when honest taxpayers feel like chumps, some of them start fudging too. And when that happens, voluntary payments drop even more, necessitating more examination and collection actions. This sense that the system is unfair can result in a vicious cycle of increased noncompliance and increased enforcement." The Taxpayer Advocate is concerned not only about the ways the increase of tax fraud and tax related internet fraud affect the honest taxpayer, but also about the ability of the IRS to do its primary duty of collecting the taxes to finance the government.

Impact of Tax Fraud and Tax-Related Identity Theft. Tax fraud and tax-related identity theft, although distinct problems, often overlap and present similar challenges for taxpayers and the IRS. Tax identity theft has decreased in prevalence in recent years. Since the pandemic, tax-related identity theft reports are up 45 percent compared to pre-pandemic years. (In 2023, there were over 1 million reports of identity theft across the country (down from 2022). Tax-related identity theft is the most common during the tax filing season, according to the Federal Trade Commission.) This is measured by the number of taxpayers who filed IRS identity theft affidavits. In spite of the reduction, it is still a large problem and the IRS has identified it as one of its "Dirty Dozen" list of tax scams. The IRS has implemented the Return Review Program (RRP) to replace its Electronic Fraud Detection System (EFDS), which it hopes will assist in detection and prevention of a greater number of attempts at filing fraudulent returns, and identity theft.

Tax Fraud. The report notes that the IRS's automated fraud-detection filters are inherently imperfect. Among the roughly two million refund claims the IRS held, tens of thousands were legitimate. "As the IRS develops [its] filters," the report says, "it must also create procedures that would allow honest taxpayers with legitimate refund claims to receive their money without unnecessary delay."

Where the IRS seeks to verify suspect wage and withholding information, its procedures until recently required it to make a final determination within 11 weeks or release the claimed refund. Because of the combination of more cases and budget limitations, the IRS is now placing "hard freezes" on cases it cannot handle within that time, meaning that claimed refunds must be manually released or will not be paid. The report expresses concern that the IRS has little incentive to prioritize a case once a hard freeze has been imposed, resulting in harm to honest taxpayers whose returns inadvertently tripped a filter. Impact of the coronavirus pandemic delayed refunds even longer. For example, the IRS reported that on average, it took 257 days to resolve identity theft cases. The Taxpayer Advocate says identity theft inventories have increased and on average it is taking up to two years to resolve identity theft cases. The IRS is committed to resolving identity theft cases as quickly as possible, and is taking steps to reduce this time frame to 120 days or less.

Identity Theft. Resource constraints also are limiting the IRS's ability to assist victims of tax-related identity theft. Tax-related identity theft typically arises when an identity thief uses the Social Security number of another person to file a false tax return with the intent of obtaining an improper refund. Identity theft can impose a significant burden on its victims, whose legitimate refund claims are blocked and who often must spend months or longer trying to convince the IRS that they are, in fact, victims and then working with the IRS to untangle their account problems.

Balancing Speedy Refunds, Fraud Prevention, and Victim Assistance. The report notes the IRS faces competing pressures to issue refunds quickly and investigate suspicious claims. During 2023, the IRS processed more than 271.4 million returns for more than $4.7 trillion in collections and more than $659 million in tax refunds. Many families depend on these funds and need them quickly, sometimes to pay rent or high winter heating bills. At the same time, the IRS needs time to investigate the more than two million potentially fraudulent claims it identifies.

The IRS now notifies certain affected taxpayers by letter when it has a problem processing their returns and instructs them to call the new Taxpayer Protection Unit (TPU) to provide more information. However, this unit has been unable to answer about two out of every three calls it has received from taxpayers so far this year. At times during the filing season, it was answering only about one out of every nine calls it received—and those who managed to get through waited an average of over an hour to speak with an employee.

While Congress and taxpayers rightfully demand that the IRS stop payment on fraudulent refund claims, Congress and taxpayers also rightfully demand that the IRS pay refunds out to legitimate taxpayers immediately the Tax Advocate wrote. Tax fraud and identity theft will continue to be key areas of focus for TAS during the upcoming fiscal year.

.03   Taxpayer Assistance Orders (TAOs) and Taxpayer Advocate Directives (TADs)

To ensure that the concerns of the National Taxpayer Advocate and Taxpayer Advocate Service are adequately addressed, Congress gave the Advocate the authority to issue TAOs to the IRS ordering it to take an action or refrain from taking an action in taxpayer cases. Over the past year, the report says, the IRS has ignored and sought to limit the Advocate's authority to issue TADs.

The report also raises concerns about the level of attention the IRS has given recently to TAOs and TADs. The Advocate has also been given parallel administrative authority to issue TADs to the IRS, directing it to take action on systemic issues to "protect taxpayer rights, prevent undue burden, ensure equitable treatment, or provide an essential service to taxpayers."

TAD to Improve Audit Process Challenged. In January 2012, the National Taxpayer Advocate issued a TAD to address problems taxpayers were facing in connection with the correspondence examination process as described in a TAS study, including problems caused by obsolete regulations. The IRS challenged the National Taxpayer Advocate's authority to issue a TAD to the Chief Counsel or to interpret the law. Interpreted broadly, this conclusion would severely limit the National Taxpayer Advocate's authority to issue TADs generally. The report explains that because nearly everything the IRS does is governed by law, it is very difficult for a TAD to address problems that taxpayers are facing without making a recommendation as to how the law should be interpreted. For example, if a TAD seeks to prevent the IRS from infringing taxpayer rights, which are embodied in law, the IRS may decline to respond to the TAD on the basis that it interprets law. The IRS's position significantly reduces the utility of these directives and undermines the purpose for which they were created.

TAOs and TADs Are Important Tools to Elevate Taxpayer Rights Issues to the IRS Leadership. TAS generally uses TAOs and TADs as part of a strategic approach to issues that arise in multiple TAS cases, are the focus of projects and teams, and for which TAS has repeatedly sought solutions from the IRS, the report says. The report points out that the IRS Commissioner and Deputy Commissioner may overturn any TAO or TAD, which in practice means that TAOs and TADs are primarily vehicles the National Taxpayer Advocate may use to raise priority concerns to the IRS leadership.

The Advocate wrote that the purpose of TAOs and TADs is to ensure that issues that may impinge on taxpayer rights or impose excessive taxpayer burden are elevated for consideration to the highest levels of the IRS leadership in a formal way that requires a written response, so that the issues and competing considerations are made transparent to Congress and other stakeholders. For that reason, it is utterly mystifying to me why the IRS would seek to squelch the authority of the National Taxpayer Advocate to raise taxpayer rights and taxpayer burden issues to the senior IRS leadership in this way, and we certainly will not accede to attempts to constrain our advocacy efforts on behalf of our nation's taxpayers.

¶44,002   Advocate's Annual Report to Congress

The 2019 Annual Report was the first since 2000 that has not been submitted by Nina Olson. Ms. Olson retired on July 31, 2019, after leading the Taxpayer Advocate Service for over 18 years. Ms. Olson fought tirelessly for taxpayer rights and created an organization of advocates who will carry on her legacy. Ms. Olson was replaced by Erin M. Collins in March 2020, and Ms. Collins submitted the 2020 report, as well as the subsequent reports in 2021, 2022, and 2023.

.01   The IRS Needs to Develop a Comprehensive Customer Service Strategy

Under the Taxpayer First Act, the IRS was required to create and submit a comprehensive customer service strategy to Congress by July 1, 2020. The IRS submitted the Taxpayer First Act Report to Congress in January 2021 and subsequent years. In this regard, the National Taxpayer Advocate has identified several concerns with how IRS is currently handling customer service that should be addressed.

Customer service has always been an issue at the IRS for years. Taxpayers had to wait for hours for a phone call to be picked up or months for a correspondence to be addressed. The biggest issue that NTA addressed was that IRS does not view itself as a service organization. The IRS does not take into consideration the taxpayers' needs and preferences. Forcing taxpayers to use digital avenues undermines taxpayer rights. NTA also pointed out that service strategy should include services to the practitioners.

.02 Information Technology Modernization of IRS

The IRS's Integrated Modernization Business Plan ("Plan"), which aims to improve the taxpayer experience, by modernizing core tax administration systems, IRS operations and cybersecurity was identified as having some issues. While the Plan will greatly improve the IRS's IT infrastructure, make tax administration more efficient, and enable the IRS to provide better taxpayer service, the Plan does not address all its IT issues. Further, for the IRS to make any progress in modernizing its systems, its efforts must be fully funded.

.03 IRS Funding

The IRS struggled to provide quality service with the level of funding it had been receiving. The IRS expects to bring on about 30,000 new employees over the next two years as it begins spending the $80 billion in new funds Congress provided.

Modern technology would substantially improve service. For example, only a few of the IRS's phone lines use customer callback technology, which frees callers from waiting on hold. Because the IRS lacks an enterprise-wide case management system, each function's employees must transcribe or import information from other electronic systems, and mail or fax it to other functions. All these delay due process to the taxpayers.

.04 Delays in Processing Returns

Filtering the refund fraud that was rampant in previous years continue to cause delay taxpayer refunds for legitimate returns, potentially causing financial hardship. The IRS has designed a number of filters to assist in the detection and prevention of non-identity theft (non-IDT) refund fraud. Despite improvements to this program, issues persisted that affected both taxpayers and TAS, including: delays in releasing legitimate refunds; false positive rates (FPR) as high as 71 percent; and inadequate information as to the reasons for refund delays and what steps taxpayers can take to expedite the process.

Taxpayers whose returns are selected into the non-IDT refund fraud program often experience delays in receiving the refunds claimed on their original returns. In addition to the filters used related to refund fraud, there are a number of other contributing factors to the delays in processing returns. For three years, the IRS has struggled with a backlog of work. During the 2022 filing season, the IRS focused on reducing its correspondence backlog, which left most phone calls from taxpayers unanswered. The IRS also prioritized processing its backlog of returns from 2021, but had more than 12 million returns to process as of late September 2022. In mid-2024, there was a backlog of about 500,000 identify theft cases and 1.4 million EITC claims. As of April 20, 2024, there were still around 11.7 million tax returns awaiting processing.

¶44,003 Systemic Advocacy Management System (SAMS)

As an independent organization within the IRS, the Systemic Advocacy Management System (SAMS) helps taxpayers solve problems with the IRS and recommend changes that will prevent problems from occurring.

The National Taxpayer Advocate invites taxpayers, practitioners, professional organizations, and all interested citizens to help identify and recommend solutions to problems with the IRS and the tax code. Individuals can do this by submitting advocacy issues to the Taxpayer Advocate Service through SAMS: a web-based method of receiving issues, suggestions and ideas, and using them to help reduce or eliminate the burdens facing taxpayers. The Systemic Advocacy Management System acts as a database of issues and information submitted by IRS employees and the public. Systemic issues do not apply to just one taxpayer. Following are characteristics of systemic issues:

- They always affect multiple taxpayers.
- They impact segments of the taxpayer population, locally, regionally or nationally.
- They relate to IRS systems, policies, and procedures.
- They require study, analysis, administrative changes or legislative remedies.
- They involve protecting taxpayer rights, reducing or preventing taxpayer burden, ensuring equitable treatment of taxpayers or providing essential services to taxpayers.

Many issues and problems should be handled by means other than SAMS. These include:

- Individual problem cases.
- Tax law questions.
- Free online filing questions.
- Requests for IRS forms and publications.

An individual may submit an issue for consideration by going to the SAMS Help page for instructions. After a review of all submission on the database, each is ranked to determine whether it becomes an advocacy project; if so, it is scheduled to be resolved.

¶44,004   Taxpayer Advocacy Panel

The Taxpayer Advocacy Panel (TAP) is a federal advisory committee charged with providing direct taxpayer feedback to the IRS. TAP helps identify tax issues of importance to taxpayers and provide a taxpayer perspective to the IRS on key programs, products, and services. It also serves as a focus group that makes recommendations to the IRS and the National Taxpayer Advocate. There are presently 75 citizen volunteers.

According to the IRS Commissioner, TAP members play an important role for the nation's taxpayers. The panelists provide the IRS with insights that help make the tax administration process better for all taxpayers.

The TAP listens to taxpayers, identifies issues and makes suggestions for improving IRS service and customer satisfaction. Oversight and program support for the TAP are provided by the Taxpayer Advocate Service, an independent organization within the IRS that helps resolve taxpayer problems and make recommendations to avoid future problems.

TAP members work with IRS executives on priority topics, primarily those involving the Wage & Investment and Small Business/Self-Employed operating divisions. Members also serve as a conduit for bringing grassroots concerns raised by the taxpaying public to the attention of the IRS.

TAP members are U.S. citizens who volunteer to serve a three-year appointment and are expected to devote 300 to 500 hours per year to panel activities. TAP members are demographically and geographically diverse, providing balanced representation from all 50 states, the District of Columbia and Puerto Rico.

Taxpayers can contact the TAP representative for their geographic area by calling 888-912-1227 (a toll-free call) or via the Internet at *www.improveirs.org*. Taxpayers can also send written correspondence to the TAP at the following address:

Taxpayer Advocacy Panel (TAP)
TA: TAP, Room 1314
1111 Constitution Avenue, NW
Washington, D.C. 20224

¶44,005   2024 and 2023 Purple Book

The National Taxpayer Advocate released the National Taxpayer Advocate 2024 Purple Book containing a concise summary of 66 legislative recommendations that she believes will strengthen taxpayer rights and improve tax administration. The Purple Book is updated each year. The 2023 revision had 65 recommendations, similar to those in 2022. The recommendations in the 2024 version of the Purple Book are:

STRENGTHEN TAXPAYER RIGHTS AND TAXPAYER SERVICE

1. Elevate the Importance of the Taxpayer Bill of Rights by Redesignating It as Section 1 of the Internal Revenue Code
2. Require the IRS to Timely Process Claims for Credit or Refund

IMPROVE THE FILING PROCESS

3. Treat Electronically Submitted Tax Payments and Documents as Timely If Submitted on or Before the Applicable Deadline
4. Authorize the IRS to Establish Minimum Competency Standards for Federal Tax Return Preparers and Revoke the Identification Numbers of Sanctioned Preparers
5. Extend the Time for Small Businesses to Make Subchapter S Elections
6. Adjust Individual Estimated Tax Payment Deadlines to Occur Quarterly
7. Eliminate Duplicative Reporting Requirements Imposed by the Bank Secrecy Act and the Foreign Account Tax Compliance Act

IMPROVE ASSESSMENT AND COLLECTION PROCEDURES

8. Require That Math Error Notices Describe the Reason(s) for the Adjustment With Specificity, Inform Taxpayers They May Request Abatement Within 60 Days, and Be Mailed by Certified or Registered Mail
9. Continue to Limit the IRS's Use of "Math Error Authority" to Clear-Cut Categories Specified by Statute
10. Require Independent Managerial Review and Written Approval Before the IRS May Assert Multiyear Bans Barring Taxpayers From Receiving Certain Tax Credits and Clarify That the Tax Court Has Jurisdiction to Review the Assertion of Multiyear Bans
11. Give Taxpayers Abroad Additional Time to Request Abatement of a Math Error Assessment
12. Give Taxpayers Abroad Additional Time to Request a Collection Due Process Hearing and to File a Petition Challenging a Notice of Determination in the U.S. Tax Court
13. Provide That Assessable Penalties Are Subject to Deficiency Procedures
14. Direct the IRS to Implement an Automated Formula to Identify Taxpayers at Risk of Economic Hardship
15. Provide That "an Opportunity to Dispute" an Underlying Liability Means an Opportunity to Dispute Such Liability in the U.S. Tax Court

16. Prohibit Offset of the Earned Income Tax Credit (EITC) Portion of a Tax Refund to Past-Due Federal Tax Liabilities
17. Eliminate Installment Agreement User Fees for Low-Income Taxpayers and Those Paying by Direct Debit
18. Improve Offer in Compromise Program Accessibility by Repealing the Up-front Payment Requirements
19. Require the IRS to Consider a Taxpayer's Current Income When Determining Whether to Waive an Installment Agreement User Fee
20. Modify the Requirement That the Office of Chief Counsel Review Certain Offers in Compromise
21. Require the IRS to Mail Notices at Least Quarterly to Taxpayers With Delinquent Tax Liabilities
22. Clarify When the Two-Year Period for Requesting Return of Levy Proceeds Begins
23. Protect Retirement Funds From IRS Levies, Including So-Called "Voluntary" Levies, in the Absence of "Flagrant Conduct" by a Taxpayer
24. Provide Taxpayer Protections Before the IRS Recommends the Filing of a Lien Foreclosure Suit on a Principal Residence
25. Provide Collection Due Process Rights to Third Parties Holding Legal Title to Property Subject to IRS Collection Actions
26. Extend the Time Limit for Taxpayers to Sue for Damages for Improper Collection Actions
27. Revise the Private Debt Collection Rules to More Accurately Identify and Protect Taxpayers With Incomes Below 200 Percent of the Federal Poverty Level

REFORM PENALTY AND INTEREST PROVISIONS

28. Convert the Estimated Tax Penalty Into an Interest Provision to Properly Reflect Its Substance
29. Apply One Interest Rate Per Estimated Tax Underpayment Period
30. Pay Interest to Taxpayers on Excess Payments of Estimated Tax to the Same Extent Taxpayers Must Pay a Penalty on Underpayments of Estimated Tax
31. Extend the Reasonable Cause Defense for the Failure-to-File Penalty to Taxpayers Who Rely on Return Preparers to E-File Their Returns
32. Authorize a Penalty for Tax Return Preparers Who Engage in Fraud or Misconduct by Altering a Taxpayer's Tax Return
33. Clarify That Supervisory Approval Is Required Under IRC § 6751(b) Before Proposing Penalties

34. Require an Employee to Determine and a Supervisor to Approve All Negligence Penalties Under IRC § 6662(b)(1)
35. Modify the Definition of "Willful" for Purposes of Determining Report of Foreign Bank and Financial Accounts Violations and Reduce the Maximum Penalty Amounts

STRENGTHEN TAXPAYER RIGHTS BEFORE THE OFFICE OF APPEALS

36. Require Taxpayers' Consent Before Allowing IRS Counsel or Compliance Personnel to Participate in Appeals Conferences

STRENGTHEN THE OFFICE OF THE TAXPAYER ADVOCATE

37. Clarify That the National Taxpayer Advocate May Hire Legal Counsel to Enable Her to Advocate More Effectively for Taxpayers
38. Clarify the Authority of the National Taxpayer Advocate to Make Personnel Decisions to Protect the Independence of the Office of the Taxpayer Advocate
39. Clarify the Taxpayer Advocate Service's Access to Files, Meetings, and Other Information
40. Authorize the National Taxpayer Advocate to File *Amicus* Briefs
41. Authorize the Office of the Taxpayer Advocate to Assist Certain Taxpayers Experiencing Economic Hardships During a Lapse in Appropriations
42. Repeal Statute Suspension Under IRC § 7811(d) for Taxpayers Seeking Assistance From the Taxpayer Advocate Service

STRENGTHEN TAXPAYER RIGHTS IN JUDICIAL PROCEEDINGS

43. Expand the U.S. Tax Court's Jurisdiction to Hear Refund Cases
44. Authorize the Tax Court to Order Refunds or Credits in Collection Due Process Proceedings Where Liability Is at Issue
45. Promote Consistency With the Supreme Court's Boechler Decision by Making the Time Limits for Bringing All Tax Litigation Subject to Equitable Judicial Doctrines
46. Extend the Deadline for Taxpayers to Bring a Refund Suit When They Have Requested Appeals Reconsideration of a Notice of Claim Disallowance But the IRS Has Not Acted Timely to Decide Their Claim
47. Authorize the Tax Court to Sign Subpoenas for the Production of Records Held by a Third Party Prior to a Scheduled Hearing

48. Provide That the Scope of Judicial Review of "Innocent Spouse" Determinations Under IRC § 6015 Is *De Novo*
49. Clarify That Taxpayers May Raise Innocent Spouse Relief as a Defense in Collection, Bankruptcy, and Refund Cases
50. Fix the Donut Hole in the Tax Court's Jurisdiction to Determine Overpayments by Non-Filers With Filing Extensions

MISCELLANEOUS RECOMMENDATIONS

51. Restructure the Earned Income Tax Credit (EITC) to Make It Simpler for Taxpayers and Reduce Improper Payments
52. Adopt a Consistent and More Modern Definition of "Qualifying Child" Throughout the Internal Revenue Code
53. Permanently Give Taxpayers Affected by Federally Declared Disasters the Option of Using Prior Year Earned Income to Claim the Earned Income Tax Credit (EITC)
54. Amend the Lookback Period for Allowing Tax Credits or Refunds to Include the Period of Any Postponement or Additional or Disregarded Time for Timely Filing a Tax Return
55. Protect Taxpayers in Federally Declared Disaster Areas Who Receive Filing and Payment Relief From Inaccurate and Confusing Collection Notices
56. Exclude Taxpayers in Specific Circumstances From the Requirement to Provide a Social Security Number for Their Children to Claim the Child Tax Credit
57. Clarify Whether Dependents Are Required to Have Taxpayer Identification Numbers for Purposes of the Credit for Other Dependents
58. Allow Members of Certain Religious Sects That Do Not Participate in Social Security and Medicare to Obtain Employment Tax Refunds
59. Remove the Requirement That Written Receipts Acknowledging Charitable Contributions Must Be Contemporaneous
60. Establish a Uniform Standard Mileage Deduction Rate for All Purposes
61. Eliminate the Marriage Penalty for Nonresident Aliens Who Otherwise Qualify for the Premium Tax Credit
62. Encourage and Authorize Independent Contractors and Service Recipients to Enter Into Voluntary Withholding Agreements
63. Require the IRS to Specify the Information Needed in Third-Party Contact Notices
64. Enable the Low Income Taxpayer Clinic Program to Assist More Taxpayers in Controversies With the IRS
65. Compensate Taxpayers for "No Change" National Research Program Audit
66. Establish the Position of IRS Historian Within the Internal Revenue Service to Record and Publish Its History

Appendix 1: Additional Reference Materials for Legislative Recommendations in This Volume

Appendix 2: Prior National Taxpayer Advocate Legislative Recommendations Enacted Into Law

.01   TAS Blueprint

The Blueprint is designed to describe the future TAS organization and the goals, foundations, strategic themes, and capabilities necessary for success.

It serves as the base for the strategic planning process by presenting a vision of how TAS should operate, while connecting current and planned initiatives to the future.

.02   TAS Guiding Principles

In conjunction with the Blueprint, TAS developed the Guiding Principles shown below to govern the way TAS does business and to represent the essence of what TAS customers need, want, and expect from the Service.

> *Advocacy* The willingness and ability to see the situation from a taxpayer's perspective, advocate for the taxpayer's rights, and assist IRS leadership in integrating the taxpayer's perspective into tax administration.
>
> *Independence* The ability to advocate objectively for the taxpayer separately from the IRS.
>
> *Impartiality* An unbiased assessment of the taxpayer's situation in light of existing tax law.
>
> *Confidentiality* The discretion not to disclose certain information to the IRS.
>
> *Competency* The knowledge and ability to understand the taxpayer's issue and how to resolve it.
>
> *Empathy* The understanding of and compassion for the taxpayer's situation and feelings.
>
> *Communications* The commitment to engage in clear and open communications, listen to taxpayers and stakeholders, understand their perspectives and issues, educate them about the tax system, and effect changes.
>
> *Improvement* The pursuit of opportunities to improve tax administration for the benefit of taxpayers.

.03   Themes Used in Planning

Within the framework of these guiding principles, TAS will use the following strategic themes to plan and accomplish their mission effectively:

> *Strategic Planning*—Refine TAS's strategic design to further associate the planning and spending processes of the office;

Implementing Advocacy—TAS functions work cohesively to identify and resolve individual and systemic issues;

Empower the Workforce—TAS's employees contribute to achieving its mission and have the necessary skills, knowledge, and tools to deliver results and serve as the voice of the taxpayer at the IRS;

Modernization—Timely, accurate, efficient, and consistent case processing and data collection information is accessible from a single source with common processes, methodologies, and data analytics; and

Process Improvement—TAS uses a standard approach in identifying and implementing process improvement initiatives.

¶44,006   Grants for Low Income Taxpayer Clinics

The Low Income Taxpayer Clinic (LITC) grant program is a federal program administered by the Office of the Taxpayer Advocate at the IRS. The LITC program awards matching grants of up to $100,000 per year to qualifying organizations to develop, expand, or maintain a low income taxpayer clinic. The LITC program funds organizations that serve individuals who have a tax controversy with the IRS, and whose income is below a certain level. Most LITCs can provide representation before the IRS or in court on audits, tax collection disputes, and other issues for free or for a small fee. If an individual's native language is not English, some clinics can provide multilingual information about taxpayer rights and responsibilities. Applicants may apply for either type of program, or both. Although LITCs receive partial funding from the IRS, LITCs, their employees, and their volunteers are independent from the IRS. Examples of qualifying organizations include:

- Clinical programs at accredited law, business or accounting schools whose students represent low income taxpayers in tax disputes with the IRS; and
- Organizations exempt from tax under IRC §501(a) that represent low-income taxpayers in tax disputes with the IRS or refer those taxpayers to qualified representatives.

Each clinic determines if prospective clients meet the income poverty guidelines and other criteria before it agrees to represent a client. Taxpayers who are experiencing economic harm or a systemic problem, or are seeking help in resolving tax problems that have not been resolved through normal channels, but do not qualify for assistance in the LITC program, may be eligible for Taxpayer Advocate Service (TAS) assistance.

Each year, on June 1st, the IRS announces the opening of the year's LITC grant application process. The grant cycle runs from January 1, through December 31. Applications must be electronically filed, postmarked, sent by private delivery service, or hand-delivered to the LITC Program Office in Washington, DC by July 15, of the year prior to the one for which they wish to be considered.

Periodically, the LITC program identifies targeted areas of need and is particularly interested in receiving applications from organizations in those areas.

¶44,007   IRS Seeks New Issues for the Industry Issue Resolution Program

The IRS encouraged business taxpayers, associations and other interested parties to submit tax issues for resolution involving a controversy, a dispute or a potentially unnecessary burden on business taxpayers to the Industry Issue Resolution (IIR) Program.

For each issue selected, an IIR team of IRS and Treasury personnel gather relevant facts from taxpayers or other interested parties affected by the issue. The goal is to recommend guidance to resolve the issue. This benefits both taxpayers and the IRS by saving time and expense that would otherwise be expended on resolving the issue through examinations.

IIR project selections are based on the criteria set forth in Rev. Proc. 2003-36. For each issue selected, a multi-functional team of IRS, Chief Counsel and Treasury personnel is assembled. The teams gather and analyze the relevant facts from industry groups and taxpayers for each issue and recommend guidance.

At any time, business associations and taxpayers may submit tax issues that they believe could be resolved through the IIR program. Submissions received are reviewed semi-annually. While issues may be submitted to *IIR@irs.gov* at any time for consideration in the IIR program, submissions should be received by August 31 for the summer screening of submissions.

The aim of the IIR program is to resolve business tax issues common to significant numbers of taxpayers through new and improved guidance. In past years, issues have been submitted by associations and others representing both small and large business taxpayers. The resulting tax guidance has affected thousands of taxpayers.

.01   Business Tax Issues Appropriate for IIR

The IIR program is available to all business taxpayers served by the Small Business and Self-Employed Division (SB/SE) and Large and Mid-Size Business Division (LMSB). Business tax issues appropriate for the IIR program must have at least two of these characteristics:

- The proper tax treatment of a common factual situation is uncertain.
- The uncertainty results in frequent, and often repetitive, examinations of the same issue. The uncertainty results in taxpayer burden.

- The issue is significant and impacts a large number of taxpayers, either within an industry or across industry lines.
- The issue requires extensive factual development.
- Learning about industry practices and views concerning the issue would assist the Service in determining the proper tax treatment.

.02   Issues Not Appropriate for IIR Treatment

The IIR Program is *not appropriate* for resolving the following types of business tax issues:

- Issues unique to one or a small number of taxpayers.
- Issues that are primarily under the jurisdiction of the Operating Divisions of the Service other than the LMSB and SB/SE Divisions.
- Issues that involve transactions that lack a bona fide business purpose, or transactions with a significant purpose of improperly reducing or avoiding federal taxes.
- Issues involving transfer pricing or international tax treaties.

.03   Recent Submissions Accepted and Guidance Issued

In December 2015, the IRS and Treasury accepted related requests for guidance from the Mortgage Bankers Association and the American Bankers Association into the Industry Issue Resolution (IIR) Program. The issue accepted for IIR was the proper reporting of interest under IRC §6050H. Interest included in payments that are made were accrued while unpaid interest has been treated for non-tax purposes as increasing the unpaid principal balance of a mortgage loan, i.e., following a significant medication of the loan.

Since its inception in 2000, the IIR program has resulted in resolution of many different tax issues cumulatively affecting thousands of taxpayers in many diverse lines of business.

Recent submissions for inclusion in the IIR program and examples of guidance issued as a result of the IIR Program include:

- Transmission and Distribution Network Assets in the Utilities (Unit of Property) Industry submitted by Edison Electric Institute.
- Power Generation Assets in the Utilities Industry (Unit of Property) also submitted by Edison Electric Institute.
- Tax Accounting Issues Important to Life Insurance Companies Issuing Variable Annuities submitted by two of the largest global accounting firms.
- Repair vs Capitalization in the Natural Gas Industry (Unit of Property) submitted by the American Gas Association and the Interstate Natural Gas

Association of America. Telecommunication Issues Included The Proper Treatment of Unit of Property For Network Assets, and the Appropriate Asset Class for Wireless Telecommunications Assets.

¶44,008   Declaration of Taxpayer Rights

The first part of this discussion explains some of a taxpayer's most important rights. The second part explains the examination, appeal, collection, and refund procedures.

I.   Protection of a Taxpayer's Rights. IRS employees will explain and protect a taxpayer's rights throughout his or her contact with the IRS.
II.   Privacy and Confidentiality. The IRS will not disclose to anyone the information given to the IRS, except as authorized by law.
III.   Professional and Courteous Service. If a taxpayer believes an IRS employee has not treated him or her in a professional, fair, and courteous manner, the employee's supervisor should be told. If the supervisor's response is not satisfactory, the taxpayer should write to the IRS District Director or Service Center Director.
IV.   Representation. A taxpayer can either represent himself or herself or, with proper written authorization, have someone else as a representative. The taxpayer's representative must be a person allowed to practice before the IRS, such as an attorney, certified public accountant, or enrolled agent.

   If a taxpayer is in an interview and asks to consult such a person, then the IRS must stop and reschedule the interview in most cases. Someone may accompany the taxpayer to an interview, and make recordings of any meetings with the IRS examining agent, appeal or collection personnel, provided the taxpayer tells the IRS in writing ten days before the meeting.
V.   Payment of Only the Correct Amount of Tax. Taxpayers are responsible for paying the correct amount of tax due under the law—no more, no less. If a responsible taxpayer cannot pay all of his or her tax when it is due, it may be possible to make monthly installment payments. Arrangements for payments are made with the IRS.
VI.   Help with Unresolved Tax Problems. The National Taxpayer Advocate's Problem Resolution Program can help a taxpayer who has tried unsuccessfully to resolve a problem with the IRS. A local Taxpayer Advocate can offer special help for a significant hardship as a result of a tax problem. The taxpayer may call toll-free or write to the Taxpayer Advocate at the IRS office that last contacted him or her.

VII. Appeals and Judicial Review. If a taxpayer disagrees with the IRS about the amount of a tax liability or certain collection actions, it is the taxpayer's right to ask the Appeals Office to review the case. The taxpayer also has the right to ask a court to review the case.

VIII. Relief from Certain Penalties and Interest. The IRS will waive penalties when allowed by law if a taxpayer can show he or she has acted reasonably and in good faith or relied on the incorrect advice of an IRS employee. The IRS will waive interest that is the result of certain errors or delays caused by an IRS employee.

PART VIII
Appendices

A few other topics of interest, that do not easily fit into other chapters, are added to Part VIII as appendices.

APPENDIX A

Financial Planning Tables

The following tables, involving the effects of interest factors, are useful in various forms of future business planning.

SIMPLE INTEREST TABLE

Example of use of this table:
  Find amount of $500 in 8 years at 6% simple interest.
  From table at 8 yrs. and 6% for $1   1.48
  Value in 8 yrs. for $500 (500 × 1.48) $740

Number of Years	Interest Rate							
	3%	4%	5%	6%	7%	8%	9%	10%
1	1.03	1.04	1.05	1.06	1.07	1.08	1.09	1.10
2	1.06	1.08	1.10	1.12	1.14	1.16	1.18	1.20
3	1.09	1.12	1.15	1.18	1.21	1.24	1.27	1.30
4	1.12	1.16	1.20	1.24	1.28	1.32	1.36	1.40
5	1.15	1.20	1.25	1.30	1.35	1.40	1.45	1.50
6	1.18	1.24	1.30	1.36	1.42	1.48	1.54	1.60
7	1.21	1.28	1.35	1.42	1.49	1.56	1.63	1.70
8	1.24	1.32	1.40	1.48	1.56	1.64	1.72	1.80
9	1.27	1.36	1.45	1.54	1.63	1.72	1.81	1.90
10	1.30	1.40	1.50	1.60	1.70	1.80	1.90	2.00
11	1.33	1.44	1.55	1.66	1.77	1.88	1.99	2.10
12	1.36	1.48	1.60	1.72	1.84	1.96	2.08	2.20
13	1.39	1.52	1.65	1.78	1.91	2.04	2.17	2.30
14	1.42	1.56	1.70	1.84	1.98	2.12	2.26	2.40
15	1.45	1.60	1.75	1.90	2.05	2.20	2.35	2.50
16	1.48	1.64	1.80	1.96	2.12	2.28	2.44	2.60
17	1.51	1.68	1.85	2.02	2.19	2.36	2.53	2.70
18	1.54	1.72	1.90	2.08	2.26	2.44	2.62	2.80
19	1.57	1.76	1.95	2.14	2.33	2.52	2.71	2.90
20	1.60	1.80	2.00	2.20	2.40	2.60	2.80	3.00
21	1.63	1.84	2.05	2.26	2.47	2.68	2.89	3.10
22	1.66	1.88	2.10	2.32	2.54	2.76	2.98	3.20
23	1.69	1.92	2.15	2.38	2.61	2.84	3.07	3.30
24	1.72	1.96	2.20	2.44	2.68	2.92	3.16	3.40
25	1.75	2.00	2.25	2.50	2.75	3.00	3.25	3.50
26	1.78	2.04	2.30	2.56	2.82	3.08	3.34	3.60
27	1.81	2.08	2.35	2.62	2.89	3.16	3.43	3.70
28	1.84	2.12	2.40	2.68	2.96	3.24	3.52	3.80
29	1.87	2.16	2.45	2.74	3.03	3.32	3.61	3.90
30	1.90	2.20	2.50	2.80	3.10	3.40	3.70	4.00
31	1.93	2.24	2.55	2.86	3.17	3.48	3.79	4.10
32	1.96	2.28	2.60	2.92	3.24	3.56	3.88	4.20
33	1.99	2.32	2.65	2.98	3.31	3.64	3.97	4.30
34	2.02	2.36	2.70	3.04	3.38	3.72	4.06	4.40
35	2.05	2.40	2.75	3.10	3.45	3.80	4.15	4.50
36	2.08	2.44	2.80	3.16	3.52	3.88	4.24	4.60
37	2.11	2.48	2.85	3.22	3.59	3.96	4.33	4.70
38	2.14	2.52	2.90	3.28	3.66	4.04	4.42	4.80
39	2.17	2.56	2.95	3.34	3.73	4.12	4.51	4.90
40	2.20	2.60	3.00	3.40	3.80	4.20	4.60	5.00

COMPOUND INTEREST TABLE

Example of use of this table:
Find amount of $1,000 now in bank will grow to in 14 years at 6% interest.
From table 14 years at 6%   2.2609
Value in 14 years of $1,000   2,260.9

Number of Years	Interest Rate							
	6%	6 1/2%	7%	7 1/2%	8%	8 1/2%	9%	9 1/2%
1	1.0600	1.0650	1.0700	1.0750	1.0800	1.0850	1.0900	1.0950
2	1.1236	1.1342	1.1449	1.1556	1.1664	1.1772	1.1881	1.1990
3	1.1910	1.2079	1.2250	1.2422	1.2597	1.2772	1.2950	1.3129
4	1.2624	1.2864	1.3107	1.3354	1.3604	1.3858	1.4115	1.4376
5	1.3332	1.3700	1.4025	1.4356	1.4693	1.5036	1.5386	1.5742
6	1.4135	1.4591	1.5007	1.5433	1.5868	1.6314	1.6771	1.7237
7	1.5030	1.5539	1.6057	1.6590	1.7138	1.7701	1.8230	1.8875
8	1.5938	1.6549	1.7181	1.7834	1.8509	1.9206	1.9925	2.0668
9	1.6894	1.7625	1.8384	1.9172	1.9990	2.0838	2.1718	2.2632
10	1.7908	1.8771	1.9671	2.0610	2.1589	2.2609	2.3673	2.4782
11	1.8982	1.9991	2.1048	2.2156	2.3316	2.4531	2.5804	2.7136
12	2.0121	2.1290	2.2521	2.3817	2.5181	2.6616	2.8126	2.9714
13	2.1329	2.2674	2.4098	2.5604	2.7196	2.8879	3.0658	3.2537
14	2.2609	2.4148	2.5785	2.7524	2.9371	3.1334	3.3417	3.5628
15	2.3965	2.5718	2.7590	2.9588	3.1721	3.3997	3.6424	3.9013
16	2.5403	2.7390	2.9521	3.1807	3.4259	3.6887	3.9703	4.2719
17	2.6927	2.9170	3.1588	3.4193	3.7000	4.0022	4.3276	4.6777
18	2.8543	3.1066	3.3799	3.6758	3.9960	4.3424	4.7171	5.1221
19	3.0255	3.3085	3.6165	3.9514	4.3157	4.7115	5.1416	5.6087
20	3.2075	3.5236	3.8696	4.2478	4.6609	5.1120	5.6044	6.1416
21	3.3995	3.7526	4.1405	4.5664	5.0338	5.5465	6.1088	6.7250
22	3.6035	3.9966	4.4304	4.9089	5.4365	6.0180	6.6586	7.3639
23	3.8197	4.2563	4.7405	5.2770	5.8714	6.5295	7.2578	8.0635
24	4.0489	4.5330	5.0723	5.6728	6.3411	7.0845	7.9110	8.8295
25	4.2918	4.8276	5.4274	6.0983	6.8484	7.6867	8.6230	9.6683
26	4.5493	5.1414	5.8073	6.5557	7.3963	8.3401	9.3991	10.5868
27	4.8223	5.4756	6.2138	7.0473	7.9880	9.0490	10.2450	11.5926
28	5.1116	5.8316	6.6488	7.5759	8.6271	9.8182	11.1671	12.6939
29	5.4183	6.2106	7.1142	8.1441	9.3172	10.6527	12.1721	13.8998
30	5.7434	6.6143	7.6122	8.7549	10.5582	11.5582	13.2676	15.2203
31	6.0881	7.0442	8.1451	9.4115	10.8676	12.5407	14.4617	16.6662
32	6.4533	7.5021	8.7152	10.1174	11.7370	13.6066	15.7633	18.2495
33	6.8408	7.9898	9.3253	10.8762	12.6760	14.7632	17.1820	19.9832
34	7.2510	8.5091	9.9781	11.6919	13.6901	16.0181	18.7284	21.8816
35	7.6860	9.0622	10.6765	12.5688	14.7853	17.3796	20.4139	23.9604
36	8.1479	9.6513	11.4239	13.5115	15.9681	18.8569	22.2512	26.2366
37	8.6360	10.2786	12.2236	14.5249	17.2456	20.4597	24.2538	28.7291
38	9.1542	10.9467	13.0792	15.6142	18.6252	22.1988	26.4366	31.4583
39	9.7035	11.6582	13.9948	16.7853	20.1152	24.0857	28.8159	34.4469
40	10.2857	12.4160	14.9744	18.0442	21.7245	26.1330	31.4094	37.7193

Appendix A

COMPOUND INTEREST TABLE (*Cont'd*)

Number of Years	6%	6 1/2%	7%	7 1/2%	8%	8 1/2%	9%	9 1/2%
1	1.1000	1.1100	1.1200	1.1300	1.1400	1.1500	1.1600	1.1700
2	1.2100	1.2321	1.2544	1.2769	1.2996	1.3225	1.3456	1.3689
3	1.3310	1.3576	1.4049	1.4428	1.4815	4.5208	1.5608	1.6016
4	1.4647	1.5180	1.5735	1.6304	1.6389	1.7490	1.8106	1.8738
5	1.6105	1.6350	1.7623	1.8424	1.9254	2.0113	2.1003	2.1924
6	1.7715	1.8704	1.9738	2.0819	2.1949	2.3130	2.4363	2.5651
7	1.9487	2.0761	2.2106	2.3526	2.5022	2.6600	2.8262	3.0012
8	2.1435	2.3045	2.4759	2.6584	2.8525	3.0590	3.2784	3.5114
9	2.3579	2.5580	2.7730	3.0040	3.2519	3.5178	3.8029	4.1084
10	2.5937	2.8394	3.1058	3.3945	3.7072	4.0455	4.4114	4.8068
11	2.8531	3.1517	3.4785	3.8358	4.2262	4.6523	5.1172	5.6239
12	3.1384	3.4984	3.8959	4.3345	4.8179	5.3502	5.9360	6.5800
13	3.4522	3.8832	4.3634	4.8980	5.4924	6.1527	6.8857	7.6986
14	3.7974	4.3104	4.8871	5.5347	6.2613	7.0757	7.9875	9.0074
15	4.1772	4.7845	5.4735	6.2542	7.1379	8.1370	9.2655	10.5387
16	4.5949	5.3108	6.1303	7.0673	8.1372	9.3576	10.7480	12.3303
17	5.0544	5.8950	6.8660	7.9860	9.2764	10.7612	12.4676	14.4264
18	5.5599	6.5435	7.6899	9.0242	10.5751	12.3754	14.4625	16.8789
19	6.1159	7.2633	8.6127	10.1974	12.0556	14.2317	16.7765	19.7483
20	6.7274	8.0623	9.6462	11.5230	13.7434	16.3665	19.4607	23.1055
21	7.4002	8.9491	10.8038	13.0210	15.6675	18.8215	22.5744	27.0335
22	8.1402	9.9335	12.1003	14.7138	17.8610	21.6447	26.1883	31.6292
23	8.9543	11.0262	13.5523	16.6266	20.3615	24.8914	30.3762	37.0062
24	9.8497	12.2391	15.1786	18.7880	23.2122	28.6251	35.2364	43.2972
25	10.8347	13.5854	17.0000	21.2305	26.4619	32.9189	40.8742	50.6578
26	11.9181	15.0793	19.0400	23.9905	30.1665	37.8567	47.4141	59.2696
27	13.1099	16.7386	21.3248	27.1092	34.3899	43.5353	55.0003	69.3454
28	14.4209	18.5799	23.8838	30.6334	39.2044	50.0656	63.8004	81.1342
29	15.8630	20.6236	26.7499	34.6158	44.6931	57.5754	74.0085	94.9270
30	17.4494	22.8922	29.9599	39.1158	50.9501	66.2117	85.8498	111.0646
31	19.1943	25.4104	33.5551	44.2009	58.0831	76.1435	99.5858	129.9456
32	21.1137	28.2055	37.5817	49.9470	66.2148	87.5650	115.5195	152.0363
33	23.2251	31.3082	42.0915	56.4402	75.4849	100.6998	134.0027	177.8825
34	25.5476	34.7521	47.1425	63.7774	86.0527	115.8048	155.4431	208.1226
35	28.1024	38.5748	52.7996	72.0685	98.1001	133.1755	180.3140	243.5034
36	30.9128	42.8180	59.1355	81.4374	111.8342	153.1518	209.1643	284.8990
37	34.0039	47.5280	66.2318	92.0242	127.4909	176.1246	242.6306	333.3319
38	37.4048	52.7561	74.1796	103.9874	145.3397	202.5433	281.4515	389.9983
39	41.1447	58.5593	83.0812	117.5057	165.6872	232.9248	326.4837	456.2980
40	45.2592	65.0008	93.0509	132.7815	188.8835	237.8635	378.7211	533.8687

COMPOUND INTEREST TABLE (*Cont'd*)

Number of Years	18%	19%	20%	21%	22%	23%	24%	25%
1	1.1800	1.1900	1.2000	1.2100	1.2200	1.2300	1.2400	1.2500
2	1.3924	1.4161	1.4400	1.4641	1.4884	1.5129	1.5376	1.5625
3	1.6430	1.6851	1.7280	1.7715	1.8158	1.8608	1.9066	1.9531
4	1.9387	2.0053	2.0736	2.1435	2.2153	2.2888	2.3642	2.4414
5	2.2877	2.3863	2.4883	2.5937	2.7027	2.8153	2.9316	3.0517
6	2.6995	2.8397	2.9859	3.1384	3.2973	3.4628	3.6352	3.8146
7	3.1854	3.3793	3.5831	3.7974	4.0227	4.2592	4.5076	4.7683
8	3.7588	4.0213	4.2998	4.5949	4.9077	5.2389	5.5895	5.9604
9	4.4354	4.7854	5.1597	5.5599	5.9874	6.4438	6.9309	7.4505
10	5.2338	5.6946	6.1917	6.7274	7.3046	7.9259	8.5944	9.3132
11	6.1759	6.7766	7.4300	8.1402	8.9116	9.7489	10.6570	11.6415
12	7.2875	8.0642	8.9161	9.8497	10.8722	11.9911	13.2147	14.5519
13	8.5993	9.5964	10.6993	11.9181	13.2641	14.7491	16.3863	18.1898
14	10.1472	11.4197	12.8391	14.4209	16.1822	18.1414	20.3190	22.7373
15	11.9737	13.5895	15.4070	17.4494	19.7422	22.3139	25.1956	28.4217
16	14.1290	16.1715	18.4884	21.1137	24.0855	27.4461	31.2425	35.5271
17	16.6722	19.2441	22.1861	25.5476	29.3844	33.7587	38.7408	44.4089
18	19.6732	22.9005	26.6233	30.9126	35.8489	41.5233	48.0385	55.5111
19	23.2144	27.2516	31.9479	37.4043	43.7357	51.0736	59.5678	69.3889
20	27.3930	32.4294	38.3375	45.2592	53.3576	62.8206	73.8641	86.7361
21	32.3237	38.5910	46.0051	54.7636	65.0963	77.2693	91.5915	108.4202
22	38.1420	45.8233	56.2061	66.2640	79.4175	95.0413	113.5735	135.5252
23	45.0076	54.6487	66.2473	80.1795	86.8893	116.9008	140.8311	169.4065
24	53.1090	65.0319	79.4968	97.0172	118.2050	143.7880	174.6306	211.7582
25	62.6686	77.3880	95.3962	117.3908	144.2101	176.8592	216.5419	264.6977
26	73.9488	92.0918	114.4754	142.0429	175.9363	217.5368	268.5120	330.8722
27	87.2597	109.5892	137.3705	171.8719	214.6423	267.5703	332.9549	413.5903
28	102.9665	130.4112	164.8446	207.9650	261.8636	329.1115	412.8641	516.9878
29	121.5005	155.1893	197.8135	251.6377	319.4736	404.8072	511.9515	646.2348
30	143.3708	184.6753	237.3763	304.4816	389.7578	497.9128	634.8199	807.7935
31	169.1773	219.7636	284.8515	368.4227	475.5046	612.4328	787.1767	1009.7419
32	199.6292	261.5187	341.8218	445.7915	580.1156	753.2923	976.0991	1262.1774
33	235.5625	311.2072	410.1862	539.4077	707.7410	926.5496	1210.3629	1577.7218
34	277.9638	370.3366	492.2235	652.6834	863.4441	1139.6560	1500.8500	1972.1522
35	327.9972	440.7006	590.6682	789.7469	1053.4018	1401.7769	1861.0540	2465.1903
36	387.0368	524.4337	708.8018	955.5938	1285.1502	1724.1855	2307.7069	3081.4879
37	456.7034	624.0761	850.5622	1156.2685	1567.8833	2120.7482	2861.5586	3851.8598
38	538.9100	742.5605	1020.6746	1399.0849	1912.8176	2608.5206	3548.3302	4814.8248
39	635.9138	883.7542	1224.8096	1692.8927	2333.6375	3208.4800	4399.9295	6018.5310
40	750.3783	1051.6675	1469.7715	2048.4002	2847.0377	3946.4304	5455.9126	7523.1638

PERIODIC DEPOSIT TABLE

Example of use of this table:
How much is $1,000 a year invested at 6% worth in 20 years?
At 6% for 20 years, the figure is   38.993
For $1,000 a year, the amount is $38,993

Number of Years	Interest Rate							
	6%	7%	8%	9%	10%	11%	12%	13%
1	1.060	1.070	1.080	1.090	1.100	1.110	1.120	1.130
2	2.183	2.215	2.246	2.278	2.310	2.342	2.374	2.407
3	3.375	3.440	3.506	3.573	3.641	3.710	3.779	3.850
4	4.637	4.751	4.867	4.985	5.105	5.228	5.353	5.480
5	5.975	6.153	6.336	6.523	6.716	6.913	7.115	7.323
6	7.394	7.654	7.923	8.200	8.487	8.783	9.089	9.405
7	8.897	9.260	9.637	10.028	10.436	10.859	11.300	11.757
8	10.491	10.978	11.488	12.021	12.579	13.164	13.776	14.416
9	12.181	12.816	13.487	14.193	14.937	15.722	16.549	17.420
10	13.972	14.784	15.645	16.560	17.531	18.561	19.655	20.814
11	15.870	16.888	17.977	19.141	20.384	21.713	23.133	24.650
12	17.882	19.141	20.495	21.953	23.523	25.212	27.029	28.985
13	20.015	21.550	23.215	25.019	26.975	29.095	31.393	33.883
14	22.276	24.129	26.152	28.361	30.772	33.405	36.280	39.417
15	24.673	26.888	29.324	32.003	34.950	38.190	41.753	45.672
16	27.213	29.840	32.750	35.974	39.545	43.501	47.884	52.739
17	29.906	32.999	36.450	40.301	44.599	49.396	54.750	60.725
18	32.760	36.379	40.446	45.018	50.159	55.939	62.440	69.749
19	34.786	39.995	44.762	50.160	56.275	63.203	71.052	79.947
20	38.993	43.865	49.423	55.765	63.002	71.265	80.699	91.470
21	42.392	48.006	54.457	61.873	70.403	80.214	91.503	104.491
22	45.996	52.436	59.893	68.532	78.543	90.148	103.603	119.205
23	49.816	57.177	65.765	75.790	87.497	101.174	117.155	135.831
24	53.865	62.249	72.106	83.701	97.347	113.413	132.334	154.620
25	58.156	67.676	78.954	92.324	108.182	126.999	149.334	175.850
26	62.706	73.484	86.351	101.723	120.100	142.079	168.374	199.841
27	67.528	79.698	94.339	111.968	133.210	158.817	189.699	226.950
28	72.640	86.347	102.966	123.135	147.631	177.397	213.583	257.583
29	78.058	93.461	112.283	135.308	163.494	198.021	240.333	292.199
30	83.802	101.073	122.346	148.575	180.943	220.913	270.293	331.315
31	89.890	109.218	133.214	163.037	200.138	246.324	303.848	375.516
32	96.343	117.933	144.951	178.800	221.252	274.529	341.429	424.463
33	103.184	127.252	157.627	195.982	244.477	305.837	383.517	481.903
34	110.435	137.237	171.317	214.711	270.024	340.590	430.663	545.681
35	118.121	147.913	186.102	235.125	298.127	379.164	483.463	617.749
36	126.268	159.337	202.070	257.376	329.039	421.982	542.599	699.187
37	134.904	171.561	219.316	281.630	363.043	469.511	608.831	791.211
38	144.058	184.640	237.941	308.066	400.448	522.267	683.010	895.198
39	153.762	198.635	258.057	336.882	441.593	580.826	766.091	1012.704
40	164.048	213.610	279.781	368.292	486.852	645.827	859.142	1145.486

Appendix A

COMPOUND DISCOUNT TABLE

This table shows the present or discounted value of $1 due at a given future time. For example, assume property which will revert to a lessor in 10 years will then be worth $1,000. The present value of this reversion, computed at an assumed rate of 4% on the investment, is found by finding the factor on the 10-year line in the 4% column. The factor .6756 is multiplied by 1000 to obtain the answer of $675.60.

Years	4%	4 1/2%	5%	5 1/2%	6%	6 1/2%	7%	7 1/2%	8%	9%	10%	11%
1	.9615	.9569	.9524	.9479	.9434	.9390	.9346	.9302	.9259	.9174	.9091	.9009
2	.9246	.9157	.9070	.8985	.8900	.8817	.8734	.8653	.8573	.8417	.8264	.8116
3	.8890	.8763	.8638	.8516	.8396	.8278	.8163	.8050	.7938	.7722	.7513	.7312
4	.8548	.8386	.8277	.8072	.7921	.7773	.7629	.7488	.7350	.7084	.6830	.6587
5	.8219	.8025	.7835	.7651	.7473	.7299	.7130	.6966	.6806	.6499	.6209	.5935
6	.7903	.7679	.7462	.7252	.7050	.6853	.6663	.6480	.6302	.5963	.5645	.5346
7	.7599	.7343	.7107	.6874	.6651	.6435	.6227	.6027	.5835	.5470	.5132	.4816
8	.7307	.7032	.6768	.6516	.6274	.6042	.5820	.5607	.5403	.5019	.4665	.4339
9	.7026	.6729	.6446	.6176	.5919	.5673	.5439	.5216	.5002	.4604	.4241	.3909
10	.6756	.6439	.6139	.5854	.5584	.5327	.5083	.4852	.4632	.4224	.3855	.3522
11	.6496	.6162	.5847	.5549	.5268	.5002	.4751	.4514	.4289	.3875	.3505	.3173
12	.6246	.5897	.5568	.5260	.4970	.4697	.4440	.4199	.3971	.3555	.3186	.2858
13	.6006	.5643	.5303	.4986	.4688	.4410	.4150	.3906	.3677	.3262	.2897	.2575
14	.5775	.5400	.5051	.4726	.4423	.4141	.3878	.3633	.3405	.2992	.2633	.2320
15	.5553	.5167	.4810	.4479	.4173	.3888	.3624	.3380	.3152	.2745	.2394	.2090
16	.5339	.4945	.4581	.4246	.3936	.3651	.3387	.3144	.2919	.2519	.2176	.1883
17	.5134	.4732	.4363	.4024	.3714	.3428	.3166	.2924	.2703	.2311	.1978	.1696
18	.4936	.4528	.4155	.3815	.3503	.3219	.2959	.2720	.2502	.2120	.1799	.1528
19	.4746	.4333	.3957	.3616	.3305	.3022	.2765	.2531	.2317	.1945	.1635	.1377
20	.4564	.4146	.3769	.3427	.3118	.2838	.2584	.2354	.2145	.1787	.1486	.1240
21	.4388	.3968	.3589	.3249	.2942	.2665	.2415	.2190	.1987	.1637	.1351	.1117
22	.4220	.3797	.3418	.3079	.2775	.2502	.2257	.2037	.1839	.1502	.1228	.1007
23	.4057	.3633	.3256	.2919	.2618	.2349	.2109	.1895	.1703	.1378	.1117	.0907
24	.3901	.3477	.3101	.2766	.2470	.2206	.1971	.1763	.1577	.1264	.1015	.0817
25	.3751	.3327	.2953	.2622	.2330	.2071	.1842	.1640	.1460	.1160	.0923	.0736
26	.3607	.3184	.2812	.2486	.2198	.1945	.1722	.1525	.1352	.1064	.0829	.0663
27	.3468	.3047	.2678	.2356	.2074	.1826	.1609	.1419	.1252	.0976	.0763	.0597
28	.3335	.2916	.2551	.2233	.1956	.1715	.1504	.1320	.1159	.0895	.0693	.0538

COMPOUND INTEREST TABLE (*Cont'd*)

Years	11%	10%	9%	8%	7 1/2%	7%	6 1/2%	6%	5 1/2%	5%	4 1/2%	4%
29	.0485	.0630	.0822	.1073	.1228	.1406	.1610	.1846	.2117	.2429	.2790	.3207
30	.0437	.0573	.0754	.0994	.1142	.1314	.1512	.1741	.2006	.2314	.2670	.3083
31	.0394	.0521	.0691	.0920	.1063	.1228	.1420	.1643	.1902	.2204	.2555	.2965
32	.0354	.0474	.0634	.0852	.0988	.1147	.1333	.1550	.1803	.2099	.2445	.2851
33	.0319	.0431	.0582	.0789	.0919	.1072	.1251	.1462	.1709	.1999	.2340	.2741
34	.0288	.0391	.0534	.0730	.0855	.1002	.1175	.1379	.1620	.1904	.2239	.2636
35	.0259	.0356	.0490	.0676	.0796	.0937	.1103	.1301	.1535	.1813	.2142	.2534
36	.0234	.0323	.0449	.0626	.0740	.0875	.1036	.1227	.1455	.1727	.2050	.2437
37	.0210	.0294	.0412	.0580	.0688	.0818	.0973	.1158	.1379	.1644	.1962	.2343
38	.0189	.0267	.0378	.0537	.0640	.0765	.0914	.1092	.1307	.1566	.1878	.2253
39	.0171	.0243	.0347	.0497	.0596	.0715	.0858	.1031	.1239	.1491	.1797	.2166
40	.0154	.0221	.0318	.0460	.0554	.0668	.0805	.0972	.1175	.1420	.1719	.2083
41	.0139	.0201	.0292	.0426	.0515	.0624	.0756	.0917	.1113	.1353	.1645	.2003
42	.0125	.0183	.0268	.0395	.0480	.0583	.0710	.0865	.1055	.1288	.1574	.1926
43	.0112	.0166	.0246	.0365	.0446	.0545	.0667	.0816	.1000	.1227	.1507	.1852
44	.0101	.0151	.0225	.0338	.0412	.0509	.0626	.0770	.0948	.1169	.1442	.1780
45	.0091	.0137	.0207	.0313	.0386	.0476	.0588	.0726	.0899	.1113	.1380	.1712
46	.0082	.0125	.0190	.0290	.0359	.0445	.0552	.0685	.0852	.1060	.1320	.1646
47	.0074	.0113	.0174	.0269	.0334	.0416	.0518	.0647	.0807	.1009	.1263	.1583
48	.0067	.0103	.0160	.0249	.0311	.0389	.0487	.0610	.0765	.0961	.1209	.1522
49	.0060	.0094	.0147	.0230	.0289	.0363	.0457	.0575	.0725	.0916	.1157	.1463
50	.0054	.0085	.0134	.0213	.0269	.0339	.0429	.0543	.0688	.0872	.1107	.1407
51	.00488	.0077	.0123	.0197	.0250	.0317	.0403	.0512	.0652	.0831	.1059	.1353
52	.00440	.0070	.0113	.0183	.0233	.0297	.0378	.0483	.0618	.0791	.1014	.1301
53	.00396	.0064	.0104	.0169	.0216	.0277	.0355	.0456	.0586	.0753	.0970	.1251
54	.00357	.0058	.0095	.0157	.0201	.0259	.0333	.0430	.0555	.0717	.0928	.1203
55	.00322	.0053	.0087	.0145	.0187	.0242	.0313	.0406	.0526	.0683	.0888	.1157
56	.00290	.0048	.0080	.0134	.0174	.0226	.0294	.0383	.0499	.0651	.0850	.1112
57	.00261	.044	.0073	.0124	.0162	.0211	.0276	.0361	.0473	.0620	.0814	.1069
58	.00235	.040	.0067	.0115	.0151	.0198	.0259	.0341	.0448	.0590	.0778	.1028
59	.00212	.0036	.0062	.0107	.0140	.0185	.0243	.0321	.0425	.0562	.0745	.0989
60	.00191	.0033	.0057	.0099	.0130	.0173	.0229	.0303	.0403	.0535	.0713	.0951

PRESENT WORTH TABLE—SINGLE FUTURE PAYMENT

Example of use of this table:
Find how much $10,000 payable in 12 years is worth now at an interest rate of 6%.
From table for 12 years 6%   .4970
Present value of $10,000 in 12 years $4,970

Number of Years	Interest Rate							
	6%	7%	8%	9%	10%	11%	12%	13%
1	.9434	.9346	.9259	.9174	.9091	.9009	.8929	.8850
2	.8900	.8734	.8573	.8417	.8264	.8116	.7972	.7831
3	.8396	.8163	.7938	.7722	.7513	.7312	.7118	.6931
4	.7921	.7629	.7350	.7084	.6830	.6587	.6355	.6133
5	.7473	.7130	.6806	.6499	.6209	.5935	.5674	.5428
6	.7050	.6663	.6302	.5963	.5645	.5346	.5066	.4803
7	.6651	.6227	.5835	.5470	.5132	.4816	.4523	.4251
8	.6274	.5820	.5403	.5019	.4665	.4339	.4039	.3762
9	.5919	.5439	.5002	.4604	.4241	.3909	.3606	.3329
10	.5584	.5083	.4632	.4224	.3855	.3522	.3220	.2946
11	.5268	.4751	.4289	.3875	.3505	.3173	.2875	.2607
12	.4970	.4440	.3971	.3555	.3186	.2858	.2567	.2307
13	.4688	.4150	.3677	.3262	.2897	.2575	.2292	.2042
14	.4423	.3878	.3405	.2992	.2633	.2320	.2046	.1807
15	.4173	.3624	.3152	.2745	.2394	.2090	.1827	.1599
16	.3936	.3387	.2919	.2519	.2176	.1883	.1631	.1415
17	.3714	.3166	.2703	.2311	.1978	.1696	.1456	.1252
18	.3503	.2959	.2502	.2120	.1799	.1528	.1300	.1108
19	.3305	.2765	.2317	.1945	.1635	.1377	.1161	.0981
20	.3118	.2584	.2145	.1784	.1486	.1240	.1037	.0868
21	.2942	.2415	.1987	.1637	.1351	.1117	.0926	.0768
22	.2775	.2257	.1839	.1502	.1228	.1007	.0826	.0680
23	.2618	.2109	.1703	.1378	.1117	.0907	.0738	.0601
24	.2470	.1971	.1577	.1264	.1015	.0817	.0660	.0532
25	.2330	.1842	.1460	.1160	.0923	.0736	.0588	.0471
26	.2198	.1722	.1352	.1064	.0829	.0663	.0525	.0417
27	.2074	.1609	.1252	.0976	.0763	.0597	.0470	.0369
28	.1956	.1504	.1159	.0895	.0693	.0538	.0420	.0326
29	.1846	.1406	.1073	.0822	.0630	.0485	.0374	.0289
30	.1741	.1314	.0994	.0754	.0573	.0437	.0334	.0256
31	.1643	.1228	.0920	.0691	.0521	.0394	.0298	.0226
32	.1550	.1147	.0852	.0634	.0474	.0354	.0266	.0200
33	.1462	.1072	.0789	.0582	.0431	.0319	.0238	.0177
34	.1379	.1002	.0730	.0534	.0391	.0288	.0212	.0157
35	.1301	.0937	.0676	.0490	.0356	.0259	.0189	.0139
36	.1227	.0875	.0626	.0449	.0323	.0234	.0169	.0123
37	.1158	.0818	.0580	.0412	.0294	.0210	.0151	.0109
38	.1092	.0765	.0536	.0378	.0267	.0189	.0135	.0096
39	.1031	.0715	.0497	.0347	.0243	.0171	.0120	.0085
40	.0972	.0668	.0460	.0318	.0221	.0154	.0107	.0075

Appendix A

PRESENT WORTH TABLE—PERIODIC FUTURE PAYMENT

Example of use of this table:
To find the cost now of $1,000 of income per year for 20 years at 7%.
From table for 20 years 7%   10.5940
Cost of $1,000 per year ($1,000 × 10.5940) $10,594

Number of Years	Interest Rate							
	6%	7%	8%	9%	10%	11%	12%	13%
1	0.9434	0.9346	0.9259	0.9174	0.9091	0.9009	0.8929	0.8850
2	1.8334	1.8080	1.7833	1.7591	1.7355	1.7125	1.6901	1.6681
3	2.6730	2.6243	2.5771	2.5313	2.4869	2.4437	2.4018	2.3612
4	3.4651	3.3872	3.3121	3.2397	3.1699	3.1024	3.0373	2.9745
5	4.2124	4.1002	3.9927	3.8897	3.7908	3.6959	3.6048	3.5172
6	4.9173	4.4665	4.6229	4.4859	4.3553	4.2305	4.1114	3.9975
7	5.5824	5.3893	5.2064	5.0330	4.8684	4.7122	4.5638	4.4226
8	6.2098	5.9713	5.7466	5.5348	5.3349	5.1461	4.9676	4.7988
9	6.8017	6.5152	6.2469	5.9952	5.7590	5.5370	5.3282	5.1317
10	7.3601	7.0236	6.7101	6.4177	6.1446	5.8892	5.6502	5.4262
11	7.8869	7.4987	7.1390	6.8052	6.4951	6.2065	5.9377	5.6869
12	8.3838	7.9427	7.4361	7.1607	6.8137	6.4924	6.1944	5.9176
13	8.8527	8.3577	7.9038	7.4869	7.1034	6.7499	6.4235	6.1218
14	9.2950	8.7455	8.2442	7.7862	7.3667	6.9819	6.6282	6.3025
15	9.7122	9.1079	8.5595	8.0607	7.6061	7.1909	6.8109	6.4624
16	10.1059	9.4466	8.8514	8.3126	7.8237	7.3792	6.9740	6.6039
17	10.4773	9.7632	9.1216	8.5436	8.0216	7.5488	7.1196	6.7291
18	10.8276	10.0591	9.3719	8.7556	8.2014	7.7016	7.2497	6.8399
19	11.1581	10.3356	9.6036	8.9501	8.3649	7.8393	7.3658	6.9380
20	11.4699	10.5940	9.8181	9.1285	8.5136	7.9633	7.4694	7.0248
21	11.7641	10.8355	10.0168	9.2922	8.6487	8.0751	7.5620	7.1016
22	12.0416	11.0612	10.2007	9.4424	8.7715	8.1757	7.6446	7.1695
23	12.3034	11.2722	10.3711	9.5802	8.8832	8.2664	7.7184	7.2297
24	12.5504	11.4693	10.5288	9.7066	8.9847	8.3481	7.7843	7.2829
25	12.7834	11.6536	10.6748	9.8226	9.0770	8.4217	7.8431	7.3299
26	13.0032	11.8258	10.8100	9.9290	9.1609	8.4881	7.8957	7.3717
27	13.2105	11.9867	10.9352	10.0266	9.2372	8.5478	7.9426	7.4086
28	13.4062	12.1371	11.0511	10.1161	9.3066	8.6016	7.9844	7.4412
29	13.5907	12.2777	11.1584	10.1983	9.3696	8.6501	8.0218	7.4701
30	13.7648	12.4090	11.2575	10.2737	9.4269	8.6938	8.0552	7.4957
31	13.9291	12.5318	11.3498	10.3428	9.4790	8.7331	8.0850	7.5183
32	14.0840	12.6466	11.4350	10.4062	9.5264	8.7686	8.1116	7.5383
33	14.2302	12.7538	11.5139	10.4644	9.5694	8.8005	8.1354	7.5560
34	14.3681	12.8540	11.5869	10.5178	9.6086	8.8293	8.1566	7.5717
35	14.4982	12.9477	11.6546	10.5668	9.6442	8.8552	8.1755	7.5856
36	14.6210	13.0352	11.7172	10.6118	9.6765	8.8786	8.1924	7.5979
37	14.7368	13.1170	11.7752	10.6530	9.7059	8.8996	8.2075	7.6087
38	14.8460	13.1935	11.8289	10.6908	9.7327	8.9186	8.2210	7.6183
39	14.9491	13.2649	11.8786	10.7255	9.7569	8.9357	8.2330	7.6268
40	15.0463	13.3317	11.9246	10.7574	9.7791	8.9511	8.2438	7.6344

APPENDIX B
Tax Terminology

A

accountant's report. When used regarding financial statements, a document in which an independent public or certified public accountant indicates the scope of the audit (or examination) which has been made and sets forth an opinion regarding the financial statements taken as a whole, or an assertion to the effect that an overall opinion cannot be expressed. When an overall opinion cannot be expressed, the reasons must be stated.

accounting method. A set of rules used to determine when and how income and expenses are reported. Examples are accrual, cash and hybrid.

adjusted issue price. The issue price increased by any amount of discount deducted before repurchase, or, in the case of convertible obligations, decreased by any amount of premium included in gross income before repurchase.

adverse party. Any person having a substantial beneficial interest in the trust which would be adversely affected by the exercise or nonexercise of the authority which he/she possesses regarding the trust.

affiliate. An affiliate of, or a person affiliated with, a specific person is one who directly or indirectly, through one or more intermediaries, controls, or is controlled by, or is under common control with, the person specified. (See person below)

affiliated group. One or more chains of includable corporations connected through stock ownership with a common parent corporation which is an includable corporation. (See includable corporation below). The ownership of stock of any corporation means the common parent possesses at least 80 percent of the total voting power of the stock of such corporation and has a value equal to at least 80 percent of the total value of the stock of that corporation.

agent. A person authorized by another, the principal, to act on behalf of the principal. An employee may be an agent of his or her employer.

alien. A foreigner is an alien who has filed his/her declaration of intention to become a citizen, but who has not yet been admitted to citizenship by a final order of a naturalization court.

allowed or allowable. When an business asset is sold or disposed of, its basis is computed (or recomputed) by recognizing the amount of depreciation allowed or allowable. Allowed refers to the amount of depreciation reported for the asset on the entity's tax return (whether correctly computed or not). Allowable refers to the amount of depreciation that should have been taken if the depreciation had been computed correctly. If the proper amount of depreciation is reported each year on the tax return, then the amount allowed will be the same as the amount allowable. If the two amounts are not the same, then the greater amount for each year is used in computing the basis of the asset disposed of.

amount. When used regarding securities, the principal amount if relating to evidences of indebtedness the number of shares if relating to shares, and the number of units if relating to any other kind of security.

amount loaned. The amount received by the borrower.

annual accounting period. The annual period, calendar year or fiscal year, on the basis of which the taxpayer regularly computes his/her income in keeping the books.

annual compensation. Includes an employee's average regular annual compensation, or such average compensation over the last five years, or such employee's last annual compensation if reasonably similar to his or her average regular annual compensation for the five preceding years.

annuity contract. A contract which may be payable in installments during the life of the annuitant only.

applicable installment obligation. Any obligation which arises from the disposition of personal property under the installment method by a person who regularly sells or otherwise disposes of personal property of the same type on the installment plan. The disposition of real property under the installment method which is held by the taxpayer for sale to customers in the ordinary course of the taxpayer's trade or business, or the disposition of real property under the installment method which is property used in the taxpayer's trade or business, or property held for the production of rental income, but only if the sale price of such property exceeds $150,000.

arm's length transaction. A transaction entered into by unrelated parties each acting for his or her own self interest.

assignment of income. Who is the taxpayer? You put money in a certificate of deposit at the bank. The certificate will come due and pay interest in a year. Three days before the interest is to be paid to you, you give the CD to your child who is in a lower tax bracket. You have attempted to assign your income to someone else and it won't fly. Similarly if you asked that your paycheck be made out to your child who is in a lower tax bracket.

associate. Indicates a relationship with any person, and means 1) any corporation or organization of which such person is an officer or partner or is directly or indirectly the beneficial owner of 10 percent or more of any class of equity securities, 2) any trust or other estate in which such person has a substantial beneficial interest or for which such person serves as trustee or in a similar fiduciary capacity, and 3) any relative or spouse of such person, or any relative of such spouse, who has the same home as such person or who is a director or officer of the registrant or any of its parents or subsidiaries.

B

balance. With respect to a reserve account or a guaranteed employment account, the amount standing to the credit of the account as of the computation date.

bank holding company. A person who is engaged, either directly or indirectly, primarily in the business of owning securities of one or more banks for the purpose, and with the effect, of exercising control. (See person below)

basis of obligation. The basis of an installment obligation is the excess of the face value of the obligation over an amount equal to the income which would be returnable were the obligation satisfied in full.

below-market loan. Any demand loan for which the interest is payable on the loan at a rate less than the applicable Federal rate, or in the case of a term loan (see term loan below) the amount loaned exceeds the present value of all payments due under the loan.

bond. Any bond, debenture, note, or certificate or other evidence of indebtedness, but does not include any obligation which constitutes stock in trade of the taxpayer or any such obligation of a kind which would properly be included in the inventory of the taxpayer if on hand at the close of the taxable year, or any obligation held by the taxpayer primarily for sale to customers in the ordinary course of trade or business.

brother-sister corporations. Two or more corporations owned by five or fewer individuals having at least a 50% common ownership. The result is a sharing of the tax brackets and other tax items.

C

C corporation. With respect to any taxable year, a corporation which is not an S corporation for such year.

calendar year. A period of 12 months ending on December 31. A tax-payer who has not established a fiscal year must make his/her tax return on the basis of a calendar year.

capital asset. Property held by a taxpayer, whether or not connected with a trade or business. The term does not include stock in trade of the taxpayer or other property of a kind which would properly be included in the inventory of the taxpayer if on hand at the close of the taxable year, or property held for sale to customers in the ordinary course of a trade or business.

capital expenditure. Any cost of a type that is properly chargeable to a capital account under general Federal income tax principles. Whether an expenditure is a capital expenditure is determined at the time the expenditure is paid with respect to the property. Future changes in law do not affect whether an expenditure is a capital expenditure. Capital expenditures do not include expenditures for items of current operating expense that are not properly chargeable to a capital account–so called working capital items.

capital gain. The excess of the gains from sales or exchanges of capital assets over the losses from sales or exchanges.

carrier. An express carrier, sleeping car carrier, or rail carrier providing transportation.

casualty loss. When a taxpayer suffers a loss to property resulting from an earthquake, tornado, hurricanes, volcanoes, fires, hail or other sudden and unexpected disaster, special tax rules may allow a deduction for loss of value.

charitable contribution. A contribution or gift to or for the use of a corporation, trust, community chest, fund, or foundation operated exclusively for religious, charitable, scientific, literary, or educational purposes, or to foster national or international amateur sports competition if no part of its activities involves the provision of athletic facilities or equipment. A contribution or gift is deductible only if it is used within the United States or any of its possessions.

charter. Articles of incorporation, declarations of trust, articles of association or partnership, or any similar instrument affecting, either with or without filing with any governmental agency, the organization or creation of an incorporated or unincorporated person (see person below).

child. Son, stepson, daughter, stepdaughter, adopted son, adopted daughter, or for taxable years after December 31, 1958, a child who is a member of an individual's household if the child was placed with the individual by an authorized placement agency for legal adoption pursuant to a formal application filed by the individual with the agency.

child care facility. Any tangible property which qualifies as a child care center primarily for children of employees of the employer, except that the term does not include any property not of a character subject to depreciation, or located outside the United States.

citizen. Every person born or naturalized in the United States and subject to its jurisdiction.

claim of right. In a dispute—if you have been paid but you might have to refund part of the money back, it is still income to you and the later repayment will be a deduction.

collapsible corporation. A corporation formed or availed of principally by the manufacture, construction, or production of property, for the purchase of property which is in the hands of the corporation, or for the holding of stock in a corporation so formed or availed of with a view to the sale or exchange of stock by its shareholders. The term includes distribution to its shareholders, before the realization by the corporation manufacturing, constructing, producing, or purchasing the property of 2/3 of the taxable income to be derived from such property, and by the realization by such shareholders of gain attributable to such property.

common equity. Any class of common stock or an equivalent interest including, but not limited to a unit of beneficial interest in a trust or a limited partnership interest.

common trust fund. A fund maintained by a bank exclusively for the collective investment and reinvestment of moneys contributed thereto by the bank in its capacity as a trustee, executor, administrator, or guardian, or as a custodian of accounts which the Secretary determines are established pursuant to a State law, and which bank has established that it has duties and responsibilities similar to the duties and responsibilities of a trustee or guardian.

company. Corporations, associations, and joint-stock companies.

complete liquidation. (See distribution below)

computation date. The date, occurring at least once each calendar year and within 27 weeks prior to the effective date of new rates of contributions, as of which such dates are computed.

conduit debt securities. Certain limited-obligation revenue bonds, certificates of participation, or similar debt instruments issued by a state or local governmental entity for the express purpose of providing financing for a specific third party (the conduit bond obligor) that is not a part of the state or local government's financial reporting entity. Although conduit debt securities bear the name of the governmental entity that issues them, the governmental entity often has no obligation for such debt beyond the resources provided by a lease or loan agreement with the third party on whose behalf the securities are issued. Further, the conduit bond obligor is responsible for any future financial reporting requirements.

constructive dividend. A dividend attributed to the owner of a corporation (usually as the result of an IRS audit) based on personal use by the shareholder of company assets without adequate compensation to the corporation. A constructive dividend may also arise from a non-arm's length transaction between the shareholder of a closely held corporation and the corporation.

constructive receipt. A doctrine applicable to cash basis tax payers requiring the inclusion in income of cash not actually received by the taxpayer, but for which there was no significant restriction on the taxpayer receiving the cash. An example would be declining the receipt of a payment due to the taxpayer for services performed and requesting the payment be remitted after the tax year-end.

constructive sale price. An article sold at retail, sold on consignment, or sold otherwise than through an arm's length transaction at less than the fair market price.

contributions. Payments required by a State law to be made into an unemployment fund by any person on account of having individuals in his/her employ, to the extent that such payments are made without being deducted or deductible from the remuneration of the employed individuals.

control. The ownership of stock possessing at least 80% of the total combined voting power of all classes of stock entitled to vote and at least 80% of the total number of shares of all other classes of stock of the corporation.

controlled foreign corporation. Any foreign corporation if more than 50%of the total combined voting power of all classes of stock of such corporation entitled to vote, or the total value of the stock of such corporation, is owned, directly or indirectly, by and for a foreign corporation, foreign partnership, foreign trust, or foreign estate shall be considered as being owned proportionately by its shareholders, partners, or beneficiaries.

controlled group of corporations. One or more chains of corporations connected through stock ownership with a common parent corporation if stock possessing at least 80% of the total combined voting power of all classes of stock entitled to vote or at least 80% of the total value of shares of all classes of stock of each of the corporations, and the common parent corporation is owned by one or more of the other corporations.

convertible obligation. An obligation which is convertible into the stock of the issuing corporation, or a corporation which, at the time the obligation is issued or repurchased, is in control of (see control above) or controlled by the issuing corporation.

cooperative bank. An institution without capital stock organized and operated for mutual purposes and without profit, which is subject by law to supervision and examination by State or Federal authority having supervision over such institutions.

cooperative housing corporation. A corporation having one and only one class of stock outstanding, each of the stockholders of which is entitled, solely by reason of ownership of stock in the corporation, to occupy for dwelling purposes a house, or an apartment in a building, owned or leased by the cooperative housing corporation. No stockholder of the housing corporation is entitled to receive any distribution that is not out of earnings and profits of the corporation except on a complete or partial liquidation of the corporation.

corporate acquisition indebtedness. Any obligation evidenced by a bond, debenture, note, or certificate or other evidence of indebtedness issued by a corporation to provide consideration for the acquisition of stock in another corporation; or the acquisition of the assets of another corporation in accordance with a plan under which at least two-thirds in value of all the assets (excluding money) is used in trades and businesses carried on by the corporation.

corporation. Includes associations, joint-stock companies, and insurance companies.

currency swap contract. A contract involving different currencies between two or more parties to exchange periodic interim payments on or prior to maturity of the contract. The swap principal amount is an amount of two different currencies which, under the terms of the currency swap contract, is used to determine the periodic interim payments in each currency and which is exchanged upon maturity of the contract.

D

date of original issue. The date on which the issue was first issued to the public, or the date on which the debt instrument was sold by the issuer. In the case of any debt instrument which is publicly offered, it is the date on which the debt instrument was issued in a sale or exchange.

debt instrument. A bond, debenture, note, or certificate or other evidence of indebtedness.

deficiency. The amount by which the tax imposed exceeds the sum of the amount shown as the tax by the taxpayer upon his/her return, if a return was made by the taxpayer and an amount indicated as the tax. Deficiency includes the amounts previously assessed or collected without assessment as a deficiency over the amount of rebates.

deficiency dividends. The amount of dividends paid by the corporation on or after the date of the determination (see determination below),before filing claims which would have been includable in the computation of the deduction for dividends paid for the taxable year with respect to which the liability for personal holding company tax exists, if distributed during such taxable year. No dividends are considered as deficiency dividends unless distributed within 90 days after the determination.

deficiency dividend deduction. No deduction is allowed unless the claim therefore is filed within 120 days after the determination.

demand loan. Any loan which is payable in full at any time on the demand of the lender.

dependent. Any of the following individuals over half of whose support for the calendar year in which the taxable year of the taxpayer begins was received from the taxpayer or treated as received from the taxpayer:

1. A son or daughter of the taxpayer, or a descendant of either.
2. A stepson or stepdaughter of the taxpayer.
3. A brother, sister, stepbrother, or stepsister of the taxpayer.
4. The father or mother of the taxpayer, or an ancestor of either.

5. A stepfather or stepmother of the taxpayer.

6. A son or daughter of a brother or sister of the taxpayer.

7. A brother or sister of the father or mother of the taxpayer.

8. A son-in-law, daughter-in-law, father-in-law, mother-in-law, brother-in-law, sister-in-law, of the taxpayer.

9. An individual, other than an individual who at any time during the taxable year was the spouse, who, for the taxable year of the taxpayer, has as his/her principal place of abode the home of the taxpayer and is a member of the taxpayer's household.

depositary share. A security, evidenced by an American Depositary Receipt, that represents a foreign security or a multiple of or fraction thereof deposited with a depositary.

determination. A decision by the Tax Court or a judgment, decree, or other order by any court of competent jurisdiction, which has become final.

development stage company. A company which is devoting substantially all its efforts to establishing a new business and either of the following conditions exists:

1. Planned principal operations have not commenced.

2. Planned principal operations have commenced, but there has been no significant revenue therefrom.

distiller. Any person who produces distilled spirits from any source or substance.

distribution. A distribution is treated as in complete liquidation of a corporation, if the distribution is one of a series of distributions in redemption of all of the stock of the corporation pursuant to a plan.

dividend. Any distribution of property made by a corporation to its shareholders out of earnings and profits of the taxable year, or from the most recently accumulated earnings and profits, computed at the close of the taxable year, without regard to the amount of earnings and profits at the time the distribution was made.

domestic. When applied to a corporation or partnership, created or organized in the United States or under the laws of the United States or of any State.

domestic building and loan association. A domestic building and loan association, a domestic savings and loan association, or a federal savings and loan association.

E

earned income. Wages, salaries, or professional fees, and other amounts received as compensation for personal services rendered by an individual to a corporation which represent a distribution of earnings or profits rather than a reasonable allowance as compensation for the personal services actually rendered. Earned income includes net earnings from self-employment to the extent such net earnings constitute compensation for personal services actually rendered.

earnings and profits (E & P). A calculation, for tax purposes, of the amount available for paying dividends. A corporation's earnings and profits is derived from its income adjusted for resources that were not taxable, but which are available for the payment of dividends and for expenses or deductions that did not expend resources. Earnings and profits are segregated between current earnings and profits and accumulated earnings and profits.

educational organization. An organization which normally maintains a regular faculty and curriculum and normally has regularly organized body of students in attendance at the place where its educational activities are carried on.

employee. Any officer of a corporation; any individual who, under the usual common law rules applicable to determining the employer-employee relation-ship, has the status of an employee; any individual who performs services for remuneration for any person as an agent-driver engaged in distributing products; a full-time life insurance salesperson; a home worker performing work; a traveling or city salesperson.

employee stock purchase plan. A plan which provides that options are to be granted only to employees of the employer corporation, or of its parent or subsidiary corporation, to purchase stock in any such corporation; and such plan is approved by the stockholders of the granting corporation within 12 months before or after the plan is adopted. Under the terms of the plan, no employee can be granted an option if the employee, immediately after the option is granted, owns stock amounting to 5%or more of the total combined voting power or value of all classes of stock of the employee corporation or of its parent or subsidiary corporation. Under the plan, options are to be granted to all employees of any corporation whose employees are granted any of such options by reason of their employment by such corporation, except employees who have been employed less than 2 years, or employees whose customary employment is 20 hours or less per week, or employees whose customary employment is for not more than 5 months in any calendar year.

employee versus independent contractor. Many tax issues depend on whether someone is self-employed (an independent contractor) or an employee. Among the issues are whether the employer is required to withhold and remit Social Security and federal and state income taxes. Also at issue are fringe benefits such as retirement coverage.

employer. With respect to any calendar year, any person who during any calendar quarter in the calendar year or the preceding calendar year, paid wages of $1500 or more, or on each of some 20 days during the calendar year or during the preceding calendar year (each day being in a different calendar week) employed at least one individual in employment for some portions of the day.

employment. Any service of whatever nature performed by an employee for the person employing him or her, irrespective of the citizenship or residence of either within the United States; or any service in connection with an American vessel or American aircraft under a contract of service which is entered into within the United States or during the performance of which and while the employee is employed on and in connection with such vessel or aircraft when outside the United States. The term also includes any service of whatever nature performed outside the United States by a citizen or resident of the United States as an employee of an American employer, or if it is service, regardless of where or by whom performed, which is designated as employment or recognized as equivalent to employment under an agreement entered into under the Social Security Act.

endowment contract. A contract with an insurance company which depends in part on the life expectancy of the insured, which may be payable in full during the insured's life.

energy property. Property that is described in at least one of 6 categories:
1. Alternative energy property.
2. Solar or wind energy property.
3. Specifically defined energy property.
4. Recycling equipment.
5. Shale oil Equipment.
6. Equipment for producing natural gas from geopressured grime.

Property is not energy property unless depreciation or amortization is allowable and the property has an estimated useful life of 3 years or more from the time when the property is placed in service.

enrolled actuary. A person who is enrolled by the Joint Board for the Enrollment of Actuaries.

enrolled agent. A tax professional, often a former IRS employee, who has passed an examination given by the IRS and is thereby qualified to represent taxpayers before the IRS on audit and collection matters.

equity security. Any stock or similar security, or any security convertible, with or without consideration, into such a security, or carrying any warrant or right to subscribe to or purchase such security, or any such warrant or right.

exchanged basis property. Property having a basis determined in whole or in part by reference to other property held at any time by the person for whom the basis is determined.

executor. The administrator of the decedent, or, if there is none appointed, qualified, and acting within the United States, then any person in actual or constructive possession of any property of the decedent.

F

farm. Includes stock, dairy, poultry, fruit and truck farms; also plantations, ranches, and all land used for farming operations.

farmer. All individuals, partnerships, or corporations that cultivate, operate, or manage farms for gain or profit, either as owners or tenants.

fiduciary. A guardian, trustee, executor, administrator, receiver, conservator, or any person acting in any fiduciary capacity for any person.

fifty-percent-owned person. A person approximately 50% of whose outstanding voting shares is owned by the specified person either directly or indirectly through one or more intermediaries (see person).

financial statements. Include all notes to the statements and all related schedules.

financial statements are available to be issued. Financial statements are considered available to be issued when they are complete in a form and format that complies with U.S. GAAP and all approvals necessary for issuance have been obtained, for example, from management, the board of directors, and/or significant shareholders. The process involved in creating and distributing the financial statements will vary depending on an entity's management and corporate governance structure as well as statutory and regulatory requirements.

fiscal year. An accounting period of 12 months ending on the last day of any month other than December; the 52–53 week annual accounting period, if such period has been elected by the taxpayer. A fiscal year is recognized only if it is established as the annual accounting period of the taxpayer and only if the books of the taxpayer are kept in accordance with such fiscal year.

foreign. A corporation or partnership which is not domestic or which is domestic but which is operating in a state different from the one in which it was formed.

foreign currency contract. A contract which requires delivery of, or settlement of, and depends on the value of, a foreign currency which is a currency in which positions are also traded through regulated futures contracts. The contract is traded in the interbank market, and is entered into at arm's length at a price determined by reference to the price in the interbank market.

foreign earned income. The amount received by any individual from sources within a foreign country or countries which constitutes earned income attributable to services performed by such individual. Amounts received are considered to be received in the taxable year in which the services to which the amounts are attributable are performed.

foreign estate (foreign trust). An estate or trust, as the case may be, the income of which comes from sources without the United States which are not materially connected with the conduct of a trade or business within the United States.

foreign insurer or reinsurer. One who is a non-resident alien individual, or a foreign partnership, or a foreign corporation. The term includes a non-resident alien individual, foreign partnership, or foreign corporation which will become bound by an obligation of the nature of an indemnity bond. The term does not include a foreign government, or municipal or other corporation exercising the taxing power.

foreign investment company. Any foreign corporation which is registered under the Investment Company Act of 1940, as amended, either as a management company or as a unit investment trust, or is engaged primarily in the business of investing, reinvesting, or trading in securities, commodities, or any interest in property, including a futures or forward contract or option.

FSC (foreign sales corporation). Any corporation which was created or organized under the laws of any foreign country, or under the laws applicable to any possession of the United States, has no more than 25 shareholders at any time during the taxable year, does not have any preferred stock outstanding at any time during the taxable year, and during the taxable year maintains an office located outside the United States in a foreign country, or in any possession of the United States. The term FSC does not include any corporation which was created or organized under the laws of any foreign country unless there is in effect between such country and the United States a bilateral or multilateral agreement, or an income tax treaty which contains an exchange of information program to which the FSC is subject.

foreign trading gross receipts. The gross receipts of any FSC which are from the sale, exchange, or other disposition of export property, from the lease or rental of export property for use by the lessee outside the United States, or for services which are related and subsidiary to any sale, exchange, lease, or rental of export property by such corporation.

forgiveness of debt. Having a loan or other debt forgiven or erased is the same as receiving income and paying off the debt. If someone loans you money and you are later not required to pay back the entire amount, the forgiven amount is income. Unless a specific tax provision makes the forgiven income non-taxable it must be reported as income.

foundation manager. With respect to any private foundation, an officer, director, or trustee of a foundation responsible for any act, or failure to act, and for the employees of the foundation having authority or responsibility, and for their failure to act.

G

general partner (see partner). The person or persons responsible under state law for directing the management of the business and affairs of a partnership that are subject of a roll-up transaction (see roll-up transaction) including, but not limited to, a general partner(s), board of directors, board of trustees, or other person(s) having a fiduciary duty to such partnership.

general power of appointment. The power which is exercisable in favor of the decedent, his/her estate, his/her creditors, or the creditors of the estate.

generation-skipping transfer. A taxable distribution, a taxable termination, and a direct skip. The term does not include any transfer to the extent the property transferred was subject to a prior tax imposed; and such transfers do not have the effect of avoiding tax.

gift. The lifetime transfer of something of value from one taxpayer to another with no strings attached, giving rise to a potential gift tax. An annual gift tax exclusion applies to gifts below the annual threshold (indexed for inflation) permitting gifts without incurring a gift tax.

gift loan. Any below-market loan where the forgoing of interest is in the nature of a gift (see below-market loan).

gross income. All income derived from whatever source; income realized in any form, whether in money, property, or services; income realized in the form of services, meals, accommodations, stock, or other property, as well as in cash. Gross income, however, is not limited to the items enumerated.

H

head of household. An individual is considered a head of household if, and only if, such individual is not married at the close of his/her taxable year, is not a surviving spouse, (see surviving spouse), maintains as his or her home a household that constitutes, for more than one-half of such taxable year, the principal place of abode of a dependent relative. However, an unmarried child, grandchild, stepchild, or adopted child need not be a dependent. In addition, if the taxpayer maintains a separate home for his or her parent or parents, head of household status may be claimed if at least one of the parents is a dependent.

holder. Any individual whose efforts created property held; any other individual who has acquired an interest in such property in exchange for consideration in money or money's worth paid to such creator of the invention covered by the patent, if such individual is neither the employer of the creator, nor related to the creator.

hot assets. Assets such as inventory and accounts receivable that normally produce ordinary income. In the context of a partnership distribution, for example, taxpayers may attempt to achieve beneficial capital gains treatment for the receipt of assets otherwise producing ordinary income.

housing expenses. The reasonable expenses paid or incurred during the taxable year by or on behalf of an individual for housing in a foreign country for the individual, spouse and dependants.

I

includable corporation. Any corporation except those exempt from taxation, foreign corporations, insurance companies subject to taxation, regulated investment companies, and real estate investment trusts subject to tax.

income recognition. Dividends are included in income on the ex-dividend date; interest is accrued on a daily basis. Dividends declared on short positions existing on the record date are recorded on the ex-dividend date and included as an expense of the period.

income tax return preparer. Any person who prepares for compensation, or who employs one or more persons to prepare for compensation, any return of tax or any claim for refund of tax. The preparation of a substantial portion of a return or claim for refund is treated as if it were the preparation of such return or claim for refund. A person is not an income tax return preparer merely because such person furnishes typing, reproducing, or other mechanical assistance, or prepares a return or claim for refund of the employer, or of an officer or employee of the employer, by whom the person is regularly and continuously employed.

Indian tribal government. A governing body of a tribe, band, pueblo, community, village, or a group of native American Indians, or Alaska Native.

individual retirement account. A trust created or organized in the United States for the exclusive benefit of an individual or his/her beneficiaries, but only if the written governing instrument creating the trust meets the following requirements:

1. The trustee is a bank, or such other person who demonstrates that the manner in which such other person will administer the trust will be consistent with the requirements of this section.
2. No part of the trust funds will be invested in life insurance contracts.
3. The interest of the individual in the balance of the account is nonforefeitable.
4. The assets of the trust will not be commingled with other property except in a common trust fund or common investment fund.

individual retirement annuity. An annuity contract, or an endowment contract issued by an insurance company which meets the following requirements:
1. The contract is not transferable by the owner.
2. Under the contract, the premiums are not fixed.
3. Any refund of premiums will be applied before the close of the calendar year following the year of the refund toward the payment of future premiums or the purchase of additional benefits.
4. The entire interest of the owner is nonforfeitable.

influencing legislation. Any attempt to have an effect on legislation by trying to impact the opinions of the general public or any segment thereof through communication with any member or employee of a legislative body, or with any government official or employee who may participate in the formulation of the legislation. It does not include any communication with a government official or employee other than one whose principal purpose is to affect legislation.

insurance company. A company whose primary and predominant business activity during the taxable year is the issuing of insurance or annuity contracts, or the reinsuring of risks underwritten by insurance companies. It is the character of the business actually done in the taxable year which determines whether a company is taxable as an insurance company. Insurance companies include both stock and mutual companies, as well as mutual benefit insurance companies. A voluntary unincorporated association of employees, including an association formed for the purpose of relieving sick and aged members, and the dependants of deceased members, is an insurance company.

installment sale. A sale where the proceeds will be received over two or more accounting periods. The amount of income to be reported each year is based on a computation of the gross profit percent from the original sale times the amount received each year to determine the amount of income to be reported. So the basis of what is sold is spread over the periods during which the payments are to be received.

interest. Return on any obligation issued in registered form, or of a type issued to the public, but does not include any obligation with a maturity (at issue) of not more than 1 year which is held by a corporation.

international organization. A public international organization entitled to the privileges, exemptions, and immunities as an international organization under the International Organizations Immunities Act.

investment in the contract. As of the annuity starting date, the aggregate amount of premiums or other consideration paid for the contract, minus the aggregate amount received under the contract before such date, to the extent that such amount was excludable from gross income under prior income tax laws.

itemized deductions. Those allowable other than the deductions allowable in arriving at adjusted gross income and the deduction for personal exemptions.

J

joint return. A single return made jointly by a husband and wife.

L

life insurance contract. An endowment contract which is not ordinarily payable in full during the life of the insured.

like-kind exchange. An exchange of assets under the rules of IRC §1031 wherein the basis of the respective assets exchanged is adjusted rather than currently recognizing income resulting from the transaction.

limited liability company (LLC). An entity created by state law for conducting business. Like a corporation an LLC provides legal protection to the owners (referred to as members) but like a partnership it provides flexibility in organization.

limited liability partnership (LLP). An entity created by state law for the operation of a professional organization (such as a group of doctors or accountants). It provides protection for is owners from the malpractice of other owners but not against an owner's own malpractice.

lobbying expenditures. Amounts spent for the purpose of influencing legislation (see Influencing Legislation).

long-term capital gain. A gain from the sale or exchange of a capital asset held for more than 1 year, if and to the extent such gain is taken into account in computing gross income.

long-term capital loss. A loss from the sale or exchange of a capital asset held for more than 1 year, if and to the extent that such loss is taken into account in computing taxable income.

long-term contract. A building, installation, construction or manufacturing contract (see manufacturing contract) which is not completed within the taxable year in which it is initiated.

lowest price. Determined without requiring that any given percentage of sales be made at that price, and without including any fixed amount to which the purchaser has a right as a result of contractual arrangements existing at the time of the sale.

M

majority-owned subsidiary company. A corporation, stock of which represents in the aggregate more than 50%of the total combined voting power of all classes of stock of such corporation entitled to vote, is owned wholly by a registered holding company, or partly by such registered holding company and partly by one or more majority-owned subsidiary companies, or by one or more majority-owned subsidiary companies of the registered holding company.

managing underwriter. An underwriter(s) who, by contract or otherwise, deals with the registrant, organizes the selling effort, receives some benefit, directly or indirectly, in which all other underwriters similarly situated do not share in proportion to their respective interests in the underwriting, or represents any other underwriters in such matters as maintaining the records of the distribution, arranging the allotments of securities offered, or arranging for appropriate stabilization activities, if any.

manufacturing contract. A long-term contract which involves the manufacture of unique items of a type which is not normally carried in the finished goods inventory of the taxpayer, or of items which normally require more than 12 calendar months to complete regardless of the duration of the actual contract.

material. Information required for those matters about which an average prudent investor ought reasonably to be informed.

mathematical or clerical error:

1. An error in addition, subtraction, multiplication, or division shown on any return.
2. An incorrect use of any table provided by the IRS with respect to any return, if such incorrect use is apparent from the existence of other information on the return.
3. An entry on a return of an item which is inconsistent with another entry of the same or another item on the return.
4. An omission of information which is required to be supplied to substantiate an entry on the return.
5. An entry on a return of a deduction or credit in amount which exceeds a statutory limit, if such limit is expressed as a specified monetary amount, or as a percentage, ratio, or fraction, and if the items entering into the application of such limit appear on the return.

member. The owner of a limited liability company.

municipal bond. Any obligation issued by a government or political subdivision thereof, if the interest on such obligation is excludable from gross income. It does not include such an obligation if it is sold or otherwise disposed of by the taxpayer within 30 days after the date of its acquisition.

N

net capital gain. The excess of the net long-term capital gain for the taxable year over the net short-term capital loss for that year.

net capital loss. For corporations, the excess of the losses from sales or exchanges of capital assets only to the extent of gains from such sales or exchanges. For taxpayers other than a corporation, losses from sales or exchanges of capital assets are allowable only to the extent of the gains from such sales or exchanges, plus the lower of $3,000 ($1,500 in the case of a married individual filing a separate return), or the excess of such losses over such gains.

net earnings from self-employment. The gross income derived by an individual from any trade or business carried on by such individual, less the deductions allowed which are attributable to such trade or business.

net long-term capital gain. The excess of long-term capital gains for the taxable year over the long-term capital losses for such year.

net long-term capital loss. The excess of long-term capital losses for the taxable year over the long-term capital gains for such year.

net operating loss. The excess of the deductions allowed over the gross income. In the case of a taxpayer other than a corporation, the amount deductible on account of losses from sales or exchanges of capital assets cannot exceed the amount includable on account of gains from sales or exchanges of capital assets.

net short-term capital gain. The excess of short-term capital gains for the taxable year over the short-term capital losses for such year.

net short-term capital loss. The excess of short-term capital losses for the taxable year over the short-term capital gains for such year.

nonadverse party. Any person who is not an adverse party (see adverse party, above).

nongovernmental entity. An entity that is not required to issue financial reports in accordance with guidance promulgated by the Governmental Accounting Standards Board or the Federal Accounting Standards Advisory Board.

nonpublic entity. Any entity that does not meet any of the following conditions:
   a. Its debt or equity securities trade in a public market either on a stock exchange (domestic or foreign) or in an over-the-counter market, including securities quoted only locally or regionally.
   b. It is a conduit bond obligor for conduit debt securities that are traded in a public market (a domestic or foreign stock exchange or an over-the-counter market, including local or regional markets).

   c.   It files with a regulatory agency in preparation for the sale of any class of debt or equity securities in a public market.

   d.   It is required to file or furnish financial statements with the Securities and Exchange Commission.

   e.   It is controlled by an entity covered by criteria (a) through (d).

not-for-profit entity. An entity that possesses the following characteristics, in varying degrees, that distinguish it from a business entity:

   a.   Contributions of significant amounts of resources from resource providers who do not expect commensurate or proportionate pecuniary return.

   b.   Operating purposes other than to provide goods or services at a profit.

   c.   Absence of ownership interests like those of business entities.

Entities that clearly fall outside this definition include the following:

   a.   All investor-owned entities.

   b.   Entities that provide dividends, lower costs, or other economic benefits directly and proportionately to their owners, members, or participants, such as mutual insurance entities, credit unions, farm and rural electric cooperatives, and employee benefit plans.

nonrecognition transaction. Any disposition of property in a transaction in which gain or loss is not recognized in whole or in part.

notional principal contract. A contract that provides for the payment of amounts by one party to another at specified intervals calculated by reference to a specified index upon a notional principal amount in exchange for a specified consideration or a promise to pay similar amounts.

O

obligation. Any bond, debenture, note, certificate, or other evidence of indebtedness.

operating foundation. Any private foundation which makes distributions directly for the conduct of the activities constituting the purpose or function for which the foundation is organized and operated, equal to substantially all of the lesser of its adjusted net income, or its minimum investment return.

option. The right or privilege of an individual to purchase stock from a corporation by virtue of an offer of the corporation continuing for a stated period of time, whether or not irrevocable, to sell such stock at a price determined under an option price, or price paid under the option. Option Price means the consideration in money or property which, pursuant to the terms of the option, is the price at which the stock subject to the option is purchased. The individual owning the option is under no obligation to purchase, and the right or privilege must be evidenced in writing. While no particular form of words is necessary, the written option should express, among other things, an offer to sell at the option price and the period of time during which the offer will remain open. The individual who has the right or privilege is the optionee and the corporation offering to sell stock under such an arrangement is referred to as the optionor.

organizational expenditures. Any expenditure which is incident to the creation of a corporation, chargeable to capital accounts, and is of a character which, if expended incident to the creation of a corporation having a limited life, would be amortizable over such life.

overpayment. Any payment of an Internal Revenue tax which is assessed or collected after the expiration of the period of limitation properly applicable thereto.

owner-employee. An owner of a proprietorship, or, in the case of a partnership, a partner who owns either more than 10% of the capital interest, or more than 10% of the profits interest, of the partnership.

P

paid or incurred (paid or accrued). Defined according to the method of accounting upon the basis of which the taxable income is computed. Paid refers to cash basis while incurred applies to accrual basis.

parent. Of a specified person, (see person) is an affiliate controlling such person directly, or indirectly, through one or more intermediaries.

parent corporation. Any corporation, other than the employer corporation, in an unbroken chain of corporations ending with the employer corporation if each of the corporations other than the employer corporation owns stock possessing 50% or more of the total combined voting power of all classes of stock in one of the other corporations in the chain.

partially pooled account. A part of an unemployment fund in which all contributions thereto are mingled and undivided. Compensation from this part is payable only to individuals to whom compensation would be payable from a reserve account or from a guaranteed employment account but for the exhaustion or termination of such reserve account or of a guaranteed employment account. (See pooled fund.)

partner. An owner member of a partnership.

partner's interest, liquidation thereof. The termination of a partner's entire interest in a partnership by means of a distribution, or a series of distributions, to the partner by the partnership. A series of distributions means distributions whether they are made in one year or in more than one year. Where a partner's interest is to be liquidated by a series of distributions, the interest will not be considered as liquidated until the final distribution has been made. One which is not in liquidation of a partner's entire interest is a current distribution. Current distributions, therefore, include those in partial liquidation of a partner's interest, and those of the partner's distributive share.

partnership. A syndicate, pool, group, joint venture or other unincorporated organization through or by means of which any business, financial operation, or venture is carried on, and is not a corporation, trust, or estate.

partnership agreement. Includes the original agreement and any modifications thereof agreed to by all the partners or adopted in any other manner provided by the partnership agreement. The agreements or modifications can be oral or written.

payroll period. A time frame for which a payment of wages is ordinarily made to the employee by the employer. The term miscellaneous payroll period means one other than a daily, weekly, biweekly, semimonthly, monthly, quarterly, semiannual, or annual period.

pension plan contracts. Any contract entered into with trusts which at the time the contracts were entered into were deemed to be trusts and exempt from tax. Includes contracts entered into with trusts which were individual retirement accounts, or under contracts entered into with individual retirement annuities.

person. Includes an individual, a trust, estate, partnership, association, company, or corporation, an officer or employee of a corporation or a member or employee of a partnership, who is under a duty to surrender the property or rights to property to discharge the obligation. The term also includes an officer or employee of the United States, of the District of Columbia, or of any agency or instrumentality who is under a duty to discharge the obligation.

personal holding company. Any corporation if at least 60% of its adjusted ordinary gross income for the taxable year is personal holding company income, and at any time during the last half of the taxable year more than 50% in value of its outstanding stock is owned, directly or indirectly, by or for not more than 5 individuals. To meet the gross income requirement, it is necessary that at least 80% of the total gross income of the corporation for the taxable year be personal holding company income (see personal holding company income).

personal holding company income. The portion of the adjusted ordinary gross income which consists of dividends, interest, royalties (other than mineral, oil, or gas royalties or copyright royalties), and annuities.

political organization. A party, committee, association, fund, or other organization, whether or not incorporated, organized and operated primarily for the purpose of directly or indirectly accepting contributions or making expenditures for an exempt function activity. A political organization can be a committee or other group which accepts contributions or makes expenditures for the purpose of promoting the nomination of an individual for an elective public office in a primary election, or in a meeting or caucus of a political party:

1. exempt function activity. Includes all activities that are directly related to and support the process of influencing or attempting to influence the selection, nomination, election, or appointment of any individual to public office, or office in a political organization.

2. segregated fund. A fund which is established and maintained by a political organization or an individual separate from the assets of the organization or the personal assets of the individual. The amounts in the fund must be for use only for an exempt function, or for an activity necessary to fulfill an exempt function. A segregated fund established and maintained by an individual may qualify as a political organization.

pooled fund. An unemployment fund or any part thereof other than a reserve account (see reserve account) or a guaranteed employment account, into which the total contributions of persons contributing thereto are payable, in which all contributions are mingled and undivided, and from which compensation is payable to all eligible individuals.

predecessor. A person from whom another person acquired the major portion of the business and assets in a single succession, or in a series of related successions. In each of these successions the acquiring person received the major portion of the business and assets of the acquired.

previously filed or reported. Previously filed with, or reported in, a definitive proxy statement or information statement, or in a registration statement under the Securities Act of 1933.

principal holder of equity securities. Used regarding a registrant or other person named in a particular statement or report, a holder of record or a known beneficial owner of more than 10 percent of any class of equity securities of the registrant or other person, respectively, as of the date of the related balance sheet filed.

principal underwriter. An underwriter in privity of contract with the issuer of the securities as to which he or she is underwriter.

promoter. Any person who, acting alone or in conjunction with others, directly or indirectly, takes initiative in founding and organizing the business or enterprise of an issuer. Any person who in so doing received in consideration of services or property, or both services and property, 10 percent or more of any class of securities of the issuer or 10 percent or more of the proceeds from the sale of any class of securities. However, a person who receives such securities or proceeds with or solely as underwriting commissions or solely in consideration of property will not be deemed a promoter within the meaning of this paragraph if such person does not otherwise take part in founding and organizing the enterprise.

property used in the trade or business. That property used in a trade or business of a character which is subject to an allowance for depreciation, held for more than 1 year, and real property used in a trade or business, held for more than 1 year, and which is not a copyright, a literary work, musical, artistic composition, or similar property. Also not included in the definition is property of a kind which would properly be includable in the inventory of the taxpayer if on hand at the close of the taxable year, nor property held by the taxpayer primarily for sale to customers in the ordinary course of the trade or business.

public business entity. A public business entity is a business entity meeting any one of the criteria below. Neither a not-for-profit entity nor an employee benefit plan is a business entity.

    a.   It is required by the U.S. Securities and Exchange Commission (SEC) to file or furnish financial statements, or does file or furnish financial statements (including voluntary filers), with the SEC (including other entities whose financial statements or financial information is required to be or are included in a filing).

    b.   It is required by the Securities Exchange Act of 1934 (the Act), as amended, or rules or regulations promulgated under the Act, to file or furnish financial statements with a regulatory agency other than the SEC.

    c.   It is required to file or furnish financial statements with a foreign or domestic regulatory agency in preparation for the sale of or for purposes of issuing securities that are not subject to contractual restrictions on transfer.

    d.   It has issued, or is a conduit bond obligor for, securities that are traded, listed, or quoted on an exchange or an over-the-counter market.

    e.   It has one or more securities that are not subject to contractual restrictions on transfer, and it is required by law, contract, or regulation to prepare U.S. GAAP financial statements (including notes) and make them publicly available on a periodic basis (for example, interim or annual periods). An entity must meet both of these conditions to meet this criterion.

An entity may meet the definition of a public business entity solely because its financial statements or financial information is included in another entity's filing with the SEC. In that case, the entity is only a public business entity for purposes of the financial statements that are filed or furnished with the SEC.

Q

qualified assets. The nature of any investments and other assets maintained, or required to be maintained, by applicable legal instruments in respect of outstanding face-amount certificates. If the nature of the qualifying assets and amount thereof is not subject to the provisions of the Investment Company Act of 1940, a statement to that effect should be made.

qualified individual. An individual whose tax home is in a foreign country and who is a citizen of the United States and establishes that he/she has been a bona fide resident of a foreign country (or countries) for an uninterrupted period which includes an entire taxable year, or a citizen or resident of the United States and who, during any period of 12 consecutive months, is present in a foreign country (or countries) during at least 330 full days in such period.

qualified pension, profit-sharing, stock bonus plans and annuity plans. Compensation is paid under a deferred payment plan, and bond purchase plan. The plan is a definite written program and arrangement which is communicated to the employees and which is established and maintained by an employer.

In the case of a pension plan, to provide for the livelihood of the employees or their beneficiaries after the retirement of such employees through the benefits determined without regard to profits.

In the case of a profit-sharing plan, to enable employees or their beneficiaries to participate in the profits of the employer's trade or business, or in the profits of an affiliated employer who is entitled to deduct any contributions to the plan pursuant to a definite formula for allocating the contributions and for distributing the funds accumulated under the plan.

In the case of a stock bonus plan, to provide employees or their beneficiaries benefits similar to those of profit-sharing plans, except that such benefits are distributable in stock of the employer, and that the contributions by the employer are not necessarily dependent upon profits.

R

real estate investment trust (REIT). A corporation, trust, or association which meets the following conditions:

1. Is managed by one or more trustees or directors. A trustee means a person who holds legal title to the property of the real estate investment trust, and has such rights and powers as will meet the requirement of centralization of management. The trustee must have continuing exclusive authority over the management of the trust, the conduct of its affairs, and the disposition of the trust property.

2. Has beneficial ownership which is evidenced by transferable shares or by transferable certificates of beneficial interest and must be held by more than 100 persons determined without reference to any rules of attribution.

3. In case of a taxable year beginning before October 5, 1976, does not hold any property, other than foreclosure property, primarily for sale to customers in the ordinary course of its trade or business.

4. Is neither a financial institution, nor an insurance company.

5. Beneficial ownership of the REIT is held by 100 or more persons.

6. The REIT would not be a personal holding company if all of its gross income constituted personal holding company income.

realized versus recognized. Income or a loss is realized when a transaction takes place. But not all income is taxable, so only taxable income is also recognized (reported to the IRS). Likewise not all losses are deductible, for example, losses on the sale of personal use personal property are not deductible. In this case a loss can be realized in a transaction (you sell your car) but not recognized (you don't report it to the IRS).

recomputed basis. With respect to any property, its adjusted basis recomputed by adding to it all adjustments reflected on account of deductions allowed or allowable to the taxpayer or to any other person for depreciation or amortization.

recovery. Regarding the recovery of tax benefit items, gross income does not include income attributable to the recovery during the taxable year of any amount deducted in any prior taxable year to the extent such amount did not reduce the amount of tax imposed.

recovery exclusion. Regarding a bad debt, prior tax, or delinquency amount, it is the amount determined in accordance with regulations of the deductions or credits allowed, on account of such bad debt, prior tax, or delinquency amount, which did not result in a reduction of the taxpayer's tax under corresponding provisions of prior income tax laws.

registrant. The issuers of the securities for which an application, a registration statement, or a report is filed.

related parties. All affiliates of an enterprise, including its management and their immediate families, its principal owners and their immediate families, its investments accounted for by the equity method, beneficial employee trusts that are managed by the management of the enterprise, and any party that may, or does, deal with the enterprise and has ownership of, control over, or can significantly influence the management or operating policies of another party, to the extent that an arm's-length transaction may not be achieved.

reorganization, a party to. Includes a corporation resulting from a reorganization, and both corporations in a transaction qualifying as a reorganization where one corporation acquires stock or properties of another corporation. A corporation remains a party to the reorganization although it transfers all or part of the assets acquired as a controlled subsidiary. A corporation controlling an acquiring corporation is a party to the reorganization when the stock of the controlling corporation is used in the acquisition of properties.

repurchase premium. The excess of the repurchase price paid or incurred to repurchase the obligation over its adjusted issue price (see adjusted issue price).

restricted securities. Investment securities which cannot be offered for public sale without first being registered under the Securities Act of 1933.

return. Any return, statement, schedule, or list, and any supplement thereto, filed with respect to any tax imposed by the law.

return of capital. You sell a car that cost $4000 for $4500. The first $4,000 is return of your original investment (capital) and is not taxed – only the $500 additional would be taxable. You always get to recover your investment before you have to start paying tax on a transaction.

roll-up transaction. Any transaction or series of transactions that, directly or indirectly, through acquisition or otherwise, involve the combination or reorganization of one or more partnerships and the offer or sale of securities by a successor entity, whether newly formed or previously existing, to one or more limited partners of the partnerships to be combined or reorganized.

rules and regulations. All needful rules and regulations approved by the Commissioner for the enforcement of the Code. Includes all rules and regulations necessary by reason of the alterations of the law in relation to Internal Revenue.

S

S corporation. Regarding any taxable year, a small business corporation for which an election is in effect for such year (see small business corporation).

section 1245 property. Any property, other than livestock, which is or has been property of a character subject to an allowance for depreciation or subject to an allowance for amortization and is personal property, or other property if such property is tangible, but not including a building or its structural components.

section 1250 property. Any real property, other than Section 1245 property, which is or has been property of a character subject to an allowance for depreciation.

security. A share, participation, or other interest in property or in an entity of the issuer or an obligation of the issuer that has all of the following characteristics:

a. It is either represented by an instrument issued in bearer or registered form or, if not represented by an instrument, is registered in books maintained to record transfers by or on behalf of the issuer.

b. It is of a type commonly dealt in on securities exchanges or markets or, when represented by an instrument, is commonly recognized in any area in which it is issued or dealt in as a medium for investment.

c. It either is one of a class or series or by its terms is divisible into a class or series of shares, participations, interests, or obligations.

self-employment income. The net earnings from self-employment derived by an individual during any taxable year, except if such net earnings for the taxable year are less than $400.

sham transaction. A transaction done only to save taxes with no business purpose.

share. A unit of stock in a corporation, or unit of interest in an unincorporated person. short-term capital gain A gain from the sale or exchange of a capital asset held for not more than 1 year, if and to the extent such gain is taken into account in computing gross income.

short-term capital loss. A loss from the sale or exchange of a capital asset held for not more than 1 year, if and to the extent that such loss is taken into account in computing gross income.

short tax year. A tax year of less than twelve months either in the first or last year of a corporation's operation (or other tax entity) or resulting from a change in year-end.

significant subsidiary. A subsidiary, including its subsidiaries, which meets any of the following conditions:

1. The registrant's and its other subsidiaries' investments in and advances to the subsidiary exceed 10 percent of the total assets of the registrant and its subsidiaries consolidated as of the end of the most recently completed fiscal year for a proposed business combination to be accounted for as a pooling-of-interests. This condition is also met when the number of common shares exchanged by the registrant exceeds 10 percent of its total common shares outstanding at the date the combination is initiated.

2. The registrant's and its other subsidiaries' proportionate share of the total assets, after intercompany, eliminations, of the subsidiary exceeds 10 percent of the total assets of the registrant and its subsidiaries consolidated as of the end of the most recently completed fiscal year.

3. The registrant's and its other subsidiaries' equity in the income from continuing operations before income taxes, extraordinary items and cumulative effect of a change in accounting principle of the subsidiary exceeds 10 percent of such income of the registrant and its subsidiaries consolidated for the most recently completed fiscal year.

small business corporation. A domestic corporation which is not an ineligible corporation, e.g., a member of an affiliated group, and which does not have more than 75 shareholders, does not have as a shareholder a person, other than an estate or trust, who is not an individual, and does not have a non-resident alien as a shareholder.

standard deduction. The sum of the basic standard deduction and the additional standard deduction.

step transaction. You want to buy a car for cash in the amount of $36,000. The dealer informs you that he will have to report the receipt of that much cash to the IRS (payments of $10,000 or more in cash must be reported). So you decide to buy the car by giving the dealer $9,000 down, then the next day an additional $9,000 and so on until the car is paid for. The step transaction doctrine requires the dealer to collapse these individual transactions into one $36,000 transaction.

straight debt. Any written unconditional promise to pay on demand or on a specified date a sum certain in money if the interest rate and interest payment dates are not contingent on profits or the borrower's discretion, not convertible into stock, and the creditor is an individual, an estate, or a trust.

substance over form. The owner of a small business (corporation) writes himself a check and calls it a loan (so it will not be taxable income to him) – but there is no note, no interest rate, no collateral, no time when due – it is really a dividend and he must pay tax. The form of a transaction is how it is characterized or outwardly structured. The form of a transaction might be a sale because the parties filled out a form that says Bill of Sale. The substance of a transaction is what is actually occurring and may be different from the form. What is structured like a sale might actually be a bribe or a gift or a dividend, depending on the specific circumstances. The idea is that the IRS can "look behind" a transaction to see what its real nature or affect is.

subsidiary corporation. (see parent corporation.)

substituted basis property. Property which is transferred basis property, or exchanged basis property.

summarized financial information. The presentation of summarized information as to the assets, liabilities and results of operations of the entity for which the information is required.

support. Includes food, shelter, clothing, medical and dental care, education, etc. The amount of an item of support will be the amount of expense incurred by the one furnishing such item. If the item of support furnished an individual is in the form of property or lodging, it is necessary to measure the amount of such item of support in terms of its fair market value.

surviving spouse. A taxpayer whose spouse died during either of his/her two taxable years immediately preceding the taxable year, and who maintains as his/her home a household which constitutes for the taxable year the principal place of abode as a member of such household.

T

tax benefit rule. If you deduct an item in one year and receive a refund in a later year (e.g. insurance) the refund is taxable to the extent you received a benefit in the year of deduction.

tax court. The United States Tax Court.

tax-exempt obligation. Any obligation if the interest on such obligation is not includable in gross income.

tax shelter. In general a transaction where the amount paid will result in deductions greater than the amount paid is potentially a tax shelter. Such transactions are scrutinized by the IRS and their use is subject to restrictions.

taxable gifts. The total amount of gifts made during the calendar year, less the deductions provided.

taxable income. Gross income minus the deductions allowed, other than the standard deduction (see standard deduction). For individuals who do not itemize deductions for the taxable year, it is adjusted gross income, minus the standard deduction, and the deductions for personal exemptions.

taxable transportation. Transportation by air which begins and ends in the United States or in the 225-mile zone. The term 225-mile zone means that portion of Canada and Mexico which is not more than 225 miles from the nearest point in the continental United States. The term Continental United States means the District of Columbia and the States other than Alaska and Hawaii.

taxable year. The taxpayer's annual accounting period if it is a calendar year or a fiscal year, or the calendar year if the taxpayer keeps no books or has no accounting period. (See annual accounting period and calendar year.)

term loan. Any loan which is not a demand loan (see demand loan).

tips. Wages received while performing services which constitute employment, and included in a written statement furnished to the employer.

totally held subsidiary. A subsidiary substantially all of whose outstanding equity securities are owned by its parent and/or the parent's other totally held subsidiaries, and which is not indebted, in an amount which is material in relation to the particular subsidiary, excepting indebtedness incurred in the ordinary course of business which is not overdue and which matures within 1 year from the date of its creation whether evidenced by securities or not. Indebtedness of a subsidiary which is secured by its parent by guarantee, pledge, assignment, or otherwise, is excluded.

tract of real property. A single piece of real property, except that two or more pieces of real property should be considered a tract if at any time they were contiguous in the hands of the taxpayer, or if they would be contiguous except for the imposition of a road, street, railroad, stream, or similar property.

trade or business. Includes the performance of personal services within the United States at any time within the taxable year. Includes the performance of the functions of a public office.

transferred basis property. Property having a basis determined in whole or in part by reference to the basis in the hands of the donor, grantor, or other transferor.

trust. As used in the Internal Revenue Code, an arrangement created either by a will or by an inter vivos declaration whereby trustees take title to property for the purpose of protecting or conserving it for the beneficiaries under the ordinary rules applied in chancery or probate courts. Usually the beneficiaries of such a trust do no more than accept the benefits thereof and are not the voluntary planners or creators of the trust arrangement.

U

undistributed foreign personal holding company income. The taxable income of a foreign personal holding company.

undistributed personal holding company income. The amount which is subject to the personal holding company tax.

united states property. Any property which is a tangible property located in the United States, stock of a domestic corporation, an obligation of a United States resident, or any right to the use in the United States of a patent or copyright, an invention, model, or design (whether or not patented).

unrealized receivables. Any rights, contractual or otherwise, to payments for goods delivered, or to be delivered, to the extent that such payment would be treated as received for property other than a capital asset. Includes services rendered, or to be rendered, to the extent that income arising from such right to payment was not previously includable in income under the method of accounting employed. The basis for unrealized receivables includes all costs or expenses attributable thereto paid or accrued, but not previously taken into account under the method of accounting employed.

unrecognized gain. Any position held by the taxpayer as of the close of the taxable year, the amount of gain which would be taken into account with respect to such position if such position were sold on the last business day of such taxable year at its fair market value.

V

valuation of assets. The balance sheets of registered investment companies, other than issuers of face-amount certificates, which reflect all investments at value, with the aggregate cost of each category of investment and of the total investments reported shown parenthetically.

voting shares. The sum of all rights, other than as affected by events of default, to vote for election of directors; the sum of all interests in an unincorporated person (see person).

W

wages. All remuneration for services performed by an employee for an employer, including the cash value of all remuneration, including benefits.

welfare benefits fund. Any fund which is part of a plan of an employer, and through which the employer provides welfare benefits to employees or their beneficiaries.

wherewithal to pay. This general doctrine says that before someone should be asked to pay taxes on a transaction, they should have received the cash to do so. An example is an installment sale. An individual who sells some property, say a house, and is to receive payments over a number of years, is not required to report (recognize) the income from the sale until the payments are actually received. Contrast this with ordinary business accrual accounting where a business would credit sales and debit a note receivable. There all the income is recorded in the year of sale.

wholly owned subsidiary. A subsidiary substantially all of whose outstanding voting shares (see voting shares) are owned by its parent and/or the parent's other wholly owned subsidiaries.

Y

year. Any 12 consecutive months.

APPENDIX C
Investment Vocabulary

Any language has a core vocabulary of about 700 words—English, French or Russian—it doesn't matter which one. In addition, all professions have vocabularies of similar size. What we hope to accomplish here is to give basic definitions of words that crop up in most media treatments of securities and investment. While this is not an exhaustive vocabulary, nor are these complete definitions, they are most certainly working definitions of the most common words. They will help the CPA/PFS get through almost any article or conversation without feeling hopelessly confused and left out by the nomenclature of the discussion.

A

account. The formal relationship between a securities entity and a client wherein the client buys and sells securities.

account executive. The person responsible for executing your securities transactions.

account statement. Monthly written record of a securities client's positions and transactions.

across the board. Activity in the stock market where seemingly everything goes up or everything goes down in tandem.

acquisition. One company buying out another.

active market. Large trading volume for a period of time in either a specific security or in investment vehicles per se.

against the box. Short sale of a security that the holder owns with a long position already.

American Depository Receipt (ADR). U.S. versions of foreign stocks traded domestically, mitigating against relying upon foreign exchanges to invest in their securities.

American Depository Share (ADS). Shares that make up an ADR and are the underlying security of that ADR.

American Stock Exchange (AMEX). Stock exchange in New York that is second only to the New York Stock Exchange (NYSE) in volume. It largely specializes in small and middle capitalization stocks, options, bonds and some over-thecounter (OTC) issues.

annual meeting. Annual recounting of a company's activities held in a public place with management, directors, shareholders, and the press.

Annual Percentage Rate (APR). Simple annual percentage expression of the costs of a loan to consumers that must be disclosed per the Truth In Lending Act.

annual report. Annual accounting in print of all the activities of a company required by the SEC.

annual return. Pre-tax and expense figure resulting from total income and gain or loss being combined to create one total return figure for the year.

annualize. Conversion of a return to an annual basis.

appreciation. Increase in value of a security.

asset. Something of measurable value.

asset allocation. Determining the percentage of funds invested between cash, stock and bonds.

B

back-ended load. A vanishing deferred sales charge common in mutual funds and annuities that enables investors to have their entire investment working for them at the onset of their investment.

balanced mutual fund. Asset allocation fund that has a blend of stocks, bonds and cash—usually, consistent with a conservative investment pattern.

basis. Cost of a security including all expenses related to the acquisition of that security.

bear market. Market in which prices go down for an extended period of time.

bid and offer. The prices at which people are willing to buy (bid) and sell (offer) securities to someone else.

big board. Slang name for the New York Stock Exchange.

block. Large number of securities.

blue chip. Stock of a household-name company that has done very well over an extended number of years.

bond. A debt security obligating the issuer to pay the holder interest for some period of time.

bond rating. A measurement of a bond issuer's ability to pay its bondholders their interest and principal.

bottom. Lowest point of something (stock, market, yield) at some measured time (day, quarter, year).

bottom-up. Micro to macro look at a subject.

breakpoint. Mutual fund dollar commitment that results in a lower sales fee.

breakup value. Market value of the parts of a company separated from its whole.

broker. Same as account executive; colloquial rather than official term.

brokered CD. Certificates of deposit (CDs) sold at brokerages rather than at the bank and having the same characteristics as bank CDs.

budget. Estimate of cash flow and expenses.

bull market. Market in which prices go up for an extended period of time.

business cycle. Recurring periods of expansion and recession in the economy.

buy. Make an investment.

buy and hold. Long-term investment.

buyer's market. A market in which investment in securities predominates.

buying on margin. Investing in securities on credit.

buyout. Take over the control of a company.

C

call feature. Bond issuer's ability to claim back a bond before it matures as stated in the schedule of redemption for that bond.

call option. Opportunity to buy a certain amount of a security at a certain price for a certain amount of time.

callable. The ability of an issuer to redeem securities before their stated maturity.

called. Security is redeemed prior to maturity.

capital gain. Profit realized on sale of a security.

capital gains distribution. Distribution of profit, usually in December, from a mutual fund's successful trading.

capital loss. Loss realized on sale of a security.

capital markets. Markets where stocks and bonds are traded, both public and private.

capitalization. The value of a company based on its total stock shares multiplied by the price of the stock.

cash. Currency.

cash dividend. Dividend paid out to shareholders in cash.

cash equivalent. Securities so safe and liquid that they are just removed from being cash.

central bank. A country's bank; in the U.S., the Federal Reserve System.

certificate of deposit (CD). Interest-paying debt instrument issued by banks.

certified financial planner (CFP). Financial planner who has completed the program of the Institute of Certified Financial Planners.

certified public accountant (CPA). Accountant who has completed the program required to obtain certification in the state in which he or she works as an accountant.

chairman of the board. Highest ranking officer in a corporation, who presides over board meetings.

charitable remainder trust. Trust that is irrevocable and that gives money to a charity, generates an income for life to the grantor, and creates tax benefits for the grantor.

chief executive officer (CEO). Actual manager of a company, as opposed to a ceremonial title, responsible for its day-to-day operation.

chief financial officer (CFO). Person who controls the purse strings of a company.

churning. Excessive trading in a brokerage account.

closed-end mutual fund. Mutual fund with a finite number of shares traded on a stock exchange.

common stock. An equity security of a public company.

company. A business.

compliance department. Entity set up to see that securities activities are in accordance with the law.

confirmation. Paper slip used to inform clients in writing of a securities transaction.

constant dollar plan. Dollar cost averaging.

contrarian. Person who does the opposite of what he or she perceives everyone else is doing.

controlling interest. Enough shares to control a company.

convertible securities. Securities that can be converted from one security into another; usually from a bond into stock.

cornering a market. Illegally gaining control of a security.

corporate bond. Bond issued by a company.

corporation. Chartered legal company.

correction. Downward price adjustment in a security or market.

cost basis. Acquisition price of a security.

coupon. Rate of return on a bond as expressed by a percentage of the face value of the bond.

crash. Extraordinary drop in stock prices, usually in one day.

credit rating. A measurement of an entity's ability to pay its creditors.

credit risk. Chance that a debt will not be repaid.

custodial account. Account created for a minor.

custodian. Entity that holds securities for another entity, such as a bank holding securities for a mutual fund.

cyclical stock. Stock whose price reflects the state of the economy.

D

debt instrument. Written document that is issued to cover a debt.

debt security. Security that is issued to cover a debt.

debt service. Loan payments.

defined benefit pension plan. Pension plan that pays a specific amount to a participant after a given employment tenure for the life of that participant.

defined contribution pension plan. Pension plan in which there is a specific contribution allowed and the ultimate benefits are dependent upon the investment results of the plan.

delisting. Removal of a security from an exchange.

denomination. Face value of some financial instrument stated in currency.

derivative. Security whose value is based on the value of some other security.

devaluation. Lowering the value of a currency relative to the value of some other currency.

disclosure. Positive and negative information required by the SEC for determination of an investment decision.

discount bond. Bond selling at below its par value.

discount broker. Brokerage that charges commissions below the full-service brokerage commissions.

discounting the news. Price fluctuations based on anticipated news about a company.

discount rate. The rate the Federal Reserve charges member banks for loans secured by various acceptable securities.

discretionary account. Account in which trades may be made without first consulting with the client.

discretionary income. Income left over after all obligations have been met.

disintermediation. Taking funds out of a bank.

disposable income. Income left over after all government tax obligations have been met.

diversification. Spreading risk by investing in multiple types of investment.

dividend. Earnings distribution.

dividend investment plan. Reinvesting stock dividends in that company's stock to add more stock to a position on a regular basis.

dollar cost averaging. Securities investment of a given amount of money at a given time interval for an indefinite period, where volatility is lessened because of the time factor.

downside risk. Estimate as to how low the value of an investment can go.

downtick. Trade at lower price than previous one.

down trend. Security moving downward in price.

dumping. Selling large amounts of stock regardless of the price offered.

E

early withdrawal penalty. Fee paid to terminate a time deposit contract, usually with bank CDs.

earned income. Income actively earned.

earnings momentum. Accelerated earnings that tend to provoke upward price movement in stocks.

earnings per share. Post-tax, post-bond and preferred stock payment amount of earnings expressed on a per-share basis.

Employee Retirement Income Security Act (ERISA). Private pension and benefit plans law enacted in 1974.

employee stock ownership plan (ESOP). Stock purchase plan set up for the employees of a company to buy their company's stock.

encumbered. Owned by one party but another party has a justified claim for ownership.

endorse. Transfer ownership.

entrepreneur. Risk-oriented investor.

equity. Ownership.

equivalent taxable yield. Adjustment made to compare tax-exempt yields on an equivalent basis to taxable ones.

estate. What a person owns at death.

estate planning. Orderly addressing of the documentation and tax planning for the disposition of an estate.

Eurodollar. Dollars in banks in Europe.

event risk. Risk that something will happen to cause a lower rating of a security and a subsequent decline in price.

excess reserves. Reserves of money above Federal Reserve requirement by a member bank.

exchange rate. Price one currency can be bought at with another currency.

ex-dividend. Time between declaration and payment of a dividend.

execution. Consummate a trade.

executor/executrix. Administrator of an estate.

exercise. Utilize right to do something by contract, usually, with options or futures.

expense ratio. A mutual fund's operating expenses expressed as a percentage of the fund's assets that are used to pay expenses plus its 12b-1 fees divided by the fund's net asset value.

F

face value. Stated denomination of a security on the certificate of that security.

family of funds. List of funds managed by the same company.

favorable trade balance. Occurs when you export more than you import.

federal deficit. Shortfall of revenue relative to expenses of the federal government.

Federal Deposit Insurance Corporation (FDIC). Federal agency that insures bank deposits.

federal funds. Commercial bank deposits at the Federal Reserve Bank.

federal funds rate. Bank-to-bank loan rates charged on excess deposits at the Federal Reserve.

Federal Open Market Committee (FOMC). Federal Reserve committee that sets government short-term monetary policy.

Federal Reserve Banks. Group of banks making up the Federal Reserve System.

Federal Reserve Board (FRB). Board that governs the Federal Reserve.

Federal Reserve System. Regulator of U.S. monetary policy and banking system.

fiduciary. Entity responsible for another's assets.

fill. Complete a customer's order.

Financial Accounting Standards Board (FASB). Establishes and interprets accounting terms and rules.

financial markets. The total of the different markets of all types.

financial planner. Person who analyzes clients' financial circumstances and prepares a plan for them to realize their goals.

financial pyramid. Graphic representation of investments going from least (base) to most (peak) speculative investments.

financial statement. Written financial record including balance sheet and income statement.

financial supermarket. A large number of financial products sold at one company.

fiscal year. A 365-day accounting period.

fixed annuity. An annuity that guarantees a specific rate of return.

fixed cost. Cost that remains the same regardless of outside sales effects.

fixed income investment. A security whose payout rate is set.

fixed rate. Loan or security whose interest rate does not change.

flat. Bonds trading without interest payment accruing.

flight to quality. Rush to high-grade securities in difficult times.

floating rate. Loan or security whose interest rate changes.

floor broker. Agent who acts for clients of a member firm on an exchange floor.

floor trader. Trader who acts for him- or herself on an exchange floor.

forecasting. Predicting the future.

foreclosure. Seizure of property.

foreign exchange. Payments between countries.

forward. Buy or sell contract for a commodity.

401(K) plan. Elective pre-tax contributions to a qualified tax-deferred retirement plan.

fraud. Illegal detrimental behavior to obtain advantage.

front-ended load. Up-front mutual fund sales charge.

full-service brokerage. A financial supermarket where many financial products are available.

fully invested. Asset allocation involving no cash but only stocks and bonds.

fully valued. Stock prices at exactly what a company's earnings justify.

fundamental analysis. Determination of the price movement of a stock based on earnings expectations as suggested by balance sheet and income statement data.

futures contract. A buy or sell agreement for a specific amount of a product at a specific price for a specific time.

futures exchanges. Markets where future contracts are traded.

G

general obligation (GO) bond. Municipal bond backed by the full faith and credit of its issuer.

general partner. Managing partner of a limited partnership with theoretically limitless liability.

going long. Purchasing a security.

going private. Removing a company from public ownership by buying up all its stock.

going public. Making a public sale of a company.

going short. Selling a security that is not owned by the seller.

gold fixing. Setting of the cash (spot) price of one ounce of gold.

gold mutual fund. Mutual fund made up primarily of gold and other mining shares.

gold standard. Monetary system whereby currency is convertible to bullion on demand.

goldbug. Someone who believes in the appreciation potential of gold.

golden handcuffs. Incentives to keep a person from leaving a company.

golden parachute. Corporate takeover protection for a key employee.

good faith deposit. Earnest money for a securities trade.

government securities. Securities issued by the U.S. government and its agencies.

grandfather clause. Exemption from a new rule by virtue of prior involvement.

green shoe. Provision to issue additional shares of an underwriting if demand is strong enough.

H

hard dollar fee. Payment in cash for services.

high-yield bond. Bonds rated BB or lower.

holding period. Amount of time an owner has held an asset.

hot issue. New stock issue everyone wants because these stocks tend to go up sharply in price.

hot stock. Stock that is trading large relative volume and often is going up sharply in price.

hypothecation. Using securities as loan collateral.

I

illiquid. Cannot be immediately converted to cash.

in-the-money option. Option where the underlying security is trading at a price that would be advantageous to exercise the option.

inactive security. Illiquid security owing to scarcity of trading activity for any reason.

income tax. Tax on income imposed by country, state or city.

indemnify. Agree to pay for loss.

index. Compilation of statistics (economy) or prices (securities) as a measurement standard.

index fund. Fund made up of the constituents of a securities index.

index option. Put or call on an index.

individual retirement account (IRA). Personally created retirement account subject to various regulations that are often altered and amended over the years.

individual retirement account rollover (IRA Rollover). Lump sum distribution deposited into an IRA account to avoid current tax consequences.

inflation. Increase in prices caused by excessive demand for limited supply of goods and services.

inflation rate. Rate of increase in prices of goods and services attributable to excessive demand and limited supply.

initial public offering (IPO). New stock issue that is publicly traded for the first time.

inside information. Significant corporate information that has not yet been made public.

insider. Person who has access to inside information about a company.

insolvent. Unable to pay obligations.

institution. Bank, mutual fund, pension fund, corporation, insurance company, college or union.

insurance. Contract to reimburse for a loss.

insured account. Accountant at a financial entity with government or private insurance coverage.

interest sensitive. Reacts to upward or downward movement of rates.

intermediate term. In stocks or bonds, a year or more.

intermediation. Putting money on deposit at a bank.

inverted yield curve. Yield curve where short-term rates are higher than long-term rates.

investment banker. Firm that intermediates as broker between issue and buyers.

investment company. Entity that manages mutual funds.

investment grade. Bonds rated BBB or better.

investment history. Pattern of investment practice through time.

investment income. Income from securities.

investment strategy. Asset allocation plan.

Investor Relations Department. Corporate office responsible for addressing investor needs.

irrevocable trust. A trust in which the beneficiary must agree to any changes in, or the termination of, that trust.

issuer. Entity that issues and promotes sale of its securities.

J

joint account. Account opened and owned by two or more people.

joint venture. Two or more parties in contract on a project together.

jumbo certificate of deposit (jumbo CD). Usually, a certificate of $100,000 or more.

junk bond. Bond rated BB or lower.

K

Keogh plan. Type of tax-deferred pension plan.

kicker. Usually, equity partnership in a bond deal to enhance appeal of the bond.

kiddie tax. Tax filed for children's accounts as they generate taxable income or gains.

know your customer. Obligation on the part of the broker to determine client suitability.

L

labor intensive. Industry that requires a high number of workers.

ladder. Succession of fixed income maturities set up to diversify risks associated with timing or reinvestment.

last sale. Most recent sale of a security in a trading period.

last trading day. Last day a futures contract can settle.

late tape. Heavy trading volume that causes the tape to lag behind transactions.

lay off. Usually, risk reduction.

leader. Stock or group of stocks that leads an advance or decline, usually in volume activity.

leverage. Borrowing.

leveraged buyout. Takeover relying on borrowed funds.

liability. Claim on assets.

lien. Creditor's claim against an asset.

limit order. Order to buy or sell at a specific price or better than the current market level.

limit price. Price set in a limit order.

limited partnership. Investors who have invested in a partnership, but who do not have liability beyond their investment for losses.

liquid asset. Asset that can immediately be converted to cash.

liquidity. Measurement of an asset's convertibility to cash.

listed security. Security traded on a recognized U.S. exchange.

listing requirements. Standards for inclusion on a given exchange.

load. Mutual fund sales charge.

loan. Borrowing of an asset by one entity from another entity.

loan value. Value of collateral.

long bond. The U.S. 30-Year Treasury Bond.

long position. Owning a security.

long term. Holding period of more than six months for a security.

long-term debt. Debt issued for more than one year.

loophole. Way to legally, but not always ethically, get around a rule or law.

lump sum distribution. Cashing out an entire vehicle for one payment.

M

macroeconomics. National economic view and study.

maintenance fee. Brokerage account fee to cover costs of services and generate revenue for the brokerage.

make a market. Willing to buy or sell a given security at its current price.

managed account. Discretionary account where a manager allocates the asset for a fee.

management. The organizational structure of a company.

management fee. Comprises internal fees of a mutual fund established to cover costs of services and generate revenue for the fund.

managing underwriter. Lead underwriter of an offering.

manipulation. False appearance of price movement, volume or any kind of activity in a security.

margin. Borrowing capability of a security.

margin account. An account set up to facilitate margin trades if the customer so desires.

margin agreement. Mutual agreement between brokerage and client regarding margin activity rules.

mark to the market. Timely adjusted price of a security.

market. Public area to buy and sell.

market analysis. Study of different markets in order to project the future behavior of one particular market.

market capitalization. Value of a company as determined by outstanding shares of its stock multiplied by the stock's current price.

market letter. Research publication directed toward market projections.

market maker. Person who will buy and sell at current prices of a security.

market order. Order to buy or sell at current prices.

market price. Most recent price of a security.

market research. Research to evaluate a market for a product.

market risk. Risk attached to a market as a whole, as reflected in any one security.

market share. The part of a market that a given security or product makes up.

market timing. Buying or selling of securities based on a perception of what the market as a whole may do.

market tone. Psychological status of a market.

market value. Security's value based on current price.

marketability. Liquidity.

marketable security. Liquid security.

marketing. Selling.

marketplace. Market.

mature economy. Economy of a major nation that is in its later stages of growth.

maturity date. Date on which a security comes due for payment to the holder.

medium term. Intermediate-term maturity of a note.

medium-term notes (MTNs). Notes of 2-to-10-year duration that often pay monthly.

member bank. A Federal Reserve Bank.

member firm. Firm that has a seat on an exchange.

merchant bank. Bank that facilitates investment activities.

merger. The joining of two or more companies.

microeconomics. Study of primary units of an economy.

missing the market. Failure to execute an order in a timely fashion that is to the client's disadvantage.

momentum. Rate of flow, price, or volume of a security.

monetary policy. Money supply policy set by the Federal Reserve.

money center bank. Bank located in one of the major financial centers of the world.

money market. Trading market for short-term debt securities.

money market fund. Open-ended mutual fund made up of short-term debt securities.

money supply. Cash or cash deposits in the economy.

monopoly. Control of something to the extent that competition is precluded.

mortgage-backed security. A security issued with mortgages as its backing.

mortgage pool. Collection of similar mortgage into one lot.

most active list. Highest volume of traded shares on a per day basis.

moving average. Trend analysis of a security price using a preset period of time as a scale.

multinational corporation. Domestic company with at least one foreign branch established to operate as a foreign subsidiary.

municipal bond. Bond issued without federal tax consequence by a nonfederal government entity.

municipal bond insurance. Private insurance for municipal debt bought by the issuer for the benefit of the bondholder to cover interrupted payments in default or ultimately to pay off defaulted principle payments.

mutual fund. Pooled money managed by an investment company for the benefit of shareholders invested in stocks, bonds, cash or other securities.

mutual fund custodian. Bank where mutual fund assets are deposited for safety reasons.

N

narrow market. Illiquid and low-volume market.

narrowing the spread. Reducing the gap between the bid and offer on a security.

National Association of Securities Dealers (NASD). Regulators of OTC securities dealers.

National Association of Securities Dealers Automated Quotation System (NASDAQ). A price quotation system for OTC securities.

national bank. Bank with a U.S. charter.

national debt. Money owed by the U.S. government.

nationalization. Government takeover of a company.

negative cash flow. Spending in excess of income.

negotiable. Transferable.

net asset value (NAV). Bid price of a mutual fund established daily after the close by adding the value of the fund's assets, subtracting its liabilities and dividing by the number of shares outstanding.

net change. Change in price of a security from one day to the next.

net current assets. Working capital.

net earnings. Net income.

net proceeds. Amount left from a transaction after all costs have been subtracted.

net sales. Sales less all costs after they have been subtracted.

net transaction. Securities trade with no fees attached.

net worth. Amount left in assets after all liabilities have been removed by subtraction.

new account page. Form filled out by broker to fulfill know-your-client regulations.

New York Stock Exchange (NYSE). Oldest and largest U.S. securities exchange.

niche. Area of a company's business that distinguishes it from other companies of its type.

Nikkei Stock Exchange. Tokyo stock exchange.

no-load fund. Mutual fund with no front-end sales charge.

non-callable. Bond or preferred stock that cannot be redeemed at the option of the issuer.

non-public information. Information of a significant nature that will affect the current price of a company's securities once it becomes public.

note. Usually, intermediate-term debt issues.

not rated. Security unrated by any type of rating service, often simply by choice, and neither a positive nor a negative event.

O

offer. Asked buy price.

offering price. Price per share for an IPO or secondary offering.

offset transaction. Closing trade to eliminate a position.

one-decision stock. A buy-and-hold stock.

144A bonds. Junk-debt private placements of low issuer cost.

open-end management company. Mutual fund sales company that sells open-ended funds.

open-end mutual fund. Mutual fund with an unlimited number of shares issued through a management company.

opening trade. Establishes a position.

operations department. Department in a brokerage firm that handles custom-errelated clerical functions.

option. Opportunity to buy or sell a certain number of securities at a certain price for a certain amount of time.

option agreement. Account document required to activate an option trading account for a client.

Options Clearing Corporation (OCC). Corporation dealing in customer-related clerical functions that manages options exchanges.

option writer. Entity that sells options.

order. Request for a securities transaction.

order ticket. Form with request for a securities transaction written on it.

ordinary income. Earned income.

organizational chart. Company employment positions chart.

original cost. All costs bundled together to determine price for an asset acquisition.

originator. Investment banker.

OTC. See over the counter.

other income. Not normal income.

out of favor. Currently unpopular with analysts and investors for performance reasons.

out-of-the-money option. Options whose price does not warrant exercising the option at current levels.

overbought. Unnaturally high price for a security.

overhanging supply. Excessive quantity of securities available awaiting price to sell opportunity.

overheating. Excessive economic expansion.

oversold. Unnaturally low price for a security.

oversubscribed. Banking issue with demand in excess of the available supply.

over the counter (OTC). Securities not traded on an organized exchange.

overvalued. Unnaturally high price for a security from a price/earnings standpoint.

P

paper gain. Unrealized gain, as no transaction has been made to take the gain.

paper loss. Unrealized loss, as no transaction has been made to take the loss.

par. Face value.

parent. Company that owns other companies.

partnership. Two or more people in business together.

passive income. Income from investments deemed by the IRS to be passive investments.

passive loss. Losses from investments deemed by the IRS to be passive investments.

pass-through security. Security that is a packaged income product that passes through the income to the security's holders.

payment date. Income payment date to security holder.

pay up. To pay above the currently perceived value of a security on the belief that the security will trade still higher.

penny stocks. Usually, stocks that trade at less than $10 per share are OTC and are quite speculative.

pension fund. Retired workers' retirement fund.

physical commodity. The underlying tangible item upon which a futures contract is based.

pink sheets. Listing of thousands of OTC stocks, their current bid/offer prices and who trades them.

pledging. Surrendering collateral as security for a loan or other obligation.

plow back. Usually with aggressive growth stocks, to retain rather than distribute earnings.

point. One percent, as it relates to debt securities; one dollar, as it relates to stocks.

poison pill. Securities transaction that is activated by hostile takeover to make a company both less attractive and less susceptible to takeover.

portfolio. All securities assets held.

portfolio manager. Professional securities manager.

portfolio theory. Risk/reward approach to evaluating securities.

position. Security holding.

position building. Accumulating a security holding.

power of attorney (POA). Permission to act for another in a brokerage relationship.

preferred stock. Nonvoting, income producing dividend-oriented stock.

premium. Payment above norm.

premium bond. Bond priced above par.

premium income. Option-writing income.

prepayment. Debt payoff before maturity or due date has arrived.

prerefunding. Replacing one bond with another before the first is due by using proceeds of the replacement bond to pay it off.

present value. Future income measured in today's dollars.

price/earnings ratio (P/E). Price of a stock divided by its most recent annual earnings.

price range. Usually, the 52-week high/low price of a security.

price support. Usually, government support levels for commodities prices.

pricey. Too high an offer price or too low a bid price.

primary dealer. Entities that can deal directly with the Federal Reserve to buy government securities.

primary issue. New issue of securities.

primary market. New-issue market.

prime rate. Rate banks charge their most creditworthy customers.

principal. Total amount invested (including all costs of acquisition) in a security.

principal amount. Face amount of a bond.

probate. Process by which a will is administered through court system with executor.

producer price index (PPI). Wholesale price index calculated once per month.

profit. Selling price minus purchase price, if to the advantage of the seller.

profit center. Area of a company that on its own is expected to make money.

profit sharing. Corporate plan to distribute some of its profits internally to employees.

profit taking. Usually, sharp responses to broad-based selling by traders who made some money, often quickly, on a security, industry group or even a market.

program trading. Buying and selling by computer-driven price-monitoring schemes.

progressive tax. Tax system under which the more one makes, the more taxes one pays.

projection. Prediction.

pro rata. Proportionate share.

prospectus. SEC-required informational publication on securities offered for sale.

proxy. Vote designation.

proxy fight. Usually, takeover-related vote designation battle.

proxy statement. SEC-required informational publication on securities vote.

Prudent Man Rule. State-by-state determination of fiduciary rules.

publicly held. Shares owned by the public.

public ownership. Shares owned by the public.

purchasing power. Margin credit line at a brokerage.

pure play. Security that is without any diversification from its stated industry group.

put option. Opportunity to sell a certain amount of a security at a certain price for a certain amount of time.

pyramid. Leverage.

Q

qualified annuity. Annuity purchased in a qualified plan.

qualified plan. Tax-deferred retirement plan.

quantitative analysis. Numbers-related analysis that depends on statistical interpretation of price movement.

R

raider. Investor oriented toward takeover and new management.

rally. Upward movement of securities prices, especially after a decline.

random walk. The notion that the past is no indication of the future as securities respond only to the random-pattern current events, and these are in no way predictable.

range. High/low quotes on a security over some given period of time.

rate of return. Measurement of performance.

rating. Credit ranking assessing default risk to debt and investment grade to equity as assigned by rating agencies.

Real Estate Investment Trust (REIT). Usually, publicly traded packaged real estate portfolio.

real rate of return. Inflation-adjusted return.

rebate. Purchase inducement by refund.

recession. Usually, two quarters in a row of downside economic activity.

recovery. Upward economic or market movement after a decline.

redemption. Payoff of a debt security.

refinancing. Refunding a debt issue by issuing another.

regional bank. Local bank.

regional stock exchange. A local exchange that for a non-New York market.

registered representative. Broker.

regressive tax. Tax system under which the more one makes, the fewer taxes one pays.

regulated investment company. Mutual fund that conforms to IRS regulations under Regulation M.

reinsurance. Insurance company risk diversification.

reinvestment. Returning dividends into the original investment to grow or compound at the rate of return of the investment itself.

relative strength. Price movement comparing one security to another.

reorganization. Redoing a firm under bankruptcy laws.

rescind. Cancel.

research and development (R&D). Creating and preparing for sale a product.

research department. Security analysis area of a securities-oriented company.

retail deposit notes (RTNs). Monthly pay senior-debt notes of 5 to 20 years with 2 to 5 years of call protection that are bank issued and FDIC insured.

retail investor. Person who invests.

return. Profit or loss on an investment.

return on equity (ROE). Percent earnings based on price of a stock.

reversal. Change of direction in a security price or market.

rich. Security that is overpriced relative to past history, other stocks in its group or the market.

right of survivorship. Ability to take title of something when an owner dies.

risk. Downside potential.

risk adverse. Avoids risk.

risk-free return. Usually, short-term U.S. Treasury Bill returns.

riskless transaction. Transaction in which the maker cannot lose money.

risk premium. Total return potential minus a risk-free return.

rollover. Investment transfer from one investment to another.

run. Usually, a rapid rising price.

S

salary reduction plan. Tax-deferred retirement plan so named because the contributions are pre-tax.

sale. Completed transaction.

sales charge. Fee paid for securities purchase.

sales literature. Marketing material.

sales load. Mutual fund sales charge.

savings bank. Retail bank.

savings bond. U.S. government bonds in $10,000 or smaller denominations; typically used for a child's savings plans.

screening. Computer scanning for securities of a given parameter.

seasonal. Securities that go up or down in some relationship to the time of year.

seat. Euphemism for securities exchange membership.

secondary. Public distribution of existing shares in a publicly traded company.

secondary market. Post-original-issue markets.

secondary stock. Small- or middle-capitalization stock.

sector. Stock group.

sector fund. Mutual fund of stock group.

secured debt. Debt with collateral attached.

securities analyst. Securities prognosticator.

Securities and Exchange Commission (SEC). Public protection agency that regulates the securities industry.

Securities Industry Association (SIA). Securities industry lobby.

Securities Investor Protection Corporation (SIPC). Corporations that insure customer accounts against non-market-related brokerage losses, such as default of the house.

security. Investment instrument.

security ratings. Investment and/or credit evaluation of companies.

sell off. Dumping securities with the premise that they will go lower in price sooner than they will rise.

sell out. Usually, to cover a margin debit, liquidation of a position or an account.

sell short. Selling a security not owned, with the theory in mind that it will go lower in price and can be bought to close the position at a profit on a later date.

seller's market. Demand exceeds supply.

selling climax. Usually, market bottom induced by a drop in volume and price.

selling group. Underwriters who market an issue to the public.

sentiment indicators. Gauge of public investor confidence.

settle. Pay.

settlement date. Payment date for a securities purchase.

shakeout. Elimination of secondary-level competition in an industry.

share. Usually, equity unit of ownership of a security.

shareholder. Owner of shares.

share repurchase plan. Corporate stock buyback.

shelf registration. Two-year window of opportunity to issue a public offering.

shop. Retail brokerage office.

short covering. Buying shares to close out a short position.

short position. Shares sold short and not yet covered.

short squeeze. Rising securities prices go up so far and so fast that many shortsellers, particularly those who sell on margin, are forced to cover because of the magnitude of their losses.

short term. One year or less.

short-term debt. Paper maturing in one year or less.

short-term gain or loss. Gain or loss realized in six months or less.

simple interest. Stated rate of interest divided by principal invested.

simplified employee pension (SEP) plan. Plan combining aspects of an IRA and a 401(K).

single-premium deferred annuity. Lump sum payment annuity that earns without tax consequences until distributions begin.

single-premium life insurance. Lump sum payment whole life insurance.

Small Business Administration (SBA). Federal loan agency established to help start up businesses of risk.

small-capitalization stocks. Stocks of companies with less than $500 million capitalization that are often, because of their size, more volatile than large-capitalization stocks ($1 billion or more, often quite a bit more).

small investor. Usually, the stock odd-lot and modest mutual fund investor who does not have significantly large investments.

soft currency. Usually, currency of an economy that has no hard assets to back up that currency and thus lacks liquidity in the currency exchange markets.

soft dollars. Commission fees paid to a brokerage.

soft landing. Slow but not collapsing economy.

soft market. One in which supply exceeds demand.

soft spot. Weak stock in a group or weak group in a market.

solvency. Ability to pay debt obligations.

sovereign risk. Political risk.

specialist. Exchange market maker.

speculation. Assumption of significant risk for unusually significant return.

spin-off. Company that is removed from another company and becomes independent.

split. Dividing shares without influencing capitalization with the idea that a stock will be more attractive to investors if it is at a lower price.

spread. Difference between bid and offer.

squeeze. Forced short-sale-position closing due to sharply rising prices.

stabilization. Leveling.

staggered maturity. Reinvestment risk reduction in bond portfolios by laddered maturities.

stagnation. Arrested or declining economic growth.

Standard and Poor's Index (S&P 500). Widely held bundle of 500 stocks that is the generally accepted index of U.S. stock performance.

standard deviation. Margin of error in a calculation.

start-up. New business.

state bank. State-chartered rather than federally chartered bank.

statement. Client's written periodic account record.

staying power. Pain tolerance in a declining market.

stock. Equity ownership of shares.

stock average. Standard of market measurement to gauge market performance.

stock buyback. Corporation buys its own stock for an assortment of purposes.

stock certificate. Piece of paper that represents equity ownership shares.

stock dividend. A share rather than cash dividend.

stock exchange. Organized securities trading place.

stock index. Standard of market measurement to gauge market performance.

stock market. Usually, Dow Jones Industrial Averages; or, an exchange where securities are traded.

stock option. Opportunity to buy or sell a given amount of stock for a given amount of time at a given level of price.

stock purchase plan. Internal corporate buying plan for employees.

stock symbol. Series of letters to identify companies, usually, one to three letters for listed stocks and four to five letters for OTC stocks.

stockholder. Entity that owns shares.

stockholder of record. Owner of a share on a given day.

strategic buyout. Buyout with what is perceived as an organized plan and purpose.

street. Wall Street.

street name. Brokerage term for collective positions of customers' securities held by their securities firm for safekeeping and convenience in the name of the firm.

strip. Zero coupon treasury security.

subject. Quote on a security that can be changed and is therefore not firm.

suitability rules. Know-your-client requirements related especially to higher-risk securities.

support level. Area in which a declining security price is expected to stabilize.

suspended trading. Trading halt generated by some announcement of significance or important information.

swap. One security is replaced with another.

syndicate. Underwriting group.

syndicate manager. Underwriting manager.

synergy. The notion that the sum of the various parts of a corporate merger will somehow exceed their separate values.

synthetic. Artificially created securities.

systematic investment. Dollar cost averaging of mutual funds by contracted agreement with the fund family.

systematic risk. Market risk.

T

take a position. Long or short position in a security.

takeover. Assumed control of a corporation.

taking delivery. Getting a security certificate in hand and assuming possession of it.

tangible asset. Real asset, such as collectibles, real estate or other physically formed property.

target. Takeover candidate.

target price. Stated price goal of an investor at which he or she might want to sell.

tax basis. Total cost basis of an investment.

tax bracket. Maximum rate of tax on a given income.

tax credit. Dollar-for-dollar offset of income tax liability with a credit.

tax deferred. Tax liability postponed but not avoided until effective possession has been secured.

tax-exempt security. Usually, municipal bond whose interest is not taxable federally or by the state or city in which the issuer is located.

tax planning. Systematic and orderly look at a tax situation with the design of reducing tax liability to a minimum.

tax selling. Usually, generating losses at year-end to utilize as an offset against gains.

taxable equivalent yield. Taxable yield that nets the same to a bondholder as a tax-free municipal bond would.

taxable income. Total income remaining at the bottom line of the tax form after all credits and deductions.

technical analysis. Price and volume indicators used as a predictor of future securities performance.

technical rally. Usually, a bounce-up of prices in a downtrend perceived as being based upon technical factors.

APPENDIX D
The Going Concern Concept

The concept that financial statements are prepared on the basis of a "going concern" is one of the basics relating to financial accounting. The word "concern" in this context does not refer to worry. It is from an older usage of the word. A concern is defined as a worry, but it is also defined as something of interest to someone. So, in earlier days, it was used to refer to a business. Therefore, a "going concern" is a business that is expected to continue forward and stay in business. There is an underlying presumption in the standards set for financial accounting that a business, once started, will continue functioning and operating. For example, the use of historical costs for building and property, which are currently more valuable, presupposes that the use of that property will generate more advantages than disposing of the property. Deferrals to future periods through systematic allocations, such as depreciation, depletion, or amortization, also indicate a presumption of longevity.

This presumption of continuance as a going concern was historically never stated by the independent auditor—never worded in his or her own opinion. On the *contrary*, it was when there appeared to be danger of the entity's *not* being able to continue as a going concern that the auditor added an emphasis-of-matter paragraph stating there was substantial doubt about the entity's ability to continue as a going concern. Therefore, the actual use of the terminology, "going concern," in the auditor's opinion indicated trouble. This recently changed. In the "new" audit opinion now required, several changes have been made. One of those changes is to add to the paragraph describing the responsibilities of management, a statement that management is required to evaluate whether there are conditions or events that raise substantial doubt about the entity's ability to continue as a going concern. Similarly, in the section describing the auditor's responsibilities, wording is required to explain the auditor's conclusion whether, in the auditor's judgment, there are conditions or events that raise substantial doubt about the entity's ability to continue as a going concern. In addition to the audit opinion, footnote disclosure is required to provide more information if substantial doubt does exist.

Several types of problems may indicate problems with an entity's continuation as a going concern:

1. Operational uncertainties which may present two different types of situations giving cause for concern:

a. Progressive deterioration of a firm's financial stability resulting from changing markets, outmoded or inefficient plant and facilities, or inept management. This, in turn, leads to declining earnings or actual losses, reduced cash balances and eventually an inability to meet current liabilities. Such uncertainties may result in gradual deterioration or, less frequently, in a very sudden turnaround of a previously profitable firm.

b. A start-up business that may never get off the ground. This is the enterprise that begins with high hopes but has not yet met with success nor achieved a solid financial footing. In the event of even a minor setback at this juncture, the firm's continuation may be open to question particularly in relation to the liquidity of its assets. What assets it has may very well be tied up in inventories, specialized plant and equipment or deferred charges.

2. External difficulties beyond the control of an entity. These may be as a result of governmental controls, natural disasters such as earthquakes or floods, mandatory product recalls or devastating lawsuits. Any of these or other potential catastrophes could drain an entity beyond its financial capacity to recover.

Following is a random listing of factors which could be indicative of *possible* failure to continue as a going concern:

1. Inability to satisfy obligations on due dates.
2. Inability to perform contractual obligations.
3. Inability to meet substantial loan covenants.
4. A substantial deficit.
5. A series of continued losses.
6. The presence of major contingencies which could lead to heavy losses.
7. Catastrophes which have rendered the business inoperable.
8. Negative cash flows from operations.
9. Adverse key financial ratios.
10. Denial of usual trade credit from suppliers.
11. Necessity of finding new sources of financing.
12. Loss of key personnel.
13. Loss of a principal customer.
14. Work stoppage and labor disputes.

Statement of Auditing Standards (SAS) No. 59 was effective for audits of financial statements for periods beginning on or after January 1, 1989. It was redrafted as part of the Auditing Standards Board (ASB) of the AICPA clarity project, as SAS 126 in 2012. Up to that point, there were no accounting standards related to the going concern concept—it was only an audit standard. Even though there was no related accounting standard, auditors required their clients to include footnote disclosure so the auditors could be in compliance with their audit standards. SAS 132 was issued in 2017, after the FASB had issued an accounting standard.

The FASB issued ASU No. 2014-15 in August 2014 to give guidance to financial statement preparers related to disclosures of uncertainties about an entity's ability to continue as a going concern.

Guidance for auditors of public companies may be found in PCAOB AS 2415.

It should be noted that this discussion relates to situations where there is "substantial doubt" about an entity's ability to continue as a going concern. If applicable factors make it *certain* that the entity will not continue as a going concern, it is likely that the liquidation method of accounting will be used instead of U.S. GAAP.

In a nutshell, management is required to evaluate whether there are conditions or events, such as those listed above, that raise substantial doubt about the entity's ability to continue as a going concern within one year after the date that the financial statements are issued or available to be issued. When such conditions or events are identified, management should consider whether its plans to mitigate the conditions or events will alleviate the substantial doubt. When those conditions or events are identified, whether or not plans are expected to effectively mitigate substantial doubt, disclosure should be made about the relevant details.

APPENDIX E
Guidelines for Interim Reporting

Guidelines for interim reporting by publicly traded companies have been established by the AICPA (and the SEC). Interim reporting is much more applicable to public companies due to the requirement to file Form 10-Q each quarter. For private companies, which do not bear the same responsibility for full and adequate disclosure to public shareholders, the guidelines for interim reporting are found in FASB ASC 270, *Interim Reporting*.

Following are the standards for determining applicable information and the appropriate guidelines for minimum disclosure:

1. Results should be based on the same principles and practices used for the latest annual statements (subject to the modifications below).
2. Revenue should be recognized as earned for the interim on the same basis as for the full year. Losses should be recognized as incurred or when becoming evident.
3. Costs may be classified as:
    a. Those associated with revenue (cost of goods sold);
    b. All other costs expenses based on:
        (i) Those actually incurred, or
        (ii) Those allocated, based on: time expired, or benefits received, or other period activity.
4. Costs or losses (including extraordinary times) should not be deferred or apportioned unless they would be at year-end. Advertised costs may be apportioned in relation to sales for interims.
5. With respect to inventory and cost of sales:
    a. LIFO basis should not be liquidated if expected to be replaced later, but should be based on expected replacement factor;
    b. Inventory losses should not be deferred because of cost or market rule; and conversely, later periods should then reflect gains on market price recoveries. Inventory losses should be reflected if resulting from permanent declines in market value in the interim period in which they occur; recoveries of such losses would be gains in a later interim period. If a change in inventory value is temporary, no recognition is given.
    c. With standard costs, variances which are expected to be absorbed by year-end should be deferred for the interim, not expensed. Unplanned purchase price or volume variance, not expected to turn around, is to be absorbed during the period;
    d. The estimated gross profit method may be used, but must be disclosed.

6. The seasonal nature of activities should be disclosed, preferably including additional 12-month-to-date information with prior comparative figures.

7. Income taxes:
   a. Effective yearly tax rate (including year-end applicable tax-planned advantages) should be applied to interim taxable income;
   b. Extraordinary items applicable to the interim period should be shown separately net of applicable tax and the effect of the tax not applied to the tax on ordinary net income.

8. Extraordinary and unusual items including the effects of segment disposals should be disclosed separately, net of tax, for the interim period in which they occur, and they should not be apportioned over the year.

9. Contingencies should be disclosed the same as for the annual report.

10. Changes in accounting practices or principles from those allowed in prior periods should be disclosed and, where possible, those changes should be made in the first period of the year.

11. Retroactive restatement and/or prior period adjustments are required under the same rules applying to annual statements.

12. The effect of a change in an accounting estimate, including a change in the estimated effective annual tax rate, should be accounted for in the period in which the change in estimate is made. No restatement of previously reported interim information should be made for changes in estimates, but the effect on earnings of a change in estimate made in a current interim period should be reported in the current and subsequent interim periods, if material in relation to any period presented, and should continue to be reported in interim financial information of the subsequent year, for as many periods as necessary to avoid misleading comparisons.

Minimum Data to Be Reported on Interim Statements

1. Sales or gross revenues, provisions for income taxes, extraordinary items (including related tax), cumulative effect of changes in accounting principles or practices, and net income;

2. Primary and fully diluted earnings per share data for each period presented;

3. Seasonal revenue, costs and expenses;

4. Disposal of business segments and extraordinary items, as well as unusual or infrequent items;

5. Contingencies;

6. Changes in estimates, changes in accounting principles or practices;

7. Significant changes in balance sheet items;

8. Significant changes in tax provisions;

9. Current year-to-date, or the last 12 months, with comparative data for prior periods;

10. In the absence of a separate fourth-quarter report, special fourth-quarter adjustments and extraordinary, infrequent or unusual items which occurred during that fourth quarter should be disclosed in a note to the annual financial statement;
11. Though not required, condensed balance sheet data and funds flow data are suggested to provide better understanding of the interim report.
12. If a fourth quarter is not presented, any material adjustment to that quarter must be commented upon in the annual report.

Interim reports are usually prepared by management and issued with that clear stipulation.

Accounting firms which issue reports for interim periods are to be guided by auditing standards set for "Reports on a Limited Review of Interim Financial Information" in Section 722 of Statements on Auditing Standards, April, 1981.

Accounting Changes in Interim Statements

ASC 270, *Interim Reporting*, provides guidance with respect to reporting an accounting change in interim financial reports. Any change in accounting principle from the principles applied in the comparable interim period of the prior annual period, preceding interim periods in the current annual period, or the prior annual report shall be indicated in a report of interim financial information. Changes are to be reported in the period in which the change is made, in accordance with guidance in ASC 250, *Accounting Changes and Error Corrections*. Similar indication should be made for changes in estimates, except no restatement of previously reported information shall be made, also in accordance with ASC 250. Whenever possible, entities should adopt accounting changes in the first interim period of a fiscal year.

APPENDIX F

Reporting Cash Payments of Over $10,000

Often smugglers and drug dealers use large cash payments to "launder" money from illegal activities. Laundering means converting "dirty" money or illegally gained money to "clean" money. Congress passed the Tax Reform Act of 1984 and the Anti-Drug Abuse Act of 1988 requiring the payment of certain cash payments of over $10,000 to be reported to the Internal Revenue Service. Any person in a trade or business who receives more than $10,000 in a single transaction or in related transactions must report the transaction to the IRS. The government can often trace the laundered money through payments that are reported. Compliance with the law provides valuable information that can stop those who evade taxes and those who profit from the drug trade and other criminal activities.

Receipt of such a payment should be reported on Form 8300. IRS Publication 1544 explains why, when, and where to report these cash payments. It also discusses the substantial penalties for not reporting them.

A "person" includes an individual, a company, a corporation, a partnership, an association, a trust, or an estate. A report does not have to be filed if the entire transaction, including the receipt of cash, takes place outside of:

1. The 50 states.
2. The District of Columbia.
3. Puerto Rico.
4. A possession or territory of the United States.

However, a report must be filed if the transaction, including the receipt of cash, occurs in Puerto Rico or a possession or territory of the United States and the person is subject to the Internal Revenue Code.

A transaction occurs when:

1. Goods, services, or property are sold.
2. Property is rented.
3. Cash is exchanged for other cash.
4. A contribution is made to a trust or escrow account.
5. A loan is made or repaid.
6. Cash is converted to a negotiable instrument such as a check or bond.

Payments to be reported include:

1.   A sum over $10,000.
2.   Installment payments that cause the total cash received within one year of the initial payment to total more than $10,000.
3.   Other previously unreportable payments that cause the total cash received within a 12-month period to total more than $10,000.
4.   Those received in the course of a trade or business.
5.   Those received from the same buyer or agent.
6.   Those received in a single transaction or in related transactions.

A Designated Reporting Transaction

A designated reporting transaction is the retail sale of any of the following:

1.   A consumer durable, such as an automobile or boat. A consumer durable is property other than land or buildings that is suitable for personal use and can reasonably be expected to last at least one year under ordinary usage.
2.   Has a sales price of more than $10,000.
3.   Tangible property.
4.   A "collectible," including works of art, rugs, antiques, gems, stamps, coins.
5.   Travel or entertainment, if the total sales price of all items sold for the same trip or entertainment event in one transaction, or related transactions, is more than $10,000. The sales price of items such as air fare, hotel rooms, and admission tickets are all included.

Retail Sales

The term "retail sales" means any sale made in the course of a trade or business that consists mainly of making sales to ultimate consumers. Thus, if a business consists mainly of making sales to ultimate consumers, all sales made in the course of that business are retail sales. This includes sales of items that will also be resold.

Definition of Cash

In this context, cash is considered to be:

1.   The coins and currency of the U.S. and any other recognized country.
2.   Cashier's checks, bank drafts, traveler's checks, and money orders received if they have a face value of $10,000 or less and were received in:
     a.   A designated reporting transaction.
     b.   Any transaction in which the receiver knows the payer is trying to avoid the reporting of the transaction.

A check drawn on an individual's personal account is not considered cash; however, a cashier's check, even when labeled a "treasurer's check" or "bank check," is considered cash.

Exceptions to Definition of Cash

A cashier's check, bank draft, traveler's check, or money order received in a designated transaction is not treated as cash if:

1. It is the proceeds from a bank loan. As proof that it is proceeds from a bank loan, a copy of the loan document, a written statement or lien instructions from the bank, or similar proof are acceptable as evidence,
2. If received in payment on a promissory note or an installment sales contract, including a lease that is considered a sale for federal tax purposes. This exception applies if:
   a. The receiver uses similar notes or contracts in other sales to ultimate consumers in the ordinary course of trade or business.
   b. Total payments for the sale are received on or before the 60th day after the sale, and are 50 percent or less of the purchase price.
3. For certain down payment plans in payment for a consumer durable or collectible, or for travel and entertainment, and all three of the following statements are true:
   a. It was received under a payment plan requiring one or more down payments, and payment of the remainder before receipt of goods or service.
   b. It was received more than 60 days before final payment was due.
   c. Similar payment plans are used in the normal course of the trade or business.

Taxpayer Identification Number (TIN)

The receiver must furnish the correct TIN of the person or persons from whom the cash is received. If the transaction is conducted on behalf of another person or persons, the receiver must furnish the TIN of that person or persons. There are three types of TINs:

1. The TIN for an individual, including a sole proprietor, is the individual's social security number (SSN).
2. The TIN for a nonresident alien individual who needs a TIN, but is not eligible to get an SSN, is an IRS individual taxpayer identification number (ITIN). An ITIN has nine digits, similar to an SSN.
3. The TIN for other persons, including corporations, partnerships, and estates, is the employer identification number.

A nonresident alien individual or a foreign organization does not have to have a TIN, and so a TIN does not have to be furnished for them, if all the following are true:

1. The individual or organization does not have income effectively connected with the conduct of a trade or business in the United States, or an office or place of business or a fiscal or paying agent in the United States, at any time during the year.
2. The individual or organization does not file a federal tax return.
3. In the case of a nonresident alien individual, the individual has not chosen to file a joint federal income tax return with a spouse who is a U.S. citizen or resident.

Related Transactions

Any transaction between a buyer, or an agent of the buyer, and a seller that occurs within a 24-hour period are related transactions. If a person receives over $10,000 in cash during two or more transactions with one buyer in a 24-hour period, he or she must treat the transactions as one transaction and report the payments. For example, if two products are sold for $6,000 each to the same customer in one day, and the customer pays the seller in cash, they are related transactions. Because they total $12,000, they must be reported.

Transactions can be related if they are more than 24 hours apart if the person knows, or has reason to know, that each is one of a series of connected transactions. For example, a travel agent receives $8,000 from a client in cash for a trip. Two days later, the same client pays the agent $3,000 more in cash to include another person on the trip. These are related transactions and must be reported.

When a person receives $10,000 or less in cash, the person may voluntarily report the payment if the transaction appears to be suspicious. A transaction is suspicious if it appears that a person is trying to cause the receiver not to report, or is trying to cause a false or incomplete report, or if there is a sign of possible illegal activity.

The amount received and when it was received determines when it must be reported to the IRS. Generally, a report must be filed within 15 days after receiving payment. If the first payment is not more than $10,000, the seller must add the first payment and any later payments made within one year of the first payment. When the total cash payments are more than $10,000, the buyer must file within 15 days. After a report is filed, a new count of cash payments received from that buyer within a 12-month period must be reported to the IRS within 15 days of the payment that causes the additional payments to total more than $10,000. The report can be filed in the seller's local IRS office.

A written statement must be given to each person named on the report to the IRS. The statement must show the name and address of the person who receives the payment, the name and telephone number of a contact person, and the total amount of reportable cash received from the person during the year. It must state that the information is being reported to the IRS. The statement must be sent to the buyer by January 31 of the year after the year in which the seller receives the cash that caused the information to be filed with the IRS. The individual making the report must keep a copy of every report filed for five years.

Penalties

There are civil penalties for failure to:

1. File a correct report by the date it is due.
2. Provide the required statement to those named in the report.
3. If the person receiving the cash payment intentionally disregards the requirement to file a correct form by the date it is due, the penalty is the larger of:
   a. $25,000.
   b. The amount of cash the person received and was required to report, up to $100,000.

There are criminal penalties for:

1. Willful failure to file a report.
2. Willfully filing a false or fraudulent report.
3. Stopping or trying to stop a report from being filed.
4. Setting up, helping to set up, or trying to set up a transaction in a way that would make it seem unnecessary to file a report.

Interference with or prevention of the filing of a report as well as actual willful failure to file a report may result in a substantial fine, imprisonment, or both. The fine can be up to $250,000 ($500,000 for corporations). An individual may also be sentenced to up to five years in prison. Both a fine and a prison sentence may be imposed.

The penalties for failure to file can also apply to any person, including a payer, who attempts to interfere with or prevent the seller, or business, from filing a correct report. This includes any attempt to structure the transaction in a way that would make it seem unnecessary to file a report by breaking up a large cash transaction into small cash transactions.

APPENDIX G
Goodwill

Goodwill is an intangible asset that represents the advantage or benefits acquired in a business in excess of the value of the other assets. Goodwill can be internally generated as a result of earnings, or it can be purchased as part of the cost of acquiring a group of assets in the purchase of another business. Goodwill is an intangible asset because it is difficult to determine its value directly, despite it being associated with aspects of a business, such as its value as a going concern, skilled employees, expected continued customer patronage, name or reputation, effective management, and future expected profits. For both financial accounting and tax accounting, goodwill is recognized only when there is a purchase of another business. Thus, no accounting or tax recognition is given to internally generated goodwill.

In the acquisition of a business, the purchase price is compared with the fair market values of the identifiable tangible and intangible assets acquired, and the difference is assigned to goodwill if the purchase price exceeds the values of the individual assets, or to a gain on acquisition, if the value of the assets exceeds the purchase price. The underlying assets in a business purchase must be individually assigned a fair value at the date of acquisition; this normally requires an appraisal of the tangible and intangible assets purchased (excluding goodwill).

Accountants who have been practicing for some time, have seen a complete reversal of position on the amortization of goodwill by the IRS, Congress, and the FASB. Internal Revenue Code (IRC) sec. 197 was enacted as part of the *Revenue Reconciliation Act of 1993* allowing business intangibles, including goodwill, acquired after August 10, 1993 to be amortized over a 15-year period. Before that, any amortized goodwill was strictly nondeductible.

The FASB in 2002 issued FASB 142, *Goodwill and Other Intangible Assets*, effective for fiscal years beginning after December 15, 2001, putting a halt to the amortization of goodwill for financial reporting purposes. The result for corporate tax returns is that whereas the amortization of goodwill was formerly an M-1 item that was deductible for book purposes but not for tax purposes, it is now an M-1 item that is deductible for tax purposes but not for financial reporting.

The fundamental reasoning of the Board in issuing FASB 142 was to make the amortization of intangibles dependent upon their measurable lives or their benefits to the business. It addresses acquired intangible assets but leaves the former coverage of internally developed intangibles as directed in APB Opinion No. 17, *Intangible Assets*. The FASB concluded that the benefits of goodwill are too indeterminable to be assigned a definite life, and hence are not subject to amortization.

Tax Treatment of Goodwill

IRC sec. 1060 sets out the method for allocating the purchase price of an ongoing business to its assets. The IRS requires Form 8594, *Asset Acquisition Statement Under Section 1060*, to be filed by both the buyer and seller. This form records the allocation of the purchase price to various classes of assets, including goodwill. This requirement applies regardless of the form of the business (sole proprietorship, partnership, LLC, C Corporation, S Corporation, or trust). The form is attached to the first tax return filed following the sale-purchase.

IRS Form 8594 requires dividing the acquired assets into classes:

- Class I assets include cash and cash equivalents.
- Class II assets include publicly traded stocks and securities (but not the stock of the target company), certificates of deposit, U.S. government securities and foreign currency.
- Class III assets include accounts receivable and other debt assets that the taxpayer marks-to-market at least annually for federal income tax purposes.
- Class IV assets include inventory or stock in trade of the purchased business, or other assets held for sale to customers in the ordinary course of business.
- Class V assets are all assets not included in another class, including class VI.
- Class VI assets are all IRC sec. 197 intangibles except goodwill and going concern value. IRC sec. 197 assets include workforce in place, business books and records, customer-based intangibles, licenses, permits, covenants not to compete, franchises, interest in land, certain computer software, interests under leases of tangible property, certain separately acquired interests in patents or copyrights, professional sports franchises and certain transaction costs. The basis of intangible assets is the cost to buy or create them, including legal fees to defend them when applicable.
- Class VII assets are goodwill and going concern value (whether or not the goodwill or going concern value qualified as sec. 197 intangibles).

The IRS requires the residual method for allocating the sales price of the purchased assets. Based on the fair market value of the assets purchased, the residual method allocates the sales price beginning with Class I assets and working up the classes to Class VI. Any remaining balance after the allocation to all other assets may be allocated to Class VII, goodwill and going concern value.

The fair market value (to be assigned to assets in Classes I-VI) is the price at which property would change hands between a buyer and a seller, neither under a compulsion to buy or sell, and both having reasonable knowledge of all relevant facts.

Amortization is a ratable deduction for the cost of certain intangible property over the period specified by law, 15 years, in the case of sec. 197 intangibles, including goodwill and going concern value. Intangibles are amortized on a straight-line basis, by the month in the year of acquisition and annually thereafter.

If the acquisition of an ongoing corporation is accomplished through the purchase of its stock, consideration should be given to an IRC sec. 338 election, treating the deal as an asset purchase for tax purposes.

Financial Reporting Treatment of Goodwill

For financial reporting, although amortization of goodwill is no longer allowed, except as an option described elsewhere for private companies, identifiable reductions in the value of goodwill are subject to write-downs if the asset becomes impaired. Specific rules are provided by FASB ASC 350, *Intangibles—Goodwill and Other*, for goodwill and for determining when impairment has occurred.

FASB ASC 350 provides that goodwill shall be tested for impairment at least annually and at the same time of the year each time, though it may be done anytime during the year. Impairment is the condition that exists when the carrying amount of goodwill exceeds its "implied fair value." The use of the term *implied fair value* indicates that the value of goodwill cannot be measured directly but is always a residual amount. The testing for impairment of goodwill was formerly done in two steps but that has changed with recent standards. Before any steps are taken, an entity may first assess qualitative factors to determine if it is necessary to perform the quantitative impairment test. Examples of such qualitative factors are listed in ASC 350-20-35-3C as macroeconomic conditions, industry and market considerations, cost factors, overall financial performance, other relevant entity-specific events, changes affecting a reporting unit, or a sustained decrease in share price. If an entity determines it is more likely than not that the fair value of a reporting unit is less than its carrying amount, it shall then perform the quantitative impairment test.

The quantitative test involves comparing the fair value of the business, or reporting unit, to its carrying amount, including goodwill. As long as the fair value of the business exceeds its carrying amount, there is no impairment and no further measures are required.

If the fair value is less than the carrying amount, then an impairment loss is recognized equal to the difference. The loss from the impairment of goodwill is reported on the income statement as a separate line item before the subtotal *income from continuing operations*. An exception is made if the impairment is identified with a discontinued operation, in which case the loss is reported net of tax in the subtotal for results of discontinued operations.

APPENDIX H
Foreign Currency Translations

FASB ASC 830, *Foreign Currency Matters*

ASC 830 covers accounting for the translation of foreign currency statements and the gain and loss on foreign currency transactions. Foreign currency transactions and financial statements of foreign entities include branches, subsidiaries, partnerships and joint ventures, which are consolidated, combined, or reported under the equity method in financial statements prepared in accordance with U.S. generally accepted financial principles.

Why is translation necessary? It is not arithmetically possible to combine, add, or subtract measurements expressed in different currencies. It is necessary, therefore, to translate assets, liabilities, revenues, expenses, gains, and losses that are measured or denominated in a foreign currency.

Definitions

An understanding of this rather complex accounting rule can be aided by becoming familiar with the terms used in the Statement. The following list of definitions will enable the accountant to apply the accounting procedures and methods outlined below.

Attribute. For accounting purposes, the quantifiable element of an item.

Conversion. Exchanging one currency for another.

Currency Exchange Rate. The rate at which one unit of a currency can be exchanged or converted into another currency. For purposes of translation of financial statements, the current exchange rate is the rate at the end of the period covered by the financial statements, or the dates of recognition in the statements for revenues, expenses, gains and losses.

Currency Swap. An exchange between enterprises of the currencies of two different countries with a binding commitment to reverse the exchange of the two currencies at the same rate of exchange on a specified future date.

Current Rate Method. All assets and liabilities are translated at the exchange rate in effect on the balance sheet date. Capital accounts are translated at *historical exchange rates*.

Discount or Premium on a Forward Contract. The foreign currency amount of a contract multiplied by the difference between the contracted forward rate and the spot rate at the date of inception of the contract.

Economic Environment. The nature of the business climate in which an entity *primarily* generates and expends cash.

Entity. In this instance, a party to a transaction which produces a monetary asset or liability denominated in a currency other than its functional currency.

Exchange Rate. The ratio between a unit of one currency and the amount of another currency for which that unit can be exchanged at a particular time. The appropriate exchange rate for the translation of income statement accounts is the rate for the date on which those elements are recognized during the period.

Foreign Currency. A currency other than the functional currency of the entity being referred to. For example, the dollar could be a foreign currency for a foreign entity. Composites of currencies, such as the Special Drawing Rights (SDRs), used to set prices or denominate amounts of loans, etc., have the characteristics of foreign currency for purposes of applying ASC 830.

Foreign Currency Transaction. A transaction in which the terms are denominated in a currency other than an entity's functional currency. Foreign currency transactions arise when an enterprise buys or sells goods or services on credit at prices which are denominated in foreign currency; when an entity borrows or lends funds and the amounts payable or receivable are denominated in foreign currency; acquires or disposes of assets, or incurs or settles liabilities denominated in a foreign currency.

Foreign Currency Translation. Amounts that are expressed in the reporting currency of an enterprise that are denominated in a foreign currency. An example is the translation of the financial statements of a U.S. company from the foreign currency to U.S. dollars.

In the translation of balance sheets, the assets and liabilities are translated at the *current exchange rate*, e.g., rate at the balance sheet date. Income statement items are translated at the *weighted-average exchange rate* for the year.

There are two steps in translating the foreign country's financial statements into U.S. reporting requirements:

1. Conform the foreign country's financial statements to U.S. GAAP.
2. Convert the foreign currency into U.S. dollars, the reporting currency.

Foreign Entity. An operation (subsidiary, division, branch, joint venture, etc.) whose financial statements are prepared in a currency other than the currency of the reporting enterprise. The financial statements are combined and accounted for on the equity basis in the financial statements of the reporting enterprise.

Foreign Exchange Contract. An agreement to exchange, at a specified future date, currencies of different countries at a specified rate, which is the *forward rate*.

Functional Currency. The currency of the primary economic environment in which an entity operates; that is, the currency of the environment in which an entity primarily generates and expends cash.

Hedging. An effort by management to minimize the effect of exchange rate fluctuations on reported income, either directly by entering into an exchange contract to buy or sell one currency for another, or indirectly by managing exposed net assets or liabilities' positions by borrowing or billing in dollars rather than the local currency. An agreement to exchange different currencies at a specified future date and at a specified rate is referred to as *the forward rate*.

Highly Inflationary Economy. Economies of countries in which the *cumulative* local inflation rate over a three-year period exceeds approximately 100 percent, or more.

Historical Exchange Rate. A rate, other than the current or a forward rate, at which a foreign transaction took place.

Inflation. Not defined by specific reference to a commonly quoted economic index. Management can select an appropriate method for measuring inflation. An annual inflation rate of about 20 percent for three consecutive years would result in a cumulative rate of about 100 percent.

Intercompany Balance. The foreign currency transactions of the parent, the subsidiary, or both. An intercompany account denominated in the local foreign currency is a foreign currency transaction of the parent. An intercompany account denominated in dollars is a foreign currency transaction of a foreign entity whose functional currency is a currency *other than* the U.S. dollar.

Local Currency. The currency of a particular country.

Measurement. Measurement is the process of measuring transactions denominated in a unit of currency (e.g., purchases payable in British pounds).

Remeasurement. Measurement of the functional currency financial statement amounts in other than the currency in which the transactions are denominated.

Reporting Currency. The currency used by an enterprise in the preparation of its financial statements.

Reporting Enterprise. An entity or group whose financial statements are being referenced. In ASC 830, those financial statements reflect a) the financial statements of one or more foreign operations by combination, consolidation, or equity accounting; b) foreign currency transactions; c) both a) and b).

Self-Contained Operations. Operations which are integrated with the local economic environment, and other operations which are primarily a direct or integral component or extension of a parent company's operations.

Speculative Contracts. A contract that is intended to produce an investment gain (not to hedge a foreign currency exposure).

Spot Rate. An exchange for *immediate delivery* of the currencies exchanged.

Transaction Date. The date at which a transaction, such as a purchase of merchandise or services, is recorded in accounting records in conformity with U.S. GAAP. A long-term commitment may have more than one transaction date; for example, the due date of each progress payment under a construction contract is an *anticipated transaction date* credited to shareholders' equity.

Transaction Gain or Loss. Gains or losses from a change in exchange rates between the functional currency and the currency in which a foreign transaction is denominated.

Translation Adjustment. Translation adjustments translate financial statements from the entity's functional currency into the reporting currency. The amount necessary to balance the financial statements after completing the translation process. The amount is charged or credited to shareholder's equity.

Unit of Measure. The currency in which assets, liabilities, revenues, expenses, gains and losses are measured.

Weighted Average Rates. Determined on a monthly basis by an arithmetic average of daily closing rates, and on a quarterly and an annual basis by an arithmetic average of average monthly rates.

Discussion of ASC 830

ASC 830 applies to the financial reports of most companies with foreign operations. The essential requirements of the Statements are:

1. Translation adjustments arising from consolidating a foreign operation *are* not included in net income. Adjustments should be disclosed separately and accumulated in a separate classification as other comprehensive net income, in accordance with ASC 220, *Income Statement—Reporting Comprehensive Income.*
2. Exchange rate changes on a foreign operation which directly affect the parent's cash flows must be included in net income.
3. Hedges of foreign exchange risks are accounted for as hedges without regard to their form.
4. Transaction gains and losses result from exchange rate changes on transactions denominated in currencies other than the functional currency.
5. The balance sheet translation uses the exchange rate prevailing as of the date of the balance sheet.
6. The exchange rate used for revenues, expenses, gains and losses is the rate on the date those items are recognized, though it is common practice to use

an average rate for the period as an estimate, if not materially different from what would be calculated on each transaction date.

7. Upon sale (or liquidation) of an investment in a foreign entity, the amount accumulated inother comprehensive net income is removed and reported as a gain (or loss) on the disposal of the entity.

8. Intercompany transactions of a long-term investment nature are not included in net income.

9. The financial statements of a foreign entity in a highly inflationary economy must be remeasured as if the functional currency were the reporting currency. A "highly inflationary economy" is defined in the Statement to be an economy that has had a cumulative inflation rate of 100 percent, or more, over a three-year period.

10. If material change in an exchange rate has occurred between year-end and the audit report date, the change should be reported as a subsequent event.

Background. Even several decades ago, the rapid expansion of international business activities of U.S. companies and dramatic changes in the world monetary system created the need to reconsider the accounting and reporting for foreign currency translation. In considering this topic, the FASB issued FASB Statement 52, which, in effect, became ASC 830 and related to the following four areas:

1. Foreign currency transactions including buying or selling on credit goods or services whose prices are denominated in a foreign currency; i.e., currency other than the currency of the reporting entity's country.

2. Being a party to an unperformed foreign exchange contract.

3. Borrowing or lending funds denominated in a foreign currency.

4. For other reasons, acquiring assets or incurring liabilities denominated in foreign currency.

ASC 830 also applies to a foreign enterprise which reports in its currency in conformity with U.S. Generally Accepted Accounting Principles. For example, a French subsidiary of a U.S. parent should translate the foreign currency financial statements of its Italian subsidiary in accordance with ASC 830. The objective of translation is to measure and express in dollars, and in conformity with U.S. Generally Accepted Accounting Principles, the assets, liabilities, revenues, or expenses that are measured or denominated in foreign currency. In achieving this objective, translation should remeasure these amounts in dollars without changing accounting principles. For example, if an asset was originally measured in a foreign currency under the historical cost concept, translation should remeasure the carrying amount of the asset in dollars at historical cost, not replacement cost or market value.

The most common foreign currency transactions result from the import or export of goods or services, foreign borrowing or lending, and forward exchange contracts. Import or export transactions can be viewed as being composed of two elements—a sale or purchase and the settlement of the related receivable or payable. Changes in the exchange rate, which occur between the time of sale or purchase and the settlement of the receivable or payable, should not affect the measurement of revenues from exports or the cost of imported goods or services.

Foreign currency statements should be translated based on the exchange rate at the end of the reporting year. Translation gains and losses are presented as other comprehensive income or loss. Also important is the accounting treatment of gains and losses resulting from transactions denominated in a foreign currency. These are shown in the current year's income statement.

Because of the proliferation of multinational companies, expanding international trade, business involvement with foreign subsidiaries, and joint ventures, ASC 830 was established, in effect, by popular demand. The stated aims of ASC 830 are to (a) provide information that is generally compatible with the expected effects of a rate change on an enterprise's cash flows and equity, and (b) reflect in consolidated statements the financial results and relationships of the individual consolidated entities as measured in their functional currencies, whether the U.S. dollar or a specified foreign currency, in conformity with U.S. Generally Accepted Accounting Principles.

The method adopted to achieve these aims is termed the *functional currency approach* which is the currency of the primary economic environment in which the entity carries on its business; in substance, where it generates and expends cash. The Statement permits a multiple measurement basis in consolidated financial statements (depending upon the country in which the subsidiary operates) because business enterprises made up of a multinational enterprise operate and generate cash flows in diverse economic environments, each with its own functional currency. When an enterprise operates in several of these environments, the results of business transactions are measured in the functional currency of the particular environment. "Measured in the functional currency" has the specific meaning that gains and losses comprising income are determined only in relation to accounts denominated in the functional currency.

Mechanically, the functional currency approach calls for eventual translation of all functional currency assets and liabilities into dollars at the current exchange rate. Under ASC 830, use of the current rate for all accounts resolves both the economically compatible results and operating margins distortions. In the past, these distortions came about with the translation of nonmonetary accounts at historical rates. The volatility of earnings distortions is alleviated by recording the translation adjustments directly into shareholders' equity.

The functional currency approach presumes the following:

1. Many business enterprises operate and generate cash flows in a number of different countries (different economic environments).
2. Each of these operations can usually be identified as operating in a single economic environment: the local environment or the parent company's environment. The currency of the principal economic environment becomes the functional currency for those operations.
3. The enterprise may be committed to a long-term position in a specific economic environment and have no plans to liquidate that position in the foreseeable future.

Because measurements are made in multiple functional currencies, decisions relating to the choice of the functional currency of a specific foreign operation will in all likelihood have a significant effect upon reported income. Even though the management of the business enterprise is entitled to a degree of latitude in its weighing of specific facts, the thinking behind adoption of this Statement is that the functional currency is to be determined based on the true nature of the enterprise and not upon some arbitrary selection which management feels might be of particular advantage to the reporting entity.

Determining the Functional Currency. Multinational companies are involved with foreign business interests either through transactions or investments in foreign entities operating in a number of different economic environments. Each of these endeavors may be associated with one primary economic environment whose currency then becomes the functional currency for that operation. On the other hand, in a foreign country where the economic and/or political environment is so unstable that a highly inflationary economy is likely, it may be deemed wise to carry on the enterprise with the dollar as the functional currency. If the operations in situations of this nature are re-measured on a dollar basis, further erosion of nonmonetary accounts may be avoided.

When there is a reasonably stable economic situation, the national environment of each operation should be considered as the primary economic environment of the particular operation since national sovereignty is a primary consideration in relation to currency control.

Industry practice, on the other hand, may in some instances be instrumental in the determination of a primary economic environment and functional currency. If it is an industry-wide practice that pricing or other transaction attributes are calculated in a specific currency, such as prices set in dollars on a worldwide basis, that fact may be more of a determinant than local currency considerations.

The actual decisions in determining a functional currency depend to a large extent upon the operating policy adopted by the reporting company. Two broad classes of foreign operations are to be considered:

1. Those in which a foreign currency is the functional currency. This designation will have been made after receiving the facts and determining that this particular aspect of foreign business operations is largely autonomous and confined to a specific foreign economic environment. That is, ordinary operations are not dependent upon the economic environment of the parent company's functional currency, nor does the foreign operation primarily generate or expend the parent's functional currency.

2. When the workaday business of the foreign operation is deemed to be in actuality just an extension of the parent company's operation and dependent upon the economic environment of the parent company, the dollar may be designated as the functional currency. In substance, most transactions can reasonably be in dollars, thus obviating the need for foreign currency translation.

One of the objectives of ASC 830 is to provide information that is generally compatible with the expected economic effects of a rate change on an enterprise's cash flow and equity in a readily understood manner. If a foreign operation's policy is to convert available funds into dollars for current or near-term distribution to the parent, selection of a dollar functional currency may be expedient.

Therefore, reporting for investments expected to be of short-term duration, such as construction or development joint ventures, the dollar should probably be designated the functional currency. If the nature of an investment changes over a period of time, future redetermination of the appropriate functional currency may become necessary. Such redetermination is permissible only when, in actual fact, significant changes in economic facts and/or circumstances have occurred. The operative functional currency cannot be redetermined merely because management has "changed its collective mind." It becomes evident that functional currency determination should be carefully considered with the decision weighted in favor of the long-term picture rather than short-term expectations.

In the event that redetermination is necessary, three procedures should be kept in mind:

1. When the functional currency has been changed, ASC 830 provides that the prior year's financial statement need not be restated for a change in functional currency.

2. When the functional currency change is from the local currency to the dollar, historical costs and exchange rates are to be determined from translated dollar amounts immediately prior to the change.

3. When the functional currency change is from the dollar to the local currency, nonmonetary assets are to be translated at current exchange rates, charging the initial translation adjustment to equity similar to that produced when ASC 830 was adopted.

Translation. Translation is the process of converting financial statements expressed in one unit of currency to a different unit of currency (the reporting currency). In short, translation as used in ASC 830 is the restatement into the reporting currency (the U.S. dollar) of any/all foreign currency financial statements utilized in preparing the consolidated financial statements of the U.S. parent company.

Thus, the focus for the preparation and subsequent translation of the financial statements of individual components of an organization is, as previously stated, to:

1. Provide information that is generally compatible with the expected economic effects of a rate change on the enterprise's cash flows and equity, and
2. Reflect in consolidated statements the financial results and relationships of the individual consolidated entities as measured in their functional currencies in conformity with U.S. Generally Accepted Accounting Principles.

Measurement is the process of stating the monetary value of transactions denominated in a particular unit of currency (e.g., purchases payable in British pounds). These transactions may also be figured in a unit of currency other than that in which they are denominated. This process then becomes remeasurement and is accomplished by assuming that an exchange of currencies will occur at the exchange rate in effect at the time of the remeasurement. As is evident, should the exchange rate fluctuate between the date of the original transaction and the date of the exchange, a foreign exchange gain or loss will result. The gains or losses so recorded vary little from other trading activities and are, therefore, included in income.

Foreign Currency Transactions. Foreign currency transactions are those denominated in a currency other than the entity's functional currency. These transactions include:

1. Buying or selling goods priced in a currency other than the entity's functional currency.
2. Borrowing or lending funds (including intercompany balances) denominated in a different currency.
3. Engaging in an unperformed forward exchange contract.

As becomes evident, companies with foreign subsidiaries can readily become engaged in foreign currency transactions which must be considered when financial statements are prepared. But, in addition, companies which have no foreign branches may also in the everyday course of business become involved in foreign currency transactions.

Regardless of whether the company is entirely domestic-based or not at the transaction date, each resulting asset, liability, revenue, expense, gain, or loss not already denominated in the entity's functional currency must be so measured and recorded. At the close of each subsequent accounting period, all unsettled monetary balances are to be remeasured using the exchange rates in effect on the balance-sheet date. Gains and losses from remeasuring or settling foreign currency transactions are accounted for as current income.

APPENDIX I
Whistleblower Program

Fiscal Year (FY) 2023 continued to build on the record-breaking success of previous years for the U.S. Securities and Exchange Commission's (SEC's) Whistleblower Program. In 2023, the SEC awarded nearly $600 million to 68 individual whistleblowers, including a single award for almost $279 million—the largest in the history of the Program. The following information provides background on this Program. Since the beginning of the Program, the SEC has paid more than $1.9 billion in 397 awards.

The Commission also received a record high number of whistleblower tips alleging wrongdoing. In Fiscal Year 2023, the Commission received 18,354 whistleblower tips—the largest number of whistleblower tips received in a fiscal year.

The Program is already a success, according to the Chairman of the SEC. The SEC is seeing high-quality tips that are saving investigators substantial time and resources.

The SEC Whistleblower Program, implemented under Section 922 of the Dodd-Frank Act, is primarily intended to reward individuals who act early to expose violations and who provide significant evidence that helps the SEC bring successful cases.

To be considered for an award, the SEC's rules require that a whistleblower must voluntarily provide the SEC with original information that leads to the successful enforcement by the SEC of a federal court or administrative action in which the SEC obtains monetary sanctions totaling more than $1 million.

"For an agency with limited resources like the SEC, it is critical to be able to leverage the resources of people who may have first-hand information about violations of the securities laws," according to the SEC. "While the SEC has a history of receiving a high volume of tips and complaints, the quality of the tips we have received has been better since Dodd-Frank became law. We expect this trend to continue, and these final rules map out simplified and transparent procedures for whistleblowers to provide us critical information."

Section 922 of the Dodd-Frank Wall Street Reform and Consumer Protection Act authorizes the SEC to pay rewards to individuals who provide the Commission with original information that leads to successful SEC enforcement actions and certain related actions.

In passing the Dodd-Frank Act, Congress substantially expanded the agency's authority to compensate individuals who provide the SEC with information about violations of the federal securities laws. Prior to the Act, the agency's bounty program was limited to insider trading cases and the amount of an award was capped at 10 percent of the penalties collected in the action.

Rules Requirements

The final rules define a whistleblower as a person who provides information to the SEC relating to a possible violation of the securities laws that has occurred, is ongoing or is about to occur.

To be considered for an award, the final rules require that a whistleblower must:

Voluntarily provide the SEC...

- In general, a whistleblower is deemed to have provided information voluntarily if the whistleblower has provided information before the government, a self-regulatory organization or the Public Company Accounting Oversight Board asks for it directly from the whistleblower or the whistleblower's representative.

... with original information ...

- Original information must be based upon the whistleblower's independent knowledge or independent analysis, not already known to the Commission and not derived exclusively from certain public sources.

... that leads to the successful enforcement by the SEC of a federal court or administrative action ...

- A whistleblower's information can be deemed to have led to a successful enforcement action if:
  a. The information is sufficiently specific, credible and timely to cause the Commission to open a new examination or investigation, reopen a closed investigation, or open a new line inquiry in an existing examination or investigation.
  b. The conduct was already under investigation when the information was submitted, and the information significantly contributed to the success of the action.
  c. The whistleblower reports original information through his or her employer's internal whistleblower, legal, or compliance procedures before or at the same time it is passed along to the Commission; the employer provides the whistleblower's information (and any

subsequently-discovered information) to the Commission; and the employer's report satisfies prongs (1) or (2) above.

... in which the SEC obtains monetary sanctions totaling more than $1 million.

- The rules permit aggregation of multiple Commission cases that arise out of a common nucleus of operative facts as a single action. These may include proceedings involving the same or similar parties, factual allegations, alleged violations of the federal securities laws, or transactions or occurrences.

The final rules further define and explain these requirements.

Avoiding Unintended Consequences:

Certain people generally will not be considered for whistleblower awards under the final rules. These include:

- People who have a pre-existing legal or contractual duty to report their information to the Commission.
- Attorneys (including in-house counsel) who attempt to use information obtained from client engagements to make whistleblower claims for themselves (unless disclosure of the information is permitted under SEC rules or state bar rules).
- People who obtain the information by means or in a manner that is determined by a U.S. court to violate federal or state criminal law.
- Foreign government officials.
- Officers, directors, trustees or partners of an entity who are informed by another person (such as by an employee) of allegations of misconduct, or who learn the information in connection with the entity's processes for identifying, reporting and addressing possible violations of law (such as through the company hotline).
- Compliance and internal audit personnel.
- Public accountants working on SEC engagements, if the information relates to violations by the engagement client.

However, in certain circumstances, compliance and internal audit personnel as well as public accountants could become whistleblowers when:

- The whistleblower believes disclosure may prevent substantial injury to the financial interest or property of the entity or investors.

- The whistleblower believes that the entity is engaging in conduct that will impede an investigation.
- At least 120 days have elapsed since the whistleblower reported the information to his or her supervisor or the entity's audit committee, chief legal officer, chief compliance officer—or at least 120 days have elapsed since the whistleblower received the information, if the whistleblower received it under circumstances indicating that these people are already aware of the information.

Certain other people—such as employees of certain agencies and people who are criminally convicted in connection with the conduct—are already excluded by Dodd-Frank.

Under the final rules, the Commission also will not pay culpable whistleblowers awards that are based upon either:

- The monetary sanctions that such culpable individuals themselves pay in the resulting SEC action.
- The monetary sanctions paid by entities whose liability is based substantially on conduct that the whistleblower directed, planned or initiated.

The purpose of this provision is to prevent wrongdoers from benefitting by, in effect, blowing the whistle on themselves.

Providing Information to the Commission and Seeking a Reward

The rules also describe the procedures for submitting information to the SEC and for making a claim for an award after an action is brought. The claim procedures provide opportunities for whistleblowers to fairly present their claim before the Commission makes a final award determination.

Under the final rules, the SEC also will pay an award based on amounts collected in related actions brought by certain agencies that are based upon the same original information that led to a successful SEC action.

Clarifying Anti-Retaliation Protection

Under the rules, a whistleblower who provides information to the Commission is protected from employment retaliation if the whistleblower possesses a reasonable belief that the information he or she is providing relates to a possible securities law violation that has occurred, is ongoing, or is about to occur. In addition, the rules make it unlawful for anyone to interfere with a whistleblower's efforts to communicate with the Commission, including threatening to enforce a confidentiality agreement.

Supporting Internal Compliance Programs

The final rules do not require that employee whistleblowers report violations internally in order to qualify for an award. However, the rules strengthen incentives that had been proposed and add certain additional incentives intended to encourage employees to utilize their own company's internal compliance programs when appropriate to do so. For instance, the rules:

- Make a whistleblower eligible for an award if the whistleblower reports internally and the company informs the SEC about the violations.
- Treat an employee as a whistleblower, under the SEC Program, as of the date that employee reports the information internally – as long as the employee provides the same information to the SEC within 120 days. Through this provision, employees are able to report their information internally first while preserving their "place in line" for a possible award from the SEC.
- Provide that a whistleblower's voluntary participation in an entity's internal compliance and reporting systems is a factor that can increase the amount of an award, and that a whistleblower's interference with internal compliance and reporting is a factor that can decrease the amount of an award.

Whistleblower Web page

With its Whistleblower Program officially becoming effective on August 12, 2011, the SEC launched a Web page for people to report a violation of the federal securities laws and apply for a financial award. Prior to the enactment of Dodd-Frank, the SEC had authority to reward whistleblowers only in insider trading cases.

The Dodd-Frank Wall Street Reform and Consumer Protection Act provided the SEC with the authority to pay financial rewards to whistleblowers who provide new and timely information about any securities law violation. Among other things, to be eligible, the whistleblower's information must lead to a successful SEC enforcement action with more than $1 million in monetary sanctions.

The SEC's whistleblower Web page at www.sec.gov/whistleblower includes information on eligibility requirements, directions on how to submit a tip or complaint, instructions on how to apply for an award, and answers to frequently asked questions.

The SEC's Whistleblower Program strengthens the SEC's ability to protect investors in several ways:

- **Better Tips:** Over the past several months, the SEC has seen an increase in the quality of tips that it has been receiving from individuals since Congress created the Program.

- **Timely Tips:** Potential whistleblowers are more likely to come forward sooner rather than later with "timely" information not yet known to the SEC.
- **Maximizes Outside Resources:** With fewer than 4,000 employees to regulate more than 35,000 entities, the SEC cannot be everywhere at all times. With a robust Whistleblower Program, the SEC is more likely to find and deter wrongdoing at firms it may not have otherwise discovered were breaking the law.
- **Protections Against Retaliation:** Employees who come forward are provided with tools to protect themselves against employers who retaliate.
- **Bolsters Internal Compliance:** The rules provide significant incentives for employees to report any wrongdoing to their company's internal compliance department before coming to the SEC. Therefore, companies that would prefer their employees report internally first are more likely to have a credible, effective compliance program in place.

Individuals wishing to be considered for an award under the Whistleblower Program are required to submit an online questionnaire or on Form-TCR.

Submitting Tip, Complaint or Referral

In addition to whistleblower rules, the Dodd-Frank Act called upon the SEC to create an Office of the Whistleblower. That office, works with whistleblowers, handles their tips and complaints, and helps the Commission determine the awards for each whistleblower. The staffing of the office has been completed and the Investor Protection Fund, which will be used to pay awards to eligible whistleblowers, has been fully funded.

To qualify for an award under the Whistleblower Program, an individual must submit information regarding possible securities law violations to the Commission in one of the following ways:

- Online through the Commission's Tip, Complaint or Referral Portal;
- By mailing a Form TCR to: SEC Office of the Whistleblower at 100 F Street NE, Mail Stop 5971, Washington, DC 20549; or
- By Fax: to (703) 813-9322.

To submit information anonymously, i.e., without providing identity or contact information, the whistleblower must be represented by, and provide contact information for an attorney in connection with the submission in order to be eligible for an award.

Index

All references are to paragraph (¶) numbers.

All references are to paragraph (¶) numbers.

All references are to paragraph (¶) numbers.

All references are to paragraph (¶) numbers.

All references are to paragraph (¶) numbers.

All references are to paragraph (¶) numbers.

C

All references are to paragraph (¶) numbers.

All references are to paragraph (¶) numbers.

All references are to paragraph (¶) numbers.

All references are to paragraph (¶) numbers.

E

All references are to paragraph (¶) numbers.

All references are to paragraph (¶) numbers.

All references are to paragraph (¶) numbers.

All references are to paragraph (¶) numbers.

All references are to paragraph (¶) numbers.

All references are to paragraph (¶) numbers.

All references are to paragraph (¶) numbers.

G

All references are to paragraph (¶) numbers.

All references are to paragraph (¶) numbers.

All references are to paragraph (¶) numbers.

All references are to paragraph (¶) numbers.

All references are to paragraph (¶) numbers.

H

All references are to paragraph (¶) numbers.

All references are to paragraph (¶) numbers.

All references are to paragraph (¶) numbers.

IES

All references are to paragraph (¶) numbers.

All references are to paragraph (¶) numbers.

All references are to paragraph (¶) numbers.

All references are to paragraph (¶) numbers.

All references are to paragraph (¶) numbers.

All references are to paragraph (¶) numbers.

All references are to paragraph (¶) numbers.

All references are to paragraph (¶) numbers.

All references are to paragraph (¶) numbers.

All references are to paragraph (¶) numbers.

All references are to paragraph (¶) numbers.

All references are to paragraph (¶) numbers.

All references are to paragraph (¶) numbers.

All references are to paragraph (¶) numbers.

All references are to paragraph (¶) numbers.

All references are to paragraph (¶) numbers.

All references are to paragraph (¶) numbers.

All references are to paragraph (¶) numbers.

All references are to paragraph (¶) numbers.